The United States

★ National Capital   ⊙ State Capital   • Largest City in State

0   100   200   300   400 Miles

American History:
A Survey

Richard N. Current

University of North Carolina at Greensboro

T. Harry Williams

Louisiana State University

Frank Freidel

Harvard University

New pictorial essays on "The Course of American Art"
by Gerald Bernstein, Brandeis University

Fourth Edition

American History
A Survey

ALFRED · A · KNOPF

New York

To the Memory of William Best Hesseltine
(1902 – 1963)

THIS IS A BORZOI BOOK   PUBLISHED BY ALFRED A. KNOPF, INC.

Fourth Edition
9876543
Copyright © 1959, 1961, 1964, 1966, 1971, 1975 by Richard N. Current, T. Harry
Williams, Frank Freidel
All rights reserved under International and Pan-American Copyright Conventions.
No part of this book may be reproduced in any form or by any means, electronic
or mechanical, including photocopying, without permission in writing from the
publisher. All inquiries should be addressed to Alfred A. Knopf, Inc., 201 East
50th Street, New York, N.Y. 10022. Published in the United States by Alfred A.
Knopf, Inc., New York, and simultaneously in Canada by Random House of
Canada Limited, Toronto. Distributed by Random House, Inc., New York.

Library of Congress Cataloging in Publication Data

Current, Richard Nelson.
  American history: a survey.

  Based on A history of the United States, by
T. H. Williams, R. N. Current, and F. Freidel.
  Includes bibliographical references.
  1. United States—History. I. Williams, Thomas
Harry, 1909–   joint author. II. Freidel, Frank
Burt, joint author. III. Williams, Thomas Harry,
1909–   A history of the United States. IV. Title.
E178.1.C93   1975   973   74-18435
ISBN 0-394-31863-3

MANUFACTURED IN THE UNITED STATES OF AMERICA

**Published 1961, reprinted five times   Second edition, 1966; reprinted
three times   Third edition, 1971; reprinted four times
Fourth edition, 1975**

Cartographic consultants:
David Ward
Randall Sale
University of Wisconsin

Douglas McManis
Columbia University

Cartographic additions and revisions:
Jean Paul Tremblay

Cover art by Gerald McConnell

Preface

During the four years since the previous edition of this book appeared, a good deal of new history has been made—new history both in the sense of actual events and in the sense of scholarly writings. In revising the book, we have extended our account to include recent events, and we have made numerous changes throughout in order to reflect developments in historical scholarship. In particular, we have given increased attention to the role of minorities and of women in American history.

We have revised not only the text itself but also the special features. We have replaced a number of the "boxes" containing excerpts from historical records of various kinds and thus introducing the student to aspects of the past as it was experienced by people of the time. We have incorporated some of the latest views in our historiographical essays, "Where Historians Disagree," which acquaint the student with some of the continuing conflicts of interpretation among historians. To this series we have added an essay, "Why Historians Disagree," to suggest reasons for and limits to the differences in interpretation. Gerald Bernstein, an expert in art history, has provided a completely new series of pictorial essays on "The Course of American Art." These inserts, with pictures in full color and with a running commentary, provide a synopsis of trends in art and architecture.

In the text proper, over half of the illustrations have been freshly chosen for this edition. Several new maps have been drawn, and some of the others have been redrawn in the interest of clarity and informativeness. A few of the charts and graphs are new. Bibliographies and appendices have been brought up to date.

In the work of revision we have had the benefit of editorial expertise provided by Alfred A. Knopf, Incorporated. We wish particularly to thank Helen D. Litton, who as project editor of this edition has had a truly creative part in its production. We have been immeasurably aided by historical scholars, experts in their respective fields, who have examined and criticized parts of our earlier editions. For the sake of objectivity, some of these scholars have made their critiques without our being informed of their names. Since it is impossible to identify all the critics, we have decided to identify none of them, but we cannot forgo this opportunity to extend to all of them our most sincere thanks. We have been greatly helped also by users of the text, students as well as instructors, who have sent us criticisms and corrections. To these sharp-eyed and well informed readers, too, we wish to express our profound gratitude. We shall continue to be grateful for suggestions regarding corrections or other improvements to be made in future reprintings and revisions.

Contents

THE COURSE OF AMERICAN ART

WHERE HISTORIANS DISAGREE

Illustrations

Maps

Charts

American History:
A Survey

From the Old World to the New

One

The history of the United States from its colonial beginnings is fairly short. It covers a period of less than 400 years, a period that can be spanned by the overlapping lifetimes of a mere half-dozen men. Yet the roots of American civilization go deep into the human past. These roots are to be traced mostly to the Old World, not the New.

There is no evidence that human life originated in the New World. No bones or fossils of the apelike ancestors of man, such as those unearthed on other continents, have ever been found in either North or South America. The earliest remains of humanity so far discovered here are, at the most, only about 25,000 years old.

The American continents were peopled as a result of two long-continuing immigration movements, the first from Asia, the second from Europe and Africa. Probably the first began thousands of years ago when Siberian tribes, in search of new hunting grounds or of refuge from pursuing enemies, crossed over the Bering Strait to Alaska. Crossings by Asians, a few at a time, went on for centuries, then finally ceased. From Alaska the newcomers and their descendants fanned out to populate both the continents. By 1492 there were perhaps a million people north of Mexico, 3 million in Mexico and Central America, and 6 million (some estimates run much higher) in South America.

The Stone Age forefathers of these people brought little with them from Asia. Over the centuries the first Americans developed for themselves such tools and customs as they possessed when the Europeans arrived. At that time the aboriginal cultures ranged from the simple to the complex, from those of primitive, acorn-gathering tribes to that of the Aztecs, the inheritors of the Mayas who by A.D. 1000 had created in Central America one of the most brilliant civilizations

English Wigwams
The first English settlers were unfamiliar with the log cabin that later became typical of the American frontier. They constructed temporary shelters of various kinds, including wigwams patterned after those of the Indians. Shown are reconstructions of such buildings in Salem, Massachusetts. (The Society for the Preservation of New England Antiquities)

then existing anywhere in the world. Technological development in America, however, lagged behind that in Europe and Asia. As late as 1492 none of the Indians were using wheeled vehicles or machines or, indeed, wheels of any kind.

The second peopling of the Americas began with the expansion of Europe at the end of the medieval and the start of the modern period. The history of the United States is an extension of European and particularly English history. The new Americans had much to learn from those already here, and they were to be influenced a good deal by the wilderness environment they found, but their way of life was to be based mainly on the European traditions they brought with them.

The Epoch of Discovery

Between the time when those first Siberian tribesmen descried the headlands of Alaska and the time thousands of years later when Christopher Columbus sighted a West Indian island, no doubt other wanderers from abroad—certainly from Scandinavia and possibly from Egypt and elsewhere—caught at least a glimpse of some part of America. If so, these "discoveries" did not lead to any general knowledge that such a place existed, and still less to any systematic effort to explore it. The rest of the world was not yet ready for such an enterprise. The great age of exploration had to wait for developments in Europe.

THE QUICKENING OF EUROPE

During the Middle Ages (roughly from A.D. 500 to A.D. 1500) the civilization of Western Europe was in many ways inferior to that of ancient Greece or Rome. After Germanic barbarians had overrun the Roman Empire, the dream of Roman peace and unity lingered on. The countries of medieval Europe were thought to form a single whole, under the spiritual authority of the Roman Catholic Church and the political authority of what was called the Holy Roman Empire. But kings often asserted power independently of the emperor, and nobles asserted power independently of the kings. Ordinary people, the serfs, tied by custom to the soil, worked the fields while their lords engaged in desultory warfare and chivalric games. Merchants and craftsmen were handicapped by the disorders that prevailed much of the time. Except within the Church, art and learning had

few practitioners, and it fell to the monasteries to keep alive the memory of past greatness.

Medieval Europe was backward even by comparison with certain other areas of the contemporary world. Though India and China, like the Roman Empire, had suffered from invasion and conquest, they had fallen upon no "dark age" comparable to that of Europe. The land of the Moslems, extending around the southern rim of the Mediterranean and on to the east of it, supported science, industry, and commerce such as no country of Christian Europe could match. Moslem scholars were familiar with classical learning and far surpassed it in such fields as mathematics, with their Arabic numerals and their decimal system (based on a concept of early India). The wonders of the Far East dazzled the few Europeans who, like the Venetian merchant Marco Polo, got a chance to visit them, and the wonders of the Near East amazed the crusading knights who set out to recover the Holy Land from the infidels.

Forces leading to the awakening of Europe and the discovery of America were set in motion around A.D. 1000 by an outpouring of the Norsemen from Denmark, Norway, and Sweden. These Vikings made conquests as far east as Russia, as far south as France and the British Isles, and as far west as Iceland and Greenland. Two of them, Biarni Heriulfson and Leif Ericson, on separate voyages, even touched upon the coast of North America, but later attempts at colonization failed, and neither of these men is generally considered the effective discoverer of the New World. Indirectly, however, the Norse did contribute to the subsequent discovery or rediscovery by Columbus.

They pioneered in the construction of ocean-going ships, stimulated trade over the area of their widespread conquests, and infused into the life of Europe much of their own energy and daring. Their descendants in France, the Normans (who set up kingdoms in England, Italy and Sicily, and northern Africa), provided outstanding leadership in the Crusades.

The Crusades further encouraged ship-building and commerce. In Syria and Egypt the Crusaders got acquainted with a number of exotic goods — spices, perfumes, drugs, silks, china, glassware, gems — which were brought by land and by sea all the way from the Orient. In the Near East some Europeans, especially the Italians, set up trading posts where they exchanged for Oriental commodities the gold, silver, copper, lead, and tin from the mines of Western Europe. These traders sent their imports on to such wholesaling centers as Pisa, Genoa, and Venice, which distributed the goods among merchants from other towns and ultimately among the consumers, remote from the original sources of supply in China, India, or the "Spice Islands" of the East Indies.

This commerce fostered the growth of towns and gave a new importance to town life in Europe. The townsmen or bourgeosie came to form a substantial "middle" class between the nobles and the clergy above them and the serfs below. They accumulated capital in larger and larger amounts, making possible trading ventures of increasing size and profit. Desiring peace and security, such as would be good for business, the merchants breathed a spirit quite out of harmony with feudalism and its disorders. In the contests between kings and turbulent nobles, the bourgeoisie came to the support of the kings and thus aided in the rise of centralized national governments.

Increased wealth, leisure, and security made possible a greater cultivation of the things of the mind and prepared the way for the Renaissance in Europe. The Renaissance was marked by a changing outlook on life. Formerly, preoccupied with their own sinfulness and weakness, men had viewed their earthly lives as contemptible and had tried to concentrate their thoughts upon eternity. Now, with increasing human self-confidence, they began to show more and more interest in the world about them. Formerly they had relied for their ideas mostly on the authority of the Bible and the works of Aristotle as expounded by the churchmen. Now many became willing to observe, experiment, and test truths for themselves. This changing attitude was involved both in the renewed study of Greek and Roman classics and in the creation of vernacular literatures. It was related also to the multiplication of efforts to control the natural environment through applied science and technology rather than through prayer or magic.

Among the inventions coming into use after the twelfth century were guns and gunpowder, bellows and blast furnaces, various machines powered by water or wind, movable type and the printing press, the mechanical clock, improvements in ship design and construction, and several devices intended to aid the art of navigation. The compass, at first only a needle magnetized with lodestone and floated in water, told the navigator his direction. He could obtain his latitude by sighting a fixed star with the quadrant, the cross-staff, or the astrolabe. Theoretically he could calculate his longitude by means of the clock, but in actual practice this was not accurate enough to help him much (until the invention of the chronometer in the eighteenth century). So he continued to follow the coasts when feasible, and when he ventured out of sight of land, he proceeded (as Columbus did) mainly by dead reckoning, setting his course by the compass, and finding his position by elapsed time and estimated speed.

Geographical knowledge was still, as in ancient times, a mixture of fable and fact, even though map making had improved remarkably. Mariners, foremost among them the Italians, carefully charted the shorelines along which they sailed, until the coastal areas of almost all the known world had been accurately mapped. On the high seas away from the familiar routes, however, everything remained a matter of speculation. Practical sailors and educated men believed that the earth was a sphere, but many of them underestimated its size. The first globe ever made, the work of a Nuremberg cartographer in 1492, showed an unbroken ocean stretching westward from Europe around to Asia and occupying only about a third of the earth's surface.

On the European edge of this sea of darkness stood the rising nation-states of England, France, Holland, Portugal, and Spain, each with a strong government and a consciousness

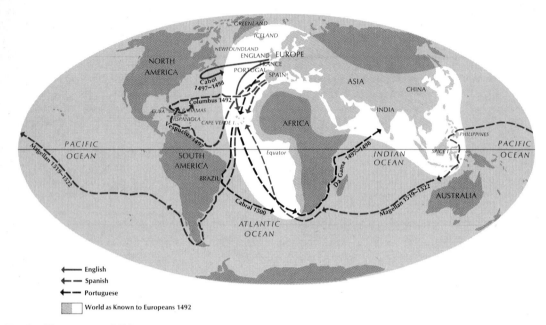

Early Voyages of Discovery

of national unity. These countries, while the most powerful in Europe, were also the most distant from the rich sources of the Oriental trade. In the process of this trade, Italian and Arab merchants added their profits and commissions, and various rulers added their tolls and taxes, so that by the time Oriental wares reached the Atlantic nations the price was outrageously high, and excessive amounts of money were drained away to the East. If the middlemen somehow could be by-passed, the Western merchants could gain larger profits for themselves and the Western nations could end the troublesome loss of specie. Here was an adequate motive for finding new routes, entirely by sea, that could be controlled from home. The search for new approaches to the East led to the discovery of new lands in the West, in that presumably empty ocean that lay at the back of Europe.

WESTWARD TO THE EAST

Without the wealth of the merchants and the organizing power of the nation-states, the glorious age of exploration would have been un-

thinkable. But it would also have been inconceivable without patriotic and religious zeal, skillful seamanship, bold imagination, and courageous leadership.

Portugal early took the lead as an exploring nation. Its maritime supremacy owed a great deal to one man, Prince Henry the Navigator, who devoted his life to nautical studies and to the promotion of exploration. Concentrating upon the western coast of Africa, with the visionary aim of establishing a Christian empire to aid in war against the Moors, and with the more practical object of finding gold, Prince Henry sent out expedition after expedition, some of his mariners going as far south as Cape Verde. After his death in 1460 his work was carried on by intrepid explorers advancing still farther south. At last, in 1486, Bartholomeu Diaz went clear around the southern tip of the continent, and in 1497–1498 Vasco da Gama proceeded all the way to India. In 1500 the next fleet bound for India, that of Pedro Cabral, was blown off its southward course and happened upon the coast of Brazil. So America would have been discovered within a decade even if Columbus had never made his famous voyage of 1492.

Christopher Columbus, who was born and reared in Genoa, got most of his seafaring knowledge and experience in the service of the Portuguese. He was not the first man to think of reaching the East by sailing west, but he was the first to do something about it. Though an industrious student of geography, he was convinced of the feasibility of his plan as a result of errors rather than special insight. From his reading of Marco Polo's wondrous travel book, from his correspondence with the Florentine geographer Toscanelli, and from other studies and his own calculations, he gathered that the world was smaller than it actually is and that the Asian continent extended farther eastward than it actually does. So he concluded that the western ocean was narrow enough to be crossed on a relatively brief voyage. But he failed to convince the King of Portugal, and as the Portuguese progressed with their own route to the East around Africa, they complete-ly lost interest in the idea of a westward crossing.

Columbus then turned from Portugal to Spain. Though not a maritime people like the Portuguese, the Spaniards were proud, energetic, and zealous. They were being unified under the strongest monarchy in Europe after the marriage of Ferdinand of Aragon and Isabella of Castile. To Queen Isabella the importunate Columbus appealed for money, men, and ships with which to carry out his project and thereby extend the sway of Christianity and the power and glory of Spain. For several years the Queen withheld her aid, partly because her advisers doubted Columbus' theories and partly because she was busy with Christianizing and conquering Spain itself. In 1492, with the fall of the Moorish stronghold of Granada, the Mohammedans were practically eliminated from Spanish soil, and during that same year the Jews who rejected conversion were

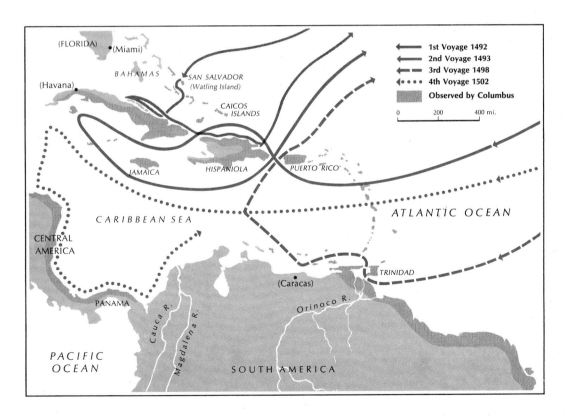

The Lands That Columbus Saw on His Four Voyages

forced to leave the country. At last Isabella granted Columbus his request.

On his first voyage, with the *Pinta,* the *Niña,* and the *Santa Maria* and with ninety men, Columbus steered as straight as he could for Japan. He thought he had arrived there when, ten weeks after embarking, he landed on Watling Island in the Bahamas, and he thought he had reached the China coast when he pushed on to Cuba. He returned to Spain with a few natives – he called them "Indians" – but he brought no news of the great Khan's court in China and no samples of the famous wealth of the Indies. The next year, with a much larger expedition, he discovered other islands and left a colony on one of them, Hispaniola. On a third voyage, in 1498, cruising along the northern coast of South America, he passed the mouth of the Orinoco River and surmised that such a large fresh-water stream must emerge from a continent, one separate from Asia. On his last voyage, in 1502, he tried to sail around the northwestern end of the continent so as to find the rich and civilized part of the Indies, but he was blocked by the Isthmus of Panama and succeeded only in exploring the Caribbean coast of Central America. He died still thinking he had been in at least the fringes of the Far East.

At first a hero, then a man in disgrace, Columbus was not even honored in the naming of the land he had discovered. Disregarding Columbus' promised monopoly, Spain itself licensed numerous explorers after him, and rival governments sent out expeditions of their own. The Portuguese, who claimed the whole region of his discoveries, promptly dispatched a fleet to the scene (1501). A Florentine merchant, Americus Vespucius, who was aboard, afterward wrote partly fictitious letters describing several visits to the new continent, and a German geographer, Martin Waldseemüller, published one of the letters with the suggestion that the land be named for Americus. The name stuck.

Yet Columbus, for all his misconceptions, deserved the fame that ultimately came to him. He dispelled the terrors of the unknown ocean and led the way to the New World. The explorers of many nations who followed him were only carrying on the work he had begun. Just as he had done on his final voyage, they concentrated their efforts mainly on the search for a water passage that would lead through or around the new lands and on to the riches of the Far East. They never found the kind of passage they sought (because it did not exist until 1914, when the Panama Canal was opened), but they revealed the outlines of both continents and made known the vastness of the territory available for European use.

Spain, turning to the sea as a result of Columbus' initiative, replaced Portugal as the foremost exploring nation. Vasco de Balboa fought his way across the Isthmus of Panama (1513) and gazed upon the great ocean that separated America from China and the Indies. Seeking access to that ocean, Ferdinand Magellan, a Portuguese in Spanish employ, found the strait that now bears his name at the southern end of South America, struggled through the stormy narrows and into the ocean, so calm by contrast that he christened it the Pacific, then proceeded to the Philippines. There Magellan himself fell at the hands of natives, but his expedition went on to complete the first circumnavigation of the globe (1519–1522). By 1550 the Spaniards had explored the coasts of North America as far north as Oregon and Labrador.

England followed Spain as a sponsor of voyages westward in search of the East. John Cabot, Genoa-born like Columbus and inspired by the latter's unsuccessful efforts to reach the Orient, sailed twice to the northeastern coast of North America under the auspices of King Henry VII, the first time in 1497. Columbus never laid eyes upon the North American continent; Cabot was the first to leave a record of having viewed it, and he may therefore be considered its effective discoverer. Much later, after failing to find a northeast passage around Europe, Englishmen began to look for a northwest passage around North America. Martin Frobisher made three trips, the last one in 1578, and discovered Frobisher's Bay, Baffin's Land, and the Eskimos, but not the strait he was after. Year after year, other Englishmen kept up the search.

Meanwhile, under Francis I, the government of France promoted a series of expeditions to the New World. In 1523–1524 Giovanni Verrazano, a Florentine navigator, followed the shore northward from North Carolina in quest of an opening to Asia for France. Between 1534 and 1541 Jacques Cartier and Jean François Roberval, on separate voyages, tried to find the much-sought passage by pushing up the St. Lawrence River. The Dutch govern-

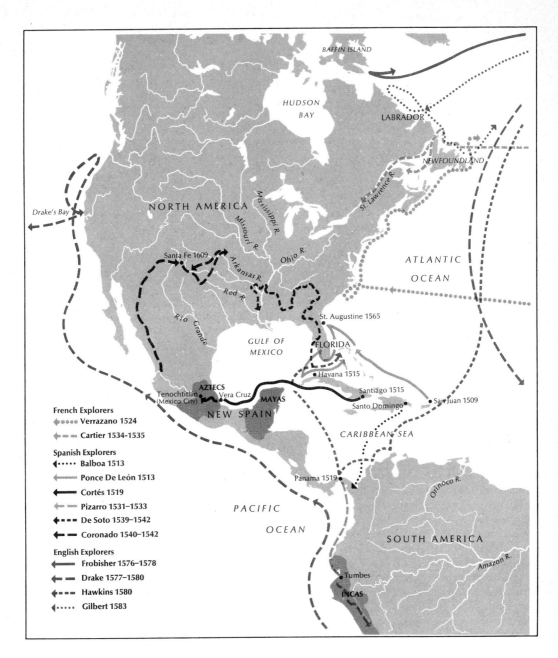

Explorations of Sixteenth-Century America

ment, a latecomer, commissioned the English- man Henry Hudson to find an all-Dutch route to Asia. He was looking for it when, in 1609, he entered the river that afterward was named for him. Though much valuable information came from all this activity by men of several national- ities sailing under diverse flags, often not their own, the precise relationship of the Asian and North American continents remained some- thing of a mystery until 1728, when Vitus Ber- ing, a Dane in Russian employ, voyaged through the strait that separates the two.

The Colonizing Impulse

While remaining an obstacle to those preoccupied with routes to the East, the New World became for others a goal in itself, a possible source of wealth rivaling and even surpassing the original Indies. The Spaniards soon were building themselves an American empire. On the basis of Columbus' discoveries and a papal decree, they claimed the whole of the New World, except for a chunk of it (Brazil) which they left to the Portuguese. Other nations waited a century or more to grow into successful colonizing powers. During this time the English (and the French as well) were developing the national strength and unity that would enable them to compete with Spain. Finally the English and others challenged the Spanish monopoly at least in North America.

THE SPANISH COLONIES

Awaiting the Spaniards were the riches of the native Aztec and Inca empires. The Aztecs were the heirs of Mayan civilization, which had reached its height at about A.D. 1000. In Central America the Mayas had built elaborately carved stone temples and pyramids, bred corn from a kind of wild grass, devised an accurate calendar from astronomical observations, and invented a number system similar to the Arabic and superior to the Roman. After conquering the Mayas and other, less highly civilized peoples, the Aztecs ruled them all through their emperor, whose capital was on the present site of Mexico City. From Cuzco in the mountains of Peru the Incas ruled a more highly centralized and even larger empire, one of the largest of all history, and they constructed thousands of miles of paved roads (or rather pathways, for they had no wheeled vehicles) to hold their empire together.

The early Spanish colonists, beginning with those Columbus brought on his second voyage, settled in the islands of the Caribbean, where they tried without much luck to enslave the Indians and uncover gold. Then (during the same years, 1519–1522, that Magellan's fleet was on its way around the world) Hernando Cortés destroyed the Aztec empire and looted its treasure. The news of silver to be found in Mexico turned the attention of the Spaniards to the mainland. From the island colonies and from the mother country fortune hunters descended upon Mexico in a movement comparable in some ways to the nineteenth-century gold rushes elsewhere in the world. When Francisco Pizarro conquered Peru and revealed the wealth of the Incas (1532–1538), the way was opened for a similar advance into South America.

Exploration and colonization in Spanish America was primarily a work of private enterprise, carried on by individual leaders, with little direct support from the government at home. Before a man could undertake the job he had to get a royal license. By its terms the King was to have a tenth of the wealth to be produced in the new colony, and the colonizer was to have a tenth in addition to a generous estate, other lands to divide among his followers, and the right for himself and for them to the use of native labor. But he had to equip and finance his own expedition and take the risk of loss or ruin. He might succeed and make a fortune, or through shipwreck or other accident he might lose everything including his life, as many an adventurer did.

The colonial population came only in small part from Spain itself and scarcely at all from other countries in Europe, for few Spaniards were able or willing to emigrate, and foreigners with a few exceptions were excluded from the colonies. Colonial officials were supposed to bring their wives with them, but among the ordinary settlers men outnumbered women by at least ten to one. Naturally, then, most of the Spanish men married Indian women, and a sizable mixed population grew up. There was nevertheless a manpower shortage, which the Spaniards tried to overcome by forcing the Indians to work for wages. The first experiments with forced labor, as on the island of Hispaniola, resulted in the near extermination of the natives, but Indians continued to work in the mines or on the ranches of the mainland for centuries. As workers on the plantations of the islands and coastal areas, Negro slaves began to be imported as early as 1502, the African slave trade having been established by the Portuguese more than fifty years before that.

The whites exploited the colored peoples, yet the Spanish conquerors were not peculiarly

Tenochtitlán — The Aztec Capital

This is a model reconstructing the central square. Tenochtitlán, located on the site of the present Mexico City, had a population of about 100,000 in 1502 when the last of the emperors, Montezuma II, began his reign. His empire, covering much of central and southern Mexico, was a rather loose association of city-states from which he collected heavy tribute. The Aztecs developed a complex and magnificent civilization, made up largely of elements adapted from the Mayas and other neighboring peoples. In Tenochtitlán there were surgeons and physicians who are believed to have been as skillful as the best in contemporary Europe, and there were hospitals and nurses. There were also human sacrifices. To appease the Aztec gods, young men and women captives were slaughtered on top of the pyramids. These structures, like those of the Mayas, were comparable in size to the pyramids of ancient Egypt but were used as temples rather than burial monuments. When Hernando Cortés, the Spanish conqueror of Mexico, entered Tenochtitlán in 1519, he found in the central square a rack which held the skulls of about 100,000 sacrificial victims. (Courtesy of The American Museum of Natural History)

cruel and predatory, no more so than the later English colonists. The millions of Indians who died in Spanish America were mostly victims of the white man's diseases. The Spanish reputation for harsh treatment of the natives arose originally from the writings of a sensitive friend of the Indians in the colonies who was himself a Spaniard — Bartolomeo de las Casas.

And if the Spaniards seemed at times to have a monomania for gold and silver, they were in this respect little different from Englishmen such as those at Jamestown who spent their first precious weeks prospecting feverishly for gold. The difference was that the Spaniards, or many of them at least, were fabulously successful. Over a period of three centuries the mines in Spanish America yielded more than ten times as much gold and silver as all the rest of the mines in the world.

The Spanish settlers farmed as well as mined, and they brought in elements of European civilization which, over the centuries, proved far more valuable to the New World than all the gold and silver they took out. They transferred their language and learning, their tools and mechanical arts, from the homeland to the colonies. They transplanted grains and fruits and vegetables, including wheat, oranges, lemons, grapes, bananas, olives, and sugar cane. They introduced domestic animals such as cows, pigs, mules, and especially horses, which soon multiplied and ran wild even beyond the colonial frontiers, becoming accessible to the Indians far north on the Great Plains and revolutionizing their way of life. And though the Spaniards brought the sword, they also brought the cross. Priests or friars accompanied every colonizing venture, making each settlement a Christian community and carrying the gospel bravely to the heathen.

The government of the colonies was reasonably efficient and highly centralized. But the Spanish empire did have weaknesses. For one thing, its commercial policy was unusually inflexible and strict. To enforce the collection of duties and provide protection against pirates, the government required all trade with the colonies to be carried on through a single Spanish port and only a few colonial ports, in fleets making but two voyages a year. This system checked the prosperity of many of the colonists, such as those in Argentina, who had to import their European manufactures and export their own agricultural products through distant Porto Bello on the Isthmus of Panama.

One of the most serious weaknesses of the empire resulted from the facts of geography. Above Mexico the colonial domain widened out into the whole continent of North America, with no natural barrier such as would limit the aspirations of the Spaniards or provide them with an easily defensible boundary. They could not people the area within this wide border arc thickly enough to make it secure, yet they kept expending energy and resources in trying to hold and even to advance beyond it. The mo-

Mission San Xavier del Bac
During the eighteenth century the Spaniards established numerous missions on the northern frontiers of New Spain. One of the finest and best preserved of the churches is San Xavier del Bac, which is located near the present city of Tucson, Arizona. Spaniards visited this area as early as 1539. They were looking for the fabled Seven Cities of Cibola which, according to Indian reports, were full of gold. Eventually missionaries arrived, to Christianize the Indians. (Wayne Andrews)

tives for this northward push varied. Such early explorers as Coronado, De Soto, and Ponce de Leon looked for fabled treasures in the wilderness. Men of religious orders, Jesuit or Franciscan, went out to save souls, the Franciscans establishing a chain of missions, which by 1776 extended through California as far north as San Francisco Bay. Frontiersmen moved into New Mexico and Texas to prospect for silver or engage in the Indian trade. Viceroyal expeditions set up remote military outposts, as at St. Augustine in Florida (1565). Indeed, the requirements of defense were always a consideration—defense against the raids of wild tribes and against the colonial thrusts of rival European nations—and *presidios* or fortresses dotted the frontier. But it was a wasting struggle, and in the end a losing one.

These outer reaches of the empire, eventually incorporated into the United States, brought elements of Spanish culture directly into the amalgam of American civilization. Many of these elements are indicated by Spanish words that have become Americanized, words like *ranch, rodeo, corral, lariat, patio,* and *calaboose.*

ENGLAND AGAINST SPAIN

While Spain was building her American empire, the religious unity of Western Europe disappeared, with profound consequences for the colonization of America. As of 1500, the Christian world already was divided between East and West, between the Church of Constantinople and the Church of Rome. But virtually all of Western Europe was Roman Catholic and, in spiritual matters, recognized the supremacy of the Pope. Soon Western Europe itself was divided, between Catholics and those who protested, or Protestants, of whom there came to be many sects. The Protestant leaders intended to reform the Church, and so their movement is known as the Reformation.

The Reformation began in 1517 when Martin Luther, a German professor of theology, challenged the right of the Pope to sell "indulgences" for the remission of sins. Before long, Luther broke completely with the Roman Church. He concluded that man could not find salvation through the Church, its priests, or its sacraments, that man could be saved only by faith, by a thoroughgoing belief in redemption through Christ. Advancing beyond strictly religious matters, Luther advised German rulers to seize Church lands. Rapidly he won converts among both rulers and people.

While Luther was getting his revolt under way, a second great Protestant leader arose, one who was to have a far more direct and important influence upon American civilization. This man was John Calvin. A Frenchman by birth, Calvin studied law and theology in Paris. About 1533 he left the Catholic Church, and then the country. Fleeing to Switzerland, he settled in Geneva, and there he set up a kind of church-state.

In his *Institutes of the Christian Religion* (1536), one of the great theological works of all time, Calvin expounded his religious views. The main points, much simplified, were these: God is all-knowing, all-powerful. Man is weak, helpless, born in sin, and cannot save himself by his own efforts: he must rely upon God. The future of every soul is foreordained from the beginning of things, long before the soul is born. God's elect would give evidence of their future glory by the upright, moral life they lived in this world. Others had a duty to honor God and, regardless, had no choice but to conform. Calvin insisted upon hard work and strict morality. The Calvinist doctrines, stern and even terrifying as they appear, appealed to many people because of their very forthrightness and puritanical austerity.

Neither Calvin nor Luther, however, caused England to leave the Church of Rome. England broke away because of the political ambitions and marital difficulties of one of her kings, Henry VIII. He coveted the monastery wealth, disliked the loss of money in English contributions to the Pope, desired a male heir (which his wife Catherine, daughter of Ferdinand and Isabella of Spain, failed to give him), and fell in love with Anne Boleyn. When the Pope refused to grant a dispensation permitting him to marry Anne, Henry VIII with the cooperation of Parliament made himself (1534) "the supreme head of the Church of England." He was no theological reformer: he kept the main tenets of Roman Catholic doctrine.

After the death of Henry VIII (1547) the Church of England went first to Protestant and then, under "Bloody Mary," to Catholic extremes, with persecutions and martyrdoms on both sides. Finally the Anglican Church straightened out upon a steady middle course during the long and glorious reign of Anne Boleyn's fiery, red-headed, able daughter, Elizabeth I (1558–1603). Under Elizabeth, the Church was given a theology more Protestant than it had had under her father, Henry VIII.

While losing many lands to Lutheranism, Calvinism, or Anglicanism, the Church of Rome undertook to reform itself and win back as much of the world as possible. This undertaking is known as the Catholic Reformation or the Counter Reformation. King Philip II of Spain assumed the task of leading the Roman Catholic forces of the world against the Protestants.

In 1568 the Dutch revolted against Philip II, their Spanish overlord. They fought as Dutchmen for national independence, and as Calvinists for religious freedom. They were an industrial and maritime people, noted for their linen and woolen cloth, their ships, their fisheries, and their trade. Holding an advantage upon the sea, they robbed the galleons bringing treasure from the New World to Spain. When Spain agreed to a truce (1609), the Dutch turned to planning American colonies of their own.

In their forays against Spanish shipping the Dutch received encouragement and aid from England. Queen Elizabeth had to fend against the machinations of Philip II as he sought to enhance the power of Spain and win back for Rome the areas of Christendom that had been lost. English Catholics were ready to collaborate with a foreign king in forwarding this presumably holy work. With Philip's encouragement they plotted to get rid of Elizabeth and put Mary Stuart, "Queen of Scots," on the throne. Elizabeth, foiling them, had Mary executed.

In this undeclared war England did not remain on the defensive. Seamen loyal to the Queen—urged on by patriotism, piety, and plunder—struck at the colonial sources of Spanish strength in every way they could. Roving the waters of Spanish America, these "sea dogs" smuggled slaves, pirated treasure ships, and robbed unprotected towns. The greatest of them all, Francis Drake, followed Magellan's route into the Pacific, looted his way northward along the American coast, went on around the world, and returned a profit of several thousand percent to the Queen, who secretly had backed his venture. When she knighted him, instead of rebuking him as the Spanish ambassador demanded, she indicated plainly enough that England was ready to challenge Spain upon the sea.

The decisive test soon came. After England had made an alliance with the rebels of the United Netherlands, Philip II declared war. Determining to invade and conquer England, he assembled an unprecedented fleet of his best and largest warships, an "Invincible Armada." But the Spaniards thought of themselves as soldiers more than sailors, and they applied their ideas of land warfare to naval combat, loading troops on their unwieldy vessels to board the enemy craft and grapple at close range with the latter's men. The English, islanders that they were, relied upon their navy and their privateers, not upon an army. They had fast, maneuverable ships that could sail into the Spanish fleet, fire destructive broadsides, and escape to return and fire again. When, in 1588, the Armada appeared in the English Channel, the new naval tactics did not have a chance to show fully their superiority, for a terrible storm helped to scatter the invaders and destroy most of their ships.

England, having become the world's foremost sea power, could not be kept from colonial enterprises of her own on the other side of the Atlantic. Already Englishmen had made their first, rather tentative efforts to start settlements in the New World. Soon the English were to people the Atlantic coast of North America with colonies which eventually would grow into a great continental nation.

ENGLISHMEN LOOK OVERSEAS

The dream of America as a place of unique opportunity—for liberty, abundance, security, and peace—appeared in England soon after Columbus' discovery. This dream found a classic expression in *Utopia*, a book written by Sir Thomas More and published in Latin in 1516 (translated, 1551), which described society on an imaginary island supposedly discovered by a companion of Americus Vespucius in the waters of the New World. Life in Utopia was as nearly perfect as human beings guided by reason and good will could make it. Though the Utopians lived comfortably enough, they scorned the mere accumulation of material things, and while all were expected to keep busy, none was oppressed or overworked. They enjoyed complete freedom of thought but were careful not to offend one another in the expression of their beliefs. True lovers of peace, they went to war only to defend their neighbors and thereby ensure their own ultimate safety. In presenting such a picture of an ideal community, the book commented by indirection upon the social and economic evils of More's England.

The Tudor age, for all its literary glory and its swashbuckling spirit, was not a happy time for most of the common people, who suffered not only from war and religious strife but also from the effects of economic change. While the population of England grew steadily — from 3 million in 1485 to 4 million in 1603 — the food supply did not increase proportionately. Landowners concentrated on the production of wool. Neither cotton nor silk being yet in general use, wool was in great demand for making cloth. Land tilled at one time by serfs and later by rent-paying tenants, much of it better suited to sheep raising than to the production of crops, was steadily enclosed for sheep runs and taken away from the farmers on it.

Thousands of evicted tenants roamed the countryside in gangs, to the alarm of more fortunate householders, whose feelings are preserved in the nursery rhyme: "Hark, hark! The dogs do bark: the beggars are coming to town." The Elizabethan government passed rather ineffectual laws for halting enclosures, relieving the worthy poor, and compelling the able-bodied or "sturdy beggars" to work. Relatively few of these could find reemployment in raising or manufacturing wool. All the while the cost of living rose, mainly because of an increased money supply arising from the output of Spanish gold and silver mines in America. England, it seemed, contained either too many sheep or too many people.

Amid the widespread distress, a rising class of merchant capitalists prospered from the expansion of foreign trade as they turned from the export of raw wool to the export of woolen cloth. These merchant capitalists gathered up the raw material, put it out for spinning and weaving in individual households, and then sold the finished product both in England and abroad.

At first each exporter did business on his own, though he might belong to the Company of Merchant Adventurers. This company regulated the activities of its members, secured trading privileges for them, and provided protection for their voyages. In time chartered companies sprang up, each with a monopoly from the sovereign of England for trading in a particular region, among them the Muscovy Company (1555), the Levant Company (1581), the Barbary Company (1585), the Guinea Company (1588), and the East India Company (1600). Some of these were regulated companies, similar to the Merchant Adventurers, each member doing business separately. Others were joint-stock companies, much like modern corporations, with stockholders sharing risk and profit either on single ventures or, as became more common, on a permanent basis. These investors often made fantastic profits from the exchange of English manufactures, especially woolens, for exotic goods, and they felt a powerful urge to continue with the expansion of their profitable trade.

To further this drive, spokesmen for the merchant capitalists developed a set of ideas about the proper relation of government and business — ideas supporting the argument that (notwithstanding the sufferings of the dispossessed) the whole nation benefited from the activities of the overseas traders. The trade of England as a whole, it was said, was basically like that of any individual or firm: transactions were worthwhile if sales exceeded purchases in value. The difference in value would have to be paid in money (gold and silver), and the inflow of money into England would stimulate business and strengthen the national economy by raising commodity prices and lowering interest rates. Merchant capitalists depended upon loans to carry on their business, and interest was considered now as a cost of production, whereas in medieval times it had been regarded as sinful usury. According to their theory, the government should act to encourage a "favorable" balance of trade — that is, an excess of exports over imports.

This economic philosophy, restated by Thomas Mun in his book *England's Treasure by Forraign Trade* (1664), came to be known in the eighteenth century as "mercantilism." It guided the economic policies not only of England but also of Spain, France, and other nation-states.

Colonies would fit well into this mercantilistic program, would also alleviate poverty and unemployment, and would serve other useful purposes, or so it seemed to a number of thoughtful Englishmen in the late sixteenth and early seventeenth centuries. The Oxford clergyman Richard Hakluyt, who published a series of explorers' narratives and an essay (1584) on "western planting," made himself the outstanding propagandist for the establishment of colonies. He and others argued that colonies would provide an additional market for English manufacturers and that the colonial demand would give employment in the mother country to the poor who lived there "idly to the annoy of the whole state." Colonial commerce, while yielding profit for shipowners, would bring from the colonies products for which England previously had depended upon foreigners — products such as lumber, naval stores, and above all, silver and gold.

Colonies might also serve as bases for finding and controlling a westward passage to Asia, attacking the Spanish empire, and converting the Indians to Protestantism so that the Catholic revival, the Counter Reformation, would not spread to the New World.

There was yet another reason for the growing interest in colonies. The Church of England, in the form it took under Queen Elizabeth, by no means satisfied all her subjects. It was much too Protestant to suit those Englishmen who held on to the Roman Catholic faith, and at the same time it seemed too "popish" to many who opposed the ways and influence of Rome. Among these were the Puritans, who, affected in varying degrees by the teachings of John Calvin, wished to "purify" the Church. The majority of the Puritans were content to remain within the Anglican fold but hoped to simplify the forms of worship and lessen the power of the bishops, who were appointed by the throne. A minority, the Separatists, were determined to worship as they pleased in their own independent congregations. Like all subjects, however, they were forbidden by law to absent themselves from regular Anglican services or to hold unauthorized religious meetings, and they were taxed to support the established Church.

The discontent of the Puritans and other dissenters increased after the death of Queen Elizabeth, the last of the Tudors, and the accession of James I, the first of the Stuarts, in 1603. A Scotsman, James I was looked upon as a foreigner. He was a learned man but a poor politician — the "wisest fool in Christendom," it was said. Convinced that kings ruled by divine right, he let his subjects know at the outset that he intended to govern as he pleased. He soon anatagonized the Puritans, who included most of the rising businessmen, by resorting to illegal and arbitrary taxation and also by favoring English Catholics and supporting "high church" forms of elaborate ceremony. More and more religious nonconformists began to look for places of refuge outside the kingdom.

The Wilderness Setting

The fate of the English colonies — their success or failure, the kind of development they took — was to depend in large measure upon the environment in which they were planted along the Atlantic seaboard of North America. This environment consisted not only of geographical conditions such as soil and climate, flora and fauna, but also of the human inhabitants apart from the English themselves, that is, the Indian natives and the European intruders.

THE EASTERN WOODLANDS

Three thousand miles and more from England, the colonies were to be separated from the mother country, and yet connected with it, by the Atlantic Ocean. The overseas crossing took from four to twelve weeks or more, in close-packed and often disease-ridden ships which sailed at irregular intervals depending on wind and weather. The distance and the difficulty of ocean travel put the colonists very much upon their own resources once they had landed on the American shore. Nevertheless, the nature of the shoreline and of the terrain behind it inclined them toward the sea, and they kept in touch with the homeland by means of the same ocean they had crossed.

Along much of its extent the coast had been submerged, and the rivers emptying into the ocean had been "drowned" by the prehistoric sinking of the continent's edge. So there was, and is, an indented coastline with a number of bays and harbors, into each of which flows one or more rivers, giving access for varying distances to and from the interior. For instance, the Charles leads to Boston harbor at its mouth, the much longer Hudson to New York harbor, the Delaware to Delaware Bay, the Susquehanna and the Potomac and the York and the James (among others) to Chesapeake Bay, and the Ashley and the Cooper to Charleston harbor. At a time when travel and transportation by water were easier and more economical than by land, the rivers with their tributaries largely determined the lines of settlement and the course of trade.

The topography of the area in which the colonies were located divides it lengthwise into three belts at different levels: the coastal plain, the piedmont plateau, and the Appalachian highland. The plain, very narrow in New England but increasing southward from New York to a width of 200 miles in Georgia, is so low that the rivers traversing it flow backward with the incoming tides, and hence it is known (in the South) as the "tidewater" region. The piedmont, 150 miles across at its widest, is several hundred or more feet higher than the plain and is set off from it by the "fall line," an imaginary line drawn through the points at which the rivers descend to the lowland over falls or rapids. From the piedmont the Appalachian Mountains rise to elevations as high as 6,000 feet in New Hampshire and North Carolina. The mountain barrier is unbroken from New England to Georgia except along the course of the Hudson and the Mohawk rivers, but between the various parallel ranges are valleys that allow fairly easy movement along the highland southwestward from Pennsylvania.

Depending upon latitude, elevation, and distance from the sea, the climate in what was English America varies a great deal from place to place, providing most though not all kinds of weather to be found within the Temperate Zone. There is a remarkable contrast between the steamy summers of the South Carolina coast and the snowy winters of the New England interior. Yet the climate on the whole was fairly similar to what Englishmen had known at home, similar enough that they could easily adapt themselves to it. The unfamiliar features—the greater extremes of heat and cold, the more violent storms, the more brilliant and abundant sunshine—generally

appealed to the newcomers and no doubt stimulated them to unwonted activity.

Soils in America resembled those in England enough to permit the growing of most of the familiar crops, in one place or another. But the soils varied considerably, from the silted river bottoms of the tidewater to the sandy pine barrens on the edge of the upcountry in the South, and from the rich lands of the Susquehanna Valley to the thin topsoil of glacier-scoured New England in the North. Subsoil minerals abounded, especially in the mountains, but most of them—coal, oil, gas—were left for later exploitation. Available in the colonial period were widely scattered deposits of iron ore, both in the mountains and in the lowland bogs. But at that time the most valuable natural resource, other than the soil itself, was the wood that grew upon it and that then served hundreds of industrial uses.

To the first colonists, America was trees. From the Atlantic to the Appalachians and beyond stretched a great forest, unbroken except for occasional small clearings made by the elements or by the Indians, and thick with tall pines, maples, oaks, and countless other varieties of trees as well as shrubs. Even before sighting land the early voyagers to America could sometimes smell the fresh and invigorating forest scent, and once they had disembarked they found themselves in a veritable Garden of Eden, full of birds and beasts for game; flowers, berries, and fruits; and infinite resources of wood. All this made a refreshing contrast with comparatively treeless England, rapidly being deforested to meet the needs of industry.

And yet the friendly forest—so green and beautiful, so rich in materials for food and shelter and manufactures of many kinds—also had its uninviting and even hostile aspects. In its shadows lurked the wolves and panthers that devoured the settler's livestock, lurked also the red men who often threatened his and his family's lives. It stood in the way of the frontiersman eager to cultivate the soil, and he had to convert forest into fields by the slow and laborious effort of girdling or else chopping down the trees, burning the dead or downed timber, and eventually uprooting the stumps.

Apart from the great forest, the geographical fact that most distinguished the new from the old country and most influenced the economic development of the colonies was sheer space, the vast extent of the land. Not that all the land was readily accessible. The need for clearing the forest, the presence of hostile tribes, the dependence upon water transport, and ultimately the difficulty of crossing the mountain barrier—all these considerations hindered the actual occupation of the land, and they operated more and more effectively in proportion to remoteness from the seaports. Hence the English settlements, scattered though they might seem, remained on the whole fairly compact throughout the colonial period, at least in comparison with the Spanish and French settlements in the New World, though not in comparison with the crowded towns and countryside of the Old World. There populations teemed and lacked sufficient room. Here land was plentiful and people relatively scarce.

THE WOODS INDIANS

The North American Indians had the general features of their Mongoloid ancestors—yellow or brown skin, straight and coarse black hair, and high cheekbones—but there were minor variations in physical appearance among the numerous tribes. There were greater differences in modes of living and ways of speaking. Hundreds of languages were spoken, but most of these belonged to one or another of about a dozen linguistic stocks. Men of different tribes with related languages could not always understand each other, any more than Frenchmen could understand Spaniards, nor were such tribes necessarily alike in their cultural patterns.

In 1600 along the Atlantic seaboard south of the St. Lawrence River there lived about

Work of the Forest Indians
A Frenchman, J. F. Lafitau, visited North America, studied the customs of the Indians, and described them in a book that was published in Paris in 1724. This one of his sketches shows members of a southeastern tribe weaving, preparing hides, cooking, grating roots, and making corn meal by pounding and winnowing corn. (Bibliothèque Nationale, Paris)

Indians Greet the White Man [1524]

In most cases the American natives were very hospitable to the European upon his first approach. Thus Verrazano, exploring for the King of France, reported of his visit to the North Carolina coast:

While at anchor on this coast, there being no harbor to enter, we sent the boat on shore with twenty-five men, to obtain water; but it was not possible to land without endangering the boat, on account of the immense high surf thrown up by the sea, as it was an open roadstead. Many of the natives came to the beach, indicating by various friendly signs that we might trust ourselves on shore. One of their noble deeds of friendship deserves to be made known to your Majesty. A young sailor was attempting to swim ashore through the surf, to carry them some knickknacks, as little bells, looking glasses, and other like trifles; when he came near three or four of them he tossed the things to them, and turned about to get back to the boat; but he was thrown over by the waves; and so dashed by them that he lay, as it were, dead upon the beach. When these people saw him in this situation, they ran and took him by the head, legs, and arms, and carried him to a distance from the surf. The young man, finding himself borne off in this way, uttered very loud shrieks in fear and dismay, while they answered as they could in their own language, showing him that he had no cause for fear. Afterwards they laid him down at the foot of a little hill, when they took off his shirt and trousers and examined him, expressing the greatest astonishment at the whiteness of his skin. Our sailors in the boat, seeing a great fire made up and their companion placed near it—full of fear, as in all cases of novelty—imagined that the natives were about to roast him for food. But as soon as he had recovered his strength, after a short stay with them, showing by signs that he wished to return aboard, they hugged him with great affection, and accompanied him to the shore, then leaving him that he might feel more secure, they withdrew to a little hill, from which they watched him until he was safe in the boat.

125,000 Indians. They were most heavily concentrated in southern New England and around Chesapeake Bay. The largest group, as classified by language type, were the Algonquins, who were scattered from Canada south to Virginia. Next in numbers were the Iroquois, centering in New York and forming a wedge between the northern and southern Algonquins. The Iroquois included the "five nations"—Seneca, Cayuga, Onondaga, Oneida, and Mohawk—and also, far to the south, the Cherokees and the Tuscaroras. Still farther south roamed the tribes of the third largest language group, the Muskogean. These were the Chickasaws, Choctaws, Creeks, and Seminoles.

Most of the tribes carried on a primitive form of agriculture. They made clearings by cutting into trees to kill them and by setting fires in the forest. Among the dead and blackened trunks they planted pumpkins, squash, beans, and corn—crops they had learned of indirectly from the Indians of Mexico and South America. A tribe abandoned its clearing and made a new one when the yields fell, or when the accumulated filth of the village became too deep to endure. The Indian "old fields," especially in New England, attracted incoming settlers as convenient places to begin settlement, and the newcomers eagerly adopted the cultivation of native crops, above all corn. Without the clearings and the crops that the Indians provided, the Englishmen would have had much greater difficulty than they did in getting a start in the New World.

None of the Indians of the eastern woodlands (or, for that matter, of the entire continent north of Mexico) showed a talent for political organization at all comparable to that of the Aztecs or the Incas. The nearest thing to it was found in the Iroquois league of five nations (which became six nations in 1713 when the Tuscaroras moved north and joined the league). Other tribes had their own separate and rudimentary governments and were often at war with one another or with the Iroquois. From time to time they made alliances or temporary confederations.

The primitive tribal system offered both advantages and disadvantages for the invading Englishmen. On the one hand, the divisions and rivalries among the red men made it easier for the whites to deal with them than would otherwise have been the case. If the Indians had been united, they could possibly have driven out the invaders. On the other hand, the disunity of the tribes prevented the English from making such a quick and easy conquest as the Spaniards had made when they got control of Mexico and Peru by killing or capturing the native imperial rulers.

To Englishmen the Indians were of interest as customers for English goods and as suppliers of woodland commodities, especially hides and skins. Trade brought the white man and the red man together. It weakened the Indian, for while he obtained guns, knives, blankets, and iron pots, he also received firewater, and he became increasingly dependent upon the white man and his commerce.

As viewed from a distance in England, the Indian in the American wilderness seemed like a strong and innocent creature, a noble savage, awaiting only an opportunity to be civilized and Christianized. Some of the colonists, after their arrival in America, continued to look upon him in that way, and by 1619 about fifty missionaries had already entered the wilds to convert native souls. But most of the colonists soon changed their image of the Indian. After a few bloody conflicts they began to consider him a wild beast fit only to be slaughtered.

In English America there was not to be the fusion of Indian and European peoples and cultures that developed in the Spanish empire. The reasons for this were various, but one of them was the fact that the Englishmen, unlike the Spaniards (and the Frenchmen), almost always came as family men, with their womenfolk, and hence had much less occasion to intermarry with the aborigines.

Nevertheless, American history without the Indians would have lacked much of its special character. Not only did the colonists receive from them a number of new things to eat, such as corn, but the English language in America was enriched by words of native origin (*moccasin* and *succotash*, to mention only two), and American thought was colored by numerous elements of Indian lore. Yet on the whole the aboriginal influence on American civilization was more negative than positive. Despite their kindly aid to the first European arrivals, the Indians formed an obstacle to the advance of white settlement, and life on the frontier derived many of its peculiarly "American" qualities from the Indian danger and the Indian wars.

EUROPEAN RIVALS

In the wilderness the English were to encounter threats not only from the Indians but also from rival Europeans. To the south and southwest were scattered the outposts of the Spaniards who, despite a peace that Spain and England made in 1604, continued to look upon the English as intruders. The English in their settlements along the coast could not for many years feel entirely safe from attack by Spanish ships.

On the north and northwest were beginning to appear the outposts of another and eventually even more dangerous rival, France. The French founded their first permanent settlement in America at Quebec in 1608, less than a year after the English had started their first at Jamestown. New France grew in population very slowly. Few Roman Catholics felt any inclination to leave their beloved homeland, and the discontented Protestants who desired to emigrate were excluded from the colony. To the English in America, however, the French presented a danger disproportionate to their numbers, largely because of their influence upon the Algonquin Indians.

In the Indian trade the English had the advantage of cheaper goods, but the French had an offsetting advantage. While the English in the region generally bought from the Iroquois, who as middlemen secured furs from more remote tribes, the French by-passed the Iroquois and dealt directly with the Algonquins. *Coureurs de bois*, foot-loose and fearless fur traders and trappers, penetrated deep into the interior, made friends with the Indians, lived among them, and took squaws for wives. Thus the French gained the backing of the Hurons and other Algonquin tribes.

At the same time the French antagonized the Algonquins' traditional foes, the Iroquois. When Samuel de Champlain, founder of Quebec, discovered Lake Champlain and came upon a band of Iroquois (1609), some of his men fired. Terrified by their first experience with guns, the Indians fled. Thus began a historic enmity between the Iroquois and the French. The anti-French feeling of the Iroquois persist-

ed because the Iroquois as middlemen resented the competition of the French in the fur trade. For many years the Iroquois were to look upon their English customers as allies.

Besides the Spaniards and the Frenchmen, the English were soon to find in the New World another European rival, the Dutch. Shortly after the planting of the first two English colonies, at Jamestown and Plymouth, the Dutch began to wedge themselves in between, when the Dutch West India Company established posts on the Hudson, Delaware, and Connecticut rivers.

The First English Settlements

The English colonies in America did not result from deliberate governmental planning. They originated in a variety of responses to the economic changes and religious and political struggles going on in England at the end of the sixteenth and the beginning of the seventeenth century. England was advancing out of feudalism and into capitalism faster than any other country. Her colonization was essentially a business enterprise, a product of the new age. But it was motivated by ideals of a better life as well as by the search for power and profit.

EARLY ATTEMPTS

The pioneers of English colonization were Sir Humphrey Gilbert and his half-brother Sir Walter Raleigh, though neither of them succeeded in founding a permanent colony. Both were friends of Queen Elizabeth. While Drake and other sea dogs were harrying the Spaniards in the New World and on the high seas, Gilbert kept insisting at court that English bases in America would give still greater opportunities for sapping the power of Spain. In 1578 he obtained from Elizabeth a patent conferring upon him, for six years, the exclusive right "to inhabit and possess at his choice all remote and heathen lands not in the actual possession of any Christian prince."

That same year Gilbert and Raleigh, with seven ships and nearly 400 men, set out to establish a base in the New World. Storms turned

them back before they had crossed the ocean. Gilbert waited five years while he sought to raise enough money to try again. Then, in 1583, he sailed with a second and smaller expedition, reached Newfoundland, and took possession of

Early English and Dutch Settlements, About 1630

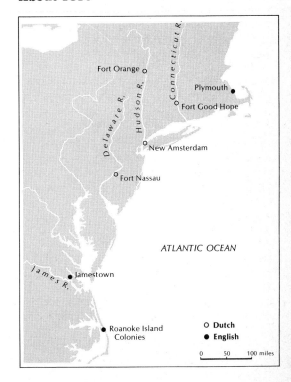

Arrival at Roanoke

John White, a "skilful painter," sailed with the first colonizing expedition to Roanoke Island, in 1585. He recorded the country and its inhabitants in a series of pictures which Thomas Hariot, another member of the expedition, published in a Briefe and True Report of the New Found Land of Virginia. *The illustration reproduced above was entitled "The Arrival of the Englishmen." It shows the sheltered position of Roanoke Island behind the Outer Banks of the North Carolina coast. After the failure of the first colonizing attempt, White went to Roanoke as governor of the second colony, in 1587. Returning to England for supplies, he was unable to get back to Roanoke again until 1590. He then could find no trace of the colonists, including his daughter and his granddaughter, Virginia Dare.*

---

it in the Queen's name. He proceeded southward along the coast, looking for a good place to build a military outpost that might eventually grow into a profitable colony, of which he would be proprietor. Once more a storm defeated him; this time his ship sank and he was lost at sea.

The next year Raleigh, securing from Elizabeth a six-year grant similar to Gilbert's, sent out men to look over the American coast. They returned with two Indians and with glowing reports of an island the natives called Roanoke, and of its environs (in what is now North Caro-

lina). With her permission Raleigh named the area "Virginia" in honor of Elizabeth, the "Virgin Queen." He expected financial aid in return, but she said she could not afford it. So he had to raise money from private investors to finance another voyage to Roanoke. The hundred men he sent out in 1585 spent a year in America, exploring as far north as Chesapeake Bay, which they recommended as the best location for a settlement.

In 1587 Raleigh sponsored still another expedition, this one carrying ninety-one men, seventeen women (two of them pregnant), and nine children as colonists. He directed them to Chesapeake Bay, but the pilot nevertheless landed them on Roanoke Island. Here one of the women gave birth to Virginia Dare, the first American-born child of English parents. A relief ship, delayed until 1590 by the hostilities with Spain, found the island utterly deserted. What had become of the "lost colony" is still a mystery.

The colonizing efforts of Gilbert and Raleigh taught lessons and set examples for later and more successful promoters of colonization. After sending out his ill-fated settlers, Raleigh again sought financial aid from merchants, to whom he sold rights of trading with his proposed colony. He realized that the undertaking was too big for the purse of one man alone. Some of the colonizers after him raised funds for their ventures by forming companies and selling stock, but others, as individuals or unincorporated groups, depended on their own resources.

After the accession of James I, Raleigh was accused of plotting against the King. Raleigh was deprived of his monopoly, imprisoned, and eventually executed. None of his successors received grants so vast and undefined as both his and Gilbert's had been. Thereafter the crown, in theory the owner as well as the sovereign of lands to be occupied by Englishmen, granted and regranted territory to companies or proprietors, on terms that imposed varying conditions and set boundaries that often were conflicting and vague.

A group of London merchants, to whom Raleigh had assigned his charter rights, planned to renew his attempts at colonization in Virginia, which still consisted of an undefined stretch along the Atlantic seaboard. A rival group of merchants, who lived in Plymouth and other West Country towns, were also interested in American ventures. They were already sponsoring voyages of exploration to the coast farther north, up to Newfoundland, where West Country fishermen had been going for many years.

In 1606 James I issued a new charter, which divided America between the two groups. The London Company got the exclusive right to colonize in the south (between the 34th and the 41st parallels), and the Plymouth Company the same right in the north (between the 38th and the 45th parallels). These areas overlapped, but neither company was allowed to start a colony within a hundred miles of where the other already had put a settlement. Each company, as soon as it had begun actual colonization, was to receive a grant of land a

---

Flora and Fauna of the New World
Europeans were much impressed by the strangeness of some of the plants and animals they found in the New World. John White, the artist who accompanied the Roanoke expedition, carefully recorded many of the wonders he saw. While the expedition was in the Caribbean, on the way to Roanoke, White drew an "allagatto" and a "pyne frute," among other things. (Courtesy Trustees of the British Museum)

hundred miles wide and a hundred miles deep. The settlers themselves were to retain all the "liberties, franchises, and immunities" that belonged to Englishmen at home.

Through the efforts of the London Company (or Virginia Company of London, its full name), the first enduring English colony was about to be planted in America. The merchants, taking the East India Company as their model, intended at the outset to found not an agricultural settlement but a trading post. To it they expected to send English manufactures for barter with the Indians, and from it they hoped to bring back American commodities procured in exchange or produced by the labor of their own employees.

JAMESTOWN AND VIRGINIA

The London Company's first expedition of three small ships (the *Godspeed*, the *Discovery*, and the *Sarah Constant*), with about 100 men, the survivors among 144 who had embarked from England, sailed into Chesapeake Bay and up the James River in the spring of 1607. The men had instructions from the company to avoid the mistakes of Roanoke and pick an easily defended site well inland and on high ground. They disembarked and began to build a palisaded town—which, like the river, they named for their King—at a point that seemed to meet most of the requirements. But the place

The First Ships at Jamestown
The Godspeed, *the* Discovery, *and the* Sarah Constant *prepare to anchor in the James River, 1607. These double-decked, three-masted ships were similar in size and shape to the* Mayflower *and other English merchantmen of the time. They were less than one hundred feet long and provided extremely close quarters for passengers, crew, equipment, and cargo. From a pencil study for a painting in the Virginia State Capitol, Richmond. (The Mariners Museum, Newport News, Va.)*

Suffering at Jamestown [1607–1608]

An expedition under Captain Christopher Newport began the Jamestown settlement in May 1607. In June, Captain Newport sailed for England, leaving behind 104 settlers. In September only 46 of these were still living. One of the survivors, George Percy, wrote an account of the terrible time at Jamestown:

There were never Englishmen left in a foreign country in such misery as we were in this new discovered Virginia. We watched every three nights, lying on the bare cold ground, what weather soever came; and warded all the next day; which brought our men to be most feeble wretches. Our food was but a small can of barley, sodden in water, to five men a day. Our drink, cold water taken out of the river; which was at flood very salt; at low tide full of slime and filth, which was the destruction of many of our men. Thus we lived for the space of five months [from August 1607 to January 1608] in this miserable distress, not having five able men to man our bulwarks upon any occasion. If it had not pleased God to put a terror in the savages' hearts we had all perished by those wild and cruel pagans, being in that weak estate as we were; our men night and day groaning in every corner of the fort most pitiful to hear. . . .
It pleased God after a while to send those people which were our mortal enemies, to relieve us with victuals, as bread, corn, fish, and flesh in great plenty, which was the setting up of our feeble men; otherwise we had all perished.

---

was low and swampy, it was surrounded by thick woods which were hard to clear for cultivation, and it was soon threatened by hostile Indians of a confederation led by the imperial chief Powhatan.

The colonists, too many of whom were adventurous gentlemen and too few of whom were willing laborers, ran into serious difficulties from the moment they landed. They faced an overwhelming task in trying to sustain themselves, and the promoters in London complicated the task by demanding a quick return on their investment. When the men in Jamestown ought to have been growing food, they were required to hunt for gold and to pile up lumber, tar, pitch, and iron ore for export. By January 1608, when ships appeared with additional men and supplies, all but thirty-eight of the first arrivals were dead.

Jamestown, already facing extinction, was carried through the crisis mainly by the efforts of twenty-seven-year-old Captain John Smith, hero of his own narratives of hairbreadth escapes from both Turks and Indians but a sensible and capable man nevertheless. Leadership in the colony had been divided among the several members of a council who quarreled continually until Smith, as council president, as-

serted his will. He imposed work and order on the community. During the next winter, fewer than a dozen (in a population of about 200) succumbed. By the summer of 1609, when Smith was deposed from the council and returned to England for the treatment of a serious powder burn, the colony was showing promise of survival, though in fact its worst trials were yet to come.

Already the promoters in London were making a strenuous effort to build up the Virginia colony. To raise money and men, they sold company stock to "adventurers" remaining at home, gave shares to "planters" willing to migrate at their own expense, and provided passage for poor men agreeing to serve the company for seven years. Under a new communal plan, the company would hold all land and carry on all trade for a seven-year period. The settlers would contribute their labor to the common enterprise and draw upon a company storehouse for their subsistence. At the end of the period the profits would be divided among the stockholders. The London merchants obtained a new charter (1609), which increased their power over the colony and enlarged its area (to a width of 400 miles north and south and a length extending all the way "from sea to sea, west and northwest"). In the spring of 1609 the company sent off to Virginia a "great fleet" of nine vessels with about 600 men, women, and children aboard.

Disaster followed. One of the Virginia-bound ships sank in a hurricane, and another ran aground on the island of Bermuda. Many of those who reached Jamestown, still weak from their long and stormy voyage, succumbed to fevers before winter came. That winter of 1609–1610 turned into a "starving time" worse than anything before. While Indians killed off the livestock in the woods and kept the settlers within the palisade, these unfortunates were reduced to eating "dogs, cats, rats, snakes, toadstools, horsehides," and even the "corpses of dead men," as one survivor recalled. When the migrants who had been stranded on Bermuda arrived at Jamestown the following May, they found about 60 scarcely human wretches still alive (there had been nearly 500 people there the previous summer). No one could see much point in staying, and soon all were on their way downriver, leaving the town to its decay.

Yet the colony was to begin again. The refugees met a relief ship coming up the river and were persuaded to go back to Jamestown. This ship was part of a fleet bringing supplies and the colony's first governor, Lord De La Warr. He reestablished the settlement and imposed strict discipline, then went home on account of illness, while new relief expeditions with hundreds of colonists began to arrive. De La Warr's successors Thomas Dale and Thomas Gates continued his harsh rule, sentencing offenders to be flogged, hanged, or broken on the wheel. Under Dale and Gates the colony spread, with new settlements lining the river above and below Jamestown. The communal system of labor was not functioning very well, for despite the governors' strictness the lazy often evaded work, "presuming that howsoever the harvest prospered, the general store must maintain them." Before the seven years of the system were up, Dale changed it to allow the private ownership and cultivation of land, in return for part-time work for the company and contributions of grain to its storehouse. Meanwhile the cultivators were discovering, in tobacco, a saleable crop.

Tobacco had come into use in Europe soon after Columbus' first return from the West Indies, where he had seen the Cuban natives smoking small cigars *(tabacos)*, which they inserted in the nostril. In England Sir Walter Raleigh popularized the smoking habit, and the demand for tobacco soared despite objections on both hygienic and economic grounds. Some critics denounced it as a poisonous weed, the cause of many diseases. King James I himself led the attack with *A Counterblaste to Tobacco* (1604), in which he urged his people not to imitate "the barbarous and beastly manners of the wild, godless, and slavish Indians, especially in so vile and stinking a custom." Other critics were concerned because England's tobacco imports came from the Spanish colonies and resulted in the loss of English gold. In 1612 the Jamestown planter John Rolfe began to experiment with the West Indian plant. It grew well in Virginia soil and, though rated less desirable than the Spanish-grown, found ready buyers in England. Tobacco cultivation quickly spread up and down the James.

When the seven-year communal period was up (1616), the company had no profits to divide, but only land and debts. Still, the promoters were rather optimistic because of their success with tobacco. In 1618 they launched a last great campaign to attract settlers and make the colony profitable. They offered a "headright" of fifty acres to anyone who paid his own or someone else's passage to Virginia, and another fifty for each additional migrant whose way he paid. Thus a wealthy man could send or take servants to work for him and receive, in turn, a sizable plantation. The company expected to add to its income by charging the headright landholder a small quitrent (one shilling a year for every fifty acres). Old investors and settlers were given grants of one hundred acres apiece. To make life in the colony more attractive, the company promised the colonists the rights of Englishmen (as provided in the original charter of 1606), an end to the strict and arbitrary rule, and even a share in self-government. To diversify the colonial economy, the company undertook to transport ironworkers and other skilled craftsmen to Virginia.

On July 30, 1619, in the Jamestown church, delegates from the various communities met as the House of Burgesses to consider, along with the governor and his council, the enactment of laws for the colony. This was a bright example for the future – the first meeting of an elected legislature, a representative assembly, within what was to become the United States. A month later there occurred in Virginia another event with a far less happy outcome. As John Rolfe recorded, "about the latter end of August" a Dutch ship brought in "20 and odd Negroes." These black persons were bought, it seems, not as slaves but as servants to be held for a term of years and then freed, like the white servants with whom the planters already were familiar. In any case, a start had been made toward the enslavement of Africans within what was to be the American republic.

For several years the Indians had given the Virginia colonists little trouble. A kind of truce had resulted from the capture of the great chief Powhatan's daughter Pocahontas and her marriage (1614) to John Rolfe. Going with her husband on a visit to England, Pocahontas as a Christian convert and a gracious lady stirred up interest in projects to civilize the Indians. She died while abroad. Then Powhatan also died, and his brother Opechancanough replaced him as head of the native confederacy. Under Opechancanough the Indians pretended to be friendly while he laid plans to eliminate the English intruders. On a March morning in 1622 the tribesmen called on the white settlements as if to offer goods for sale, then suddenly turned to killing and were not stopped until 347 whites of both sexes and all ages, including Rolfe, lay dead or dying. The surviving Englishmen struck back with merciless revenge and gave up all thought of civilizing the aborigines.

The massacre came as a final blow to the London Company, which soon faced bankruptcy. In 1624 James I revoked the company's charter and took control of the colony. By that time the white population of Virginia was less than 1,300; thousands more had come over, but most of these had died and many had gone back to England. Still, the remaining colonists had a cash crop, a representative government (which was to continue), and a hope for future growth and prosperity. Though a failure as a profit-making enterprise, Virginia was at last succeeding as a colonizing venture.

PLYMOUTH PLANTATION

While the London Company was starting the colonization of Jamestown, the Plymouth Company attempted to found a colony far to the north, at the mouth of the Kennebec River (on the coast of what is now Maine), but in a year the surviving colonists returned to England. The Plymouth Company made no further effort to colonize. The most it did was to send Captain John Smith, after his return from Jamestown, to look over its territory. He drew a map of the area, wrote an enthusiastic pamphlet about it, and named it "New England." Eventually the Plymouth merchants reorganized as the Council for New England and, with a new, sea-to-sea land grant from the King, proceeded to deal in real estate on a tremendous scale.

The first enduring settlement in New England—the second in English America—resulted from the discontent of a congregation of Puritan Separatists. From time to time Separatists had been imprisoned and even executed for persisting in their defiance of the government and the Church of England. A band of them in the hamlet of Scrooby looked to Holland as a country where they might worship as they pleased, though it was against the law to leave the realm without the King's consent. Slipping away a few at a time, members of the Scrooby congregation crossed the English Channel and began their lives anew in Holland. Here they were allowed to meet and hold their services without interference. But, as aliens, they were not allowed to join the Dutch guilds of craftsmen, and so they had to work long and hard at unskilled and poorly paid jobs. They were further troubled as their children began to speak Dutch, marry into Dutch families, and lose their Englishness. Some of the Puritans decided to move again, this time across the Atlantic, where they might find opportunity for happier living and also for spreading "the gospel of the Kingdom of Christ in those remote parts of the world."

Leaders of this group got permission from the London Company to settle as an independent community with land of its own in Virginia. They tried, and failed, to get from James I a guarantee of religious freedom, but they were assured that he would "not molest them, provided they carried themselves peaceably." This was a historic concession on the part of the King, for it opened English America to settlement by dissenting Protestants. The next step was to arrange financing for the voyage. Several English merchants agreed to advance the necessary funds, on the condition that a

The Mayflower Compact [1620]

In the name of God, Amen. We, whose names are underwritten, the Loyal Subjects of our dread Sovereign Lord King James, by the Grace of God, of Great Britain, France, and Ireland, King, Defender of the Faith, &c. Having undertaken for the Glory of God, and Advancement of the Christian Faith, and the Honour of our King and Country, a Voyage to plant the first colony in the northern Parts of Virginia; Do by these presents, solemnly and mutually in the Presence of God and one another, covenant and combine ourselves together into a civil Body Politick, for our better Ordering and Preservation, and Furtherance of the Ends aforesaid; And by Virtue hereof do enact, constitute, and frame, such just and equal Laws, Ordinances, Acts, Constitutions, and Offices, from time to time, as shall be thought most meet and convenient for the general Good of the Colony; unto which we promise all due Submission and Obedience.

---

communal plan like that of Jamestown be put into effect, with the merchants to share the profits at the end of seven years.

The migrating Puritans "knew they were pilgrims" when they left Holland, their leader and historian William Bradford later wrote. The sailing from Plymouth was delayed, and it was not until September that the *Mayflower,* with thirty-five "saints" (Puritan Separatists) and sixty-seven "strangers" aboard, finally put out to sea. Their destination was probably the mouth of the Hudson River, in the northeast corner of the London Company's Virginia grant, but when they sighted Cape Cod in November, it was too late in the year to go on. After reconnoitering, they chose a site in an area that John Smith had labeled "Plymouth" on his map. Since this lay outside the London Company's territory, they would be without a government once ashore, and some of the "strangers" began to show a lawless spirit. One of the "saints" therefore drew up an agreement, which forty-one of the passengers signed. This Mayflower Compact was like the church covenant by which the Separatists formed congregations, except that it set up a civil government, and it professed allegiance to the King. Then, December 21, 1620, the Pilgrims landed at Plymouth Rock.

Here they settled on cleared land that had been an Indian village until, several years earlier, an epidemic swept the place. During the first winter half of the colonists perished from scurvy and exposure, but the rest managed to put the colony on its feet. Among the neighboring Indians, whose military power had been weakened by the recent plague, the Pilgrims discovered friends—Squanto, Samoset, Massasoit—who showed them how to obtain seafood and cultivate corn. After the first harvest the settlers invited the Indians to join them in an October festival, the original Thanksgiving. They could not aspire to rich farms on the sandy and marshy soil, but they soon developed a profitable trade in fish and furs. From time to time new colonists arrived from England, and in a decade the population reached the modest total of 300.

The people of "Plymouth Plantation" elected their own governor, and they chose the great-hearted William Bradford again and again. As early as 1621 he cleared their land title with a patent from the Council for New England, but he never succeeded in his efforts to secure a royal charter giving them indisputable rights of government. Terminating the communal labor plan ahead of schedule, the governor distributed land among the families, thus making "all hands very industrious." He and a group of fellow "undertakers" assumed the colony's debt to its financiers in England and, with earnings from the fur trade, finally paid it off, even though the financiers had not lived up to their agreement to keep on sending supplies.

The Pilgrims remained poor; as late as the 1640s they had only one plow among them. Yet they clung to the belief that God had put them in the New World for a reason. Governor Bradford wrote in retrospect: "As one small candle may light a thousand, so the light here kindled hath shone to many, yea in some sort to our whole nation."

Selected Readings

The American Indians
W. T. Hagan, *American Indians* (1961); Kenneth MacGowan, *Early Man in the New World** (1950); Clark Wissler, *Indians of the United States: Four Centuries of Their History and Culture* (1940); Paul Radin, *The Story of the American Indian* (1927); Francisco Guerra, *The Pre-Columbian Mind* (1971); W. R. Jacobs, *Dispossessing the American Indian: Indians and Whites on the Colonial Frontier* (1972).

The European Background
W. H. McNeill, *The Rise of the West* (1963); Wallace Notestein, *The English People on the Eve of Colonization, 1603–1630** (1954); Alan Simpson, *Puritanism in Old and New England* (1955); K. E. Knorr, *British Colonial Theories, 1570–1850* (1944); Maurice Powicke, *The Reformation in England** (1941); R. H. Tawney, *Religion and the Rise of Capitalism** (1926); J. U. Nef, *Industry and Government in France and England, 1540–1640* (1940); Lawrence Stone, *The Crisis of Aristocracy* (1965).

Discovery and Exploration
C. E. Nowell, *The Great Discoveries and the First Colonial Empires** (1954); J. B. Brebner, *The Explorers of North America, 1492–1806** (1933); Gwyn Jones, *The Norse Atlantic Saga* (1964); R. A. Skelton, T. E. Marston, and G. D. Painter, *The Vinland Map and the Tartar Relation* (1965); S. E. Morison, *Admiral of the Ocean Sea* (2 vols., 1942), a classic biography of Columbus; Paul Horgan, *Conquistadors in North American History* (1963); Charles Gibson, *Spain in America* (1966); W. L. Cook, *Flood Tide of Empire: Spain and the Pacific Northwest, 1543–1819* (1973).

Early English Colonizing Efforts
A. L. Rowse, *Sir Walter Raleigh* (1962); D. B. Quinn, *The Roanoke Voyages, 1584–1590* (2 vols., 1955).

Jamestown
G. F. Willison, *Behold Virginia* (1951); Bradford Smith, *Captain John Smith: His Life and Legend* (1953); Philip L. Barbour, *The Three Worlds of Captain John Smith* (1964).

Plymouth
William Bradford, *Of Plymouth Plantation,* ed. by S. E. Morison (1952); George Langdon, *Pilgrim Colony: A History of New Plymouth, 1620–1691* (1966); G. F. Willison, *Saints and Strangers** (1945).

*Titles available in paperback.

Transplanted Englishmen

Two

The colonists who came to English America in the seventeenth century were transplanted Englishmen. They had no desire to lose their Englishness. Rather, they hoped to build in the New World a better England, one that would be free from the imperfections of their native land, one that would give them greater opportunities for personal happiness. They disagreed among themselves as to what was good and what was bad at home. Depending on their religion and their station in life, they saw their fortunes and prospects in England rising or falling as one side or the other gained the upper hand in a long-continuing struggle between King and Parliament.

King James I died in 1625, before actually coming to blows with Parliament, but his son Charles I was more extreme in his autocratic tendencies and in his Roman Catholic sympathies. From 1629 to 1640, Charles I ruled as an absolute monarch, refusing to call Parliament into session, imposing high-church forms upon the people, and imprisoning Puritan leaders. Finally he called Parliament because he needed money and hoped the members would vote taxes for him. This "Long Parliament" remained in session almost twenty years.

During that time, civil war broke out between the King's followers, the Cavaliers, and the Parliament forces, the Roundheads, who were largely Puritans. After Charles I had been defeated and beheaded, the stern Roundhead leader Oliver Cromwell governed England as "Protector" from 1649 until his death in 1658. There was no strong man to succeed him, and after his son had been Protector for less than a year, the Protectorate came to an end.

In 1660 the Stuart dynasty was restored. Parliament accepted Charles II as King on the condition that he govern in partnership with its members and not in the high-handed way of his father and grandfather. The handsome and debonair Charles II, tired of his travels in exile, desired above all to stay in England and keep

Earliest Known View of Manhattan
At what is now the Battery, in New York City, on the southern tip of Manhattan Island, the Dutch built a fort, a large windmill, and a number of houses during the 1620s, as shown in this contemporary Dutch drawing. (Stokes Collection, New York Public Library)

his throne. His less clever brother James II, who succeeded him in 1685, appointed Catholics to high office and attempted to dictate to Parliament and the courts. He quickly lost popular support.

James II fled to France, without resisting, when Parliament offered the throne to his Protestant daughter Mary and her husband William of Orange, ruler of the Netherlands and Protestant champion of Europe. William and Mary became joint sovereigns of England in 1688. By this "Glorious Revolution" the long struggle between King and Parliament was finally settled in Parliament's favor.

These events of seventeenth-century England form an essential part of the background of colonization during the period when most of her American colonies were founded.

New England

New England from the 1620s to the 1670s took its character as a colony in part from the Pilgrims who settled at Plymouth, but in a much larger measure from the Puritans who later landed at nearby Massachusetts Bay and then spread out from there. These Puritans would have liked to remake the institutions of England, but they faced too much opposition there. In the wilderness of America they saw an opportunity to create society anew.

MASSACHUSETTS BAY

Englishmen were first attracted to Massachusetts Bay by its fisheries, and as early as 1623 a group of merchants tried to set up a permanent fishing and trading post on Cape Ann. Some of the settlers later moved to Salem. In 1628 another group of merchants—Puritans—obtained from the Council for New England a grant of land lying between the Merrimac and Charles rivers and extending from sea to sea. These wealthy Puritans bought the equipment of the defunct fishing and trading business and sent to Salem a ship with supplies and forty passengers to lay the groundwork for a large settlement. In 1629 the new enterprisers organized the Massachusetts Bay Company, secured a royal charter confirming their land grant and giving the company the right to govern its colony, and sent out nearly 400 additional settlers.

Some members of the company, alarmed by the high-church and anti-Parliament atti-

The Tenth Muse [1650] The first woman poet in America was Anne Bradstreet, who had come to Massachusetts Bay in 1630, and whose husband served for a time as the colony's governor. Mrs. Bradstreet wrote more than seven thousand lines of verse. Much of it is didactic and dull (though no more so than the poetry of her male contemporaries). The amazing thing is that she managed to write at all, considering the hardships of colonial life, the eight children she had to care for, and the prevailing view that a woman ought to confine herself to household duties. She became famous as "The Tenth Muse" after her first collection of poems, under that title, was published in London (1650). Nevertheless, she felt the antifeminist prejudice of the time as she indicated in the following lines:

I am obnoxious to each carping tongue
Who says my hand a needle better fits,
A poet's pen all scorn I should thus wrong,
For such despite they cast on female wits:
If what I do prove well, it won't advance,
They'll say it's stol'n, or else it was by chance.

tudes of the new King, Charles I, were beginning to look upon the colony less as a business venture and more as a Puritan refuge. Some were eager to migrate themselves if they could do so and still control the company. They arranged to buy the stock of those who preferred to stay at home. Then, in 1630, they sailed under the lead of the company's governor, John Winthrop, a gentleman of means, with a university education, a deep but narrow piety, a cool and calculating way, and a remarkably forceful and stubborn character. The expedition, with seventeen ships and 1,000 people, was the largest of its kind in the seventeenth century. These colonists founded a number of new towns, among them Boston, which was to be both the company's headquarters and the colony's capital.

The Massachusetts Bay Company soon was transformed into the Massachusetts colonial government. Governor Winthrop brought with him the company charter. According to its terms, the "freemen" (the stockholders) were to meet as a General Court to choose officers and adopt rules for the corporation. After their arrival in America the freemen proceeded to elect officials and pass laws for the colony. At their first meeting the freemen, eight of them, voted to concentrate power in their own and the governor's hands. At their next meeting, in 1631, they increased the number of freemen (the word now meaning voters or citizens, not necessarily stockholders) by more than a hundred, so as to include about half of the family heads in the colony at that time. Governor Winthrop continued to dominate colonial politics, but in 1634 he agreed to an arrangement by which the freemen would elect from year to year the governor, the deputy governor, the council of governor's assistants, and two "deputies" from each town—all of whom would constitute the General Court. In 1644 this became a bicameral legislature, with a lower House of Deputies and an upper chamber consisting of the governor and his council.

To be a freeman, to take any part in the colonial government, a man had to be a member of the Puritan Church. This was not easy. The Puritans in England (and the Pilgrims in Plymouth) had required for church membership only that a person profess the faith, sign the covenant, and live an upright life. The Puritans in Massachusetts, however, soon began to limit membership to the "visible saints," that is, to those who could demonstrate that they had experienced God's saving grace and hence belonged to the elect, the group whom He had chosen for eventual salvation. Churches were formed by persons covenanting with one another and with God, and these members, once in, decided who else could enter the fold. Whether admitted to membership or not, everyone in the community was a part of the congregation and was required by law to attend religious services.

Unlike the Separatist founders of Plymouth, the Puritan founders of Massachusetts had come with no intention of breaking away from the Church of England. They only wished, at first, to rescue the Church from what they saw as the evil influence of Rome. Nevertheless, they soon were acting as if they were religiously independent. As the prominent preacher John Cotton said, the Church in every town had "complete liberty to stand alone." Each congregation chose its own minister and regulated its own affairs. Thus there arose in Massachusetts—as well as in Plymouth—what came to be known as the Congregational Church.

These Massachusetts Puritans were not necessarily grim, joyless, or "puritanical," despite their belief in predestination. They enjoyed the ordinary pleasures of life, and they appreciated beauty in plain and simple forms. They strove to lead a useful, conscientious life of thrift and hard work. They honored material success, for if a person did well it was possible evidence that God favored him as one of the elect. If his ways were upright, this was another possible indication of divine grace. Many were hopeful that they were among the chosen, but no one could be entirely sure. So people searched their hearts, and those of their neighbors so far as possible, to look for signs of salvation.

"We here enjoy God and Jesus Christ," Winthrop wrote to his wife soon after his arrival; "is this not enough?" He and the other Massachusetts founders saw themselves as starting a holy commonwealth, a model for the corrupt world to see. The problem was to keep it holy. In this effort the preachers and the politicians worked together. The ministers did not run the government, but they supported it, and they exerted great influence upon the church members who alone could vote or hold office in it. The government in turn protected the ministers, taxed the people (members and nonmembers alike) to support the Church, and enforced the law requiring attendance at services. In this Puritan oligarchy the dissidents had no more freedom of worship than the Puritans themselves had had in England.

The Lord seemed to smile upon the Massachusetts enterprise. After the first winter (1629–1630), when nearly 200 died and many others decided to leave, the colony grew and prospered. The nearby Pilgrims helped with food and advice. Incoming settlers, many of them well-to-do, brought needed tools and other goods, which they exchanged for the cattle, corn, and other produce of the established colonists. During the 1630s, while Charles I ruled England without a Parliament, Puritans escaping from his tyranny migrated in such numbers that by 1643 the colony had a population of about 15,000. Then, during the war against King and Cavaliers, quite a few of the colonists went back to aid the Puritan cause at home, and for a while those returning to England outnumbered those newly arriving in Massachusetts.

EXODUS FROM THE BAY COLONY

Meanwhile, an outpouring from Massachusetts Bay to various parts of New England (and to other places in English America) had begun. This exodus was motivated generally by one or both of two considerations: the unproductiveness of the stony soil around Boston, and the oppressiveness of the Massachusetts government. Not all the incoming settlers were saints, and as the population increased, the proportion of those who could vote or hold office declined. To the Puritan authorities, opposition to their Church seemed like a threat to the government, like both heresy and treason. Independent thinkers—and Puritanism somehow bred them—had little choice but to give in or get out. Such thinkers were responsible for new settlements north and south, in New Hampshire and Rhode Island. Families seeking richer lands as well as greater religious and political independence began new settlements in the west, in Connecticut.

The Connecticut Valley, one hundred miles beyond the settled frontier, contained fertile meadows that invited pioneering despite the presence of warlike Indians and the claims of the already fortified Dutch. By the early 1630s a few Englishmen were already living there. Well up the river was a post that Pilgrims going out from Plymouth had founded. Near the river's mouth was the post of Saybrook, started by a group of English Puritans who had a large though vague land grant from the Council for New England.

The Connecticut Valley appealed to Thomas Hooker, a minister of Newtown (Cambridge), who questioned the fairness of government by the General Court, arguing that "a general council, chosen by all," would be "most suitable to rule and most safe for the relief of the whole people." When, in 1634, Newtown petitioned the General Court for permission to occupy the Connecticut Valley before it was "possessed by others," Governor Winthrop and his associates turned down the request. In 1635 a number of families from other Massachusetts towns moved west with the General Court's approval, on the understanding that they would "continue still under this government." The next year Hooker led his congregation through the wilds and established the town of Hartford.

Disregarding the claims of the Dutch, the English grantees, and the Massachusetts General Court, the people of Hartford and two other newly founded upriver towns, Windsor

---

Colonies That Grew Out of Massachusetts Bay

The New England Confederation [1643]

The said United Colonies [Massachusetts, Plymouth, Connecticut, and New Haven] for themselves and their posterities do jointly and severally hereby enter into a firm and perpetual league of friendship and amity for offence and defence, mutual advice and succor upon all just occasions both for preserving and propagating the truth and liberties of the Gospel and for their own mutual safety and welfare.

The United Colonies further agreed:
1. To provide men and provisions and to share in all costs in proportion to their abilities.
2. To send immediate aid to any of their confederates that might be invaded or in danger.
3. To appoint two commissioners apiece for managing the affairs of the confederation.
4. To begin no war, and to involve the confederation in no war, without the consent of at least six of the eight commissioners.

---

and Wethersfield, decided to set up a colonial government of their own. In 1639 they adopted a kind of constitution known as the Fundamental Orders of Connecticut. This provided for a government similar to that of Massachusetts Bay, but gave a larger proportion of the people the right to vote and hold office.

A separate colony, the project of a Puritan minister and a wealthy merchant from England, grew up around New Haven on the Connecticut coast. The Fundamental Articles of New Haven (1639) set up a Bible-based government even stricter than that of Massachusetts Bay. Eventually the governor of Connecticut obtained a royal charter (1662) that not only authorized his colony but also extended its jurisdiction over the New Haven settlements.

Rhode Island had its origin in the religious dissent of Roger Williams, a likeable but troublesome young minister of Massachusetts Bay. Even John Winthrop, who considered him a heretic, called Williams a "sweet and amiable" man, and William Bradford described him thus: "A man godly and zealous, having many precious parts, but very unsettled in judgement." Williams was an extreme Separatist who at first advocated not religious freedom but rather a church made even more pure and strict. Making friends with the neighboring Indians, he concluded that the land belonged to them and not to the King or to the Massachusetts Bay Company. The colonial government, considering Williams a dangerous man, decided to deport him, but he escaped. He took ref-

úge with Narragansett tribesmen during a bitter winter, then bought a tract of land from them and in 1636, with a few of his friends, created the town of Providence on it.

By that time another menace to the established order had appeared in Massachusetts Bay. Anne Hutchinson, the charming and strongminded wife of a substantial Bostonian, attracted many more followers than Williams with her heretical doctrine that the Holy Spirit dwelled within and guided every true believer. If this were so, the Bible would have no more authority than anyone's personal revelation, and both the church and the government would be exposed to anarchy, or so it seemed to Governor Winthrop and his associates. Mrs. Hutchinson's followers were numerous and influential enough to prevent Winthrop's re-election as governor in 1636, but the next year he got back into office and set the orthodox ministers to proving that she was a heretic. In 1638, after a trial at which Winthrop himself presided, she was convicted of sedition and banished as "a woman not fit for our society." With her family and some of her followers she moved to a point on Narragansett Bay not far from Providence.

In time other communities of dissidents arose in that vicinity. They quarreled with one another and with Roger Williams, who, having paid the Indians for the land, looked upon himself as its proprietor. As he matured he modified some of his views on religion. He began to advocate complete freedom of worship and absolute separation of church and state. Eventually he turned into a "seeker," one who respected but doubted all religions while he sought the true one. Rhode Island reflected his changing ideas. In 1644 he got from Parliament a charter authorizing a government for the combined settlements. The government, though based on the Massachusetts pattern, did not restrict the vote to church members nor did it tax the people for church support. A royal charter of 1663 confirmed the existing arrangement and added a guarantee of "liberty in religious concernments."

New Hampshire and Maine had become the separate possessions of two proprietors, Captain John Mason and Sir Ferdinando Gorges. In 1629 they divided their grant from the Council for New England along the Piscataqua River. Despite lavish promotional efforts, especially on the part of Gorges, few settlers were drawn to these northern regions until the religious disruption of Massachusetts Bay. In 1639 John Wheelwright, a disciple of Anne Hutchinson, led some of his fellow heretics to Exeter, in New Hampshire. Thereafter a number of towns in that province and in Maine were peopled by orthodox and unorthodox Puritans from Massachusetts or by new colonists from abroad. The Massachusetts Bay Company extended its authority over the whole territory in the north but ultimately lost its cases against the heirs of both Mason and Gorges in the highest courts of England. New Hampshire was then set up as a separate colony in 1679. The Gorges family having sold their rights to it, Maine remained a part of Massachusetts until admitted to the Union as a state in 1820.

FRONTIER DEFENSE

As New England spread, the settlers ran into trouble with the Indians. With a few exceptions like Roger Williams and John Eliot, a saintly missionary who translated the Bible into an Indian language, the Puritans viewed the red men as "pernicious creatures" who deserved extermination unless they would adopt the white man's ways. In 1637 the exasperated Pequots went on the warpath in the Connecticut Valley. The Connecticut frontiersmen marched against a palisaded Pequot stronghold and set it afire. About 400 Indians were burned to death or killed when trying to escape, and most of the survivors were hunted down, captured, and sold as slaves. The Pequot tribe was almost wiped out.

The New England colonies faced danger not only from the Indians but also from the Dutch and the French, who claimed the territory on which some of the outlying settlements were made. The colonies could not expect help from England at the time when the mother country was distracted by the civil war between Cavaliers and Roundheads. To provide frontier protection, to adjust boundary disputes among themselves, and to further their mutual interests in other ways, four of the colonies joined to form "The Confederation of the United Colonies of New England" (1643). These four were Massachusetts, Plymouth, Connecticut, and New Haven. The other settlements—those of Rhode Island, New Hampshire, and Maine—were excluded, since Massachusetts aspired to annex them and objected to recognizing them as equals.

By 1675, when King Philip's War began, the New England Confederation had deteriorated so much that it could no longer be relied upon for organizing frontier defense. King Philip and the Wampanoags, with their Indian allies, destroyed or depopulated twenty towns and caused the deaths of a sixteenth of the white male population in three years of gloom and terror for New England. The war did not end until Massachusetts had called upon the aid of "praying" Indians, thousands of whom John Eliot and other missionaries had converted and who had settled down in or near the white man's towns. One of these Indians shot and killed King Philip. Other leaders were executed after their surrender, and many warriors again were sold into slavery (in the West Indies), but danger still remained. The French, who had given little aid to King Philip's hosts, were later to back the Indians in revengeful attacks upon the New England frontier.

CHANGING WAYS

In New England the early settlers almost always took up land in groups. A congregation arriving from England received from the General Court the grant of a town (township), an area of twenty-five square miles or so. Its distribution was left to the leaders of the new settlement. They laid out a village, in which they set aside a "common" as pasture and timberland, chose a site for a meeting house (church) and for a fort, and assigned each family a strip of land as a home lot on either side of the one village street. They also divided up the outlying fields in the town, the size of a field and the desirability of its location depending on the family's numbers, wealth, and social standing. Wherever he went to work his fields, the typical seventeenth-century New Englander lived not in a lonely farmhouse but in a village with neighbors close by, and he maintained a strong sense of community.

Once established, the town was left to go pretty much its own way, with little interference from the colonial government except in cases where the townspeople could not agree among themselves. They held a yearly "town meeting" in the meeting house to decide important local questions and to choose a group of "selectmen" who governed the town until the next general gathering. The town meeting itself decided who could participate in its sessions and who was eligible for election to a town office. As a rule it qualified all adult males, even in Massachusetts, instead of limiting the local suffrage to church members. The town (not the county) was the basic unit of local government.

One thing the Massachusetts government attempted to require of the towns was provision for education. An early statute called upon parents to see to their children's "ability to read and understand the principles of religion and the capital laws of the country." A law of 1647 — designed to circumvent "that old deluder Satan" — required each town of fifty householders to hire a schoolmaster to teach reading and writing, and each town of one hundred householders to set up a Latin grammar school (high school). Connecticut adopted somewhat similar legislation. The laws could not always be enforced, especially in the frontier settlements, which often preferred paying a fine to undergoing the expense of maintaining schools.

The villagers were fairly self-sufficient, producing most of what they consumed. They needed crops, however, that they could sell or exchange for goods they could not themselves produce. They experimented unsuccessfully with hemp, wine grapes, and sassafras (then in demand abroad as a supposed cure for syphilis). Some trapped or traded for furs, and others

set up sawmills, both furs and lumber being valuable items for export. The Massachusetts government helped to promote an iron furnace at Saugus, to lessen the need for imports by making possible the colonial manufacture of pots, kettles, plows, and guns. This experiment lasted only from 1652 to 1676.

Coastal towns meanwhile developed an overseas trade through fishing, shipping, shipbuilding, and related enterprises. For New England, the ocean proved more productive than the land. Locally built vessels soon were busy taking ship's timbers and naval stores to England, fish to Spain, and lumber products and African slaves to the West Indies; in return they brought back sugar and a variety of manufactured goods. Since money was scarce, imports were commonly bartered for domestic products. Massachusetts, alone among all the English colonies, minted a coin of its own, the "pine-tree shilling," but only for about three decades (1652–1684).

With the growth of commerce, the colonial shipowning merchants came to dominate the New England economy. Some of these merchants diversified their holdings, investing part of their profits in timberlands, sawmills, shipyards, rum distilleries, and properties of various kinds. The rich businessmen might be good Puritans — though many were not — and yet their way to wealth inevitably created tensions within Puritan society. Such men looked outward to the world of the Atlantic, and their activities brought in sophisticated, cosmopolitan attitudes as well as exotic commodities. These activities changed New England life, especially in the port towns. Here dwelled not only the merchants in their mansions but also the upstart blacksmiths, carpenters, and other artisans who demanded and got higher and higher pay for their indispensable skills. The ports were overrun, besides, with rowdy sailors and longshoremen and with the gaudy women who catered to them. Old and orthodox Puritans resented the changes taking place, and at the same time the rising merchants longed for further changes of a kind that would give them a greater voice in colonial government.

The Puritan oligarchy gradually lost some of its political power, even in Massachusetts, and the ministers lost some of their authority, while the merchants gained in influence. John Winthrop, the dominant figure of early Massachusetts and most of the time its governor, died

Day of Doom
[1662]

The earliest book-publishing centers in English America were Cambridge and Boston. From their presses came more than two hundred titles between 1640 and 1700. The very first of these was *The Whole Book of Psalms,* popularly known as the "Bay Psalm Book." Another best seller, published in 1662 and reprinted many times thereafter, was *The Day of Doom, Or a Poetical Description of the Great and Last Judgment,* written by Michael Wigglesworth, a Harvard graduate and Puritan divine. Two of its 224 dreary stanzas describe the eternal punishment of the damned as follows:

> *Whom having brought, as they are taught,*
>   *unto the brink of Hell,*
> *(That dismal place far from Christ's face*
>   *where Death and Darkness dwell;*
> *Where God's fierce ire kindleth the fire,*
>   *and vengeance feeds the flame*
> *With piles of Wood, and Brimstone Flood,*
>   *that none can quench the same,)*
>
> *With Iron bands they bind their hands*
>   *and cursed feet together,*
> *And cast them all, both great and small,*
>   *into that Lake for ever,*
> *Where day and night, without respite,*
>   *they wail, and cry, and howl*
> *For tort'ring pain, which they sustain*
>   *in Body and in Soul.*

---

in 1649. As he and others of the first generation of American Puritans passed away, the number of church members declined, for few of the second generation could show the saving grace that church membership required.

The Puritans faced a dilemma. If they continued to admit no one except "visible saints," the Church would go on shrinking, but if they opened the door to others, the Church would lose its purity. To meet this problem, the Puritans allowed the children of saints to be baptized as partial members even without proof of a conversion experience. But what about the unconverted children of these partial members? By the Half-Way Covenant, which a conference of ministers approved in 1662, such men and women of the third generation were given the right to be baptized, though not the right to partake of communion or vote in church affairs. As time passed, the difference between full and half membership was forgotten, and in most communities the Congregational Church came to include all who cared to join and could profess the faith. As the number of church members rose, so did the number of

men who could take part in colonial politics as voters and officeholders.

Orthodox Puritans continued to oppose the transformation that was coming over the erstwhile land of the saints. Sabbath after Sabbath the ministers preached sermons (as of course ministers still do) deploring the signs of waning piety. "Truly so it is," one minister lamented in 1674, "the very heart of New England is changed and exceedingly corrupted with the sins of the times." There was, he said, a growing spirit of profaneness, pride, worldliness, sensuality, gainsaying and rebellion, libertinism, carnality, formality, hypocrisy, "and a spiritual idolatry in the worship of God."

Yet Puritanism remained an important element in the life of New Englanders, and it was in some degree to affect the outlook of most Americans for many generations. It left its lasting mark not in the form of theological doctrines or religious practices but in the form of attitudes that were real though hard to define — a sense of duty, of hard work and of success as its reward, and of mission to make the world a better place.

The Chesapeake Country

The Massachusetts Bay Colony began as a planned society, and early New England continued to be characterized by a sense of collective interest and social purpose. The Chesapeake Bay colonies — Virginia and Maryland — developed in a somewhat different way. "The most noticeable feature of the Chesapeake settlements," the historian Wesley Frank Craven has written, "is the absence of a common purpose and goal except such as was dictated principally by the requirements of individual interest."

MARYLAND

One of the stockholders of the London Company, George Calvert, Lord Baltimore, after taking part in the promotion of Virginia, conceived the idea of undertaking a new colony on his own. Himself a convert to the Roman Catholic faith, Calvert had in mind primarily a gigantic speculation in real estate, and incidentally the establishment of a refuge for Roman Catholics, victims of political discrimination in England. After getting a Newfoundland grant from James I and spending a winter on it, he looked over Virginia and decided to relocate his colony in the warmer climate to the south of his previous location. From Charles I he obtained a patent to a wedge of Virginia's territory which lay north of the Potomac and east of Chesapeake Bay, and which the King now christened Maryland in honor of his Roman Catholic wife, the Frenchwoman Henrietta Maria. George Calvert died before the grant was made official, and it was then issued (1632) to his son Cecilius, the second Lord Baltimore.

The Maryland charter contained some curious provisions which revived in the colony a feudal concept long dead in the mother country. Calvert and his heirs were to hold their province as "true and absolute lords and proprietaries," acknowledging the suzerainty of the King by the annual payment of two Indian arrowheads and a fifth of all the gold and silver to be mined. The proprietor, exercising within Maryland a power comparable to that of the King in England, was to have the privilege of subinfeudating his land — that is, granting it in parcels to men who would become his vassals. But he was to make no laws incompatible with those of England, and none without the consent of the freemen or their representatives.

Since the London Company (which still claimed its land rights in Virginia) objected to the Calvert grant, Lord Baltimore remained at home to defend his interests at court. He appointed his brother Leonard Calvert governor and sent him with another brother to see to the settlement of the family's province. In March of 1643 the *Ark* and the *Dove*, bearing 200 or 300 passengers, most of them Protestants, entered the Potomac and turned into one of its eastern tributaries. On a high and dry bluff these first arrivals laid out the village of St. Mary's, while the neighboring Indians, already withdrawing to avoid native enemies, assisted by selling land and providing stocks of corn. The early Marylanders knew no massacres, no plagues, no starving time.

Spending a large part of the family fortune in the development of their American possessions, the Calverts had to attract many thousands of settlers if their venture was to pay. They encouraged the immigration of Protestants as well as Roman Catholics, and since relatively few of the latter were inclined to leave England, the Protestant settlers (mostly Anglicans) soon far outnumbered the Catholics.

The Calverts drew on the experience and example of Virginia. To the early arrivals they offered land on even more generous terms — one hundred acres for each man, another one hundred for his wife and for every servant he brought along, and fifty for each of his children. The landholders were expected to pay the same modest quitrent as those in Virginia (one shilling for every fifty acres). The Virginia governor welcomed the newcomers and offered them his aid, but not all the Virginians were so friendly. One of them, William Claiborne, made continual trouble for the Maryland proprietors by his claim to Kent Island, which lay within the Maryland boundaries. In Claiborne's absence Leonard Calvert invaded the island and took it by force (1637).

At the insistence of Maryland settlers, the proprietor agreed (1635) to the calling of a representative assembly — the House of Delegates, as it came to be known — which based its proceedings on the rules of Parliament. By the 1650s Maryland had a bicameral legislature, with the governor and his council constituting the upper house. The governor was appointed by the proprietor, Lord Baltimore. This was similar to the government that was developing in Virginia, except that there the governor was appointed by the King.

Politics in Maryland from the beginning were complicated by the hostility of the Protestants toward the Catholic minority and the Catholic proprietor. To appease the majority, he appointed a Protestant as governor in 1648. To further calm the colony, he sent over from England the draft of an "Act Concerning Religion," which assured freedom of worship to all who believed in Jesus Christ. Before passing this as part of the Maryland Toleration Act (1649), the legislature added a series of religious offenses with drastic penalties for them, including the death penalty for cursing God. The act did not end the political turbulence in Maryland.

TOBACCO AND SOCIETY

Tobacco growing quickly spread throughout the Chesapeake settlements — in Maryland as well as Virginia — and provided the basis for the society that grew up in the region. Accounting for tobacco's primacy were not only the soil and climate but also the long and irregular shoreline, with dozens of deep creeks and rivers emptying into the bay. To transport heavy hogsheads overland was difficult and damaging to the leaf, but for the man with a farm on one of the natural waterways it was easy enough to roll the hogsheads to his own landing, from which ocean-going ships could carry them to markets abroad. The early settlers therefore took up land along the bay and the navigable streams, and many acquired extensive tracts. Thus most of the people came to be widely scattered, living on isolated farms. Villages or towns were few.

Even if a man owned a thousand acres or more, he actually farmed only a small part of

---

Virginia Tobacco Land [1686]

In 1686 the Reverend John Clayton of Yorkshire, England, visited the Virginia tobacco country. Two years later he reported to the Royal Society of London (a society of Englishmen and colonials devoted to scientific inquiry):

And yet in truth 'tis only the barrenest parts that they have cultivated, by tilling and planting only the highlands, leaving the richer vales unstirred, because they understand not anything of draining. So that the richest meadow lands, which is one third of the country, is boggy, marsh, and swamp, whereof they make little advantage, but lose in them abundance of their cattle, especially at the first of the spring, when the cattle are weak, and venture too far after young grass. Whereas vast improvements might be made thereof, for the generality of Virginia is sandy land with a shallow soil, so that after they have cleared a fresh piece of ground out of the woods, it will not bear tobacco past two or three years, unless cowpenned [and thus manured]. . . . Therefore every three or four years they must be for clearing a new piece of ground out of the woods, which requires much labour and toil, it being so thick grown all over with massy timber. Thus their plantations run over vast tracts of ground, each ambitious of engrossing as much as they can, that they may be sure to have enough to plant, and for their stocks and herds of cattle to range and to feed in. Plantations of 1,000, 2,000 or 3,000 acres are common, whereby the country is thinly inhabited, the living solitary and unsociable, trading confused and dispersed, besides other inconveniences. Whereas they might improve 200 or 300 acres to more advantage, and would make the country much more healthy. For those that have 3,000 acres have scarce cleared 600 acres thereof, which is peculiarly termed the plantation, being surrounded with the 2,400 acres of wood, so that there can be no free or even motion of the air.

Tobacco Preparation: Eighteenth Century

When tobacco was harvested, the stalks were hung in a well-ventilated barn to cure. After several months, in damp weather when the leaves were pliable, they were stripped from the stalks, sorted, and tied into "hands," then packed tightly in hogsheads. These were stored in public warehouses until examined by official inspectors. Eventually the hogsheads were carried by boat or wagon or were rolled to the nearest ship landing. Ships from England ascended the rivers of the tobacco country to pick up cargoes. From William Tatham, An Historical and Practical Essay on the Culture and Commerce of Tobacco *(London, 1800).*

his land, because of the difficulty of clearing it. On his clearing he raised not only tobacco but also corn, fruit, vegetables, cattle, hogs, and other things for his own and his family's use, so that the farm was fairly self-sufficient. His life was hard. He lived in no elegant mansion but in a small and often crude house, and he worked in his fields alongside his boys and his servants or slaves — if he had any.

His servants might have come with him from England. If he brought them along and paid their way, he received not only a headright of land for each of them but also their services for a term of years, usually four or five. Or the servants might have come later, binding themselves to their master in return for their passage over. Some were sold into servitude against their will. From time to time, beginning as early as 1617, the English government dumped shiploads of convicts in America, though according to Captain John Smith "some did chuse to be hanged ere they would go thither, and were." The government also transported prisoners taken in battles with the Scots and with the Irish in the 1650s. Likewise it got rid of other groups deemed undesirable: orphans, vagrants, paupers, and those who were simply "lewd and dangerous." Still other involuntary immigrants were neither dangerous nor dependent but were victims of kidnaping, or "impressment."

The system of temporary servitude grew naturally out of existing practices in England, such as that of apprenticeship by which a youth bound himself to a master for seven years to learn a trade. Men and women binding themselves to a master in America were commonly known as "indentured" servants because of the papers recording the contract, papers which were cut or torn with an indented or indentured edge, so that the two copies, one going to the master and the other to the servant, would correspond. Upon completing his term the servant was entitled to certain benefits—clothing, tools, and occasionally land—in addition to his freedom and the privilege, if he could afford it, of acquiring servants of his own.

Relatively few of the indentured servants landed in New England, where the economy was not such as to create much of a demand for them. During the seventeenth century they flocked to Virginia and Maryland, where the laborious processes of cultivating tobacco required many hands.

Throughout this period, the number of black workers on the tobacco farms increased rather slowly. "Most of the Negroes came from the Spanish Indies or directly from Africa," the historian David Hawke explains, "and were of small use to a farmer with little time to spare in directing an untrained man who spoke a strange tongue." In Virginia there were fewer than 300 Negroes in 1640, and only about 2,000 in 1670, when the total population of the colony had reached 40,000. By that time blacks were being treated as permanent slaves and no longer as temporary servants. But the day of the great tobacco plantation, with its labor force consisting almost entirely of Negro slaves, still lay in the future.

As early as 1640 the price of tobacco had begun to fall because of overproduction and because of the poor quality of much of the product. In that year the Virginia government made an attempt at crop control, ordering the farmers of the colony to plant less. This directive was hard to enforce throughout Virginia, and it had no effect at all in Maryland, which refused to cooperate. While Virginians complained about the "trash" that Marylanders were exporting, the price continued on a fluctuating downward trend. To maintain their incomes, planters tried to grow more tobacco, not less. Those who could acquired additional land and labor and enlarged their fields. Thus the price decline contributed to the eventual development of great plantations.

In the Chesapeake region, with its scattered population, the English county was adapted as the basic unit of local government. In Virginia the House of Burgesses created eight counties in 1634. The governor and his council appointed the sheriffs, justices of the peace, and other county officials. In Maryland the proprietor originally intended to set up vast feudalistic estates, each with a baron who would be responsible for governing the settlers on his land. But a county system similar to that of Virginia grew up instead. Though Virginians and Marylanders did not elect their county officers, they could exert considerable influence in county affairs. Still, these people had a smaller role in local government than did contemporary New Englanders.

Though there was more religious diversity in Maryland than in Virginia, Anglicans predominated in both colonies, but in both of them Anglicanism soon ceased to be quite the same thing that it was in England. Virginia laws dating from 1643 directed all members to conform to the Church of England, ordered the expulsion of nonconformists, and required the payment of tithes to support the established church. The Bishop of London was supposed to watch over the far-flung American parishes, but he left the responsibility to the colonial governors, who most of the time were preoccupied with political affairs. Actual control gravitated to the parishes themselves. They worked out relatively democratic and independent church organizations of their own. Local vestries (governing boards of laymen) hired pastors on a yearly basis and provided salaries. These were paid in tobacco, and the amount remained the same while the price fluctuated. The living was uncertain, and to qualify as a pastor a candidate had to cross the ocean and be ordained by a bishop in England, there being no bishops in America. Fewer and fewer able and well-trained men were attracted to the ministry, and the numbers of idle and profligate "fox-hunting parsons" increased. Even the most conscientious parsons found it next to impossible to give adequate care to the souls of their parishioners, so far apart did the planters live and so extensive were the parish boundaries. Often the elaborate rituals of the Church had to be simplified or omitted altogether.

In Virginia, as in Massachusetts, laws were passed as early as the 1640s to encourage schooling. A Virginia statute ordered county officials to "take up" children whose parents were "disabled to maintain and educate them." In promoting schools, Massachusetts had the advantages of fairly compact settlement, a comparatively large number of university graduates among the early settlers, and a religion that strongly emphasized the ability to read the Bible. Education in the seventeenth-century tobacco colonies was left mainly to individual families, who, when they could afford to do so, imported servants as tutors or endowed "old field schools" on worn-out tobacco lands.

POLITICAL TURBULENCE

The political history of Virginia from the 1640s to the 1670s centered on the career of Sir William Berkeley, a strong-willed Oxford graduate who at the age of thirty-six arrived in 1642 with an appointment as governor from King Charles I.

In the beginning Governor Berkeley was popular. He helped to open up the interior by sending out explorers who crossed the Blue Ridge Mountains. He directed a force that put down the Indians in 1644 when old Chief Opechancanough led them in a bloody attack comparable to the massacre of twenty-two years earlier. Opechancanough was captured and, against Berkeley's orders, was shot and killed. The defeated Indians agreed to a treaty ceding all the land between the York and the James rivers to the east of the fall line, and prohibiting white settlement to the west of that line.

This attempt to delimit Indian territory — like many such attempts later in American history — was a failure from the start. Virginia was growing fast, especially after Cromwell's victo-

ry in the English civil war and the flight of many of the defeated Cavaliers to the colony. By 1650 its population (16,000) was twice as large as in 1640, and by 1660 five times as large (40,000). As the choice lands along the tidewater were taken up, new arrivals and servants completing their terms or escaping from their masters pressed on beyond the falls into the piedmont. By 1652 three counties had been formed in the territory recently set aside for the Indians. Clashes frequently occurred between the Indians and the frontiersmen.

When Cromwell seized power in England, Berkeley had to give up the governorship of Virginia, but King Charles II reappointed him after the Stuart Restoration. Once back in office, Berkeley, by the force of his personality, and by corrupting the council and the House of Burgesses, made himself practically an autocrat. Originally the Virginia government had been remarkably democratic. When the first burgesses were elected in 1619, all men aged seventeen or older were entitled to vote. After 1670 the vote was restricted to landowners, and elections were seldom held, the same burgesses remaining in office year after year. Each county continued to have only two representatives, even though the new counties of the back country contained many more people than some of the old ones of the tidewater area. Thus the more recent settlers on the frontier were underrepresented — if indeed they were represented at all.

Popular discontent, made worse by the low price of tobacco, was already widespread when, in 1673, the young, bold, handsome Cambridge graduate Nathaniel Bacon arrived in Virginia. His wealthy family gave him the money to buy a good farm in the back country and got him a place on the governor's council. A few years later the Indians raised the war cry on the frontier, killing several hundred whites, among them Bacon's overseer. Bacon and other concerned landholders demanded that Governor Berkeley send the militia out to pursue and chastise the marauders. But Berkeley preferred not to antagonize the Indians — he and many of his political associates were profiting from a large-scale trade with them — and so he ordered the militia merely to guard the edge of settlement. Bacon then led a force of his own to attack the Indians, whereupon Berkeley dismissed him from the governor's council and proclaimed him and his men rebels.

Thus, in 1676, began Bacon's Rebellion. When Berkeley, to gain popular support, called for a new election of burgesses, Bacon ran and was overwhelmingly elected. Going to Jamestown for the session, the rebel, not yet thirty years old, confronted the governor, now seventy. Berkeley had Bacon arrested but, hesitating to hang such a "darling of the people," pardoned him and gave him a commission to fight the Indians. While Bacon went off with his army, the House of Burgesses passed a series of reforms, known as Bacon's Laws, to lessen the authority of the governor and give greater powers of self-government to the counties. Now Berkeley again denounced Bacon as a rebel, and Bacon turned back from the frontier and marched with his army toward Jamestown, while Berkeley fled. Bacon captured the town and burned it, but when he was on the point of taking command of Virginia, he died of dysentery. Berkeley returned, recovered control, secured the repeal of most of Bacon's Laws, and saw to the execution of thirty-seven of the leading rebels before he was recalled to England, where he too died.

Later generations of Americans, looking back and finding a parallel between 1676 and 1776, were to view Bacon as a forerunner of the Patriots who championed the cause of Independence. He was not that, though his example helped to inspire the rebels who came long after him. He had advocated reform of the colonial government, not separation from England. He represented a disaffected group of the ruling class, but he also gained a following among the common people of Virginia.

His rebellion aroused the discontented of Maryland also. These people objected not only to Lord Baltimore's religion but also to his economic exploitation and arbitrary rule of his domain. From quitrents, export duties, and other sources, the proprietor was making out of the colony the present-day equivalent of more than a third of a million dollars a year. In 1670 he copied Virginia and limited the suffrage to landholders, then undertook to get control of the legislature. At the time Bacon was burning Jamestown, two Marylanders tried to rouse a mob to overthrow the proprietor's government. Both men were hanged.

More Proprietary Colonies

After Lord Baltimore had received his Maryland grant, no new colonization projects got under way from England for approximately thirty years, until the Stuart Restoration. Then Charles II, having returned from his wandering exile (1660) to reign as the Merry Monarch, proceeded to reward his faithful courtiers with truly regal gifts of American land. He not only acknowledged with royal charters the various colonies that had broken off from the (to him) detestable Puritan commonwealth of Massachusetts, but he also gave rise within a quarter of a century to four additional colonies: Carolina, New York, New Jersey, and Pennsylvania. All these, like Maryland, were founded by proprietors rather than companies. By this time, companies had lost interest in colonization and had turned to more profitable ventures; meanwhile, because of the presence of already thriving settlements, proprietors were finding colonization much easier than it had been in the days of Sir Humphrey Gilbert and Sir Walter Raleigh.

CAROLINA

Carolina (after the Latin *Carolinus*, meaning Charles), partly taken like Maryland from the Virginia grant, was awarded by Charles II to a group of eight of his favorites, all prominent politicians active in colonial affairs. One was the Virginia governor, Sir William Berkeley, but the man who was to do the most for the development of Carolina was Sir Anthony Ashley Cooper, about to become the Earl of Shaftesbury. In successive charters (1663, 1665) the eight proprietors received joint title to a vast territory stretching south to the Florida peninsula and west to the Pacific Ocean. Like Lord Baltimore in respect to Maryland, they were given almost kingly powers over their grant.

Like him, they expected to profit as landlords and land speculators, reserving tremendous estates for their own development, selling or giving away the rest in smaller tracts, and collecting annual payments as quitrents from the settlers. Though committed to the

advancement of the Church of England, the
Carolina proprietors welcomed customers
whether Anglican or not. Indeed, the charter
guaranteed religious freedom to all who would
worship as Christians. The proprietors also
promised political freedom — at least as much of
it as was to be found anywhere else in America — with laws to be made by a representative
assembly. They hoped to attract settlers from
the existing American colonies and thus to
avoid the expense of financing expeditions
from England.

The proprietors, four of whom had investments in the African slave trade, also intended
to introduce slaves into the colony so as to profit
both from selling them and from using their
labor. Early settlers were offered a bonus of
extra land for every black bondsman or woman they brought in. Negro slavery existed from
the outset in Carolina, with no transitional period of temporary servitude as in Virginia.

The leading proprietor, the Earl of Shaftesbury, desired a planned society and a uniform
pattern of settlement for the colony. With the
aid of the philosopher John Locke he drew up
the Fundamental Constitution for Carolina in
1669. According to this document, the territory
was to be divided into 12,000-acre squares, with
counties consisting of forty squares apiece. In
each county, eight of the squares would belong to the proprietors, or "seigneurs," eight
others would go to newly created nobles, who
would bear the title of "landgrave" or "ca-
cique," and the remaining twenty-four would
be distributed among ordinary settlers, or
"leet-men." At the bottom of this stratified society would be the blacks, whose subjection
would be complete, regardless of their possible
conversion to Christianity: "Every freeman of
Carolina shall have absolute power and authority over his Negro slaves, of what opinion or religion soever." Proprietors, nobles, and other
landholders would have a voice in the colonial
parliament in proportion to the size of their
land holdings.

While the Fundamental Constitution, with
occasional revisions, remained in effect (at
least on paper) for thirty years, Carolina was
slow to develop, and when it did, it took a pattern much less regular and artificial. In fact, the
colony developed along two natural but quite
different lines in its two widely separated areas
of settlement — the one in its northeastern corner, around Albemarle Sound; and the other

The Carolinas and Georgia

far to the southwest, on the Ashley and Cooper
rivers and in their hinterland.

The northern part of Carolina, the first
part to be settled, suffered in the early years
from geographical handicaps, the coastal region being isolated by the Dismal Swamp, by
the southeastwardly flow of the rivers, and by
the lack of natural harbors usable for ocean-
going ships. As a Carolina proprietor, Virginia's
Governor Berkeley worked hard to induce
Virginians to take up land on the other side of
the colonial boundary, and gradually the Albemarle settlements grew. Virginians were inclined to look upon the neighboring Carolinians
as a lazy and immoral set of runaway servants,
debtors, thieves, and pirates. Actually, most of
these people — like many in the Virginia they
had left behind — were honest but poor tobac-
co-growing farmers, though they showed the
marks of their primitive, backwoods existence,
having few roads and practically no villages,
churches, schools — or slaves. The settlers disliked paying quitrents, and when one of Nathaniel Bacon's lieutenants, John Culpeper,
took refuge in Albemarle County, some of them
followed him in overthrowing the Albemarle
governor, in 1677, and took temporary control
themselves.

The southern part of Carolina was favored
with an excellent harbor at the point where the
Ashley and Cooper rivers joined (as local boost-

ers eventually were to say) "to form the Atlantic Ocean." Here in 1670 a fleet bringing colonists arrived whom the Earl of Shaftesbury had sent out after realizing that settlers from existing colonies were not going to flock in. Then in 1680 he saw to the laying-out of the city of Charleston, which soon had its wharves, fortifications, and fine houses, and its wide streets running at right angles to one another. Settlers took up land along the two rivers, down which they began to send large quantities of corn, lumber, cattle, pork, and (in the 1690s) some rice to Charleston, for shipment to Barbados in the British West Indies. To Charleston also came furs, hides, and Indian slaves obtained by traders who were advancing farther and farther into the interior, around the southern end of the Appalachians, to deal with the southwestern tribes.

In Charleston and its vicinity there developed a stratified society that embodied the spirit, though not the letter, of Shaftesbury's Fundamental Constitution. Many of the early inhabitants had moved here from the declining sugar plantations of Barbados and other West Indian islands. These people, already familiar with African slavery, brought their blacks with them. Large planters, often with homes in Charleston as well as plantations nearby, and city merchants occupied more or less the position of the nobles in the Shaftesbury plan. Ordinary farmers, many of them located at some distance inland, corresponded roughly to the "leet-men." The wealthy planters and merchants, centering in Charleston, dominated the region's economy, social life, and politics. Charleston became the capital of Carolina in 1690, when the governor took up his residence there, leaving a deputy to take charge of the Albemarle settlements.

Already there were in fact two Carolinas, each having a distinctive way of life, long before the colony was formally divided (1729) into North and South Carolina, with completely separate governments.

NEW YORK

The year after making his Carolina grant, Charles II bestowed (1664) upon his brother, the Duke of York, all the territory lying between the Connecticut and Delaware rivers. A large part of this land presumably belonged to the Massachusetts Bay Company by virtue of the company's sea-to-sea grant. The whole region was claimed by the Dutch, who occupied strategic points within it.

The Dutch republic, after winning independence from Spain, had launched upon its own career of overseas trading and empire building in Asia, Africa, and America. On the basis of Hudson's explorations, the Dutch staked an American claim and proceeded promptly to exploit it with a busy trade in furs. To add permanence to the business, the Dutch West India Company began to encourage settlement, transporting whole families on such voyages as that of the *New Netherland* in 1624, and later offering vast feudal estates to "patroons" who would bring over immigrants to work the land. So developed the colony of New Netherland. It centered on New Amsterdam with its blockhouse on Manhattan Island and included thinly scattered settlements on the Hudson, the Delaware, and the Connecticut, with forts for their protection. In 1655 the Dutch extended their sway over the few Swedes and Finns settled along the lower Delaware. In the Connecticut Valley, they had to give in to the superior numbers of the English moving out from Massachusetts Bay.

Three Anglo-Dutch wars arose from the commercial and colonial rivalry of England and the Netherlands throughout the world and particularly in America, where the English resented the foreign stronghold that wedged apart their own northern and southern colonies and provided smuggling bases for the Dutch. In 1664 troop-carrying vessels of the English navy put in at New Amsterdam and extracted a surrender from the arbitrary and unpopular governor, the peglegged Peter Stuyvesant. During the final conflict the Dutch reconquered and briefly held their old provincial capital (1673–1674), then lost it again for good.

New York, formerly New Netherland, already the property of the Duke of York and renamed by him, was his to rule as virtually an absolute monarch. Since he was himself a Roman Catholic, and the inhabitants of his province included Anglicans from England and Puritans from New England as well as Calvinists from Holland, he found it expedient to be broad-minded with regard to religion and politics.

The Stadt Huys, New Amsterdam

The government building, together with the adjoining buildings in a typically Dutch style, made New Amsterdam look much like a town in Holland. It continued to have much the same appearance when this drawing was made, about 1679, after the English had established control and renamed the place New York. From the Journal of a Voyage to New York, 1679–1682, *by Jasper Dankers and Peter Stuyler. (Courtesy of the Long Island Historical Society)*

Like other proprietors before him, instead of going to America he delegated powers to a governor and a council. The Duke's Laws, which the first governor issued, basing them on some of the laws of Massachusetts and Connecticut, provided for no town meetings but for the election of certain local officials and for the gubernatorial appointment of others. These laws also directed each town to set up a church and to give tax support both to it and to any other church that residents of the town might organize. Thus there was to be a variety of established churches. On the Duke's instructions, a later governor, who took office in 1683, consulted with representatives of the people and with them adopted a Charter of Liberties and Privileges, which guaranteed the rights of Englishmen and called for an elected assembly.

The Duke's concessions failed to satisfy all New Yorkers. Many people complained about the inequality of property holding and political power. The Duke confirmed the Dutch patroonships already in existence, the most notable of them being Rensselaerswyck with its 700,000 acres around Albany, and he gave comparable estates to Englishmen in order to create a class of influential landowners loyal to him. Wealthy English and Dutch landlords, shipowners, and fur traders, along with the Duke's political appointees, actually dominated the colonial government.

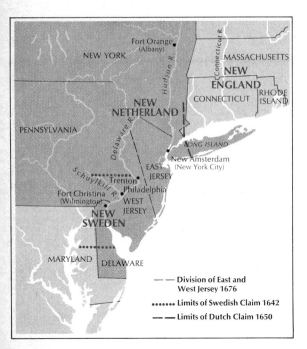

The Middle Colonies in the Seventeenth Century

and Connecticut. On the south it was enlarged somewhat by his claim (based on conquest from the Dutch) to land west of the lower Delaware, but was diminished even more by his generosity in parting with his possessions. He gave what became New Jersey to a couple of cronies, both Carolina proprietors, Sir George Carteret and Sir John Berkeley. The latter sold his half interest to two enterprising members of the Society of Friends, thus bringing the Quakers into the colonization business. The Duke gave what became Delaware to another Quaker, the greatest colonizer of all, William Penn.

THE QUAKER COLONIES

The Society of Friends originated in mid-seventeenth-century England in response to the preachings of George Fox, a Nottingham shoemaker, whose followers came to be known as Quakers from his admonition to them to "tremble at the name of the Lord." The essence of Fox's teachings was the doctrine of the Inner Light, the illumination from God within each soul, the divine conscience, which when rightly heeded could guide human beings along the paths of righteousness.

Of all the Protestant sectarians of the time, the Quakers were the most anarchistic and the most democratic. They had no church government except for their monthly, quarterly, and annual meetings at which the congregations were represented on a local, regional, and national basis. They had no traditional church buildings—only meeting houses. They had no paid clergy, and in their worship they spoke up one by one as the spirit moved them. Disregarding social distinctions such as those of sex and class, they treated women as equals and addressed one another with the "thee" and "thou" then commonly used in speaking to servants and inferiors. Defying other accepted conventions, they refused to participate in taking oaths or in fighting wars. The Quakers were unpopular enough as a result of these beliefs and practices, and they increased their unpopularity by occasionally breaking up other religious groups at worship. Many of them were jailed from time to time.

The system of landholding turned away from New York some settlers who preferred living on their own farms to working as tenants on someone else's estate. Under English rule the population nevertheless grew much faster than under the Dutch regime. By 1685, when the Duke ascended to the throne as James II, New York contained about four times as many people (around 30,000) as when he had taken it over some twenty years before. Most of them still lived within the Hudson Valley, close to the river itself, with the largest settlement at its mouth, in the town of New York. The colony had become predominantly English in both population and customs, yet Dutch traditions lingered on to leave a distinctive regional flavor.

On the north and west the Duke's dominions were extended as far as Lake Ontario by means of a protectorate over the Iroquois. On the east, however, his territory was trimmed in a boundary compromise with Massachusetts

Naturally, like the Puritans earlier, George Fox and his followers looked to America for asylum. A few of them went to New England, but there (except in Rhode Island) they were greeted with fines, whippings, and orders to leave, and three men and a woman who persisted in staying were actually put to death. Many migrated to northern Carolina, and there, as the fastest-growing religious community, they soon were influential in colonial politics. Yet the Quakers desired a colony of their own, and Fox himself visited America (1671–1672) to look over the land. As the head of a sect despised in England, however, he could not get the necessary grant without the aid of someone influential at the court. Fortunately for his cause, his teachings had struck the hearts of a number of wealthy and prominent men, one of whom in particular made possible a large-scale effort to realize the Quaker dream.

William Penn—whose father was Sir William Penn, an admiral in the Royal Navy and a landlord of valuable Irish estates—received a gentleman's education at his father's expense but could not overcome his mystical inclina-

tions despite his father's discipline. Converted to the doctrine of the Inner Light, the younger Penn took up evangelism and, though always moderate and soft-spoken, was repeatedly put in prison, where he wrote a powerful tract, *No Cross, No Crown.* With George Fox he visited the European continent and found Quakers there, as in the British Isles, who longed to emigrate.

New Jersey, half of which two of his fellow Quakers owned, received Penn's attention when he was asked to assist them with their debts. In their behalf he helped to see to the division of the province into East and West Jersey, Carteret as one of the original proprietors keeping the East, and the Quakers the West. West Jersey soon began to fill up with Friends from England while East Jersey was being populated mostly by Puritans from New England. Before long Penn together with other wealthy Quakers purchased the eastern property from Carteret (1682), and eventually the

Quakers Going to Meeting

The meeting house, at which these members of the Society of Friends are arriving on a summer day, was in a Welsh settlement near Cambria, Pennsylvania. Though made in the early nineteenth century, this print depicts a scene not very different from that in similar communities of the previous century. (Library of Congress)

Penn's Treaty with the Indians
William Penn entered into a number of treaties with the Indians for the purchase of land. These treaties were scrupulously observed by the Pennsylvania Quakers. Benjamin West's painting, one of the best known of his many historical canvases, probably represents negotiations that were carried on in June 1683. (Library of Congress)

two Jerseys were reunited as one colony (1702), second in Quaker population only to Pennsylvania itself.

Pennsylvania—which Charles II insisted on naming for his old ally the admiral—was based on the King's grant of 1681. Penn, reconciled with his father, had inherited the latter's Irish lands and also his claim to a small fortune owed by the King. Charles II, possessing more real estate than ready cash, paid the debt with a grant of territory, between New York and Maryland, which was larger than England and Wales combined and which (unknown to him) contained more value in soil and minerals than any other province of English America. Within this fabulous estate Penn was to have the rights of both landlord and ruler while acknowledging the feudal suzerainty of the King by the token payment of two beaver skins a year.

Like the Calverts, the Carolina proprie-

tors, and the Duke of York, Penn intended to make money from land sales and quitrents and from private property to be worked for him. He promptly sold several large tracts to rich Quaker associates and one tract of 15,000 acres to a group of German immigrants led by Francis Daniel Pastorius. Through his informative and honest advertising—as in his pamphlet entitled *A Brief Account of the Province of Pennsylvania*, which was translated into several European languages—Penn made Pennsylvania the best-known and most cosmopolitan of all the colonies. But he and his descendants were to find almost hopeless the task of collecting quitrents.

Much more than a mere real-estate promoter, Penn undertook in Pennsylvania what he called a Holy Experiment. Colonies, he said, were the "seeds of nations," and he proposed to plant the seeds of brotherly love. Closely supervising the planting, he devised a liberal Frame of Government with a representative assembly. He personally voyaged to Pennsylvania (1682) to oversee the laying-out, between the Delaware and Schuylkill rivers, of the city he appropriately named Philadelphia ("Brotherly Love"), which with its rectangular streets, like those of Charleston, helped to set the pattern for most later cities in America. Penn believed, as had Roger Williams, that the land belonged to the Indians, and he was careful to see that they were reimbursed for it, as well as to see that they were not debauched by the fur traders' firewater. With the Indians, who honored him as a rarity, an honest white man, his colony had no trouble during his lifetime. It prospered from the outset because of his thoughtful planning and also because of favorable circumstances, including the mildness of the climate and the fertility of the soil. The settlers were well-to-do and well equipped, and they received assistance from the people of other colonies and from the Hollanders and Swedes and Finns already there — for Pennsylvania when Penn first saw it was not as much of a wilderness as Virginia had been when John Smith arrived.

Delaware, after its transfer to Penn from the Duke of York (1682), was treated as a part of Pennsylvania (and was known as "the lower counties") but was given the privilege of setting up its own representative assembly. The three counties did so in 1703, and thereafter Delaware was considered a separate colony, though until the Revolution it continued to have the same governor as Pennsylvania.

Experiment in Union

The colonies, for the most part, had originated as quite separate projects and had grown up in rather independent ways, with little thought for a long time that they belonged, or ought to belong, to a unified empire. To be sure, a step toward intercolonial union had been taken with the forming of the New England Confederation, but that was the doing of some of the colonies themselves for their own purposes, and these did not include the strengthening of imperial control. A very different kind of union, one imposing the King's authority on the colonies, was attempted in the 1680s with the establishment of the Dominion of New England. This was intended to help enforce the mercantile system.

THE MERCANTILE SYSTEM

One of the arguments for colonization in the first place had been that colonies would increase the wealth of the mother country and lessen her dependence on other nations. According to the mercantile theory, she would prosper and grow strong by exporting more and more to foreigners and importing less and less from them. Colonies would aid by providing a market for her manufactured goods and a source of supply for raw materials she could not produce at home. To get the full benefit, she would have to exclude foreigners (as Spain had done) from her colonial trade.

On the whole, such a mercantile system would meet the needs of the colonies as well as those of the mother country. The colonies stood to gain by concentrating on the crude products of the field and forest, and exchanging these for the finer goods of manufacturers abroad who had the capital and skilled labor to produce them economically. In actual practice, the colonies did turn out products that the mother country needed for her own consumption or for resale to foreigners — products such as tobacco, furs, lumber, and naval stores. But the colonies also produced surpluses of commodities like wheat, flour, and fish that competed with commodities produced in the mother country. And whether the goods were complementary or competitive, the colonial producers sometimes found that they could make a better bargain with Spaniards, Frenchmen, or Hollanders than with Englishmen. Hence a considerable trade early developed between the English colonists and foreigners, especially the Dutch.

At first the English government, distracted as it was by the conflict between King and Parliament, made only half-hearted efforts to regulate the colonial trade in accordance with mercantilist principles. Once Oliver Cromwell was in power, he secured laws from Parliament (1650, 1651) to keep Dutch ships out of the English colonies. After the Restoration, under Charles II, the government went much further, adopting legislation that had the positive aim of directing colonial trade as well as the negative one of excluding foreigners from it.

This legislation consisted of three Navigation Acts. The first of these (1660) closed the colonies to all trade except that carried in English ships, which were defined as ships built in England or the colonies and manned by sailors of whom three-fourths were Englishmen or colonists. This law also required that certain enumerated items, among them tobacco, be exported from the colonies only to England or to an English possession. The second act (1663) provided that all goods sent from Europe to the colonies had to go by way of England and that taxes could be put on the goods during their transshipment. The third act (1673) was designed to prevent colonists from evading the export control (in regard to the enumerated items) by clearing from one colonial port for another and then actually heading for a foreign port. The new act levied a duty on cargoes bound for the intercolonial coastal trade. It also provided for the appointment of customs officials to collect the duties and administer the Navigation Acts. These acts, with later amendments and additions, were to form the legal basis of England's mercantile system for a century.

THE DOMINION OF NEW ENGLAND

If the Navigation Acts were to be strictly enforced, the King would have to do more than dispatch customs officials to America. With the cooperation of Parliament, he would have to set up in London some kind of agency to oversee colonial affairs. He would also have to get more direct control over the colonial governments than he had.

Only in Virginia, a "royal colony" since 1624, did the King as yet have the right to appoint the governor. In Massachusetts, a "cor-

porate colony," the people elected their own governor, as they also did in Plymouth. In Maryland, a "proprietary colony," the appointing power had been delegated to the proprietor. When Charles II created other proprietary colonies — Carolina, New York, New Jersey, Pennsylvania — he himself followed the Maryland example. And when he gave royal charters to Connecticut and Rhode Island, he accepted these two as "corporate colonies" by allowing them to go on choosing their officials. Moreover, he and his predecessors had permitted the development of an assembly representing the people (or some of the people) in each of the colonies — royal, corporate, or proprietary. And the assemblies were claiming more and more power for themselves.

For help in enforcing the new trade regulations, Charles II could not place much reliance on the colonial governments. Least of all could he depend on Massachusetts, the worst offender, which dared to behave practically like an independent republic, even usurping the sovereign's prerogative of coining money. The Puritan oligarchs, whose religion in itself was obnoxious to him, persisted in maintaining their own established church instead of the Church of England, thus violating the terms of the Massachusetts Bay Company's charter, which obliged the colony to conform to English law. Many of the Massachusetts merchants, disregarding the Navigation Acts as well, evaded the payment of duties and made smuggling a regular business.

After a royal investigating commission had visited the Bay Colony and reported back to London the extent of the colony's illegal business, Charles II decided to take action for controlling and chastising Massachusetts in particular, and tightening control over the American empire in general. In 1675 he set up a special committee, the Lords of Trade (consisting of some of his official advisers on the Privy Council), to make recommendations for imperial reform. The Lords of Trade recommended that the King participate more directly in colonial government. He did so, and at the same time struck a blow at Massachusetts when, in 1679, he denied her authority over New Hampshire and chartered a separate, royal colony whose governor he would himself appoint.

Charles II wished to make a royal colony of Massachusetts as well, but her corporate charter was one he could not revoke without a lawsuit. He soon had grounds for action. When the Lords of Trade ordered Massachusetts to see that the Navigation Acts were obeyed, the General Court replied that, in view of the charter's provisions for self-government, Parliament had no power to legislate for the colony. When the Lords of Trade sent over a customs official to see to the enforcement of the acts, the General Court not only refused to recognize him but arrested the local agents he appointed. Finally the King started legal proceedings that led, in 1684, to the revocation of the charter.

His brother and successor, James II, went much further when he came to the throne in 1685. He combined Massachusetts and the rest of the New England colonies into one Dominion of New England, and later he added New York and New Jersey to it. Within this dominion he eliminated the existing assemblies, and over it he placed a single governor, Sir Edmund Andros, with headquarters in Boston. An able but stern and tactless administrator, Andros thoroughly antagonized the people as he proceeded to levy taxes and enforce the Navigation Acts. When colonists protested on the basis of their rights as Englishmen—especially their right to be taxed only with the consent of their representatives—he retorted that they had no rights.

THE "GLORIOUS REVOLUTION"

Soon after the Bostonians heard of the 1688 movement to overthrow James II in England, they determined to overthrow his viceroy in New England. A mob set out after Andros and other royal officials; he escaped but later surrendered and was imprisoned.

The Massachusetts leaders now hoped to get back their old corporate charter, but they were to be disappointed. Despite the persuasive efforts of Increase Mather, an outstanding Puritan divine who was on a lobbying mission in London, the new sovereigns, William and Mary, combined Plymouth with Massachusetts and claimed the land as a royal colony (1691). Under the new charter, they themselves appointed the governor, but they restored the General Court with its elected lower house and allowed the General Court to choose the mem-

bers of the upper house. This charter also did away with the religious test for voting and officeholding. Though there remained a property requirement, the great majority of Massachusetts men could meet it. Thus the Massachusetts government, no longer a Puritan oligarchy, began to be fairly democratic. Quakers, Baptists, and other sectarians now were free to worship as they pleased in what once had been the exclusive land of the Puritans, though all had to pay tithes in support of the established (Congregational) church.

The politico-religious crisis in Massachusetts gave rise to an atmosphere of tension and uncertainty in which public hysteria could thrive. This, together with the efforts of preachers to revive the Puritan sense of sin, led to the worst witch craze ever to occur in the English colonies (though others as bad or worse occurred in various parts of contemporary Europe).

None of the seventeenth-century ministers labored harder to keep up the old faith than did Increase Mather and his son Cotton. Puritanism demanded a well-educated ministry, and the Mathers were intellectual giants. Like most scientists of the period, they believed in witches. In one of the many learned books he wrote, *Illustrious Providences* (1684), Increase Mather undertook to show that God had a special concern for New England and that the people should note carefully any evidence of "Witchcrafts, Diabolical Possessions, Remarkable Judgements upon noted Sinners," and the like. There later arose a widespread hysteria, which went to its greatest extremes in the Massachusetts town of Salem, where it was stimulated by the antics of two West Indian slaves who were steeped in voodoo lore. Hundreds of people were accused as witches, many of them were sentenced to die, and nineteen were actually put to death before the witchcraft trials were stopped in 1692.

Afterward almost all the witch hunters publicly repented their part in the affair. The Mathers often were blamed for it, though in fact they had pleaded for moderation during the trials and had helped to bring them to an end. Still, the net effect was to diminish the prestige and authority of the Church and its leaders.

Andros had been ruling New York through a lieutenant governor, Captain Francis

Confession of a Witch [1692]

Mrs. Mary Osgood, of Andover, Massachusetts, was examined for witchcraft, September 8, by a group of judges. They reported:

She confesses that, about 11 years ago, when she was in a melancholy state and condition, she used to walk abroad in her orchard; and upon a certain time she saw the appearance of a cat, at the end of the house, which yet she thought was a real cat. However, at that time, it diverted her from praying to God, and instead thereof she prayed to the devil; about which time she made a covenant with the devil, who, as a black man, came to her and presented her a book, upon which she laid her finger, and that left a red spot: and that upon her signing, the devil told her he was her God, and that she should serve and worship him, and she believes she consented to it. She says, further, that about two years agone, she was carried through the air, in company with deacon Frye's wife, Ebenezer Baker's wife, and Goody Tyler, to five mile pond, where she was baptised by the devil, who dipped her face in the water and made her renounce her former baptism, and told her she must be his, soul and body, forever, and that she must serve him, which she promised to do.

About six weeks later, on October 19, she was visited by Increase Mather, who reported:

Mrs. Osgood freely and relentingly said that the confession which she made upon her examination for witchcraft, and afterwards acknowledged before the honourable judges, was wholly false, and that she was brought to the said confession by the violent urging and unreasonable pressings that were used toward her; she asserted that she never signed the devil's book, was never baptised by the devil, never afflicted any of the accusers, or gave her consent for their being afflicted.

Nicholson, who enjoyed the support of the wealthy merchants and fur traders of the province. The same groups had shared in political power while New York was a proprietary colony of the Duke of York and after it became a royal colony upon the Duke's accession to the English throne as James II. The groups that were excluded from a fair share in the government—farmers, mechanics, small traders, and shopkeepers—already had a long accumulation of grievances when news came of James' fall and Andros' arrest. Rebellious militiamen seized the New York City fort, and Lieutenant Governor Nicholson sailed away to England.

The leadership of the New York rebels fell to Jacob Leisler, who had come from Germany, succeeded as a merchant, and married into a prominent Dutch family, but had never gained acceptance as one of the colony's ruling class. Leisler's followers proclaimed him commander in chief, and he declared his loyalty to William and Mary. He claimed, as intended for him, the dispatches arriving from the King and Queen and addressed to "Our Lieutenant-Governor and Commander-in-Chief of our Province of New York, or in his absence to such as for the time being take care to keep the peace and administer the laws." Assuming the title of lieutenant governor, Leisler with the aid of the militia kept the peace and administered the laws for two years (1689–1691), until William and Mary finally appointed a new governor, who was given authority to call an elected assembly. When, ahead of the new governor, a British officer appeared with a contingent of troops, Leisler refused to surrender the fort to him. Leisler afterward yielded, but the delay gave his political enemies, soon back in power, a pretext for charging him with treason. He and a son-in-law were hanged, drawn, and quartered.

In Maryland the people at first assumed (erroneously) that the Catholic Lord Baltimore had sided with the Catholic James II and had opposed the accession of William and Mary. So, in 1689, an old opponent of the proprietor's government, John Coode, started a new revolt as head of an organization calling itself "An Association in Arms for the Defense of the Protestant Religion, and for Asserting the Right of King William and Queen Mary to the Province of Maryland and All the English Dominions." The insurgents drove out Lord Baltimore's officials and, through an elected convention, chose a committee to run the government for the time being. In 1691 William and Mary took advantage of their opportunity to deprive the proprietor of his authority and transform Maryland into a royal colony. (It became a proprietary colony again in 1715, after the fifth Lord Baltimore had joined the Anglican Church.)

Thus the Glorious Revolution of 1688 in England touched off revolutions, mostly blood-less, in the colonies. Under the new regime the representative assemblies that had been abolished were revived, but not the scheme for colonial unification from above. Several of the provinces, however, were now royal colonies in which the King appointed the governor, and over which he potentially had greater direct control than he once had had. The colonists had not yet challenged the ultimate authority of the King. "What had been won (possibly the word should be 'preserved')," W. F. Craven has written, "was the practical right of the colonists to determine very largely for themselves questions of public policy fundamentally affecting their domestic life. In this large measure of self-government the colonists were to find with time good cause for remembering the Revolution as a glorious one and, by remembering it, fresh and potent defenses for their rights of self-government."

Selected Readings

General Accounts
C. M. Andrews, *The Colonial Period of American History** (4 vols., 1934–1938); Clarence L. Ver Steeg, *The Formative Years, 1607–1763* (1964).

New England
C. M. Andrews, *The Fathers of New England* (1919); S. E. Morison, *Builders of the Bay Colony** (1930); A. T. Vaughan, *New England Frontier: Puritans and Indians, 1620–1675* (1965); Perry Miller, *The New England Mind: The Seventeenth Century** (1939); R. Middlekauff, *The Mathers: Three Generations of Puritan Intellectuals, 1596–1728* (1971); Bernard Bailyn, *The New England Merchants in the Seventeenth Century** (1955); E. S. Morgan, *The Puritan Dilemma: The Story of John Winthrop** (1958); S. H. Brockunier, *The Irrepressible Democrat: Roger Williams* (1940); Edith Curtis, *Anne Hutchinson* (1930); M. J. A. Jones, *Congregational Commonwealth: Connecticut, 1636–1662* (1968); R. E. Wall, Jr., *Massachusetts Bay: The Crucial Decade, 1640–1650* (1972).

The Middle Colonies
T. J. Wertenbaker, *The Founding of American Civilization: The Middle Colonies* (1938); T. J. Condon, *New York Beginnings: The Commercial Origins of New Netherland* (1968); George L. Smith, *Religion and Trade in New Netherland: Dutch Origins and American Development* (1973); A. W. Trelease, *Indian Affairs in Colonial New York: The Seventeenth Century* (1960); E. B. Bronner, *William Penn's "Holy Experiment": The Founding of Pennsylvania, 1681–*

1701 (1962); M. M. Dunn, *William Penn: Politics and Conscience* (1967); W. W. Comfort, *William Penn, 1644–1718* (1944); J. E. Pomfret, *The Province of West New Jersey, 1609–1702* (1956) and *The Province of East New Jersey* (1962).

The South
W. F. Craven, *The Southern Colonies in the Seventeenth Century, 1607–1689* (1949) and *White, Red, and Black: The Seventeenth-Century Virginian* (1971); Verner Crane, *The Southern Frontier, 1670–1732** (1956); M. P. Andrews, *The Founding of Maryland* (1933); R. L. Morton, *Colonial Virginia* (2 vols., 1960); T. J. Wertenbaker, *Torchbearer of the Revolution* (1940), on Nathaniel Bacon as a democratic hero; W. E. Washburn, *The Governor and the Rebel: A History of Bacon's Rebellion in Virginia* (1958), a less sympathetic account.

Imperial Control
G. L. Beer, *The Origins of the British Colonial System* (1908) and *The Old Colonial System* (2 vols., 1912); Michael Kammen, *Deputyes and Libertyes: The Origins of Representative Government in Colonial America** (1969); L. A. Harper, *The English Navigation Laws* (1939); Viola Barnes, *The Dominion of New England* (1923); J. R. Reich, *Leisler's Rebellion* (1953); M. G. Hall, L. H. Leder, and M. G. Kammen, eds., *The Glorious Revolution** (1964), a collection of contemporary writings; D. S. Lovejoy, *The Glorious Revolution in America* (1972).

*Titles available in paperback.

Provincial Americans

Three

The seventeenth-century colonists remained essentially transplanted Englishmen, though even the first arrivals had begun to depart from many of their accustomed ways. As new generations grew up in America, they developed a more and more distinctive character. In the course of the eighteenth century they became provincial "Americans" — a term that had been applied to them even before 1700 but did not come into general use until after 1750.

There were three main reasons for the divergence between the culture of the colonies and that of the homeland. First, English society was not transplanted as a whole. The people who left for America were not entirely typical of England: usually they were the more discontented or the more adventurous; they were themselves in some degree "different." Second, they found in the New World a new environment with new challenges and opportunities. Certain elements of the English inheritance flourished and adapted themselves to the strange surroundings, while others withered or never took root at all. Third, some of the early colonists (the Dutch, for example) had come from countries other than England, and during the eighteenth century new

The John Ward House
The left-hand portion of this house in Salem, Massachusetts, was built in 1684. The right-hand portion, with another gable, was added later, and the lean-to in the rear still later. Note the second-story overhang. This was characteristic of many seventeenth-century dwellings in New England. It was copied from medieval English houses, but its origin and purpose are uncertain. The most likely theories are these: (1) It was a technical matter of construction: separate, offset posts for the two stories made possible a stronger framing than did one long post; (2) It was a matter of aesthetics: people liked the way the overhang looked. Note too the casement windows with their diamond-shaped panes, also typical of the time. (Essex Institute, Salem, Mass.)

The John Ward House: Kitchen
In colonial New England the kitchen usually was located either in an ell of the house or in a lean-to at the rear (in the South, the kitchen often was located in a separate outbuilding). The kitchen, with its large fireplace, was used not only for the preparation of meals but also as a dining room, a general workroom, and to a considerable extent a living room. Its furniture included a trestle table, chairs, a wash-bench, meat tubs, a cheese press, a churn, a spinning wheel, often a loom, and sometimes a pallet bed for an indentured servant or an apprentice. (Essex Institute, Salem, Mass.)

arrivals in much larger numbers came from other places — from Scotland and Ireland, the European continent, and Africa. Hence, in America, there was a mixture of peoples and cultures, though the English continued to predominate.

Provincial Americans were affected by new currents of thought coming from abroad during the eighteenth century. This was the Age of the Enlightenment, when the ideas of the Englishman Sir Isaac Newton and other scientists (or "natural philosophers") gave a fresh conception of God's universe. They saw it as a universe that God had fashioned like a clock and set to operate with regularity. It followed natural laws that could be understood by the use of man's reason. The spirit of the Enlightenment spread from England and Europe to America.

In the developing American character there were variations from colony to colony and from region to region. The New England colonies had much in common with one another, less in common with the middle colonies (Pennsylvania, New Jersey, New York), and still less in common with the Southern colonies. These last fell into two subgroups with important differences between the two: the tobacco colonies (Maryland, Virginia, and North Carolina) and the others (South Carolina and, after its founding in 1733, Georgia).

The Expanding Settlements

The population of English America increased tenfold between 1700 and 1776. This mainly reflected the growth of existing colonies; only one new colony was founded during these years.

THE FOUNDING OF GEORGIA

Georgia, the last of the mainland colonies, was unique in its origins. It was founded by neither a corporation nor a proprietorship, and its guiding purpose was neither to make profits nor to create a sectarian refuge. In the beginning Georgia was the work of trustees serving without pay. Their main purpose was twofold: to provide a new start in life for Englishmen imprisoned for debt, and to erect a military barrier against the Spaniards on the southern border of English America.

As claimants to the whole continent, the Spaniards had looked suspiciously upon the encroachment at Jamestown, and had taken one captive while giving up three of their own men in a half-hearted attempt to frighten the English away. In a treaty of 1676 Spain recognized England's title to lands already occupied by English subjects. Ten years later Spanish forces from Florida attacked and destroyed an outlying South Carolina settlement south of the treaty line. When Spain and England went to war in Europe (1701–1713) hostilities were renewed in America, and thereafter another European conflict with American repercussions was continually expected.

General James Oglethorpe, a hero of the late war with Spain, was much concerned about the need for a buffer colony between South Carolina and Florida. As head of a parliamentary committee investigating English prisons, Oglethorpe also knew at first hand the plight of honest debtors rotting in confinement. He conceived the idea of solving both problems at once by resettling such prisoners as farmer-soldiers on the faraway frontier.

The charter from George II (1732) transferred the land between the Savannah and Altamaha rivers to the administration of Oglethorpe and his fellow trustees for a period of twenty-one years. In their colonization policies they were to keep in mind the needs of military security. Landholdings were limited in size so as to make settlement compact. Negroes — free or slave — were excluded, and Roman Catholics also, to forestall the danger of wartime insurrection and of collusion with enemy coreligionists. And the Indian trade was strictly regulated, with rum prohibited, to lessen the risk of Indian complications.

Oglethorpe himself led the first expedition, building a fortified town at the mouth of the Savannah in 1733, and later constructing additional forts south of the Altamaha. Only a few debtors were released from jail and sent to Georgia, but hundreds of needy tradesmen and artisans from England and Scotland and religious refugees from Switzerland and Germany were brought to the new colony at the expense of the trustees, who raised funds from charitable individuals as well as from Parliament. Though other settlers came at their own expense, immigrants were not attracted in large numbers during the early years. Newcomers generally preferred to settle in South Carolina, where there were no laws against big plantations, slaves, and rum. Before the twenty-one years of the trusteeship were up, these restrictions were repealed, and after 1750 Georgia developed along lines similar to those of South Carolina.

THE LABOR SUPPLY

After 1700 few white servants headed for the South, even for Virginia or Maryland, where they once had flocked. The largest numbers

An Eighteenth–Century Indenture
This contract, dated May 13, 1784, was made late in the history of indentured servitude and typifies the standardized form that developed. Note that it is printed, with spaces left blank to be filled in. In this particular case, the contract was made between the master and his servant before either of them sailed for America. Originally, a contract was written in two identical parts on a single sheet, which was torn in two, leaving an indented or indentured edge—hence the term "indenture."

now went to Pennsylvania, where opportunities and working conditions were most attractive, and they continued to go to Pennsylvania and New York, though in dwindling numbers, until long after the American Revolution. Many of these people were "free willers" or "redemptioners" from Europe, who gave their indentures to the captain of the ship they boarded. He auctioned off their contracts after putting in at an American port, and each buyer then claimed his servants.

In Virginia and Maryland white servitude was being replaced by Negro slavery, which had advantages for the master. It gave him a constant labor supply and practically complete control over it. Identifiable by their color, black slaves could not run away and merge themselves with the mass of free humanity as white servants could. Nor could slaves rise out of their bondage to compete with their masters for wealth and political influence as the servants sometimes did. Moreover, considering the length of their service, slaves were cheaper, especially with the fall of slave prices after 1697, when the monopoly of the Royal African Company was broken and the slave trade was opened to English and colonial merchants on a competitive basis.

This trade was dominated by ships owned in England but was shared by others owned in New England. The latter often followed a "triangular" route. That is, a ship took rum and other items from a New England port to the Guinea Coast of Africa, slaves from Africa to the West Indies, and sugar and molasses as well as specie and bills from the West Indies to the home port. There the molasses would be distilled into rum for another voyage of the same kind. On the African coast the slave marts were kept supplied by native chieftains who made a business of capturing enemy tribesmen in warfare and bringing them, tied together in long lines known as "coffles," out of the jungle. Then, after some haggling on the seashore, came the horrors of the "middle passage" – so-called because it was the second of the three legs of the voyage – during which the slaves were packed in the dark and stinking hold, with no sanitary facilities, no room to stand up, and scarcely air enough to breathe. Those who died en route were thrown overboard, and the losses from disease were sometimes high.

Slavery in colonial times was not confined to any single region. Slaves labored as domestics and occasionally as farm hands for wealthy families in the North. As of 1763 there were about 230,000 Negroes in all the colonies, most of them slaves. About 16,000 lived in New England, 29,000 in the middle colonies, and the rest in the South. By 1775 nearly half of the people of Virginia and more than two-thirds of those of South Carolina were black.

POPULATION GROWTH

Besides the Africans, other non-English peoples came in large numbers to the colonies after the end of the seventeenth century, while immigration from England itself fell off. Recovering from a prolonged depression in the 1630s, England thereafter began to develop more and more industries that demanded workmen, so that the talk of overpopulation ceased to be heard. Instead of encouraging emigration from its own shores, the government tried to check the loss of English manpower by prohibiting the departure of skilled artisans, while continuing to unload the unemployable or the undesirable upon the defenseless colonies. Although, during the eighteenth century, the colonies received relatively few newcomers from England, the populations of several of them were swelled by vast numbers of arrivals from France, Germany, Switzerland, Ireland, and Scotland.

Of these immigrants the earliest though not the most numerous were the French Calvinists, or Huguenots. Under the Edict of Nantes (1598) they had enjoyed liberties and privileges that enabled them to constitute practically a state within the state in Roman Catholic France. In 1685 the edict was revoked, and singly and in groups the Huguenots took the first opportunity to leave the country, until a total of about 300,000 had left for England, the Netherlands, America, and elsewhere, only a small minority of them going to the English colonies. These émigrés were mostly artisans, merchants, and men of letters and science who enriched their new homes with both their talents and their wealth. In America they settled in the towns along the coast from Charleston to Boston, to become the ancestors of Americans like Paul Revere (Rivoire).

Like the French Protestants, many German Protestants suffered from the arbitrary enactments of their rulers, and German Catho-

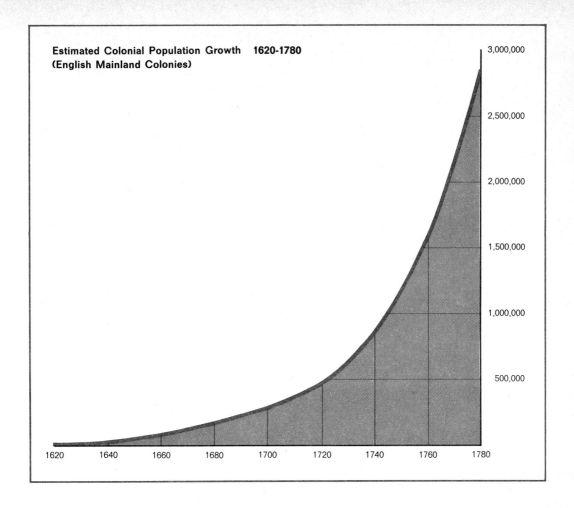

**Estimated Colonial Population Growth   1620-1780
(English Mainland Colonies)**

3,000,000

2,500,000

2,000,000

1,500,000

1,000,000

500,000

1620   1640   1660   1680   1700   1720   1740   1760   1780

lics as well as Protestants suffered even more from the devastating wars of the Sun King of France, Louis XIV. The Rhineland of south-western Germany, the area known as the Palatinate, was especially exposed to the slaughter of its people and the ruin of its farms. For the Palatine Germans, the unusually cold winter of 1708–1709 came as the last straw, and more than 12,000 of them sought refuge in England. The Catholics among them were shipped back to Germany and the rest were resettled in England, Ireland, or the colonies.

Arriving in New York, approximately 3,000 of them tried to make homes in the Mohawk Valley, only to be ousted by rapacious colonial landlords. Some of the Palatines moved farther up the Mohawk, but most of them made their way to Pennsylvania, where they received a hearty welcome. After that, the Quaker colony was the usual destination of Germans, who sailed for America in growing numbers, including some Moravians and Mennonites with religious views similar to those of the Quakers. But quite a few of the German Protestants went to

North Carolina, especially after the founding of New Bern (1710) by a company of 600 German-speaking Swiss. All together, the Germans comprised the largest body of eighteenth-century white immigrants except for the Scotch-Irish.

The Scotch-Irish, the most numerous of the newcomers, were not Irishmen at all, though coming from Ireland, and they were distinct from the Scots who came to America directly from Scotland. In the early 1600s King James I, to further the conquest of Ireland, had seen to the peopling of the northern county of Ulster with his subjects from the Scottish Lowlands, who as good Presbyterians might be relied upon to hold their ground against the Irish Catholics. These Ulster colonists—the Scotch-Irish—eventually prospered despite the handicap of a barren soil and the necessity of border fighting with the Irish tribesmen. Then, after about a century, the English government destroyed their prosperity by prohibiting the export of their woolens and other products, and at the same time threatened their religion

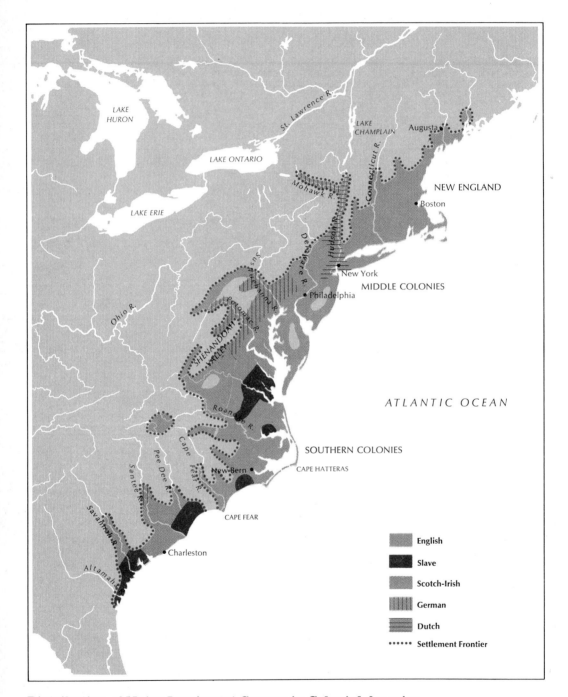

Distribution of Major Immigrant Groups in Colonial America

by virtually outlawing it and insisting upon conformity with the Anglican Church. As the long-term leases of the Scotch-Irish terminated, in the years after 1710, the English landlords doubled and even tripled the rents. Rather than sign new leases, thousands upon thousands of the ill-used tenants embarked in successive waves of emigration.

Understandably a cantankerous and troublesome lot, these people often were coldly received at the colonial ports, and most of them pushed out to the edge of the American wilderness. There they occupied land with scant regard for ownership, believing that "it was against the laws of God and nature that so much land should be idle while so many Christians wanted it to labor on and to raise bread." There also they fought the Indians as earlier they had fought the Irish. Among their illustrious descendants was the characteristically Scotch-Irish Andrew Jackson.

The Scots and the Irish, as migrants to America, had no connection with the Scotch-Irish. Scottish Highlanders, some of them Roman Catholics frustrated in the rebellions of 1715 and 1745, went with their tartans and kilts and bagpipes to more than one of the colonies, but mostly to North Carolina. Presbyterian Lowlanders, afflicted with high rents in the country and unemployment in town, left in largest numbers shortly before the American Revolution. These Scots, Lowlanders and Highlanders alike, with few exceptions became Loyalists after the outbreak of the Revolutionary War, but the Scotch-Irish were Patriots almost to the man, as were the Irish. The Irish had migrated in trickles over a long period and, by the time of the Revolution, were about as numerous as the Scots, though less conspicuous, many of them having lost their Roman Catholic religion and their identity as Irishmen.

All these various immigrants contributed to the remarkable growth of the colonies. In 1700 the colonial population totaled a quarter of a million or less; by 1775 it was nearly ten times as large, more than 2 million. The number practically doubled every twenty-five years, as Benjamin Franklin observed, leading the English clergyman Thomas Malthus to his pessimistic conclusion (1798) that any population, if unchecked, would increase in a geometrical progression while the means of subsistence (except in a new and favored country like America) could not be increased nearly so fast. Important as the continuing immigration was, the rapid growth of the colonial population was mainly due to natural increase, to the excess of births over deaths. In the colonies, with their abundance of land and opportunity, large families were an asset rather than a liability, and husbands and wives heeded the Biblical advice: "Be ye fruitful and multiply."

Hence the colonists of English origin, those who had arrived earliest and had had the longest time to multiply, continued greatly to outnumber those of non-English origin. Yet the proportion of non-English ancestry increased year by year, from a tenth in 1700 to a third (including the people from Africa) in 1760. The most homogeneous and most purely English part of the colonies was New England, while the most cosmopolitan part was the middle colonies, above all Pennsylvania. By the 1770s the Pennsylvania population was in origin roughly a third English, a third German, and a third Scotch-Irish. These groups did not intermix very much but were concentrated in separate areas—the English around Philadelphia, the Germans to the north and west, and the Scotch-Irish still farther out on the frontier. Many of the Germans continued to speak their native language, which eventually was corrupted into a German-English dialect known as "Pennsylvania Dutch." Nevertheless, in the colonies as a whole, there was a good deal of intermarriage between the different nationalities, and even before the Revolution thousands of Americans could trace their ancestry to two or more nations of the Old World.

As compared with the population of England, that of the colonies was not only mixed but also youthful and masculine, containing somewhat fewer old persons and women, especially along the frontier. And the colonial population was surprisingly mobile, New Englanders resettling in New Jersey and other colonies to the south, and Pennsylvanians (Scotch-Irish and Germans) swarming up the Shenandoah Valley to people the back country of the Carolinas. In all the colonies men and women pushed upstream toward the unsettled wilderness, until with Daniel Boone leading the way into Kentucky (1769) they began even to occupy the land beyond the mountains.

Along the seacoast a number of villages grew into small cities. For more than a century after its founding, Boston remained the largest town, but eventually it was overtaken by both Philadelphia and New York. In 1760 Philadelphia had more than 23,000 people, New York about 18,000, and Boston nearly 16,000. Next in order were Charleston, S.C., with approximately 8,000 and Newport, R.I., with 7,500. After 1700 these colonial towns increased more rapidly than most English cities, yet not always so rapidly as did the American population as a

Baltimore in 1752
*Though founded in 1729, Baltimore remained a small settlement at the time this
painting was made. The town had not developed as a port, since most of the Maryland
tobacco growers shipped their crops from their own wharves along the rivers. (The
Maryland Historical Society, Baltimore)*

whole. Eight out of a hundred Americans lived
in towns in 1720, and only about five or six out
of a hundred in 1742. The rest of the people —
the overwhelming majority throughout the colonial period — were scattered over the countryside and lived upon farms of one description
or another.

The Economic Basis

In the shaping of the provincial economy — that
is, in the determination of the ways the colonists made their living — three forces were especially important. One of these was the policy
of the British government, which discouraged
certain occupations and encouraged others, in
accordance with mercantilist principles. A
second and more important influence derived
from the geographical conditions in America,
which favored some lines of activity and made
others impracticable. A third consisted of the
aims and energies of the individual settlers,
who brought with them from the British Isles
and the European continent (and, in the case
of the slaves, from Africa) their own skills and
habits and aspirations for personal success. As
a result of these diverse factors, there flourished in the eighteenth century a variety of
agricultural, industrial, and commercial pursuits, not all of which conformed to the broad
mercantilistic plan.

AGRICULTURE

Though there were regional differences, farming throughout the colonies had certain characteristics in common. In all the colonies it was a

matter of adapting European plants and animals to American conditions or applying European techniques to the cultivation of native crops. The colonist's tools and methods, while an improvement on those of the Indian, continued to be extremely primitive. The ground was still broken with hoe and mattock or with a crude wooden plow, usually drawn by oxen because of their slower and steadier pull than horses could provide, and often requiring two men to hold and guide it. Harvesting was back-breaking work with sickle or scythe. Grain was threshed with a flail or by the trampling of oxen, and it was winnowed by being tossed in the air for the breeze to carry away the chaff. In George Washington's time these processes were not much advanced beyond what they had been in the day of the Pharaohs, and in colonial America there was even less care of the soil than there had been in ancient Egypt. Most of the colonists gave little thought to conserving their land by rotating crops, applying fertilizers, or checking erosion. Their attitude was reasonable enough in their circumstances: it paid them to economize on labor, not on land.

Near the frontier—that ever-expanding arc from Maine to Georgia, which bounded the area of settlement—subsistence farming was the rule. The frontiersman planted his corn and beans amid the stumps in patches he had incompletely reclaimed from the forest, and with his crops and his catch of wild game he fed himself and his family. Eventually some of the backwoodsmen went in for cattle raising on a fairly large scale, especially in Pennsylvania and the Carolinas. In these areas, long before the day of the cowboy on the Great Plains, herders let their branded cattle roam over an open range and, after the annual roundup, drove them to distant cities. The town of Cowpens, South Carolina, derived its name from its origin as a cattle-raising center. As the line of settlement moved outward, so did the frontier kind of farm and ranch life. Within that line—in areas that, beginning with the seacoast itself, had shared most of the frontier characteristics at one time or another—arose patterns of agriculture increasingly more elaborate, more productive, and more diverse.

In New England—where farmers once had lived on village lots, shared the "commons" as pasture and timberland, and tilled outlying fields—the system of landholding gradually changed. After 1700 the commons were partly divided into private property, and the fields were consolidated into separate farms. The typical farm became one that was small enough to be worked by the farmer, his sons, and perhaps an occasional hired hand, with the aid of neighbors at harvests and at house or barn raisings. It was bounded by fences made of stones that had been laboriously cleared off the fields. A fairly self-sufficient unit, producing mainly for use rather than for sale, it contained a variety of scrawny livestock, apple and other orchards, and fields devoted chiefly to hay and corn, the prevalence of the "blast" or black-stem rust having discouraged the cultivation of wheat.

An exception to the usual New England farm scene was to be found on the shores and islands of Narragansett Bay. Here were rich and extensive farms on which were bred fine sheep, cattle, and horses, notably the Narragansett pacer. And here gangs of Negro slaves were used.

In New York, despite the abundance of excellent soil, agricultural productivity lagged because of the engrossment of the land in great estates, running to thousands and even hundreds of thousands of acres, on which few people were willing to work as tenants when they could get farms of their own in other colonies. The Dutch and their descendants set examples of careful tillage on the freeholds they had acquired at an early date.

In Pennsylvania, of all the colonies the most favored by nature for farming, the Germans likewise applied the intensive cultivation they had learned in the old country. Their neat and substantial barns were their pride, but the work of their womenfolk in the fields was sometimes shocking to non-Germans. With fairly large holdings, these farmers needed all the labor they could get, and in addition to their wives and daughters they employed indentured servants, women as well as men.

In New York and Pennsylvania the farmers concentrated upon the production of staples to be sold abroad and at home. After ceasing to produce enough food to feed all its own people, New England depended upon these "bread colonies" for its wheat. So, to some extent, did those Southern colonies that were preoccupied with the growing of tobacco.

In the Chesapeake region there still existed tobacco farms as small as a hundred acres, cultivated by the owners, their families, and perhaps a servant or a slave or two. Such farms, however, had come to be overshadowed by large plantations with thousands of acres and dozens of Negroes. The Maryland plantation of Charles Carroll of Carrollton, reputedly the wealthiest man in the colonies, covered 40,000 acres and contained 285 slaves. On the tobacco plantations slave labor was easily adapted to the simple and repetitive round of tasks that the crop required — sowing, transplanting, weeding, worming, picking, curing, stripping, and packing.

Slave labor was also fairly well suited to rice culture along the Georgia and Carolina coasts. Here dikes and ditches leading from the tidal rivers permitted the necessary flooding and draining of the paddies, while care was taken to see that no salt water reached the rice with the incoming tide. To cultivate the growing rice, men had to stand knee-deep in mud, their bare backs exposed to malarial mosquitoes and to the broiling sun. Since white men could not be hired to do it, Negroes were compelled to perform this torturing and unhealthful work. But the rice plantations were smaller than the tobacco plantations and did not provide a similar year-round routine that would utilize slave labor to the full.

Indigo supplemented rice after the successful cultivation of the dye plant (1743) by Eliza Lucas, the daughter of a West Indian planter. Grown on high ground, the indigo did not get in the way of the rice on the river bottoms, and it occupied the slaves at times when they were not busy with the rice. They tended the indigo fields, cut the leaves, soaked them in vats, and extracted the residue as a blue powder. Glad for a chance to be freed from foreign sources of the dye, Parliament granted a bounty of sixpence a pound.

The British government tried to encourage the production of other crops that would meet the needs of mercantilism. It gave bounties for hemp, and a little was grown in the colonies, particularly in North Carolina, but not enough to make the experiment pay. The government also attempted to force the growth of grapes for wine and of mulberry trees for silk, but had even less success with these than with hemp. Too much skilled labor was required for such products. Obstinately the colonial farmers and planters stuck to those lines of production in which they had a comparative advantage over producers elsewhere in the world. In some cases, as with tobacco and indigo, the colonial products happened to supplement those grown in England and thus fit the mercantilistic pattern. In other cases, as with wheat, the produce of the colonies competed with that of the mother country and was either irrelevant to the mercantile system or incompatible with it.

INDUSTRIES

In the 1700s, as in earlier times, farm families produced nearly all their necessities within the household. Here the women did most of the work, baking, churning, spinning, weaving, dyeing, sewing, and making soap, candles, and other things for home consumption. An increasing quantity of goods, however, was manufactured outside the home, in shops. Specialists in various arts and crafts had come to America in the seventeenth century but found it hard to make a living from their specialties. These men had to turn to farming, and their skills deteriorated from disuse. Even after 1700 there were few opportunities for craftsmen in rural areas, particularly in the colonies to the south of Pennsylvania. On many a plantation, slaves were trained to produce the needed manufactures that it was not feasible to import from England.

In the rising towns, artisans of many kinds appeared — carpenters, chandlers (candlemakers), coopers (barrelmakers), cordwainers (shoemakers), weavers, tailors, wheelwrights, and dozens of others. Except in such lines as millinery and dressmaking, women artisans were rare, though now and then a widow took over her husband's work and succeeded as a cobbler, tinworker, or even blacksmith. By the year 1750 almost a third of the people of Philadelphia owed their living to a craft of some kind.

The craft usually was a family enterprise, and the shop was on the ground floor of the master craftsman's home. The master was assisted by his sons and by one or more journeymen and apprentices, who lived as members of his household, and who aspired eventually to become masters with shops of their own. In some ways the craftsman was like the small businessman of the present. He had to procure and train workers, provide materials, supervise the work (while taking an active part in it), and find a market. When possible, he made goods to order, or, as he called them, "bespoke" goods, but in slack times he might produce a stock of articles for general sale. In newspaper advertisements he sometimes made exaggerated and even fraudulent claims for his wares, while running down the wares of his competitors. He sold on credit or for barter, seldom for cash.

In America the guild, or association of craftsmen, which in England regulated each of the trades, did not take root. Regulations regarding apprenticeship, the quality of goods, and other matters were provided by the colonial and municipal governments. Despite the laws intended to maintain high standards, some of the products were shoddy and most of them were inferior to the machine-made goods of today. By 1750, however, American artisans were turning out some articles that compared with the best of that time or of any time. For instance, the gunsmiths of Lancaster, Pennsylvania, were justly famous for the Pennsylvania rifle (also known as the Kentucky rifle), and the wagonmakers of the same town for the Conestoga wagon (the original "covered wagon," with ends up-curved to hold the load securely on hills and rough roads). American silversmiths, such as Paul Revere, did work as fine as that of England or France and finer than that of the rest of Europe. The same was true of American cabinetmakers.

Colonial craftsmanship became notable for quantity as well as quality. As late as 1700 all but a tiny fraction of the manufactures that the colonists bought were made in England. Before the Revolution, more than half of the manufactures were made in America. The rise of the colonial craftsman was watched with concern by men in London who took the doctrines of mercantilism seriously.

When colonial merchants began to organize the work of shops and households on a larger and more efficient scale, there arose the "putting-out" system, which was a forerunner of the later factory system. The merchant supplied materials to workers in homes or shops, then gathered up and marketed the finished product. Before the Revolution, Lynn, Massa-chusetts, was already famous for shoemaking and Germantown, Pennsylvania, for producing knit goods. Under the putting-out system the workers were not drawn together as in post-Revolutionary factories.

Water power was widely used in various kinds of colonial mills. At the rapids of streams small enough to be easily dammed, grist and fulling mills were set up to take some of the heavier labor out of the household, grinding grain and fulling cloth (shrinking and tightening the weave by a process of soaking and pounding) for the farmers in the area. The mill-owner was usually a farmer himself in his spare time. He frequently used his water wheel to power a sawmill for cutting his neighbors' logs. Other and busier sawmills accompanied the lumber industry, which followed the retreating forest. Circular saws were as yet unknown, and the up-and-down powered saw, while it would do the work of twenty men in cutting soft pine, was not very efficient in cutting hardwoods, particularly if the trees were large. So it had to be supplemented by the large "pit saw" operated by two men, one down in a pit and the other on the ground above, and also by the ax and the adze, the hammer and the wedge. Other forest industries yielded pitch, tar, resin, turpentine, and potash for a number of industrial uses.

Like lumbering, the fur trade and the fisheries were extractive industries, depending closely upon the resources provided by nature. Both fishing and fur trading became big businesses employing what were, by colonial standards, large amounts of capital. It was expensive to provide fur traders with goods for bartering with Indian trappers—guns, knives, blankets, looking-glasses, and beads to exchange for furs and hides—and most of the business came to be controlled by English merchants in London and colonial merchants in Albany, Philadelphia, and Charleston. It was costly also to outfit fleets for the fishing industry, which concentrated mainly in New England waters, though almost every farmer near a stream or pond was at least a part-time fisherman.

The fisheries led to shipbuilding, the first colonial-built ships being put together on the New England coast for the use of fishermen, and the abundance of timber and naval stores enabled the industry in the colonies to expand to the point of outdoing that of England itself. So cheap and yet so seaworthy were the materials that, despite the high wages of colonial labor, excellent ships could be produced at as little as half the cost of those built in English yards. Usually a master shipwright contracted for the construction of a vessel, and he procured, paid, and directed the laborers who did the work. While New England kept its early lead in shipbuilding, New York and Pennsylvania also had their shipyards, and Virginia and the Carolinas, with their fine supply of live-oak timber, became important centers of the industry in the latter half of the eighteenth century.

Some undertakings on a still larger scale than ship construction were to be found in the iron industry. From almost the very beginnings of Virginia and Massachusetts, small bloomeries and forges were erected to utilize the bog ores in those colonies, and eventually sizable furnaces were erected to smelt either bog or rock ores in almost all the colonies. The most extensive industrial enterprise anywhere in English America was that of the German iron-master Peter Hasenclever, in northern New Jersey. It was founded in 1764 with British capital and was operated thereafter with a labor force of several hundred, many of whom were brought over from ironworks in Germany. It included not only furnaces and forges but also sawmills and a gristmill.

From the beginning of colonization, the home government encouraged the colonial production or iron in a crude form, as a raw material for English mills and foundries. When colonial ironmakers began to produce more than merely the crude metal, their competitors in England induced Parliament to pass the Iron Act of 1750, which removed the English duty on pig and bar iron but forbade the colonists to erect new mills for the secondary processing of iron or steel. This prohibition was in line with other acts intended to limit the rise of advanced manufactures in America. The Woolen Act (1699) prohibited the export of wool or woolens from a colony to any place outside its boundaries, and the Hat Act (1732) similarly prohibited the export of hats, which could be cheaply made in America because of the availability of beaver skins. But the colonists usually disregarded such legislation when it was in their interest to do so.

MONEY AND COMMERCE

Though the colonists produced most of what they consumed, they by no means achieved economic self-sufficiency. The colonies as a whole could not supply their entire wants from their own agriculture and industry. Neither could any of the separate colonies, nor could an individual household except at an extremely low level of living. To maintain and raise their living standards the mainland colonists had to have the benefits of trade with one another and with people overseas.

Intercolonial trade was fairly extensive and diversified. In the busy coastal traffic the surplus products of each region were exchanged — such products as the fish and rum of New England, the flour and meat of the middle colonies, and the tobacco and indigo of the South. The trade between the seaports and their hinterland involved some of these same products, besides many others, including the variety of small articles carried by the pack-horse peddler. A large proportion of the commodities distributed upriver from the seaports had their origin abroad, and a large proportion of those gathered in the interior were destined for export. Much of the intercolonial and inland trade was thus a part of overseas commerce.

Foreign trade provided indispensable consumer and capital goods that the colonists could not manufacture for themselves in suitable quantity or quality. From abroad the mill-owner had to get his machinery, the shipwright his hardware and navigating instruments, the farmer his spades and other tools, the Indian trader most of his supplies. Even a modest home included kitchen utensils, tableware, needles and thread, lanterns, and other equipment of European make. Wealthier families bought additional imports, luxury items such as mirrors, paper, books, fine furniture, and fancy cloth. The more the colonists prospered, whether individually or collectively, the more they demanded goods of foreign manufacture.

The central problem in the overseas commerce of the colonies was to find the means of payment for these increasing imports. Money was scarce in the colonies. They did not mine their own gold or silver, and the mercantilist policy was intended to drain them of such specie as they might acquire. They did obtain a

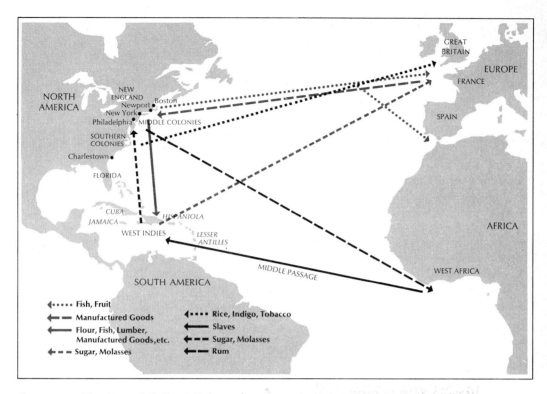

Fish, Fruit ◄······
Manufactured Goods ◄ ─ ─
Flour, Fish, Lumber,
Manufactured Goods, etc. ◄────
Sugar, Molasses ◄ ─ ─

Rice, Indigo, Tobacco ◄ ▪▪▪▪
Slaves ◄────
Sugar, Molasses ◄ ▪ ─
Rum ◄ ▪ ▪

Overseas Trades of Colonial America

motley collection of Spanish and other European coins from their dealings with pirates and from certain routes of overseas trade. Generally, in their transactions with one another, the colonists resorted to barter or else used money substitutes, though always calculating in terms of pounds, shillings, and pence. Beaver skins circulated widely as a medium of exchange and so did tobacco—not the leaves but warehouse certificates representing tobacco in storage. All the colonies experimented at one time or another with paper currency, often securing it with land. But Parliament suppressed this expedient by legislating against the Massachusetts land bank in 1740, and by outlawing paper money as legal tender in New England in 1751 and in the rest of the colonies later on. Anyhow, this kind of paper was not acceptable in payment for imported goods and services, which had to be bought with specie or with bills of exchange arising from colonial exports. In short, the colonies had to sell abroad in order to

buy from abroad, but British policy attempted to limit and control their selling opportunities.

Though the tobacco planters had an abundant staple for export, they were not allowed to dispose of it to the highest bidder in the markets of the world. According to the Navigation Acts, tobacco was one of the "enumerated items" that must be exported only to the British Isles, whence more than half of it was reexported to other places. The laws also prohibited the growing of tobacco in the British Isles, but protection against competition in the mother country did not quite offset the disadvantages of the colonial planter.

He usually sold his annual crop to an English merchant (or after the mid-eighteenth century to a Scottish merchant) either directly or through a factor in the colonies, and the merchant credited him with its value, after deducting charges for shipping, insurance, and a merchant's commission. Through the merchant he bought slaves and manufactured goods, and the merchant deducted the cost of these from the planter's credit on the books. After tobacco prices had begun to fall, the planter often found at the end of a year that his crop did not pay for all the goods he had ordered in return. The merchant then carried him until the next year and charged interest on the extension of credit. As the years went by, the planter went more and more deeply into debt, eventually leaving his indebtedness to his heirs.

The colonial merchant in such ports as Boston, New York, and Philadelphia did not have the same difficulties as the tobacco planter, though he had others of his own. He was favored by the Navigation Acts, passed in 1650 and after, which excluded foreign ships from practically all of the colonial carrying trade. And he found a market in England for the furs, timber, naval stores, and vessels produced in the Northern colonies. But he could not profitably sell in England all the fish, flour, wheat, and meat which the colonies produced for export. He had to find other markets for these commodities if he was to obtain adequate means of paying for his imports from England. Wherever he traded, his profits would be reduced if he obeyed the laws and paid the duties imposed on most of the colonial goods that went to England and on all the European goods that went through England to the colonies.

In the English island colonies of the West Indies the colonial merchant found a ready outlet for mainland products. In the French, Dutch, and Spanish islands of the Caribbean he also got eager customers—and often better prices. Responding to pressure from English sugar planters, who wished to monopolize the mainland trade, Parliament in the Molasses Act of 1733 put a high duty on foreign sugar taken to the continental colonies. The molasses duty was intended to discourage commerce with the foreign islands. But the Northern merchant could evade the tax by smuggling, and he often did.

From the ports of New England and the middle colonies went cargo after cargo of lumber, horses, wheat, flour, biscuits, corn, peas, potatoes, fruit, beef, pork, bacon, and fish. From the West Indies were obtained sugar, molasses, rum, dyewoods, cotton, ginger, coffee, Spanish coins and bills of exchange (these were drafts drawn by planters in the West Indies on merchants in England; they served much the same purpose as checks drawn on a bank). Sometimes West Indian products were carried directly to England; more commonly they were brought back to American ports, where part was sold in the domestic market and the rest exported to England. These exports, together with bills of exchange and Spanish money, helped to pay for the English goods imported into the thirteen colonies.

To and from England, to and from the West Indies—these were much the most important routes of trade for the Northern merchant. He also worked out a number of routes of indirect trade with the mother country, some of them complex and frequently changing, others fairly stable and somewhat "triangular" in their simplicity. Thus he might direct his ships to Catholic southern Europe with fish, then to England with wine and other proceeds in cash or bills of exchange, and then back home with manufactured goods.

Aspects of Society

In provincial America the generous economic basis of life supported a society in which the benefits of physical well-being were more widely diffused than anywhere else in the world. It was a comparatively open society, in which people had more opportunity than elsewhere to rise in economic and social status. Yet it was also a society with great inequalities, one that offered only hardship and poverty to many of its members and especially to those of African descent.

THE CLASS STRUCTURE

In England, as in Europe, class lines were sharply marked during the seventeenth and eighteenth centuries. The chances for any Eng-

A Slave Coffle

A slave ship off the African coast awaits her cargo. One slave trader wrote: "The negroes are so wilful and loth to leave their own country, that they have often leap'd out of the canoos, boat and ship, into the sea, and kept under water till they were drowned, to avoid being taken up and saved by our boats. . . ." The historian Philip D. Curtin has estimated that, between 1701 and 1810, more than 6 million slaves from Africa arrived in North and South America. Of these, fewer than 350,000 (less than 6 per cent) went to the British mainland colonies of North America or to the United States. Illustration from Freedman's National and Family Record *(1873). (Library of Congress)*

A Slave Ship

The plan of the Brookes, *an eighteenth-century English vessel built especially for the slave trade, shows how little space was wasted. Pictured here is only one of two lower decks. The slaves were packed in so tightly that they had no room to stand or even to sit. During part of the day (except in bad weather) they were allowed on the main deck to get food, air, and exercise. (New York Public Library)*

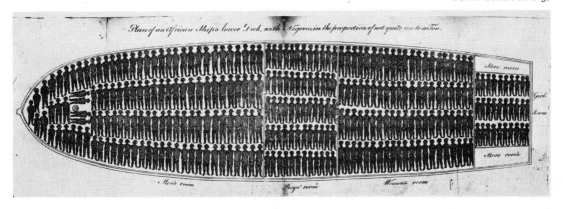

lishman to rise above the station of his father and grandfather were rather slim — unless he went to America.

In the colonies the English class arrangement was not reproduced. Few or none of the nobility became colonists, though some of them were colonial enterprisers. A relatively small number of untitled gentlemen and a great many members of the middle and lower orders migrated to Virginia, Massachusetts, and other colonies. Some of these arrivals doubtless hoped to reconstruct in America something like the social system they had known in England, only here they hoped to occupy the higher levels themselves. A fortunate few did acquire extensive landholdings and proceeded to mimic the aristocrats back home, but no true aristocracy was transplanted to the colonies.

A colonial class system nevertheless grew up. Once social differentiation was well developed, as it was by the middle of the eighteenth century, the upper classes in the colonies consisted of the royal officials, the proprietary families, the great landholders in the North and the planters in the South, and the leading merchants with their investments mostly in forms of property other than land. The middle classes included most of the landowning farmers and, in the towns, the lesser merchants, shopkeepers, ship captains, professional men, and self-employed artisans. The lower classes comprised the indentured servants and the poorest farmers, together with the comparatively small number of wage earners, including farm hands, sailors, and fishermen. Forming a separate class or caste, though often working in the fields alongside white servants and even alongside men of the master class, were the Negro slaves, the lowliest of all.

All except the slaves could aspire to a higher place for themselves or at least for their children. Once a man had made a fortune, he was usually accepted by those who theretofore had considered him their social inferior. The colonists, believing in enterprise and material success, honored the self-made man. Afterward his descendants were inclined to forget the humble and even grubby origins of the family fortune and to think of themselves as thoroughgoing aristocrats. For example, one of the "first families" of eighteenth-century Virginia, the Byrds, enjoyed a fortune that William Byrd I had put together in the seventeenth century by

selling pots, pans, guns, and rum to the Indians in exchange for furs and hides, as well as by dealing in Indian and African slaves.

Class consciousness and class distinctions came to be quite noticeable in provincial America. Usually a person's place in society was obvious from his appearance and dress. An ordinary farmer in his coarse linen homespun or a town craftsman in his leather apron made a sharp contrast with a planter or merchant in buckle shoes, knee breeches, colorful waistcoat, starched ruffles, and powdered wig. A farm girl, her faced parched by winter fire or summer sun, her buxom figure clothed in homemade linsey-woolsey, was not likely to be mistaken for a planter's or merchant's daughter, whose delicate form was clad in imported silks and satins, and whose complexion was protected by a dainty parasol.

As some of the rich grew richer, some of the poor became more impoverished. There was a widening of extremes. If many of the early indentured servants acquired valuable land and respectable status after completing their servitude, many of the later ones either took up subsistence farming on the frontier or sank to the level of the "poor whites" on worn-out lands in the neighborhood of the planters. Yet, especially in New England, the vast majority of the people came to form a self-respecting, property-owning middle class.

A few humanitarians began to take note of what they considered the wrongs of the society they knew. Of these reformers the foremost was a New Jersey Quaker, John Woolman, who wrote appealingly and traveled widely in a patient effort to better the condition of workers, especially slaves. In *Some Considerations on the Keeping of Negroes* (Part I, 1754; Part II, 1762) he took up an antislavery crusade which had been preached before him, but never so earnestly.

The pleas of Woolman and other reformers did little to soften the institution of slavery, which during the first half of the eighteenth century had become more and more rigid, with slave codes that were more and more severe. This was especially true in South Carolina, where whites had reason to fear the blacks who greatly outnumbered them. There, slave conspiracies or mere rumors of them brought savage retribution and further tightenings of the already strict laws governing slavery. Near

Charleston several slaves accused of conspiring to revolt were burned to death in 1720. In the city itself fifty were hanged in 1740, and when a disastrous fire followed, two more were executed for arson.

Such events were not confined to the South. In New York City a Negro insurrection led in 1712 to the execution of twenty-one participants, one of whom was chained up without food or drink until he died. Again, in 1741, 101 Negroes were convicted of plotting with poor whites to burn the city; 18 of the blacks were hanged, 13 burned alive, and the rest banished; 4 whites, 2 of them women, went to the gallows. Even in New England, where slaves were relatively few and slavery relatively mild, there were occasional instances of blacks attacking whites. In 1723 several Negroes were suspected of starting a series of fires in Boston, and in 1741 a black man and woman schemed to set the torch to neighboring Charlestown. But the threat from Negroes caused no mass hysteria or wholesale vengeance in New England.

HOME AND FAMILY

From the beginning, the family shelters of the colonists were fairly close imitations of those already familiar to them, yet houses (like almost everything else) were more or less altered

---

Westover
In 1688 William Byrd I began the construction of a house on land he had bought along the James River, not far from the place where Richmond, Virginia, later was to be located. His son, the brilliant William Byrd II, lived here during much of his life (when he was not in England). In 1749 the house burned down, and William Byrd III had it rebuilt. He failed, however, to maintain the fortune his father and grandfather had accumulated, and eventually the estate passed out of the family's possession. A French traveler, the Marquis de Chastellux, who was a guest at Westover in 1782, wrote: "There are magnificent houses at every view, for the banks of the James River form the garden of Virginia. That of Mrs. Byrd surpasses them all in the magnificence of the buildings, the beauty of its situation, and the pleasures of society." Westover is one of the finest examples of the Georgian style, as applied to domestic architecture, in America. (Photograph by Thomas T. Waterman, Library of Congress)

by Americanizing trends. The first English pioneers built thatched huts rather than log cabins of the kind now considered peculiarly American. Introduced by the early Swedish settlers along the Delaware, the log cabin did not become the typical frontier dwelling until the eighteenth century. By that time a variety of building materials and architectural styles had appeared in the older settled areas. Though a higher proportion of colonial than of English houses were built of wood, a considerable number were built of stone or brick, some of which was imported. In New England a common type of farmhouse was the "salt-box," two stories high in front and one in back, and sided with unpainted clapboards. In the middle colonies the redbrick house with a Dutch gambrel roof and the substantial farmhouse of native stone were characteristic. In the South the more prosperous planters erected Georgian mansions, which as a rule were copies of English models, reduced in size and simplified in ornament.

Crowded into the generally small houses were comparatively large families, at least in the early years of settlement. The family often included not only numerous children but also a varying number of dependent relatives, such as elderly grandparents or unmarried aunts. The household was further enlarged in many cases by the presence of servants, domestic slaves, or hired hands living under the same roof.

As head of the household, the father traditionally wielded strong authority over its members. He was entitled to whatever property his wife had owned before her marriage to him, but he was responsible also for her debts and misdeeds. The position of women, however, was somewhat higher in the colonies than in the homeland. Since they were relatively scarce, colonial women were proportionately valued for reasons of supply and demand. They were, for instance, more free than Englishwomen to travel about without male escorts or female chaperones, though Sarah Knight's journey from Boston to New York by herself (1704) was rather exceptional, at least in regard to distance.

In the life of the colonial family there was much more than congeniality and companionship to hold a married couple together. The family as a unit performed many functions which, since that time, have been taken over by business enterprises or by the state. It had economic functions as the producer of most of what its members consumed. It performed educational services, many a child learning his ABCs at his mother's knee from the family Bible. The family served as a welfare agency in caring for the aged, the unemployable, and the sick. It was even a defense organization, at least on the frontier, where the lonely farmstead became a fortress to be manned by the whole family at the sound of the war-whoop. Having all these forces of cohesion, families were rarely broken, except by death. Divorces were seldom sought and, except in New England, were difficult or impossible to obtain. Occasionally, it is true, husbands deserted or wives absconded, as advertisements in contemporary newspapers reveal.

Nevertheless, the patriarchal family, with its enlarged household, proved difficult to maintain under the conditions of life in eighteenth-century America. Here, where land was so much more abundant and labor so much scarcer than in England, separate and smaller families could manage to survive much more easily. "Dependent kin, servants, and sons soon left the patriarchal household, setting up their own reduced establishments which would never grow to the old proportions," as the historian Bernard Bailyn has observed. Elders were shocked by what seemed to them the breakup of the very foundation of the social order. In a futile effort to restore parental authority, the colonies passed laws demanding obedience from children and providing severe penalties for filial disrespect.

Immorality in provincial America would be hard to measure. Among their contemporaries in neighboring colonies, the countryfolk of North Carolina had a reputation for loose morals, but as a whole these Carolinians were probably no worse than their critics. The church and court records of New England contain much evidence of premarital relations in that part of the country, but what the evidence most likely proves is that the Puritans were prone to confess their sins and to keep careful records, rather than that these people were especially given to fornication. Furthermore, the Puritan betrothal was itself such a solemn and binding ceremony that some New Englanders doubted whether intercourse between engaged couples was really wrong, and in the early eighteenth century Harvard students discussed that very question in public debate. In the rural South, as in the rural North, prostitutes were almost unheard of, but in the seaports commercialized vice grew with the growth of commerce itself.

Among indentured servants nonmarital relations were a common evil, or so it was believed — and no doubt correctly, since servants usually were forbidden to marry during their servitude. As for the slaves, their marriages were not recognized by law, and few masters were as much concerned with the identity of a slave father as they were with the fecundity of a slave mother. The offspring of white fathers and black mothers, and vice versa, began to appear at an early date and, despite the intensification of race prejudice, became more numerous as time went on. Though indentured servants were blamed for the racial intermixture, men of the master class were responsible for much of it.

The Mind and Spirit

The new scientific spirit of the Enlightenment was quite out of keeping with old beliefs, such as the notion of witchcraft or even the idea of a personal God who kept watch over individual lives. Nevertheless old attitudes persisted and often were intermingled with the new. In provincial America the diverging points of view were represented by two outstanding figures: Benjamin Franklin, a superb example of the Enlightenment man, and Jonathan Edwards, a latter-day expounder of the old-time Puritan faith. Yet Edwards, along with many other religious leaders, also shared the growing interest in science and reason.

THE PATTERN OF RELIGIONS

Though originating abroad, religions developed a new and distinctive pattern in America. With the immigration of diverse sectarians from several countries, the colonies became an ecclesiastical patchwork made up of a great variety of churches. Toleration flourished to a degree remarkable for the time, not because it was deliberately sought but because conditions favored its growth. No single religious establishment predominated in the colonies as the Church of England did in the British Isles and as other state churches, Lutheran or Roman Catholic, did in Western Europe.

By law, the Church of England was established in Virginia, Maryland, New York, the Carolinas, and Georgia. In these colonies everyone regardless of belief or affiliation was supposed to be taxed for the support of the Church. Actually, except in Virginia and Maryland, the Church of England succeeded in maintaining its position as the established church only in certain localities.

To strengthen Anglicanism in America, the Bishop of London began in 1689 to delegate the supervision of the colonial churches to his personal representatives, or commissaries. When the first commissary, James Blair, was appointed in Virginia, more than half of the parishes in the colony had no minister. When Blair died in 1743, after more than fifty years of devoted labor, there were only two unsupplied parishes.

Further to strengthen Anglicanism, in America and elsewhere, the Church of England in 1701 set up the Society for the Propagation of the Gospel in Foreign Parts. Missionaries of the SPG founded a number of new Anglican communions in the colonies, especially in Massachusetts and Connecticut. Seeing that Anglicanism in America was handicapped by the lack of a bishop, the missionaries agitated for the appointment of one. But Congregationalists and others opposed this as a step toward tyranny, and the Anglican clergy of Virginia and Maryland agreed with them. No bishop was appointed.

Not all the Puritans were Congregationalists: some of them became Presbyterians. In belief, these two groups were essentially the same, but they differed in ecclesiastical organization, the Presbyterians having a more highly centralized government, with a governing body of presbyters (made up of ministers and

Christ Church, Cambridge, Massachusetts

Peter Harrison, who designed Christ Church, has been called "America's first architect." Born in England, Harrison became a ship captain when only twenty-three. He married an American woman with considerable property and prospered as a merchant of Newport, Rhode Island. In versatility, though not in genius, he rivaled Benjamin Franklin. He was not a jack of all trades, according to his biographer Carl Bridenbaugh, but was "rather a master of ten — ship-handling, navigation, ship-building, woodcarving, drafting, cartography, surveying, military engineering and construction, commerce, and the new agriculture," in addition to architecture. He acquired the largest and best selected architectural library in colonial America. Among the notable structures he designed were King's Chapel in Boston, Touro Synagogue in Newport, St. Michael's in Charleston, and Christ Church in Cambridge. The building committee for Christ Church insisted upon the most simple and inexpensive construction. Though he did not manage to keep within the cost limit, Harrison succeeded in creating a charmingly original design, in the spirit of the late Georgian style, at a remarkably low cost. On the interior, he produced an effect of considerable spaciousness for so small a church by leaving out the usual gallery, or balcony, on each side. (Library of Congress)

lay elders) for the churches of each district. In the early 1700s many of the Puritan churches of Connecticut, and most of those founded in other colonies by emigrants from New England, adopted the Presbyterian form of government. The number of Presbyterians in America was greatly increased by the immigration of the Scotch-Irish. At first, most of these people lacked churches and pastors. Francis Makemie, often called the father of Presbyterianism in America, organized the first American presbytery (1705) and for twenty years traveled up and down the coast from New York to South Carolina to set up churches for the churchless.

Another Calvinist group, numerous in parts of New York and New Jersey, was the Dutch Reformed. Originally the American Baptists, of whom Roger Williams is considered the first, were also Calvinistic in their theology. Then, in Rhode Island and in other colonies, a bewildering variety of Baptist sects sprang up. They had in common a belief that infant baptism did not suffice and that rebaptism, usually by total immersion, was necessary. Some remained Calvinists, believers in predestination, and others came to believe in salvation by man's free will.

Quite different from the Calvinists were the Quaker mystics and the German pietists, such as the Mennonites, Dunkers, and Moravians. The Quakers (Society of Friends) abandoned their early enthusiasm, which once had caused them to disturb other religious gatherings when they first settled in America. As their wealth increased, many of the Friends lost still more of their old-time fervor, the rich Philadelphia merchants dividing their allegiance between meeting house and counting house. Though politically dominant in Pennsylvania from the beginning, the Quakers did not use their power to compel conformity. Of all the colonies, Rhode Island and Pennsylvania were characterized by the greatest religious diversity and freedom. In Pennsylvania and other places where Germans settled, the Lutherans as well as the pietist sects added variety to the colonial religious scene.

Protestants extended toleration to one another more readily than to Roman Catholics. To strict Puritans the Pope seemed no less than Antichrist. Their border enemies in New France, being "papists," seemed agents to the devil bent on frustrating the divine mission of the wilderness Zion in New England. In most of the English colonies, however, the Roman Catholics were far too small a minority to occasion serious conflict. They were most numerous in Maryland, and even there they numbered no more than 3,000. Ironically, they suffered their worst persecution in that colony, which had been founded as a refuge for them and had been distinguished by its Toleration Act of 1649. According to Maryland laws passed after 1691, Catholics not only were deprived of political rights but also were forbidden to hold religious services except in private houses.

Even fewer than the Catholics, the Jews in provincial America totaled no more than about 2,000 at any time. The largest community lived in New York City, smaller groups in Newport and Charleston, and dispersed families in all the colonies. There was relatively little social discrimination against the Jews, but there was political discrimination: in no colony could they vote or hold office. In New England they enjoyed a certain esteem because of the Puritans' interest in the Old Testament and in Hebrew culture.

THE GREAT AWAKENING

During the early 1700s the pious outlook gave way more and more to a worldly view. With the westward movement and the wide scattering of the colonial population, many of the frontiersmen lost touch with organized religion. With the rise of towns and the multiplication of material comforts, the inhabitants of the more densely settled areas were inclined toward an increasingly secular outlook. With the appearance of numerous and diverse sects, some people were tempted to doubt whether any particular denomination, even their own, possessed a monopoly of truth and grace. And with the progress of science and free thought in Europe, at least a few Americans began to adopt a rational and skeptical philosophy.

For thousands of the colonists, the trend away from religion was reversed by a revival movement known as the Great Awakening, which reached a climax in the 1740s. Wandering exhorters from abroad did much to stimulate the revivalistic spirit. John and Charles Wesley, founders of Methodism, which began as a reform movement within the Church of England, visited Georgia and other colonies in the 1730s with the intention of revitalizing religion and converting Indians and Negroes. George Whitefield, a powerful open-air preacher from England and for a time an associate of the Wesleys, made several evangelizing tours through the colonies. Everywhere he went, Whitefield drew tremendous crowds, and it was said (with some exaggeration) that he could make his hearers weep merely by uttering, in his moving way, the word "Mesopotamia."

"Sinners in the Hands of an Angry God"
[1741]

Jonathan Edwards (1703–1758) was the most original and systematic theologian of colonial America. Edwards argued that God's grace is the only way that any man can be redeemed from the original sin committed by Adam; poor sinners could yield themselves up to God's grace if their hearts were "filled with love to him who has loved them." The extremes of terror and salvation that he posed were undeniably effective: when he preached this sermon at Enfield, Connecticut, in 1741, it produced great "breathing of distress, and weeping."

Your wickedness makes you as it were heavy as lead, and to tend downwards with great weight and pressure towards hell; and if God should let you go, you would immediately sink and swiftly descend and plunge into the bottomless gulf . . .

O sinner! Consider the fearful danger you are in: it is a great furnace of wrath, a wide and bottomless pit, full of the fire of wrath, that you are held over in the hand of God . . . You hang by a slender thread, with the flames of divine wrath flashing about it, and ready every moment to singe it, and burn it asunder . . .

And now you have an extraordinary opportunity, a day wherein Christ has thrown the door of mercy wide open, and stands in the door calling and crying with a loud voice to poor sinners . . .

And let everyone that is yet out of Christ, and hanging over the pit of hell, . . . now hearken to the loud calls of God's word and providence. This acceptable year of the Lord, a day of such great favours to some, will doubtless be a day of as remarkable vengeance to others. . . .

Though itinerants like Whitefield contributed to the rousing of religious excitement, the Great Awakening could hardly have occurred without the work of regular ministers with an evangelizing bent. One of the most important of these was Theodore J. Frelinghuysen, a youthful German-born pastor of three Dutch Reformed congregations in central New Jersey. Frelinghuysen preached the necessity of spiritual rebirth not only to the Dutch Reformed but also to the Scotch-Irish Presbyterian settlers of the Raritan Valley. His emotional preaching divided his own parishioners. The older and more well-to-do among them were scandalized; the young and the poor rallied to his support.

The Puritans of New England also were divided on the issue of revivalism. A majority of the Congregational ministers of Massachusetts denounced the "errors" and "disorders" arising from revival meetings. Among the errors and disorders was the practice of uneducated men "taking upon themselves to be preachers of the word of God," creating confusion and tumult, and leading members away from their regular churches.

Yet the outstanding preacher of the Great Awakening in New England was Jonathan Edwards—a Puritan of the Puritans and one of the most profound theologians in the history of American religious thought. From his pulpit in Northampton, Massachusetts, Edwards attacked the new doctrines of easy salvation for all. He called upon his people to return to the faith of their fathers. He preached afresh the old Puritan ideas of the absolute sovereignty of God, the depravity of man, predestination, the necessity of experiencing a sense of election, and election by God's grace alone. Describing hell as vividly as if he had been there, he brought his listeners to their knees in terror of divine wrath. Day after day the agonized sinners crowded his parsonage to seek his aid; at least one committed suicide.

The Great Awakening spread over the colonies like a religious epidemic. It was most contagious in frontier areas and among the comparatively poor and uneducated folk, especially in the South. In the Southern back country it affected the largest number of people, prevailed the longest, and had the most lasting consequences. The Presbyterian Church was split by the formation of a large and rapidly growing group of revivalistic, "New Light" Presbyterians. Converts flocked to various free-will Baptist sects; the Baptists were on the way to eventually becoming one of the two most numerous denominations in the United States.

The Great Awakening not only led to the division of existing congregations and the founding of new sects, but it also had a number of other results. Some of the revivalists denounced book learning as a snare and a delusion, a positive hindrance to salvation, but others saw education as a means of furthering their own brand of religion, and so they founded schools for the preparation of ministers. Many believed that revivalism, through its emphasis on righteous conduct, brought about an improvement in manners and morals, and no doubt it did so, at least temporarily. To some extent, too, it aroused a spirit of humanitarianism, a concern for the physical as well as the spiritual welfare of the poor and oppressed. The widely preached doctrine of salvation for all—of equal opportunity to share in God's grace—encouraged the notion of equal rights to share also in the good things on earth. Thus it stimulated feelings of democracy.

Though the Great Awakening had these important and lasting consequences, many of the converted soon backslid, and by the end of the colonial period English America contained fewer church members for its population than did any other Christian country of the time, and fewer than the United States has today.

READING AND WRITING

As an American variant of English culture developed in the colonies, it was reflected in the partial Americanization of the English language. New words originated in borrowings from the Indians (such as *skunk* and *squash*), from the French *(portage, prairie),* and from the Dutch *(boss, cooky).* Americanisms also arose from the combining of words already in the English language *(bull-frog, snow-plow),* from the formation of new adjectives based on existing nouns *(kinky, chunky),* from the adoption of unfamiliar uses for familiar words *(branch,* meaning *stream; ordinary,* meaning *inn),* and from the retention of old English expressions that were being dropped in England *(cater-corner; bub,* for *boy).* After 1700 English travelers in America began to notice a strangeness in accent as well as vocabulary,

and in 1756 the great lexicographer Dr. Samuel Johnson mentioned the existence of an "American dialect."

Dr. Johnson thought of Americans as barbarians, and some no doubt were, but from the beginning many had been concerned lest civilization be lost in the wilderness. They continued to provide schooling for their children as best they could, particularly in New England. In various colonies, the advancement of religion being one motive for education, the Quakers and other sects operated church schools. Here and there a widow or an unmarried woman conducted a "dame school," holding private classes in her home. In some of the cities master craftsmen set up evening schools for their apprentices, at least a hundred such schools appearing between 1723 and 1770. To the end of the colonial period (and beyond it) numberless children with no school available were still learning to read and write from their father or mother at the family fireside.

Far more people learned to read than ever attended school, yet a great many never learned to read at all. The literacy rate, which is unknown, must have varied a good deal from place to place. It seems to have been very low in some of the thinly settled areas, especially in the South. It was highest in the towns, especially in New England. Nevertheless, the Connecticut legislature stated in 1690 that many people in Connecticut were "unable to read the English tongue," and of the thirteen town proprietors of Manchester, New Hampshire, in 1716, eight could not write. Colonial wills and other legal documents often were signed with a mark, by people who could not write even their own names. On the whole, literacy doubtless improved during the eighteenth century, and by the time of the Revolution probably a majority of Americans could read.

Books were available in numerous collections. Several of the wealthy colonists owned hundreds of volumes apiece; William Byrd II had one of the largest private libraries, with more than 3,600 volumes, at Westover, his plantation home. A dozen or more subscription libraries were established, most of them in Pennsylvania, and a few small endowed public libraries, one of the earliest at Bath, North Carolina. Harvard College, in 1723, possessed 3,200 volumes. Much the larger proportion of all these books were printed abroad and imported, but several American cities were active book-publishing centers.

Founded in 1704, the first regular newspaper in the colonies, though not a very newsy one, was the weekly Boston *News-Letter,* a small folded sheet of four pages with two columns to a page. By the 1760s one or more weekly papers were being published in each of the colonies except New Jersey and Delaware, both of which were well enough supplied by the presses of New York and Philadelphia. Several monthly magazines, notably the *American Magazine* of Philadelphia, were started after about 1750, with hopes of wide circulation. One after another they appeared for a year or two and then expired. More successful and more widely read were the yearly almanacs. Originally mere collections of weather data, these turned into small magazines of a sort, containing a great variety of literary fare. *Poor Richard's Almanac,* now well remembered, was only one of many, though a superior one.

Its publisher, Benjamin Franklin, was one of a few colonial-born men of letters who wrote works of lasting literary merit. The titles of some of his essays — *Advice to a Young Man on Choosing a Mistress* (1745), *Reflections on Courtship and Marriage* (1746), *Observations Concerning the Increase of Mankind* (1755), and *Advice to a Young Tradesman* (1762) — suggest his pragmatic and worldly wise outlook. Quite different was the sternly logical and other-worldly view of Jonathan Edwards, whose treatise *On the Freedom of the Will* (1754) is considered, by those who can understand it, as perhaps the most brilliant of American theological studies. John Woolman in his *Journal* (published in 1775, after his death) related a life as spiritual as Edwards' and as humanitarian as Franklin's but more humble and sensitive than either. A writer rivaling Franklin in charm, though not in productivity, was William Byrd II, whose breezy *History of the Dividing Line* (not published till 1841) recounted his experiences as one of the commissioners who, in 1728, marked off the boundary between Virginia and North Carolina.

As a rule, colonial authors had no time for belles-lettres, for fiction, poetry, drama, and the like. Writers concentrated upon sermons, religious tracts, and subjects of urgent, practical concern. Puritans, Quakers, and many other Protestants condemned playacting as sin-

ful. The first theaters opened in the South, one at Williamsburg in 1718 and the famous Dock Street Theater at Charleston in 1736. By the middle of the century plays could be seen in all the larger seaport cities except Boston, where the Puritan ban remained.

HIGHER LEARNING

Of the six colleges in actual operation by 1763, all but two were founded by religious groups primarily for the training of preachers. Harvard (1636) was established by Congregationalists, William and Mary (1693) by Anglicans, and Yale (1701) by conservative Congregationalists who were dissatisfied with the growing religious liberalism of Harvard. The College of New Jersey (1746), later known as Princeton, was set up by Presbyterians in response to the Great Awakening. At any of these institutions a student with secular interests could derive something of a liberal education from the prevailing curricula, which included logic, ethics, physics, geometry, astronomy, rhetoric, Latin, Hebrew, and Greek. From the beginning Harvard was intended not only to provide an educated ministry but also to "advance learning and perpetuate it to posterity." King's College (1754), afterward Columbia, had no theological faculty and was interdenominational from the start. The Academy and College of Philadelphia (1755), which grew into the University of Pennsylvania, was a completely secular institution, founded by a group of laymen under the inspiration of Benjamin Franklin. It offered courses in utilitarian subjects as well as the liberal arts — in mechanics, chemistry, agriculture, government, commerce, and modern languages. Though the colonies thus were well supplied with colleges, at least in comparison with other countries at the time, some Americans continued to go to English universities. But the great majority of colonial leaders, after 1700, received their entire education in America.

Until a medical school was opened in Philadelphia (1765) there was no opportunity for aspiring physicians to get academic training on this side of the Atlantic. Those who desired to attend a medical school had to go abroad, and usually they went to the University of Edinburgh. Most of the practicing physicians had no medical degrees. Some put in a sort of internship with an older practitioner, and others took up the healing art entirely on their own. Some colonial physicians and, surprising though it seems, churchmen like Cotton Mather and Jonathan Edwards advocated as earnestly as anyone in the world the most controversial medical innovation of their time — inoculation against smallpox. There was no law school in the colonies, and men prepared themselves for a legal career by independent study, by working with an established lawyer, or, in comparatively few cases, by attending one of the Inns of Court (law schools) in London.

In the colonial colleges, considerable attention was given to scientific subjects. Chairs in "natural philosophy," or physical science, were endowed at William and Mary and at Harvard. The most advanced scientific thought of Europe — Copernican astronomy and Newtonian physics — eventually made its way into American teaching. But scientific speculation and experiment were not the exclusively academic, professional occupations that they later became.

Mather, Edwards, and many other ministers, merchants, and planters in America were active as amateur scientists. The Royal Society of London, founded in 1662 for the advancement of science, honored a number of them by electing them as fellows. To this society the American members and nonmember correspondents sent samples and descriptions of plants, animals, and remarkable phenomena. By means of their contributions the colonial amateurs added a good deal to the accumulation of data upon which later scientific progress was to be based. They also sent in plans for

Nassau Hall at Princeton

At the left is Nassau Hall, completed in 1756, ten years after the founding of the College of New Jersey (which became Princeton University in 1896). It is the oldest building now standing on the Princeton campus. At the right is the president's house. From a drawing made in 1763. (Princeton University Library)

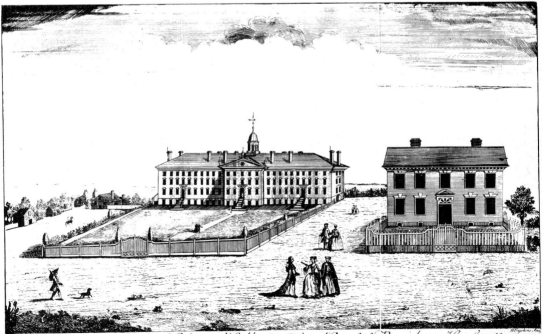

A North-West Prospect of Nassau-Hall, with a Front View of the Presidents House, in New Jersey.

mechanical inventions and helped to start the reputation of Americans as a mechanically ingenious people.

Though women were excluded from the colleges and the professions, a few of them gained the equivalent of a higher education through their own exertions. Notable examples were Abigail Smith (who married John Adams) and Mercy Otis (who married James Warren), both of whom belonged to learned, book-loving Massachusetts families. Relying on traditional cures and Indian remedies, most women served as nurses and, to some extent, even as doctors within their own households. Midwives delivered babies. At least one woman, Mrs. Hannah Williams of South Carolina, emulated the men who were making modest contributions to science. As early as 1705 she was collecting specimens of "some of our vipers and several sorts of snakes, scorpions, and lizards," besides insects, wild bees' nests, and various kinds of native plants.

The greatest of colonial scientists and inventors, Benjamin Franklin, gained worldwide fame with his kite experiment (1752) which demonstrated that lightning and electricity are one and the same. Showing their respect for experimental science, Harvard, Yale, and William and Mary honored themselves by honoring Franklin as a Master of Arts. The University of St. Andrews in Scotland and Oxford University in England conferred doctoral degrees upon him. Thereafter he took satisfaction in being known as "Dr. Franklin." He interested himself in countless subjects besides electricity, and he was a theoretical or "philosophical" scientist as well as a practical one. He also was a promoter of science. In 1727 he and his Philadelphia friends organized the Junto, a club for the discussion of intellectual and practical matters of mutual interest. In 1744 he led in the founding of the American Philosophical Society, the first learned society in America.

CONCEPTS OF LAW

As with social and intellectual life, the legal and political institutions inherited from England also were more or less modified in their transmission to the colonies. Changes in the law resulted in part from the scarcity of English-trained lawyers, who were almost unknown in America before 1700. Not till a generation after that did the authorities in England make a deliberate effort to impose the common law and the statutes of the realm upon the provinces. By that time the legal standards on this side of the ocean had become pretty well fixed, and a number of variant legal systems had come into being through a lack of acquaintance or sympathy with English law, though all these systems embodied many of its essentials, including such ancient rights as trial by jury.

Pleading and court procedure were simplified in America, and punishments were made less severe. Instead of the gallows or the prison, the colonists more commonly resorted to the whipping post, the branding iron, the stocks, and the ducking stool (for gossipy women). Crimes were redefined. In England a printed attack on a public official, whether true or false, was considered libelous. In the colonies, at the trial (1734) of the New York publisher John Peter Zenger, who was powerfully defended by the Philadelphia lawyer Andrew Hamilton, it was held that criticisms of the government were not libels if factually true—a verdict that brought some progress toward freedom of the press. Legal philosophy itself was changed as colonists came to think of law as a reflection of the divine will or the natural order, not as an expression of the power of an earthly sovereign. Provincial lawyers, who became an influential class during the eighteenth century, were less closely attached to English tradition than the legal profession in the United States was afterward to be.

Selected Readings

Expanding Settlements
T. R. Reese, *Colonial Georgia: A Study in British Imperial Policy in the Eighteenth Century* (1963); R. L. Meriwether, *The Expansion of South Carolina, 1729–1765* (1940); A. H. Hirsch, *The Huguenots of Colonial South Carolina* (1928); I. C. C. Graham, *Colonists from Scotland* (1956); J. G. Leyburn, *The Scotch-Irish: A Social History* (1962); A. B. Faust, *The German Element in the United States* (2 vols., 1909); Frederic Klees, *The Pennsylvania Dutch* (1950).

Labor
M. W. Jernegan, *Laboring and Dependent Classes in Colonial America, 1607–1783* (1932); R. B. Morris, *Government and Labor in Early America* (1946); A. E. Smith, *Colonists in Bondage* (1947); Samuel McKee, *Labor in Colonial New York, 1664–1776* (1935); C. A. Herrick, *White Servitude in Pennsylvania* (1926); J. C. Ballagh, *A History of Slavery in Virginia* (1902); L. J. Greene, *The Negro in Colonial New England* (1942); W. D. Jordan, *White over Black: American Attitudes Toward the Negro, 1550–1812** (1968).

Economic Life
Lyman Carrier, *The Beginnings of Agriculture in America* (1923); A. C. Bining, *British Regulation of the Colonial Iron Industry* (1933) and *Pennsylvania Iron Manufacture in the Eighteenth Century* (1938); R. McFarland, *A History of the New England Fisheries* (1911); R. G. Albion, *Forests and Sea Power* (1926); F. B. Tolles, *Meeting House and Counting House** (1948).

Aspects of Society
Carl Bridenbaugh, *Myths and Realities: Societies of the Colonial South** (1952), *The Colonial Craftsman* (1950), *Cities in the Wilderness, 1625–1742** (1938), *Cities in Revolt, 1743–1776** (1955), and, with Jessica Bridenbaugh, *Rebels and Gentlemen: Philadelphia in the Age of Franklin* (1942); E. S. Morgan, *Virginians at Home** (1952); L. B. Wright, *The First Gentlemen of Virginia** (1940); T. J. Wertenbaker, *The Planters of Colonial Virginia* (1922); Sumner Powell, *Puritan Village** (1963); M. Zuckerman, *Peaceable Kingdoms: New England Towns in the Eighteenth Century** (1970).

Culture in General
L. B. Wright, *The Cultural Life of the American Colonies, 1607–1763** (1957) and *The Atlantic Frontier: Colonial American Civilization* (1947); D. J. Boorstin, *The Americans: The Colonial Experience** (1958); C. M. Andrews, *Colonial Folkways* (1919); Hugh Morrison, *Early American Architecture from the First Colonial Settlements to the Early National Period* (1952); L. A. Cremin, *American Education: The Colonial Experience, 1607–1783* (1971); R. Hofstadter, *America at 1750* (1972).

Religion
W. W. Sweet, *Religion in Colonial America* (1942); Perry Miller, *The New England Mind: From Colony to Province** (1953); M. L. Starkey, *The Devil in Massachusetts** (1949); E. S. Gaustad, *The Great Awakening in New England* (1957); Perry Miller, *Jonathan Edwards** (1949); O. E. Winslow, *Jonathan Edwards, 1703–1758* (1940); Janet Whitman, *John Woolman, American Quaker* (1942); J. T. Ellis, *Catholics in Colonial America* (1965); J. R. Marcus, *Early American Jewry* (1951).

Science
Brook Hindle, *The Pursuit of Science in Revolutionary America, 1735–1789* (1956); Carl Van Doren, *Benjamin Franklin** (1938), an extensive biography; V. W. Crane, *Benjamin Franklin and a Rising People** (1954), a compact account; O. T. Beall, Jr., and R. H. Shryock, *Cotton Mather, First Significant Figure in American Medicine* (1954); John Duffy, *Epidemics in Colonial America* (1953).

*Titles available in paperback.

Thursday, *October* 31, 1765.

THE
PENNSYLVANIA J
AND
WEEKLY ADVER⸺

EXPIRING: In Hopes of a Resurrectior

I AM forry to be obliged to acquaint my Readers, that as The STAMP-ACT, is fear'd to be obligatory upon us after the *First of November* enfuing, (the *fatal To-mor-row*) the Publiher of this Paper unable to bear the Burthen, has thought it expedient to STOP a while, in order to deliberate, whether any Methods can be found to elude the chains forged for us, and efcape the infupportable Slavery; which it is hoped, from the juft Reprefentations now made againft that Act, may be effected. Mean while, I muft earneftly Requeft every Individual of my Subfcribers, many of whom have been long behind Hand, that they would immediately Difcharge their refpective Arrears, that I may be able, not only to fupport myfelf during the Interval, but be better prepared to proceed again with this Paper, whenever an opening for that Purpofe appears, which I hope will be foon. WILLIAM BRADFORD.

Remember, O *my friends!* the Laws, the Rights,
The generous plan of power deliver'd down,
From age to age, by your renown'd fore-fathers;
O let it never perifh in your hands!
But pioufly tranfmit it to your children.
Do thou, great Liberty, infpire our fouls,
And make our lives in thy poffeffion happy;
Or our deaths glorious in thy defence. ADDISON's Cato.

L IBERTY is one of the greateft Bleffings, which human beings can poffibly enjoy: When we are deprived of this earthly happinefs, we are fettered with the Chains of inimical fervitude. Nations, who are born for the mutual fupport of each other, fhould preferve a fteady attachment to the welfare and happinefs of that nation with whom they are united, that their mutual alliance of friendfhip might be fincere and permanent. When this union is feparated by the illegal encroachments on that Liberty, which is the Soul of Commerce, and the Support of Life, it degenerates into implacable Enmity, which in time grows inveterate, and finally recoils upon

And in all political Diforders the more contented we are under them, fo much the worfe are they, and fo much the worfe are we for them. It is a very happy Circumftance attending public Virtue and public Spirit, that the more it is vilified, the more illuftrious it always appears. No Falfhood formed againft it can profper, for it at once detects and confutes the darkeft and moft inveterate Calumny. But although public Virtue cannot be affected by the Indulgence of the moft unlimited Freedom of fpeaking or writing, yet Oppreffion and Tyranny as it derives all its Influence from its Secrecy, may be extremely benefited by the Reverfe. For this reafon, in Countries fubjected to the infatiable Demands of Power and Avarice, the firft Attempts to infpire People with a juft Senfe of their Condition, are commonly nipt in the Bud. It is of the laft Importance to the Views of defigning Men to fhut up the moft fuccefsful and univerfal Channel of Information from the People, when they are forming fuch Schemes as need only to be known in order to be Oppofed. Befides the Deprivation of our whole Liberty may be juftified on the fame Principles as the Deprivation of any individual Part, fuch as the Liberty of the Prefs undoubtedly is.

How amiable is the Enjoyment of Liberty! But how deteftable are the Bonds of Servitude! 'Tis therefore fincerly to be hoped, that the old *New-England* Spirit fo exemplarily free in former Times, will never condefcend in Submiffion to new and unwarrantable Reftrictions.

A Day, an Hour of virtuous Liberty,
Is worth a whole Eternity in Bondage.

May we all as loyal Subjects, and free born Britons exert our utmoft to preferve the Rights and Liberties of our Country, in a Manner that fnall add Honour to our Endeavours; that future Pofterity may reap the Benefit, and blefs the Hands which were the Inftruments of procuring it.⸺

That Glory then, the brighteft Crown of Praife,
Which every Lover of his Country's Wealth,
And every Patron of Mankind deferves;
Will gracefully adorn fuch Patriot's Deeds, ·
And leave behind an Honour that will laft
With Praife immortal to the End of Time.

Thurfday laft arrived here the fhip Philadelphia Packet, Capt. Budden, from London, by whom we have the following advices.

ROME, *July* 24.

T HE harveft in this country hath not proved fo good as we hoped. This event hath engaged the congregation eftablifhed for infpecting into the fupplies of provifions for this capital, to feek all poffible means to prevent a frefh fcarcity.

St. James's, Auguft 17. The king has been pleafed to appoint the moft honourable the Marquis of Rockingham to be lord lieutenant of the weft-ridings of the county of York, and of the city of York, and county of the fame city: and alfo Cuftos Rotulorum of the north and weft-ridings in the faid county of York and of the city of York, and county of the fame city; and Ainfty, other-

Four

Looking back two centuries later, it is easy enough to see that the people of the thirteen colonies, for all their diversity, had come to share some distinctive characteristics by the middle of the eighteenth century. From the point of view of England at that time, these people seemed already to be Americans rather than, in a strict sense, Englishmen. As yet, however, few of the colonists thought of themselves as Americans. Their "country," as they saw it, was first of all their particular colony, and then perhaps their region (at least in the case of Southerners and New Englanders), and finally the British Empire.

As of 1763 the Empire appeared to be an imposing success, having just disposed of its last great imperial rival in America—France. Yet is was about to prove a failure, at least so far as its ability to hold the thirteen colonies was concerned. After the great victory over the French, the policy makers in London undertook to bind the outlying provinces more closely than ever to the metropolitan center. Instead of consolidating the Empire, however, its rulers unwittingly prepared the way for its early disruption.

The colonies by then had long been used to a large measure of self-rule, and to preserve this they resisted the imperial program of George III's government. In the course of their resistance they developed a new sense of common cause and new forms of political cooperation. They were not yet conscious of belonging to, or of desiring to create, a separate country, but they eventually found themselves engaged in the first battles of a war that was to lead to independence.

War came in consequence of a real clash of interests, economic and political, between the groups dominant in England and those dominant in the colonies. This conflict was the result of a century and a half of

---

Response to the Stamp Act
This issue of a Pennsylvania newspaper, for October 31, 1765, has the heavy black rules and the death's head insignia as signs of mourning—mourning for the loss of popular liberties as a result of the Stamp Act and for the death of the paper itself, which is ceasing publication rather than pay the tax. (New York Public Library)

divergence in the development of English and American ways. As the historian Charles M. Andrews has said, "New soil had produced new wants, new desires, new points of view, and the colonists were demanding the right to live their own lives in their own way."

A Loosening of Ties

After England's Glorious Revolution of 1688 and the collapse of the Dominion of New England, the English government (or, after 1707, the British government when Great Britain was created by the union of England and Scotland) made no serious or sustained effort for more than seventy years to tighten its control over the colonies. During that time, it is true, additions were made to the list of royal colonies (New Jersey, 1702; North and South Carolina, 1729; Georgia, 1754) until they numbered eight, in all of which the King had the power of appointing governors and other colonial officials. During that time, also, Parliament passed new laws supplementing the original Navigation Acts and elaborating on the mercantilist program—laws restricting colonial manufactures, prohibiting paper currency, and regulating trade. Nevertheless, the British government itself remained uncertain and divided about the extent to which it ought to interfere in colonial affairs. The colonies were left, within broad limits, to go their separate ways, and they were able to assert fairly extensive rights of self-government.

TOWARD SELF-RULE

During the first half of the eighteenth century, though the colonies continued to be governed in the King's name, Parliament more and more asserted its supremacy over the King. Theoretically Parliament represented the interests of the whole kingdom and indeed the whole Empire. Actually it represented best the interests of the great merchants and landholders in England. Most of them objected to any ambitious scheme for imperial reorganization that would require large expenditures, increase taxes, and diminish the profit of the colonial trade.

During the reigns of George I (1714–1727) and George II (1727–1760), both of whom were German-born, the real executive in England was beginning to be the prime minister and his fellow cabinet ministers, who held their places not by the King's favor but by their ability to control a majority in Parliament. The first of the prime ministers, Robert Walpole, believed that a relaxation of trade restrictions against the colonies would enable them to buy more English goods and would thus benefit England and her merchants. Walpole therefore deliberately refrained from attempting a very strict enforcement of all Navigation Acts. His policy of "salutary neglect" was to continue until after the outbreak of the French and Indian War.

Meanwhile the day-to-day administration of colonial affairs remained decentralized and inefficient. In England there was no separate and full-fledged colonial office. The nearest equivalent was the Board of Trade and Plantations, set up in 1696. The board, a mere advisory body, made recommendations to the Privy Council (the central agency of all administration), while the Privy Council, the war department, the lords of the admiralty, or the treasury officials made most of the actual decisions. All these agencies, except for the board itself, had responsibility for administering laws at home as well as overseas; none could concentrate upon colonial affairs alone. To complicate matters further, there was a certain amount of overlapping and confusion of authority among the departments. And very few of the London officials ever visited America and obtained firsthand knowledge of conditions there.

Some information could be obtained from colonial agents in England. Though the colonists did not elect official representatives to sit in Parliament, some of the assemblies sent unofficial representatives or lobbyists to London to encourage the passage of desired legislation and discourage the enactment of unwanted laws. The best known of these colonial agents, Benjamin Franklin, looked out for the interests of not only Pennsylvania but also Georgia, New Jersey, and Massachusetts.

The conflicts of administrative authority in London, together with the ministerial policy of salutary neglect, weakened the hold of England upon the colonies, and so did the character of the officials who were sent to America. These included the officials placed in charge of each royal colony—governor, councillors, secretary, attorney general, receiver general, surveyor general, supreme court justices—and the agents of the London administrative departments, such as collectors of customs and naval officers, who were located in all the colonies. Some of these officeholders were able and devoted men, but the majority were not. There being no merit system, appointments often were made on the basis of bribery or favoritism rather than ability or integrity. Many an appointee remained in England and, with part of his salary, hired another man to take his place in America. Such a deputy, poorly paid as he was, found it hard to resist opportunities to augment his income with bribes. For example, a customs collector seldom hesitated, for a fee smaller than the duty itself, to pass the goods of a smuggling colonial merchant. Even honest and well-paid officials, desiring to get along with the people among whom they had to live, usually found it expedient to yield to popular resistance in the colonies.

This resistance to imperial authority centered in the colonial assemblies. By the 1750s they had established the right to levy taxes, make appropriations, approve appointments, and pass laws for their respective colonies. Their legislation was subject to veto by the governor and to disallowance by the Privy Council, but they could often sway the governor by means of their money powers, and they could get around the Privy Council by repassing disallowed laws in slightly altered form. The assemblies came to look upon themselves as little parliaments, each practically as sovereign within its colony as Parliament itself was in England. In 1754 the Board of Trade reported to the King, regarding the members of the New York assembly: They "have wrested from Your Majesty's governor the nomination of all offices of government, the custody and direction of the public military stores, the mustering and direction of troops raised for Your Majesty's service, and in short almost every other part of executive government."

INTERCOLONIAL DISUNITY

Despite their frequent resistance to British authority and evasion of British laws, the colonists continued to think of themselves as loyal British subjects. They had much to gain from keeping their imperial connection. They enjoyed access to the markets of the Empire, bounties on the production of certain goods, the protection afforded by British naval and military forces, and the pride of belonging to the most powerful aggregation of peoples on the globe.

In some respects the colonists had more in common with Englishmen than with one another. To New Englanders Virginia seemed almost a foreign land, and to Virginians New England was just as strange. A Connecticut man denounced the merchants of New York for their "frauds and unfair practices," while a New Yorker condemned Connecticut because of the "low craft and cunning so incident to the people of that country." An English traveler wrote: "Fire and water are not more heterogeneous than the different colonies in North America."

Meanwhile some developments were laying a basis for the eventual growth of a sense of intercolonial community. The increase of population, which produced an almost continuous line of settlement along the seacoast, brought the people of the various colonies into closer and closer contact, as did the gradual construc-

---

The Need for Colonial Unity
Probably the first American editorial cartoon, this sketch appeared in Benjamin Franklin's newspaper, the Pennsylvania Gazette *of Philadelphia, for May 9, 1754. The cartoon was intended to illustrate the need for colonial unity and, in particular, for the adoption of Franklin's Albany Plan.*

tion of roads, the rise of intercolonial trade, and the improvement of the colonial post office. In 1691 the postal service operated only from Massachusetts to New York and Pennsylvania. In 1711 it was extended to New Hampshire on the north, in 1732 to Virginia on the south, and ultimately all the way to Georgia. After 1753 Franklin, a deputy postmaster, improved the service, providing weekly instead of biweekly posts and speeding them up so that, for example, mail was delivered from Boston to Philadelphia in about three weeks instead of six. Post riders carried newspapers as well as letters and thus enlarged and unified the colonial reading public.

Still, the colonists were loath to cooperate even when, in 1754, they faced a new threat from old and dreaded enemies, the French and their Indian allies. At the call of the Board of Trade, a conference of colonial leaders—with delegates on hand from Pennsylvania, Maryland, New York, and the New England colonies—was meeting in Albany to negotiate a treaty with the Iroquois. The delegates stayed on to talk about forming a colonial federation for defense. Benjamin Franklin proposed to his fellow delegates a plan by which Parliament would set up in America "one general government" for all the colonies, each of which would "retain its present constitution" except for the powers to be given the general government. The King would appoint a President-General, and the colonial assemblies would elect representatives to a Grand Council. The President-General in consultation with the Council would take charge of all relations with the Indians; the Council, subject to his veto, would make laws and levy taxes for raising troops, building forts, waging war, and carrying on other Indian affairs.

War with the French and Indians was already beginning when this Albany Plan was presented to the colonial assemblies for their consideration. Yet none of them approved it, and none except the Massachusetts assembly even gave it very serious attention. "Everyone cries, a union is necessary," Franklin wrote to the Massachusetts governor, "but when they come to the manner and form of the union, their weak noodles are perfectly distracted."

Struggling for a Continent

Spacious though it was, the continent of North America seemed too small to contain both the English and the French. The English, as Protestants, and the French, as Roman Catholics, eyed each other with suspicion and fear. As fishermen and fur traders they competed for the profits of the forest and the sea. Each national group began ultimately to feel that its very survival in America depended upon the elimination of the other's influence.

NEW FRANCE

The French greatly extended their sway in America after the Grand Monarch, Louis XIV, took the government into his own hands (1661) and, with a program of centralization at home and expansion abroad, proceeded to live up to his supposed remark, "I am the state." His finance minister and economic planner, Jean Colbert, conceived of an integrated empire consisting of four parts: France itself as the center and the source of capital and manufactured goods; her West Indian islands (especially Martinique and Guadeloupe) as suppliers of sugar and other exotic products; posts along the African coast as aids in carrying on the slave trade; and the settlements in Canada as a market for exports from France and a granary for provisioning the West Indies. The colonies were to be governed directly from Paris, pretty much as if they were local subdivisions of France itself. New France was to have a governor, an intendant, and a bishop, each to be appointed by the King and each to serve as a check upon the other two. In practice this arrangement led to jealousies and cross-purposes which often frustrated the colonial administration—except when some individual official in America had the character and will to assert his preeminence. Such a man was Jean Talon, the first of the intendants, and even more outstanding was Count Frontenac, the greatest of the governors (1672–1698).

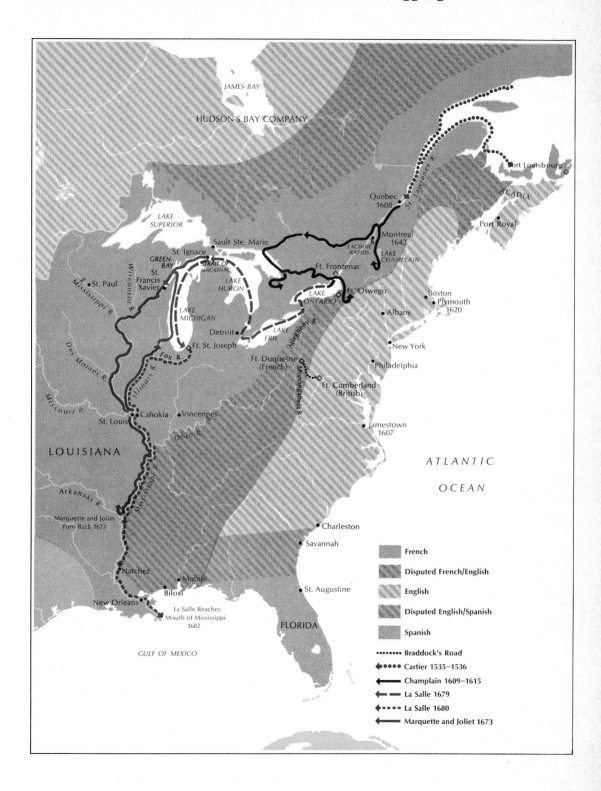

JAMES BAY

HUDSON'S BAY COMPANY

Port Louisbourg

ACADIA

LAKE
SUPERIOR

Quebec
1608

St. Lawrence R.

Port Royal

Montreal
1642

LACHINE
RAPIDS

LAKE
CHAMPLAIN

Sault Ste. Marie

St. Ignace

GREEN
BAY

STRAIT OF
MACKINAC

Ft. Frontenac

St.
Francis
Xavier

LAKE
HURON

Ft. Oswego

Boston

Plymouth
1620

Wisconsin R.

St. Paul

LAKE
MICHIGAN

LAKE
ONTARIO

Albany

Mississippi R.

Detroit

LAKE
ERIE

New York

Ft. St. Joseph

Fox R.

Allegheny R.

Des Moines R.

Illinois R.

Ft. Duquesne
(French)

Philadelphia

Monongahela R.

Ft. Cumberland
(British)

Missouri R.

Cahokia

Vincennes

St. Louis

Ohio R.

Jamestown
1607

LOUISIANA

ATLANTIC

OCEAN

Arkansas R.

Marquette and Joliet
Turn Back 1673

Mississippi R.

Charleston

Savannah

Natchez

Mobile

Biloxi

New Orleans

La Salle Reaches
Mouth of Mississippi
1682

St. Augustine

FLORIDA

GULF OF MEXICO

▨	French
▨	Disputed French/English
▨	English
▨	Disputed English/Spanish
▨	Spanish
••••••••	Braddock's Road
◄•••••	Cartier 1535–1536
◄━━━	Champlain 1609–1615
◄━ ━	La Salle 1679
◄■■■■	La Salle 1680
◄━━━	Marquette and Joliet 1673

The French in America

Though Colbert intended to make Canada a compactly settled agricultural province, the aspirations of Talon and Frontenac for the glory of France caused them to expand New France beyond Colbert's limits; other forces also tended to disperse the colonial population. The lure of the forest and its furs drew immigrant peasants into the wilderness where they often married Indian squaws and adopted tribal ways. Another group, the Jesuits, were impelled onward by their missionary zeal in the search for savage souls to save. And the bottom lands of the Mississippi attracted farmers discouraged by the short growing season in Canada.

The nature of the Illinois country had been made known by adventuresome explorers. In 1673 Louis Joliet and Father Marquette journeyed together by canoe from Green Bay along the Fox, Wisconsin, and Mississippi rivers as far as the mouth of the Arkansas, then returned with assurance that the Mississippi empties into the Gulf of Mexico, not the Gulf of California as previously thought. The next year René Robert Cavelier, Sieur de La Salle, a supremely romantic and at the same time a shrewdly practical man, began the explorations that finally, in 1682, took him to the delta of the Mississippi, where he took possession of the surrounding country for the King of France, naming it Louisiana in the King's honor. Subsequently traders and missionaries wandered to the southwest as far as the Rio Grande, and the explorer La Vérendrye (1743) pushed westward from Lake Superior to a point within sight of the Rocky Mountains. Eventually Frenchmen revealed the outlines of the whole continental interior and marked its boundaries with the cross and the fleur-de-lis.

To secure their hold upon the territory thus staked out, they founded a string of widely separated communities, strategically located fortresses, and far-flung missions and trading posts. On Cape Breton Island they established Fort Louisbourg, one of the most redoubtable strongholds in all the New World, to guard the approach to the Gulf of St. Lawrence. From both banks of the St. Lawrence River the strips of land ("seigneuries") of would-be feudal lords stretched to the edge of the clearings. On a high bluff above the river stood Quebec, the pride of the French empire in America. Farther up the river was Montreal, even more "provincial"

and less sophisticated than Quebec. Hundreds of miles to the west, near the juncture of Lake Superior with Lakes Michigan and Huron, was the tiny outpost of Sault Sainte Marie. Hundreds of miles to the southeast of this, at the juncture of Lakes Huron and Erie, was the well-fortified Detroit. Farther to the southwest, along the Mississippi between the Missouri and the Ohio, was a cluster of hamlets—Cahokia, Kaskaskia, Fort Chartres, Sainte Genevieve— each with its outlying common fields of black earth under cultivation. Over on the Wabash was the fifth tiny settlement of the Illinois country, Vincennes.

On the lower Mississippi were plantations much like those in the Southern colonies of English America, plantations worked by Negro slaves and supporting a race-conscious class of "Creoles," who had far more pretensions to grandeur than did the comparatively poor and necessarily democratic seigneurs of Canada. Louisiana became relatively populous, especially after thousands of settlers had been brought in by the land-speculation schemes of John Law, whose "Mississippi Bubble" burst in 1721, to the ruin of investors in Europe and the disillusionment of recently arrived Louisianans. Founded in 1718, New Orleans soon grew into a city comparable in size with some of those on the Atlantic seaboard but quainter than most, with its houses built of cypress logs and bark roofs and set upon stilts above the swampy ground. To the east of New Orleans, along the Gulf of Mexico, were the towns of Biloxi (founded 1699) and Mobile (1702), completing the string of mainland settlements which stretched all the way around from Fort Louisbourg.

ANGLO-FRENCH CONFLICT

No serious trouble between English and French colonists occurred so long as their homelands remained at peace. Charles II and James II of England persisted in their friendship for Louis XIV of France despite the fact that Louis, with his wars of French aggrandizement, ran directly counter to the traditional English policy of maintaining a balance of power on the European continent. In the Treaty of Whitehall (1686) James II and Louis XIV pledged themselves to refrain from hostilities in

Advantages of the French Threat [1748–1749]

Peter Kalm, a university professor in Swedish Finland, toured some of the English colonies during 1748–1749. He reported:

I have been told by Englishmen . . . that the English colonies in North America, in the space of thirty or fifty years, would be able to form a state by themselves, entirely independent of Old England. But as the whole country which lies along the sea-shore is unguarded, and on the land side is harassed by the French, in times of war these dangerous neighbors are sufficient to prevent the connection of the colonies with their mother country from being quite broken off. The English government has therefore sufficient reason to consider the French in North America as the best means of keeping their colonies in due submission.

America even if ("which God forbid") they should find themselves at war with one another in Europe. This was an early and interesting attempt to keep America out of Europe's wars, but in just a few years it was a dead letter.

When James II was deposed, he was replaced by Louis XIV's enemy, William III, who continued to be stadholder (chief magistrate) of the Netherlands as well as King of England, and who soon resumed his stubborn resistance to the European aggressions of the French. His successor, Queen Anne, with the aid of alliances he had formed before his death, carried on the struggle against France and her newly found ally, Spain.

These wars spread from Europe to America, where they were known to the English colonists as King William's War (1689–1697) and Queen Anne's War (1701–1713). The first, which involved few of the colonists except in northern New England, led to no decisive result. The second, which entailed border fighting with the Spaniards in the South as well as the French and their Indian allies in the North, ended in one of the great and far-reaching international settlements of modern history – the Treaty of Utrecht (1713). At Utrecht the English were awarded some sizable territorial gains in North America at the expense of the French: Acadia (Nova Scotia), Newfoundland, and the shores of Hudson Bay.

After about a quarter of a century of European and American peace, England went to war with Spain over the question of English trading rights in the Spanish colonies, and the English in Georgia came to blows with the Spaniards in Florida. The Anglo-Spanish conflict soon merged in a general European war when Frederick the Great of Prussia seized some of the territory of Maria Theresa of Austria. Louis XV of France joined the Prussians against the Austrians in the hope of getting the Austrian Netherlands (Belgium), and George II of England came to the aid of Maria Theresa so as to keep the French out of the Low Countries. Again New England and New France were involved in the hostilities – in what the English colonists referred to as King George's War (1744–1748). New Englanders captured the French bastion at Louisbourg on Cape Breton Island, but to their bitter disappointment they had to abandon it in accordance with the peace treaty, which provided for the mutual restoration of conquered territory.

This war and the two preceding it had arisen primarily from European causes, and only a small fraction of the people in the English colonies had taken any part. To the colonists these were foreign wars – King William's, Queen Anne's, King George's – rather than their own. But the next conflict was different. Known to the colonists as the French and Indian War, it was in fact a "Great War for the Empire." Unlike the preliminaries, this climactic struggle originated in the interior of North America.

THE GREAT WAR FOR THE EMPIRE

Within the American wilderness a number of border disputes arose, but the most serious of them concerned the ownership of the Ohio Val-

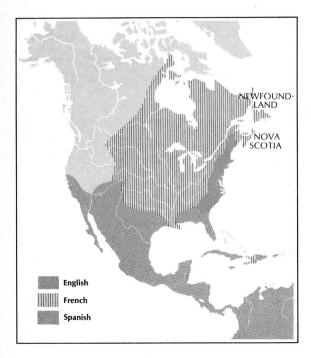

North America in 1700

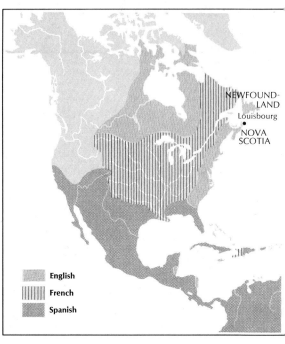

North America After 1713

ley. The French, desiring to control this direct route between Canada and Louisiana, began to build a chain of fortifications to make good their claim. Pennsylvania fur traders and Virginia land speculators (the latter organized as the Ohio Company) looked to the country across the Alleghenies as a profitable field for their operations, and the British government, aroused to the defense of its territorial rights, gave instructions to the colonial governors to resist French encroachments. Acting on these instructions, the governor of Virginia sent George Washington, then only twenty-one, to protest to the commanders of the French forts newly built between Lake Erie and the Allegheny River, but these commanders politely replied that the land was French. While Washington was on his fruitless mission, a band of Virginians tried to forestall the French by erecting a fort of their own at the strategic key to the Ohio Valley—the forks of the Ohio, where the Allegheny and Monongahela rivers join. A stronger band of Canadians drove the Virginians away, completed the work, and named it Fort Duquesne. Arriving with the advance

guard of a relief force from Virginia, Washington met a French detachment in a brief but bloody skirmish. He then fell back to a hastily constructed stockade, Fort Necessity, where he was overwhelmed by troops from Fort Duquesne and compelled to surrender (July 4, 1754). The first shots of the French and Indian War had been fired.

For the English colonists, the war had begun inauspiciously, and it continued to go badly for them during the next few years. They received aid from the home government, but this aid was inefficiently and unintelligently applied. The British fleet failed to prevent the landing of large French reinforcements in Canada, and the newly appointed commander in chief of the British army in America, General Edward Braddock, failed to retake the forks of the Ohio. Brave but aged, wise in the ways of European warfare but unused to the American woods, Braddock wore out his men by having them cut a long military road through the forest toward Fort Duquesne, and he exposed them to attack from the tree-hidden enemy by marching them in the accepted European for-

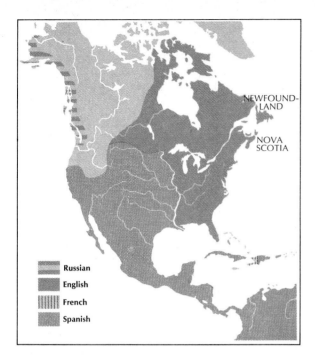

North America After 1763

one, but were by no means that much stronger militarily. The French had numerous and powerful Indian allies, many of them newly attracted to the French by the latter's early victories in the war. The English had few such allies; the Iroquois, traditionally friendly to the English and hostile to the French, now remained firmly neutral. Furthermore, the French government kept its colonists in a fairly good state of military discipline and readiness, and could count upon the loyal services of a high proportion of its colonial manpower. The British government, on the other hand, exercised much less control over its thirteen colonies, which often acted as if they were autonomous. Only where and when they were exposed to immediate danger did the English colonists wholeheartedly support the war effort.

At first the overall direction of British strategy was weak. Then, in 1757, William Pitt, as prime minister, was allowed to act as practically a wartime dictator of the Empire. Pitt reformed the army and the navy, replacing bureaucratic deadwood with young and eager officers. He gave generous subsidies to Frederick the Great, who thus was enabled to keep the French fairly busy in Europe. And he turned from the defensive to the offensive in America, with a determination to drive the French out of the continent.

With Pitt as organizer, the British regulars in America, together with colonial troops, proceeded to take one French stronghold after another, including Fort Duquesne in 1758. The next year, after a siege of Quebec, supposedly impregnable atop its towering cliff, the army of General James Wolfe struggled up a hidden ravine, surprised the larger forces of the Marquis de Montcalm, and defeated them in a battle in which both commanders were slain. The fall of Quebec marked the climax of the American phase of the war, and the decisive battle was afterward remembered as a romantic and tragic encounter between two high-minded, able men.

Some other phases of the war were less romantic, less high-minded. In the course of it the British resorted to such expedients as population dispersal. Fearing trouble from the French inhabitants of Nova Scotia, the British uprooted several thousand of them and scattered them throughout the English colonies; some of these Acadians eventually made their

mation. Seven miles from the fort he ran into a French and Indian ambush (July 9, 1755); he himself and large numbers of his men were killed, and the survivors fled all the way back to Fort Cumberland in Maryland. The frontier from Pennsylvania to Virginia was left exposed to Indian raids, and many frontier settlers withdrew to the east of the Allegheny Mountains.

After about two years of fighting in America, the governments of France and England finally declared hostilities, and a world war (known in Europe as the Seven Years' War, 1756–1763) began. France and England now changed partners, France allying herself with her former enemy, Austria, and England joining France's former ally, Prussia. Henceforth battles were fought not only on the American mainland but also in the West Indies, in Europe, and around the world in India.

In this global contest the British had the advantage of the mightiest navy on the seas and, with Frederick the Great on their side, the finest army in Europe. In America the people of the English colonies outnumbered those of the French colonies by approximately fifteen to

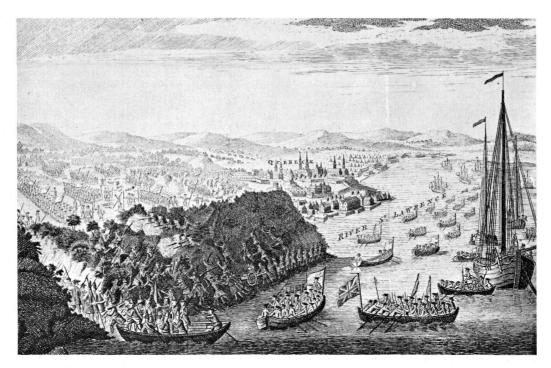

The Taking of Quebec

In 1759 the capture of Quebec was the main objective of the British campaign in America. General James Wolfe, only thirty-two, commanded an army that proceeded up the St. Lawrence River on navy transports. General Jeffrey Amherst, commander in chief of the British armies in America, was to take forts Crown Point and Ticonderoga, then join Wolfe before Quebec. Amherst was delayed, and Wolfe decided to go ahead alone, though his army was smaller than that of the French at Quebec under the Marquis de Montcalm. The Quebec defenses were too strong for a direct attack from the river. After a few months' siege, Wolfe daringly landed his troops above the town, led them up an insufficiently guarded ravine, and reached the heights known as the Plains of Abraham. Now the cautious Montcalm had no choice but to fight. He attacked without waiting to assemble all his available forces, and in about fifteen minutes he was compelled to retreat. The contemporary English engraving portrays in the one scene a whole succession of events—the landings, the climb up the ravine, and the battle itself. (Library of Congress)

way to Louisiana, where they became the ancestors of the present-day Cajuns. Meanwhile the French and their savage allies were committing worse atrocities, and hundreds of defenseless families along the English frontier fell before the hatchet and the scalping knife.

Peace finally came after the accession of the peace-minded George III and the resignation of Pitt, who disagreed with the new King and wished to continue hostilities. Yet Pitt's aims were pretty well realized in the treaty signed at Paris in 1763. By its terms the French ceded to Great Britain some of their West Indian islands and all their colonies in India except two. The French also transferred Canada and all other French territory east of the Mississippi, except the island of New Orleans, to Great Britain, and New Orleans and the French claims west of the Mississippi to Spain. Thus the French gave up all title to the mainland of North America.

The New Imperialism

As the war ended, the London policy makers faced a dilemma, though they were not fully aware of it. On the one hand, they could revert to the old colonial system with its half-hearted enforcement of the mercantilist program, but that would mean virtual independence for the colonies. On the other hand, the men in London could renew their efforts to reform the Empire and enforce the laws, but that would lead to revolt and absolute independence. The problem was further complicated by both the costs and the rewards of the war — the debts and the territory that it brought.

BURDENS OF EMPIRE

So strong had grown the colonial feeling against direct legislation by Parliament that, during the French and Indian War, the English government did not attempt to tax or draft the colonists directly but called upon the assemblies to provide quotas of soldiers and supplies. This requisition system, itself a concession to provincial prejudice, heightened the self-importance of the assemblies, and most of them further asserted their autonomy by complying in a slow and niggardly way. Some of them, unwilling to be taxed by Parliament, also refused to tax themselves; they issued paper money instead.

In Virginia the legislature not only issued paper money but, when the price of tobacco rose, also passed a law to deprive the Anglican clergy (who were paid in tobacco) of the benefits of the price rise. When this law was disallowed (1759), one of the ministers sued his vestrymen for his full pay. At the trial of the "parson's cause" the young lawyer Patrick Henry, defending the vestrymen, denounced the Privy Council for its tyranny and told his fellow Virginians to ignore its action. Roused by Henry's oratory, the jurors awarded the parson damages of only one penny. Thus did they defy the authority of the British government.

In Massachusetts the merchants disregarded the laws of the Empire even more flagrantly than did the planters in Virginia. Throughout the war these merchants persisted in trading with the enemy in Canada and in the French West Indies. British officials resorted to general search warrants — "writs of assistance" — for discovering smuggled goods and stamping out the illegal and unpatriotic trade. As attorney for the Massachusetts merchants, James Otis maintained that these searches violated the ancient rights of Englishmen and that the law of Parliament authorizing the warrants was therefore null and void. With eloquence as stirring as Henry's, Otis insisted that Parliament had only a limited power of legislating for the colonies.

The thirteen continental colonies were only a part of the British possessions scattered throughout the Americas and the world, and before 1763 they were not considered (except in their own eyes) as the most valuable part. Some of them, such as Virginia and Maryland with their tobacco production, fitted in fairly well with the aims of mercantilism; but on the whole the island colonies contributed a great deal more than those of the mainland to the profits of English merchants and the prosperity of the English homeland. The "sugar islands" in particular — Barbados and the Windward Islands, the Leeward Islands, Jamaica — yielded remarkable opportunities for the investment of English capital. They also complemented the economies of some of the mainland colonies by providing a market for the output of fisheries, farms, and forest industries.

Believing in a kind of commercial imperialism, most English merchants opposed the acquisition of territory for its own sake. But some Englishmen and Americans began to believe that land itself should be acquired for the Empire because of the population the land would support, the taxes it would produce, and the sense of imperial greatness it would confer. Both William Pitt and Benjamin Franklin were among the advocates of this new territorial imperialism. Franklin wrote powerfully upon the future greatness of the British Empire in America, stressing the need for vast spaces to accommodate the rapid and limitless growth of the American people. Old-fashioned mercantilists, however, continued to think of trade as the essence of empire, and of island and coastal possessions as bases for trade. The issue came to a head with the peacemaking at the end of

the French and Indian War. Commercial imperialists urged that Canada be returned to
France in exchange for the most valuable of
her sugar islands, Guadeloupe. Territorial
imperialists, Franklin among them, argued in
favor of keeping Canada. The decision to retain
Canada marked a change in the emphasis of
imperial policy.

With the acquisition of Canada and the
other fruits of war in 1763, the area of the British Empire was more than doubled and the
problems of governing it were made many
times more complex. The war had left the British government with a staggering burden of
debt, and English landlords and merchants
objected violently to increased taxes. The rather half-hearted war effort of the colonists had
shown the cumulative evils of salutary neglect.
And, by giving Great Britain undisputed title to
the transmontane West as well as Canada, the
peace had brought new problems of administration and defense. British statesmen feared
that France, by no means crushed, might soon
launch an attack somewhere in America for the
recovery of her lost territories and prestige.

POLICIES OF GEORGE III

Responsibility for the solution of these postwar
problems fell to the young monarch George III,
who had come to the throne in 1760. Unlike the
first two Georges, who had remained essentially German in point of view, George III was
thoroughly British and proud of it. He was determined to follow the advice of his mother to
be King in fact as well as name. Shrewdly, he
took care not to upset the recently developed
constitutional practice according to which the
party controlling Parliament made and un-
made ministries. Instead, becoming a politician
himself, the King created a party of his own
through patronage and bribes and thus took
control of Parliament away from the Whigs.
Though not at all the ogre he was once pictured in American schoolbooks, George III
achieved his aim of personal government and
therefore deserves much of the credit or blame
for the acts that followed.

More immediately responsible was George
Grenville, whom the King made prime minister
in 1763. Grenville, a brother-in-law of William
Pitt, did not share Pitt's sympathy with the co-

lonial point of view. He agreed with the prevailing British opinion that the colonists should be
compelled to obey the laws and to pay a part of
the cost of defending and administering the
Empire. He fancied himself something of an efficiency expert, and he was indeed an able administrator. Furthermore, as chancellor of the
exchequer and first lord of the treasury, he was
well acquainted with matters of public finance.
Promptly he undertook to impose system upon
what had been a rather unsystematic aggregation of colonial possessions in America.

The Western problem was the most urgent. With the repulse of the French, frontiersmen from the English colonies had begun
promptly to move over the mountains and into
the upper Ohio Valley. Objecting to this intrusion, an alliance of Indian tribes, under the
remarkable Ottawa chieftain Pontiac, raised
the war cry. As an emergency measure the
British government issued a proclamation forbidding settlers to advance beyond a line
drawn along the mountain divide between the
Atlantic and the interior.

Though the emergency passed, the principle of the Proclamation Line of 1763 remained—
the principle of controlling the westward
movement of population. This was something
new. Earlier the government had encouraged
the rapid peopling of the frontier for reasons of both defense and trade. In time the
official attitude had begun to change, because
of a fear that the interior might draw away so
many people as to weaken markets and investments nearer the coast, and because of a desire
to reserve land-speculating and fur-trading opportunities for English rather than colonial enterprisers. Then, having tentatively announced
a new policy in 1763, the government soon extended and elaborated it. A definite Indian
boundary was to be located, and from time to
time relocated, in agreement with the various
tribes. Western lands were to be opened for
occupation gradually, and settlement was to be
carefully supervised to see that it proceeded in
a compact and orderly way.

To provide further for the defense of the
colonies, and to raise revenue and enforce imperial law within them, the Grenville ministry
with the cooperation of Parliament meanwhile
instituted a series of measures, some of which
were familiar in principle and others fairly
novel. Regular troops were now to be stationed

permanently in the provinces, and by the Mutiny Act (1765) the colonists were called upon to assist in provisioning and maintaining the army. Ships of the navy were assigned to patrol American waters and look out for smugglers. The customs service was reorganized and enlarged, and vice-admiralty courts were set up in America to try accused smugglers without the benefit of sympathetic local juries. Royal officials were ordered to take up their colonial posts in person instead of sending substitutes. The Sugar Act (1764), designed in part to eliminate the illegal trade between the continental colonies and the foreign West Indies, lowered the high molasses duty of the Molasses Act of 1733, but imposed new duties on a number of items and made provision for more effective collection. The Currency Act (1764) forbade the colonial assemblies to issue any more paper money and required them to retire on schedule all the paper money issued during the war. And, most momentous of all, the Stamp Act (1765) imposed a tax to be paid on every legal document in the colonies, every newspaper, almanac, or pamphlet, and every deck of cards or pair of dice.

Thus the new imperial program with its reapplication of old mercantilist principles began to be put into effect. In a sense it proved highly effective. British officials soon were collecting more than ten times as much annual revenue in America as before 1763. But the new policy was not a lasting success.

COLONIAL SELF-INTEREST

The colonists still had much to gain by remaining within the Empire and enjoying its many benefits. They still held grievances against one another as well as against the authorities in London. In 1763, for example, a band of Pennsylvania frontiersmen known as the Paxton Boys descended on Philadelphia to demand defense money and changes in the tax laws, and bloodshed was averted only by concessions from the colonial government.

In 1771 a small-scale civil war broke out as a consequence of the Regulator movement in North Carolina. The Regulators were farmers of the Carolina upcountry who organized to oppose the extortionate taxes that the sheriffs

collected. These sheriffs, along with other local officials, were appointed by the governor. At first the Regulators tried to redress their grievances peaceably, by electing their leaders to the colonial assembly. The western counties were badly underrepresented in the assembly, and the Regulators were unable to get control of it. They finally armed themselves and undertook to resist tax collections by force. To suppress the revolt, Governor William Tryon raised an army of militiamen, mostly from the eastern counties. The militiamen met and defeated the Regulators, some 2,000 strong, in the Battle of Alamance, in which nine on each side were killed and many others wounded. Afterward, six Regulators were hanged for treason.

Though such bloodshed was exceptional, the people of the colonies were divided by numerous conflicts of interest. After 1763, however, the policies of the British government increasingly offset the divisive tendencies within the colonies and caused Americans to look at the disadvantages of empire more closely than at its benefits. These policies threatened, in some degree or other, the well-being of nearly all classes in America.

Northern merchants would suffer from the various restraints upon their commerce, from the closing of the West to their ventures in land speculation and fur trading, from the denial of opportunities in manufacturing, and from the increased load of taxation. Southern planters, already burdened with debts to English merchants, would not only have to pay additional taxes but would also be deprived of the chance to lessen their debts by selling Western land, in which George Washington and others were much interested. Professional men—preachers, lawyers, and professors—considered the interests of merchants and planters to be identical with their own. Small farmers, clearly the largest group in the colonies, stood to lose as a result of reduced markets and hence lower prices for their crops, together with an increase in their taxes and other costs, not to mention the difficulty of getting paper-money loans. Town workers faced the prospect of narrowing opportunities, particularly because of the restraints on manufacturing and paper money.

At the end of the French and Indian War, the colonists already were beginning to feel the pinch of a postwar depression. Previously the British government, pouring money into their

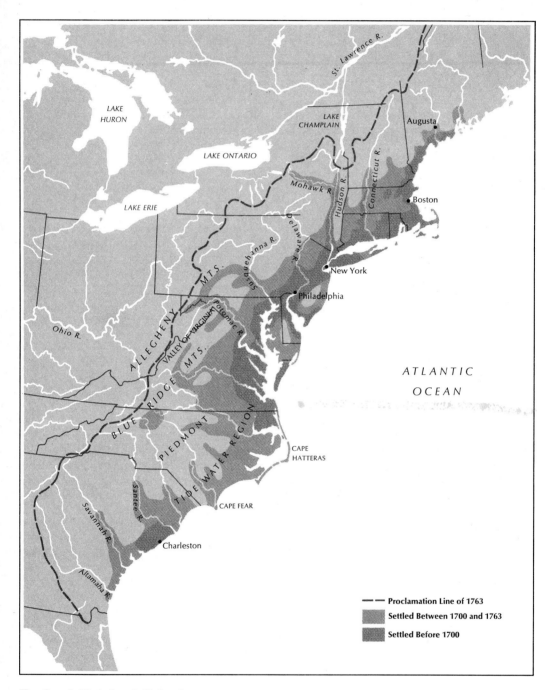

England Mainland Colonies

midst to finance the fighting, had stimulated a wartime boom. Now the government was going to take money out of the colonies instead of putting it in. If the government's measures should be strictly enforced, the immediate effect would be to aggravate the hard times. The long-term effect would be to confine the enterprising spirit of the colonists and condemn them to a fixed or even a declining level of living.

Grievous as were the economic consequences of George III's program, its political consequences would be as bad or worse. While colonial democracy was far from all-inclusive, the colonists were used to a remarkably wide latitude in self-government. Nowhere else in the world at that time did so large a proportion of the people take an active interest in public affairs. The chief centers of American political activity were the provincial assemblies, and here the people (through their elected representatives) were able to assert themselves because the assemblies had established the right to give or withhold appropriations for the costs of government within the colonies. If, now, the British authorities should succeed in raising extensive revenues directly from America, the colonial voters and their representatives would lose control over public finance, and without such control their participation in politics would be very nearly meaningless.

Home rule was not something new and different that these Americans were striving to get. It was something old and familiar that they desired to keep. They would lose it if the London authorities were allowed to carry out the program of raising revenues from colonial taxation and providing unconditional salaries for royal officials. The discontented Americans eventually prepared themselves to lay down their lives for a movement that was both democratic and conservative—a movement to conserve the liberties they already possessed.

Stirrings of Revolt

The experience of the French and Indian War, while convincing prominent Englishmen of the need for tighter imperial control, had exerted an opposite effect on the attitude of colonials. Rightly or wrongly, they had gained a heightened sense of self-confidence in their own military prowess, along with a certain contempt for British regulars and especially their officers, such as the unfortunate General Braddock. The French threat having been removed from the frontier forest, many of the colonists felt a new surge of expansive energy and daring. In short, they concluded that they needed not more but rather less of imperial guidance and protection than they had previously received.

Through its very different influences on the thinking of English and colonial leaders, the grand victory of the Empire led to a period of unprecedented tension between the mother country and the colonies.

THE STAMP ACT CRISIS

If Prime Minister Grenville had wished deliberately to antagonize and unify some of the most influential groups in the colonies (which, of course, he did not) he could have chosen no means more effective than the Stamp Act. The tax fell upon all Americans, of whatever section, colony, or class. In particular, the stamps required for ship's papers and legal documents offended merchants and lawyers. Tavern owners, often the political oracles of their neighborhoods, now were supposed to buy stamps for their licenses; and printers, for their newspapers and other publications. Thus the tax antagonized those who could play most effectively upon public opinion.

Nevertheless, it occurred to few colonists that they could do more than grumble and buy the stamps, until the Virginia House of Burgesses sounded a "trumpet of sedition" that aroused Americans to action almost everywhere. In the House of Burgesses a group of young aristocrats aspired to exert themselves against the oligarchy of tidewater planters who, with the royal governor, dominated Virginia politics. Foremost among these young malcontents was Patrick Henry, who was ambitious to enlarge the fame he had gained in the "parson's cause." Henry made a fiery speech in the House (May 1765), concluding with a hint that George III like earlier tyrants might lose his head. There were shocked cries of "Treason!" and, according to a man who was present, Henry apologized, though many years afterward he was quoted as having made the defiant reply: "If *this* be treason, make the most of it." In any case, he proceeded to introduce a set of resolutions declaring that Americans possessed all the rights of Englishmen,

The Stamp Act Congress: Resolutions [1765]

I. That His Majesty's subjects in these colonies owe the same allegiance to the Crown of Great Britain that is owing from his subjects born within the realm, and all due subordination to that august body the Parliament of Great Britain.

II. That His Majesty's liege subjects in these colonies are intitled to all the inherent rights and liberties of his natural born subjects within the kingdom of Great Britain.

III. That it is inseparably essential to the freedom of a people, and the undoubted right of Englishmen, that no taxes be imposed on them but with their own consent, given personally or by their representatives.

IV. That the people of these colonies are not, and from their local circumstances cannot be, represented in the House of Commons in Great Britain.

V. That the only representatives of the people of these colonies are persons chosen therein by themselves, and that no taxes ever have been, or can be constitutionally imposed on them, but by their respective legislatures. . . .

---

especially the right to be taxed only by their own representatives; moreover, that Virginians should pay no taxes except those voted by the Virginia assembly, and that anyone advocating the right of Parliament to tax Virginians should be deemed an enemy of the colony. The House of Burgesses did not adopt the most extreme of Henry's resolutions, but all of them were printed and circulated as the "Virginia Resolves," thus giving the impression in other colonies that the people of Virginia were both more daring and better unified than was the fact.

Stirred by the Virginia Resolves, mobs in various places began to take the law into their own hands, and during the summer of 1765 riots broke out in various places, the worst of them in Boston. Men belonging to the newly organized "Sons of Liberty" went about terrorizing stamp agents and burning the stamps. The agents, themselves Americans, hastily resigned, and very few stamps were sold in the continental colonies. In Boston the mob got out of hand and went about harrying pro-British "aristocrats" such as the lieutenant governor, Thomas Hutchinson, whose house was wrecked (though privately he had opposed the passage of the Stamp Act).

At about the time that Patrick Henry presented his resolutions to the Virginia assembly, James Otis proposed to his fellow legislators in Massachusetts that they call an intercolonial congress for concerted action against the new tax. In October 1765 the Stamp Act Congress met in New York, with delegates from nine of the colonies present. The delegates decided to petition both the King and the two houses of Parliament. Though admitting that Americans owed to Parliament "all due subordination," the congress denied that they could rightfully be taxed except by their provincial assemblies.

If the British government had tried to enforce the Stamp Act, possibly the Revolutionary War would have begun ten years earlier than it actually did. The government was not deterred by resolves, riots, and petitions, but the Americans also used something more persuasive than any of these—economic pressure. Already, in response to the Sugar Act of 1764, many New Englanders had quit buying English goods. Now the colonial boycott spread, and the Sons of Liberty intimidated those colonists who were reluctant to participate in it. The merchants of England, feeling the loss of much of their colonial market, begged Parliament to repeal the Stamp Act, while stories of unemployment, poverty, and discontent arose from English seaports and manufacturing towns.

Having succeeded Grenville as prime minister, the Marquis of Rockingham used his influence in favor of appeasing both the English merchants and the American colonists, and King George III himself finally was convinced that the act must be repealed. Opponents of

The Declaratory Act [1766]

While repealing the Stamp Act, Parliament denied the arguments put forth by Americans at the meeting of the Stamp Act Congress and on other occasions. The constitutional issue was sharply drawn, as may be seen by comparing the resolutions of the Stamp Act Congress with these words of Parliament's "declaratory" act:

Whereas several of the houses of representatives in his Majesty's colonies and plantations in America have of late, against law, claimed to themselves, or to the general assemblies of the same, the sole and exclusive right of imposing duties or taxes upon his Majesty's subjects in the said colonies and plantations; and have, in pursuance of such claim, passed certain votes, resolutions, and orders, derogatory to the legislative authority of parliament, and inconsistent with the dependency of said colonies and plantations upon the crown of Great Britain: . . . be it declared . . . That the said colonies and plantations in America have been, are, and of right ought to be subordinate unto and dependent upon the imperial crown and parliament of Great Britain; and that the King's majesty, by and with the advice and consent of the lords spiritual and temporal and commons of Great Britain in parliament assembled, had, hath, and of right ought to have full power and authority to make laws and statutes of sufficient force and validity to bind the colonies and people of America, subjects of the crown of Great Britain, in all cases whatsoever.

---

repeal, and they were strong and vociferous, insisted that unless the colonists were compelled to obey the Stamp Act, they would soon cease to obey any laws of Parliament. So Parliament passed the Declaratory Act, asserting parliamentary authority over the colonies in "all cases whatsoever," and then repealed the Stamp Act (1766). In their rejoicing over the repeal, most Americans paid little attention to the sweeping declaration of Parliament's power.

THE TOWNSHEND PROGRAM

The appeasement policy of the Rockingham government was not so well received in England as in America. English landlords protested that the government had "sacrificed the landed gentlemen to the interests of traders and colonists." Soon the King dismissed the unpopular Rockingham and called upon William Pitt to form a new ministry. A critic of the Stamp Act, Pitt had a reputation in America as the colonists' friend, though his reputation suffered somewhat when he accepted a peerage as Lord Chatham. He continued as prime minister after gout and mental illness had laid him low, and the actual leadership of his administration

fell to the chancellor of the exchequer, Charles Townshend, "Champagne Charlie," a brilliant man but a sort of playboy of British politics.

Townshend had to deal with imperial problems and colonial grievances still left over from the Grenville ministry. Now that the Stamp Act was gone, the worst of these grievances was the Mutiny Act of 1765, which required the colonists to provide quarters and supplies for the British troops in America. The Massachusetts assembly, refusing to vote the supplies, was the first to defy the Mutiny Act, but the New York assembly, when it did the same thing, presented a more serious challenge to imperial authorities, since the army headquarters were in New York.

To enforce the Mutiny Act and raise a revenue in the colonies, Townshend proposed two measures to Parliament. First, New York was to be punished by the suspension of its assembly until the law was obeyed there. By thus singling out New York, Townshend thought he would avoid Grenville's mistake of arousing all the colonies at once. Second, duties were to be laid upon colonial imports of glass, lead, paint, paper, and tea. Townshend reasoned that the colonists could not logically object to taxation of this kind. For Benjamin

Franklin, as a colonial agent in London trying to prevent the passage of the Stamp Act, had drawn a distinction between "internal" and "external" taxes and had denounced the stamp duties as internal taxation. While Townshend laughed at this distinction he was now recom-

mending duties that, without question, were to be collected externally. In 1767 Parliament approved the Townshend duties and suspended the New York assembly.

To the colonists, however, the Townshend duties were scarcely more acceptable than the

Though the Stamp Act (1765) apparently had little effect on imports from England, the Townshend Act (1767) led to a considerable reduction in them in 1769. After this law's almost complete repeal (1770), imports rose dramatically in 1771. The Tea Act (1773) and the nonimportation agreement (1774) helped to bring on another decline, and the subsequent outbreak of hostilities resulted in an almost complete stoppage of trade.

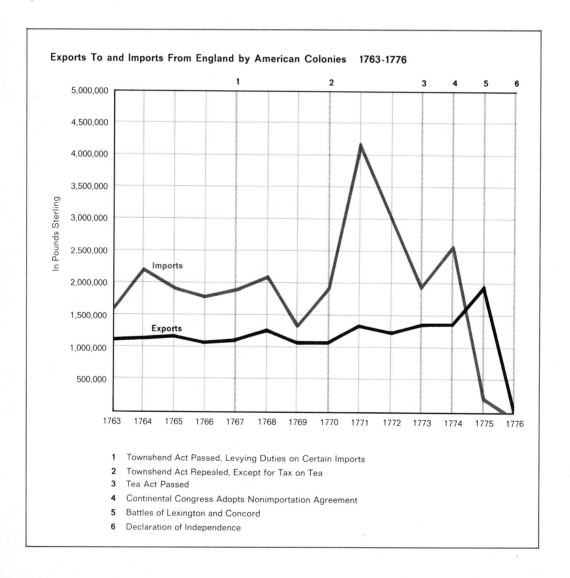

Exports To and Imports From England by American Colonies   1763-1776

1   Townshend Act Passed, Levying Duties on Certain Imports
2   Townshend Act Repealed, Except for Tax on Tea
3   Tea Act Passed
4   Continental Congress Adopts Nonimportation Agreement
5   Battles of Lexington and Concord
6   Declaration of Independence

stamp tax, and the suspension of the one assembly threatened the annihilation of all. Taking up New York's cause as well as its own, the Massachusetts assembly sent out a circular letter urging all the rest to stand up against every tax, external or internal, imposed by Parliament. At first the Massachusetts circular evoked little response in some of the legislatures and ran into strong opposition in at least one of them, that of Pennsylvania. Then Lord Hillsborough, in the new office of Secretary of State for the Colonies, issued a circular letter of his own in which he warned that assemblies endorsing the Massachusetts letter would be dissolved. Promptly the other colonies, even Pennsylvania, rallied to the support of Massachusetts.

Besides inducing Parliament to levy import duties and suspend the New York assembly, Townshend also took steps to enforce commercial regulations in the colonies more effectively than ever. The most fateful of these steps was the establishment of a board of customs commissioners in America. In doing so, he intended to stop the leaks in the colonial custom houses. His commissioners, with headquarters in Boston, virtually ended the smuggling at that place, though smugglers continued to carry on a busy trade in other colonial seaports.

Naturally the Boston merchants were the most indignant, and they took the lead in organizing another boycott. In 1768 the merchants of Philadelphia and New York joined those of Boston in a nonimportation agreement, and later some of the Southern merchants and planters also agreed to cooperate. Throughout the colonies, crude American homespun became suddenly fashionable, while English luxuries were frowned upon. Some enthusiasts, advocating the development of colonial manufactures of all kinds, looked forward to the creation of a self-sufficient America, with an economy independent of the Empire's.

Before the consequences of his program were fully apparent, Townshend died, leaving the question of revising his import duties to his successor, Lord North. Hoping to break the nonimportation agreement and divide the colonists, Lord North secured the repeal (1770) of all the Townshend duties except the tea tax.

Meanwhile the presence of the customs commissioners in Boston led to violence. The Boston mob had the most aggressive leader of all, Samuel Adams. The impoverished son of a once wealthy brewer, Adams had taken to politics after he himself had failed in business. As a rabble-rouser he had no equal in the colonies, and from the time of the Stamp Act troubles he was the guiding spirit of Massachusetts radicalism, even outdoing James Otis. Adams' success as a politician depended upon his finding suitable topics for agitation, and the British government, having repeatedly supplied him with topics, obliged him again by locating the customs commissioners in Boston and then stationing troops there.

To the Boston "liberty boys," the presence of the customs commissioners was a standing invitation to violence, and before long the terrified officials were driven to take refuge in Castle William, out in the harbor. So that they could return safely to their duties, the British government placed four regiments (afterward reduced to two) within the city. The presence of the redcoats antagonized Samuel Adams and his followers more than ever. While his men ragged the soldiers and engaged them in brawls, Adams filled the newspapers with imaginary stories of rapes and other atrocities committed by the troops, and he spread throughout Boston a rumor that the soldiers were preparing for a concerted attack upon the citizens. On the night of March 5, 1770, a mob of dockworkers and other "liberty boys" fell upon the sentry at the custom house. Hastily Captain Preston lined up several of his men in front of the building to protect it. There was some scuffling, and one of the soldiers was knocked down. Other soldiers then fired into the crowd, killing five of its members.

These events quickly became known as the "Boston Massacre" through the efforts of Samuel Adams and his adherents, who published an account bearing the title *Innocent Blood Crying to God from the Streets of Boston* and giving the impression that the dead were victims of a deliberate plot. The soldiers, tried before a jury of Bostonians and defended by Samuel Adams' cousin John Adams, were found guilty of no more than manslaughter and were given only a token punishment. Nevertheless, through newspapers and pamphlets, Samuel Adams convicted the redcoats of murder in the minds of many contemporary Americans, and year after year on March 5 he revived the people's memory with orations recalling the events of 1770. Later generations accepted his version of the "massacre" and thus, without knowing it, honored his skill as the foremost propagandist of the pre-Revolutionary decade.

The "Bloody Massacre"

This broadside, "Engrav'd Printed & Sold by Paul Revere, Boston," pictures the Patriot version of the Boston incident of March 5, 1770. At the extreme right, Captain Thomas Preston, in command of the Custom House guards, leers as he orders his grinning men to fire on the unarmed citizens. The Custom House, Preston's headquarters, is sarcastically labeled "Butcher's Hall." Accompanying the picture were the names of the dead and eighteen lines of verse. One of the dead was Crispus Attucks, a tall, brawny, forty-seven-year-old man, reputed to be a Negro with some Indian blood who had escaped from slavery and taken up the life of a sailor. When, in 1888, a monument was erected to the fallen, a poem was recited honoring Attucks as "leader and voice that day; /The first to defy and the first to die. . . ." (Courtesy of the Metropolitan Museum of Art, gift of Mrs. Russell Sage, 1910)

THE PHILOSOPHY OF REVOLT

Though America quieted down for a while after 1770, Americans did not abandon their principles, and these principles were revolutionary, at least in implication. "The Revolution was effected before the war commenced," one of the greatest of the Revolutionary leaders, John Adams, afterward remarked. "The Revolution was in the minds and hearts of the people." Of course, very few of the people thought of outright independence till after the war had begun, and even those few (among them Samuel Adams) considered it best not to admit that independence was their ultimate aim. For the time being, most politically conscious Americans desired no more, and no less, than autonomy within the Empire. They argued that the English Constitution, correctly interpreted, supported their claims to individual liberty and colonial self-rule, and that the laws of nature and of God justified them in resisting infringements upon their rights.

In the course of the argument the Americans came to the conclusion that they were better Englishmen than the English themselves, better acquainted with the Constitution and more devoted to the liberties it guaranteed. Some of the Whig politicians in England, such as William Pitt and above all Edmund Burke, who spoke eloquently in favor of conciliation, were more or less inclined to agree. But other Englishmen, like the famous lexicographer and literary critic Samuel Johnson, looked upon the Americans as a deluded and indeed a barbarized offshoot of the English people. The majority in England were outraged rather than convinced by all the speechmaking and pamphleteering on the other side of the Atlantic.

To Englishmen the Constitution, though worthy of the highest respect, was an assortment of laws and usages that had developed through many centuries and that were rather elastic and vague. To Americans, on the other hand, it was a fixed and definite body of principles, which ought to be written down so as to avoid disagreements. Americans believed the colonies did have written constitutions — the colonial charters, which supposedly guaranteed to Americans all the traditional rights of Englishmen.

Of these rights the most fundamental, according to the colonists, was the right to be taxed only with their own consent. When Townshend levied his "external" duties, the Philadelphia lawyer John Dickinson maintained in the *Letters of a Pennsylvania Farmer* that even external taxation was legal only when designed to regulate trade and not to raise a revenue. But Americans did not like trade regulations, either, when the regulations began to be enforced. Eventually the discontented colonists took an unqualified stand upon the slogan "No taxation without representation."

This clamor about "representation" made little sense to Englishmen. Only about one in twenty-five of them was entitled to vote for members of Parliament, and some populous boroughs in England had no representatives at all. According to the prevailing English theory, however, Parliament did not represent individuals or geographical areas. Instead, it represented the interests of the whole nation and indeed the whole Empire, no matter where the members happened to come from. The unenfranchised boroughs of England, the whole of Ireland, and the colonies 3,000 miles away — all were represented in the Parliament at London.

That was the theory of "virtual" representation, but Americans believed in actual representation. They felt they could be represented in Parliament only if they sent their quota of members to it. Some of them, even James Otis, considered proposals for electing American representatives, but most of the colonists realized that if they should participate in the action of Parliament they would be bound by that action, even though they were outnumbered and outvoted. So they reverted to the argument that they could be fairly represented only in their own colonial assemblies.

According to the American view of the Empire, and according to actual fact, these assemblies were little parliaments, as competent to legislate for their respective colonies as Parliament was for England. The Empire was a sort of federation of commonwealths, each with its own legislative body, all tied together by common loyalty to the King (much as in the British Commonwealth of Nations today). This being their conception of the Empire, the Americans protested bitterly against the pretensions of Parliament but had nothing except kind words for George III — until they decided to cut their imperial ties completely and declare for independence. According to the English view, the Empire was a single, undivided unit, and everywhere within it the King and Parliament together were supreme.

The American doctrine of resistance to unconstitutional and tyrannical laws was based chiefly upon the Bible and the writings of John Locke. For generations the preachers of New England had taught that no man need obey a government when it violated the will of God as set forth in the Scriptures. Now, to show that rebellion against tyranny was lawful in God's sight, they retold such Bible stories as the one about a King of Israel who burdened his people with unjust taxes and was overthrown.

John Locke (1632–1704) would probably have been shocked if he had lived to see the use that Americans made of his doctrines. In his *Two Treatises of Government* (1690) Locke attempted to justify the English revolution of 1688–1689 by which Parliament had won supremacy over the King. According to Locke's theory, men originally lived in a state of nature and enjoyed complete liberty, then agreed to a "compact" by which they set up a government to protect their "natural rights," especially their right to the ownership and enjoyment of private property. The government was limited by the terms of the compact and by "natural law." It was contrary to natural law for a government to take property without the consent of the owners, Locke wrote, and Americans noted in particular his sentence: "If any one shall claim a power to lay and levy taxes on the people by his own authority, and without such consent of the people, he thereby invades the fundamental law of property, and subverts the end of government." To Americans of the 1760s and 1770s it was clear that the British government was flouting the law of nature as well as the will of God. And, according to Locke, if a government should persist in exceeding its rightful powers, men would be released from their obligation to obey it. What was more, they would have the right to make a new compact and establish another government.

THE TEA EXCITEMENT

From time to time after 1770 Americans resisting British law broke the comparative stillness in America with such deeds as the seizure of a revenue ship on the lower Delaware, the burning of another (the *Gaspee*) in Narragansett Bay, and the tarring and feathering of a customs officer on the streets of Boston. Not till 1773, however, did Americans reassert their revolutionary principles with anything approaching the unity and vigor of former years.

Tea revived the dispute. The East India Company, with a large stock of unsalable tea on hand, was nearly bankrupt, and Lord North induced Parliament to go to the company's relief with the Tea Act of 1773. This law permitted the company to export its product to America without paying any of the usual taxes except the tea tax still remaining from the original Townshend duties. With these privileges the company could undersell American merchants who bought their tea supplies in England.

Lord North, like others in his office before him, was surprised by the reaction of the Americans. He had not expected the tea-importing merchants in the colonies to like the new law, for it threatened to drive them out of business and replace them with a giant monopoly. But the colonists—especially the women—were excessively fond of tea. Lord North thought they would be so glad to get it cheap that they would swallow the hated tea tax along with it. Instead, they renounced their beloved beverage and turned for the time being to such substitutes as coffee and chocolate.

Meanwhile, with strong popular support, leaders in various colonies made plans to prevent the East India Company from landing its cargoes in colonial ports. In Philadelphia and New York determined men kept the tea from leaving the company's ships, and in Charleston they stored it away in a public warehouse. In Boston, having failed to turn back the three ships in the harbor, the followers of Samuel Adams staged a spectacular drama. On the evening of December 16, 1773, three companies of fifty men each, masquerading as "Mohawks," passed between the protecting lines of a tremendous crowd of spectators, went aboard, broke open the tea chests, and heaved them into the water. As the electrifying news of the Boston "tea party" spread, other seaports followed the example and held tea parties of their own.

When the Bostonians refused to pay for the property they had destroyed, George III and Lord North decided upon a policy of coercion, to be applied not against all the colonies but only against Massachusetts—the chief

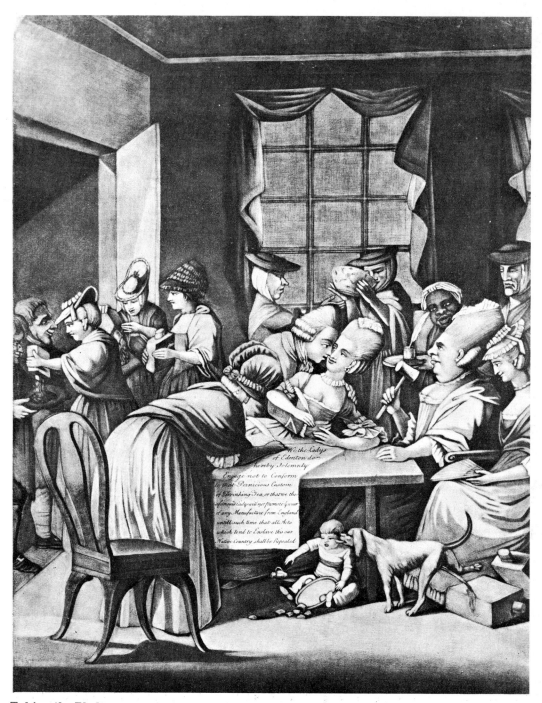

Taking the Pledge

*This British caricature, entitled "A Society of Patriotic Ladies, at Edenton in North Carolina,"
was published in London in March 1775. It ridicules the American buy-at-home movement. The
women are emptying their tea canisters and signing a pledge, which reads: "We the Ladies of
Edenton do hereby Solemnly Engage not to Conform to that Pernicious Custom of Drinking Tea,
or that we the aforesaid Ladies will not promote the Wear of any Manufacture from England until
such time that all Acts which tend to Enslave this our Native Country shall be Repealed."
(Courtesy of the Metropolitan Museum of Art, bequest of Charles Allen Munn, 1924)*

center of resistance. In four acts of 1774 Parliament proceeded to put this policy into effect. One of the laws closed the port of Boston, another drastically reduced the local and provincial powers of self-government in Massachusetts, still another permitted royal officers to be tried in other colonies or in England when accused of crimes, and the last provided for the quartering of troops in the colonists' barns and empty houses.

These Coercive Acts were followed by the Quebec Act, which was separate from them in origin and quite different in purpose. Its object was to provide a civil government for the French-speaking, Roman Catholic inhabitants of Canada and the Illinois country. The law extended the boundaries of Quebec to include the French communities between the Ohio and Mississippi rivers. It also granted political rights to Roman Catholics and recognized the legality of the Roman Catholic Church within the enlarged province. In many ways it was a liberal and much needed piece of legislation.

To many Protestants in the thirteen colonies, however, the Quebec Act was anathema. They were already alarmed by rumors that the Church of England schemed to appoint a bishop for America with the intention of enforcing Anglican authority upon all the various sects. To them the line between the Church of England and the Church of Rome always had seemed dangerously thin. When Catholics ceased to be actively persecuted in the mother country, alarmists in the colonies began to fear that Catholicism and Anglicanism were about to merge, and at the passage of the Quebec Act they became convinced that a plot was afoot in London for subjecting Americans to the tyranny of the Pope. Moreover, those interested in Western lands believed that the act, by extending the boundaries of Quebec, would reinforce the land policy of the Proclamation Line of 1763 and hinder westward progress.

Had it not been for the Quebec Act, Lord North might have come close to succeeding in his effort to divide and rule the colonies by isolating Massachusetts. As it was, the colonists generally lumped the Quebec law with the Massachusetts measures as the fifth in a set of "Intolerable Acts." From New Hampshire to South Carolina the people prepared to take a united stand.

Cooperation for War

Revolutions do not just happen: they must be led and organized. From 1765 on, colonial leaders provided a variety of organizations for converting popular discontent into action, organizations that in time formed the basis for an independent government.

THE CONTINENTAL CONGRESS

Some of these organizations were local, some colony-wide, and some intercolonial. In many cases the provincial assemblies themselves served as centers of resistance, and sometimes they were replaced or supplemented by extralegal meetings, as when (in 1768) Sam Adams called a convention of delegates from the Massachusetts towns to sit in place of the General Court, which the royal governor had dissolved. Adams and others in various places organized mobs as Sons of Liberty and also set up committees of prominent citizens for a number of specific purposes. The most famous and most effective were the committees of correspondence. Massachusetts took the lead (1772) with such committees on the local level, a network of them connecting Boston with the rural towns, but Virginia was the first to establish committees of correspondence on an intercolonial basis. These made possible cooperation among the colonies in a more continuous way than had the Stamp Act Congress, the first effort at intercolonial union for resistance against imperial authority. Virginia took the greatest step of all toward united action in 1774 when, the governor having dissolved the assembly, a rump session met in the Raleigh Tavern at Williamsburg, declared that the Intolerable Acts menaced the liberties of every colony, and issued a call for a Continental Congress.

Variously elected by the assemblies or by extralegal meetings, delegates from all the thirteen colonies except Georgia were present when, in September 1774, the Continental

Congress convened in Philadelphia. The delegates divided into moderates and extremists, and the more extreme members seized the upper hand. At the outset they showed their strength by designating Carpenters' Hall as the meeting place. This was the headquarters of the Philadelphia Carpenters' Company, and some members complained that its selection was an unseemly attempt to curry favor with the city's artisans. In the ensuing sessions of the Congress, however, the extremists were unable to carry through a program quite so thorough as some of them would have liked.

A majority of the delegates in Carpenters' Hall agreed upon five major decisions. First, in a very close vote, they defeated the plan of Joseph Galloway for a colonial union under British authority, a plan (much like the Albany Plan) which included a legislative council made up of representatives from the colonial assemblies and a president-general to be appointed by the King. Second, they drew up a somewhat self-contradictory statement of grievances, conceding to Parliament the right to regulate colonial trade but demanding the elimination of all oppressive legislation passed since 1763, and they addressed a petition to George III as their "Most Gracious Sovereign." Third, they approved a series of resolutions from a Suffolk County (Massachusetts) convention recommending, among other things, that military preparations be made for defense against possible attack by the British troops in Boston. Fourth, they agreed to nonimportation, nonexportation, and nonconsumption as means of stopping all trade with Great Britain, and they formed a "Continental Association" to see that these agreements were carried out. Fifth, the delegates adjourned to meet again the next spring, thus indicating that they conceived of the Continental Congress as a continuing organization.

Through their representatives in Philadelphia the colonies had, in effect, reaffirmed their autonomous status within the Empire and declared economic war to maintain that position. The more optimistic of the Americans supposed that economic warfare alone would win a quick and bloodless victory, but the more pessimistic had their doubts. "I expect no redress, but, on the contrary, increased resentment and double vengeance," John Adams said to Patrick Henry; "we must fight." And Henry replied, "By God, I am of your opinion."

During the winter of 1774–1775 the enforcement of the nonimportation, nonexportation, and nonconsumption agreements proved increasingly difficult as people in the middle colonies and in the South, viewing the Continental Association as hardly less tyrannical than the British government, began to complain against the sacrifices they were compelled to make— all for the sake of those troublemakers in Massachusetts!

During the winter the Parliament in London debated proposals for conciliating the colonists. Lord Chatham (William Pitt) urged the withdrawal of troops from America, Edmund Burke urged the repeal of the Coercive Acts, but in vain; and not even Chatham and Burke thought of renouncing parliamentary authority over the colonies. Lord North, conceding less than Burke or Chatham, introduced a set of proposals of his own, and Parliament approved them early in 1775. The essence of these so-called Conciliatory Propositions was that the colonies, instead of being taxed directly by Parliament, should tax themselves at Parliament's demand. With this offer Lord North intended to redivide Americans by appealing to the disgruntled moderates. But his offer was too grudging, and it came too late. It did not reach America till after the first shots of war had been fired.

LEXINGTON AND CONCORD

For months the farmers and townspeople of Massachusetts had been gathering arms and ammunition and training as "minutemen," ready to fight on a minute's notice. The Continental Congress had approved preparations for a defensive war, and these citizen-soldiers only waited for an aggressive move by the British regulars in Boston.

In Boston, General Thomas Gage, commanding the British garrison, knew of the warlike bustle throughout the countryside but thought his army too small to do anything until reinforcements should arrive, though some of his less cautious officers assured him that Americans were cowards, and Major John Pitcairn insisted that a single "small action" with the burning of a few towns would "set everything to rights." When General Gage received orders to arrest the rebel leaders Sam Adams

The Battle of Lexington

A contemporary engraving by Amos Doolittle. It pictures the American version of the affair of April 19, 1775, at Lexington. In the center is shown "the party who fired first," at the command of Major Pitcairn, on horseback. In the foreground are some of the fallen and the fleeing members of the "Provincial Company of Lexington" (minutemen). The more prominent buildings on the edge of the square, or green, are the Public Inn at the left of the large tree and the Meeting House at the right of it. Behind the Meeting House are companies of British regulars marching along the road to Concord. (Courtesy of the New York Public Library, Stokes Collection)

and John Hancock, known to be in the vicinity of Lexington, he still hesitated, but when he heard that the minutemen had stored a large supply of gunpowder in Concord (eighteen miles from Boston) he at last decided to act. On the night of April 18, 1775, he sent a detachment of about 1,000 men out from Boston on the road to Lexington and Concord. He intended to surprise the colonials with a bloodless coup.

But during the night the hard-riding horsemen William Dawes and Paul Revere warned the villages and farms, and when the redcoats arrived in Lexington the next day, several dozen minutemen awaited them on the common. Shots were fired and some of the minutemen fell, eight of them killed and ten more wounded. Advancing to Concord, the British burned what was left of the powder supply after the Americans hastily had removed most of it to safety. On the road from Concord back to Boston the 1,000 troops, along with 1,500 more who met them at Lexington, were harassed by the continual gunfire of farmers hiding behind trees, rocks, and stone fences. Before the day was over, the British had lost almost three times as many men as the Americans.

The first shots had been fired, but who had fired the first shot? According to the Lexington minutemen, Major Pitcairn upon his arrival had shouted, "Disperse, ye rebels!" and when this command was disregarded he had given the order to fire. According to the British officers and soldiers, one of American guns had flashed first. The truth is still unknown, but the fact remains that the rebels succeeded in circulating their account well ahead of the British version, and they adorned it with horrible tales of redcoat atrocities. The effect was to rally to the rebel cause thousands of colonists, North and South, who previously had been lukewarm in its support. A war was on, and most Americans believed the enemy had started it.

Selected Readings

The French and the Frontier
H. I. Priestley, *France Overseas Through the Old Regime* (1939); J. A. Caruso, *The Mississippi Valley Frontier: The Age of French Exploration and Settlement* (1966); Francis Parkman, *A Half Century of Conflict* (2 vols., 1892) and *The Parkman Reader,* ed. by S. E. Morison (1955); L. H. Gipson, *The British Empire Before the American Revolution* (13 vols., 1936–1967), vols. 6 and 7: *The Great War for the Empire*; H. H. Peckham, *The Colonial Wars, 1689–1762* (1964) and *Pontiac and the Indian Uprising* (1947); C. H. Ambler, *George Washington and the West* (1936); D. E. Leach, *The Northern Colonial Frontier, 1607–1763* (1966) and *Flintlock and Tomahawk* (1958); J. M. Sosin, *Whitehall and the Wilderness: The Middle West in British Colonial Policy, 1760–1775* (1961); T. P. Abernethy, *Western Lands and the American Revolution* (1937); C. W. Alvord, *The Mississippi Valley in British Politics* (2 vols., 1916).

Revolutionary Backgrounds in General
J. C. Miller, *Origins of the American Revolution* (1957); L. H. Gipson, *The Coming of the Revolution, 1763–1775* (1954); C. M. Andrews, *The Colonial Background of the American Revolution* (1924).

Commercial Policy and Colonial Government
Sir Lewis B. Namier, *England in the Age of the American Revolution* (1930); Herbert Butterfield, *George III and the Historians* (1959); L. W. Labaree, *Royal Government in America: A Study of the British Colonial System Before 1783* (1930); F. B. Wickwire, *British Subministers and Colonial America, 1763–1783* (1966); A. G. Olson, *Anglo-American Politics, 1660–1775: The Relationship Between Parties in England and Colonial America* (1973); G. L. Beer, *British Colonial Policy, 1754–1765* (1907); J. P. Greene, *The Quest for Power: The Lower Houses of Assembly in the Southern Royal Colonies, 1689–1776* (1963); O. M. Dickerson, *American Colonial Government, 1696–1765* (1912) and *The Navigation Acts and the American Revolution* (1951); A. M. Schlesinger, *The Colonial Merchants and the American Revolution, 1763–1776* (1917); J. M. Sosin, *Agents and Merchants: British Colonial Policy and the Origins of the American Revolution, 1763–1776* (1965); R. L. Schuyler, *Parliament and the British Empire* (1929), a defense of British policy; C. H. McIlwain, *The American Revolution: A Constitutional Interpretation* (1923), a brief for the discontented colonists.

Developments in Individual States
Carl Becker, *The History of Political Parties in the Province of New York, 1760–1776* (1909); C. A. Barker, *The Background of the Revolution in Maryland* (1940); Oscar Zeichner, *Connecticut's Years of Controversy, 1750–1776* (1949); Theodore Thayer, *Pennsylvania Politics and the Growth of Democracy, 1740–1776* (1953); R. E. Brown, *Middle-Class Democracy and the Revolution in Massachusetts, 1691–1780* (1955) and, with B. K. Brown, *Virginia, 1705–1786: Democracy or Aristocray?* (1964); D. S. Lovejoy, *Rhode Island and the American Revolution, 1760–1776* (1958).

The Revolutionary Crisis
E. S. and H. M. Morgan, *The Stamp Act Crisis* (1953); A. M. Schlesinger, *Prelude to Independence: The Newspaper War on Britain, 1764–1776* (1958); J. C. Miller, *Sam Adams, Pioneer in Propaganda* (1936); Jacob Axelrod, *Patrick Henry, The Voice of Freedom* (1947); D. S. Freeman, *George Washington* (7 vols., 1949–1957), vols. 1 and 2; C. C. Currey, *Road to Revolution: Benjamin Franklin in England, 1765–1775* (1968); B. W. Labaree, *The Boston Tea Party* (1964); John Shy, *Toward Lexington: The Role of the British Army in the Coming of the American Revolution* (1965); P. Maier, *From Resistance to Revolution: Colonial Radicals and the Development of American Opposition to Britain, 1765–1776* (1972); J. K. Martin, *Men in Rebellion: Higher Governmental Leaders and the Coming of the American Revolution* (1973).

*Titles available in paperback.

The American Revolution

Five

"The Revolution was effected before the war commenced," the Patriot leader John Adams said afterward. "The Revolution was in the minds and hearts of the people." What Adams meant was that long before 1775 Americans had come to take for granted a high degree of political and economic liberty, and they were bound to resist, by force if necessary, any serious infringement of it. He did not mean they had already decided upon complete independence, for that decision was not made until after the fighting had begun. Nor did he mean that all the people ever made up their minds in favor of the revolutionary cause, for according to his own estimate a third of the people opposed it.

The actual fighting seems insignificant in comparison with more recent wars. Battle deaths on the American side totaled less than 5,000. Cannons tossed out iron balls that did no damage unless they made a direct hit, and an alert soldier could see them coming and get out of the way. The Pennsylvania rifle, which some of the Patriots carried, was fairly accurate at a range of one hundred yards, but the more common smoothbore musket was not, and its flintlock misfired when wet. A military campaign was almost out of the question except in good weather.

Yet the war as the Patriots fought it, old-fashioned though it was in some respects, had one feature that made it new and revolutionary in itself. In previous wars comparatively small numbers of professional soldiers had served for pay. In this one the people on the American side took up arms in their own cause. Though their armies seldom numbered more than a few thousand at any one time, a total of almost 400,000 men enlisted (most of them for short terms) during the eight years that the war lasted.

George Washington
From 1772 to 1795 the Maryland-born artist and taxidermist Charles Willson Peale painted from life more than a dozen portraits of George Washington, under whom he served as a soldier during the Revolutionary War. This portrait, which conveys something of the moral as well as the physical grandeur of Washington, shows him in the uniform of commander in chief at his Princeton headquarters in 1776. (The Pennsylvania Academy of the Fine Arts)

Its consequences also were revolutionary. The first of the modern wars against colonialism, it brought into being a new nation which, though weak and insecure at the start, was eventually to grow into one of the greatest powers of all time. The ideals the war aroused provided inspiration for future generations not only in the United States but also in other countries. One of the leading revolutionaries of 1776, Thomas Paine, averred that the war "contributed more to enlighten the world, and diffuse a spirit of freedom and liberality among mankind, than any human event . . . that ever preceded it."

The States United

In the American Revolution a war for autonomy on the part of the united colonies soon turned into a war for independence on the part of the United States. This inchoate nation, with a population less than a third as large as the nine million of Great Britain, and with economic and military resources proportionately still smaller, faced a tremendous task of mobilizing for the war. The task was further complicated by divisions among the people, who persisted in disagreeing about war aims.

ORIGINAL WAR AIMS

Three weeks after the battles of Lexington and Concord, when the Second Continental Congress met in the State House in Philadelphia, the delegates (again from every colony except Georgia, which was not represented until the following autumn) agreed in their determination to support the war but disagreed about its objects. At one extreme the Adams cousins, John and Samuel, leaned toward independence (though they did not yet avow it), and at the other extreme John Dickinson of Pennsylvania hoped for an early reconciliation with Great Britain. Most of the delegates, holding views that ranged between those of Dickinson and the Adamses, disregarded Lord North's Conciliatory Propositions as insincere but voted reluctantly for one last appeal to the King in the Olive Branch Petition. Then, on July 6, 1775, they adopted a Declaration of the Causes and Necessity of Taking up Arms, announcing that the British government had left the American people with only two alternatives, "unconditional submission to the tyranny of irritated ministers or resistance by force," and that the people had decided to resist.

So, for the first year of the war, the Americans were fighting for a redress of grievances within the British Empire, not for independence. During that year, however, many of them began to change their minds, for various reasons. For one thing, they were making sacrifices so great — as in the Battle of Bunker Hill, the bloodiest engagement of the entire war and one of the most sanguinary anywhere in the eighteenth century — that their original war aims seemed incommensurate with the cost. For another thing, they lost much of their lingering affection for the mother country when she prepared to use Indians, Negro slaves, and foreign mercenaries (the hated "Hessians") against them. And, most important, they felt that they were being forced into independence when the British government replied to the Olive Branch Petition with the Prohibitory Act, which closed the colonies to all overseas trade and made no concession except an offer of pardon to repentant rebels. The Americans desperately needed military supplies to continue the war, and now they could get them from abroad in adequate amounts only if they broke completely with Great Britain and proceeded to behave in all respects as if they comprised a sovereign nation.

These feelings in America were not caused, but were clarified and crystallized, by the publication, in January 1776, of the pamphlet *Common Sense*. Its author, unmentioned on the title page, was Thomas Paine, who with letters of introduction from Benjamin Franklin

COMMON SENSE;

ADDRESSED TO THE

INHABITANTS

O F

A M E R I C A,

On the following interesting

S U B J E C T S.

I. Of the Origin and Design of Government in general, with concise Remarks on the English Constitution.

II. Of Monarchy and Hereditary Succession.

III. Thoughts on the present State of American Affairs.

IV. Of the present Ability of America, with some miscellaneous Reflections.

Man knows no Master save creating HEAVEN,
Or those whom choice and common good ordain.
THOMSON.

P H I L A D E L P H I A;
Printed, and Sold, by R. BELL, in Third-Street.

M DCC LXX VI.

had emigrated from England to America less than two years before. Though long a failure in various trades, Paine now proved a brilliant success as a revolutionary propagandist. In his pamphlet he argued with flashing phrases that it was plain common sense for Americans to separate from an England rotten with the corrupt monarchy of George III, brutal as an unnatural parent toward her colonies, responsible for dragging them in to fight her wars in the past, and no more fit as an island kingdom to rule the American continent than a satellite was fit to rule the sun. "O! ye that love mankind! ye that dare oppose not only the tyranny but the tyrant, stand forth!" Month after month the pamphlet was reprinted until many thousands of copies were in circulation, passing from hand to hand and being read and reread.

DECLARATION OF INDEPENDENCE

Despite the persuasion of *Common Sense*, the American people were far from unanimous, and they entered upon a bitter debate over the merits of dependence and independence. While the debate raged, the Continental Congress advanced step by step toward a final break. Congress opened the ports of America to all the world except Great Britain, entered into communication with foreign powers, and recommended to the various colonies that they establish governments without the authority of the Empire, as in fact they already were doing. Congress also appointed a committee to draft a formal declaration and, on July 2, 1776, before approving the declaration, adopted a resolution "That these United Colonies are, and, of right, ought to be, free and independent states; that they are absolved from all allegiance to the British crown, and that all political connexion between them and the state of Great Britain is, and ought to be, totally dissolved." Two days later Congress approved the Declaration of Independence, which gave reasons for the action already taken.

The thirty-three-year-old Virginian Thomas Jefferson wrote the Declaration of Independence, his fellow committeemen Benjamin Franklin and John Adams revised the wording a little, and Congress made more drastic changes, striking out passages that condemned the British people and the slave trade. As Adams afterward observed, Jefferson said nothing new in composing the document. Its very virtue, in fact, lay in his noble phrasing of beliefs already widespread in America. He planned the document in two main parts. In the first part he restated the familiar contract theory of John Locke, who had held that governments were formed to protect the rights of life, liberty, and property, but Jefferson gave the theory a more humane twist by referring instead to the rights of "life, liberty and the pursuit of happiness." In the second part he listed the alleged crimes of the King who, with the backing of Parliament, had violated his contract with the colonists and thus had forfeited all claim to their loyalty.

Once adopted, the Declaration of Independence exerted an incalculable influence upon later history. With its democratic principle that "all men are created equal," it stimulated humanitarian movements of various kinds in the United States, and abroad it helped to inspire the French Revolution with its Declaration of the Rights of Man. More immediately, it led to increased foreign aid for the struggling rebels and prepared the way for France's all-out intervention on their side. It steeled American Patriots to carry on without regard to offers of a peace short of the stated goal. And at the same time it divided Americans more cruelly and more extensively than they ever had been divided before.

At the news of the Declaration of Independence, crowds gathered to cheer, fire guns and cannons, and ring church bells in Philadelphia, Boston, and other places, but there were many people in America who did not rejoice. Some had disapproved of the war from the beginning, and others had been willing to support it only so long as its aims did not conflict with their basic loyalty to the King. These people, numerous but in the minority, refused to cross the new line that had been drawn. Either openly or secretly they remained Loyalists, as they chose to call themselves, or Tories, as they were known to the Whig or Patriot majority. Among the Loyalists were rich families and poor ones, highly educated men (like the scientist Benjamin Thompson) and illiterates, townspeople, and backwoodsmen. Among the Loyalist leaders were royal officials and Anglican clergymen who had sided with the British government throughout the prewar decade of controversy, plus a few of the wealthy merchants and large planters who earlier had belonged to the Patriot party but who seceded from it after the Declaration of Independence.

The remaining Patriots continued to be divided among themselves. On the one hand were men like John Adams and George Washington who wished to see independence achieved with comparatively little social change in America, but whose ranks were thinned by the loss of their former allies, now Loyalists. On the other hand were men like Thomas Jefferson who desired to accomplish democratic and humanitarian reforms along with independence. Thus (as in other wars, including World War II) patriotic Americans held different as well as common aims, some intending only to smite the foreign enemy, others aspiring also to lead a popular crusade at home.

STATE GOVERNMENTS

While waging war, the Patriots also busied themselves with providing a government for the new nation. With the outbreak of war they set up provisional governments based upon existing assemblies or emergency conventions as the royal officials fled from their positions in one colony after another. When the colonies became states, the Patriots formed permanent governments with written constitutions. The constitution-making procedure varied from state to state. In Rhode Island and Connecticut the legislatures merely revised the old colonial charters, and in most of the other states the legislatures, though not elected for that purpose,

Slavery in Massachusetts [1783]

In the case of Quork Walker, who was a slave suing his master, the Chief Justice of Massachusetts gave the following charge to the jury:

As to the doctrine of slavery and the right of Christians to hold Africans in perpetual servitude, and sell and treat them as we do our horses and cattle, that (it is true) has been heretofore countenanced by the Province Laws formerly, but nowhere is it expressly enacted or established. It has been a usage — a usage which took its origin from the practice of some of the European nations, and the regulations of British government respecting the then Colonies, for the benefit of trade and wealth. But whatever sentiments have formerly prevailed in this particular or slid in upon us by the example of others, a different idea has taken place with the people of America, more favorable to the natural rights of mankind, and to that natural, innate desire of Liberty, with which Heaven (without regard to color, complexion, or shape of noses) has inspired all the human race. And upon this ground our Constitution of Government, by which the people of this Commonwealth have solemnly bound themselves, sets out with declaring that all men are born free and equal — and that every subject is entitled to liberty, and to have it guarded by the laws, as well as life and property — and in short is totally repugnant to the idea of being born slaves. This being the case, I think the idea of slavery is inconsistent with our own conduct and Constitution; and there can be no such thing as perpetual servitude of a rational creature, unless his liberty is forfeited by some criminal conduct or given up by personal consent or contract.

took it upon themselves to draft new constitutions. Thomas Jefferson, for one, insisted that the fundamental law should come from the people of each state, who should elect constitutional conventions and then vote on ratification. Actually, conventions were held in only three states, referendums in only five, and both a convention and a referendum in only one — Massachusetts.

The new constitutions, all pretty much alike in general outline though different in detail, were both conservative and democratic. They were conservative in retaining essentially the same structure as the old colonial governments. Except in Georgia and Pennsylvania, both of which experimented with a unicameral legislature, each constitution provided for a two-house legislature, with an elected senate taking the place of the former governor's council. All the constitutions except Pennsylvania's continued the office of governor, though most of them denied the holder of this position the bulk of the executive powers he had enjoyed in colonial days. All of the new documents confirmed and extended the ideas of popular rule that long had been put into practice; every one of them included a bill of rights, and some had

preambles stating that sovereignty (the ultimate power of government) resided in the people. To vote in any state a man had to own only a modest amount of property, in some states just enough so that he could qualify as a taxpayer. To hold office he had to meet a somewhat higher property requirement, essentially as in pre-Revolutionary times. Only in New Jersey were women allowed to vote, and eventually they were deprived of the suffrage even there. But, considering the widespread ownership of property, something approaching universal manhood suffrage existed from the beginning in all the states.

Once in operation, the new states proceeded to make advances in social as well as political democracy. In one way or another they multiplied opportunities for land ownership and thus enlarged the voting population. For instance, they eliminated the legal rights of primogeniture and entail, which before the war had helped to maintain a landed aristocracy by transferring an entire estate to the oldest son (when a man died without a will) and by keeping the estate intact from generation to generation (when a man by entailment willed that the property never be sold). The new states

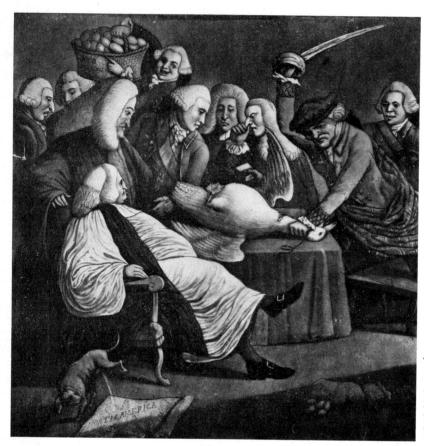

Killing the Goose
This cartoon, which appeared in a colonial newspaper early in 1776, shows the British government's ministers killing the American goose that laid the Empire's golden eggs. The point of the cartoon is hardly an exaggeration, for the government's policies were, indeed, having the effect of destroying England's profitable trade with the colonies. (John Carter Brown Library, Brown University)

also made considerable progress toward religious freedom, though some retained religious tests for officeholding. New York and the Southern states, in which the Church of England had been tax-supported, soon saw to its complete disestablishment, and the New England states stripped the Congregational Church of some of its privileges. Virginia, in its Declaration of Rights, boldly announced the principle of complete toleration and, in 1786, enacted the principle in the Statute of Religious Liberty, which Jefferson long had championed.

The new states took steps toward personal as well as religious freedom. All of them except South Carolina and Georgia prohibited the importation of slaves, and even South Carolina laid temporary wartime bans on the slave trade. After the first antislavery society in America (founded in 1775) began its agitation, and prominent Southerners including Jefferson and Washington declared their opposition to slavery, Virginia and other Southern states changed their laws so as to encourage manumission, Pennsylvania passed a gradual-emancipation act (1780), and Massachusetts through a decision of its highest court (1783) held that the state's bill of rights outlawed the ownership of slaves. Besides all this, five of the new states put provisions into their constitutions for the establishment of public schools, and all soon began to revise their criminal codes so as to make the punishment more nearly fit the crime.

THE CONFEDERATION

While the separate states were fashioning constitutions and recasting their legal systems, the Second Continental Congress tried to create a

The Articles of Confederation [1781]

1. [Article II] "Each state retains its sovereignty, freedom and independence, and every Power, Jurisdiction and right, which is not by this confederation expressly delegated to the United States, in Congress assembled."

2. [Article IV] The free inhabitants of each state "shall be entitled to all privileges and immunities of free citizens in the several states," and "full faith and credit" shall be given by each state to the judicial and other official proceedings of other states.

3. [Article V] Each state shall be represented in Congress by no less than two and no more than seven members, shall pay its own delegates, and shall have one vote (regardless of the number of members).

4. [Article VI] No state, without the consent of Congress, shall enter into diplomatic relations or make treaties with other states or with foreign nations, or engage in war except in case of actual invasion.

5. [Article VIII] A "common treasury" shall be supplied by the states in proportion to the value of their land and improvements; the states shall levy taxes to raise their quotas of revenue.

6. [Article IX] Congress shall have power to decide on peace and war, conduct foreign affairs, settle disputes between states, regulate the Indian trade, maintain post offices, make appropriations, borrow money, emit bills of credit, build a navy, requisition soldiers from the states, etc.—but nine states must agree before Congress can take any important action.

7. [Article X] A "Committee of the States," consisting of one delegate from each state, shall act in the place of Congress when Congress is not in session.

8. [Article XIII] No change shall be made in these Articles unless agreed to by Congress and "afterwards confirmed by the legislatures of every state."

---

written form of government for the states as a whole. No sooner had the Congress appointed a committee to draft a declaration of independence than it appointed another to draft a plan of union, and after much debate and many revisions the Congress, in November 1777, adopted the committee's plan, the Articles of Confederation.

The Articles of Confederation provided for a central government very similar to the one already in actual operation, though it increased the powers of Congress somewhat. Congress was to have the powers of conducting war, carrying on foreign relations, and appropriating, borrowing, and issuing money, but not the powers of regulating trade, levying taxes, or drafting troops. For troops and taxes it would have to make requisitions upon the states. There was to be no separate, single, strong executive (the "President of the United States"

was to be merely the presiding officer at the sessions of Congress), but Congress itself was to see to the execution of the laws through an executive committee of thirteen, made up of one member from each state, through ad hoc and standing committees for specific functions, and through such administrative departments as it might choose to create. There were to be no Confederation courts, except for courts of admiralty, but disputes among the states were to be settled by a complicated system of arbitration. These states were to retain their individual sovereignty, each of the legislatures electing and paying the salaries of two to seven delegates to Congress, and each delegation, no matter how numerous, having only one vote. At least nine of the states (through their delegations) would have to approve any important measure, such as a treaty, before Congress could pass it, and all thirteen state legislatures would have to approve before the Articles could be ratified or amended.

Ratification was delayed by differences of opinion about the proposed plan. Some Americans were willing enough to accept a relatively weak central government, but others preferred to see it strengthened. The people of all the small states insisted upon equal state representation, but those of the large states thought they should be represented in proportion to their population. Above all, the states claiming Western lands wished to keep them, but the rest of the states demanded that the whole territory be turned over to the Confederation government. The "landed" states, among which Virginia had the largest and best claim, founded their claims upon colonial charters, with the exception of New York, which based its rights upon a protectorate over the Iroquois Indians. The "landless" states, particularly Maryland, maintained that as the fruit of common sacrifices in war the Western land had become the rightful property of all the states. In this dispute selfish interests as well as high principles were involved, for rival groups of land speculators schemed to secure the cancellation or confirmation of private grants already made. At last New York gave up its rather hazy claim, and Virginia made a qualified offer to cede its lands to Congress. Then Maryland, the only state still holding out against ratification, approved the Articles of Confederation, and they went into effect in 1781.

The Confederation government came into being in time to conclude the war and make the peace. Meanwhile, during the years of fighting from 1775 to 1781, the Second Continental Congress served as the agency for directing and coordinating the war effort of the people of the thirteen states.

MOBILIZING FOR WAR

Congress and the states faced overwhelming tasks in raising and organizing armies, providing the necessary supplies and equipment, and paying the costs of war.

Supplies of most kinds were scarce at the outset, and shortages persisted to the end. Though America, being a land of hunters, contained numerous gunsmiths, they were not able to meet the wartime demand for guns and ammunition, nor were they able to produce heavy arms. Some of the states offered bounties for the encouragement of manufactures, especially for the production of guns and powder, and Congress in 1777 established a government arsenal at Springfield, Massachusetts. Even so, the Americans themselves managed to manufacture only a small fraction of the equipment they used. They supplemented their own manufactures with matériel that fell into their hands upon the seizure of forts like Crown Point and Ticonderoga (in 1775), the surrender of British armies, and the capture of supply ships by American privateers. But they got most of their war materials through importations from Europe, particularly from France.

In trying to meet the expenses of war, Congress had no power to tax the people, and the states had little inclination to do so. Indeed, cash was scarce in the country, as it always had been. When Congress requisitioned the states for money, none of them contributed more than a tiny part of its share. At first Congress hesitated to requisition goods directly from the people, but finally allowed army purchasing agents to take supplies from farmers and pay with certificates of indebtedness. Congress could not raise much money by floating long-term loans at home, since few Americans could afford war bonds and those few usually preferred to invest their funds in more profitable ventures, such as privateering. So Congress had no choice but to issue paper money, and Continental currency came from the printing presses in large and repeated batches. The states added sizable currency issues of their own.

With goods and coin so scarce and paper money so plentiful, prices rose to fantastic heights and the value of paper money fell proportionately. There quickly appeared all the usual evils of wartime profiteering, and more too. One reason why Washington's men suffered from shortages of food and clothing at Valley Forge during the terrible winter of 1777–1778 was that American farmers and merchants preferred to do business with the British forces occupying nearby Philadelphia, since the British could pay in gold or silver coin. To check the inflationary trend, Congress advised the states to pass laws for price control, but soon saw the futility of such measures and recommended that they be dropped. Eventually, in 1780, Congress decided that the states should accept Continental currency from taxpayers at the rate of forty paper dollars to one silver dollar, then send it to Congress to be destroyed. If the currency was not turned in for taxes at a fortieth of its face value, it became utterly worthless, hence the expression "Not worth a Continental." By this time Congress was able to meet the most pressing of its financial needs by borrowing from abroad.

The states added to their financial resources by seizing lands belonging to the Crown and to colonial proprietors. In 1777 Congress recommended that the states also confiscate and sell the property of Loyalists active in the British cause, then lend the proceeds to the central government. The states were eager enough to expropriate the Loyalists, though not to make the requested loan. Already Patriots were punishing Tories in various ways, taking from them the rights of citizenship, barring them from certain occupations, and imposing special taxes and heavy fines upon them. The seizure and sale of Loyalist property, resulting incidentally in a widened distribution of land ownership among the buyers, netted the states a total of several million pounds, in value if not in actual cash. Around 100,000 of the Loyalists themselves, either voluntarily or because of banishment, left the country during the course of the war, the most numerous group going to Quebec and laying the foundations of English-speaking Canada.

The willingness of the remaining Tories to aid the British depended somewhat on the proximity of British troops and the prospects for the British cause. As for the Patriots, only a small proportion of them were willing to volunteer for the American armies once the first surge of patriotism at the start of the war had passed. The states had to resort to persuasion and force, to bounties and the draft, the bounties being commonly in the form of land scrip, since land was an asset with which the states were well supplied. Thus recruited, militiamen remained under the control of their respective states. Many of the recruits were expert marksmen and on the average they were physically bigger and stronger than the British regulars. Yet man for man they were no match for the redcoats in battle, since they lacked the regulars' fine training, discipline, and esprit de corps.

Foreseeing some of the disadvantages of separately organized militias, Congress called upon the states (while they were still colonies) to raise troops for a regular force, the Continental army, and agreed that it should have a single commander in chief. George Washington, forty-three years old, sober and responsible by nature, possessed more command experience than any other American-born officer available. And he had political as well as military qualifications. An early advocate of independence, he was admired and trusted by nearly all the Patriots. A Virginian, he had the support not only of Southerners but also of Northerners who feared that the appointment of a New Englander might jeopardize sectional harmony. As the unanimous choice of the delegates, he took command in June 1775.

Congress chose well. Throughout the war Washington kept faithfully at his task, despite difficulties and discouragements that would have daunted a lesser man. With the aid of foreign military experts such as the Marquis de Lafayette and the Baron von Steuben he succeeded in building and holding together the Continental army, though at no time did it number as many as 10,000 men (not counting the militia of the separate states). The morale of the soldiers, who were getting short rations and low pay, became so bad that mutinies broke out (in 1781) among the Pennsylvania and New Jersey troops. Meanwhile, during the dark winter of Valley Forge, some congressmen and army officers, conspiring together in the so-called Conway Cabal, hinted at replacing Washington as commander in chief. He, on the other hand, complained often and bitterly against his employers, the delegates in Congress, who seemed to do too little in supplying him with manpower and equipment, and too much in interfering with his conduct of military operations. The faults were not all on the side of Congress, which had its difficulties too. Washington had his shortcomings as a military commander and he lost more battles than he won. Yet he was a great war leader. For all his faults and failures, he led the army and the nation to ultimate victory with his supreme steadiness and courage, his sacrificial devotion to the cause of independence.

The War for Independence

In their war for independence the Americans had the advantage of fighting on their home terrain, far from the center of British might. They also had the benefit of tremendous foreign aid, especially after the American war merged with a world contest in which Great Britain faced the strongest powers of Europe as actual or potential foes. But the success of the Americans was also due to their own patriotic effort. Though losing battle after battle, they avoided catastrophes and gained at least a few decisive victories through the exertions of thousands of armed men under the majestic generalship of George Washington. And, having held their own in war, they won the peace because their diplomats shrewdly made the most of the opportunities that the world situation offered.

THE FIGHTING, TO 1777

For about the first year of the fighting (1775–1776) the colonial armed forces took the offensive. After the British retreat from Concord and Lexington, the Americans besieged the army of General Gage in Boston, and though suffering severe casualties in the Battle of Bunker Hill (actually fought on Breed's Hill, June 17, 1775), they inflicted even greater losses upon the enemy and thereafter they continued to tighten the siege. Far to the south, at Moore's Creek Bridge in North Carolina, a band of Patriots crushed an uprising of Tories (February 27, 1776) and thereby discouraged British plans for invading the Southern states with Loyalist aid. Far to the north the Americans themselves undertook an invasion of Canada. The fearless Benedict Arnold threatened Quebec after a winter march of incredible hardship. He was joined by Richard Montgomery, who took command of the combined forces. When they launched an attack, Montgomery was killed and Arnold wounded; though the latter kept up a siege for a time, the Quebec campaign ended in frustration. In the spring a civilian commission headed by the seventy-year-old Franklin returned from the north without success in its efforts to secure the allegiance of Canada as

The War in the North   1775

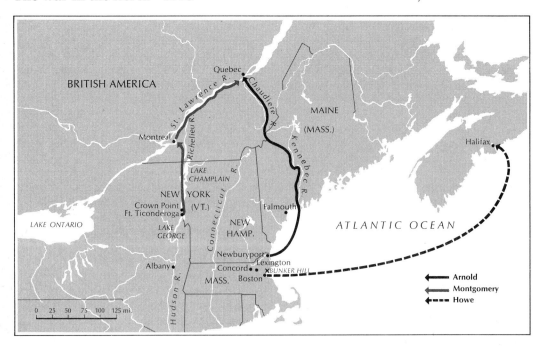

the fourteenth state. Already, however, the British had given up their attempt to hold Boston and had departed with hundreds of Loyalist refugees (March 17, 1776) for Halifax. Within a year from the firing of the first shots, the enemy had been driven from American soil.

The enemy soon returned, to put the Americans on the strategic defensive for the remainder of the war. During the summer of 1776, in the weeks immediately following the Declaration of Independence, the waters around the city of New York became filled with the most formidable military force Great Britain ever had sent abroad. Here were hundreds of men-of-war and troopships and a host of 32,000 disciplined soldiers under the command of the tall and affable Sir William Howe. Having no grudge against the Americans, Howe would rather awe them into submission than shoot them, and he believed that most of them, if given a chance, would show that they were at heart loyal to the King. In a parley with commissioners from Congress he offered the alternatives of submission with royal pardon or battle against overwhelming odds.

To oppose Howe's awesome array, Washington could muster only about 19,000 poorly armed and trained soldiers, including both Continentals and state troops, and he had no navy at all. Yet without hesitation the Americans chose continued war, which meant inevitably a succession of defeats. The British pushed the defenders off Long Island, compelled them to abandon Manhattan Island, and drove them in slow retreat over the plains of New Jersey, across the Delaware River, and into Pennsylvania.

Warfare being for eighteenth-century Europeans a seasonal activity, the British settled down for the winter with occupation forces at various points in New Jersey and with an outpost of Hessians at Trenton on the Delaware. But Washington did not content himself with sitting still. On Christmas night 1776, he daringly recrossed the icy river, surprised and scattered the Hessians, and occupied the town. Then he advanced and drove off a force of redcoats at Princeton. Unable to hold either Princeton or Trenton, he finally took refuge for the rest of the winter in the hills around Morristown. As the campaign of 1776 came to an end, the Americans could console themselves with the thought that they had won two minor victo-

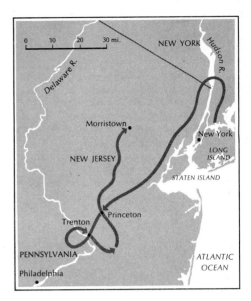

Washington's Retreat   1776

ries, that their main army was still intact, and that the invaders were really no nearer than ever to the decisive triumph that Howe so confidently had anticipated.

For the campaign of 1777 the British devised a strategy that, if Howe had stuck to it, might have cut the United States in two and prepared the way for final victory by Great Britain. According to this plan, Howe would move from New York up the Hudson to Albany, while another force, in a gigantic pincers movement, would come down from Canada to meet him. One of Howe's ambitious younger officers, the dashing John Burgoyne, "Gentleman Johnny," secured command of this northern force and elaborated upon the plan by preparing for a two-pronged attack along both the Mohawk and the upper Hudson approaches to Albany.

Then, fortunately for the United States, Howe adopted a different plan for himself, intending to dispirit the Patriots and rally the Loyalists by seizing the rebel capital, Philadelphia. Taking the bulk of his forces away from New York by sea, Howe landed at the head of Chesapeake Bay, brushed Washington aside at the Battle of Brandywine (September 11), and proceeded to occupy Philadelphia. Meanwhile, Washington after an unsuccessful attack at

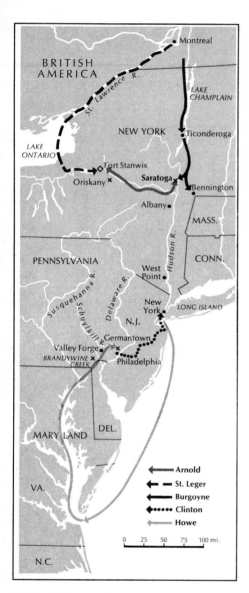

British Campaigns   1777

Mohawk, Burgoyne with his own army advanced directly down the upper Hudson Valley. He got off to a flying start, easily taking Fort Ticonderoga and an enormous store of powder and supplies, and causing such consternation that Congress removed General Philip Schuyler from command in the north and replaced him with Horatio Gates, in response to the demands of New Englanders.

By the time Gates took command, Burgoyne already faced a sudden reversal of his military fortunes in consequence of two staggering defeats. In one of them, at Oriskany, New York (August 6), Nicholas Herkimer with his German farmers checked a force of St. Leger's Indians and Tories, so that Benedict Arnold had time to go to the relief of Fort Stanwix and close off the Mohawk Valley to St. Leger's advance. In the other battle, at Bennington, Vermont (August 16), the Bunker Hill veteran John Stark with his New England militiamen severely mauled a detachment that Burgoyne had sent out to seek supplies. Short of materials, with all help cut off, Burgoyne fought a couple of costly engagements and then withdrew to Saratoga, where Gates surrounded him. Burgoyne was through, and he knew it. On October 17, 1777, he ordered what was left of his army, nearly 5,000 men, to lay down their arms.

Not only the United States but also Europe took note of the amazing news from the woods of upstate New York, and France in particular was impressed. The British surrender at Saratoga, a great turning point in the war, led directly to an alliance between the United States and France.

Germantown (October 4) went into winter quarters at Valley Forge, and the scattered Congress resumed its sittings in York, Pennsylvania.

Up north, Burgoyne was left to carry out his twofold campaign without aid from Howe. Sending Colonel Barry St. Leger with a fast-moving force up the St. Lawrence River toward Lake Ontario and the headwaters of the

FOREIGN FRIENDS

Shortly after the fighting had begun, Congress appointed a secret committee with Franklin as chairman for the purpose of corresponding with "our friends" in Great Britain and, more significantly, in "other parts of the world." Later Congress replaced this agency with a Committee for Foreign Affairs and then (1781) with a Department of Foreign Affairs, the immediate ancestor of the State Department. As far as possible, however, Congress as a whole conducted foreign relations, often overruling or by-passing the agencies it created.

Was the American Revolution essentially a civil war, in which the ordinary people of the colonies were struggling to get democracy at home? Did slaves in the Old South keep alive their African culture and maintain cohesive, well-knit families? Was the United States to blame for the start of the Cold War with the Soviet Union?

On these and many other questions, American historians have disagreed among themselves. Conflicting points of view on several of these issues are presented in this book in a series of essays entitled "Where Historians Disagree." Why do they disagree?

In totalitarian countries there are few controversies of this kind. In the Soviet Union, for example, historians are required to follow the official, Marxist-Leninist interpretation of history. They cannot openly discuss such questions as their own government's responsibility for the Cold War. Only in a free society do scholars have the right to seek to know the past as it actually was. In the search for truth they are obligated only to the impartial standards of historical scholarship. They are limited only by their personal infirmities and biases.

American historians, in writing about their country, have come to agree on most of the "facts." But there are countless facts, and historians have differed as to which are the most important and should therefore be emphasized. Hence the differences in the interpretation of certain phases of American history.

Historians may disagree because of differences in their personal backgrounds (geographic, social, religious, racial, ethnic) or in their historical philosophies (their theories or assumptions about the nature of history and about historical methods) — which lead them to focus on particular aspects of a subject. From one period to another the prevailing view of historians on some phase of the past may change as a result of new evidence coming to light or new public issues rising to prominence. Since the study of the past helps us to understand the problems of the present, it is only natural that historians in each generation should emphasize those features of earlier times that seem most relevant to contemporary preoccupations.

This is not to say that present concerns should dictate historical views. Present concerns can provide only the questions, not the answers. Nor is it to say that all interpretations are equally valid. In time one view may prove to be right and the opposing view wrong. More commonly there is something of value in both, or in several, interpretations. Often it is a matter of each of the contending historians getting hold of only one part of the subject — like the blind men examining the elephant in the fable. Usually the controversies lead to further research and to deepened understanding, if not also to a new consensus.

In these controversies (with few exceptions) the historians are, to repeat, not disputing the facts. The question is not "What happened?" but "What is the *significance* of what happened?" Even where historians disagree the most, they agree much more than they disagree.

Even before the Declaration of Independence, Congress drew up a treaty plan for liberal commercial arrangements with other countries and prepared to send representatives to the capitals of Europe for negotiating treaties—which necessarily would mean European recognition of the United States as one of the sovereign nations of the world. "Militia diplomats," John Adams called the early American representatives abroad, and unlike the diplomatic regulars of Europe they knew little of the formal art and etiquette of Old World diplomacy. Yet most of them were well acquainted with certain fundamentals, for they had gained much diplomatic experience through their dealings with one another in intercolonial affairs, with the Indian tribes in war and peace, and with the British government as colonial

agents in London. Since overseas communication was slow and uncertain (it took from one to three months to cross the Atlantic), these representatives abroad sometimes had to interpret the instructions of Congress very freely and make crucial decisions entirely on their own.

Of all the possible foreign friends of the United States, the most promising and most powerful was France, who still resented her defeat at the hands of Great Britain in 1763. France, under King Louis XVI, who came to the throne in 1774, had an astute and determined foreign minister in the Count de Vergennes, an expert practitioner of Machiavellian principles, thoroughly trained in the cutthroat diplomacy of eighteenth-century Europe. Vergennes soon saw that France had a vital interest in the outcome of the American war. If the

The Continental Army at Valley Forge

Many foreigners served as officers in the Continental army—too many, it seemed to General Washington. Most of them received their commissions from Congress, not from the commander in chief. Once he referred to the foreigners as "hungry adventurers." But he deeply appreciated the assistance of a few of the volunteers from abroad, especially the Marquis de Lafayette and the Baron von Steuben. A veteran of the Prussian army, Steuben came to the United States in 1777, and Washington appointed him inspector general, with overall charge of military discipline, instruction, and supply. Steuben reorganized the Continental army, provided for improved training and drill of soldiers, and wrote a manual of army regulations. The painting by Edwin A. Abbey, which hangs in the Pennsylvania House of Representatives, shows Steuben instructing troops in Washington's camp at Valley Forge, near Philadelphia, during the winter of 1777–1778. After the war he settled in New York. (Courtesy of the Pennsylvania Department of Commerce)

In their accounts of the American Revolution, historians at one time concentrated on the Patriot aim of autonomy within the British Empire and then complete independence from it. These historians differed among themselves in regard to revolutionary motivation; some of them emphasized political ideals, others stressed economic interests. But all of them took as their central theme the struggle between the American colonies and the British government.

Eventually, a number of writers began calling attention to struggles *within* the colonies as well. These writers maintained that the Revolution involved not only the question of home rule but also the question who should rule at home. It was, according to them, a movement toward both independence and democracy. Thus, in a study of New York politics from 1770 to 1776 (1909) and in *The Eve of the Revolution* (1918), Carl L. Becker described the Revolution as, in part, a kind of civil war, a contest for power between American radicals and conservatives, one that led to the "democratization of American politics and society." J. F. Jameson elaborated upon the idea in his slim but influential volume *The American Revolution Considered as a Social Movement* (1926). "The stream of revolution, once started, could not be confined within narrow banks, but spread abroad upon the land," Jameson wrote. "Many economic desires, many social aspirations were set free by the political struggle, many aspects of colonial society profoundly altered by the forces thus let loose." The social changes tended "in the direction of levelling democracy."

This view long prevailed, but recently it has been sharply challenged. The most forceful attack on it comes from Robert E. Brown, who shows in *Middle Class Democracy and the Revolution in Massachusetts, 1691–1780* (1955) that, before 1776, Massachusetts was already "very close to a complete democracy," with practically all men enjoying the right to vote. Brown argues that, at least in Massachusetts and probably also in other colonies, the aim of the Revolutionary leaders was to preserve the democratic liberties that already existed. And E. S. Morgan, in a bold and concise reinterpretation, *The Birth of the Republic, 1763–1789* (1956), holds that most Americans were in basic agreement on political principles; thus he endorses the older view of the Revolution as a struggle between the colonies and the British government.

The debate goes on, with no final decision on points of interpretation, but the net result is greatly to broaden our knowledge of the Revolutionary period.

colonies should assert and maintain their independence, the power of Great Britain would be seriously weakened by the loss of a good part of her empire, and the power of France would be correspondingly increased.

From the start of the troubles between England and her colonies, the French had maintained observers in America to report the course of events, and after the shooting began both Americans and Frenchmen put out diplomatic feelers. In London the Massachusetts colonial agent Arthur Lee met the French dramatist and political genius Caron de Beaumarchais, and the two discussed the possibilities of secret assistance to the colonies. Beaumarchais reported to Vergennes, and Vergennes dispatched an army officer to America to encourage the rebellion, urge independence, and promise supplies. After several meetings with Vergennes' spokesman, Franklin's committee of secret correspondence sent Silas Deane to France as a "merchant" to make "commercial" arrangements. In consequence of these arrangements, Beaumarchais shipped large quantities of munitions to America through a fictitious trading firm that he had rigged up to disguise the fact that most of the shipments were financed by the King of France and the King of Spain. Whether this sort of lend-lease was a gift or a loan later became a question of bitter dispute between Congress and Beaumarchais.

After the Declaration of Independence, Franklin himself went to France to get further aid and outright recognition of the United States. A natural diplomat, the equal if not the superior of the world's best at that time, Franklin immediately captivated Frenchmen of all classes — and Frenchwomen too. But Vergennes hesitated. At the first news of the American Declaration, he was inclined to make a treaty recognizing United States independence, but he did not wish to act without Spain; and when reports came of Washington's defeat on Long Island, he decided to wait and watch the military developments in America. If and when the Americans should show that they had a real chance of winning, then France would intervene. Meanwhile Vergennes was willing to go on financing the American war. He initiated a series of subsidies which in time amounted to nearly $62 million and a series of loans which totaled over $6 million.

The news that Vergennes and Franklin were waiting for — the news from Saratoga — arrived in London on December 2 and in Paris on December 4, 1777. In London the knowledge of Burgoyne's surrender caused Lord North to decide in favor of a peace offensive, an offer of complete home rule within the Empire for Americans if they would quit the war. In Paris, learning of Lord North's intentions from a British spy, Franklin let the word get out for Vergennes to hear. Vergennes worried. If the Americans should accept the British offer, his opportunity to weaken France's traditional enemy would be gone, and if they could not get what they wanted from France, they might accept. Without waiting for Spain to go along with France, Vergennes on February 6, 1778, signed two treaties with Franklin and Deane, one a treaty of commerce and amity, and the other, which was supposed to be secret, a treaty of conditional and defensive alliance, to take effect if Great Britain should go to war with France. Congress and the King quickly ratified the treaties, and Congress received and banqueted a minister from France while the King welcomed Franklin as minister from the United States.

France soon drifted into war with Great Britain, and in 1779 Spain, with objectives of her own, declared war as an ally of France though not of the United States; Spain refused even to receive officially the American representative in Madrid, John Jay. A year later the Netherlands, persisting in its profitable trade with both the French and the Americans, found itself also at war with Britain and agreed to a treaty with the United States. The League of Armed Neutrals — Russia, Denmark, Sweden — assumed a defiant attitude toward Britain, but refrained from considering war and refused to have any official dealings with the upstart nation in America.

Indirectly all the countries arrayed in hostility to Britain contributed to the ultimate success of the United States by complicating the task of the latter's foe. Directly, the Netherlands provided loans to the Americans but was powerless to give military or naval support, and Spain gave unofficial subsidies but confined her military and naval activities to strictly Spanish objectives. France (for her own reasons, of course) was the true friend in need of the Americans. Not only did she furnish them

I. THE COLONIAL PERIOD:
Pattern Books and Indigenous Invention

Plate 1: Anonymous,
MRS. ELIZABETH FREAKE
AND BABY MARY
*(Worcester Art Museum,
Worcester, Massachusetts)*

In adjusting to the difficult conditions of their new environment, the early settlers of the American colonies had little time for luxuries. And yet from almost the very moment of their arrival, the colonists began to create a distinctly personal artistic heritage. In architecture and painting, as well as in toolmaking, American craftsmen produced objects based on European precedent but modified to achieve an art uniquely American in character.

With the relaxation of strict Puritan injunctions against painting, portraiture flourished in seventeenth-century New England. For those who could afford it, primarily the wealthy merchants, portraits were among the few luxuries to be found in the colonial home. Little is known of the itinerant portrait painters, for they generally left their works unsigned. The artist was simply referred to as a limner or liner (from an archaic word meaning "to draw or paint"), and is identified today by associating him with the family name of his subject; the anonymous craftsman who painted "Mrs. Elizabeth Freake and Baby Mary" *(Plate 1)* is known as the Freake limner.

The linear style of the Freake limner had its basis in medieval Tudor tradition, which, although no longer practiced at the English court, had been imported from rural England to the colonies. The essentially flat, linear portrait lacks a feeling of movement or perspective, but the untrained artist conveys an instinctive sense of design. By reducing the background to a dark unbroken area and emphasizing the intricate patterns of lace, ribbon and embroidery, the artist documents with precision how a wealthy merchant's wife and child might have dressed in seventeenth-century New England.

In the German and Dutch settlements of rural New York and Pennsylvania, craftsmen continued to work in the idiom of their native countries. Their furniture design is particularly noteworthy for its simple, sturdy construction and colorful painted decoration. The brightly ornamented "Marriage Chest of Margaret Kernen," 1788 *(Plate 2)*, was built and decorated by German immigrants who settled in eastern Pennsylvania. This richly carved bridal chest, a common article of furniture in German and Dutch colonial homes, was made of tulipwood and painted in vivid colors with stylized flowers and birds. The upper section is divided into three arched niches, with the two flanking the central inscription panel featuring gaily painted prancing unicorns — symbols of virginity — surrounded by the popular tulip motif. Similar use of stylized flowers can be found in other contemporary crafts, including silver and needlework. A particularly fine example is the crewelwork embroidery done by Mary Bulman for a bed hanging in the late eighteenth century *(Plate 3)*.

In the southern colonies, especially Virginia, cultural ties to the mother country were very strong. The great plantation homes around Williamsburg were undoubtedly suggested by the palatial mansions of contemporary England. "Carter's Grove" in James City County, constructed between 1750 and 1753, was designed and executed by local builders relying extensively on pattern books which had been brought from England to the colonies. These pattern books, written by contemporary Englishmen, provided models from which Americans could adapt their own designs. The elegant entrance hall *(Plate 4)* presents in scale and proportion, as well as richly detailed ornament, one of the finest examples of colonial craftsmanship.

In the New England area also, architectural designs drew upon England for inspiration. At first, copying what they remembered from their provincial background, the earliest settlers adapted medieval forms to the colder climate of New England. By the beginning of the eighteenth century, the northern colonists began to borrow directly from contemporary English sources, making such necessary modifications as reducing the size of the houses and substituting easily worked wood for stone.

One of the leading architects of the colonial

Plate 2: Anonymous,
MARRIAGE CHEST
OF MARGARET KERNEN
*(Courtesy, The Henry Francis
du Pont Winterthur Museum)*

Plate 3: Mary Bulman,
CREWEL BED HANGING
(Old Gaol Museum, York, Maine)

Plate 4: Anonymous, CARTER GROVE: ENTRANCE HALL *(Photo by Sandak, 1960)*

Plate 5: Peter Harrison, TOURO SYNAGOGUE: INTERIOR *(Society of Friends of Touro Synagogue; Photo by Sandak)*

period was Peter Harrison. Although a merchant by profession, Harrison's interest in architecture led him to collect a library of architectural pattern books from which he borrowed various designs for buildings in Newport, Cambridge, and Boston. One of his most remarkable commissions was for the Touro Synagogue in Newport, Rhode Island. For the interior, Harrison's inspiration was the English architect Inigo Jones's two-story hall in Whitehall Palace, London, which he ingeniously adapted to the requirements of a Jewish congregation. The elaborately carved columns and ornate pulpit *(Plate 5)* were based on plates found in the pattern books of Englishmen James Gibbs and Batty Langley. The richly decorated building, erected between 1759 and 1763, has survived as the oldest extant American synagogue and is a credit to the superbly trained woodcarvers and carpenters of the colonies.

With most woodcarvers actively engaged in architectural decoration and detail, sculpture in the colonies was largely restricted to signs, gravestones, and weather vanes. The wooden figure of a felon *(Plate 6)*, which hung outside the jail in East Greenwich, Rhode Island, is crudely carved; but the execution is forceful, and severe facial features and clenched fists add a touch of originality to this traditional folk rendering.

Although most of the early artists were immigrants, born and sometimes trained in Europe, by the middle of the eighteenth century America produced its first major native-born painter. Born in Long Island, Robert Feke became one of the leading portrait painters traveling between Boston and Philadelphia. Little is known of his early life and training, but between 1741 and 1750 he received many commissions from the mercantile aristocracy of the north. Though his opportunity to see original English painting was limited by his isolation in the colonies, his work shows a strong influence of the English Baroque style, and he was undoubtedly aware of contemporary European taste through the engravings and mezzotints which were then being imported into America. In Feke's portrait of Isaac Winslow, done in 1748 *(Plate 7)*, the figure is set in a light-filled outdoor environment. Through contrasting patterns of lights and darks, Feke achieves a sense of monumentality.

Also around the middle of the eighteenth century, in response to the growing affluence of the merchant class, there appeared in the colonies a style of painting characterized by a lighter and more graceful manner. Placing greater emphasis on material objects and their tactile values, it reflected the then dominant mode of the French and English courts. One practitioner of this style — known as the Rococo — was Joseph Blackburn, who came to Boston from London. In 1755 Blackburn was commissioned to paint a large family group for the same Isaac Winslow whom Robert Feke had painted seven years earlier. In contrast to Feke's formal linear structure, Blackburn's family portrait *(Plate 8)* attempts to achieve an air of elegance through animated — though artificial — poses. The glossy surface treatment of the fine materials and fabrics and the use of pastel

Plate 6: Anonymous,
KENT COUNTY JAIL SIGN
(The Rhode Island Historical Society; Photo by Sandak)

Plate 7: Robert Feke, ISAAC WINSLOW *(Courtesy Museum of Fine Arts, Boston)*

tones were consistent with the Rococo ideal.

The influence of Blackburn on the next generation of American artists is particularly apparent in the work of John Singleton Copley, the most important colonial painter of the eighteenth century. Copley was born in Boston in 1738 and was trained by his stepfather, an engraver, in the traditional Baroque style. The appearance of Blackburn and his elegant treatment of surface and subject must have been a revelation to the young artist. Although Copley was handicapped by lack of firsthand experience with major European painting, he began to develop a purely personal style based on the nuances of light and shade and the contour of line. His 1769 portrait of the Connecticut merchant Isaac Smith *(Plate 9)* captures the vibrant energy of the sitter and provides an exciting color contrast between the subject's plum suit and the brilliant blue drapery behind him.

Copley, however, became dissatisfied with life in provincial New England. His desire to paint historical and religious subjects was thwarted by the absence of patronage. Just before the outbreak of the Revolution he traveled to Europe and eventually settled in London. There he developed his painting technique in accordance with contemporary Rococo taste. Although he became a respected member of the English artistic establishment, his later paintings, on a more grandiose scale, lacked the freshness of his earlier, American, works.

The departure of Copley from the colonies on the eve of the Revolution was not typical of American artists and craftsmen. Many of the country's leading artisans were among the new nation's most ardent supporters. The famous patriot Paul Revere was a highly respected silversmith who took over his father's shop in 1754. A few years before the Revolution Revere had sat for a portrait by Copley, in which the craftsman is seen at his workbench contemplating one of his creations.

Plate 8: Joseph Blackburn, ISAAC WINSLOW AND HIS FAMILY *(Courtesy Museum of Fine Arts, Boston)*

Plate 9:
John Singleton Copley,
ISAAC SMITH
(Yale University Art Gallery)

Revere's ability as a silversmith is exemplified by his "Liberty Bowl" (Plate 10), a silver punch bowl he executed in 1768 for the Massachusetts House of Representatives, in commemoration of their decision not to rescind a seditious letter. The smooth surface and elegant shape were inspired by Chinese porcelain bowls which had been recently imported to the Colonies. Revere, like many of his compatriots in the arts, continued to contribute after the birth of the United States to a newly emerging national style.

Plate 10: Paul Revere, LIBERTY BOWL
(Courtesy Museum of Fine Arts, Boston)

most of their money and munitions, but she also provided a navy and an expeditionary force that, with Washington's army, made possible the decisive victory at Yorktown.

VICTORY AT YORKTOWN

During the first two years of the war the important campaigns and battles had taken place in the North, but after Saratoga the fighting in that part of the country developed into a stalemate. Replacing General Howe, Sir Henry Clinton withdrew from Philadelphia and took

what had been Howe's army back to New York. Washington used most of his army to keep watch around New York while (1778–1779) sending part of it to chastise the Indians along the frontier for their horrible massacres in the Cherry Valley (New York) and the Wyoming Valley (Pennsylvania). During that same winter George Rogers Clark, with orders from the state of Virginia and not from Washington or Congress, led a heroic expedition over the mountains and redeemed the settlements of the Illinois country from the British and their Indian allies. In 1779 the treason of Benedict Arnold shocked Washington and Pa-

John Paul Jones

A Scot by birth, a Virginian by adoption, Jones became for Americans the greatest naval hero of the Revolutionary War. As captain of the sloop of war Ranger, *he took to France the official news of the Saratoga victory and then proceeded to harry the British coast, boldly sinking ships within sight of the land and occasionally going ashore to raid. In France, through Franklin's influence, he obtained a small fleet with the Bonhomme Richard (named for the "Poor Richard" of Franklin's famous almanac) as the flagship. The Bonhomme Richard under Jones' command defeated the British frigate Serapis in a spectacular duel (September 23, 1779). Captain Jones created such a nuisance for the British that he compelled them to keep a part of their naval force close to home. This is an early portrait by an unknown artist. (Library of Congress)*

triots everywhere but did little military damage except for the transfer of Arnold's services to the British, since his scheme for betraying the Hudson River stronghold of West Point was frustrated in the nick of time. During the final two years of fighting, all the significant action occurred in the South.

Sir Henry Clinton, a rather timid strategist, planned a Southern offensive that was supposed to end the American will to resist, but he put the command of the operation in the hands of Lord Cornwallis, an able general but one as rash as Clinton himself was cautious, and capable of changing plans and disobeying orders in mid-campaign. Clinton and Cornwallis based their strategy on assumptions that were not to prove facts. They assumed that seapower would enable them to move their troops from point to point along the coast with ease, that the difficulties of overland travel would make American counteraction ineffectual, and that Loyalists would rise en masse to welcome and assist the redcoats as liberators. With the conquered South as a base, Clinton and Cornwallis thought they could dispose of the rest of the country at their leisure.

While it was true that in Georgia and the Carolinas there were numerous Tories, some of them disgruntled veterans of the Regulator movement, it was also true that in Virginia as in Massachusetts the mass of the people were fiercely patriotic and that even in the lower South the Loyalist strength was grossly overestimated. Actually, having the support of most of the countryside, the Patriot forces were to be better off than the British in matters of logistics and supply. And the French, while far from able to maintain consistent control of the coastal waters, were finally to have a fleet in the right place at the right time.

The British succeeded in taking Savannah (December 29, 1778) and Charleston (May 20, 1780), inspiring many Loyalists to take up arms, and advancing far into the interior. At every turn they were harassed, however, by Patriot guerrillas led by such resourceful fighters as Thomas Sumter, Andrew Pickens, and Francis Marion, the "Swamp Fox." Penetrating to Camden, well up the Wateree River in South Carolina, Cornwallis met and crushed (August 16, 1780) a combined force of militiamen and Continentals under Horatio Gates, who did not quite deserve his fame as the hero of Saratoga.

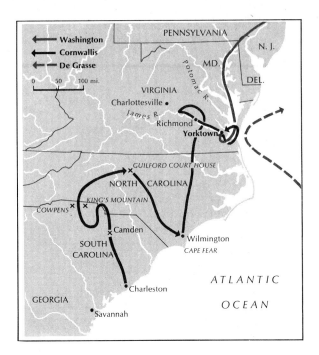

Road to Yorktown   1780–1781

Congress recalled Gates, and Washington gave the Southern command to Nathanael Greene, a former Quaker blacksmith of Rhode Island and probably the ablest of all the American generals of the time next to Washington himself.

Before Greene arrived in the war theater along the North and South Carolina line, the tide of battle already had begun to turn against Cornwallis. At King's Mountain (October 7, 1780) a band of Patriot riflemen from the backwoods killed, wounded, or captured an entire force of 1,100 New York and South Carolina Tories, upon whom Cornwallis had depended as auxiliaries. Once arrived, Greene confused and exasperated Cornwallis by dividing the American forces into fast-moving contingents while refraining from a showdown in open battle. One of the contingents inflicted what Cornwallis admitted was "a very unexpected and severe blow" at Cowpens (January 17, 1781). At last, having received the reinforcements he awaited, Greene combined all his forces and arranged to meet the British on ground of his own choosing at Guilford Court House, North Carolina. After a hard-fought battle (March 15, 1781) Greene was driven from the field, but Cornwallis lost so many men that he decided at last to abandon the Carolina campaign.

Cornwallis withdrew to Wilmington, where he hoped to get supplies by sea, and then he moved north to carry on raids in the interior of Virginia. But Clinton, concerned for the army's safety, ordered him to take up a position on the peninsula between the York and James rivers and wait for water transport to New York or Charleston. So Cornwallis retreated to Yorktown and began to build fortifications there.

Washington made plans with the Count de Rochambeau, commander of the French expeditionary force in America, and with Admiral de Grasse, commander of a French fleet in American waters, for trapping Cornwallis. Washington and Rochambeau marched a Franco-American army from the New York vicinity to join Lafayette in Virginia while de Grasse sailed with additional troops for Chesapeake Bay and the York River. These joint operations, perfectly timed and executed, caught Cornwallis between land and sea. After a few shows of resistance, he asked for terms on October 17, 1781, four years to the day after the capitulation of Burgoyne, and two days later he surrendered his whole army of more than 7,000.

The fighting was over, but the war was not quite won. The United States continued to be something of an occupied country, with British forces holding the seaports of Savannah, Charleston, Wilmington, and New York. Before long a British fleet met and defeated Admiral de Grasse's fleet in the West Indies, ending Washington's hopes for further seapower assistance. So far as the naval and military situation was concerned, the British still held the upper hand in America. And peace was yet to be made.

WINNING THE PEACE

Until Yorktown, peace had been for Americans an illusory and at times a dangerous proposition; and the prospects even after that victory, though improved, were not ideal. The trouble was with Spain. She entered the war solely to recover lost territories in America and Europe, above all Gibraltar, and she had an alliance

binding France to make no separate peace. The United States had promised in its treaty of alliance to conclude no peace without France. Now, if Spain should fight on till she won Gibraltar back, and if France should stick by Spain, and the United States by France, the Americans might be at war forever. That, however, was not the real danger to American interests. The danger was that Spain, to get Gibraltar or American territory, might enter into a deal with Great Britain at the expense of the United States and that France might feel compelled to go along with Spain. In making peace, the United States had as much to fear from its allies as from its enemy.

When, in 1779, Spain in the role of mediator proposed a peace conference, Congress promptly named John Adams as the American delegate and sent him instructions to enter into no negotiations unless Great Britain first recognized the United States as "sovereign, free, and independent." Adams, already abroad as a militia diplomat, proceeded to Paris and remained there waiting for new peace opportunities after the Spanish proposal had been forgotten. The blustery Adams did not get along with Vergennes as well as the soft-spoken Franklin did. Vergennes sent to America a new minister, La Luzerne, to do something about the Adams nuisance. Lobbying with congressmen and playing up to the Secretary for Foreign Affairs, La Luzerne secured the replacement of the single delegate with a whole delegation, including Franklin and John Jay as well as Adams, and La Luzerne virtually dictated the delegation's instructions. These instructions told the prospective peacemakers to keep in close touch with the French government, tell it everything, follow its advice. Thus the United States was put into the hands of Vergennes by the time (1781) Austria and Russia made their joint mediation offer that led eventually to a general peace settlement.

Then the victory at Yorktown, by giving the Americans new bargaining power, rescued them from the worst of their dependence upon Vergennes. In England, Cornwallis' defeat provoked outcries against continuing the war and demands for cultivating American friendship as an asset in international politics. Lord North resigned and Lord Shelburne emerged from the political wreckage as prime minister. British emissaries appeared in France to talk

Treaty of Paris [1783]

1. "His Britannic Majesty acknowledges the said United States . . . to be free, sovereign and independent States."

2. Boundaries shall run, as described in some detail, from Nova Scotia to and through the Great Lakes and the Lake of the Woods, "thence on a due west course to the river Mississippi," down the Mississippi to the thirty-first parallel, and then east to the Atlantic Ocean.

3. The people of the United States shall have fishing rights and liberties in the waters of British North America.

4. Creditors on either side "shall meet with no lawful impediment to the recovery of the full value, in sterling money, of all *bona fide* debts heretofore contracted."

5. Congress "shall earnestly recommend to the legislatures of the respective States" that they make restitution for confiscated Loyalist property.

6. There shall be no future confiscations or prosecutions on account of the part that anyone may have taken in the war.

7. Hostilities shall cease, and "His Britannic Majesty shall, with all convenient speed, and without causing any destruction, or carrying away any negroes or other property of the American inhabitants, withdraw all his armies, garrisons and fleets from the said United States, and from every post, place and harbour within the same."

---

informally with Franklin. He suggested what he called "necessary" terms of peace, including independence and the establishment of the Mississippi as the western boundary of the United States, and "desirable" terms including the cession of Canada for the purpose of "reconciliation," a "sweet word," as he said. But John Jay, recently arrived from his fruitless mission to Spain, where he had acquired reason to be suspicious of Spaniards and all Europeans, objected to continuing the negotiations on the grounds that the Americans were addressed not as plenipotentiaries of a sovereign nation but as "persons" from "colonies or plantations." The negotiations were delayed until Jay was satisfied.

All along Franklin, Jay, and Adams had kept Vergennes informed of their conversations with British agents, in accordance with the instructions from Congress. Then, one day, Jay learned that Vergennes' private secretary was off on a secret mission to England. Jay feared that Vergennes was going to leave the United States in the lurch and make a separate peace by which Great Britain and Spain would divide between themselves the territory west of the Alleghenies and east of the Mississippi. Such a deal, as Franklin exclaimed, would have "cooped us up within the Allegheny Mountains." Though Jay was mistaken as to the details of the secret mission, he was right in thinking that Vergennes was suggesting separate negotiations that were to be kept from the American peacemakers and that might have proved disadvantageous to the United States. From that day on, Franklin, Jay, and Adams ceased to inform Vergennes of their diplomacy but went ahead on their own and soon drew up a preliminary treaty with Great Britain. In doing so, they may have violated the spirit but they did not violate the letter of the Franco-American alliance, since they were not making a separate final peace. Of course, they disregarded their instructions from Congress, but those instructions had come originally from Vergennes himself.

After the preliminary articles were signed (November 30, 1782), Jay and Adams left to Franklin the delicate task of telling Vergennes what had been done. Franklin admitted to Vergennes that the Americans perhaps had violated etiquette in failing to keep the French informed, but he trusted that the incident would cause no rift in the Franco-American alliance. Cleverly Franklin observed: "The English, I just now learn, flatter themselves they have already divided us. I hope this little misunderstanding will therefore be kept a secret, and that they will find themselves totally mistaken." Vergennes, dealing with a fellow master of diplomacy, could not say much and was doubtless glad to have an excuse for ending the war regardless of the wishes of his Spanish ally. Franklin coolly asked for another loan from France – and got it!

The final treaty was signed September 3, 1783, when Spain as well as France agreed to end hostilities. It included a number of provisions that Franklin and Jay and Adams had opposed, and some of these were to lead to serious friction with Great Britain and with Spain in the years ahead. Yet it also included essentially the "necessary" terms that Franklin originally had indicated, though not his "desirable"

ones such as the cession of Canada. On the whole the peace was remarkably favorable to the United States in granting a clear-cut recognition of independence and a generous, though ambiguous, delimination of territory – from the southern boundary of Canada to the northern boundary of Florida and from the Atlantic to the Mississippi. Indeed, by playing off the powers of Europe against one another, Franklin and his colleagues had achieved the greatest diplomatic success in the history of the United States. With good reason the American people celebrated as the last of the British occupation forces embarked from New York and General Washington at the head of his troops rode triumphantly in.

The Confederation's Problems

As usually happens at the end of a long and hard-fought war, peace in 1783 brought to the American people tasks almost as trying as those of the war itself. Congress, with the inadequate powers granted to it in the Articles of Confederation, did not quite succeed in solving its postwar problems of diplomacy and public finance, though it made a good beginning toward organizing its territories in the West. The states, too, had difficulties with debts and taxes and, in the case of Massachusetts, with an armed uprising.

A DISPUTED TREATY

The peace treaty of 1783 recognized the independence of the United States and granted the new nation a vast domain – on paper – but Americans found it hard to exercise their full sovereignty in fact. At once they ran into serious conflict with both Great Britain and Spain, yet they could not count upon the support of France even though France remained technically America's ally.

Despite the treaty provision calling upon the British to evacuate American soil, British forces continued to occupy a string of frontier posts along the Great Lakes within the United

States. Secret orders to hold these forts went from the Colonial Office in London to the governor general of Canada on April 8, 1784, just one day before King George III proclaimed the peace treaty as being in final effect and called upon all his subjects to obey its terms! The real reason for the secret orders was the Canadian and British desire to maintain points of contact with Indian tribes in the Northwest for the conduct of the fur trade and the continuance of defensive alliances with them. The avowed reason, which was an afterthought, was the alleged failure of the United States to carry out its treaty obligations, particularly in regard to private debts.

These debts, dating from pre-Revolutionary days, were owed by American citizens, mostly Southern planters, to merchants and other creditors in England. The American debtors had no intention of paying – many of them had supported the Revolution in order to gain independence and thus throw off their old obligations. The treaty provided only that the United States should place no obstacle in the way of the collection of the debts, and the United States did place no obstacle in the way. True, the individual states interfered with debt collections, through the passage of debtor stay laws, the issuance of paper money as legal tender, and the rulings of courts sympathetic with local debtors.

According to the ill-founded British complaints, the United States was violating not only the article regarding private debts but also the one regarding Loyalist property. On this point the treaty said merely that Congress should recommend to the various states that they make restitution to certain categories of Loyalists whose possessions had been confiscated during the war. Congress did recommend, but the states did not respond. The British had not really expected them to. The article was put into the treaty as a gesture of the King's concern for the fate of his faithful subjects. Anticipating that the states would do little or nothing for Loyalist refugees, Parliament itself appropriated money for their relief.

To British allegations of bad faith, Americans countered with the charge that Great Britain, besides refusing to abandon the frontier posts, was disregarding the treaty provision that obligated her to compensate American slaveowners whose slaves had been carried off by the British armies at the end of the war. And the two countries disputed the meaning and application of still another article, the one defining the northeastern boundary of the United States. Over part of its course the boundary was supposed to follow the St. Croix River, but unfortunately the river had two major branches, and the treaty did not specify which of the two was meant.

The peace arrangements led also to a boundary dispute between the United States and Spain. In her settlement with Spain, Great Britain gave back Florida (which had been British from 1763 to 1783) with the Atlantic and the Mississippi specified as its eastern and western limits but with no precise definition of its northern border. In the preliminary treaty with the United States, however, Great Britain had agreed secretly that, if she herself were to keep Florida, its boundary would be set at latitude 32° 28′ and that, if she ceded it to Spain, its boundary would be located farther south, at the thirty-first parallel. Afterward the United States insisted upon the more southerly of these lines, but Spain demanded the additional northern strip as rightfully a part of Florida. Spain also claimed extensive territory even north of that, as belong-

ing to her by virtue of her (rather small-scale) military operations in the American West during the Revolutionary War.

There was another conflict between Anglo-American arrangements and the claims of Spain. In their treaty of peace Great Britain and the United States recognized the right of subjects and citizens of both countries to navigate the Mississippi River to its mouth. But Spain, possessing Louisiana as well as Florida and thus occupying both banks of the lower Mississippi, denied that Great Britain had any rights there to grant to the United States. In 1784 Spain exercised her lawful power over her territorial waters by closing the lower Mississippi to American navigation.

FAILURES IN FOREIGN AFFAIRS

Thus several provisions of the peace with Great Britain failed to give Americans the benefits they desired and expected, and the treaty omitted entirely still other provisions they had hoped for. Above all, American shippers and traders wanted commercial arrangements that would give them privileges of trading and shipping on equal terms with British subjects in all parts of the British Empire.

No longer colonists, these businessmen, it is true, now had opportunities for exploiting world-wide routes of trade, which before the war had been legally closed to them. Congress proceeded to make satisfactory commercial treaties with the nations of Europe—with France (1778), the Netherlands (1782), Sweden (1783), and Prussia (1785). Congress also agreed to pay protection money to the Sultan of Morocco (1786) so that American merchantmen in the Mediterranean would be free from the depredations of at least some of the Barbary pirates. Without benefit of treaty, American enterprisers opened fabulously profitable trade routes to the Orient, beginning with the voyage of the *Empress of China* in 1784–1785.

Yet, though commerce flourished in new directions, most American trade persisted as much as possible in the old, prewar patterns. In the United States the bulk of imports continued to come from British sources, for Americans were used to British goods, and British merchants knew and catered to American tastes, offered attractive prices, and extended long and easy credit. To earn the British funds needed to pay for these imports, Americans desired free access to more British markets than were open to them after the war.

In 1784 Congress sent John Adams as minister to London with instructions to get a commercial treaty and speed up the evacuation of the frontier posts. Taunted by the query whether he represented one nation or thirteen, Minister Adams made no headway in England, partly because Congress had no power to retaliate against the kind of commercial warfare that Great Britain was pursuing against the United States. Throughout the 1780s the British government refused even to return the courtesy of sending a minister to the American capital.

The Spanish government, by contrast, was willing to negotiate its differences with the United States, and in 1785 its representative, Don Diego de Gardoqui, arrived in New York (where Congress had moved from Philadelphia) to deal with the Secretary for Foreign Affairs, John Jay. After months of the most friendly conversations, Jay and Gardoqui initialed a treaty (1786). By its terms, the Spanish government would have granted Americans the right to trade with Spain but not with her colonies; would have conceded the American interpretation of the Florida boundary; and (in a secret article) would have joined in an alliance to protect American soil from British encroachments. The United States, besides guaranteeing Spanish possessions in America, would have agreed to "forbear" the navigation of the Mississippi for twenty years, though not to abandon the right of navigation. Jay found it hopeless, however, to secure the necessary nine state votes for the ratification of his treaty by Congress, since the delegates from the five Southern states objected bitterly and correctly that the interests of Southerners in Mississippi navigation were being sacrificed to the interests of Northerners in Spanish trade.

THE NEEDS OF THE WEST

Into the areas of postwar border conflict with Great Britain and Spain moved an unprecedented horde of American settlers during and after the Revolution. When the war began, only a few thousand lived west of the Appalachian divide; by 1790 their numbers had increased to 120,000. Most of the migrants made the mountain crossing under the auspices of able and far-seeing land promoters. James Robertson and John Sevier led pioneers from North Carolina to the Watauga settlements (1770) and later to the Cumberland Valley (1779), thus laying the foundations for the future state of Tennessee. Richard Henderson, promoter of the Transylvania Company and employer of Daniel Boone, stimulated the growth of Kentucky by selling lands, organizing a provisional government (1776), and having the Wilderness Road hewn out. The managers of the Vandalia Company encouraged migration to what eventually became West Virginia. And the Allen brothers—Ethan, Ira, and Levi—attracted purchasers for their regal holdings of real estate in the Green Mountains of Vermont. The frontiersman usually had to depend upon such speculators for his land title and for other favors, yet he was characteristically an individualist determined to make a future for himself. He and his family, together with thousands of others like him, comprised what was potentially the strongest single factor for redeeming the West for the United States.

But the United States could realize this potentiality only if the government were able to meet the needs of the frontier settler and keep him loyal to its distant authority. The settler needed protection from the Indians, access to outside markets for his surplus crops, and courts with orderly processes of law. In dealing with the West, Congress inherited responsibilities that formerly had baffled King and Parliament.

At first Congress lacked clear-cut jurisdiction over the trans-Appalachian region, and for several years conflicts of authority persisted among Congress, the states, and the frontier settlements themselves. Of course, with Virginia's cession in 1781, the landed states had begun to yield their Western claims to the Confederation. But Virginia had ceded her territory to the north of the Ohio River on the condition that private grants within it be canceled, and for a few years the grantees lobbied successfully to keep Congress from accepting the territory with that stipulation. North Carolina temporarily took back its ceded land, other states postponed

State Claims to Western Lands   1781

their cessions, and not till 1802 did the last of them, Georgia, give up its claim. Meanwhile these states transferred the actual ownership of most of the land south of the Ohio River to private individuals and companies, and impatient settlers proceeded to set up their own state governments for Frankland or Franklin (Tennessee) and for Kentucky. North Carolina attempted to incorporate Tennessee, and Virginia tried to make Kentucky a Virginia county.

PLANNING FOR THE TERRITORIES

In 1784, having persuaded Virginia to make a new cession without specific restrictions, Congress accepted Virginia's Western lands (not including Kentucky), and began to make policy for the national domain. The most momentous decision, already resolved upon, was that settlements in the territory should not be held in permanent subjection as colonies but should be transformed ultimately into states equal with the original thirteen. In the Ordinance of 1784 Congress temporarily adopted Thomas Jefferson's very democratic plan for the transition to statehood of the territory between the Ohio River and the Great Lakes. This territory was to have been divided into ten districts, each to be self-governing from the start, to be represented by a delegate in Congress as soon as its population reached 20,000, and to be admitted as a state when its population equaled the number of free inhabitants of the smallest existing state.

Having thus prepared a scheme of territorial government, Congress in the Ordinance of 1785 provided a system of land survey and sale. The land to the north of the Ohio was to be surveyed and marked off in a rectangular pattern before any of it was sold. This program derived from the practice of New England towns rather than from that of the South, where the settler located a choice plot and afterward determined its boundaries, usually following topographical irregularities. The land ordinance of Congress provided for east-west base lines, north-south "ranges," and townships with sides paralleling the ranges and base lines. Each township was to contain thirty-six square-mile sections. In every township four sections were to be set aside for the United States and one for a public school. The rest of the sections were to be sold at auction for not less than $1 an acre. Since there were 640 acres in a section, the prospective buyer of government land had to have at least $640 in ready cash or in United States certificates of indebtedness.

These terms favored the large speculators too much and the ordinary frontiersman too little to suit Jefferson, who believed that the West ought to belong to actual settlers on the ground. But the large speculators desired still further advantages, and Congress, in a hurry to realize returns from its domain, soon gave in to lobbying groups composed of some of its own members and various former army officers. To the Ohio and Scioto companies and the associates of John Cleves Symmes, Congress disposed of several million acres at only a few cents an acre. Millions of acres besides had been reserved at the time of cession by Virginia and Connecticut as bounty lands for their Revolutionary soldiers. Thus, before the government surveys had been well started, most of the

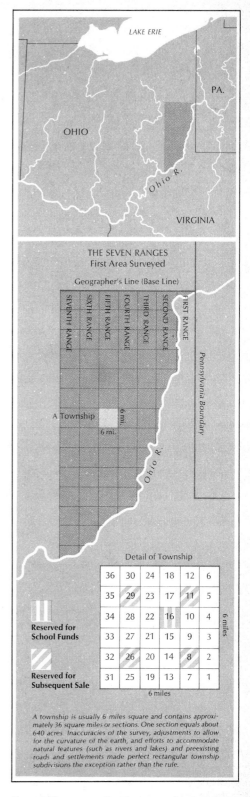

A township is usually 6 miles square and contains approximately 36 square miles or sections. One section equals about 640 acres. Inaccuracies of the survey, adjustments to allow for the curvature of the earth, and efforts to accommodate natural features (such as rivers and lakes) and preexisting roads and settlements made perfect rectangular township subdivisions the exception rather than the rule.

Land Survey: Ordinance of 1785

The Northwest Ordinance [1787]

1. Congress shall appoint a governor, a secretary, and three judges for the Northwest Territory. These officials shall adopt suitable laws from the original states. When the territory has "five thousand free male inhabitants of full age," they shall be allowed to elect representatives. These, together with the governor and a legislative council of five, shall form a general assembly to make laws for the territory.

2. The inhabitants shall be entitled to the benefits of trial by jury and other judicial proceedings according to the common law.

3. "Religion, morality, and knowledge being necessary to good government and the happiness of mankind, schools and the means of education shall forever be encouraged."

4. "There shall be formed in the said territory not less than three nor more than five States. . . . And, whenever any of the said States shall have sixty thousand free inhabitants therein, such State shall be admitted, by its delegates, into the Congress of the United States, on an equal footing with the original States."

5. "There shall be neither slavery nor involuntary servitude in the said territory, otherwise than in the punishment of crimes whereof the party shall have been duly convicted."

---

choicest land north of the Ohio River was already spoken for (as was all the land south of the Ohio, to which the ordinances of Congress did not apply).

To protect their interests in the Northwest, the directors of the Ohio and Scioto companies demanded a territorial government that would give less influence to the inhabitants than would the one outlined in Jefferson's Ordinance of 1784, and the companies' skillful lobbyist Manasseh Cutler carried their case to Congress. Some of the congressmen themselves disliked Jefferson's idea of creating as many as ten new states north of the Ohio, since these states in time might gain political ascendancy. Soon Congress replaced the original law — which had never gone into actual effect — with the Ordinance of 1787. This famous "Northwest Ordinance" established one Northwest Territory for the time being, provided for its subsequent division into several territories, not fewer than three nor more than five, and laid out three stages for the evolution of each territory into a state. In the first stage, Congress-appointed officials would govern the territory, in the second an elected legislature would share power with them, and in the third, when the people numbered 60,000 or more, they might frame a constitution and apply for statehood. The Northwest Ordinance, em-

bodying as it did the views of conservative Easterners, failed to satisfy the restless inhabitants of the Ohio country.

The Indian policy of Congress fell short of the requirements of land speculators as well as of frontier settlers. In 1785 and 1786 congressional commissioners made treaties with representatives of the Iroquois and other tribes, who thereby surrendered their claims to a stretch of land north of the Ohio in return for comparatively worthless trinkets. Repudiating the treaties, many of the tribesmen went on the warpath. Congress vainly instructed Colonel Josiah Harmar, commanding the federal troops in the Ohio country, to drive the Indians back, then in desperation called upon the aging hero George Rogers Clark to save the frontier. While the campaign against the Indians in the Northwest faltered, a new threat arose in the Southwest, where the Creeks under the half-breed Alexander McGillivray not only repudiated their treaties ceding land but also formed an alliance with the Spaniards to resist the advance of American frontiersmen.

Some of the frontier leaders in the Southwest, instead of fighting the Spaniards, turned to collaborating with them. These leaders and their followers thought for a time that they saw advantages for themselves in the possible creation of a Southwestern confederacy under

Spanish tutelage. They might thus get what the United States seemed unable to give them— protection from the Indians, cheap or free land, and an outlet to Eastern and foreign markets through the navigation of the Mississippi. After the collapse of the Jay-Gardoqui negotiations, the "Spanish Conspiracy" began to hum, attracting not only unscrupulous adventurers like General James Wilkinson but also such prominent politicians as William Blount of Kentucky and John Sevier of Tennessee. At the same time another underground separatist movement was afoot on the far northern frontier. The aspirations of Vermont for statehood having been frustrated by the rival claims of New York and New Hampshire to its soil, the Allen brothers intrigued with British agents for returning the Green Mountain country to the British Empire.

DEBTS, TAXES, AND DANIEL SHAYS

At the end of the war foreign ships crowded into American seaports with cargoes of all kinds, and the American people bought extravagantly with cash or credit. In consequence the wartime accumulations of specie were drained out of the country, consumer indebtedness to importing merchants was multiplied, and a postwar depression lasting from 1784 to 1787 was made worse than it might otherwise have been. The depression, with its money scarcity, bore heavily upon debtors both public and private, complicating the financial problems of many citizens and of the Confederation and state governments.

The Confederation government had canceled most of its war debt to Americans by repudiating hundreds of millions of dollars in Continental currency. Yet it still owed a domestic debt estimated at about $34 million in 1783; and through continued borrowings from abroad, mostly from the Netherlands, its foreign debt increased to more than $10 million by 1788. During the 1780s the government had to make do with uncertain and fluctuating revenues. It could only make requisitions on the states; it never got around to assessing the real property in the states but merely estimated the proper quota for each of them to contribute. Often the states complained of unfairness and refused to comply; as a whole, they paid an average of only about one-sixth of the total that was requested. This was barely enough to meet the government's ordinary operating expenses. To pay the interest on the foreign debt, the Secretary of the Treasury, Robert Morris, used the proceeds from the new loans. Thus he maintained an excellent credit rating with Dutch and other foreign bankers. But he could not keep up with the domestic obligations, and the government lost credit at home. At a fraction of the face value, shrewd speculators bought up Confederation certificates of indebtedness from former Revolutionary soldiers and others who lost hope of payment from Congress and who needed ready cash.

The states, too, came out of the war with large debts, and one by one they added to their obligations by taking over parts of the Confederation debt owed to their respective citizens. Taxable resources varied a good deal from state to state. The chief reliance everywhere was upon the direct tax on land and its improvements, the income tax then being exceptional, though Maryland had one. The states supplemented their revenues by means of customs duties and harbor fees, though these tariff and navigation laws served also to protect the states' manufacturers and shippers from foreign competition. To some extent the tariffs interfered with trade between states, but with a few exceptions they were designed to limit importations of foreign and not American goods.

Suffering seriously from the postwar deflation and from the tax burden upon their land, the debtor farmers of the country demanded relief in the form of paper money, and seven of the states responded by issuing such currency. Of these seven, Rhode Island went to the greatest extremes, not only designating its paper as legal tender but compelling creditors to accept it or lose the right to collect their debts. While creditors fled from debtors eager to pay in Rhode Island currency, the highest court in the state, in the case of *Trevett* v. *Weeden* (1786), held that the monetary legislation was unconstitutional, and the legislature summoned the judges before it and censured them for their action.

The other six states refused to yield to the advocates of inflation and pursued policies of unrelieved taxation to support their public debts. To the state creditors—that is, the bondholders—all this was sound and honest public finance. But it seemed like robbery and tyranny to many of the poverty-stricken farmers, especially in New England, who felt that money was being extorted from them to swell the riches of the wealthy bondholders in Boston and other towns. At a time when cash was not to be had, these farmers were called upon to pay in specie not only state tax collectors but also mortgage holders and other private creditors. Debtors who failed to pay found their mortgages foreclosed and property seized, and sometimes they found themselves in jail.

Mobs of distressed farmers rioted in various parts of New England but caused the most serious trouble in Massachusetts. There the malcontents of the Connecticut Valley and the Berkshire Hills, many of them Revolutionary veterans, found a leader in Daniel Shays, himself a former captain in the Continental army. Organizing and drilling his followers, Shays put forth a program of demands including paper money, tax relief, a moratorium on debts, the removal of the state capital from Boston to the interior, and the abolition of imprisonment for debt. During the summer of 1786 the Shaysites concentrated upon the immediate task of preventing the collection of debts, private or public, and went in armed bands from place to place to break up court sittings and sheriff's sales. In Boston, members of the legislature, including Samuel Adams, denounced Shays and his men as rebels and traitors. When winter came these rebels, instead of laying down their arms, advanced upon Springfield to get more of them from the arsenal there. From Boston approached an army of state militiamen financed by a loan from wealthy merchants who feared a new revolution. In January 1787, this army met the ragged troops of Shays, killed several of them, captured many more, and scattered the rest to the hills in a blinding snowstorm.

As a military enterprise, Shays' Rebellion was a fiasco, yet it had important consequences for the future of the United States. In Massachusetts it resulted in a few immediate gains for the discontented groups. Shays and his lieutenants, at first sentenced to death, were soon pardoned, and some concessions to Shays' earlier demands were granted in the way of tax relief and the postponement of debt payments. Far more significant, the rebellion also affected the country as a whole by giving added urgency to the movement for a new Constitution.

Selected Readings

The Revolution in General
J. R. Alden, *The American Revolution, 1775–1783** (1954) and *History of the American Revolution* (1969); J. C. Miller, *Triumph of Freedom, 1775–1783** (1949); J. F. Jameson, *The American Revolution Considered as a Social Movement* (1926).

Independence and Loyalism
C. L. Becker, *The Declaration of Independence** (1922); R. G. Adams, *The Political Ideas of the American Revolution* (1922); P. H. Smith, *Loyalists and Redcoats: A Study in British Revolutionary Policy* (1964); W. H. Nelson, *The American Tory** (1961); C. H. Van Tyne, *The Loyalists in the American Revolution* (1905); R. M. Calhoon, *Loyalists in the American Revolution* (1973).

Campaigns and Battles
Christopher Ward, *The War of the Revolution* (2 vols., 1952); W. M. Wallace, *Appeal to Arms** (1951); Lynn Montross, *Rag, Tag, and Bobtail* (1952); H. H. Peckham, *The War for Independence: A Military History* (1958); G. F. Scheer and H. F. Rankin, *Rebels and Redcoats** (1957); Bernard Knollenberg, *Washington and the Revolution* (1940); Carl Berger, *Broadsides and Bayonets: The Propaganda War of the American Revolution* (1961).

The Naval War
G. W. Allen, *Naval History of the American Revolution* (2 vols., 1913); S. E. Morison, *John Paul Jones: A Sailor's Biography** (1959); W. B. Clark, *Ben Franklin's Privateers* (1956).

Diplomacy
S. F. Bemis, *The Diplomacy of the American Revolution** (1935); R. B. Morris, *The Peacemakers: The Great Powers and American Independence* (1965); A. O. Aldridge, *Franklin and His French Contemporaries* (1957); Gerald Stourzh, *Benjamin Franklin and American Foreign Policy* (1954); B. Graymont, *The Iroquois in the American Revolution* (1971).

War Finance
C. L. Ver Steeg, *Robert Morris, Revolutionary Financier* (1954); E. J. Ferguson, *The Power of the Purse: A History of American Public Finance, 1776–1790* (1961).

The Continental Congress
Lynn Montross, *The Reluctant Rebels: The Story of the Continental Congress, 1774–1789* (1950); E. C. Burnett, *The Continental Congress** (1941).

The "Critical Period"
Merrill Jensen, *The Articles of Confederation** (1948) and *The New Nation: A History of the United States During the Confederation, 1781–1789** (1950); E. P. Douglass, *Rebels and Democrats: The Struggle for Equal Political Rights and Majority Rule During the American Revolution** (1955); R. P. McCormick, *Experiment in Independence: New Jersey in the Critical Period, 1781–1789* (1950); Irving Brant, *James Madison: The Nationalist, 1780–1787* (1948); M. L. Starkey, *A Little Rebellion* (1955), on the Shays uprising.

From Independence to the Constitution
G. S. Wood, *The Creation of the American Republic, 1776–1787* (1969) and *Rising Glory of America* (1972); B. F. Wright, *Consensus and Continuity, 1776–1787* (1958); E. S. Morgan, *The Birth of the Republic, 1763–89** (1956).

*Titles available in paperback.

Beginnings Under the Constitution

Six

William E. Gladstone, a nineteenth-century British statesman, once described the Constitution of the United States as the "most wonderful work ever struck off at a given time by the brain and purpose of man." Of course, the Constitution was not the result of a sudden stroke of genius. It was the product of years of experience with colonial and state governments and with the Articles of Confederation. It took form in the heat of political controversy and was adopted in the face of bitter opposition. Yet, though far from flawless, it was indeed a wonderful work. Certainly it created, as it was intended to do, a "more perfect union" than existed at the time it was written. More than that, it provided a fundamental law capable of growth and adaptation to meet the needs of the nation for centuries to come.

From the beginning the Constitution took on some of the characteristics of a sacred writing, a holy mystery of the Americans. Among its virtues was its brevity (only about 7,000 words), but the defect of that virtue was a considerable ambiguity, which left room at certain points for a variety of interpretations. Political differences, no matter what the interests that underlay them, came to be expressed in constitutional terms. In discussing a governmental policy, men asked not only whether it was to their particular advantage, or whether it contributed to the public good, but also whether it was in accord with the Constitution. Those who had opposed the adoption of the Constitution joined the discussion instead of advocating repeal. All were willing to obey the fundamental law, but not all agreed on just what it permitted them to do.

Two basic lines of interpretation quickly appeared. According to one of them, the words of the document were to be liberally construed, so as to give the new government "implied powers" beyond those literally specified. According to the other line of interpretation, the words were to be strictly followed, so as to leave to the states all powers not plainly delegated to the new

The Constitutional Convention
While the presiding officer, George Washington, stands at the desk, delegates to the convention sign the final draft of the Constitution in Independence Hall, Philadelphia, late in the summer of 1787. This painting, done much later, is by Howard Chandler Christie, a popular illustrator of the twentieth century. (Library of Congress)

government. Alexander Hamilton was the first great exponent of liberal or loose construction, and Thomas Jefferson of strict construction and state rights.

It has been said that the shadows of Hamilton and Jefferson fall across the whole of subsequent American history, that to this day all Americans are either Hamiltonians or Jeffersonians. This is an oversimplification. Hamilton and Jefferson and their respective followers disagreed on other things besides the reading of the Constitution, and even on that subject their views changed before long. It would be nearer the truth to say that, over the years, the people in whichever party happened to be in control of the federal government have wished to use its powers to achieve their aims and hence have favored a liberal construction. To oppose those aims the people out of power have resorted to the doctrine of state rights.

Toward a New Government

During the 1780s the Confederation Congress steadily lost prestige while leading a rather waiflike existence. Its members timidly withdrew from Philadelphia in 1783 to escape the clamor of army veterans demanding back pay. After taking refuge for a while in Princeton, the delegates moved on to Annapolis and then to New York (1785), which for the time being remained the capital. With some difficulty a quorum had been rounded up to ratify the treaty ending the Revolutionary War. Only eighteen members, representing eight of the states, were on hand to pass the Northwest Ordinance.

ADVOCATES OF CENTRALIZATION

Weak though the Confederation government was, it satisfied a great many—probably a majority—of the people. They did not want a strong central government. Having just fought the Revolutionary War to avert the danger of remote and, to them, tyrannical authority, they desired to keep the centers of political power close to home in the thirteen states.

Others, however, either disliked the Articles of Confederation from the outset or came eventually to desire something different. Disgruntled at the refusal of Congress to grant them half pay for life, some of the military men through their exclusive and hereditary Society of the Cincinnati hoped to control and to invigorate the government, some of them even aspiring to a kind of army dictatorship. Artisans or "mechanics," the manufacturers of the time, preferred a uniformly high national tariff to the varying state tariffs. Merchants and shippers preferred a single and effective commercial policy to thirteen different and ineffective ones. Land speculators wished to see the "Indian menace" finally removed from their Western tracts, and creditors desired to stop the state issues of paper money. Investors in Confederation securities hoped to have the Confederation debt made good and the value of their securities enhanced. Large property owners in general looked for a reliable means of safety from the threat of mobs.

The issue was not whether the Confederation should be changed but how drastic the changes should be. Even its defenders reluctantly came to agree that the government needed strengthening at its weakest point—its lack of power to tax. To save the Articles of Confederation, its friends backed the impost amendment of 1782, which would have authorized Congress to levy customs duties. All the states ratified the amendment except Rhode Island, whose single veto was enough to kill it. The next year a similar amendment was accepted by Rhode Island but defeated by New York. Later the state-rights advocates proposed that the states make to Congress a temporary and qualified grant of taxing authority (not an amendment to the Articles), but most of the centralizers had begun to lose interest in such remedies. They insisted upon a much more thoroughgoing change.

The 1780s once seemed to historians like a "critical period," one of impending collapse and chaos from which the newly independent republic was rescued only by the timely adoption of the Constitution. This was the theme of a widely read book that John Fiske, a popularizer of both science and history, wrote a century afterward (1888). Fiske and other writers emphasized the difficulties and failures of the 1780s — the business depression, the weaknesses of the central government under the Articles of Confederation, the threats to American territory from Great Britain and Spain, the debts of the Confederation and of the states, the interstate jealousies and barriers to trade, the widespread resort to paper-money inflation, and the disorders and lawlessness culminating in Shays' Rebellion. All this, according to Fiske and those who followed him, represented the darkness before the dawn. The dawn supposedly came with the establishment of the new government under the Constitution, when conditions suddenly began to improve.

One of the greatest of American historians, Charles A. Beard, challenged the prevailing view in an arresting and controversial work, *An Economic Interpretation of the Constitution of the United States* (1913). Beard maintained that the 1780s had been a "critical period" only for certain business interests, not for the people as a whole. According to him, these interests desired a central government strong enough to promote industry and trade, safeguard private property, and make good the public debt. Many of the delegates to the constitutional convention, he said, stood to gain directly as well as indirectly from their efforts, for they had bought up the Confederation's "certificates of indebtedness" cheaply, and these would rise in value if a strong central government were set up. He added that the advocates of the Constitution succeeded in obtaining its ratification despite the indifference or opposition of a majority of the people. In a later book (1927) Beard suggested that the Articles of Confederation might still be serving quite satisfactorily as our twentieth-century frame of government if a comparatively small group of impatient and determined men had not managed to bring about a drastic change in 1787 – 1788.

Most historians promptly adopted Beard's conclusions, and some proceeded to elaborate upon his work. Merrill Jensen, for one, in *The Articles of Confederation* (1940) and *The New Nation* (1950), produced additional evidence to show that the 1780s were a time of hopeful striving rather than black despair, of economic recovery and not persisting depression, of governmental progress under the Articles despite temporary failures. Other historians disagreed with Beard, however, and in recent years the dissenters, notably Robert E. Brown and Forrest McDonald, have criticized his methods and findings with increasing effectiveness. Today, few if any historians accept the Beard thesis without qualification.

The Virginia Plan
[1787]

The following branches of government were recommended in the Virginia Plan:

1. A "National Legislature," with the states represented in proportion either to their "quotas of contribution" or to "the number of free inhabitants." Two branches, the members of the first to be elected by the people, the members of the second to be nominated by the state legislatures and elected by the first. Powers: To "legislate in all cases to which the separate states are incompetent," to "negative all laws passed by the several states, contravening in the opinion of the National Legislature the articles of Union," and to use force against recalcitrant states.

2. A single "National Executive" to be chosen by the National Legislature.

3. A "National Judiciary" to be chosen by the National Legislature.

4. A "Council of Revision," consisting of the National Executive and part of the National Judiciary, with power to "examine" and reject state and national laws before they went into effect.

The most resourceful of the reformers was the political genius, New York lawyer, one-time military aide to General Washington, and illegitimate son of a Scottish merchant in the West Indies—Alexander Hamilton. From the beginning he had been dissatisfied with the Articles of Confederation, had seen little to be gained by piecemeal amendments, and had urged the holding of a national convention to overhaul the entire document. To this end he took advantage of a movement for interstate cooperation that began in 1785 when a group of Marylanders and Virginians met in Alexandria to settle differences between the two states.

One of the Virginians, James Madison, who was as eager as Hamilton to see a stronger government, induced the Virginia legislature to invite all the states to send delegates to a larger conference on commercial questions. This group met at Annapolis in 1786, but representatives from only five states appeared at the meeting. Hamilton, a delegate from New York, took satisfaction in seeing the conference adopt his report and send copies to the state legislatures and to Congress. His report recommended that Congress call a convention of special delegates from all the states to gather in Philadelphia the next year and consider ways to "render the constitution of the Federal government adequate to the exigencies of the union."

At the moment, in 1786, there seemed little possibility that the Philadelphia convention would be any better attended or would accomplish any more than the previous meeting at Annapolis. The leadership of Washington would be essential for success. One of the wealthiest men in the country, but temporarily short of cash, Washington doubted whether he would undertake the trouble and expense of a trip to Philadelphia.

Then, early in 1787, the news of commotion and bloodshed in Massachusetts spread throughout the country and the world, news which seemed to foretell other and more dangerous insurrections than that of Shays. In Paris the American minister, Thomas Jefferson, was not alarmed. "I hold," he confided in a letter to his Virginia friend James Madison, "that a little rebellion, now and then, is a good thing, and as necessary in the political world as storms in the physical." At Mount Vernon, however, Washington did not take the news so calmly. "There are combustibles in every State which a spark might set fire to," he exclaimed. "I feel infinitely more than I can express for the disorders which have arisen. Good God!" Washington refused to listen to renewed suggestions that he make himself a military dictator, but after Congress had issued its call for a constitutional convention he borrowed money for the journey and, in May, left Mount Vernon for Philadelphia.

**The
New Jersey
Plan
[1787]**

The main features of the New Jersey Plan were:

1. The continuance of the existing one-house Congress, with one vote for each state. but with the following additional powers: to raise a revenue from import duties, stamp taxes, and postage; to regulate interstate and foreign commerce; and to provide for the collection of taxes within any state failing to pay its share of the requisitions upon the states.

2. A plural "Federal Executive" to be elected by Congress.

3. A "Federal Judiciary" to be appointed by the Executive.

4. The establishment of acts of Congress and federal treaties as the "supreme law" of the states, and the authorization of the Federal Executive to "call forth the power of the Confederated States . . . to enforce and compel an obedience."

A DIVIDED CONVENTION

Fifty-five men, representing all the states except Rhode Island, attended one or more sessions of the convention that sat in the Philadelphia State House from May to September, 1787. Never before or since has there been a more distinguished gathering in America. These "Founding Fathers," instead of being graybearded ancients as the term implies, were on the whole relatively young men, many of them in their twenties and thirties and only one (Benjamin Franklin) extremely old; his eighty-one years raised the average age from forty-three to forty-four. Despite their comparative youth, the delegates were men of vast practical experience in business, plantation management, and politics; and they were well educated for their time, more than a third of them being college graduates. Practically all of them represented, both directly and indirectly, the great property interests of the country. Many feared what one of them called the "turbulence and follies" of democracy.

Most of the constitution makers agreed that the United States needed a stronger central government. There were differences of opinion, however, as to how much stronger the government should be, what specific powers it should have, and what structure it should be given. There were differences, in particular, over the relative influence the large and small states should exert in the new system, and over the provisions to be included for the protection and promotion of economic interests in different sections of the country.

Among the states, Virginia was then much the largest in population—more than twice as large as New York, more than four times as large as New Jersey, more than ten times as large as Delaware. Among the delegations at Philadelphia, the Virginians were also the best prepared for the work of the convention. And among the Virginians, James Madison (aged thirty-six) was the intellectual leader. Already, before the convention met, he had done his homework well, having devised in some detail a plan for a new "national" government. The Virginians took the initiative from the moment the convention began.

Washington was easily elected to preside, and then a resolution was passed to keep the proceedings absolutely secret. Next, Edmund Randolph of Virginia proposed that "a *national* government ought to be established, consisting of a *supreme* Legislative, Executive, and Judiciary." This being approved, Randolph introduced the plan that Madison already had worked out. The Virginia Plan, if adopted, would give the larger influence to the richer and more populous states. It would also mean abandoning the Articles of Confederation and building the government anew.

But the existing Congress had called the convention "for the sole and express purpose of revising the Articles of Confederation," and the states in commissioning their "deputies" had authorized them to do no more than revise the Articles. Some of the delegates—especially those from the smaller states—now raised doubts whether the convention properly could entertain such proposals as were embodied in the Virginia Plan. At first, however, these men had nothing to offer in its stead. After some delay, William Paterson of New Jersey submitted an alternative scheme for a "federal" as opposed to a "national" government. The New Jersey Plan was intended only to revise and strengthen the Articles.

The stage was now set for a full debate between large-state and small-state delegates — between advocates of a national system (nationalists) and of a federal system (federalists). The Virginia Plan went much too far to suit the federalists. To them, one of its worst features was the system of representation in the proposed two-house legislature. In the lower house, if the states were to be represented in proportion to their population, the largest state (Virginia) would have about ten times as many representatives as the smallest (Delaware). In the upper house, if its members were to be elected by the lower house, some of the smaller states at any given time might have no members at all! To the small-state delegates the Congress of the Articles of Confederation, as well as the Congress of the New Jersey Plan, at least had the merit of equal representation for all the states, regardless of size. But the New Jersey Plan gained the support of only a minority in the convention and, after much argument, was tabled.

The Virginia Plan was left as the basis for discussion. Its proponents realized that they would have to make concessions to the small-state men if the convention were ever to reach a general agreement. The majority soon conceded an important point by consenting that the members of the upper house should be elected by the state legislatures rather than by the lower house of the national legislature. Thus each state would be sure of always having at least one member in the upper house, but there remained the question of how many members each state should have.

There remained also the question of the number of representatives each state should have in the lower house. If the number was to depend upon population, were slaves to be included in the population figure? The delegates from the states where slavery seemed a permanent institution — especially those from South Carolina — insisted that slaves should be counted as persons (though not, of course, entitled to vote) in determining a state's representation. But these delegates argued that slaves ought to be considered as property, not as persons, when it was proposed that the new legislature be allowed to levy a direct tax (such as a land or poll tax) upon each state in proportion to its population. Men who came from states where slavery had disappeared or was expected to disappear argued that slaves should be included in calculating taxation but not representation. Thus an issue between slave and free states was added to the one between large and small states.

DIFFERENCES COMPROMISED

On these and other matters, the delegates bickered day after day. By the end of June, as both temperature and tempers rose to uncomfortable heights, the convention seemed in danger of breaking up, with nothing accomplished. If this should happen, the men at Philadelphia would "become a reproach and by-word down to future ages," said the venerable Franklin, the voice of calmness and conciliation throughout the summer. "And what is worse, mankind may hereafter, from this unfortunate instance, despair of establishing governments by human wisdom, and leave it to chance, war and conquest."

Through the calming influence of Franklin and others, especially Oliver Ellsworth of Connecticut, the delegates managed to settle the most serious of their disputes and go on with their work. A committee of twelve, with one member from each state, brought in a report that culminated in what afterwards was known as the "Great Compromise" (adopted on July 16, 1787). One part of this report provided that the states should be represented in the lower house in proportion to their population, and that three-fifths of the slaves should be included in determining the basis for both representation and direct taxation. The three-fifths formula, though seemingly rather arbitrary, gained some degree of logic from the assumption that, in contributing his labor to the wealth of a state, a slave was on the average three-fifths as productive as a freeman. Another part of the Great Compromise provided that in the upper house, the states should be represented equally with two members apiece.

In the ensuing weeks, while committees busied themselves with various parts of the document that was beginning to take shape, the convention as a whole effected another compromise, this one having to do with the legislative power to impose tariffs and regulate commerce. The men from some of the Southern states feared that this power might be used for levying export duties on their crops, interfering with the slave trade, and making commercial agreements (as in the recent Jay-Gardoqui treaty) which would sacrifice the interests of rice and tobacco growers. The South Carolinians proposed that a two-thirds vote in the legislature be required not only to approve commercial treaties but also to pass commercial laws. Though not accepting that proposal, the convention made concessions by forbidding the legislature to levy a tax on exports, to put a duty of more than ten dollars a head on imported slaves, or to prohibit slave importations until twenty years had elapsed.

Some differences of opinion the convention was unable to harmonize, and it disposed of them by evasion or omission. One of these concerned the question whether the new courts or some special agency should be empowered to review legislative acts and set them aside. The "council of revision," a part of the original Virginia Plan, was dropped, and no provision was added to confer the power of judicial review explicitly upon the courts.

The Constitution, as it finally took form at the end of summer in 1787, though an outgrowth of the Virginia Plan, was in some respects so different that Randolph himself refused to sign it. Yet it differed even more from the New Jersey Plan, and several refused on that account to give it their approval. Indeed, the completed document did not entirely satisfy any of the delegates. Nevertheless, thirty-nine of them affixed their signatures to it, doubtless with much the same feeling that Franklin expressed. "Thus I consent, Sir, to this Constitution," he said, *"because I expect no better, and because I am not sure that it is not the best."*

THE CONSTITUTION OF 1787

Madison, who was responsible for most of the actual drafting, observed that it was, "in strictness, neither a national nor a federal Constitution, but a composition of both."

Certainly it possessed some strongly national features. The Constitution and all laws and treaties made under it were to be the "supreme law" of the land, regardless of anything to the contrary in the constitution or laws of any state. Broad powers were granted to the central government, including the congressional powers of taxation, regulation of commerce, control of money, and the passage of laws "necessary and proper" for carrying out its specific powers. At the same time, the states were deprived of a number of the powers — such as the issuance of money and the passage of laws "impairing the obligation of contracts," for example, laws postponing the payment of debts — which they had been free to exercise under the Articles of Confederation. Now all state officials were to be required to take an oath of allegiance to the Constitution, and the state militias were to be made available, upon call, for enforcing the new "supreme law." Nowhere were the former claims of the states to individual sovereignty recognized. Gone was the stipulation of the Articles that "each State shall retain every power, jurisdiction, and right not *expressly* delegated to the United States in Congress assembled." Lacking was any bill of rights to limit the central government as the state bills limited the state governments.

On the other hand, the Constitution was federal in setting up a government that presupposed the existence of separate states and left wide powers to them. For instance, the states were to be represented as separate and equal entities in one of the two branches of the new legislature.

Within the allotted sphere of its powers, the new government was authorized to act directly upon the people of the United States. It would not have to act upon them solely through the member states, as the previous Confederation government, and indeed all confederation governments of the past, had done. Here, then, was something new and unique, something for which old terms were hardly adequate. It was a combination of two kinds of government, state and central, with each of them intended to be supreme within its respective sphere.

Next to the distinctive federal arrangement (the "division of powers"), the most striking feature of the new system was the complex organization and operation of the central government itself, with its checks and balances among the legislative, executive, and judicial branches (the "separation of powers"). There was the new Congress, with its two chambers, the Senate and the House of Representatives, each of the two with members elected in a different way and for different terms, and each checking the other, since both must agree before any law could be passed. There was the single executive, the President, who was to be chosen in a roundabout way, by special electors who themselves were to be chosen in whatever way the separate states might designate. The electors, meeting in isolated groups, state by state, were to cast their ballots as they saw fit, and if any man should receive a majority of the electoral votes, he would be President. It was assumed, however, that usually no man would get a majority, and then the final selection among the leading candidates would be up to the House of Representatives. Thus the election of a President would be far removed from the mass of the people. Yet the President, in addition to other powers, would have the power of vetoing acts of Congress. There was also the Supreme Court, which was still further removed from the ordinary voters since the President with the consent of the Senate was to appoint the judges for life. And while nothing was said in the Constitution itself about the power of reviewing and disallowing presidential actions or congressional acts, the Supreme Court could be expected to have some authority over them.

This complicated structure resulted from accident – that is, from the compromising of contradictory views – as much as from deliberate planning. Nevertheless, the complexity was such as to give the Founding Fathers hope that no single group or combination of groups in the country could ever gain absolute and unchecked power. A government so divided against itself ought to frustrate tyranny from whatever source. When the Founding Fathers spoke of tyranny, they usually had in mind the rule of mobs and demagogues – the threat of such leaders as Daniel Shays.

Adoption and Adaptation

Since the delegates at Philadelphia had exceeded their instructions from Congress and the states, they had reason to doubt whether the Constitution would ever be ratified if they followed the procedures laid down in the Articles of Confederation, which required *all* of the state *legislatures* to approve alterations in the form of the government. So the convention changed the rules, specifying in the Constitution that the new government should go into effect among the ratifying states when only *nine* of the thirteen had ratified, and recommending to Congress that the Constitution be submitted to specially called state *conventions* rather than to the legislatures of the states.

"FEDERALISTS," "ANTIFEDERALISTS"

The Congress in New York, completely overshadowed by the convention in Philadelphia, accepted the latter's work and submitted it to the states for their approval or disapproval. The state legislatures, again with the exception of Rhode Island, arranged for the election of delegates to ratifying conventions, and sooner or later each of these conventions got down to business. Meanwhile, from the fall of 1787 to the summer of 1788, the merits and demerits of the new Constitution were debated in the legislatures, in mass meetings, and in the columns of newspapers, as well as in the convention halls. For the most part the struggle, though intense, was peaceful and deliberative, yet the opposing factions sometimes came to blows, and death and injury resulted in at least one place (Albany, New York).

Despite the reference of its preamble to "We the people," the Constitution was not in literal fact ordained and established by the whole people of the United States. As is shown by the elections for the state conventions, something like three-fourths of the adult white males in the country as a whole failed to vote for delegates, mainly because of indifference, and therefore exercised no real influence upon the outcome. Of those who did vote, a large majority favored ratification. The voters, however, did not have a clear-cut choice between a "federal" and a "national" government. The issues were confused, both because of the "mixed" character of the Constitution itself and because of the

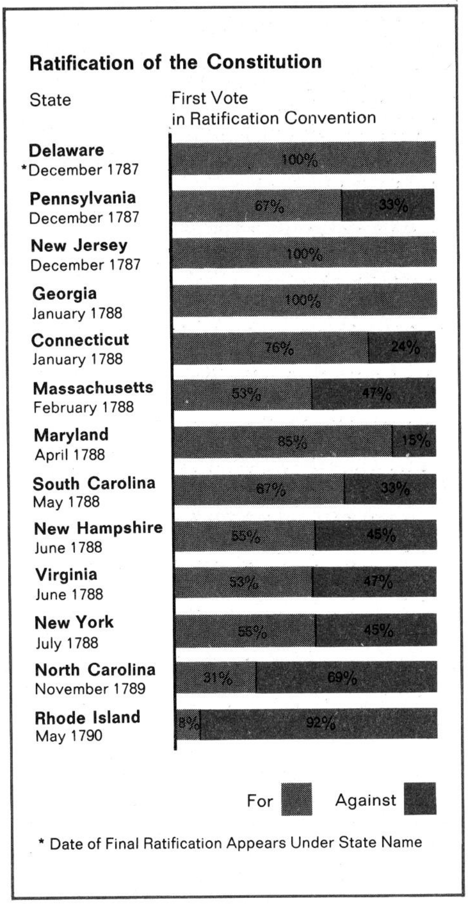
Ratification of the Constitution
State
First Vote in Ratification Convention
Delaware
*December 1787
100%
Pennsylvania
December 1787
67%
33%
New Jersey
December 1787
100%
Georgia
January 1788
100%
Connecticut
January 1788
76%
24%
Massachusetts
February 1788
53%
47%
Maryland
April 1788
85%
15%
South Carolina
May 1788
67%
33%
New Hampshire
June 1788
55%
45%
Virginia
June 1788
53%
47%
New York
July 1788
55%
45%
North Carolina
November 1789
31%
69%
Rhode Island
May 1790
8%
92%
For
Against
* Date of Final Ratification Appears Under State Name

The Constitution was promptly and overwhelmingly approved by the ratifying conventions of some of the smaller states, such as Delaware, New Jersey, and Georgia. But it barely got by in the large states of Massachusetts, Virginia, and New York. It was approved by North Carolina and Rhode Island only after it had already gone into effect. The conventions in these two states waited until they were sure a bill of rights would be added.

---

terminology that was employed in the ratification debates. Since the idea of a strongly national government was thought to be unpopular, the advocates of the new Constitution chose to call themselves "Federalists" and to call their opponents "Antifederalists." These misnomers stuck, despite the insistence of opponents of ratification that they were "Federal Republicans," the true federalists of the time.

The friends of the Constitution had a number of advantages. They possessed a positive program and an appealing name, while the Antifederalists by that very word were made to stand for nothing constructive, for chaos itself. The Federalists were the better-organized group and had the weight of fame and superior leadership on their side. They could point to the support of the two most eminent men in America, Franklin and Washington. And Washington himself declared that the choice lay between the Constitution and disunion. The Federalists also included some of the most profound political philosophers of any period or place in Hamilton, Madison, and Jay, who under the joint pseudonym "Publius" wrote a long series of newspaper essays expounding the meaning and virtues of the Constitution. Afterwards published in book form as *The Federalist,* these papers have been considered as the most authoritative of all constitutional commentaries and, indeed, as one of the greatest of all treatises on political science.

The opponents of ratification produced no comparable set of Antifederalist papers, yet these men too were able and sincere and they made a vigorous case for themselves in their own speeches and newspaper propaganda. Necessarily, the Antifederalists resorted mainly to negative argument. The Constitution, they protested, was illegal—as indeed it was if judged by the Articles of Confederation, the existing fundamental law. The new government would increase taxes, obliterate the states, wield dictatorial powers, favor the "well-born" over the common people, and put an end to individual liberty, the Antifederalists added. Of all their specific criticisms the most compelling was this: the Constitution lacked a bill of rights.

For all the efforts of the Antifederalists, ratification proceeded during the winter of 1787–1788. Delaware, the first to act, did so unanimously, as did two others of the smallest states, New Jersey and Georgia. In the large states of Pennsylvania and Massachusetts the Antifederalists put up a determined struggle but lost in the final vote. By June 1788, when the New Hampshire convention at last made up its mind, nine of the states had ratified and thus had made it possible for the Constitution to go into effect among themselves.

A new government could hardly hope to succeed, however, without the participation of Virginia and New York, whose conventions remained closely divided. Before the end of the month Virginia and then New York consented to the Constitution by rather narrow votes. The New York convention yielded to expediency— even some of the most staunchly Antifederalist delegates feared that the state's commercial interests would suffer if, once the other states had got together under the "New Roof," New York were to remain outside. Massachusetts, Virginia, and New York all ratified on the assumption, though not on the express condition, that certain desired amendments would be added to the Constitution, above all a bill of rights. Deciding to wait and see what became of these hopes for amendment, the North Carolina convention adjourned without taking action. Rhode Island, for the time being, did not even call a convention to consider ratification.

FILLING IN THE GAPS

When the first elections under the Constitution were held, in the early months of 1789, the results showed that the new government was to be in the hands of its friends. Few if any of the newly elected congressmen and senators had been extreme Antifederalists; almost all had favored ratification, and many had served as delegates to the Philadelphia convention. The President-elect, George Washington, had presided at the convention; many who had favored ratification did so because they expected him to preside over the new government also. He received the votes of all the presidential electors whom the states, either by legislative action or by popular election, had named. John Adams, a firm Federalist, though not a member of the

Ratification Banquet, New York
The New York convention ratified the Constitution on July 26, 1788. Three days earlier, confident that the convention was going to act favorably, six thousand citizens of New York City gathered to celebrate. After parades, they took their places in a gigantic pavilion to feast and to listen to speeches. From a contemporary drawing. (Courtesy of the New-York Historical Society, New York City)

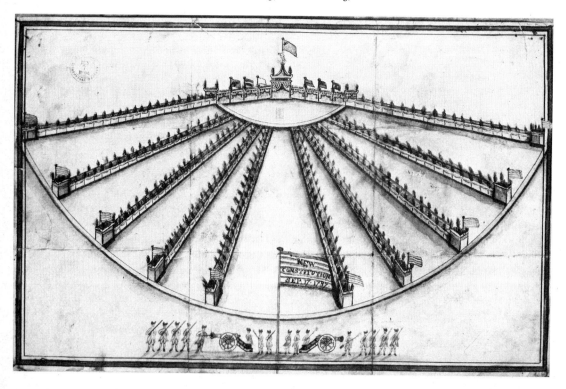

convention, received the next highest number of electoral votes and hence was to be Vice President.

For the time being the seat of government was to continue to be the city of New York, and thus the sensibilities of the geographical sections were neatly balanced, the President being from the South, the Vice President from New England, and the capital in one of the middle states. Congressmen were so slow to reach New York that not until April was a quorum on hand to make an official count of the electoral vote and send a messenger to notify General Washington of his election. After a journey from Mount Vernon marked by elaborate celebrations along the way, Washington was inaugurated on April 30.

The responsibilities facing the first President and the first Congress were in some ways greater than those facing any President or Congress to follow. Though these men of 1789 had the Constitution as a guide, that document provided only a general plan that had yet to be applied to specific situations as they arose. It left many questions unanswered. What, for example, should be the rules of the two houses for the conduct of their business? What code of etiquette should govern the relations between the President on the one hand and Congress and the people on the other? Should he have some high-sounding title, such as "His Highness the President of the United States and Protector of Their Liberties"? (John Adams, who would probably have been horrified at the thought of a later Vice President being called "The Veep," thought both he and the President ought to have dignified forms of address.) What was the true meaning of various ambiguous phrases in the Constitution? In answering these and other questions, Washington and his colleagues knew they were setting precedents that, in many cases, would give lasting direction to the development of the Constitution in actual practice.

By filling certain gaps in the Constitution, the first Congress served almost as a continuation of the constitutional convention. The work of the convention had been incomplete in various respects, especially in that it had omitted a bill of rights. Dozens of amendments intended to make up for this lack had been proposed in the state ratifying conventions, and Congress now undertook the task of sorting these, reduc-

ing them to a manageable number, and sending them to the states for ratification. Of the twelve sent out, ten were ratified, and these took effect in 1791. The first nine of them limited Congress by forbidding it to infringe upon certain basic rights, such as freedom of religion, of speech, and of the press, immunity from arbitrary arrest, and trial by jury. The Tenth Amendment, reserving to the states all powers except those specifically withheld from them or delegated to the federal government, bolstered state rights and changed the emphasis of the Constitution from nationalism to federalism.

In regard to the structure of the federal courts, the Constitution had only this to say: "The judicial power of the United States shall be vested in one Supreme Court, and in such inferior courts as the Congress may from time to time ordain and establish." Thus the convention had left up to Congress the number of Supreme Court judges to be appointed and the kinds of lower courts to be organized. In the Judiciary Act of 1789 Congress provided for a Supreme Court of six members, with one chief justice and five associate justices; for thirteen district courts with one judge apiece; and for three circuit courts, each to consist of one of the district judges sitting with two of the Supreme Court justices. In the same act Congress gave the Supreme Court the power to make the final decision in cases involving the constitutionality of state laws. If the Constitution was in fact to be the "supreme law of the land," the various state courts could not be left to decide for themselves whether the state legislatures were violating that supreme law.

As for executive departments, the Constitution referred indirectly to them but did not specify what or how many they should be. The first Congress created three such departments—state, treasury, and war—and also the offices of attorney general and postmaster general.

In appointing department heads and other high officials, President Washington selected men who were qualified by character and experience, who were well disposed toward the Constitution (no Antifederalists) and who as a group would provide a balanced representation of the different sections of the country. To the office of secretary of the treasury he appointed Alexander Hamilton of New York, who had taken the lead in calling the constitutional convention and who, though only thirty-two, was an expert in public finance. For secretary of war he chose the Massachusetts Federalist, General Henry Knox. As attorney general he named Edmund Randolph of Virginia, sponsor of the plan upon which the Constitution had been based. He picked as secretary of state another Virginian, Thomas Jefferson, who had not opposed the Constitution though he had had nothing to do with its framing or adoption, having been away from the country as minister to France.

From time to time Washington called upon these four men for advice, usually as individuals. They did not form a cabinet in the sense of a group of presidential counselors holding regular meetings (the cabinet in this sense began to develop during the presidency of Jefferson).

When Washington took office he supposed, as did many others, that the Senate would act for certain purposes as an advisory council, since according to the Constitution the Senate was to give its advice and consent for the appointment of high officials and for the ratification of treaties. With only twenty-two members in the beginning, the Senate was small enough so that Washington could expect to consult personally with it. He changed his mind, however, after taking a treaty draft to the senators for their advice. They demanded that he leave the document for them to inspect and change at their leisure, and he refused, resolving never again to submit a treaty to the senators until its negotiation had been completed. Thus he set a precedent in treaty making which for the most part his successors have followed.

Hamilton Against Jefferson

During George Washington's first term he and his followers infused vigor into the government—the *national* government, as he always called it. As President, he thought it his duty to see that the laws of Congress, if constitutional, were faithfully carried out. A man of strong will, he was the master of his own administration, but (unlike later Presidents such as Andrew Jackson and Franklin D. Roosevelt) he did not conceive of himself as a popular leader who should find out the will of the people and then see that Congress enacted it into law. One of his department heads, Secretary of the Treasury Hamilton, provided the legislative leadership that Washington himself lacked. Hamilton exerted a greater positive influence than anyone else upon both domestic and foreign policies during Washington's presidency, continuing to be influential even after his resignation in 1794.

HAMILTON'S FINANCIAL PLANS

Of all the leading men of his time, Hamilton was one of the most aristocratic in his personal tastes and in his political philosophy. He distrusted the common people. An admirer of the British political system, with its rule by King

and upper classes, he wished to adapt its principles as closely as he could to government in the United States. What the country most needed, he thought, was order and stability; the people already had enough liberty, indeed too much of it. He thought the new government could be strengthened and made to succeed if the support of the wealthy men of the country could be brought to it. And, believing that all men were motivated by self-interest, he assumed that the way to gain the support of the wealthy was to give them a stake in the success of the new government. He therefore planned a program of legislation that, among other things, was intended to cause the propertied classes to look to the federal government for profitable investments and for the protection and promotion of their property interests.

If men of means were to have faith in the government, then it must keep faith with them by paying its debts and establishing its credit on a sound basis. Therefore, first of all, Hamilton proposed that the existing public debt be "funded," or in other words that the miscellaneous, uncertain, depreciated certificates of indebtedness that the old Congress had issued during and since the Revolution be called in and exchanged for uniform, interest-bearing bonds, payable at definite dates. Next he recommended that the Revolutionary state debts be "assumed" or taken over by the United States, his object being to cause the state as well as the federal bondholders to look to the central government for eventual payment. His plan was not to pay off and thus eliminate the debt, either state or federal, but just the opposite: to create a large and permanent public debt, new bonds being issued as old ones were paid off.

Hamilton also planned the establishment of a national bank. At the time, there were only a few banks in the country, located in Boston, Philadelphia, and New York. A new, national bank would serve several purposes. It would aid business by providing loans and currency — in the form of bank notes, which in those days were used instead of checks. It would aid the government by making a safe place available for the deposit of federal funds, by facilitating the collection of taxes and the disbursement of the government's expenditures, and by keeping up the price of government bonds through judicious bond purchases. The kind of institution that Hamilton had in mind was to be "national" in the sense that it was to be chartered by the federal government, was to have a monopoly of the government's own banking business, and was to be government-controlled to some degree, one-fifth of the directors being appointed by the government.

The funding and assumption of the debts, together with the payment of regular interest on them, would cost a great deal of money, and so Hamilton had to find adequate sources of revenue. He thought the government should depend mainly upon two kinds of taxes (in addition to the receipts to be anticipated from the sales of public land). One of these was an excise to be paid by distillers of alcoholic liquors. This tax would hit most heavily the whiskey distillers of the back country, especially in Pennsylvania, Virginia, and North Carolina. These were small farmers who converted part of their corn and rye crop into whiskey, so as to have a concentrated and valuable product that they could conveniently take to market by horseback or muleback over poor mountain roads.

The other tax upon which Hamilton relied was the tariff on imports. Such a tax would not only raise a revenue, but also protect and encourage American manufactures by raising the price of competing manufactured goods brought in from abroad. In the old Articles of Confederation, according to its defenders as well as its critics, the worst defect had been Congress' lack of power to levy customs duties. One of the first acts of the new Congress, in 1789, was the passage of a tariff law designed to foster industries while raising a revenue, but the average level of duties under this law was extremely low. Hamilton advocated a higher and more decidedly protective tariff. In his Report on Manufactures he glowingly set forth the advantages, as he saw them, of stimulating the growth of industry in the United States. Factories, he said, would make the nation more nearly self-sufficient in wartime, would increase prosperity by creating a home market for the produce of the farms, and would make possible the fuller utilization of all kinds of labor, including the labor of women and children, even those (to quote Hamilton himself) of "tender years."

ENACTING THE PROGRAM

Between 1789 and 1792 Hamilton succeeded in persuading Congress to pass the necessary laws for erecting his financial system — but only after a bitter struggle with a rising opposition group.

As for the funding of the public debt, very few of the congressmen objected to the plan itself, for they agreed with Hamilton that the government must make its credit good. Many of them disagreed, however, with his proposal to fund the debt *at par*, that is, to exchange new bonds for old certificates of indebtedness on a dollar-for-dollar basis. These old certificates had been issued to merchants and farmers in payment for war supplies during the Revolution, or to officers and soldiers of the Revolutionary army in payment for their services. Many of these original holders had been forced to sell at a sacrifice during the hard times of the 1780s, to speculators who bought up the securities at a fraction of their face value.

Admitting that the government should arrange to pay every cent it owed, to *whom* should it arrange to pay? Many congressmen believed that the original holders deserved some consideration, and James Madison, now a representative from Virginia, argued for a plan by which the new bonds would be divided

Constitutionality of the Bank: Jefferson

The incorporation of a bank, and the powers assumed by this bill, have not, in my opinion, been delegated to the United States by the Constitution.

I. They are not among the powers specially enumerated. . . .

II. Nor are they within either of the general phrases, which are the two following:—

1. "To lay taxes to provide for the general welfare of the United States." . . . They [Congress] are not to do anything they please, to provide for the general welfare, but only to lay taxes for that purpose. . . . It was intended to lace them up straitly within the enumerated powers, and those without which, as means, these powers could not be carried into effect. . . .

2. The second general phrase is, "to make all laws necessary and proper for carrying into execution the enumerated powers." But they can all be carried into execution without a bank. A bank, therefore, is not necessary, and consequently not authorized by this phrase.

It has been much urged that a bank will give great facility or convenience in the collection of taxes. Suppose this were true; yet the Constitution allows only the means which are "necessary," not those which are merely "convenient," for effecting the enumerated powers.

---

between the original holders and the later purchasers. But the friends of Hamilton insisted that such a plan was impracticable and that the honor of the government required a literal fulfillment of its earlier promises to pay. Congress finally passed the funding bill in the form that Hamilton desired.

His assumption bill ran into even greater difficulty. Its opponents had a very good case, for if the federal government took over the state debts, the people of one state would have to pay federal taxes for servicing the debts of other states, and some of these debts, such as that of Massachusetts, were much larger than others, such as that of Virginia. Naturally, Virginians did not think it fair for them to have to pay a share of the large Massachusetts debt, and their representatives in Congress balked at the assumption bill.

Finally the bill got the support of some of them and so managed to pass, but only because of a logrolling deal. The Virginians wanted the national capital to be permanently located near them in the South. After Jefferson's return from France, Hamilton appealed to him, and Jefferson held a dinner at which arrangements were made to barter Virginia votes for the assumption bill in return for Northern votes for a Southern location of the capital. In 1790 the

capital was changed back to Philadelphia for a ten-year period, and after that a new capital city was to be built on the banks of the Potomac River, on land to be selected by Washington himself.

When Hamilton's bank bill was introduced into Congress, Madison and others opposed it on the grounds that is was unconstitutional, and though a majority voted for it, President Washington himself had his doubts. He therefore asked his official advisers for written opinions on the subject. In Hamilton's opinion the establishment of a bank was a fitting exercise of the powers of Congress, though the Constitution nowhere explicitly gave Congress the right. But Jefferson, with the support of his fellow Virginian, Randolph, argued that the Constitution should be construed in a strict sense and that Congress should be allowed no powers not clearly given to it. Washington found Hamilton's case more convincing, and he signed the bank bill when it came to him. The Bank of the United States began operations in 1791, under a charter that granted it the right to continue in business for twenty years.

Hamilton also had his way with the excise tax, though after its passage the law was altered somewhat, in response to protests from farmers, so as to bear less heavily on the

Constitutionality of the Bank: Hamilton

It is conceded that implied powers *are to be considered as delegated equally with* express ones. *Then it follows, that as a power of erecting a corporation may as well be* implied *as any other thing, it may as well be* employed *as an* instrument *or* mean *of carrying into execution any of the specified powers, as any other* instrument *or* mean *whatever.* . . . .

It is objected that none but necessary and proper means are to be employed; and the Secretary of State maintains that no means are to be considered as necessary *but those without which the grant of the power would be* nugatory. . . .

It is certain that neither the grammatical nor popular sense of the term requires that construction. According to both, necessary *often means no more than* needful, requisite, incidental, useful, *or* conducive to. . . .

If the end be clearly comprehended within any of the specified powers, and if the measure have an obvious relation to that end, and is not forbidden by any particular provision of the Constitution, it may safely be deemed to come within the compass of the national authority. . . .

A bank has a natural relation to the power of collecting taxes—to that of regulating trade—to that of providing for the common defence. . . . *[Therefore] the incorporation of a bank is a constitutional measure.* . . .

---

smaller distillers. He did not succeed in getting from Congress a tariff as highly protective as he had hoped for, yet the tariff law of 1792 did raise the rates somewhat.

Once enacted, Hamilton's program worked as he had intended. The public credit quickly was restored; the bonds of the United States were soon selling at home and abroad at prices even above their par value.

At the same time, speculators got rich and corruption was rife. Many congressmen had bought up large amounts of the old certificates of indebtedness, and these men profited by their own legislation in funding the debt at par. Directly or indirectly, properly or improperly, thousands of wealthy merchants in the seaports also gained from the Hamilton program.

The mass of the people—the farmers scattered over the countryside—profited much less. While these people shared some of the benefit of national strength and prosperity, they bore most of the burden of paying for it. The financial program required taxes, and these came mostly from the farmers, who had to pay not only land taxes to their state governments but also the excise and, indirectly, the tariff to the federal government. The feeling grew that the Washington administration was not treating all the people fairly, and out of this feeling an organized political opposition arose.

RISE OF POLITICAL PARTIES

The Constitution made no reference to political parties, and the Founding Fathers, George Washington in particular, believed that such organizations were evil and should be avoided. Yet parties soon arose from a division between the followers of Hamilton and those of Madison and Jefferson.

Jefferson and Madison were such close collaborators that it is sometimes difficult to separate the contributions of the two. To describe the political philosophy of one is, in the main, to describe the political philosophy of both. Jefferson, himself a farmer, believed that farmers were God's chosen people and that an ideal republic would consist of sturdy citizens each tilling his own soil. Though an aristocrat by birth, his mother belonging to one of the first families of Virginia, the Randolphs, he had faith in the good intentions of such farmer-citizens and thought that, if properly educated, they could be trusted to govern themselves through the election of able and qualified men. But, in the 1790s, he feared city

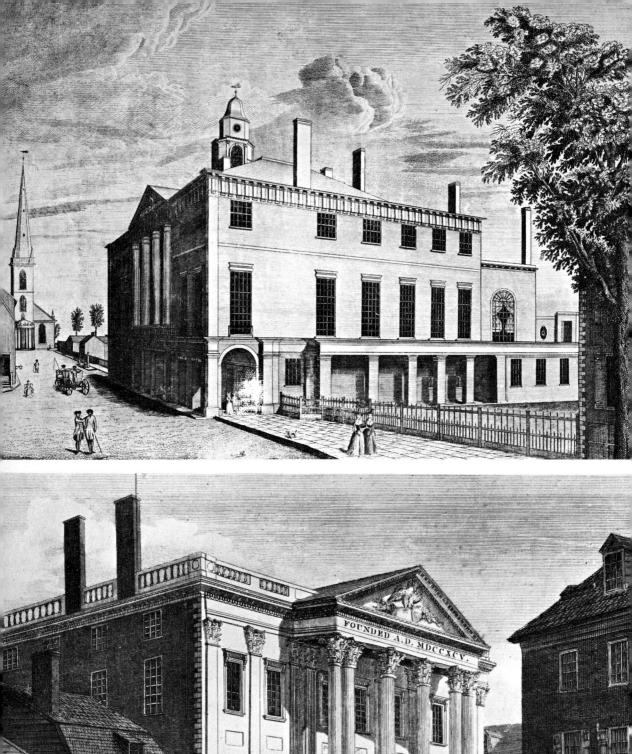

FOUNDED A.D. MDCCXCV.

Federal Hall, New York
*Here George Washington was inaugurated as President on April 30, 1789, taking
his oath of office on the balcony that overlooks Wall Street. The building was
originally constructed as the City Hall in 1699–1700. It was extensively
remodeled and enlarged after the Revolution and was renamed Federal Hall
when it served as the temporary capitol of the United States, in 1789–1790. At the
end of Wall Street is the Gothic-styled Trinity Church (Anglican). It was built in
1688, destroyed in a great fire following the British occupation of the city in 1776,
and rebuilt in 1788. Behind the church was a meadow sloping down to the
Hudson River. (Top left)*

The First Bank of the United States
*The headquarters of the Bank of the United States, which was founded through
Alexander Hamilton's efforts, were in Philadelphia. The bank building on Third
Street was completed in 1795. It is a good example of Early Republican architecture,
with its rather boxlike shape, its balustrade along the roof edge, its quoins at the
angle of the walls, and its Roman pediment and columns in front. From a drawing and
engraving by W. Birch & Son of Philadelphia, published in 1799. (Bottom left)*

---

mobs as "sores upon the body politic." He then
opposed the development of extensive manufactures because they would lead to the growth
of cities packed with propertyless workers.
While Hamilton emphasized the need for order
and stability, Jefferson stressed the importance
of individual freedom.

As a member of President Washington's
official circle, Jefferson differed so strongly
with his colleague Hamilton on particular issues such as the Bank that he soon offered to
resign. But Washington preferred to keep both
men in office to preserve national unity if possible. His became a coalition government, though
he himself agreed more often with Hamilton
than with Jefferson. The two secretaries continued to work against each other, and each
began to organize a following in Congress and
in the country at large. Hamilton's followers
came to be known as Federalists, Jefferson's
as Republicans.

The Federalists of the 1790s were not entirely the same men as the Federalists of 1787–
1788 who had campaigned for the ratification of
the Constitution, nor were the Republicans
exactly the same men as the old Antifederalists.
There were numerous exceptions, the most
noteworthy being Madison, who had played a
leading role at the constitutional convention
and in the ratification effort, then had broken
with Hamilton on the questions of funding and
the Bank, and had become one of the founders
of the Republican party. Both of the parties
contained members in all sections of the coun-

try, but the Federalists were most numerous in
the commercial centers of the Northeast,
though also strong in such Southern seaports
as Charleston, while the Republicans were
most numerous in the rural areas of the South
and the West.

Unlike the old Antifederalists, the new
Republicans did not denounce the Constitution. On the contrary, they professed to be its
special friends and accused their opponents of
violating it.

Republicans and Federalists differed in
their social philosophies as well as in their economic interests and their constitutional views.
Their differences in social outlook are seen in
their reactions to the progress of the revolution
in France. When that revolution first began, as
a rather mild movement in favor of constitutional monarchy and the rights of man, practically all Americans hailed it as a step in the
right direction. But when the revolution went
to radical extremes, with attacks on organized
religion, the overthrow of the monarchy, and
eventually the guillotining of the King and
Queen, Americans adoped different views
about the events in France, the Federalists
denouncing and the Republicans applauding
them. Indeed, many of the Republicans imitat-
ed the French radicals (the Jacobins) by cutting their hair short, wearing pantaloons, and
addressing one another as "Citizen" Smith or
"Citizeness" Jones. Thus, for a time, it was
possible to tell a man's party by his manners
and appearance, for the Federalists kept the

old-fashioned long hair or powdered wig, knee breeches, and traditional etiquette of the gentleman. Republicans accused the Federalists of being aristocratic and even "monarchical." Federalists referred to the Republicans, in horrified tones, as "Jacobins" and as "Jacobinical rabble"—terms that then had much the same implication as the word "communist" was to have many years later.

The two parties had different leanings in foreign affairs. Both were pro-American, but Jefferson and the Republicans believed that American interests would best be served by maintaining close relations with France, while Hamilton and the Federalists believed that friendship with Great Britain was essential for the success of the United States.

When the time came for the election of 1792, the Republicans had no candidate to put up against Washington. Jefferson as well as Hamilton urged him to run for a second term, and the President consented for the good of the country, though he would have preferred to retire to Mount Vernon.

Asserting National Sovereignty

Under the Federalists the new government disposed of questions that the old government of the Confederation had scarcely begun to deal with, questions not only of public finance but also of the frontier and diplomacy.

SECURING THE FRONTIER

During the early 1790s, while the American people began to be divided between two political parties, they became more strongly united than ever in their loyalty to the government itself. Previously, during the 1780s, the old Congress had been powerless to tie the outlying parts of the country firmly to the United States, as farmers in western Massachusetts rose in revolt and settlers in Vermont, Kentucky, and Tennessee toyed with the idea of separating these territories from the Union. Now, however, the Washington administration made the power of the federal government felt even on the farthest reaches of the frontier.

The federal authority was challenged when, in 1794, the farmers of western Pennsylvania refused to pay the whiskey excise and terrorized the would-be tax collectors, much as the colonists had done throughout America at the time of the Stamp Act. The so-called Whiskey Rebellion was not left to the authorities of Pennsylvania as Shays' Rebellion had been left to the authorities of Massachusetts. Urged on by Hamilton, Washington took drastic steps. Calling out the militia of three states, he raised an army of nearly 15,000, a larger force than he had commanded against the British during most of the Revolution, and he personally accompanied this army as far as the town of Bedford. At the approach of the militiamen, the farmers around Pittsburgh, where the rebellion centered, either ran for cover or stayed home and professed to be law-abiding citizens. The rebellion quickly collapsed.

While the whiskey rebels were intimidated into obedience, other frontiersmen were made loyal to the government by its acceptance of new states as members of the Union. First to be admitted were two of the original thirteen, North Carolina (1789) and Rhode Island (1790), both of which had ratified the Constitution when they found that a bill of rights was definitely to be added and that they could not conveniently go on as independent commonwealths. Then Vermont, which had had its own state government since the Revolution, was accepted as the fourteenth state (1791) after New York and New Hampshire finally agreed to give up their claims to sovereignty over the Green Mountain country. Next came Kentucky (1792) with the consent of Virginia, which previously had governed the Kentucky counties as its own. After North Carolina finally ceded its Western lands to the Union, these were given a territorial government similar to that of the Northwest Territory and after six years became the state of Tennessee (1796). With the admission of these frontier states, the schemes for separating Vermont, Kentucky, and Tennessee from the Union soon came to an end.

In the more remote areas of the Northwest and the Southwest, meanwhile, the government had to contend with the Indians and their foreign allies, British and Spanish, in order to get a firm grasp upon all the territory belonging to the United States. The Indians of the Southwest—Cherokees, Creeks, Choctaws, and Chickasaws—were led by the colorful and vengeful Alexander McGillivray, a half-breed Creek chieftain who had fought as a Tory during the Revolution and who continued to hate Americans. In his efforts to resist the advance of American frontiersmen into the lower Mississippi Valley, McGillivray received the support and encouragement of Spain. In 1790 President Washington tried to buy peace with the Southwestern Indians by inviting McGillivray to New York and agreeing to pay him $100,000. Despite McGillivray's treaty with the United States, the Indians continued to accept subsidies from the Spaniards and to raid American settlements along the border. At last, in 1793–1794, the Tennesseans went on the warpath themselves, their militia invading the Indian country and chastising several of the tribes. Thus the Southwestern frontier was made safe for the time being.

In the Northwest the government pursued a policy of force against the Indians, even at some risk of becoming involved in hostilities with their protector and ally, Great Britain. Two expeditions failed before a third one finally succeeded in the conquest of the Ohio country. Washington gave the frontier command to General Wayne, who, despite his nickname "Mad Anthony," was a careful planner as well as a dashing soldier. With over 4,000 men, including a large contingent of Kentucky sharpshooters, Wayne moved cautiously toward the Maumee River, building forts as he went. The British officials in Canada, who were providing the Indians with supplies, themselves ordered the construction of a fort about twenty miles from the mouth of the river, well within the boundary of the United States. Near the British fort, at a place where trees had been blown over by a windstorm, Wayne in the summer of 1794 met and decisively defeated the Indians in the Battle of Fallen Timbers, the British garrison prudently keeping out of the fight. Next summer the Indians agreed in the Treaty of Greenville to abandon to the white men most of what afterward became the state of Ohio.

Before the government could be sure of its hold upon the border areas, it had to bring to terms the foreign powers that persisted in exerting influence there—Great Britain and Spain. In its diplomacy the Washington administration, by taking advantage of the opportunities that arose from the accidents of international politics, managed to reassert American independence and redeem the West.

MAINTAINING NEUTRALITY

When Washington became President, Great Britain had not yet sent a minister to the United States, though all the other powers of Europe (except Russia) had entered into normal diplomatic relations with the young republic. In Congress Madison and the Republicans argued that Great Britain, in refusing to make a commercial treaty with the United States, was waging a kind of economic warfare against this country, and that the United States should retaliate by imposing special customs duties and harbor dues, in excess of the regular rates, upon her goods and ships. Though this legislation did not pass, the threat of it induced the British government finally, in 1791, to dispatch a regular minister to America.

A new crisis in foreign affairs faced the Washington administration when the French revolutionary government, after guillotining King Louis XVI, went to war in 1793 with Great Britain and her allies. Should the United States recognize the radical government of France by accepting a diplomatic representative from it? Was the United States obligated by the alliance of 1778 to go to war on the side of France? These questions Washington put to his official advisers, and both Hamilton and Jefferson recommended a policy of neutrality, though they presented quite different arguments for it. Washington decided to recognize the French government and to issue a proclamation announcing the determination of the United States to remain at peace. The proclamation (1793), though it did not mention the word "neutrality," was generally interpreted as a neutrality statement, which it actually was. Next year Congress passed a Neutrality Act, forbidding American citizens to participate in the war and prohibiting the use of American soil as a base of operations for either side.

The first challenge to American neutrality came from France. Not that the French revolutionaries asked for a declaration of war: they did not, for they supposed that the United States would be of more use to them as a nonbelligerent. Their purposes became apparent when their first minister to this country arrived. Instead of landing at Philadelphia and presenting himself immediately to the President, the youthful and brash Citizen Edmond Genêt disembarked at Charleston. There he made plans for using American ports to outfit French warships, issued letters of marque and reprisal authorizing American shipowners to serve as French privateers, and commissioned the aging George Rogers Clark to undertake an overland expedition against the possessions of Spain, which at the moment was an ally of Great Britain and an enemy of France. In all these steps, Genêt brazenly disregarded Washington's proclamation and flagrantly violated the Neutrality Act. When he finally reached Philadelphia, after being acclaimed by pro-French crowds on a tour through the interior, he got a stony reception from the President. He then assumed that the people were behind him, and he repeatedly appealed to them over the President's head. His conduct not only infuriated Washington and the Federalists but also embarrassed all except the most ardent Francophiles among the Republicans. At last Washington demanded that the French government recall him, but by that time Genêt's party, the Girondins, were out of power in France and the still more extreme Jacobins in control, so it would not have been safe for him to return. Generously the President granted him political asylum in the United States, and he settled down to live to a ripe old age with his American wife on a Long Island farm. Meanwhile the neutrality policy had survived its first great test.

The second challenge, an even greater one, came from Great Britain. Early in 1794 the Royal Navy suddenly seized hundreds of American ships engaged in trade in the French West Indies. The pretext for these seizures was a British interpretation of international law — known as the Rule of 1756 — which held that a trade prohibited in peacetime (as American trade between France and the French overseas possessions had been) could not be legally opened in time of war. At the news of the seizures, the prevalent opinion in the United States became as strongly anti-British as it had recently been anti-French, and the anti-British feeling rose still higher at the report that the Governor-General of Canada had delivered a rousing and warlike speech to the Indians on the northwestern frontier. With peace thus endangered, Hamilton grew concerned, for war would mean an end to imports from England, and most of the revenue for maintaining his financial system came from duties on those imports.

JAY'S TREATY

To Hamilton and to other Federalists it seemed that this was no time for ordinary diplomacy. Jefferson had resigned in 1793 to devote himself to organizing a political opposition, and the State Department was now in the hands of an even more ardently pro-French Virginian, Edmund Randolph. By-passing the State Department, Washington named as a special commissioner to England the staunch New York Federalist, former Secretary for Foreign Affairs under the old Confederation, and current Chief Justice of the Supreme Court, John Jay. Jay was instructed to secure damages for the recent spoliations, withdrawal of British forces from the frontier posts, and a satisfactory commercial treaty, without violating the terms of the existing treaty of amity and commerce with France, signed at the time of the alliance in 1778.

The treaty that Jay negotiated (1794) was a long and complex document, dealing with frontier posts, boundaries, debts, commerce, ship seizures, and neutral rights. It yielded more to Great Britain and obtained less for the United States than Jay had been authorized to give or instructed to get. When the terms were published in the United States, the treaty was denounced more than any treaty before or since, and Jay himself was burned in effigy in various parts of the country. The Republicans were unanimous in decrying it; they said it was a departure from neutrality, favoring Great Britain and unfair to France. Even some of the Federalists were outraged by its terms, those in

Jay's Treaty [1794]

Frontier Posts. "His Majesty will withdraw all his troops and garrisons from all posts and places within the boundary lines assigned by the treaty of peace to the United States."

Boundaries. Joint surveys will be made to locate the United States-Canadian boundary west of the Lake of the Woods and at the northeast, between Maine and New Brunswick.

Debts. The United States "will make full and complete compensation" for uncollectable debts owed by Americans to British creditors.

Commerce. There shall be freedom of commerce and navigation between the United States and Great Britain and the British East Indies. (Article XII, permitting the United States to trade with the British West Indies also, but only in relatively small ships, was stricken out before ratification.)

Ship Seizures. The British government will compensate Americans for ships and cargoes illegally captured in the past, the amount of payment to be determined by arbitration.

Neutral Rights. American ships carrying enemy (French) property, when captured by the British, shall be taken to British ports and the enemy property removed. (This was inconsistent with the usual American principle that "free ships make free goods.")

---

the South objecting to its provision for the payment of the pre-Revolutionary debts. Opponents of the treaty went to extraordinary lengths to defeat it in the Senate, and French agents aided them and cheered them on. The American minister to France, James Monroe, and even the Secretary of State, Edmund Randolph, cooperated closely with the French in a desperate attempt to prevent ratification. Nevertheless, after amending the treaty a bit, the Senate gave its consent.

There was much to be said for Jay's Treaty, despite its very real shortcomings. By means of it the United States gained valuable time for continued peaceful development, obtained undisputed sovereignty over all the Northwest, and secured a reasonably satisfactory commercial agreement with the nation whose trade was most important. More than that, the treaty led immediately to a settlement of the worst of the outstanding differences with Spain.

In Madrid the Spanish foreign minister feared that the understanding between Great Britain and the United States might prove a prelude to joint operations between those two countries against Spain's possessions in North America. Spain was about to change sides in the European war, abandoning Great Britain for France, and it was therefore to Spain's interest to appease the United States. The relentless pressure of American frontiersmen advancing toward the Southwest made it doubtful whether Spain could long hold her borderlands in any event. And so, when Thomas Pinckney arrived in Spain as a special negotiator, he had no difficulty in gaining practically everything that the United States had sought from the Spaniards for over a decade. Pinckney's Treaty (1795) recognized the right of Americans to navigate the Mississippi to its mouth and to deposit goods at New Orleans for reloading on ocean-going ships; fixed the northern boundary of Florida where Americans always had insisted it should be, along the thirty-first parallel; and bound the Spanish authorities to prevent the Indians in Florida from raiding across the border.

Thus, before Washington had completed his second term in office, the United States had freed itself from the encroachments of both Great Britain and Spain.

Downfall of the Federalists

After George Washington had left the Presidency, the Federalists overreached themselves in their grasp for power. They faced the dilemma of all rulers in a government that depends upon the will of the people — that is, the dilemma of choosing between governmental strength and individual freedom — and they made their choice in favor of strong government at the expense of popular liberty and popular support. The Federalists never won another presidential election after 1796, yet their main achievements endured and, in one form or another, still endure.

ELECTION OF 1796

As the time approached for the election of 1796, some of the party friends of Washington urged him to run again. Already twice elected without a single vote cast against him in the electoral college, he could be counted upon to hold the Federalist party together and carry it to a third great victory. But Washington, weary of the burdens of the presidential office, disgusted with the partisan abuse that was being heaped upon him, longed to retire to his beloved home, Mount Vernon. Though he did not object to a third term in principle, he did not desire one for himself. To make his determination clear, he composed, with Hamilton's assistance, a long letter to the American people and had it published in a Philadelphia newspaper.

When Washington in this "Farewell Address" referred to the "insidious wiles of foreign influence," he was not writing merely for rhetorical effect. He had certain real evils in mind. Lately he had dismissed the Secretary of State, Edmund Randolph, and had recalled the minister to France, James Monroe, for working hand in hand with the French to defeat Jay's Treaty. The French were still interfering in American politics with the hope of defeating the Federalists in the forthcoming presidential election.

There was no doubt that Jefferson would be the candidate of the Republicans, and he chose as his running mate the New York Republican leader, Aaron Burr. With Washington out of the running, there was some question as to who the Federalist candidate would be. Hamilton, the very personification of Federalism, was not "available" because his forthright views had aroused too many enemies. John Jay was too closely identified with his unpopular treaty, and Thomas Pinckney, though *his* treaty had been enthusiastically received, had the handicap of being a South Carolinian at a time when party leaders thought the next candidate should be a Northerner. John

John Adams
When elected to the Presidency, Adams was almost thirty years younger than the man depicted in this portrait, painted when he was past eighty. The artist was Samuel F. B. Morse. Afterward best known as the inventor of the magnetic telegraph, Morse did not give up painting for invention until he was in his forties. He was born in Massachusetts, the son of Jedidiah Morse, who was America's foremost geographer of the late eighteenth and early nineteenth centuries. The younger Morse graduated from Yale, studied art under Benjamin West and Washington Allston in England, and in 1823 opened a studio in New York. He helped to found and was the first president of the National Academy of Design. (In the Brooklyn Museum Collection)

Adams, who as Vice President was directly associated with none of the Federalist measures, finally got the nomination for President at a caucus of the Federalists in Congress, and Pinckney received the nomination for Vice President.

With Washington stepping aside, the Federalist party became torn by fierce factional rivalries. Hamilton disliked Adams and preferred Pinckney, as did many other Federalists, especially in the South. New Englanders, on the other hand, had no particular liking for Pinckney and feared a plot to make him President instead of Adams. The result was a near disaster for the Federalists. They elected a majority of their presidential electors, despite the electioneering tactics of the French government, whose efforts may have boomeranged and helped the Federalists. But when the electors balloted in the various states, some of the Pinckney men declined to vote for Adams, and a still larger number of the Adams men declined to vote for Pinckney. So Pinckney received fewer votes than Jefferson, and Adams only three more than Jefferson. The next President was to be a Federalist, but the Vice President was to be a Republican!

By virtue of his diplomatic services during the Revolution, his writings as a conservative political philosopher, and his devotion to the public weal as he saw it, "Honest John" Adams ranks as one of the greatest American statesmen. Like most prominent members of the illustrious Adams family afterward, however, he lacked the politician's touch which is essential for successful leadership in a republican society. Even Washington, remote and austere as he sometimes seems to have been, was fairly adept at conciliating factions and maintaining party harmony. Unwisely, the new President chose to continue Washington's department heads in office. Most of them were friends of Hamilton, and they looked to him for advice, though he held no official post.

QUASI-WAR WITH FRANCE

As American relations with Great Britain and Spain improved in consequence of Jay's and Pinckney's treaties, relations with France, now under the government of the Directory, went from bad to worse. Despite the victory of the Federalists in the election of 1796, the leaders of the Directory assumed that France had the sympathy and support of the mass of the American people and could undermine the Adams administration by frustrating it in foreign affairs. Therefore the French, asserting that they were applying the same principles of neutral rights as the United States and Great Britain had adopted in Jay's Treaty, continued to capture American ships on the high seas and, in many cases, to imprison the crews. When Minister Monroe left France after his recall, the French went out of their way to show their affection for him and for the Republican party. When the South Carolina Federalist Charles Cotesworth Pinckney, a brother of Thomas Pinckney, arrived in France to replace Monroe, the Directory considered him *persona non grata* and refused to receive him as the official representative of the United States.

War seemed likely unless the Adams administration could settle the difficulties with France. Some of the President's advisers, in particular his Secretary of State, the stiff-backed New England Francophobe Timothy Pickering, favored war. Others urged a special effort for peace, and even Hamilton approved the idea of appointing commissioners to approach the Directory. Adams, himself a peace man, appointed a bipartisan commission of three: C. C. Pinckney, the recently rejected minister; John Marshall, a Virginia Federalist, afterward famous as the great Chief Justice of the United States; and Elbridge Gerry, a Massachusetts Republican but a personal friend of the President's. In France, in 1797, the three Americans were met by three agents of the Directory's foreign minister, Prince Talleyrand, who had a reputation as the wizard of European diplomacy but who did not understand the psychology of Americans, even though he had lived for a time in the United States. Talleyrand's agents demanded a loan for France and a bribe for French officials before they would deal with Adams' commissioners. The response of the commissioners was summed up in Pinckney's laconic words: "No! No! Not a sixpence!"

When Adams received the commissioners' report, he sent a message to Congress in which he urged readiness for war, denounced the French for their insulting treatment of the United States, and vowed he would not appoint

The X Y Z Affair
*In this American cartoon of 1799, the five-man directory of France is represented by
the five-headed creature in the center. He is demanding a bribe from the American
commissioners, John Marshall, C. C. Pinckney, and Elbridge Gerry. Actually the
hint of a money payment had come from three of the French foreign minister
Talleyrand's agents, whom President Adams later designated as Messrs "X," "Y,"
and "Z." (The Henry E. Huntington Library)*

another minister to France until he knew the minister would be "received, respected and honored as the representative of a great, free, powerful and independent nation." The Republicans, doubting the President's charge that the United States had been insulted, asked for proof. Adams then turned the commissioners' report over to Congress, after deleting the names of the three Frenchmen and designating them only as Messrs. X., Y., and Z. When the report was published, the "X. Y. Z. Affair" provoked even more of a reaction than Adams had bargained for. It aroused the martial spirit of most Americans, made the Federalists more popular than ever as the party of patriotism, and led to a limited and undeclared war with France (1798–1800).

With the cooperation of Congress, which quickly passed the necessary laws, Adams cut off all trade with France, abrogated the treaties of 1778, and authorized public and private vessels of the United States to capture French armed ships on the high seas. Congress set up a Department of the Navy (1798) and appropriated money for the construction of warships to supplement the hundreds of privateers and the small number of government vessels already built for the protection of American shipping in the Mediterranean against the Barbary pirates. The new United States Navy soon gave a good account of itself. Its warships won a number of duels with French vessels of their own class and captured a total of eighty-five ships including armed merchantmen.

Having abandoned neutrality, the United States now was cooperating so closely with Great Britain as to be virtually a cobelligerent, though technically at peace. When the British offered to lend a part of their fleet to the United States, President Adams declined to borrow, since he preferred to build up a navy of his own. Nevertheless, the British provided shot and shell to make up for the deficient American supplies, furnished officers to help with the training and direction of American crews, and exchanged signaling information so that British and American ships could communicate readily with one another. Thus the United States was involved in the world war as a kind of associate member of the coalition against France.

The French foreign minister, Talleyrand, finally began to see the wisdom of an accommo-

---

Building the Navy

After the Revolutionary War the United States abandoned the warships it had accumulated, and from 1783 to 1798 there was no American navy. Then, with the outbreak of undeclared hostilities with France, the Department of the Navy was established and a naval building program begun. In that age of wooden sailing ships, there were three main categories of war vessels: (1) ships of the line, or line-of-battle ships, which were the largest and most heavily armed (roughly corresponding to twentieth-century battleships or dreadnoughts); (2) frigates, which were smaller and faster and had fewer guns (comparable to modern cruisers); (3) corvettes, sloops of war, and other relatively small craft (somewhat like the light cruisers, destroyers, and gunboats of the present). At the outset the United States navy eschewed line-of-battle ships and placed its chief reliance on specially designed frigates which were faster, more maneuverable, and more heavily gunned than their European counterparts. In 1798 the frigates United States, Constitution, *and* Constellation, *already partly built, were completed, and the* Philadelphia *and several others were started. The illustration shows work in progress on the* Philadelphia *in a Philadelphia shipyard. This frigate was not finished in time to be used against the French, but it saw plenty of action later (1803) in the war with Tripoli. Tripolitan pirates captured the ship, and Americans in a daring raid destroyed her to prevent the enemy's using her against them. (The Historical Society of Pennsylvania)*

dation with the Americans. He took notice of the rapprochement between the United States and Great Britain, the successes of the American Navy, and the failure of the American people to show the expected enthusiasm for the cause of France. He was enlightened in regard to American public opinion by George Logan, a Philadelphia Quaker who, with no official authorization but with a letter of introduction from Vice President Jefferson, visited France to work for peace in the midst of the undeclared war. After Logan returned, President Adams gave him a sympathetic hearing, though the Federalists in Congress passed a law, the so-called Logan Act, to prohibit citizens from engaging in private and unofficial diplomacy with foreign governments in the future.

When, in 1800, Adams' new three-man commission arrived in France, Napoleon Bonaparte was in power as First Consul. The Americans requested that France terminate the treaties of 1778 and pay damages for seizures of American ships. Napoleon replied that, if the United States had any claim to damages, the claim must rest upon the treaties, and if the treaties were ended, the claim must be abandoned. Napoleon had his way. The Americans agreed to a new treaty that canceled the old ones, arranged for reciprocity in commerce, and ignored the question of damages. When Adams submitted this treaty to the Senate, the extreme Federalists raised so many objections that its final ratification was delayed until after he had left office. Nevertheless, the "quasiwar" had come to an honorable end, and the United States at last had freed itself from the entanglements and embarrassments of the "perpetual" alliance with France.

REPRESSION AND PROTEST

The outbreak of hostilities in 1798 had given the Federalists an advantage over the political opposition, and in the congressional elections of that year they increased their majorities in both houses. Meanwhile their newly found power went to their heads. Some of them schemed to go on winning elections by passing laws to weaken and to silence the opposition. They had as an excuse the supposed necessity of protecting the nation from dangerous foreign

influence in the midst of the undeclared war. By persecuting their critics, the Federalists produced a crop of Republican martyrs, gave rise to protests against their disregard of the Constitution, and provoked a reaction that helped to bring their party to defeat.

Since many Republican critics of the administration were foreigners by birth, especially Irish or French, the Federalists in Congress thought it desirable to limit the political rights of aliens and make it more difficult for them to become citizens of the United States. The Federalists struck at the civil liberties of both native Americans and the foreign-born in a series of laws commonly known as the Alien and Sedition Acts.

President Adams did not invoke the Alien Act nor deport any aliens, but this law together with the Naturalization Act doubtless had some effect in discouraging immigration and encouraging many foreigners already here to leave. The administration did enforce the Sedition Act, arresting about two dozen men and convicting ten of them. Most of these were Republican newspaper editors whose writings, while tending to bring the Federalists into disrepute, were not truly seditious at all. One of the editors merely had expressed the wish that, when a salute was fired in honor of the President, the wadding of the cannon had "struck him in the rear bulge of the breeches."

The Republicans had no reason to look to the Supreme Court for relief. Indeed, the Court never yet had declared an act of Congress unconstitutional, and the Republicans denied that it had the power to do so. They believed, however, that the recent Federalist legislation, particularly the Sedition Act, was unconstitutional, for the First Amendment stated that Congress should pass no law abridging freedom of speech or of the press.

What agency of government should decide the question of constitutionality? The Republican leaders Jefferson and Madison concluded that the state legislatures should decide. They ably expressed their view in two sets of resolutions, one written (anonymously) by Jefferson and adopted by the Kentucky legislature (1798, 1799), and the other drafted by Madison and approved by the Virginia legislature (1798). These Kentucky and Virginia resolutions asserted the following doctrines. The federal government had been formed by a "compact" or contract among the states. It was a limited government, possessing only certain delegated powers. Whenever it exercised any additional and undelegated powers, its acts were "unauthoritative, void, and of no force." The parties to the contract, the states, must decide for themselves when and whether the central government exceeded its powers. And "nullification" by the states was the "rightful remedy" whenever the general government went too far. The resolutions urged all the states to join in declaring the Alien and Sedition Acts null and void and in requesting their repeal at the next session of Congress, but none of the others went along with Virginia and Kentucky.

ELECTION OF 1800

In the election of 1800 Jefferson and Burr, representing the alliance of Virginia and New York, were again the Republican candidates. Adams was running for reelection on the Federalist ticket, and his running mate was C. C. Pinckney.

During the nearly twelve years of Federalist rule, the party had created numerous political enemies in consequence of Hamilton's financial program, the suppression of the Whiskey Rebellion, Jay's Treaty, and the Alien and Sedition Acts. Denouncing these measures, and especially the last of them, the Republicans made state rights and constitutional liberties the main issues of their campaign in 1800. They pictured Adams as a tyrant and a man who wanted to be King. The Federalists, on the other hand, described Jefferson as a dangerous radical and his followers as wild men who, if they should get into power, would bring on a reign of terror comparable to that of the French Revolution at its worst.

The contest was close, and the outcome in the electoral college depended upon the voting in one state, New York. In New York City the vice-presidential candidate, Burr, was the organizer of Republican victory. The Revolutionary veterans of the city had formed the Tammany Society to maintain their wartime fellowship and to combat the pretensions of the Society of the Cincinnati, the exclusive and aristocratic organization of Revolutionary officers. Though not himself a member of Tammany, Burr converted it into a political machine

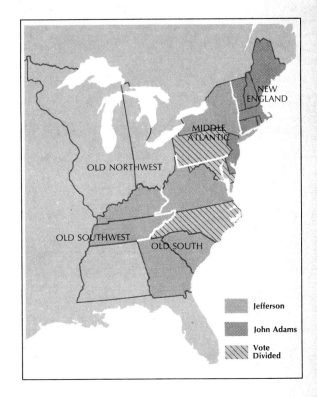

Election of 1800

and, with its aid, carried the city for the Republicans by such a large majority as to carry the state also. The Republicans gained control of the legislature, and since New York was one of the states in which the legislature cast the electoral vote, the Republicans could count upon that vote in the presidential election.

When the state electors cast their votes, Adams received a total of 65 and Pinckney 64. Jefferson got 73 and so did Burr. To avoid such a tie, Republican leaders had meant for at least one of their electors to refrain from giving Burr his vote. But through a misunderstanding—some said that Burr himself was secretly responsible—the plan went awry. And so the election was not yet over: in accordance with the Constitution the decision between the two highest—between Burr and Jefferson—was up to the House of Representatives, with the delegation from each state casting a single vote.

Since the Federalists controlled a majority of the states' votes in the existing Congress, they had the privilege of deciding which of their opponents was to be the next President, though the Republicans, in making their nominations, had clearly intended for Jefferson to have the first place on their ticket. Some of the more extreme of the Federalists now hoped to postpone or to prevent any breaking of the tie and, instead, to make new arrangements for the presidential succession so that the highest office in the land would still fall to a Federalist. Others, fearing chaos and possible civil war if no election were made, thought it would be better to come to an understanding with Burr and elect him. Hamilton disapproved of both proposals. Though he had a low opinion of Jefferson, he had a still lower one of Burr, his bitter rival in law and politics in New York. Burr himself remained strangely silent, neither electioneering openly for himself nor publicly refusing to accept office at the hands of the Federalists.

During the winter of 1800–1801 the House balloted again and again without mustering a majority for either candidate. Finally, only a few weeks before inauguration day, some of the Federalist die-hards gave in, the tie was broken, and Jefferson was named as President, Burr as Vice President. Afterward one of the Federalists claimed that he had given in because Jefferson's friends had assured him that Jefferson, if elected, would appoint him to a government job and would preserve the main Federalist policies with respect to commerce, the navy, and the public debt, while making no wholesale removals of Federalists from the lower offices of the government.

In addition to winning a majority of the presidential electors in 1800, the Republicans also won a majority of the seats in both houses of the next Congress. The only branch of the government left in Federalist hands was the judiciary, and Adams and his fellow partisans during his last months in office took steps to make their hold upon the courts secure.

By the Judiciary Act of 1801 the Federalists succeeded in reducing the number of Supreme Court justiceships by one but at the same time greatly increasing the number of federal judgeships as a whole. The act created a separate system of circuit courts of appeal, between the federal district courts and the Supreme Court. Formerly (in accordance with the Judiciary Act of 1789) a district judge had sat with two Supreme Court justices to hear appeals on the circuit. The new law also provided for ten additional district judgeships.

To these newly created positions Adams proceeded to appoint deserving Federalists. It was said that he stayed up until midnight on his last day in office, March 3, 1801, in order to complete the signing of the judges' commissions, and so these officeholders were known as his "midnight appointments." Since federal judges held office for life—that is, with good behavior—Jefferson as the incoming President would be powerless to remove Adams' appointees. Or so the Federalists assumed.

Selected Readings

The Constitution
Max Ferrand, *The Framing of the Constitution of the United States** (1913); C. A. Beard, *An Economic Interpretation of the Constitution of the United States** (1913); R. E. Brown, *Charles Beard and the Constitution** (1956); Forrest McDonald, *We the People: The Economic Origins of the Constitution** (1958) and *E Pluribus Unum: The Formation of the American Republic, 1776–1790* (1965); Clinton Rossiter, *The Grand Convention* (1966); Max Farrand, ed., *Records of the Federal Convention of 1787** (4 vols., 1911–1937).

Ratification
J. T. Main, *The Anti-Federalists: Critics of the Constitution, 1781–1788* (1961); A. T. Mason, *The State Rights Debate: Antifederalism and the Constitution* (1964); R. A. Rutland, *The Ordeal of the Constitution:*

The Antifederalists and the Ratification Struggle of 1787–1788 (1966); L. G. DePauw, *The Eleventh Pillar: New York State and the Federal Constitution* (1966); J. E. Cooke, ed., *The Federalist** (1961).

The Federalist Regime
J. C. Miller, *The Federalist Era, 1789–1801** (1960); Leonard White, *The Federalists** (1948); M. J. Dauer, *The Adams Federalists* (1953); Nathan Schachner, *The Founding Fathers** (1954); Stephen Kurtz, *The Presidency of John Adams** (1957).

The Jeffersonian Opposition
C. A. Beard, *The Economic Origins of Jeffersonian Democracy** (1915); Joseph Charles, *The Origins of the American Party System** (1956); W. N. Chambers, *Political Parties in a New Nation: The American Experience, 1776–1809** (1963); Noble Cunningham,

The Jeffersonian Republicans (1957); M. D. Peterson, *Thomas Jefferson and the New Nation* (1970); Bernard Bailyn, *Origins of American Politics* (1969); J. T. Main, *Political Parties Before the Constitution* (1972).

Rights and Repression
Irving Brant, *The Bill of Rights* (1965); L. W. Levy, *Legacy of Suppression: Freedom of Speech and Press in Early American History** (1960); J. M. Smith, *Freedom's Fetters: The Alien and Sedition Laws and American Civil Liberties* (1956); J. C. Miller, *Crisis in Freedom: The Alien and Sedition Acts** (1951); L. D. Baldwin, *Whiskey Rebels: The Story of a Frontier Uprising* (1939).

Diplomacy
S. F. Bemis, *Jay's Treaty** (1923) and *Pinckney's Treaty** (1926); A. P. Whitaker, *The Spanish-American Frontier, 1783–1795* (1927) and *The Mississippi Question, 1795–1803* (1934); Alexander De Conde, *Entangling Alliance: Politics and Diplomacy Under*

George Washington (1958) and *The Quasi-War: The Politics and Diplomacy of the Undeclared War with France, 1797–1801* (1966); Bradford Perkins, *The First Rapprochement: England and the United States, 1795–1805* (1955); P. A. Varg, *Foreign Policies of the Founding Fathers* (1963); Felix Gilbert, *To the Farewell Address** (1961); L. S. Kaplan, *Jefferson and France* (1967).

Biographies
D. S. Freeman, *George Washington* (7 vols., 1948–1957); C. P. Smith, *John Adams* (1962); Gilbert Chinard, *Honest John Adams** (1933); J. C. Miller, *Alexander Hamilton: Portrait in Paradox* (1959); Dumas Malone, *Jefferson and His Time* (3 vols., 1948–1962); Irving Brant, *James Madison: Father of the Constitution, 1787–1800* (1950); F. B. Tolles, *George Logan of Philadelphia* (1953).

*Titles available in paperback.

The Jeffersonian Era

Seven

Thomas Jefferson and the Republicans, while out of power, had championed the rights of the states against the powers of the federal government. They denounced the Federalists for stretching those powers too far and interpreting the Constitution too loosely. Jefferson stood for governmental principles that were appropriate to the kind of country he envisaged — a country made up mostly of independent farmers and happily free from the workshops, the industrial towns, and the city mobs of Europe. He favored France and the French influence against England and English ways. A man of the Enlightenment like Franklin, he took a rational and skeptical approach to life both here and hereafter.

But during those years the young republic was beginning to develop in directions that would eventually make some (but by no means all) of Jefferson's views seem obsolete. New machinery, derived from England or devised at home, gave a little start to the growth of an industrial society, with factories and factory towns dotting the American countryside. The English tone prevailed over the French in most things of the mind. To the extent that American writers resisted the English influence, they tended to arouse a national feeling and thus to diminish the particularist sentiment, the sense of identification with an individual state. And a renewal of religious revivalism, coinciding with Jefferson's taking office, almost submerged the rational philosophy that had been rampant for some time.

Moreover, once Jefferson and his party followers were in control of the government, they had to deal with situations that seemed to demand strong, unfettered action. Soon the Republicans were going even further, in some respects, than the Federalists had gone in the exercise of federal authority. If Jefferson appeared to be inconsistent, so did many of his opponents, for they now adopted the theory of state rights and turned his former arguments against him.

Thomas Jefferson
Jefferson was sixty-one years old when this portrait was painted, in 1805, at the President's mansion in Washington, by Rembrandt Peale, son of Charles Willson Peale. (Courtesy of the New-York Historical Society, New York City)

But the idea of state rights was not the whole of the Jeffersonian philosophy. He stood primarily for the interests of the majority as he conceived them. As President, he did much to advance those interests, his greatest achievement being to double the territory of the United States.

Spirit of the Young Republic

Having won political independence, the American people—or at least some of them—also aspired to a kind of cultural independence. More than that, they looked forward to a time when (as a "Poem on the Rising Glory of America" had foretold in 1772) their "happy land" would

A School in Session About 1800
In such a one-room school, children of practically all ages were brought together. While one group recited, the rest learned their lessons—or were supposed to. Paper and ink were scarce; a slate and a slate pencil were commonly used instead. There was little in the way of furnishings except for backless benches and a few desks, usually placed under the windows, where the light was best. The teacher had to look out for the fire and perform the other chores of a janitor. Often the teacher was a college student, earning money during the long winter vacation from his own studies, or he was a recent college graduate supporting himself while he prepared for the law and politics. Daniel Webster and Thaddeus Stevens once taught school, and so did many another young man who afterward became prominent in public life. (Library of Congress)

be the "seat of empire" and the "final stage" of civilization, with "glorious works of high invention and of wond'rous art." The United States, as Joel Barlow saw it in his *Vision of Columbus* (1787), was destined to be "the last and greatest theatre for the improvement of mankind."

EDUCATION AND THE PROFESSIONS

In certain respects the Revolutionary War temporarily handicapped American intellectual life. Some learned men turned from science and scholarship to military or political service. The noted astronomer David Rittenhouse, for example, left his telescopes and devoted himself to a Revolutionary committee, the Pennsylvania Council of Safety, while advising his countrymen to abandon schools and concentrate on defense. Many schools did close, especially in rural areas, and most of the colleges were disrupted. Harvard buildings were used as American army barracks; Nassau Hall at Princeton was damaged during Washington's New Jersey campaign; and the William and Mary campus became the military headquarters of Cornwallis before the Battle of Yorktown.

But the Revolution also stimulated intellectual activity and brought forth ideas that were to have lasting consequences. Through military service thousands of young men got better acquainted with their own country, and by reading patriotic pamphlets, or at least hearing them discussed, these soldiers received something of a political education. With the French alliance there came from France not only troops and supplies but also ideas — giving further spread to the skeptical, experimental, scientific notions of the Enlightenment. And, with independence as an accomplished fact, it seemed to thoughtful Americans that widespread literacy and learning were absolutely essential to the success of the new republic. Thomas Jefferson, for one, called for a "crusade against ignorance."

The friends of learning advocated not merely education as such but a special kind of education, one that would fill the minds of youth with patriotic, republican thoughts. The Massachusetts geographer Jedidiah Morse, author of *Geography Made Easy* (1784), said the country must have its own textbooks so that the

people would not be infected with the monarchical and aristocratic ideas of England. The Connecticut schoolmaster and lawyer Noah Webster likewise contended that the American schoolboy should be educated as a patriot. "As soon as he opens his lips," Webster wrote, "he should rehearse the history of his own country; he should lisp the praise of liberty, and of those illustrious heroes and statesmen who have wrought a revolution in her favor."

To foster a distinctive culture and unify the nation, Webster insisted upon a simplified and Americanized spelling — "honor" instead of "honour," for example. His *American Spelling Book* (1783), commonly known as the "blue-backed speller," eventually sold over 100 million copies to become the best-selling book (except for the Bible) in the entire history of American publishing. Webster also wrote grammars and other schoolbooks. His school dictionary (1806) was republished in many editions and eventually was much enlarged to form *An American Dictionary of the English Language* (1828). By means of his speller and his dictionary he succeeded in establishing a national standard of words and usages for the United States.

In their first constitutions, several of the states endorsed the principle of public education, but none actually required the establishment of free schools. A Massachusetts law of 1789 reaffirmed the colonial laws providing for the support of schools by the various towns. Jedidiah Morse observed later that the enforcement of the law was lax in many places. Even in Boston only seven public schools existed in 1790, and most of these were poorly housed; more than twice as many private schools were in operation. In Virginia, Jefferson as wartime governor proposed a plan by which the elements of reading and writing should be provided for all children, and secondary and higher education for the gifted, with state scholarships for the needy. The plan was not enacted into law. As late as 1815 none of the states (not even Massachusetts) had a comprehensive public school system in actual operation.

Outside of New England, schooling continued to be viewed as the responsibility of the family and the church rather than the state. In the Middle Atlantic region and the South, most schools were run by religious groups, by pro-

prietary schoolmasters, or by philanthropic societies. Though requiring tuition from parents
who could afford it, many schools accepted the
poor without pay. In the cities, special organizations were formed for the education of the
poor. One of these, the New York Free School
Society, introduced the Lancastrian method
from England (1806), to economize on instruction costs: the teacher taught a lesson to several
superior pupils, and then these "monitors"
drilled groups of their fellow pupils.

During and after the Revolution, private
academies sprang up in increasing numbers.
Many were patterned after the academies
founded by the Phillips family at Andover,
Massachusetts (1778), and at Exeter, New
Hampshire (1781). By 1815 there were thirty
private secondary schools in Massachusetts,
thirty-seven in New York, and more than one

hundred in the country as a whole. Most of
these admitted only boys, but a few academies
or seminaries were provided for girls. Salem
Female Academy, established in 1772 by North
Carolina Moravians, was one of the earliest.

At the outbreak of the Revolution there
had been a total of nine colleges in all the colonies; in 1800 there were twenty-two in the various states, and the number continued steadily
to increase thereafter. Whereas all but two of
the colonial colleges were sectarian in origin
and spirit, a majority of those founded during
the first three decades of independence were
nondenominational. Especially significant in
foreshadowing the future pattern of higher
education was the fact that five were state institutions: the universities of Georgia (1785),
North Carolina (1789), Vermont (1791), Ohio
(1804), and South Carolina (1805). For the time

View of New Bedford
*New Bedford, Massachusetts, a seaport about fifty miles south of Boston, began to
concentrate on the whaling industry in the 1760s, gained a reputation as the whaling
capital of the world, and prospered at the business for a century, until the
discovery of petroleum ruined the market for whale oil. This painting, by William
Wall, shows the village as it appeared in 1807. (The Whaling Museum, New Bedford,
Mass.)*

being, none of these was either quite public or a university in the modern sense. Their offerings were limited, and their financial support was derived mainly from private endowments, gifts, and tuition fees rather than appropriations by the rather niggardly legislatures. Scarcely more than one man in a thousand (and no women at all) had the benefit of such college education as was available.

Jefferson, John Adams, and a few other statesmen nourished the ideal of a true university, providing the best of training in the professions as well as the liberal arts. Nothing came of Jefferson's hope that a national university might be established. As wartime governor of Virginia, he managed to expand the work of William and Mary by adding professorships of law, medicine, and modern languages. George Wythe, the first law professor at the college, taught a remarkable number of youths who afterward became distinguished lawyers and statesmen. Before 1800 the University of Pennsylvania and Columbia College instituted law courses, and Judge Tapping Reeve opened a private law school in Litchfield, Connecticut. As a rule, lawyers got their training, as in colonial times, by "reading law" in the office of a practicing attorney.

Most physicians likewise still studied medicine and gained experience by working with an established practitioner, but several medical schools were in existence by the early 1800s, the oldest of them at the University of Pennsylvania. Its most distinguished professor, and the outstanding physician in America, was Benjamin Rush, who had received his medical degree at Edinburgh. As an army surgeon during the Revolutionary War, Dr. Rush protested against improper sanitation and medical care, which caused many more soldiers to die of camp diseases than of battle wounds. Afterward he interested himself in the effects of diet and drink upon health, and he also made pioneering studies of psychosomatic and psychiatric disorders. As educators, Rush and other physicians had to struggle against age-old superstitions and against popular hostility to the dissection of corpses. In 1788 a riot was provoked when a human limb was hung out of a New York hospital window to dry, and from time to time medical students got into trouble for body snatching, since cadavers seldom were available by legal means.

The science of public as well as private health remained in its infancy. In the summer of 1793 an epidemic of yellow fever raged unchecked in Philadelphia, bringing death to a tenth of the population in one of the worst disasters ever to befall an American city. The physicians were helpless, though Dr. Rush came near to guessing the cause of the epidemic when he explained it as being due to the miasma arising from decomposed matter. The Philadelphia experience stimulated programs for improving sanitation and making cities cleaner, and thus unwittingly the number of breeding places for the mosquito that transmits yellow fever were reduced. In many cases the prevailing medical practices hastened death instead of prolonging life. George Washington probably need not have died from a throat infection in 1799, but his physicians, doing their best according to their knowledge, bled and purged him so thoroughly as to impair his resistance to the disease.

THE RIGHTS OF WOMEN

The Declaration of Independence, with its emphasis on the rights of man, provoked some thought about the rights of women. "By the way," Abigail Adams wrote to her husband John Adams in 1776, "in the new code of laws which I suppose it will be necessary for you to make, I desire you would remember the ladies and be more generous and favorable to them than your ancestors. Do not put such unlimited power into the hands of the husbands." But Adams gently laughed off his wife's suggestion.

Women earned some consideration through their contributions to the revolutionary cause. They joined willingly in sacrificing their comforts and boycotting British goods. Mercy Otis Warren, sister of James Otis and friend of Abigail Adams, rivaled her brother as a pamphleteer, composing satires and farces that ridiculed British pretensions. Afterwards she wrote a history of the Revolution. During the war, women managed farms and businesses for their absent husbands, or they followed them with the army to cook, wash, and do other chores around the camp. On a hot summer day one wife busied herself on the battlefield, carrying pitchers of water to

Mercy Otis Warren
Mercy Otis (Mrs. James Warren), born in Barnstable, Massachusetts, in 1728, was about thirty-five years old when John Singleton Copley painted this portrait of her. Mrs. Warren was to be a leading propagandist of the Revolution. Copley, of Boston, was an outstanding American portraitist and at first a sympathizer with the Patriot cause and an admirer of Samuel Adams, whose portrait he also painted. In 1774, however, Copley left America to continue his distinguished artistic career in England for the rest of his life. (Courtesy, Museum of Fine Arts, Boston)

thirsty soldiers (and thus winning legendary fame as "Molly Pitcher"). When her husband fell she took his place at a field gun.

An outstanding American feminist of the time, along with Mrs. Adams and Mrs. Warren, was Judith Sargent Murray, who had shared the studies of her brother while he was preparing for Harvard and who, at the age of eighteen, had married a Massachusetts sea captain. In a 1779 essay Mrs. Murray argued that girls had minds as good as boys'. In a 1784 magazine article, the first of her works to be published, she maintained that education, by making young women self-confident and self-dependent, would keep them from rushing into early marriage for fear of spinsterhood or insecurity. Her trenchant writings on religion, politics, and

manners and customs as well as education, collected in three volumes under the title *The Gleaner* (1798), proved her an essayist at least equal to her leading male contemporaries such as Noah Webster and Philip Freneau.

The women's cause received some support from a few prominent men, among them Benjamin Franklin, Benjamin Rush, and Thomas Paine. The immediate aim was not legal or political rights so much as educational opportunities that, the reformers hoped, would lead to eventual equality, though Yale students in the 1780s debated the question "Whether women ought to be admitted into the magistracy and government of empires and republics." Women gained no new rights, of course, in the Constitution of 1787.

The discussion of women's place, in America and in the world, got added stimulus with the appearance of the English feminist Mary Wollstonecraft's provocative book *A Vindication of the Rights of Women* (1792). After reading this, Mrs. Murray rejoiced that "the Rights of Women" were beginning to be understood in the United States, and she predicted that girls then growing up would inaugurate "a new era in female history."

No such new era arrived in Mrs. Murray's lifetime (she died in 1820). In the young republic other women achieved individual success as writers. Susanna H. Rowson, for one, wrote a novel, *Charlotte: A Tale of Truth* (1791), that was to be the most popular of all American novels until the appearance sixty years later of another woman author's work, *Uncle Tom's Cabin*. With the passing of the revolutionary generation, however, interest in the women's revolution declined, though it never disappeared.

LITERATURE AND MUSIC

During the first decades of independence, the most widely read American writings – and some of the greatest ones (such as *The Federalist*) – were polemical and political, not esthetic. In pamphlets and newspapers the literate American followed the arguments about British colonial policy, the aims of the Revolution, the question of a new Constitution, and the party contests of the young republic. He became a "newspaper-reading animal," as an English visitor observed. This preoccupation with the news of the day drew attention away from literature of a more artistic and permanent kind. Thus, in one way, the newspapers handicapped literary development. Yet, in another way, they helped it, for they created a reading public and produced a potential market for literary works.

There was a more serious handicap to the rise of American authorship. An aspiring author found it hard to get his manuscript published, or to get it sold after it was in print. Until well into the nineteenth century, there were in America no book publishers in the modern sense, no firms that would bear the cost and take the risk of publishing. The author himself had to pay all or at least the larger part of the expenses. He could find few printers willing to share the burden with him, for they could reprint the works of popular English authors without paying a royalty. No author in the young republic could support himself by means of his writing alone. The first to try it was the novelist Charles Brockden Brown. He produced a series of well-written horror stories but had to take a job as a magazine editor in order to supplement his income.

The American author, if he looked to periodicals or the theater for a market, did little if any better than with books. In the late eighteenth century, several magazines were published in the United States, the most important being the *Columbian,* the *American Museum,* the *Massachusetts Magazine,* and the *New-York Magazine.* All of these filled their pages chiefly by clipping material from English publications. Meanwhile the theater had grown into an accepted, permanent institution in American cities, with substantial buildings and regular schedules of performances. George Washington himself attended plays, and opposition to the theater as "the house of the devil" declined, though it by no means disappeared. But the American dramatist, like the writer of books and the contributor to magazines, had to compete with English authors, who did not have to be paid royalties.

Under the circumstances, it is surprising that the young republic contained so many able and active poets, essayists, novelists, and playwrights as it did. Among the most active poets and essayists were the "Hartford Wits," a group of Connecticut writers who met together for sociability and mutual encouragement. The leaders were Joel Barlow, Timothy Dwight, and John Trumbull (not to be confused with the contemporary painter of the same name). These men wrote epics on American greatness and satires on American foibles – as seen from a solid, Federalist, New England point of view. Barlow eventually went over to the Jeffersonian side, but the ablest and most thoroughgoing Jeffersonian poet, a hardy foe of the Hartford Wits, was Philip Freneau of New Jersey.

Novels became the rage in England during the last half of the eighteenth century, and their popularity spread to the United States, where the latest English successes were promptly imported, reprinted, and eagerly read. The most fashionable themes were sex and sentimentality, satire, and terror. When novelists finally appeared in America, they hoped to produce a native, original kind of fiction, but they had to appeal to the prevailing taste. They used essentially the same themes as the English novelists, though substituting American scenes and situations for English ones.

Most of the songs popular during and after the Revolution consisted of new and patriotic words set to familiar English tunes. "Yankee Doodle" was written during the French and Indian War by a British army surgeon with the intention of poking fun at the ragged colonial troops. It became a favorite with the Yankees themselves, and during the Revolution they added many variations, some of them unsuitable for polite company. Other popular music was written by Francis Hopkinson, the first notable American composer and a man of amazing versatility. The first student to be graduated from the College of Philadelphia, Hopkinson practiced law, served in the first Continental Congress and signed the Declaration of Independence, wrote verse, essays, and Revolutionary pamphlets, painted, gave public performances on the harpsichord, and sat as a judge in Pennsylvania and federal courts, besides composing music. A collection of his best work was published under the title of *Seven Songs* (1788). His son, the eminent lawyer Joseph Hopkinson, wrote the words for "Hail, Columbia" during the undeclared war with France (1798); for many years, this stirring song remained the nearest equivalent to a national anthem.

CHURCHES AND RELIGION

Americans of the young republic might have been patriotic enough but, from the point of view of many a religious leader, they were insufficiently pious. The religious excitement of the Great Awakening had passed, and sermons of the Revolutionary era lamented the "decay of vital piety," the "degeneracy of manners," and the luxurious growth of "vice."

Certainly large numbers of the people were turning away from familiar faiths. Many interested themselves in deism, the rational religion of Enlightenment philosophers, especially those in France. The deists believed in God but considered Him a rather remote being who had created the universe, not an intimate presence who was concerned with human individuals and their sins. Franklin, Jefferson, and others among the Founding Fathers held deistic views. Such views, at first confined to the well educated, finally spread among the people at large. By 1800, books and articles attacking religious "superstitions" found eager readers all over the country. The most influential of such writings, Thomas Paine's *The Age of Reason* (1794–1796), was discussed in homes, colleges, taverns, stagecoaches, everywhere. Paine once declared that Christianity was the "strangest religion ever set up," for "it committed a murder upon Jesus in order to redeem mankind from the sin of eating an apple." No wonder the preachers regularly denounced Paine and deism and called for a new revival of religious faith.

While resisting the spread of free thought, the churches also had to deal with other problems. After the Declaration of Independence the groups with foreign ties had to reconsider their position, and even those without such ties faced the task of reorganizing on a national basis. As population moved westward, the churches had to follow the frontier if they were to grow with the country's growth. In responding to the challenges of the time, some denominations succeeded much better than others. New sects arose. The grim doctrines of Calvinism gave way to more optimistic faiths, and the religious pattern of the young republic became even more variegated than that of colonial America had been.

The Congregationalists, who led in numbers and influence at the close of the colonial period, soon lost their preeminence. They continued to be tax supported in Massachusetts, Connecticut, and New Hampshire even after those colonies were transformed into states. But the Congregationalists lacked the missionary zeal, appealing theology, and strong, centralized organization that were essential for winning and holding converts.

In New England, its home ground, the Congregational Church was weakened by the growing popularity of universalist and unitarian doctrines. Many of its members rejected not only the idea of predestination but also the idea of the Trinity. They believed that salvation was available to all, and that God was one (not three), Jesus being only a great religious teach-

A Camp Meeting

Originating in 1800, the camp meeting soon became a popular American religious institution in rural areas, especially in the South and West. By 1820, about 1,000 meetings a year were held. The painting reproduced here was made in the 1830s. A typical camp meeting (in Maryland, in 1806) was described by a participant who wrote of the tents, the wagons, the plank seats, the covered stand for the preacher, and the daily schedule. "At day break the trumpets were blown round the camp for the people to rise 20 minutes afterward for family prayer at the door of every tent—if fair weather—at sunrise they blew at the stand for public prayer, and then breakfasted. At 10 oclock they blew for preaching—by 2 ocl. dinner was to be over in every tent. At 3 ocl. preaching again, and again at night." After several days of this, "hundreds were prostrate upon the earth before the Lord. . . .Will I ever see anything more like the day of Judgment on this side of eternity—to see the people running, yes, running, from every direction to the stand, weeping, shouting, and shouting for joy. Prayer was then made—and every Brother fell upon the neck of his Brother, and the Sisters did likewise. Then we parted. O! glorious day they went home singing and shouting." (Courtesy of the New-York Historical Society, New York City)

er and not the son of God. The Universalist Church came into existence (1779) when believers in universal salvation began to hold meetings in Gloucester, Massachusetts. A little later the Unitarian Church was founded in Boston (1782).

American Presbyterians adopted a constitution (1789) by which the whole country was divided into sixteen presbyteries and four synods, with a general assembly that served as the highest ecclesiastical court. Already well entrenched on the frontier, where so many of the Scotch-Irish had settled before the Revolution,

the Church expanded with the expanding nation. Indeed, it grew too fast for the maintenance of internal harmony. Bickering reappeared between Old and New Lights, between traditional Calvinists and believers in salvation for all. New sects splintered off, as did the followers of Thomas and Alexander Campbell, who in the early 1800s rejected the Calvinist dogma of limited election. Later the Campbellites formed a separate church known as the Disciples of Christ.

Among the Baptists, as among the Presbyterians, there were disputes about the question of predestination or free will, but theological differences did not prevent the Baptists from growing more rapidly than any other denomination except one (the Methodist) during the late eighteenth and early nineteenth century. Scattered over the whole country, they were especially numerous in Virginia and the Carolinas. Long the most militant advocates of the separation of church and state, they ceased to impress others as dangerous radicals after this principle was adopted in the Virginia statute of religious liberty and in the federal Bill of Rights.

More than the Baptists or any other religious group, the Roman Catholics gained in prestige (though not in numbers) as a consequence of the Revolution. On the advice of Charles Carroll of Carrollton, a Maryland statesman and Catholic lay leader, most of the Catholics in America supported the Patriot cause during the war. The French alliance brought Catholic troops and chaplains to this country. In such times as these, Catholic Americans no longer seemed, as in colonial days, like agents of the devil. After the war the Vatican provided for the United States a church government separate from that of England. In 1784 Father John Carroll was appointed head of Catholic missions in this country, and with the elaboration of the American hierarchy he was made the first American bishop (1789) and finally Archbishop of Baltimore (1808).

The Anglicans suffered more than any other religious group as a result of the Revolution. They were badly divided on the issues of the war, the clergy being mostly Loyalist in the states where Anglicans were few, and partly Loyalist in Virginia and Maryland. In these two states the Anglican Church had benefited from tax support, which was lost when the Church was disestablished. In other states the Church had depended upon aid from the mother country, and that aid was withdrawn. By the end of the war a large proportion of the parishes lacked clergymen, for there were few recruits to take the places of those who had died or had left the country as Loyalist refugees. Since there never had been an American bishop or an intercolonial organization of the Church, postwar Anglican leaders had to start from scratch in setting up an independent, national hierarchy. By 1789 they had succeeded in organizing the Protestant Episcopal Church. Until after the War of 1812 the Church re-

mained weak, gaining few members and losing many with the departure of the Methodists.

John Wesley, the founder of Methodism, did not set up a new church in England, nor did he intend to do so in America. In 1776, ten years after his lay ministers had begun to organize Methodist "classes" in the colonies, American Methodists insisted that they were not "common dissenters" but "a religious society in communion with the Church of England." But the war changed their attitude. When peace came, the greatest of Wesley's agents in America, Francis Asbury, concluded that American conditions required the formation of a separate body. In 1784 Asbury called a meeting of Methodist preachers at Baltimore, and launched the Methodist Church, with himself as the first bishop.

The Methodists had a unique and effective organization. It was authoritarian, with power concentrated at the top in the hands of the bishops. The preachers were itinerants: each of them had charge of several widely scattered congregations and rode the rounds from one to another. Every year the preachers met in a conference (by 1796 there were six annual conferences in different parts of the country) where a bishop conferred with them, ordained new ministers, and assigned all the riders to their circuits, making frequent changes. This system was well adapted to a growing, moving, frontier society. As the historian W. W. Sweet has said, the Presbyterian minister in the West "was called by the people," the Baptist farmer-preacher "came with the people," and the Methodist circuit-rider "was sent to the people." The circuit-rider brought a message of individual responsibility for eternal happiness. It was a welcome message. The Methodist Church, within sixty years after its foundation, became the largest in the United States.

Along with the Baptists and the Presbyterians, the Methodists gained many converts in the Second Awakening, a new wave of revivalism that swept the country at the turn of the century. This revivalism had two distinct phases. It began among the Presbyterians in certain colleges of the East and South, reaching its height at Yale under the leadership of President Timothy Dwight (1797–1817). Then, with zealous graduates carrying the evangelical spirit to the West, it went to even greater extremes on the frontier. In 1800, in Kentucky, the Presbyterians held the first camp meeting, an outdoor revival that lasted several days. The Methodists soon took up the camp-meeting technique, and the circuit-rider Peter Cartwright won fame as the most effective soul-saver of all backwoods revivalists. The camp meeting was a Methodist "harvest time," as Bishop Asbury said. It became increasingly popular, the bishop noting with satisfaction in 1811 that 400 camp meetings were to be held that year. Crowds of sinners as well as salvation seekers attended these open-air get-togethers, and the atmosphere sometimes was far from churchlike. Many Presbyterians, especially Campbellites, came to frown on the camp meeting. Even Cartwright deplored the worst outbreaks of frenzy, when men and women had fits, rolled in the dust, and lay twitching with the "holy jerks."

After 1800 the devil and the deists were on the run. Freethinkers by no means disappeared (the young Abraham Lincoln took up free thought in frontier Illinois), but they were put upon the defensive. The great majority of Americans subscribed to some variant of revealed Christianity, though it usually was not quite the same as the predominant faith of their forefathers. The churches in the nineteenth century placed more emphasis on the New Testament and the saving grace of Jesus and less emphasis on the Old Testament and the stern decrees of Jehovah than those of the seventeenth or even the eighteenth century had done.

Emerging Industrialism

While religious patterns were changing, so were industrial techniques, even more fundamentally. A new technology was developing, which was to have profound effects upon the future of the United States.

SOME NEW TECHNOLOGY

In part, the new technology came from England, where the Industrial Revolution was beginning at the time the American Revolution occurred. The essence of the Industrial Revolution was simply this: more rapidly and extensively than ever before, power-driven machines were taking the place of hand-operated tools. To tend the machines, workers were brought together in factories or mills located at the sources of power. New factory towns arose, with a new class of dependent laborers and another of millowners or industrial capitalists. The factory system was adapted most readily to the manufacture of cotton thread and cloth. In textile making, invention called forth invention. Improvements in weaving made necessary improvements in spinning so that the spinners could keep up with the weavers, and these improvements required new devices for carding, that is, combing and straightening the fibers for the spinner. Water, wind, and animal power continued to be used but began to be supplemented and replaced by steam. This was especially true after the appearance of James Watt's steam engine (patented in 1769), which, though cumbersome and inefficient, was a great improvement upon Thomas Newcomen's earlier "atmospheric" engine.

Though Americans copied all they could from England, the Industrial Revolution in the United States was largely an indigenous growth, with roots extending far back into the colonial period.

When English imports were cut off by the prewar boycott and then by the Revolutionary War, desperate efforts were made to stimulate the manufacture of certain necessities in America. Homespun became both patriotic and fashionable, and to speed up the output of linens and woolens a few of the states gave loans or bounties for the making of wire for card teeth. Several of the states offered loans or bounties for the production of cannon, gunpowder, camp kettles, and other war material. Public efforts to encourage industry continued after the war, and to these a bit of tariff protection was added after the adoption of the Constitution. Private companies were formed, and one of these with Alexander Hamilton as a sponsor founded the town of Paterson, New Jersey

(1791), to exploit the available water power for manufacturing.

Still, the American textile industry lagged behind that of England. Capital was scarce in the United States, even after certain American shipowners began to invest some of their shipping profits in textile mills. For years, prospects of profit were dim because of the abundance of cheap English imports, and the machinery available remained inferior to the steadily progressing English inventions. To protect England's superior position as a manufacturing nation, the British government tried to prevent the export of textile machinery and the emigration of skilled mechanics. Nevertheless, a number of mechanics and millwrights made their way to the United States, the most impor-

tant of them being Samuel Slater. In 1790, with the aid of American mechanics, Slater built a spinning mill for the Quaker merchant Moses Brown at Pawtucket, Rhode Island. Though a few inferior spinning mills already were in operation, Slater's work is generally considered as the beginning of the factory system in America.

In textiles and in some other manufactured goods the young republic did not measure up to England. Americans generally produced the coarser kinds of yarn and cloth, and though they supplied their own needs in common metalware, they still imported the finer grades of cutlery and other metal products. Yet in certain respects American industry was neither imitative nor inferior, and some American inventors

Slater Mill
Samuel Slater left England in the disguise of a farm boy, since English law prohibited the emigration of mechanics with a knowledge of textile machinery. At Pawtucket, Rhode Island in 1790, he designed what became the first successful cotton spinning mill in the United States. In 1815 he added facilities for weaving woolen cloth. This watercolor-and-ink drawing represents the Pawtucket bridge, falls, and mill as they were sometime between 1810 and 1819. (The Rhode Island Historical Society)

and engineers were equal to the greatest in the world. They were especially advanced in certain new techniques of mass production.

One of the most ingenious mechanics of his time was Oliver Evans, a Delaware farmer's son. Evans invented a card-making machine, constructed an automatic flour mill, improved upon the steam engine, and combined theory and practice in America's first textbook of mechanical engineering, *The Young Mill-Wright's and Miller's Guide* (1795). In his flour mill, which he put into operation the same year the constitutional convention met (1787), all the work was done by a variety of machines geared to the same water wheel. Only two men were needed. At one end of the mill a man emptied bags of wheat, and at the other end a man closed and rolled away barrels full of flour. Here was history's first continuous automatic production line, the beginning of automation.

Another pioneer in mass production was the Massachusetts-born, Yale-educated Eli Whitney. He is best known for the cotton gin, but he is even more important for the revolution he accomplished in the manufacture of guns.

The rise of the textile industry in England and America created a tremendous demand for the cotton that planters had begun to grow in the American South. But the planters were faced with the problem of separating the seeds from the cotton fast enough to meet the demand. There was a variety of cotton with smooth black seeds and long fibers that were easily cleaned, but this "long-staple" or "sea-island" variety could be grown successfully only along the coast or on the offshore islands of Georgia and South Carolina. There was also a short-staple cotton that could be raised almost anywhere in the South, but its sticky green seeds were very difficult to remove, a skilled slave being able to clean no more than a few pounds a day by hand. The planters were casting about for a machine or "gin" (that is, an engine) to clean the short-staple cotton when Whitney, then serving as a tutor on the Georgia plantation of General Nathanael Greene's widow, made his famous invention in 1793.

The gin was quite simple. A toothed roller caught the fibers of the cotton boll and pulled them between the wires of a grating, which held back the seeds, and a revolving brush removed the lint from the roller's teeth. But the gin had momentous consequences. With it, one slave could clean cotton as fast as several could by hand. Soon cotton growing spread into the upland South, and within a decade the total crop increased eightfold. Slavery, which with the decline of tobacco production had become a dying institution, was now revived, expanded, and firmly fixed upon the South.

During the undeclared war with France (1798–1800) all-out war was expected, and so the army needed many thousands of muskets in a hurry. Muskets then were made one at a time, and no two of them exactly alike, by skilled gunsmiths. There were not enough gunsmiths, and there was not enough time to meet the army's anticipated need. But Whitney had a plan. He made a contract with the government for the delivery of 10,000 muskets within two years. He designed a machine to make each of the parts exactly according to a pattern. Then all he had to do was to assemble the guns. This was the beginning of standardized quantity production through the manufacture of interchangeable parts. Before long, the same system was used for making clocks, and eventually it was applied to sewing machines and many other complicated products.

By fastening cotton and slavery upon the South, Whitney's gin contributed to the coming of the Civil War. His techniques of mass production, by building up the industrial strength of the North, helped the Union to win the war that the gin did so much to bring on. Such were some of the aftereffects of the industrial developments in the period of the young republic. There were also other political and social consequences of the changes then just getting under way. In America as in England, though somewhat more slowly, the Industrial Revolution created new classes and class conflicts, hastened the growth of crowded manufacturing towns, and gave rise to troublesome political issues, such as the perennial issue of the protective tariff.

TRANSPORTATION AND TRADE

Before the full potential of the Industrial Revolution could be realized in the United States, transportation had to be improved. What was needed was a system of roads and waterways

Fulton's Famous Voyage [1807]

In August, 1807, Robert Fulton wrote this letter to his friend Joel Barlow, a diplomat and poet, one of the group of authors known as the "Hartford Wits":

My steamboat voyage to Albany and back has turned out rather more favourable than I had calculated. The distance from New York to Albany is 150 miles; I ran it up in thirty-two hours, and down in thirty hours; the latter is just five miles an hour. I had a light breeze against me the whole way going and coming, so that no use was made of my sails, and the voyage has been performed wholly by the power of the steam engine. I overtook many sloops and schooners beating to windward, and passed them as if they had been at anchor.

The power of propelling boats by steam is now fully proved. The morning I left New York, there were not perhaps thirty persons in the city who believed that the boat would ever move one mile an hour, or be of the least utility; and while we were putting off from the wharf, which was crowded with spectators, I heard a number of sarcastic remarks. This is the way, you know, in which ignorant men compliment what they call philosophers and projectors.

Having employed much time, and money and zeal, in accomplishing this work, it gives me, as it will you, great pleasure to see it so fully answer my expectations. It will give a cheap and quick conveyance to merchandise on the Mississippi and Missouri, and other great rivers, which are now laying open their treasures to the enterprise of our countrymen. And although the prospect of personal emolument has been some inducement to me, yet I feel infinitely more pleasure in reflecting with you on the immense advantage that my country will derive from the invention.

---

that would connect all parts of the country and create a market extensive enough to justify production on a reasonably large scale. In the late eighteenth and early nineteenth century, goods still moved far more cheaply by water than by land. For the Atlantic seaports, ocean commerce with other continents was more easily carried on than overland trade with American settlements west of the Appalachian range. As Charles and Mary Beard have written, "the streets of London, the quays of Lisbon, and the Hong of Canton were more familiar sights to the merchants of the coast than were the somber forests and stump-studded clearings of Western America."

Temporarily, the Revolutionary War unsettled merchant shipping, as the British navy drove American merchantmen and fishing vessels from the seas. But, before the war was over, Americans learned to evade the enemy with light, fast, maneuverable ships. Indeed, the Yankees began to prey upon British commerce with hundreds of privateers. For many a

shipowner, privateering proved to be more profitable than ordinary peacetime trade.

When, in 1785, the *Empress of China* returned to New York from Canton, she brought back a cargo of silk and tea, which yielded a fabulous profit. Within five years Yankee ships were trading regularly with the Far East. Generally these ships carried various manufactured goods around Cape Horn to California, exchanged them for hides and furs, and with these proceeded on across the Pacific, to barter them in China.

Not only in China but also in Europe and the Near East enterprising Yankees from Salem and other ports sought out every possible opportunity for commerce. These Yankees were aided by two acts of the new Congress (1789) giving preference in tariff rates and port duties to homeowned ships. American shipping was greatly stimulated (despite the loss of ships and cargoes seized by the belligerents) by the outbreak of European war in the 1790s. Yankee vessels took over most of the carrying trade between Europe and the European colonies in the Western Hemisphere.

As early as 1793, the young republic had come to possess a merchant marine and a foreign trade larger than those of any other country except England. In proportion to its population, the United States had more ships and commerce than any other nation in the world. And the shipping business was growing fast. Between 1789 and 1810 the total tonnage of American vessels engaged in overseas traffic rose from less than 125,000 to nearly 1 million. The country's exports carried in American ships increased from 30 to 90 percent, and imports from 17.5 to 93 percent.

Transportation and trade within the United States labored under handicaps, but improvements were steadily being made. In river transportation a new era began with the development of the steamboat. Oliver Evans' high-pressure engine, lighter and more efficient than James Watt's, made steam more feasible for powering boats as well as mill machinery and eventually the locomotive. Even before the high-pressure engine was available, a number of inventors experimented with steam-powered craft, and John Fitch exhibited to some of the delegates at the constitutional convention a forty-five-foot vessel with paddles operated by steam. The perfecting of the steamboat was chiefly the work of the inventor Robert Fulton and the promoter Robert R. Livingston. Their *Clermont*, equipped with paddle wheels and an English-built engine, voyaged up the Hudson in the summer of 1807, demonstrating the practicability of steam navigation even though taking thirty hours to go 150 miles. In 1811 a partner of Livingston's, Nicholas J. Roosevelt, introduced the steamboat to the West by sending the *New Orleans* from Pittsburgh down the Ohio and Mississippi. The next year this vessel entered upon a profitable career of fairly regular service between New Orleans and Natchez.

Meanwhile, in land transportation, the turnpike era had begun. In 1792 a corporation constructed a toll road the sixty miles from Philadelphia to Lancaster, with a hard-packed surface of crushed rock. This venture proved so successful that similar turnpikes (so named from the kind of tollgate frequently used) were laid out from other cities to neighboring towns. Since the turnpikes were built and operated for private profit, construction costs had to be low enough and the prospective traffic heavy enough to assure an early and ample return. Therefore these roads, radiating from Eastern cities, ran for comparatively short distances and through rather thickly settled areas. If similar highways were to be extended over the mountains, the state governments or the federal government would have to finance the construction, at least in part.

CITY AND COUNTRY

The young republic was a land of remarkable diversity—in learning, in literary tastes, in religion, and in economic and social development. Much of the country remained a wilderness, yet its leading cities ranked in size and urban sophistication with the largest of England and Europe, except for such national capitals as London and Paris. The United States had no comparable capital of politics, science, literature, and art.

The total population rose from less than 4 million by the first census (1790) to well over 5 million by the second (1800). At this time, only three people in a hundred lived in towns of more than 8,000. Ten in a hundred lived west of the Appalachian Mountains. Though Virginia was still the most populous of the states, it contained none of the largest cities. Philadelphia (70,000) ranked first; New York (60,000) was close behind; and next in order were Baltimore (26,000), Boston (24,000), and Charleston (20,000).

Washington City, the newly founded national capital, was only a raw and straggling village, the entire District of Columbia containing no more than 3,200 people. Its broad but unpaved avenues radiated from the uncompleted Capitol and the President's house in accordance with the elaborate plan of the French architect, P. C. L'Enfant. This small town provided a new focus for the growing nationalism of Americans, and it symbolized their grand hopes for the future of their country. President Adams and his wife Abigail, sacrificing the comforts and attractions of Philadelphia, moved to Washington in 1800. And here President-elect Jefferson was inaugurated the following year.

Jefferson in Power

Long afterward Jefferson referred to his party's victory as "the revolution of 1800," but in his inaugural address of 1801, trying to sweeten the bitterness of the recent campaign, he emphasized the common principles of the two parties while restating the principles of his own. Noting that the country was separated by a wide ocean from the "devastating havoc" of the European war, he recommended a foreign policy of "peace, commerce, and honest friendship with all nations, entangling alliances with none"—much as George Washington had done in his Farewell Address. With respect to domestic affairs, Jefferson proposed a "wise and frugal government" that would leave men free to "regulate their own pursuits of industry." Yet he also favored the "encouragement of agriculture and of commerce as its handmaid."

The Unfinished Capitol, 1800
When Jefferson was inaugurated as President, the magnificent plan for the federal city of Washington still remained for the most part on paper. Two edifices had appeared in the Maryland woods—the president's "palace" and the new Capitol, with one wing completed. These two centers of government, about a mile and a half apart, were connected by Pennsylvania Avenue, a muddy road cut through swamps, and by a stone sidewalk bordering the avenue. Stonecutters are still busy in this view of the Capitol's east front. From a contemporary watercolor. (Library of Congress)

Jefferson's First Inaugural [1801]

We are all Republicans, we are all Federalists. If there be any among us who would wish to dissolve this Union or to change its republican form, let them stand undisturbed as monuments of the safety with which error of opinion may be tolerated where reason is left free to combat it. . I know, indeed, that some honest men fear that a republican government can not be strong, that this Government is not strong enough; but would the honest patriot, in the full tide of successful experiment, abandon a government which has so far kept us free and firm on the theoretic and visionary fear that this Government, the world's best hope, may by possibility want energy to preserve itself? I trust not. I believe this, on the contrary, the strongest Government on earth. I believe it the only one where every man, at the call of the law, would fly to the standard of the law, and would meet invasions of the public order as his own personal concern. Sometimes it is said that man can not be trusted with the government of himself. Can he, then, be trusted with the government of others? Or have we found angels in the forms of kings to govern him? Let history answer this question.

PRESIDENT AND PARTY LEADER

From the outset Jefferson acted in a spirit of democratic simplicity, which was quite in keeping with the frontierlike character of the raw city of Washington, but which was very different from the ceremonial splendor of former Federalist administrations in the metropolis of Philadelphia. He walked like an ordinary citizen to and from his inauguration at the capital, instead of riding in a coach at the head of a procession. In the presidential mansion he disregarded the courtly etiquette of his predecessors, widower that he was, without a First Lady to take charge of social affairs. At state dinners, adopting the "rule of pell-mell," he let his guests scramble for places at the table. He did not always bother to dress up, and the fastidious minister from Great Britain complained of being received by the President in slippers that were down at the heels, and coat and pantaloons that were "indicative of utter slovenliness and indifference to appearances."

Even at his best, the tall, freckle-faced sandy-haired Jefferson did not make a very impressive appearance, what with his shyness, his awkward posture, and his shambling gait. Yet, though a rather ineffective public speaker, he charmed his guests in conversation and he wrote with greater literary skill than any President before or since, with the possible exceptions of Abraham Lincoln and Woodrow Wilson. More than that, he was a genius with a wider diversity of talents than any other President, without exception. Besides being a politician and a diplomat, he was an architect, educator, inventor, scientific farmer, and philosopher-scientist, who diverted himself with such pastimes as sorting the bones of prehistoric animals. As a shrewd and practical politician, he was excelled by no other President, though he was equaled by Lincoln and by Franklin D. Roosevelt.

Jefferson was a strong executive, but neither his principles nor his nature inclined him to dictate to Congress. To avoid even the semblance of dictation, and to indulge his distaste for public speaking, he decided not to deliver his messages to Congress in person as Presidents Washington and Adams had done. Instead, he submitted his messages in writing, thus setting a precedent that was followed for more than a century, until President Wilson revived the practice of addressing Congress in person. Yet Jefferson, as party leader, gave direction to his fellow partisans among the senators and representatives, by quiet and sometimes by rather devious means.

To his cabinet he appointed a group of Republicans who were like-minded with him but were more than mere yes-men. Two of the ablest were the Secretary of State, James Madison, and the Secretary of the Treasury, Albert Gallatin. Madison, Jefferson's long-time neighbor and friend, continued to be so close a collaborator that, throughout Jefferson's presidency, it is hard to tell how much of the impetus to policy came from the President himself and how much from the Secretary of State, particularly in foreign affairs. Gallatin, born in Switzerland, his speech marked by a French accent, was as able a public financier as the great Hamilton had been and was, in addition, a thoroughgoing democrat, who at the time of the Whiskey Rebellion had used his talents as a lawyer to defend the tax-resisting farmers of the Pennsylvania frontier.

Jefferson used patronage as a political weapon. Like Washington before him, he believed that federal offices should be filled with men loyal to the principles and policies of the administration. True, he did not attempt a sudden and drastic removal of Federalist office-holders, possibly because of assurances to the contrary that had been given in his name when Federalist votes in Congress were needed to break the tie with Burr. Yet, at every convenient opportunity, he replaced the holdovers from the Adams administration with his own trusted followers. By the end of his first term about half the government jobs, and by the end of his second term practically all of them, were held by good Republicans. The President punished Burr and the Burrites by withholding patronage from them; he never forgave the man whom he believed guilty of plotting to frustrate the intentions of the party and the ambitions of its rightful candidate.

A tie vote between the presidential and vice-presidential candidates of the same party could not occur again. The Twelfth Amendment, added to the Constitution in 1804 before the election of that year, by implication recognized the function of political parties; it stipulated that the electors should vote for President and Vice President as separate and distinct candidates. Burr had no chance to run on the ticket with Jefferson a second time. In place of Burr, the congressional caucus of Republicans nominated his New York factional foe, George Clinton. The Federalist nominee, C. C. Pinckney, made a poor showing against the popular Jefferson, who carried even the New England states except Connecticut and was reelected by the overwhelming electoral majority of 162 to 14, while the Republican membership of both houses of Congress was increased.

During his second term Jefferson lost some of his popularity, and he had to deal with a revolt within the party ranks. His brilliant but erratic relative John Randolph of Roanoke, the House leader, turned against him, accused him of acting like a Federalist instead of a state-rights Republican, and mustered a handful of anti-Jefferson factionalists who called themselves "Quids."

Randolph became a fanatic on the subject of the Yazoo land claims. These arose from the action of the Georgia legislature, which, before ceding its territorial rights to the federal government, had made and then canceled a grant of millions of acres along the Mississippi to the Yazoo Land Companies. Jefferson favored a compromise settlement that would have satisfied both the state of Georgia and the Yazoo investors, many of whom were Northern Republicans whose support he needed. But Randolph, insisting that the claims were fraudulent, charged the President and the President's friends with complicity in corruption. A number of Randolph's colleagues in Congress were investors in the land companies or supporters of their claims, and time and again the tall, skinny Virginian would point his bony finger at one or another of these men and shriek "Yazoo!" He prevented the government from making any settlement of the question until after both he and Jefferson were out of office.

Randolph had a special antipathy toward Madison, whom he considered as one of the worst of the Yazoo men. He did all he could, which was not enough, to prevent Madison's nomination for the presidency in 1808. Jefferson refused to consider a third term for himself, for he was opposed to it in principle, unlike Washington, who had declined to run again in 1796 only because he was weary of public office. Jefferson's refusal established a tradition against a third term for any President, a tradition that remained unbroken until Franklin D. Roosevelt was elected for a third time in 1940 (and then for a fourth time in 1944). Though unwilling himself to be a candidate in 1808, Jefferson was determined that his alter ego, Madison, should succeed him and carry on his policies without a break.

CONFLICT WITH THE COURTS

The Federalists had used the courts as a means of strengthening their party and persecuting the opposition, or so it seemed to the Republicans, and soon after Jefferson's first inaugura-

Marbury v. Madison [1803]

Chief Justice Marshall:

It is emphatically the province and duty of the judicial department to say what the law is. Those who apply the rule to particular cases must of necessity expound and interpret that rule. If two laws conflict with each other, the courts must decide on the operation of each.

So if a law be in opposition to the constitution; if both the law and the constitution apply to a particular case, so that the court must either decide that case conformably to the law, disregarding the constitution, or conformably to the constitution, disregarding the law, the court must determine which of these conflicting rules governs the case. This is of the very essence of judicial duty.

If, then, the courts are to regard the constitution, and the constitution is superior to any ordinary act of the legislature, the constitution, and not such ordinary act, must govern the case to which they both apply.

---

tion his followers in Congress launched a counterattack against the Federalist-dominated judiciary. They repealed the Naturalization Act, changing the residence period for citizenship of foreigners from fourteen to five years, and they allowed the hated Alien and Sedition Acts to expire. Then they repealed the Judiciary Act of 1801, abolishing the new circuit courts and arranging for each of the Supreme Court justices to sit with a district judge on circuit duty. As President, Jefferson did not have the power to remove Adams' "midnight appointees" from their newly created jobs, but Congress achieved the same object by pulling their benches out from under them, despite Federalist protests that the repeal violated the constitutional provision that judges should hold office during good behavior for life.

In the debate on the question of the Judiciary Act of 1801 the Federalists maintained that the Supreme Court had the power of reviewing acts of Congress and disallowing those that conflicted with the Constitution. The Constitution itself said nothing about such a power of judicial review, but Hamilton in one of *The Federalist* papers had argued that the Supreme Court should have the power, and the Court actually had exercised it as early as 1796, though upholding the law of Congress then in question. In 1803, in the case of *Marbury* v. *Madison,* the Court for the first time declared a congressional act, or part of one, unconstitutional. (Not for more than half a century, in the Dred Scott case of 1857, did the Court do so a second time.)

William Marbury, one of President Adams' "midnight appointments," had been named as a justice of the peace in the District of Columbia, but his commission, though duly signed and sealed, had not been delivered to him at the time Adams left the presidency. Madison, as Jefferson's secretary of state, refused to hand over the commission, and so Marbury applied to the Supreme Court for an order (writ of mandamus) directing Madison to perform his official duty.

The Chief Justice of the United States was John Marshall, a leading Federalist and prominent lawyer of Virginia, whom President Adams had appointed in 1801. (For the remainder of Adams' term, Marshall had continued to serve also as secretary of state. It was he himself who, in that capacity, had neglected to see that Marbury's commission was delivered.) Marshall never forgot his experiences with Washington's army during the Revolution. Having shared the sufferings at Valley Forge, he retained a vivid impression of the evils of a weak, divided, and inefficient form of government. As chief justice, he did his best to give the government unity and strength.

In the case of *Marbury* v. *Madison,* Marshall decided that Marbury had a right to the commission but that the Court had no power to issue the order. True, the original Judiciary Act of 1789 had conferred such a power upon the Court, but, said Marshall, the powers of the Court had been defined in the Constitution itself, and Congress could not rightfully enlarge them. Marshall did not claim, however, that only the federal judges could decide what the Constitution meant; he implied that each of the three branches of the federal government could decide for itself. In delivering his opinion, he went out of his way to discredit the Jefferson administration, yet shrewdly avoided an open conflict. Since he decided the immediate question (whether Madison should be ordered to deliver Marbury's commission) in Madison's favor, the administration had no opportunity to defy the Chief Justice by disobeying his decision.

While the case of *Marbury* v. *Madison* was still pending, President Jefferson prepared for a renewed assault upon that Federalist stronghold, the judiciary. If he could not remove the most obnoxious of the judges directly, perhaps he could do so indirectly through the process of impeachment. According to the Constitution, the House of Representatives was empowered to bring impeachment charges against any civil officer for "high crimes and misdemeanors," and the Senate sitting as a court was authorized to try the officer on the charges. Jefferson sent evidence to the House to show that one of the district judges, John Pickering of New Hampshire, was unfit for his position. The House accordingly impeached him, and the Senate, despite his obvious insanity, found him guilty of high crimes and misdemeanors. He was removed.

Later the Republicans went after bigger game, one of the justices of the Supreme Court itself. Justice Samuel Chase, a rabidly partisan Federalist, had applied the Sedition Act with seeming brutality and had delivered political speeches from the bench, insulting President Jefferson and denouncing the Jeffersonian doctrine of equal liberty and equal rights. In doing so, Chase was guilty of no high crime or misdemeanor in the constitutional sense, and he was only saying what thousands of Federalists believed. Some of the Republicans came to the conclusion, however, that impeachment should not be viewed merely as a criminal proceeding, and that a judge could properly be impeached for political reasons—for obstructing the other branches of the government and disregarding the will of the people. As for Justice Chase, he could easily be shown to be out of step with Congress, the President, and public opinion, especially after the overwhelming victory of the Republicans in the election of 1804.

At Jefferson's own suggestion, the House of Representatives set up a committee to investigate Chase's conduct. Impeached on the basis of the committee's findings, the justice was brought to trial before the Senate early in 1805. Jefferson did his best to secure a conviction, even temporarily cultivating the friendship of Aaron Burr, who as Vice President presided over the trial. But Burr performed his duties with aloof impartiality, and John Randolph as the impeachment manager bungled the prosecution for the House of Representatives. A majority of the senators finally voted for conviction, but not the necessary two-thirds majority. Chase was acquitted.

From the Republican point of view, the Pickering and Chase impeachments, though only half successful, did considerable good, for they caused the federal judges as a whole to be more discreet and less partisan in statements from the bench. If the Republicans had succeeded in getting rid of Chase, they might have been emboldened to take action against the Chief Justice himself. As things stood, Marshall remained secure in his position, and the political duel between the Chief Justice and the President continued.

DOLLARS AND SHIPS

According to the Republicans, the administrations of Washington and Adams had been extravagant. Yearly expenditures had risen so much that by 1800 they were almost three times as high as they had been in 1793, and the public debt also had grown, though not so fast, since revenues had increased considerably. A part of these revenues came from internal taxation, including the hated whiskey excise. In 1802 the Republicans in Congress abolished the whole system of internal taxes, leaving customs duties and land sales as practically the only sources of revenue. Despite the tax cut, the new administration was determined to reduce the public debt by economizing on federal expenses. Secretary of the Treasury Gallatin proceeded to carry out a drastic retrenchment plan, scrimping as much as possible on expenditures for the ordinary operations of the government and effecting what Jefferson called a "chaste reformation" in the army and the navy. The tiny army of 4,000 men was reduced to only 2,500. The navy was pared down from twenty-five ships in commission to seven, and the number of officers and men was cut accordingly.

These reductions in the armed forces reflected other Jeffersonian principles as well as the desire for government economy. Jefferson feared that anything except the smallest of standing armies might become a menace to civil liberties and to civilian control of government. He believed that the navy, while no such threat to the principle of civilian supremacy, was likely to be misused as a means of forcing the expansion of overseas commerce, which he thought should be kept subordinate to agriculture. Yet, though he once said "peace is our passion," Jefferson was far from being a pacifist fanatic. He desired an efficient if small military force, and his administration deserves credit for founding the United States Military Academy at West Point (1802). He also contributed to the efficiency of the navy, even while reducing the size of it, for most of the decommissioned ships were outmoded, and many of the discharged officers were incompetent. And, in spite of himself, he was compelled to reverse his small-navy policy and build up the fleet because of trouble with pirates in the Mediterranean.

For years the Barbary states of North Africa — Morocco, Algiers, Tunis, and Tripoli — had made piracy a national enterprise. They demanded protection money from all nations whose ships sailed the Mediterranean, and even the mistress of the seas, Great Britain, gave regular contributions (she did not particularly desire to eliminate the racket, since it hurt her naval rivals and maritime competitors more seriously than it did her). During the 1780s and 1790s the United States agreed to treaties providing for annual tribute to Morocco and the rest, and from time to time the Adams administration ransomed American sailors who had been captured by the corsairs and were being held as slaves. Jefferson doubted the wisdom of continuing the appeasement policy. "Tribute or war is the usual alternative of these Barbary pirates," he said. "Why not build a navy and decide on war?"

The decision was not left to Jefferson. In 1801 the Pasha of Tripoli, dissatisfied with the American response to his extortionate demands, had the flagpole of the American consulate chopped down, that being his way of declaring war on the United States. Jefferson concluded that, as President, he had a constitutional right to defend the United States without a war declaration by Congress, and he sent a squadron to the relief of the ships already at the scene. Not until 1803, however, was the fleet in the Mediterranean strong enough to take effective action, under Commodores Edward Preble and Samuel Barron. In 1805 the Pasha, by threatening to kill captive Americans, compelled Barron to agree to a peace that ended the payment of tribute but exacted a large ransom ($60,000) for the release of the prisoners. This was hardly a resounding victory for the United States.

Though the war in Tripoli cost money, Secretary Gallatin pressed on with his plan for diminishing the public debt. He was aided by an unexpected increase in tariff revenues. By the time Jefferson left office, the debt had been cut almost in half (from $83 million to $45 million), despite the expenditure of $15 million to buy Louisiana from Napoleon Bonaparte.

Doubling the National Domain

In the year that Jefferson was elected President of the United States, Napoleon made himself dictator of France with the title of First Consul, and in the year that Jefferson was reelected, Napoleon assumed the name and authority of Emperor. These two men, the democrat and the dictator, had little in common, yet they were good friends in international politics until Napoleon's ambitions leaped from Europe to America and brought about an estrangement.

JEFFERSON AND NAPOLEON

Napoleon failed in a grandiose plan to seize the British Empire in India, though he succeeded in the conquest of Italy. Then he was reminded that France at one time had possessed a vast empire of her own in North America. In 1763 her possessions east of the Mississippi had gone to Great Britain, and those west of it to Spain. The former were lost for good, but the latter might be recovered. In 1800 (on the very day after the signing of the peace settlement with the United States) Napoleon arranged for Spain to cede these possessions to him in the secret treaty of San Ildefonso. Thus he got title to Louisiana, which included roughly the whole of the Mississippi Valley to the west of the river, plus New Orleans to the east of the river near its mouth. He intended Louisiana to form the continental heartland of his proposed empire.

Other essential parts of his empire-to-be were the sugar-rich and strategically valuable West Indian islands which still belonged to France — Guadeloupe, Martinique, and above all Santo Domingo. Unfortunately for his plans, the slaves on Santo Domingo had been inspired by the French Revolution to rise in revolt and create a republic of their own, under the leadership of the remarkable Negro, Toussaint L'Ouverture. Taking advantage of a truce in his war with England, Napoleon sent to the West Indies an army led by his brother-in-law, Charles Leclerc, to put down the insurrection and restore French authority.

Meanwhile, unaware of Napoleon's ultimate aim, Jefferson pursued the kind of foreign policy that was to be expected of such a well-known friend of France. He appointed as the American minister to Paris the ardently pro-French Robert R. Livingston. Continuing and hastening the peace policy of Adams, he carried through the ratification of the Franco-American settlement of 1800 and put it into effect even before it was ratified. With respect to Santo Domingo, however, he did not continue the policy of Adams, who had cooperated with the British in recognizing and supporting the rebel regime of Toussaint. Jefferson assured the French minister in Washington that the American people, especially those of the slave-holding states, did not approve of the Negro revolutionary who was setting a bad example for their own slaves. He even led the French minister to believe that the United States would join with France in putting down the rebellion.

Jefferson began to reappraise the whole subject of American relations with France when he heard rumors of the secret retrocession of Louisiana. "It completely reverses all the political relations of the U.S.," he wrote to Minister Livingston (April 18, 1802). Always before, we had looked to France as our "natural friend." But there was on the earth "one single spot" the possessor of which was "our natural and habitual enemy." That spot was New Orleans, the outlet through which the produce of the fast-growing West was shipped to the markets of the world. If France should actually take and hold New Orleans, Jefferson said, then "we must marry ourselves to the British fleet and nation."

Jefferson was even more alarmed when, in the fall of 1802, he learned that the Spanish intendant in charge at New Orleans had prohibited Americans from continuing to deposit their goods at that port for transshipment from river craft to ocean-going vessels. By the Pinckney Treaty (of 1795) Spain had guaranteed to Americans the right to deposit either at New Orleans or at some other suitable place. Without such a right, Spain's permission to use the lower Mississippi was of little value to the United States.

Westerners suspected, as did Jefferson himself, that Napoleon had procured the closing of the river for sinister purposes of his own. They demanded that something be done to reopen the river, and some of the more extreme among them clamored for war with France, the supposed source of all their troubles. The Federalists of the Northeast, though they had no real concern for the welfare of the West, played upon the discontent of the frontiersmen and encouraged the war cry for political reasons. The more the Federalists could arouse the West, the more they could embarrass the Jefferson administration. The President faced a dilemma. If he yielded to the frontier clamor and sought satisfaction through force, he would run the risk of renewed war with France. If, on the other hand, he disregarded the clamor, he would stand to lose the political support of the West.

There was possibly a way out of the dilemma, and that was to purchase from Napoleon the port so indispensable to the United States. Or, assuming that the First Consul should prove unwilling to sell New Orleans, and assuming also that he had acquired East and West Florida along with Louisiana in the secret treaty with Spain, it might be possible to obtain from him all or part of the Floridas, or at least the rights of navigation and deposit on some river flowing into the Gulf of Mexico to the east of New Orleans. Jefferson did not think of trying to buy any part of Louisiana to the west of the Mississippi; he was content, for the time being, to let that river form the boundary between the French empire and the United States. Soon after hearing rumors of the Louisiana retrocession, he instructed Livingston in Paris to negotiate for the purchase of New Orleans, and Livingston on his own authority proceeded to suggest to the French that they might be glad to be rid of the upper part of Louisiana as well.

Jefferson also induced Congress to provide an army and a river fleet, and he allowed the impression to get out that American forces, despite his own desire for peace, might soon descend upon New Orleans. Then he sent a special envoy to work with Livingston in persuading the French to sell. For this extraordinary mission he chose an ideally suited man, James Monroe, who was well remembered in France and who, at the same time, had the confidence of the American frontiersmen; his appointment would reassure them that the President was looking after their interests. Jefferson told Monroe that if he and Livingston could not obtain even the minimum needs of the United States — even the use of the Mississippi or some other river emptying into the Gulf — they were to cross the Channel to England and there discuss some kind of understanding with the British government. Whether Jefferson, in his hints at an attack on New Orleans and an alliance with Great Britain, merely meant to bluff the French, he had no chance to show. While Monroe's coach was still rumbling on its way to Paris, Napoleon suddenly made up his mind to dispose of the entire Louisiana Territory.

Startling though this decision seemed to some of his advisers, Napoleon had good reasons for it. His plans for an American empire had gone awry partly because of certain mischances, which might be summarized in two words — *mosquitoes* and *ice*. The mosquitoes brought yellow fever and death to General Leclerc and to thousands of the soldiers whom Napoleon had sent to reconquer Santo Domingo. The ice, forming earlier than expected in a Dutch harbor as winter came in 1802, delayed the departure of an expeditionary force that Napoleon was readying to reinforce Leclerc's army and also to take possession of Louisiana. By the spring of 1803 it was too late. Napoleon then was expecting a renewal of the European

war, and he feared that he would not be able to hold Louisiana if the British, with their superior naval power, should attempt to take it. He also realized that, quite apart from the British threat, there was danger from the United States: he could not prevent the Americans, who were pushing steadily into the Mississippi Valley, from sooner or later overrunning Louisiana.

THE LOUISIANA PURCHASE

Napoleon left the negotiations over Louisiana to his finance minister, Barbé-Marbois, rather than his foreign minister, Talleyrand, since Talleyrand was remembered for the X. Y. Z. Affair and was distrusted by Americans, while Barbé-Marbois had their respect, having lived for some time in the United States and having married an American girl. Livingston and Monroe, after the latter's arrival in Paris, had to decide first of all whether they should even consider making a treaty for the purchase of the entire Louisiana Territory, since they had not been authorized by their government to do so. They dared not wait until they could get new instructions from home, for Napoleon in the meantime might change his mind as suddenly as he had made it up. They decided to go ahead, realizing that Jefferson could reject their treaty if he disapproved what they had done. After a little haggling over the price that Barbé-Marbois asked — and he asked and got somewhat more than Napoleon's minimum — Livingston and Monroe put their signatures to the treaty, on April 30, 1803.

By the terms of the purchase arrangement, the United States was to pay 60 million francs directly to the French government and up to 20 million more to American citizens who held claims against France for ship seizures in the past — or a total of approximately $15 million. The United States was also to give France certain commercial privileges in the port of New Orleans, privileges not extended to other countries. Moreover, the United States was to incorporate the people of Louisiana into the Union and grant them as soon as possible the same rights and privileges as other citizens. This seemed to imply that the Louisiana inhabitants were to have the benefits of statehood in the near future. The boundaries were not defined,

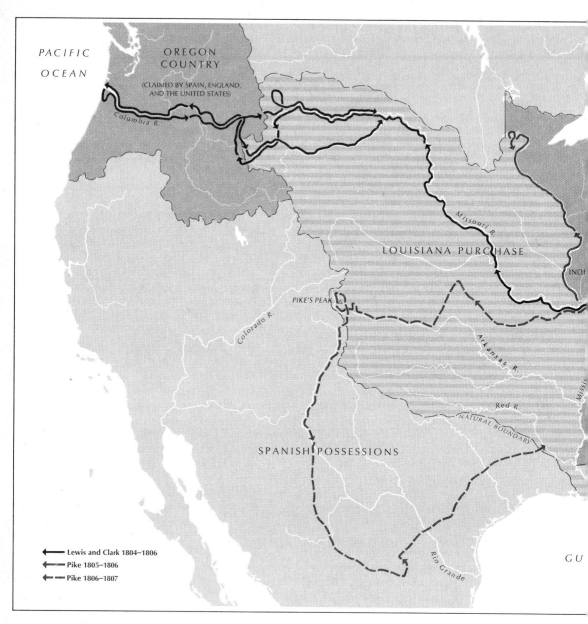

The United States at the Time of the Louisiana Purchase

Louisiana being transferred to the United States simply with the "same extent" as when owned by France and earlier by Spain. When Livingston and Monroe appealed to Talleyrand for his opinion about the boundary, he merely replied: "You have made a noble bargain for yourselves, and I suppose you will make the most of it."

In Washington, the President was both pleased and embarrassed when he received the treaty. He was glad to get such a "noble bargain," but, according to his oft-repeated views on the Constitution, the United States lacked the constitutional power to accept the bargain. In the past he had always insisted that the federal government could rightfully exer-

might be long delayed or possibly defeated, and they assured him that he already possessed all the constitutional power he needed: the President with the consent of the Senate obviously could make treaties, and the treaty-making power would justify the purchase of Louisiana. Years afterward (in 1828) the Supreme Court upheld this view, but Jefferson — strict constructionist that he had been — continued to have doubts about it. Finally he gave in, trusting, as he said, "that the good sense of our country will correct the evil of loose construction when it shall produce ill effects." Thus, by implication, he left the question of constitutional interpretation to public opinion, and he cut the ground from under his doctrine of state rights.

When Jefferson called Congress into special session, a few of the die-hard Federalists of New England raised constitutional and other objections to the treaty, but the Senate promptly gave its consent and the House soon passed the necessary appropriation bill. The Spanish minister in Washington protested to Secretary Madison that the transaction was illegal, since Napoleon when acquiring Louisiana had promised never to part with it and also had agreed to provide an Italian kingdom for the son of the Spanish king but had never done so. Madison easily disposed of the protest by reminding the Spanish minister that the latter once had advised the United States to apply to France, not Spain, in response to a query whether Spain would be willing to sell a part of Louisiana.

Though Madison and Jefferson had a good case for the American title to Louisiana itself, they had considerably less justification when, taking advantage of the vagueness of the boundaries, they also claimed part of West Florida as American by virtue of the treaty with France. The Spaniards denied that any of Florida was included in Louisiana, and indeed the two provinces had had separate histories and had been separately administered. To persuade the Spaniards to give up Florida, Jefferson tried both promises of money and threats of force. Despite John Randolph's outraged opposition, the President obtained from Congress an appropriation for secret purposes, one of which was to bribe France to bring pressure upon Spain. It was no use. All of Florida remained in Spanish hands until after Jefferson left the presidency.

cise only those powers assigned to it in so many words, and nowhere did the Constitution say anything about the acquisition of new territory. Now he thought, at first, that an amendment should be adopted to give the government the specific right to buy additional land; he even went so far as to draft a suitable amendment. But his advisers cautioned him that ratification

When the United States concluded the purchase treaty with France, Spain was still administering Louisiana, the French never having taken actual possession. They did not take possession until late in 1803, and then only to turn the territory over to General James Wilkinson, the commissioner of the United States and the commander of a small occupation force. In New Orleans, beneath a bright December sun, the recently raised French tricolor was brought down and the Stars and Stripes run up. For the time being, Louisiana Territory was given a semimilitary government with officials appointed by the President; later it was organized on the general pattern of the Northwest Territory, with the assumption that it would be divided into states. The first of these was admitted to the Union as the state of Louisiana in 1812.

EXPLORING THE WEST

Meanwhile the geography of the far-flung territory was revealed by a series of explorations. Even before he became President, Jefferson as a scientist had been interested in finding out all he could about the nature and extent of the North American continent, and he had encouraged explorers interested in the Far West. After becoming President he renewed his efforts. In 1803, before Napoleon's offer to sell Louisiana, Jefferson planned an expedition that was to cross all the way to the Pacific Ocean and gather not only geographical facts but also information about the prospects for Indian trade. Congress having secretly provided the necessary funds, Jefferson named as leader of the expedition his private secretary and Virginia neighbor, the thirty-two-year-old Meriwether Lewis, who as a veteran of Indian wars was skilled in wilderness ways. Lewis chose as a colleague the twenty-eight-year-old William Clark, who, like George Rogers Clark, his older brother, and like Lewis himself, was an experienced frontiersman and Indian fighter.

Lewis and Clark, with a chosen company of four dozen hardy men, set up winter quarters in St. Louis at about the time the United States took formal possession of Louisiana. In the spring of 1804 they started up the Missouri River, and with the Shoshoni squaw Sacaja-

The Lewis and Clark Expedition   1804–1806
Patrick Gass, one of the men who accompanied Lewis and Clark, wrote A Journal of the Voyages and Travels of a Corps of Discovery *(1811), which was the first account of the expedition to be published. This book was illustrated with crude drawings. The one here reproduced was captioned "Captain Lewis & Clark holding a Council with the Indians."*

wea as their guide, her papoose on her back, they eventually crossed the Rocky Mountains, descended the Snake and the Columbia rivers, and in the late autumn of 1805 encamped on the Pacific coast. In September 1806 they were back again in St. Louis, bringing with them carefully kept records of what they had observed along the way. No longer was the Far West a completely unknown country.

While Lewis and Clark were on their epic journey, Jefferson sent out other explorers to fill in the picture of the Louisiana Territory. The most important of these was Lieutenant Zebulon Montgomery Pike. In the fall of 1805, then only twenty-six, Pike led an expedition from St. Louis up the Mississippi River in search of its source, and though he did not find it, he learned a good deal about the upper Mississippi Valley. In the summer of 1806 Pike was sent out again, this time by Wilkinson instead of Jefferson, to proceed up the valley of the Arkansas. He discovered, but failed in his attempt to climb, the peak that now bears his name. Then he turned southward into Mexico and ran into a Spanish army; he was compelled to surrender his maps and papers and return to the United States. His account of his Western travels left the impression that the land between the Missouri and the Rockies was a desert that American farmers could never cultivate and that ought to be left forever to the nomadic Indian tribes.

THE BURR CONSPIRACY

In the long run the Louisiana Purchase prepared the way for the growth of the United States as a great continental power. Immediately, however, the purchase provoked reactions that threatened or seemed to threaten the very existence of the Union. From both the Northeast and the Southwest there soon arose rumors of secession plots.

Most of the American people heartily approved the acquisition of the new territory, as they indicated by their presidential votes in 1804, but some of the New England Federalists raged against it. Their feelings are understandable enough. Both their party and their section stood to lose in importance with the growth of the West. From their point of view the existence of the Northwest Territory was bad enough, for they would soon be outnumbered in national politics with the creation of new

states, the first of which in that area was admitted to the Union as the state of Ohio in 1803. The addition of Louisiana Territory, with its potential for still more new states, only made the evil worse in the minds of New England Federalists. A group of the most extreme of these men, known as the Essex Junto, concluded that the only recourse for New England was to secede from the Union and form a separate "Northern Confederacy." They justified such action by means of state-rights arguments similar to those Jefferson had used only about five years earlier in opposition to the Alien and Sedition Acts.

If a Northern Confederacy were to have any hope for lasting success as a separate nation, it would have to include New York as well as New England, or so the prospective seceders believed. But the prominent New York Federalist Alexander Hamilton had no sympathy with the secessionist scheme. He wrote: "Dismemberment of our empire will be a clear sacrifice of great positive advantages without any counterbalancing good, administering no relief to our real disease, which is *democracy*." He feared that disorders like those of the French Revolution were about to sweep over the United States. Then, he thought, the country would need a military dictator, a sort of American Napoleon, to bring order out of chaos, and he imagined that he himself would emerge as the man of the hour. He had no future so far as ordinary politics was concerned.

His New York Republican rival, Aaron Burr, was another politician without prospects, at least within the party of the vengeful Jefferson. When some of the Federalists approached Burr, he agreed to run with their support for governor in 1804. Rumor had it that he was implicated in the disunion plot and that, if elected, he would lead the state into secession along with New England, but the rumor lacked proof and the plot itself was fantastic, an impossible dream. Nevertheless, Hamilton accused Burr of plotting treason and cast slurs upon his personal character. Burr lost the election, then challenged Hamilton to a duel. Hamilton dared not refuse; if he did, he would sacrifice his reputation for honor and manliness, a reputation that would be indispensable to the career supposedly awaiting him as the savior of his country. And so the two men with their seconds met at Weehawken, New Jersey, across the Hudson River from New York City, on a July morning in 1804. Hamilton was mortally wounded; he died the next day.

Burr, indicted for murder in both New Jersey and New York, presided over the United States Senate the following winter and then, at the end of his term as Vice President, faced a political outlook more hopeless than ever. He was ambitious and resourceful, with almost magical powers of attracting people to him. What could he do? During the next year he busied himself with mysterious affairs in the Southwest. He talked and corresponded with prominent men of the region, especially with General James Wilkinson, now governor of Louisiana Territory. Burr was up to something, and Wilkinson was his partner in it, but no one except Burr and Wilkinson themselves knew just what it was, and Burr told different stories. Some people believed (and some historians still believe) that he intended to separate the Southwest from the Union and rule it as an empire of his own. His ultimate aim most probably was the conquest of Spanish territory beyond the boundaries of Louisiana rather than the division of the United States.

In the fall of 1806 the armed followers of Burr, with Blennerhassett's Island as their rendezvous, started by boat down the Ohio River, Burr himself joining them after they were well under way. Wilkinson, suddenly turning against Burr, sent a messenger to tell Jefferson that treason was afoot and that an attack upon New Orleans was expected. Jefferson then issued a proclamation calling for the arrest of Burr and his men as traitors. Eventually Burr was captured and brought to Richmond for trial.

Jefferson, not present in Richmond but managing the prosecution by remote control from Washington, was determined to convict his one-time running mate. The prosecution relied hopefully upon its star witness, General Wilkinson, though Wilkinson was a despicable character who accepted pay as a spy for the Spaniards and who demanded extra money from them on the grounds that, in heading off the Burr expedition, he had saved their territory from attack! But Chief Justice Marshall, presiding over the case on circuit duty, had political as well as judicial reasons for insisting that Burr be given a fair hearing.

At the trial (1807–1808) Marshall applied quite literally the clause of the Constitution that says no one shall be convicted of treason except upon the testimony of at least two witnesses to the same "overt act." He excluded all evidence not bearing directly upon such an act, and so the jury had little choice but to acquit Burr, since not even one witness had actually seen him waging war against the United States or giving aid and comfort to its enemies.

Though freed, Burr gained lasting notoriety as a traitor; after exiling himself abroad for a few years, he returned and lived long enough to hail the Texas revolution (1836) as the fruition of the same sort of movement that he had hoped to start. The trial had given the Chief Justice another chance to frustrate the President. It had set a precedent that made it almost impossible to convict anyone of treason against the United States. And the loyalty of the Southwestern frontiersmen had been proved beyond a doubt by their patriotic reaction to the cry of treason in their midst.

Selected Readings

The Young Republic
J. A. Krout and D. R. Fox, *The Completion of Independence, 1790–1830* (1944); R. B. Nye, *The Cultural Life of the New Nation, 1776–1830** (1960); C. P. Nettels, *The Emergence of a National Economy, 1775–1815* (1962); J. T. Main, *The Social Structure of Revolutionary America** (1965); Harry Warfel, *Noah Webster, Schoolmaster to America* (1936); G. A. Koch, *Republican Religion: The American Revolution and the Cult of Reason* (1938); N. J. Goodman, *Benjamin Rush* (1934); C. M. Green, *Eli Whitney and the Birth of American Technology** (1956) and *Washington: Village and Capital, 1800–1878* (1962); C. F. Ware, *The Early New England Cotton Manufacture* (1931); P. D. Jordan, *The National Road* (1948); J. A. Durrenburger, *Turnpikes: A Study of the Toll Road Movement in the Middle Atlantic States and Maryland* (1931); J. T. Flexner, *Steamboats Come True* (1944).

Politics and Administration
Henry Adams, *History of the United States During the Administrations of Jefferson and Madison* (9 vols., 1889–1891), also available in a 2-vol. abridged ed. by

Herbert Agar (1947), and *John Randolph** (1882); Edward Channing, *The Jeffersonian System* (1906); C. G. Bowers, *Jefferson in Power* (1936); L. D. White, *The Jeffersonians: A Study in Administrative History, 1801–1829* (1951); N. E. Cunningham, Jr., *The Jeffersonian Republicans in Power: Party Operations, 1801–1809* (1963); D. H. Fischer, *The Revolution of American Conservatism: The Federalist Party in the Era of Jeffersonian Democracy* (1965); N. K. Risjord, *The Old Republicans: Southern Conservatism in the Age of Jefferson* (1965); Morton Borden, *Parties and Politics in the Early Republic, 1789–1815** (1967); Russell Kirk, *Randolph of Roanoke: A Study in Conservative Thought* (1951).

Jefferson and Colleagues
Nathan Schachner, *Thomas Jefferson: A Biography* (2 vols., 1951); Dumas Malone, *Jefferson and the Ordeal of Liberty* (1962); L. W. Levy, *Jefferson and Civil Liberties: The Darker Side* (1963); M. D. Peterson, *The Jefferson Image in the American Mind** (1960); Adrienne Koch, *The Philosophy of Thomas Jefferson** (1943) and *Jefferson and Madison: The Great Collaboration* (1950); Irving Brant, *James Madison: Secretary of State, 1800–1809* (1953); Raymond Walters, Jr., *Albert Gallatin: Jeffersonian, Financier, and Diplomat* (1957).

Territorial Expansion
E. W. Lyon, *Louisiana in French Diplomacy, 1789–1804* (1934) and *The Man Who Sold Louisiana: The Life of Francois Barbé-Marbois* (1942); R. W. Irwin, *Diplomatic Relations of the United States with the Barbary Powers* (1931); John Bakeless, *Lewis and Clark, Partners in Discovery** (1947); Bernard De Voto, ed., *The Journals of Lewis and Clark** (1953); Donald Jackson, ed., *Letters of the Lewis and Clark Expedition* (1963); Nathan Schachner, *Aaron Burr** (1937), a sympathetic biography; T. P. Abernethy, *The Burr Conspiracy* (1954), an unfriendly account.

*Titles available in paperback.

Free Seas and Fresh Lands

Eight

The European war, renewed in 1803, was both a blessing and a curse for the United States. The continual conflict abroad enabled Americans to develop a profitable trade with the belligerents on both sides and at times to play them off against each other to the diplomatic advantage of this country, as in the cases of the Pinckney Treaty with Spain and the Louisiana treaty with France. Yet the war in Europe jeopardized the policy proclaimed by Washington and endorsed by Jefferson—the policy of neutrality and peace. Twice the United States got involved in the European struggle; the first time in opposition to France (1798), the second time in opposition to Great Britain (1812).

The War of 1812 was anomalous in many ways. Though avowedly waged for free seas and sailors' rights, it was opposed by the group most directly interested in seagoing commerce, the New England merchants, who sneeringly referred to it as "Mr. Madison's war," not theirs. Peace overtures began before the fighting did, and the peace treaty was signed before the last and greatest of the battles had been fought. The treaty did not even mention the most important of the war aims—the conquest of Canada and the elimination of impressment. Indeed, the war was at best a draw, and the United States was lucky to avoid surrendering some of its own territory.

Yet the war had important consequences. It broke the Indian barriers that had stood in the way of the northwestward and southwestward expansion of settlement. It gave a boost to the spirit of nationalism, which discredited the antiwar party and helped to overcome the divisive forces of postwar sectionalism. Perhaps most important of all, it stimulated the growth of manufactures, thus accelerating the progress of the nation toward industrial greatness.

The year the war ended, 1815, marks a turning point in the relations of the United States with the rest of the

The Burning of Washington
After the British had invaded Washington, in August 1814, Admiral Sir George Cockburn gave orders to burn the government buildings but to spare private property. His superior, Admiral Sir Alexander Cochrane, afterward wrote him: "I am sorry you left a house standing in Washington—depend upon it, it is mistaken mercy." This picture is from a contemporary British woodcut. (Library of Congress)

203

world. Previously, this country had become involved again and again in the broils of Europe, and much of the time the requirements of diplomacy had dictated domestic policies. Afterward, for almost a century, domestic politics held a clear priority over foreign affairs as the country entered upon a period of comparative "isolation."

Causes of Conflict

The causes of the War of 1812 were debated by politicians at the time and have been disputed by historians ever since. One view emphasizes the question of frontier lands, and another the question of freedom of the seas. Actually, these matters were interrelated, and both must be taken into account.

NEUTRAL RIGHTS

In the early 1800s the warring nations of Europe found it impossible to take care of their own shipping needs. The merchant ships of France and Spain seldom ventured far upon the ocean, dominated as it was by the sea power of Great Britain, and the merchant marine of Britain herself was too busy in the waters of Europe and Asia to devote much attention to those of America. To some degree or other, all the belligerents had to depend upon the neutrals of the world for cargoes essential to effective war-making, and in the size and activity of its merchant marine the United States was the most important of the neutrals. American shipowners prospered as, year after year, they engrossed a larger and larger proportion of the carrying trade between Europe and the West Indies. Farmers shared in the prosperity, for exports from the United States to the West Indies and Europe also increased prodigiously.

In the Battle of Trafalgar (1805) a British fleet practically destroyed what was left of the French navy. Thereafter the supremacy of Great Britain upon the seas was unchallenged, while Napoleon proceeded to extend his domination over the continent of Europe. Powerless to invade the British Isles, Napoleon devised a scheme, known as the Continental System, which he hoped would bring the enemy to terms. The British, he reasoned, were a nation of shopkeepers who depended for their existence upon buying and selling in the rest of the world, especially in Europe. If he could close the continent to their trade, he thought, they ultimately would have to give in. So, in a series of decrees beginning with those of Berlin (1806) and Milan (1807), he proclaimed that British ships and neutral ships touching at British ports were not to land their cargoes at any European port controlled by France or her allies.

The British government replied to Napoleon's decrees with a succession of orders-in-council. These announced an unusual kind of blockade of the European coast. The blockade was intended not to keep goods out of Napoleon's Europe but only to see that the goods were carried either in British vessels or in neutral vessels stopping at a British port and paying for a special license. Thus, while frustrating the Continental System, Britain would compel the neutrals to contribute toward financing her war effort, and she would limit the growth of her maritime rivals, above all the United States.

Caught between Napoleon's decrees and Britain's orders, American vessels sailing directly for Europe took the chance of capture by the British, and those going by way of a British port ran the risk of seizure by the French. Both of the warring powers disregarded American rights and sensibilities, yet to most Americans the British seemed like the worse offender of the two. Possessing effective sea power, they pounced upon Yankee merchantmen all over the wide ocean; the French could do so only in European ports. True, Napoleon's officials sometimes imprisoned and brutally mistreated the crews of confiscated ships, but the British navy far more often infringed upon personal liberty and national sovereignty, stopping American ships on the high seas and taking sailors off the decks as victims of impressment.

IMPRESSMENT

The British navy—with its floggings, its low pay, and its dirty and dangerous conditions on shipboard—was a "floating hell" to its sailors. They had to be impressed (forced) into the service and at every good opportunity they deserted, many of them joining the merchant marine of the United States and even its navy. To check this loss of vital manpower, the British claimed the right to stop and search American merchantmen, though not naval vessels, and reimpress deserters. They did not claim the right to take native-born Americans, but they did seize naturalized Americans born on British soil, for according to the laws of England a true-born subject could never give up his allegiance to the King: once an Englishman, always an Englishman. In actual practice the British often impressed native as well as naturalized Americans, and thousands upon thousands of sailors claiming the protection of the Stars and Stripes were thus kidnapped. To these hapless men, impressment was little better than slavery. To their shipowning employers it was at least a serious nuisance. And to millions of proud and patriotic Americans, even those living far from the ocean, it was an intolerable affront to the national honor.

In the summer of 1807, in the *Chesapeake-Leopard* incident, the British went to more outrageous extremes than ever. The *Chesapeake* was a public and not a private vessel, a frigate of the United States navy and not an ordinary merchantman. Sailing from Norfolk, with several alleged deserters from the British navy among the crew, the *Chesapeake* was hailed by His Majesty's Ship *Leopard*, which had been lying in wait off Cape Henry, at the entrance to Chesapeake Bay. Commodore James Barron refused to allow the *Chesapeake* to be searched, and so the *Leopard* opened fire and compelled him, unprepared for action as he was, to strike his colors. A boarding party from the *Leopard* dragged four men off the American frigate.

This was an attack upon the United States! When news of the outrage got around the country, most of the people cried for a war of revenge. Not since the days of Lexington and Concord had Americans been so strongly aroused; never again were they to be so solidly united in opposition to Great Britain. Even the "most temperate people and those most attached to England," the British minister reported home, "say that they are bound as a people and that they must assert their honor on the first attack upon it." If Congress had been in session, or if President Jefferson had called a special session, as he was urged to do, the country might have stampeded into war. But, as the French minister in Washington informed Talleyrand, "the President does not want war," and "Mr. Madison dreads it now still more."

Instead of assembling Congress and demanding a war declaration, Jefferson made a determined effort to maintain the national honor with peace. First, he issued an order expelling all British warships from American waters, so as to lessen the likelihood of future incidents. Then he sent instructions to his minister in England, James Monroe, to get satisfaction from the British government and to insist again upon the complete renunciation of impressment. On the whole the British government was conciliatory enough. It disavowed the action of Admiral Berkeley, the officer primarily responsible for the *Chesapeake-Leopard* affair, recalled him, and offered to indemnify the wounded and the families of the killed and to return the captured sailors (only three were left; one had been hanged). But the British cabinet refused to concede anything to Jefferson's main point; instead, the cabinet issued a proclamation reasserting the right of search to recover deserting seamen.

Thus the impressment issue stood between the British and American governments and prevented a compromise that might have led away from war. Though by 1812 the British had made a money settlement, the *Chesapeake* outrage meanwhile remained an open sore in Anglo-American relations. This incident, together with the impressment issue involved in it, was probably the most important single cause of the War of 1812, even though its final effect was delayed for five years.

Seaman's Protection Paper

To protect American sailors from British impressment, Congress authorized the issuance of certificates of American citizenship, which came to be known as "protection" papers. These papers were not always respected by British naval officers. To them a certificate of naturalization was meaningless, for the British government claimed the allegiance of all British subjects for life. A certificate of American birth was not dependable, for it could be obtained by fraud. Some Americans made a business of selling forged documents. One woman, it is said, had an oversized cradle built, for British deserters to climb into, so that she could honestly swear that she had known them from the cradle. (Essex Institute, Salem, Mass.)

"PEACEABLE COERCION"

Even at the height of the excitement over the *Chesapeake,* Jefferson made no preparations for a possible war. He and Madison believed that, if worse came to worst, the United States could bring Great Britain to terms, and France as well, through the use of economic pressure instead of military or naval force. Dependent as both nations were upon the Yankee carrying trade, they presumably would mend their ways if they were completely deprived of it.

Hence, when Congress met for its regular session, Jefferson hastily drafted an embargo bill, Madison revised it, and both the House and the Senate promptly enacted it into law. The embargo prohibited American ships from leaving this country for any port in the world; if it had specified only British and French ports it could have been evaded by means of false clearance papers. Congress also passed a force act to make the embargo effective.

Though the law was nevertheless evaded in various ways, it was effective enough to be felt in France, much more in Great Britain, and still more in the United States itself. Throughout the United States—except in the frontier areas of Vermont and New York, which soon doubled their overland exports to Canada—the embargo brought on a serious depression. The planters of the South and the farmers of the West, though deprived of foreign markets for their crops, were willing to suffer in comparative silence, devoted Jeffersonian Republicans that most of them were. But the Federalist merchants and shipowners of the Northeast, still harder hit by the depression, made no secret of their rabid discontent.

Though the Northeastern merchants disliked impressment, the orders-in-council, and Napoleon's decrees, they hated Jefferson's embargo much more. Previously, in spite of risks, they had kept up their business with excellent and even fabulous returns; now they lost money every day their ships idled at the wharves. Again, as at the time of the Louisiana Purchase, they concluded that Jefferson had violated the Constitution (as indeed he had—if judged by the principles he had advocated before becoming President).

In the midst of the embargo-induced depression came the election of 1808. The Federalists, with C. C. Pinckney again their candidate, made the most of the embargo's unpopularity and won a far larger proportion of the popular and electoral votes than in 1804, yet

---

Commercial Warfare [1806–1810]

Napoleon's Berlin Decree, 1806 No vessel coming from or touching at a British port shall be received in any European port of France or her allies.

British Orders-in-Council, 1807 All vessels trading to or from enemy ports shall be subject to capture unless they first put in at a British port, pay a fee, and obtain a certificate.

Napoleon's Milan Decree, 1807 Any vessel submitting to search by an English ship, or paying any fee to the English government, shall be considered as an English vessel and shall be liable to seizure.

The U.S. Embargo Act, 1807 No ship shall clear from the United States for any foreign port. No ship shall depart even for another American port without first giving bond, of twice the value of ship and cargo, that the goods will be relanded within the United States.

The U.S. Non-Intercourse Law, 1809 All shipping and trade between the United States and British- or French-controlled ports (but not the rest of the world) are prohibited. If either Great Britain or France "shall cease to violate the neutral commerce of the United States," trade and shipping will be resumed with the nation so doing.

Macon's Bill No. 2, 1810 Intercourse with France and Great Britain is renewed, but if either nation ceases its violations of American rights, and the other refuses to do so, the provisions of the Non-Intercourse Law will be reimposed against the nation thus refusing.

Madison was safely elected as Jefferson's successor. The Federalists also gained a number of seats in the House and the Senate, though the Republicans continued to hold a majority in both houses. To Jefferson and Madison the returns indicated plainly enough that the embargo was a growing liability in politics. A few days before going out of office, Jefferson approved a bill terminating his and Madison's first experiment with what he called "peaceable coercion." But Jefferson's succession by Madison meant no basic change in policy, and other experiments with measures short of war were soon to be tried.

By the time he entered upon his presidential duties, James Madison already had a career behind him that would assure him immortality in history books. He was not only experienced in affairs of government; he was also a more profound and original thinker than he was credited with being by his contemporaries and by later generations who have assumed that he was merely Jefferson's echo. Unfortunately for his reputation, he was not an impressive figure of a man, but was small and wizened, with a scholarly frown. Nor was he equipped with the personal charm or politician's skill needed for strong presidential leadership. What he lacked in personality, his wife more than supplied. Dolley Madison, North Carolina born, was as gay and gracious a First Lady as ever adorned the White House.

Just before Madison's inauguration, Congress passed a modified embargo bill known as the Nonintercourse Act. The Nonintercourse Act was soon replaced by another expedient commonly called Macon's Bill No. 2 (1810). This freed commercial relations with the whole world, including Great Britain and France, but authorized the President to prohibit intercourse with either belligerent if it should continue its violations after the other had stopped. The freeing of American trade was more to the advantage of the British than the French, since it fitted in with the efforts of the former to pierce and weaken the Continental System. Napoleon had every incentive to induce the United States to reimpose the embargo against his enemy. He succeeded in doing so by means of a trick, the Cadore letter, which pretended to revoke the Berlin and Milan decrees as far as they interfered with American commerce. Madison accepted the Cadore letter as evi-

dence of Napoleon's change of policy, even though the French continued to confiscate American ships. He announced that early in 1811, an embargo against Great Britain alone would automatically go into effect, in accordance with Macon's Bill, unless Britain meanwhile rescinded her orders-in-council.

In time the new embargo, though less well enforced than the earlier, all-inclusive one had been, hurt the economy of England enough to cause influential Englishmen to petition their government for repeal of the orders-in-council. Eventually the orders were repealed—too late to prevent war, even if they had been the only grievance giving rise to the martial spirit in the United States. But there were other grievances, namely, impressment and a border conflict between the British Empire and the expanding American frontier.

RED MEN AND REDCOATS

Ever since the days of the Revolution the Indians generally had looked to their old "white father," the King of England, for protection against the relentlessly advancing Americans. And the British in Canada had relied upon Indian friendship to keep up their fur trade, even within the territory of the United States, and to maintain potentially useful allies. At one time, in 1794, this country nearly went to war with Great Britain because of her Indian policy, but Anthony Wayne's victory over the tribes at Fallen Timbers and the conclusion of Jay's Treaty dispelled the war danger and brought on a period of comparative peace. Then, in 1807, the border quiet was disturbed by an event occurring far away—the British assault upon the *Chesapeake*. The ensuing war crisis had repercussions that, as will be seen, terribly aggravated the frontier conflict between tribesmen and settlers. Much of this conflict of red men and white was personified in the two opposing leaders, Tecumseh and William Henry Harrison.

The Virginia-born Harrison, already a veteran Indian fighter at twenty-six, went to Washington as the congressional delegate from the Northwest Territory in 1799. He was largely responsible for the passage of the Harrison Land Law (1800), which enabled settlers to acquire farms from the public domain on much easier terms than before. Land in the Northwest Territory soon was selling fast. The growth of population led to a division of the area into the state of Ohio and the territories of Indiana, Michigan, and Illinois. By 1812 Ohio contained 250,000 people and was beginning to look like an Eastern state, as paths widened into roads, villages sprang up and in some cases grew into cities, and the forests receded before the spreading cornfields. By 1812 Michigan had few settlers, but Illinois contained a scattered population of about 13,000, and Indiana 25,000.

Receiving from Jefferson an appointment as governor of Indiana Territory, Harrison devoted himself to carrying out Jefferson's policy of Indian removal. According to the Jeffersonian program, the Indians must give up their claims to tribal lands and either convert themselves into settled farmers or migrate to the west of the Mississippi. Playing off one tribe against another, and using whatever tactics suited the occasion—threats, bribes, trickery—Harrison made treaty after treaty with the separate tribes of the Northwest. By 1807 the United States claimed treaty rights to eastern Michigan, southern Indiana, and most of Illinois. Meanwhile, in the Southwest, millions of acres were taken from other tribes in the states of Georgia and Tennessee and in Mississippi Territory. Having been forced off their traditional hunting grounds, the Indians throughout the Mississippi Valley seethed with discontent. But the separate tribes, helpless by themselves against the power of the United States, probably would have quieted down and accepted their fate if two complicating factors had not arisen.

One complication was the policy of the British authorities in Canada. For years they had neglected their Indian friends across the border to the south. Then came the *Chesapeake* incident and the surge of anti-British feeling throughout the United States. Now the Canadian authorities, expecting war and an attempted invasion of Canada, began to take desperate measures for their own defense. "Are the Indians to be employed in case of a rupture with the United States?" asked the lieutenant governor of Upper Canada (December 1, 1807). And Sir James Craig, the governor general of the entire province, replied: "If we do not employ them, there cannot exist a moment's

doubt that they will be employed against us." Craig at once took steps to renew friendship with the Indians and provide them with increased supplies. Thus the trouble on the sea over the question of impressment intensified the border conflict hundreds of miles inland.

The second factor intensifying this conflict was the rise of a remarkable native leader, one of the most admirable and heroic in Indian history. Tecumseh, "The Shooting Star," chief of the Shawnees, aimed to unite all the tribes of the Mississippi Valley, resist the advance of white settlement, and recover the whole Northwest, making the Ohio River the boundary between the United States and the Indian country. He maintained that Harrison and others, by negotiating with individual tribes, had obtained no real title to land in the various treaties, since the land belonged to all the tribes and none of them could rightfully cede any of it without the consent of the rest. "The Great Spirit gave this great island to his red children. He placed the whites on the other side of the big water." So Tecumseh eloquently told Harrison. "They were not contented with their own, but came to take ours from us. They have driven us from the sea to the lakes—we can go no farther."

In his plans for a united front, Tecumseh was aided by his brother, a one-eyed, epileptic medicine man know as the Prophet. The Prophet, visiting the Great Spirit from time to time in trances, inspired a religious revival that spread through numerous tribes and helped bring them together. Few Indians doubted his supernatural powers after, having secretly learned from Canadian traders of a forthcoming eclipse, he commanded the sun to be dark on the appointed day. The Prophet's town, at the confluence of Tippecanoe Creek and the Wabash River, became the sacred place of the new religion as well as the headquarters of Tecumseh's confederacy. Leaving his brother there after instructing him to avoid war for the time being, Tecumseh journeyed down the Mississippi in 1811 to bring the Indians of the South into his alliance. At that time a great earthquake occurred centering at New Madrid, Missouri, and rumbling up and down the Mississippi Valley, causing much of the river to change its course. To many of the Indians, this seemed another awesome sign that a new era was at hand for them.

During Tecumseh's absence, Governor Harrison saw a chance to destroy the growing influence of the two Indian leaders. With 1,000 soldiers he camped near the Prophet's town, provoked an attack (November 7, 1811), and though suffering losses as heavy as those of the enemy, succeeded in driving off the Indians and burning the town. This, the Battle of Tippecanoe, disillusioned many of the Prophet's followers, for they had been led to believe that his magic would protect them from the white man's bullets. Tecumseh returned to find his confederacy shattered, yet there were still plenty of warriors eager for the warpath, and by the spring of 1812 they were busy with hatchet and scalping knife all along the frontier, from Michigan to Mississippi.

Westerners blamed Great Britain for the bloodshed along the border. Her agents in Canada encouraged Tecumseh, used the Prophet as a "vile instrument," as Harrison put it, and provided the guns and supplies that enabled the Indians to attack. To Harrison and to most of the frontiersmen, there seemed only one way to make the West safe for Americans. That was to drive the British out of Canada and annex that province to the United States.

While frontiersmen in the North demanded the conquest of Canada, those in the South looked to the acquisition of Florida. In Spanish hands, that territory was a perpetual nuisance, with slaves escaping across the line in one direction and Indians raiding across it in the other. Through Florida ran rivers like the Alabama, the Apalachicola, and others which in American possession would give access to the Gulf of Mexico and the markets of the world. In 1810 American settlers in West Florida took matters into their own hands, fell upon the Spanish fort at Baton Rouge, and requested that the territory be annexed to the United States. President Madison unhesitatingly proclaimed its annexation, then schemed to get the rest of Florida too. With Madison's connivance, the former Georgia governor George Mathews attempted to foment a revolt in East Florida (1811). Spain protested, and Madison backed down, but the desire of Southern frontiersmen for all of Florida did not abate. Spain was Britain's ally, and a war with Britain would give these frontiersmen an excuse for taking Spanish as well as British territory.

Thus the war fever was raging on both the Northern and the Southern frontiers by 1812. The denizens of these outlying regions were not numerous as compared with the population of the country as a whole, and for the most part they were not directly represented in Congress, except by a few territorial delegates. Nevertheless, they were ably represented at the national capital by a group of determined young congressmen who, with good reason, soon gained the name of "war hawks."

THE WAR HAWKS

Three days before the Battle of Tippecanoe a new Congress met in Washington for the session of 1811–1812. In the congressional elections of 1810, most of the voters had indicated their disgust with such expedients as Macon's Bill No. 2 by defeating large numbers of Republican advocates of measures short of war, as well as Federalist advocates of continued peace. Of the newly elected congressmen and senators, the great majority were warlike Republicans, and after the news of Tippecanoe they became more eager than ever for a showdown with the power that seemed to threaten both the security of the frontier and the freedom of the seas.

A new generation had arrived upon the political scene, a group of daring young men of whom the most influential came from the new states in the West or from the back country of the old states in the South. Two of the natural leaders were Henry Clay and John C. Calhoun, whose careers were to provide much of the drama of American politics for the next four decades. The tall, magnetic Clay, barely thirty-four, was a Virginian by birth but had made Kentucky his home. Already, while still under the legal age for a senator, he had appeared briefly in the United States Senate. As handsome as Clay though less appealing, the twenty-nine-year-old Calhoun was the son of Scotch-Irish pioneers in the South Carolina hills.

When Congress organized in 1811, the war faction of young Republicans got control of both the House and the Senate. As Speaker of the House, Clay held a position of influence then second only to that of the President himself. Clay filled the committees with the friends of force, appointing Calhoun to the crucial Committee on Foreign Affairs, and launched a drive toward war for the conquest of Canada. This would bring Great Britain to terms and avenge the wrongs that Clay recited eloquently and at length. Or at least he supposed it would, and he further imagined that the conquest would be quick and easy.

The Federalists in Congress, representing the commercial interests of the Northeast, deprecated the clamor for Canada and war. But they were powerless to stem the drive toward hostilities, even with the aid of dissident Republicans like the eccentric "Quid," John Randolph of Roanoke. Dubbing the Clay men "war hawks," Randolph ridiculed their cry as being like that of the whippoorwill, "one eternal monotonous tone—Canada! Canada! Canada!"

While Congress debated, President Madison moved reluctantly toward the conclusion that war was necessary. In May the war faction took the lead in the caucus of Republican congressmen who renominated him for the presidency, and on June 1 he sent his war message to Congress.

In his message the President maintained that Great Britain—by impressing American citizens, interfering with American trade, and inciting the Indians along the frontier—was already waging war against the United States. He recommended that Congress declare war in return. Congress responded with a declaration of hostilities on June 18, two days after a new ministry had announced in Parliament that the orders-in-council were to be suspended, but before the news could reach Washington. The close vote on the declaration, 19 to 13 in the Senate and 79 to 49 in the House, showed how badly the American people were divided.

The division of public opinion was again revealed in the election of 1812. Opposing Madison and the war, a peace faction of the Republicans nominated a rival candidate, De Witt Clinton of New York, and the Federalists gave their support to him. Most of the electors in the

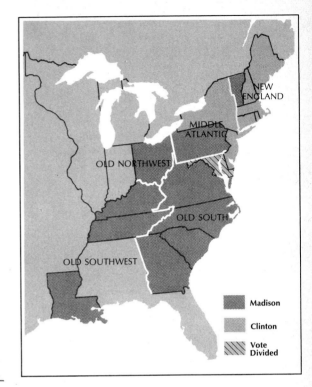

Election of 1812

Northeast voted for Clinton and peace, but all of those in the South and the West sustained Madison and war, the President being reelected, 128 to 89.

With the people thus divided, the country as a whole was not psychologically prepared for war, nor was it financially or militarily prepared. Congress had adjourned without increasing the army and navy, voting war taxes, or renewing the charter of the government's indispensable financial agency, the Bank of the United States, which expired in 1811. The war hawks, however, were not worried. On to Canada!

The War of 1812

At first Great Britain, preoccupied with her mighty struggle against Napoleon, paid little attention to the American war, a mere annoyance to her. Then, in the fall of 1812, Napoleon launched the Russian campaign that, before the

winter was over, was to bring him disaster and prepare the way for his ultimate defeat. As the months passed, Great Britain was able to divert more and more of her military and naval power to America. Only for about a year did the

United States undertake the offensive; thereafter this country was forced to fight a defensive war, a war to protect its own territory.

THE COURSE OF BATTLE

The conquest of Canada, supposedly a "mere matter of marching," as Jefferson himself put it, soon proved to be an exercise in frustration. A three-pronged invasion was planned to strike into Canada by way of Detroit, the Niagara River, and Lake Champlain, with the greatest concentration of force at Detroit. At Detroit, however, after marching into Canada, the elderly General William Hull, Governor of Michigan Territory, retreated and surrendered the fort (August 1812). The other invasion efforts also failed, and Fort Dearborn (Chicago) fell before an Indian attack.

During the year of disaster and defeat on land, the Madison administration and its supporters took what consolation they could in the news of successes on the sea. American frigates engaged British warships in a series of duels and won some spectacular victories, one of the most renowned being the victory of the *Constitution* over the *Guerrière*. American privateers destroyed or captured one British merchant ship after another, occasionally braving the coastal waters of the British Isles and burning vessels within sight of the shore. After that first year, however, the score was evened by the British navy, which not only drove the American frigates to cover but also instituted a close blockade of the United States and harried the coastal settlements from Virginia to Maine.

While British sea power dominated the ocean, American fleets arose to control the Great Lakes. First, the Americans took command of Lake Ontario, enabling troops to cross over to York (Toronto), the capital of Canada. At York (April 27, 1813) the invaders ran upon a cunningly contrived land mine, the explosion of which killed more than fifty, including General Zebulon M. Pike. Some of the enraged survivors, without authorization, set fire to the capital's public buildings, which burned to the ground. After also destroying some ships and military stores, the Americans returned across the lake.

Next, Lake Erie was redeemed for American use, mainly through the work of the youthful Oliver Hazard Perry. Having constructed a fleet at Presqu' Isle (Erie, Pennsylvania), Perry took up a position at Put-in-Bay, near a group of islands off the mouth of the Maumee River. With the banner "Don't Give up the Ship" flying on his flagship, he awaited the British fleet, whose intentions he had learned from a spy. He smashed the fleet upon its arrival (September 10, 1813) and established American control of the lake.

This made possible, at last, an invasion of Canada by way of Detroit. The post had been hard to reach overland, for supply wagons either had to struggle through the almost impassable Black Swamp of the Maumee Valley or had to make a long detour around it. After Perry's victory at Put-in-Bay, supplies as well as men could be quickly and easily transported by water. William Henry Harrison, who had replaced Hull in the Western command, now pushed up the River Thames into Upper Canada and won a victory (October 5, 1813), notable for the death of Tecumseh, who had been commissioned a brigadier general in the British army. The Battle of the Thames resulted in no lasting occupation of Canadian soil, but it disheartened the Indians of the Northwest and eliminated the worst of the danger they had offered to the frontier.

While Harrison was harrying the tribes of the Northwest, another Indian fighter was striking an even harder blow at the Creeks in the Southwest. The Creeks, aroused by Tecumseh on his Southern visit, were supplied by the Spaniards in Florida. These Indians had fallen upon Fort Mims, on the Alabama River just north of the Florida border, and had massacred the frontier families taking shelter within its stockade. Andrew Jackson, Tennessee planter and militia general, turning from his plans for invading Florida, tracked down the Creeks. In the Battle of Horseshoe Bend (March 27, 1814) Jackson's men took frightful vengeance, slaughtering squaws and children along with warriors. Then Jackson went into Florida and seized the Spanish fort at Pensacola.

After the Battles of the Thames and Horseshoe Bend, the Indians were of little use to the British. But, with the surrender of Napoleon in Europe, the British could send their veterans of the European war to dispose of the "dirty shirts," the unkempt Americans. In 1814 the

Victory at Sea

As of 1812, the British in the course of the Napoleonic Wars had fought 200 naval battles and won 200 victories, in engagements between individual ships or whole fleets. Great Britain seemed invincible on the ocean. Then the United States frigate Constitution *met and defeated three British vessels in a row. The third victim, off the coast of Brazil on December 19, 1812, was the Java, which was blown up after surrender and the removal of her crew, as shown in this sketch by an American naval lieutenant. (The Mariners Museum, Newport News, Va.)*

British prepared to invade the United States by three approaches—Chesapeake Bay, Lake Champlain (the historic route of Burgoyne), and the mouth of the Mississippi.

An armada under Admiral Sir George Cockburn, a hard-bitten old sea dog, sailed up the Patuxent River from Chesapeake Bay and landed an army that marched a short distance overland to Bladensburg, on the outskirts of the District of Columbia. Hastily drawn up to oppose this army was a much more numerous force of poorly trained militiamen. When the firing started they gave more than they received, but they were unnerved by the repeated assaults of the well-disciplined redcoats and finally broke formation and ran. The British marched on into Washington (August 24, 1814), putting the government to flight. Then they deliberately burned the public buildings, including the White House, in retaliation for the earlier unauthorized incendiarism at York. The sack of Washington marked the low point of American fortunes in the war; better days were coming.

Leaving Washington in partial ruins, the invading army reembarked and proceeded up the bay, toward Baltimore. But Baltimore, guarded by Fort McHenry, was ready. To block the river approach, the garrison had stretched a chain across the Patapsco and had sunk several boats in the river. From a distance the British bombarded the fort (September 12, 1814) while through the night an American, Francis Scott Key, watched from one of the enemy ships where he had gone to secure the release of a prisoner. At the "dawn's early light," as Key wrote the next day, the flag on the fort was still flying "o'er the land of the free and the home of the brave." The British withdrew, and Key's words, set to the tune of an old drinking song, quickly became popular.

Meanwhile another invasion force was descending upon northern New York. On Lake Champlain the British mustered a fleet about the size of the American fleet drawn up to oppose it, and near by they had an army three times as large as the mixed force of regulars and militia facing it. Yet, in the Battle of Plattsburg (September 11, 1814), the defenders destroyed the invading fleet, and the invading army then retreated to Canada. The northern border was safe.

Far to the south the most serious threat of all soon materialized. In December 1814, a formidable array of battle-hardened veterans, fresh from the Duke of Wellington's peninsular campaign against the French in Spain, landed below New Orleans. On Christmas, Wellington's brother-in-law Sir Edward Pakenham arrived to take command. Neither he nor anyone else in America knew that a treaty of peace between the British and American governments had been signed in faraway Belgium the day before. Awaiting Pakenham's advance up the Mississippi was Andrew Jackson with a motley collection of Tennesseans, Kentuckians, Creoles, Negroes, and pirates drawn up behind breastworks. For all their drill and bravery, the redcoats advancing through the open (January 8, 1815) were no match for Jackson's well-protected men. Making good use of artillery as well as rifles, the Americans held their fire as each wave of attackers approached, then sent out deadly volleys at close range. Finally the British retreated while an American band struck up "Hail Columbia!" Left behind were 700 dead, including Paken-

ham himself, 1,400 wounded, and 500 other prisoners. Jackson's losses: 8 killed, 13 wounded.

NEW ENGLAND OBJECTIONS

With notable exceptions, such as the Battle of New Orleans, the military operations of the United States, 1812–1815, were rather badly bungled. This should cause little surprise. What is surprising is the fact that American arms succeeded as well as they did. After all, the government was woefully unprepared for the war at the outset and faced increasing popular opposition as the contest dragged on. The opposition centered in New England, and it went to remarkable extremes. Some of the Federalists there celebrated British victories, sabotaged their own country's war effort, and even plotted disunion and a separate peace.

Until 1814 the blockade did not extend north of Newport, Rhode Island, the British government deliberately cultivating the New England trade. Goods carried in Yankee ships helped to feed British troops in Canada as well as Spain, and for a time many a shipowner grew rich by trading with the enemy while denouncing Madison and the war, though eventually the business of the shipowners as a whole fell far below the level of the prosperous prewar years.

Though most of the money in the nation was concentrated in New England, only a small part of the government's war bonds could be sold there. One of the Treasury loans, desperately needed to keep soldiers in the field, almost fell through because of the refusal of the New England banks to lend. Secretary of the Treasury Gallatin had to turn to his friend John Jacob Astor of New York and two foreign-born bankers of Philadelphia for the necessary funds. On several occasions the governors of New England states refused to allow the state militia to take orders from the President or to fight outside the country.

In Congress the Republicans had continual trouble with the Federalist opposition. The leadership of the administration party fell to Calhoun, who devoted himself to justifying the war and raising men and money with which to fight it. At every step he ran against the obstructionists, foremost among them the young congressman from New Hampshire, Daniel

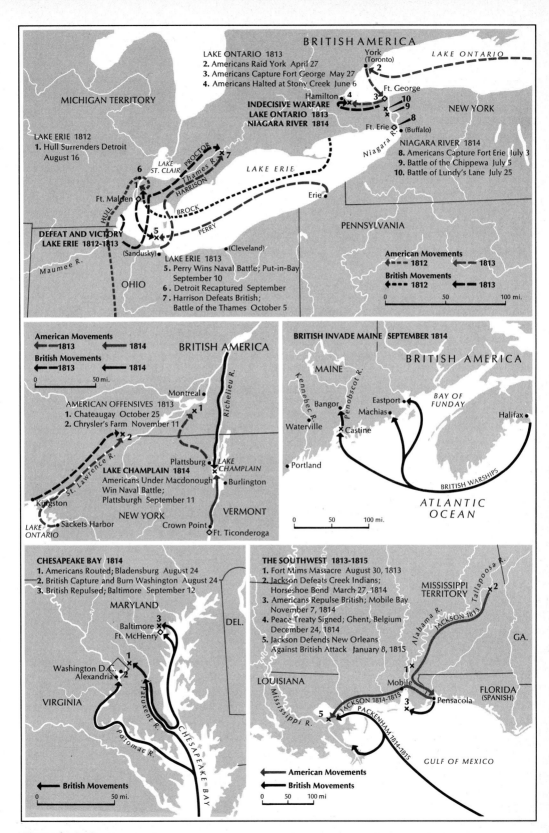

War of 1812

LAKE ONTARIO 1813
2. Americans Raid York April 27
3. Americans Capture Fort George May 27
4. Americans Halted at Stony Creek June 6

INDECISIVE WARFARE
LAKE ONTARIO 1813
NIAGARA RIVER 1814

LAKE ERIE 1812
1. Hull Surrenders Detroit
   August 16

NIAGARA RIVER 1814
8. Americans Capture Fort Erie July 3
9. Battle of the Chippewa July 5
10. Battle of Lundy's Lane July 25

DEFEAT AND VICTORY
LAKE ERIE 1812-1813

LAKE ERIE 1813
5. Perry Wins Naval Battle; Put-in-Bay
   September 10
6. Detroit Recaptured September
7. Harrison Defeats British;
   Battle of the Thames October 5

American Movements
◄---- 1812   ◄---- 1813
British Movements
◄···· 1812   ◄---- 1813
0   50   100 mi.

MICHIGAN TERRITORY
BRITISH AMERICA
York (Toronto)
LAKE ONTARIO
Ft. George
NEW YORK
Hamilton
Ft. Erie (Buffalo)
Niagara R.
LAKE ST. CLAIR
PROCTOR
Thames R.
HARRISON
BROCK
LAKE ERIE
Erie
HULL
Ft. Malden
PERRY
(Sandusky)
(Cleveland)
Maumee R.
OHIO
PENNSYLVANIA

American Movements
◄---- 1813   ◄---- 1814
British Movements
◄---- 1813   ◄---- 1814
0   50 mi.

BRITISH AMERICA
Montreal
Richelieu R.

AMERICAN OFFENSIVES 1813
1. Chateaugay October 25
2. Chrysler's Farm November 11

LAKE CHAMPLAIN 1814
Americans Under Macdonough
Win Naval Battle;
Plattsburgh September 11

St. Lawrence R.
Kingston
LAKE ONTARIO
Sackets Harbor
Plattsburg
LAKE CHAMPLAIN
Burlington
NEW YORK
VERMONT
Crown Point
Ft. Ticonderoga

BRITISH INVADE MAINE SEPTEMBER 1814
BRITISH AMERICA
MAINE
Kennebec R.
Penobscot R.
Bangor
Waterville
Castine
Eastport
Machias
BAY OF FUNDY
Halifax
Portland
BRITISH WARSHIPS
ATLANTIC OCEAN
0   50   100 mi.

CHESAPEAKE BAY 1814
1. Americans Routed; Bladensburg August 24
2. British Capture and Burn Washington August 24
3. British Repulsed; Baltimore September 12

MARYLAND
Baltimore
Ft. McHenry
Washington D.C.
Alexandria
DEL.
VIRGINIA
Patuxent R.
Potomac R.
CHESAPEAKE BAY
British Movements
0   50 mi.

THE SOUTHWEST 1813-1815
1. Fort Mims Massacre August 30, 1813
2. Jackson Defeats Creek Indians;
   Horseshoe Bend March 27, 1814
3. Americans Repulse British; Mobile Bay
   November 7, 1814
4. Peace Treaty Signed; Ghent, Belgium
   December 24, 1814
5. Jackson Defends New Orleans
   Against British Attack January 8, 1815

MISSISSIPPI TERRITORY
Tallapoosa R.
Alabama R.
JACKSON 1813
GA.
LOUISIANA
Mobile
FLORIDA (SPANISH)
JACKSON 1814-1815
Pensacola
PACKENHAM 1814-1815
Mississippi R.
GULF OF MEXICO
American Movements
British Movements
0   50   100 mi

Webster. Introducing resolution after resolution to embarrass the administration, Webster demanded reasons for the war and intimated that Napoleon had tricked the President into antagonizing England, as in fact Napoleon had. Every measure to finance the fighting — by loans, taxes, tariffs, or a national bank — Webster and his Federalist allies vehemently denounced. At a time when volunteering lagged and the army was seriously undermanned, he opposed a bill to encourage enlistments. In its extremity the administration decided to draft men into the regular army from the state militia. Helping to defeat the conscription bill, Webster warned that no such law could be enforced in his part of the country.

As new states in the South and West, strongly Republican, were added to the Union, the Federalists had become more and more hopelessly a minority party in the country as a whole. But they were the majority in New England. If that section were to become a separate confederacy, they could control its destinies and escape the dictation of slaveholders and backwoodsmen. The talk of secession, heard before at the time of the Louisiana Purchase and again at the time of Jefferson's embargo, was revived during the war and reached a climax in the winter of 1814–1815, when the Republic appeared to be on the verge of ruin.

On December 15, 1814, while the British were beginning their invasion by way of New Orleans, delegates from the New England states met in Hartford, Connecticut, to consider the grievances of their section against the Madison administration. The would-be seceders were overruled by the comparatively moderate men who were in the overwhelming majority at the Hartford Convention. The convention's report reasserted the right of nullification but only hinted at secession, observing that "the severance of the Union by one or more States, against the will of the rest, and especially in time of war, can be justified only by absolute necessity." But the report proposed seven essential amendments by the Constitution, presumably as the condition of New England's remaining in the Union. These amendments were intended to protect New England from the growing influence of the South and the West.

The Federalists, apparently in a strong bargaining position, assumed that the Republicans would have to give in to the Hartford Convention terms, since the government was in such dire extremity. Soon after the convention adjourned, however, the news of Jackson's smashing victory at New Orleans reached the cities of the Northeast. While most Americans rejoiced, the Federalists were plunged into gloom. A day or two later came tidings from abroad concerning the conclusion of a treaty of peace. Of course, the treaty had been signed before the Battle of New Orleans, but the people heard of the battle first. They got the impression that the United States had won the war. "Peace is signed in the arms of victory!" *Niles's Register* exclaimed. The Hartford Convention and the Federalist party were discredited as not only treasonable but also futile.

THE PEACE SETTLEMENT

During the War of 1812 peace talks began before the battles did. President Madison, reluctant to ask for a declaration of war and "regretting the necessity which produced it," looked hopefully toward an early end to hostilities. Soon after the declaration the British government, wishing to liquidate a minor war and concentrate upon the major one, against Napoleon, sent an admiral to Washington with armistice proposals, but negotiations failed to develop because of Madison's continued insistence upon the renunciation of impressment. Britain's ally Russia, eager to get supplies from America as well as unhampered military aid from England, twice offered to mediate, the first time on the day before Napoleon's invading forces entered Moscow (September 13, 1812). The British politely declined both of the Czar's offers but finally agreed to meet the Americans in direct negotiations on neutral ground. After prolonged delays the peacemakers got together in Ghent, Belgium, on August 8, 1814.

The American peace delegation at Ghent happened to be composed of men of exceptional ability, men who were more than a match for their opposite numbers around the peace table. The delegation included men of both parties and all sections. At the head of it was John Quincy Adams, a former Federalist who had broken with his party to support Jefferson's

The Hartford Convention [1815]

New England opponents of the war, meeting at Hartford, Connecticut, late in 1814, demanded the following amendments to the federal Constitution in their report, published early in the following year:

1. "Representatives and direct taxes shall be apportioned among the several states . . . according to their respective numbers of free persons. . . ."

2. "No new state shall be admitted into the Union by Congress . . . without the concurrence of two thirds of both houses."

3. "Congress shall not have power to lay any embargo . . . for more than sixty days."

4. "Congress shall not have power, without the concurrence of two thirds of both houses, to interdict the commercial intercourse between the United States and any foreign nation. . . ."

5. "Congress shall not make or declare war, or authorize acts of hostility against any foreign nation, without the concurrence of two thirds of both houses, except such acts of hostility be in defence of the territories of the United States when actually invaded."

6. "No person who shall hereafter be naturalized, shall be eligible as a member of the senate or house of representatives of the United States, nor capable of holding any civil office under the authority of the United States."

7. "The same person shall not be elected president of the United States a second time; nor shall the president be elected from the same state two terms in succession."

---

embargo, and a diplomat of varied experience who recently had been minister to Russia. One of his colleagues was Henry Clay, once a war hawk, now a peace dove. Another was the Secretary of the Treasury in both Jefferson's and Madison's administrations, Albert Gallatin. A natural diplomat, Gallatin held the delegation together by moderating the disputes of Adams and Clay.

At Ghent the two sets of peacemakers at first presented fantastically extreme demands, then gradually backed down and finally agreed to a compromise. The Americans, in accordance with their instructions, originally demanded the renunciation of impressment as a necessary condition to peace, and they also asked for all or part of Canada and for British aid in acquiring Florida from Spain. The Englishmen, contrary to their instructions, presented an ultimatum requiring the United States to cede territory in the Northwest for the formation of an Indian buffer state. Then, when their home government refused to sustain them in the ultimatum, they withdrew it and proposed that peace be made on the principle of *uti possidetis*. This meant that each of the belligerents

should keep the territory it actually held whenever the fighting stopped. Expecting large territorial gains from the invasion of America, the Englishmen at Ghent tried to delay negotiations so as to maximize the gains. But the government in London, becoming more and more alarmed by developments in Europe, decided to hasten the settlement with the United States and recommended peace on the basis of the *status quo ante bellum*, which meant a return to things as they had been before the war began. Already President Madison had advised his delegation that they need no longer make an issue of impressment. A treaty providing for the status quo, hastily drawn up, was signed on Christmas Eve 1814.

According to the Treaty of Ghent, the war was to end not immediately, but when the document had been ratified and proclaimed on both sides (hence it is not exactly true, as is sometimes said, that the battle of New Orleans was fought after the war was over). Each of the belligerents was to restore its wartime conquests to the other. Four commissions with both American and British members were to be appointed to agree upon disputed or undetermined segments of the boundary between Canada and the United States.

The Treaty of Ghent was followed by other settlements that contributed to the improvement of Anglo-American relations. A separate commercial treaty (1815) gave Americans the right to trade freely with England and the British Empire except for the West Indies. A fisheries convention (1818) renewed the privileges of Americans to catch and dry fish at specified places along the shores of British North America. The Rush-Bagot agreement (1817) provided for mutual disarmament on the Great Lakes. Gradually disarmament was extended to the land, and eventually (though not till 1872) the Canadian-American boundary became the longest "unguarded frontier" in the world.

Though the British had not renounced impressment in principle, they ceased to apply it in practice after 1815. With the final end of the Napoleonic wars after the battle of Waterloo, the nations of Europe entered upon a century of comparative peace, broken only by wars of limited scale. So the British no longer had occasion to violate American sovereignty on the high seas, and the government and people of the United States could afford to devote their energies primarily to affairs at home.

FREE SEAS AGAIN

No sooner had peace come in 1815 than Congress declared war again, this time against Algiers, which had taken advantage of the War of 1812 to loose its pirates once more against American shipping in the Mediterranean. Two American squadrons now proceeded to North African waters. One of the two, under the command of Stephen Decatur, a naval hero of the late war with England, captured a number of corsair ships, blockaded the coast of Algiers, and forced the Dey to accept a treaty that not only ended the payment of tribute by the United States but required the Dey to pay reparations to this country. Going on to Tunis and Tripoli, Decatur collected additional indemnities in both of those places. This naval action in the Mediterranean brought a more clear-cut victory for the freedom of the seas than had the War of 1812 itself. Of course, the victory was made possible by the growth in naval strength and national spirit which the war with England had occasioned. After 1816, when the Dey of Algiers began to make trouble again, only to have his entire fleet destroyed by combined British and Dutch forces, the United States had no further difficulties with the Barbary pirates.

Postwar Expansion

Americans could now give their full attention to domestic problems as the country, during a postwar boom, expanded its economy, its territory, and its population. Suddenly the boom terminated in a bust.

BANKS, TARIFFS, ROADS

The War of 1812 led to chaos in shipping and banking, as well as stimulating the growth of manufactures, and exposed dramatically the inadequacy of the existing transportation system. Hence arose the postwar issues of reestablishing the Bank of the United States, protecting the new industries, and providing a nationwide network of roads and waterways. On these issues the former war hawks Clay and Calhoun became the leading advocates of the

national as opposed to the local or sectional point of view. The party of Jefferson now sponsored measures of a kind once championed by the party of Hamilton. In regard to the Bank and the tariff the new nationalists were completely successful; in regard to internal improvements, only partly so.

The wartime experience seemed to make necessary another national bank. After the first Bank's charter expired (1811), a large number of state banks sprang up. These issued vast quantities of banknotes (promises to pay, which then served much the same purpose as bank checks were later to do) and did not always bother to keep a large enough reserve of gold or silver to redeem the notes on demand. The notes passed from hand to hand more or less as money, but their actual value depended upon the reputation of the bank that issued them, and the variety of issues was so confusing as to make honest business difficult and counterfeiting easy. This bank money was not legal tender, and it was not issued directly by the state governments, yet its issuance hardly conformed with the clause of the Constitution giving Congress the exclusive power to regulate the currency and forbidding the states to emit bills of credit.

Congress struck at the currency evil not by prohibiting state banknotes but by chartering a second Bank of the United States in 1816. Except that it was allowed a larger capital, this institution was essentially the same as the one founded under Hamilton's leadership in 1791. In return for the charter, the Bank had to pay a "bonus" of $1.5 million to the government. Though its potentialities were not fully realized

The Embargo Act (1807) reduced trade in 1808 and 1809 to about half of what it had been in the years immediately preceding, when it was stimulated by the war in Europe. The War of 1812 caused trade to shrink still further in 1813 and 1814. During the postwar recovery, imports considerably exceeded exports, creating an "unfavorable balance of trade" and provoking demands for increased tariff protection.

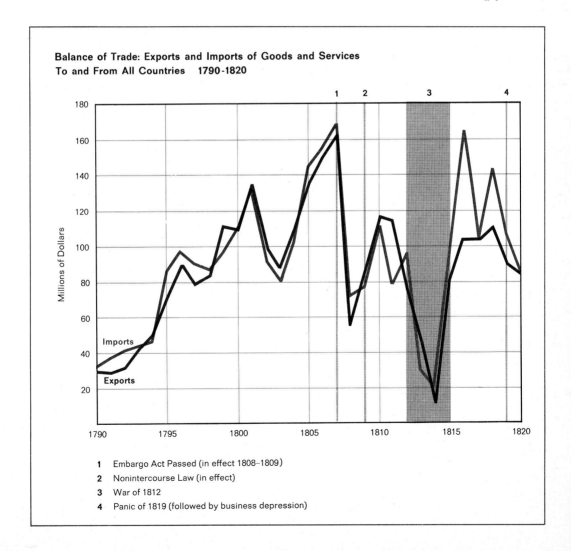

Balance of Trade: Exports and Imports of Goods and Services To and From All Countries   1790-1820

Millions of Dollars

Imports

Exports

1   Embargo Act Passed (in effect 1808–1809)
2   Nonintercourse Law (in effect)
3   War of 1812
4   Panic of 1819 (followed by business depression)

during the first few years of its existence, this national bank possessed the power of controlling the state banks by presenting their notes from time to time and demanding payment either in cash or in its own notes, which were as good as gold. Once the Bank of the United States began to exercise its power, the state banks had to stay on a specie-paying basis or risk being forced out of business.

The war had a disastrous effect upon American shipping, especially after the British blockade was extended to include the New England coast. Between 1811 and 1814 exports dropped from $61 million to $7 million, and imports from $53 million to $13 million. The total tonnage of American vessels engaged in foreign trade declined from about 950,000 to less than 60,000 tons. Some ships managed to escape the blockade but others were caught and confiscated, altogether about 1,300 of them.

Farmers, unable to get their produce out to the markets of the world, suffered from the ruin of the carrying trade, but manufacturers prospered as foreign competition almost disappeared in consequence of the embargoes and the blockade. Much of the capital and labor formerly employed in commerce and shipbuilding was diverted to manufacturing. Goods were so scarce that, even with comparatively unskilled labor and poor management, new factories could be started with an assurance of quick profits.

The American textile industry had grown rather slowly until English imports were checked by Jefferson's Embargo of 1807 and then by the War of 1812. The first census of manufacturing, in 1810, counted 269 cotton and 24 woolen mills in the country. From 1807 to 1815 the total number of cotton spindles increased from 8,000 to 130,000. Most of the factories were located in New England. Until 1814 they produced only yarn and thread: the weaving of cloth was left to families operating hand looms at home. Then the Boston merchant Francis C. Lowell, after examining textile machinery in England, perfected a power loom that was an improvement on its English counterpart. Lowell organized the Boston Manufacturing Company and founded at Waltham, Massachusetts, the first mill in America to carry on the processes of spinning and weaving under a single roof.

As the war came to an end, the manufacturing prospects of the United States were suddenly dimmed. British ships swarmed alongside American wharves and began to unload their cargoes of manufactured goods at cut prices, even selling below cost. As Lord Brougham explained to Parliament, it was "well worth while to incur a loss upon the first exportation, in order, by the glut, to stifle in the cradle those rising manufactures in the United States, which war had forced into existence, contrary to the natural course of things." Thus, though the war was over, Great Britain persisted in a kind of economic warfare against the United States.

The "infant industries" needed protection if they were to survive and grow strong enough to stand upon their own feet against foreign competition. So the friends of industry maintained, reviving the old arguments of Hamilton. In 1816 the protectionists brought about the passage of a tariff law with rates high enough to be definitely protective, especially on cotton cloth.

The war had delayed the extension of steamboat lines on both eastern and western waters. Not until 1816 did a river steamer, the *Washington*, make a successful voyage upstream as far as Louisville, at the falls of the Ohio. Within a few years steamboats were carrying far more cargo on the Mississippi than all the flatboats, barges, and other primitive crafts combined.

When Ohio was admitted as a state (1803) the federal government agreed that part of the proceeds from the sale of public lands there should be used for building roads. In 1807 Jefferson's Secretary of the Treasury, Albert Gallatin, proposed that a national road, financed partly by Ohio land sales, be built from the Potomac to the Ohio, and both Congress and the President approved. The next year Gallatin presented a comprehensive plan of internal improvements, requiring an appropriation of $20 million, but Jefferson doubted the constitutionality of such an expenditure, and the plan was shelved. Finally, in 1811, construction of the National Road began, at Cumberland, Maryland, on the Potomac. By 1818 this highway, with a crushed stone surface and massive stone bridges, was completed to Wheeling, Virginia, on the Ohio. Meanwhile the state of

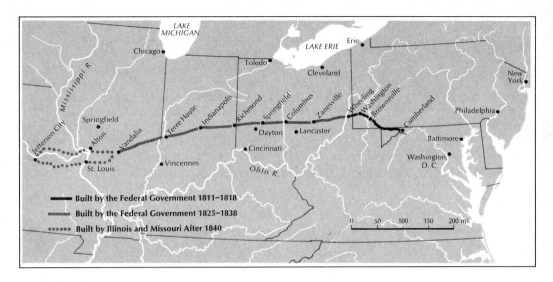

The National Road

Pennsylvania contributed $100,000 to a private company which extended the Lancaster pike westward to Pittsburgh.

Over both of these roads moved a heavy traffic of stagecoaches, Conestoga wagons, private carriages, and other vehicles, as well as droves of cattle. Despite the high tolls, freight rates across the mountains now were lower than ever before. They were not low enough to permit the long-distance hauling of bulky loads like wheat or flour. But commodities with a high value in proportion to their weight, especially manufactures, moved from the Atlantic seaboard to the Ohio Valley in unprecedented quantities.

Despite the progress being made with steamboats and turnpikes, there remained serious gaps in the transportation network of the country, as experience during the War of 1812 had shown. Once the coastwise shipping had been cut off by the British blockade, the coastal roads became choked by the unaccustomed volume of north-south traffic. At the river ferries, long lines of wagons waited for a chance to cross. Oxcarts, pressed into emergency service, took six or seven weeks to go from Philadelphia to Charleston. In various localities there appeared serious shortages of goods normally carried by sea, and prices rose to new heights,

rice costing three times as much in New York as in Charleston, flour three times as much in Boston as in Richmond. On the northern and western frontiers the military campaigns of the United States were frustrated partly by the absence of good roads.

With this wartime experience in mind, President Madison in 1815 called the attention of Congress to the "great importance of establishing throughout our country the roads and canals which can be best executed under the national authority," and he suggested that a constitutional amendment would resolve any doubts about the authority of Congress to provide for the construction of canals and roads. Representative Calhoun promptly espoused a bill by which the moneys due the government from the Bank of the United States—both the "bonus" and the government's share of the annual profits—would be devoted to internal improvements. "Let us, then, bind the republic together with a perfect system of roads and canals," Calhoun urged. "Let us conquer space."

Congress passed the bonus bill, but President Madison, on his last day in office (March 3, 1817), returned it with his veto. While he approved its purpose, he still believed that a constitutional amendment was necessary. And so, with some exceptions, the tremendous task of internal improvements was left to the state governments and to private enterprise.

"ERA OF GOOD FEELINGS"

After 1800 the presidency seemed to have become the special possession of Virginians, who passed it from one to another in unvarying sequence. After two terms in office Jefferson named his Secretary of State, James Madison, to succeed him, and after two more terms Madison secured the nomination of *his* Secretary of State, James Monroe. Many in the North already were muttering against this succession of Virginians, the so-called Virginia Dynasty, yet the Republicans had no difficulty in electing their candidate in the remarkably listless campaign of 1816. Monroe received 183 ballots in the electoral college; his opponent, Rufus King of New York, only 34, from the states of Massachusetts, Connecticut, and Delaware.

At the time he became President, Monroe was sixty-one years old. Tall and dignified, he wore the old-fashioned garb of his youthful days, including knee-length pantaloons and white-topped boots. He had reached the peak of a long and varied career as Revolutionary soldier, diplomat, and cabinet officer. Although when young he had been regarded as impulsive and changeable, he now was noted for his caution and patience. He was neither so subtle nor so original as his gifted predecessors from Virginia, Jefferson and Madison, yet he was more able than posterity generally has considered him. He had a mind of his own, and he was the master of his administration, even though he picked a group of exceptionally strong men for his advisers.

In choosing his cabinet, Monroe intended to recognize and harmonize the major interests of the country. For the first and most important position, that of secretary of state, he selected the New Englander and former Federalist, John Quincy Adams. This choice was significant in view of the well-established custom that made the State Department a stepping stone to the presidency: Monroe appeared to be announcing that he would be the last of the Virginia Dynasty and that the next President (after a second term for Monroe) would be a Massachusetts man. For secretary of war, Monroe

James Monroe
When Monroe was governor of Virginia (1799–1802) an acquaintance said of him: "To be plain, there is often in his manner an inartificial and even an awkward simplicity, which, while it provokes the smile of a more polished person, forces him to the opinion that Mr. Monroe is a man of most sincere and artless soul." In 1825, when Monroe was in his last year as President, a Virginia lady gave her impression of him after attending a New Year's reception at the White House: "From the frank, honest expression of his eye . . . I think he well deserves the encomium passed upon him by the great Jefferson, who said, 'Monroe is so honest that if you turned his soul inside out there would not be a spot on it.'" The portrait here reproduced was done by Gilbert Stuart, who painted portraits of all the men who served as President during his lifetime— Washington, Adams, Jefferson, Madison, Monroe, and John Quincy Adams. (The Pennsylvania Academy of the Fine Arts)

chose the forceful South Carolinian, John C. Calhoun, after Henry Clay had declined the office, preferring to continue as Speaker of the House.

Soon after his inauguration Monroe did what no other President since Washington had done: he made a goodwill tour through the country, eastward to New England, westward as far as Detroit. In New England, so recently the scene of rabid Federalist discontent, he was greeted everywhere with enthusiastic demonstrations. The *Columbian Centinel*, a Federalist newspaper of Boston, commenting on the "Presidential Jubilee" in that city, observed that an "era of good feelings" had arrived. This phrase soon became popular; it spread throughout the country, and eventually it came to be almost synonymous with the presidency of Monroe.

There was a good deal of hidden irony in this phrase of 1817, for the "good feelings" did not last long, and the period over which Monroe presided turned into one of very bad feelings indeed. Yet he was reelected in 1820 with the nearest thing to a unanimous electoral vote that any presidential candidate, with the exception of George Washington, has ever had. Indeed, all but one of the electors cast their ballots for Monroe. The lone dissenter, a strong-minded Yankee from New Hampshire who thought Monroe unfit for the presidency, voted for John Quincy Adams. The Federalists had not even bothered to put up an opposing candidate.

FLORIDA AND THE FAR WEST

The first big problem facing John Quincy Adams as Secretary of State was that of Florida. Already the United States had annexed West Florida, but Spain still claimed the whole of the province, East and West, and actually held most of it, though with a grasp too feeble to stop the abuses against which Americans long had complained—the escape of slaves across the border in one direction, the marauding of Indians across it in the other. In 1817 Adams began negotiations with the Spanish minister, Don Luis de Onís, for acquiring all of Florida (or rather for acquiring that part of it which the United States did not already claim). Talks between the cantankerous puritan and

the wily don progressed haltingly, then were broken off when the hot-tempered Andrew Jackson took matters forcefully into his own hands.

Jackson, in command of American troops along the Florida frontier, had orders from Secretary of War Calhoun to "adopt the necessary measures" to end the border troubles. Jackson also had an unofficial hint—or so he afterward claimed—that the administration would not mind if he undertook a punitive expedition into Spanish territory. At any rate he invaded Florida, seized the Spanish forts at St. Marks and Pensacola, and ordered the hanging of two British subjects on the charge of supplying the Indians and inciting them to hostilities. News of these events provoked a sharp discussion behind the scenes in Monroe's cabinet. Calhoun and others insisted that the general should be punished or at least reprimanded for exceeding his authority, but Adams defended Jackson so ably as to prevent any action against him.

Instead of blaming Jackson or disavowing the raid, Adams wished the government to assume complete responsibility for it, for he saw in it a chance to further his Florida diplomacy. Rejecting a Spanish protest, he demanded reparations from Spain to pay the cost of the expedition, though he did not press this demand. He pointed out that Spain had promised in Pinckney's Treaty to restrain the Indians in her territory but had failed to live up to her treaty obligations. The United States, he argued, was justified by international law in taking drastic measures for self-defense. He implied that this country would be justified in going even farther than it had done.

Jackson's raid demonstrated that the United States, if it tried, could easily take Florida by force, unless Spain could get aid from some other power. The only power to which she could look was Great Britain.

Unable to obtain British support, Spain had little choice but to come to terms with the United States, though the resourceful Onís made the most of a bad situation for his country. In the treaty of 1819 it was agreed that the King of Spain should cede "all the territories which belong to him situated to the eastward of the Mississippi and known by the name of East and West Florida." This ambiguous wording was used so as to evade the troublesome question whether Spain was ceding both East and West Florida or whether West Florida already belonged to the United States. In return the United States assumed the claims of its citizens against the Spanish government to the amount of $5 million. This money was to be paid to American citizens, not to the Spanish government: we did not "purchase" Florida, as is sometimes said. The United States also gave up its claims to Texas, and Spain her claims to territory north of the forty-second parallel from the Rockies to the Pacific. Thus a line was drawn from the Gulf of Mexico northwestward across the continent delimiting the Spanish empire and transferring to the United States the Spanish title to the West Coast north of California. Adams and Onís had concluded something more than a Florida agreement: it was a "transcontinental treaty."

President Monroe, with the approval of the Senate, promptly ratified the treaty, but the coming of a revolution delayed ratification by Spain. The treaty finally went into effect in 1821. Thereafter the whole of Florida was, without question, territory belonging to the United States. And for the first time the area of the Louisiana Purchase had a definite southwestern boundary.

At the time of his negotiations with Onís, Adams showed much more interest in the Far West than did most of his fellow countrymen. Few Americans were familiar with the Oregon coast except for New Englanders engaged in Pacific whaling or in the China trade. Only the fur traders and trappers knew intimately any of the land between the Missouri and the Pacific. Before the War of 1812 John Jacob Astor's American Fur Company had established Astoria as a trading post at the mouth of the Columbia River. But when war came Astor sold his interests to the Northwestern Fur Company, a British concern operating from Canada, and after the war he centered his own operations in the Great Lakes area, from which he eventually extended them westward to the Rockies. Manuel Lisa's Missouri Fur Company, founded in 1809, with headquarters in St. Louis, sent traders and supplies up the Missouri and its tributaries and brought back peltries obtained from the Indians. The Rocky Mountain Fur Company, which Andrew Henry and William Henry Ashley organized in 1822, pushed the trade farther north and west and revolution-

ized the business by sending out white trappers who procured their furs directly and brought them to an annual "rendezvous" in the mountains to be sold to the company's agents.

The trappers or "mountain men," notably Jedediah S. Smith, explored the Far West and gained an intimate knowledge of it, but they did not write books. General information about the region was increased in consequence of the explorations of Major Stephen H. Long. In 1819 and 1820, with instructions from the War Department to find the sources of the Red River, Long with nineteen soldiers ascended the Platte and South Platte rivers, discovered the peak named for him, and returned eastward by way of the Arkansas River, but failed to find the headwaters of the Red. "In regard to this extensive section of country between the Missouri River and the Rocky Mountains," Long said in his report, "we do not hesitate in giving the opinion that it is almost wholly unfit for cultivation, and of course uninhabitable by a people depending upon agriculture for their subsistence." On the published map of his expedition the Great Plains were marked as the "Great American Desert." Thus he gave increased currency to the idea earlier put forth by Pike that the farming frontier would run against a great natural barrier beyond the Missouri. Meanwhile the vacant lands to the east, between the Appalachians and the Mississippi, were rapidly being converted into plantations and farms.

THE GREAT MIGRATION

One of the central themes of American history, for nearly three centuries after the founding of Jamestown, was the movement of population from the Atlantic coast to the interior and ultimately across the continent. This was no steady march, uniform along a broad front. It proceeded in irregular waves, following the lines of greatest attraction and least resistance, and accelerating in times of prosperity and peace. A sudden surge, greater than any preceding it, swept westward during the boom years that followed the War of 1812.

Weakened though it had been, the Indian threat still had to be taken into account. In a series of treaties forced upon the tribes after 1815, the federal government resumed the poli-

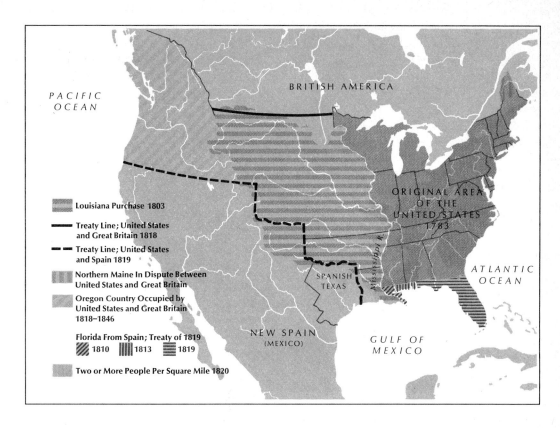

Louisiana Purchase 1803

Treaty Line; United States and Great Britain 1818

Treaty Line; United States and Spain 1819

Northern Maine In Dispute Between United States and Great Britain

Oregon Country Occupied by United States and Great Britain 1818–1846

Florida From Spain; Treaty of 1819
1810   1813   1819

Two or More People Per Square Mile 1820

PACIFIC OCEAN

BRITISH AMERICA

ORIGINAL AREA OF THE UNITED STATES 1783

ATLANTIC OCEAN

SPANISH TEXAS

NEW SPAIN (MEXICO)

GULF OF MEXICO

MISSISSIPPI R.

Boundary Settlements   1818–1819

cy of compelling the redmen to choose between settling down as civilized farmers and migrating beyond the Mississippi. Along the Great Lakes and the upper Mississippi a chain of stockaded forts was erected to protect the frontier. A "factory" system, by which government factors or agents traded with the Indians, supplying them with goods at cost, was instituted in an effort to drive out of business the Canadian traders who persisted in carrying on their activities on American soil. After several years the government factories were abandoned because of the opposition of American fur companies who objected to government competition with private enterprise. By that time the Canadian traders had retreated across the border, and foreign influence over the American tribes finally came to an end.

The land abandoned by the Indians in the Northwest had been richly favored by nature, though its qualities were not entirely recog-

nized by the early pioneers. Over most of the Northwest extended the great primeval forest, but in central Illinois the forest gave way to a grand prairie billowing with wild grass as tall as six feet. The first settlers avoided this treeless stretch, for they saw unfamiliar problems in its tough sod and scarcity of wood, and they little knew the productivity of its black loam.

"Old America seems to be breaking up and moving westward," remarked an Englishman who joined the throng. Some were Kentucky and Tennessee frontiersmen, restless spirits who had begun to feel crowded as their states became increasingly populous. Others were small farmers from the back country of Virginia and the Carolinas who fled the encroachment of slavery and the plantation system. Still others came from the middle states, New England, and foreign countries, but the great majority were Southerners. Whatever the starting point, the Ohio River was for most of the mi-

From Forest to Farm

First (top left), a clearing is begun and a rude cabin is built. The stream remains unbridged and has to be forded. Second (bottom left), the cabin is fenced in (note the "worm" fence), more trees are cut, stumps are burned, a small crop is put in, and the stream is spanned by a log bridge. Third (top right), the cabin is enlarged,

a barn is built, the fencing is improved, fields are widened, and a bridge is erected. Finally (bottom right), all trace of the wilderness is gone, an imposing house has replaced the cabin, a village has grown up nearby, and an arched stone bridge has been built. These illustrations are from O. Turner, Pioneer History of the Holland Land Purchase of Western New York *(1850).*

grants the main route, the "grand track," until the completion of the Erie Canal in 1825. They took the turnpike to Pittsburgh or the National Road to Wheeling and thus reached the river, or they took one of its tributaries such as the Kanawha, the Cumberland, or the Tennessee. Downstream they floated on flatboats bearing all their worldly goods. Then, leaving the Ohio at Cincinnati or at some place farther down, they pressed on overland with wagons, handcarts, packhorses, cattle, and hogs.

Once having arrived at his destination, preferably in the spring or early summer, the settler built a lean-to or cabin for his family, then hewed a clearing out of the forest and put in a crop of corn to supplement the wild game he caught and the domestic animals he had brought with him.

These frontier folk knew loneliness and poverty and dirt, suffered much from the forest fevers and from malnutrition, commonly had a lean and sallow look. Yet they were on the whole remarkably proud, bold, and independent. They were "half wild and wholly free."

To the Southwest moved people from Kentucky, from Tennessee, and from as far away as New England. Most numerous among the settlers on the Southern frontier, however, were farmers and planters from the South Atlantic states, especially from the piedmont of Georgia and the Carolinas. Their motive for migrating was, in a word, cotton. With the spread of cotton cultivation throughout the uplands of the older South, the soil there lost much of its natural fertility from repeated croppings, or washed away as torrential rains gullied the hillsides. Seeking fresh soil with a climate suitable for cotton, the planters naturally looked to the Southwest, around the end of the Appalachian range, where there stretched a broad zone within which cotton could thrive. Included in this zone was the Black Belt of central Alabama and Mississippi, a prairie with a fabulously productive soil of rotted limestone.

The advance of the Southern frontier meant the spread of cotton and slavery. Usually the first arrivals were ordinary frontiersmen like those farther north, small farmers who made rough clearings in the forest. Then came planters who bought up the cleared or partially cleared land, while the original settlers moved on west and started over again. As a rule the planters made the westward journey in a style quite different from that of the other pioneers. Over the alternately dusty and muddy roads came great caravans consisting of herds of livestock, wagonloads of household goods, long lines of slaves, and, bringing up the rear, the planter and his family riding in carriages. Soon the clearings expanded into vast fields white with cotton, and the cabins of the pioneers gave way to more sumptuous log dwellings and ultimately to imposing mansions that demonstrated the rise of a class of the newly rich.

Though by 1819 settlers already were pushing beyond the Mississippi, much of the area to the east of the river, around the Great Lakes and along the Gulf of Mexico, was yet to be occupied. Despite the gaps in settlement, the population of the Mississippi Valley had increased far more rapidly than that of the nation as a whole. The census of 1810 indicated that only one American in seven lived to the west of the Appalachian Mountains; the census of 1820, almost one in four. During the immediate postwar years four new states were created in this region—Indiana (1816), Mississippi (1817), Illinois (1818), and Alabama (1819). Meanwhile Missouri had grown populous enough for statehood, and the struggle over her admission indicated how important, politically and otherwise, the West was becoming in the eyes of the rest of the nation. For the time being, however, the westward movement was slowed down by the onset of the depression following the Panic of 1819.

THE PANIC OF 1819

In part the Panic of 1819 was a delayed reaction to the War of 1812 and to the preceding years of warfare in Europe. Since 1793 the continual fighting had drawn manpower from European fields, disrupted business as well as agriculture, and created an abnormal demand for the produce of American plantations and farms. The whole period was one of exceptionally high prices for American producers, and though some prices fell with the decline of trade in 1814, they recovered with the resumption of exports to Europe after the war.

Public Lands: Terms of Sale [1785–1820]

Ordinance of 1785 Allowed a minimum purchase of 640 acres and set a minimum price of $1 an acre. Made no provision for credit.

Act of 1796 Raised the minimum price to $2 an acre but allowed a year's credit on half of the amount due.

Act of 1800 Reduced the minimum purchase from 640 to 320 acres and extended credit to four years, with a down payment of one-fourth of the whole amount and three later installments.

Act of 1804 Further reduced the minimum purchase to 160 acres. (Now a man with as little as $80 on hand could obtain a farm from the government, although he would still owe $240 to be paid within four years.)

Act of 1820 Reduced the minimum purchase still further, to 80 acres, and the minimum price to $1.25 an acre, but abolished the credit system. *NOTE:* Under each of these laws, the land was first offered for sale at auction, and much of it sold for more than the minimum price.

Rising prices for farm products stimulated a land boom in the United States, particularly in the West. After the war the government land offices did a bigger business than ever before; not for twenty years were they to do as good a business again. In 1815 sales totaled about a million acres and in 1819 more than 5 million. Many settlers bought on credit: under the land laws of 1800 and 1804 they could pay as little as $80 down, and they hoped to raise the remaining three installments within four years from the proceeds of their farming. Speculators bought large tracts of choice land, hoping to resell it at a profit to incoming settlers. At the land-office auctions, bidding became so spirited that much of the public land sold for prices far above the minimum of $2 an acre, some in the Black Belt of Alabama and Mississippi going for $100 and more. Still higher prices sometimes were paid by optimistic real-estate promoters who laid out town sites, even in swamps, and expected to make fortunes through the sale of city lots. Until 1817 neither the settlers nor the speculators needed hard cash to buy government land: they could borrow from the state banks and pay the government with banknotes.

Even after the refounding of the Bank of the United States in 1817, wildcat banks continued to provide easy credit for a few years. In-deed, the United States Bank itself at first offered easy loans. Then in 1819, under new management, it suddenly began to tighten up. It called in loans and foreclosed mortgages, acquiring thousands of acres of mortgaged land in the West. It gathered up state banknotes and presented them to the state banks for payment in cash. Having little money on hand, many of these banks closed their doors. Most of the rest soon had to follow suit, for they were beset by depositors with notes to be cashed. The panic was on.

Six years of depression followed. Prices fell rapidly. With the prices of farm products so low, those settlers buying land on credit could not hope to keep up their payments. Some stood to lose everything—their land, their improvements on it, their homes. They demanded relief from their congressmen, and Congress responded with the land law of 1820 and the relief act of 1821. The new land law abolished the credit system, but lowered the minimum price from $2.00 to $1.25 and the minimum tract from 160 to 80 acres. Hereafter a purchaser would have to buy his farm outright, but he could get one for as little as $100. The relief act allowed a previous buyer to pay off his debt at the reduced price, to accept the reduced acreage and apply the payments to it, and to have more time to meet his installments.

Selected Readings

Backgrounds of Conflict
J. W. Pratt, *Expansionists of 1812* (1925); A. L. Burt, *The United States, Great Britain, and British North America from the Revolution to the Peace After the War of 1812* (1940); Bradford Perkins, *Prologue to War: England and the United States, 1805–1812* (1961); Reginald Horsman, *The Causes of the War of 1812** (1962); R. H. Brown, *The Republic in Peril: 1812* (1964); J. F. Zimmerman, *Impressment of American Seamen* (1925); L. M. Sears, *Jefferson and the Embargo* (1927).

War and Peace
F. F. Beirne, *The War of 1812* (1949); H. L. Coles, *The War of 1812** (1965); William Wood, *The War with the United States* (1915), a Canadian viewpoint; J. R. Jacobs, *The Beginning of the United States Army, 1783–1812* (1947); A. T. Mahan, *Sea Power in Its Relation to the War of 1812* (2 vols., 1919); Fletcher Pratt, *Preble's Boys: Commodore Preble and the Birth of American Sea Power* (1950); F. L. Engelman, *The Peace of Christmas Eve* (1962).

Postwar Expansion
George Dangerfield, *The Era of Good Feelings** (1952); F. J. Turner, *Rise of the New West** (1906); F. S. Philbrick, *The Rise of the West, 1754–1830** (1965), anti-Turner; T. P. Abernethy, *The South in the New Nation, 1789–1819* (1961); A. L. Kohlmeier, *The Old Northwest as the Keystone of the Arch of the American Federal Union* (1938); R. C. Buley, *The Old Northwest: Pioneer Period, 1815–1840* (2 vols., 1950); Dale Van Every, *The Final Challenge: The American Frontier, 1804–1845** (1964); E. B. Wesley, *Guarding the Frontier: A Study of Frontier Defense from 1818 to 1825* (1935); H. P. Beers, *The Western Military Frontier, 1815–1846* (1935); R. M. Robbins, *Our Landed Heritage: The Public Domain** (1942); P. C. Brooks, *Diplomacy and the Borderlands: The Adams-Onís Treaty of 1819* (1939); L. C. Hunter, *Steamboats on the Western Rivers* (1949); M. N. Rothbard, *The Panic of 1819: Reactions and Policies* (1962).

Biographies
Irving Brant, *James Madison: The President, 1809–1812* (1956) and *James Madison: Commander in Chief, 1812–1836* (1961); C. M. Wiltse, *John C. Calhoun: Nationalist, 1782–1828* (1944); Bernard Mayo, *Henry Clay, Spokesman of the New West* (1937); Freeman Cleves, *Old Tippecanoe* (1939), William Henry Harrison; Marquis James, *Andrew Jackson, Border Captain** (1933); Glenn Tucker, *Tecumseh: Vision of Glory* (1956); S. F. Bemis, *John Quincy Adams and the Foundations of American Foreign Policy* (1949).

*Titles available in paperback.

Sectionalism and Patriotism

Nine

The westward movement of population led, five years after the end of the War of 1812, to a sectional crisis. The specific question was whether Missouri should be admitted as a slaveholding state, but also involved was the larger question whether the North or the South should control the rising West. Though the Missouri controversy was settled by a compromise, the spirit of sectionalism persisted, awaiting other occasions to flare up.

For the time being, however, there were countervailing forces of nationalism. The ideal of a strong national government was vigorously reasserted in the Supreme Court decisions of Chief Justice John Marshall (though these provoked widespread criticism, especially in the South) and in the foreign policies of President James Monroe. Significantly, both Marshall and Monroe were Southerners. National unity was further strengthened by the revival of the system of two political parties, each of which had members in all parts of the country, so that partisan lines cut across and weakened sectional divisions. Meanwhile, an eventual economic basis for national unity was promised by improvements in transportation—canals and railroads—which began to link the coastal cities with the interior, the East with the West. Business could now be conducted on something approaching a truly nationwide scale.

Still another bond of union was the heritage of patriotism, the heroic memories of the Revolution, annually recalled with fife and drum and flamboyant speechmaking on the Fourth of July. The War of 1812 was too recent for the unpatriotic factionalism it had engendered to be entirely forgotten, but the earlier war with Great Britain, as it receded into the past, was more and more suffused with a haze of heroic legend. When General Lafayette, the French hero of the Revolution, revisited the United States in 1824–1825, the glorious past was revived as never before. Everywhere the beloved general went, crowds without

Fourth of July   1819
The public celebration in Center Square, Philadelphia, as shown in this detail from a painting by J. L. Krimmel, was typical of Independence Day festivities throughout the country. Here militiamen parade, women prepare picnic lunches, and some of the men get drunk. (The Historical Society of Pennsylvania)

distinction of section or party cheered him in frenzied celebrations.

The Revolutionary heritage was most dramatically brought home to the American people by news of the deaths of Thomas Jefferson and John Adams.
Jefferson, the author of the Declaration of Independence, and Adams, "its ablest advocate and defender" (as Jefferson said), who at one time were bitter political rivals, had become friendly correspondents in their old age. They died on the same day, and that day was July 4, 1826, exactly half a century after the adoption of the Declaration. To some, this appeared to be more than a coincidence, perhaps a sign from God instructing the American people to cherish the nationality their ancestors had so dearly won.

The Canal Age

More than ever, with the improvements in transportation and the broadening of business, each part of the country could concentrate on the production of a particular kind of goods, since it could depend upon other parts of the country to buy its surplus and supply its needs. This geographical specialization made the East and the West, the North and the South, increasingly interdependent, though at the same time it also intensified differences of economic interest and thus accounted for much of the persisting sectionalism in politics.

THE PEOPLE 1820–1840

During the 1820s and 1830s, as during the whole of American history, three trends of population were fairly obvious: rapid increase, migration to the West, and movement to towns and cities.

Americans continued to multiply almost as fast as in the colonial period, the population still doubling every twenty-five years or so. The total figure, lower than 4 million in 1790, approached 10 million by 1820 and rose to nearly 13 million in 1830 and to about 17 million in 1840. The United States was growing much more rapidly in population than the British Isles or Europe: by 1860 it had gone ahead of the United Kingdom and had nearly overtaken Germany and France.

The Negro population increased more slowly than the white. After 1808, when the importation of slaves was made illegal, the proportion of blacks to whites in the nation as a whole steadily declined. In 1820 there was one Negro to every four whites; in 1840, one to every five. The slower increase of Negroes was due to their comparatively high death rate, not to a low birth rate. Slave mothers had large families, but life was shorter for both slaves and free Negroes than for whites.

The mortality rate for whites slowly declined. Public health improved a little, though epidemics continued to take their periodic toll, among them a cholera plague that swept the country in 1832. On the average, people lived somewhat longer than in earlier generations. The population increase, however, was due less to lengthened life than to the maintenance of a high birth rate, which more than offset the death rate.

Immigration accounted for little of the population growth before the 1840s. The long years of war in Europe, from 1793 to 1815, had kept the number of newcomers to America down to not more than a few thousand a year, and then the Panic of 1819 checked the immigrant tide that had risen after Waterloo. During the 1820s arrivals from abroad averaged about 14,000 annually. Of the total population of nearly 13 million in 1830, the foreign-born numbered less than 500,000, mostly naturalized citizens. Soon immigration began to grow, reaching a total of 60,000 for 1832 and nearly 80,000 for 1837.

Since the United States exported more goods than it imported, returning ships often had vacant space and filled it with immigrants as ballast, so to speak. Competition among shipping lines reduced fares so that, by the 1830s, the immigrant could get passage across the Atlantic for as little as $20 or $30. No longer did he need to sell his services to a temporary

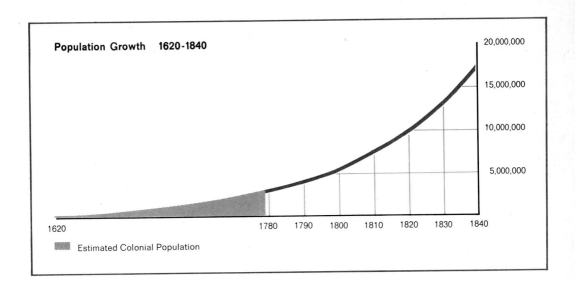

Population Growth   1620-1840

Estimated Colonial Population

The United States was the first country to undertake a complete and periodic population count, beginning with the census of 1790. From 1790 to 1840 the American population grew, by actual count, from a little less than 4 million to a little more than 17 million. Meanwhile the world population grew, according to estimate, from about 700 million to more than 1 billion. During this period the population of the United States was increasing by about 3 per cent a year, that of the United Kingdom less than 1 per cent, and that of France less than one-half of 1 per cent.

master in America in order to pay for the voyage. And so the system of indentured servitude, which had dwindled steadily after the Revolution, disappeared entirely after the Panic of 1819.

Until the 1830s most of the new arrivals came from the same sources as had come the bulk of the colonial population—from England and the northern counties of Ireland. In the 1830s, however, the number arriving from the southern counties of Ireland began to grow, anticipating the tremendous influx of Irishmen that was to occur in the next two decades. Generally the newcomers, the Irish as well as others, were welcomed in the United States. They were needed to provide labor for building canals and railroads, manning ships and docks, and performing other heavy work essential to the expanding economic system. But the Irish, as Roman Catholics, excited Protestant prejudices in some communities. In 1834 an anti-Catholic mob set fire to a convent in Charlestown, Massachusetts, and the next year Samuel F. B. Morse (who is better remem-

bered as a portrait painter and as the inventor of the telegraph) published his *Foreign Conspiracy*, which served thereafter as a textbook for nativists crusading against what they imagined was a popish plot to gain control of the United States. Still, the federal government did nothing to check immigration, and shipowners, employers, and some of the states took measures to encourage it.

The West (including both Northwest and Southwest) continued to grow much more rapidly than the rest of the country. By 1830 more than a fourth of the American people lived to the west of the Appalachians; by 1850, nearly a half. Some of the seaboard states suffered serious losses of manpower and womanpower, not to mention the personal property that departing migrants took away. Year after year the Carolinas gave up nearly as much in human resources as they gained by natural increase; their populations remained almost stationary. The same was true of Vermont and New Hampshire. Many a village in these two states was completely depopulated, its houses and barns left to rot, as its people scattered over the country in search of an easier life than the granite hills afforded.

Not all the migrating villagers and farmers sought the unsettled frontier: some moved instead to increasingly crowded population centers. Cities (considered as communities of 8,000 or more) grew faster than the nation as a whole. In 1820 there were more than twice as many cities, and in 1840 more than seven times as many, as there had been in 1790. While the vast majority of Americans continued to reside in the open country or in small towns, the number of city dwellers increased remarkably. In 1790 one person in thirty lived in a community of 8,000 or more; in 1820, one in twenty; and in 1840, one in twelve.

The rise of New York City was phenomenal. By 1810 it had surpassed Philadelphia, which earlier had replaced Boston as the largest city in America. New York steadily increased its lead in both population and trade. Its growth was based on the possession of a superior natural harbor and on several historical developments after the War of 1812. After the war the British chose New York as the chief place to "dump" their manufactured goods and thus helped make it an import center. State laws, which were liberal with regard to auction sales, encouraged inland merchants to do their buying in New York. The first packet line, with regularly scheduled monthly sailings between England and the United States, made New York its American terminus (1816) and hence a more important center of overseas commerce than ever. And the Erie Canal (completed in 1825) gave the city unrivaled access to the interior.

NEW WATERWAYS

Despite the road improvements of the turnpike era (1790–1830) Americans continued as in colonial times to depend wherever possible on water routes for travel and transportation. The larger rivers, especially the Mississippi and the Ohio, became increasingly useful as steamboats grew in number and improved in design.

A special kind of steamboat evolved to meet the problems of navigation on the Mississippi and its tributaries. These waters were shallow, with strong and tricky currents, shifting bars of sand and mud, and submerged logs and trees. So the boat had to have a flat bottom, paddle wheels rather than screw propellers, and a powerful, high-pressure engine, which meant a dangerously explosive one. To accommodate as much cargo and as many passengers as possible, the boat was triple-decked, its superstructure rising high in the air. Such a "floating palace" at its best was an impressive sight, elaborately ornamented with gilt and "gingerbread."

River boats carried to New Orleans the corn and other crops of Northwestern farmers, the cotton and tobacco of Southwestern planters. From New Orleans, ships took the cargoes on to Eastern ports. Neither the farmers of the West nor the merchants of the East were completely satisfied with this pattern of trade. Farmers could get better prices for their crops if the alternative existed of sending them directly eastward to market, and merchants could sell larger quantities of their manufactured goods if these could be transported more directly and more economically to the West.

True, the highways across the mountains, such as the Philadelphia-Pittsburgh turnpike and the National Road, provided a partial solution to the problem. But the costs of hauling goods overland, though lower than before these roads were built, were too high for anything except the most compact and valuable merchandise. New waterways were needed in addition to highways. It was calculated that four horses could pull a wagon weight of one ton twelve miles a day over an ordinary road and one and a half tons eighteen miles a day over a turnpike. On the other hand, four horses could draw a boatload of a hundred tons twenty-four miles a day on a canal.

Sectional jealousies and constitutional scruples stood in the way of action by the federal government, and necessary expenditures were too great for private enterprise. If extensive canals were to be dug, the job would be up to the various states.

New York was the first to act. It had the natural advantage of a comparatively level route between the Hudson River and Lake Erie, through the only break in the entire Appalachian chain. Yet the engineering tasks were imposing. The distance was more than 350 miles, several times as long as any of the existing canals in America, and there were ridges to cross and a wilderness of woods and swamps to penetrate. For many years New Yorkers debated whether the scheme was practical. The canal advocates finally won the debate after De Witt Clinton, a late but ardent convert to the cause, was elected governor. Digging began on the Fourth of July, 1817.

This, the Erie Canal, was by far the greatest construction job that Americans ever had undertaken, and it was the work of self-made engineers. Though one of them made a careful study of English canals, he and his associates did more than merely copy what he saw abroad. They devised ingenious arrangements of cables, pulleys, and gears for bringing down trees and uprooting stumps. Instead of the usual shovels and wheelbarrows, they used specially designed plows and scrapers for moving earth. To make watertight locks they produced an ideal cement from native limestone. The canal itself was simply a big ditch, forty feet wide and four feet deep, with towpaths along the banks for the horses or mules that were to draw the canal boats. (Steamboats were not to be used: the churning of a paddle wheel or propeller would cave in the earthen banks.) Cuts and fills, some of them enormous, enabled the canal to pass through hills and over valleys;

New York Port 1828

A view of South Street, from the intersection with Maiden Lane, which got its name from the fact that Dutch washermaidens in New Amsterdam used to come here to do their laundry in a brook outside of town. The East River docks lined South Street; there were other docks along the Hudson River on the opposite side of Manhattan Island. Below Maiden Lane, the city by 1828 was almost solidly built up. Above the Lane, there were gardens around the houses, and there were vacant lots which in some cases ran out into open fields. In summer boys swam nude in the East River. The population of the city was approaching 150,000. Note the cobblestone pavement. From a contemporary print. (Courtesy of the New York Public Library, Stokes Collection)

The Erie Canal
Canal boats, loaded with migrants on their way to the West, arrive at the landing at Little Falls, New York. Note the tandem team of horses on the towpath. The boats moved so slowly that passengers could lighten their tedium from time to time by getting off and walking alongside. From a contemporary pencil sketch. (Courtesy of the New-York Historical Society, New York City)

stone aqueducts carried it across streams; and eighty-eight locks, of heavy masonry, with great wooden gates, took care of the necessary ascents and descents.

Not only was the Erie Canal an engineering triumph; it quickly proved a financial success as well. It was opened for through traffic in October 1825, with fitting ceremonies. Governor Clinton at the head of a parade of canal boats made the trip from Buffalo to the Hudson and then downriver to New York City, where he emptied a keg of Erie water into the Atlantic to symbolize the wedding of the lake and the ocean. Soon traffic was so heavy that, within about seven years, the tolls brought in enough

to repay the whole construction cost. The prosperity of the Erie encouraged the state to enlarge its canal system by building several branches. An important part of the system was the Champlain Canal, begun at about the same time as the Erie and completed in 1822, which connected Lake Champlain with the Hudson River. Though some of the branches did not pay for themselves, they provided useful water connections between New York City and the larger towns of the state. The main line, giving access to Lake Erie as it did, led beyond the state's borders, to the West.

The range of the New York canal system was still further extended when the states of

Ohio and Indiana, inspired by the success of the Erie Canal, provided water connections between Lake Erie and the Ohio River. In 1825 Ohio began the building of two canals, one between Portsmouth and Cleveland and the other between Cincinnati and Toledo, both of which were in use by 1833. In 1832 Indiana started the construction of a canal that was to connect Evansville with the Cincinnati-Toledo route. These canals made it possible to ship or to travel by inland waterways all the way from New York to New Orleans, though several changes among canal, lake, and river craft would be necessary. By way of the Great Lakes it was possible to go by water from New York to Chicago. After the opening of the Erie

Canal, shipping on the Great Lakes by sail and steam rapidly increased.

The consequences of the development of this transportation network were far-reaching. One of the immediate results was the stimulation of the settlement of the Northwest, not only because it had become easier for migrants to make the westward journey but also, and more important, because it had become easier for them, after taking up their farms, to ship their produce to markets. Towns boomed along the Erie and other canals, New York City benefiting the most of all. Though much of the Western produce, especially corn, continued to go downriver to New Orleans, an increasing proportion of it and most of the wheat of the North-

Canals in the Northeast   1840

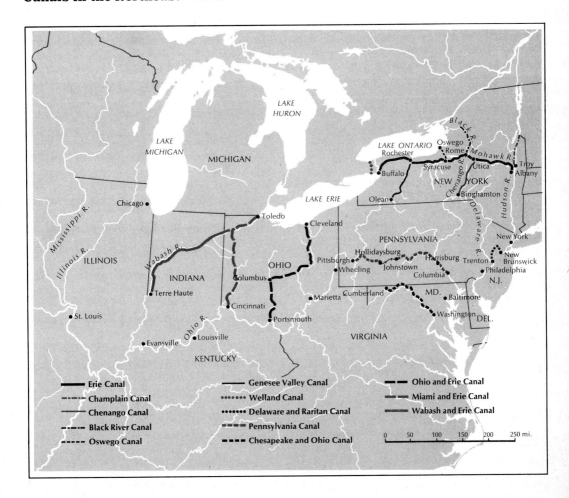

west went toward New York. And manufactured goods now went in growing volume from New York by the comparatively direct and economical new routes to the West.

Rival cities along the Atlantic seaboard took alarm at the prospect of New York's acquiring so vast a hinterland, largely at their expense. If they were to hold their own, they too must find ways of tapping the Western market. Boston, remote from the West, her way to the Hudson River impeded by the Berkshire Hills, seemed out of the running, at least so far as a canal was concerned. Philadelphia and Baltimore, though they had the still more formidable Allegheny Mountains to contend with, did not give up without an effort at canal building. Beginning in 1834, the commonwealth of Pennsylvania invested in a complicated and costly system of waterways and railways—with an arrangement of "inclined planes," stationary engines, and cable cars to take canal boats over the mountains—intending thus to connect Philadelphia with Pittsburgh. This "Pennsylvania system" proved a failure, financially and otherwise. From Baltimore a canal was projected to ascend the Potomac Valley and tunnel through the mountains, thus achieving essentially the same object as George Washington once had hoped to accomplish. The digging of this grandly conceived Chesapeake and Ohio Canal began in 1828, but it never got farther west than Cumberland. In the South, Richmond and Charleston also aspired to reach the Ohio Valley; Richmond, planning at first to join the James and the Kanawha rivers, eventually saw a canal built as far as Lynchburg.

For none of these rivals of New York did canals provide a satisfactory way to the West. Some cities, however, saw their opportunity in a different and newer means of transportation. Before the canal age had reached its height, the era of the railroad already was beginning.

THE FIRST RAILROADS

It is hard to date the beginning of railroads, since they resulted from a combination of different elements, each of which had a separate history. One of these was the use of rails, wooden or iron, laid on a prepared roadbed to make a fairly straight and level track. Another was the employment of steam-powered locomotives, and a third was the operation of trains as public carriers of passengers and freight. For nearly 200 years before the nineteenth century opened, railways with cars pulled by men (and women) or by animals had been used to haul coal from English mines, and in the early 1800s similar railways appeared in the United States. By 1804 both English and American inventors had experimented with steam engines for propelling land vehicles as well as boats. In 1820 John Stevens ran a locomotive and cars around a circular track on his New Jersey estate. Finally, in 1825, the Stockton and Darlington Railroad in England began to operate with steam power over a short length of track and to carry general traffic.

This news quickly aroused the interest of American businessmen, especially in those seaboard cities that sought better communications with the West. First to organize a railroad company was a group of New Yorkers, who in 1826 obtained a charter for the Mohawk and Hudson and five years later began running trains the sixteen miles between Schenectady and Albany. First to begin actual operations was the Baltimore and Ohio; the only living signer of the Declaration of Independence, Charles Carroll of Carrollton, dug a spadeful of earth in the ceremonies to start the work on July 4, 1828, and a thirteen-mile stretch opened for business in 1830. In that same year the Charleston and Hamburg ran trains over a segment of its track in South Carolina; when this line was completed, in 1833, it was the longest in the world (136 miles). The next year the commonwealth of Pennsylvania finished its line from Philadelphia to the Susquehanna River as part of the "Pennsylvania system" of rail and waterways. Meanwhile, in Massachusetts, three companies received charters for routes radiating out from Boston, the most important of these being the Western Railroad, which reached Worcester in 1836. Not only the seaboard but also the Mississippi Valley became the scene of railroad building. By 1836 a total of more than 1,000 miles of track had been laid in eleven states.

There did not yet exist what could be called a railroad system. Even the longest of the lines was comparatively short, and most of them served mainly to connect water routes and supplement water transportation.

**Traveling
by Railroad
[1835]**

In her widely read work on *Society in America* (1836) the scholarly Englishwoman Harriet Martineau recalled railroad trips she had taken in South Carolina and Pennsylvania:

My journeys on the Charleston and Augusta railroad were by far the most fatiguing of any I underwent in the country. The motion and the noise are distracting. Whether this is owing to its being on piles in many places, whether the fault is in the ground or the construction, I do not know. Almost all the railroad traveling in America is very fatiguing and noisy. . . .

One great inconvenience of the American railroads is that, from wood being used for fuel, there is an incessant shower of large sparks, destructive to dress and comfort, unless all the windows are shut, which is impossible in warm weather. Some serious accidents from fire have happened in this way; and during my last trip on the Columbia and Philadelphia railroad, a lady in the car had a shawl burned to destruction on her shoulders; and I found that my own gown had thirteen holes in it; and my veil, with which I saved my eyes, more than could be counted.

During the 1830s the railroad underwent a rapid technological development. At first the track consisted of strap-iron rails laid on wooden stringers, which were anchored to granite blocks set in the ground, but this kind of track proved too rigid to absorb the shocks of actual use and was soon replaced by heavier iron rails on wooden ties ballasted with crushed rock. The tracks of different companies varied in width, so that when too different lines connected, the cars and engines of the one might not fit on the tracks of the other. In the early years experiments were made with various forms of motive power—horses, sails, and stationary steam engines with windlasses and cables (for steep grades), as well as steam locomotives. The very first locomotives were imported from England, but as early as 1830 engines of American manufacture like the Charleston and Hamburg's *Best Friend of Charleston* were put into use, and before long only American locomotives were used on American roads; some were even exported. Since railroads in this country were built with sharper curves and steeper grades, the locomotives had to be both more flexible and more powerful than in England. Passenger cars, originally mere stagecoaches adapted to rails, took the form of an elongated box with two rows of reversible seats and a center aisle soon after 1840. Schedules were erratic and wrecks frequent, as the roadbeds and bridges were poorly constructed.

From the outset railroads and canals were bitter competitors. For a time the Chesapeake and Ohio Canal Company blocked the advance of the Baltimore and Ohio Railroad through the narrow gorge of the upper Potomac, and the state of New York prohibited railroads from hauling freight in competition with the Erie Canal and its branches. But railroads had the advantages of speed and year-round operation (canals closed down for the winter freeze) and could be located almost anywhere, regardless of terrain and the availability of water. Where free competition existed, railroads took most of the passenger traffic and the light freight.

The future, in fact, belonged to the towns and cities along the path of the "iron horse," not to those that continued to depend exclusively upon waterways.

BROADENING OF BUSINESS

While mills and factories multiplied, the household and the workshop slowly declined as producers of manufactured goods. In the textile industry the use of machinery and the dependence on water power (occasionally steam power) made it necessary to bring operations together under a single roof. Yet a good deal of spinning and weaving continued to be done in the home, either for sale or for home use. Though shoes were still made by hand and not by machines, shoe manufacture was increasingly the work of men and women who, in a careful division of labor, specialized in one or another of the various tasks. Mass-produced shoes, in ungraded sizes and without distinction as to rights or lefts, came in the 1830s chiefly from eastern Massachusetts and were bought mostly by frontier emigrants, sailors, and Southern planters, who used them for their slaves. Other people still made their own shoes or had them made to order by a cobbler. Iron came largely from Pennsylvania, where it was produced in furnaces using local sources of ore, limestone, and charcoal. Other furnaces were scattered over the country, however, and finished iron products were wrought in thousands of local blacksmith shops.

The expansion of business was not simply an automatic result of transportation improvements or other technological changes. It was also the result of daring and imagination on the part of businessmen and their employees. Two industries, one old and one new, illustrate the capacities of Yankee enterprise. One was the whaling industry, which was reaching its heyday in the 1830s. From New Bedford and other New England ports, bold skippers and their crews, having driven most of the whales from the Atlantic, voyaged far into the Pacific in their hazardous tracking of the source of spermaceti for candles, whale oil for lamps, and whalebone for corset stays and other uses. Another example of Yankee enterprise was the ice industry. Though for years Northeastern farmers had harvested winter ice from ponds and stored it for the summer, the large-scale transportation and sale of ice as a commodity began in the 1830s. The New England ice harvest then found a ready market in Northern cities, on Southern plantations, and around the world in India, where it was carried in fast-sailing ships; a voyage was considered highly successful if no more than half the cargo melted on the way.

The distribution of goods, whether of foreign or of domestic origin, continued to be rather haphazard by present-day standards, though it was becoming more and more systematic. Stores specializing in groceries, dry goods, hardware, or other lines appeared in the larger cities, but smaller towns and villages depended on the general store, like the one where Abraham Lincoln once clerked in New Salem, Illinois. The storekeeper did much of his business by barter, taking country eggs and other produce in exchange for such things as pins and needles, sugar and coffee. Many customers, living remote from any store, welcomed the occasional visits of the peddler, who came afoot or by horse, with his pack or with his peddler's wagon equipped with sloping sides which opened to reveal his racks of wares. A special variety of peddler, the Connecticut Yankee, toured the West and the South as a factory agent to sell clocks, at one time made of wood (including the works) but in the 1830s and after usually made of brass.

The organization of business was undergoing a gradual change. Most of it was, and continued to be, operated by individuals or partnerships operating on a small scale. The dominating figure was the great merchant capitalist, who owned and directed much of the big business of the time. He owned his own ships, and he organized certain industries—for example, that of shoe manufacturing—on the putting-out system, according to which he provided the materials, directed the work, and sold the finished product. In the larger enterprises, however, the individual merchant capitalist was giving way before the advance of the corporation. Corporations had the advantage of combining the resources of a large number of shareholders, but their development was long held back by handicapping laws. A corporation had to have a charter, granted by the state, and at first a special act of the legislature was required. By the 1830s the states were beginning to pass general incorporation laws according to which any group meeting certain requirements could secure a charter merely by paying a fee. Moreover, the laws began to grant the privilege of limited liability, which meant that the individual stockholder was liable only to the extent of losing the value of his stock if the corporation should fail.

Corporations made possible the accumulation of larger and larger amounts of capital for manufacturing enterprises as well as for banks, turnpikes, and railroad companies. Some of this capital came from the profits of wealthy merchants who turned from shipping to newer ventures, some from the savings of men of only moderate means, and some from tax collections, since state governments often bought shares in turnpike, canal, and railroad companies. A considerable part was supplied by foreign, especially English, investors. From all these sources too little was derived to meet the demands of promoters with ambitious schemes of personal profit or community improvement. Hence the banks, which should have confined their long-term lending to the limit of their savings deposits, often were induced to issue excessive amounts of bank notes as a means of providing capital for expanding business ventures. As a result of this practice, bank failures were more frequent and bank deposits less secure than they might otherwise have been.

WORKERS AND UNIONS

The growth of industry required labor as well as capital. From the colonial beginnings, labor had been scarce in America. At the opening of the nineteenth century nearly ninety of every one hundred Americans still lived and worked on the land: they were farmers. City workers were comparatively few, and many of them were skilled artisans who owned and managed their shops: they were small businessmen, not employees. There were also some unskilled laborers—longshoremen and the like—but there was no sizable reservoir of manpower for new industries to draw upon. In response to the needs of industry a considerable class of wage earners finally began to form. Its members came mostly from the marginal farms of

Girls in Cotton Mills

In cotton mills, such as this one in Lowell, Massachusetts, about 1850, most of the employees were farm girls from the surrounding countryside who worked for a few years as factory hands and then returned to their homes to marry and settle down. With respect to Lowell, it was said: "Visitors will be agreeably surprised by the neat and respectable appearance of the operatives of this industrious city; and equally so with their moral condition." (Prints Division, The New York Public Library, Astor, Lenox and Tilden Foundations)

the East (those farms least able to compete with the fertile fields of the West) and somewhat later from the British Isles and Europe.

In the textile mills two different methods of labor recruitment were used. One of these, which prevailed in the middle states and parts of New England, brought whole families to the mill. Father, mother, and children, even those no more than four or five years old, worked together in tending the looms. The second, the Waltham or Lowell system, which was common in Massachusetts, enlisted young women in their late teens and early twenties. These unmarried girls went from farms to factories to work for only a few years and returned, with their savings, to settle down as housewives. They did not form a permanent working class.

Labor conditions in American mills seemed very good in comparison with conditions in English factories and mines. Child labor, indispensable for supplementing the manpower supply, entailed fewer evils in the United States, where the working children remained under the control of their parents, than in England, where asylum authorities hired out orphans to factory employers. The lot of the working woman in mills like those of Lowell appeared idyllic in contrast with the plight of contemporary women who worked in British mines. A parliamentary investigation revealed that some of these unfortunates, naked and filthy, crawled on their hands and knees to pull coal carts through narrow tunnels. No wonder that English visitors considered Lowell a female paradise. The Lowell girls lived in pleasant boarding houses (much like college residence halls) where their morals were carefully supervised. They were well paid by the standards of the period. They found time to write and publish a monthly magazine, the *Lowell Offering,* even though working hours were long—from sunup to sundown six days a week. In the early days of the factory these hours seemed natural enough to people who were used to the daylong labor of the farm.

Much worse off were the construction gangs who performed the heavy, unskilled work on turnpikes, railroads, and canals. A large and growing number of these men were Irish immigrants. They received low pay and, since their work was seasonal and uncertain,

did not make enough in a year to maintain a family at what was generally considered a decent living standard; many of them lived in the most unhealthful of shanties. After about 1840 Irish men and women began to be employed in textile mills. As these newcomers replaced the native farm girls, the earlier paternalistic system broke down and working conditions deteriorated somewhat. Piece rates were paid instead of a daily wage; these and other devices were used to speed up production and exploit the labor force more efficiently.

Neither ditchdiggers nor mill hands, however, were the first to organize and act collectively to improve the conditions of their work. Skilled artisans formed the earliest labor unions and arranged the first strikes (shortly before 1800). From the 1790s on, the printers and cordwainers took the lead. The cordwainers—makers of high-quality boots and shoes, each man fashioning his entire product—suffered from the competition of merchant capitalists who put out work to be performed in separate tasks. These artisans sensed a loss of security and status with the development of mass-production methods, and so did members of other skilled trades, such as carpenters, joiners, masons, plasterers, hatters, and shipbuilders. In cities like Philadelphia, Baltimore, Boston, and New York, the skilled workers of each craft formed societies for mutual aid. During the 1820s and 1830s the craft societies began to combine on a city-wide basis and set up central organizations known as trade unions. Since, with the widening of the market, workers of one city competed with those at a distance, the next step was to federate the trade unions or to establish craft unions of national scope. In 1834 delegates from six cities founded the National Trades' Union, and in 1836 the printers and the cordwainers set up their own national craft unions.

This labor movement soon collapsed. Labor leaders struggled against the handicap of hostile laws and hostile courts. By the common law, as interpreted by judges in the industrial states, a combination among workers was viewed as, in itself, an illegal conspiracy. But adverse court decisions did not halt, though they handicapped, the rising unions. The death blow came from the Panic of 1837 and the ensuing depression.

Sectional and National Trends

While the divisive spirit of sectionalism came to a head in the Missouri controversy, Chief Justice Marshall, in a series of his greatest decisions, was strengthening the national sovereignty against the rights of the states. In 1823, announcing what was later to be known as the Monroe Doctrine, the President appealed to patriotism with an assertion of American leadership in the Western Hemisphere against the pretensions of European powers.

THE MISSOURI COMPROMISE

When Missouri applied for admission as a state, slavery already was well established there. The French and Spanish inhabitants of the Louisiana Territory (including what became Missouri) had owned slaves, and in the Louisiana Purchase treaty of 1803 the American government promised to maintain and protect the inhabitants in the free enjoyment of their property as well as their liberty and religion. By 1819 approximately 60,000 people resided in Missouri Territory, of whom about 10,000 were slaves. In that year, while Missouri's application for statehood was being considered in Congress, Representative James Tallmadge, Jr., of New York, moved to amend the enabling bill so as to prohibit the further introduction of slaves into Missouri and to provide for the gradual emancipation of those already there. This Tallmadge amendment provoked a controversy that was to rage for the next two years.

Though the issue arose suddenly, waking and terrifying Thomas Jefferson like "a fire bell in the night," as he said, sectional jealousies that produced it had been accumulating for a long time. Already the concept of a balance of power between the Northern and Southern states was well developed. From the beginning, partly by chance and partly by design, new states had come into the Union more or less in pairs, one from the North, another from the South. With the admission of Alabama in 1819, the Union contained an equal number of free and slave states, eleven of each. Thus the free and slave states were evenly balanced in

the Senate, though the free states with their more rapidly growing population had a majority in the House. If Missouri should be admitted as a slave state, not only would the existing sectional balance be upset but also a precedent would be established which, in the future, would still further increase the political power of the South.

In the North the most active antislavery people were well-to-do philanthropists and reformers who generally supported the Federalist party. They opposed the extension of slavery on both humanitarian and political grounds. On the eve of the dispute over Missouri the Manumission Society of New York was busy with attempts to rescue runaway slaves, and the Quakers were conducting a campaign to strengthen the laws against the African slave trade and to protect free Negroes from kidnappers who sold them into slavery. In the South there were still a large number of critics of slavery and its abuses, but here the humanitarian impulse was not reinforced by political interest as it was in the North. Northerners, in particular the Federalists, never tired in their denunciations of the Virginia Dynasty and the three-fifths clause which, they charged, gave the Southern states a disproportionate weight in national politics.

Once the Missouri controversy had arisen, it provided the opportunity, which Federalist leaders such as Rufus King had awaited, to attempt a revival and reinvigoration of their party. By appealing to the Northern people on the issue of slavery extension, the Federalists could hope to win many of the Northern Republicans away from their allegiance to the Republican party's Southern leadership. In New York the De Witt Clinton faction of the Republicans, who had joined with the Federalists in opposition to the War of 1812 and who were outspoken in their hostility to "Virginia influence" and "Southern rule," were more than willing to cooperate with the Federalists again. The cry against slavery in Missouri, Thomas Jefferson wrote, was "a mere party trick." He explained: "King is ready to risk the union for any chance of restoring his party to power and wriggling himself to the head of it,

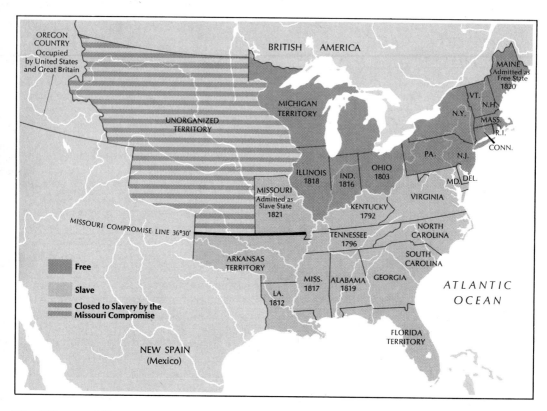

The Missouri Compromise   1820–1821

nor is Clinton without his hopes nor scrupulous as to the means of fulfilling them." Though Jefferson himself took a biased, partisan view of the subject, there seems little reason to doubt that some of the Federalists desired to use the Missouri controversy for creating a new, sectional alignment of parties, the North against the South.

The Missouri question soon was complicated by the application of Maine for admission as a state. Massachusetts had consented to the separation of the northern part of the commonwealth but only on the condition that Maine be granted statehood before March 4, 1820. The Speaker of the House, Henry Clay, informed Northerners that if they refused to consent to Missouri's becoming a slave state Southerners would deny the application of Maine. In the House the Northern majority nevertheless insisted on the principle of the Tallmadge amendment, but in the Senate a few of the Northern-

ers sided with the Southerners and prevented its passage.

A way out of the impasse opened when the Senate combined the Maine and Missouri bills, without prohibiting slavery in Missouri. Then, to make the package more acceptable to the House, Senator Jesse B. Thomas of Illinois proposed an amendment prohibiting slavery in all the rest of the Louisiana Purchase territory north of the southern boundary of Missouri (latitude 36° 30'). The Senate adopted the Thomas amendment, and Speaker Clay undertook to guide the amended Maine-Missouri bill through the House. Eventually, after the measure had been broken up into three separate bills, he succeeded. A group of Northern Republicans, some of them suspecting the political designs of the Federalists, voted with the Southerners to make the compromise possible.

The first Missouri Compromise (1820) did not end the dispute; a second compromise was necessary. In 1820 Maine was actually admitted as a state, but Missouri was only authorized to form a constitution and a government. When the Missouri constitution was completed, it contained a clause forbidding free Negroes or mulattoes to enter the state. Several of the existing states, denying the right of citizenship to "free persons of color," already had laws against their immigration. Other states, among them New York, recognized colored persons as citizens. According to the federal Constitution, "The citizens of each State shall be entitled to all privileges and immunities of citizens in the several States." This meant that a citizen of such a state as New York, whether he was white or black, was entitled to all the privileges of a citizen of Missouri, including of course the privilege of traveling or residing in the state. The anti-Negro clause was clearly unconstitutional, and a majority in the House of Representatives threatened to exclude Missouri until it was eliminated. Finally Clay offered a resolution that Missouri should be admitted to the Union on the condition that the clause should never be construed in such a way as to deny to any citizen of any state the privileges and immunities to which he was entitled under the Constitution of the United States. In the circumstances, this resolution was meaningless, yet Clay secured its passage and enhanced his reputation as the "Great Pacificator," a reputation he was again and again to confirm during his long career. Clay's resolution made possible the admission of Missouri as a state in 1821.

Though the Missouri controversy did not unite the North, as some of the Federalists hoped it would, it made at least a beginning toward the creation of a solid South. At that time the most disaffected of the Southern states was Virginia and not, as later on, South Carolina. The Carolinian Calhoun hailed the compromise as a means of preserving the Union. The Virginian Jefferson looked to the fateful day when the South might have to defend itself in a civil war.

In this perspective the subject of education, always one of Jefferson's chief concerns, became even more crucial. He was afraid that Southern youths attending Northern colleges might be indoctrinated with "lessons of anti-Missourianism." Already the University of Virginia, the favorite project of his old age, was under construction. He hoped that this university, devoting itself to sound Southern doctrines, would attract from Virginia and other Southern states a large number of students who otherwise would have pursued their studies in the North. For him, education once had been a means of liberating the human mind; now it became also a means of enabling slaveholders to protect their interests. Henceforth, in the South, the liberal and equalitarian philosophy that we think of as Jeffersonian declined in popularity and respect. Jefferson himself, in response to the Missouri controversy, had done much toward launching the new conservative trend.

MARSHALL AND THE COURT

John Marshall remained as chief justice for almost thirty-five years, from 1801 to 1835. During these years Republican Presidents filled vacancies with Republican justices, one after another, and yet Marshall continued to carry a majority with him in most of the Court's decisions. He was a man of practical and penetrating mind, of persuasive and winning personality, and of strong will. The members of the Court boarded together, without their families, during the winter months when the Court was in session, and Marshall had abundant opportunity to bring his talents to bear upon his younger associates. He not only influenced their ways of thinking; he also molded the development of the Constitution itself. The net effect of the hundreds of opinions delivered by the Marshall Court was to strengthen the judicial branch at the expense of the other two branches of the government; increase the power of the United States and lessen that of the states themselves; and advance the interests of the propertied classes, especially those engaged in commerce.

No state, the Constitution says, shall pass any law "impairing the obligation of contracts." The first Supreme Court case involving this provision was that of *Fletcher* v. *Peck* (1810), which arose out of the notorious Yazoo Land frauds. The Court had to decide the question whether the Georgia legislature of 1796 could rightfully repeal the act of the previous legislature granting lands under shady circumstances to the Yazoo Land Companies. In the decision, which was unanimous, Marshall held that a land grant was a contract and therefore, regardless of any corruption involved, the repeal was invalid. This was the first time the Supreme Court had voided a state law on the ground that it conflicted with a provision of the United States Constitution, though the Court previously had declared state laws unconstitutional because they were inconsistent with federal laws or treaties.

Dartmouth College v. *Woodward* (1819) was an even more famous case concerning the contract clause. The case had originated in a quarrel between the trustees and the president of the college, and it became a hot political issue in New Hampshire when the Republicans championed the president, and the Federalists took the side of the trustees. Getting control of the state government, the Republicans undertook to revise Dartmouth's charter (granted by King George III in 1769) so as to convert the private college into a state university. Daniel Webster, a Dartmouth graduate, represented the trustees when the case came before the Supreme Court in Washington. The Court, he reminded the judges, had decided in *Fletcher* v. *Peck* that "a *grant* is a contract." The Dartmouth charter, he went on, "is embraced within the very terms of that decision," since "a grant of corporate powers and privileges is as much a *contract* as a grant of land." Then, according to a later story, he brought tears to the eyes of the justices with an irrelevant peroration concluding: "It is, sir, as I have said, a small college. And yet there are those who love it—" After delaying a year, while some of the justices made up their minds, the Court gave its decision in favor of Webster and the trustees. While the importance of the case often has been exaggerated, it had a significant bearing upon the development of business corporations. It proclaimed the principle that corporation charters were contracts and contracts were inviolable; thereafter the states had to contend against this doctrine in their efforts to control corporate activity.

Did the Supreme Court rightfully have the power to hear appeals from the state courts, as in the Dartmouth College case? The Judiciary Act of 1789 provided that whenever the highest state court decided against a person claiming rights under the federal Constitution, laws, or treaties, the judgment could be reviewed and possibly reversed by the Supreme Court. But

Virginia state-rightists denied the constitutionality of the Judiciary Act. They insisted that the federal government, of which the Supreme Court was a branch, could not be the final judge of its own powers, for, they said, it would then be a consolidated government instead of a true federal one such as the Constitution had intended. In the case of *Cohens* v. *Virginia* (1821) Marshall gave the Court's reply to the dissident Virginians. A Virginia court had convicted the Cohens of selling lottery tickets in violation of a state law, and the Cohens had appealed their case under the disputed provision of the Judiciary Act. Though Marshall decided against the Cohens, he did not satisfy the state of Virginia. He affirmed the constitutionality of the Judiciary Act, explaining that the states no longer were sovereign in all respects, since they had given up part of their sovereignty in ratifying the Constitution. The state courts, he insisted, must submit to federal jurisdiction; otherwise the government would be prostrated "at the feet of every state in the Union."

Meanwhile, in *McCulloch* v. *Maryland* (1819), Marshall had confirmed the "implied powers" of Congress by upholding the constitutionality of the Bank of the United States. The Bank, with headquarters in Philadelphia and branches in various cities throughout the country, became so unpopular in the South and the West that several of the states tried to drive the branches out of business by outright prohibition or by prohibitory taxes. Maryland, for one, laid a heavy tax on the Baltimore branch of the Bank. This case presented two constitutional questions to the Supreme Court: Could Congress charter a bank and, if so, could one of the states thus tax it? As one of the Bank's attorneys, Webster first repeated the arguments used originally by Hamilton to prove that the establishment of such an institution came within the "necessary and proper" clause. Then, to dispose of the tax issue, Webster added an ingenious argument of his own. The power to tax, he said, involved a "power to destroy," and if the states could tax the Bank at all, they could tax it to death. But the Bank with its branches was an agency of the federal government: no state could take an action tending to destroy the United States itself. Marshall adopted Webster's words in deciding for the Bank.

The case of *Gibbons* v. *Ogden* (1824) brought up the question of the powers of Con-

**McCulloch
v. Maryland
[1819]**

Chief Justice Marshall used the following argument in his decision that a state, such as Maryland, could not constitutionally tax a branch of the United States Bank:

That the power to tax involves the power to destroy; that the power to destroy may defeat and render useless the power to create; that there is a plain repugnance in conferring on one government a power to control the constitutional measures of another, which other, with respect to those very measures, is declared to be supreme over that which exerts the control, are propositions not to be denied. . . .

If the States may tax one instrument, employed by the [federal] government in the execution of its powers, they may tax any and every other instrument. They may tax the mail; they may tax the mint; they may tax patent rights; they may tax the papers of the customhouse; they may tax judicial processes; they may tax all the means employed by the government, to an excess which would defeat all the ends of government. This was not intended by the American people. They did not design to make their government dependent on the States.

---

gress, as against the powers of the states, in regulating interstate commerce. The state of New York had granted Robert Fulton's and Robert Livingston's steamboat company the exclusive right to carry passengers on the Hudson River to New York City. From this monopoly Aaron Ogden obtained the business of navigation across the river between New York and New Jersey. Thomas Gibbons, with a license granted under an act of Congress, went into competition with Ogden, who brought suit against him and was sustained by the New York courts. When Gibbons appealed to the Supreme Court, the justices faced the twofold question whether "commerce" included navigation and whether Congress alone or Congress and the states together could regulate interstate commerce. Marshall replied that "commerce" was a broad term embracing navigation as well as the buying and selling of goods. Though he did not exactly say that the states had no authority whatever regarding interstate commerce, he asserted that the power of Congress in regard thereto was "complete in itself" and might be "exercised to its utmost extent." He concluded that the state-granted monopoly was void.

Here was a grant that neither Marshall nor Webster, Gibbons' attorney, considered sacred. The decision, the last of Marshall's great pronouncements, was the first conspicuous one in which the Marshall Court appeared to be on

the popular side. Most people, then as always, hated monopolies and he had declared a monopoly unconstitutional! The lasting significance of *Gibbons* v. *Ogden* was that it freed internal transportation from restraints by the states, and thus prepared the way for the unfettered economic development of the nation. More immediately, it had the effect of helping to head off a movement that was under way for hamstringing the Supreme Court.

For some time Virginia Republicans like Thomas Jefferson, Spencer Roane, and John Taylor of Caroline (a Virginia county) had protested against the views of their fellow Virginian John Marshall. In *Construction Construed and Constitutions Vindicated* (1820) Taylor argued that Marshall and his colleagues were not merely interpreting but were actually changing the nature of the Constitution, which should properly be changed only by the amending process, requiring the approval of three-fourths of the states. In Congress some critics of the Court, mostly from the South and the West, proposed various means of curbing what they called judicial tyranny. A Kentucky senator suggested making the Senate, not the Court, the agency to decide the constitutionality of state laws and to settle interstate disputes. Other senators and congressmen introduced bills to increase the membership of the Court (from seven to ten) and to require more than a mere majority to declare a state law unconstitutional. The Court reformers did not succeed, however, in passing any of their various panaceas, and after the *Gibbons* v. *Ogden* decision the hostility to the judicial branch of the government gradually died down, to be revived in later years.

LATIN AMERICAN INDEPENDENCE

To most people in the United States, South and Central America had been "dark continents" before the War of 1812. Suddenly they emerged into the light, and Americans looking southward beheld a gigantic spectacle: the Spanish empire struggling in its death throes, a whole continent in revolt, new nations in the making with a future no man could foresee.

Already a profitable trade had developed between the ports of the United States and those of the Río de la Plata in South America, of Chile, and above all of Cuba, with flour and other staples being exported in return for sugar and coins. This trade was small in comparison with that of Great Britain, whose exports to Latin America were several times as large as those of the United States, but the trade was growing steadily, and during the depression after 1819 it held up better than business in general did. Presumably the trade would increase much faster once the United States had established regular diplomatic and commercial relations with the countries in revolt.

In 1815 the United States proclaimed its neutrality in the wars then raging between Spain and her rebellious colonies. This neutrality in itself was advantageous to the rebels, since it implied a recognition of them as belligerents, as nations for the purposes of waging war, though not as nations for all purposes. It meant, for example, that their warships would be treated as bona-fide belligerent vessels, not as pirate ships. Moreover, even though the neutrality law was revised and strengthened in 1817 and 1818, it still permitted the revolutionists to obtain unarmed ships and supplies from the United States. It prohibited the purchase of arms or armed vessels and the enlistment of men in this country, but these prohibitions could be evaded and often were. In short, the United States was not a strict and impartial neutral but a nonbelligerent whose policy,

though cautious, was intended to help the insurgents and actually did.

Secretary Adams and President Monroe hesitated to take the risky step of recognition unless Great Britain would agree to do so at the same time. In 1818 and 1819 the United States made two bids for British cooperation, and both were rejected. Finally, in 1822, President Monroe informed Congress that five nations — La Plata (Argentina), Chile, Peru, Colombia, and Mexico — were ready for recognition, and he requested an appropriation for sending ministers to them. This was a bold stroke: the United States was going ahead alone as the first country to recognize the new governments, in defiance of the rest of the world.

ORIGIN OF THE MONROE DOCTRINE

In 1823 President Monroe stood forth as an even bolder champion of America against Europe. Presenting to Congress his annual message on the state of the Union, he announced a policy which afterward — though not for thirty years — was to be known as the "Monroe Doctrine." One phase of this policy had to do with the relationship of Europe to America. "The American continents," Monroe declared, ". . . are henceforth not to be considered as subjects for future colonization by any European powers." Furthermore, "we should consider any attempt on their part to extend their system to any portion of this hemisphere as dangerous to our peace and safety." And we should consider any "interposition" against the sovereignty of existing American nations as an unfriendly act. A second aspect of the President's pronouncement had to do with the relationship of the United States to Europe. "Our policy in regard to Europe," said Monroe, ". . . is not to interfere in the internal concerns of any of its powers."

How did the President happen to make these statements at the time he did? What specific dangers, if any, did he have in mind? Against what powers in particular was his warning directed? To answer these questions, it may be well to consider first the relations of the United States with the European powers as of 1823, and then the main steps in the decision of the Monroe administration to make an announcement to Congress and the world.

Monroe Doctrine [1823]

. . . The American continents, by the free and independent condition which they have assumed and maintain, are henceforth not to be considered as subjects for future colonization by any European powers. . . .

In the wars of the European powers in matters relating to themselves we have never taken any part, nor does it comport with our policy to do so. . . . We should consider any attempt on their part to extend their system to any portion of this hemisphere as dangerous to our peace and safety. With the existing colonies or dependencies of the European powers we have not interfered and shall not interfere. But with the Governments who have declared their independence and maintained it, and whose independence we have, on great consideration and on just principles, acknowledged, we could not view any interposition for the purpose of oppressing them, or controlling in any other manner their destiny, by any European power, in any other light than as the manifestation of an unfriendly disposition toward the United States.

After Napoleon's defeat the powers of Europe combined in a "concert" to uphold the principle of "legitimacy" in government and to prevent the overthrow of existing regimes from within or without. When Great Britain withdrew from the concert, it became a quadruple alliance with Russia and France as the strongest of its four members. Tsar Alexander I of Russia also sponsored the "Holy Alliance," which eventually was joined by all the European sovereigns except the Pope and the King of England, and which was supposed to put into practice the Tsar's rather fuzzy ideal of peace and justice based upon Christian principles. Though the quadruple alliance and the Holy Alliance were separate, most Americans made no distinction between them, commonly referring to the European concert as the "Holy Alliance." In 1823, after assisting in the suppression of other revolts in Europe, the European allies authorized France to intervene in Spain to restore the Bourbon dynasty that revolutionists had overthrown. Some observers in England and the Americas wondered whether the allies next would back France in an attempt to retake by force the lost Spanish empire in America.

Actually, France was still a relatively weak power, not yet recovered from the long and exhausting Napoleonic wars. Though France disliked Latin American independence, she was willing to accept it as one of the realities of the world, especially if it should result in the creation of monarchies instead of republics. France endeavored to bring about the establishment of pro-French kingdoms in Latin America by means of intrigue, but dared not challenge British sea power with an expedition to subvert the new governments by force.

Russia, the great land power of Europe, lacked naval strength. She desired the friendship of the United States because of her world-wide conflicts with Great Britain. When the Tsar expressed his wish that the United States become a member of the Holy Alliance, Secretary Adams politely let him know that this country could best serve the exalted purpose of the alliance by remaining apart from it. While American pacifists admired the Tsar as a friend of brotherhood and peace, Adams grew sarcastic about the supposedly peace-loving Tsar who sold warships to Spain to assist her war against her revolting colonies. Besides the vague threat Russia offered to Latin American independence, there were other causes of friction between her and the United States. Russia owned Alaska, and Russian fur traders ranged as far south as California. In 1821 the Tsar issued a ukase (imperial order) requiring foreign ships to keep approximately one hundred miles from the Northwest coast above the 51st parallel. This order perturbed Adams not only because it interfered with the activities of American traders and whalers in the North Pacific but also because it implied a Russian territorial claim that would enlarge the area of Russian

America. Adams protested strongly to the Russians. Instead of taking offense, they agreed to negotiate regarding the southern boundary of their possessions. The settlement was not completed until 1824, when the Russians abandoned their claim south of 54° 40′. But in 1823 the negotiations were already under way and, for the time being, Russian-American relations were reasonably good.

In the minds of most Americans, certainly in the mind of their secretary of state, Great Britain at that time seemed a serious threat to American interests. Adams was much concerned about supposed British designs upon Cuba. Like Jefferson and others before him, Adams opposed the transfer of Cuba from a weak power like Spain, its owner, to a strong power like Great Britain. He thought Cuba eventually should belong to the United States, for the "Pearl of the Antilles" had great economic and strategic value and, because of its location, was virtually a part of the American coastline. Adams did not desire to seize the island; he wanted only to keep it in Spanish hands until, by a kind of political gravitation, it should fall naturally to the United States. Despite his worries over the supposed British threat to Cuba, he and other American leaders were pleased to see the rift between Great Britain and the concert of Europe. He was willing to cooperate with her, but only to the extent that her policies and his own coincided in regard to this hemisphere.

These policies did not exactly coincide, however, as was shown by the British rejection of the American overtures for joint recognition of Latin American independence in 1818 and 1819, and as was shown again by the American reaction to a British proposal for a joint statement in 1823. That summer, the British Secretary for Foreign Affairs, George Canning, suggested to the American minister in London, Richard Rush, that Great Britain and the United States should combine in announcing to the world their opposition to any European movement against Latin America. Though Rush lacked instructions to act, he was ready to go ahead with Canning on one condition—that Great Britain agree to recognize the Latin American nations as the United States already had done. When Canning declined to promise recognition, Rush wrote home for instructions. During the summer Canning remained eager

for Rush's cooperation, but in the fall, having been assured by the French minister that France had no intention of "acting against the colonies by force of arms," Canning suddenly lost interest in his idea of a joint statement with the United States.

Meanwhile the Monroe administration was considering the proposal that Canning had made earlier. Monroe sent the Rush correspondence to former Presidents Madison and Jefferson for their advice, and both of them recommended that Rush be authorized to sign a joint statement with Canning. Adams objected. For one thing, he did not like the statement that Canning had proposed: it included a pledge by Great Britain and the United States that neither of the two would seek further territory in this hemisphere, and Adams did not wish to stop this country from future territorial acquisitions. For another thing, he believed it would be more honorable for the American government to speak out on its own instead of following along like a "cockboat in the wake of the British man-of-war." Actually, when the time arrived for Monroe's message to Congress, the President no longer faced a question of acting with Great Britain or alone. He had the choice of acting alone or not at all, since Canning had changed his mind about cooperation with the United States.

Though Canning's overture led to Monroe's announcement, the message was directed against all the powers of Europe, including Great Britain, which seemed at least as likely as Russia to undertake further colonizing ventures in America. The message was intended to head off the threat of European schemes against Latin American independence, but the most serious threat was one of undermining that independence by subtle influences rather than overt military action. The message aimed to rally the people of Latin America to look to their own security. It also aimed to stir the people of the United States. In issuing his challenge to Europe, Monroe had in mind the domestic situation as well as the international scene. At home the people were bogged down in a business depression, divided by sectional politics, and apathetic toward the rather lackluster administration of Monroe. In the rumors of European aggression against this hemisphere lay a chance for him to arouse and unite the people with an appeal to national pride.

The Two-Party System Revived

After 1816 the Federalist party offered no presidential candidate and soon ceased to exist as a national organization. Presidential politics was carried on within the Republican party alone until the campaign of 1828, when the Republicans divided into two groups and thus set going a party system comparable to the one that had operated before 1820.

"CORRUPT BARGAIN!"

From 1796 to 1816, presidential candidates had been nominated by caucuses of the members of each of the two parties in Congress. In 1820, when the Federalists declined to oppose his candidacy, Monroe ran as the Republican nominee without the necessity of a caucus nomination. If the caucus system were revived and followed in 1824, this would mean that the nominee of the Republicans in Congress would run unopposed, as Monroe had done. Several men aspired to the presidency, however, and they and their followers were unwilling to let a small group of congressmen and senators determine which one was to win the prize.

In 1824 "King Caucus" was overthrown. Fewer than a third of the Republicans in Congress bothered to attend the gathering that went through the motions of nominating a candidate (William H. Crawford) and he found the caucus nomination as much a handicap as a help in the campaign. The rest of the candidates received nominations from state legislatures and endorsements from irregular mass meetings throughout the country.

John Quincy Adams, secretary of state for two terms, had made a distinguished record in the conduct of foreign affairs, and he held the office that had become traditionally the stepping stone to the presidency. But, as he himself ruefully realized, he was a man of cold and forbidding manners, not a candidate with strong popular appeal. Contending against Adams was the Secretary of the Treasury, William H. Crawford of Georgia, an impressive giant of a man who seemed to have a promising future in national politics. The caucus candidate, Crawford had the backing of the extreme state-rights faction of the Republican party. In mid-

campaign, however, he was stricken by a paralyzing illness.

Challenging the cabinet contenders was Henry Clay, the Speaker of the House. This tall, black-haired Kentuckian, with his broad smile and his ready handshake, had a personality that gained him a devoted following. He also stood for a definite and coherent program, which he called the "American System." His plan, a familiar one but attractive to citizens just recovering from a business depression, was to create a great home market for factory and farm producers by means of raising the tariff to stimulate industry, maintaining the national bank to facilitate credit and exchange, and spending federal funds on internal improvements to provide transportation between the cities and the farms.

Election of 1824

Jackson

Adams

Crawford

Clay

Andrew Jackson offered no such clear-cut program as did Clay. Though Jackson had served briefly as a representative in Congress and was a member of the United States Senate, he had no legislative record to run on. Nevertheless, he had the inestimable advantages of a military hero's reputation and a campaign shrewdly managed by the Tennessee politician friends who had put him forward as a candidate. To some of his contemporaries he seemed a crude, hot-tempered frontiersman and Indian fighter. Actually, though arising from a humble background as an orphan in the Carolinas, he had become a well-to-do planter who lived in an elegant mansion ("The Hermitage") near Nashville and was a gentleman, at least by the standards of the West.

Once the returns were counted, there was no doubt that the next Vice President was to be Calhoun, who ran on both the Adams and the Jackson tickets. But there was considerable doubt as to who the next President would be. In those states where the people chose the presidential electors, Jackson led all the rest at the polls. In the electoral college also he came out ahead, with 99 votes to Adams' 84, Crawford's 41, and Clay's 37. He lacked the necessary majority, however. So, in accordance with the Twelfth Amendment, the final decision was left to the House of Representatives, which was to choose among the three candidates with the highest electoral vote. Clay, for all his charm, was out of the running.

If Clay, in 1825, could not be President, he could at least be President maker, and perhaps he could lay the ground for his own election later on. As Speaker, he was in a strategic position for influencing the decision of the House of Representatives. In deciding among the three leading candidates, the House was to vote by states, the delegation from each state casting one vote. Clay, as the winner of the recent election in Kentucky, Ohio, and Missouri, could swing the congressional delegations of those three states at least.

Before Congress got around to making the decision, the friends of Jackson, Crawford, and Adams approached Clay in behalf of their respective candidates. To which of the three should he give his support? Jackson's followers insisted that Jackson, with his popular and electoral pluralities, was really the people's choice and that Congress had no rightful alternative but to ratify the people's will. But Jack-

son was Clay's most dangerous rival for the political affections of the West, and he could not be depended upon to champion Clay's legislative program. Crawford was out of the question, for he was now a paralytic, incapable of discharging the duties of the presidency. Only Adams was left. Personally, he was no friend of Clay and had clashed with him repeatedly when both were peace delegates at Ghent and afterward. Politically, however, Adams was similar to Clay in cherishing nationalistic principles such as those of the "American System." Finally Clay gave his support to Adams, and the House elected him.

The Jacksonians were angry enough at this, but they became far angrier when the new President made known his appointments. Clay was to be the secretary of state! The State Department being the well-established route to the presidency, Adams thus appeared to be naming Clay as his own successor. The two must have agreed to make each other President—Adams now, Clay next—or so the Jacksonians exclaimed, and they pretended to be horrified by this "corrupt bargain." Very likely there had been some sort of understanding, and though there was nothing improper in it, it proved to be politically unwise for both Adams and Clay.

Soon after Adams' inauguration as President, Jackson resigned from the Senate to accept a renomination for the presidency from the Tennessee legislature and to begin a three-year campaign for election in 1828. Politics now overshadowed everything else. Throughout his term in the White House, Adams and his policies were to be thoroughly frustrated by the political bitterness arising from the "corrupt bargain."

THE SECOND PRESIDENT ADAMS

The career of John Quincy Adams divides naturally into three parts. In the first part, as befitted the son of John Adams, he made a brilliant record in diplomacy, serving as the American minister in one foreign capital after another and then as one of the most successful of all secretaries of state. In the second phase of his career, as President (1825–1829), he endured four ineffectual years that amounted to a mere interlude between the periods of his greatness. In the third, as a congressman from Massachusetts, he served his constituents and the nation with high distinction, gaining fame as "Old Man Eloquent," the foremost congressional champion of free speech. His frustration in the White House shows that the presidency demands more than exceptional ability and high-mindedness, for John Quincy Adams possessed both. The presidency also requires political skill and political luck, and these he did not have.

In his inaugural address and in his first message to Congress he boldly stated a broad conception of the powers and duties of the federal government. He recommended "laws promoting the improvement of agriculture, commerce, and manufactures, the cultivation of the mechanic and of the elegant arts, the advancement of literature, and the progress of the sciences, ornamental and profound." He had no chance of getting an appropriation from Congress to improve the minds of his countrymen. The most he could get was a few million dollars for improving rivers and harbors and for extending the National Road westward from Wheeling. This amount was more than Congress had appropriated for internal improvements under all his predecessors together, but it was far less than he hoped for.

Even in the field of diplomacy, where Adams had more experience than any other President before or since, he failed in the major efforts of his administration. Yielding to Secretary of State Clay's wish for cooperation with the Latin American governments, Adams appointed two delegates to attend an international conference which the Venezuelan liberator, Simon Bolívar, had called to meet at Panama in 1826. Objections arose in Congress for two reasons. One was that Southerners hated to think of white Americans mingling in Panama with colored delegates from Haiti, the independence of which the United States refused to recognize. The other reason for obstruction was simply politics—the determination of Jacksonians to discredit the administration. They charged that Adams aimed to sacrifice American interests and involve the nation in an entangling alliance. While the Jacksonians filibustered, Congress delayed the Panama mission so long that it became futile. One of the American delegates died on the way to the conference, and the other arrived after it was over. The United States had accomplished nothing to offset British influence, which prevailed in Latin America.

John Quincy Adams

When this photograph was taken, shortly before his death in 1848, Adams was more than eighty years old and was a congressman from Massachusetts. He had left the Presidency almost twenty years earlier. During his White House days, as always, he was a hard, conscientious worker. He rose at four in the morning and built a fire before the servants were up. Then he made a long entry in his diary for the previous day. He wrote so much that his right hand sometimes became paralyzed with writer's cramps, so he taught himself to use his left hand also. (Brown Brothers)

Adams was worsted also in a contest with the state of Georgia. That state attempted to remove the remaining Creek and Cherokee Indians so as to gain additional soil for cotton planters. The Creeks, however, had a treaty with the United States (1791) that guaranteed them the possession of the land they occupied. A new treaty (1825) ceded the land to the state, but Adams refused to enforce this treaty, believing that it had been obtained by fraud. The Georgia governor defied the President of the United States and went ahead with plans for Indian removal. At last the Creeks agreed to still another treaty (1827) in which they yielded their claims. Adams' stand had been honorable but unpopular. Southerners condemned him for encroaching upon state rights, and Westerners as well as Southerners disapproved of his interfering with efforts to get rid of the Indians.

Southerners again denounced the administration and its supporters on account of the tariff of 1828. This measure originated in the demands of Massachusetts and Rhode Island woolen manufacturers, who complained that the British were dumping woolens on the American market at prices with which the domestic mill owners could not compete. Petitioning Congress, the distressed mill owners expected relief from the Woolens Bill of 1827. It passed the House but was defeated in the Senate when Vice President Calhoun cast his negative vote to break a tie. Thus frustrated, the protectionists of New England combined with those of the middle and Western states to put more pressure on Congress, after gathering in a grand convention at Harrisburg, Pennsylvania.

The bill of 1828 contained high duties not only on woolens but also on a number of other items, such as flax, hemp, iron, lead, molasses, and raw wool. Thus it displeased New England manufacturers, for it would raise the cost of their raw materials as well as the price of their manufactured goods. A story arose that the bill had taken its shape from a Jacksonian plot to embarrass New Englanders and discredit Adams. The bill related to "manufactures of no sort or kind but the manufacture of a President of the United States," John Randolph said. Supposedly it was intended to put Adams in a dilemma that would lose him friends whether he signed or vetoed it. While some politicians did see the measure as an electioneering device, others intended it seriously as a means of benefiting the farmers and manufacturers of the middle states and the West.

When the bill was considered item by item, Southerners voted against reductions in the hope that some of its outrageous duties would so antagonize New Englanders that they would help defeat it. But when it came to a final test, Daniel Webster voted for it despite its duties on raw materials, and he carried with him enough New England votes to enable it to pass. Adams signed it. The Southerners, whose tactics had backfired, cursed it as the "tariff of abominations."

JACKSON VINDICATED

By 1828, the Republican party having split completely, there were again two parties in the campaign—the Adamsites, who called themselves National Republicans, and the Jacksonians, who took the name of Democratic Republicans. Adams himself once had been a Federalist, and most of the old Federalists joined his party, though some became followers of Jackson.

Issues figured little in the campaign of 1828, though much was said about the "corrupt bargain" and something was said about the West Indian trade and the "tariff of abominations." Regarding the tariff, Adams was on record, having signed the abominations bill, but nobody knew exactly where Jackson stood. Again, as in 1824, more was made of personalities than of policies, and this time there was far worse mudslinging than ever before. Indeed, one would have thought that two criminals were running for the highest office in the land.

As for Adams, the Jacksonians charged

Election of 1823

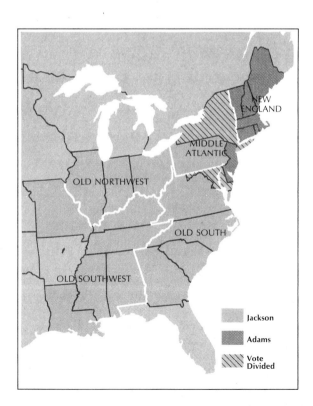

Jackson

Adams

Vote Divided

that as President he had been guilty of gross waste and extravagance, using public funds to buy gambling devices (a chess set and a billiard table) for the White House. But that was not the worst of Adams' alleged crimes. Once, as minister to Russia, he had tried to procure a beautiful American girl for the sinful pleasures of the Tsar, or so the Jacksonians said. Of course, these charges were wholly false. Indeed, they were fantastic things to say about a man as conscientious and puritanical as John Quincy Adams.

As for Jackson, the Adamsites had accusations even worse. He was a murderer and an adulterer, according to the speeches, handbills, and pamphlets of his party foes. A "coffin handbill" listed within coffin-shaped outlines the names of militiamen whom Jackson was said to have shot in cold blood during the War of 1812. Actually, these men had been deserters

who were executed after due sentence by a court martial. It was also rumored that Jackson knowingly had lived in sin with the wife of another man. Actually, he had married the woman, his beloved Rachel, at a time when the pair honestly though mistakenly supposed her first husband had divorced her.

Though the majority voted for Jackson, a large minority (44 percent) favored Adams, who received all but one of the electoral votes from New England, all from New Jersey and Delaware, and some from New York and Maryland. These totaled only 83, however, as compared with 178 for Jackson, who carried the rest of the country. His victory was decisive enough, even though not quite so sweeping as it seemed. In the eyes of his followers, he — and they — were vindicated in their claim that he had been wrongfully deprived of the presidency in 1825.

Selected Readings

Canals and Railroads

G. R. Taylor, *The Transportation Revolution, 1815–1860* (1951); R. E. Shaw, *Erie Water West: A History of the Erie Canal, 1792–1854* (1966); Nathan Miller, *The Enterprise of a Free People: Aspects of Economic Development in New York State During the Canal Period, 1792–1828* (1962); Carter Goodrich and others, *Canals and American Economic Development* (1961); W. S. Sanderlin, *The Great National Project* (1947), the Chesapeake and Ohio Canal; A. D. Trumbull, *John Stevens: An American Record* (1928); F. W. Stevens, *The Beginnings of the New York Central Railroad* (1926); Edward Hungerford, *The Story of the Baltimore and Ohio Railroad, 1827–1927* (2 vols., 1928); S. M. Derrick, *Centennial History of the South Carolina Railroad* (1930).

Industry and Trade

A. H. Cole, *The American Wool Manufacture* (2 vols., 1926); C. A. Ware, *The Early New England Cotton Manufacture* (1931); S. E. Morison, *The Maritime History of Massachusetts, 1783–1860** (1921); F. R. Dulles, *The Old China Trade* (1930).

Urban Development

R. G. Albion, *The Rise of New York Port, 1815–1860* (1939); Blake McKelvey, *Rochester, the Water-Power City, 1812–1854* (1945); L. D. Baldwin, *Pittsburgh: The Story of a City* (1938); J. W. Livingood, *The Philadelphia-Baltimore Trade Rivalry, 1780–1860* (1947); R. C. Wade, *The Urban Frontier: The Rise of Western Cities, 1790–1830** (1959); N. M. Blake, *Water for the Cities* (1956); A. R. Pred, *Urban Growth and the Circulation of Information: The United States System of Cities, 1790–1840* (1973).

Nationalism and Sectionalism

George Dangerfield, *The Awakening of American Nationalism, 1815–1828** (1965); Merle Curti, *The Roots of American Loyalty* (1946); W. E. Davies, *Patriotism on Parade: The Story of Veterans' and Hereditary Organizations in America, 1783–1900* (1955); W. F. Craven, *The Legend of the Founding Fathers** (1956); P. C. Nagel, *One Nation Indivisible: The Union in American Thought, 1776–1861* (1964); Glover Moore, *The Missouri Controversy, 1819–1821* (1953).

The Marshall Court

A. J. Beveridge, *The Life of John Marshall* (4 vols., 1916–1919); R. K. Faulkner, *The Jurisprudence of John Marshall* (1968); M. G. Baxter, *Daniel Webster and the Supreme Court* (1966).

The Monroe Doctrine

A. P. Whitaker, *The United States and the Independence of Latin America, 1800–1830** (1941); E. H. Tatum, *The United States and Europe, 1815–1823* (1936); Dexter Perkins, *The Monroe Doctrine, 1823–1826* (1927); C. C. Griffin, *The United States and the Disruption of the Spanish Empire* (1937); Bradford Perkins, *Castlereagh and Adams: England and the United States, 1812–1823* (1964); J. H. Powell, *Richard Rush, Republican Diplomat, 1780–1859* (1942); Frank Thistlethwaite, *The Anglo-American Connection in the Early Nineteenth Century* (1959).

Party Politics

S. F. Bemis, *John Quincy Adams and the Union* (1956); R. V. Remini, *The Election of Andrew Jackson** (1964); Shaw Livermore, Jr., *The Twilight of Federalism: The Disintegration of the Federalist Party, 1815–1830* (1962).

*Titles available in paperback.

Jacks

Jacksonian Democracy

DEMOCRACY,

"*The Union must be P-*

Ten

In 1831–1832 a twenty-six-year-old French nobleman, Alexis de Tocqueville, made a tour of the United States, talking with people of all kinds, from President Jackson in the White House to Negro slaves in the cotton fields of the South. Tocqueville's aim was to study the workings of democracy—or, more specifically, the idea of equality—in what he considered the most democratic country on earth. He believed that democracy was the way of the future, that it was bound to come sooner or later to France. He wanted to find its good and bad and its essential and unessential features so that his own country could be prepared to adopt the best and avoid the worst. His two-volume study of *Democracy in America* (1835–1840) still stands as the most perspicacious general account of American institutions ever to be written by a foreigner.

"The government of democracy," Tocqueville wrote, "brings the notion of political rights to the level of the humblest citizens, just as the dissemination of wealth brings the notion of property within the reach of all the members of the community; and I confess that, to my mind, this is one of its greatest advantages." But he feared that, with the continued growth of factories, there might eventually arise in the United States a large group of dependent workingmen and a small group of new aristocrats, an industrial plutocracy. For "at the very moment at which the science of manufactures lowers the class of workmen, it raises the class of masters."

With this prospect of widening class differences, some Americans wondered about the wisdom of extending political rights to larger and larger numbers. President Jackson and his followers, however, generally endorsed and aided the extensions of democratic thought and practice that preceded, accompanied, and followed his rise to power. Viewing himself as the real

Jackson Poster
Running for reelection in 1832, Andrew Jackson was hailed as a great democrat because of his opposition to the monopolistic Bank of the United States and as a great patriot because of his resistance to the doctrine of nullification and secession. This campaign handbill stresses both the democratic and the patriotic theme. (Tennessee State Library and Archives, Manuscripts Section, Andrew Jackson Papers)

representative of the people, Jackson dominated American politics for a time. Like a powerful magnet, he attracted a majority of the voters to him, and he polarized the others into a pattern of opposition — anti-Jacksonians against Jacksonians or, as they came to be known, Whigs against Democrats. He took a decisive part in the major controversies that arose. These concerned not only the role of the common man in government but also the rights of the states and the rights of the Indians, the nullification threat from South Carolina, and the alleged danger to

democracy arising from a great financial monopoly, the Bank of the United States.

The Jacksonians made strenuous efforts to arouse and organize the citizens and bring them out to vote. Then, stealing the Jacksonians' thunder, the Whigs came into office in 1840 by stirring up the electorate as not even Jackson had been able to do. This, rather than 1828, was the year of a "mighty democratic uprising." Politicians now developed new techniques of mass manipulation, and politics took on a modern look.

Advent of Mass Politics

On March 4, 1829, unprecedented thousands of Americans attended the inaugural ceremonies at the Capitol, and then the noisy crowd followed their hero to the White House, where at a public reception they trampled one another and even the elegantly upholstered sofas and chairs in their eagerness to shake his hand. "It was a proud day for the people," one of the Jacksonians, Amos Kendall, reported to his newspaper in Kentucky. "General Jackson is *their own* president." But most old Federalists and all lovers of political decorum were horrified. John Marshall's friend and colleague Justice Joseph Story disgustedly remarked: "The reign of King 'Mob' seemed triumphant."

THE COMMON MAN'S PRESIDENT

Though the new President was no democratic philosopher like Jefferson, he nevertheless held certain democratic convictions, notably the conviction that government should offer "equal protection and equal benefits" to all the people. His enemies denied that he ever really championed the people's cause, but they could not deny that he became a living symbol of democracy or that, far more than any of his predecessors, he gave a sense of participation in government to the common man.

As President, Jackson promptly set about to "reform" the personnel procedures of the federal government. For a generation, ever

since the downfall of the Federalists in 1800, there had been no complete party turnover in Washington. Officeholders accordingly stayed on year after year and election after election, many of them growing gray and some of them growing corrupt in office. "Office is considered as a species of property," Jackson told Congress, "and government rather as a means of promoting individual interests than as an instrument created solely for the service of the people." He believed that official duties could be made "so plain and simple that men of intelligence may readily qualify themselves for their performance." According to him, offices belonged to the people, not to the entrenched officeholders. Or, as one of his henchmen, William L. Marcy of New York, more cynically put it, "To the victors belong the spoils."

A corollary to the spoils system was the doctrine of rotation in office. Since ordinary men ("of intelligence") presumably were fit or could easily be fitted for government service, and since loyal members of the victorious party deserved government jobs, a particular position should not be held too long by any one person but should be passed around, or rotated, among several deserving applicants.

In actual practice, Jackson did not make such drastic removals as his partisan critics then and afterward asserted. During the entire eight years of his presidency he removed a total of no more than one-fifth of the federal officeholders, and many of these he removed for

Jackson's Inaugural Reception [1829]

Andrew Jackson's inauguration impressed a Washington society woman, Mrs. Samuel H. Smith, as a solemn and sublime event. Afterward Mrs. Smith went with a party of friends to the inaugural reception at the White House. "But what a scene did we witness!" she wrote a few days later, in a letter to an out-of-town relative.

The Majesty of the People had disappeared, & a rabble, a mob, of boys, negros, women, children, scrambling, fighting, romping. What a pity, what a pity! No arrangements had been made, no police officers placed on duty & the whole house had been inundated by the rabble mob. We came too late. The President, after having been literally nearly pressed to death & almost suffocated & torn to pieces by the people in their eagerness to shake hands with Old Hickory, had retreated through the back way or south front & had escaped to his lodgings at Gadsby's. Cut glass & china to the amount of several thousand dollars had been broken in the struggle to get the refreshments, punch & other articles had been carried out in tubs & buckets, but had it been in hogsheads it would have been insufficient, ice-cream, & cake & lemonade, for 20,000 people, for it is said that number were there, tho' I think the estimate exaggerated. Ladies fainted, men were seen with bloody noses & such a scene of confusion took place as is impossible to describe,—those who got in could not get out by the door again, but had to scramble out of windows.

---

cause, such as misuse of government funds. Proportionally, Jackson dismissed no more of the jobholders than Jefferson had done. Nor did he appoint illiterate coon-hunters or the like to positions requiring special training or skill. The fact remains, nevertheless, that the Jackson administration, adapting the spoils system from some of the states, fixed it firmly upon national politics.

Eventually the Jacksonians adopted another instrument of democratic politics—the national nominating convention—which was originated by the earliest of the third parties in American history, the Anti-Masonic party. This party was a response to widespread resentment against the secret and exclusive, hence supposedly undemocratic, Society of Freemasons. Feeling rose to new heights when, in 1826, a man named William Morgan mysteriously disappeared from his home in Batavia, New York. Since Morgan had been about to publish a book purporting to expose the secrets of freemasonry, his friends believed that vengeful Masons had done away with him. The excitement spread, and politicians in New York, Pennsylvania, and several other states seized upon it to organize a party with popular appeal. The party was anti-Jackson as well as Anti-Mason, Jackson being a high-ranking member of the lodge. In 1831 the Anti-Masons held a national convention in Harrisburg, Pennsylvania, to nominate a candidate for the next year's presidential campaign.

MORE AND MORE VOTERS

When Ohio and other new states in the West joined the Union, they adopted constitutions that gave the vote to all adult white males and allowed all voters the right to hold public office. Thus the new states set an example for the older ones. These older states became concerned about the loss of their population to the West, and they began slowly and haltingly to grant additional political rights to their people so as to encourage them to stay at home. Even before the War of 1812 a few of the Eastern states permitted white men to vote whether or not they owned property or paid a tax. After 1815 the states began to revise their constitutions by calling conventions that served as grand committees of the people to draw up new documents and submit them for public approval.

An Argument Against Universal Suffrage [1821]

According to the original constitution of New York, the state senate was elected by owners of land worth at least $250 and the assembly by owners of land worth at least $50. At the constitutional convention of 1821 the radicals proposed to abolish all property qualifications for voting. A conservative delegate, James Kent, objected. Then chancellor of the state chancery court, Kent was one of the nation's foremost legal authorities. Later he wrote a classic four-volume work entitled *Commentaries on American Law* (1826–1830). In 1821 he was willing to abolish the property qualification for assembly elections, but he wished to "preserve our Senate as the representative of the landed interest." He told his fellow delegates:

By the report before us, we propose to annihilate, at one stroke, all those property distinctions and to bow before the idol of universal suffrage. That extreme democratic principle, when applied to the legislative and executive departments of the government, has been regarded with terror, by the wise men of every age, because in every European republic, ancient and modern, in which it has been tried, it has terminated disastrously, and been productive of corruption, injustice, violence, and tyranny. . . .

The apprehended danger from the experiment of universal suffrage applied to the whole legislative department, is no dream of the imagination. It is too mighty an excitement for the moral constitution of men to endure. The tendency of universal suffrage is to jeopardize the rights of property and the principles of liberty. There is a constant tendency . . . in the poor to covet a share in the plunder of the rich; in the debtor to relax or avoid the obligation of contracts; in the majority to tyrannize over the minority, and trample down their rights; in the indolent and profligate to cast the whole burthens of society upon the industrious and the virtuous; and there is a tendency in ambitious and wicked men to inflame these combustible materials.

Eventually all the states (some of them not till after the Civil War) changed their constitutions in the direction of increased democracy.

Change was resisted, and at times the democratic trend was stopped short of the aims of the more radical reformers, as, for example, when Massachusetts held its convention in 1820. The reform-minded delegates complained that in the Massachusetts government the rich were better represented than the poor, both because of the restrictions on voting and officeholding and because of the peculiar system of property representation in the state senate. The number of senators from each district of the state depended not upon the number of people in the district but upon the amount of its taxable wealth. The reformers urged an amendment apportioning senators according to population alone. Daniel Webster, one of the conservative delegates, opposed the change on the grounds that "power *naturally* and *necessarily* follows property" and that "property as such should have its weight and influence in political arrangement." Webster and the rest of the conservatives could not prevent the reform of senate representation, nor could they prevent elimination of the property requirement for voting. But, to the disgust of the radicals, the new constitution required that every voter be a taxpayer and that the governor be the owner of considerable real estate.

In the New York convention of 1821 the conservatives, led by Chancellor James Kent, insisted that a taxpaying requirement for suffrage was not enough and that, at least in the election of state senators, the property qualification should be retained. Kent argued that society "is an association for the protection of property as well as of life" and that "the individual who contributes only one cent to the common stock ought not to have the same power and influence in directing the property concerns of the partnership as he who contributes his thousands.'' The reformers, appealing to the Declaration of Independence, maintained that life, liberty, and the pursuit of happiness, not property, were the main concerns of society and government. The property qualification was abolished in New York.

Other states proceeded more slowly in the broadening of democracy, none of them going to radical extremes. Progress was peaceful, except in Rhode Island. There the constitution was the old colonial charter, little changed, and it disqualified as voters more than half of the adult males of the state. Thomas L. Dorr and his suffragist followers, despairing of reform by legal processes, held a convention of their own, drew up a new constitution, and tried to set up an administration with Dorr as governor. When the existing state government began to imprison his followers he led a band of his men in an attack upon the Providence arsenal (1842). The Dorr Rebellion was quickly put down, yet it hastened the reforms that came afterward in Rhode Island.

In the South reformers criticized the overrepresentation of the tidewater areas and the underrepresentation of the back country in the legislatures. When the Virginia constitutional convention met, in 1829, the delegates from the western counties gained some slight concessions but not enough to satisfy them. Elsewhere in the Southeast the planters and politicians of the older counties continued to dominate the state governments.

With few exceptions, free Negroes could not vote anywhere in the South, nor could they vote in most of the Northern states. Pennsylvania at one time allowed Negro suffrage but eventually (1838) amended the constitution so as to prohibit it. In North and South, women continued to be denied the vote, regardless of the amount of property they might own. Everywhere the ballot was open, not secret, and often it was cast as a spoken vote rather than a written one. The lack of secrecy meant that voters could be, and sometimes were, bribed or intimidated.

In most of the states there was at first no popular vote for President. As late as 1800, the legislature chose presidential electors in ten of the states, and the people in only six. The trend was toward popular election, however, and after 1828 the legislature made the choice in only one state, South Carolina. There the people had no chance to vote in presidential elections till after the Civil War.

Despite the persisting limitations, the number of voters increased far more rapidly than did the population as a whole. In the presidential election of 1824 fewer than twenty-seven in one hundred of adult white males voted (though previously, in some of the states, more than fifty had done so). In the election of 1828 the proportion rose to about fifty-five in one hundred—more than twice the figure for 1824—and in the elections of 1832 and 1836 the proportion remained approximately the same as in 1828. Then, in 1840, people flocked to the polls as never before, seventy-eight in one hundred white men casting their ballots. The multiplication of voters was due only in part to the widening of the electorate. It was due in greater measure to a heightening of interest in politics and a strengthening of party organization. Citizens now were aroused and brought out to vote who in former times had seldom bothered with elections.

Not only did the number of voters increase; so did the number of elective offices in the states. The first state constitutions had provided for the appointment of high state officials by the governor or by the legislature. The newer constitutions put the election of these officials, including judges in some cases, into the hands of the people. Supposedly the people thus were to have increased control over government. Actually, with authority so divided and diffused, it was harder than ever for the people to locate and hold to account the officials responsible for particular policies.

Political parties became more important as both the electorate and the elections grew in number and complexity. Parties were necessary for bringing together voters of diverse interests and providing common goals so that the will of the people could express itself in a united and meaningful way. Parties were also necessary to give central direction to governments made up of independently elected officials. Hence, as the states became more democratic, political organizations within them became more tightly knit. Political machines and party bosses appeared in states like New

York and Pennsylvania which had large and heterogeneous electorates with a variety of conflicting interests. In New York and Pennsylvania the spoils system was introduced before it was transplanted to the federal government. State jobs were awarded to loyal workers of the victorious party, and job-seeking came to be the motive that held together and infused spirit into the core of the party membership.

"Our Federal Union"

President Jackson had taken office with no clearly announced program to carry out. His followers — who soon began to call themselves simply Democrats — had interests so diverse that a statement of definite aims would have alienated many of the party at the outset. This is not to say that Jackson himself was wishy-washy or lacking in convictions. Far from it. Besides believing in government by and for the common man, he stood for strong presidential leadership and, while respecting what he considered the legitimate rights of the states, he was devoted to the national Union. He did not hesitate to assert his principles when South Carolina tried to put into effect the nullification (or interposition) theory of John C. Calhoun.

CALHOUN: HIS THEORY

At the age of forty-six (in 1828) Calhoun had a promising future as well as a distinguished past. A congressional leader during the War of 1812, afterward head of the War Department for eight years (making a record that entitles him to rank as one of the few truly great secretaries of war), then Vice President in John Quincy Adams' administration, he now was running as the vice-presidential candidate on the Jackson ticket. And he could look forward to the presidency itself after a term or two for Jackson — if all went well.

But the tariff question placed Calhoun in a dilemma. Once he had been a forthright protectionist, coming out strongly for the tariff of 1816, but since that time many South Carolinians had changed their minds on the subject, and so had he. Carolina cotton planters were disturbed because their plantations did not pay, or at least were less profitable than it seemed they should have been. The whole state appeared to be stagnating, its population remaining almost stationary, its countryside showing signs of ruin and decay. One reason was the exhaustion of the South Carolina soil, which could not well compete with the newly opened, fertile lands of the Southwest. But the Carolinians blamed their trouble on quite another cause — the tariff, in particular the "tariff of abominations," the law of 1828. They reasoned that protective duties raised the prices of the things they had to buy, whether they bought them at home or from abroad, and lowered the price of the cotton they sold, most of which was exported. They had a point: in order to export, a nation has to import, and to the extent that the tariff kept foreign goods out of the United States it also reduced the foreign market for American cotton. Some exasperated Carolinians were ready to seek escape from the hated law through revolution — that is, through secession. Here was a challenge Calhoun had to meet in order to maintain his leadership in the state and make a future for himself in national politics.

Quietly he worked out a theory to justify state action in resisting the tariff law. He intended for this action, if and when it became necessary, to be strictly legal and constitutional, not revolutionary. So he had to find a basis for his plan in the Constitution itself. In his earlier career, as a nationalist, he had said the Constitution was not a thing for logicians to exercise their ingenuity upon, but should be construed with plain good sense. Now he himself resorted to subtle and ingenious logic, discovering implications in the Constitution that were not obvious to everybody — not even to the "father of the Constitution," James Madison, who denounced the Calhoun theory when he heard of it. Calhoun believed, however, that he was following the lines laid down by Madison and Jefferson in their Virginia and Kentucky resolutions of 1798–1799. Indeed, his

Many of the early biographers of Andrew Jackson and historians of the Jackson period were upper middle-class Easterners who sympathized with his opponents, the Whigs. These unfriendly, Whiggish authors described him as a "barbarian" whose election was a "mistake" and whose policies on the whole were "deplorable." Such views prevailed until the end of the nineteenth century.

Then a new generation of scholars, nearly all of them from the West or the South, began to rewrite history in a manner highly favorable to Jackson. They saw him as a true democrat who, much like the progressives of their own time, strove to make government responsive to the will of the people rather than the desires of the special interests. The most influential of the newer historians, Frederick Jackson Turner, in his famous essay "The Significance of the Frontier in American History" (1893) and in later writings, maintained that Jacksonian Democracy had originated in the "frontier democratic society" of the West. Turner's "frontier interpretation" soon became predominant, though one authority on early Tennessee politics (Thomas P. Abernethy) insisted that Jackson actually had been a frontier aristocrat and had opposed the democratic trend in his own state.

In recent years historians have emphasized social classes rather than geographical sections in seeking to explain Jackson and his program, but they have disagreed about which class he represented. Arthur M. Schlesinger, Jr., contended in *The Age of Jackson* (1945) that Jacksonian Democracy was an effort "to control the power of the capitalistic groups, mainly Eastern, for the benefit of noncapitalist groups, farmers and laboring men, East, West, and South." Critics of Schlesinger, however, argued that Jackson was antilabor rather than prolabor and that he really reflected the interests of the rising businessmen. In *Banks and Politics in America from the Revolution to the Civil War* (1957) Bray Hammond described the Jacksonian cause as "one of enterpriser against capitalist, of banker against regulation, and of Wall Street against Chestnut"—that is, of New York City bankers against the Philadelphia-based Bank of the United States.

Disagreeing with both Hammond and Schlesinger and also with earlier historians such as Turner, Lee Benson maintained that the very term "Jacksonian Democracy" had "obscured rather than illuminated" our understanding of the period. In *The Concept of Jacksonian Democracy: New York as a Test Case* (1961) Benson showed that, at least in the state of New York, both the Jackson and the anti-Jackson parties included the same kinds of big as well as small businessmen in addition to farmers and city workers and that politicians on both sides made use of similar "agrarian" rhetoric. According to Benson, the democratic movement was much broader than the Democratic party. Therefore, he suggested, we could take a step toward clarification by "discarding the old caption for the period" and substituting "the Age of Egalitarianism" for "the Age of Jackson."

reasoning was quite similar to theirs, but he carried it further than they had done, and he provided a definite procedure for state action, which they had not.

Calhoun started his reasoning with the assumption that sovereignty, the ultimate source of power, lay in the states considered as separate political communities. He went on to assume that these separate peoples had created the federal government, through their conventions that ratified the Constitution after it had been drawn up. Putting this in legal terminology, he described the states (meaning their peoples, not their governments) as the "principals," the federal government as their "agent," and the Constitution as a "compact" containing instructions within which the agent was to operate.

From these assumptions the rest of his theory followed logically enough. The Supreme Court was not competent to judge whether acts of Congress were constitutional, since the Court, like the Congress, was only a branch of an agency created by the states. No, Calhoun reasoned, the principals must decide, each for itself, whether their instructions were violated. If Congress enacted a law of doubtful constitutionality—say, a protective tariff—a state could "interpose" to frustrate the law. That is, the people of the state could hold a convention, and if (through their elected delegates) they decided that Congress had gone too far, they could declare the federal law null and void within their state. In that state the law would remain inoperative until three-fourths of the whole number of states should ratify an amendment to the Constitution specifically assigning Congress the power in question. And if the other states should ever get around to doing this, the nullifying state would then submit—or it could secede.

The legislature of South Carolina published Calhoun's first statement of his theory, anonymously, in a document entitled *The South Carolina Exposition and Protest* (1828). This condemned the recent tariff as unconstitutional, unfair, and unendurable—a law fit to be nullified. Calhoun had good reason for not wishing to be identified publicly as the author of the document. It was bound to arouse a certain amount of opposition in parts of the country, and of course he hoped to be reelected

Vice President and later to be elected President.

After the Jackson-Calhoun ticket had won its victory at the polls, Calhoun was no more eager than before to see nullification put into effect. He waited, hoping that Jackson as President would persuade Congress to make drastic reductions in tariff rates and thus mollify the outraged Carolina planters. It remained to be seen what chance Calhoun would have for the presidency as Jackson's friend and successor. As soon as the major appointments had been made, he gained an inkling of his importance, or unimportance, in the new administration. He then realized he had a powerful rival for Jackson's favor in the person of Martin Van Buren.

VAN BUREN TO THE FORE

Van Buren, about the same age as Calhoun and equally ambitious, was quite different in background and personality. Born of Dutch ancestry in the village of Kinderhook near Albany, New York, he advanced himself through skillful maneuvering to the position of United States senator (1820–1828). He also made himself the party boss of his state by organizing and leading the Albany Regency, the Democratic machine of New York. Though he supported Crawford for President in 1824, he afterward became one of the most ardent of Jacksonians, doing much to carry his state for Jackson in 1828 while getting himself elected as governor. By this time he had a reputation as a political wizard. Short and slight, with reddish gold sideburns and a quiet manner, he gained a variety of revealing nicknames, such as "the Sage of Kinderhook," "the Little Magician," and "the Red Fox." Never giving or taking offense, he was in temperament just the opposite of the choleric Jackson, yet the two were about to become the closest of friends. Van Buren promptly resigned the governorship and went to Washington when Jackson called him to head the new cabinet as secretary of state.

Except for Van Buren, this cabinet contained no one of more than ordinary talent. It was intended (as cabinets usually are) to represent and harmonize the sectional and factional interests within the party. No Virginian was included: for the first time since 1789 Virginia provided neither the President nor any of the secretaries. Friends of both Van Buren and Calhoun were given places. This cabinet was not intended to form a council of advisers: Jackson did not even call cabinet meetings.

Instead, he relied on an unofficial circle of political cronies who came to be known as the "Kitchen Cabinet." Noteworthy in this group were several newspaper editors, among them Isaac Hill, a hunchbacked master of invective from New Hampshire, and Amos Kendall and Francis P. Blair from Kentucky. After 1830 Blair edited the administration's official organ, the Washington *Globe*. The close-mouthed, asthmatic, "invisible" Kendall was said to be the genius who, behind the scenes, really ran the administration. While doubtless influential, he was no more so than several others, especially Jackson's old Tennessee friend and political manager William B. Lewis, who roomed at the White House and had ready access to the President. Soon to be the most important of all was Van Buren, a member of both the official and the unofficial cabinet.

Vice President Calhoun, to his dismay, saw signs of Van Buren's growing influence when he viewed the division of the spoils. Not only did Van Buren get cabinet places for himself and his friends; he also secured the appointment of his followers to most of the lesser offices. Already, beneath the surface, there was the beginning of a rift between the Vice President and the President. Then Calhoun and Jackson were further estranged, and at the same time Jackson and Van Buren were brought closer together, in consequence of a curious quarrel over a woman and etiquette.

Peggy O'Neil, the bright-eyed, vivacious daughter of a Washington tavern-keeper, was the kind of woman whom men admire and women dislike. Jackson's Tennessee friend Senator John H. Eaton took the young widow as his wife, with Jackson's blessing. Washington gossips told and retold scandalous stories about her relationship with Eaton while her former husband had been still alive. All the talk would have amounted to little if Jackson had not appointed Eaton as his secretary of war and thus made Mrs. Eaton a cabinet wife. The rest of the administration wives, led by Mrs. Calhoun, snubbed Mrs. Eaton. Jackson was furious. His own wife, the dead Rachel, had been slandered by his political enemies, and he was confident that Peggy too was virtuous, an innocent victim of dirty politics. He not only defended her virtue: he demanded that his secretaries and associates concede it and treat her with respect. But they had their wives to contend with. Calhoun, for one, had no choice but to take sides against Mrs. Eaton, which meant taking sides against her champion, Jackson. With Van Buren the case was different. A widower, without daughters, he had no womenfolk to worry about. From the outset he befriended the Eatons and thus ingratiated himself with the President.

The Eaton affair dragged on, and finally Jackson decided to get rid of his uncooperative secretaries and reorganize his cabinet (1831). Van Buren resigned and so did two of his friends; the others took the hint and submitted their resignations too. Jackson appointed a new cabinet which on the whole was considerably stronger than the first one. Thereafter he relied more on his official advisers, less on the Kitchen Cabinet. As for Van Buren, he was sent to England as American minister, the appointment being made while the Senate was not in session. When the Senate met, there was a tie vote on the question of confirming the appointment, and Calhoun as the presiding officer broke the tie by casting his own ballot against Van Buren. This brought Van Buren home but gave no advantage to Calhoun.

Already Jackson had picked Van Buren for the presidential succession and had marked Calhoun as the worst of foes. The final break came when Jackson learned the inside story of a Monroe cabinet meeting years earlier. At the time of Jackson's Florida raid (1817) and for a long time afterward he supposed that Calhoun, as Monroe's secretary of war, had stood up for him when others in the administration proposed to punish him for his action. The truth, as Calhoun's enemies at last convinced Jackson, was quite otherwise.

THE WEBSTER-HAYNE DEBATE

If there had been only personal differences between Jackson and Calhoun, their parting would have been less significant than it actually was. But there were also differences of principle. At the height of the Eaton affair the opposing views of the two men were dramatically revealed in consequence of a great debate on the nature of the Constitution.

The Webster-Hayne debate, in January 1830, grew out of a Senate discussion of public lands, a discussion provoked when a senator from Connecticut suggested that all land sales and surveys be discontinued for the time being. This suggestion immediately aroused Senator Thomas Hart Benton of Missouri, once Jackson's antagonist in a wild frontier brawl, now the Jacksonian leader in the Senate and a sturdy defender of the West. Always suspicious of New England, he charged that the proposal to stop land sales was intended to keep New England workers from going West and thus to choke off the growth and prosperity of the frontier.

A young, debonair senator from South Carolina, Robert Y. Hayne, took up the argument after Benton. Hayne and other Southerners hoped to get Western support for their drive to lower the tariff, and at the moment they were willing to grant abundant and cheap lands to the Westerners in exchange for such support. He hinted that the South and the West might well combine in self-defense against the Northeast.

Daniel Webster, now a senator from Massachusetts, once had been a state-rights and antitariff man but, like Calhoun, only in reverse, he had changed his position with the changing interests of his section. The day after Hayne's speech he took the floor in an effort to head off the threatened rapprochement of the West and the South and thus to protect the interests of New England, including the tariff interest. Ignoring Benton, he directed his remarks to Hayne and, through him, to Calhoun in the Vice President's chair. He reviewed much of the history of the republic, with occasional disregard for historical facts, to prove

Webster Replying to Hayne
Hayne is sitting in the front center, with his hands together. Calhoun, presiding as Vice President, leans intently on his desk, in the shadow at the extreme left. Note the bonneted ladies in the gallery and the page in the left foreground. From G. P. A. Healy's painting, which hangs in Faneuil Hall, Boston. (Courtesy of Edward J. Kennedy and the Frick Art Reference Library)

that New England always had been the friend of the West. Referring to the tariff of 1816 he said that New England was not responsible for beginning the protectionist policy but had accepted it after other sections had fixed it upon the nation. Then, changing the subject, he spoke gravely of disunionists and disunionism in South Carolina.

Thus he challenged Hayne to meet him, not on the original grounds of the public lands and the tariff, but on the issue of state rights versus national power, an issue that could be made to seem one of treason versus patriotism. And in due time Hayne, coached by Calhoun, came back with a flashing defense of the nullification theory. It took Webster two afternoons to deliver what schoolboys were afterward to know as the second reply to Hayne. "I go for the Constitution as it is, and for the Union as it is," he declaimed, as he turned to an exposition of the "true principles" of the Constitution. "It is, Sir, the people's Constitution, the people's government, made for the people, made by the people, and answerable to the people." And he meant one people, the whole nation. He concluded with the ringing appeal: "Liberty *and* Union, now and for ever, one and inseparable!"

Calhoun's followers were sure that Hayne had the better of the argument. The important question at the moment, however, was what President Jackson thought and what side, if any, he would take.

An answer soon was given at a Democratic banquet that was supposed to honor Thomas Jefferson as the founder of the party. At the banquet the friends of Calhoun hoped to build up the alliance of South and West and strengthen his presidential prospects by identifying his principles with those of Jefferson. As was customary at such affairs, the guests settled down after dinner to an evening of drinking toasts. The President, forewarned by Van Buren, was ready with a toast of his own, which he had written down, underscoring certain words. When his turn came, he stood up and proclaimed: "Our *Federal* Union—It must be preserved." While he spoke he looked sternly at Calhoun. Van Buren, who stood on his chair to see better from the far end of the table, thought he saw Calhoun's hand shake and a trickle of wine run down the outside of his glass. Calhoun responded to Jackson's toast with his own:

"The Union—next to our liberty most dear. May we always remember that it can only be preserved by distributing evenly the benefits and the burthens of the Union."

STATE RIGHTS AND THE VETO

Jackson's pro-Union and antinullification feelings, as expressed in his Jefferson's birthday toast, did not mean that he was opposed to state rights as such. On the contrary, as he had declared in his inaugural address, he believed in none but "constitutional" undertakings by the federal government. During his administration he readily vetoed laws that he thought exceeded the powers originally granted to Congress by the states; in fact, he used the veto more freely than any President before him.

The Maysville Road Bill (1830) brought on the most significant of Jackson's vetoes. This bill, by authorizing the government to buy stock in a private company, would have given a federal subsidy for the construction of a turnpike from Maysville to Lexington, within the state of Kentucky. The Maysville pike was a segment of a projected highway that was to form a great Southwestern branch of the National Road. Nevertheless, since the pike itself was an intrastate and not an interstate project, Jackson doubted whether Congress constitutionally could give aid to it. Earlier (in 1822) President Monroe, vetoing the Cumberland Road Bill, had declared that the federal government should support only those improvements that were of general rather than local importance, and Jackson then had agreed with Monroe. Now, with Van Buren's assistance, Jackson prepared a veto message based on similar grounds. He also urged economy, denounced the selfish "scramble for appropriations," and stressed the desirability of paying off the national debt. Though Jackson also refused to sign other appropriation bills, he did not object to every proposal for federal spending to build roads or improve rivers and harbors. During his two terms such expenditures continued to mount, far exceeding even those of the John Quincy Adams administration.

The Maysville veto was not popular in the West, where better transportation was a never-ending demand, but Jackson's Indian policy was wholeheartedly approved in both the West and the South.

INDIAN REMOVAL

As an old Indian fighter, Jackson was no lover of the red man, and he desired to continue and expedite the program, which Jefferson had begun, of removing all the eastern tribes to the west of the Mississippi. The land between the Missouri and the Rockies, according to such explorers as Lewis and Clark and Stephen H. Long, was supposed to be a vast desert, unfit for white habitation. Why not leave that land for the Indians? By the Indian Removal Act of 1830 Congress proposed to exchange tribal lands within the states for new homes in the West, and by the Indian Intercourse Act of 1834 Congress marked off an Indian country and provided for a string of forts to keep the Indians inside it and the whites outside. Meanwhile the President saw that treaties, nearly a hundred in all, were negotiated with the various tribes and that reluctant tribesmen along with their women and children were moved west, with the prodding of the army.

In the process of Indian removal there was much tragedy and a certain amount of violence. When (in 1832) Chief Black Hawk with a thousand of his hungry Sac and Fox followers—men, women, and children—recrossed the Mississippi into Illinois to grow corn, the frontiersmen feared an invasion. Militiamen and regular troops soon drove the unfortunate Indians into Wisconsin and then slaughtered most of them as they tried to escape. Such was the Black Hawk War, in which Abraham Lincoln was a captain of militia (he saw no action) and Jefferson Davis a lieutenant in the regular army.

More serious was the Seminole War. It began when Chief Osceola led an uprising of his tribesmen (including runaway Negroes), who refused to move west in accordance with a treaty of 1833, and the fighting lasted off and on for several years. Jackson sent troops to Florida, but the Seminoles with their Negro associates were masters of guerrilla warfare in the jungly Everglades. Even after Osceola had been treacherously captured under a flag of truce and had died in prison, the red and black rebels continued to resist.

Unlike the Sacs and Foxes or the Seminoles, the Cherokees in Georgia were a civilized people, with a written language of their own (invented by the half-breed Sequoyah in

1821) and with a settled way of life as farmers. Yet the state of Georgia, after getting rid of most of the Creeks, was eager to remove the Cherokees also and open their millions of acres to white occupation. In 1827 these Indians adopted a constitution and declared their independence as the Cherokee Nation. Promptly the Georgia legislature extended its laws over them and directed the seizure of their territory. Hiring a prominent lawyer, the Cherokees appealed to the Supreme Court. In the case of *Cherokee Nation* v. *Georgia* (1831) Chief Justice Marshall gave the majority opinion that the Indians were "domestic dependent nations" and had a right to the land they occupied until they voluntarily ceded it to the United States. In another case, *Worcester* v. *Georgia* (1832), Marshall and the Court held that the Cherokee Nation was a definite political community with territory over which the laws of Georgia had no force and into which Georgians could not enter without permission.

President Jackson did not sympathize with the Cherokees as President Adams had done with the Creeks. Vigorously supporting Georgia's position, Jackson did nothing to aid the Indians or to see that the rulings of the Supreme Court were carried out. The Chief Justice had implied that it was the President's duty to uphold the rights of the Indians. Jackson's attitude is well expressed in the comment attributed to him: "John Marshall has made his decision; now let him enforce it." The decision was never enforced.

In 1835 a few of the Cherokees, none of them a chosen representative of the Cherokee Nation, were induced to sign a treaty giving up the nation's Georgia land in return for $5 million and a reservation in Indian Territory (Oklahoma). The great majority of the 17,000 Cherokees were unwilling to leave their homes, so Jackson sent an army of 7,000 under General Winfield Scott to drive them westward at bayonet point. About a thousand fled across the state line to North Carolina, where eventually the federal government provided a reservation for them.

Most of the rest—along with others of the "Five Civilized Tribes": Choctaws, Chickasaws, Creeks, and Seminoles—made the long, forced trek to the West, beginning in midwinter, 1838. Along the way a Kentuckian observed: "Even aged females, apparently nearly

ᏣᎳᎩ ᏚᎳᏚᎳ
CHEROKEE PHŒNIX.

VOL. I.   NEW ECHOTA, THURSDAY FEBRUARY 21, 1828.   **NO. 1.**

EDITED BY ELIAS BOUDINOTT.

PRINTED WEEKLY BY

ISAAC H. HARRIS,

FOR THE CHEROKEE NATION.

At $2 50 if paid in advance, $3 in six months, or $3 50 if paid at the end of the year.

To subscribers who can read only the Cherokee language the price will be $2,00 in advance, or $2,50 to be paid within the year.

Every subscription will be considered as continued unless subscribers give notice to the contrary before the commencement of a new year.

The Phœnix will be printed on a Super Royal sheet, with type entirely new procured for the purpose. Any person procuring six subscribers, and becoming responsible for the payment, shall receive a seventh gratis.

Advertisements will be inserted at seventy-five cents per square for the first insertion, and thirty-seven and a half cents for each continuance; longer ones in proportion.

☞ All letters addressed to the Editor, post paid, will receive due attention.

A GOOD CONSCIENCE.

WHAT is there, in all the pomp of the world, the enjoyments of luxury, the gratification of passion, comparable to the tranquil delight of a good conscience? *It is the health of the mind.* It is a sweet perfume, that diffuses its fragrance over every thing near it without exhausting its store. Unaccompanied with this, the gay pleasures of the world are like brilliants to a diseased eye, music to a deaf ear, wine to an ardent fever, or dainties in the languor of an ague. To lie down on the pillow, after a day spent in temperance in beneficence, and piety, how sweet is it! How different from the state of him, who reclines, at an unnatural hour, with his blood inflamed, his head throbbing with wine and gluttony, his heart aching with rancorous malice, his thoughts totally estranged from Him who has protected him in the day, and will watch over him, ingrateful as he is, in the night season! A good conscience is, indeed, the peace of God, passions lulled to sleep, clear thoughts, cheerful tempers, a disposition to be pleased with every object around, and innocent object around; these are the effects of a good conscience; these are the things which constitute happiness; and these condensed to dwell with the poor man, in his humble cottage in the vale of obscurity. In the magnificent mansion of the proud and vain, glitter the exteriors of happiness, the gilding, the trapping, the show, the pomp; but in the direct, by his little piety is oftener found than ease or real heartfelt peace: that each of which the peace of the vain, the freedom, and voluptuous, is but a shadowy semblance.

Christian Philosophy.

Flattery.—Few things are more universally condemned than flattery yet there are few men, who are above its influence, and still fewer, who have received sufficient to guard it with a faithful rebuke. The following anecdote is recommended, as affording a specimen of a good answer to flatterers. A certain city clergyman in New England, eminent both for his learning and humility, was one day sent for by a parishioner, who [?] commended some of his performances. "A braver and indelicate right to their respective improvements, as expressed in this article, shall possess an old one power to dispose of their improvements in any manner whatever to the United States, individual States, nor to individuals, citizens thereof, and that, whenever any such citizens or citizens shall remove with their effects out of the limits of this Nation, and become citizens of any other Government, shall [?]..."

CONSTITUTION OF THE CHEROKEE NATION,

Formed by a Convention of Delegates from the several Districts, at New Echota, July 1827.

WE, THE REPRESENTATIVES of the people of the CHEROKEE NATION in Convention assembled, in order to establish justice, ensure tranquility, promote our common welfare, and secure to ourselves and our posterity the blessings of liberty; acknowledging with humility and gratitude the goodness of the sovereign Ruler of the Universe, in offering us an opportunity so favorable to the design, and imploring his aid and direction in its accomplishment, do ordain and establish this Constitution for the Government of the Cherokee Nation.

ARTICLE I.

Sec. 1. THE BOUNDARIES of this nation, embracing the lands solemnly guarantied and reserved forever to the Cherokee Nation by the Treaties concluded with the United States, are as follows; and shall forever hereafter remain unalterably the same—to wit—Beginning on the North Bank of Tennessee River at the upper part of the Chickasaw old fields; thence along the main channel of said river, including all the islands therein, to the mouth of the Hiwassee river, thence up the main channel of said river, including Islands, to the first hill which closes in on said river, about two miles above Hiwassee old Town; thence along the ridge which divides the waters of the Hiwassee and little Tellico, to the Tennessee river at Talassee; thence along the main channel, including Islands, to the junction of the Cowee and Nanteyalee; thence along the ridge in the fork of said river, to the top of the blue ridge; thence along the blue ridge to the Unicoy Turnpike road; thence by a straight line to the main source of the Chestatee; thence along its main channel, including Islands, to the Chattahoochy; and thence down the same to the Creek boundary at Buzzard Roost; thence along the boundary line which separates this and the Creek Nation, to a point on the Coosa river opposite the mouth of Wills Creek; thence down along the South bank of the same to a point opposite to Fort Strother; thence up the river to the mouth of Wills Creek; thence up along the East bank of said creek, to the West branch thereof, and on the same to its source; and thence along the ridge which separates the Tombeckbee and Tennessee waters, to a point on the top of said ridge; thence due North to Camp Coffee on Tennessee river, which is opposite the Chickasaw Island; and thence to the place of beginning.

Sec. 2. The Sovereignty and Jurisdiction of this Government shall extend over the Country within the boundaries above described, and the lands therein are, and shall remain, the common property of the Nation; but the improvements made thereon, and in the possession of the citizens of the Nation, are the exclusive and indefeasible property of the citizens respectively who made, or may rightfully be in possession of them: *Provided*, That the citizens of the Nation, possessing exclusive and indefeasible right to their respective improvements, as expressed in this article, shall possess no right nor power to dispose of their improvements in any manner whatever to the United States, individual States, nor to individuals, citizens thereof; and that, whenever any such citizens or citizens shall remove with their effects out of the limits of this Nation, and become citizens of any other Government, all their rights and privileges as citizens of this Nation shall cease: *Provided nevertheless,* That the Legislature shall have power to re-admit by law to all the rights of citizenship, any such person or persons who may at any time desire to return to the Nation on their memorializing the General Council for such readmission. *Moreover*, the Legislature shall have power to adopt such laws and regulations, as its wisdom may deem expedient and proper, to prevent the citizens from monopolizing improvements with the view of speculation.

ARTICLE II.

Sec. 1. THE POWER of this Government shall be divided into three distinct departments;—the Legislative, the Executive, and the Judicial.

Sec. 2. No person or persons, belonging to one of these Departments, shall exercise any of the powers properly belonging to either of the others, except in the cases hereinafter expressly directed or permitted.

ARTICLE III.

Sec. 1. THE LEGISLATIVE POWER shall be vested in two distinct branches; a Committee, and a Council; each to have a negative on the other, and both to be styled, the General Council of the Cherokee Nation; and the style of their acts and laws shall be,

"RESOLVED by the Committee and Council in General Council convened."

Sec. 2. The Cherokee Nation, as laid off into eight Districts, shall so remain.

Sec. 3. The Committee shall consist of two members from each District, and the Council shall consist of three members from each District, to be chosen by the qualified electors of their respective Districts for two years; and the elections to be held in every District on the first Monday in August for the year 1828, and every succeeding two years thereafter; and the General Council shall be held once a year, to be convened on the second Monday of October in each year, at New Echota.

Sec. 4. No person shall be eligible to a seat in the General Council, but a free Cherokee Male citizen, who shall have attained to the age of twenty-five years. The descendants of Cherokee men by all free women, except the African race, whose parents may be or have been living together as man and wife, according to the customs and laws of this Nation, shall be entitled to all the rights and privileges of this Nation, as well as the posterity of Cherokee women by all free men. No person who is of negro or mulatto parentage, either by the father or mother side, shall be eligible to hold any office of profit, honor or trust, under this Government.

Sec. 5. The Electors, and members of the General Council shall, in all cases except those of treason, felony, or breach of the peace, be privileged from arrest during their attendance at election, and at the General Council, and in going to, and returning from, the same.

Sec. 6. In all elections by the people, the electors shall vote viva voce. Electors for members to the General Council for 1828, shall be held at the places of holding the several courts, and at the other two precincts in each District which are designated by the law under which the members of this Convention were elected; and the District Judges shall superintend the elections within the precincts of their respective Court Houses, and the Marshals & Sheriffs shall superintend within the precincts which may be assigned them by the Circuit Judges of their respective Districts, together with one other person, who shall be appointed by the Circuit Judges for each precinct within their respective Districts; and the Circuit Judges shall appoint a clerk to each precinct.— The superintendents and clerks shall, on the Wednesday morning succeeding the election, assemble at their respective Court Houses and proceed to examine and ascertain the true state of the polls, and shall issue to each member, duly elected, a certificate and also make an official return of the state of the polls of election to the principal Chief, and it shall be the du...

[Cherokee syllabary text appears in parallel columns throughout the Constitution section.]

A Cherokee Newspaper

The front page of the Cherokee Phoenix for February 21, 1828, presents the Constitution of the Cherokee Nation in both English and Cherokee. Sequoya (who is believed to have been the son of a part-Cherokee mother and a white father) had only recently, in 1821, completed the work of devising a Cherokee alphabet after twelve years of effort. (American Antiquarian Society)

ready to drop in the grave, were travelling with heavy burdens attached to their backs, sometimes on frozen ground and sometimes on muddy streets, with no covering for their feet." Several thousand perished before reaching their undesired destination. In Indian Territory the survivors were never to forget the hard way by which they had arrived there. They called it "The Trail Where They Cried," the trail of tears.

SOUTH CAROLINA INTERPOSES

In a sense Georgia nullified federal authority when, proclaiming state rights, she flouted the rulings of the highest court of the United States. In doing so, nevertheless, the state had the backing of the President. But when, in the midst of the Georgia controversy, another state attempted out-and-out nullification of an act of Congress, Jackson reacted quite differently.

After waiting four years for Congress to undo the "tariff of abominations," the South Carolina followers of Calhoun had little patience left, and they lost that when Congress denied them any real relief in the tariff of 1832.

Though making certain changes in individual rates, the new law did not lower the tariff, as a whole, enough to satisfy the cotton planters of the state. And the rice growers, though not concerned about the tariff, were apprehensive that slavery might be threatened if federal power remained unchecked.

Some of the South Carolinians now were ready for revolt, and had it not been for Calhoun's program and leadership, they might have taken even more drastic action than they did. Having ceased to be Jackson's friend and prospective successor, Calhoun had come out openly for nullification, elaborated the doctrine further, and induced the extremists to adopt it as their remedy. To nullify or not to nullify — that was the question in the state election of 1832. The nullifiers proved to be the majority, but their opponents (who called themselves Unionists) made up a large minority, the vote being approximately 23,000 to 17,000. Without delay the newly elected legislature called for the election of delegates to a state convention. The convention adopted an ordinance of nullification that declared null and void the tariffs of 1828 and 1832 and forbade the collection of duties, within the state. The legislature then

---

Nullification Ordinance [1832]

Having failed to obtain relief from what most planters considered an oppressive and unfair tariff, South Carolina put Calhoun's theory into practice with the following resolutions:

Whereas the Congress of the United States, by various acts, purporting to be acts laying duties and imports on foreign imports, but in reality intended for the protection of domestic manufactures, and the giving of bounties to classes and individuals engaged in particular employment, at the expense and to the injury and oppression of other classes and individuals, . . . hath exceeded its just powers under the Constitution, which confers on it no authority to afford such protection, and hath violated the true meaning and intent of the Constitution, which provides for equality in imposing the burthens of taxation upon the several States and portions of the Confederacy. . . .

We, therefore, the people of the State of South Carolina, in Convention assembled, do declare and ordain . . .

That the several acts and parts of acts of the Congress of the United States, purporting to be laws for the imposing of duties and imposts on the importation of foreign commodities . . . [especially the tariff acts of 1828 and 1832] . . . are unauthorized by the Constitution of the United States, and violate the true meaning and intent thereof, and are null, void, and no law, nor binding upon this State. . . .

passed laws to enforce the ordinance and make preparations for military defense. Needing a strong man to take command at home, and another to present the South Carolina case ably in Washington, the nullifiers arranged for Hayne to become governor and for Calhoun to replace Hayne as senator. So Calhoun resigned as Vice President.

While the nullifiers prepared for war they hoped for peace. According to the Calhoun theory the federal government had no rightful recourse, and the rest of the states could do nothing except to amend the Constitution. When the theory was put to the test, however, not a single state came to South Carolina's support.

Unofficially the President threatened to hang Calhoun. Officially he proclaimed that nullification was treason and its adherents traitors. Jackson did not confine himself to mere words. Cooperating closely with the Unionists of South Carolina, he also took steps to strengthen the federal forts in the state, ordering General Winfield Scott and a warship and several revenue cutters to Charleston.

When Congress met, the President asked for specific authority with which to handle the crisis. His followers introduced a "force bill" authorizing him to use the army and navy to see that acts of Congress were obeyed. The force bill, like Jackson's proclamation, further antagonized the South Carolina extremists. Violence seemed a real possibility early in 1833, as Calhoun took his place in the Senate to defend his theory and its practice. He introduced a set of resolutions on the "constitutional compact" and then made a speech against the force bill.

Webster's reply to Calhoun (February 16, 1833), if less colorful than his reply to Hayne three years earlier, dwelt more fully and more cogently upon the constitutional issues at stake. The Constitution, Webster argued, was no mere compact among sovereign states that might secede at will. It was an "executed contract," an agreement to set up a permanent government, supreme within its allotted sphere and acting directly upon the people as a whole. Webster dismissed secession as a revolutionary but not a constitutional right, then denounced nullification as no right at all. The nullifiers, he said, rejected "the first great principle of all republican liberty; that is, that the majority must govern." They pretended to be con-

---

Jackson's Proclamation [1832]

Our present Constitution was formed . . . in vain if this fatal doctrine [nullification] prevails. It was formed for important objects that are announced in the preamble, made in the name and by the authority of the people of the United States, whose delegates framed and whose conventions approved it. The most important among these objects—that which is placed first in rank, on which all the others rest—is "to form a more perfect union." Now, is it possible that even if there were no express provision giving supremacy to the Constitution and laws of the United States over those of the States, can it be conceived that an instrument made for the purpose of "forming a more perfect union" than that of the Confederation could be so constructed by the assembled wisdom of our country as to substitute for that Confederation a form of government dependent for its existence on the local interest, the party spirit, of a State? Every man of plain, unsophisticated understanding who hears the question will give such an answer as will preserve the Union. Metaphysical subtlety, in pursuit of an impracticable theory, could alone have devised one that is calculated to destroy it. . . .

The laws of the United States must be executed. I have no discretionary power on the subject; my duty is emphatically pronounced in the Constitution.

cerned about minority rights, but did they practice what they preached? "Look to South Carolina, at the present moment. How far are the rights of minorities there respected?" Obviously the nullificationist majority was proceeding with a "relentless disregard" for the rights of the Unionist minority — "a minority embracing, as the gentleman himself will admit, a large portion of the worth and respectability of the state."

At the moment Calhoun was in a predicament. South Carolina, standing alone, itself divided, could not hope to prevail if a showdown with the federal government should come. If the nullifiers meekly yielded, however, they would lose face and their leader would be politically ruined. Calhoun was saved by the timely intervention of the Great Pacificator, Henry Clay. Newly elected to the Senate, Clay in consultation with Calhoun devised a compromise scheme by which the tariff would be lowered year after year, reaching in 1842 approximately the same level as in 1816. Finally Clay's compromise and the force bill were passed on the same day (March 1, 1833). Webster consistently opposed any concessions to the nullifiers, but

Jackson was satisfied: he signed the new tariff measure as well as the force bill.

In South Carolina the convention reassembled and repealed its ordinance of nullification as applied to the tariffs of 1828 and 1832. Then, as if to have the last word, the convention adopted a new ordinance nullifying the force act. This proceeding meant little, since the force act would not go into effect anyhow, the original ordinance (against which it was directed) having been withdrawn. The second nullification was intended to reinforce the impression that Calhoun's program was a success and was still to be reckoned with. Though Calhoun and his followers, having brought about tariff reduction, claimed a victory for nullification, the system had not worked out in the way its sponsors had intended. Calhoun had learned a lesson: no state could assert and maintain its rights by independent action. Thereafter, while continuing to talk of state rights and nullification, he devoted himself to building up a sense of Southern solidarity so that, when another trial should come, the whole section might be prepared to act as a unit in resisting federal authority.

Jackson and the Bank

The Bank of the United States was a private corporation with a charter from the federal government, which owned one-fifth of the stock. It was a monopoly, having an exclusive right to hold the government's deposits. With its headquarters in Philadelphia and its branches in twenty-nine other cities, it also did a tremendous business in general banking, totaling about $70 million a year. Its services were important to the national economy because of the credit it provided for profit-making enterprises, because of its banknotes that circulated throughout the country as a dependable medium of exchange, and because of the restraining effect that its policies had upon the less well-managed banks chartered by the various states.

BIDDLE'S INSTITUTION

Nicholas Biddle, president of the Bank from 1823 on, had done much to put the company on a sound and prosperous basis. A member of an aristocratic Philadelphia family, Biddle was educated at the University of Pennsylvania and thereafter devoted himself to a number of intellectual interests, including poetry. He personally owned a large proportion of the Bank's stock, so much of it that together with two other large stockholders he controlled the Bank. He could and did choose the officials of the branches, decide what loans were to be made, and set the interest rates. For several years after he took charge he made these decisions according to financial considerations. A banker, not a politician, he had no desire to mix in politics. But he finally concluded it was necessary to do so in self-defense when, with the encouragement of Jackson, popular opposition to the Bank rose to a threatening pitch.

Opposition came from two very different groups, the "soft-money" and the "hard-money" men. The former, consisting largely of state bankers and their friends, objected to the Bank of the United States because it restrained the state banks from issuing notes as freely as some of them would have liked, through its policy of collecting such notes and presenting them for payment in cash. These critics of the Bank desired more paper money (that is, bank notes circulating as money), not less. The other set of critics, the hard-money people, had the opposite complaint. Believing in coin as the only safe currency, these people condemned all banks of issue — all banks issuing bank notes — whether chartered by the states, as all but one of them were, or by the federal government, as the Bank alone was.

Jackson himself was a hard-money man. At one time in his life he had dealt in grandiose land and mercantile speculations based on paper credit. Then a financial panic (1797) ruined his business and put him deeply into debt.

The Second Bank of the United States
Architecturally, the home office of the Bank, in Philadelphia, was an excellent example of the Greek Revival style. In 1818 architects were invited to submit competitive plans for "a chaste imitation of Grecian architecture." William Strickland won the competition with a design modeled on that of the Parthenon of ancient Athens. Benjamin H. Latrobe, who had submitted a similar plan, charged that Strickland had stolen the Latrobe design. After the expiration of the Bank's charter, the building became the Philadelphia Custom House.
(The Granger Collection)

Thereafter he was suspicious of all banks. After he became President he raised the question, in his inaugural address and in other statements, whether the charter of the Bank of the United States should be renewed. Unless renewed, it would expire in 1836.

To preserve the institution, Biddle began to grant banking favors to influential men in the hope of winning them to his side. At first he sought to cultivate Jackson's friends, with some success in a few instances. Then he turned more and more to Jackson's opponents. He extended loans on easy terms to several prominent newspaper editors, to a number of important state politicians, and to more than fifty congressmen and senators. In particular, he relied upon Senators Clay and Webster, the latter of whom was connected with the Bank in various ways—as legal counsel, director of the Boston branch, frequent and heavy borrower, and Biddle's personal friend.

Clay, Webster, and other advisers persuaded Biddle to apply to Congress for a recharter bill in 1832, four years ahead of the expiration date. After investigating the Bank and its business, Congress passed the recharter bill. At once Jackson vetoed it, sending it back to Congress with a stirring message in which he denounced the Bank as unconstitutional, undemocratic, and un-American. The veto stood, for the Bank's friends in Congress failed to obtain the two-thirds majority necessary for overriding it. And so the Bank question emerged as the paramount issue of the coming election, just as Clay had fondly hoped it would.

In 1832 Clay ran as the unanimous choice of the National Republicans, who had held a nominating convention in Baltimore late in the previous year. Jackson, with Van Buren as his running mate, sought reelection as the candidate of the Democratic Republicans, or Democrats. Still another candidate was in the field, representing a third party for the first time in American history. He was William Wirt, a prominent Baltimore lawyer and man of letters, the nominee of the Anti-Masonic party. Though he preferred Clay to Jackson, Wirt drew more votes away from the former than from the latter, though he did not draw a great many from any source, carrying only the state of Vermont. The legislature of South Carolina gave that state's electoral vote in protest to a man who was not even a candidate, John Floyd, one of Calhoun's Virginia followers. Of the remaining electoral votes, Jackson received more than five times as many as Clay.

THE "MONSTER" DESTROYED

Jackson took his decisive reelection as a sign that the people endorsed his views on the Bank of the United States. As soon as the nullification crisis had been disposed of, he determined to strike a blow at this banking "monster," this dangerous money power, as he saw it. He could not put an end to the Bank before the expiration of its charter, but at least he could lessen its power by seeing to the removal of the government's deposits. By the law establishing the Bank, the secretary of the treasury had to give the actual order for removing them. When the incumbent secretary refused to give the order, Jackson appointed a new one, and when this man procrastinated, Jackson named a third, Roger B. Taney, previously the attorney general and a member of the Kitchen Cabinet. Taney was more than willing to cooperate.

With Taney at the head of the Treasury Department, the process of removing the government's deposits was immediately begun. The government stopped putting new funds in the Bank, but continued paying its bills by drawing on its existing deposits, which steadily dwindled. Meanwhile the government opened accounts with a number of state banks, depositing its incoming receipts with them. These banks, including one in Baltimore with which Taney himself was associated, were chosen presumably on the basis of their financial soundness but not always without consideration of their political leanings. Jackson's enemies called them his "pet banks." By 1836 there were 89 of them.

The proud and poetic Biddle, "Czar Nicholas" to Jacksonians, was not the man to give in without a fight. "This worthy President," he wrote sarcastically, "thinks that because he has scalped Indians and imprisoned Judges, he is to have his way with the Bank. He is mistaken." Biddle struck back when the Jackson administration began to transfer funds directly from the Bank of the United States to the pet banks. He felt that the loss of government deposits, amounting to several millions, made it necessary for him to call in loans and raise interest rates, since the government deposits had

"The Downfall of Mother Bank"
*This 1832 cartoon shows President Jackson destroying the Bank of the
United States and driving away its corrupt supporters by means of
his order withdrawing government deposits from the Bank. (Library of
Congress)*

served as the basis for much of the Bank's
credit. He realized that, by making borrowing
more difficult, he was bound to hurt business
and cause unemployment, but he consoled
himself with the belief that a short depression
would help to bring about a recharter of the
Bank. "Nothing but the evidence of suffering,"
he told the head of the Boston branch, would
"produce any effect in Congress."

During the winter of 1833–1834, with interest high and money scarce, there was suffering
indeed, as many businessmen failed and thousands of workers lost their jobs. All over the
country, friends of the Bank organized meetings to adopt petitions begging for relief from
Congress, petitions that delegates then brought
in person to Washington and that pro-Bank
senators or representatives introduced with
appropriately lugubrious speeches. But Jackson and the Jacksonians denied responsibility.

When distressed citizens appealed to the President he answered, "Go to Biddle."

The banker finally carried his contraction
of credit too far to suit his own friends among
the anti-Jackson businessmen of the Northeast,
and some of them did go to Biddle. A group of
New York and Boston merchants protested (as
one of them reported) that the business community "ought not and would not sustain him in
further pressure, which he very well knew was
not necessary for the safety of the bank, and in
which his whole object was to coerce a
charter." To appease the business community
he at last reversed himself and began to grant
credit in abundance and on reasonable terms.

The "Bank War" was over, and Jackson
had won it. But, with the passing of the Bank of
the United States (in 1836), the country lost an
indispensable financial institution. Economic
troubles lay ahead.

Whigs Against Democrats

During the Bank War the opponents of Jackson not only formally censured him in the Senate but also denounced him throughout the country for his allegedly high-handed and arbitrary actions. His opponents often referred to him as a tyrant, "King Andrew I," and they began to call themselves "Whigs," after the party which in England stood traditionally for limiting the power of the King. At the end of a single term for Jackson's hand-picked successor, who had the misfortune to preside over the worst business depression yet, the Whigs outdid the Democrats in demagoguery and turned them out of office.

PARTY PRINCIPLES

The Whig party, organized in time for the congressional elections of 1834 and the presidential election of 1836, was an aggregation of dissimilar groups. It included the National Republicans who had opposed Jackson in 1828 (some of these were old Federalists, others former Jeffersonian Republicans), and it also included many people who had supported Jackson in 1828 but had turned against him afterward because of his stand on internal improvements, nullification, or the Bank. Some of the Whigs, as in Virginia, were really state-rights Democrats who had broken with the President when he threatened to use force against a sister state, South Carolina. On the whole the new party was strongest among the merchants and manufacturers of the Northeast, the wealthier planters of the South, and the farmers most eager for internal improvements in the West. But the party as a rule did not appeal very strongly to the mass of voters. Throughout its existence of twenty years or so the party was able to win only two presidential elections (1840 and 1848), both of them with military heroes as its candidates.

In Jackson the Democrats had a military hero and popular leader whom no Whig could match. True, each of the two foremost Whigs, Clay and Webster, had a devoted following. The glamorous Clay, "Harry of the West," won friends throughout the country—but not enough friends ever to elect him President,

though he was a candidate three times. The eloquent Webster gained fame and respect for his speeches expounding the Constitution and upholding the Union, and some of his businessman admirers thought him a greater man than any President. But his close connection with the unpopular Bank of the United States and his dependence on rich men for his financial support disqualified him in the minds of many voters. He and Clay were bitter rivals, and their rivalry weakened the party, though at times they cooperated in politics. Sometimes associated with them and sometimes opposing them was Calhoun, the third member of what came to be known as the Great Triumvirate. Calhoun did not consider himself a Whig: after his break with Jackson he thought of himself as a no-party man. Nevertheless he joined with Webster and Clay on the Bank issue. One thing the three men and all Whigs had in common was their opposition to Jackson and most of what he stood for.

Jackson and his party, in the course of his two presidential terms, developed a fairly definite and coherent political philosophy. The Jacksonians believed in laissez faire. That is, they believed that the government should let economic activities pretty much alone. They proposed the elimination of governmental favors to private enterprise, the destruction of government-granted monopolies and other corporate privileges. Then in theory the people through free and fair competition would be able to take care of themselves, each prospering in accordance with his own labor and skill. The worst of poverty and of social inequality would thus be done away with when the government ceased to help the rich and hinder the poor. While the Democrats did not advocate social revolution, the more radical of them (known as "Loco Focos") maintained that revolutionary violence might unfortunately appear unless economic inequalities were removed.

Calhoun agreed with the Loco Focos that the dangers of class struggle were very real, and he explored the nature and prospects of the struggle more thoroughly than anyone else of his time. Long before Karl Marx and Friedrich Engels published their *Communist Mani-*

festo (1848) he elaborated a similar view, though he hoped to prevent revolution whereas they intended to hasten it. In his *South Carolina Exposition and Protest* (1828) and in later writings he predicted that capitalist society would tend to divide into only two classes, "capitalists" and "operatives," that the former would expropriate and impoverish the latter, and that a revolutionary crisis would eventuate. "There is and always has been in an advanced stage of wealth and civilization," he insisted (1837), "a conflict between labor and capital." He hoped that the revolutionary danger would cause Northern businessmen to join with Southern planters in self-defense.

Webster, the leading Whig philosopher, stoutly denied the contentions of Calhoun and the radical Democrats. "In the old countries of Europe there is a clear and well-defined line between capital and labor," Webster conceded, but he declared there was no line so "broad, marked, and visible" in the United States. If there was any revolutionary discontent among the American people, he charged, it was due to the policies of the Jackson administration and the clamor of Democratic agitators. He maintained that the people had common interests rather than conflicting ones, at least so long as the government pursued the correct policies. He believed that a wise and active federal government, by stimulating and regulating economic activity through a national banking system, a protective tariff, and expenditures for internal improvements, could assure the economic well-being of all the people and thereby harmonize the interests of every section and class.

Thus both parties thought of themselves as representing the best interests of the whole country, though they differed in their notions of the appropriate means of achieving the general welfare. For the time being the Democrats were in power and their policies prevailed.

Party feeling affected opinions on foreign as well as domestic affairs. The Whigs opposed Jackson on an issue of foreign policy when he became involved in a dispute with France. A number of American citizens held claims against the French government on account of ships seized or destroyed under Napoleon's decrees before the War of 1812. In 1831 the French government agreed to pay 25 million francs in partial satisfaction of these so-called

spoliation claims. The French Chamber of Deputies, however, failed to appropriate money for making the payment. Demanding that France make good its acknowledged debt, Jackson recommended to Congress the confiscation of French property in this country. The French took this as an insult to their national honor and insisted upon an apology. Though he refused to apologize, Jackson explained that he had meant no insult. As if expecting war he asked Congress (1835) for appropriations to build up the navy and the fortifications along the coast. The Whigs, denouncing him as a warmonger, voted against such appropriations. Despite political opposition at home, he won a diplomatic victory when the Chamber of Deputies at last provided funds and the debt was paid.

THREE AGAINST ONE   1836

At stake in the party contests of the time were not only issues of foreign and domestic policy but also questions of federal jobholding and other prerequisites of political power. The Democrats had the power and the jobs; the Whigs wanted them. As the presidential election of 1836 approached, the Democrats had the advantages of patronage, Jackson's prestige, and a superior party organization. Jackson, not desiring a third term for himself, was able to choose the President to succeed him. The Democratic convention readily nominated his favorite, Van Buren.

The Whigs in 1836 could boast no such unity and discipline. Indeed, they could not even agree upon a single candidate. Their strategy, masterminded by Biddle, was to run several candidates, each of them supposedly strong in part of the country. Webster was the man for New England, and Hugh Lawson White of Tennessee was to seek the votes of the South. The former Indian fighter and hero of the War of 1812 from Ohio, William Henry Harrison, was counted upon in the middle states and the West. As Biddle advised: "This disease is to be treated as a local disorder—apply local remedies—if General Harrison will run better than anybody else in Pennsylvania, by all means unite upon him." None of the three candidates could expect to get a majority in the electoral college, but separately they might draw enough votes from Van Buren to prevent his getting a majority. The election would then devolve, as in 1824–1825, upon the House of Representatives, where conceivably the Whigs might be able to elect one of their men.

The three Whigs proved to be no match for the one Democrat. When the returns were in, Van Buren had 170 electoral votes to 124 for all his opponents. Again the South Carolina legislature gave the state's 11 electoral votes to a man who was not a regular candidate – Willie P. Mangum, of North Carolina. One of the Whig leaders of New York, William H. Seward, explained the victory of Van Buren thus: "The people are for him. Not so much for him as for the principle they suppose he represents. That principle is Democracy."

THE PANIC OF 1837

At the time of the election of 1836 a nationwide boom was reaching its height. Canal enterprisers and railroad builders were busy digging ditches and laying tracks here, there, and everywhere. Prices were high and going higher, as people indulged in an orgy of spending and speculating. Money was plentiful. Much of it came from abroad, English investors buying large amounts of American corporation securities and state bonds. Most of it was manufactured by the banks, which multiplied their loans and notes with little regard to their reserves of cash, until, by 1837, bank loans outstanding amounted to five times as much as in 1830. Never had the nation seemed so prosperous.

Land as usual was a favorite speculation, especially the land sold by the federal government. After the act of 1821 had abolished installment buying and set the minimum price at $1.25 an acre, sales of public lands reached an average of 300,000 to 400,000 acres a year in the late 1820s and early 1830s. Then the business suddenly boomed. Between 1835 and 1837 nearly 40 million acres were disposed of, and the expression "doing a land-office business" came into use to describe fast selling of any kind. Nearly three-fourths of the land being sold went to speculators – men acquiring large tracts in the hope of reselling at a profit – and only about a fourth of it to actual settlers. Spec-

Election of 1836

ulators generally borrowed from the banks to make payment at the land offices.

For the time being the government profited. Receipts from land sales, which had averaged less than $2.4 million annually for the ten years preceding 1835, rose to more than $24 million in 1836. This was the government's largest source of revenue, but customs duties under the compromise tariff of 1833 added considerably to total income. The government received more money than it paid out. Steadily the national debt was reduced, as Jackson insisted it should be, and finally from 1835 to 1837 the government for the first and only time in its history was out of debt. Not only that: there was also a large and growing surplus in the federal treasury.

The question for Congress and the administration was how to get rid of the treasury surplus. Tampering with the tariff was not to be considered, since the recent compromise had put to rest that touchy subject and few wanted to reopen it.

Why not give the federal surplus to the states? This would be an effective way of getting rid of it, and the idea appealed to Congress. In 1836 Congress passed and Jackson signed a distribution act providing that the surplus accumulated by the end of the year (estimated at $40 million) be paid to the states in four quarterly installments as a loan without security or interest, each state getting a share proportional to its representation in Congress. No one seriously expected the "loan" to be repaid. As the states began to receive their shares, they promptly spent the money, mainly to encourage the construction of highways, railroads, and canals. The distribution of the surplus thus gave further stimulus to the speculative boom. At the same time the withdrawal of federal funds strained the "pet banks," for they had to call in a large part of their own loans in order to make the transfer of funds to the state governments.

Congress did nothing to check the speculative fever, with which many congressmen themselves were badly infected, Webster for one buying up thousands of acres in the West. But the President was much concerned. Though money continued to pour into the trea-

The Panic of 1837
The banner beneath the flag reads: "July 4th 1837. 61st Anniversary of Our Independence." Militiamen parade to observe the occasion, but the people, instead of watching, are preoccupied with their troubles. Mechanics stand idle with their tools. The only busy places are the shop of "Shylock Graspall, Licensed Pawnbroker," where the unemployed seek loans with which to buy liquor; the "Mechanics' Bank," where depositors try to get cash for their worthless bank notes; and the "Sheriff's Office," where property is being sold for unpaid taxes. From a contemporary lithograph. (Courtesy of the New-York Historical Society)

sury from the land offices, most of it was money of dubious value. The government was selling good land and was receiving in return a miscellaneous collection of state bank notes, none of them worth any more than the credit of the issuing bank. Jackson finally decided to act. He issued his Specie Circular (1836) announcing that in the future only hard money or the notes of specie-paying banks would be accepted in payment for public lands. This was but one sign of trouble ahead for prosperity-crazed Americans.

Van Buren had been President less than three months when the panic broke. The banks of New York, followed by those of the rest of the country, suddenly suspended specie payments (that is, they stopped paying cash on demand for their bank notes and other obligations). During the next few years hundreds of banks failed, and so did hundreds of other business firms. As unemployment grew, bread riots occurred in some of the larger cities. Prices fell, especially the price of land, which now became a burden to the recently optimistic speculators, Webster being only one of a great many who all at once found themselves "land-poor." Many railroad and canal schemes were abandoned; several of the debt-burdened state governments ceased to pay interest on their bonds and a few repudiated their debts, at least temporarily. The depression, the worst the American people ever had experienced, lasted for about five years.

The Whigs blamed Jackson for the depression. It had come, they said, because of his destruction of the national bank and his mismanagement of public finance. But they were also in part to blame. The distribution of the treasury surplus was a Whig measure, though Jackson signed it (with the onset of the panic, the distribution was halted before the entire surplus had been transferred to the states). This step, by weakening the pet banks, helped to bring on the crash. So did Jackson's Specie Circular, which started a general run on the banks as land buyers rushed to get cash in return for banknotes to make land-office payments. Distribution of the surplus and the Specie Circular only precipitated the depression, however; they did not cause it.

While the Bank of the United States, if continued, could have lessened the overexpansion of credit, a period of financial stringency doubtless would have come anyhow, sooner or later. For the depression was international, affecting England and Western Europe as well as the United States. As English investors faced a financial crisis at home, they began to withdraw funds from America, thus accounting for part of the strain on American banks. A succession of crop failures on American farms not only reduced the purchasing power of farmers but also necessitated imports of foodstuffs; to pay for these imports, additional money was drawn out of the country.

Besides its economic consequences, the Panic of 1837 had other significant results. Hard times increased social, sectional, and economic tensions. Want in the cities heightened the feeling that there existed even in America a real and dangerous class conflict—a struggle between the poor and the rich. Heavy losses suffered by Southern planters confirmed them in their conviction that national policies worked to their disadvantage, while the decline of business profits in the North intensified the belief of manufacturers that the compromise of 1833 must be undone and the tariff raised. Defaults on interest payments and outright repudiation of state bonds, many of them held by Englishmen, added to difficulties in the relations between the United States and Great Britain. Distress among the people was turned into dissatisfaction with the administration, so that the predominance of the Democrats was brought temporarily to an end after Van Buren had served but a single term.

THE VAN BUREN PROGRAM

The modern concept that government can successfully fight depressions, and has an obligation to do so, simply did not exist in President Van Buren's time. The only tradition of government intervention in economic matters was the Federalist-National Republican-Whig program of aid to business, to which Democrats were fiercely opposed. Consequently Van Buren recommended but few direct antidepression measures. He advised Congress to authorize the borrowing of $10 million to meet expenses during the emergency, and Congress did so. He also urged that the government should accept only specie for taxes and other due payments, a policy that would not raise either prices or confidence in the banking system.

In formulating a program of permanent legislation, the administration clearly reflected the wishes of the dominant farmer-labor segment of the party. The President urged Congress to reduce the price of public lands, and he recommended passage of a general preemption bill giving settlers the right to buy 160 acres at a set minimum price before land in any particular area was opened for public sale. A bill graduating land prices downward passed the Senate three times but was blocked in the House. A similar fate befell the preemption bill. His program of agrarian reform foiled by legislative opposition, Van Buren had to resort to executive action to please his urban followers. By presidential order he established a ten-hour work day on all federal works. For the first time in the nation's history the government thus took direct action to aid the rising labor class.

The most important measure in the President's program, and the most controversial, was his proposal for a new fiscal system. With the Bank of the United States destroyed and with Jackson's expedient of "pet banks" discredited, some kind of new system was urgently needed. Van Buren's fiscal ideas demonstrate both his mental ingenuity and his sincere devotion to Democratic principles. The plan he suggested, known as the "Independent Treasury" or "Subtreasury" system, was simplicity itself. Government funds would be placed in an independent treasury at Washington and in subtreasuries in specified cities throughout the country. Whenever the government had to pay out money, its own agents would handle the funds. No bank or banks would have the government's money or name to use as a basis for speculation. The government and the banks would be "divorced."

Van Buren placed the Independent Treasury proposal before Congress in a special session he called in 1837. It encountered the immediate and bitter opposition of most Whigs and of many conservative Democrats. Twice a bill to establish an independent treasury passed the Senate only to fail in the House. Not until 1840, the last year of Van Buren's presidency, did the administration succeed in driving the measure through both houses of Congress.

THE LOG CABIN CAMPAIGN

As the campaign year of 1840 approached, the Whigs scented victory. The effects of the depression still gripped the country, and the Democrats, the party in power, could be blamed for the depression. So reasoned the Whigs, who now realized that a party representing the upper-income groups must, if it expected to win, pose as a party of the people.

The Whigs also realized that they would have to achieve more unity and a stronger organization than they had demonstrated in 1836. They would have to settle on one candidate who could appeal to all segments of the party and to all sections of the country. Obviously the easiest way to coordinate the party was through the new mechanism of the national nominating convention, already used by the Democrats. Accordingly the Whigs held their first convention in Harrisburg, Pennsylvania, in December 1839. Their veteran leader, Henry Clay, "Mr. Whig," expected the nomination, but the party bosses decided otherwise. Clay had too definite a record; he had been defeated too many times; he had too many enemies. Passing him over, the convention nominated William Henry Harrison of Ohio, and for Vice President, John Tyler of Virginia.

William Henry Harrison was a descendant of the Virginia aristocracy, but he had spent all his adult life in the Northwest, where he first went as a young army officer in General Wayne's campaign against the Indians. Though he had little governmental experience, he was a renowned Indian fighter (like Jackson) and a popular national figure.

The Democrats, meeting in national convention at Baltimore, nominated Van Buren, pointed proudly to their record, especially the Independent Treasury, and condemned all the works of Whigs, especially the Bank of the United States. Demonstrating that their party was, in some respects, no more united than the Whigs, the Democrats failed to nominate a vice-presidential candidate, declaring vaguely that they would leave the choice of that office to the wisdom of the voters.

Whig Broadside of 1840

This Whig campaign document depicts the principal episodes in the career of General Harrison — from his humble log cabin beginnings to fame as soldier and statesman. (Library of Congress)

The campaign of 1840 set a new pattern in American politics. It inaugurated the circus-carnival atmosphere that would mark presidential elections for years in the future and that would awe or amuse European beholders—vast meetings, shouting parades, party badges and other insignia, and campaign songs.

Throughout the campaign the eager Whigs were on the offensive. They depicted themselves as the party of the people and the party that could save the nation from depression. They said Van Buren was an aristocrat who used cologne, drank champagne, and engaged in other undemocratic and un-American practices. A Democratic newspaper unwisely sneered that Harrison was a simple soul who would be glad to retire to a log cabin if provided with a pension and plenty of hard cider. In a country where many people lived or had lived in log cabins, this was almost handing the election to the Whigs, and they took the cue. Yes, their candidate was a simple man of the people, they proclaimed, and he loved log cabins and cider (actually he was a man of substance and lived in a large and well-appointed house).

Thereafter the log cabin was an established symbol at every Whig meeting, and hard cider an established beverage. Hundreds of Whig orators bragged that they had been born in log cabins or apologized for having been brought into the world in more sumptuous edifices. Thousands of Whig auditors listened to these effusions and happily chanted the songs that turned every Whig gathering into a frenzy of enthusiasm: "Tippecanoe and Tyler too" and "Van, Van is a used-up man." Against such techniques and the lingering effects of the depression the Democrats could not avail. When the votes were counted in November, Harrison had 234 electoral votes to 60 for Van Buren. The Whig victory was not as sweeping as it seemed; of the popular vote, Harrison had 1,275,000 to Van Buren's 1,129,000, a majority of less than 150,000.

THE TANEY COURT

Though the Democrats had lost control of the executive branch, they kept their hold on the Supreme Court. Jackson had been able to appoint seven new justices; and so, of the nine members, seven were Democrats. And the Chief Justice after 1835, Roger B. Taney, was a Jacksonian of the Jacksonians.

Between the Marshall-dominated Court and the Taney-dominated Court there was no sharp break in constitutional interpretation. But there was a marked change in emphasis. Taney and the majority of his colleagues were moderate agrarian liberals. In general they tended to recognize the right of popular majorities, acting through state legislatures, to regulate private property rights and the activities of corporations. In general, without adhering at all to the doctrines of Calhoun, they were inclined to modify the nationalism of the Marshall Court.

The attitude of the Court was revealed in the case of *Charles River Bridge* v. *Warren Bridge* (1837). In briefest essence, the background of this case was as follows: one company had a charter from Massachusetts to operate a toll bridge for a specified period of years; the legislature authorized another corporation to erect a bridge that would be toll-free; the first company contended that the state's action was invalid because it was a breach of contract. It was the old question—Could a state alter an agreement with a corporation?—which in the Dartmouth College case Marshall had decided against the state. But now Taney, speaking for the Democratic majority, supported Massachusetts. Though he advanced legal precedents to justify the decision, Taney based his position broadly on Jacksonian social doctrine. The object of government, he said, was to promote happiness, and this purpose was superior to property rights: a state had power to regulate corporations if such action was necessary to achieve the well-being of the community. Although the decision opened the way to increased state control and was wildly denounced by conservatives, it really aided the development of business. Industry was not going to grow if older corporations could maintain monopolies and choke off the competition of newer companies.

Another Taney case that enlarged state powers was *Bank of Augusta* v. *Earle* (1839). The question here was whether a corporation chartered in one state could do business in another that wished to exclude it. The Court held that under interstate comity a corporation had a general right to operate in other states, but that a state could, if it wished, exclude a foreign corporation or establish regulations for its entrance. This decision led many states to enact regulatory laws for outside corporations. In the absence of any federal regulation of interstate commerce, these measures were the only restrictions on companies engaged in business on a regional or on a national scale.

Selected Readings

Democratic Trends

Alexis de Tocqueville, *Democracy in America** (2 vols., 1945); M. Ostrogorski, *Democracy and the Organization of Political Parties** (2 vols., 1902); Chilton Williamson, *American Suffrage from Property to Democracy, 1760–1860* (1960); C. R. Fish, *The Civil Service and the Patronage* (1905); Louis Hartz, *The Liberal Tradition in America** (1955).

Jacksonian Democracy

G. G. Van Deusen, *The Jacksonian Era, 1828–1848** (1959); A. M. Schlesinger, Jr., *The Age of Jackson** (1945); R. P. McCormick, *The Second American Party System: Party Formation in the Jacksonian Era* (1966); C. G. Bowers, *The Party Battles of the Jackson Period* (1922); L. D. White, *The Jacksonians: A Study in Administrative History, 1829–1861* (1954); R. V. Remini, *Andrew Jackson* (1966); H. C. Syrett, *Andrew Jackson: His Contribution to the American Tradition* (1953); J. W. Ward, *Andrew Jackson: Symbol for an Age** (1955); Edward Pessen, *Jacksonian America* (1970).

Leading Jacksonians

W. N. Chambers, *Old Bullion Benton, Senator from the New West* (1956); E. B. Smith, *Magnificent Missourian: The Life of Thomas Hart Benton* (1958); I. D. Spencer, *The Victor and the Spoils: A Life of William L. Marcy* (1959); C. G. Sellers, Jr., *James K. Polk, Jacksonian, 1795–1843* (1957); C. B. Swisher, *Roger B. Taney* (1936); R. V. Remini, *Martin Van Buren and the Making of the Democratic Party* (1959); J. A. Garraty, *Silas Wright* (1949).

Indian Policy

F. P. Prucha, *American Indian Policy in the Formative Years* (1962); Grant Foreman, *Indian Removal: The Emigration of the Five Civilized Tribes* (1923); A. H. Abel, *A History of Events Resulting in Indian Consolidation West of the Mississippi* (1908); U. B. Phillips, *Georgia and State Rights* (1902); Donald Jackson, ed., *Black Hawk: An Autobiography* (1955); B. W. Sheehan, *Seeds of Extinction: Jeffersonian Philanthropy and the American Indian* (1973); A. H. De Rosier, Jr., *The Removal of the Choctaw Indians* (1971); Angie Debo, *And Still the Waters Run: The Betrayal of the Five Civilized Tribes* (1973); J. K. Mahon, *History of the Second Seminole War, 1835–1842* (1967); John Tebbel, *The Compact History of the Indian Wars* (1966); Cecil Eby, *"That Disgraceful Affair," the Black Hawk War* (1973).

Nullification

C. S. Sydnor, *The Development of Southern Sectionalism* (1948); W. W. Freehling, *Prelude to Civil War: The Nullification Controversy in South Carolina, 1816–1836* (1966); Frederick Bancroft, *Calhoun and the South Carolina Nullification Movement* (1928); C. M. Wiltse, *John C. Calhoun, Nullifier, 1829–1839* (1949); M. L. Coit, *John C. Calhoun: American Portrait** (1950); G. M. Capers, *John C. Calhoun—Opportunist: A Reappraisal** (1960); R. N. Current, *John C. Calhoun** (1963).

The Bank and the Panic

Bray Hammond, *Banks and Politics in America from the Revolution to the Civil War* (1957); W. B. Smith, *Economic Aspects of the Second Bank of the United States* (1953); T. P. Govan, *Nicholas Biddle, Nationalist and Public Banker, 1786–1844* (1959); R. C. McGrane, *The Panic of 1837** (1924); W. B. Smith and A. H. Cole, *Fluctuations in American Business, 1790–1860* (1935).

The Whigs

E. M. Carroll, *Origins of the Whig Party* (1925); A. C. Cole, *The Whig Party in the South* (1913); C. M. Fuess, *Daniel Webster* (2 vols., 1930); R. N. Current, *Daniel Webster and the Rise of National Conservatism** (1955); S. Nathans, *Daniel Webster and Jacksonian Democracy* (1972); G. R. Poage, *Henry Clay and the Whig Party* (1936); G. G. Van Deusen, *The Life of Henry Clay** (1937); R. G. Gunderson, *The Log Cabin Campaign* (1957).

State Studies

T. P. Abernethy, *From Frontier to Plantation in Tennessee* (1932); D. R. Fox, *The Decline of Aristocracy in the Politics of New York** (1919); Walter Hugins, *Jacksonian Democracy and the Working Class: A Study of the New York Workingmen's Movement, 1829–1837* (1960); Lee Benson, *The Concept of Jacksonian Democracy: New York as a Test Case** (1961); D. T. Miller, *Jacksonian Aristocracy: Class and Democracy in New York, 1830–1860* (1967); R. P. McCormick, *The History of Voting in New Jersey* (1953); A. B. Darling, *Political Changes in Massachusetts, 1824–1848* (1925).

*Titles available in paperback.

Eleven

Sectionalism – the rivalry of one part of the country against another – had its origins early in American history. Even in colonial times there were three great areas (New England, the middle colonies, and the South) that developed characteristics different enough to set them apart as distinct sections. As the country grew after independence, the composition of the sections changed, and sectional feelings were intensified. By the 1840s and 1850s three sections that could be distinguished were the Northeast, the Northwest, and the South. These were gradually reduced to two – the North and the South – and the antagonism between them increasingly threatened to disrupt the nation.

If the sectional division had been a mere matter of geography, the dividing line might have run in a different direction. The Appalachian range, a great natural barrier, separated the East from the West, and beyond it the Mississippi Valley formed a vast geographic unit. In the minds of statesmen of the early republic, these geographical facts seemed to indicate that a new trans-Appalachian nation might someday arise and declare its independence.

With the elimination of slavery in New England and the middle states, however, all these states came to constitute a single, more or less homogeneous area, the Northeast. The new states of the Northwest, where the Northwest Ordinance prohibited slavery, developed a somewhat similar free-labor economy, and these states were connected with the Northeast through the construction of canals and railroads. Those of the original states where slavery persisted comprised an increasingly distinctive South, and this section, with the westward spread of slavery, included the newer states of the Southwest. Thus the slave boundary cut across both the Appalachian Mountains and the Mississippi Valley. So terribly potent was the slavery issue that it distorted the natural lines of separation and cohesion.

Hoe's Printing Press
The rotary press, which Robert Hoe and his son Richard patented in 1846, carried the type on a steam-powered revolving cylinder. Printing much more rapidly than the previous flat-bed press, the new "lightning press" revolutionized journalism by making possible the mass circulation of newspapers. (Collection of Business Americana, NMHT, Smithsonian Institution)

There nevertheless remained strong forces tending to hold the North and the South together. Groups within each section had conflicting interests, which weakened sectional loyalties, and groups in both sections had common interests, which led to intersectional cooperation. Improvements in transportation and communication provided a better and better technological basis for national unity. And cultural nationalism persisted. Many people, especially in the North, while priding themselves on the intellectual attainments of the United States, continued to call for a civilization no longer imitative of Europe but distinctively American.

The Northern Economy

Even without the moral question of slavery, the political and economic issues involved in the sectional controversy would have strained the national fabric. Many of the political questions of the 1840s and 1850s were economic in origin, and the economy of each section had much to do with determining its social and cultural as well as political views. In each section a particular economic activity predominated, and hence a particular class tended to control the wealth and lead the other classes in politics. In the Northeast, where industry and overseas commerce predominated, the manufacturers and bankers were the leaders. In the Northwest, where most of the people were small farmers, they themselves were uppermost in both economic and political life. In the South, by contrast, though small farmers were the most numerous group, they yielded to the large planters, who exercised a controlling influence.

THE NORTHEAST: BUSINESS

Between 1840 and 1860 American industry experienced a steady and, in some fields, a spectacular growth. In 1840 the total value of manufactured goods produced in the United States stood at $483 million; ten years later the figure had climbed to over $1 billion; and in 1860 it reached close to $2 billion. For the first time the value of manufactured goods was approximately equal to that of agricultural products. In the cotton textile industry the number of spindles in operation doubled during this twenty-year period.

Industrial growth was greatest in the states of the Northeast. Most conspicuous in this part of the country were the change from domestic or household manufactures to the factory system, the shift of economic power from merchant capitalism to industrial capitalism, the spread of the corporate organization in business, and other innovations that heralded the coming of modern America. A few figures will illustrate the industrial predominance of the Northeast. Of the approximately 140,000 manufacturing establishments in the country in 1860, 74,000 were located in this section; they represented well over half the total national investment in manufactures, and the annual value of their products was two-thirds of the national figure. Of the 1,311,000 workers in the entire country, about 938,000 were employed in the mills and factories of New England and the middle states.

Even the most highly developed industries still showed qualities of immaturity and were still far away from the production goals they would attain after 1865. The cotton manufacturers, for example, concentrated on producing goods of coarse grade, making little attempt to turn out fine items, which continued to be imported from England. A similar situation existed in the woolens industry, which because of a short American supply of raw wool could not even meet the domestic demand for coarse goods. As yet, American industry, which exported very little, was unable to satisfy fully the wants of American consumers.

Technology and industrial ingenuity were, however, preparing the way for future American industrial supremacy. The machine tools used in the factories of the Northeast, such as the turret lathe, the grinding machine, and the universal milling machine, were better than those in European factories. The principle of interchangeable parts, applied earlier in gun factories by Eli Whitney and Simeon North, was being introduced into other lines of manufacturing. Coal was replacing wood as an industrial fuel, particularly in the smelting of iron. Coal was also being used in increasing amounts to generate power in the steam engines that were replacing the water power that had driven most of the factory machinery in the Northeast. The production of coal, most of it mined in the Pittsburgh area of western Pennsylvania, leaped from 50,000 tons in 1820 to 14 million tons in 1860.

The great technical advances in American industry owed much to American inventors. The patent records reveal the growth of Yankee ingenuity. In 1830 the number of inventions patented was 544; in 1850 the figure rose to 993; and in 1860 it stood at 4,778. In 1839 Charles Goodyear, a New England hardware merchant, discovered a method of vulcanizing rubber; his process had been put to 500 uses by 1860, and the rubber industry was firmly established. In 1846 Elias Howe of Massachusetts constructed a sewing machine, upon which improvements were soon made by Isaac Singer. The Howe-Singer machine was soon employed in manufacturing ready-to-wear clothing. A little later, during the Civil War, it would supply the Northern troops with uniforms.

In an earlier period the dominant economic figure in the Northeast had been the merchant capitalist – the man who engaged in foreign or domestic trade, who invested his surplus capital in banks, and who sometimes financed small-scale domestic manufacturers. By 1840 merchant capitalism was in a state of decline, though the merchant by no means disappeared. In cities like New York, Philadelphia, and Boston, there were important and influential mercantile groups that operated shipping lines to Southern ports – carrying away cotton, rice, and sugar – or dispatched fleets of trading vessels to the ports of Europe and the Orient. Many of these vessels were the famous clippers, the most beautiful and the fastest-sailing ships afloat. In their heyday in the late forties and early fifties, the clippers were capable of averaging 300 miles a day, which compared favorably with the best time then being made by steamships. Though the value of American exports, almost entirely agricultural in nature, increased from $124 million in 1840 to $334 million in 1860, American merchants in the 1850s saw much of their carrying trade fall into the hands of British competitors, who enjoyed the advantages of steam-driven iron ships and government subsidies.

It was not foreign rivalry, however, that caused the decline of the merchant capitalist, but rather the rise of the factory system in the

---

John Murray Forbes

The migration of New England capital from overseas trade to manufacturing is mirrored in the career of John Murray Forbes (1813–1898). This cultured and charming merchant made a fortune in the China trade while still a young man. Returning to the United States, he continued his mercantile activities, but began to shift his interest and eventually his investments into textiles and other industries. In 1846 he turned his attention to railroads in the Mississippi Valley. He was the leading figure in the group of Eastern merchants who purchased and completed the Michigan Central Railroad from Detroit to Chicago. Forbes was also allied with New York capitalists who controlled the Illinois Central, the north-south route in Illinois that by 1858 linked Chicago and Cairo. At the same time Forbes and his associates took over and combined several lines into the Chicago, Burlington and Quincy Railroad, the first line to enter Iowa from the east. Still another road that came under his guiding hand was the Hannibal and St. Joseph. In the Civil War and postwar period Forbes devoted his major energies to public service, but railroads continued to be his dominating economic interest. The railroad king had permanently replaced the merchant prince.

United States. The merchants saw greater opportunities for profit in manufactures than in trade. They shifted their capital from mercantile investments to industry, becoming owners and operators of factories or placing their money in companies operated by others. Indeed, one reason why industries developed soonest in the East was that the merchant class had the money and the will to finance them.

Many business concerns were owned by one man, by a family, or by partners. But, particularly in the textile industry, the corporation form of organization spread rapidly. In their overseas ventures the merchants had been accustomed to diversifying their risks by buying shares in a number of vessels and voyages. They employed the same device when they moved their capital from trade to manufacturing, purchasing shares in several textile companies.

Regardless of the forms of business organization, the industrial capitalists became the ruling class, the aristocrats of the Northeast. As they had sought and secured economic dominance, they reached for and grasped political influence. In politics, local or national, they liked to be represented by highly literate lawyers who could articulate their prejudices and philosophy. Their ideal of a representative was Daniel Webster of Massachusetts, whom the businessmen of the section, at considerable financial cost to themselves, supported for years in the United States Senate.

THE NORTHEAST: FARMS AND LABOR

The story of agriculture in the Northeast after 1840 is largely one of economic deterioration. The reason for the worsening situation is simple: the farmers of this section could not produce goods in competition with the new and richer soil of the Northwest. Eastern farmers turned to a system of production that aimed at a rude self-sufficiency or to the cultivation of products that would not suffer from Western competition. Many went West and took up new farms or moved to mill towns and became laborers. As a result, the rural population in many parts of the Northeast continued to decline.

The centers of production shifted westward for wheat, corn, grapes, cattle, sheep, and hogs. In 1840 the leading wheat-growing states were New York, Pennsylvania, Ohio, and Virginia; in 1860 they were Illinois, Indiana, Wisconsin, Ohio, and Michigan. In the case of corn, Illinois, Ohio, and Missouri supplanted New York, Pennsylvania, and Virginia. In 1840 the most important cattle-raising areas in the country were in New York, Pennsylvania, and New England, but by the 1850s the leading cattle states were Illinois, Indiana, Ohio, and Iowa, in the West, and Texas in the South.

In some lines of agriculture the Northeast held its own or even surpassed the Northwest. As the Eastern urban centers increased in population, many farmers turned profitably to the task of supplying foods to the city masses, engaging in truck gardening (vegetables) or fruit raising. New York led all other states in apple production. Also stimulated by the rise of cities was dairy farming. The profits to be derived from supplying milk, butter, and cheese to local markets attracted many farmers in central New York, southeastern Pennsylvania, and various parts of New England. Approximately half of the dairy products of the country were produced in the East; the other half came from the West, with Ohio being the dairy center of that section. Partly because of the expansion of the dairy industry, the Northeast led other sections in the production of hay. New York was the leading hay state in the nation, and large crops were grown in Pennsylvania and New England. The Northeast also exceeded other areas in producing potatoes.

Most of the workers in Northeastern factories during the decade of the forties came from the native population of the section—from the farming classes that were being pinched off the land by Western competition. Almost half of the laborers were women and children, and in some industries, notably textiles, the percentage was much higher. The rural people who flocked to the mill towns in the hope of finding a better life soon discovered that their situation there was little if any better than it had been back on the farms. Most mill towns were cheerless, ugly places in which to live, and most factories were unsanitary, unhealthful buildings in which to work. The average workday was twelve to fourteen hours. The wages of skilled workers ranged from $4 to $10 a week; unskilled workers and women and children received $1 to $6 per week.

Workers attempted, with little success, to

persuade state legislatures to pass laws setting a maximum workday. New Hampshire, in 1847, enacted a statute providing that no person be required to work more than ten hours in one day unless he agreed to an "express contract" calling for greater time; in the following year Pennsylvania adopted a similar law for the textile and paper industries. These measures were largely inoperative because many employers forced prospective employees to sign agreements for longer hours. Three states— Massachusetts, New Hampshire, and Pennsylvania—passed laws regulating child labor, but the statutes merely forbade the employment of minors for more then ten hours in a day without the consent of their parents. Probably the greatest legal victory achieved by labor was in a judicial case in Massachusetts. The supreme court of that state, in *Commonwealth* v. *Hunt* (1842), declared that unions were lawful organizations and that the strike was a lawful weapon. Other state courts gradually accepted the principles of the Massachusetts decision.

During the 1840s the factory labor supply of the Northeast was augmented by immigrants from Europe. The immigrant flood helped to delay the development of the labor organizations that had experienced a vigorous growth in the thirties but had been hard hit by the depression after 1837. Generally the newcomers were willing to work for less than the wages demanded by native workers. Labor never recovered, before 1860, the ground it had lost in the lean depression years. By the 1850s several national craft unions had been formed by such groups as machinists, hat workers, printers, molders, stone cutters, and a few others. But these were organizations of skilled workers, representing only a tiny minority of labor and manifesting almost no class awareness. The mass of laborers remained unorganized.

THE NORTHWEST

There was some industry in the Northwest, more than in the South, and in the two decades before the Civil War the section experienced a steady industrial growth. By 1860 it had 36,785 manufacturing establishments employing 209,909 workers. Along the southern shore of Lake Erie was a flourishing industrial and commercial area of which Cleveland was

the center. Another manufacturing locality was in the Ohio River Valley, with the meat-packing city of Cincinnati as its nucleus. Farther west, the rising city of Chicago, destined to be the great metropolis of the section, was emerging as the national center of the agricultural machinery and meat-packing industries. The most important industrial products of the West were farm machines, flour, meats, distilled whiskey, and leather and wooden goods.

But the West predominantly was a land of family farms and small farmers. The average size of Western farms was 200 acres, and the great majority of the farmers owned their own land.

In concentrating on corn, wheat, cattle, sheep, and hogs, the Western farmer was motivated by sound economic reasons. As the Northeast became more industrial and urban, it enlarged the domestic market for farm goods. At the same time England and certain European nations, undergoing the same process, started to import larger amounts of food from the outside. This steadily increasing world-wide demand for farm products resulted in steadily rising farm prices. For the farmers, the forties and early fifties were years of prosperity.

The expansion of agricultural markets had profound effects on sectional alignments in the United States. Of the Northwest's total output, by far the greatest part was disposed of in the Northeast; only the surplus remaining after domestic needs were satisfied was exported abroad. The new well-being of Western farmers, then, was in part sustained by Eastern purchasing power. Eastern industry, in turn, found an augmenting market for its products in the prospering West. Between the two sections there was being forged a fundamental economic relationship that was profitable to both.

To meet the increasing demands for its products, the Northwest had to enlarge its productive capacities. The presence of large blocks of still unoccupied land made it possible to enlarge the area under cultivation during the 1840s. By 1850 the growing Western population had settled the prairie regions east of the Mississippi and was pushing beyond the river. Stimulated to greater production by rising prices and conscious of the richness of his soil, the average Western farmer engaged in wasteful, exploitative methods of farming that often resulted in rapid soil exhaustion.

St. Louis in the 1850s

As the West grew in population and expanded its economy, its cities became larger. They began to assume the form and to exercise the functions of metropolitan centers in the East. This print shows one of the principal Western cities, St. Louis, as it appeared in the 1850s. Of the three major cities of the West, St. Louis and Cincinnati were older than Chicago and for years were more populous. But by 1860 the Lake Michigan city, experiencing a spectacular growth, was hard on their heels, and after the Civil War it would emerge as the metropolis of the section. (Courtesy Chicago Historical Society)

Some improvements in farming methods did, however, find their way into use. New varieties of seed, notably Mediterranean wheat, which was hardier than the native type, were introduced in some areas; better breeds of animals, such as hogs and sheep from England and Spain, were imported to take the place of native stock. In nearly every case these and similar innovations were first tried out on Eastern farms, and later won whole or partial acceptance in the West.

Of greater importance were the improvements that Americans continued to introduce in farm machines and tools. During the forties more efficient grain drills, harrows, mowers, and hay rakes were placed in wide use. The cast-iron plow, devised earlier, continued to be popular because its parts could be replaced

when broken. An even better implement appeared in 1847 when John Deere established at Moline, Illinois, a factory to manufacture plows with steel moldboards, which were more durable than those made of iron and were also self-scouring.

Two new machines heralded a coming revolution in grain production. The most important was the automatic reaper, invented by Cyrus H. McCormick of Virginia. The reaper, taking the place of sickle, cradle, and hand labor, enabled a crew of six or seven men to harvest in a day as much wheat (or any other small grain) as fifteen men could harvest using the older methods. McCormick, who had patented his device in 1834, established in 1847 a factory at Chicago in the heart of the grain belt. By 1850 he was turning out 3,000 reapers a year; by

1860, over 100,000 were in use on Western farms. Almost as helpful an aid to the grain grower was the thresher, which appeared in large numbers after 1840. Before that time, grain was flailed out by hand (seven bushels a day was a good average) or trodden out by farm animals (twenty bushels a day on the average). The threshing machines could thresh twenty-five bushels or more in an hour. Most of the threshers were manufactured at the Jerome I. Case factory in Racine, Wisconsin.

The Northwest was the most democratic of the three sections in the sense that the farmers, the majority, were the dominant economic class and generally had their way in politics. Theirs was a capitalistic, property-conscious, middle-class kind of democracy. Abraham Lincoln, an Illinois Whig, voiced the economic opinions of many of the people of his section. "I take it that it is best for all to leave each man free to acquire property as fast as he can," said Lincoln. "Some will get wealthy. I don't believe in a law to prevent a man from getting rich; it would do more harm than good. . . . When one starts poor, as most do in the race of life, free society is such that he knows he can better his condition; he knows that there is no fixed condition of labor for his whole life."

Cyrus McCormick's Reaper
In 1831 McCormick demonstrated the first successful mechanical reaper near the town of Steele's Tavern, Virginia. Two men were required to operate the machine, one to ride the horse and the other to rake the grain stalks off the platform. Other workers followed to bind the grain. (Library of Congress)

The democratic conservatism of the West was apparent in the program it advocated in national politics: internal improvements, cheap or preferably free lands, and territorial expansion.

UNIFYING AND DIVISIVE FORCES

Between 1850 and 1860 the population of the United States rose by more than a third, from 23 million to over 31 million, as the nation continued its phenomenal human as well as material growth. Much of this increase was due to immigration. On the one hand, the immigrants stimulated a sense of nationalism, both because of their attachment to their new homeland as a whole (they had no inherited loyalty to any of the particular states) and because of the anti-foreigner and self-consciously "American" feeling that some of them aroused on the part of many of the native Americans. On the other hand, the new arrivals contributed to social differentiation between North and South, since they did not distribute themselves evenly throughout the country but settled in much the larger numbers in the North.

A more positive unifying force was to be found, at least potentially, in the development of railroads and the introduction of the telegraph. "The fifties," writes the historian A. C. Cole, "saw the emerging outlines of a genuinely national system of transportation and communication."

RISING IMMIGRATION

Between 1830 and 1840 only about 500,000 immigrants had entered the country, with the highest yearly figure, 84,000, being reached in 1840. Then the floodgates opened. From 1840 to 1850 over 1.5 million Europeans moved to

Population Density   1860

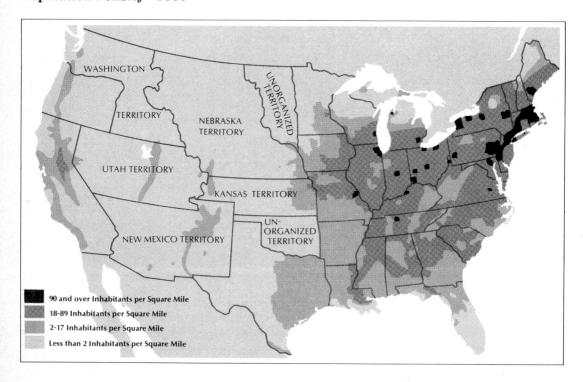

Urban Growth [1840–1860]

In 1840 the largest cities in the country were in the Northeast and the South. But in the next two decades, as the East became increasingly industrialized, cities there shot ahead of their Southern rivals. The following figures show the comparative rates of growth:

	1840	1850	1860
New York	312,000	515,000	805,000*
Philadelphia	220,000	340,000	565,000
Boston	93,000	136,000	177,000
Baltimore	102,000	169,000	212,000
New Orleans	100,000	116,000	165,000

*Or 1,200,000 including Brooklyn.

The most spectacular population gains were scored by the new Western cities. From 40,000 in the 1830s, Cincinnati climbed to 161,000 in 1860. In the same period St. Louis went from 10,000 to 160,000, and Chicago, astonishing everybody but itself, from 250 to 109,000.

America; in the last years of the decade the average number arriving yearly was almost 300,000. Of the 23 million people in the United States in 1850, 2,210,000 were foreign-born; of these almost 1 million were Irish and over 500,000 were German. Special reasons accounted for the prevalence of immigrants from Ireland and Germany: widespread poverty caused by the economic dislocations of the Industrial Revolution; famines resulting from the failure of the potato and other crops; dislike of English rule by the Irish; and the collapse of the liberal revolutions of 1848 in Germany. The great majority of the Irish settled in the Eastern cities where they swelled the ranks of unskilled labor. Not until after 1850, however, when the tide of immigration reached even greater heights, did foreigners outnumber the native-born in the labor population. Most of the Germans, having a little more money than the Irish, who had practically none, moved on to the Northwest, where they became farmers or went into business in the Western towns.

The number of immigrants who came in the fifties exceeded even that of the previous decade, reaching an estimated aggregate of over 2.5 million. As before, the overwhelming majority of the newcomers hailed from Ireland and Germany. By 1860 more than 1.5 million Irishmen had migrated to the United States, and approximately 1 million Germans. Other nationalities represented in the immigrant tide were Englishmen, Frenchmen, Italians, Scandinavians, Poles, and Hollanders. Most of the foreigners collected in the urban centers of the Northern states. Almost half of the population of New York City consisted of aliens, and in St. Louis, Chicago, and Milwaukee the foreign-born outnumbered those of native birth. Few immigrants settled in the South. Only 500,000 lived in the slave states in 1860, and a third of these were concentrated in Missouri; of the Southern cities, only New Orleans contained a large number of foreign-born residents. Immigrants avoided the South partly because of the climate, partly because most of them were opposed to slavery or feared the competition of slave labor, but mostly because the bulk of them landed at Northern ports and from these points gravitated easily to areas in the North that attracted them.

In some cities and states the foreign vote assumed pivotal importance. Existing laws in many states permitted aliens to vote if they had been in the country for a year and had declared intention to seek citizenship. Particularly in the large cities, the politicians courted the immigrant voters with material favors, including outright money payments, and in some places it became common to buy votes in blocks. In general, the immigrants tended to affiliate with the Democrats, whose party they regarded as the representative of the common man.

THE NATIVIST MOVEMENT

The presence of huge numbers of aliens occasioned the first important organized nativist movement in American history. While some natives recognized the contribution that the newcomers were making to the cultural and material development of their adopted land, many others disliked their ways and feared their influence. These critics contended that many of the immigrants were mentally and physically defective, that they created slums, and that they corrupted politics by selling their votes. Laborers complained that the aliens, willing to work for low wages, were stealing their jobs. Protestants, impressed by the aptitude that the Catholic Irish demonstrated for politics, believed, or affected to believe, that the Church of Rome was attaining an undue power in American government. Many Americans of older stock were honestly concerned that the immigrants would not assimilate into national life or would inject new and radical philosophies into national thought.

Out of these tensions and prejudices emerged a number of secret societies to combat the "alien menace." Originating in the East and later spreading to the West and South, these groups combined in 1850 to form the Supreme Order of the Star-Spangled Banner. Included in the official program of the order were opposition to Catholics or aliens holding public office and support of stricter naturalization laws and literacy tests for voting. When members were asked to define their platform, they replied, because of the secrecy rule, "I know nothing," and hence were dubbed "Know-Nothings."

Soon the leaders, deciding to seek their objectives by political methods, formed the so-called American party. In the East the new organization scored an immediate and astonishing success in the elections of 1854, casting a large vote in Pennsylvania and New York and winning control of the state government in Massachusetts. Elsewhere the progress of the Know-Nothings was more modest and tempered by local conditions. Western members of the party, because of the presence of many German voters in the area, found it expedient to proclaim that they were not opposed to naturalized Protestants. In the South, where Catholics were few, the leaders disavowed any religious bias, and Catholics participated in the movement. The party's spectacular growth would soon be interrupted by the rise of the larger issue of slavery.

DEVELOPMENT OF RAILROADS

The swelling domestic trade between East and West could not have developed without an adequate transportation system. In the 1830s most of the goods exchanged between the two sections were carried on the Erie Canal. After 1840 railroads gradually supplanted canals and all other modes of transport. In 1840 the total railroad trackage of the country was only 2,818 miles. There was a speed-up of construction in the forties, and by the end of the decade the trackage figure had risen to 9,021 miles. Most of the new lines ran east and west and several of them crossed New York State. The railroads enabled the Western farmers to ship their products cheaply and quickly to Eastern markets and thus helped to force many Eastern farmers out of business.

An outburst of railroad construction without previous parallel occurred in the fifties. The amount of trackage tripled between 1850 and 1860. The Northeast had the most efficient system, with twice as much trackage per square mile of land as the West and four times as much as the South. Railroads were reaching even west of the Mississippi, which at several points was spanned by iron bridges. One line ran from Hannibal to St. Joseph on the Missouri River, and another was being built from St. Louis to Kansas City. As for the South, many of its lines were short ones, and there were few through lines. Nevertheless, such towns as Charleston, Atlanta, Savannah, and Norfolk had direct connections with Memphis, and thus with the Northwest; and Richmond was connected, via the Virginia Central, with the Memphis and Charleston railroad. In addition, several independent lines furnished a continuous connection between the Ohio River and New Orleans.

A new feature in railroad development—and one that would profoundly affect the nature of sectional alignments—was the trend toward the consolidation of short lines into trunk lines. By 1853 four roads had surmounted the Appalachian barrier to connect the North-

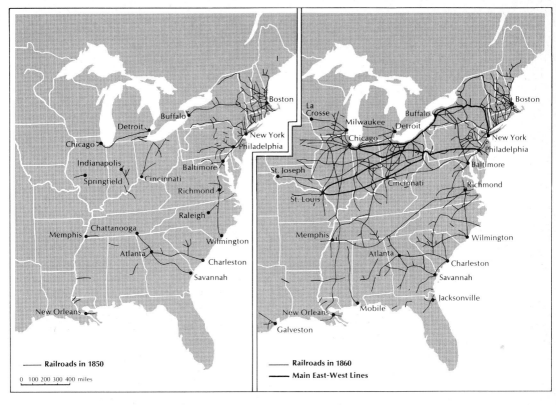

The Growth of Railroads 1850-1860

east with the Northwest. Two, the New York Central and the New York and Erie, gave New York City access to the Lake Erie ports. The Pennsylvania road linked Philadelphia and Pittsburgh, and the Baltimore and Ohio connected the Maryland metropolis with the Ohio River at Wheeling. From the terminals of these lines, other railroads into the interior touched the Mississippi River at eight points. Other important trunk routes were the Michigan Central and the Michigan Southern, which entered Chicago from the East, and the Rock Island and Chicago, which connected the Great Lakes and the Mississippi. Chicago became the rail center of the West, served by fifteen lines and over a hundred daily trains. The appearance of the great trunk lines tended to divert traffic from the water routes—the Erie Canal and the Mississippi River. By lessening the dependence of the West upon the Mississippi, the railroads helped to weaken the connection between the Northwest and the South. By binding more

closely the East and West, they prepared the way for a coalition of those sections.

At the opening of the century the average freight rate by wagon had been 33 cents per ton mile; the average passenger rate was 6 cents per mile. In the stagecoach era of the 1830s a trip from Boston to New York consumed forty-one hours; from New York to St. Louis, a distance of 1,600 miles, over three weeks were required. The average coach fare for 300 miles was $15. The principal result of the advent of water transportation was to reduce freight charges. According to one estimate, the costs of traffic on the various means of transportation in 1840 were as follows: roads, 10 to 20 cents per mile; canals, 1½ cents; lake steamers, 2 to 4 cents; river steamers, 1½ cents; railroads, 2½ cents. Water transportation continued to be cheaper than railroad transportation, but the railroads could move goods in about half the time required on water. Railroad freight rates continued to decrease,

A Railroad Train in the 1850s

*By the 1850s locomotives in this country had become
standardized according to what was known as the "American
type." This had a cowcatcher, a four-wheel leading truck, two
pairs of drive wheels, and a funnel-shaped smokestack with a
screen to check the escape of sparks from the wood-burning
boiler. Note the wood stacked in the tender. Posing on the
locomotive are artists taking an excursion from Baltimore
to Wheeling in June 1858. (Baltimore and Ohio Railroad
Company)*

**Speed
by Water
and by Rail
[1850s]**

The following table indicates the rapidity of rail as compared with water
travel and transportation between New York City and Western cities:

From New York To	Distance in Miles	Time by Water	Time by Railroads
Cleveland	700	9 days	3 days
Detroit	825	10 days	4 days
Chicago	1,500	14½ days	6½ days
St. Louis	1,600	———	12½ days

reaching by the decade of the 1860s an average of slightly less than 2 cents per ton mile.

Capital to finance the railroad boom came from various sources. Part of it was provided by American investors, and large sums were borrowed abroad. Substantial aid was provided by local governmental units—states, cities, towns, counties—eager to have a road to serve their needs. This support took the form of loans, stock subscriptions, subsidies, and donations of land for rights of way. The railroads also obtained assistance from the federal government in the shape of public land grants. In 1850 Senator Stephen A. Douglas and other railroad-minded politicians persuaded Congress to grant lands to the state of Illinois to aid the Illinois Central, then building toward the Gulf of Mexico; Illinois was to transfer the land to the Central as it carried its construction forward. Other states and their railroad promoters demanded the same privileges, and by 1860 Congress had allotted over 30 million acres to eleven states.

The operation of railroads was facilitated by the magnetic telegraph, the lines of which were extended along the tracks to connect one station with another.

THE TELEGRAPH

Culminating several years of experimentation with an electric (magnetic) telegraph, Samuel F. B. Morse in 1844 transmitted from Baltimore to Washington the news of James K. Polk's nomination for the presidency. The Morse telegraph seemed, because of the relatively low cost of constructing wire systems, the ideal answer to the problems of long-distance communication. By 1860 over 50,000 miles of wire connected most parts of the country, and a year later the Pacific telegraph, with 3,595 miles of wire, was open between New York and San Francisco. Nearly all of the independent lines had been absorbed into one organization, the Western Union Telegraph Company. American enthusiasm for wire communication was not limited to the confines of the nation. Cyrus W. Field, a New York businessman, conceived the project of laying an Atlantic cable between Newfoundland and Ireland. With financial aid from associates and encouragement from the British and American governments, he completed a cable in 1858. Messages between Great Britain and the United States were exchanged, and man seemed to have accomplished another conquest of distance. But within a few weeks the cable went dead, nor could Field, who continued to believe in his idea, get it to work again. (After the Civil War, Field returned to his labors, and in 1866 succeeded in laying a permanent cable.)

THE NEW JOURNALISM

In 1846 Richard Hoe invented the steam cylinder rotary press, making it possible to print newspapers at a much faster rate and a much lower cost. The development of the telegraph, together with the introduction of the rotary press, made possible much speedier collection and distribution of news than ever before. In 1846 the Associated Press was organized for the purpose of cooperative news gathering by wire; no longer did publishers have to depend on exchanges of newspapers for out-of-town reports.

Other changes in journalism also occurred. Originally Washington had been the national news center, and the papers published there had been government or party organs that filled their columns with dull documents and speeches. With the advent of the telegraph and the railroad and with the government's assumption of the function of public printing, the center of news transmission shifted to New York. A new type of newspaper appeared, one that was more attuned to the spirit and the needs of the new America. Although newspapers continued to concentrate on politics, they came to report more human interest stories and to record the most recent news, the happenings of yesterday, which they could not have done before the telegraph. The New York papers, and to a lesser degree those of other Northern cities, maintained corps of special correspondents to go into all parts of the country to cover any event that seemed newsworthy.

Most of the metropolitan journals were owned in whole or in part by their editors, who were also in many cases their founders; unlike modern newspapers they bore the imprint of a single personality and are often referred to as "personal" organs. The leading Northern papers were Horace Greeley's *Tribune,* James Gordon Bennett's *Herald,* and Henry J. Raymond's *Times,* all of New York. The *Herald* specialized in scandal and crime, the *Tribune* in self-improvement and social uplift. With a separate weekly edition, the *Tribune* served as a national or at least a sectional paper, having mail subscribers scattered throughout the Northeast and Northwest. Southern papers, with smaller budgets, tended to follow the older pattern of reporting mainly rather stale political news. The combined circulation of the New York *Tribune* and *Herald* exceeded that of all the dailies published in the South. In the country as a whole, there were more than 3,000 newspapers by 1860.

During the fifties Americans experienced the impact of a new kind of magazine journalism. In increasing numbers the upper and middle classes were reading monthly magazines that featured fiction and news articles by some of the country's outstanding writers. Easily the leader in this field was *Harper's New Monthly Magazine*, with 170,000 subscribers, but competition was furnished by *Putnam's Magazine* and the *Atlantic Monthly,* both founded in the fifties. Another organ that appealed to the more literate groups was the New York religious-political weekly, the *Independent,* with a circulation of nearly 100,000. For the edification of the masses there appeared the pictorial weeklies, lavishly illustrated with drawings by America's best popular artists. The pioneer among the picture journals was the *National Police Gazette*, established in 1845 by George Wilkes. It was also the most sensational, reporting "horrid murders, outrageous robberies, bold forgeries, astounding burglaries, hideous rapes, vulgar seductions." Other picture magazines reaching huge audiences were *Leslie's Illustrated Newspaper* (1855) and *Harper's Weekly* (1857).

In one sense, the new journalism helped to feed the fires of sectional discord. The rapid reporting of detailed information regarding differences between the North and the South prompted people to anger more quickly and more often than otherwise would have been the case. But viewed in a longer perspective, the revolution in news was a unifying factor in American life. As one historian of journalism (L. M. Starr) has pointed out, the ultimate result of the news revolution was to endow the American people with that mystic sense of common destiny that is conveyed only by news of great events being reported everywhere simultaneously and soon after their occurrence.

Persisting Cultural Nationalism

"In the four quarters of the globe, who reads an American book? or goes to an American play? or looks at an American picture or statue?" So asked the English wit Sydney Smith in the *Edinburgh Review* (1820), and he assumed that the answer was obvious—nobody. Like him, many cultivated Europeans believed that the American democracy was a cultural vacuum.

DEMOCRACY AND CIVILIZATION

On the whole, British travelers in the United States confirmed Smith's impression of American culture. Occasionally these book-writing tourists had a kind word about the American and his habits. One of the most sympathetic, Harriet Martineau, author of *Society in Ameri-* ca (1837), admitted that the American people already had realized many ideals for which the rest of the world still strove. Though Americans had their faults, she added, they could not be discouraged by them, for they "are in possession of the glorious certainty that time and exertion will infallibly secure all wisely desired objects." Even when the British were complimentary, however, they were inclined to be condescending. Much of the time they were highly critical. To them the typical Yankee seemed filthy, rude, ignorant, quarrelsome, boastful, and greedy, as well as sickly and sallow. The Southerner seemed even worse, tyrannical and brutal, a beater of slaves. North, South, and West, the American male according to the British visitors was an inveterate tobacco chewer and spitter, with an aim that was none too good.

What these writers saw in America reflected their own prejudices as well as the objective facts. English authors, including Charles Dickens, were personally aggrieved because American publishers "pirated" their works, that is, reprinted them without paying royalties. Along with other Englishmen, men of letters also lost money by investing in state bonds that proved worthless or nearly so with the defaults and repudiations following the Panic of 1837. Quite often the interpreters of the United States to the English public were Tories who feared democracy at home and therefore wished to discredit it abroad. They were fighting against the campaign to widen the suffrage in England, a campaign that culminated in the Reform Bill of 1832 and in the Chartist movement of 1848. Reviewers of the travel books in British quarterlies gave much attention to the criticisms of American democracy and pointed out the

The Park Theater
A comedy was being performed to a full house in the Park Theater, New York City, when John Searles made this watercolor drawing in November 1822. (Courtesy of The New-York Historical Society, New York City)

seemingly obvious conclusion: true morality and real culture could have no place in a country where the will of the majority prevailed.

Quite different was the attitude of the young French visitor Alexis de Tocqueville, who welcomed political equality as the way of the future for France and the world. Even though he disapproved of much that he saw, he sought to understand American behavior, not to denounce it. Like the British observers, he concluded that Americans were backward in respect to science, literature, and the arts, but he did not blame their backwardness upon democracy. He wrote: "Their strictly Puritanical origin—their exclusively commercial habits—even the country they inhabit, which seems to divert their minds from the pursuit of science, literature and the arts—the proximity of Europe, which allows them to neglect these pursuits without relapsing into barbarism—a thousand special causes, of which I have only been able to point out the most important—have singularly concurred to fix the mind of the American upon purely practical objects."

Colonial attitudes persisted in America so far as things of the mind were concerned. Seldom was an American author appreciated at home until he had been praised by critics abroad, and sometimes not even then. In 1830, it has been estimated, 70 percent of the books sold in America were published in England. By 1840 this percentage had been drastically reduced, to only about 30. In the space of one decade the American book industry had grown tremendously, though most of the books had to be subsidized or else produced for advance orders secured by subscriptions. Despite the rise of book publishing in several American cities, especially in New York, the great majority of books published and sold were written, as before, by English authors. The romantic novels of Charles Dickens and Sir Walter Scott were as much the rage in the United States as in the British Isles. Scott was a special favorite among Southerners, who often applied Scott's word "Southron" to themselves, and who viewed their own section as the contemporary land of chivalry and romance.

American writers had other outlets for their wares in the hundreds of magazines that appeared and disappeared, their average life being about two years. In the best of these magazines some of the greatest of native authors found a market for their works. In many other magazines, however, neither the writers nor their stories were great by any standard except popular appeal. The taste of most readers, especially women, was little different from that of their descendants who a century later were to listen to soap operas on radio or television. Sentimental tales of struggling womanhood were as popular a hundred years ago as now.

As in the Revolutionary era, the question of literary independence continued to draw much discussion from American writers. Some responded to British criticisms by declaring war again—the so-called war of the quarterlies—in which magazine replied to magazine, the Americans defending life in the United States and denouncing the customs of England. Instead of joining in such recriminations, a few thoughtful Americans called upon their countrymen for increased originality and creative effort. "The more we receive from other countries, the greater the need of an original literature," said William Ellery Channing (1830). He went on to contend: "A people into whose minds the thoughts of foreigners are poured perpetually, needs an energy within itself to resist, to modify this mighty influence, and without it will inevitably sink under the worst bondage, will become intellectually tame and enslaved." And Ralph Waldo Emerson, in his notable Phi Beta Kappa address at Harvard (1837), urged scholars, philosophers, and men of letters to do all they could toward developing a self-reliant nationhood. But there were also arguments on the other side. Confessing that American literature was largely derivative, James Russell Lowell said (1849), "There is no degradation in such indebtedness"; and he suggested, "It may not be our destiny to produce a great literature."

LITERATURE: A GOLDEN AGE

Foreign critics were too severe and native commentators too modest in their appraisals of American letters. In retrospect the period from the 1820s to the 1850s has seemed, indeed, a kind of golden age of literature in the United States. It was the time of Washington Irving, James Fenimore Cooper, Herman Melville, and Walt Whitman (all New Yorkers); Edgar

Allan Poe (a Southerner by affirmation though not by birth); and Ralph Waldo Emerson, Henry David Thoreau, and Nathaniel Hawthorne (New Englanders). All these writers contributed to world literature: sooner or later they won lasting renown abroad as well as at home. Besides them, a number of others gained the esteem at least of their own countrymen and their own generation.

Irving, author of the earliest American literary "classics," was the first to achieve foreign recognition. His *History of New York* (1809) aimed, in his words, "to embody the traditions of the city in an amusing form," and did so in the stories of an imaginary historian of Dutch descent, Diedrich Knickerbocker. Irving's most famous work, *The Sketch Book* (1819–1820), containing "Rip Van Winkle" and "The Legend of Sleepy Hollow," made further use of the Dutch folklore of New York. Afterward Irving lived for a number of years in Spain and found story materials there, and still later he wrote historical works about the American West. A conservative in politics, he avoided contemporary political and social problems as literary themes. He did not disturb his readers with philosophical challenges but charmed them with his easy style and graceful art.

Cooper, a less polished but more prolific writer, turned out more than thirty novels in thirty years (1820–1850). Born into a well-to-do family, Cooper grew up in Cooperstown, New York, at a time when the frontier was not far away. He served for several years in the navy. Thus he knew the forest and the sea, the settings of his adventure stories. Among the most successful were *The Spy* (1821), a novel of the Revolutionary War, and several "Leatherstocking" tales, including *The Last of the Mohicans* (1826) and *The Deerslayer* (1841). Over and over Cooper used the same formula of heroic action, breathless pursuit, and narrow escape. A born storyteller, he held his readers' attention despite the stilted dialogue of his stylized characters—the noble red man, the resourceful pioneer, the virtuous maid, and the enemy villain. He created an enduring character in the frontiersman Natty Bumppo ("Leatherstocking"). In some of his novels and also in his essays Cooper turned to social criticism. As a Democrat with aristocratic ideals, he condemned the pushing, go-getting spirit of his fellow Americans.

Walt Whitman

This picture of the youthful, jaunty, bearded poet appeared as the frontispiece in the first edition of Leaves of Grass *(1855). It is an engraving made from a painting by Francis B. Carpenter. Born in Homer, New York, and largely self-taught, Carpenter became one of the most successful portrait painters of the second half of the nineteenth century. He lived in the White House from February to July 1864 while doing a canvas of Lincoln reading his emancipation proclamation to the cabinet. He afterward wrote* Six Months at the White House *(1866), giving an inside view of Lincoln at home. (New York Public Library)*

Melville, once a sailor and a resident of the South Seas, had a background even more adventurous than Cooper's, and he too wrote narratives of adventure. But Melville was vastly more subtle and sophisticated in his writing, and he filled his stories with discursive philosophizing and extraordinary symbolism. The greatest of his books, *Moby Dick* (1851), is both an epic of man's industry and courage and a tragedy brought on by overweening pride. A great hero, Captain Ahab, destroys his ship, his crew, and himself in a mad attempt to get revenge on the white whale, Moby Dick, which has maimed him and has thus become for him the embodiment of universal evil. For all the vividness of Melville's scenes, the depth and complexity of his characters, and the richness of his style, his plots move too slowly and his meaning was too obscure for the reading public of his time. A century later he was recognized as one of the greatest novelists ever to write in the English language.

Whitman, the self-proclaimed poet of American democracy, likewise was more widely appreciated by posterity than by his contemporaries, though some of them hailed him as the most original and authentic voice of the United States. The son of a Long Island carpenter, Whitman roamed the country and supported himself by odd jobs while composing his first poems. When he hired a printer to put out a thin volume of his work, *Leaves of Grass* (1855), he could find few buyers or readers, and he scandalized most of them. His verse, unconfined by rhyme, praised democracy and sang exuberantly of the flesh as well as the spirit. Whitman identified himself with the American people. He wrote:

> I celebrate myself, and sing myself,
> And what I assume you shall assume,
> For every atom belonging to me as good
>   belongs to you.

Five more editions of *Leaves of Grass*, with added poems, appeared before Whitman's death (1892), and so did other volumes of poetry and essays, the most notable of which was *Democratic Vistas* (1871). His work eventually was translated into many languages. Today he is looked upon as a forerunner of twentieth-century poetry, a bold experimenter who liberated verse from restrictive conventions of form and content on the assumption that the "old forms must be fitted to the new age."

Poe, in a short and unhappy life that ended in 1849, made himself an even more controversial figure than Whitman. After briefly attending the University of Virginia and the United States Military Academy, Poe made a living as best he could by editing literary magazines and selling an occasional bit of writing. He devised a theory of aesthetics—supposedly based on music and mathematics—which he put into practice in his haunting onomatopoetic verse, his macabre, personality-probing tales (he invented the detective story), and his sharp literary criticism. His first book, *Tamerlane and Other Poems* (1827), published anonymously, brought him little money and no fame, but he gained a national reputation with "The Raven" when it appeared in a newspaper in 1845. Some critics were contemptuous of his musical effects, and Emerson referred to him sneeringly as the "jingle man." In England, however, Alfred Lord Tennyson hailed Poe as a true, original poet, and in France Charles Baudelaire took him as an inspiration and a model. Indeed, Poe's writings influenced European literature far more than did those of any other nineteenth-century American.

THE FLOWERING OF NEW ENGLAND

New York, where Poe spent his last years, had become the literary capital of the nation after 1820. Then during the 1840s and 1850s New York, as a center of authorship, was largely eclipsed by New England, if not by the one village of Concord, Massachusetts. Why there should have been such a literary "flowering" in New England is hard to explain. Of course, there was a long tradition of literacy and scholarship in the region. Ships returning from exotic ports throughout the world, including the Far East, brought in stimulating ideas along with profitable cargoes. Travelers, among them students attending German universities, returned with the stimulus of European romanticism. And the rise of industry altered society and the countryside, unsettling old habits and beliefs and, perhaps, provoking the imagination.

Emerson, leader of the Concord literary circle, began his career as a Unitarian minister, then resigned (1832) and devoted himself to the exposition of a transcendental philosophy. He derived his ideas partly from wide reading in the works of Plato, Plotinus, seventeenth-century Neoplatonists, and writers of China, Persia, and India. He was inspired even more by European travel and by conversation with English romantic authors such as Samuel Taylor Coleridge and Thomas Carlyle. From various sources Emerson put together a distinctively American philosophy of optimism, which saw reality as essentially good, and individualism, which stressed the capability of self-reliant man. Though he also wrote poetry, Emerson was most noted for his platform lectures, some of which were condensed and revised for publication under the title *Essays* (1841–1844). Through both the printed and the spoken word, he reached and influenced a wide audience, though he did not convince all who read or heard him, not even all his friends. One admirer, Melville, thought him full of "oracular gibberish" at times.

Thoreau, a friend and disciple of Emerson's, built a shack in the woods on Emerson's property and lived there, beside Walden Pond, for two years. Afterward he explained: "I went to the woods because I wished to live deliberately, to front only the essential facts of life, and see if I could not learn what it had to teach, and not, when I came to die, discover that I had not lived." He was delayed five years in finding a publisher for his account of the experience, which finally appeared as *Walden* (1854). A man of ruggedly honest principles as well as ruggedly honest prose, Thoreau meanwhile spent a night in jail for refusing to pay taxes for the support of what he considered an unjust government (the United States then being at war with Mexico). He justified his stand in *Resistance to Civil Government* (1849), an essay on "civil disobedience" or "passive resistance" that afterward influenced a number of revolutionaries abroad, among them Mahatma Gandhi in India.

Hawthorne, at different times a friend and neighbor of Emerson's and of Melville's, had an outlook more like Melville's than Emerson's. A latter-day Puritan, Hawthorne dwelt upon somber themes from the Puritan past, with a conviction that evil was a grim reality. In a series of magazine stories, collected in *Twice-Told Tales* (1837), he probed the psychology of sin, much as Jonathan Edwards might have done if Edwards had written fiction instead of theological treatises. Hawthorne's greatest success was *The Scarlet Letter* (1850), which is still regarded as one of the most nearly perfect of American novels. Treating the familiar triangle in an unfamiliar way, this psychological novel tells of the beautiful Hester Prynne, her husband, and her lover, and their very different responses to the evil in their lives.

Besides Emerson, Thoreau, and Hawthorne, there were other New England authors who, in their own time, enjoyed reputations as high or higher than any of those three. William Cullen Bryant, as a young man in the Berk-shire Hills, wrote "Thanatopsis" and other poems that brought him a reputation as America's foremost poet by 1832, after he had moved to New York to edit a newspaper, the *Evening Post*. Henry Wadsworth Longfellow, a sedate Harvard professor, appealed to popular tastes with his short poems on familiar subjects, like the village blacksmith, and his long poems elaborating historic traditions, such as *Evangeline* (1847), *The Song of Hiawatha* (1855), and *The Courtship of Miles Standish* (1858). His books sold well—a total of 300,000 copies by 1857. Oliver Wendell Holmes, another Harvard professor, a physician who taught in the Medical School, had time to write light verse and witty essays. James Russell Lowell, the first editor of the *Atlantic Monthly,* was a leading critic, essayist, and versifier. John Greenleaf Whittier, the "Quaker Poet," composed gentle, homespun verse about rural life in New England—and not so gentle verse attacking slavery in the South.

Though each section had its historians, New England had the ablest. George Bancroft celebrated the successes of what he considered God's chosen people in his ten-volume *History of the United States* (1834–1882). Like many of the intellectuals of the time, Bancroft was a Jacksonian, and his political feelings were apparent when the first volume came out, though it dealt with the colonial beginnings and not with contemporary events. The book, critics said, voted for Jackson. Works of more enduring value, because of their literary quality and their critical use of evidence, were written by William H. Prescott, Francis Parkman, and John Lothrop Motley. These writers looked outside the United States for their subject matter—to Mexico and Peru, New France, and the Dutch republic.

ARTS AND SCIENCES

In the arts of drama, painting, sculpture, and music, and in the sciences, Americans produced much less of originality and lasting value than in literature. Yet, even in those fields, Americans were not always wholly imitative during the four decades from 1820 to 1860.

The theater became increasingly popular, though not entirely respectable, despite its efforts to appear on the side of morality through the presentation of temperance dramas like *The Drunkard* and *Ten Nights in a Bar-room*. Regular stock companies, English and American, toured the cities and larger towns. The companies depended on their stars to attract audiences. Fanny Kemble and William Charles Macready, both English, were outstanding attractions. So were the Americans Joseph Jefferson, who played the role of Rip Van Winkle before countless applauding audiences after 1859, and Edwin Forrest, famous for Shakespearean parts. Intense rivalries developed among celebrities and among their respective fans. In 1849 a mob of Forrest's admirers marched upon a New York theater where Macready was playing, and in the ensuing riot twenty-two persons were killed and many more injured. The legitimate stage often resorted to cheap showmanship to compete with such spectacles as circuses, minstrel shows, and "museums," containing freaks and oddities like the midget Tom Thumb. In the 1840s P. T. Barnum rose to become the leading promoter of these kinds of mass amusement.

Painters generally conformed to the sentimental taste of their customers, who demanded soft landscapes, flattering portraits, and storytelling pictures. Among the better artists, Asher B. Durand and others of the "Hudson School" concentrated upon natural scenery, William Sidney Mount portrayed his fellow Long Islanders at work and play, and George Caleb Bingham recorded everyday scenes of life in Missouri. The most successful sculptor was Hiram Powers, whose statue of a naked woman, entitled "The Greek Slave," attracted attention and provoked controversy on moral rather than esthetic grounds.

By the 1840s New York, Philadelphia, and Boston possessed orchestras of their own, and Americans flocked to the performances of such foreign celebrities as the Norwegian violinist Ole Bull and the "Swedish Nightingale" Jenny Lind. But American composers were rare, the most successful (judged by their enduring popularity) being John Howard Payne, Lowell Mason, and Stephen C. Foster. Payne, an actor and playwright, wrote "Home, Sweet Home" for an opera (1823). Mason, a Boston music teacher, composed the tunes for "Nearer, My God, to Thee," "From Greenland's Icy Mountains," and other stately hymns. Foster wrote "Oh! Susanna," "Old Black Joe," and more

than 200 other melodies, most of them to accompany his own verse. Many of these songs, written for blackface minstrel bands, convey a sense of genuine nostalgia for the plantation, though Foster was born in Pennsylvania and spent his brief and tragic life (1826–1864) in the Northeast.

Americans were more noted for applied science than for scientific theory. Nevertheless, from observation and experiment, some of them made significant contributions to scientific knowledge. John J. Audubon, pioneer ornithologist, published his exquisite sketches in *Birds of America* (1827–1838). Joseph Henry, the most original American scientist since Benjamin Franklin, made important discoveries in electromagnetism (thus preparing the way for Morse's invention of the telegraph). A Georgia physician, Crawford W. Long, demonstrated the practicability of ether as an anesthetic (1842).

The federal government sponsored some kinds of scientific work, though not as generously as it might have done had congressmen not opposed expenditures on grounds of thrift and state rights. Geographical knowledge was increased by the United States Coast Survey, begun in 1832, and by the United States Exploring Expedition, which between 1838 and 1842 surveyed extensive areas of the Pacific Ocean, under the leadership of Lieutenant Charles Wilkes. In the 1840s Congress voted funds to support the Naval Observatory and Hydrographical Office, an agency to study and report on nautical and astronomical subjects. Matthew Fontaine Maury became its director and began a monumental investigation of oceanography. In 1846 the Smithsonian Institution was founded in Washington, after an Englishman had willed his fortune of $500,000 to the United States "for the increase and diffusion of knowledge." Appropriately the noted physicist Joseph Henry became the first head of the institution.

The leading colleges, Yale and Harvard, also served as important patrons of science. At Yale Benjamin Silliman taught chemistry and mineralogy for a half-century after his appointment in 1802, and for many years he edited the *American Journal of Science and Art*, after founding it in 1818. Though not a notable researcher, Silliman was an outstanding teacher who kept American students and scholars informed of scientific developments throughout the world. At Harvard the zoologist and geologist Louis Agassiz and the botanist Asa Gray not only taught but also carried on important research in their respective fields. Through his studies of plant distribution Gray assisted the English scholar Charles Darwin in formulating the theory of evolution. When Darwin's epoch-making book *On the Origin of Species* appeared (1859), Gray endorsed and Agassiz rejected the idea that plants and animals, instead of remaining unchanged since God created them, had developed through a process of natural selection.

Selected Readings

The Economy in General

D. C. North, *The Economic Growth of the United States, 1790–1860** (1961); Stuart Bruchey, *The Roots of American Economic Growth** (1965); T. C. Cochran and William Miller, *The Age of Enterprise** (1942); L. M. Hacker, *The Triumph of American Capitalism** (1940); Roger Burlingame, *The March of the Iron Men** (1938); E. W. Martin, *The Standard of Living in the United States in 1860* (1942).

Agriculture, Industry, Trade

P. W. Gates, *The Farmer's Age* (1960); P. W. Bidwell and J. I. Falconer, *History of Agriculture in the Northern United States, 1620–1860* (1925); V. S. Clark, *History of Manufactures in the United States* (3 vols., 1928); Allan Nevins, *Abram S. Hewitt, with Some Account of Peter Cooper* (1935); J. R. Commons and others, *History of Labour in the United States* (4 vols., 1918–1935); Norman Ware, *The Industrial Worker, 1840–1860* (1924); E. R. Johnson and others, *History of the Domestic and Foreign Commerce of the United States* (2 vols., 1915).

Transportation and Communication

Seymour Dunbar, *A History of American Travel* (4 vols., 1915; 1-vol. edition, 1937); G. R. Taylor, *The Transportation Revolution, 1815–1860* (1951); J. F. Stover, *American Railroads** (1961); T. C. Cochran, *Railroad Leaders, 1845–1890* (1953); E. C. Kirkland, *Men, Cities, and Transportation, 1820–1900* (2 vols., 1948), on New England; U. B. Phillips, *A History of Transportation in the Eastern Cotton Belt to 1860* (1908); P. W. Gates, *The Illinois Central Railroad and Its Colonization Work* (1934); R. W. Fogel, *Railroads and American Economic Growth* (1964); Albert Fishlow, *American Railroads and the Transformation of the Ante-Bellum Economy* (1965); C. C. Cutler, *The Story of the American Clipper* (1930); R. L. Thompson, *Wiring a Continent* (1947).

Immigration and Nativism

M. L. Hansen, *The Immigrant in American History** (1940) and *The Atlantic Migration, 1607–1860** (1940); Carl Wittke, *Refugees of Revolution: The German Forty-Eighters in America* (1952) and *The Irish in America* (1956); Oscar Handlin, *Boston's Immigrants** (1941); Robert Ernst, *Immigrant Life in New York City, 1825–1863* (1949); R. A. Billington, *The Protestant Crusade, 1800–1860** (1938); Sister M. E. Thomas, *Nativism in the Old Northwest, 1850–1860* (1936); W. D. Overdyke, *The Know-Nothing Party in the South* (1950).

Journalism

F. L. Mott, *American Journalism* (1950) and *A History of American Magazines*, vol. 1, *1741–1850* (1930), vol. 2, *1850–1865* (1938); E. F. Brown, *Raymond of the Times* (1951); D. C. Seitz, *The James Gordon Bennetts* (1928); G. G. Van Deusen, *Horace Greeley* (1953).

Cultural Trends

Max Berger, *The British Traveller in America, 1836–1860* (1943); Van Wyck Brooks, *The Flowering of New England, 1815–1865** (1936); F. O. Matthiessen, *American Renaissance* (1941); Lewis Mumford, *The Golden Day** (1926); R. L. Rusk, *The Life of Ralph Waldo Emerson* (1949); Neil Harris, *The Artist in American Society: The Formative Years, 1790–1860* (1966); Carleton Mabee, *The American Leonardo: A Life of Samuel F. B. Morse* (1943); Carl Bode, *The Anatomy of American Popular Culture, 1840–1861* (1959); S. K. Schultz, *The Culture Factory: Boston Public Schools, 1789–1860* (1973).

*Titles available in paperback.

Slavery and the South

Twelve

America, the scene of Thomas More's sixteenth-century book *Utopia*, still seemed in the nineteenth century a land of utopian possibilities, at least to a great many Americans. To them, progress was a profound faith. As invention followed invention, they were confirmed in the belief that they lived in a wondrous age of increasing ease and plenty. Some assumed that progress in material things led automatically to progress in government and society as well. Others came to the conclusion that active effort would be needed to keep social improvement abreast of technological advance.

These progress-minded Americans were convinced that their country led the rest of the world in moral as well as material development. They sprang to the defense whenever foreigners criticized American ways, as foreigners often did. The Americans themselves, however, readily found fault with conditions in their own country when these conditions seemed to hinder the perfecting of society and man. There resulted a tumultuous and many-sided movement for social reform, which picked up momentum in the 1830s and continued through the 1850s.

From the reformers' point of view, one social evil came to stand out above all others. This was the plight of the more than 4 million Americans of African descent, most of whom were slaves, and the rest of whom were less than wholly free. Eventually the reform drive concentrated its main force on a single goal, the elimination of slavery.

Since all the slaves and nearly all the Negroes were concentrated in one section, the reform movement took on a sectional aspect. The economy and society of the South were based largely on the enslavement of the blacks, and most Southern whites feared the economic and social consequences of the slaves' liberation. The reform spirit — a "freedom's ferment" — had never stirred the South so much as it had the North, and with

"Overseer Doing His Duty"
An ironic commentary on slavery, in which a white man takes his ease with a cigar while two black girls busy themselves with hoes. From a water color by the famous architect Benjamin H. Latrobe, who designed the Second Bank of the United States. He died in 1820. (The Papers of Benjamin Henry Latrobe)

the development of an antislavery crusade white Southerners resisted more strongly than ever the radical "isms" of the day as they rallied to a defense of their "peculiar institution." Thus the nation began increasingly to divide on moral as well as economic and political grounds.

Freedom's Ferment

"In no country in the world has the principle of association been more successfully used, or more unsparingly applied to a multitude of different objects, than in America," Tocqueville observed. "Societies are formed to resist enemies which are exclusively of a moral nature, and to diminish the vice of intemperance: in the United States associations are established to promote public order, commerce, industry, morality, and religion; for there is no end which the human will, seconded by the collective exertions of individuals, despairs of attaining."

Indeed, Americans organized reform societies of all kinds, not only for temperance but also for education, world peace, the care of the poor and the handicapped, the improvement of prisons, women's rights, the abolition of slavery, and dozens of other idealistic purposes.

SPIRIT OF SOCIAL REFORM

This reform spirit derived from a variety of sources, religious and rational, domestic and foreign. The Christian doctrine of human worth, the Revolutionary philosophy of the equality of man—these were part of the general background. More immediately, the rise of industrialism in the British Isles and Western Europe as well as the United States produced social dislocations and suffering but at the same time gave promise of a more abundant life for all. No doubt, with some people, a determination to improve human welfare was stimulated by the contrast between what actually was and what apparently might be. The humanitarian stirrings of the time were to be found in many lands at once, and most conspicuously in those countries that were being most rapidly industrialized.

In Europe the agitation was in some ways quite different from that in this country. There, it led to violent outbreaks, to the revolutionary attempts of 1830 and 1848. In America, where (except in the Southern states) there was no repressive government to contend with, the reformers had to fear violence only at the hands of unsympathetic mobs: reform did not mean revolt, though it culminated in the Civil War. Despite the differences in the American and European movements, American reformers often consulted and cooperated with their European counterparts, particularly with Englishmen. When it came to human betterment, cultural nationalism gave way to cosmopolitanism.

In Protestant countries the reform ethic was stronger than in Roman Catholic countries, which for the most part were less highly industrialized. Protestantism and reformism were closely related. In the United States the stimulus to reform came largely from two quite different Protestant trends—from the revivalistic, hellfire teachings of "New Light" Calvinists, on the one hand, and on the other hand from optimistic, salvation-for-all ideas of Universalists, Unitarians, and others who completely repudiated the tenets of Calvinism.

Emerson's philosophy of transcendentalism contributed to the reform spirit. Emerson evolved the doctrine of the Oversoul or spiritual essence from which all things derived, including the soul of man. Since all humanity shared in this essential Being, this all-in-all, there existed a very real brotherhood of mankind. And since the Oversoul was good, there could be no such thing, in the last analysis, as evil. (The later teachings of Mary Baker G. Eddy, founder of Christian Science, were in some respects similar to those of Emerson.) This philosophy, for all its obscurities and inconsistencies, had practical consequences for its believers. It made them optimistic. It taught them that they were potentially divine and could increase their divinity by identifying

Transcendentalism and Reform [1837]

In his Phi Beta Kappa address, "The American Scholar," which he delivered at Harvard College on August 31, 1837, Ralph Waldo Emerson presented a kind of intellectual declaration of independence for the United States. He also adumbrated his transcendentalist philosophy, speaking of the "human mind" as "one central fire," "one light which beams out of a thousand stars," and "one soul which animates all men." He suggested a relationship between transcendentalism and reform in the following passage:

It is a mischievous notion that we are come late into nature; that the world was finished a long time ago. As the world was plastic and fluid in the hands of God, so it is ever to so much of his attributes as we bring to it. To ignorance and sin, it is flint. They adapt themselves to it as they may; but in proportion as a man has any thing in him divine, the firmament flows before him and takes his signet and form. Not he is great who can alter matter, but he who can alter my state of mind. They are the kings of the world who give the color of their present thought to all nature and art, and persuade men by the cheerful serenity of their carrying the matter, that this thing which they do is the apple which the ages have desired to pluck, now at last ripe, and inviting nations to the harvest. The great man makes the great thing.

---

themselves more and more fully with the Over-soul, with Being, with Truth. It led them to believe in the perfectibility of man.

Still more important as a call to reform were the preachings of the revivalist Charles G. Finney, who was at first a Presbyterian and later a Congregationalist. In upstate New York and in Ohio, beginning in the 1820s, Finney delivered many a memorable sermon on the dangers of damnation and the possibilities of salvation—through good works as well as faith. "The church," he maintained, "must take right ground on the subject of Temperance, and Moral Reform, and all the subjects of practical morality which come up for decision from time to time." Not all the churches did so, and some reformers (known as "come-outers") left the fold and even turned against organized religion, denouncing it as a bulwark to the status quo. Yet many churches heeded Finney's call, especially Presbyterian and Congregational churches, which provided more reform leaders than did any of the other Protestant sects, even the Quakers.

These leaders implied by their activities that they believed in a sort of earthly millennium as well as a heavenly one. Going a step further, one religious prophet together with his thousands of followers expected and awaited the actual second coming of Christ. From his studies of the Bible and from other signs and calculations, William Miller of Low Hampton, New York, predicted that on a certain day in 1843 Christ would appear and all true believers would ascend bodily to heaven. After new predictions and repeated disappointments he made the date indefinite. His followers formed a lasting sect, the Seventh-Day Adventists.

Miller and other prophets of the time, such as Finney and also Joseph Smith, the founder of Mormonism, were New Englanders by birth and residents of upstate New York at some stage in their careers. So, too, the great majority of reform leaders were New England-born, and a large number of them lived at least temporarily in New York State. Most were descended from substantial New England families, neither rich nor poor, whose heads once had been highly respected as preachers, doctors, teachers, and farmers. With the rise of commerce and industry these families lost status in comparison with the upcoming merchants and manufacturers. The families who migrated to New York settled in counties that at first were economically dominant but that by the 1830s had fallen behind the rest of the state. These family backgrounds suggest that the typical reformer was unconsciously a product of social changes under way in the North.

The reform spirit was far more prevalent among Whigs than among Democrats. Though it affected some of the latter too, it cannot be considered as essentially an extension of Jacksonian Democracy. The Jacksonians advocated political and economic reforms, such as the widening of the suffrage and the destruction of monopoly, but were far from unanimous in supporting social reforms, such as the abolition of slavery. Nor can the reform spirit be viewed as an outgrowth of the labor movement, except in certain cases, notably the drive for free public schools. Most reform leaders disbelieved in unions, opposed strikes, and were indifferent to the plight of the unemployed. William Lloyd Garrison, the abolitionist, denounced labor agitators for trying "to inflame the minds of our working classes against the more opulent, and to persuade men that they are contemned and oppressed by a wealthy aristocracy." A few of the "more opulent," such as the merchants Arthur and Lewis Tappan of New York and Amos and Abbott Lawrence of Boston, contributed vast sums to finance various reforms. This is not to say, however, that big business in general was favorable to the reform movement. More often than not, reform was resisted by both the laborer and the capitalist. It was essentially a middle-class movement, receiving its greatest support from the reasonably well-to-do farmers, shopkeepers, and professional people of the North and the West.

FREE PUBLIC SCHOOLS

As of 1830 no state could yet boast a general system of free public education in the modern sense—with full tax support, compulsory attendance, and enforced maintenance of schools—though Massachusetts, as in earlier times, came fairly close to it. A very high proportion of American children had the benefit of the three Rs, but most of them still got their learning from church schools, proprietary institutions, private tutors, or members of their own families.

Then, during the 1830s, a widespread demand for state-supported primary education arose. This demand came from reformers who feared the consequences of allowing every man to vote, including in many cases even the newly arrived immigrant, without making public provision for his literacy at least. The demand came also from workingmen who hoped that book learning would enable their children

to rise in the world. Opposition was forthcoming, however, from taxpayers (especially childless ones) who objected to paying for the education of other people's families, and from Lutherans, Roman Catholics, and other religious groups who already supported their own church schools and did not wish to be taxed for public education besides.

Educational reformers made considerable headway against such opposition in several of the states. The greatest of these leaders was Horace Mann, the first secretary of the Massachusetts board of education, which was established in 1837. He reorganized the state's school system, lengthened the school year (to six months), doubled teachers' salaries, enriched the curriculum, and improved teacher training and teaching methods. Henry Barnard led the way to better schools in Connecticut and Rhode Island. In Pennsylvania a school law was passed in 1835, making state funds available for the education of all children and not merely the children of paupers, as formerly; but only the exertions of Thaddeus Stevens in the legislature saved the law from an early repeal. In New York, after William H. Seward became governor in 1839, the upstate system of school districts supporting their own schools was extended to the metropolis. This step aroused much opposition, since it gave control of some new districts to the local Roman Catholic majorities.

By the 1850s the principle of tax-supported elementary schools was accepted in all the states, and all of them were making at least a start toward putting the principle into practice. Still, there were vast differences in the quantity and quality of public schools from place to place, the poorest performances and the lowest literacy rates being found in the newly settled areas of the West and in the more sparsely populated parts of the South. In the country as a whole, only a small proportion of children of school age were actually going to school—one white child out of every seven in the South and one out of every six elsewhere (1860).

Most teachers were poorly paid and poorly prepared, and many of them were scarcely able to read, write, and cipher. In rural district schools, containing husky youths along with tender tots, what the schoolmaster needed was a strong arm rather than a well-stocked mind. If he could not thrash the most obstreperous of

Horace Mann on Education [1848]

Now surely nothing but universal education can counterwork this tendency to the domination of capital and the servility of labor. If one class possesses all the wealth and the education, while the residue of society is ignorant and poor, it matters not by what name the relation between them may be called: the latter, in fact and in truth, will be the servile dependents and subjects to the former. But, if education be equally diffused, it will draw property after it by the strongest of attractions; for such a thing never did happen, and never can happen, as that an intelligent and practical body of men should be permanently poor. Property and labor in different classes are essentially antagonistic; but property and labor in the same class are essentially fraternal.

his pupils, he could get nowhere with his lessons. Reformers like Mann and Barnard, believing that human nature was essentially good, advocated gentleness and understanding as practiced by progressive educators in Switzerland (notably Johann Pestalozzi). Most teachers—and parents too—subscribed to the old Calvinist doctrine of inborn wickedness: they did not wish to spare the rod.

Under the circumstances the majority of teaching positions continued to be filled by men, even in the elementary schools. Seldom did these men look upon teaching as a career; often they were aspiring lawyers or preachers who worked their way through college by doubling as schoolmasters in vacation periods. Nevertheless, teaching was beginning to be looked upon as a profession, and an increasing number of young women were going into it. With Mann taking the lead, Massachusetts in 1839 established the first American state-supported teacher-training or "normal" school, at Lexington. In 1845 he organized a state association of teachers.

Since so many teachers were poorly prepared, both they and their pupils had to rely heavily upon textbooks. Noah Webster's spellers and grammars continued to be widely used. Supplementing them and rivaling them in popularity were the six graded *Eclectic Readers* (1835–1857) prepared by William Holmes McGuffey, who was an Ohio professor and college president and then for many years a professor at the University of Virginia. The McGuffey readers were filled with moral lessons, patriotic declamations, sentimental verse, and fascinating facts. A favorite recitation piece was the following:

Woodman, spare that tree;
Touch not a single bough.
In youth it sheltered me,
And I'll protect it now.

Eventually adopted in thirty-seven states, the McGuffey books gave thousands of schoolchildren a shared background of popular culture and helped to mold the literary tastes of the reading public.

The principle of state support was applied later to secondary than to elementary schools. By 1860 there were 22 tax-supported "free academies" in New York, more than 100 public high schools in Massachusetts, and a total of about 300 such institutions in the nation as a whole. At the same time there were approximately 6,000 private academies. Most of them were open to boys only, a few were coeducational, and a growing number were female seminaries.

HIGHER EDUCATION

While the private academies were multiplying, so were the private colleges, though at a slower rate, about eighty being founded between 1830 and 1850. Almost all of these were denominational colleges, with close church connections, and their chief though not their only purpose was to prepare a learned clergy. These institutions became too numerous for their own good. Their enrollments were small, in many cases fewer than 100 in the 1850s (even Harvard and Yale had only 400 or 500 students apiece, though the College of William and Mary had nearly 1,000). Generally endowments were scanty, facilities poor, salaries low, and professors unscholarly, though self-sacrificing and sincere.

None of these institutions admitted women until, in 1837, Oberlin accepted four girls as regular students and thus became the first coeducational college. Some outsiders feared that coeducation was a rash experiment approximating free love, but the Oberlin authorities were confident that "the mutual influence of the sexes upon each other is decidedly happy in the cultivation of both mind & manners." Only a few other institutions copied Oberlin's example before the Civil War. Some of the young ladies' seminaries—notably Mount Holyoke, which the most famous of all women educators, Mary Lyon, founded in Massachusetts in 1837—eventually became full-fledged women's colleges.

The idea of state support for higher education had to contend against the prevailing concept of private, denominational control. Besides the older states with public universities (Vermont, North Carolina, Georgia, Ohio, Virginia) many of the newer states of the Northwest and Southwest committed themselves to the support of higher learning. State universities were established in Indiana, Michigan, Kentucky, Missouri, Mississippi, Iowa, Wisconsin, Minnesota, and Louisiana before the Civil War. None of these, whether old or new, was a true university in the European sense of an institution devoted to high-level, graduate training.

The standard curriculum, whether in the private college or the state university, still emphasized the old-fashioned liberal arts. A young man who desired training for a professional career (other than the ministry) had few institutions to choose from. He could study engineering at the United States Military Academy, Rensselaer Polytechnic Institute (1824), or at Yale or Harvard, which set up engineering schools in 1846 and 1847. He could study law or medicine at one of several institutions, but no American medical school compared with the best ones abroad. In most cases, as in earlier times, he apprenticed himself to a practicing physician, learned engineering on the job (the Erie Canal was a most productive "school" for engineers), or "read law" in the office of some successful lawyer.

Adult education was furthered by the founding of numerous libraries, study clubs, and self-improvement societies of various kinds. Noteworthy was the Lyceum, which was started by Josiah Holbrook in Massachusetts (1826) and spread rapidly throughout the North. "The first step to form a Lyceum," Holbrook explained, "is for a few neighbors or citizens to agree to hold meetings for their mutual improvement." Next, they could acquire books, scientific apparatus, specimens of rocks and plants, and the like. Then they could conduct experiments, carry on discussions among themselves, and sponsor public lectures. The sponsorship of lectures soon became their principal activity. Though the Lyceum many thousands of Americans were able to hear scientists like Agassiz, foreign authors like Dickens, exemplars of self-culture like the "learned Blacksmith" Elihu Burritt, popular philosophers like Emerson, and social reformers like the abolitionist Garrison or the repentant drunkard John B. Gough.

MODEL COMMUNITIES

While many reformers hoped to make possible a better life by creating opportunities through education or by eliminating specific social evils, some of the more advanced thinkers aspired to start afresh and remake society by founding ideal, cooperative communities. America still seemed a spacious and unencumbered country where models of a perfect society could be set up with a good chance to succeed. Presumably success would lead to imitation, until communities free of crime, poverty, and other evils would cover the land. A number of religious groups, notably the Shakers, practiced a kind of socialism as a means of realizing what they considered a truly Christian life. But the impetus to communitarianism as a way of perfecting earthly society came chiefly from nonreligious, rationalistic thinkers.

Among the communitarian philosophers, three of the most influential were Robert Owen, Charles Fourier, and John Humphrey Noyes. Owen, famous for his humanitarian policies as owner of prosperous textile mills in Scotland, reached the conclusion that faulty environment was to blame for human failings, and hence that poverty and crime would not appear in a rationally planned society. In 1825 he put his principles into practice at New Harmony, on the banks of the Wabash in Indiana.

The Oneida Community
Members of the Oneida Community, in upstate New York, believed in "complex marriage," according to which all the men were considered as married to all the women. Women enjoyed the same rights as men, and the whole community took care of the children. The members looked upon all kinds of work as honorable. Here, on the lawn at Oneida, some of them are taking part in a "working bee," in which (like many other Americans of the time) they combined labor with conversation and merrymaking. (Library of Congress)

Within a few years New Harmony failed as an economic enterprise, though in other respects it was a success. Fourier, a mere commercial employee in France, never visited the United States. His theories of cooperative living, however, influenced many Americans through the writings of Albert Brisbane, whose *Social Destiny of Man* (1840) explained the principles of Fourierism with its self-sufficient associations, or "phalanxes." One or more of these phalanxes was organized in every Northern state, the most famous of them being Brook Farm, a community of intellectuals including Hawthorne, near Boston. Noyes, a native Vermonter and a former Yale divinity student, founded the most bizarre and most enduring of all the

utopian colonies, the Oneida Community in upstate New York (1848), where his followers carried out his unorthodox sexual theories, old men mating with young women and vice versa, all changing partners at his direction, supposedly in the interest of scientific breeding. Needless to say, none of these experiments set a pattern for American life.

REMEDYING SOCIAL ILLS

Less thoroughgoing reforms, however, did much to alleviate the ills of society as it actually was. No evil was more glaring than the treatment of social offenders and unfortunates.

Criminals of all kinds, debtors unable to pay their debts, senile paupers, and the mentally ill were crowded indiscriminately into prisons and jails which in many cases were literally holes, one jail in Connecticut being an abandoned mine shaft.

From the 1820s on, the states one by one abolished imprisonment for debt, and some of them greatly improved their handling of the criminal and the insane. New York, with the erection of its new prison at Auburn (1821), introduced a system of solitary confinement by night and group work with absolute silence by day; Pennsylvania tried solitary confinement for both day and night. Though both of these systems now seem harsh, they were then hailed as progressive steps, since they gave each prisoner an opportunity to meditate upon his wrongdoing and also checked the tendency for old convicts to corrupt the young. Public hangings, supposedly a deterrent to crime, used to attract spectators by the thousands, including thieves and pickpockets busily plying their trade. In the 1830s several states began to hold executions within the privacy of prison walls, and a few states did away with capital punishment entirely. While a few mental hospitals already existed, the insane (unless cared for at home) generally were kept in jail and treated brutally. The Boston schoolmistress, Dorothea Dix, shocked by her chance visit to the Cambridge jail (1841), devoted her life to securing the establishment of insane asylums in Massachusetts and other states.

In looking for causes of insanity, pauperism, and crime, many reformers concluded that these evils could be traced largely to strong drink. Americans of earlier generations had been an alcoholically convivial people, with a remarkable per capita consumption of whiskey, hard cider, and rum. The Puritans had been hard drinkers and many respectable preachers continued to resort to stimulants. Few Americans supposed that a birth, a wedding, or a funeral could be properly observed without plenty of liquor—the story is told of drunken pallbearers who lost their way to the grave. From colonial times on, however, a few men like Cotton Mather and Dr. Benjamin Rush had spoken out against intemperance.

In the early 1800s an organized temperance movement began with the formation of local societies in New England, and in 1826 the

American Society for the Promotion of Temperance appeared as a coordinating agency for the various groups. The movement gained in sensationalism when six reformed drunkards of Baltimore organized the Washington Temperance Society in 1840 and began to draw crowds to hear their intriguing confessions. As the temperance forces grew and spread over the country, the crusaders diverged, some advocating total abstinence and others seeing no harm in wine or beer; some favoring prohibition laws and others relying on the individual conscience. Massachusetts and other states experimented with legislation for local option, allowing communities to regulate or prohibit liquor sales, and Maine passed a statewide prohibition law in 1851. Prohibitionists in a few other states gained similar victories, but the laws were unpopular and soon were repealed except in Maine.

To some it seemed that not only alcoholic beverages but also tobacco, coffee, and unnatural foods hindered the full realization of man's perfectionist possibilities. A leading health faddist, Dr. Sylvester Graham, believed that one way to social happiness was through the eating of coarse, whole-wheat bread (the "Graham cracker" is a faint reminder of him). Other health reformers relied on hydropathy with its regimen of bathing and water drinking; spas like the Hot Springs in Virginia became fashionable places for taking the "water cure." Orson Fowler, the foremost exponent of phrenology (a "science" based on the notion that character and personality are revealed in the contour of the cranium), expected to bring about a "renovating of mankind" through the self-understanding that was supposed to result from the examination of bumps on the head. This science became so popular that practically everyone turned into an amateur phrenologist.

Recalling the Napoleonic Wars and the War of 1812, many reformers agreed with the Quakers that one of the worst ills of the world was war. By 1819 more than a dozen local peace societies had sprung up in various parts of the United States, and in 1828 the Maine merchant William Ladd undertook to coordinate the movement by founding the American Peace Society with headquarters in New York. Later (1840) Ladd devised a peace plan embracing a Congress of Nations and a Court of Nations whose decisions were to be enforced by public opinion rather than economic or military sanctions. Meanwhile the pacifists disagreed, some approving defensive but not offensive wars, others taking a pledge of complete nonresistance. To most of the peace workers in New England, the Mexican War (1846–1848) seemed an act of proslavery aggression on the part of the United States, and they took their stand against it, Henry David Thoreau refusing to pay taxes for its support, and James Russell Lowell writing in the *Bigelow Papers:* "Ez fer war, I call it murder,—there you hev it plain an' flat." But the Civil War put the pacifists in a dilemma, at least momentarily, since most of them were also abolitionists. Finally the antislavery cause took precedence over the antiwar cause, as it already had taken precedence over the rest of the reform crusades.

"The Drunkard's Progress"
From the first casual glass, the young man rises step by step to the summit of drunken jollification and then declines to desperation and suicide, while his wife and child mourn. This lithograph was published in 1846 by Nathaniel Currier, who later joined with James M. Ives to form the most famous American firm of lithographers. Currier and Ives turned out thousands of color prints of artwork reflecting manners, movements, and events in the days before photographs could be accurately reproduced by means of halftone engravings.
(Library of Congress)

IMPROVING WOMAN'S LOT

Whatever the social handicaps that beset man as man, those that a woman had to face in early nineteenth-century America were considerably worse. Legally she remained an inferior. According to both common and statute law, a husband still had almost absolute authority over the person and property of his wife: what was his was his, and what was hers was his also. In case of divorce he was far more likely than she to get custody of the children. Though women worked hard in household and mill, they could not look forward to careers in medicine, the ministry, politics, or law. By custom they were forbidden to speak in public to a mixed audience, lest they "unsex" themselves and lose their feminine charm. As long as women kept their expected place, men in America generally treated them with great deference—with much greater deference, foreign travelers noted, than men in Europe did.

Women, Dorothea Dix among them, took an active and often a leading part in the various reform movements, but most of the male reformers tried to confine the women to a subor-

A Social Reformer
Dorothea Dix (1802–1887) was born in Maine and brought up in Massachusetts. She taught school and wrote books for children before starting her campaign to establish public hospitals for the mentally ill (and also to make prisons less inhumane). Until she was eighty she continued to travel the United States and Europe in furtherance of this cause. (Library of Congress)

The Course of American Art
II. THE NEW REPUBLIC:
The Search for an American Style

Plate 1: STATE HOUSE, BOSTON, MASSACHUSETTS *(Photo by Sandak)*

The period immediately after the Revolution witnessed the rejection of many of the old cultural ties to England and the desire on the part of many American artists and architects to create a style expressive of the ideals and achievements of the new republic. Under the influence of Thomas Jefferson, ancient Roman architecture—monumental in size and symbolic of the concepts of justice and liberty connoted by Roman republican government— became a model for government buildings from the city to the federal level. His own design for the state capitol building of Virginia, 1789, was inspired by a Roman temple.

Not all architects, however, were ready to turn their backs on their English heritage. Charles Bulfinch was influenced by current English practice in his design for the Massachusetts State House *(Plate 1)*. The large red brick structure, with its colonnaded façade and golden dome, was designed by Bulfinch after a trip to Europe in 1785. The arcade below the columns is modeled after a house in London, and the arched windows on the second story are derived from traditional English pattern books.

The conflict between those like Jefferson who advocated a new national style based on classical precedents, and those like Bulfinch who remained under the influence of the former mother country, was also seen in the development of American painting. Since the middle of the eighteenth century colonial artists had gone to England to study their craft. Such painters as Benjamin West, John Singleton Copley, and Charles Willson Peale had traveled to London in search of a more refined technique. With the coming of independence, artists like Ralph Earle and Thomas Sully continued to make the pilgrimage. But as the nineteenth century began, a new style of painting, featuring a

Plate 2: John Vanderlyn, MARIUS AMID THE RUINS OF CARTHAGE (*The Fine Arts Museums of San Francisco; Photo by Sandak*)

revival of classical characteristics, began to gain prominence in Europe, and Paris, the center for the study of neoclassicism, attracted a number of American artists. The first American to study under the founder of neoclassicism, Jacques Louis David, was John Vanderlyn. Vanderlyn's "Marius amid the Ruins of Carthage" *(Plate 2)*, painted in 1807, was shown at the Paris Salon and was awarded a gold medal by the Emperor Napoleon. The subject, taken from Roman history, was found to have the proper didactic and allegorical qualities to meet the strict requirements of the Parisian artistic establishment; and the painting showed a masterful treatment of the careful drawing, clear color, and firm modeling which characterized the neoclassical style.

For all of Vanderlyn's European triumphs, his severe neoclassic style met with only limited success on his return to America. In architecture, however, the classical revival did dominate the scene for domestic and public buildings during the first half of the nineteenth century. By 1820 Jefferson's architectural style of republican Rome had given way to more severe Greek forms. The new generation of architects who practiced in the Greek revival style relied for inspiration on such English publications as Stuart and Revett's *Antiquities of Athens*, which contained a series of black-and-white engravings illustrating individual buildings. One of the principal architects of the style was William Strickland, who based his most important commissions on Greek precedent. Strickland's Second Bank of the United States, 1819 (see page 275), is taken directly from an engraving illustrating the Parthenon in Stuart and Revett's book. The monumental façade with porticos of Doric columns became a symbol of strength and stability, well suited to banks and governmental buildings.

In sculpture, the enthusiasm for the Greco-Roman style reached its height with the commission in 1832 for a monumental statue of George Washington to be placed in the rotunda of the United States Capitol. Horatio Greenough's conception *(Plate 3)* was that of a huge seated figure, nude to the waist and gesturing like the Olympian Zeus. Carved in Rome, the twenty-ton marble statue was brought to America for its installation in the Capitol. The monument was found to be too heavy for the foundation of its indoor setting, so it was moved outdoors to a makeshift shelter on the Mall, and fifty years later moved again to its present home, the Smithsonian Institution. The public questioned the "nakedness" of their beloved first President, but the ideals of classicism, with its basic principles of restraint, precision, and self-containment were popularly accepted and thought to be consistent with the growing spirit of self-confidence in the new nation.

In most major cities, from Boston to Baltimore, furniture making continued after the Revolution on the highest levels of skill and refinement. Inspiration was still derived largely from European sources, particularly pattern books of the English designers Hepplewhite and Sheraton. By the turn of the century, American craftsmen such as Duncan Phyfe and John Seymour had evolved from the imported models a uniquely American Federal style, and had added patriotic motifs such as eagles to traditional decorative devices. An elegant mahogany "Tall Clock" *(Plate 4)*, made in 1818, features delicate inlays of satinwood and, in the upper section above the clock face, twenty inlaid stars representing the number of states in the

Plate 3: Horatio Greenough, GEORGE WASHINGTON *(Courtesy of National Collection of Fine Arts, Smithsonian Institution)*

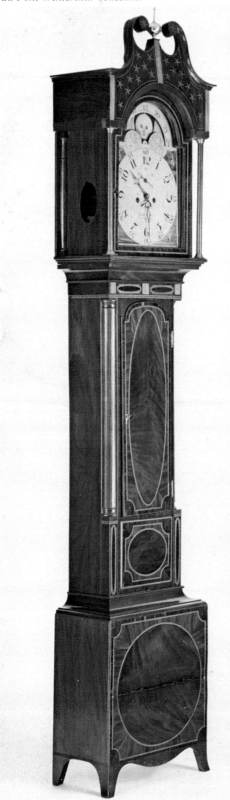

Plate 4: Anonymous, TALL CLOCK
*(Courtesy, The Henry Francis
du Pont Winterthur Museum)*

Union at the time the clock was made.

Painting too offered American artists an opportunity to express a sense of confidence in the American experiment. Samuel F. B. Morse (later to be the inventor of the telegraph), whose early training had been in Italy, painted a large canvas depicting a scene in the Old House of Representatives (now Statuary Hall) *(Plate 5)*. Completed in 1822, the painting captures a quiet and reflective moment when the chandelier has been lowered for the lighting of the lamps. A soft reddish glow pervades the majestic chamber with light flickering off the marble columns and coffered ceiling. Morse has successfully combined the grandiose proportions of the legislative hall with intimate details of the people within it.

As mid-century approached, American taste moved away from the severe classicism which had dominated the first six decades of independence, toward a romantic eclecticism — a kind of artistic escapism characterized by the borrowing of historical and exotic styles. In all the arts the tradition of patriotic sentiment persisted, but it was no longer expressed exclusively in classical forms. During this period landscape painting came of age in America. The formation of the first native American school of painting was rooted in a new awareness on the artists' part of the unlimited continent that stretched out before them. Working primarily in the mountains of New York and New England, these painters — whom later critics dubbed the "Hudson River School" — glorified the natural environment, making the wilderness a symbol of national pride.

The leader of the school was Thomas Cole, born in England but brought to America as a small child. His 1840 painting entitled "The Architect's Dream" *(Plate 6)* was, like many of his works, commissioned by a wealthy businessman. Although the subject of the "Dream" differs from Cole's usual American landscape panoramas, the artist's intention was, as always, symbolic and romantic. For the painting includes a vast vocabulary of architectural styles ranging from Egyptian to Gothic, which would serve American eclectic taste in architecture for the remainder of the century.

Another painter associated with the Hudson River School was Asher B. Durand. Beginning his career as an engraver, Durand perfected a landscape style of meticulous detail and precision. In his "Kindred Spirits" *(Plate 7),*

Plate 5: Samuel F. B. Morse, THE OLD HOUSE OF REPRESENTATIVES *(In the Collection of the Corcoran Gallery of Art)*

Plate 6: Thomas Cole, THE ARCHITECT'S DREAM *(The Toledo Museum of Art; Gift of Florence Scott Libbey)*

Plate 7: Asher B. Durand, KINDRED SPIRITS *(Collection of The New York Public Library; Astor, Lenox and Tilden Foundations)*

which he painted in 1849 as a memorial to Thomas Cole, Durand sees in the landscape both the wildness and the grandeur of nature. The two figures represent Cole and the poet William Cullen Bryant. The picturesque woodland and the mood of sentimental reverence reflect the artist's romantic tendencies.

Another landscape painted in the 1840s also evoked a mood of contemplation, but this time the setting was not the Hudson River valley but the Missouri River frontier. In George Caleb Bingham's "Fur Traders Descending the Missouri," ca. 1845 (Plate 8), the artist captures the quiet of early morning, as the two boatmen glide through the mist on the mirror-like surface of the river. Bingham communicates the quality of frontier life without resorting to anecdote or sentimentality.

The change from portraiture to landscapes as the most popular form of American painting was paralleled by an equally dramatic change in interior design and furnishings. Classical motifs, which had dominated the first half of the century, gave way to the exuberant forms of Rococo curvilinear rhythms and richly polished surfaces. An excellent example of a Rococo interior is the parlor of the Colonel Robert J. Milligan House from Saratoga, New York, 1853 (Plate 9), which is now installed in the Brooklyn Museum. Although some classical elements such as pilasters and moldings still persist, the overall appearance of the room is one of Rococo opulence. The elaborately carved marble mantelpiece and the richly upholstered chairs contribute to the lush setting.

In architecture, as in the other arts and crafts, the influence of Greece and Rome faded in the romantic wave that swept across the country. The dream of the architect in Cole's painting was fulfilled as Gothic churches, Renaissance villas, and Egyptian

Plate 8: George Caleb Bingham, FUR TRADERS DESCENDING THE MISSOURI *(The Metropolitan Museum of Art, Morris K. Jesup Fund, 1933)*

Plate 9: Anonymous, MILLIGAN HOUSE: PARLOR *(The Brooklyn Museum)*

gateways replaced classical forms. The
reliance on pattern books continued, but
many were now published in America. As the
taste for romantic styles increased, even
examples of Near Eastern designs were
included in publications. In Samuel Sloan's
The Model Architect, 1852, plate 63
represented an "Oriental Villa." This design
was chosen by a wealthy southern planter,
and under Sloan's direction "Longwood"
(Plate 10), with its Moorish arches, onion-
shaped dome, and intricate decoration began
to be built near the shores of the Mississippi
River in 1860. Unfortunately the outbreak of
the Civil War prevented completion of this
intriguing example of eclectic design, and it
remains to this day unfinished.

Plate 10: Samuel Sloan, LONGWOOD
*(The Mississippi Department of Archives
and History)*

Equal Rights for Women [1848]

After declaring that "all men and women are created equal" and listing the "injuries and usurpations on the part of man toward woman," the Seneca Falls women's rights convention adopted a series of resolutions for constructive action, among them the following:

Resolved, *That the same amount of virtue, delicacy, and refinement of behavior that is required of woman in the social state, should also be required of man, and the same transgressions should be visited with equal severity on both man and woman.*

Resolved, *That the objection of indelicacy and impropriety, which is so often brought against women when she addresses a public audience, comes with a very ill grace from those who encourage, by their attendance, her appearance on the stage, in the concert, or in feats of the circus.*

Resolved, *That it is the duty of the women of this country to secure to themselves their sacred right to the elective franchise.*

Resolved, *That the equality of human rights results necessarily from the fact of the identity of the race in capabilities and responsibilities.*

Resolved, *That the speedy success of our cause depends upon the zealous and untiring efforts of both men and women, for the overthrow of the monopoly of the pulpit, and for the securing to women an equal participation in the various trades, professions, and commerce.*

---

dinate role, though some husbands gave them every encouragement, a few even going so far as to omit the word "obey" from the wedding ceremony. When, in 1840, a world antislavery convention met in London, the men in charge refused to allow women delegates to participate. One of the rejected American delegates was Lucretia Mott, the happily married wife of a Massachusetts sea captain and eventually the mother of six children. Another was Elizabeth Cady Stanton, an abolitionist's wife, who had set out to prove herself the equal of any man after her father, on the death of his only son, had said to her: "Oh, my daughter, I wish you were a boy." The rebuff in London helped to convince Mrs. Mott and Mrs. Stanton that their first duty, as reformers, was to raise the status of women. Finally they called a women's rights convention, which met in Seneca Falls, New York, in 1848. This convention adopted resolutions (patterned on the Declaration of Independence) to the effect that all men *and women* are created equal and endowed with certain inalienable rights.

While the feminists failed to obtain the right to vote or hold office, they made noticeable gains before the Civil War. As early as 1839, Mississippi had recognized the right of married women to control their own property, and during the next two decades several other states did the same. Meanwhile a number of women from well-to-do and well-educated families, in addition to Mrs. Mott and Mrs. Stanton, broke the barriers that had kept women from professional and public careers. For example, Dr. Elizabeth Blackwell, born in England, gained acceptance and fame as a physician. Her sister-in-law Antoinette Brown Blackwell became the first ordained woman minister (Congregational and Unitarian) in the United States. Another sister-in-law, Lucy Stone, who was determined to "call no man master," kept her maiden name with her husband's approval. A graduate of Oberlin College, where she was not allowed to take part in public speaking, she rose to be one of the country's most popular and successful lecturers. Emma Willard, founder of the Troy Female Seminary (1821), and Catharine Beecher, founder of the Hartford Female Seminary (1823), made great contributions to progressive education, especially for girls.

For a time, in the 1850s, many of the feminists adopted a distinctive style of dress, a skirt

The Bloomer Costume

*An enterprising Philadelphia music
publisher, taking advantage of a timely
topic, brought out "The New Costume Polka"
and dedicated it to Mrs. "Lydia" (it should
have been "Amelia") Bloomer. The cover of
the sheet music was adorned with this picture
of a demure young lady wearing the clothes
that in the 1850s Mrs. Bloomer recommended
as a means of giving women greater freedom.
The clothes came to be known as "bloomers."
(Library of Congress)*

and pantalettes combination that allowed freedom of movement without loss of modesty. This
outfit, introduced by the famous actress Fanny
Kemble, came to be called the "bloomer" costume after one of its advocates, Mrs. Amelia
Bloomer, a postmistress and newspaper editor
in upstate New York. It provoked so much controversy that Mrs. Bloomer and other women's
rights leaders concluded it was distracting attention from their more important aims and
decided to give it up.

The Antislavery Crusade

Mid-nineteenth-century Americans would have
had some justification for boasting of their
democratic society if they could have ignored
the Negro—the freeman as well as the slave.
But they could not ignore him. Reformers
black and white would not let them.

THE NEGRO IN THE NORTH

In the 1850s there were more than 4 million
black Americans, of whom about 95 percent
were confined to the South. That left nearly a
quarter of a million of them living in the North.
These people were concentrated mainly in the
cities, about 22,000 in Philadelphia and about
12,000 in New York. Many were fugitives from
slavery.

In some respects the free Negroes of the
North were little if any better off than the free
Negroes or even the slaves of the South. An
English traveler, who was acquainted with the
treatment of the black man in both sections,
reported in 1854 that he was "utterly at a loss to
imagine the source of that prejudice which
subsists against him in the Northern states, a
prejudice unknown in the South, where the
relations between the African and the European [white American] are so much more intimate." This confirmed an earlier observation
of Tocqueville's: "the prejudice which repels
the Negroes seems to increase in proportion as
they are emancipated."

Certainly the Northern Negro faced severe
handicaps in even managing to exist. He had
little or no political influence: he could vote
only in New England (not including Connecticut), and in New York only if he owned a certain amount of property, which was not required of white voters. In most places he was
excluded from the public schools that whites
attended. He faced the constant danger of being attacked by white mobs or kidnapped by
slave dealers and sold, or resold, into slavery.

Usually he had no choice but to take a low-paying job as a domestic servant or unskilled laborer. Seafaring offered him one of his best opportunities; in the 1850s, when the American merchant marine was at its height, nearly half of the sailors in it were blacks. The typical city Negro lived in squalor in a segregated neighborhood. He was eleven times as likely as a white man to be jailed on a charge of theft, robbery, or other crime.

Despite the almost hopeless odds, a number of Northern Negroes managed to succeed in business or the professions. James Forten, for example, started out as an errand boy around the Philadelphia docks, became a sailmaker, and accumulated a small fortune. The Negroes of New York City, as early as 1837, owned $1.4 million worth of taxable real estate and had $600,000 on deposit in savings banks. But what most distinguished the free Negroes of the North from those of the South (some of whom also acquired property) was the opportunity to speak out, to protest the plight of black people both free and slave, and to try and do something about it.

In the early 1800s a Massachusetts free Negro, Paul Cuffe, tried to begin a back-to-Africa movement so as to give his people a new life in their ancestral homeland. Cuffe had spent $4,000 on the project, without success, when he died in 1817. That same year a group of prominent white Virginians organized the American Colonization Society to "colonize" freed slaves in Africa. Some Northern Negroes feared this was a scheme to get rid of them, and James Forten called a mass meeting of Philadelphia blacks to object to it. Many well-meaning Northern whites favored it as a step toward emancipation; they thought it would encourage slaveowners to free at least some of their slaves. The American Colonization Society received private contributions and appropriations from Congress and the Virginia and Maryland legislatures to carry on the work. Though shipping out of the country fewer Negroes in a decade than were being born in it each month, the society succeeded in founding and governing on the west coast of Africa the colony of Liberia, which it converted into an independent black republic in 1846.

Meanwhile, in Massachusetts, a new note of black militancy had been struck. David Walker, born free in North Carolina, made his living by selling second-hand clothes in Boston. There, in 1829, he published a pamphlet entitled *Walker's Appeal . . . to the Colored Citizens*. In it he declared: "America is more our country than it is the whites'—we have enriched it with our *blood and tears*." He warned: "The whites want slaves, and want us for their slaves, but some of them will curse the day they ever saw us." He ridiculed the "Christian" pretensions of the slaveholders and urged slaves to cut their masters' throats. "Kill, or be killed!"

A number of other black critics of slavery, most of them less bitterly outspoken than Walker, appeared in the North. The greatest of all—and one of the most electrifying orators of his time, black or white—was Frederick Douglass. Born a slave in Maryland, Douglass ran off to

Black Leader
The most prominent American Negro of the pre-Civil War era, and indeed of the nineteenth century, was Frederick Douglass. He was born in Maryland, of an unknown white father and a slave mother. In 1838 he escaped from slavery and went to the Northeast. There he shortly became a leader in the abolitionist movement, appearing on the lecture platform, editing a newspaper, the North Star, and publishing his autobiography, Narrative of the Life of Frederick Douglass *(1845). Douglass demanded not only emancipation for his race but also social and economic equality.*
(United Press International)

The Liberator: First Issue [1831]

William Lloyd Garrison made clear his fiery spirit and his uncompromising aim in the very first number of his abolitionist newspaper, *The Liberator*. He told his readers:

I am aware that many object to the severity of my language; but is there not cause for severity? I will be as harsh as truth, and as uncompromising as justice. On this subject, I do not wish to think, or speak, or write with moderation. No! No! Tell a man whose house is on fire, to give a moderate alarm; tell him to moderately rescue his wife from the hands of the ravisher; tell the mother to gradually extricate her babe from the fire into which it has fallen;—but urge me not to use moderation in a cause like the present. I am in earnest—I will not equivocate—I will not excuse—I will not retreat a single inch—AND I WILL BE HEARD.

Massachusetts in 1838, made a name for himself as an antislavery leader, and lectured for two years in England, where he was lionized. (More than a dozen other black abolitionists also visited the British Isles and made a strong impression there.) After returning to the United States in 1847, Douglass purchased his freedom from his Maryland owner and founded an antislavery newspaper, the *North Star*, in Rochester, New York.

As early as 1830, black abolitionists had held their first national convention. They were ready to cooperate with white reformers when some of these launched an agressive antislavery movement.

THE WHITE ABOLITIONISTS

During the 1820s the most active white crusader against slavery was the New Jersey Quaker Benjamin Lundy, who published the leading antislavery newspaper of the time, the *Genius of Universal Emancipation*, in Baltimore. Lundy used moderate language and advocated a mild and gradual program.

In 1831 his helper, the young Massachusetts-born printer William Lloyd Garrison, sounded a much more strident note when he presented the first issue of his own weekly, *The Liberator*, in Boston. From the outset Garrison condemned the thought of gradual, compensated emancipation and demanded immediate abolition, without reimbursement for slaveholders. He denounced the American Colonization Society as no emancipationist agency

but the reverse, a group whose real aim was to strengthen slavery by ridding the country of Negroes already free. He got support from free Negroes, who bought most of the subscriptions to *The Liberator*. Despite his strong language, he was no advocate of slave rebellions, and he criticized *Walker's Appeal* as a "most injudicious publication."

Under the leadership of Garrison the New England Antislavery Society was founded in 1832 and the American Antislavery Society the following year. But he shocked many friends of freedom, including Frederick Douglass, by the extremes to which he went. He opposed the government, characterizing the Constitution as "a covenant with death and an agreement with hell," and he opposed the churches on the grounds that they were bulwarks of slavery. In 1840 he split the American Antislavery Society by insisting upon the right of women to participate fully in its activities, even to speak before audiences that included men as well as women.

By that time there were in existence nearly 2,000 local societies with a total of almost 200,000 members. These societies remained alive, active, and growing after the disruption of the national organization.

Another outstanding leader, busy in New York and the Northwest, was Theodore Weld. Converted to reform by Charles G. Finney's preaching, Weld worked within the churches, especially the Presbyterian and Congregational. He married Angelina Grimké, a South Carolina planter's daughter who, with a sister, had turned against slavery. With the aid of his wife, Weld compiled an overwhelming factual indictment of the institution in the book *American Slavery As It Is: Testimony of a Thousand Witnesses* (1839).

But the most powerful of all abolitionist propaganda was a work of fiction, Harriet Beecher Stowe's novel *Uncle Tom's Cabin.* This first appeared as a serial in an antislavery weekly (1851–1852). It was then published as a book, which sold more than 300,000 copies in the year of its publication and was later reissued again and again, to become one of the most remarkable best sellers in American publishing history. Dramatized in various versions, and presented by countless theatrical companies throughout the North, the story brought its emotional message to many thousands besides those who read it. Mrs. Stowe belonged to a famous New England ministerial family (her father and seven brothers were preachers). While living in Cincinnati she had made several excursions into Kentucky to view slavery and plantation life. In her novel she intended no personal attack upon Southern whites, and she made the worst of her villains a New England native, Simon Legree. Her aim was to show the brutalizing effect that slavery had upon all who were connected with it.

Through *Uncle Tom's Cabin* and other antislavery writings and speeches, a great many Northerners who never joined an abolitionist society came to disapprove strongly of slavery. Hence it is hard to say how many antislavery people there were at any given time, especially since "antislavery" was a term broad enough to include all kinds and degrees of opposition.

THE CAMPAIGN FOR LIBERATION

Most of the active members of organized societies were "abolitionists" in the sense that they favored immediate abolition. But this did not mean precisely what it seemed to mean. The abolitionists aimed at what they called "immediate abolition gradually accomplished." That is, they hoped to bring about a sudden and not a gradual end to slavery, but they did not expect to achieve this for some time. At first, they counted on "moral suasion": they were going to appeal to the conscience of the slaveholder and convince him that slaveholding was a sin. Later they turned more and more to political action, seeking to induce the Northern states

and the federal government to aid the cause where possible. They helped runaway slaves find refuge in the North or in Canada, though in doing so they did not set up any such highly organized system as the term "Underground Railroad" implies. After the Supreme Court (in *Prigg* v. *Pennsylvania,* 1842) held that the states need not aid in enforcing the federal fugitive slave law of 1793, abolitionists secured the passage of "personal liberty laws" in several of the Northern states. These laws forbade state officials to assist in the capture and return of runaways. Above all, the antislavery societies petitioned Congress to abolish slavery in places where the federal government had jurisdiction—in the territories and the District of Columbia—and to prohibit the interstate slave trade. Only a very few of the abolitionists supposed that Congress constitutionally could interfere with a "domestic" institution like slavery within the Southern states themselves.

While the abolitionists engaged in pressure politics, they never formed a political party with an abolition platform. In 1840 the Liberty party was launched, with the Kentucky antislavery leader James G. Birney as its presidential candidate, but this party and its successors did not campaign for outright abolition: they stood for "free soil," that is, for keeping slavery out of the territories. Some free-soilers were friends of the slave; others were Negrophobes who cared nothing about slavery but desired to make the West a white man's country. Garrison said free-soil-ism was really "white-man-ism."

The real friends of the Negro were quite aware that, to be consistent, they would have to help the free as well as the enslaved, since so-called freedom was "but an empty name—but the debasing mockery of true freedom." Garison assured his "free colored brethren" that the attainment of equal rights for them was "a leading object." He and other abolitionists did try to open new opportunities for them. They had little success in appealing to employers to hire additional Negroes and give them training as apprentices. But the reformers made other rather modest gains. They established schools for Negroes (by 1837 there were a hundred young white women teaching black children in Ohio) and even colleges (Wilberforce in Ohio, Avery in Pennsylvania). They opened Oberlin College to black students. They brought about the desegregation of all Massachusetts public schools in 1855, six years after Charles Sumner had argued in a Boston lawsuit (as opponents of segregation elsewhere were to do a century later) that, no matter how good the facilities provided for Negro pupils, "the separate school is not an equivalent." The reformers also secured the repeal of Massachusetts and Ohio laws requiring separate Negro cars on railroads.

The abolitionists might have accomplished more reforms in the North if it had not been for the widespread anti-Negro if not proslavery feeling there. Prejudice was reinforced by the desire of many Northern businessmen to keep on good terms with Southern customers or suppliers, and by the fear on the part of wage-earning Northern whites that Negroes, if freed and given equal opportunities, would be dangerous competitors for jobs. The antislavery movement provoked much hostility in the North, especially during the early years. When Prudence Crandall undertook to admit Negro girls to her private school in Connecticut, local citizens had her arrested and threw filth into her well, forcing her to close the school. A mob burned the Philadelphia abolitionists' "temple of liberty" and started a bloody race riot (1834). Another mob seized Garrison on the streets of Boston and threatened to hang him, and a member of still another group shot and killed the antislavery editor Elijah Lovejoy in Alton, Illinois (1837). Throughout the North antislavery lecturers, risking their health if not their lives, time and again were attacked with rotten eggs or stones.

In the South the reaction was far stronger, and if no abolitionists were killed there, it was only because (from the 1830s on) very few of them dared even venture into that part of the country.

The Southern Way of Life

Of the three great sections of the country, the South was the one that possessed the highest degree of cultural unity, the one that presented the strongest appearance of solidarity to the outside world. The South (defined as the area of the slave states) was an entity even though within its vast expanse it exhibited immense differences in climate, soil, and people—more perhaps than were to be found in any other region.

ELEMENTS OF SOUTHERNISM

The qualities that gave the South its distinctive flavor are not easy to define. Generally, the climate is warm and mild; on the lower Gulf coast, it is subtropical. The growing seasons are longer than in the North, varying from six months in the upper South to nine months in the Gulf states. The economy, predominantly agricultural, was characterized by the presence of the large plantation as well as the small farm. Farming was largely commercial, concentrating on producing certain staple crops—cotton, tobacco, sugar, and rice—for sale to outside areas. Unlike the West, the South disposed of the bulk of its products in England and Europe rather than the domestic market; it felt closer economic ties with England than with the Northeast. The South was a rural land, with fewer cities, towns, and villages than there were in the Northern states, and its population was more diffused (about thirteen persons per square mile in 1860 as compared with twenty in the North). The great majority of the Southern white people were Anglo-Saxon in origin and in cultural ideals and Protestant in religion.

The South was the only area in the United States (indeed in all the Western world except for Brazil and Cuba) where slavery still existed. It was the only section that contained vast numbers of a race other than white. Southerners might differ among themselves on political and economic questions, but by the 1850s they had closed ranks on the issue of race. They were determined to keep the South a white man's country, and they viewed slavery as the best means to that end. Thus slavery was more than a labor system. It was also a white-supremacy device, and as such it finally enlisted the support of the Southern white masses, including the great majority who did not own slaves. Race consciousness, then, helped to account for the oneness of the South.

An ever mounting condemnation of slavery came not only from the Northern states but also from the Latin American countries that had outlawed it, and from Great Britain, whose government had abolished it throughout the British Empire in 1833. The South was an area of Western civilization—not a nation but a section of a nation (and in point of population a minority section)—that cherished an institution at variance with the culture of the civilization of which it was a part.

Thoughtful Southerners realized that slavery isolated them from most of the rest of mankind. Said William Harper of South Carolina: "The judgment is made up. We can have no hearing before the tribunal of the civilized world. Yet, on this very account, it is more important that we, the inhabitants of the slaveholding States, insulated as we are by this institution, and cut off, in some degree, from the communion and sympathies of the world by which we are surrounded, . . . and exposed continually to their animadversions and attacks, should thoroughly understand this subject, and our strength and weakness in relation to it."

Was slavery profitable? On the whole, the planters themselves believed they were making very satisfactory profits. At the same time there can be no doubt that the slave system, or rather the economic system of which slavery was a part, retarded Southern development and posed some grave problems for the section. Because of the concentration on agriculture, the South had to purchase its finished goods from the outside. Thoughtful Southerners realized the economic subordination of their region. "From the rattle with which the nurse tickles the ear of the child born in the South to the shroud that covers the cold form of the dead, everything comes to us from the North," exclaimed Albert Pike. Said a writer in *De Bow's Review:* "I think it would be safe to estimate the amount which is lost to us annually by our vassalage to the North at $100,000,000. Great God!" The antebellum South had a colonial economy.

The white Southerners' sense of being exploited by the North, together with their race consciousness and their minority status in the nation and in the world, intensified their feeling of sectional unity.

GRADATIONS OF WHITE SOCIETY

Only a minority of Southern whites owned slaves. In 1850, when the total white population of the South was over 6 million, the number of slaveholders was 347,525. In 1860, when the white population was just above 8 million (the slave population was 3,950,513), the number of slaveholders had risen to only 383,637. These figures, taken in themselves, give a somewhat misleading impression. Each slaveholder was normally the head of a family averaging five members. To arrive at the number of whites having a proprietary interest in slavery, it is necessary to multiply by five the number of slaveholders. This formula shows 1,737,625 whites connected with slave ownership in 1850, and 1,937,625 in 1860. Broadly speaking, one family in four owned slaves. Of the minority of whites holding slaves, only a small proportion owned substantial numbers.

At the apex of society stood the large planters—the cotton magnates and the sugar, rice, and tobacco nabobs—who owned at least forty or fifty slaves and 800 or more acres. Next came the small and medium planters, with ten to forty slaves apiece. Farmers with from one to nine slaves outranked those more numerous farmers who owned none at all.

The total number of planters—large, medium, and small—was 92,257 in 1850. The large planters represented the social ideal of the South. Enriched by vast annual incomes, dwelling in palatial homes, surrounded by broad acres and many black servants, they were the class to which all others paid a certain deference. Enabled by their wealth to practice the leisured arts, they cultivated gracious living, good manners, learning, and politics. Their social pattern determined to a considerable degree the tone of all Southern society.

The Southern planters constituted the closest approach to an aristocracy to be found in the United States. They enjoyed in their section a higher social position, a greater political power, a more unquestioned leadership than did the factory owners of the Northeast.

Class distinctions were more sharply drawn in the South than in other sections. Some Southerners spoke scornfully of democracy. Yet, particularly in the newer states, an ambitious person could move from one class to another. Farmers nursed the hope of becoming small slaveholders, and small planters aimed to

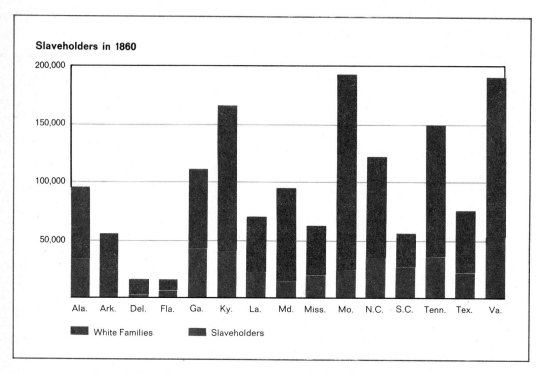

Slaveholders in 1860

The proportion of slaveholding families in relation to the total white families tended to be higher in the cotton states of the Deep South than in the border states. For example, the number of slaveholders in Georgia and Kentucky was approximately the same, yet in Georgia they constituted almost half of the white population while in Kentucky they represented less than one-third.

become large ones. Many achieved their goal. In fact, the great majority of the cotton lords of the Mississippi Valley states had come from the ranks of the obscure and the ordinary. Planters who wished to exercise political influence, whether or not they believed in majority rule, had to affect democratic manners and mouth principles that would please the multitudes.

The farmers, those who owned a few slaves and the greater number who owned none, lived lives of rude plenty, devoting more attention to subsistence farming than did the planters. Most of them owned their land. During the 1850s the number of nonslaveholding landowners increased much faster than the number of slaveholding landowners.

In Southern society the business classes— the manufacturers and merchants—were of considerable importance, though comparatively few. Flour milling and textile and iron manu-

facturing were the main Southern industries, with the principal mill areas being located in Virginia, the Carolinas, and Georgia. The Tredegar Iron Works in Richmond compared favorably with the best iron mills in the Northeast. The value of Southern textile goods increased from $1.5 million in 1840 to $4.5 million in 1860. Despite some promising beginnings, however, Southern industry before 1860 remained largely in a formative stage. Most Southerners showed a distaste for industrialism, and those with surplus capital usually preferred to invest it in slaves and land.

More important than the budding manufacturers were the merchants, particularly the brokers or factors who marketed the planters' crops. These individuals, in towns like New Orleans, Charleston, Mobile, and Savannah, acted as selling agents for the planters, and sometimes also as purchasing agents. Frequently the broker became a banker to the planter, furnishing money or goods on credit. In such cases the planter might be in debt to his factor for a long period, during which time he would have to consign his entire crop to the broker. The merchant-broker, dominating as he did the credit facilities of the rural South, was in a position to exert great economic pressure on the planter.

Closely linked economically with the planters were the professional classes—lawyers, editors, doctors, and others. Because their well-being largely depended on planter prosperity, the professional groups usually agreed with and voiced the ideals of the dominant class.

In the Southern mountains—the Appalachian ranges east of the Mississippi and the Ozarks west of the river—lived the Southern highlanders, the white groups set most apart from the mainstream of Southern life. These mountaineers practiced a crude form of subsistence agriculture, with practically no slaves. They had a proud sense of seclusion, and they held to old ways and old ideals, which included the ideal of loyalty to the nation as a whole. The mountain region was the only part of the South that defied the trend toward sectional conformity.

Occupying the lowest position in Southern white society was that tragic and degraded class known as the poor whites, who in 1850 totaled perhaps half a million. The poor whites were distinct from the ordinary farmers and from the highlanders. The "crackers," "sand hillers," or "white trash" occupied the infertile lands of the pine barrens, the red hills, and the swamps. Here they lived in miserable cabins surrounded by almost unbelievable squalor. Their degradation resulted partly from dietary deficiencies and disease. Afflicted by pellagra, hookworm, and malaria, the poor whites resorted to eating clay, a practice which in itself indicated a serious shortcoming in their diet.

KING COTTON

The Southern agricultural system was organized around the great staples: tobacco, rice, sugar, and above all cotton. These were the section's money crops, but they did not constitute by any means its only forms of agricultural effort. What might be termed general or diversified farming was carried on in many areas, notably in the Shenandoah Valley of Virginia and the Bluegrass region of central Kentucky. Most planters aimed to produce on the plantation the foodstuffs needed by the family and the slaves. On some large plantations, more acres were planted in corn than in cotton, and in 1850 half the corn crop of the country was raised in the South. The section produced 87 percent of the nation's hemp supply (in Kentucky and Missouri) and 80 percent of its peas and beans. Other important products of Southern husbandry were apples, peaches, peanuts, sweet potatoes, hogs, and mules. Despite the planters' efforts to achieve self-sufficiency, they could not supply all the needs of their slaves, and large amounts of corn and pork had to be imported annually from the Northwest.

But the staples dominated the economic life of the section and absorbed the attention of the majority of the people. Climatic and geographical conditions dictated the areas where each was produced. Tobacco, which needed only a fairly short growing season (six months), was grown in tidewater Maryland west of the Chesapeake, in piedmont Virginia and adjacent North Carolina, in northern and western Kentucky, in northwestern Tennessee, and in the Missouri River Valley of Missouri. Rice demanded a growing season of nine months and irrigation, and hence was restricted to the coastal region of South Carolina and Georgia. Sugar, with a similar period necessary for maturation, was concentrated in southern Louisiana and a small area in eastern Texas (around Galveston). Cotton, which required a growing season of seven to nine months and could be produced in a variety of soil formations, occupied the largest zone of production. The Cotton Kingdom stretched from North Carolina to Texas.

From the sale of the great staples, the South derived its chief sources of revenue. Into the markets of the world in the 1850s the section poured annually over 400,000 pounds of tobacco, over 360,000 hogsheads of sugar, and over 240,000 pounds of rice. But the big money crop was cotton. From 1 million bales in 1830, Southern production of cotton steadily increased until it reached 4 million bales in 1860. In that year Southern cotton brought $191 million in the European markets and constituted

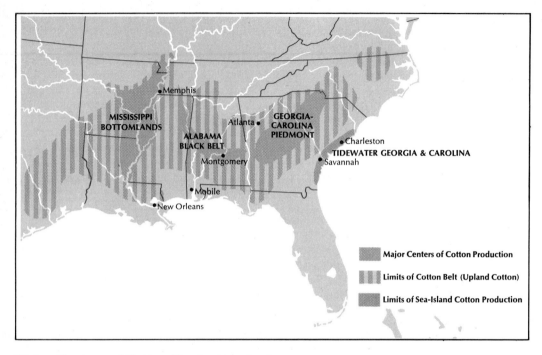

Major Centers of Cotton Production in the Antebellum South

Legend:
- Major Centers of Cotton Production
- Limits of Cotton Belt (Upland Cotton)
- Limits of Sea-Island Cotton Production

almost two-thirds of the total export trade of the United States. (By way of contrast, the annual value of the rice crop was $2 million.) No wonder that Southerners said smugly, "Cotton is King."

As cotton culture expanded, the centers of production moved westward into the fresher lands of Alabama, Mississippi, Arkansas, Louisiana, and Texas. The extension of the Cotton Kingdom into this area bore certain resemblances to the rush of gold seekers into a new frontier. The prospect of tremendous profits quickly drew settlers by the thousands. Some who came were wealthy planters from the older states who transferred their assets and slaves to a cotton plantation. Most were small slaveholders or slaveless farmers who intended to become planters.

A similar shift occurred in slave population. The number of slaves in Alabama leaped from 41,000 in 1820 to 435,000 in 1860, and in Mississippi from 32,000 to 436,000. In the same period in Virginia, the increase was only from 425,000 to 490,000. It has been estimated that between 1840 and 1860, 410,000 slaves were moved from the upper South to the cotton states.

Like the farmers of the Northwest, those of the South employed methods that exhausted the soil. They gave little attention to crop rotation, the use of fertilizers, or deep plowing. Like other Americans, they considered it easier to migrate to new lands than to restore old ones. Still, there were agricultural societies and journals in the South, as in the other sections, and there were dedicated individuals who labored to improve farm techniques. Such a man was the famous Edmund Ruffin of Virginia, advocate of fertilization, rotation, and deep plowing. The author of a work on calcareous manures and the founder of the excellent *Farmers' Register*, Ruffin was one of the best agricultural experts in the country during the 1850s. Through his efforts and those of others, some progress in checking soil depletion was made in the older states.

THE MIND OF THE SOUTH

Most Southerners took their literary cues from English or New York sources. Though the planters bought books in large numbers, they usually chose the works of English and Northern writers, almost ignoring the authors of their own section. They showed the same lack of appreciation for Southern magazines. Of the one hundred magazines founded in the South, only nine survived for any length of time. And of the nine, only three attained much vogue: the excellent literary journals, *The Southern Literary Messenger* (Richmond, 1834–1864) and *The Southern Quarterly Review* (New Orleans and Charleston, 1842–1857), and the magazine of Southern commercial and agricultural expansion, *De Bow's Review* (New Orleans, 1846–1880). Even these periodicals had to take second place to Northern productions. In that hotbed of Southern sentiment, Charleston, *De Bow's Review* sold an average of 173 copies, while *Harper's Magazine* was regularly purchased by 1,500 Carolinians.

Considering the bleak reception accorded local authors, it is surprising that the section contained as many fine writers as it did. In the 1830s most of the outstanding authors had been from the Virginia-Maryland area: Nathaniel Beverly Tucker *(The Partisan Leader)*, William Alexander Caruthers *(The Cavaliers of Virginia)*, and John Pendleton Kennedy *(Swallow Barn* and *Horseshoe Robinson)*. They were novelists who wrote historical romances or romantic eulogies of the plantation system in the upper South. After 1840 the Southern literary capital shifted to Charleston. Here lived and wrote the antebellum South's most distinguished man of letters, William Gilmore Simms. Primarily a novelist, although he composed some tolerable poetry, Simms wrote over thirty works of fiction, some of them novels (such as *The Yemassee)* glorifying Charleston and South Carolina, others historical romances of the Revolution. He had a rare talent for earthy description of common folk, and his better work compares favorably with that of James Fenimore Cooper. Other Charlestonians were Hugh Swinton Legaré, perhaps the best linguist in America and authority on the history of law, and the young poets Henry Timrod and Paul Hamilton Hayne, who would achieve their chief renown after the Civil War.

Producing works more distinctively American were the writers of the Southern frontier. These men depicted the society of the backwoods rural areas; they described ordinary people and poor whites instead of aristocratic cavaliers; they were deliberately and sometimes painfully realistic; and they seasoned their sketches with a robust, vulgar humor that was something new in American literature. The leading frontier writer was Augustus B. Longstreet of Georgia *(Georgia Scenes)*. Others who wrote in the same vein were Joseph G. Baldwin *(Flush Times of Alabama and Mississippi)* and Johnson J. Hooper *(Some Adventures of Captain Simon Suggs)*. Together, these Southern realists established a tradition of humor that was uniquely American and that was ultimately to find a supreme exponent in Mark Twain.

It has been said (by H. C. Nixon) that in the South there were more people who could read Latin and fewer who could read English than in any other part of the country. The educational system of the section reflected the aristocratic ideals of the plantation regime. In 1860 there were 260 Southern colleges and universities, public and private, with 25,000 students enrolled in them, or more than half the total number of students in the United States. The South had twice as many students per 1,000 of white population in college as any other section. The lower South had 11,000 students in its institutions of higher learning, while New England, with approximately the same population, could boast of only 3,748. Below the college level, the schools of the South were not only fewer but also inferior to those of the East, but about as good as those of the West. Libraries where an enterprising individual might educate himself also were fewer in the South. In Louisiana there were only one hundred books to each 1,218 white people, while in Massachusetts there were one hundred to each 118 persons. The South had over 500,000 white illiterates, or more than half of the country's total.

In the fields of belles-lettres and science, the South was primarily a section of consumers rather than producers. The section did not produce a literature or a body of scientific findings to compare with those of the Northeast. Among the reasons for the relative backwardness of the South was the rural character of the region. There were few cities, and not one like

New York or Boston that could act as a focal point of culture, and there were few publishing facilities. The high illiteracy rate among white adults decreased the potential reading audience. In the simple nature of Southern society there were few complexities to intrigue the writer and impel him to find an explanation. The planters, the class that might have patronized a Southern literature, considered oratory and statesmanship to be much more significant activities. At a time when writing was becoming a recognized and respected profession in the North, Southern authors, as so many of them bitterly testified, were regarded as amusing fellows who had little to offer their society.

Furthermore, after 1830 much of the creative energy of the South was channeled into the defense of slavery. Under criticism from the outside, the section felt a compulsion to glorify its image of itself and to enforce conformity to that image. Freedom of thought, which was largely accepted in the North and which Jefferson and other former Southern leaders had said was necessary in a good society, was stifled in the South.

The "Peculiar Institution"

When slaveowners referred to the "peculiar institution" of the South, they did not mean to imply that slavery was somehow odd or queer. Rather, they indicated their belief that it was special and distinctive.

THE REGIMEN OF SLAVERY

Slavery was an institution established by law and regulated in detail by law. The slave codes of the Southern states forbade a slave to hold property, to leave his master's premises without permission, to be out after dark, to congregate with other slaves except at church, to carry firearms, to strike a white man even in self-defense. The codes prohibited teaching a slave to read or write, and denied the right of a slave to testify in court against a white person. They contained no provisions to legalize slave marriages or divorces. Any person showing a strain of African ancestry was presumed to be a slave unless he could prove otherwise. If an owner killed a slave while punishing him, the act was not considered a crime.

These and dozens of other restrictions and impositions indicate that the slaves lived under a harsh and dismal regime, which would have been unrelieved had the laws been drastically enforced. In fact, they were applied unevenly. Sometimes slaves did acquire property, were taught to read and write, and assembled with other slaves, the laws to the contrary notwithstanding. Most slave offenses were tried by the master, who might inflict punishments ranging from some mild disciplinary action to flogging or branding for running away. Major offenses, including crimes, were generally referred to the courts. Slaves faced the death penalty for the following offenses: killing or even resisting a white person and inciting to revolt or even participating in what was suspected to be an insurrectionary plot.

The routine of plantation life was governed by a system of rules created by custom and the planters. A small planter directly supervised the work on his place. A medium or large planter hired an overseer and perhaps an assistant overseer to represent him. The "head driver," a trusted and responsible slave, acted under

Slave Scenes
Photographs of slaves at work or performing any function are almost impossible to obtain. But during the Civil War and after it photographs of Negroes on plantations were taken, and these often reproduce the conditions of labor and life under slavery. Thus the picture of the cotton pickers (top right) is postwar, but the harvesting techniques were the same as those used before the war. The other picture (bottom right) shows Negro, or slave, quarters on a South Carolina plantation. (Courtesy of the New-York Historical Society, New York City)

the overseer as a kind of foreman. Under him might be several subdrivers. Two methods or systems of assigning slave labor were employed. One was the task system, most widely used in rice culture. Here a slave was allotted a particular task in the morning, say to hoe one acre; when he completed his job he was free for the rest of the day. The other was the gang system, employed on the cotton, sugar, and tobacco plantations. Here the slaves were simply divided into groups, each of which was directed by a driver, and were worked for as many hours as the overseer considered a reasonable work day.

Slaves were provided with at least enough necessities to enable them to live and work. They were furnished with an adequate if rough diet, consisting mainly of corn meal, salt pork, and molasses. Many were allowed to raise gardens for their own use and were issued fresh meats on special occasions. They received issues of cheap clothes and shoes. They lived in rude cabins, called the slave quarters. Medical care was provided by the plantation mistress or a doctor retained by the owner. The slave worked hard, beginning with light tasks as a child, and his workday was longest at harvest time. He sometimes had time off to hunt and fish, and he attended the church services and some of the social festivities of his white family.

The master had an economic interest in taking reasonably good care of his slaves. He was likely to use hired labor, when available, for the most unhealthful or dangerous tasks. A traveler in Louisiana noted, for example, that Irishmen were employed to clear malarial swamps and to handle cotton bales at the bottom of chutes extending from the river bluff down to a boat landing. If an Irishman died of disease or was killed in an accident, the master could hire another for a dollar a day or less. But he would be out perhaps a thousand dollars or more if he lost a prime field hand. Still, a cruel master might forget his pocketbook in the heat of momentary anger. And slaves were often left to the discipline of an overseer, who had no pecuniary stake in their well-being; he was paid in proportion to the amount of work he could get out of them.

Household servants had a somewhat easier life than did field hands. On a small plantation the same persons might serve in both capacities, but on a large one there would be a separate staff of nursemaids, housemaids, cooks, butlers, coachmen, and the like. These people lived close to the master and his family, eating the leftovers from the family table, and in some cases even sleeping in the "big house." Between the blacks and whites of such a household, there might develop an affectionate, almost familial relationship.

Slavery in the cities differed significantly from slavery in the country. On the more or less isolated plantation the slaves were kept apart from free Negroes and lower-class whites. The master, his family, and his overseers maintained a fairly direct and effective control. A deep and unbridgeable chasm yawned between slavery and freedom. In the city, however, the master often could not supervise his slaves closely and at the same time use them profitably. Even if they slept at night in carefully watched backyard barracks, they went about by day on errands of various kinds. Others were hired out, and after hours they fended for themselves, neither the owner nor the employer caring to look after them. Thus the urban slaves gained numerous opportunities to mingle with free Negroes and with whites, including fair-complexioned prostitutes. A line between slavery and freedom remained, but it became less and less distinct.

Indeed, slavery was basically incompatible with city life, and as Southern cities grew, the number of slaves in them dropped, relatively if not absolutely. The reasons were social rather than economic. Fearing conspiracies and insurrections, urban slaveowners sold off much of their male property to the countryside. The cities were left with an excess of Negro women while continuing to have an excess of white men (a circumstance that helped to account for the birth of many mulattoes). While slavery in the cities declined, segregation of Negroes both free and slave increased. Segregation was a means of social control intended to make up for the loosening of the discipline of slavery itself.

The transfer of slaves from one part of the South to another (when the slaves were not carried by their migrating owners) was accomplished through the medium of professional slave traders. In long-distance traffic the slaves were moved on trains or on river or ocean steamers. Or they were moved on foot, trudging in coffles of hundreds along the dusty highways. Eventually they arrived at some central market like Natchez, New Orleans, Mobile, or Galveston, where purchasers collected to bid for them. At the auction the bidders checked the slaves like livestock, watching them as they were made to walk or trot, inspecting their teeth, feeling their arms and legs, looking for signs of infirmity or age. It paid to be careful, for traders were known to deceive buyers by blacking gray hair, oiling withered skin, and concealing physical defects in other ways. A sound young field hand would fetch a price that, during the 1840s and 1850s, varied from $500 to $1,700, depending mainly on fluctuations in the price of cotton. The average figure was about $800. A good-looking "fancy girl," desirable as a concubine, might bring several times that much.

The domestic slave trade, while essential to the growth and prosperity of the whole system, was one of the least defensible aspects of it. Not only did the trade dehumanize all who were involved in it; it also separated children from parents, and parents from one another. Even in the case of a kindly master who had kept families together, they might be broken up in the division of his estate after his death. Planters condoned the trade and eased their consciences by holding the traders in contempt and assigning them a low social position—except those who invested their profits in plantations (like Nathan Bedford Forrest, a slave trader and then a planter and eventually a war hero of the Confederacy).

The foreign slave trade was as bad or worse. Though federal law had prohibited the importation of slaves from 1808 on, they continued to be smuggled in as late as the 1850s. The numbers can only be guessed at. They were not large enough to satisfy all planters, and the Southern commercial conventions, which met annually to consider means of making the South economically independent, began to discuss the legal reopening of the trade. "If it is right to buy slaves in Virginia and carry them to New Orleans," William L. Yancey of Alabama asked his fellow delegates at the 1858 meeting, "why is it not right to buy them in Cuba, Brazil, or Africa and carry them there?" The convention that year voted to recommend the repeal of all laws against slave imports. Only the delegates from the states of the upper South, which profited from the domestic trade, opposed the opening of foreign competition.

THE SLAVE'S RESPONSE

Slaves reacted to slavery in a variety of ways. Some, especially among favored domestic servants, identified with the master and accepted their subservient position with little difficulty, perhaps with real contentment. Others learned to adjust to necessity by acting out, in the white man's presence, the expected role of shuffling, grinning, head-scratching deference. Still others could never quite bring themselves to either acceptance or accommodation. They harbored an unquenchable spirit of rebelliousness, and from the frustration it brought them they sometimes developed personality disorders (signs of these were seen in newspaper advertisements for runaways who were described as having a stutter or other behavioral quirks).

For the vast majority, there was no way out of their predicament. A few were allowed to earn money with which they managed to buy their own and their families' freedom. Some had the good luck to be set free by their master's will after his death—like the more than 400 slaves belonging to John Randolph of Roanoke (1833). From the 1830s on, however, state laws made it more and more difficult, and in some cases practically impossible, for an owner to manumit his slaves. The laws, when permitting manumission, often required the removal of the freed slaves from the state. The masters objected to the very presence of free Negroes, who by their existence set a disturbing example for the slaves.

By 1860 there nevertheless were about 250,000 free Negroes in the slaveholding states, more than half of them in Virginia and Maryland. A few, as in the North, attained wealth and prominence. A few themselves owned slaves, usually relatives whom they had bought in order to assure their ultimate emancipation. Most lived in abject poverty, even worse than in the North. Law or custom closed many occupations to them, forbade them to assemble without white supervision, and placed numerous other restraints upon them. They were only quasi-free, and yet they had all the burdens of freedom, including the obligation of paying taxes.

Great as were the hardships of freedom, Negroes generally preferred them to the hardships of slavery. Occasionally slaves sought freedom through flight. They might succeed in hiding out for a time, but the chance of escaping to the North or to Canada was exceedingly slim except for those who lived fairly close to the free-state border and who got help from free Negroes and friendly whites on the so-called Underground Railroad. For fugitives from the deep South, the hazards of distance and geographical ignorance, of white patrols and bloodhounds, were hard if not impossible to overcome, especially since every Negro at large was presumed to be a runaway slave unless he carried documentary proof to the contrary.

The discontented slave could express his feelings through individual acts of resistance. He might be deliberately careless with his master's property, losing or breaking tools, setting fire to houses or barns. He might make himself useless by cutting off his fingers or even committing suicide. Or, despite the terrible consequences, he might turn upon the master and kill him.

The idea of combining with other blacks, rising up, and overthrowing the masters occurred to slaves and free Negroes from time to time. In 1800 Gabriel Prosser gathered a thousand rebellious slaves outside of Richmond, but two blacks gave the plot away, and the Virginia militia were called out in time to head it off. Gabriel and thirty-five others were executed. In 1822 the Charleston free Negro Denmark Vesey and his followers—rumored to total 9,000—made preparations for revolt, but again

the word leaked out and retribution followed. In 1831 Nat Turner, a slave preacher, led a band of Negroes who armed themselves with guns and axes and, on a summer night, went from house to house in Southampton County, Virginia. They slaughtered sixty white men, women, and children before being overpowered by state and federal troops. More than a hundred Negroes were put to death in the aftermath. Nat Turner's was the only actual slave insurrection in the nineteenth-century South, but slave conspiracies and threats of renewed violence continued throughout the section as long as slavery lasted.

THE PROSLAVERY REACTION

By the 1830s slavery was being threatened from three directions—from the slaves themselves, from Northern abolitionists, and from Southern slaveless farmers. There were still antislavery societies in the South, and as late as 1827 there had been a larger number than in the North. They were most numerous in the border slave states, where a few antislavery men, notably Cassius M. Clay of Kentucky, kept up their campaign through the 1850s. Between 1829 and 1832 a Virginia constitutional convention and then the state legislature, responding to demands from nonslaveholders in the western part of the state, seriously considered ending slavery through compensated emancipation but were discouraged by the tremendous expense it would have required.

Calhoun on Slavery [1837]

I hold that in the present state of civilization, where two races of different origin, and distinguished by color, and other physical differences, as well as intellectual, are brought together, the relation now existing in the slaveholding States between the two is, instead of an evil, a good—a positive good. I feel myself called upon to speak freely upon the subject where the honor and interests of those I represent are involved. I hold then, that there never has yet existed a wealthy and civilized society in which one portion of the community did not, in point of fact, live on the labor of the other. . . . I may say with truth that in few countries so much is left to the share of the laborer, and so little exacted from him, or where there is more kind attention paid to him in sickness or infirmities of age. Compare his condition with the tenants of the poor houses in the more civilized portions of Europe— look at the sick and the old and infirm slave, on one hand, in the midst of his family and friends, under the kind superintending care of his master and mistress, and compare it with the forlorn and wretched condition of the pauper in the poor house.

The Slave's Response to Slavery

For many years after its publication in 1918, Ulrich B. Phillips' *American Negro Slavery* was accepted as the standard authority on the subject. A Georgian by birth and upbringing, Phillips assumed (as defenders of slavery had done before the Civil War) that the typical plantation Negro was lazy, childlike, irresponsible, contented, and submissive – all because of his African racial make-up. "The wrench from Africa and the subjection to the new discipline had little more effect upon his temperament than upon his complexion." Phillips believed, however, that the American Negro kept little if any of his African cultural inheritance (his native customs, language, and the like, as distinct from his "temperament"). On this point, even black scholars long felt compelled to agree. As late as 1939 the black sociologist E. Franklin Frazier wrote: "Probably never before in history has a people been so nearly stripped of its social heritage as the Negroes who were brought to America."

Eventually strong dissenters appeared. In *The Myth of the Negro Past* (1941) the white anthropologist Melville J. Herskovits emphasized the number of "Africanisms" that survived through slavery times and after. In *American Negro Slave Revolts* (1943) the Marxist historian Herbert Aptheker claimed to have discovered "approximately two hundred and fifty revolts and conspiracies in the history of American Negro slavery" besides countless "individual acts of resistance." Aptheker concluded that "discontent and rebelliousness were not only exceedingly common, but, indeed, characteristic of American Negro slaves." In *The Peculiar Institution* (1956) Kenneth M. Stampp viewed the black slaves as "ordinary human beings" who reacted to slavery in a variety of ways, much as white people would have done in the same circumstances.

Then, in 1959, Stanley M. Elkins provoked continuing controversy with his *Slavery: A Problem in American Institutional and Intellectual Life.* Elkins agreed with Phillips that the typical slave had a "Sambo" personality but accounted for it on a quite different basis. According to Elkins, it was due to the psychological shock of enslavement and the enforced "adjustment to absolute power" in the hands of the master. The result was infantilism, much like the effect that a Nazi concentration camp had upon many of its inmates. In the process the slaves lost the tribal or cultural identity that might have helped them to maintain their personal independence. Slave rebels, such as Denmark Vesey and Nat Turner, stand out because they were, in Elkins' words, "so exceptional" and "so few."

The black historian John Blassingame agreed with Herskovits and completely disagreed with Elkins. "The most remarkable aspect of the whole process of enslavement," Blassingame declared in *The Slave Community* (1973), "is the extent to which the American-born slaves were able to retain their ancestors' culture." According to Blassingame, they retained it largely through the slave family, which, even though it had no legal basis, served as an "important survival mechanism" and enabled its members to "cooperate with other blacks" and maintain their self-esteem.

On the basis of an elaborate quantitative study, Robert W. Fogel and Stanley L. Engerman concluded, in *Time on the Cross: The Economics of American Negro Slavery* (1974), that planters themselves, out of self-interest, encouraged stable family relationships among the slaves. These authors also found the slaves to have been typically not lazy, inefficient "Sambo" types, but very productive workers, many of them skilled.

Meanwhile the news of the Turner insurrection terrified whites in Virginia and all over the South. They had always been uneasy, always mindful of the horrors of the successful slave uprising in Santo Domingo (in the 1790s). Now they were reminded of their insecurity, and they were especially horrified because there had been long-trusted house servants among Nat's followers who, axe in hand, had suddenly confronted their masters' sleeping families. Who among the blacks could the whites really depend upon? Many of the master class now blamed Garrison and the abolitionists for the slaves' defection. Planters were determined to make slavery secure against all dangers.

While the Southern states strengthened their slave codes, controlling the movement of slaves and prohibiting their being taught to read, Southern leaders proceeded to elaborate an intellectual defense of slavery. In 1832 Professor Thomas R. Dew of the College of William and Mary published a pamphlet outlining the slavery case. In subsequent years many others added their contributions to the cause, and in 1852 the defense was summed up in an anthology, The Pro-Slavery Argument.

As early as 1837 John C. Calhoun boasted that Southerners had ceased to apologize for slavery as a necessary evil and had been convinced that it was "a good — a positive good." According to the proslavery argument it was good for the slave because he was an inferior creature who needed the master's guidance and who was better off — better fed, clothed, and housed, and more secure — than the Northern factory worker. It was good for Southern society because it was the only way two races so different as the black and the white could live together in peace. It was good for the nation as a whole because the entire Southern economy depended on it, and the prosperity of the nation depended on the prosperity of the South. It was good in itself because the Bible sanctioned it — did not the Hebrews of the Old Testament own bondsmen, and did not the New Testament apostle Paul advise, "Servants, obey your masters"? These and other arguments convinced most Southerners, even those (the great majority) who owned no slaves and had no direct interest in the peculiar institution.

Some proslavery propagandists concluded that slavery was such a good thing it should be extended to include white workers in the North as well as black laborers in the South. In *Sociology for the South, or the Failure of Free Society* (1854) George Fitzhugh, of Virginia, praised slavery as the only workable form of socialism and urged the whole world to adopt it, at once, as the sole cure for class conflict and the other ills of competitive society.

While spreading proslavery propaganda, Southern leaders tried to silence the advocates of freedom. Southern critics of slavery found it healthful to leave home, among them Hinton Rowan Helper of North Carolina, whose *Impending Crisis of the South* (1857) contended that slavery hurt the welfare of the nonslaveholder and made the whole region backward. In 1835 a mob destroyed sacks containing abolition literature in the Charleston post office, and thereafter Southern postmasters generally refused to deliver antislavery mail. Southern state legislatures passed resolutions demanding that Northern states suppress the "incendiary" agitation of the abolitionists. In Congress, Southern representatives with the cooperation of Northerners secured the adoption of the "gag rule" (1836) according to which antislavery petitions were automatically laid on the table without being read.

As a champion of freedom of speech and petition, John Quincy Adams led a struggle against the gag rule, finally (1844) securing its repeal. Throughout the North many people who were not abolitionists began to feel that civil liberties were endangered in the entire country, not just the South. These people were inclined to sympathize with the abolitionist as a martyr for freedom in the broadest sense. They came to suspect that there really existed, as the abolitionist claimed, a kind of "Slave Power Conspiracy" to destroy the liberties of the country as a whole. They began to wonder, as Abraham Lincoln did, whether the nation could long continue to be half slave and half free — whether the nation might not become all slave. Thus the majority of Northerners, though not necessarily for love of the Negro, eventually came to sympathize in varying degrees with the antislavery cause, while an even larger and more determined majority of Southerners rallied to the defense of the peculiar institution, thereby laying the foundation for a "solid South."

Selected Readings

The Reform Spirit
A. M. Schlesinger, *The American as Reformer* (1950);
W. R. Cross, *The Burned-Over District** (1950); A. A.
Ekirch, *The Idea of Progress in America, 1815–1860*
(1944); C. C. Cole, Jr., *The Social Ideals of the North-
ern Evangelists, 1826–1860* (1954); T. L. Smith, *Reviv-
alism and Social Reform in Mid-Nineteenth-Century
America* (1957); C. S. Griffin, *Their Brothers' Keepers:
Moral Stewardship in the United States, 1800–1865*
(1960).

Miscellaneous Reforms
A. F. Tyler, *Freedom's Ferment: Phases of American
Social History to 1860** (1940); M. E. Curti, *The American Peace Crusade* (1929); Paul Monroe, *The Found-
ing of the American Public School System* (1949); Arthur Bestor, *Backwoods Utopias: The Sectarian and
Owenite Phases of Communitarian Socialism in
America, 1663–1829** (1950); M. L. Carden, *Oneida:
Utopian Community to Modern Corporation* (1971);
Carl Bode, *The American Lyceum* (1956); N. K. Tee-
ters and J. D. Shearer, *The Prison at Philadelphia*
(1957); J. D. Davies, *Phrenology: Fad and Science*
(1955); H. S. Commager, *Theodore Parker, Yankee
Crusader** (1936); H. E. Marshall, *Dorothea Dix, For-
gotten Samaritan* (1937); Otelia Cromwell, *Lucretia
Mott* (1958); F. O. Gatell, *John Gorham Palfrey and the
New England Conscience* (1963); I. H. Bartlett, *Wen-
dell Phillips, Brahmin Rebel* (1961); R. V. Harlow,
Gerrit Smith, Philanthropist and Reformer (1939).

The Negro in the North
L. F. Litwack, *North of Slavery: The Negro in the Free
States, 1790–1860* (1961); Benjamin Quarles, *Black
Abolitionists* (1969); William Stanton, *The Leopard's
Spots: Scientific Attitudes Toward Race in America,
1815–59* (1960); E. J. McManus, *Black Bondage in
the North* (1973).

The Antislavery Movement
Louis Filler, *The Crusade Against Slavery, 1830–
1860** (1960); F. L. Dumond, *Antislavery: The Crusade for Freedom in America* (1961); G. H. Barnes,
The Antislavery Impulse, 1833–1844* (1933); D. B.
Davis, *The Problem of Slavery in Western Culture**
(1966); Bertram Wyatt-Brown, *Lewis Tappan and the
Evangelical War Against Slavery* (1969); Martin
Duberman, ed., *The Antislavery Vanguard* (1965);
Larry Gara, *The Liberty Line: The Legend of the Un-
derground Railroad* (1961); R. B. Nye, *Fettered Free-
dom: Civil Liberties and the Slavery Controversy,
1830–1860* (1949) and *William Lloyd Garrison and the
Humanitarian Reformers** (1955); W. M. Merrill,
*Against Wind and Tide: A Biography of Wm. Lloyd
Garrison* (1963); J. L. Thomas, *The Liberator: Wil-
liam Lloyd Garrison* (1963); A. S. Kraditor, *Means

and Ends in American Abolitionism: Garrison and
His Critics on Strategy and Tactics, 1834–1850* (1969);
B. P. Thomas, *Theodore Weld, Crusader for Freedom*
(1950); M. L. Dillon, *Benjamin Lundy and the Struggle
for Negro Freedom* (1966); Betty Fladeland, *James
Gillespie Birney: Slaveholder to Abolitionist* (1955)
and *Men and Brothers: Anglo-American Antislavery
Cooperation* (1972); D. L. Smiley, *Lion of White Hall:
The Life of Cassius M. Clay* (1962); Benjamin
Quarles, *Black Abolitionists* (1969); L. L. Richards,
*"Gentlemen of Property and Standing": Anti-Aboli-
tion Mobs in Jacksonian America* (1971).

The Southern Economy
L. C. Gray, *History of Agriculture in the Southern
United States to 1860* (2 vols., 1933); U. B. Phillips,
Life and Labor in the Old South* (1929); F. L. Olm-
sted, *The Cotton Kingdom*, ed. by A. M. Schlesinger
(1953); R. R. Russel, *Economic Aspects of Southern
Sectionalism, 1840–1861* (1924); F. L. Owsley, *Plain
Folk of the Old South** (1949).

Southern Thought
Clement Eaton, *Freedom of Thought in the Old South**
(1940), *The Growth of Southern Civilization, 1790–
1860** (1961), and *The Mind of the Old South** (1964);
W. J. Cash, *The Mind of the South** (1941); W. R. Taylor, *Cavalier and Yankee: The Old South and American National Character** (1961); J. H. Franklin, *The
Militant South* (1956); R. G. Osterweis, *Romanticism
and Nationalism in the Old South** (1949); J. B. Hub-
bell, *The South in American Literature, 1607–1900*
(1954); Frank Freidel, *Francis Lieber* (1947); Harvey
Wish, *George Fitzhugh, Propagandist of the Old South*
(1943); W. S. Jenkins, *Pro-Slavery Thought in the Old
South* (1935).

Slavery
U. B. Phillips, *American Negro Slavery** (1918); K. M.
Stampp, *The Peculiar Institution: Slavery in the
Ante-Bellum South** (1956); S. M. Elkins, *Slavery: A
Problem in American Institutional and Intellectual
Life** (1959); E. D. Genovese, *The Political Economy
of Slavery** (1965); R. C. Wade, *Slavery in the Cities**
(1964); Frederic Bancroft, *Slave-Trading in the Old
South* (1931); W. K. Scarborough, *The Overseer: Plan-
tation Management in the Old South* (1966); W. D.
Jordan, *White over Black* (1969); R. S. Starobin, *Industrial Slavery in the Old South* (1970); C. N. Degler,
*Neither Black nor White: Slavery and Race Relations
in Brazil and the United States* (1971); J. W. Blassingame, *The Slave Community: Plantation Life in the
Antebellum South* (1973); G. P. Rawick, *From Sundown to Sunup: The Making of the Black Community**
(1973).

*Titles available in paperback.

Fruits of Manifest Destiny

Thirteen

In the time of James K. Polk the egalitarian spirit of Jacksonian Democracy broadened into a nationalistic demand for military conquest. Expansionism seemed a corollary of egalitarianism to Democratic party intellectuals who rationalized the demand. Conquest was "Manifest Destiny," a phrase coined by a party journalist who, in 1845, prophesied "the fulfillment of our manifest destiny to overspread the continent allotted by Providence for the free development of our yearly multiplying millions." In other words, the United States had a divine mission to take the whole of North America, by force if necessary, and thus make room for its own rapidly growing people while carrying the blessings of democracy to less favored peoples who happened to occupy attractive lands nearby.

Not all Americans of the time agreed with that view. Many, especially among the Whigs, believed their country had a mission to encourage the American brand of democracy and civilization throughout the continent and, indeed, the entire world—but only by peaceful means. "I have always wished," said Daniel Webster, for one, "that this country should exhibit to the nations of the earth the example of a great, rich, and powerful republic which is not possessed by a spirit of aggrandizement."

Even the forceful expansionists were not motivated merely by the grandiose notion of Manifest Destiny. They usually had fairly specific goals in mind. Polk himself focused his attention on the two great natural harbor areas of the Pacific Coast: Puget Sound and San Francisco Bay. Nor did the expansionists press their conquests to include the entire North American continent. During the expansionist flurry of the 1840s and 1850s the United States attained essentially the size and shape that it still has (so far as the forty-eight contiguous states are concerned). It might have

Migrants Crossing the Missouri
The Mormon Trail and one branch of the Oregon Trail crossed the Missouri River between Council Bluffs, Iowa, and Omaha, Nebraska, a town that a ferry company laid out in 1854. Here westward migrants with their covered wagons are being ferried over. From an illustration in James Linforth's Route from Liverpool to the Great Salt Lake Valley *(1855). (Library of Congress)*

341

added other territories—including overseas possessions such as Cuba and the Hawaiian Islands—if the expansionists had remained sufficiently united in their aims. But they came to be divided on the question of slavery in the new acquisitions.

Expansion arose from nationalism and ultimately was to strengthen it. But the immediate result was to endanger national unity, for expansion provoked and intensified sectional conflict. And because of this conflict the acquisition of an overseas empire was to be postponed for half a century.

The Tyler Administration

The fruition of Manifest Destiny was not to come until after the election of 1844 had brought the Democrats back into power. Meanwhile, the Whigs found themselves divided and frustrated despite their overwhelming victory in the "log cabin" campaign of 1840, which had brought into office their appealing ticket of "Tippecanoe and Tyler too."

"Old Tippecanoe," William Henry Harrison, was never to have a chance to demonstrate what sort of President he would have made. Though he seemed to be in good health, he was sixty-eight years old in 1841, and the strain of the campaign and the inauguration and the pressing demands of his office-seeking supporters were apparently too much for him. He contracted a cold which turned into pneumonia, and he died on April 4, 1841, exactly one month after he had been inaugurated—the first President to die in office. In his brief presidential tenure he had looked for advice to the accepted leaders of the party, particularly to Clay and Webster. Webster became secretary of state, and four of Clay's friends went into the cabinet. Clay and Webster had expected to guide the old soldier through the political jungle, but now Tippecanoe was dead. "Tyler too," a practicing politician and a Southern Whig, was in the White House.

FRUSTRATION OF THE WHIGS

Vice President John Tyler, though some contended he was merely the second officer acting as the first, immediately assumed the title as well as the powers of the presidency. For the time being, he kept Harrison's cabinet. A member of an aristocratic Virginia family, Tyler had left the Democratic party in protest

against Jackson's overly equalitarian program and imperious methods. One reason the Whigs had put him on the ticket with Harrison was the hope that he would attract the votes of similar conservative former Democrats. Nevertheless, Clay apparently had the impression that the new President would support a national bank and other Whig projects, but Tyler soon broke with Clay.

A part of Clay's program was enacted without causing serious division in the party. With near unanimity the Whigs passed a measure, which Tyler signed, abolishing the Independent Treasury system. They also agreed on a bill, the Tariff of 1842, which raised the rates to approximately the same level as in 1832. Tyler accepted this bill, too, but with no great show of enthusiasm.

Part of the Whig legislative program made a bid for the approval of Western settlers and farmers. The frontier was continuing its steady expansion. Arkansas became a state in 1836, Michigan in 1837, and Florida in 1845. The greatest rush of settlers was into the future states of Wisconsin, Iowa, and Minnesota. To attract Western voters the Whig leadership put through the Preemption Act of 1841, which made it possible for a man to claim 160 acres of land before they were offered publicly for sale and to pay for them later at $1.25 an acre. This "log cabin bill" was hailed by the Whigs as a relief measure for sufferers from the depression and as a proof of their party's devotion to the welfare of the common man.

The Whig leadership was committed to restoring a financial system similar to the Bank of the United States. But Tyler desired a kind of "state-rights national bank," one that would confine its operations to the District of Columbia and establish branches in the states only with their consent. He twice vetoed bills for setting up what the Whigs tried to disguise as a "Fiscal Corporation."

Lacking a sufficient majority to override the veto, the Whigs fumed with rage at the President, who added to their anger by vetoing a number of internal improvement bills. In an unprecedented action, a conference of congressional Whigs read Tyler out of the party. All the cabinet members resigned except Webster, who had some diplomatic business with Great Britain that he wished to settle. To fill their places, the President appointed five men of his own stripe — former Democrats.

A portentous new political alignment was taking shape. Tyler and a small band of conservative Southern Whigs who followed him were getting ready to rejoin the Democrats. When the office of secretary of state became vacant in 1844, Tyler appointed John C. Calhoun — who had left the Democratic party in the 1830s and had since rejoined it. Into the common man's party of Jackson and Van Buren came a group of men who had aristocratic ideas about government, who thought that government had an obligation to protect and even expand the institution of slavery, and who believed in state rights with a single-minded, almost fanatical devotion.

WEBSTER'S DIPLOMACY

Starting in the late 1830s a series of incidents brought Great Britain and the United States close to actual war. In 1837 rebellion broke out in the eastern provinces of Canada, and many Americans applauded the rebels and furnished them with material aid. The rebels chartered a small American steamship, the *Caroline*, to carry supplies across the Niagara River from New York. One night while the ship was moored at a wharf on the American side, the Canadian authorities sent over a force that took possession of the *Caroline* and burned her; in the melee one American was killed. Excitement flared on both sides of the border. President Van Buren issued a proclamation asking Americans to abide by the neutrality laws, and he sent General Winfield Scott to the border to act as a pacifier. The State Department demanded an apology and reparations from Great Britain, but the British government neither disavowed the attack nor offered compensation for it.

While the *Caroline* affair simmered, the troublesome issue of the Maine boundary came up. As defined by the Treaty of 1783, this line was impossible to locate. Previous attempts to fix it by mutual agreement and by arbitration had failed. In 1838 Americans and Canadians, mostly lumberjacks, began to move into the Aroostook River region in the disputed area. A head-smashing brawl between the two parties — the "Aroostook War" — threatened more trouble between England and America.

Soon a Canadian named Alexander McLeod was arrested in New York and charged with the murder of the American who had died in the *Caroline* incident. The British government reacted with majestic rage, contending that McLeod could not be accused of murder because he had acted under official orders. The foreign secretary, the bellicose Lord Palmerston, demanded McLeod's release and threatened that his execution would bring "immediate and frightful" war. Webster as secretary of state did not think McLeod was worth a war but could do nothing to release him. The prisoner was under New York jurisdiction and had to be tried in the state courts, a peculiarity of American jurisprudence that the British did not seem to understand. Fortunately for the cause of peace — and for himself — McLeod was able to establish an alibi and was acquitted.

Festering points of disagreement still remained. In an attempt to stamp out the African slave trade, Great Britain was asking for the right to search American merchant ships suspected of carrying black cargoes. Since the American government, sensitive on the matter of search, had always refused the British request, slavers of other nations frequently sought to avoid capture by hoisting the American flag. Complicating the issue was the domestic slave trade, in which slaves were carried by sea from one American port to another. Sometimes the ships in this trade were blown off their course to the British West Indies, where the authorities, acting under English law, freed the slaves. In 1841 an American brig, the *Creole*, sailed from Virginia for New Orleans with over a hundred slaves aboard. En route the slaves mutinied, took possession of the ship, and took it to the Bahamas. Here British officials declared the bondsmen free. Although

Webster protested, England refused to return the slaves. Many Americans, especially Southerners, were infuriated.

At this critical juncture a new government came to power in Great Britain, one that was more disposed to conciliate the United States and to settle the outstanding differences between the two countries. The new ministry sent to America an emissary, Lord Ashburton, to negotiate an agreement on the Maine boundary and other matters. Ashburton liked Americans, and Webster admired the English. To avoid war, both were willing to compromise. The result of their deliberations was the Webster-Ashburton Treaty of August 9, 1842.

By the terms of this arrangement, the United States received about seven-twelfths of the disputed area, which was about as much as it could expect. Minor rectifications in the boundary were made in the Lake Champlain area and from Lake Superior to the Lake of the Woods. The boundary was now established as far west as the Rocky Mountains. Other issues disposed of were the extradition of criminals and the slave trade. Seven crimes were listed for which the United States and Canada would extradite accused citizens of the other country. It was agreed that both Great Britain and the United States would maintain naval squadrons off the African coast, the American ships being charged with chasing slavers using the American flag.

Through exchanges of notes that were not part of the treaty, Webster and Ashburton also eased the memory of the *Caroline* and *Creole* affairs. Ashburton expressed "regret" for the raid on the *Caroline*, and he pledged that in the future there would be no "officious interference" with American ships forced by "violence or accident" to enter British ports—presumably meaning there would be no repetition of the *Creole* episode.

Webster used secret funds to inspire newspaper propaganda favorable to his arrangements with Ashburton, and the treaty proved quite popular. War talk was forgotten for a time, as Anglo-American relations suddenly looked better than they had for many years.

During the Tyler administration the United States established diplomatic relations with China. In 1842 Britain forced China to open certain ports to foreign trade. Eager to share the new privileges, American mercantile interests persuaded Tyler and Congress to send a commissioner to China to negotiate a trade treaty. Webster wrote the instructions for the first commissioner, Caleb Cushing. In the Treaty of Wanghia, concluded in 1844, Cushing secured most-favored-nation provisions giving Americans the same privileges as Englishmen. He also persuaded the Chinese to grant Americans the right of extraterritoriality—the right, if accused of crimes, to be tried by American officials rather than by Chinese judges. In the next ten years American trade with China steadily increased.

Polk and Expansion

During the James K. Polk administration (1845–1849) over a million square miles of new territory came under American control, and the western boundary of the United States advanced from the Louisiana Purchase line to the Pacific Ocean. Well might the ordinary-looking little man from Tennessee feel proud of his work. No other President except Jefferson had acquired so much for his country.

ELECTION OF 1844

In 1844 Henry Clay expected to be the Whig candidate, and Van Buren the Democratic nominee. Both wanted to avoid taking a stand on the annexation of Texas, because a stand, no matter on which side, was certain to lose some votes. Consequently, they issued separate statements, so similar in tone as to indicate

Manifest Destiny [1845]

The phrase "manifest destiny" was put into circulation by a Jacksonian journalist, John L. O'Sullivan (1813–1895), writing in the *Democratic Review,* of New York, in July 1845, and again in the New York *Morning News* in December of the same year. The essence of his idea is suggested by the following passages from his *Morning News* editorial:

Texas has been absorbed into the Union in the inevitable fulfillment of the general law which is rolling our population westward; the connexion of which with that ratio of growth in population which is destined within a hundred years to swell our numbers to the enormous population of two hundred and fifty millions (if not more), is too evident to leave us in doubt of the manifest design of Providence in regard to the occupation of this continent. . . .

A population will soon be in actual occupation of California, over which it will be idle for Mexico to dream of dominion. They will necessarily become independent. All this without agency of our government, without responsibility of our people—in the natural flow of events, the spontaneous working of principles, and the adaptation of the tendencies and wants of the human race to the elemental circumstances in the midst of which they find themselves placed.

---

previous consultation between the authors. They both favored annexation, but only with the consent of Mexico. Since this consent was most unlikely to be forthcoming, the statements had little or no meaning.

Clay's action did not harm his candidacy. The Whig convention nominated him unanimously, although the platform discreetly omitted any reference to Texas. But Van Buren had destroyed his chances with the Democrats, particularly with those from the South, who were enraged by his equivocal stand on annexation. The Democratic convention threw him aside, and nominated James K. Polk, a champion of expansion. The platform caught the prevailing mood in its key resolution: "that the re-occupation of Oregon and the re-annexation of Texas at the earliest practicable period are great American measures." The words "re-occupation" and "re-annexation" were intended to imply that, in taking Oregon and Texas, the United States would only be confirming its claim to territories that had already belonged to it. By combining Oregon and Texas, the Democrats hoped to appeal to both Northern and Southern expansionists.

Too late Clay realized that he had muffed the expansion issue. In mid-campaign he announced that under certain circumstances he might be for the acquisition of Texas. His tardy straddling probably cost him more votes than it gained. Polk carried the election by 170 electoral votes to 105, though his popular majority was less than 40,000. The Liberty party, running James G. Birney a second time, polled 62,000 votes (as compared with 7,000 in 1840), most of which were cast by Whigs who turned against Clay.

"Who is James K. Polk?" the Whigs had sarcastically asked during the campaign. Actually, he was not so obscure as all that. Born in North Carolina, he had moved, when in his mid-twenties, to Tennessee, thus following the pattern of the man who became his political mentor, Andrew Jackson. Elected to the national House of Representatives, he held his seat for fourteen consecutive years, serving for four of them as Speaker. He was thin, worn, even grim-looking, and his public manners comported with his appearance. But he had a good mind, he worked hard at his job, and above all he had an iron, implacable will. Probably no other President entered office with so clearly defined a program and accomplished so much of it as did Polk.

PARTITIONING OF OREGON

The ownership of Oregon was long in dispute, but its boundaries were clearly defined—on the north the latitude line of 54° 40′, on the east the crest of the Rocky Mountains, on the south the 42nd parallel, and on the west the Pacific Ocean. Included in its half-million square miles were the present states of Oregon, Washington, and Idaho, parts of Montana and Wyoming, and half of British Columbia.

At various times in the past the Oregon country had been claimed by Spain, Russia, France, England, and the United States. By the 1820s only the last two nations remained in contention. The others had withdrawn and surrendered their rights to Britain or to the United States or to both. The American and British claims were equally valid—or invalid. Both countries could assert title on the basis of the activities of their explorers, maritime traders, and fur traders. The English had one solid advantage: they were in actual possession of a part of the area. In 1821 the powerful British fur trading organization, the Hudson's Bay Company, under the leadership of its factor, John McLoughlin, established a post at Fort Vancouver, north of the Columbia River.

Several times the English government proposed the Columbia as a suitable line of division. The United States, also showing a desire to compromise, countered by suggesting the 49th parallel. This difference in official views prevented a settlement of the Oregon question in the Treaty of 1818. Unable to agree on a demarcation line, the diplomats of the two powers negotiated a compact whereby the citizens of each were to have equal access to Oregon for ten years. This arrangement, called joint occupation, was renewed in 1827 for an indefinite period, with either nation empowered to end it on a year's notice.

The first real American interest in Oregon came as a result of the activities of missionaries, notably Jason Lee, Marcus Whitman, and Father Pierre Jean de Smet. All the missionaries located their posts east or south of the Columbia River, mostly in the fertile Willamette Valley. They described their work in reports and letters that were published in influential religious journals and widely reprinted in secular newspapers. These reports dwelt as much on the rich soil and lovely climate of Oregon as on the spiritual condition of the Indians.

Beginning in 1841, thousands of pioneers set out for Oregon. Amazed observers remarked upon the "Oregon fever." Two thousand miles in length, the Oregon Trail penetrat-

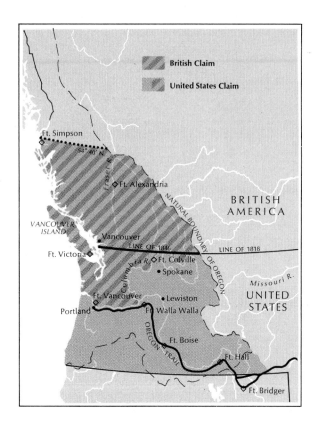

British Claim

United States Claim

American Expansion in Oregon

ed Indian country and crossed mountains and semidesert regions. To the emigrants, traveling in caravans of covered wagons and accompanied by huge herds of cattle, it presented enormous problems in transportation. The average period required for the journey was from May to November. Some never lived to complete it. But the great majority got through. By 1845, 5,000 Americans were living south of the Columbia—and demanding that their government take possession of Oregon.

When Polk assumed office, though in his inaugural address he seemed to reassert American title to all of Oregon, he was in reality willing to compromise—to effect a division on the line of the 49th parallel. The British minister in Washington rejected Polk's offer without referring it to London.

Abruptly Polk took a more militant attitude. Saying America should look John Bull "straight in the eye" and hinting at war, he asserted claim to all of Oregon. In his annual message to Congress, in December 1845, he asked leave to give notice to England that joint occupation would end in a year. The United States, he said, would not permit further European colonization. This was a restatement of the Monroe Doctrine, which had been largely forgotten since 1823. Congress, with some Whigs dissenting, complied with the President's request.

Though there was loose talk of war on both sides of the Atlantic, neither nation really wished to resort to force. The British government now offered to divide Oregon at the 49th parallel—that is, to accept Polk's original proposal. The President affected to believe the offer should be rejected, but he was easily persuaded by his cabinet to submit it to the Senate for advice. Probably he was relieved to shift the responsibility for making a decision to the senators. They accepted the proposed agreement, and on June 15, 1846, a treaty was signed fixing the boundary at the 49th parallel. The United States had secured the larger and better part of the Oregon country and certainly all that it could have legitimately expected to get.

ANNEXATION OF TEXAS

Southwest of the United States stretched the northern provinces of Mexico—Texas, New Mexico, and Upper California—once parts of Spain's colonial empire in North America but, since 1822, states in the independent republic of Mexico. Under Spanish rule the provinces had been subject to only the lightest supervision from the government of the viceroyalty in Mexico, and only a few thousand white men had settled in them. The same conditions prevailed under the republic, which lacked the power and the population to govern and settle such distant areas. At one time the United States had advanced a claim to Texas as a part of the Louisiana Purchase, but had renounced the claim in 1819. Twice thereafter, however, in the presidencies of John Quincy Adams and Jackson, the United States had offered to buy Texas, only to meet with indignant Mexican refusals.

The Mexican government invited the inevitable in Texas. In the early 1820s it encouraged American immigration by offering land grants to men like Stephen Austin who promised to colonize the land. Probably the motive of the government was to build up the economy of Texas, and hence its tax revenues, by increasing the population with foreigners, but the experiment was to result in the loss of Texas to the United States. Thousands of Americans, attracted by reports of the rich soil in Texas, took advantage of Mexico's welcome. The great majority, by the very fact of geography, came from the Southern states, sometimes bringing with them slaves. By 1835 approximately 35,000 Americans were living in Texas.

Almost from the beginning there was friction between the settlers and both the Mexicans and the Mexican government. Finally the Mexican government, realizing that its power over Texas was being challenged by the settlers, moved to exert control. A new law reduced the powers of the various states of the republic, a measure that the Texans took to be aimed specifically at them. In 1836 the Texans proclaimed their independence.

The Mexican dictator, Santa Anna, advanced into Texas with a large army. Even with the aid of volunteers, money, and supplies from private groups in the United States, the Texans were having difficulty in organizing a resistance. Their garrison at the Alamo mission in San Antonio was exterminated; another at Goliad suffered substantially the same fate when the Mexicans murdered most of the force after it surrendered. But General Sam Houston, emerging as the national hero of Texas, kept a small army together, and at the battle of San Jacinto (April 21, 1836, near present-day Houston) he defeated the Mexican army and took Santa Anna prisoner. Although the Mexican government refused to recognize the captured dictator's vague promises to withdraw Mexican authority from Texas, it made no further attempts to subdue the province. Texas had won its independence.

The new republic desired to join the United States and through its president, Sam Houston, asked for recognition, to be followed by annexation. Though President Andrew Jackson favored annexation, he proceeded cautiously.

Abolitionism was beginning to make its influence felt in politics. Many Northerners expressed a conviction that it would be im-

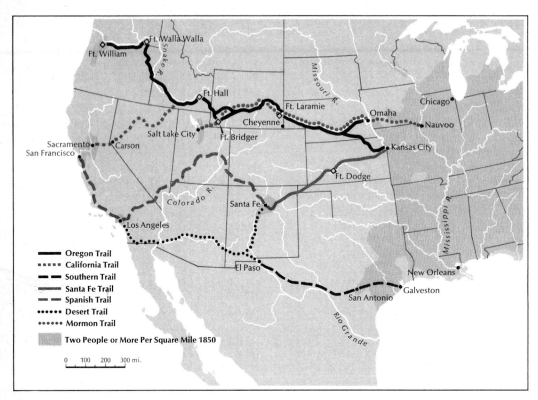

Western Trails

moral to extend the dominion of slavery. Others were opposed to incorporating a region that would add to Southern votes in Congress and in the electoral college. Jackson feared that annexation might cause an ugly sectional controversy and bring on a war with Mexico. He did not, therefore, propose annexation and did not even extend recognition to Texas until just before he left office in 1837. His successor, Van Buren, also refrained, for similar reasons, from pressing the issue.

Refused by the United States, Texas sought recognition, support, and money in Europe. Her leaders talked about creating a vast southwestern nation, stretching to the Pacific, which would be a rival to the United States. It was the kind of talk that Europe, particularly England, was charmed to hear. An independent Texas would be a counterbalance to the United States and a barrier to further American expansion; it would supply cotton for European industry and provide a market for European exports. England and France hastened to recognize Texas and to conclude trade treaties with her. The English government played with the idea of guaranteeing Texan independence. President Tyler, eager to increase Southern power, persuaded Texas to apply again, and Secretary of State Calhoun submitted an annexation treaty to the Senate in April 1844. Unfortunately for Texas, Calhoun presented annexation as if its only purpose were to extend and protect slavery. The treaty was soundly defeated.

President Tyler, who remained in office until March 1845, viewed the election returns of 1844 as a mandate to carry annexation through. He proposed to Congress that Texas be annexed by a joint resolution of both houses, a device that would get around the necessity of obtaining a two-thirds majority in the Senate for a treaty. In February 1845, Congress voted to admit Texas to the Union. Conditions were affixed: Texas could be subdivided into not more than four additional states; it had to pay its own public debts but was to retain its public lands; and it had to submit to the United States any boundary disputes in which it became involved. After Polk's inauguration Texas accepted the conditions. It became a state in December 1845.

Promptly, the Mexican government broke diplomatic relations with the United States. To make matters worse, a dispute over Texas' boundary with Mexico now developed. The Texans claimed that the Rio Grande constituted the western and southern border, an assertion that would place much of what is now New Mexico in Texas. Mexico, while not formally conceding the loss of Texas, replied that the border had always been the Nueces River.

Polk recognized the Texan claim, and in the summer of 1845 he sent a small army under General Zachary Taylor to the Nueces line to protect Texas, he said, against the Mexicans.

LANDS BEYOND TEXAS

New Mexico, another of Mexico's frontier provinces, supported a scanty population on a semi-primitive economy. Its small metropolis and trade center, Sante Fe, was 300 miles from the most northern settlements in Mexico. Under Spanish rule the New Mexicans had to export their few products over 1,000 miles to Mexico City and Vera Cruz and from these economic centers import their meager finished goods.

American Expansion into the Southwest

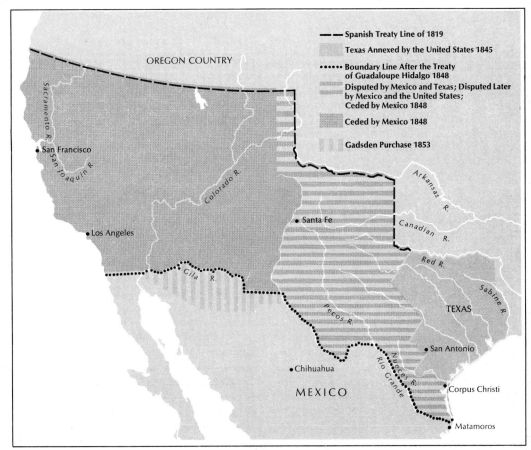

When Mexico became independent, she let it be known that traders from the United States would be welcome in New Mexico.

An American, William Becknell, wagoned a load of merchandise to Santa Fe in 1821 and sold it at a high profit. Out of his success arose the famous and colorful "Santa Fe trade." Every year traders with a stock of manufactured goods gathered at Independence, Missouri, and traveled in an organized caravan over the Sante Fe Trail, more than 800 miles long. The merchants brought back gold, silver, furs, and mules. The Santa Fe trade opened up another route to the West and pointed another direction for expansion.

Even more distant from Mexico City and even freer from Mexican supervision was the third of the northern provinces, California. In this vast, rich region lived perhaps 7,000 Mexicans, descendants of Spanish colonists, who engaged in agricultural pursuits, chiefly ranching, lived lives of primitive plenty, and carried on a skimpy trade with the outside world.

The first Americans to enter California were maritime traders and captains of the Pacific whaling ships, who stopped to barter goods or acquire supplies. Following them came merchants, who established stores, imported merchandise, and conducted a profitable trade with the Mexicans and Indians. Thomas O. Larkin, who set up business in Monterey in 1832, soon attained the status of a leading citizen. Although Larkin maintained close and friendly relations with the Mexican authorities, he secretly longed for the day when California would become an American possession. In 1844–1845 he accepted an appointment as United States consul, with instructions to arouse sentiment among the Californians for annexation.

As reports spread of the rich soil and mild climate, immigrants began to enter California from the east by land. These were pioneering farmers, men of the type who were penetrating Texas and Oregon in search of greener pastures. By 1845 there were 700 Americans in California, most of them concentrated in the valley of the Sacramento River. The overlord of this region was John A. Sutter, once of Germany and Switzerland, who had moved to California in 1839 and had become a Mexican citizen. His headquarters at Sutter's Fort was the center of a magnificent domain where the owner ranched thousands of cattle and horses and maintained a network of small manufacturing shops to supply his armed retainers.

President Polk feared that Great Britain wanted to acquire or dominate California as well as Texas — a suspicion that was given credence by the activities of British diplomatic agents in the province. His dreams of expansion went beyond the Democratic platform. He was determined to acquire for his country New Mexico and California and possibly other parts of northern Mexico.

At the same time that he sent Taylor to the Nueces, Polk also sent secret instructions to the commander of the Pacific naval squadron to seize the California ports if he heard that Mexico had declared war. A little later Consul Larkin was informed that, if the people wanted to revolt and join the United States, they would be received as brethren. Still later an exploring expedition led by Captain John C. Frémont, of the army's corps of topographical engineers, entered California. The Mexican authorities, alarmed by the size of the party and its military aspects, ordered Frémont to leave. He complied, but moved only over the Oregon border.

After preparing measures that looked like war, Polk resolved on a last effort to achieve his objectives by diplomacy. He dispatched to Mexico a special minister, John Slidell, a Louisiana politician, with instructions to settle with American money all the questions in dispute between the two nations. If Mexico would acknowledge the Rio Grande boundary for Texas, the United States would assume the damage claims, amounting to several millions, which Americans held against Mexico. If she would cede New Mexico, the United States would pay $5 million. And for California, the United States would pay up to $25 million. Slidell soon notified his government that his mission had failed. Immediately after receiving Slidell's information, on January 13, 1846, Polk ordered Taylor's army to move across the Nueces to the Rio Grande.

If Polk was hoping for trouble, he was disappointed for months. Finally, in May, he decided to ask Congress to declare war on the grounds that Mexico had refused to honor its financial obligations and had insulted the United States by rejecting the Slidell mission. While Polk was working on a war message, the news arrived from Taylor that Mexican troops had crossed the Rio Grande and attacked a unit of American soldiers. Polk now revised his message. He declared: "Mexico has passed the boundary of the United States . . . and shed American blood upon the American soil"—"war exists by the act of Mexico herself." Congress accepted Polk's interpretation of events and on May 13, 1846, declared war by votes of 40 to 2 in the Senate and 174 to 14 in the House.

Although Congress had accepted war with near unanimity, there was more opposition than appeared on the surface. Opposition increased and intensified as the war continued and costs and casualties came home to the people. The Whigs in Congress supported the military appropriation bills, but they became ever bolder and more bitter in denouncing "Mr. Polk's war" as aggressive in origin and objectives.

WAR WITH MEXICO

In the opening phases of the war President Polk assumed the planning of grand strategy, a practice that he continued almost to the end of the war. His basic idea was to seize key areas on the Mexican frontier and then force the Mexicans to make peace on American terms. Accordingly, he ordered Taylor to cross the Rio Grande and occupy northeastern Mexico, taking as his first objective the city of Monterrey. Polk seems to have had a vague idea that from Monterrey Taylor could advance southward, if necessary, and menace Mexico City. Taylor, "Old Rough and Ready," beloved by his soldiers for his courage and easy informality but ignorant of many technical aspects of war, attacked Monterrey in September 1846. After a hard fight he captured it, but at the price of agreeing to let the garrison evacuate without pursuit. Although the country hailed Taylor as a hero, Polk concluded that he did not possess the ability to lead an offensive against Mexico City. Also, Polk began to realize that an advance south through the mountains would involve impossible problems of supply.

Two other offensives planned by Polk were aimed at New Mexico and California. In the summer of 1846 a small army under Colonel Stephen W. Kearny made the long march to Santa Fe and occupied the town with no opposition. Kearny sent part of his army (Missouri volunteers under Colonel A. W. Doniphan) south to join Taylor, and disposed other parts to garrison the province. Then, acting under instructions from Polk, Kearny proceeded with a few hundred troopers to California to take charge of operations there. In California a combined revolt and war was being staged by the settlers, Frémont's exploring party, and the American navy. The settlers had proclaimed California an independent state in the "Bear Flag Revolution." Frémont had returned from Oregon to lead the rebels, and the navy had landed forces and annexed California to the United States. When Kearny arrived, the Americans were fighting under the direction of Commodore R. F. Stockton of the navy. With some difficulty, Kearny brought the disparate American elements under his command, and by the autumn of 1846 completed the conquest of California.

In addition to northeastern Mexico, the United States now had possession of the two provinces for which it had gone to war. In a sense, the objectives of the war had been achieved. The only trouble was that Mexico refused to recognize realities; she would not agree to a peace and cede the desired territory. At this point Polk turned to General Scott, the commanding general of the army and its finest soldier, for help.

Together Polk and Scott devised a plan to force the Mexicans to accept peace. Scott would assemble at Tampico an army to be made up partly of troops from Taylor's army and partly of forces from other areas. The navy would transport this army down the coast to Vera Cruz, which would be seized and made into a base. From Vera Cruz, Scott would move west along the National Highway to Mexico City. Late in 1846 Scott went to Mexico to organize his forces. Taylor, who lost about half of his army to Scott, was instructed to stand on the defensive.

While Scott was assembling his army off the coast, General Santa Anna, the Mexican dictator, decided to take advantage of the division of American forces by marching northward and crushing Taylor and then returning to deal with Scott. With an army much larger than Taylor's, Santa Anna attacked the Americans at Buena Vista (February 1847). Santa Anna could not break the American line and had to return to defend Mexico City.

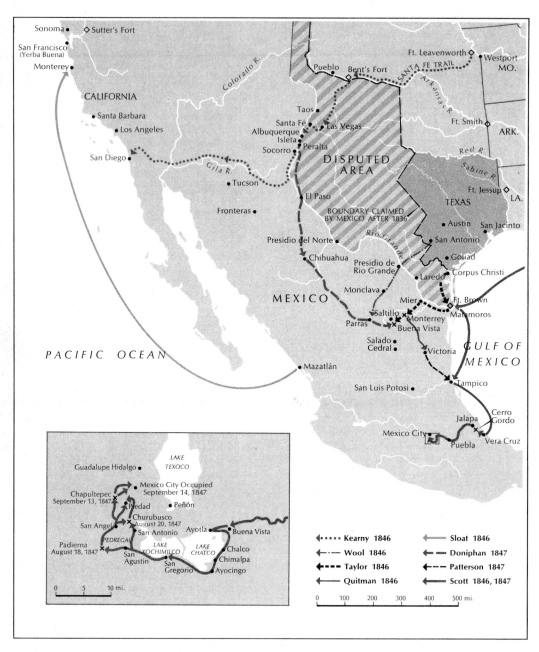

The Mexican War   1846–1848

In the meantime Scott had taken Vera Cruz by siege and was moving inland, in one of the most brilliant campaigns in American military annals. With an army that never numbered more than 14,000, he advanced 260 miles into enemy territory, conserved the lives of his soldiers by using flanking movements instead of frontal assaults, and finally achieved his objec-

Entrance of Scott's Army into Mexico City
This print of the American army taking possession of the Mexican capital in 1847 appeared in a history of the war written by George W. Kendall of the New Orleans Picayune. Kendall was one of the first war correspondents ever to accompany an army on its campaigns. (Library of Congress)

tive without losing a battle. At Cerro Gordo, in the mountains, he inflicted a smashing reverse on the Mexicans. He met no further resistance until he was within a few miles of Mexico City. After capturing the fortress of Chapultepec in a hard fight, the Americans occupied the enemy capital. A new Mexican government came into power, one that recognized the fact of defeat and that was willing to make a peace treaty.

Polk, in his growing anxiety to get the war finished, had sent with the invading army a presidential agent who was authorized to negotiate an agreement. On February 2, 1848, the agent concluded the Treaty of Guadalupe Hidalgo. Mexico agreed to cede California and New Mexico and to acknowledge the Rio Grande boundary of Texas. In return, the United States contracted to assume the claims of its citizens against Mexico and to pay $15 million to Mexico.

Some expansionists in the United States were demanding that the government hold out for the annexation of *all* Mexico. This permitted the antislavery leaders to charge that Southern slaveholders were running the government for their own ends. (Actually, some antislavery men, convinced that slavery could never thrive in Mexico, favored taking the whole country.) Polk acted quickly to silence the extremists on both sides. He submitted the treaty to the Senate, and by a vote of 38 to 14, it was approved.

A New Sectional Crisis

The Mexican War, with the vast territory it yielded, led directly to the most serious threat of disunion yet to confront the United States.

SETTLERS IN THE FAR WEST

When the war ended, a portion of the territory acquired from Mexico was already settled by Americans who, oddly enough, had left their country because they were unhappy there. These people were adherents of a religious sect formally known as the "Church of Jesus Christ of Latter Day Saints" and more commonly known as Mormons. The Mormon faith, one of the numerous new religions that flowered in America in the 1820s and 1830s, had originated in western New York. The Mormons believed in a tightly knit and disciplined community life directed by the church elders. Seeking a more congenial environment, under the leadership of their prophet, Joseph Smith, they moved to Ohio, then to Missouri, and finally to Nauvoo, Illinois. Everywhere they met with resentment, largely caused by their economic and community organization. At Nauvoo they particularly outraged the opinions of their neighbors by introducing polygamy. Their troubles came to a climax when a mob lynched Smith.

Smith's successor, Brigham Young, now decided that if the Mormons were to escape further persecution they would have to move outside the United States. In 1846 almost the entire Mormon community left Nauvoo. Their destination, picked out by Young, was the Great Salt Lake basin in Utah, so arid that no other people would have the courage to live there. By 1850 over 11,000 people were settled in and around the Mormon metropolis of Salt Lake City. With the aid of irrigation they made the desert bloom. They established thriving home industries, and they built up a profitable trade with emigrants on the way to California.

In January 1848, gold was accidentally discovered in the Sacramento Valley in California. As word of the strike spread, inhabitants of California and the whole Far West, fired by hopes of becoming immediate millionaires, stampeded to the area to stake out claims. By the end of summer the news had reached the Eastern states and Europe. Then the gold rush really started. From the United States and all the world, thousands of "Forty-Niners" poured into California. Those who left from the older states could choose among three routes of travel: overland by covered wagon, inexpensive but involving a long journey over the Great Plains and across the Rockies; by ship around Cape Horn, quicker but more expensive; or the dangerous, difficult shortcut across the Isthmus of Panama. By all three routes, disdaining hunger, thirst, disease, and even death, the seekers after gold came — more than 80,000 of them in 1849. By the end of that year, California had a population of approximately 100,000, more than enough to entitle her to statehood.

WARTIME AND POSTWAR POLITICS

In domestic politics President Polk was as aggressive — and successful — as he was in foreign policy. At his insistence Congress reestablished the Independent Treasury system, thus pleasing all sections of the Democratic party and redeeming one of its platform promises. Again at his demand, Congress fulfilled another platform pledge by lowering the tariff. The Tariff of 1846 reduced the average rates enough to delight the South, but it could not have been passed without the votes of Northwestern Democrats.

Naturally, the Westerners expected something in return, and specifically they expected Southern support for internal improvements. Two internal improvements bills passed Congress, but Polk, who sincerely believed that the national government had no legal power to finance such projects, vetoed both of them. The Westerners were disappointed and angered. As in the case of Oregon, they thought that Polk was sacrificing their interests to those of the South.

Before Polk left office, a much more dangerous issue emerged. In August 1846, while the war was in progress, he had asked Congress to provide him with $2 million that he could use to purchase peace with Mexico. When the appropriation was introduced in the House, David Wilmot of Pennsylvania, an antislavery Democrat from a high-tariff state,

Mormon Leader
*Brigham Young was born in
Vermont and grew up in western
New York in an area known,
because of the fiery religious
revivals that swept across it, as
the "burnt-over district." Here
the Mormon faith originated,
and here Young was converted to
it. He quickly became a leader in
the church and became its
president on Smith's death in
1844. He led his people to Utah
and on seeing the grim and
forbidding Great Salt Lake
basin, he exclaimed: "This is
the place." (Library of Congress)*

moved an amendment that slavery should be prohibited in any territory secured from Mexico. The so-called Wilmot Proviso passed the House but failed in the Senate. It would be called up again and be debated and voted on for years.

Diametrically opposed to the Wilmot Proviso was the formula of the Southern extremists. They contended that the states jointly owned the territories and that the citizens of each state possessed equal rights in them, including the right to move to them with their property, particularly slave property. According to this view, Congress, which was the only agent for the joint owners, had no power to prohibit the movement of slavery into the public domain or to regulate it in any way except by extending protection. Neither could a territorial legislature, which was a creature of Congress, take any action to ban slavery.

Two compromise plans were presented. One, which numbered President Polk among its advocates, proposed to run the Missouri Compromise line of 36° 30′ through the new

territories to the Pacific coast, banning slavery north of the line and permitting it south. The other, first prominently espoused by Lewis Cass, Democratic senator from Michigan, was originally called "squatter sovereignty." Later, when taken up by Stephen A. Douglas, an Illinois senator of the same party, it was given the more dignified title of "popular sovereignty." According to this formula, the question of slavery in each territory should be left to the people there, acting through the medium of their territorial legislature.

Congress and the country debated the various formulas, but at the end of Polk's administration a decision had still not been reached. No territorial government had been provided for California or New Mexico (New Mexico included most of present New Mexico and Arizona, all of Utah and Nevada, and parts of Colorado and Wyoming). Even the organization of Oregon, so far north that obviously slavery would never enter it, was held up by the controversy. Southern members of Congress, hoping to gain some advantage in the regions farther south, blocked a territorial bill for Oregon until August 1848, when a free-soil government was finally authorized.

The debate was partially stilled by the presidential campaign of 1848. Both the Democrats and the Whigs tried to avoid definite and provocative references to the slavery question. The Democrats nominated as their candidate Lewis Cass of Michigan, an elderly, honest, dull wheel horse of the party. Although the platform was purposely vague, it was capable of being interpreted as an endorsement of squatter sovereignty. The Whigs adopted no platform and presented as their candidate a military hero with no political record—General Zachary Taylor of Louisiana.

Ardent abolitionists and even moderates who merely opposed the expansion of slavery found it difficult to swallow either Cass or Taylor. The situation was ripe for the appearance of a third party. The potential sources for such a group were the existing Liberty party and the antislavery members of the old organizations. Late in the campaign, third-party promoters held a national convention, adopted a platform endorsing the Wilmot Proviso, free homesteads, and a higher tariff, and nominated former President Van Buren for the presidency. Thus was launched the Free Soil party.

Taylor won a narrow victory. Though Van Buren failed to carry a single state, he polled an impressive 291,000 votes, and the Free-Soilers elected ten members to Congress. It is probable that Van Buren pulled enough Democratic votes away from Cass, particularly in New York, to throw the election to Taylor.

TAYLOR AND THE TERRITORIES

Zachary Taylor was the first man to be elected President with no previous political training or experience. He was also the first professional soldier to sit in the White House. Though a

Washing for Gold
These miners in a Western gold camp are engaging in placer mining. The gold found in the first strikes was located in the form of particles along stream beds. Prospectors separated the gold from sand or gravel by washing the deposit in a swirl of water. Washing was done in pans or boxes. From Samuel Bowles, Our New West.

Southerner and a slaveholder, he had acquired a national outlook from his long years in the army.

Since Congress had failed to provide civil government for the area annexed from Mexico, those regions were being administered by military officials who were responsible to the President. The situation was unsatisfactory to everybody concerned with it. To President Taylor, statehood seemed to be the solution to California's problem and to the controversy over slavery in the territories. Let California and also New Mexico frame state constitutions and apply for admission to the Union. Once they had become states, nobody could deny their right to dispose of slavery as they wished. So Taylor directed military officials in the territories to expedite statehood movements.

California promptly ratified a constitution in which slavery was prohibited. When Congress assembled in December 1849, Taylor rather proudly described his efforts. He recommended that California be admitted as a free state and that New Mexico, when it was ready, be permitted to come in with complete freedom to decide the status of slavery as it wished. But Congress was not about to accept the President's program.

Complicating the situation was the emergence of side issues generated by the conflict over slavery in the territories. One such issue concerned slavery in the District of Columbia. Antislavery people, charging that human servitude in the capital was a national disgrace, demanded that it be abolished there. Southerners angrily replied that the institution could not be touched without the consent of Maryland, which had originally donated the land, and that to abolish it would place a stigma on the entire South.

Another disturbing question concerned the rendition of fugitive slaves. Northern "personal liberty laws," forbidding courts and police officers to assist in the return of runaways, provoked Southerners to call for a new, more stringent *national* fugitive slave law.

A third issue related to the boundary between Texas and New Mexico. Texas claimed the portion of New Mexico east of the Rio Grande, although the national government during the Mexican War had assigned this region to New Mexico. To Texans it seemed that Washington was trying to steal part of their ter-

ritory. They also resented the government's refusal to assume the Texas war debt. Southern extremists supported the pretensions of Texas, while Northerners, eager to cut down the size of a slave state, upheld New Mexico.

But the biggest obstacle in the way of the President's program was the South—angered and frightened by the possibility that two new free states would be added to the Northern majority. Only in the Senate did the South still maintain equality. The number of free and slave states was equal in 1849—fifteen of each. But now the admission of California would upset the balance, and New Mexico, Oregon, and Utah were yet to come.

Responsible Southern leaders declared that if California was to be admitted, and if slavery was to be prohibited in the territories, the time had come for the South to secede from the Union. At the suggestion of Mississippi, a call went out for a Southern-rights convention to meet in June 1850 at Nashville, Tennessee, to consider whether the South should resort to the ultimate act of secession. In the North excitement ran equally high. Every Northern state legislature but one adopted resolutions demanding that slavery be barred from the territories. Public meetings all through the free states called for the passage of the Wilmot Proviso and the abolition of slavery in the District of Columbia. Such was the crisis that confronted Congress and the country as the tense year of 1850 opened.

THE COMPROMISE OF 1850

Moderates and lovers of the Union turned their thoughts, during the winter of 1849–1850, to the framing of a great congressional compromise that would satisfy both sections and restore tranquillity. The venerable statesman from Kentucky, Henry Clay, headed the forces of conciliation. To Clay's way of thinking, no compromise would have any lasting effect unless it settled all the issues in dispute between the sections. Accordingly, he took a number of separate measures, which had been proposed before, combined them into one set of resolutions, and on January 29, 1850, presented these to the Senate. He recommended (1) that California be admitted as a free state; (2) that, in the rest of the Mexican cession, territorial gov-

**An Extreme
Southern
View on
Compromise
in 1850**

In his last speech Calhoun insisted that the North should either agree to everything that the South demanded as its rights or permit the minority section to depart the Union:

It is time, Senators, that there should be an open and manly avowal on all sides, as to what is intended to be done. If the question is not now settled, it is uncertain whether it ever can hereafter be; and we, as the representatives of the States of this Union, regarded as governments, should come to a distinct understanding as to our respective views, in order to ascertain whether the great questions at issue can be settled or not. If you, who represent the stronger portion, cannot agree to settle them on the broad principle of justice and duty, say so; and let the States we both represent agree to separate and part in peace, tell us so; and we shall know what to do, when you reduce the question to submission or resistance. If you remain silent, you will compel us to infer by your acts what you intend.

---

ernments be formed without restrictions as to slavery; (3) that Texas yield in her boundary dispute with New Mexico and be compensated by the federal government's taking over her public debt; (4) that the slave trade, but not slavery itself, be abolished in the District of Columbia; and (5) that a new and more effective fugitive slave law be passed.

These resolutions started a debate that raged for months in Congress and throughout the country. Clay himself opened the oratorical tournament with a defense of his measures and a plea to North and South to be mutually conciliatory and forebearing.

Early in March, Calhoun, who had less than a month to live, presented the views of the Southern extremists. Too ill to speak, he sat grimly in his seat while a colleague read his speech. Almost ignoring Clay's proposals, he devoted his argument to what to him was the larger and the only subject—the minority South—and he asked more for his section than could be given. Because of Northern aggressions, the cords that bound the Union were snapping, he said. What would save the Union? The North must admit that the South possessed equal rights in the territories, must agree to observe the laws concerning fugitive slaves, must cease attacking slavery, and must accept an amendment to the Constitution guaranteeing a balance of power between the sections. The amendment he had in mind provided for the election of dual Presidents, one from the North and one from the South, each possessing a veto power. In short, nothing would satisfy Calhoun except abject surrender by the North.

After Calhoun came the third of the elder statesmen, Webster. His "Seventh of March address" was probably the greatest forensic effort of his long oratorical career. Still nourishing White House ambitions, he now sought to calm angry passions and to rally Northern moderates to support Clay's compromise. The voice of the Northern extremists was the New York Whig William H. Seward, who maintained extremely cordial personal relations with President Taylor. There was a higher law than the Constitution, Seward proclaimed, the law of God, which required men to oppose slavery.

Popular sentiment in all sections was slowly swinging in favor of some kind of compromise. The country was entering upon a period of prosperity—the result of an expanding foreign trade, the flow of gold from California, and a boom in railroad construction—reminiscent of the flush days of the 1830s. Conservative economic interests everywhere wanted to terminate the sectional dispute and concentrate the attention of the nation upon internal expansion. Even in the South excitement seemed to be abating. The Nashville convention met in June, and after adopting some tame resolutions, adjourned to await final action by Congress.

For a time, however, it seemed that Congress was not going to act. One reason was the opposition of Taylor. The President persisted in his stand that the admission of California, and possibly New Mexico, must come first. After that, it might be possible to discuss other measures. In the meantime, if the South want-

An Extreme Northern View on Compromise in 1850

William H. Seward, Senator from New York, expressed the feelings of those Northerners who refused to make any further concessions to the South in 1850:

I AM OPPOSED TO ANY SUCH COMPROMISE, IN ANY AND ALL THE FORMS IN WHICH IT HAS BEEN PROPOSED. *Because, while admitting the purity and the patriotism of all from whom it is my misfortune to differ, I think all legislative compromises radically wrong and essentially vicious. They involve the surrender of the exercise of judgment and conscience on distinct and separate questions, at distinct and separate times, with the indispensable advantages it affords for ascertaining truth. They involve a relinquishment of the right to reconsider in future the decisions of the present, on questions prematurely anticipated. And they are a usurpation as to future questions of the province of future legislators.*

---

ed to try anything like secession, "Old Zack" was ready to use force against his native section and to lead the armed forces in person.

On July 9, President Taylor suddenly died, the victim of a violent stomach disorder following an attack of heat prostration. He was succeeded by the Vice President, Millard Fillmore of New York. The new chief executive was a handsome, dignified man of no great abilities, but he was also a practical politician who understood the importance of give and take. He ranged himself on the side of the Compromise, using his powers of persuasion and patronage to swing Northern Whigs into line. Clay, exhausted by his labors, temporarily left Congress, and Stephen A. Douglas took over the leadership of the Compromise forces. Douglas broke up Clay's "omnibus bill" into separate measures and presented them one by one. By mid-September, all had been enacted by both houses of Congress and signed by the President.

It was one thing to pass the Compromise through Congress and another to persuade the country to accept it. In the North the most objectionable of the measures was the Fugitive Slave Act. By this law, a Negro accused of being a runaway was denied trial by jury and the right to testify in his own behalf. His status was to be decided by a federal judge or by a special commissioner appointed by the federal circuit courts. He could be remanded to slavery on the bare evidence of an affidavit presented by the man who claimed to be his owner.

But the Fugitive Slave Act was the only part of the Compromise that most Southerners could approve. The adjourned session of the Nashville convention met in November 1850 (with only about a third of the original delegates present) and condemned the Compromise. Eventually, the South brought itself to accept the settlement, but only after much agonizing, and then only conditionally. Epitomizing the feelings of its people was the "Georgia Platform." This declared that Georgia would acquiesce in the Compromise—but if the North disregarded the Fugitive Slave Act, or attempted to abolish slavery in the District of Columbia, or denied admission to a state because it wished to have slavery, then Georgia would consider the compact broken and would protect its rights even to the point of seceding.

An Uneasy Truce

The Compromise of 1850 proved to be only a truce, and a short and uneasy one at that. During the next few years the sectional conflict continued to smolder. It was reflected in both domestic politics and foreign policy.

RENEWED AGITATION

At their national convention in 1852 the Democrats adopted a platform pledging their unswerving devotion to the Compromise of 1850

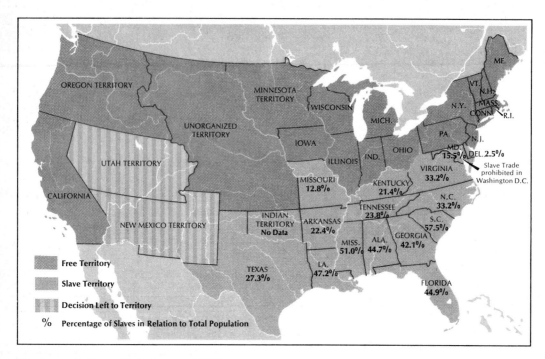

OREGON TERRITORY
MINNESOTA TERRITORY
WISCONSIN
MICH.
UNORGANIZED TERRITORY
IOWA
OHIO
PA.
N.Y.
ME.
VT.
N.H.
MASS.
CONN.
R.I.
N.J.
MD. 15.5%
DEL. 2.5%
UTAH TERRITORY
ILLINOIS
IND.
VIRGINIA 33.2%
Slave Trade prohibited in Washington D.C.
CALIFORNIA
MISSOURI 12.8%
KENTUCKY 21.4%
N.C 33.2%
TENNESSEE 23.8%
S.C. 57.5%
NEW MEXICO TERRITORY
INDIAN TERRITORY No Data
ARKANSAS 22.4%
GEORGIA 42.1%
MISS. 51.0%
ALA. 44.7%
TEXAS 27.3%
LA. 47.2%
FLORIDA 44.9%

Free Territory
Slave Territory
Decision Left to Territory
%   Percentage of Slaves in Relation to Total Population

Slave and Free Territory   1850

and their united opposition to all attempts in any "shape or color" to renew the agitation of the slavery question. Not so unanimous when it came to choosing a candidate, they wrangled through forty-nine ballots, with no one of the leading contenders—Cass, Douglas, or James Buchanan of Pennsylvania—being able to secure a two-thirds majority. Finally, the prize went to one of the more obscure aspirants, a "dark horse," Franklin Pierce of New Hampshire. The Whigs likewise endorsed the Compromise but in much milder terms and over the opposition of many antislavery, or "Conscience," Whigs. Instead of nominating a man connected with and committed to the Compromise, they named, after fifty-three ballots, General Winfield Scott, whose views were unknown and whose support by Northern delegates made him suspect to Southerners even though he was a Virginian. He was to be the last Whig candidate. Only the Free-Soilers, with John P. Hale of New Hampshire as their candidate, repudiated the Compromise.

Probably because the Democrats had taken the strongest stand in favor of the Compro-

mise, they won at the polls. When Franklin Pierce was inaugurated in 1853, he was, at the age of forty-nine, the youngest man up to that time to become President. Amiable and charming, he had been selected as the Democratic nominee largely for reasons of party harmony. In his short political career he had upheld few opinions and made few enemies. As President, he was dominated by the strong men of his cabinet, especially Secretary of State William L. Marcy of New York and Secretary of War Jefferson Davis of Mississippi.

The Compromise did not dissolve the abolitionist organizations nor stop their crusade to convince the Northern masses that slavery was a sin. In the 1850s the abolitionists found new allies and more effective media of expression. Several Free-Soilers now sat in Congress, and these men—such as Charles Sumner of Massachusetts in the Senate and Joshua R. Giddings of Ohio in the House—could denounce slavery from the vantage point of the national forum.

Northern hostility to the new Fugitive Slave Act was intensified when Southerners appeared in the Northern states to pursue fugitives or to claim as slaves Negroes who had been living for years in Northern communities. Mobs attempted to impede enforcement of the law. In 1851 a crowd in Boston took from a federal marshal a runaway named Shadrach and sent him on his way to Canada. Later in the same year at Syracuse, New York, there was a similar rescue of a slave named Jerry McHenry. In 1854 a Boston mob led by respectable and prominent men tried unsuccessfully to take Anthony Burns from the custody of federal officers.

These displays of violence alarmed the South, and so did the new personal-liberty laws passed by several Northern legislatures. The frank purpose of the statutes was to render the Fugitive Slave Act a nullity. They interposed state power between the accused fugitive and the federal authority. In Wisconsin and Massachusetts, state courts were instructed to issue writs of habeas corpus (requiring an appearance before a judge) against any person detaining a fugitive and to grant the fugitive a judicial hearing in which the burden of proof was placed on the pursuer. The supreme court of Wisconsin, in the case of *Ableman* v. *Booth* (1857), declared the national law void. When the Supreme Court of the nation decided against the state, the Wisconsin court ignored the decision. Thus legal and judicial barriers were being thrown in the way of the one provision of the Compromise that the South considered a positive victory, and Southerners were deeply angered.

"YOUNG AMERICA"

In Europe the great liberal and nationalist revolutions of 1848 were running their course, some succeeding, others petering out in failure. A vision of a republican Europe, with governments to be based on the model of the United States, stirred the American imagination. A group of Democrats started a "Young America" movement with vague ideas of aiding revolutionaries abroad. These adventurous Democrats also aimed to promote American commerce in the Pacific and elsewhere and to extend the sweep of Manifest Destiny with new acquisitions in this hemisphere. Other politicians in both parties caught the "Young America" spirit, and it influenced the foreign policies

of both the Fillmore and the Pierce administrations. At first these aggressive policies abroad were intended to offset the divisive, sectional feelings at home. Before long, however, the interest in additional territories complicated the relations between the sections as well as the relations between the United States and foreign governments.

The Whig Daniel Webster, secretary of state a second time, under Fillmore, saw a chance to play upon the national pride when the Austrian representative in Washington protested against the apparent readiness of the United States to recognize the independence of the Hungarians, who were revolting against Austrian rule. In reply, Webster dismissed the protest and added the gratuitous observation that, in comparison with the vast extent of the United States, the domain of Austria was "but as a patch on the earth's surface." And when (after the collapse of the Hungarian revolt) the rebel leader Louis Kossuth visited the United States, Webster joined in Kossuth's enthusiastic reception by speaking at a banquet in his honor.

Showing concern for Pacific commerce, the Fillmore administration sent out an expedition under Commodore Matthew C. Perry to open trade relations with Japan, which for two centuries had been a hermit nation. Perry touched at Japan in 1853 and reappeared there the following year with an impressive display of naval might. He obtained a treaty opening two ports and providing for the residence of an American consul in one of them. The first consul, Townsend Harris, after years of patient labor, secured a new treaty (1858) with additional trading rights.

The Fillmore administration was cautious about American schemes for taking Cuba, the rich "pearl of the Antilles," which Polk once had tried to purchase from Spain. Later a Venezuelan adventurer, General Narciso López, proposed to conquer the island with a force of American volunteers and present it to the United States. On his third attempt, in 1851, López landed in Cuba with about 400 men, mostly Americans, but ran into a much stronger army of Spaniards. They defeated and captured him and most of his followers, then executed him and more than fifty others. While a retaliating mob wrecked the Spanish consulate in New Orleans, the governments of Great

THE LAND OF LIBERTY.

RECOMMENDED TO THE CONSIDERATION OF "BROTHER JONATHAN."

"The Land of Liberty"
*A British view of the United States. Americans are committing aggression in Mexico
after taking Texas and Oregon and are dueling, engaging in drunken brawls,
repudiating their state debts and thus robbing foreigners, and enslaving and
lynching blacks while preoccupying themselves with money and trampling on their
own Revolutionary ideals. From an 1847 issue of the British humor magazine* Punch.

Britain and France took alarm at the American filibustering. They proposed that the United States join them in a tripartite agreement guaranteeing Cuba to Spain. Edward Everett, Webster's successor as secretary of state, declined the proposal. He explained that his government could make no pledge never to acquire Cuba, since the island, so close by, was of immense strategic importance to the United States and someday "might be almost essential to our safety."

The Pierce administration, though more aggressive, was frustrated in its expansionist hopes because of sectional jealousies. Schemes to get new slave territories aroused opposition in the North, and the acquisition of lands unsuited to slavery was unpopular in the South. Though the kingdom of Hawaii agreed to join the United States (1854), the annexation treaty had no chance for Senate approval, since it contained a clause prohibiting slavery.

The old idea of adding Canada to the United States had never died out among Americans, and it was beginning to appeal to more and more Canadians. Some of them saw a union as the only way out of their economic difficulties. As a result of British free-trade policy (after 1846) and the American tariff, Canadians had lost much of their export trade. Annexation would open the American market to them. To deal with Canada's economic problem, and to settle a revived quarrel over American fishing rights along the Newfoundland and Labrador coasts, the British government sent Lord Elgin on a special mission to Washington in 1854. Lord Elgin and Secretary of State William L. Marcy negotiated a treaty specifying fishing rights and providing for tariff reciprocity. Canada was to accept certain American commodities, and the United States certain Canadian commodities, duty free. Thus Canadians, without annexation, would have access to American markets. The Elgin Treaty was promptly ratified. A Vermont senator explained that many of his fellow senators, those from the South, had been in a hurry to head off the union movement.

Central America had attracted attention for several years, ever since the California gold rush, when many gold-seekers crossed the isthmus on their way to the West Coast. With the rapid settlement of California, some Americans began to think of improving communications by constructing a canal somewhere across Central America. But Great Britain also had strong interests in that part of the world. A possible clash was averted by the Clayton-Bulwer Treaty (1850), in which Great Britain and the United States agreed that, if and when a canal were ever built, it would be a joint Anglo-American project.

New trouble with Britain in Central America arose from the filibustering activities of William Walker, the "gray-eyed man of destiny," an American of tremendous drive in a tiny body (he weighed just 100 pounds). With a band of American soldiers of fortune, most of them veterans of the war with Mexico, Walker made himself dictator of Nicaragua (1855) and had visions of heading a federation of Central American states. The British government, along with antislavery Americans, supposed that he was acting as an agent for President Pierce and was preparing the way for American annexation. This suspicion, though unfounded, seemed to be confirmed when Pierce recognized Walker's government. When Walker, after having been driven out of Nicaragua, attempted to return by way of Honduras, a British naval officer seized him and turned him over to the Honduran authorities. They disposed of him with a firing squad.

Meanwhile the Pierce administration had made all too clear its determination to obtain Cuba. In 1854 Secretary Marcy instructed the minister to Spain, Pierre Soulé of Louisiana, to make a new offer to buy the island. If this was refused he was to try to "detach" Cuba from Spain. Soulé was plotting with Spanish revolutionaries to overthrow the Spanish monarchy when he received new instructions: he was to consult with the ministers to England and France, James Buchanan and John Y. Mason. The three embodied their recommendations in a diplomatic dispatch that shortly found its way into the newspapers and became notorious as the Ostend Manifesto. This remarkable document stated that if Spain should persist in refusing to sell Cuba, and if disturbances there should threaten American security, the United States would be justified in "wresting" the island from Spain.

Antislavery Northerners now charged the administration with violating the spirit of the Compromise of 1850. They said that Pierce, acting as the tool of the South, was conspiring to bring in a new slave state even at the risk of war with Spain and other European powers.

Selected Readings

From Harrison to Polk
J. A. Green, *William Henry Harrison* (1941); O. P. Chitwood, *John Tyler* (1939); Robert Seager II, *And Tyler Too: A Biography of John and Julia Gardiner Tyler* (1963); O. D. Lambert, *Presidential Politics in the United States, 1841–1844* (1936); Frederick Merk, *Fruits of Propaganda in the Tyler Administration* (1971); C. G. Sellers, *James K. Polk, Continentalist, 1843–1846* (1966).

The Expansionist Urge
R. A. Billington, *The Far Western Frontier, 1830–1860** (1956); N. A. Graebner, *Empire on the Pacific* (1955); A. K. Weinberg, *Manifest Destiny** (1935); Frederick Merk, *Manifest Destiny and Mission in American History: A Reinterpretation* (1963) and, with L. B. Merk, *The Monroe Doctrine and American Expansion, 1843–1849* (1966); Bernard De Voto, *The Year of Decision, 1846** (1943).

Far Western Trade and Exploration
P. C. Phillips, *The Fur Trade* (2 vols., 1961); R. G. Cleland, *This Reckless Breed of Men: The Trappers and Fur Traders of the Southwest* (1950); G. G. Cline, *Exploring the Great Basin* (1963); Allan Nevins, *Frémont, Pathmarker of the West* (1955); Donald Jackson and M. L. Spence, eds., *The Expeditions of John Charles Frémont* (3 vols., 1970); R. L. Duffus, *The Santa Fe Trail* (1930).

Texas
E. C. Barker, *Mexico and Texas, 1821–1835* (1928); W. C. Binkley, *The Texas Revolution* (1952); W. R. Hogan, *The Texas Republic* (1946); J. W. Schmitz, *Texan Statecraft, 1836–1845* (1945); Frederick Merk, *Slavery and the Annexation of Texas* (1972).

Oregon and California
Francis Parkman, *The Oregon Trail** (1849 and later editions); C. M. Drury, *Marcus Whitman, M.D., Pioneer and Martyr* (1937); W. J. Ghent, *The Road to Oregon* (1929); Jay Monaghan, *The Overland Trail* (1937); R. G. Cleland, *From Wilderness to Empire: A History of California, 1542–1900* (1944); R. W. Paul, *California Gold: The Beginning of Mining in the Far West** (1947); J. W. Caughey, *Gold Is the Cornerstone* (1948).

The Mormons
F. M. Brodie, *No Man Knows My History: The Life of Joseph Smith* (1945); Preston Nibley, *Brigham Young: The Man and His Work* (1936); Wallace Stegner, *The Gathering of Zion: The Story of the Mormon Trail* (1964); Nels Anderson, *Desert Saints: The Mormon Frontier in Utah** (1942); N. F. Furniss, *The Mormon Conflict, 1850–1859* (1960).

The Mexican War
J. S. Reeves, *American Diplomacy Under Tyler and Polk* (1907); D. M. Pletcher, *The Diplomacy of Annexation: Texas, Oregon, and the Mexican War* (1973); J. H. Smith, *The War with Mexico* (2 vols., 1919); A. H. Bill, *Rehearsal for Conflict: The War with Mexico, 1846–1848* (1947); O. A. Singletary, *The Mexican War** (1960); Holman Hamilton, *Zachary Taylor, Soldier of the Republic* (1941); C. W. Elliott, *Winfield Scott* (1937).

Crisis and Compromise
Holman Hamilton, *Prologue to Conflict: The Crisis and Compromise of 1850** (1964) and *Zachary Taylor, Soldier in the White House* (1951); Allan Nevins, *Ordeal of the Union* (2 vols., 1947); R. H. Shryock,

Georgia and the Union in 1850 (1926); C. M. Wiltse, *John C. Calhoun, Sectionalist, 1840–1850* (1951); F. B. Woodford, *Lewis Cass* (1950); Clement Eaton, *Henry Clay and the Art of American Politics** (1957); G. F. Milton, *The Eve of Conflict: Stephen A. Douglas and the Needless War* (1934); G. M. Capers, *Stephen A. Douglas, Defender of the Union* (1959); R. W. Johannsen, *Stephen A. Douglas* (1973); R. J. Rayback, *Millard Fillmore* (1959).

Postwar Diplomacy

S. F. Bemis, ed., *American Secretaries of State*, vols. 5 and 6 (1928); A. A. Ettinger, *The Mission to Spain of Pierre Soulé* (1932); Basil Rauch, *American Interest in Cuba, 1848–1855* (1948); M. W. Williams, *Anglo-American Isthmian Diplomacy, 1815–1915* (1916); J. B. Brebner, *North Atlantic Triangle* (1945).

*Titles available in paperback.

The Breaking of the Union

Fourteen

George Washington on leaving the presidency had cautioned his fellow citizens that it might "disturb our Union" if political parties should ever be organized on a geographical basis — Eastern against Western or Northern against Southern — "whence designing men may endeavour to excite a belief that there is a real difference of local interests and views." He explained: "One of the expedients of party to acquire influence, within particular districts, is to misrepresent the opinions and aims of other districts."

From the beginning the parties had been national, not sectional. From the 1830s on, Whigs from North and South cooperated against Democrats from North and South. Partisan loyalties cut across geographical lines and served as bonds of union. So did denominational loyalties at a time when Northerners and Southerners belonged to the same national churches.

But bonds of union began to break. In the 1840s the Methodists and Baptists divided, because of the slavery question, into separate Northern and Southern organizations, and thereafter other churches were torn by sectional quarrels. Then, during the 1850s, the Whig party disintegrated. In the North it was replaced by a new party, the Republican, which had no members in the South. For a while the Democratic party continued to have a nationwide membership, but the party was weakened by sectional strains, and in 1860 it split into Northern and Southern wings. The time against which George Washington had warned was at hand.

No doubt some of the politicians of each section had misinterpreted the "opinions and aims" of the other. Still, the sectionalization of parties was due not merely to the influence of "designing men" but also to a "real

A Union Army Camp
This photograph of an encampment of the Army of the Potomac gives an impression of the huge, sprawling expanse of a Civil War army at rest — the array of tents, artillery, and wagons. This particular camp occupied a space of 20 square miles. (Top left, Library of Congress)

A Recruiting Poster for Negro Soldiers
This poster was typical of many put out by organizations in the North to induce Negroes to join the Union armies. Negro units were nearly always commanded by white officers. (Bottom left, Library of Congress)

difference of local interests and views." The breaking of the bonds of union and of the Union itself could hardly have occurred without real and substantial causes—the rise of opposition to slavery on moral grounds, the rapid industrialization of the North, the westward movement of population. The political disputes that led to national disruption centered on the question of future slavery in the West, not present slavery in the South, but that was largely due to the nature of the American Constitution. Opponents of slavery could hardly contend that the Constitution gave the federal government power to abolish it in the states where it already existed. These people did maintain—though defenders of slavery denied—that the federal government could, and should, prevent its spread to new territories.

New Territorial Controversy

By the 1850s the line of frontier settlement had reached the great bend of the Missouri. Beyond the western boundaries of Minnesota, Iowa, and Missouri stretched the vast expanse of plains earlier called the Great American Desert and designated as an Indian reserve. Now it was known that large sections of this region were suited to farming, and in the Northwest people were saying that the national government should open the area to settlement, provide it with territorial government, and remove the Indians. The problem of communication between the older states and the trans-Mississippi West had become urgent.

THE KANSAS-NEBRASKA ACT

The idea of a transcontinental railroad had been discussed in and out of Congress for years. Disagreement arose when people talked about the eastern terminus of the road and its specific route. Several cities pressed their claims, but the leading contenders were Chicago, St. Louis, Memphis, and New Orleans. The transcontinental railroad, like nearly everything else in the fifties, became entangled in sectionalism. It became a prize that the North and South struggled to secure.

One argument against a southern route had been removed through the foresight of Secretary of War Jefferson Davis. Surveys had indicated that a road from a southern terminus would probably have to pass through an area south of the Gila River, in Mexican territory. At Davis' suggestion, Pierce appointed James Gadsden, a Southern railroad builder, to negotiate with Mexico for the sale of this region. Gadsden persuaded the Mexican government to dispose of a strip of land that today comprises a part of Arizona and New Mexico, the so-called Gadsden Purchase (1853), which cost the United States $10 million.

Particularly interested in a transcontinental railroad was Senator Stephen A. Douglas, and his interest influenced him to introduce in Congress a fateful legislative act, one that accomplished the final destruction of the Compromise of 1850. As a senator from Illinois and a resident of Chicago and, above all, as the acknowledged leader of the Northwestern Democrats, Douglas naturally wanted the transcontinental railroad for his own city and section. He realized too the potency of the principal argument urged against the northern route: that west of the Mississippi it would run largely through unsettled Indian country. In January 1854, as chairman of the Committee on Territories, he acted to forestall this argument. He introduced a bill to organize a huge new territory, to be known as Nebraska, west of Iowa and Missouri.

Douglas seemed to realize that his bill would encounter the opposition of the South, partly because it would prepare the way for a new free state, the proposed territory being in the Louisiana Purchase area north of the 36° 30′ line of the Missouri Compromise and hence closed to slavery. In an effort to make the measure acceptable to Southerners, Douglas inserted a provision that the status of slavery in the territory would be determined by the territorial legislature, that is, according to popular sovereignty. Theoretically at least, this would open the region to slavery. The concession was not enough to satisfy extreme Southern Democrats, particularly those from Missouri who feared that their state would be surrounded by free territory. They demanded more, and Douglas had to give more to get their support. He agreed to two additions to his bill: a clause specifically repealing the antislavery provision of the Missouri Compromise, and another creating two territories, Nebraska and Kansas, instead of one. Presumably Kansas would become a slave state. In its final form the measure was known as the Kansas-Nebraska Act.

Douglas induced President Pierce to endorse his bill, and so it became an official Democratic measure. But even with the backing of the administration, it encountered stiff opposition and did not become a law until May 1854. Nearly all the Southern members of Congress, whether Whigs or Democrats, supported the bill, and nearly all the Northern Whigs opposed it. The Northern Democrats split, with half of their votes in the House going for the act and half against it.

Of greater importance than the opposition to the Kansas-Nebraska Act in Congress was the reaction against it in the Northern states. The whole North seemed to blaze with fury at this latest demonstration of the power of the slavocracy, and much of the fury was directed at Douglas, who, in the eyes of many Northerners, had acted as a tool of the slaveholders. No other piece of legislation in congressional history produced as many immediate, sweeping, and ominous changes as the Kansas-Nebraska Act. It destroyed the Whig party in the South except in the border states. At the same time, as many Southern Whigs became Democrats, it increased Southern influence in the Democratic party. It destroyed the popular basis of Whiggery in the North, with the result that by 1856 the national Whig party had disappeared and a conservative influence in American politics had been removed. It divided the Northern Democrats and drove many of them from the party. Most important of all, it called into being a new party that was frankly sectional in composition and creed.

Men in both the major parties who opposed Douglas' bill took to calling themselves Anti-Nebraska Democrats and Anti-Nebraska Whigs. In 1854 these men formed a new party and began to call themselves "Republicans." Originating in a series of spontaneous popular meetings throughout the Northwest, the Republican movement soon spread to the East. In the elections of 1854 the Republicans, often acting in concert with the Know-Nothings, elected a majority to the House and won control of a number of Northern state governments. For the moment the new party was a one-idea organization: its only platform was opposition to the expansion of slavery into the territories. Composed mainly of former Whigs and Free-Soilers but also including a substantial number of former Democrats, it represented in large part the democratic idealism of the North. But it contained, in addition, Northern power groups who felt that the South—the champion of a low tariff, the enemy of homesteads and internal improvements—was blocking their legitimate economic aspirations.

"BLEEDING KANSAS"

The pulsing popular excitement aroused in the North by the Kansas-Nebraska Act was sustained by events occurring during the next two years in Kansas. Almost immediately settlers moved into this territory. Some went as dedicated men who were determined to make Kansas free—or slave. Those from the North were encouraged by press and pulpit and the powerful organs of abolitionist propaganda. Often they received financial help from organizations like the New England Emigrant Aid Company, which had been created to render such assistance. Those from the South often received financial contributions from the communities they left.

In the spring of 1855 elections were held for a territorial legislature. Thousands of Missourians, some traveling in armed bands, moved into Kansas and voted. Although there were probably only some 1,500 legal votes in the territory, over 6,000 votes were counted. With such conditions prevailing, the proslavery forces elected a majority to the legislature, which proceeded immediately to enact a series of laws legalizing slavery. The outraged free-staters, convinced that they could not get a fair deal from the Pierce administration, resolved on extralegal action. Without asking permission from Congress or the territorial governor, they elected delegates to a constitutional convention

FREE STATE CONVENTION!

All persons who are favorable to a union of effort, and a permanent organization of all the Free State elements of Kansas Territory, and who wish to secure upon the broadest platform the co-operation of all who agree upon this point, are requested to meet at their several places of holding elections, in their respective districts on the 25th of August, instant, at one o'clock, P. M., and appoint five delegates to each representative to which they were entitled in the Legislative Assembly, who shall meet in general Convention at

Big Springs, Wednesday, Sept. 5th '55,

at 10 o'clock A. M., for the purpose of adopting a Platform upon which all may act harmoniously who prefer Freedom to Slavery.

The nomination of a Delegate to Congress, will also come up before the General Convention.

Let no sectional or party issues distract or prevent the perfect co-operation of Free State men. Union and harmony are absolutely necessary to success. The pro-slavery party are fully and effectually organized. No jars nor minor issues divide them. And to contend against them successfully, we also must be united.— Without prudence and harmony of action we are certain to fail. Let every man then do his duty and we are certain of victory.

All Free State men, without distinction, are earnestly requested to take immediate and effective steps to insure a full and correct representation for every District in the Territory. "United we stand; divided we fall."

By order of the Executive Committee of the Free State Party of the Territory of Kansas, as per resolution of the Mass Convention in session at Lawrence, Aug 15th and 16th, 1855.

J. K. GOODIN, Sec'y.   **C. ROBINSON, Chairman.**

Herald of Freedom, Print.

Free Soilers Organize in Kansas

After the Kansas proslavery elements, with the aid of "border ruffians" from Missouri, had elected a proslavery legislature, the free soilers called a convention and prepared to organize their own, antislavery government. A broadside was widely posted to announce the call. (The Kansas State Historical Society, Topeka)

---

which met at Topeka and adopted a constitution excluding slavery. They then chose a governor and legislature and petitioned Congress for statehood. Pierce stigmatized their movement as unlawful and akin to treason. The full weight of the government, he announced, would be thrown behind the proslavery territorial legislature.

A few months later a proslavery federal marshal assembled a huge posse, consisting mostly of Missourians, to arrest the free-state leaders in Lawrence. The posse not only made the arrests but sacked the town. Retribution came immediately. Among the more extreme antislavery men was a fierce, fanatical old man named John Brown who considered himself an instrument of God's will to destroy slavery. Estimating that five antislavery men had been murdered, he decided that it was his sacred

duty to take revenge. He gathered six followers, and in one night murdered five proslavery settlers (the "Pottawatomie massacre"). The result was to touch off civil war in Kansas — irregular, guerrilla war conducted by armed bands, some of them more interested in land claims or loot than in ideologies.

People in the North and the South believed (and whether or not their beliefs were completely correct is historically unimportant) that the aggressive designs of the other section were epitomized by what was happening in Kansas. Thus "Bleeding Kansas" became a symbol of the sectional controversy.

In May 1856 Charles Sumner of Massachusetts arose in the Senate to discuss affairs in the strife-torn territory. He entitled his speech "The Crime Against Kansas." Handsome, humorless, sincere, doctrinaire, Sumner em-

bodied the extreme element of the political antislavery movement. In his address he fiercely
denounced the Pierce administration, the
South, and slavery; and he singled out for particular attention as a champion of slavery Senator Andrew P. Butler of South Carolina. It was
an age when orators were wont to indulge freely in personal invective, but in his allusions to
Butler and others, Sumner went further than
most.

Particularly enraged by the attack was
Butler's nephew, Preston Brooks, a member of
the House from South Carolina. He resolved to
punish Sumner by a method approved by the
Southern code—by publicly and physically
chastising him. Approaching him at his desk
when the Senate was not in session, Brooks
proceeded to beat him with a cane until Sumner fell to the floor in bloody unconsciousness.
The injured senator stayed out of the Senate
four years, and during his absence his state
refused to elect a successor. Brooks, censured
by the House, resigned and stood for reelection. He was returned by an almost unanimous
vote.
The violence in Congress, like that in Kansas, was a symbol. It showed that Americans
were becoming so agitated by their differences
that they could not settle them by the normal
political processes of debate and the ballot.

BUCHANAN AND DEPRESSION

The presidential campaign of 18   got under
way with the country convulsed by the Brooks
assault and the continuing violence in Kansas.
The Democrats adopted a platform that endorsed the Kansas-Nebraska Act and defended popular sovereignty. The leaders wanted a
candidate who had not made many enemies
and who was not closely associated with the explosive question of "Bleeding Kansas." So the
nomination went to James Buchanan of Pennsylvania, a reliable party stalwart who as minister to England had been safely out of the
country during the recent troubles, though he
was a signer of the highly controversial Ostend
Manifesto. *P. 364*

The Republicans, engaging in their first
presidential contest, faced the campaign with
confidence. They denounced the Kansas-
Nebraska Act and the expansion of slavery but

also approved a program of internal improvements, thus beginning to combine the idealism
of antislavery with the economic aspirations of
the North. Just as eager as the Democrats to
present a safe candidate, the Republicans nominated John C. Frémont, who had made a national reputation as an explorer of the Far
West. A sincere Republican, the glamorous
"Pathfinder" was selected because he had no
political record and was highly available.

The Native American or Know-Nothing
party was beginning to break apart on the inevitable rock of sectionalism. At its convention,
many Northern delegates withdrew because
the platform was not sufficiently firm in opposing the expansion of slavery. The remaining
delegates nominated former President Millard
Fillmore. His candidacy was endorsed by the
sad remnant of another party, the few remaining Whigs who could not bring themselves to
support either Buchanan or Frémont.

The campaign was the most exciting since
1840. Its frenzied enthusiasm was due largely to
the Republicans. They shouted for "Free Soil,
Free Speech, Free Men, and Frémont," depicted "Bleeding Kansas" as a sacrifice to the
evil ambitions of the slavocracy, and charged
that the South, using Northern dupes like
Buchanan as its tools, was plotting to extend
slavery into every part of the country.

The returns seemed to indicate that the
prevailing mood of the country was conservative. Buchanan, the winning candidate, polled
1,838,000 popular votes to 1,341,000 for
Frémont, and 874,000 for Fillmore. A slight shift
of votes in Pennsylvania and Illinois would
have thrown those states into the Republican
column and elected Frémont.

James Buchanan had been in public office
almost continuously since the age of twenty-
three. Nearly sixty-six at the time of his inauguration he was, except for William Henry Harrison, the oldest President ever to take office.
Undoubtedly his age and his physical infirmities had much to do with the indecision he was
often to display.

In the year Buchanan took over, a financial panic struck the country, followed by several years of stringent depression. Europe had
shown an unusual demand for American food
during the Crimean War (1854–1856) and when
the demand fell off, agricultural prices were
seriously depressed. The depression sharp-

ened sectional differences. The South was not hit as hard as the North. Southern leaders now found confirmation for their claim that their economic system was superior to that of the free states. Smarting under previous Northern criticisms of Southern society, they loudly boasted of their superiority to the North.

In the North the depression strengthened the Republican party and weakened the Democratic. Distressed economic groups—manufacturers and farmers—came to believe that the hard times had been caused by unsound policies of Southern-controlled Democratic administrations. These groups thought that prosperity could be restored by a high tariff (the tariff was lowered again in 1857), a homestead act, and internal improvements—all measures to which the South was opposed. In short, the frustrated economic interests of the North were being drawn into an alliance with the antislavery elements as represented by the Republican party.

THE DRED SCOTT CASE

The Supreme Court of the United States projected itself into the sectional controversy with its decision in the case of *Dred Scott* v. *Sanford,* handed down two days after Buchanan was inaugurated.

Dred Scott was a Missouri slave, once the property of an army surgeon who on his military pilgrimages had carried him to Illinois, a free state, and to Minnesota Territory, where slavery was forbidden by the Missouri Compro-

Dred Scott and Roger B. Taney
A former Maryland slaveowner, Taney was one of the greatest of all Chief Justices of the United States, but his reputation in the North was badly damaged by his proslavery, anti-Negro decision in the Dred Scott case. After the decision, Scott was freed by his owner and was employed as a hotel porter in St. Louis. A year later, in 1858, he died of tuberculosis. (National Archives)

mise. Scott was persuaded by some abolitionists to bring suit in the Missouri courts for his freedom on the ground that residence in a free territory had made him a free man. The state supreme court decided against him. Meanwhile, the surgeon having died and his widow having married an abolitionist, ownership of Scott was transferred to her brother, J. F. A. Sanford, who lived in New York. Now Scott's lawyers could get the case into the federal courts on the ground that the suit lay between citizens of different states. Regardless of the final decision, Scott would be freed, as his abolitionist owners would not keep him a slave. The case was intended to secure a federal decision on the status of slavery in the territories.

Of the nine justices, seven were Democrats (five of them from the South), one was a Whig, and one was a Republican. Chief Justice Taney, in the majority opinion, declared that Scott was not a citizen of Missouri and hence could not bring a suit in the federal courts. According to Taney, no Negro could qualify as a citizen. So far as the Constitution was concerned, he added, Negroes had no rights that white men were bound to respect. Having said this, Taney could simply have declined jurisdiction over the case. Instead, he went on to argue that Scott's sojourn in Minnesota had not affected his status as a slave. Slaves were property, said Taney, and the Fifth Amendment prohibited Congress from taking property without "due process of law." Consequently, Congress possessed no authority to pass a law depriving persons of their slave property in the territories. The Missouri Compromise, therefore, had always been null and void.

Few judicial opinions have stirred as much popular excitement as this one did. Southern whites were elated: the highest tribunal in the land had invested with legal sanction the extreme Southern argument. On behalf of abolitionists black and white, Frederick Douglass declared: "This very attempt to blot out forever the hopes of an enslaved people may be one necessary link in the chain of events preparatory to the complete overthrow of the whole slave system." Republicans denounced the decision. They said it deserved as much consideration as any pronouncement by a group of political hacks. They threatened that when they secured control of the national government, they would reverse the decision—by altering the personnel of the Court and "packing" it with new members.

DEADLOCK OVER KANSAS

Endorsing the decision, President Buchanan concluded that the best solution for the Kansas troubles was to force the admission of that territory as a slave state. The existing proslavery territorial legislature called an election for delegates to a constitutional convention. The free-state people refused to participate. As a result, the proslavery forces won control of the convention, which met in 1857 at Lecompton and framed a constitution establishing slavery. When an election for a new territorial legislature was called, the antislavery groups turned out to vote and won a majority. Promptly the legislature moved to submit the Lecompton constitution to the voters. The document was rejected by more than 10,000 votes.

Although both sides had resorted to fraud and violence, the Kansas picture was clear enough. The majority of the people did not want to see slavery established. Unfortunately Buchanan could not see, or did not want to see, the true picture. He urged Congress to admit Kansas under the Lecompton constitution, and he tried to force the party to back his proposal. Stephen A. Douglas and other Western Democrats refused to accept this perversion of popular sovereignty. Openly breaking with the administration, Douglas denounced the Lecompton proposition. And although Buchanan's plan passed the Senate, Western Democrats helped to block it in the House. Partly to avert further division in the party, a compromise measure, the English bill, was now offered (1858) and passed. It provided that the Lecompton constitution should be submitted to the people of Kansas for the third time. If the document was approved, Kansas was to be admitted and given a federal land grant; if it was disapproved, statehood would be postponed until the population reached 93,600, the legal ratio for a representative in Congress. Again, and for the last time, the Kansas voters decisively rejected the Lecompton constitution. Not until the closing months of Buchanan's administration, in 1861, when a number of Southern states had withdrawn from the Union, would Kansas enter the Union—as a free state.

LINCOLN AGAINST DOUGLAS

The congressional elections of 1858 were of greater interest and importance than is usually true of such mid-term contests. Not only did they have an immediate and powerful influence on the course of the sectional controversy, but they projected into the national spotlight the man who was to be the dominating figure in the tragic years just ahead.

The widest public attention was attracted by the senatorial election in Illinois. There Stephen A. Douglas, the most prominent Northern Democrat, was a candidate for reelection, and he was fighting for his political life. Since Douglas, or his successor, would be chosen by a legislature that was yet to be elected, the control of that body became a matter of paramount importance. To punish Douglas for his resistance to the Lecompton constitution, the Buchanan administration entered Democratic candidates opposed to him in many legislative districts. But Douglas' greatest worry was that he faced

Abraham Lincoln, the ablest campaigner in the Republican party.

Lincoln had been the leading Whig in Illinois. He was now the leading Republican in the state, though hardly a national figure—his reputation could not compare with that of the famous Douglas. Lincoln challenged the senator to a series of seven joint debates. Douglas accepted, and the two candidates argued their cases before huge crowds. The Lincoln-Douglas debates were widely reported by the nation's press, and before their termination the Republican who had dared to challenge the "Little Giant" of the Democracy was a man of national prominence.

Douglas, while defending popular sovereignty, accused the Republicans of promoting a war of sections, of wishing to interfere with slavery in the South, and of advocating social equality of the races. Lincoln, denying these charges (which were untrue), accused the Democrats and Douglas of conspiring to extend slavery into the territories and possibly, by

Lincoln and Douglas in Debate
This is a depiction by a later artist, R. M. Root, of the debate between Lincoln and Douglas at Charleston. Lincoln, who was beardless until 1861, is speaking, and Douglas sits at his right. Various dignitaries of both parties are on the platform. The man behind Lincoln and to the left taking notes is probably a reporter. In the 1850s speeches were frequently recorded by men known as "stenographic reporters." They used a system of shorthand devised by Isaac Pitman and described by him in a book published in 1837, Stenographic Sound Hand. (Illinois State Historical Library)

means of another Supreme Court decision, into the free states as well (a charge that also was untrue). Lincoln was particularly effective in making it appear that Douglas did not regard slavery as morally wrong. He quoted Douglas as saying he did not care whether slavery was "voted up, or voted down."

Lincoln was opposed to slavery — on moral, political, and economic grounds. He believed that it contradicted the American ideal of democracy. Let the idea be established that Negroes were not created with an equal right to earn their bread, he said, and the next step would be to deny the right to certain groups of whites, such as day laborers. His solicitude for the economic well-being of the white masses impelled Lincoln to oppose the introduction of slavery into the territories. He maintained that the national lands should be preserved as places for poor white people to go to better their condition.

Yet Lincoln was opposed to the abolitionists. The physical fact of slavery, he believed, must be taken into account. "We have a due regard to the actual presence of it amongst us and the difficulties of getting rid of it in any satisfactory way and all the constitutional obligations thrown about it." He and his party would "arrest the further spread of it," that is, prevent its expansion into the territories, and thus prepare for its "ultimate extinction." His plan, then, was to pen up slavery in the South, where he hoped it would eventually die a natural death.

In the debate at Freeport, Lincoln asked Douglas: Can the people of a territory exclude slavery from its limits prior to the formation of a state constitution? Or in other words, is popular sovereignty still a legal formula despite the Dred Scott decision? The question was a deadly trap, for no matter how Douglas answered

it, he would lose something. If he disavowed popular sovereignty he would undoubtedly be defeated for reelection and his political career would be ended. But if he reaffirmed his formula, Southern Democrats would be offended, the party split deepened, and his chances of securing the Democratic nomination in 1860 damaged if not destroyed.

Boldly Douglas met the issue. The people of a territory, he said, could, by lawful means, shut out slavery prior to the formation of a state constitution. Slavery could not exist a day without the support of "local police regulations": territorial laws recognizing the right of slave ownership. The mere failure of a legislature to enact such laws would have the practical effect of keeping slaveholders out. Thus, despite the Dred Scott decision, a territory could exclude slavery. Douglas' reply became known as the Freeport Doctrine or, in the South, as the Freeport Heresy. It satisfied his followers sufficiently to win him a return to the Senate, but throughout the North it aroused little enthusiasm.

The elections went heavily against the Democrats, who lost ground in almost every Northern state. The administration retained control of the Senate but lost its majority in the House, where the Republicans gained a plurality. In the holdover or short session of 1858–1859, in which the Democrats were in the majority, and in the regular session of 1859 (elected in 1858), every demand of the Republicans and Northern Democrats was blocked by Southern votes or by presidential vetoes. These defeated measures included a tariff increase, a homestead bill, a Pacific railroad, and federal land grants to states for the endowment of agricultural colleges. The 1859 session was also marked by an uproarious struggle over the election of a Speaker of the House.

The Separation of the Sections

During the 1850s the nation seemed at first to drift and then to rush toward disunion. The fateful goal was reached during the winter of 1860–1861. Thereafter, for more than four years, Americans were divided into what, in effect, amounted to two separate and hostile countries.

JOHN BROWN'S RAID

Hastening the trend toward disunion was a grim event of 1859. John Brown, the antislavery fanatic from Kansas, now made a spectacular appearance on the national scene. Still convinced that he was God's instrument to destroy slavery, he decided to transfer his activities from Kansas to the South itself. With encouragement and financial aid from some Eastern abolitionists, he devised a wild scheme for putting an end to slavery. His plan was to seize a mountain fortress in Virginia from which he could make raids to liberate slaves. He would arm the freedmen, set up a Negro republic, and eventually force the South to concede emancipation. He was out to lead a slave insurrection. Because he needed guns, he chose Harpers Ferry, where a United States arsenal was located, as his base of operations. In October, at the head of eighteen followers, he descended on the town and captured the arsenal. Almost immediately he was attacked by citizens and local militia companies, who were shortly reinforced by a detachment of United States marines sent to the scene by the national government. With ten of his men killed, Brown had to surrender. He was promptly tried in a Virginia court for treason against the state, found guilty, and sentenced to death by hanging. Six of his followers met a similar fate.

Probably no other event had so much influence as the Harpers Ferry raid in convincing Southerners that their section was unsafe in the Union. Despite all their eulogies of slavery, one great fear always secretly gnawed at their hearts: the possibility of a general slave insurrection. Southerners now jumped to the conclusion that the Republicans were responsible for Brown's raid. This was, of course, untrue; prominent Republicans like Lincoln and Seward condemned Brown as a criminal. But Southerners were more impressed by the words of such abolitionists as Wendell Phillips and Ralph Waldo Emerson, who now glorified Brown as a new saint. His execution made him a martyr to thousands of Northerners.

ELECTION OF LINCOLN

The election of 1860, judged by its consequences, was the most momentous in American history.

As the Democrats gathered in convention at Charleston, South Carolina, in April, most of the Southern delegates came with the determination to adopt a platform providing for federal protection of slavery in the territories: that is, an official endorsement of the principles of the Dred Scott decision. The Western Democrats, arriving with bitter recollections of how Southern influence had blocked their legislative demands in the recent Congress, were angered at the rule-or-ruin attitude of the Southerners. The Westerners hoped, however, to negotiate a face-saving statement on slavery so as to hold the party together. They vaguely endorsed popular sovereignty and proposed that all questions involving slavery in the territories be left up to the Supreme Court. When the convention adopted the Western platform, the delegations from eight lower South states withdrew from the hall. The remaining delegates then proceeded to the selection of a candidate. Stephen A. Douglas led on every ballot, but he could not muster the two-thirds majority (of the original number of delegates) required by party rules. Finally the managers adjourned the convention to meet again in Baltimore in June. At the Baltimore session, most of the Southerners reappeared, only to walk out again. The rest of the Southerners had assembled at Richmond. The rump convention at Baltimore nominated Douglas. The Southern bolters at Baltimore and the men in Richmond nominated John C. Breckinridge of Kentucky.

Sectionalism had at last divided the historic Democratic party. There were now two Democratic candidates in the field, and, although Douglas had supporters in the South and Breckinridge in the North, one was the nominee of the Northern Democrats and the other of the Southern Democrats.

The Republicans held their convention in Chicago in May. Although the divisions developing in the Democratic ranks seemed to spell a Republican triumph, the party managers were taking no chances on a slip-up. They were determined that the party, in both its platform and its candidate, should appear to the voters as representing conservatism, stability, and moderation rather than radical idealism. No longer was the Republican party a one-idea organization composed of crusaders against slavery. It now embraced, or hoped to embrace, every major interest group in the North that believed that the South, the champion of slavery, was blocking its legitimate economic aspirations.

The platform endorsed such measures as a high tariff, internal improvements, a homestead bill, and a Pacific railroad to be built with

On the causation of the Civil War, historians' views have changed with changing times, thus illustrating the fact that history reflects the period *in* which it is written as well as the period *about* which it is written. In the 1890s, when the United States was emerging as a world power, the Civil War seemed to have been concerned with fundamental issues, for it had not only destroyed slavery but also preserved the Union, thus making possible the nation's rise to greatness. Such was the implied theme of the leading authority of the time, James Ford Rhodes. In his *History of the United States from the Compromise of 1850* . . . (7 vols., 1893–1900) Rhodes saw the war as originating in the conflict between Northern opponents and Southern defenders of slavery.

This view prevailed until the 1920s, when Charles and Mary Beard challenged it in *The Rise of American Civilization* (2 vols., 1927). The Beards believed that in politics the most powerful of human motivations were economic. Like many of their contemporaries among the intellectuals, these authors were disillusioned with the efforts of progressives to curb business monopolies. The Beards maintained that the basic causes of the Civil War were economic. According to them, the war arose out of a clash between Northern industrialists and Southern planters, each group seeking to control the federal government in its own interest, and both groups using arguments about slavery and state rights only as smoke screens. The Beards had doubts about the results of the "Second American Revolution," as they called the war, for it brought on the evils associated with the rise of big business.

In the 1930s the Beardian interpretation began to be superseded by the views of the "revisionists." While these men were writing, the American revulsion against war was at its height. The recent war to "end war" and "make the world safe for democracy" had obviously done neither, and American participation in it seemed now like a great mistake. The Civil War, too, had been unfortunate and useless according to the revisionists, such as Avery Craven and James G. Randall, who blamed it on the fanaticism and political ineptitude of a "blundering generation."

After World War II, which appeared to have saved democracy from the threat of Hitlerism, historians took a new look at the Civil War and concluded, once again, that it had been necessary and worthwhile. Arthur Schlesinger, Jr., explained that violence was sometimes indispensable for clearing away obstacles to social progress and that slavery had been such an obstacle. Allan Nevins, beginning a multivolume restudy of the period 1850–1877 in *The Ordeal of the Union* and *The Emergence of Lincoln* (4 vols., 1947–1950), characterized the Civil War as "a war over slavery *and* the future position of the Negro race in North America." As the civil rights movement gained momentum in the 1950s and 1960s, historians gave more and more attention to slavery and race relations as central issues in the sectional conflict of the 1850s and 1860s. Eugene Genovese, for one, saw the war as growing out of the Southern planters' efforts to protect and expand the slave system.

federal financial assistance. On the slavery issue, the platform affirmed the right of each state to control its own institutions, which was the Republicans' way of saying that they did not intend to interfere with slavery in the South. But they also denied the authority of Congress or of a territorial legislature to legalize slavery in the territories, which was equivalent to saying that they still would oppose the expansion of slavery.

The leading contender for the nomination was William H. Seward, who faced the competition of a number of favorite-son candidates. His prominence and his long political record damaged his chances. Passing him and other aspirants over, the convention nominated on the third ballot Abraham Lincoln—who was prominent enough to be respectable but obscure enough to have few foes, and who was radical enough to please the antislavery faction in the party but conservative enough to satisfy the ex-Whigs. To complete the strategy of availability, the vice-presidential nomination went

to Hannibal Hamlin of Maine, a former Democrat.

As if three parties were not enough, a fourth entered the lists—the Constitutional Union party. Although posing as a new organization, it was really the last surviving remnant of the oldest conservative tradition in the country; its leaders were elder statesmen and most of its members were former Whigs. Meeting in Baltimore in May, this party nominated John Bell of Tennessee and Edward Everett of Massachusetts. Its platform favored the Constitution, the Union, and enforcement of the laws.

In the North the Republicans conducted a campaign reminiscent of the exciting contest of 1840, with parades, symbols, and mass meetings. For the most part, they stressed the economic promises in their platform and subordinated the slavery issue. Lincoln, following the customary practice of candidates, made no speeches, leaving this work to lesser party luminaries. Unlike previous candidates, he refused to issue any written statements of his

Election of 1860

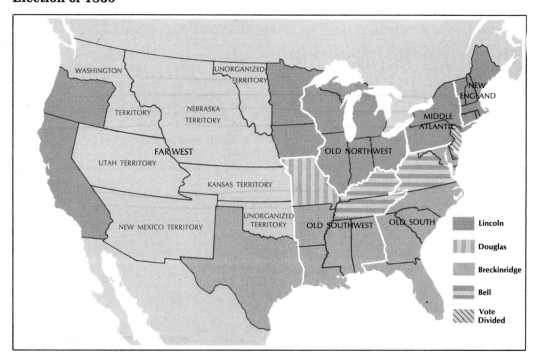

views, claiming that anything he said would be seized on by Southerners and misrepresented.

In the November election Lincoln won a majority of the electoral votes and the presidency, though only about two-fifths of the popular votes. The Republicans had elected a President, but they had failed to secure a majority in Congress; and of course they did not control the Supreme Court.

SECESSION OF THE SOUTH

During the campaign various Southern leaders had threatened that if the Republicans won the election the South would secede from the Union. Southerners had voiced secession threats at intervals since 1850, and Northerners had come to believe that the Southerners were bluffing. This time, however, some of them were in earnest.

The concept of secession was rooted in the political philosophy that the South had developed to protect its minority status. According to this doctrine, the Union was an association of sovereign states. The individual states had once joined the Union; they could, whenever they wished, dissolve their connections with it and resume their status as separate sovereignties. For a state to leave the Union was a momentous act but a lawful one, from the Southern point of view. The governor and the legislature could call an election for a special state convention and this body could pass an ordinance of secession.

South Carolina, long the hotbed of Southern separatism, led off the secession parade, its convention taking the state out of the Union on December 20, 1860, by a unanimous vote. Before Lincoln ever assumed the presidency, six other Southern states had left the Union. Not only that, but in February 1861 representatives of the seceded states met at Montgomery, Alabama, and formed a new, Southern nation — the Confederate States of America.

Something of the indecision in Northern attitudes was reflected in the thinking of President Buchanan. In his message to Congress of December 1860, he denied the right of a state to secede but did not think the federal government possessed the power to force a state back into the Union. He intended to avoid a collision of arms and to maintain the symbolic authority of the national government until his successor could take office.

As the various states seceded, they took possession of federal property within their boundaries, but they lacked the strength to seize certain offshore forts, notably Fort Sumter in the harbor of Charleston, South Carolina, and Fort Pickens in the harbor of Pensacola, Florida. South Carolina sent commissioners to Washington to ask for the surrender of Sumter, garrisoned by a small force under Major Robert Anderson. Buchanan, fearful though he was of provoking a clash, refused to yield the fort. In January 1861 he decided to reinforce it. By his direction an unarmed merchant ship, the *Star of the West*, proceeded to Fort Sumter with troops and supplies. When the vessel attempted to enter the harbor, it encountered the fire of shore batteries and turned back.

Meanwhile Buchanan recommended to Congress that it frame compromise measures to hold the Union together. The Senate and the House appointed committees to study plans of adjustment. The Senate committee concentrated on a proposal submitted by Senator John J. Crittenden of Kentucky. The Crittenden Compromise called for a series of constitutional amendments: one would have guaranteed the permanence of slavery in the states; others were designed to satisfy Southern demands on such matters as fugitive slaves and slavery in the District of Columbia. But the heart of Crittenden's plan dealt with slavery in the territories. He proposed to reestablish the Missouri Compromise line of 36° 30' in all the territory of the United States then held or *thereafter acquired.* Slavery was to be prohibited north of the line and permitted south of it. The Southern members of the committee indicated they would accept this territorial division if the Republicans also would. The Republicans, after sounding out President-elect Lincoln in Illinois, voted against the proposal. Lincoln took the position that the restoration of the Missouri Compromise line would encourage the South to embark on imperialist adventures in Latin America.

One notable attempt to effect a compromise was made outside Congress. The legislature of Virginia invited the other states to send delegates to a peace conference at Washington. Representatives from twenty-one states assembled early in February, and spent most of the

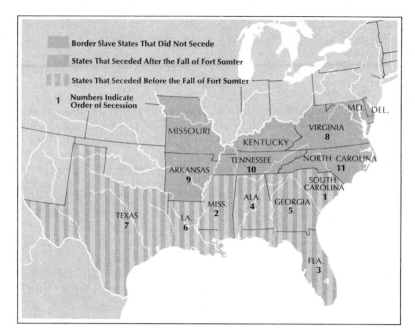

Border Slave States That Did Not Secede

States That Seceded After the Fall of Fort Sumter

States That Seceded Before the Fall of Fort Sumter

1   Numbers Indicate
     Order of Secession

MISSOURI

KENTUCKY

ARKANSAS
9

TENNESSEE
10

MD. DEL.

VIRGINIA
8

NORTH CAROLINA
11

SOUTH
CAROLINA
1

TEXAS
7

LA.
6

MISS.
2

ALA.
4

GEORGIA
5

FLA.
3

The Process of Secession

month framing compromise proposals. The plan of this Peace Convention followed closely the Crittenden scheme. The convention submitted the plan to the Senate, but it received almost no support.

And so nothing had been resolved when Abraham Lincoln was inaugurated President on March 4, 1861. In his inaugural address he laid down the following basic principles: the Union was older than the Constitution, no state could of its own volition leave the Union, the ordinances of secession were illegal, and acts of violence to support secession were insurrectionary or revolutionary. He declared that he meant to execute the laws in all the states and to "hold, occupy, and possess" the federal property in the seceded states (Forts Sumter and Pickens).

Lincoln soon found an opportunity to apply his policy in the case of Fort Sumter. Major Anderson was running short of supplies; unless he received fresh provisions the fort would have to be evacuated. If Lincoln permitted the loss of Sumter, the South and perhaps the North would never believe that he meant to sustain the Union. After much deliberation he decided to dispatch a naval relief expedition to the fort. Carefully he informed the South Carolina authorities, who, of course, would have to notify the Confederate government, that ships were on the way to bring supplies but not to land troops or munitions unless resistance was offered. His move placed the Confederates in a dilemma. If they permitted the expedition to land, they would be bowing tamely to federal authority; their people would not believe that they meant to sustain secession. But the only alternative was to reduce the fort before the ships arrived. After hours of anguished discussion, the government in Montgomery ordered General P. G. T. Beauregard, in charge of Confederate forces at Charleston, to demand Anderson's surrender and, if the demand was refused, to reduce the fort. Beauregard made the demand and Anderson rejected it. The Confederates then bombarded the fort for two days, April 12–13, 1861. On April 14, Anderson surrendered.

War had come. Lincoln moved to increase the army and called on the states to furnish troops to restore the Union. Now four more slave states seceded and joined the Confederacy: Virginia (April 17); Arkansas (May 6); Tennessee (May 7); and North Carolina (May 20). The mountain counties in northwestern Virginia refused to accept the decision of their state, established their own "loyal" government, and in 1863 secured admission to the Union as the new state of West Virginia. The four remaining slave states, Maryland, Delaware, Kentucky, and Missouri, cast their lot with the Union. Lincoln kept a keen watch on their actions, and in two, Maryland and Missouri, helped to ensure their decision by employing military force.

THE OPPOSING SIDES

A comparison of the combatants on the eve of war reveals that all the great material factors were on the side of the North. And these advantages became more significant as the conflict continued and the superior economy of the North became geared for war production. The North had a larger manpower reservoir from which to draw its armed forces. In the North, or the United States, were twenty-three states with a population of approximately 22 million. In the South, or the Confederate States, were eleven states with a population of about 9 million. Of these, approximately 3.5 million were slaves, leaving a white population of less than 6 million.

The North's greater economic potential was most formidably apparent in industrial production. Almost any set of comparative figures can be chosen to illustrate the overwhelming nature of Northern superiority. These statistics, translated into material terms, meant that the Northern armies, once the economic system had been converted to war production, would have more of everything than the Southern forces. This was not true, of course, in the first year of the war, when both sides purchased large amounts of supplies, particularly arms, from Europe. After 1862 the North was able to manufacture practically all of its war materials; its dependence on Europe ceased. The South, on the other hand, had to rely on Europe all during the war. It also tried desperately to expand its own industrial facilities. The brilliant Confederate chief of ordnance, Josiah Gorgas, accomplished wonders in building arsenals and in supplying the armies with weapons and munitions. Neverthe-

less, both the quantity and the quality of Confederate firearms were inferior. The Southern economic system was unable to provide its soldiers and civilians with the other materiel of modern war: clothes, boots, blankets, stockings, medical supplies, and the like. Its failure in this respect was one reason why Southern morale dropped badly after 1863.

In every respect the transportation system of the North was superior to that of the South. The North had more and better inland water transport (steamboats, barges), more surfaced roads, and more wagons and animals. The North had approximately 20,000 miles of railroads, while the South, containing at least as large a land area, had only 10,000 miles. The trackage figures, however, do not tell the whole story of Southern inferiority. There were important gaps between key points in the South, which meant that supplies had to be detoured long distances or carried between railheads by wagons. As the war wore on, the Confederate railroad system steadily deteriorated, and by the last year and a half of the struggle it had almost collapsed.

When the material factors are analyzed and weighed, the impression emerges that the South had absolutely no chance to win the war. Actually, the material odds were not so great as they appear at first glance. The South might have won a decision on the battlefield up to 1863. Southern inferiority in manpower and materials was partially offset by other factors. The South, for the most part, fought on the defensive in its own country and commanded interior lines. The Northern invaders had to maintain long lines of communication, to supply themselves in areas where transportation was defective, and to garrison occupied regions. Furthermore, the North had to do more than capture the enemy capital or defeat enemy armies. It had to convince the Southern civilian population that the war was hopeless by seizing and holding most of the Confederacy. The South was fighting for something very concrete, very easy for its people to understand. It simply wanted to be independent, to be let alone; it had no aggressive designs on the North. If the South could have convinced the North that it could not be conquered or that the result would not be worth the sacrifices, it might, even after 1863, have won its independence.

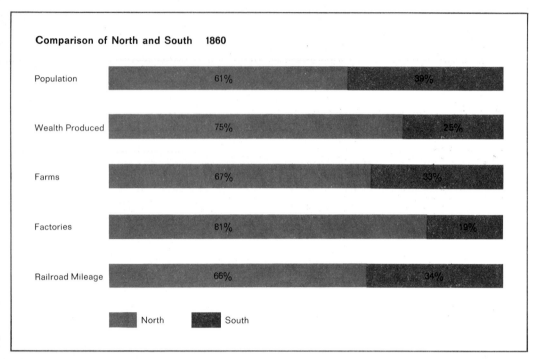

Comparison of North and South   1860

Population	61%	39%
Wealth Produced	75%	25%
Farms	67%	33%
Factories	81%	19%
Railroad Mileage	66%	34%

North   South

If the slaves were not included in the South's total population, the North's manpower advantage would appear greater than shown above. Because many of the South's so-called factories were small, the superiority of the North's industrial production was actually greater than this chart indicates.

The Aggressor, According to Lincoln

In his July 4, 1861, message to Congress, President Lincoln said with regard to Fort Sumter:

As had been intended, in this contingency, it was also resolved to notify the Governor of South Carolina, that he might expect an attempt would be made to provision the Fort; and that, if the attempt should not be resisted, there would be no effort to throw in men, arms, or ammunition, without further notice, or in case of an attack upon the Fort. This notice was accordingly given; whereupon the Fort was attacked, and bombarded to its fall, without even awaiting the arrival of the provisioning expedition.

It is thus seen that the assault upon and reduction of Fort Sumter was, in no sense, a matter of self defence on the part of the assailants. They well knew that the garrison in the Fort could, by no possibility, commit aggression upon them. They knew — they were expressly notified — that the giving of bread to the few brave and hungry men of the garrison was all which would on that occasion be attempted, unless themselves, by resisting so much, should provoke more. They knew that this Government desired to keep the garrison in the Fort, not to assail them, but merely to maintain visible possession, and thus to preserve the Union from actual and immediate dissolution. . . .

Southerners thought that even if the Southern human resources could not make up for Northern material advantages, there was still an almost certain guarantee of Confederate victory: Europe would intervene in the war on the side of the South. England and France had to have Southern cotton, and they would force the North to recognize the Confederacy.

The North Mobilizes

For the North the wartime years became a period of prosperity and expansion. Both industry and agriculture increased their productive facilities and, at the end of the war, were turning out more products than at the beginning.

ECONOMIC MEASURES

A powerful stimulant to the expanding economy was provided by the economic legislation enacted by the Republican party during the war. The Republicans represented Northern industry and agriculture, and, now that the war had removed Southern opposition, they proceeded to put into effect the kind of program their supporters expected.

The Homestead Act (1862) and the Morrill Land Grant Act (1862) were measures that the West had long sought. The first provided that any citizen or any alien who had declared his intention to become a citizen could register claim to a quarter section of public land (160 acres), and, after giving proof that he had lived on it for five years, receive title on payment of a small fee. The Morrill Law gave every state 30,000 acres of public land for each of its congressional representatives, the proceeds from the donation to be used for education in agriculture, engineering, and military science. This provided a basis for the development of the so-called land-grant colleges and universities.

Industry scored its first gain a few days before President Buchanan left office. Congress passed the Morrill Tariff Act, which provided a moderate increase in duties, bringing the rates up to approximately what they had been before 1846. Later measures enacted in 1862 and 1864 were frankly protective. By the end of the war the average of duties was 47

The Aggressor, According to Stephens

President Davis, Vice President Stephens, and indeed all good Confederates maintained that "the war was inaugurated" by Lincoln himself. Stephens expressed the Confederate view in the first volume of his postwar work entitled *A Constitutional View of the Late War Between the States* (1868):

It is a fact that the first gun was fired by the Confederates. . . . But did the firing of the first gun or the reduction of Fort Sumter inaugurate or begin the war? . . . Hallam [an authority on international law] has well said that "the aggressor in a war (that is, he who begins it) is not the first who uses force, but the first who renders force necessary."

Which side, according to this high authority (that only announces the common sentiments of mankind), was the aggressor in this instance? Which side was it that provoked and rendered the first blow necessary? The true answer to that question will settle the fact as to which side began the war.

I maintain that it was inaugurated and begun, though no blow had been struck, when the hostile fleet, styled the "Relief Squadron," with eleven ships, carrying two hundred and eighty-five guns and two thousand four hundred men, was sent out from New York and Norfolk with orders from the authorities at Washington to re-enforce Fort Sumter peaceably, if permitted — "but forcibly if they must."

percent, the highest in the nation's history, and more than double the prewar rate.

Other legislative victories for business were achieved in connection with railroad and immigration. Two laws, passed in 1862 and 1864, created two federal corporations: the Union Pacific Railroad Company, which was to build westward from Omaha, and the Central Pacific, which was to build eastward from California. The government would aid the companies by donating public lands and advancing government loans. Immigration from Europe fell off in the first years of the war, partly because of the unsettled conditions. The decrease, coupled with the military demands for manpower, threatened to cause a labor shortage, and President Lincoln and business leaders asked Congress for governmental encouragement of immigration. In 1864 Congress passed a contract labor law authorizing employers to import laborers and collect the costs of transportation from future wages.

Perhaps the most important measure affecting the business-financial community was the National Bank Act, enacted in 1863 and amended in 1864. The act created the National Banking System, which lasted without serious modification until 1913. Its architects, including Secretary of the Treasury Salmon P. Chase, argued that, both for the military present and the economic future, the country needed a uniform and standard bank-note currency. At the outbreak of the war 1,500 banks chartered by twenty-nine states were empowered to issue notes. Furthermore, Chase and his supporters claimed, national supervision of the banking system would enable the government to market its bonds more economically, thus aiding war finance.

An existing state bank or a newly formed corporation could secure a federal charter and become a national bank. Each association was required to possess a minimum amount of capital and to invest one-third of its capital in government securities. Upon depositing the securities with the national Treasury, it would receive, and could issue as bank notes, United States Treasury notes up to 90 percent of the current value of the bonds. Congress (in 1865) placed a tax on all state bank notes. This forced state notes out of existence and induced reluctant state banks to seek federal charters.

The North financed the war from three principal sources: taxation, loans, and paper money issues. From taxes, including the tariff, the government received approximately $667 million; loans, including Treasury notes, accounted for $2.6 billion; and $450 million of paper currency ("greenbacks") was issued.

Since the greenbacks bore no interest, were not supported by a specie reserve, and depended for redemption on the good faith of the government (and its ability to win the war), they fluctuated in value. In 1864 a greenback dollar, in relation to a gold dollar, was worth only 39 cents, and even at the close of the war its value had advanced to but 67 cents.

In America's previous wars, bonds had been sold only to banks and to a few wealthy investors. Through the agency of Jay Cooke, a Philadelphia banker, the Treasury now launched a campaign to persuade the ordinary man (and woman) to buy a bond. By high-pressure propaganda techniques, Cooke disposed of $400 million of bonds—the first example of mass financing of a war in our history.

Not until 1862, when mounting war expenses forced the country to face realities, did Congress adopt an adequate tax program. Then it passed the Internal Revenue Act, which placed duties on practically all goods and most occupations. For the first time, in 1861, the government levied an income tax: a duty of 3 percent on incomes above $800. Later the rates were increased to 5 percent on incomes between $600 and $5,000, and to 10 percent on incomes above the latter figure. Through the medium of the various war taxes, the hand of the government was coming to rest upon most individuals in the country. The United States was in the process of acquiring a national internal revenue system—in fact, a national tax system—one of the many nationalizing effects of the war.

RAISING THE UNION ARMIES

When hostilities started, the regular army numbered only about 16,000 troops, and many of its units were scattered throughout the West. President Lincoln, in his first call for troops to repress the "rebellion," summoned 75,000 militia for three months, the usual period of service set for state troops by existing militia law. Lincoln soon realized that the war would be of longer duration. Without constitutional sanction, he called for 42,000 volunteers for national service for three years and authorized an increase of 23,000 in the regular army. When Congress met in July 1861, it legalized the President's acts, and, at his recommendation, provided for enlisting 500,000 volunteers to serve for three years.

For a time the volunteering system served to bring out enough men to fill the armies, but not after the first flush of enthusiasm had worn off. Finally, in March 1863, Congress enacted the first national draft law in American history (the South had employed conscription almost a year earlier). Few exemptions were permitted: only high national and state officials, preachers, and men who were the sole support of a dependent family. But a drafted man could escape service by hiring a substitute to go in his place or by paying the government a fee of $300.

The purpose of the law was to spur enlistments by threatening to invoke conscription. Each state was divided into enrollment districts and was assigned a quota of men to be raised. If a state could fill the quota, it would escape the draft completely; if certain districts failed to meet their quota, a sufficient number of men were drafted to make up the difference. Some states and many districts never experienced conscription. Although the draft directly inducted only 46,000 men, it stimulated enlistments enormously. These totaled 2.9 million, but that figure includes many who enlisted several times or served short terms. Probably 1.5 million men, all together, served in the Union armies (as contrasted with 900,000 in the Confederate forces).

The casualty rate was tremendous. Not until World War I would military medicine reach a point where fewer men died from sickness than from bullets. Doubtless the death rate in camp and hospital would have been even greater but for the work of a number of private relief organizations, the largest being the United States Sanitary Commission, which provided medical care, medical supplies, and food to the armed forces.

To a people accustomed to a government that had hardly touched their daily lives, conscription seemed a strange and ominous thing. Opposition to the law was widespread, particularly from laborers, immigrants, and Peace Democrats. In places it erupted into violence. Demonstrators against the draft rioted in New York City for four days in July 1863, killed

several hundred people, mostly Negroes, and burned down Negro homes and businesses. Federal troops had to be brought in to subdue the rioters. Some Democratic governors who supported the war (like Horatio Seymour of New York) contended that the national government had no constitutional power to conscript, and they openly challenged the Lincoln administration on the issue.

POLITICS AND EMANCIPATION

When Lincoln first took over the presidency, he was widely considered a small-time prairie politician, unfit for his job. He strengthened this impression by his unpretentious air. Actually, he was well aware of his great abilities and of his superiority over other Northern leaders. His supreme confidence in himself was demonstrated by his choice of a cabinet. Representing every faction of the Republican party and every segment of Northern opinion, it was an extraordinary assemblage of advisers and a difficult set of prima donnas to manage. Three of the secretaries, Seward, Chase, and Stanton, were first-rate men. Seward and Chase thought that they were abler than Lincoln and should be in his place. At the very beginning of the administration, Seward made an attempt to dominate Lincoln, failed, and became his loyal supporter. Chase never learned that the President was a bigger man than he.

Lincoln's confidence in his inner strength was revealed by his bold exercise of the war powers of his office. In order to accomplish his purposes, he was ready to violate parts of the Constitution, explaining that he would not lose the whole by being afraid to disregard a part. In this spirit he called for troops to repress the rebellion (an act that was equivalent to a declaration of war), illegally increased the size of the regular army, and proclaimed a naval blockade of the South.

Opposition to the war came from two sources: from Southern sympathizers in the Union slave states and from the peace wing of the Democratic party. War Democrats were willing to support the war and even to accept offices from the administration. Peace Democrats or, as their enemies called them, "Copperheads," feared that agriculture and the West were being subordinated to industry and the East and that state rights were going down before nationalism. These Democrats proposed to call a truce in the fighting, invite the South to attend a national convention, and amend the Constitution to preserve both the Union and state rights. Some advocated the formation of a Western confederacy, and some joined secret societies (Knights of the Golden Circle, Sons of Liberty) which allegedly conspired to aid the Southern rebels.

To deal with opponents of the war, Lincoln resorted to military arrests. He suspended the right of habeas corpus, so that an alleged offender could be arrested and held without trial or, if tried, had to appear before a military court. At first Lincoln denied the civil process only in specified areas, but in 1862 he proclaimed that all persons who discouraged enlistments or engaged in disloyal practices would come under martial law. In all, over 13,000 persons were arrested and imprisoned for varying periods. Among those placed in custody was a Maryland secessionist leader whom Lincoln refused to release, even under a writ from Chief Justice Taney (*Ex parte Merryman*). The most prominent Copperhead in the country, Clement L. Vallandigham of Ohio, was seized by military authorities, and Lincoln exiled him to the Confederacy. (After the war, in 1866, the Supreme Court held, in *Ex parte Milligan,* that military trials in areas where the civil courts were capable of functioning were unconstitutional.)

In the Republican as well as the Democratic party there were factions—the Radicals and the Conservatives. On most questions, including economic matters, the two groups were in fundamental agreement, but they differed violently on slavery. Leaders of the Radicals were Thaddeus Stevens of Pennsylvania, master of the party machine in the House, and Senators Charles Sumner of Massachusetts and Benjamin F. Wade of Ohio. Heading the Conservatives was President Lincoln. The Radicals wanted to seize the opportunity of the war to strike slavery down—abolish it suddenly and violently. The Conservatives, who were also antislavery, wanted to accomplish the same result in a different way—easily and gradually. Lincoln made several notable although unsuccessful attempts to persuade the loyal slave states to agree to a program of compensated gradual emancipation. He feared, at first, that the introduction of abolition as a war aim would divide Northern opinion and alienate the border slave states.

A Confiscation Act, passed in August 1861, declared free all slaves used for "insurrectionary" purposes. Subsequent laws abolished slavery in the District of Columbia, with compensation to owners (April 1862), and in the national territories (June 1862). In the summer of 1862 the Radicals decided that Northern opinion had reached a point where they could move against slavery in the states. In July they pushed through Congress the second Confiscation Act, which was in essence a bold attempt to accomplish emancipation by legislative action. It declared the property of persons supporting the "rebellion" subject to forfeiture to the United States government; declared free the slaves of persons aiding and supporting the insurrection; and authorized the President to employ Negroes, including freed slaves, as soldiers.

The Republican party was coming under Radical control, and the country was beginning to accept emancipation as an aim of the war. The signs were not lost on the astute master of politics in the White House. Lincoln saw that in order to achieve his larger purpose of saving the Union he would have to yield his lesser goal of preventing the sudden destruction of slavery. To preserve the nation he had to have the support of his own party and particularly of the Radicals, who were the last-ditch Unionists, the men who would never give up the war. And if a majority of the Northern people wanted slavery destroyed, as seemed the case, he could not afford to divide popular opinion by opposing their will. In July 1862 he decided to take the leadership of the antislavery impulse away from the Radicals by putting himself at the head of it.

On September 22, 1862, after the Battle of Antietam, the President issued his preliminary Emancipation Proclamation, and on the first day of 1863 his final Emancipation Proclamation. This declared forever free the slaves in designated areas of the Confederacy. Excepted from the edict was the whole state of Tennessee, most of which was under Union control, and western Virginia and southern Louisiana, which were occupied by Federal troops. Presumably these areas were omitted because they were not enemy territory and hence were not subject to the President's war powers. For a similar reason the Proclamation did not apply to the border slave states.

The Proclamation freed immediately only a few slaves. But it indicated that henceforth there was to be a war for the emancipation of the slaves as well as for the preservation of the Union. Eventually as federal armies occupied large areas of the South, the Proclamation became a practical reality, and hundreds of thousands of slaves were freed by its operation. Equally important in the process of emancipation was the induction of many former slaves into the armed forces: some 186,000 served as soldiers, sailors, and laborers, thereby making a substantial contribution to the freeing of their race. Furthermore, the impulse to abolition which the Proclamation symbolized increased in intensity throughout the country, affecting even the border states. Before the end of the war, slavery had been abolished in two Union slave states, Maryland and Missouri, and in three "reconstructed" or occupied Confederate states, Tennessee, Arkansas, and Louisiana. The final and inevitable action was taken early in 1865 when Congress approved the Thirteenth Amendment (ratified by the required number of states several months after the war closed), which freed all slaves everywhere and abolished slavery as an institution.

Early in the war, and particularly after the election of 1862, in which the Republicans suffered heavy losses, the party leaders proceeded to form a broad coalition of all groups who supported the war, trying particularly to attract the War Democrats. The new organization, which was composed of a Republican core with a fringe of War Democrats, was known as the Union party. It encountered its major political test in the presidential election of 1864, which was the first national election held in the midst of a great war.

When the Union convention met in June, it nominated Lincoln, with the chilly assent of the Radicals, and, for Vice President, Andrew Johnson of Tennessee, a War Democrat who had refused to follow his state into secession. In August the Democratic convention nominated George B. McClellan, former Union general and an object of hatred to all good Radicals. The peace faction got a plank into the platform denouncing the war as a failure and calling for a truce to be followed by an invitation to the South to enter a national convention. Although McClellan repudiated the plank, the Democrats stood before the country as the peace party. At the same time several Northern military victories, particularly the capture of Atlanta, Georgia, early in September, rejuvenated Northern morale and gave promise of Republican success in November.

The outcome of the election was a smashing electoral triumph for Lincoln, who got 212 votes to McClellan's 21 and carried every state except Kentucky, New Jersey, and Delaware. Lincoln's popular majority, however, was uncomfortably small, 2,213,000 to 1,805,000 or an advantage of only 400,000. A slight shift of popular votes in some of the more populous states would have changed the result.

The South Mobilizes

Although the first seven Southern states to secede had left the Union as individual sovereignties, they intended from the first to come together in a common confederation, which they hoped the states of the upper South would eventually join. Accordingly, representatives of the seceded states assembled at Montgomery, Alabama, early in February 1861, to create a Southern nation. After Virginia seceded, the government moved to Richmond, partly out of deference to Virginia, partly because Richmond was one of the few Southern cities large enough to house the government.

THE CONFEDERATE GOVERNMENT

In the Confederate constitution, state sovereignty was expressly recognized, but not the right of secession. A few governmental reforms were introduced, such as the "item veto" — the President's power to veto part of a bill without rejecting the whole thing. Slavery was mentioned by name, and various provisions made its abolition (even by one of the states) practically impossible. In most other respects the constitution of the Confederate States was identical with that of the United States.

An English View of Jefferson Davis

William Howard Russell, war correspondent for the *Times* of London, visited the Confederate President at Montgomery, Alabama, in 1861. Although the Britisher had some reservations about Davis, he was favorably impressed with his freedom from the almost universal American habit of chewing tobacco:

I had an opportunity of observing the President very closely: he did not impress me as favorably as I had expected, though he is certainly a very different looking man from Mr. Lincoln. He is like a gentleman—has a slight, light figure, little exceeding middle height, and holds himself erect and straight. He was dressed in a rustic suit of slate-colored stuff, with a black silk handkerchief round his neck; his manner is plain, and rather reserved and drastic; his head is well formed, with a fine full forehead, square and high, covered with innumerable fine lines and wrinkles, features regular, though the cheekbones are too high, and the jaws too hollow to be handsome; the lips are thin, flexible, and curved, the chin square, well defined; the nose very regular, with wide nostrils; and the eyes deep-set, large and full—one seems nearly blind, and is partly covered with a film, owing to excruciating attacks of neuralgia and tic. Wonderful to relate, he does not chew, and is neat and clean-looking, with hair trimmed, and boots brushed.

Besides framing a constitution and passing temporary laws, the Montgomery convention named a provisional President and a provisional Vice President, Jefferson Davis of Mississippi and Alexander H. Stephens of Georgia. Afterward, in a general election, the same two men were chosen, without opposition, for regular six-year terms. Davis had been a firm but not extreme advocate of Southern rights in the former Union; he was a moderate but not an extreme secessionist. Stephens had been the chief among those who had contended that secession was unnecessary.

Jefferson Davis embodied the spirit of the nation he had been called to lead. His family, which was of Southern yeoman stock, had moved from Kentucky, where he was born, to the new lush cotton lands of Mississippi, where they became rich planters almost overnight. Davis was a first-generation aristocrat. So also were most of the members of his government. The Confederacy was run by the cotton nabobs of the newer "Western" South, not by the old aristocracy of the seaboard states.

Whereas Lincoln's task was to preserve a nation, Davis' was to make one. Lincoln succeeded; Davis failed. He spent too much time on routine items, on what one observer called "little trash." A good administrator, he was his own secretary of war, but he rarely rose above the secretarial level. Moreover, he proceeded on the assumption that the Confederacy was a legal and permanent organization that could fight a war in the normal fashion of older countries. The situation demanded ruthless efficiency, yet he tried to observe every constitutional punctilio. Lincoln, without clear constitutional sanction, suspended habeas corpus; Davis asked his Congress to let him suspend it and received only partial permission. One shrewd Confederate official (R. G. H. Kean) wrote: "All the revolutionary vigor is with the enemy. . . . With us timidity—hair splitting."

The Confederate cabinet displayed, at best, only average ability. The personnel changed rapidly and frequently. There were three secretaries of state, two secretaries of the treasury, four attorney generals, and five secretaries of war. Not one of them ever dared to oppose the will of President Davis.

MONEY AND MEN

In contrast to the burgeoning prosperity of the wartime North, the South in the war years underwent shortages, suffering, and sacrifice. The Southern economy, despite a frantic expansion of industrial facilities, was unable to supply the needs of its armies and civilian population.

The men seeking to devise measures for financing the Confederacy's war effort, Secretary of the Treasury Christopher G. Memminger and the congressional leaders, had to reckon with a number of hard facts. A national revenue system had to be created to collect money from a people unaccustomed to bearing large tax burdens. Southern banking houses, except in New Orleans, were fewer and smaller than those of the North. Because excess capital in the South was usually invested in slaves and land, the sum of liquid assets on deposit in banks or in individual hands was relatively small. The only specie possessed by the government was that seized in United States mints located in the South (amounting to about $1 million). In an attempt to secure more specie, the government dispatched an army column into New Mexico, but this force, after some initial success, was repelled.

The Confederate Congress, like its counterpart in the North, showed some reluctance to enact rigorous wartime taxes. In 1861 the legislators provided for a direct tax on property to be levied through the medium of the states. If a state preferred, it could meet its quota by paying as a state. Most of the states, instead of taxing their people, assumed the tax, which they paid by issuing bonds or their own notes. Moving more boldly in 1863, Congress passed a bill that included license levies and an income tax. A unique feature was "the tax in kind." Every farmer and planter had to contribute one-tenth of his produce to the government. All together, the revenue realized from taxation was relatively small—only about 1 percent of total income.

The borrowing record of the Confederacy was little better than its tax program. Eventually the government issued bonds in such large amounts that the people suspected its ability to redeem them. Congress authorized a $100 million loan to be paid in specie, paper money, or produce. The expectation was that the bulk of the proceeds would be in the form of products—"the loan in kind." The loan was subscribed, partly in paper currency and mostly in produce or pledges of produce. But many of the pledges were not redeemed, and often the promised products were destroyed by the enemy. The Confederacy also attempted to borrow money in Europe by pledging cotton stored in the South for future delivery. Its most notable venture in foreign finance was the famous Erlanger loan, which was supposed to net $15 million. Actually, Erlanger, a French financier, was interested in conducting a huge cotton speculation. The Confederate government received only $2.5 million from the loan.

Since ready revenue was needed and since cash was scarce, the government resorted to the issuance of paper money and treasury notes in 1861. Once it started, it could not stop. By 1864 the staggering total of $1 billion had been issued. In addition, states and cities issued their own notes. The inevitable result was to depreciate the value of the money. Prices skyrocketed to astronomical heights. Many people, particularly those who lived in towns or who had fixed incomes, could not pay these prices. Such people often lost some of their will to fight.

Like the United States, the Confederate States first raised armies by calling for volunteers. By the latter part of 1861 volunteering had dropped off badly. As the year 1862 opened, the Confederacy was threatened by a manpower crisis.

The government met the situation boldly. At Davis' recommendation, Congress in April enacted the First Conscription Act, which declared that all able-bodied white males between the ages of eighteen and thirty-five were liable to military service for three years. A man who was drafted could escape his summons if he furnished a substitute to go in his place. The prices for substitutes eventually went up to as high as $10,000 in Confederate currency. The purpose of this provision was to exempt men in charge of agricultural and industrial production, but to people who could not afford substitutes it seemed like a special privilege to the rich. It was repealed late in 1863 after arousing bitter class discontent.

The first draft act and later measures provided for other exemptions, mostly on an occupational basis. The government realized that conscription had to be selective, that some men had to be left on the home front to perform the functions of production. It erred in excusing men who were not doing any vital services and in permitting too many group exemptions. The provision most bitterly criticized was that exempting one white man on each plantation with twenty or more slaves. Angrily denounced as the "twenty-nigger law," it caused ordinary men to say: "It's a rich man's war but a poor man's fight."

In September 1862 Congress adopted a second conscription measure, which raised the upper age limit to forty-five. At the end of the year, an estimated 500,000 soldiers were in the Confederate armies. Thereafter conscription provided fewer and fewer men, and the armed forces steadily decreased in size. Federal armies seized large areas in the South, depriving the Confederacy of manpower in the occupied regions. Military reverses in the summer of 1863 convinced many Southerners that the war was lost, causing a kind of passive resistance to the draft as men sought to avoid it by hiding in the hills and woods, and desertions began to increase.

As 1864 opened, the situation was critical. In a desperate move, Congress lowered the age limits for drafted men to seventeen and raised them to fifty, reaching out, it was said, toward the cradle and the grave. Few men were obtained. War weariness and the certainty of defeat were making their influence felt. In 1864–1865 there were 100,000 desertions. An observant Confederate diarist (Mrs. Mary B. Chesnut) wrote in her journal in March 1865: "I am sure our army is silently dispersing. Men are moving the wrong way, all the time. They slip by with no songs and no shouts now. They have given the thing up." In a frantic final attempt to raise men, Congress in 1865 authorized the drafting of 300,000 slaves. The war ended before this incongruous experiment could be tried out.

STATE RIGHTS IN THE CONFEDERACY

In overwhelming numbers the Southern people were ready to support the war for Southern independence. The only important organized opposition to the war came from the inhabitants of the mountain areas, whose population was less than 10 percent of the Southern total. Here supporters of the national cause carried on a kind of guerrilla warfare against the occupying Confederate forces until liberated by the Federals late in 1863.

Though united in their desire to sustain the war, Southerners were bitterly divided on how it should be conducted. The differences that emerged did not take the form of party issues: the Confederacy did not last long enough for distinct parties to develop.

The great dividing force was, ironically enough, the principle of state rights—the foundation of Southern political philosophy—for whose conservation and consecration the South had left the old Union. State rights had become such a cult with Southerners that they reacted against all central controls, even those necessary to win the war. If there was an organized faction of opposition to the government, it was that group of quixotic men who counted Vice President Stephens as their leader. They had one simple, basic idea. They wanted the Confederacy to win its independence, but they would not agree to sacrificing one iota of state sovereignty to achieve that goal. If victory had to be gained at the expense of state rights, they preferred defeat. The state-righters concentrated their criticisms upon two powers that the central government sought to excerise: the suspension of habeas corpus, and conscription. Recalcitrant governors, like Joseph Brown of Georgia and Zebulon M. Vance of North Carolina, contending that the central government had no right to draft troops, tried in every way to obstruct the enforcement of conscription.

The idea of a negotiated peace fascinated the state-righters, especially Vice President Stephens. They never made it clear whether they were thinking of reunion or of Southern independence. As early as 1863 they urged a peace based on recognition of state sovereignty and the right of each state to control its domestic institutions—which implied a restored Union. At times, however, they proposed negotiations based on the independence of the Confederacy.

Selected Readings

Increasing Sectionalism
A. O. Craven, *The Coming of the Civil War* (1942);
Allan Nevins, *The Emergence of Lincoln* (2 vols.,
1950); F. J. Blue, *The Free Soilers: Third Party Poli-
tics, 1848–1854* (1973); A. W. Crandall, *The Early His-
tory of the Republican Party, 1854–1856* (1930); Eric
Foner, *Free Soil, Free Labor, Free Men: The Ideology
of the Republican Party Before the Civil War** (1970);
D. E. Fehrenbacher, *Prelude to Greatness: Lincoln
in the 1850s** (1962); H. V. Jaffa, *Crisis of the House
Divided* (1959), on the Lincoln-Douglas debates; J. A.
Isely, *Horace Greeley and the Republican Party,
1853–1861* (1947); M. B. Duberman, *Charles Francis
Adams* (1961); David Donald, *Charles Sumner and the
Coming of the Civil War* (1960); Vincent Hopkins,
*Dred Scott's Case** (1951); R. F. Nichols, *The Disrup-
tion of the American Democracy** (1948); P. S. Klein,
President James Buchanan (1962).

Kansas and John Brown
J. C. Malin, *The Nebraska Question, 1852–1854* (1953)
and *John Brown and the Legend of Fifty-Six* (1942);
O. G. Villard, *John Brown, 1800–1859* (1910); P. W.
Gates, *Fifty Million Acres: Conflicts over Kansas
Land Policy, 1854–1890** (1954); J. C. Furnas, *The
Road to Harpers Ferry* (1959).

The Crisis of 1860–1861
W. T. Baringer, *Lincoln's Rise to Power* (1937) and *A
House Dividing* (1945); R. H. Luthin, *The First
Lincoln Campaign* (1944); D. L. Dumond, *The Seces-
sion Movement, 1860–1861* (1931); R. A. Wooster, *The
Secession Conventions of the South* (1962); L. A.
White, *Robert Barnwell Rhett* (1931); P. S. Foner,
*Business and Slavery: The New York Merchants and
the Irrepressible Conflict* (1941); T. H. O'Connor,
*Lords of the Loom: The Cotton Whigs and the Coming
of the Civil War* (1968); R. G. Gunderson, *Old Gentle-
men's Convention: The Washington Peace Conference of 1861* (1961); A. D. Kirwan, *John Jordan Crittenden* (1962); D. M. Potter, *Lincoln and His Party in
the Secession Crisis, 1860–1861** (1942); K. M.
Stampp, *And the War Came: The North and the Secession Crisis, 1860–1861** (1950); R. N. Current,
*Lincoln and the First Shot** (1963); S. A. Channing,
Crisis of Fear: Secession in South Carolina (1970);

R. E. May, *The Southern Dream of a Caribbean Empire, 1854–1861* (1973).

President Lincoln
B. P. Thomas, *Abraham Lincoln* (1952); J. G. Randall,
Lincoln the President (4 vols., 1945–1955); Carl Sand-
burg, *Abraham Lincoln: The War Years** (4 vols.,
1939); David Donald, *Lincoln Reconsidered** (1956);
R. N. Current, *The Lincoln Nobody Knows** (1958).

Union Mobilization
Allan Nevins, *The War for the Union* (2 vols., 1959–
1960); F. A. Shannon, *Organization and Administration of the Union Army* (2 vols., 1928); E. P. Oberholtz-
er, *Jay Cooke, Financier of the Civil War* (2 vols.,
1907).

Wartime Politics and Emancipation
T. H. Williams, *Lincoln and the Radicals** (1941);
W. B. Hesseltine, *Lincoln and the War Governors*
(1948); Wood Gray, *The Hidden Civil War: The Story
of the Copperheads** (1942); Frank Klement, *The Copperheads in the Middle West* (1960); J. H. Franklin,
The Emancipation Proclamation (1963); V. J. Voegeli,
Free but Not Equal (1967); J. G. Randall, *Constitutional Problems under Lincoln* (1926); H. D. Hunt, *Hannibal Hamlin of Maine: Lincoln's First Vice President*
(1969).

The Confederacy
E. M. Coulter, *The Confederate States of America,
1861–1865* (1950); Clement Eaton, *A History of the
Southern Confederacy** (1954); C. P. Roland, *The
Confederacy** (1960); W. B. Yearns, *The Confederate
Congress* (1960); Hudson Strode, *Jefferson Davis,
Confederate President* (1959) and *Jefferson Davis,
Tragic Hero* (1964); R. R. Von Abele, *Alexander H.
Stephens: A Biography* (1946); B. J. Hendrick, *States-
men of the Lost Cause* (1939); R. W. Patrick, *Jefferson
Davis and His Cabinet* (1944); R. D. Meade, *Judah P.
Benjamin* (1943); A. B. Moore, *Conscription and Con-
flict in the Confederacy* (1924); F. L. Owsley, *State
Rights in the Confederacy* (1925); B. I. Wiley, *Plain
People of the Confederacy** (1943); C. W. Ramsdell,
Behind the Lines in the Southern Confederacy (1944).

*Titles available in paperback.

The War of the Rebellion

Fifteen

From the seceders' point of view, the Civil War was a war for Southern independence. Afterward (but not at the time) Southerners were to call it "the War between the States," thus implying that secession and resistance to federal authority had been legitimate, constitutional exercises of state rights. Yet the Southerners both during and after the fighting were proud to call themselves "rebels," and from the Northern point of view they were certainly engaging in rebellion as well as war. The official name that the Union government gave the conflict was "the War of the Rebellion."

This was the first great military experience of the American people. Compared to it the earlier wars—the one with Mexico, the War of 1812, even the Revolutionary struggle itself—were minor and episodic. It has been called the first of modern wars. It involved masses of men and new kinds of technology: railroads and railroad artillery, the telegraph, armored ships, balloons, the Gatling gun (precursor of the machine gun), repeating rifles, trenches, wire entanglements, water and land mines (including what then were called "infernal machines" and now would be known as "booby traps"), torpedo boats, even submarines. It compelled both sides to concentrate a high proportion of their resources on the pursuit of total victory.

For the American people, Northern and Southern, of both the wartime generation and later generations, the Civil War was the most dramatic and traumatic event in their history. More than most wars, it settled some

The North's Greatest General
One observer of Ulysses S. Grant said: "He habitually wears an expression as if he had determined to drive his head through a brick wall, and was about to do it." Of average height and small stature, slouchy in dress and manner, Grant did not look like a great general, but he was, as C. F. Adams, Jr., noted, the kind of man that all would instinctively turn to in a moment of crisis. (Left, Library of Congress)

The South's Greatest General
Robert E. Lee was a magnificent physical figure. Five feet eleven inches tall and 175 pounds in weight, he seemed larger than he was because of his massive head and wide shoulders. He was grave and reserved in manner like George Washington, his hero and model. And like Washington, he lived by a self-imposed code of high conduct. "Duty is the sublimest word in our language," he once wrote. (Right, National Archives)

issues and settled them permanently. It brought about the destruction of slavery and the preservation of the Union. After the Union victory no class or faction or section could seriously consider secession as a feasible step.

In the war's aftermath, however, difficult problems emerged to test the statesmanship of both the victors and the vanquished. What should be the status of the 4 million emancipated slaves? Upon what terms and by what process should the states of the defeated Confederacy be restored to the Union?

Thus, while the victory had decided that no state could secede and that no man could own another as his slave, it had not settled the question of the precise relationship of the states to the Union or of the blacks to the whites. These questions remained, and in one form or another they still remain, the most perplexing and tormenting issues of American life more than a century after the end of the Civil War.

Strategy and Diplomacy

So far as strategic planning was concerned, the objectives of the Union were positive and those of the Confederacy negative. To achieve a victory, the Union had to conquer the rebels and reduce them to subjection, to obedience to federal law. The Confederacy had only to stave off defeat.

In diplomacy — in relations with European powers — it was the other way around. The objectives of the Confederacy were positive and those of the Union negative. The Confederacy hoped to persuade foreign governments to recognize its independence and to step into the war and help make that independence a reality. The Union aimed to prevent foreign recognition and intervention.

THE COMMANDERS IN CHIEF

It was the responsibility of the President as commander in chief of the army and navy — of Abraham Lincoln for the Union and Jefferson Davis for the Confederacy — to see to the making and carrying out of an overall strategy for winning the war. Lincoln, a civilian all his life, had had no military education and no military experience except for a brief militia interlude. Yet he became a great war President, and a great commander in chief, superior to Davis, who was a trained soldier. Lincoln made himself a fine strategist, often showing keener insight than his generals. He recognized that numbers and matériel were on his side, and

immediately he moved to mobilize the maximum strength of Northern resources. He urged his generals to keep up a constant pressure on the whole defensive line of the Confederacy until a weak spot was found and a breakthrough could be made. At an early date he realized that the proper objective of his armies was the destruction of the Confederate armies and not the occupation of Southern territory.

During the first three years of the war, Lincoln performed many of the functions that in a modern command system would be done by the chief of the general staff or the joint chiefs of staff. He formulated policy, devised strategic plans, and even directed tactical movements. Some of his decisions were wise, some wrong, but the general effect of his so-called interfering with the military machine was fortunate for the North.

At the beginning, Lincoln was inclined to take the advice of General Winfield Scott. The old general, however, was unable to adjust his thinking to the requirements of mass war. He retired from service on November 1, 1861, and as general in chief, Lincoln replaced Scott with young George B. McClellan, who was also the commander of the Federal field army in the East, the Army of the Potomac. McClellan lacked the abilities to formulate strategy for all theaters of the war. The one grand strategic design he submitted was defective because it envisioned operations in only one theater, his own, and because it made places instead of enemy armies his objective. When McClellan took the field in March 1862, Lincoln removed him as general in chief. In July Lincoln designated General Henry W. Halleck to direct the armies. The foremost American student of the art of war, Halleck had won an undeserved reputation as a successful general in the West. Now he cast himself in the role of an adviser instead of a maker of decisions. Again Lincoln himself was forced to take up the function of forming and directing strategy, a task that he performed until March 1864, when the nation finally achieved a modern command system.

In the system arrived at in 1864, Ulysses S. Grant, who had emerged as the North's greatest general, was named general in chief. Charged with directing the movements of all Union armies, Grant, because he disliked the political atmosphere of Washington, established his headquarters with the Army of the Potomac but did not technically become commander of that army. As director of the armies, Grant proved to be the man for whom Lincoln had been searching. He possessed in superb degree the ability to think of the war in overall terms and to devise strategy for the war as a whole. Because Lincoln trusted Grant, he gave the general a relatively free hand. Grant, however, always submitted the broad outlines of his plans to the President for approval before putting them in motion. Under the new arrangement, Halleck became "chief of staff," a post in which he acted as a channel of communication between Lincoln and Grant and between Grant and the departmental commanders.

Lincoln's active command role underlines one of the most important changes occurring in modern warfare: the emergence of the civilian in strategic planning. As war became more technological and total, strategy became a problem of directing the whole resources of a nation. It was too vast a problem for any one set of leaders, especially for the military.

The most dramatic example of civilian intervention in military affairs was the Committee on the Conduct of the War, a joint investigative committee of both houses of Congress and the most powerful agency that the legislative branch has ever created to secure for itself a voice in formulating war policies. Established in December 1861, under the chairmanship of Senator Benjamin F. Wade of Ohio, it became the spearhead of the Radical attack on Lincoln's war program. The Radicals sensed that many of the Northern generals were not animated by a driving, ruthless desire for victory. The generals at first were influenced by the eighteenth-century concept of war as a kind of game — as chessboard maneuvers conducted in leisurely fashion and without heavy casualties. The Radicals ascribed the generals' hesitancy to a secret sympathy for slavery, which the professionals were supposed to have imbibed at West Point. The generals whom the committee favored — most of them incompetent amateurs — would have been no improvement, but the spirit represented by the committee helped to infuse a hard, relentless purpose into the conduct of the war.

Southern command arrangements centered on President Davis. The Confederacy failed to achieve a modern command system. Early in 1862 Davis assigned General Robert E. Lee to duty at Richmond, where, "under the direction of the President," he was "charged" with the conduct of the Confederate armies. Despite the fine words, this meant only that Lee, who had a brilliant military mind, was to act as Davis' adviser, furnishing counsel when called on. After serving a few months, Lee went into the field, and Davis did not appoint another adviser until February 1864. Then he selected Braxton Bragg, whom he had been forced to remove from field command after Bragg was defeated in the West. Bragg had real strategic ability, but he understood his position and restricted his function to providing technical advice. In February 1865 the Confederate Congress, in a move directed at Davis, created the position of general in chief, which was intended for Lee. Davis named Lee to the post but took care to announce that legally he himself was still commander in chief. Lee accepted the job on the basis offered by the President: as a loyal subordinate instead of the dictator some people wanted him to be. The war ended before the new command experiment could be fully tested.

THE ROLE OF SEA POWER

The Union had the advantage of overwhelmingly preponderant sea power, and President Lincoln made the most of it. It served two main functions. One was to enforce the blockade of the Southern coast that he proclaimed at the start of the war (April 19, 1861). The other was to assist the Union armies in combined land-and-water operations.

In the Western theater of war, the vast region between the Appalachian Mountains and the Mississippi River, the larger rivers were navigable by vessels of considerable size. The Union navy helped the armies to conquer this area by transporting supplies and troops for them and joining them in attacking Confederate strong points. In defending themselves against the Union gunboats on the rivers, the Confederates had to depend mainly on land fortifications because of their lack of naval power. These fixed defenses proved no match for the mobile land-and-water forces of the Union.

At first, the blockade was too large a task for the Union navy. Even after the navy had grown to its maximum size, it was unable to seal off completely the long shoreline of the Confederacy. Though ocean-going ships were kept away, small blockade runners continued to carry goods into and out of some of the Southern ports. Gradually the Federal forces tightened the blockade by occupying stretches of the coast and seizing one port after another, the last remaining important one (Wilmington, North Carolina) early in 1865. Fewer and fewer blockade runners got through, and the blockade increasingly hurt the South.

The Battle of Mobile Bay

To strengthen the blockade, the Union navy attempted to capture Confederate ports. The port of Mobile was defended not only by warships but also by land fortifications and underwater torpedoes, or mines. "Damn the torpedoes! Full steam ahead!" Admiral David G. Farragut cried as he directed his flotilla in a victorious mission into Mobile Bay, August 5, 1864. Here he fearlessly watches as his flagship, the Hartford, *brushes past the hostile* Tennessee *in an artistic re-creation by William H. Overend. (Courtesy Wadsworth Atheneum, Hartford)*

In bold and ingenious attempts to break the blockade, the Confederates introduced some new weapons, among them an ironclad warship. They constructed this by plating with iron a former United States frigate, the *Merrimack,* which the Yankees had scuttled in Norfolk harbor when Virginia seceded. On March 8, 1862, the *Merrimack* steamed out from Norfolk to attack the blockading squadron of wooden ships in Hampton Roads. She destroyed two of the ships and scattered the rest. Jubilation reigned in Richmond, and consternation in Washington. But the federal government had already placed orders for the construction of several ironclads of its own, which had been designed by John Ericsson. One of these, the *Monitor,* arrived at Hampton Roads on the night of March 8. When the *Merrimack* emerged on the following day to hunt for more victims, the *Monitor* met her and engaged her in the first battle between ironclad ships. Neither vessel was able to penetrate the other's armor, but the *Monitor* put an end to the depredations of the *Merrimack.*

The Confederates later experimented with other new kinds of craft in the effort to pierce the blockade. One of these was a torpedo boat, which carried the torpedo (mine) on a long pole projecting out in front. Another was a small, cigar-shaped, hand-powered submarine. In 1864, in Charleston harbor, such a submarine, pulling its mine behind it on a cable, dived under a blockading vessel, exploded the mine against the hull, and then was dragged to the bottom by the sinking ship. For the first time in the history of warfare, a submarine had made a successful strike. This and other ingenious efforts, however, fell far short of breaking or even weakening the blockade.

To weaken it, the Confederates had meanwhile decided to build or buy fast ships to prey on the Northern merchant marine on the high seas. The hope was that the Union would detach ships from the blockade to pursue the commerce raiders. The Confederates also hoped to get, from abroad, a specially built "ram" with which to smash the wooden blockading ships. As a result of these efforts, the naval war became an important element in the relations of the Union with the Confederacy, on the one hand, and with the powers of Europe on the other.

EUROPE AND THE DISUNITED STATES

Judah P. Benjamin, who occupied the Confederate foreign office for the greater part of the war, was a clever and intelligent man, but he lacked strong convictions and confined most of his energy to administrative routine. Seward, on the other hand, after some initial blunders, learned his job well and went on to become one of the outstanding American secretaries of state. In the key diplomatic post at London, the North was represented by a distinguished minister, Charles Francis Adams, who seemed to have inherited the diplomatic abilities of his father (John Quincy Adams) and grandfather (John Adams).

In the relationship of Europe to the Civil War, the key nations were Great Britain and France. These two had acted together against Russia in the Crimean War and were united by an entente, one of the understandings of which was that questions concerning the United States fell within the sphere of British influence. Napoleon III, therefore, would not act in American affairs without the concurrence of Britain. Russia, the third power of Europe, was, like the United States, an up-and-coming nation that thought her aspirations were being blocked by England. Feeling a community of interest with democratic America, autocratic Russia openly expressed sympathy for the Northern cause. In 1863, when war threatened to break out between Russia and England over Poland, Russia, in order to get her navy into position to attack British commerce, dispatched two fleets to American waters. One turned up at New York and the other at San Francisco, thereby creating a legend that they had come to support the United States if England and France should attempt to break the blockade.

At the beginning of the war the sympathies of the ruling classes of England and France were with the Confederacy. But English liberals like John Bright and Richard Cobden saw the war as a struggle between free and slave labor, and they presented it in these terms to their followers. The politically conscious but unenfranchised workers in Britain expressed their sympathy for the Northern cause frequently and unmistakably—in mass meetings, in resolutions, and, through the medium of Bright and other leaders, in Parliament itself. After the issuance of the Emancipation Proclamation, these groups intensified their activities on behalf of the Union cause.

In the minds of Southern leaders, cotton was their best diplomatic weapon. Their analysis was as follows: the textile industry was basic to the economies of England and France, which depended on the South for the bulk of their cotton supply; deprived of Southern cotton, these countries would face economic collapse. Therefore they would have to intervene on the side of the Confederacy.

But this diplomacy based on King Cotton never worked as its champions envisioned. In 1861 English manufacturers had a surplus of cotton on hand. The immediate effect of the blockade was to enable the textile operators to dispose of their remaining finished goods at high prices. Thereafter the supply became increasingly short, and many mills were forced to close. Both England and France, however, managed to avoid a complete shutdown of their textile industries by importing supplies from new sources, notably Egypt and India. Most important of all, the workers, the people most seriously affected by the shortage, did not clamor to have the blockade broken. Even the 500,000 English textile workers thrown out of jobs continued to support the North.

No European nation extended diplomatic recognition to the Confederacy. Though several times England and France considered offering mediation, they never moved to intervene in the war. Neither could afford to do so unless the Confederacy seemed on the point of winning, and the South never attained a prospect of certain victory.

Immediately after the outbreak of hostilities, Great Britain issued a proclamation of neutrality, thus attributing to the Confederacy the status of a belligerent. France and other nations followed suit. Although the Northern government, which officially insisted that the war was not a war but a domestic insurrection, furiously resented England's action, the British government had proceeded in conformity with accepted rules of neutrality and in accordance with the realities of the situation. The United States was fighting a *war*, a fact that Lincoln himself had recognized in his proclamation establishing a blockade. Thereafter three crises

or near crises between Great Britain and the United States developed, any one of which could have resulted in war between the two countries.

The first crisis, and the most dangerous one—the so-called *Trent* affair—occurred late in 1861. The Confederate commissioners to England and France, James M. Mason and John Slidell, had slipped through the then ineffective blockade to Havana, Cuba, where they boarded an English steamer, the *Trent*, for England. Hovering in Cuban waters was an American frigate, the *San Jacinto*, commanded by Captain Charles Wilkes, an impetuous officer who knew that the Southern diplomats were on the *Trent*. Acting without authorization from his government, Wilkes stopped the British vessel, arrested the commissioners, and bore them off in triumph to Boston. The British government drafted a demand for the release of the prisoners, reparation, and an apology. Lincoln and Seward, well aware that war with England would be suicidal, spun out the negotiations until American opinion had cooled off, then returned the commissioners with an indirect apology.

The second issue—the case of the Confederate commerce destroyers—generated a long-lasting diplomatic problem. Lacking the resources to construct the vessels, the Confederacy contracted to have them built and equipped in British shipyards. Six cruisers, of which the most famous were the *Alabama*, the *Florida*, and the *Shenandoah*, were sold to the Confederacy. The British government knew what was going on, being regularly and indignantly informed by Minister Adams, but winked at the practice. The United States protested that it was in violation of the laws of neutrality. The protests formed the basis, after the war, for damage claims which the United States served on Great Britain.

The third incident—the affair of the Laird rams—could have developed into a crisis, but did not because the British government suddenly decided to mend its ways. In 1863 the Confederacy placed an order from the Laird shipyards for two powerful ironclads with pointed prows for ramming and sinking Union vessels and thus breaking the blockade. Adams was instructed to inform the British that if the rams, or any other ships destined for the Confederacy, left port, then there would be danger of war. Even before Adams delivered his message, the British government acted to detain the rams and to prevent the Confederacy from obtaining any other ships.

If Napoleon III had had his way, France and England would have intervened at an early date. Unable to persuade Britain to act, he had to content himself with expressing sympathy for the Southern cause and permitting the Confederates to order commerce destroyers from French shipyards. The Emperor's primary motive for desiring an independent South was his ambition to establish French colonial

power in the Western hemisphere: a divided America could not block his plans. He seized the opportunity of the war to set up a French-dominated empire in Mexico.

Napoleon's Mexican venture was a clear violation of the Monroe Doctrine, perhaps the greatest one that had ever occurred. The United States viewed it in such a light, but for fear of provoking France into recognizing the Confederacy, it could do no more than register a protest. Only after the Civil War was ended did the United States feel strong enough to put pressure on France to get out of Mexico.

Campaigns and Battles

Since the powers of Europe refrained from direct intervention in the war, the two contestants in America were left to fight it out on their own.

THE OPENING CLASHES   1861

The year 1861 witnessed several small battles that accomplished large results and one big battle that had no important outcome. The small engagements occurred in Missouri and in western Virginia, the mountainous region that shortly would become the state of West Virginia.

In Missouri the contending forces were headed on the one hand by Governor Claiborne Jackson and other state officials, who wanted to take the state out of the Union, and on the other by Captain (later General) Nathaniel Lyon, commanding a small regular army force at St. Louis. Lyon led his column into southern Missouri, where he was defeated and killed by a superior Confederate force at the Battle of Wilson's Creek (August 10). He had, however, seriously blunted the striking power of the Confederates, and Union forces were able to hold most of the state.

Into western Virginia came a Federal force that had been assembled in Ohio under the command of George B. McClellan. Crossing the Ohio River, the invaders succeeded by the end of the year in "liberating" the mountain people. Although possession of the region placed the

Federals on the flank of Virginia, they could not, because of the transportation obstacles presented by the mountains, use it as a base from which to move eastward. The occupation of western Virginia was, however, an important propaganda victory for the North: a Union-sympathizing area in the Confederacy had been wrenched from Southern control.

The one big battle of the year was fought in Virginia in the area between the two capitals. On the Virginia front the Federals occupied three positions. A small force held Fort Monroe on the coast between the York and James rivers. Just south of Washington was an army of over 30,000 under the command of General Irvin McDowell. In the northern end of the Shenandoah Valley (usually called in Civil War literature simply the Valley) were 14,000 Federals commanded by General Robert Patterson, a venerable veteran of the War of 1812 and the Mexican War. Confronting the semicircle of Union armies were three Confederate armies: a small force opposite Fort Monroe; an army of over 20,000 under P. G. T. Beauregard based at Manassas in northern Virginia about thirty miles southwest of Washington; and 9,000 troops in the Valley, commanded by Joseph E. Johnston.

The Federals had larger forces in Virginia than the Confederates, and if McDowell's army could knock out Beauregard's (the principle Confederate force), the war might be ended immediately. The problem was to prevent other Confederate forces from coming to

Beauregard's aid. The plan, as worked out, called for Patterson to contain Johnston so that McDowell could deal with Beauregard alone. But Patterson failed.

In mid-July McDowell marched his inexperienced troops toward Manassas, his movement well advertised to the Confederates by Northern newspapers and Southern spies. Beauregard retired behind Bull Run, a small stream north of Manassas, and called on the government to order Johnston to join him. Most of Johnston's army reached Beauregard the day before the battle, making the Northern and Southern armies approximately equal in size, each numbering something over 30,000.

The Battle of Bull Run, or Manassas (July 21), might be summarized by saying that Beauregard never got his offensive into motion and that McDowell's attack almost succeeded. The Confederates stopped a last strong Union assault. Beauregard then ordered a counterattack. As the Confederates slashed forward, a sudden wave of panic struck through the Union troops, wearied after hours of hot, hard fighting and demoralized by the abrupt change of events. They gave way and crossed Bull Run in a rout. Unable to get them in hand north of the stream, McDowell had to order a retreat to Washington.

The Confederates, as disorganized by victory as the Federals were by defeat, and lacking supplies and transport, were in no condition to undertake a forward movement. Lincoln replaced McDowell with General McClellan, the victor of the fighting in western Virginia, and took measures to increase the army. Both sides girded themselves for real war.

THE WESTERN THEATER 1862

The first decisive operations in 1862 were in the Western theater. Here the Federals were trying to secure control of the Mississippi line by moving on the river itself or parallel to it. Most of their offensives were combined land-and-naval operations. To achieve their objective, the Federals advanced on the Mississippi from the north and south, moving down from Kentucky and up from the Gulf of Mexico toward New Orleans.

In April a Union squadron of ironclads and wooden vessels commanded by David G. Farragut, destined to be the first American admiral, appeared in the Gulf. Smashing past the weak forts near the mouth of the river, Farragut ran up to New Orleans, defenseless because the Confederate high command had expected the attack to come from above, and forced the civil authorities to surrender the city (April 28–May 1). For the rest of the war the Federals held New Orleans and the southern part of Louisiana. They closed off the mouth of the great river to Confederate trade, grasped the South's largest city and greatest banking center, and secured a base for future operations.

Federal land forces in the West, meanwhile, were under the direction of two departmental commanders. One army, with its base at Louisville, was led by General Don Carlos Buell. West of the Mississippi, Henry W. Halleck, with headquarters in St. Louis, was in command. An army subject to Halleck's control was stationed in western Kentucky under Ulysses S. Grant. All Confederate troops in the West were under the command of one general, Albert Sidney Johnston. A fatal weakness marked the Confederate line in Kentucky. The center, through which flowed the Tennessee and Cumberland rivers, was thrown back (southward) from the flanks, and was defended by two forts, Henry on the Tennessee and Donelson on the Cumberland. The forts had been built when Kentucky was trying to maintain a position of neutrality, and were located just over the Tennessee line. If the Federals, with the aid of naval power, could pierce the center, they would be between the two Confederate flanks and in position to destroy either.

This was exactly what the Federals did in February. Grant secured permission from Halleck to attack Fort Henry, whose defenders, awed by the ironclad river boats accompanying the Union army, surrendered with almost no resistance (February 6). Grant then marched to Donelson while his naval auxiliary moved to the Cumberland River. At Donelson the Confederates put up a scrap, but eventually the garrison of 20,000 had to capitulate (February 16). Grant, by the simple process of cracking the Confederate center and placing himself astride the river communications, had inflicted a near disaster on the Confederacy. As a result of his movement, the Confederates were forced out of Kentucky and had to yield half of Tennessee.

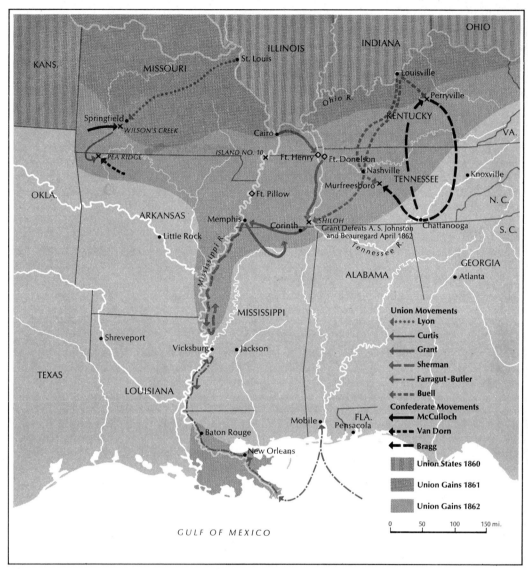

The War in the West   1861–1862

Halleck now ordered Grant, with about 40,000 troops, to proceed up the Tennessee (southward), and directed Buell, who had occupied Nashville, to march to join Grant. The immediate objective was to destroy Confederate railroad communications in the Corinth, Mississippi, area. Grant debarked his army at Pittsburg Landing, about thirty miles from Corinth. At the latter place, Johnston and Beauregard decided that their only chance to retrieve the recent reverses was to smash Grant before he was joined by Buell. Early in April they moved, 40,000 strong, toward Pittsburg Landing to attack the Federals, who were encamped between two streams flowing into the Tennessee. The battle that ensued (April 6–7) is usually known as Shiloh. The Confederates caught Grant by surprise, and by the end of the first day's fighting drove him back to the river, but here the attack was halted. At the height of the battle Johnston was killed, and Beauregard assumed command. The next day Grant, reinforced by 25,000 of Buell's troops, went over to the offensive, and regained his original lines. Beauregard then disengaged, and withdrew to Corinth. In the tactical sense, Shiloh was an extremely narrow Union victory. The most important result was strategic in nature: the Confederates had failed to prevent a concentration of the Federal armies.

After Shiloh, Halleck, bringing reinforcements with him, came to Pittsburg Landing to personally direct the advance on Corinth. Moving with excessive caution, he took almost a month to reach the town and to place his army in position to take it by siege. Beauregard, rather than risk the certain entrapment of his forces, wisely evacuated his lines. The Federals now had Corinth and the railroads of which it was the hub. Furthermore, by seizing areas parallel to the Mississippi, they flanked the Confederates out of their positions on the river. By early June the Federals had occupied the river line down as far as Memphis.

At this point Halleck was called to Washington to become general in chief. Before he left, he had assigned missions to Grant and Buell, who again became departmental commanders. To Grant, the best fighting Union general yet to appear, he gave the relatively unimportant task of guarding communications in western Tennessee and northern Mississippi. To Buell, who had done practically no fighting, he assigned the vital objective of seizing Chattanooga on the Tennessee line. For the next few months Grant did little except to repel a Confederate attempt to recover Corinth. Buell took his army to Nashville to prepare his offensive. The Confederate field army in Mississippi now commanded by Braxton Bragg (Davis had relieved Beauregard after the loss of Corinth), moved to Chattanooga, where it would be in position to undertake an offensive.

The Confederates held approximately the eastern half of Tennessee. Bragg's problem was to recover the rest of the state and, if possible, return the war to Kentucky. He was a brilliant strategist with a fatal weakness—he lacked the iron resolution to complete his plans. He now conceived a brilliant scheme. Instead of risking battle with Buell between Chattanooga and Nashville, he would rapidly invade Kentucky, forcing Buell to follow him out of Tennessee. If he could reach Kentucky first, he could place himself between Buell and

Louisville and force the Federals to fight on grounds of his own choosing. With Buell smashed, success would be at hand—Kentucky redeemed and the Western states open to invasion. Bragg did get to Kentucky first, he did stand between Buell and Louisville. But instead of fighting he withdrew. Buell went into the city and, reinforced, came out looking for Bragg. The two armies met at the indecisive Battle of Perryville (October 8), after which Bragg retired to Tennessee. Buell followed cautiously, and shortly the President relieved him. His successor was William S. Rosecrans. Toward the end of the year Bragg and Rosecrans, moving forward in simultaneous advances, came together in the hard-fought Battle of Murfreesboro or Stone's River (December 31–January 2). Again Bragg had to retire.

THE VIRGINIA FRONT 1862

In the Eastern theater in 1862 Union operations were directed by young George B. McClellan, commander of the Army of the Potomac and the most controversial general of the war. McClellan was a superb trainer of men but lacked the fighting instinct, necessary in a great captain, to commit his men to decisive battle.

During the winter of 1861–1862 McClellan had remained inactive, training his army of 150,000 men near Washington. He finally settled on a plan of operations for the spring campaign. Instead of striking for Richmond by moving southward from Washington, he would have the navy transport his army to Fort Monroe on the Virginia coast in the region between the York and James rivers known as the Peninsula. Late in March McClellan started putting his troops on transports to begin his Peninsula campaign. After the general himself had departed for Virginia, Lincoln decided, on the basis of good evidence, that McClellan had not complied with the directive to leave enough men to protect Washington. Accordingly, he ordered McDowell's corps of over 30,000 men, about to embark to join McClellan, to remain south of Washington.

McClellan was thus deprived of a substantial part of his army, leaving him with something over 100,000. He had, nevertheless, a decisive numerical superiority over the Confederates when he landed at Fort Monroe. By mid-May he was within twenty miles of Richmond, and by the latter part of the month he was approaching the gates of the city. He continued to press Lincoln to send McDowell to him, and finally the President agreed.

The Confederate high command (Davis and Lee) had misgivings about General Joseph E. Johnston's strategy of drawing McClellan closer to Richmond before fighting and they were worried by the possibility that reinforcements, particularly McDowell's corps, might join McClellan. To prevent this, Lee devised a scheme which Davis approved. The commander of the Confederate forces in the Shenandoah Valley, Thomas J. ("Stonewall") Jackson, was

directed to move northward, giving the impression that he meant to cross the Potomac. In the brilliant Valley campaign (May 4–June 9) Jackson attacked and defeated two separate Federal armies, then drove toward the northern end of the Valley. Partly to defend the approaches to Washington and partly to trap Jackson, Lincoln rushed forces to the Valley, including McDowell's corps. Jackson slipped back to safety before the various Union forces could converge on him. McDowell's troops were so fatigued by their long march that their movement to McClellan had to be suspended.

While these events were unfolding in the Valley, Johnston at last attacked McClellan at Fair Oaks or Seven Pines (May 31–June 1).

The Battle at Cedar Mountain
On August 9, 1862 – just a few weeks before suffering a disastrous defeat in the Second Battle of Bull Run – the Union army under John Pope attacked and drove off a larger Confederate force at Cedar Mountain, Virginia. In the Civil War, both sides often followed the traditional tactics of direct, frontal assault in regular lines over open ground, as illustrated here. Such tactics, with weapons of much greater range and accuracy than those used in previous wars, resulted in heavy casualties. The basic infantry weapon of the Civil War, the single-shot, muzzle-loading Springfield rifle, could kill at half a mile. From a contemporary Currier and Ives lithograph. (Library of Congress)

After the Battle of Fredericksburg
On Marye's Heights, above the town, the Federals on December 13, 1862, repeatedly attacked the Confederates, who were protected by natural fortifications. Many Union soldiers were trapped and killed in the Sunken Road on the hill, as shown in this photograph by Mathew B. Brady, the greatest American photographer of the nineteenth century. The cameras of the time used wet plates that required fairly long exposures and had to be developed on the spot, while still wet. It was almost impossible to take action pictures. (Library of Congress)

The attack failed to budge McClellan, and Johnston was so seriously wounded that he had to relinquish the command. To replace him Davis named the man who would lead the Army of Northern Virginia for the rest of the war, Robert E. Lee.

Lee, a brilliant field commander, realized that the Confederacy could not win its independence merely by repelling offensives. It would have to destroy a Union army, and to achieve this purpose Lee was ready to risk something. Informed by his cavalry leader, J. E. B. Stuart, that one-third of McClellan's army was north of the Chickahominy and two-thirds south, Lee devised a daring plan. He would call Jackson from the Valley, bringing his army up to 85,000 (as compared to McClel-

lan's 100,000), mass his forces north of the Chickahominy, and fall on the exposed Union right and destroy it. Lee's thought was that then McClellan would retreat to the York River and that he could follow and smash him before he reached his base. The risk in the plan was that McClellan would discover he confronted only a small enemy force on his left and would move into Richmond.

The operation that followed, which involved several engagements, is known as the Battle of the Seven Days (June 25–July 1). It did not proceed as Lee expected. He drove back the Union right wing but was unable to destroy it. Then McClellan, instead of retiring to the York, abandoned his base there and headed southward for the James, where he had asked the navy to set up a new base. Lee followed, trying desperately to destroy the Federals, but McClellan extricated his army, even inflicting a bloody repulse on Lee at Malvern Hill. He reached Harrison's Landing on the James, where with naval support, he was safe from any attack Lee could launch.

At Harrison's Landing the Federal army was only twenty-five miles from Richmond, and it had a secure line of water communications. But Lincoln, instead of replacing McClellan with a more aggressive commander, decided to evacuate the army to northern Virginia where it would be combined with a smaller force under John Pope — in short, to begin a new operation on the Washington-to-Richmond "overland" route.

As the Army of the Potomac left the Peninsula by water, Lee, understanding what was happening, moved his army northward with the purpose of striking Pope before he was joined by McClellan. As Lee approached, Pope retired north of the Rappahannock River. Some units of McClellan's army had reached him, and, as it developed that he might be forced into a battle, others were sent on as soon as they arrived. By a brilliant stratagem, Lee passed part of his army to Pope's rear, drawing

The death total for American soldiers was considerably higher in the Civil War than in any other war in which the United States has taken part. Considering the population of the country at the time, the Civil War total was proportionately even higher. (Many more Civil War soldiers died from disease than from battle action.) The proportion of war deaths to contemporary population, as shown in this chart, gives a truer conception of the seriousness of the losses in each war than do the absolute figures.

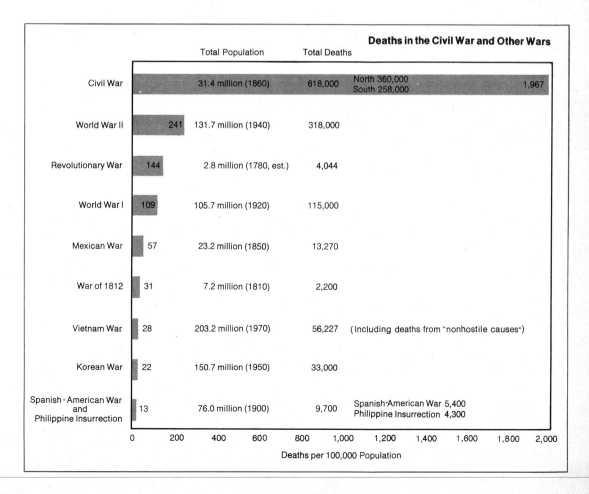

Deaths in the Civil War and Other Wars

	Total Population	Total Deaths		
Civil War	31.4 million (1860)	618,000	North 360,000 / South 258,000	1,967
World War II	131.7 million (1940)	318,000		241
Revolutionary War	2.8 million (1780, est.)	4,044		144
World War I	105.7 million (1920)	115,000		109
Mexican War	23.2 million (1850)	13,270		57
War of 1812	7.2 million (1810)	2,200		31
Vietnam War	203.2 million (1970)	56,227	(Including deaths from "nonhostile causes")	28
Korean War	150.7 million (1950)	33,000		22
Spanish-American War and Philippine Insurrection	76.0 million (1900)	9,700	Spanish-American War 5,400 / Philippine Insurrection 4,300	13

0   200   400   600   800   1,000   1,200   1,400   1,600   1,800   2,000

Deaths per 100,000 Population

the Federals north, and then followed with the remainder of his force. Pope, who was rash where McClellan was timid, was under the delusion that he faced only Jackson's corps. Although not all of McClellan's troops had joined him, he attacked the Confederates near Manassas: the Battle of Second Manassas or Second Bull Run (August 29–30). Lee easily halted the assault, and in a powerful counter-stroke swept Pope from the field. The beaten Federals retired to the Washington defenses, where Lincoln relieved Pope and placed all the troops around the city under McClellan's command.

Lee gave the Federals no respite. Early in September he went over to the offensive, invading western Maryland. With some misgivings, Lincoln let McClellan go to meet Lee. As McClellan advanced, he had a wonderful piece of luck. He captured an order by Lee showing that the Confederate army was divided, a part of it under Jackson having gone to capture Harpers Ferry. McClellan's move was to advance rapidly and attack before the enemy could concentrate. But Lee had time to pull most of his army together behind Antietam Creek near the town of Sharpsburg. Here, on September 17, McClellan, with 87,000 men, threw a series of powerful attacks at Lee's 50,000. Late in the day it seemed that the Confederate line would break, but at this moment the rest of Jackson's troops arrived from Harpers Ferry to plug the hole. Even then McClellan might have won with one more assault. But his caution asserted itself, and he called off the battle. Lee retired to Virginia, and after an interval of reorganization McClellan followed. Lincoln, disgusted by McClellan's failure to exploit his victory, removed him from command in November. It was McClellan's last military appearance in the war.

As McClellan's successor Lincoln appointed Ambrose E. Burnside, a modest mediocrity. Burnside thought that the government desired him to fight, and fight he would. He planned to drive at Richmond by crossing the Rappahannock at Fredericksburg, the strongest defensive point on that river. On December 13 he flung his army at Lee's defenses in a hopeless, bloody attack. At the end of a day of bitter failure and after suffering 12,000 casualties, he withdrew to the north side of the Rappahannock. Soon he was relieved at his own request.

YEAR OF DECISION   1863

As 1863 opened, the Union army in the East was commanded by Burnside's successor, Joseph Hooker — "Fighting Joe," as the newspapers called him. His army, which numbered 120,000, lay north of the Rappahannock opposite Fredericksburg. Hooker maneuvered opposite the town to hold Lee's attention, and crossed part of his army far up the Rappahannock. This flanking force came down on the south side, threatening to turn Lee's left. To complete his brilliant movement Hooker had only to push on to the open country around Fredericksburg — and he would have Lee in a vise. But Hooker lost his nerve. Now he hesitated, and fell back to a defensive position at Chancellorsville in the desolate area of scrub trees and brush known in Virginia as the Wilderness. Here Lee came up to attack him.

The Battle of Chancellorsville (May 1–5) was one of Lee's most brilliant exploits. With an army of only 60,000 (part of his force had been detached for other service), he took great but justified risks. Leaving a small force at Fredericksburg to contain the Federals at that point, he moved to confront Hooker. He divided his army and sent Jackson to hit the Union right, which was exposed, while he struck from in front. Finally Hooker, aided by a diversion from his troops at Fredericksburg, extricated his forces to the north side of the river. Again Lee had won, but not the decisive victory he had hoped for. And he had lost his ablest lieutenant. Jackson, wounded in the fighting, died soon afterward.

While the Federals were failing in the East, a different story was unfolding in the West, one that would influence future operations in the Eastern theater. Ulysses S. Grant was driving at Vicksburg, the most strongly fortified Confederate point on the Mississippi River. Coming down the river with naval support, he debarked his army on the Louisiana side above the city. From here he crossed to the east bank, and struck at the Confederate defenses, which were commanded by John C. Pemberton. He struck several blows, and each one failed. The terrain he was operating in north of Vicksburg was low, marshy, and laced by numerous streams and bayous, and it baffled every attempt of the army and navy to traverse it. Grant had little confidence that any of his

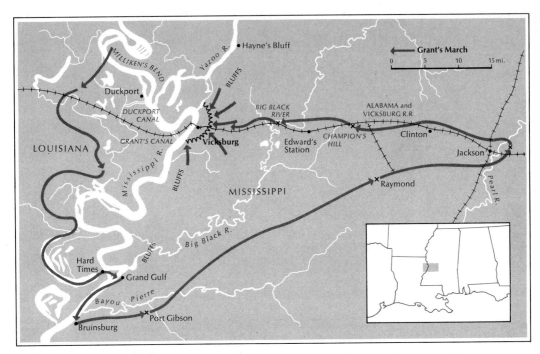

Vicksburg Campaign   1863

moves would succeed; he was keeping his forces busy until the spring, when he intended to try another route to the city.

In May he unveiled his plan. The navy ran transports past the river batteries to a point below Vicksburg. The army marched down the west side, where it was met by the navy and transported to the east side. Now Grant was south of Vicksburg on relatively high and dry ground. Moving rapidly, he defeated enemy forces barring his way at Champion's Hill and the Big Black River, and closed in on Vicksburg itself. After failing to storm the strong works, he settled down to a siege, which endured for six weeks. Pemberton, realizing that his government could not break Grant's hold and that his garrison of 30,000 was exhausted by constant fighting, surrendered on July 4. Immediately thereafter the other Confederate strong point on the river, Port Hudson (Louisiana), surrendered to a Federal force that had come up from New Orleans under N. P. Banks.

At last the Federals had achieved one of their principal strategic aims; they had gained control of the Mississippi line. The Confederacy was split into two parts, and the trans-Mississippi area was isolated from the main section. A great turning point in the war had been reached.

When the siege of Vicksburg began, the Confederate high command in Richmond was dismayed at the prospect of losing the great river fortress. Various plans to relieve the city were discussed, the principal one being a proposal to send part of Lee's army to Tennessee, possibly with Lee himself in command, to launch an offensive. But Lee demurred; he did not want to leave Virginia. He put forward a counterscheme: he would invade Pennsylvania. If he could win a victory on Northern soil, he said, great results would follow. The North might abandon the war, England and France might intervene, and the pressure on Vicksburg and other fronts would be broken. The government assented, and in June Lee started his movement, swinging his army west toward the Valley and then north through Maryland into Pennsylvania.

As Lee advanced, Hooker moved back to confront him, marching parallel to the line of Lee's route. But Hooker evidently had been

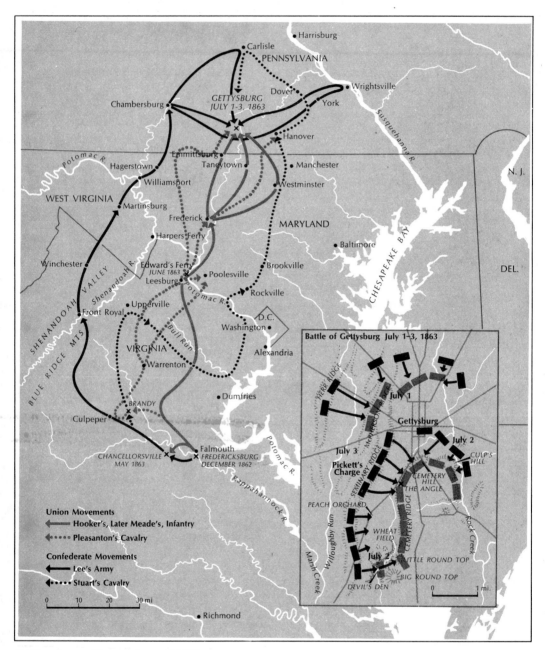

Gettysburg Campaign   1863

unnerved by his experience at Chancellorsville. He seemed to be looking for a chance to
escape his responsibility, and he soon found an
excuse to ask to be relieved. To replace him
Lincoln appointed an army corps commander,

George G. Meade, a solid if unimaginative soldier. Meade followed Lee, and approached
what might be called the strategic rear of the
Confederate army in southern Pennsylvania.
Lee, who had not expected the Federals to

move so rapidly, was astounded when he learned of their nearness. With his army marching in three columns, he was in a dangerous position; hurriedly he had to concentrate his forces. Meade, realizing that Lee in enemy country had to attack or retreat, selected a strong defensive site at the little town of Gettysburg, a road hub in the region, and Lee, seeking contact with the Federals, moved toward the same spot. Here on July 1–3 was fought the most celebrated battle of the war.

The Union army occupied a formidable position on the heights south of the town. Their line resembled an inverted fishhook, the right resting on Culp's Hill and Cemetery Hill and the front stretching along Cemetery Ridge for three miles. On the first day (July 1) the two armies jockeyed for position around Gettysburg; the tough fighting started the following day. Lee, confident of the prowess of his troops and combative by nature, decided to attack even though he was outnumbered 90,000 to 75,000. On July 2 he threw an assault at the Union left on Cemetery Ridge which crumpled up an advanced Federal corps but failed to reach the main line. On July 3 he mounted a greater effort: 15,000 men were to hit the center of the ridge and crack the Federal line wide open. The attacking force advanced over almost a mile of open space swept by enemy fire (the famous Pickett's charge). Only about 5,000 men reached the ridge, and these had to surrender or retreat. After a day of sullen waiting by both armies, Lee withdrew his shattered forces to Virginia. Meade, who had little aggressive instinct, made but a feeble pursuit. Although Meade had thrown away an opportunity to end the war, Gettysburg was another turning point. The total Confederate losses in the campaign were close to 25,000. Never again would Lee feel strong enough to fight offensively.

A third turning point against the Confederacy was reached in Tennessee. In the autumn Rosecrans moved toward Chattanooga. Bragg, in order to secure room to maneuver, evacuated the town, which was occupied by the Federals on September 9. Rosecrans, forgetting that he had not defeated Bragg, rashly plunged over the Georgia line in pursuit, where Bragg, reinforced by troops from Lee's army, was lying in wait to attack. Rosecrans barely got his scattered forces in hand before Bragg deliv-

ered his assault at Chickamauga (September 19–20). This was one of the few battles in which the Confederates enjoyed a numerical superiority (70,000 to 56,000). On the second day Bragg smashed the Union right wide open. Rosecrans and his corps generals on that flank fled to Chattanooga even though his left continued to fight under the command of George H. Thomas, who here won the nickname of "the Rock of Chickamauga." Shortly Thomas too had to retire, and the beaten army fell back into the Chattanooga defenses.

Bragg did not move rapidly to exploit his victory, partly because of his heavy casualties (17,000), but eventually he advanced and occupied the heights south of Chattanooga. Mounting batteries on these points, he commanded the roads leading into the city and virtually shut off its supplies. The Union high command, however, had ample resources to break the siege. Grant was named departmental commander of the West. Immediately he replaced Rosecrans with Thomas, and came with part of his own army to Chattanooga. The reinforced Federal army numbered 60,000, while Bragg's army was weakened by the detachment of a force for a fruitless operation against Knoxville. At the Battle of Chattanooga (November 23–25) the Federals hurled Bragg from his lines on Missionary Ridge and Lookout Mountain and back into northern Georgia. They then proceeded to occupy most of east Tennessee.

A second objective of Northern strategy had been achieved: possession of the Tennessee River line. From the Chattanooga base the Federals were in position to split the Confederacy again—what was left of it. Chattanooga deserves to be ranked with Vicksburg and Gettysburg. After 1863 the Confederacy had no chance on any front to win its independence by a military decision. Now it could hope to triumph only by exhausting the Northern will to fight.

THE ENDING   1864–1865

Grant's plans for 1864 called for two great offensives. The Army of the Potomac, commanded by Meade but accompanied and directed by Grant, was to seek to bring Lee to decisive battle in northern Virginia. From near Chattanoo-

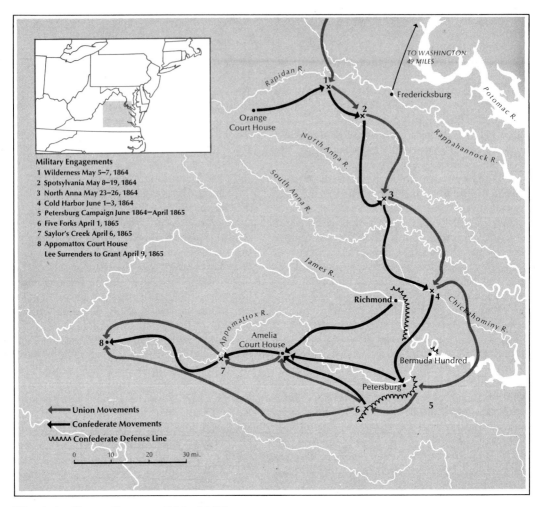

Military Engagements
1 Wilderness May 5–7, 1864
2 Spotsylvania May 8–19, 1864
3 North Anna May 23–26, 1864
4 Cold Harbor June 1–3, 1864
5 Petersburg Campaign June 1864–April 1865
6 Five Forks April 1, 1865
7 Saylor's Creek April 6, 1865
8 Appomattox Court House
  Lee Surrenders to Grant April 9, 1865

⟵ Union Movements
⟵ Confederate Movements
⩗⩗⩗⩗ Confederate Defense Line

0   10   20   30 mi.

Virginia Campaigns   1864–1865

ga the Western army, commanded by William T. Sherman, was to advance into northern Georgia, destroy the Confederate army, now commanded by Joseph E. Johnston, and wreck the economic resources of Atlanta.

The two offensives started in May. From its position in northern Virginia the Army of the Potomac, 115,000 strong, crossed the Rappahannock and Rapidan rivers and plunged into the Wilderness area. Grant's plan was to envelop Lee's right and force him to a showdown battle. Lee, whose army numbered about 75,000 at the beginning of the campaign, was determined to avoid a showdown unless he saw a chance to deal a decisive blow. In the Battle of

the Wilderness (May 5–7) each commander struck savagely at the other. Demonstrating superb defensive skill, Lee prevented Grant from turning his right. But the Federal commander, instead of retiring to reorganize as his predecessors had done after a reverse, slid off to his left and to the southeast. He turned up at Spotsylvania Court House, where Lee moved to meet him. Here another bloody, indecisive engagement was fought (May 8–19). Again Grant sidled to his left, and again Lee slid with him. In this manner, without fighting another major clash, the two armies moved until they reached Cold Harbor, a few miles north of Richmond. At this point Grant made a last attempt to destroy Lee north of Richmond (June 1–3) and was bloodily repulsed. In a month of fighting Grant had lost in total casualties 55,000 men, and Lee, 31,000.

Now Grant had to alter his strategy. If he remained where he was, Lee would retire into the Richmond defenses to stand a siege, something Grant wanted to avoid. Masking his movements from his adversary, Grant moved southward across the James heading for Petersburg, directly south of Richmond. Petersburg was the hub of all the railroads feeding into the capital; if Grant could secure it he could force Lee to come into the open to fight for his communications. He almost succeeded. Petersburg was defended only by a small force under Beauregard, who managed, however, to hold Grant off until Lee's army could arrive. Grant now realized that he would have to resort to siege operations. He dug in, and so did Lee. The trench lines of the two armies stretched for miles above and below Petersburg. Always Grant strove to extend his left around Lee's right so as to get on the railroads that were the life line of the Southern army. It would be nine months until he reached his objective.

In May, Sherman, with an army of over 90,000, moved against Johnston's army at Atlanta, which numbered 60,000 at the beginning. Johnston's plan was to delay Sherman, to fight for time, and not to commit his forces unless the conditions were exceptionally favorable. The Atlanta campaign developed primarily into a game of maneuver in which Sherman tried to trap his rival, who avoided being caught. The two armies skirmished and fought almost constantly, but the only set battle was at Kennesaw Mountain (June 27). As Sherman was approaching Atlanta, President Davis replaced Johnston with John B. Hood. Combative by nature, Hood threw two successive attacks at Sherman, both of which failed. The Union army occupied Atlanta on September 2.

Sherman had not destroyed the enemy army. Eager to strike deeper into Georgia, he

Sherman's March Through the Confederacy   1864–1865

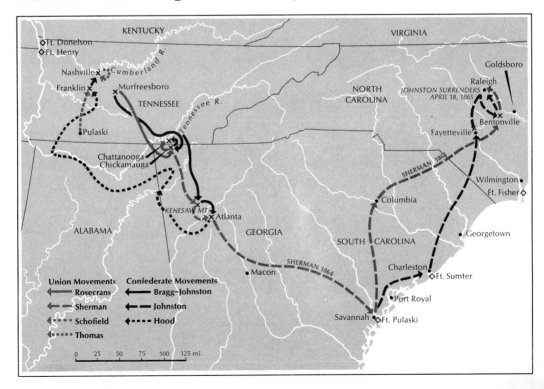

The Impact of War on the South
Because most of the fighting in the Civil War occurred in the South, that section
suffered widespread destruction of its physical resources. At the top is
Fredericksburg, Virginia, the site of a battle in 1862, and below is Columbia, South
Carolina, much of which was burned when occupied by Sherman's army in 1864.
(Library of Congress)

sent 30,000 of his army to Tennessee under Thomas, and prepared to move for Savannah on the coast. At the same time Hood decided to invade Tennessee, hoping to force Sherman to follow him.

Confronting Hood, and seeking to delay him, was a Union force of about 30,000 under John M. Schofield. Hood caught up with Schofield at Franklin, Tennessee, on November 30. With no artillery support, Hood resolved to attack across two miles of open space, though the Federals were entrenched in a strong position. In six fruitless charges he lost 6,000 men; eleven of his generals were killed or wounded. After that he might as well have gone back to Georgia. But he moved forward and took up a position south of Nashville. In the city Thomas was gathering an army that would eventually number over 60,000. When he was ready, he came out looking for Hood. At the Battle of Nashville (December 15–16) he smashed Hood from the field. As the Confederates retreated toward Mississippi, they were harried by the most merciless cavalry pursuit of the war. Only a few units reached Mississippi intact. The Confederate Army of Tennessee had, in effect, ceased to exist.

In the meantime Sherman was marching almost unopposed across Georgia, inaugurating a new kind of warfare. He was the prophet of modern total war—war against the civilian population of the enemy, war intended to break the enemy people's will to resist. His army marched on a sixty-mile front, destroying property and supplies that might be used by the Confederate forces and committing many individual depredations as well. But the greatest result of Sherman's march was psychological rather than economic. What Southerner who heard of a Union army moving at will through the heart of the South could ever believe again that the Confederacy could win the war? In Virginia soldiers in Lee's army deserted to go home to take care of their families. By December 20 Sherman was at Savannah.

Sherman then turned into South Carolina, still facing slight opposition and still ripping up enemy property. He was accomplishing two objectives: destroying both Confederate resources and the railroads that brought supplies from the lower South to Lee's army. When he advanced into North Carolina, the Confederate government got together an army of 30,000 under Johnston to oppose him, but this small force could do little more than delay his march. Nor could Lee move against him, for he was pinned down at Petersburg by Grant.

In April 1865, Grant finally passed a part of his army around Lee's right to the vital railroads. The Confederates evacuated Petersburg and Richmond, and Lee moved westward with his army, now shrunk to about 25,000. His one forlorn hope was to reach a rail line to North Carolina and unite with Johnston. But the pursuing Federal army barred his escape route. At last he realized that further fighting was hopeless, and on April 9 he met Grant at Appomattox and surrendered the Army of Northern Virginia. In North Carolina Joe Johnston reached the same conclusion, and on April 18 he surrendered to Sherman near Durham. Jefferson Davis, defiant to the last and unable to recognize defeat, fled southward, and was captured in Georgia. The war was soon over.

THE WAR'S AFTERMATH

In the North, the wartime prosperity continued into the postwar years, but Northerners who visited the South were appalled when they gazed upon the desolation left in the wake of the war—gutted towns, wrecked plantations, neglected fields, collapsed bridges, and ruined railroads. Much of the personal property of Southerners had been lost with the lost cause. Confederate bonds and currency were now worthless, and capital that had been invested in them was gone forever. And with the emancipation of the slaves, Southern whites would be deprived of property worth an estimated $2 billion.

Matching the shattered economy of the South was the disorganization of its social system. In the months that followed the end of the war, when thousands of soldiers were drifting back to their homes—258,000 never returned and other thousands went back wounded or sick—life was seriously deranged. To many people the problem of keeping alive, of securing food and shelter, seemed the only thing that mattered.

If conditions were bad for Southern whites, they were generally worse for Southern blacks—the 4 million who were emerging from the bondage that had held them and their ancestors for two and a half centuries. Many of these people, too, had seen service of one kind or another during the war. Some had served as body servants for Confederate officers or as teamsters and laborers for the Confederate armies. Tens of thousands had fought as combat troops in the Union ranks, and more than 38,000 had given their lives for the Union cause. Among the black soldiers the death rate was much higher than among the whites, partly because of the haste and poor preparation with which Negroes were sometimes sent into action, partly because of the usual Confederate practice of granting them no quarter in battle. Countless other Negroes, who never wore a uniform or drew army pay, assisted the Union forces as spies or scouts. Still others ran off from the plantations, thus depriving the South of labor, and flocked into the Union lines, often to be put to work for the Union armies. Certainly the blacks contributed a great deal of effort and sacrifice to the winning of their own freedom.

As the war ended, freedom appeared to be on the way, but its arrival was uncertain. The Thirteenth Amendment, which would make slavery unconstitutional, had yet to be ratified by the requisite number of states (it had passed Congress on February 1, 1865, and was to be proclaimed in effect on December 18, 1865). On many plantations the blacks were still being detained and forced to work. Most planters agreed with a former Confederate leader who was saying (in June 1865) that slavery had been "the best system of labor that could be devised for the Negro race" and that the wise thing to do now would be to "provide a substitute for it."

To get away from their old masters, thousands of Negroes continued to leave the plantations. Old and young, many of them feeble and ill, they trudged to the nearest town or city or they roamed the countryside, camping at night on the bare ground. Few had any possessions except the rags on their backs. Somehow they managed to stay alive.

What the Negroes wanted was, first of all, to be assured of their freedom—to feel it, to exercise it, and to know it was not going to be taken from them. Next, they needed immediate relief from the threat of starvation. Then, looking ahead, they desired land, farms of their own, a bit of economic independence. A few of the freed slaves had already settled on abandoned plantations, notably on the Sea Islands along the South Carolina coast and on land in Mississippi that had belonged to the Davis family. The Negroes also longed for schooling for their children if not for themselves. In some places, above all in New Orleans, there were well-educated and highly cultured communities of blacks who had been free for generations. But education was a rare and precious thing to the new freedmen, most of whom were as illiterate as the slave codes had intended them to be. Finally, a number of the Negroes were beginning to demand political rights. "The only salvation for us besides the power of the Government is in the *possession of the ballot*," a convention of the colored people of Virginia resolved in the summer of 1865. "All we ask is an *equal chance*."

The federal government, besides keeping troops (many of them black) in the South to preserve order and protect the Negroes, was doing something to assist them in the transition from slavery to freedom. Congress had set up (in March 1865) the Bureau of Freedmen, Refugees, and Abandoned Lands as an agency of the army. This Freedmen's Bureau was empowered to provide food, transportation, assistance in getting jobs and fair wages, and schools for former slaves, and also to settle them on abandoned or confiscated lands. Under the able direction of General Oliver O. Howard, the bureau undertook to perform its allotted functions, and more. Its agents soon distributed 20 million rations in the South, to hungry whites as well as blacks. Cooperating with the bureau, especially in its educational work, were missionaries and teachers who had been sent to the South by Freedmen's Aid Societies and other private and church groups in the North.

Nevertheless, the future of the blacks remained in doubt. The Freedmen's Bureau, according to the law creating it, was to last for only one year after the end of the war. Meanwhile, the majority of Southern whites resent-

ed the activities of the bureau and its agents. These outsiders stood in the way of the desire to set up a substitute for slavery, a substitute that would serve both as a cheap labor system and as a white supremacy device.

Selected Readings

Wartime Diplomacy
E. D. Adams, *Great Britain and the American Civil War* (2 vols., 1925); Donaldson Jordan and E. J. Pratt, *Europe and the American Civil War* (1931); F. L. Owsley, *King Cotton Diplomacy* (1931, 1959); G. G. Van Deusen, *William H. Seward* (1967); M. B. Duberman, *Charles Francis Adams, 1807–1886* (1961).

The War in General
Bruce Catton, *Mr. Lincoln's Army** (1951), *Glory Road** (1952), and *A Stillness at Appomattox** (1954); J. B. Mitchell, *Decisive Battles of the Civil War** (1955); Jay Monaghan, *Civil War on the Western Border, 1854–1865* (1955); B. I. Wiley, *The Life of Johnny Reb** (1943), *The Life of Billy Yank** (1952), and *The Road to Appomattox** (1956); Benjamin Quarles, *The Negro in the Civil War* (1953); D. T. Cornish, *The Sable Arm** (1956), an account of the black troops; David Donald, ed., *Why the North Won the Civil War** (1960); H. S. Commager, ed., *The Blue and the Gray: The Story of the Civil War as Told by Participants* (2 vols., 1950); David Donald, ed., *Divided We Fought: A Pictorial History of the Civil War* (1952); R. M. Ketchum, *The American Heritage Picture History of the Civil War* (1960).

The Union Side
T. H. Williams, *Lincoln and His Generals* (1952) and *McClellan, Sherman, and Grant* (1962); K. P. Williams, *Lincoln Finds a General: A Military History of the Civil War* (4 vols., 1949–1956); R. V. Bruce, *Lincoln and the Tools of War* (1956); Lloyd Lewis, *Sherman, Fighting Prophet* (1932); W. W. Hassler, Jr., *General George B. McClellan: Shield of the Union* (1957).

The Confederate Side
D. S. Freeman, *R. E. Lee: A Biography* (4 vols., 1934–1935) and *Lee's Lieutenants* (3 vols., 1942–1944); F. E. Vandiver, *Rebel Brass* (1956); Archer Jones, *Confederate Strategy from Shiloh to Vicksburg* (1961); T. L. Connelly, *Army of the Heartland* (1967); F. E. Vandiver, *Mighty Stonewall* (1957); T. H. Williams, *Beaure-*

*gard, Napoleon in Gray** (1955); Gilbert Govan and J. W. Livingood, *A Different Valor* (1956), on J. E. Johnston.

The Naval War
V. C. Jones, *The Civil War at Sea* (3 vols., 1960–1962); C. E. Macartney, *Mr. Lincoln's Admirals* (1956); R. S. West, Jr., *Mr. Lincoln's Navy* (1957); John Niven, *Gideon Welles, Lincoln's Secretary of the Navy* (1973); J. P. Baxter III, *The Introduction of the Ironclad Warship* (1933); R. W. Daly, *How the Merrimack Won* (1957); T. C. and Ruth White, *Tin Can on a Shingle* (1957), on the *Monitor-Merrimack* duel.

The Reconstruction Problem
Herman Belz, *Reconstructing the Union: Theory and Policy During the Civil War* (1969); W. B. Hesseltine, *Lincoln's Plan of Reconstruction** (1960); W. L. Rose, *Rehearsal for Reconstruction: The Port Royal Experiment** (1964); L. S. Gerteis, *From Contraband to Freedman: Federal Policy Toward Southern Blacks, 1861–1865* (1973); G. R. Bentley, *A History of the Freedmen's Bureau* (1955); Sidney Andrews, *The South Since the War* (1866); J. H. Trowbridge, *A Picture of the Desolated States* (1866; abridgment with title *The Desolate South*, ed. by Gordon Carroll, 1956); F. W. Klingberg, *The Southern Claims Commission* (1955); G. S. Henig, *Henry Winter Davis, Antebellum and Civil War Congressman from Maryland* (1973).

Johnson and the Radicals
David Donald, *The Politics of Reconstruction, 1863–1867** (1965); H. K. Beale, *The Critical Year: A Study of Andrew Johnson and Reconstruction* (1930); E. L. McKitrick, *Andrew Johnson and Reconstruction* (1960); La Wanda and J. H. Cox, *Politics, Principles, and Prejudice, 1865–1867* (1963); R. N. Current, *Old Thad Stevens: A Story of Ambition* (1942); F. N. Brodie, *Thaddeus Stevens, Scourge of the South* (1959); R. H. Abbott, *Cobbler in Congress: The Life of Henry Wilson, 1812–1875* (1971).

*Titles available in paperback.

Reconstructing the Nation

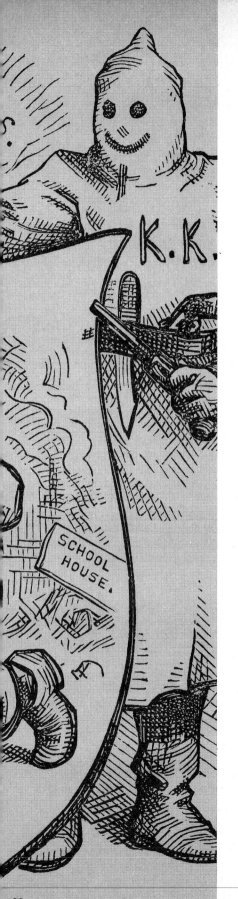

Sixteen

When Americans of a later generation looked back on the 1860s and 1870s, it seemed to many of them that there had been a sharp break between the Civil War and the ensuing period of Reconstruction. The war itself, for all its suffering and sacrifice, was remembered on the whole as an ennobling experience, one of high purpose and gallantry on both sides. The postwar years, by contrast, appeared to have been a time of low, unscrupulous politics, a time when vengeful men among the victors disgraced the country while unnecessarily delaying a real, heartfelt reunion of the North and the South.

That view contains elements of historical reality, but it misses an essential truth about the troubled postwar period. The struggle over Reconstruction was, in part, a continuation of the Civil War. It was a struggle, as the war had been, that involved (among other things) the question of both state rights and human rights. The victory for Union and emancipation had not been completely won at Appomattox. In the postwar years an effort was made to confirm the supremacy of the national government over the Southern states and to assure the benefits of freedom to the millions of emancipated slaves. This effort, provoking resistance as it did, had the effect of keeping the country psychologically divided.

Politicians on both sides added to the divisive effect by playing upon the hatreds left over from the war. Republicans implied that all Democrats, Northern as well as Southern, had been traitors. "Every man that shot Union soldiers was a Democrat," a typical Republican orator declaimed. "The man that assassinated Abraham Lincoln was a Democrat." This technique of reviving wartime emotions in order to win postwar elections came to be known, among Democrats, as "waving the bloody shirt." But in the South the Democrats waved a bloody shirt of their own. They denounced their opponents, black and

"Worse than Slavery"
During Reconstruction the blacks of the South suffered at the hands of white supremacists, as depicted in this 1874 wood engraving by Thomas Nast. The greatest American political cartoonist of the nineteenth century, Bavarian-born Nast made the elephant and donkey the symbols respectively of the Republican and Democratic parties. (Library of Congress)

white, as desecrators of the Confederate cause. The Ku Klux Klan, an anti-Republican terrorist group, pretended that its members were ghosts of the Confederate army.

The struggle over Reconstruction ended in the Compromise of 1877. This arrangement, a combination of "reunion and reaction," brought the sections together at the expense of the Negro. The federal government gave up the attempt to enforce the Negro's rights and left the Southern states in the hands of the Democrats. Yet two great charters of human liberty still stood as documents of the Reconstruction era—the Fourteenth and Fifteenth amendments to the federal Constitution—which had been intended to assure citizenship and the suffrage to the former slaves. For the time being, these documents were disregarded, but a day was to come, several decades later, when they would provide the legal basis for a renewed drive to bring true freedom and equality to all Americans.

The Problem of Peacemaking

The Constitution provides for peacemaking at the end of a foreign war. The President, with the advice and consent of the Senate, ratifies a treaty of peace. But the Constitution naturally makes no provision for ending a civil war. And Lincoln could not negotiate a treaty with Confederate leaders, for that would mean recognizing the legal existence of the Confederacy. Yet, once the armies had stopped fighting, a peace arrangement somehow had to be made.

RECONSTRUCTION: THE ISSUES

The word "Reconstruction," as contemporaries used it, referred to the process by which peace was to be made, that is, the process by which the states of the defeated Confederacy were to be brought back to their former places in the Union. One possibility would be to grant easy terms, permitting the states to return promptly and with little internal change except for the elimination of slavery. Another possibility would be to make a harsh peace, delaying the readmission of the states until they had been reconstructed in such a way as to reduce the power of the rebel leaders.

A quick and easy restoration of the Union would be to the advantage of the former Confederates and the Democratic party North and South. Ironically, the abolition of slavery would increase the power of the Southern states in national politics. In the past, under the "three-fifths clause" of the Constitution, only three-fifths of the slaves had been counted in determining a state's representation in Congress and its electoral votes in presidential elections. In the future, *all* the former slaves would be counted, whether or not they themselves were given political rights. A state such as South Carolina, where about half of the population was black, would have its congressional representation increased, for example, by approximately 20 percent. With this added strength the Southern Democrats could rejoin the Northern Democrats and get control of both Congress and the presidency.

The consequences of an easy peace, by the same token, could be disastrous for the Republican party. The Republicans had gained control of the federal government in 1860–1861 only because of the split in the Democratic party and the secession of the Southern states. Once these had been restored and the Democratic party had been reunited, the Republicans would face the uncomfortable prospect of being reduced to a minority group once again. The outlook was disturbing also for Northern businessmen who during the war had obtained favors from the federal government—a high tariff, railroad subsidies, the national banking system—which might be ended once the Democrats were back in power.

For the Negroes emerging from slavery, a quick restoration of the Southern states would be catastrophic. The master class, which had dominated the state governments before and during the war, would continue to do so. The Negroes then could expect to be kept in a position that, at best, would be somewhere between slavery and freedom.

Thus the issues of Reconstruction were very similar to those of the war itself. So far as the Southern leaders were concerned, the war had been fought for the independence of the South and for the preservation of slavery (in 1861 the Confederate Vice President, Alexander H. Stephens, had frankly proclaimed that slavery was the "cornerstone" of the Confederacy). After the war these leaders hoped to maintain a considerable degree of Southern autonomy through the assertion of state rights, and they hoped to retain much of the essence of slavery by finding some substitute for it. If they should have their way in Reconstruction, the "lost cause" they had fought for would not be completely lost.

The issues were often obscured and complicated by the emotionalism of the controversy over Reconstruction. On both sides people approached the question in a spirit of hatred left over from the four years of bloodshed. In the North there was the memory of sacrifice, suffering, and personal loss; in the South there was even more of that, plus the added bitterness of defeat. In the North there was a widespread feeling that Southerners ought to be required to acknowledge their defeat by some gesture of submission, and that at least a few of them ought to be punished for their guilt in bringing on the war and also for the atrocities which, according to Northern wartime propaganda, they had committed in the course of it. Moreover, there was a general conviction that the former slaves ought to be protected in their freedom and assured of justice. And there was a growing belief that Reconstruction offered a heaven-sent opportunity to recast the South in the image of the North—to take that supposedly backward, feudal, undemocratic section and civilize and modernize it.

The Reconstruction question was further complicated by disputes over the respective roles that the President and Congress were to play. Presumably, the task should have been one for the executive and the legislative branches, the two acting in cooperation. As it happened, however, the President and the congressional majority differed on the policy to be followed. Hence arose the issue of presidential as opposed to congressional powers.

Even among the majority in Congress—the Republicans—there was disagreement as to the kind of peace that should be imposed upon the South. The same factions of the party (the Conservatives and the Radicals) that had clashed on wartime emancipation now confronted each other on the issue of Reconstruction. The Conservatives advocated a mild peace and the rapid restoration of the defeated states to the Union; beyond insisting that the South accept the abolition of slavery, they would not interfere with race relations or attempt to alter the social system of the South. The Radicals, directed by leaders like Thaddeus Stevens of Pennsylvania and Charles Sumner of Massachusetts, stood for a hard peace; they urged that the civil and military chieftains of the late Confederacy be subjected to severe punishment, that large numbers of Southern whites be disfranchised, and that the property of rich Southerners who had aided the Confederacy be confiscated and distributed among the freedmen. From the first, some Radicals favored granting suffrage to the former slaves, as a matter of right or as a means of creating a Republican electorate in the South. Other Radicals agreed with them, but hesitated to state a position for fear of public opinion—not all Northern states permitted Negroes to vote.

Between the Radicals and the Conservatives stood a faction of uncommitted Republicans who may be termed the Moderates. They would go further than the Conservatives in demanding concessions of the South, particularly in regard to rights for Negroes, but they rejected the punitive goals of the Radicals. As the Reconstruction controversy developed, the pressure of events would inexorably force the Moderates into the Radical camp.

The various proponents of a Reconstruction policy, following an honored American tradition, attempted to buttress their position with constitutional sanction. The Conservatives, claiming that secession was illegal, contended that the seceded states had never legally been out of the Union, were still in it, and had all the rights of states. The Radicals, the uncompromising nationalists of the war, now insisted that the Southern states had in fact withdrawn from the nation and had therefore forfeited their rights as states. Sumner argued that by seceding they had committed "state suicide," and Stevens bluntly referred to them as "conquered provinces." On the other hand, Southerners who had fought to uphold the right of secession now demanded all the privileges they had previously enjoyed in the Union they had tried to dissolve.

LINCOLN'S PLAN

The process of Reconstruction was put into motion while the war was still going on, and the first plan was presented by President Lincoln. He believed there were a considerable number of actual or potential Unionists in the South. These people, most of them former Whigs, could possibly be encouraged to rejoin the old Whigs of the North and thus strengthen the Republican party, once the Union had been restored. More immediately, these men could serve as the nucleus for setting up new and loyal states in the South and thereby hastening reunion. All along, Lincoln was concerned with principle as well as politics: the principle of the inviolability of the Union. He wanted to restore the American experiment in democracy as soon as possible. Consequently, he proposed an easy mode of Reconstruction. He would subordinate to his larger goal such questions as punishment of the defeated side or determination of the status of the freedmen. The question of whether the defeated states were in or out of the Union he dismissed as a "merely pernicious abstraction." They were only out of their proper, practical relationship to the Union, he said, and they should be restored to that relationship as soon as possible.

Specifically, Lincoln's plan, which he announced to the public in a proclamation of December 1863, offered a general amnesty to all who would take an oath pledging future loyalty to the government. Temporarily excluded from the right to swear the oath were high civil and military officials of the Confederacy. Whenever in any state 10 percent of the number of voters in 1860 took the oath, they could proceed to set up a state government. The oath required acceptance of the wartime acts and proclamations of Congress and the President concerning slavery. This was the only provision in the plan that imposed on the South a condition for readmission and the only part of the plan that dealt with national supervision of race relations. Instead of demanding outright abolition (the Thirteenth Amendment had not yet been passed, and the postwar effect of the Emancipation Proclamation was uncertain, since it was a war measure), Lincoln told Southern leaders that he hoped they would provide for permanent freedom. He also urged them to give the ballot to at least a few Negroes — to those who were educated, owned property, and had served in the Union army. In three Southern states — Louisiana, Arkansas, and Tennessee — loyal governments were reestablished under the Lincoln formula in 1864.

The Radical Republicans were angered and astonished at the mildness of Lincoln's program, and they were able to induce Congress to repudiate his governments. Representatives from the Lincoln states were not admitted to Congress, and the electoral vote of those states was not counted in the election of 1864. In defeating Lincoln's plan, the Radicals were aided by a number of Moderate Republicans who thought that the President's scheme did not provide adequate protection for the freedmen. The Radicals could not stop, however, with a rejection of Lincoln's plan. The requirements of politics dictated that they produce a plan of their own. But at the moment the Radicals had not thought the Reconstruction problem through. They were not agreed as to how "hard" a peace they should enforce on the South, and they were not certain that Northern opinion would support the ideas of their more extreme leaders.

Under pressure, they prepared and passed (in July 1864) the Wade-Davis Bill, which may be considered the first Radical plan of Reconstruction. By its provisions, the President was to appoint for each conquered state a provisional governor who would take a census of all adult white males. If a majority of those enrolled — instead of Lincoln's 10 percent — swore an oath of allegiance, the governor was to call an election for a state constitutional convention. The privilege of voting for delegates to this meeting was limited to those who could swear that they had never borne arms against the United States, the so-called iron-clad oath. The convention was required to put provisions into the new constitution abolishing slavery, disfranchising Confederate civil and military leaders, and repudiating the Confederate and state war debts. After these conditions had been met, Congress would readmit the state to the Union. The Wade-Davis Bill was more drastic in almost every respect than the Lincoln plan, and it assumed that the seceded states were out of the Union and hence under the dictation of Congress. But the bill, like the President's proposal, left up to the states the question of political rights for Negroes.

The Wade-Davis Bill was passed a few days before Congress adjourned, which enabled Lincoln to dispose of it with a pocket veto. His action enraged the authors of the measure, Benjamin F. Wade and Henry Winter Davis, who issued a blistering denunciation of the veto, the Wade-Davis Manifesto, warning the President not to interfere with the powers of Congress to control Reconstruction. Lincoln could not ignore the bitterness and the strength of the Radical opposition. Practical as always, he realized that he would have to accept some of the objections of the Radicals. He began to move toward a new approach to Reconstruction, possibly one that included greater national supervision of the freedmen.

What plan he would have come up with nobody can say. On April 14, 1865, a crazed actor, John Wilkes Booth, under the delusion that he was helping the South, shot the President in a Washington theater. Lincoln died early the following morning, and because of the circumstances of his death—the heroic leader, the Great Emancipator struck down in the hour of victory by an assassin—he achieved immediate martyrdom. In the wild excitement of the hour, it was widely assumed that Booth had been instigated to his mad act by men in the South, and the Radicals played on this theme with reckless charges implicating high Confederates. Ironically, Lincoln's death helped to kill his policy of a generous peace.

JOHNSON AND "RESTORATION"

The conservative leadership in the controversy over Reconstruction fell upon Lincoln's successor, Andrew Johnson. Of all the men who accidentally inherited the presidency, Johnson was undoubtedly the most unfortunate. A Southerner and former slaveholder, he became President as a bloody war against the South was drawing to a close. A Democrat before he had been placed on the Union ticket with Lincoln in 1864, he became the head of a Republican administration at a time when partisan passions, held in some restraint during the war, were about to rule the government. As if these handicaps of background were not enough, Johnson was intemperate in language and tactless in manner, and he lacked Lincoln's skill in handling people. Unlike Lincoln, he was theoretical rather than practical, dogmatic rather than pragmatic. In dealing with Reconstruction, he stood righteously by the Constitution,

even though that document obviously did not envision the unprecedented constitutional situation that existed after the war.

Johnson revealed his plan of Reconstruction—or "Restoration," as he preferred to call it—soon after he took office, and he proceeded to execute it during the summer of 1865 when Congress was not in session. He applied it to the eight states of the late Confederacy that had not come under the Lincoln plan; he recognized as legal organizations the Lincoln governments in Louisiana, Arkansas, Tennessee, and Virginia.

In some ways Johnson's scheme resembled Lincoln's; in others it was similar to the Wade-Davis Bill. Like his predecessor, Johnson assumed that the seceded states were still in the Union, and, also like Lincoln, he an-

Andrew Johnson
Born in North Carolina, Johnson moved to Tennessee as a young man and worked as a tailor before going into politics. He had a dark complexion and piercing black eyes. A powerful orator on the stump, he easily lost his temper when heckled and used crude and intemperate language. Sincerely devoted to his principles, he was sometimes too theoretical in upholding them. (Library of Congress)

nounced his design in a proclamation of amnesty that extended pardon for past conduct to all who would take an oath of allegiance. Denied the privilege of taking the oath until they received individual pardons from the President were high-ranking Confederate officials and also men with land worth $20,000 or more; Johnson excluded a larger number of leaders than Lincoln had. For each state the President appointed a provisional governor who was to invite the qualified voters to elect delegates to a constitutional convention. Johnson did not specify that a minimum number of voters had to take the oath, as had the Lincoln and Wade-Davis proposals, but the implication was plain that he would require a majority. As conditions of readmittance, the state had to revoke the ordinance of secession, abolish slavery and ratify the Thirteenth Amendment, and repudiate the Confederate and state war debts—essentially the same stipulations that had been laid down in the Wade-Davis Bill. The final procedure before restoration was for a state to elect a state government and send representatives to Congress.

By the end of 1865 the states affected by Johnson's plan had complied with its requirements. Indeed, if the Lincoln governments are included, all of the seceded states had been reconstructed and were ready to resume their places in the Union—if Congress chose to recognize them when it met in December 1865. Recognition of the Johnson governments was exactly what the Radicals were determined to prevent. And many people in the North agreed with them that Reconstruction was being rushed too fast and was being accomplished too easily.

Northerners were disturbed by the seeming reluctance of some members of the Southern conventions to abolish slavery and by the refusal of all the conventions to grant suffrage to even a few Negroes. They were astounded that states claiming to be "loyal" should elect as state officials and representatives to Congress prominent leaders of the recent Confederacy. Particularly hard to understand was Georgia's choice of Alexander H. Stephens, former Vice President of the Confederacy, as a United States senator.

Radical Reconstruction

When Congress met in December 1865, it denied admission to the senators and representatives from the states that President Andrew Johnson had "restored." The Radical leaders explained that the Southerners should be excluded until Congress knew more about conditions in the South. Congress must first be assured that the former Confederates had accepted the results of the war and that Southern Negroes and loyal whites were safe. Accordingly, Congress set up the Joint Committee on Reconstruction to investigate opinions in the South and to advise Congress in laying down a Reconstruction policy.

CONGRESS TAKES OVER

During the next few months the Radicals, though disagreeing among themselves, advanced toward a more severe program than their first plan, the Wade-Davis Bill of 1864, which left to the states the question of what rights the freed slaves should have. The Radicals gained the support of moderate Republicans because of Johnson's intransigent attitude. Johnson insisted that Congress had no right even to consider a policy for the South until his own plan had been accepted and the Southern congressmen and senators had been admitted.

Northern opinion was aroused by the so-called Black Codes, which the Southern legislatures adopted during the sessions of 1865–1866. These measures were the South's solution for the problem of the free Negro laborer, and they were also the South's substitute for slavery as a white supremacy device. Economically, the codes were intended to regulate the labor of a race that, in the opinion of the whites, would not work except under some kind of compulsion. Although the economic provisions varied in stringency from state to state, they all authorized local officials to apprehend unemployed Negroes, fine them for vagrancy, and hire them out to private employers to satisfy the fine. Some of the codes tried to force Negroes to work on the plantations by forbidding

The Black Code of Louisiana

The sections in the Black Codes regulating Negro labor angered Northern opinion and turned many people in favor of Radical Reconstruction. The Louisiana Code had this to say:

Sec. 1. Be it enacted by the Senate and House of Representatives of the State of Louisiana in general assembly convened, That all persons employed as laborers in agricultural pursuits shall be required, during the first ten days of the month of January of each year, to make contracts for labor for the then ensuing year, or for the year next ensuing the termination of their present contracts. All contracts for labor for agricultural purposes shall be made in writing, signed by the employer, and shall be made in the presence of a Justice of the Peace and two disinterested witnesses, in whose presence the contract shall be read to the laborer, and when assented to and signed by the latter, shall be considered as binding for the time prescribed. . . .

Sec. 2. Every laborer shall have full and perfect liberty to choose his employer, but, when once chosen, he shall not be allowed to leave his place of employment until the fulfillment of his contract . . . and if they do so leave, without cause or permission, they shall forfeit all wages earned to the time of abandonment. . . .

---

them to own or lease farms or to take other jobs except as domestic servants. Socially, the codes were designed to govern relations between the races and to invest the Negroes with a legal although subordinate status. The acts conferred certain civil rights upon blacks, but they also placed special restrictions on Negroes that did not apply to whites. To the South, the Black Codes were a realistic approach to a great social problem. To the North, they seemed to herald a return to slavery.

An appropriate agency for offsetting the Black Codes was the Freedmen's Bureau, but its scheduled year of existence was about to end. It had been losing some of its original functions. With the passing of the immediate postwar emergency, there was decreasing need for the bureau's relief activities. And President Johnson had been pardoning so many former rebels—thus restoring to them their confiscated plantations—that there was less and less land available for resettling former slaves.

In February 1866 Congress passed a bill to prolong the life of the bureau and to widen its powers by authorizing special courts for settling labor disputes. Thus the bureau could set aside work agreements that might be forced upon Negroes under the Black Codes. Johnson vetoed the bill, denouncing it as unconstitutional.

In April Congress again struck at the Black Codes by passing the Civil Rights Bill, which made United States citizens of Negroes and

empowered the federal government to intervene in state affairs when necessary for protecting the rights of citizens. Johnson vetoed this bill, too. With Moderates and Radicals acting together, Congress had the necessary two-thirds majority, and it promptly overrode the veto. Then, despite another veto, Congress repassed the Freedmen's Bureau Bill.

Emboldened by their evident support in Congress, the Radicals now struck again, and harder. The Joint Committee on Reconstruction submitted to Congress in April 1866 a proposed amendment to the Constitution, the Fourteenth, which constituted the second Radical plan of Reconstruction.

The Fourteenth Amendment, which was adopted by Congress and sent to the states for approval in the early summer, is so important, both in its immediate bearing upon Reconstruction and in its future influence upon federal-state relationships, as to deserve particular analysis.

Section 1 declared that all persons born or naturalized in the United States were citizens of the United States and of the state of their residence. This clause, which set up for the first time a national definition of citizenship, was followed by a statement that no state could abridge the rights of citizens of the United States or deprive any person of life, liberty, or property without due process of law or deny to any person within its jurisdiction the equal protection of the laws.

Section 2 provided that if a state denied the suffrage to any of its adult male inhabitants, its representation in the House of Representatives and the electoral college should suffer a proportionate reduction. This clause was intended to be a corrective to the curious effect of emancipation upon the basis of representation, by which every Southern state stood to increase its influence in the national government.

Section 3 disqualified from any state or federal office persons who had previously taken an oath to support the Constitution and later had aided the Confederacy—until Congress by a two-thirds vote of each house should remove their disability.

The Southern legislatures knew that if they ratified the amendment their states would be readmitted and Reconstruction probably would be ended. But they could not bring themselves to approve the measure, mainly because of Section 3, which put a stigma on their late leaders. Johnson himself advised Southerners to defeat the amendment. Only Tennessee, of the former Confederate states, ratified it, thus winning readmittance. The other ten, joined by Kentucky and Delaware, voted it down.

The amendment thus failed to receive the required approval of three-fourths of the states and was defeated—but only temporarily. When the time was more propitious, the Radicals would bring it up again. Meanwhile, its rejection by the South strengthened the Radical cause. To many people in the North, the amendment had seemed to be a reasonable and moderate proposal.

Public acceptance of the Radical program was strikingly manifested in the elections of 1866. This was essentially a contest for popular support between Johnson and the Radicals. The Radicals could point to recent events in the South—bloody race riots in which Negroes were the victims—as further evidence of the inadequacy of Johnson's policy. Johnson harmed his own cause by the intemperate, brawling speeches he made on a stumping tour from Washington to Chicago and back. The voters returned to Congress an overwhelming majority of Republicans, most of them of the Radical variety. In the Senate the line-up of the parties was 42 Republicans to 11 Democrats; in the House, 143 Republicans to 49 Democrats. Now the Republicans could enact any kind of

Reconstruction plan they could themselves agree on. Confidently they looked forward to the struggle with Johnson that would ensue when Congress assembled in December 1866—and to their final victory over the President.

THE CONGRESSIONAL PLAN

After compromising differences among themselves and with the Moderates, the Radicals formulated their third plan of Reconstruction in three bills that passed Congress in the early months of 1867. All three were vetoed by Johnson and repassed. As these Reconstruction Acts were really parts of one piece, their provisions may be studied as a unit.

This plan was based squarely on the principle that the seceded states had lost their political identity. The Lincoln-Johnson governments were declared to have no legal standing, and the ten seceded states (Tennessee was now out of the Reconstruction process) were combined into five military districts. Each district was to be put in the charge of a military commander, supported by troops, who was to prepare his provinces for readmission as states. To this end, he was to have made a registration of voters, which was to include all adult Negro males and white males who were not disqualified for participation in rebellion. The whites who were excluded were those coming under the disability of the Fourteenth Amendment; but each voter had to swear a complicated loyalty oath, and the registrars were empowered to reject white men on the suspicion that they were not acting in good faith.

After the registration was completed in each province, the commanding general was to call on the voters to elect a convention to prepare a new state constitution that had to provide for Negro suffrage. If this document were ratified by the voters, elections for a state government could be held. Finally, if Congress approved the constitution, if the state legislature ratified the Fourteenth Amendment, and if this amendment were adopted by the required number of states and became a part of the Constitution—then the state was to be restored to the Union.

By 1868 six of the former Confederate states—Arkansas, North Carolina, South Carolina, Louisiana, Alabama, and Florida—had

Historical writing on Reconstruction, even more controversial than that on the Civil War, similarly reflects the patterns of thought that have prevailed from time to time. The first professional historian of Reconstruction, William A. Dunning, who taught at Columbia University from the 1880s to the 1920s, carried on his work during a period when scholars generally held that certain racial and ethnic groups were inherently superior to others. Dunning assumed that Negroes were inferior and hence unfit to receive the vote. Many of his students wrote books dealing with Reconstruction in particular states, and he himself provided a general account, *Reconstruction, Political and Economic* (1907), which for many years was accepted as authoritative. According to Dunning and the members of the "Dunning school," the Republicans imposed their Radical program upon the South mainly to keep their party in power. (Some later writers, notably Howard K. Beale, added an economic motive—to protect Northern business interests.) Under the Radical plan, the Southern states suffered the agonies of "bayonet rule" and "Negro rule," when with army support the blacks and their unscrupulous white accomplices plundered the people in an unbelievable orgy of corruption, ruinous taxation, and astronomical increases in the public debt.

The first historian seriously to challenge the Dunning interpretation was the Negro scholar William E. B. Du Bois. In an article in the *American Historical Review* (1910) Du Bois pointed out that the misdeeds of the Reconstruction state governments had been exaggerated and their achievements overlooked. These governments were expensive, he explained, because they undertook to provide public education and other public services on a scale never before attempted in the South. In a long book, *Black Reconstruction* (1935), Du Bois described Reconstruction politics in the Southern states as an effort on the part of the masses, black and white, to create a true democratic society. Writing under the influence of Marxism, he assumed a class consciousness for which few other historians could find much evidence.

By the 1940s the attitudes toward race, on the part of scholars at least, had drastically changed. Since that time a new generation of historians has arisen—among them C. Vann Woodward, John Hope Franklin, Eric McKitrick, and John and La Wanda Cox—who assume that the freedmen of the 1860s and 1870s, despite the handicaps of their previous servitude, were by nature quite capable of participating in self-government. According to the new historians, the Radical Republicans were motivated less by partisan or economic interests than by a determination to guarantee basic rights to the former slaves and thus to secure the war aims of reunion and freedom. There was little if anything in the South that could properly be called either military rule or Negro rule, and the Negro, carpetbagger, and scalawag politicians were at least as honest and capable as others of their time. The mistake in Reconstruction was not the attempt to confer civil and political rights upon blacks, but the failure to provide an adequate economic and educational basis and sufficient governmental protection for the assurance of those rights. The recent views are ably synthesized in Kenneth M. Stampp, *The Era of Reconstruction* (1965).

complied with the process of restoration out-lined in the Reconstruction Acts and were readmitted to the Union. Delaying tactics by the whites held up the return of Mississippi, Virginia, Georgia, and Texas until 1870. These four laggard states had to meet an additional requirement, which with the existing require-ments constituted the fourth and final congres-sional plan of Reconstruction. They had to ratify another constitutional amendment, the Fifteenth, which forbade the states and the federal government to deny the suffrage to any citizen on account of "race, color, or previous condition of servitude."

The great majority of the Northern states still denied the suffrage to Negroes at the time when the Reconstruction Acts granted it to Negroes in the Southern states. Recent at-tempts to give the vote to Northern blacks by amending the state constitutions had met with practically no success. Hence an amendment to the federal Constitution seemed necessary. Its sponsors were motivated by both idealistic and practical considerations. They would be con-sistent in extending to the Negro in the North a right they had already given to him elsewhere. At the same time they would be putting into the Constitution, where it would be safe from con-gressional repeal, the basis of Republican strength in the South. They were also con-cerned with the party's future in the North. A warning of trouble ahead had appeared in the state elections of 1867 in Pennsylvania, Ohio, and Indiana, all of which went Democratic that year. "We must establish the doctrine of na-tional jurisdiction over all the states in state matters of the franchise," the Radical leader Thaddeus Stevens now concluded. "We must thus bridle Pennsylvania, Ohio, Indiana et cet-era, or the South *being in,* we shall drift into Democracy." In several of the Northern states the Negro vote, though small, would be large enough to decide close elections in favor of the Republicans.

A number of the Northern and border states refused to approve the Fifteenth Amend-ment, and it was adopted only with the support of the four Southern states that had to ratify it in order to be readmitted to the Union. In the case of both the Fourteenth and Fifteenth amendments, the Southern states were deemed capable of ratifying even while they were not otherwise recognized as states and had no representation in Congress.

CONGRESSIONAL SUPREMACY

The Radicals thought of themselves as archi-tects of a revolution, and they did not intend to let either the executive or the judiciary get in their way. They were prepared, if necessary, to establish a kind of congressional dictatorship.

To curb the President, and also to facilitate Radical administration of the acts of 1867, Con-gress passed two remarkable laws. One, the Tenure of Office Act (1867), forbade the Presi-dent to remove civil officials, including mem-bers of his cabinet, without the consent of the Senate. Its principal purpose was to protect the job of Secretary of War Edwin M. Stanton, who was cooperating with the Radicals. The other law, the Command of the Army Act (1867), pro-hibited the President from issuing military or-ders except through the commanding general of the army (General Grant), whose headquar-ters were to be in Washington and who could not be relieved or assigned elsewhere without the consent of the Senate.

The Supreme Court, under Chief Justice Salmon P. Chase, declared in *Ex parte Milli-gan* (1866) that military tribunals were unconsti-tutional in places where civil courts were func-tioning. Although the decision was applied to a case originating in the war, it seemed to threat-en the system of military government that the Radicals were planning for the South. Radical anger at the Court was instant and intense. In Congress proposals were made to require a two-thirds majority of the justices for overrul-ing a law of Congress, to deny the Court juris-diction in Reconstruction cases, to reduce its membership to three, and even to abolish it. The judges apparently took the hint. When the state of Mississippi in 1867 asked for an injunc-tion restraining Johnson from enforcing the Reconstruction Acts, the Court refused to ac-cept jurisdiction (*Mississippi* v. *Johnson*). But the next year the Court agreed to hear argu-ments, on a writ of habeas corpus, in a case involving military courts in Mississippi (*Ex parte McCardle*) and by implication involving the legality of the Reconstruction Acts. The Radicals rushed through Congress a law deny-ing the Court appellate jurisdiction in cases concerning habeas corpus. The Court bowed by refusing to hear the case. It bowed again in *Texas* v. *White* (1869), in which Chase, while accepting the Lincoln-Johnson theory that the seceded states were still in the Union, conceded that Congress possessed the power to determine permanent conditions of Reconstruction.

Although the Supreme Court evaded the Reconstruction issue, it was not an ineffective agency during this period. In the entire history of the country before 1864 the Court had declared only two acts of Congress unconstitutional. During Chase's tenure (1864–1873), it voided ten of them.

The most aggressive move of the legislative against another branch of the government occurred when the Radicals attempted to remove the President from office. They wanted to get rid of him because of his opposition to their Reconstruction program. Early in 1867 they began searching for evidence that Johnson had committed crimes or misdemeanors in office, the only legal grounds for impeachment, but they could find nothing upon which to base charges. Then he gave them a plausible reason

for action by deliberately violating the Tenure of Office Act. He suspended Secretary of War Stanton, who had worked with the Radicals against Johnson, and named General Grant as his successor. Johnson hoped in this manner to secure a Court test case of the tenure law, which he believed to be unconstitutional. But when the Senate refused to concur in the suspension, Grant relinquished the office to Stanton. Johnson then dismissed Stanton.

In the House of Representatives the elated Radicals framed and presented to the Senate eleven charges against the President. The first nine accusations dealt with the violation of the Tenure of Office Act. The tenth and eleventh charged Johnson with making speeches calculated to bring Congress into disrespect and of not faithfully enforcing the various Reconstruction Acts. In the trial before the Senate (March 25 to May 26, 1868) Johnson's lawyers main-

The Impeachment of Andrew Johnson

In this print the Senate is voting on the charges against the President. Chief Justice Chase, the presiding officer, stands at the right. At the left Senator Ross of Kansas announces he votes "Not Guilty." From Frank Leslie's Illustrated Newspaper *(1868).*

tained that he was justified in technically violating a law in order to force a test case and that the measure did not apply to Stanton anyway: it gave tenure to cabinet members for the term of the President by whom they had been appointed, and Stanton had been appointed by Lincoln. The House managers of the impeachment stressed the theme that Johnson had opposed the will of Congress. They implied that in doing so he was guilty of crimes and misdemeanors. They brought terrific pressure upon all the Republican senators, but seven Republicans joined the twelve Democrats to vote for acquittal. On three of the charges the vote was identical, 35 to 19, one short of the required two-thirds majority. Thereupon the Radicals called off the proceedings.

THE RECONSTRUCTED STATES

In the ten states of the South that were reorganized under the congressional plan, approximately one-fourth of the white men were at first excluded from voting or holding office. The voter registration of 1867 enrolled a total of 703,000 black and 627,000 white voters. The Negro voters constituted a majority in half of the states—Alabama, Florida, South Carolina, Mississippi, and Louisiana—though only in the last three of these states did the blacks outnumber the whites in the population as a whole. However, once new constitutions had been made and new governments launched, most of these permitted nearly all whites to vote (though for several years the Fourteenth Amendment continued to keep the leading ex-Confederates from holding office). This meant that in most of the Southern states the Republicans could maintain control only with the support of a great many Southern whites.

These Southern white Republicans, whom their opponents derisively called "scalawags," consisted in part of former Whigs who, after the breakup of the Whig organization in the 1850s, had acted with the Southern Democrats but had never felt completely at home with them. Some of the scalawag leaders were wealthy (or once wealthy) planters or businessmen. James L. Alcorn, for example, had been one of the largest slaveholders in Mississippi, a Whig leader of the state, and an opponent of secession. Such men, having long controlled the Negroes as slaves, expected to control them also as vot-

ers. Many other Southern whites who joined the Republican party were farmers living in areas where slavery had been unimportant or nonexistent. These men, many of whom had been wartime Unionists, favored the Republican program of internal improvements, which would help them get their crops to market.

White men from the North also served as Republican leaders in the South. Opponents of Reconstruction referred to them as "carpetbaggers," thus giving the impression that they were penniless adventurers who had arrived with all their possessions in a carpetbag (a then common kind of valise covered with carpeting material) in order to take advantage of the Negro vote for their own power and profit. In fact, the majority of the so-called carpetbaggers were veterans of the Union army who had looked upon the South as a new frontier, more promising than the West, and at the war's end had settled in it as hopeful planters or business or professional men. They had brought with them money to invest, but many of them lost it because of their own inexperience and the hostility of their Southern white neighbors.

The most numerous Republicans in the South were the freedmen, the vast majority of whom had no formal education and no previous experience in the management of affairs. Among the Negro leaders, however, were well-educated, highly intelligent, and even brilliant men, most of whom had never been slaves and many of whom had been brought up in the North or abroad. The blacks quickly became politically self-conscious. In various states they held their own "colored conventions," the one in Alabama announcing (1867): "We claim exactly *the same rights, privileges and immunities as are enjoyed by white men*—we ask nothing more and will be content with nothing less." Negroes were organized, often with the assistance of Freedmen's Bureau agents and other Northern whites, in chapters of the Union League, which had been founded originally as a Republican electioneering agency in the North during the war. At secret night meetings, with mysterious ritual, the new members of the Union League in the South received instruction in political rights and political techniques. Another organization that gave unity and self-confidence to black people was the Negro church. Once they were emancipated, they had begun to withdraw from the white churches and form their own. "The colored preachers are *the great power* in controlling and uniting the colored vote," a carpetbagger observed in 1868.

Negroes served as delegates to the conventions that, under the congressional plan, drew up new state constitutions in the South. Then, in the reconstructed states, Negroes were elected to public offices of practically every kind. All together (between 1869 and 1901) twenty of them were sent to the House of Representatives in Washington. Two went to the United States Senate, both of them from Mississippi. Hiram R. Revels—an ordained minister of the African Methodist Episcopal Church and a former North Carolina free Negro who had been educated at Knox College in Illinois— took the Senate seat (1870) that Jefferson Davis once had occupied. Blanche K. Bruce, who

had escaped from slavery in Virginia and studied in the North, was made a senator in 1874 (he was the only Negro to be elected to a full term in the Senate until the election of Edward Brooke, of Massachusetts, in 1966).

Yet no such thing as "Negro rule" ever existed in any of the states. No Negro was elected governor, though Lieutenant-Governor P. B. S Pinchback briefly occupied the governor's chair in Louisiana. Negroes never controlled any of the state legislatures, though they held a majority in the lower house of South Carolina In the South as a whole the number of Negro officeholders was less than proportionate to the number of Negroes in the population. Nor did the state governments show much if any favoritism toward blacks as a group. Constitutions or statutes prohibited, on paper,

Hiram R. Revels
Revels was one of the few Negroes to attain high office during Reconstruction, acting as United States Senator from Mississippi from 1870–1871. Born in North Carolina of free parents, Revels became a Methodist minister and during the Civil War served as an army chaplain in Mississippi. Returning to the state after the war, he resumed his ministerial duties but entered politics. He was a moderate Republican and in 1875 joined with the Democrats to overthrow the Republican state regime. For years he was president of Alcorn College, a Negro institution. (Library of Congress)

discrimination on the basis of color, but segregation remained the common practice. Only in New Orleans were there, for a time, a few integrated schools.

The record of the Reconstruction governments is many-sided. As some of the leaders in the convention that framed the new state constitutions were Northerners, they put into these documents the most advanced provisions in those of the most progressive Northern states — provisions embodying the latest advances in local government, judicial organization, public finance, and poor relief. Generally, these changes had the effect of modernizing Southern state government and placing it in step with governmental trends in the rest of the country. But some of the provisions, which looked excellent on paper, were not suited to the peculiar environment of the rural South.

The financial program of the Republican governments was a compound of blatant corruption and well-designed, if sometimes impractical, social legislation. The corruption and extravagance are familiar aspects of the Reconstruction story. State budgets expanded to hitherto unknown totals, and state debts soared to previously undreamed of heights. In South Carolina, for example, the public debt increased from $7 million to $29 million in eight years.

In large measure, the corruption in the South was a phase of a national phenomenon, with the same social force — an expanding capitalism eager to secure quick results — acting as the corrupting agent. Included in the spending programs of the Reconstruction governments were subsidies for railroads and other internal improvements, some of which materialized and some of which did not — because the promoters and the politicians pocketed the subsidies. That much of the alleged corruption was a product of deep forces in contemporary society is demonstrated by the continuance of dishonesty in state government after Republican rule was overthrown.

The state expenditures of the Reconstruction years seem huge only in comparison with the niggardly budgets of the conservative governments of the prewar era; they do not appear large when measured against the sums appropriated by later legislatures. The reconstructed governments represented the poor Negroes, and these people had a concept, albeit a vague one, of what today would be called the welfare state. They demanded public education, public-works programs, poor relief, and other services that cost money. If there were thieving and foolish spending there were also positive and permanent accomplishments, particularly in education. One example is offered by South Carolina, which in 1860 had only 20,000 children in public schools; by 1873 some 50,000 white and 70,000 Negro students were enrolled.

The Grant Administration

The voters looked trustingly to General Ulysses S. Grant, the conquering hero of the war, to guide them through the troubled postwar years. He was President during a time (1869 – 1877) that would have taxed the abilities of a master of statecraft. Only a superb politician with profound spiritual insight - some rare leader like Lincoln – could have held the presidency at that time and escaped with an unblemished reputation. Grant, for all his fine qualities, proved to be no such political leader.

A SOLDIER PRESIDENT

At the end of the war both parties had angled to make Grant their candidate, and he could have had the nomination of either party. As he watched the congressional Radicals triumph over President Johnson, he concluded that the Radical Reconstruction policy expressed the real wishes of the people. He was receptive when the Radical leaders approached him with offers of the Republican nomination.

The Republicans placed candidate Grant on an ambiguous platform They endorsed Radical Reconstruction and Negro suffrage for the South, but declared that in the North the question of Negro voting should be determined by each state. (Thus during the campaign the Republicans opposed the suffrage amendment, the Fifteenth, which they were to pass soon after the election.) Reflecting the influence of business, the platform called for the payment of the national debt in "the spirit of the laws" under which it had been contracted, which

U. S. G. AS A RAG-PICKER.

U. S. G.—"*Why, here is Zach Chandler thrown out of the Senate Chamber as rubbish! But he may be worth something to me. I must pick him up and fling him into my basket.*"

"U. S. G. as a Rag-Picker"

One of the complaints of the anti-Grant, Liberal Republicans was the President's use of the spoils system. In this cartoon from Leslie's Illustrated Newspaper, *Grant is pictured as a rag-picker, or junkman, because of his having retrieved Zachariah Chandler and made him Secretary of the Interior. Chandler, Republican boss of Michigan, had been defeated for reelection to the Senate in 1874. (Culver)*

meant in gold instead of greenbacks; on the tariff issue, the platform was discreetly silent. Obviously the Republicans meant to make Reconstruction the big issue while subordinating economic questions that might divide the party.

Unwisely the Democrats decided to meet the Republican challenge. Their platform also emphasized Reconstruction, denouncing in extravagant terms the Radical program and demanding restoration of "home rule" in the South. Thus the Democrats chose to fight the campaign on an issue that was related to the war and its emotions — an issue that enabled their opponents to associate them with rebellion. They did, however, attempt to inject a new question of an economic nature into the contest. In 1868 approximately $356 million of the Civil War greenbacks were in circulation, and Middle Western Democrats, led by George Pendleton of Ohio, wanted to keep the paper currency and use it when legally possible to pay off the national debt. Behind this so-called Ohio idea was the larger question of retaining the greenbacks as a permanent part of the money supply. This proposal appealed to the debtor farmers of the West and also to many hard-pressed businessmen of the East. The Westerners succeeded in writing the Ohio idea into the platform, but the party nominated Horatio Seymour of New York, a gold or "sound money" man, who repudiated the currency plank.

After a bitter campaign revolving around Reconstruction and Seymour's war record as governor of New York (he had been a Peace Democrat), Grant carried twenty-six states and Seymour only eight. But Grant got only 3,012,000 popular votes to Seymour's 2,703,000, a scant majority of 310,000, and this majority was due to Negro votes in the reconstructed states of the South.

Ulysses S. Grant was the second professional soldier to be elected to the presidency (Zachary Taylor having been the first), and the last to be chosen until Dwight D. Eisenhower was selected in 1952. After graduating from West Point with no particular distinction, Grant had entered the regular army, from which after years of service he resigned under something of a cloud. In civilian life he undertook several dismal ventures that barely yielded him a living. His career before 1861 could be characterized as forty years of failure. Then came the Civil War, and Grant found at last the one setting, the one vocation for which he was supremely equipped — war.

His political naïveté as President was displayed in many of his appointments. For the important office of secretary of state he chose an old friend, the former Illinois Congressman Elihu B. Washburne. By agreement, Washburne was to hold the position only a week before resigning to become minister to France, the purpose being to enable him to brag in Par-

is that he had headed the foreign office. After offering the appointment to another man, who declined it on the grounds of expense, Grant named Hamilton Fish of New York. Like other Americans of the time, Grant inordinately admired millionaires, and he appointed A. T. Stewart, a wealthy merchant, secretary of the treasury. Stewart, however, was ineligible because of a law barring from the office any person in "trade or commerce."

In choosing his official family, Grant proceeded as if he were creating a military staff. He sent several appointments to the Senate for confirmation without asking the recipients if they would serve; they first heard the news in the papers. Fish, who had been out of politics for twenty years, wired Grant that he could not accept, but his name was already being acted on in the Senate and he was persuaded to let it go through. During his two administrations, Grant named a total of twenty-five men to the cabinet. Most of his later appointments went to men who were, at best, average, and some to men who were incompetent or corrupt, or both. Increasingly, in dispensing cabinet and executive patronage, Grant came to rely on the machine leaders in the party, on the groups most ardently devoted to the spoils system.

SUCCESSES IN FOREIGN AFFAIRS

In foreign affairs the Grant administration achieved its most brilliant successes, as the Johnson administration also had done. These were the accomplishments of two outstanding secretaries of state: William H. Seward (1861 – 1869) and Hamilton Fish (1869 – 1877).

An ardent expansionist and advocate of a vigorous foreign policy, Seward acted with as much daring as the demands of Reconstruction politics and the Republican hatred of President Johnson would permit. By exercising firm but patient pressure, he persuaded Napoleon III of France to abandon his Mexican empire, which was established during the war when the United States was in no position to protest. Napoleon withdrew his troops in 1867, his puppet Emperor Maximilian was executed by the Mexicans, and the validity of the Monroe Doctrine was strikingly reaffirmed.

When Russia let it be known that she would like to sell Alaska to the United States, the two nations long having been on friendly terms, Seward readily agreed to pay the asking price of $7.2 million. Only by strenuous efforts was he able to induce the Senate to ratify the treaty and the House to appropriate the money (1867–1868). Critics jeered that the secretary had bought a useless frozen wasteland — "Seward's Icebox" and "Walrussia" were some of the terms employed to describe it — but Alaska, a center for the fishing industry in the North Pacific and potentially rich in such resources as gold, was a distinct bargain. Seward was not content with expansion in continental

Hamilton Fish

Fish, a member of a distinguished New York family, had been out of politics for years when Grant offered him the position of Secretary of State. Accepting it reluctantly, he served for both of Grant's terms, and left a record of solid accomplishments. Fish represented the older tradition of cultivated gentlemen in politics. This sketch, almost a caricature, exaggerates some of his features but still conveys his aura of dignity. (Culver)

North America. In 1867 he engineered the annexation of the tiny Midway Islands west of Hawaii.

In contrast with its sometimes shambling course in domestic politics, the performance of the Grant administration in the area of foreign affairs was generally decisive and firm, yet showing a wise moderation. For this, Secretary Fish, to whom President Grant gave almost a free hand, deserves the major credit. A number of delicate and potentially dangerous situations confronted Fish from the beginning, but the most serious one arose out of strained relations with Great Britain.

The United States had a burning grievance against England which had originated during the Civil War. At that time the British government, according to the American interpretation, had violated the laws of neutrality by permitting Confederate cruisers, the *Alabama* and others, to be built and armed in English shipyards and let loose to prey on Northern commerce. American demands that England pay for the damages committed by these vessels became known as the "Alabama claims." Although the British government realized its diplomatic error in condoning construction of the cruisers (in a future war American-built *Alabamas* might operate against Britain), it at first hesitated to submit the issue to arbitration.

Other differences clouded Anglo-American relations. England contended that the United States should compensate British subjects who had suffered property losses in the way of cotton and ships during the war. The ancient controversy of the North Atlantic fisheries and American rights off Canadian shores had flared up again. Another dispute involved the location of the boundary between the United States and British Columbia in Puget Sound. And finally there were the Fenians — the Irish-American crusaders who thought they could free Ireland of British rule by conquering Canada. Several times during the Johnson-Grant period Fenian "armies" harassed the Canadian border. Although the American government tried to restrain these outbreaks, it refused British suggestions that it should pay for the damages committed by the Fenians.

Seward tried earnestly to settle the Alabama claims before leaving office. The American minister to England, Reverdy Johnson, negotiated an agreement, the Johnson-Clarendon Convention (1869), providing that all claims on both sides since 1853 be submitted to arbitration. The pact was distasteful to Americans because it embraced so many issues and contained no expression of British regret for the escape of the *Alabama*. Coming before the Senate immediately after Grant took office, it was rejected 54 to 1. The debate featured a speech by Charles Sumner, chairman of the Committee on Foreign Relations, denouncing Britain for her course in the Civil War and arguing that her conduct had prolonged the war by two years. Therefore, said Sumner, England owed the United States for "direct damages" committed by the cruisers and "indirect damages" for the cost of the war for two years – which would have reached the staggering total of some $2 billion. Americans who supported Sumner's position, and they were undoubtedly a majority, professed themselves willing to accept the cession of Canada as a substitute for a cash payment.

England naturally would have nothing to do with any arrangement involving indirect claims, and settlement of the problem was temporarily stalled Secretary Fish, however, continued to work for a solution, and finally in 1871 the two countries agreed to the Treaty of Washington, one of the great landmarks in international pacification, providing for arbitration of the cruiser issue and other pending controversies. The Alabama claims were to be laid before a five-member tribunal appointed by the governments of the United States, England, Italy, Switzerland, and Brazil. In the covenant Britain expressed regret for the escape of the *Alabama* and agreed to a set of rules governing neutral obligations that virtually gave the British case away. In effect, this meant that the tribunal would have only to fix the sum to be paid by Britain. Convening at Geneva in Switzerland, the arbitrators awarded $15.5 million to the United States.

The other disputes covered by the treaty were compromised just as pacifically. The question of the Puget Sound boundary was submitted to the German Emperor, who ruled in favor of the United States title to the contested San Juan Islands. An arbitration commission awarded nearly $2 million to England for damages suffered by her citizens during the Civil War. Because the treaty had extended American fishing privileges, England claimed a payment for the concessions, and a special commission, after some wrangling, decided in 1877 that the United States should compensate Britain with $5.5 million. If the value of the arbitrations were computed in money, which of course it really could not be, the United States thus netted approximately $8 million from the awards. The real and enduring significance of the procedure was that again the two countries – as they had been doing since 1818 – adjusted serious differences without resorting to force.

THE LIBERALS DEFECT

Through both his foreign and his domestic policies, President Grant antagonized and alienated a number of prominent Republicans, among them the famous Radical, Charles Sumner. Senator Sumner's extravagant demand for damages from Great Britain embarrassed Secretary Fish in the latter's diplomacy. Still worse, from the President's point of view, Sumner blocked a treaty for the annexation of Santo Domingo, a project in which Grant took a deep personal interest – indeed, it was a kind of monomania with him. The angry President got revenge by inducing his Senate friends to remove Sumner from the chairmanship of the Committee on Foreign Relations.

Sumner and other Republican leaders joined with civil-service reformers to criticize Grant for his use of the spoils system, his reliance on ruthless machine politicians. Scholarly journalists like E. L. Godkin of the *Nation* and George William Curtis of *Harper's Weekly* were arguing that the government ought to base its appointments not on services to the party but on fitness for office as determined by competitive examinations, as the British government already was doing. Grant yielded to the extent of recommending the establishment of a Civil Service Commission, which Congress authorized in 1871, to devise a system of hiring based on merit This agency, under the headship of Curtis, proposed a set of rules that seemed to meet Grant's approval. But Grant was not really much interested in reform, and even if he had been he could not have persuaded his followers to accept a new system that would undermine the very basis of party loyalty – the patronage. Congress, by neglecting to renew the commission's appropriation, soon ended its existence.

FRANK LESLIE'S ILLUSTRATED NEWSPAPER.

A REMARKABLE SACRIFICE.

U. S. G.—"*I don't want to go to Washington; I want to go to the races with Tom Murphy.*"
R. C——G.—"*Oh, but you must make a sacrifice now, and after election you can go to as many races as you like.*"

Grant Wants to Go to the Horse Races

This print depicts a widely held impression of Grant. Because the President admired fine horses, it was believed that he liked racing and gambling. Grant, shown here as an obvious weakling, is saying that he does not want to go to the White House but to the races. Two party bosses, Roscoe C. Conkling and Oliver P. Morton, are forcing him to shoulder his political responsibilities. From Frank Leslie's Illustrated Newspaper *(1872).*

Republican critics of the President also denounced him for his support of Radical Reconstruction. He continued to station federal troops in the South, and on numerous occasions he sent them to the support of Negro-and-carpetbag governments that were on the point of collapsing. To growing numbers in the North this seemed like dangerous militarism, and they were more and more disgusted by the stories of governmental corruption and extravagance that came up from the South. Some Republicans were beginning to suspect that there was corruption not only in the Southern state governments but also in the federal government itself. Still others criticized Grant because he had declined to speak out in favor of a reduction of the tariff. The high wartime duties remained substantially unchanged even though the wartime justification for them was past.

Thus, before the end of Grant's first term, members of his own party had begun to oppose him for a variety of reasons—his foreign policies, his use of the patronage, his resort to military force in the South, his high-tariff stand, and his suspected taint of corruption—all of which added up to what the critics called "Grantism." In 1872, hoping to prevent Grant's reelection, his opponents bolted the party. Referring to themselves as Liberal Republicans, they proceeded to set up their own organization for running presidential and vice-presidential candidates.

The greatest weakness of the Liberal movement lay in its diversity and disunity. This was cruelly exposed when the Liberals held their national convention and began to consider a platform. They were able to agree on resolutions that approved of civil-service reform and endorsed the basic policy of Reconstruction, but called for universal amnesty (with the restoration of full political rights to former Confederates) and the withdrawal of troops from the South. When the tariff question came up, however, the convention found itself hopelessly divided. The delegates finally compromised on an evasive plank referring the issue to the people and Congress. This evasion lessened the Liberals' chances of gaining Democratic endorsement and Southern support. They compounded their blunder in choosing a nominee. Passing over Charles Francis Adams and other able and available men, they named Horace Greeley, veteran editor and publisher of the New York *Tribune*.

Greeley over a course of thirty years had stated his position on practically every issue before the country. He had been a Whig and a Republican, a proponent of antislavery and a high tariff, an economic and political national-ist. Impulsive and erratic, he had crusaded for most of the fads that had at one time or another intrigued popular attention—spiritualism, vegetarianism, and others—and he cultivated an idiosyncratic dress and manner. With his record and personality, he was hardly the strongest candidate the Liberals could have put forward to attract the Democratic, Southern, and independent vote. The Democratic convention, seeing in his candidacy the only chance to unseat the Republicans, endorsed him with no great enthusiasm. Despite his recent attacks on Radical Reconstruction, many Southerners, remembering Greeley's own Radical past, prepared to stay at home on Election Day. The Republicans, with Grant as their standard-bearer and a platform justifying Reconstruction and calling for a high tariff, moved into the campaign with confidence.

To everybody's surprise, Greeley turned out to be a vigorous and hard-hitting campaigner. Breaking with precedent, he stumped the country advocating the Liberal cause. But the factors surrounding his candidacy made the odds against him impossible. In November Grant polled 286 electoral votes and 3,597,000 popular votes to Greeley's 62 and 2,834,000. The optimistic editor carried only two Southern and four border states. Three weeks later Greeley, apparently crushed by his defeat, died.

During the campaign the first of a series of political scandals had come to light. Although the wrongdoing had occurred before Grant took office, it involved his party and the onus for it fell on his administration. This scandal originated with the Crédit Mobilier construction company that helped build the Union Pacific Railroad. In reality, the Crédit Mobilier was controlled by a few Union Pacific stockholders who awarded huge and fraudulent contracts to the construction company, thus milking the Union Pacific, a company of which they owned a minor share, of money which in part came from government subsidies. To avert a congressional inquiry into the deal, the directors, using Oakes Ames, a Massachusetts representative, as their agent, sold at a discount (in effect gave) Crédit Mobilier stock to key members of Congress. A congressional investigation was held, and it revealed that some high-placed Republicans had accepted stock, including Schuyler Colfax, now Grant's Vice President.

One dreary episode followed another in Grant's second term. Benjamin H. Bristow, Grant's third secretary of the treasury, discovered that some of his officials and a group of distillers operating as a "Whiskey Ring" were cheating the government out of taxes by means of false reports. Among the prominent Republicans involved was the President's private secretary, Orville E. Babcock. Grant defended Babcock, appointed him to another office, and eased Bristow out of the cabinet. A House investigation revealed that William W. Belknap, secretary of war, had accepted bribes to retain an Indian-post trader in office. Belknap resigned with Grant's blessing before the Senate could act on impeachment charges brought by the House. Lesser scandals involved the Navy Department, which was suspected of selling business to contractors, and the Treasury, where John D. Sanborn, a special agent appointed to handle overdue taxes, collected $427,000 and retained a 50-percent commission for himself and the Republican bigwigs who had placed him in the job. Not to be left out of the picture, Congress passed an act doubling the annual salary of the President from $25,000 to $50,000 (the first increase since George Washington's time), and raising the salaries of members of Congress from $5,000 to $7,500 a year. The increases were justifiable, but the country was enraged to learn that its representatives had also voted themselves two years of back pay. Bowing before a storm of denunciation, the next Congress hastened to repeal the so-called "Salary Grab."

THE GREENBACK QUESTION

Meanwhile the Grant administration along with the country as a whole had suffered another blow when the Panic of 1873 struck. It was touched off by the failure of a leading investment banking firm, Jay Cooke and Company, the "financier of the Civil War," which had done well in the handling of government war bonds but had sunk excessive amounts in postwar railroad building. Depressions had come before with almost rhythmic regularity—in 1819, 1837, and 1857—but this was the worst one yet. It lasted four years, during which unemployment rose to 3 million, and agricultural prices fell so far that thousands of farmers, unable to meet mortgage payments, went more deeply into debt or lost their farms.

Debtors hoped the government would follow an inflationary, easy-money policy, which would have made it easier for them to pay their debts and would have helped to stimulate recovery from the depression. But President Grant and most Republicans preferred what they called a "sound" currency, which was to the advantage of the banks, moneylenders, and other creditors.

The money question, after figuring in the election of 1868, had confronted Grant and the Republicans in Congress from the beginning of his administration. The question was twofold: How should interest and principal of the war bonds be paid, and what should be the permanent place of the greenbacks in the national currency? Supporters of the Ohio idea, representing debtor interests, argued that the bonds had been purchased in greenbacks of depreciated value and should, unless stipulated otherwise by law, be redeemed in the same currency. The President favored payment in gold, and the Republican Congress moved speedily to promise redemption in "coin or its equivalent" and to enact a refunding act providing for long-term refinancing of the debt (1869–1870).

Approximately $450 million in greenbacks had been issued during the Civil War, and $400 million of them were still in circulation at the end of the conflict. In the Johnson administration, Congress had authorized the Treasury to reduce their quantity, but the protests of farmers and some business groups had halted further action. When Grant entered the White House, the greenback circulation was some $356 million, and the gold value of a greenback dollar was 73 cents.

Before Congress could make any disposition of the problem, the Supreme Court intervened with a decision concerning the legality of the greenbacks as legal tender. In *Hepburn* v. *Griswold* (1870), Chief Justice Chase, speaking for a divided 4-to-3 Court, declared that greenbacks were not legal tender for debts contracted prior to their issuance. This pronouncement angered agrarians and alarmed businessmen who had incurred obligations that they would now have to pay with a more valuable dollar. Demands for a reversal of the Court's decision were insistent. It so happened that Congress was about to raise the number of justices (recently reduced to seven) back to nine, and Grant appointed two men who were known to oppose the decision. It was charged that he had ascertained their opinions and was in effect packing the Court, but no proof of this exists. The government did, however, move immediately for a rehearing, and in *Knox* v. *Lee* (1871) the Court by a 5-to-4 vote reversed the previous decision.

With the legality of greenbacks established, the Treasury, as a relief measure after the Panic of 1873, increased the amount in circulation. For the same reason Congress, in the following year, voted to raise the total to $400 million. Grant, responding to pressures from the financial interests, vetoed the measure. In 1875 the Republican Congress enacted the Resumption Act, providing that after January 1, 1879, the government would exchange gold dollars for greenbacks and directing the gov-

ernment to acquire a gold reserve for redemption purposes. The law had its intended result: with the specie value of greenbacks assured, they were equal in worth to gold. The interests of the creditor classes were adequately protected, but at the same time, the debtor groups could take some comfort in the retention of the greenbacks. (Subsequently, in 1878, Congress decided that some $346 million of greenbacks should form a permanent part of the money supply.) Not all the agrarian-debtor groups accepted resumption as a satisfactory conclusion. Some dissident elements created the National Greenback party in 1875, which was active in the next three presidential elections. It failed, however, to attract wide support. After 1879 those interests favoring inflation would turn to forms of currency other than paper.

A Return to White Supremacy

The period of Republican control in the South varied from state to state. In a few states the Democrats (or Conservatives) got into power as soon or almost as soon as restoration occurred. The longest that Republican rule lasted in any of the states was about ten years. It was ended in Virginia, North Carolina, and Georgia in 1870; in Texas in 1873; in Alabama and Arkansas in 1874; in Mississippi in 1875; and in South Carolina, Louisiana, and Florida in 1877.

SOUTHERN REPUBLICANS LOSE

In the states where the whites constituted a majority—the upper South states—overthrow of Republican control was a relatively simple matter. The whites had only to organize and win the elections. Their success was facilitated by the early restoration of the suffrage to those whites who had been deprived of it by national or state action. Presidential and congressional pardons returned the privilege to numerous individuals, and in 1872 Congress, responding to public demands to forgive the penalties of the war, enacted the Amnesty Act, which restored political rights to 150,000 ex-Confederates and left only 500 excluded from political life.

In other states, where the Negroes were in the majority or the population difference be-

The Ku Klux Klan: A Southern View
This Klan broadside depicts the organization as most Southerners saw it. The figure with the flag and sword epitomizes white culture and has overthrown the Negro enemy. Note the incendiary torch in the hand of the Negro and the broken chains symbolizing his former slave status. (Rutherford B. Hayes Library)

tween the races was small, the whites resorted to intimidation and violence. Frankly terroristic were the secret societies that appeared in many parts of the South—the Ku Klux Klan, the Knights of the White Camellia, and others—which attempted to frighten or physically prevent Negroes from voting. Although the societies were effective, their influence has been exaggerated by writers intrigued by their romantic hooded and robed apparel and their elaborate ritual. Moving quickly to stamp out these societies, Congress passed two Force Acts (1870–1871) and the Ku Klux Klan Act (1871) which authorized the President to use military force and martial law in areas where the orders were active.

More potent than the secret orders were the open semimilitary organizations that operated under such names as Rifle clubs, Red Shirts, and White Leagues. After the first such society was founded in Mississippi, the idea spread to other states, and the procedure employed by the clubs was called the Mississippi Plan. Briefly stated, the plan called for the whites in each community to organize and arm, and to be prepared, if necessary, to resort to force to win elections. But the heart of the scheme was in the phrase "drawing the color

The Ku Klux Klan: A Northern View

This drawing in a Northern illustrated paper shows a group of Klansmen about to murder a carpetbagger whom they have abducted. (Library of Congress)

line." By one method or another, legal or illegal, every white man was to be forced to join the Democratic party or leave the community. By similar methods, every Negro male was to be excluded from political action; in a few states he was permitted to vote—if he voted Democratic.

Perhaps an even stronger influence than the techniques practiced by the armed bands was the simple and unromantic weapon of economic pressure. The war had freed the Negro, but he was still a laborer—a hired worker or a tenant—dependent upon the whites for his livelihood. The whites readily discovered that this dependence placed the Negro in their power. Planters refused to rent land to Republican Negroes, storekeepers refused to extend them credit, employers refused to give them work. Economic pressure was a force that the Negro could not fight. If the Radicals, in bringing the Negro to political power, had accomplished a revolution, it was a superficial one. They failed to provide the Negro with economic power, as they might have done by giving him possession of confiscated land. Hence, his political rights had no lasting basis.

Certainly the Negro's political position was hopeless without the continued backing of the Republican party and the federal government. But he was losing the support of people in the North, even of many humanitarian reformers who had worked for emancipation and Negro rights. After the adoption of the Fifteenth Amendment (1870), most of the reformers convinced themselves that their long campaign in his behalf at last was over, that with the vote he ought to be able to take care of himself. Republican disillusionment with the corruption and disorders in the Southern states helped to bring about the party split of 1872, which in turn weakened the Republicans in the South still further. They beheld the discouraging spectacle of former Radical leaders like Charles Sumner and Horace Greeley now calling themselves Liberals, cooperating with the Democrats, and outdoing even them in denunciations of what they viewed as Negro-and-carpetbag misgovernment. Most of the white Republicans of the South, including some of those who had come from the North, joined the Liberal movement and went over to the Democrats. Friction between the remaining carpetbaggers and the black Republicans grew be-

cause of a well-justified feeling on the part of the blacks that they were not receiving a fair share of the power and the jobs.

When the depression came in 1873, the hard times aggravated political discontent both North and South. In the congressional elections of 1874 the Democrats gained a majority of the seats in the national House of Representatives. After 1875, when the new House met, the Republicans no longer controlled the whole Congress, as they had done since the beginning of the war. And President Grant, in view of the changing temper of the North, no longer was willing to use military force to save from violent overthrow the Republican regimes that were still standing in the South. In 1875, when the Mississippi governor, Adelbert Ames (originally from Maine), appealed to Washington for troops to protect the Negroes from the terrorism of the Democrats, he received in reply a telegram that quoted Grant as saying: "The whole public are tired out with these annual autumnal outbreaks in the South, and the great majority are now ready to condemn any interference on the part of the government."

After the Democrats had taken Mississippi, only three states were left in the hands of the Republicans—South Carolina, Louisiana, and Florida. In the elections of 1876, again using terrorist tactics, the Democrats claimed victory in all three. But the Republicans maintained that they themselves had won, and they were able to continue holding office because federal troops happened to be on the scene. If the troops should be withdrawn, the last of the Republican regimes would fall. The future was to depend on the settlement of the presidential election of 1876, which was disputed in consequence of the electoral disputes in the South.

THE COMPROMISE OF 1877

Ulysses S. Grant was eager to run for another term in 1876, and his friends among the Republican bosses tried to secure the nomination for him. But the majority of the Republican leaders ruled Grant out. Impressed by the recent upsurge of Democratic strength, which had delivered the House of Representatives and a number of state governments to the opposition party, and fearful of the third-term issue, they

Ingersoll's Speech Nominating Blaine [1876]

At the Republican convention in 1876 Robert G. Ingersoll nominated Blaine in a speech typical of the extravagant rhetoric of the time. Like all Republican orators, Ingersoll seized the opportunity to recall the emotions of the Civil War and to equate Democrats with traitors. After this speech Blaine was known to his admirers as "the plumed knight":

This is a grand year — a year filled with recollections of the Revolution; filled with the proud and tender memories of the past; with sacred legends of liberty; a year in which the sons of freedom will drink from the fountains of enthusiasm; a year in which the people call for a man who has preserved in Congress what our soldiers won upon the field; a year in which they call for the man who has torn from the throat of treason the tongue of slander — for the man who has snatched the mask of Democracy from the hideous face of rebellion; for this man who, like an intellectual athlete, has stood in the arena of debate and challenged all comers, and who is still a total stranger to defeat. Like an armed warrior, like a plumed knight, James G. Blaine marched down the halls of the American Congress and threw his shining lance full and fair against the brazen foreheads of the defamers of his country and the maligners of her honor.

---

searched for a candidate who was not associated with the scandals of the past eight years and who could entice the Liberals back into the fold and unite the party until after the election.

Senator James G. Blaine of Maine offered himself, but he had recently been involved in an allegedly crooked railroad deal. In a remarkable display of oratory and effrontery, Blaine defended himself against the charge of corruption by reading to Congress some private letters that were supposed to incriminate him. Actually, he had carefully selected innocent portions of the correspondence, and many people were unconvinced. The so-called Mulligan letters hurt his chances in 1876 and would impede his career in the future.

The Republican convention passed over Blaine and other hopefuls and named as the standard-bearer Rutherford B. Hayes, a former Union army officer and congressman, three times governor of Ohio, and a champion of civil-service reform. The platform included the usual endorsements of Reconstruction and Republican economic legislation.

No personal rivalries divided the Democrats. Only one aspirant commanded serious attention, and with him as their candidate the Democrats were confident of returning to power. The bearer of the party's hopes was Governor Samuel J. Tilden of New York, whose name had become synonymous with governmental reform. A corporation lawyer and a millionaire, Tilden had long been a power in the Democratic organization of his state, but he had not hesitated to turn against Tammany's corrupt Tweed Ring and aid in its overthrow. His fight against Tweed brought him national fame and the governorship, in which position he increased his reputation for honest administration. The Democratic platform contained some general references to the tariff and currency problems, but its emphasis was upon reform in government. It called for an end to Reconstruction and the establishment of civil service, and declared that the primary issue of the campaign was the ejection of rascals from government and the installation in their place of "honest men."

Despite the fury of the charges flung at each other by the parties in the canvass, there were almost no differences of principle between the candidates. Hayes was on record as favoring withdrawal of troops from the South, he advocated civil service, and his record for probity was equal to Tilden's. Although the New York governor, reflecting Eastern importing interests, was amenable to some kind of tariff reduction, on other economic issues he was at least as conservative as his rival. He was a gold or "sound money" man, and he believed that government had no business interfering with economic processes. He looked on himself as a modern counterpart of Thomas Jefferson.

The November election revealed an apparent Democratic victory. In addition to the South, Tilden carried several large Northern states, and his popular vote was 4,300,000 to 4,036,000 for Hayes. But the situation was complicated by the disputed returns from Louisiana, South Carolina, and Florida, whose total electoral vote was 19. Both parties claimed to have won these states, and double sets of returns were presented to Congress. Adding to the confusion was a contested vote in Oregon, where one of the three successful Republican electors was declared ineligible because he held a federal office. The Democrats contended that the place should go to the highest Democratic elector, but the Republicans insisted that according to state law the remaining electors were to fill the vacancy. The dual and disputed returns threw the outcome of the election into doubt. As tension and excitement gripped the country, two clear facts emerged from the welter of conflicting claims. Tilden had for certain 184 electoral votes, only one short of the majority. The 20 votes in controversy would determine who would be President, and Hayes needed all of them to secure the prize.

With suprise and consternation, the nation now learned that no measure or method existed to determine the validity of disputed returns. The Constitution stated: "The President of the Senate shall, in the presence of the Senate and House of Representatives, open all the certificates and the votes shall then be counted." The question was, how and by whom? The Senate was Republican and so, of course, was its president, and the House was Democratic. Constitutional ambiguity and congressional division rendered a fair and satisfactory solution of the crisis impossible. If the president of the Senate counted the votes, Hayes would be the victor. If the Senate and House judged the returns separately, they would reach opposite decisions and checkmate each other. And if the houses voted jointly, the Democrats, with a numerical majority, would decide the result. Resort to any one of these lines of action promised to divide the country and possibly result in chaos.

Not until the last days of January 1877 did Congress act to break the deadlock. Then it created a special Electoral Commission to pass on all the disputed votes. The commission was to be composed of five senators, five representatives, and five justices of the Supreme Court. Because of the party line-up, the congressional delegation would consist of five Republicans and five Democrats. The creating law named four of the judicial commissioners, two Republicans and two Democrats. The four were to select their fifth colleague, and it was understood that they would choose David Davis, an independent Republican, thus ensuring that the deciding vote would be wielded by a relatively unbiased judge. But at this stage Davis was elected to the Senate from Illinois and suddenly resigned his seat. His place on the commission fell to a Republican. Sitting throughout February, the commission by a partisan vote of 8 to 7 decided every disputed vote for Hayes. Congress accepted the final verdict of the agency on March 2, only two days before the inauguration of the new President.

Ratification of the commission's findings was not accomplished, however, without some complicated compromising among the politicians. Behind the dealing, and partially directing it, were certain powerful economic forces with a stake in the outcome. A decision by the commission was not final until approved by Congress, and the Democrats could have prevented action by filibustering. The success of a filibuster, however, depended on concert between Northern and Southern Democrats, and this the Republicans disrupted by offering the Southerners sufficient inducement to accept the commission's findings. According to the traditional account, certain Republicans and Southern Democrats met at Washington's Wormley Hotel, and the Republicans pledged that Hayes, after becoming President, would withdraw the troops from the South. As withdrawal would mean the downfall of the last carpetbag governments, the Southerners, convinced they were getting as much from Hayes as they could get from Tilden, abandoned the filibuster.

Actually, the story behind the "Compromise of 1877" is somewhat more complex. Hayes was on record before the election as favoring withdrawal of the troops, and in any event the Democrats in the House could have forced withdrawal simply by cutting out appropriations for the army in the Reconstruction process. The real agreement, the one that brought the Southern Democrats over, was reached before the Wormley meeting. As the price for their cooperation the Southern Democrats (among them some old Whigs) exacted from the Republicans the following pledges: the appointment of at least one Southerner to the Hayes cabinet, control of federal patronage in their sections, generous internal improvements, national aid for the Texas and Pacific Railroad, and, finally, withdrawal of the troops. The Conservatives who were running the redeemed Southern states were primarily interested in economics—in industrializing the South—and they believed that the Republican program of federal aid to business would be more beneficial for their region than the archaic state-rights policy of the Democrats.

DISCRIMINATION MADE LEGAL

In his inaugural address Hayes stressed the Southern problem. While he took care to say that the rights of the Negroes must be preserved, he announced that the most pressing need of the South was the restoration of "wise, honest, and peaceful local self-government"— which meant that he was going to withdraw the troops and let the whites take over control of the state governments. Hayes laid down this policy knowing that his action would lend weight to current charges that he was paying off the South for acquiescing in his election and would strengthen those critics who referred to him as "his Fraudulency."

The President hoped to build up a "new Republican" party in the South composed of whatever conservative white groups could be weaned away from the Democrats and committed to some acceptance of Negro rights. But his efforts, which included a tour of Southern cities, failed to produce any positive results. Although many Southern leaders sympathized with the economic credo of the Republicans, they could not advise their people to support the party that had imposed Reconstruction. Nor were Southerners pleased by Hayes' bestowal of offices on carpetbaggers who now had to leave the section or by his vetoes of Democratic attempts to repeal the Force Acts. The "solid South" had come into existence, and there was nothing Hayes or any Republican could do to crack it.

The withdrawal of the troops was a symbol that the national government was giving up its attempt to control Southern politics and to determine the place of the Negro in Southern society. The surrender, it is to be noted, was made by the Republicans. They could yield with good grace because after 1877 they had no particular need for the support of the reconstructed South. The economic legislation of the war and postwar years was safe from repeal; industry was securely entrenched in the national economy; and Republican dominance could be maintained without Southern votes.

Another symbol of retreat was furnished by the Supreme Court, which in a series of decisions emasculated the Fourteenth and Fifteenth amendments of much of their significance. In the Civil Rights Cases (1883) the Court took the position that the Fourteenth Amendment prohibited states from discriminating against people on account of color but did not restrict private individuals or organizations. That is, railroads, hotels, theaters, and the like could legally practice segregation. Eventually the Court validated state legislation that discriminated against Negroes. In *Plessy* v. *Ferguson* (1896), a case involving a law that required separate seating arrangements for the races on railroads, the Court held that separate accomodations did not deprive the Negro of equal rights if the accommodations were equal. And in *Cumming* v. *County Board of Education* (1899) the Court held that laws establishing separate schools for whites and Negroes were valid if the facilities were equal for both.

The men who came to power in the South after 1877 were not in the old agrarian planter tradition. Known as "Bourbons" or "Redeemers," they were industrialists or would-be industrialists. They preached the industrialization of the South through the importation of Northern capital, a policy of low taxes to attract business, and a political alliance with the Northeast instead of with the South's traditional ally, the West. Controlling state governments through the medium of the Democratic party, which as a result of Reconstruction was the only party in the section, they practiced a program marked by economy in government, reduced taxes, and few social services. They did not attempt to abolish Negro suffrage but instead used the Negro vote to maintain white power, as men of their class had tried to use it

The Plight of the Negro [1880]

Frederick Douglass, famous as an escaped slave who had become an abolitionist orator, remained the outstanding spokesman for black Americans after the Civil War. On August 1, 1880, he said in a speech to a great convention of blacks in Elmira, New York:

We have laid the heavy hand of the constitution upon the matchless meanness of caste, as well as upon the hell-black crime of slavery. We have declared before all the world that there shall be no denial of rights on account of race, color, or previous condition of servitude. The advantage gained in this respect is immense.

It is a great thing to have the supreme law of the land on the side of justice and liberty. It is the line up to which the nation is destined to march—the law to which the nation's life must ultimately conform. It is a great principle, up to which we may educate the people, and to this extent its value exceeds all speech.

But today, in most of the Southern States, the fourteenth and fifteenth amendments are virtually nullified.

The rights which they were intended to guarantee are denied and held in contempt. The citizenship granted in the fourteenth amendment is practically a mockery, and the right to vote, provided for in the fifteenth amendment, is literally stamped out in face of government. The old master class is today triumphant, and the newly-enfranchised class in a condition but little above that in which they were found before the rebellion.

---

during Reconstruction. Negroes continued to vote after the return of white supremacy, but in reduced numbers. In some states they were prevented from voting by an implied threat of force; in others, their influence was nullified by tricky devices—tissue ballots and a complicated arrangement of ballot boxes—that disqualified their votes. But in many areas the black vote was a purchased and directed vote, paid for by the Bourbons and used by them to beat down attempts of the farmers to take over control of the Democratic party.

Not until the 1890s did the Southern states pass laws to disfranchise the Negroes, and the impetus for the attempt was furnished by the white farmers. The farmers demanded disfranchisement because they were opposed for racial reasons to Negro voting and because they objected to the Negro vote being employed against them. The rich whites acquiesced, partly out of a desire to placate the white masses and partly because in the agrarian unrest that characterized the nineties the farmers in some states had sought to get the Negro vote on their side. The threat of competition for the Negro vote frightened all whites, and there was a general feeling that the time had come to close ranks if white supremacy was to be maintained.

In devising laws to disfranchise the Negroes, the Southern states had to take care to evade the intent of the Fifteenth Amendment. That measure did not confer suffrage upon the Negroes but merely prohibited states from denying it because of color. The Southern problem, then, was to exclude Negroes from the franchise without seeming to base the exclusion on race. Two devices were widely employed before 1900. One was the poll tax or some form of property qualification. The other was the literacy and understanding test, which required a voter to demonstrate an ability to read and to interpret the Constitution. The reasoning behind the latter law was that local registrars could administer an impossible reading test to Negroes or rule that their interpretation of the Constitution was inadequate. Both of these devices could be used, and were used, to deny the franchise to poor white men, who protested against tests being applied to them. So, many states passed so-called grandfather laws, which permitted men who could not meet the literacy and property qualifications to be admitted to the suffrage if their ancestors had voted before 1867 or some date before Reconstruction began.

The Supreme Court proved as compliant in ruling on the disfranchising laws as it was in dealing with the civil-rights cases. Although the Court eventually voided the grandfather laws, it validated the literacy tests (*Williams* v. *Mississippi*, 1898) and manifested a general willingness to let the Southern states define suffrage standards—provided the evasions of the Fifteenth Amendment were not too glaring.

One Negro leader believed that his race would have to acquire economic independence before it could ask for complete social acceptance. This was Booker T. Washington, who became the head of the Tuskegee Institute in Alabama, an industrial school for Negroes, and eventually the spokesman for a large segment of his people. Washington feared that in what he called "the great leap from slavery to freedom" the Negroes had forgotten that they would have to live by the work of their hands. Therefore, he preached that education for Negroes should stress industrial and practical aspects rather than classical matters. Eventually, Washington evolved a whole new concept of race relations. He set it forth in a speech at Atlanta in 1895. Known as the Atlanta Compromise, it proposed that for the time the Negro eschew agitation for social equality and devote his efforts to achieving economic security. Upper-class whites approved Washington's philosophy and supported his endeavors, as did some wealthy whites in the North. Most Negroes also accepted the Atlanta strategy, but some were soon to reject it as too passive.

As the turn of the century approached, Southern whites seemed to have won a complete victory over the outside influences that had sought to disturb their way of life, and Reconstruction seemed to these people like a bad dream receding into the past. But the deep and turbulent forces generated in the years between 1865 and 1877 were only temporarily exhausted. They would appear again as Americans continued to search for solutions to the problems left by the Civil War and its troubled aftermath.

THE "NEW SOUTH"

With relative rapidity, the South recovered from the effects of war and restored its economic life. Since it was an agricultural society, its productive powers rested on the basis of land, and the land had survived the war. The chief problem was to get the plantations and farms under cultivation again. Work began at once (crops were harvested in 1865), and progress was steady. By 1879 the cotton crop exceeded that of 1860, part of the increase resulting from the opening of new growing areas west of the Mississippi, in Texas and Arkansas.

The rehabilitation of the South's economy was accomplished with relatively few changes in its agriculture. There was something of a shift in the distribution of land ownership, resulting in an increase in the number of small holders. In the economic travail following the war, many planters were unable to hold on to their property and were forced to offer their

---

Plessy v. Ferguson [1896]

synate but =

In this famous case the Supreme Court held that enforced separate facilities for Negroes did not imply that Negro people were inferior and did not violate the Fourteenth Amendment:

The object of the amendment was undoubtedly to enforce the absolute equality of the two races before the law, but in the nature of things it could not have been intended to abolish distinctions based upon color, or to enforce social, as distinguished from political, equality, or a commingling of the two races upon terms unsatisfactory to either. Laws permitting, and even requiring their separation in places where they are liable to be brought into contact do not necessarily imply the inferiority of either race to the other, and have been generally, if not universally, recognized as within the competency of the state legislatures in the exercise of their police power. The most common instance of this is connected with the establishment of separate schools for white and colored children, which have been held to be a valid exercise of the legislative power even by courts of states where the political rights of the colored race have been longest and most earnestly enforced. . . .

land for sale at low prices. In many cases the purchasers were white yeomen. According to the census, the number of farms in Mississippi increased from 43,000 in 1860 to 68,000 by 1870; in South Carolina from 33,000 to 52,000; and in Louisiana from 17,000 to 28,000. Actually, these figures are somewhat deceptive because some of the farms listed were under ten or twenty acres in area and were really units in a plantation, worked by tenants who were sometimes white but usually Negro.

The plantation system was modified, but it did not disappear. In the ownership of the system, however, an important change took place. The old planter (or the old type of planter who lived on the plantation) tended to disappear. More and more, the large land units were owned and administered by merchants, banks, and corporations — or by planters who lived in towns or cities where they could devote themselves to business as well as agriculture.

During the Reconstruction period, perhaps a third or more of the farmers in the South were tenants; by 1900 the figure had increased to 70 percent. Several factors accounted for the trend toward tenancy. The Negroes, when they became freedmen, had, of course, no property. They were forced, as a simple matter of survival, to become laborers or tenants, and most of them were unable to accumulate enough resources to rise above this status. As late as 1890 there were only 121,000 Negro landowners in the South. Probably the strongest influence promoting tenancy among both races was the lack of an adequate credit system, with a resulting scarcity of money. The National Bank System was slow to establish itself in the Southern states, and state banks were slow to recover from the effects of the war. Landlords did not have enough cash to hire laborers to work their land, and laborers could not secure loans to buy land or even raise sufficient currency to rent land on a cash basis.

Out of this situation developed an economic arrangement peculiar to the South, the sharecrop and crop-lien system, in which produce and labor took the place of money. There were share tenants and sharecroppers, and there was a difference between the two groups. The share tenants, most of whom were whites, worked strips of land on a large unit and paid as rent to the landlord one-fourth to one-third of their crop; they provided their own

tools, seed, stock, and other supplies. The sharecroppers, most of whom were Negroes, provided nothing but their own labor. For the average cropper, the landlord would furnish all the previously mentioned materials, and a horse or mule and a house as well. In addition, until the crop was harvested he would arrange credit facilities for the cropper and his family at a local country store owned by himself or a merchant. The cropper, for his part, agreed to consign from one-third to one-half of his crop to the landlord. Moreover, the storekeeper, the source of credit, protected his interest by taking a mortgage or lien on the tenant's share of the crop. (As time passed, the landlord and the merchant tended to become one person, and the planter-storekeeper became a major figure in the Southern credit complex.)

The lien system was a necessary credit device in the postwar years; but when it was continued and expanded after that period, it had a harmful influence upon Southern agriculture. The merchant or landlord pressed the cropper to produce a single money crop, cotton, to the neglect of diversified farming and scientific farming methods. More serious were the social results of the system. The typical sharecropper was an unlettered person who did not know how to handle his own money carefully and who did not understand the mechanics of credit. Frequently, after harvesting his crop, he found himself owing money to the storekeeper and hence forced to pledge his labor to the same source for another year. Not only did the lien system prevent tenants from rising to the owning class, but it also operated to bind them to particular pieces of land, to create a state of peonage. The Negro sharecropper was not a slave, but he was not completely free.

The Reconstruction period witnessed a restoration of Southern industrial facilities damaged or destroyed during the war, as well as some promising beginnings in new industrial activities. Most of the rehabilitation and expansion was financed with local, Southern capital, which was subscribed by the people of a town who wanted to improve their community by locating a factory in it. The only Southern enterprise that attracted Northern and European investors was the railroad. With outside aid, the war-weakened rail system was soon put in running order again, and by 1873 over 4,000 miles of new track had been constructed. Modest but noteworthy progress was recorded in tobacco manufacturing, in the lumber industry, and in iron making.

The most substantial growth occurred in textiles, which had a prewar basis to build on. Southern leaders during Reconstruction preached the economic advantage of building cotton mills where the raw material was produced, and the Southern people took this logic to heart. Practically all the mills that began to appear in Southern towns were financed by local investors. By 1880 the South could boast

of 161 textile factories housing 524,000 spindles and employing 16,000 workers.

But the great industrial development of the section, the development that created the "New South," would not come until later. And even that forward economic surge would not greatly change the nature of Southern life, would not make the South very "new." As late as 1910 only 15 percent of all the people in the region were connected with manufacturing. For many years the South would remain, as it was in the Reconstruction era, a rural and a traditional land.

Selected Readings

Reconstruction: General Accounts
W. A. Dunning, *Reconstruction, Political and Economic, 1865–1877** (1907); W. E. B. Du Bois, *Black Reconstruction** (1935); J. S. Allen, *Reconstruction: The Battle for Democracy, 1865–1876** (1937); E. M. Coulter, *The South During Reconstruction, 1865–1877* (1947); J. H. Franklin, *Reconstruction After the Civil War** (1962); W. R. Brock, *An American Crisis** (1963); K. M. Stampp, *The Era of Reconstruction** (1965).

Reconstruction: Special Studies
J. E. Sefton, *The United States Army and Reconstruction* (1967); S. I. Kutler, *Judicial Power and Reconstruction Politics* (1968); H. M. Hyman, *A More Perfect Union: The Impact of the Civil War and Reconstruction on the Constitution* (1973); M. L. Benedict, *The Impeachment and Trial of Andrew Johnson** (1972); M. E. Mantell, *Johnson, Grant and the Politics of Reconstruction* (1973); A. W. Trelease, *White Terror: The Ku Klux Conspiracy and Southern Reconstruction* (1971); R. N. Current, *Three Carpetbag Governors* (1967); R. O. Curry, ed., *Radicalism, Racism, and Party: The Border States During Reconstruction* (1972); H. L. Trefousse, *The Radical Republicans* (1969); David Donald, *Charles Sumner and the Rights of Man* (1970); Joseph Logsdon, *Horace White, Nineteenth Century Liberal* (1972); E. N. Paolino, *The Foundations of Empire: William Henry Seward and U.S. Foreign Policy* (1973).

Grant and the Republicans
L. D. White, *The Republican Era** (1958); M. R. Dearing, *Veterans in Politics* (1952); C. H. Coleman, *The Election of 1868* (1933); W. B. Hesseltine, *U. S. Grant, Politician* (1935); Allan Nevins, *Hamilton Fish: The Inner History of the Grant Administration* (1936); Goldwin Smith, *The Treaty of Washington, 1871* (1941); Sumner Welles, *Naboth's Vineyard* (2 vols., 1928), on the U.S. and Santo Domingo; A. B. Callow, Jr., *The Tweed Ring* (1966); E. D. Ross, *The Liberal Republican Movement* (1919); C. M. Fuess, *Carl Schurz, Reformer* (1932); Ari Hogenboom, *Outlawing the Spoils* (1961); R. P. Sharkey, *Money, Class,*

and Party* (1959); Irwin Unger, *The Greenback Era* (1964); W. T. K. Nugent, *Money and American Society, 1865–1880* (1968).

The Democratic Opposition
Stewart Mitchell, *Horatio Seymour* (1938); A. C. Flick, *Samuel Jones Tilden* (1939); Irving Katz, *August Belmont: A Political Biography* (1968); K. I. Polakoff, *The Politics of Inertia: The Election of 1876 and the End of Reconstruction* (1973).

The New South
C. V. Woodward, *Origins of the New South, 1877–1913** (1951) and *Reunion and Reaction: The Compromise of 1877 and the End of Reconstruction** (1951); V. P. De Santis, *Republicans Face the Southern Question: The New Departure Years, 1877–1897* (1959); S. P. Hirshson, *Farewell to the Bloody Shirt: Northern Republicans and the Southern Negro, 1877–1893* (1962); Harry Barnard, *Rutherford B. Hayes and His America* (1964); R. B. Nixon, *Henry W. Grady, Spokesman of the New South* (1943); Broadus Mitchell, *The Rise of Cotton Mills in the South* (1921); P. H. Buck, *The Road to Reunion, 1865–1900** (1937).

The Negro After 1865
William Gillette, *The Right to Vote: Politics and the Passage of the Fifteenth Amendment** (1967); R. W. Logan, *The Negro in American Life and Thought: The Nadir, 1877–1901* (1954); Paul Lewinson, *Race, Class, and Party: A History of Negro Suffrage and White Politics in the South** (1932); August Meier, *Negro Thought in America, 1880–1915** (1963); B. T. Washington, *Up from Slavery** (1901); S. R. Spencer, Jr., *Booker T. Washington and the Negro's Place in American Life** (1955); L. R. Harlan, *Booker T. Washington: The Making of a Black Leader, 1856–1901* (1973); C. V. Woodward, *The Strange Career of Jim Crow** (1966); V. L. Wharton, *The Negro in Mississippi, 1865–1900** (1947); G. B. Tindall, *South Carolina Negroes, 1877–1900** (1952); J. R. Williamson, *After Slavery: The Negro in South Carolina During Reconstruction* (1966).

*Titles available in paperback.

Industrialization and Urbanization

Seventeen

"With a stride that astonished statisticians, the conquering hosts of business enterprise swept over the continent; twenty-five years after the death of Lincoln, America had become, in the quantity and value of her products, the first manufacturing nation of the world," the historians Charles and Mary Beard have written. "What England had accomplished in a hundred years, the United States had achieved in half the time."

This rise to industrial supremacy during the last decades of the nineteenth century was due to a combination of factors. The United States was not necessarily superior in every one of them but certainly had an advantage in respect to all of them taken together.

First, this nation had an abundance of basic raw materials and sources of energy: coal, iron and other ores, timber, petroleum, water power. Second, there was a large and growing supply of willing labor, consisting in the main of American farmers and European peasants who flocked from the countryside of two continents to the rising industrial centers of the United States. Third, Americans had inherited a good deal of technological ingenuity—the "Yankee inventiveness" that had become a mark of the American character—which was capable of devising or adapting the necessary machines. Fourth, a number of remarkable business organizers, "captains of industry," had the skill to bring together raw materials, workers, and machines, to use them efficiently in the processes of production, and to distribute the resulting goods profitably in the national market. Fifth, this market itself, which was being enlarged by the growth of population and the extension of the rail network, made possible the mass consumption that is a prerequisite to mass production. Finally, the federal government, while refraining from interference with business enterprise, encouraged and assisted it by turning over public resources for private exploitation, by giving tariff protection against foreign competition, by setting up a

Tenement Street
The teeming life of a tenement district and something of its squalor are suggested in this view of Mulberry Street in New York City. (Library of Congress)

449

helpful banking and monetary system, and by providing direct subsidies of land and money.

In the United States, large-scale industry had received a start before the Civil War. The war, while temporarily setting back some industrial activities, stimulated others and — most important — removed the Southern planters as a political obstacle to governmental policies favoring Northern capitalists. The rate of industrial growth increased so rapidly in the postwar decades that these came to constitute a new age of industrialization. It was also an age of urbanization, in which cities assumed greater and greater importance. The tremendous increase in the output of goods — and the multiplication of conveniences that city life afforded — made possible a higher and higher average level of living. But all the people did not share equally in the benefits of the industrial system. There were gross inequalities, and these provoked severe criticisms of the system and led to determined and sometimes violent attempts to bring about a redistribution of income.

The Rise of Big Business

Between 1865 and 1900 American business moved in the direction of monopoly. Fewer and fewer firms produced more and more of the nation's goods. Small corporations were merged to create large ones. These often were brought together to form still larger combinations: *pools*, the members of which agreed to avoid competition and divide profits; *trusts*, in which a board of trustees controlled several corporations; or *holding companies*, which held stock in other companies and thus directed them. Regardless of their specific nature, the various combinations were popularly known as "trusts." By 1900 there were more than 300 of these trusts, and the largest ones, comprising fewer than 2 percent of the manufacturing firms, turned out almost 50 percent of all the manufactured goods in the country.

SOME BASIC INVENTIONS

This economic transformation was accompanied by a flood of inventions and technological innovations. In the entire history of the country up to 1860 only 36,000 patents had been granted, but for the period from 1860 to 1890 the figure was 440,000.

Many of the postwar inventions and discoveries were in the field of communication. In 1866 Cyrus W. Field succeeded in his project of laying a transatlantic cable to Europe. During the next decade Alexander Graham Bell developed the first practicable telephone, and by the 1890s the American Telephone and Telegraph Company, which handled his interests, had installed nearly half a million instruments in American cities. Other inventions that speeded the pace of business organization were the typewriter (by Christopher L. Sholes in 1868), the cash register (by James Ritty in 1879), and the calculating or adding machine (by William S. Burroughs in 1891).

Undoubtedly the technological innovation that had the most revolutionary effect upon industry and upon lives of the urban masses in the industrial centers was the introduction in the 1870s of electricity as a source of light and power. Among the several men who pioneered in developing a commercially practical dynamo were Charles F. Brush, who devised the arc lamp for street illumination, and Thomas A. Edison, who invented, among many other electrical contrivances, the incandescent lamp, which could be used for both street and home lighting. Edison and others designed improved generators and built central power plants to furnish electricity to office buildings, factories, and dwellings. Before the turn of the century 2,774 power stations were in operation, and some 2 million electric lights were in use in the country. Already electric power was being employed in street railway systems and in electric elevators in urban skyscrapers, as well as for driving the machines of factories. The electric power industry was dominated by two large corporations: the General Electric Company, which took over the Edison interests, and the Westinghouse Electric and Manufacturing Company.

The Edison Laboratory

Thomas A. Edison (1847–1931) operated a laboratory at Menlo Park, New Jersey, from 1876 to 1887, when he moved to a more spacious and better equipped one at West Orange. Here he is shown testing his first successful incandescent lamp, the greatest of his many inventions, in 1879. His favorite invention was the phonograph, which he had devised in 1877. (U.S. Department of the Interior, National Park Service, Edison National Historic Site)

STEEL AND OIL

The Age of Steel began in 1865. A process by which iron could be transformed into steel had been discovered simultaneously in the 1850s by an Englishman, Henry Bessemer, and an American, William Kelly (it consisted of blowing air through the molten iron to burn out the impurities), but it was not put into use until after the Civil War. In 1868 another method of making steel, the open-hearth process, was introduced from Europe by Abram S. Hewitt, a New Jersey ironmaster. Both techniques were employed in the many steel mills that began to appear—and with revolutionary effects. Hitherto steel had been used only in the manufacture of small and very expensive articles, tools and cutlery, but now it was possible to produce bulky items like locomotives and rails from steel instead of iron.

The steel industry was first concentrated where the iron industry had existed, in western Pennsylvania and eastern Ohio. Here, in a region where iron ore and coal were found in abundance, Pittsburgh reigned as the center of the steel world. But as the industry expanded, new sources of ore had to be tapped, and by the 1870s the mines of the upper peninsula of Michigan were furnishing over half of the supply. Then in the 1890s the Eastern steelmasters began to exploit the extensive Mesabi range in Minnesota, which developed into the greatest ore-producing region in the world. Another rich source was discovered around Birmingham, Alabama. Although the Michigan and Minnesota fields were located at a great distance from the Eastern plants, the ore could be transported easily and cheaply by means of railroads and Great Lakes steamers. Eventually new centers of production with ready access to ore and coal arose: Cleveland and Lorain in Ohio, Detroit, Chicago, and Birmingham.

Inevitably the high profits to be made in steel tempted consolidation, and there appeared men who had a genius for organization.

The central figure in steel was Andrew Carnegie, a Scottish immigrant boy who had worked his way up in the railroad industry. Adopting the Bessemer process, he opened in 1873 the J. Edgar Thompson Steel Works in western Pennsylvania, named in honor of his former

---

Brooklyn Bridge

As a story of persevering courage, the erection of Brooklyn Bridge by John A. and Washington Roebling can match anything in American military history. In 1866 Manhattan Island was connected with Brooklyn and the rest of Long Island only by ferries. When the East River froze, the tie was sundered. A bridge was needed. John Roebling, engineer and manufacturer of wire cables, proposed a suspension bridge with a central span of 1,600 feet — longer than had been built anywhere in the world. Other great engineers said it could not be done. But Roebling's prestige and forcefulness got approval for the idea, and he designed the bridge. Then he unexpectedly died. His son Washington Roebling was stricken by caisson bends. An invalid, he was confined to his bed at Columbia Heights. His wife watched the construction by telescope, and he supervised every detail by letter. In 1883, twelve years after work began, the bridge opened, an object of practical use which also was a thing of beauty. Here was the austere art of the Age of Steel: the massive granite towers were united in tension with the spidery cables of nineteen wire strands, and the tension held the bridge aloft. The father was dead; the son, paralyzed, growing deaf and blind; but they had shown how straightforward statement of fact could unify industrialism with aesthetics. (Currier & Ives)

PUBLISHED BY CURRIER & IVES.   158 NASSAU ST. NEW YORK.

The Bridge is to cross the river by a single span of 1600 feet, to start on the New York side from the City Hall rising by a gradual approach of 2381 feet in length, and on the Brooklyn side by an approach of 1861 feet. Its elevation above the river in the

THE GREAT EAST RIVER BRIDGE.
To Connect the Cities of New York & Brooklyn.

centre of the bridge will be 130 feet. Its floor is to be 85 feet wide with tracks for steam cars, roadway for carriages, and walks for foot passengers. It is to have an elevated promenade commanding a view of extraordinary beauty and extent, and its cost is to be about $8,000,000.

railroad employer, the head of the Pennsylvania Railroad. Soon Carnegie had built up his company to a place of dominance in the industry.

His methods were those commonly employed by other great consolidationists of the times. He obtained rebates from railroads on his shipments, so that he could cut his costs and hence his prices, and he bought out rival concerns that could not meet his competition. In collaboration with his ablest associate, Henry Clay Frick, he set up a policy of integration designed to control the processing of steel from mine to market. His company operated a fleet of ore ships on the Great Lakes, acquired railroads and coal mines, and leased part of the Mesabi range.

The machines of the Age of Steel could not run without lubrication, and so another vast enterprise came into being in the postwar era, the petroleum industry. For years before the Civil War the existence of petroleum had been known, particularly in western Pennsylvania where it often seeped to the surface of streams and springs. No one was quite sure what it was or what to do with it. Some enterprising individuals peddled it in bottles as a patent medicine. The first person to glimpse its commercial possibilities as an illuminant was George H. Bissell, who sent a sample of oil to Professor Benjamin Silliman of Yale for analysis. Silliman reported in 1855 that the substance could be used for lighting purposes, and that it would also yield such products as paraffin, naphtha, and lubricating oil. Bissell then raised enough money to begin drilling operations, and in 1859 Edwin L. Drake, employed by Bissell, put down the first oil well near Titusville, Pennsylvania. Labeled "Drake's folly" by the skeptical, it was soon producing oil at the rate of 500 barrels a month.

It also started an oil rush, as promoters searched for and found other fields, not only in Pennsylvania but in Ohio and West Virginia as well. By the 1870s nearly 40 million barrels of petroleum had been produced, oil had advanced to fourth place among the nation's exports, and the annual production was approaching 20 million barrels. Because relatively little capital was required for a man to make a start in the oil business, either as a producer or a refiner, competition at first ran wild. Refineries, which were even more profitable

than wells, dotted the Pennsylvania-Ohio region, with Pittsburgh and Cleveland constituting the two principal refining centers. Then the greatest consolidationist of the time stepped into the picture to bring order to the industry.

John D. Rockefeller was a successful businessman at an age when most boys of today would be in college. When only nineteen, he became a partner in a produce commission company in Cleveland that took solid profits selling goods to the government during the Civil War. Far sighted, highly acquisitive, and possessing abundant talents for organization, he decided that his economic future lay with oil. He also concluded that Cleveland, connected by rail and water with the Eastern and Western markets, was destined to surpass Pittsburgh, which had access only to the East through the Pennsylvania Railroad, as the oil-refining center of the country. At the end of the war he and Sidney Andrews, a Cleveland refiner, launched their own business. From the beginning Rockefeller sought to eliminate the competition and the small-scale companies that in his opinion were ruining the petroleum industry. He and Andrews enlarged their operations, took in H. M. Flagler and S. V. Harkness as allies, and proceeded methodically to buy out other refineries. In 1870 the associates formed the Standard Oil Company of Ohio, which in a few years had acquired twenty of the twenty-five refineries in Cleveland, in addition to plants in Pittsburgh, Philadelphia, New York, and Baltimore.

In its rise to dominance Standard Oil employed the familiar consolidating devices of the period, plus a few which were its own invention. The company emphasized efficient and economic operation, research, and sound financial practices. At Rockefeller's insistence, a large cash reserve was maintained to avoid reliance on banks and to purchase competitors. The company obtained rebates from railroads, and even, for a brief time, forced three of the Eastern roads to pay rebates to it on oil shipped by competing companies. Rockefeller waged price wars to drive competitors out of business and, always victorious, took over the defeated concerns.

Like Carnegie in steel, Rockefeller set up an integrated system of production. He built his own terminal warehouses and barrel factories and a network of pipelines that gave him control over most of the facilities for transporting petroleum. Standard also owned its own marketing organization, thus escaping commissions to middlemen. For sales purposes the United States was divided into districts, each of which was administered by a company executive who was assisted by a corps of agents. The salesmen were under orders to sell Standard products by almost any method, and almost always they succeeded. When the Standard Oil Trust was formed in 1882, it was only a formal recognition of the near monopoly that Rockefeller and his associates had already established.

OTHER INDUSTRIES

Three developments brought significant changes to the meat-packing business. They were the appearance of the range-cattle industry in Texas and the Great Plains, the extension of railroad lines across the Mississippi into the plains country, and the introduction of the refrigerated freight car. Chicago, situated close to the cattle supply of the trans-Mississippi area and the hog supply of the Middle West, and elaborately connected by railroads with both the producing areas and the urban markets, became the undisputed capital of the meat-packing industry. Imaginative and aggressive leaders, the counterparts of Rockefeller and Carnegie, appeared to form the inevitable combinations: Philip D. Armour, Nelson Morris, and Gustavus F. Swift. Swift sponsored the most important technological development in the industry, the refrigerator car cooled by artificial ice.

Like the meat business, flour milling was originally a localized enterprise, carried on in thousands of small mills in all parts of the country. And like meat packing, the milling industry moved west to be nearer the source of the wheat supply, adopted new technological processes, and originated large-scale organizations which turned out standardized products. By the close of the Civil War the center of wheat production had shifted to the upper Mississippi Valley, and Minneapolis, Minnesota, became the center of the milling industry. The leading millers were Cadwallader C. Washburn, Charles A. Pillsbury, and George M. Christian, the last of whom eventually merged his interests with Washburn. Two manufactur-

ing methods introduced from Europe resulted in a greatly improved product. The first, called the "middlings-purifier" or "gradual-reduction" process, preserved a higher content of gluten in finished flour than previously had been the case. The second was a process of passing wheat slowly through chilled iron rollers to achieve a flour of superior quality and unusual whiteness. By 1880 flour milling had become one of the country's largest businesses and was supplying its product to European as well as to American markets.

Many other industries, some of them antedating the war and some emerging after it, also underwent the common process of expansion and concentration. The coal industry, which supplied the bulk of the fuel used by the nation's industries, increased its output from approximately 20 million tons in 1860 to 270 million by 1900. In 1890 a near monopoly was created in tobacco manufacturing when James B. Duke fused five large corporations into the American Tobacco Company.

The prepared-foods business, concentrating on the canning of vegetables, became a major industry and in the process helped to alter the eating habits of the American people. A leader in this industry was Gail Borden. Born in rural New York, Borden had less than two years of formal schooling. After a business career in Texas, he interested himself in the possibilities of concentrated foods. He developed a process for condensing milk by evaporation and set up his first large condensary in New York State in 1861. His condensed milk was used by the Northern armies in the Civil War and thus became known to the general public. After the war he founded the town of Borden in Texas and established a plant there for concentrating fruit juices, cocoa, tea, and coffee.

Industries of a prewar origin that continued to experience growth after 1865 were boots and shoes, ready-made clothing, textiles, firearms, distilled liquors, and agricultural machinery.

RAILROAD EXPANSION

In 1860 the railroads constituted the biggest business and the most important single economic interest in the United States. Their total mileage was approximately 30,000, and in roll-

ing stock they counted 100,000 freight and passenger cars and 1,000 locomotives. Every
decade the trackage figure increased: 52,000
miles in 1870, 93,000 in 1880, 163,000 in 1890,
and 193,000 in 1900. The railroads made it possible for industry to secure its raw materials
from a national producing area and to distribute its products in a national market.

Accompanying the expansion of railroad
facilities was a host of technological improvements that made rail travel and transportation
more efficient, convenient, and safe. Among
the innovations were steel rails, heavier locomotives and cars, a uniform gauge (4 feet, $8\frac{1}{2}$
inches), and wider roadbeds. Perhaps the
most important invention affecting railroads
was the Westinghouse air brake, developed by
George Westinghouse in 1869. In 1874 interlocking block signals were introduced from
England. George Pullman had produced in
1864 the first sleeping car, and within a few
years dining, parlor, and drawing-room cars
appeared.

The major Eastern railroads were the New
York Central, the Pennsylvania, the Erie, and
the Baltimore and Ohio. By 1874 all of them had
consolidated lesser lines into their systems and
established connections with the Western market at Chicago. The creator of the New York
Central system was Cornelius Vanderbilt, a
salty, colorful character who had previously
operated a steamship line and was endearingly
known as "Commodore." A ruthless competitor but a sound railroad man, Vanderbilt improved facilities on the Central and bought up
smaller roads to complete his empire. Second
only to the Central in facilities was the Pennsylvania Railroad, whose original route ran between Philadelphia and Pittsburgh. Under the
leadership of J. Edgar Thompson, the Pennsylvania established connections with Chicago, St.
Louis, Baltimore, and Richmond, and in 1899,
by tunneling under the Hudson River, entered
New York City to compete directly with the
Central. The Erie, chartered in the 1850s to link
New York City and Lake Erie, in the postwar
years stretched its connections to Cleveland,
Cincinnati, and St. Louis. Unfortunately for the
Erie, it was controlled during the seventies by
Daniel Drew, Jay Gould, and James Fisk, three
of the most unscrupulous speculators of the
era, who were more interested in milking it of
profits than in making it into a railroad. The

Baltimore and Ohio had built lines from Baltimore as far as Wheeling on the Ohio River before the Civil War. After the war John W. Gar-
rett, its president, extended its lines to Chicago,
Cincinnati, St. Louis, and Philadelphia; it was
not able, however, to obtain access to New
York.

In the South the first railroad activity in the
years immediately after 1865 was the rehabilitation of facilities damaged in the war. Then an
outburst of construction, financed by Northern
and European capital, got under way, and by
1890 the South had increased its trackage from
9,000 to 50,000 miles. In 1893 the Southern Railway was organized, with lines extending from
Washington to New Orleans and connecting
with the Middle West at St. Louis and Cincinnati. Chief rival to the Southern was the
Atlantic Coast Line Railroad, which consolidated dozens of small roads to monopolize
transportation from Richmond to Florida. The
third big system in the South, the Illinois Central, was really a Middle Western road with a
Southern terminal. Shortly before the Civil
War it had built as far as Cairo, Illinois, at the
confluence of the Ohio and the Mississippi. In
the postwar era the Central achieved its
original purpose of reaching the Gulf of Mexico.
By gobbling up smaller lines in the South, it
increased its trackage from approximately
1,000 to 9,000 miles, reached New Orleans on
the Gulf, and eventually touched the Atlantic
at Savannah, Georgia.

From 1865 to 1873 there was more railroad
construction in the Mississippi Valley than in
any other part of the country. The Chicago and
Northwestern stretched its lines to Omaha; the
Chicago, Burlington and Quincy drove through
to Kearney, Nebraska; the Missouri Pacific
built from Kansas City to St. Louis; and the
Kansas Pacific moved from Kansas City to
Denver and then on to Cheyenne in Wyoming
Territory.

THE TRANSCONTINENTAL LINES

Of all the stupendous railroad projects of the
era between 1865 and 1900, none so gripped the
popular imagination as the great "transcontinental" lines. An act of Congress passed in 1862
and amended in 1864 chartered two railroad
corporations, the Union Pacific and the Central

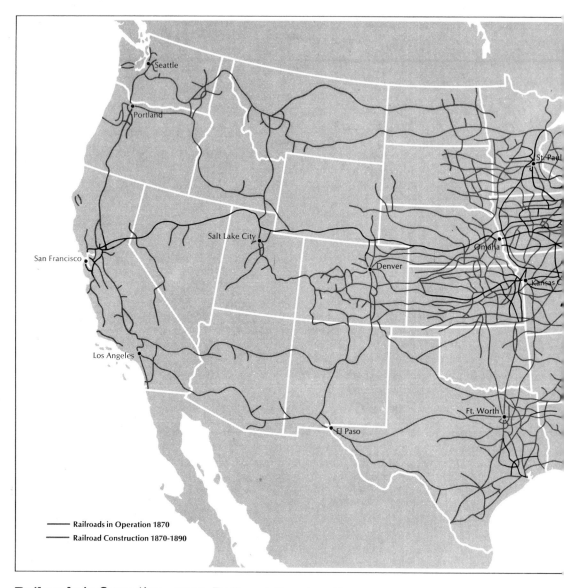

Railroads in Operation 1870; Railroad Construction 1870–1890

Pacific. The Union Pacific was to build westward from Omaha, Nebraska, and the Central Pacific eastward from Sacramento, California, until they met.

To provide the financial aid deemed necessary to initiate the roads, Congress donated a right of way across the public domain and offered the companies special benefits: for each mile of track a company laid, it would receive twenty square miles of land in alternate sec-

tions along the right of way and a thirty-year loan of $16,000, $32,000, or $48,000, depending on whether the construction was in plains, foothill, or mountain country.

Because of a scarcity of labor, the Union Pacific resorted to hiring thousands of Irish immigrants, while the Central Pacific imported several thousand Chinese workers. The builders had to cross deserts, penetrate mountain ranges, and fight off Indians. In the spring of

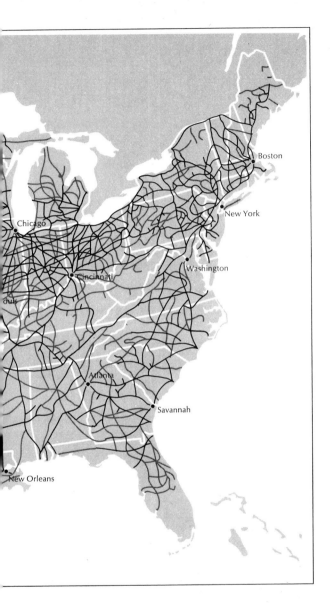

Portland, Oregon; (4) the Atchison, Topeka, and Santa Fe, running from Atchison, Kansas, to San Diego, California; and (5) the Great Northern, stretching from Duluth and St. Paul to Seattle and Tacoma, Washington. All except the Great Northern were built with some form of assistance from the national government or from state governments.

State governments put up an estimated $228 million to entice promoters into their boundaries, and in addition placed their credit at the disposal of railroads, subscribed to stock, and donated 50 million acres of land. The federal government granted over 130 million acres and provided over $60 million in loans to various Western roads. In a number of cases, the aid supplied by the government more than paid for the cost of construction. It was small wonder that many people regarded the railroads, although operated by private enterprise, as essentially public projects.

As the network of rails covered the country, it became evident that the railroad industry was being overbuilt and overextended; many railroad corporations, including some of the largest ones, were overexpanded, overcapitalized, and afflicted with impossible debt burdens. Moreover, many roads were looted and wrecked by their own directors or subjected to harassing competition by speculators like Jay Gould. In some areas of the country certain railroads enjoyed monopolies, but wherever competition existed it was savage and sustained. Competing roads fought ferocious rate wars and struggled for business by offering rebates to big shippers. The inevitable effects of overexpansion, fraudulent management, and cutthroat competition were apparent in the depression of the seventies, when 450 roads went into bankruptcy. Twenty years later, in the hard times of the nineties, 318 companies controlling 67,000 miles fell into the hands of receivers.

After the economic crisis of 1893 railroad capitalists moved to curb competition by creating larger systems. Reorganizing the railroads required huge sums of cash and credit, which could be supplied only by the big New York investment banking houses. The investment bankers, led by J. P. Morgan, were eager to finance consolidation in order to stop the railroads, with their wild financing and frenzied speculating, from ruining the investment busi-

1869, engines of the two lines met at Promontory Point in Utah Territory, and the nation was linked by rail from the Atlantic to the Pacific.

By the end of the century five transcontinental systems were in operation: (1) the Union Pacific–Central Pacific, joining Omaha to Sacramento and San Francisco; (2) the Southern Pacific, extending from San Francisco to St. Louis and New Orleans; (3) the Northern Pacific, linking St. Paul and Minneapolis to

ness. But the bankers, as the price for their aid, insisted on being given a voice in the management of the roads, a condition which the railroad promoters had to accept. By the end of the century a few major railroad systems controlled over half the mileage in the country, and these systems were wholly or partially controlled by two banking houses.

Growth of Cities

Society was being transformed along with the economy: a rural nation was being reshaped in an urban mold as cities grew with the growth of industry. The urban areas were the seats of the developing economic system, the places where most of the factories and corporate offices were located. Cities had existed from colonial times, of course, but now they assumed a new character, size, and significance.

The movement to cities was a contemporary phenomenon of much of the Western world. From countries—or parts of countries—that were industrializing slowly if at all, people moved to other countries—or to other parts of their own country—that were industrializing rapidly. Rural folk from both America and Europe made their way to the business and industrial centers of the United States.

THE CITY'S LURE

"We cannot all live in cities, yet nearly all seem determined to do so," Horace Greeley wrote soon after the Civil War. " 'Hot and cold water,' baker's bread, gas, the theatre, and the streetcars . . . indicate the tendency of modern taste." The city lured people because of its many conveniences, among them the telephone and the electric light, which it enjoyed for years before such things reached the village or the farm. It drew people because of its institutions of entertainment and culture, not only its theaters and other amusements but also its libraries and museums, its superior colleges and schools. It attracted people because, above all, it offered opportunities for employment at higher pay than the countryside afforded. The lure of the city persisted even though many who came were disappointed and urban life acquired some very unpleasant characteristics.

In the half century from 1860 to 1910 the rural population almost doubled, but the urban population increased seven times. In 1860 approximately one-sixth of the people lived in towns of 8,000 or larger; by 1900, one-third of the people. The number of cities with more than 50,000 inhabitants was 16 in 1860 and 109 in 1910. The population of the New York urban area (the city and its environs) grew from less than 1 million in 1860 to more than 3 million in 1900. Even more spectacular was the growth of Chicago, which had 100,000 inhabitants in 1860 and more than a million at the end of the century. Towns and cities were getting bigger and more numerous in all sections of the country. And this vast industrial-urban complex that was taking shape was linked in all its parts by rapid railroad transportation and instantaneous telegraphic communication.

While the cities gained, some rural parts of the country were actually losing population (as had happened to a much smaller extent in the early nineteenth century). During the 1880s, for instance, the number of inhabitants was decreasing in two-fifths of Pennsylvania's total area, three-fifths of Connecticut's, more than half of Ohio's and Illinois', and five-sixths of New York's. People seldom moved directly to a city from the farms. As the historian A. M. Schlesinger has observed, "the tendency was to move from the countryside to the nearest hamlet, from the hamlet to the town, and from the town to the city." So for a time the country town retained some importance as a market and a cultural center, but more and more the city overshadowed it. The city was the ultimate goal of restless farm and village folk. They and the immigrants, most of whom also came from rural areas, made up the great majority of urban dwellers.

THE NEWER IMMIGRANTS

Between 1860 and 1900 the total population of the United States more than doubled, rising from about 31 million to almost 76 million. Im-

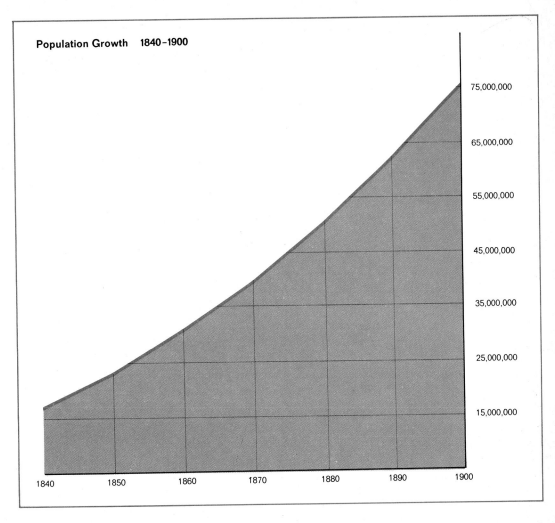

Population Growth   1840–1900

75,000,000

65,000,000

55,000,000

45,000,000

35,000,000

25,000,000

15,000,000

| 1840 | 1850 | 1860 | 1870 | 1880 | 1890 | 1900 |

The total population of the country increased significantly every decade between 1840 and 1900. At the close of the century the number of Americans was over four times the figure in 1840 and over twice that at the beginning of the Civil War.

migration accounted for a substantial portion of the increase; in this forty-year period some 14 million aliens entered the country. This was almost three times the 5 million who had come in the four decades preceding 1860, but in relation to the total population the immigrant tide was no greater after the Civil War than before. The percentage of foreign-born was about the same. In 1880 the ethnic composition of the population was substantially what it had been fifty years before. Up to that year the great majority of the immigrants had originated in

the countries of Western and Northern Europe: England, Ireland, Germany, and the Scandinavian countries.

But in the eighties the immigrant stream began to flow from another source — Southern and Eastern Europe. By the 1890s about fifty-two in one hundred immigrants were coming from this part of the world (in the 1860s it had been fewer than two in one hundred). Among the new ethnic stocks were Austrians, Hungarians, Bohemians, Poles, Serbs, Italians, Russians, and Jews from Poland and Russia.

The Mixed Crowd [1890]

In his famous book *How the Other Half Lives* (1890) the Danish-born newspaper reporter Jacob A. Riis had this to say about what he called "The Mixed Crowd" as it developed in New York City during the 1880s:

When once I asked the agent of a notorious Fourth Ward alley how many people might be living in it I was told: one hundred and forty families, one hundred Irish, thirty-eight Italian, and two that spoke the German tongue. Barring the agent herself, there was not a native-born individual in the court. The answer was characteristic of the cosmopolitan character of lower New York, very nearly so of the whole of it, wherever it runs to alleys and courts. One may find for the asking an Italian, a German, a French, African, Spanish, Bohemian, Russian, Scandinavian, Jewish, and Chinese colony. Even the Arab, who peddles "holy earth" from the Battery as a direct importation from Jerusalem, has his exclusive preserves at the lower end of Washington Street. The one thing you shall vainly ask for in the chief city of America is a distinctively American community. There is none; certainly not among the tenements. . . .

The once unwelcome Irishman has been followed in his turn by the Italian, the Russian Jew, and the Chinaman, and has himself taken a hand at opposition, quite as bitter and quite as ineffectual, against these later hordes. Wherever these have gone they have crowded him out, possessing the block, the street, the ward with their denser swarms. . . .

A map of the city, colored to designate nationalities, would show more stripes than the skin of a zebra, and more colors than any rainbow.

These people came for essentially the same reasons as earlier immigrants: the desire to escape unfavorable economic and political conditions at home. Now railroads, in order to dispose of landholdings, painted an alluring picture of America in advertisements. Industrial employers demanded cheap labor and until 1885 could import workers under the labor contract law, paying for their passage in advance and deducting the amount later from their wages. After the repeal of the law, employers continued to encourage the immigration of unskilled laborers, often with the assistance of foreign-born labor brokers such as the Greek and Italian *padrones* who provided work gangs of their fellow nationals.

Of the earlier immigrants only the Irish had tended to congregate in the Eastern cities. Most of the Germans went West to become farmers, while those that had a proclivity for urban life settled in such Middle Western centers as Milwaukee, St. Louis, and Cincinnati. Nearly all of the Scandinavians took up land in the Middle West or the Great Plains. Those earlier arrivals who became urban dwellers were, with exception of the Irish, businessmen,

professional men, or skilled laborers; and the Irish, who at first were unskilled laborers, rapidly achieved economic independence and raised their social status. In direct contrast, the later immigrants flocked in preponderant numbers to the industrial cities and became unskilled laborers. They did not have the capital to begin farming operations in the West. They had to have immediate employment, and this was offered them by the meat packers, railroads, coal producers, and steel manufacturers, hungry for cheap labor. Besides, in a strange land the newcomers felt the need of that association with their fellows that only city life could give.

The later immigrants provoked fear and resentment among native Americans, as many of the earlier arrivals had done. The newcomers were in overwhelming numbers Catholics in a predominantly Protestant country, and their influx called into existence a short-lived nativist organization, the American Protective Association, which was vaguely but bitterly antialien and anti-Catholic. Some people reacted against the immigrants out of plain prejudice, while others honestly wondered if they could be absorbed into national life. Laborers, fighting to raise their incomes and improve their working conditions, were incensed by the willingness of the immigrants to accept lower wages and to take over jobs of strikers.

With the mounting of the alien tide, the first demands for immigration restrictions rose in the land. Congress acted in 1882 to exclude the Chinese. In the same year it passed a general immigration law denying entry to certain undesirables — convicts, paupers, idiots — and placed a tax of 50 cents on every person admitted. Later legislation of the nineties enlarged the proscriptive list and increased the tax. These measures reflected a rising fear that continuing unlimited immigration would exhaust the resources of the nation and endanger its social institutions. They kept out only a small number of aliens, however, and were far from fulfilling the purposes of the extreme exclusionists. The latter group worked for a literacy test, a device intended to exclude immigrants from Eastern and Southern Europe. Congress passed a literacy law in 1897, but President Grover Cleveland vetoed it. Powerful business interests, the employers of cheap labor, continued to oppose restrictions.

THE URBAN SCENE

The city was a place of unbelievable contrasts, with the most palatial homes and the most wretched hovels, the greatest of conveniences and the worst of problems — misgovernment, poverty, overcrowding, traffic jams, filth, epidemics, and conflagrations. The basic trouble was that the city was growing too fast for planning and building to keep pace. "The problem in America," as one municipal reformer said, "has been to make a great city in a few years out of nothing."

Most city people rented the places they lived in. Landowners, to maximize the rent, encouraged as many as possible to crowd into a given space. New York was not only the largest but also the most congested city. On Manhattan Island, by 1894, the average population density had reached 143 per acre, as compared with 127 for Paris and 101 for Berlin. More than a million poor New Yorkers were jammed in tenements. (Originally the word *tenement* meant simply a multiple-family rented build-

ing; eventually the term was applied only to slum dwellings.) When the first tenement was put up (in 1850), it was hailed as a great improvement in housing for the poor. "It is built with the design of supplying the laboring people with cheap lodgings," a local newspaper commented, "and will have many advantages over the cellars and other miserable abodes, which too many are forced to inhabit." But tenements themselves became miserable abodes, three to five stories high, with many windowless rooms, little or no provision for plumbing or for central heating, and perhaps a row of privies in the basement. A New York state law of 1879 required a window in every bedroom of tenements built thereafter. Still, in 1890, the Danish immigrant and New York newspaper reporter Jacob Riis found deplorable conditions, which he described in his book *How the Other Half Lives*. A typical building was sunless and practically airless and "poisoned" by "summer stenches." "The hall is dark and you might stumble over the children pitching pennies back there."

Some of the wealthy lived in downtown mansions. Many of the rich or the reasonably well-to-do tried to combine the advantages of city and country living by moving to the city's outskirts. In the 1870s Chicago boasted of nearly one hundred residential suburbs connected with the city by railroad and offering the joys of "pure air, peacefulness, quietude, and natural scenery." The growth of the city and its suburbs — and indeed the maintenance of the very life of the city — depended on improvements in urban transportation.

Old city streets were in many cases too narrow for the heavy traffic that was beginning to move over them. A few were paved with cobblestones, but most of them lacked a hard surface and were filled alternately with mud and dust. In the last decades of the century, more and more streets were paved, usually with wooden blocks, bricks, or asphalt, but paving could not even keep up with the laying out of new thoroughfares. By 1890 Chicago had surfaced only about 600 of more than 2,000 miles of streets.

Up and down the streets of every city a variety of horse-drawn vehicles clattered — wagons and drays, hacks and omnibuses, and private carriages of many kinds — littering the ground with horse droppings that attracted

Street Scene, New York City
By 1895, horse-drawn streetcars had given way to electric trolleys, and steam-powered elevated trains to electrified lines. Cabs and other vehicles continued to be pulled by horses. From a drawing, "The Bowery at Night," by W. Louis Sonntag, Jr. (Museum of the City of New York)

flies in summer. The great cities of the time could hardly have existed without the horse, and many of them were nearly paralyzed when an epidemic of the epizootic, a horse disease, swept through the Northeast and the Midwest in the 1870s. In normal times the vehicles could scarcely move at the busiest hours of the day. As early as the 1850s New York visitors had been amazed by the frequency with which the "whole traffic of the city" came to a "deadlock."

Already streetcars drawn by horses were operating on rails laid down in many city streets; by 1866 New York had 16 lines using 800 cars and nearly 8,000 horses. Passengers found the horsecars smoother and a little faster than omnibuses, but not fast enough. In 1870 New York opened its first elevated railway, with cars pulled by steam locomotives, which were noisy and often scattered hot ashes on pedestrians below. New York, Chicago, San Francisco, and other cities experimented with cable cars, which were towed by an endless cable that moved underground and was powered by a stationary steam engine. A better solution came with the development of the electrified railway, which first appeared in Richmond, Virginia, in 1888, when 40 trolley cars began to run over a 12-mile line. Trolley systems spread rapidly, and by 1895 they were operating in 850 towns and cities, with a total of 10,000 miles of track. Interurban lines were beginning to be extended through the country-side. In 1897, putting streetcars below ground, Boston opened the first American subway, a mile and a half long.

The horsecar and then the trolley enabled cities to expand and suburbs to grow. As a rule, cities spread fastest along the radiating lines of transportation, in a kind of star-shaped pattern. They grew upward as well as outward. The technique of constructing skyscrapers, with cast-iron and then steel frames, was first perfected in Chicago, where a ten-story office building rose in 1884. By that time the electric elevator was replacing the steam-powered hoist and making possible safe and rapid vertical movement. As tall buildings became more numerous, traffic congestion increased on city streets.

Chicago had been forced to rebuild after a conflagration in 1871, and Boston suffered a disastrous fire the same year. While more fire-proof structures were appearing, wooden buildings continued to predominate in every city, and these were always in danger of going up in flames. To meet the hazard, volunteer fire fighters were beginning to give way to professional fire departments.

An even greater hazard was disease, especially in the slums, whence it often spread to the better areas of a city. Even though the germ theory was known to public-health experts, few people appreciated the relationship of sewage disposal and water contamination to such epidemic diseases as typhoid fever and cholera. To the end of the nineteenth century, most city dwellers relied on private vaults and cesspools for the disposal of human wastes. The water closet (flush toilet) had been perfected in the 1870s, and a number of cities had begun to extend their sewerage systems, but these seldom kept up with population growth. Besides, the sewer commonly emptied into an open ditch within the city limits or into a stream nearby, from which the city itself or some other city derived its drinking water. Philadelphia, for example, polluted its own water supply by pouring raw sewage into the Delaware River. By 1900 a few cities had fairly adequate sewage disposal, regular garbage collections, and water-purification systems.

Urbanization brought more than new conveniences and new insecurities. "The complex interrelationship of life in the modern city called for unprecedented precision," as the historian Oscar Handlin has written. "The arrival of all those integers who worked together, from whatever part of the city they inhabited, had to be coordinated to the moment. There was no natural span for such labor; arbitrary beginnings and ends had to be set and adhered to. The dictatorship of the clock and the schedule became absolute." Thus the modern city brought a new concept of time, which to rural Americans had been a matter of human whims and natural phenomena such as sunrises and sunsets. Rural Americans, still the great majority, had an ambivalent attitude toward the city. While a place of strong allure, it was also to them a place of poverty and sin, and of foreigners with their strange customs. However country people felt toward it, the city imposed its ways upon them as well as its own inhabitants. More and more, it set the pattern for American character and culture.

BOSS RULE

The new immigrants, like the old ones, came with high hopes to what they expected to be a land of opportunity. In New York harbor, where most of them arrived, they received a symbolic welcome from the Statue of Liberty after it was erected in 1886 as a gift from the people of France. The welcome was later to be spelled out in these words of Emma Lazarus, inscribed on the statue's base:

> *Give me your tired, your poor,*
> *Your huddled masses yearning to*
> *breathe free. . . .*

After landing, however, most of the newcomers faced frustration and bewilderment. Unused to city life, unable to speak English, scorned by native Americans and by rival immigrant groups as well, desperate for jobs, people of the various nationalities remained as "huddled masses" in the wretchedness of their separate ghettoes.

Needy families, both native and foreign-born, could look to private charitable societies for assistance, but generally these were run by middle-class humanitarians who insisted on middle-class standards of morality. Such societies operated on the belief that poverty was more commonly due to laziness and vice than to misfortune. After careful investigation they confined their help to the "deserving poor." In 1879, a year after its founding in London, the Salvation Army began its work in American cities, but at first it concentrated on religious revivals rather than on the relief of the homeless and hungry. Not till many years later was the government—local, state, or federal—to assume much responsibility for welfare work.

For most of the urban poor, especially the foreign-born and their families, the main welfare agency was the political machine, headed by a boss, who himself was typically of foreign birth or parentage, most commonly Irish. To maintain his power, the boss needed votes, and in exchange for these he offered favors of various kinds. He provided the poor with occasional relief, such as a basket of groceries or a bag of coal. He stepped in to save from jail those arrested for petty crimes. When he could, he found work for the unemployed. Most important, he rewarded his followers with political jobs, with opportunities to rise in the party organization.

The boss made money for himself and financed his machine through corruption. He awarded contracts for the construction of streets, sewers, public buildings, and other projects at prices well above the real cost, then divided the extra money with the contractors. He also sold franchises for the operation of public utilities such as street railways, waterworks, and electric light and power systems. Since many of the wealthiest and most prominent citizens profited from their dealings with him, he had strong support among the rich as well as the poor.

Boss rule was made possible if not inevitable by the weakness of city government. Within the government, no single official was given decisive power or responsibility. Power was divided among a number of officeholders—the mayor, the aldermen, and others—and was limited by the state legislature, which had the ultimate authority over municipal affairs. Centralizing power in his own hands, the boss together with his machine formed a sort of "invisible government" that made up for the inadequacy of the regular government. He might or might not hold an official position himself. Through his organization, upon which the politicians of his party depended for election, he controlled a majority of those who were in office.

From time to time middle-class reformers along with disgruntled politicians might manage to overthrow a boss, as they did with William M. Tweed of New York City's notorious "Tweed Ring" in 1871. Yet the system of boss rule continued to flourish, in New York and in other large cities, because the conditions that produced it remained essentially unchanged.

Capitalism and Its Critics

With the rise of big business, a varied rationale was developed to justify its methods and its consequences. There also appeared a variety of criticisms. Still, the philosophy of business prevailed not only among the captains of industry themselves but also among the majority of the American people.

SELF-MADE MEN

The economic revolution raised up a new ruling class in America. The industrialists and the investment bankers now sat in the seats of power formerly held by Southern planters and Northeastern merchants, by members of the old aristocracy of inherited wealth and the old middle class, by politicians and statesmen of the antebellum Webster-Clay model.

Before the Civil War there had been few millionaires in America; by 1892 there were more than 4,000 of them. Most of the new business tycoons had begun their careers from comfortable and privileged positions in the economic scale. But some—enough to invest the entire group with the aura of the American success story—had emerged from obscurity to riches. Andrew Carnegie had worked as a bobbin boy in a Pittsburgh cotton mill, James J. Hill had been a frontier clerk, John D. Rockefeller had started out as a clerk in a Cleveland commission house, and E. H. Harriman had begun as a broker's office boy. Regardless of economic background, the new millionaires were—or considered themselves to be—self-made men.

Many had gotten ahead through a ruthless disregard for the public welfare. Their attitude was epitomized by Commodore Vanderbilt's belligerent question: "Can't I do what I want with my own?" and by the much quoted statement of his son William: "The public be damned." Once, when the Commodore's lawyers warned him that a move he contemplated was illegal, he bellowed: "What do I care about the law? Hain't I got the power?" Men like Vanderbilt had the power, indeed. Through their financial contributions to politicians and to parties, by gifts of stock and outright bribes to political personages, they generally managed to get what they wanted from the national and the state governments. It was said that Standard Oil did everything to the Ohio legislature except to refine it. On one occasion a member of the Pennsylvania legislature was reported to have said: "Mr. Speaker, I move we adjourn unless the Pennsylvania Railroad has some more business for us to transact."

Wholesale bribery was a weapon in the notorious "Erie war" fought by Commodore Vanderbilt against Jay Gould and Jim Fisk for control of the Erie Railroad. Vanderbilt attempted to take over the Erie by buying stock, a move which his antagonists blocked by the simple expedient of printing more stock than he could purchase. When a bill to legalize the issue of the new stock was introduced in the New York legislature, Gould was present with $500,000, and also on hand was a Vanderbilt agent. Exactly how much money was paid out by both parties before the Commodore admitted defeat is not known. The market price of

The Modern Robber Barons

In this cartoon the millionaires of business are likened to the "robber barons" of the Middle Ages. As the serfs brought tribute to the feudal lords, so farmers, laborers, and small businessmen had to pay tribute in the form of wages and interest to the masters of the trusts. The term "robber baron" as a descriptive tag for the big businessmen of the period became popular and even passed into historical usage. From Puck *(1889).*

legislators during the fight was $15,000 a head. One influential and imaginative leader collected $75,000 from Vanderbilt and $100,000 from Gould.

Before passing judgment on the relation of business to government, however, it should be noted that in many cases the politicians deliberately created situations where they had to be bought—in effect, they blackmailed businessmen. And whatever indictments may be brought against the lords of business, these men were emphatically products of their environment; even the most crude and crass of their activities reflected prevailing mores in American society. The big corporations did a quick, if sometimes wasteful and ruthless, job of developing the country's potential economic resources. And the businessmen who headed the corporations ran various risks in whatever they did—the risk of overexpansion, the risk of unscrupulous competition. Not every businessman became a Rockefeller or a Gould.

Even the most ruthless of the tycoons were builders rather than wreckers. They were building, perhaps without realizing what they were doing, the basis of a great economic society. By integrating operations and cutting costs, they were, says Frederick Lewis Allen, opening the way to economical mass production: "In the process of playing remunerative games with the tokens that represented capital, the bankers and the steel men had introduced into America something new: twentieth-century industry, undisciplined still, but full of promise."

SURVIVAL OF THE FITTEST

Most tycoons believed that they had attained their wealth by exercising the old American and Protestant virtues of hard work, acquisitiveness, and thrift. They had gotten where they were because they deserved it; people who were not so fortunate were lazy, unintelligent, or profligate. In some way it was all connected with the moral law and with divine will. "God gave me my money," explained John D. Rockefeller.

To many businessmen, the formula of social Darwinism seemed to explain both their own success and the nature of the society in which they operated. Social Darwinism was Charles Darwin's law of evolution applied to social organization. As expounded by the Englishman Herbert Spencer, it taught that struggle was a normal human activity, especially in economic life. The weak went down, the strong endured and became stronger, and society was benefited because the unfit were eliminated and the fit survived.

Men who had risen to dominance by crushing their competitors were intrigued and comforted by a doctrine that justified any method that succeeded, and they proclaimed that wealth was a reward of competence. Carnegie, who made himself the leading disciple of Spencer in the United States, contended that the natural law of competition was responsible for the great material growth of the country: "It is here; we can not evade it; no substitutes for it have been found; and while the law may be sometimes hard on the individual, it is best for the race, because it insures the survival of the fittest in every department."

According to social Darwinism, all attempts by labor to raise its wages by forming unions and all endeavors by government to regulate economic activities would fail, because economic life was controlled by a natural law, the law of competition. This coincided with another supposed "law" that seemed to justify business practices and business dominance: the law of supply and demand as defined by Adam Smith and the classical economists. According to them, the economic system was like a great and delicate machine functioning by natural and automatic rules. The greatest among these rules, the law of supply and demand, determined all economic values—prices, wages, rents, interest rates—at a level that was just to all concerned. Supply and demand worked because man was essentially an economic creature who understood and followed his own interests, and because he operated in a free market where competition was open to all.

Businessmen mouthed the clichés of classical economics even though the combinations they were creating were undermining the foundations of the free competitive market and modifying, if not destroying, the validity of the law of supply and demand. Samuel C. T. Dodd, the lawyer who devised the trust organization for Standard Oil, spoke glowingly of the unrestrained right of competition and the unrestrained right of combination. What would happen to competition if combination triumphed, Dodd did not explain.

Leaders of Big Business

Reflecting the division of public opinion, contemporary writings about late nineteenth-century business leaders usually were either flattering or denunciatory. In the "muckraking" years of the early twentieth century, denunciation came to predominate. Thus Ida M. Tarbell, *The History of the Standard Oil Company* (1904), presented John D. Rockefeller as a predatory character who drove smaller oilmen out of business by unscrupulous means. Gustavus Myers, *The History of the Great American Fortunes* (1907), undertook to show that other successful businessmen had also amassed their wealth by crushing competitors and corrupting politicians, not by practicing the old-fashioned American virtues of honesty, thrift, and hard work.

The treatment of these businessmen became more favorable during the prosperous 1920s. In *The Rise of American Civilization* (1927) Charles and Mary Beard described them as "captains of industry" who contributed to industrial development through their remarkable powers of organization. During the depression of the 1930s, however, the pioneers of big business again fell into disrepute. Matthew Josephson gave them a name that most historians accepted in his popular book *The Robber Barons* (1934). Josephson compared them to feudal lords who got rich by preying on legitimate commerce.

Allan Nevins challenged the Josephson view in *John D. Rockefeller: The Heroic Age of American Enterprise*, which was originally published in 1940 and republished with revisions and elaborations in 1953. Nevins depicted Rockefeller as an industrial statesman who brought order and efficiency to the oil business. The Nevins interpretation reflected the changed attitude that came with World War II and the cold war, when it seemed to many Americans that the industrial greatness of the United States made possible a successful effort to save the world from totalitarianism.

Meanwhile, from the 1920s on, historians at the Harvard Business School and elsewhere were writing business history without moral judgments. These "entrepreneurial historians," among them Kenneth W. Porter and Thomas C. Cochran, were primarily interested in techniques of management, in the kinds of decision-making that had led particular companies to success or to failure. Such writers looked for object lessons in the past that might be of value to business managers in the present.

Tempering the principle of the survival of the fittest was the "gospel of wealth." If rich men held economic power, they also had responsibilities to exercise their power with Christian magnanimity. If God gave the tycoons their money, as John D. Rockefeller believed, it behooved them to use the money for social purposes.

Carnegie himself elaborated on the idea in his book *The Gospel of Wealth* (1901). The man of wealth, he wrote, ought to consider all revenues in excess of his own needs as "trust funds" that he should administer for the good of the community, "thus becoming the mere trustee and agent for his poorer brethren." Carnegie did not believe in giving directly to the poor, for he feared that such charity would have a pauperizing effect. He preferred to contribute to institutions, notably libraries, that presumably would help the poor to help themselves. He and other men of wealth devoted part of their fortunes to philanthropic works.

The notion of private wealth as a public blessing was spread by numerous popularizers. One of the most persistent was Russell H. Conwell, a Baptist minister, who delivered one lecture on the subject, *Acres of Diamonds*, over 6,000 times. "We ought to get rich if we can by honorable and Christian methods," cried Conwell (who got rich by lecturing), "and those are the only methods that sweep us quickly toward the goal of riches."

Conwell was a champion of another concept that was becoming a part of the American myth: the success story, the notion that any poor boy who was industrious and thrifty could succeed in business. Most of the millionaires in the country, Conwell claimed, had begun on the lowest rung of the economic ladder. Another promoter of the success story was Horatio Alger, a New York minister who wrote over a hundred novels of which, all together, more than 20 million copies were sold. These books rejoiced in such titles as *Andy Grant's Pluck*, *Tom the Bootblack*, and *Sink or Swim*. In every volume a poor boy from a small town went to the big city to seek his fortune, and by work, perseverance, and luck he became rich.

DOUBT AND DISSENT

Most people, poor as well as rich, accepted the rationalizations that were made by and for big business, but there were many who listened to voices of doubt and dissent. Thoughtful Americans did not agree among themselves on the lessons to be derived from Darwin's theory of evolution.

It was, perhaps, characteristic of optimistic Americans to combine the Darwinian method with the older idea of progress and come up with a hopeful prognostication. Such an analysis was attempted by Lewis H. Morgan, a pioneer anthropologist, in his *Ancient Society* (1878), in which he traced human development from its first simple beginnings to the complex but beneficent industrial order of the nineteenth century. The works of men like Morgan stressed that change was gradual and cumulative in character and that present society was safely linked with the past. Although such writers foresaw a hopeful future, they rejected the concept of unlimited progress that had marked earlier American thought. They also departed from former notions in insisting that change was evolutionary instead of revolutionary and that American development was a phase of a larger European or world scheme and not a unique experiment in a specially favored land. Opposing directions taken by American Darwinians are illustrated by the writings of two pioneers in sociology: William Graham Sumner and Lester F. Ward.

Sumner, a scholar with a tough mind and a sharp tongue, elaborated his theories in lectures at Yale, in magazine articles, and finally in a famous book, *Folkways* (1906). In contradiction to earlier thinkers who had held that man was a free agent actuated by rational powers, Sumner contended that the human mind was molded by circumstances beyond its control and that men's activities consisted of routine behavior determined by mechanistic forces. In short, man had no innate ideas and no power to reform his environment. His freedom was limited to certain narrow areas in which tradition permitted him to operate. But within these areas, Sumner insisted, man must have absolute freedom to struggle, to compete, to gratify his instinct for self-interest. The struggle for survival should be allowed to work itself out, and should not be delimited by laws or the state. Sumner's devotion to the principle of the survival of the fittest caused him to be known as the foremost champion of social Darwinism. Yet his insistence on the freedom to compete caused him to oppose protective tariffs and thus made him a critic of business policy. Essentially, he was trying to preserve the older America of truly free enterprise by employing the new insights of Darwinism.

Standing in direct opposition to Sumner was Lester Ward, though he was just as much a Darwinian as the Yale sage. Ward expressed his concepts in a number of notable books, beginning with *Dynamic Sociology* (1883). He argued that various forces altered the Darwinian process when applied to complex societies. Desire became subordinate to and controlled by intelligence. Mind thus became the master of nature, and man became capable of devising instruments to direct and improve his evolutionary future. The chief goal of modern society, Ward said, was the greatest good of all its members, and the best instrument to attain the goal was government. In contrast to Sumner, who believed that state intervention to remodel the environment was futile, Ward thought that a positive, planning government was man's only hope.

There came to be widespread acceptance of the principle that institutions should meet social needs and thus be "functional." Even in the churches there was an effort to accommodate functional concepts. Noted ministers and theologians like Washington Gladden, Walter Rauschenbusch, and Shailer Mathews proclaimed that religion had to concern itself with the material conditions in which Christ's children lived, and these men advocated such causes as industrial peace, better working conditions, slum clearance, and temperance.

SOCIALISTS AND SINGLE-TAXERS

While some Americans questioned the beneficence of capitalism, others proposed more or less drastic changes in the system, and at least a few thought it should be thrown out entirely.

Americans were less inclined than Europeans to adopt extremely radical programs such as the "scientific socialism" of Karl Marx (whose *Capital*, the first volume of which appeared in 1867, was one of the most influential books ever written) or the violent anarchism of Mikhail Bakunin. But Marxism and Anarchism had some following in America, especially among recent immigrants.

The Socialist Labor party, founded in the seventies, fell under the leadership of Daniel De Leon, an immigrant from the West Indies;

other party chiefs hailed from Eastern Europe. Although De Leon aroused something of a following in the industrial cities, the party never succeeded in polling over 82,000 votes. De Leon's somewhat theoretical and dogmatic approach pleased intellectuals but evoked no warmth among workers and seemed ill-suited to the American scene. A right-wing faction of the party sensed the fault in its approach and, seeking a more American approach, split away in 1900 to form the Socialist party.

Native radicals, with less extreme programs, gained a wider following. One of the most influential was Henry George. His angrily eloquent *Progress and Poverty*, published in 1879, was an immediate success; reprinted in successive editions, it became one of the ten best-selling nonfiction works in American publishing history. George addressed himself to the question of why poverty existed amidst the wealth created by modern industry. "This association of poverty with progress is the great enigma of our times," he wrote. "So long as all the increased wealth which modern progress brings goes but to build up great fortunes, to increase luxury and make sharper the contrast between the House of Have and the House of Want, progress is not real and cannot be permanent."

George blamed all this on monopoly, and he proposed a remedy, a "single tax" on the "unearned increment" in the value of land. An increase in the value of land resulted from the growth of society around it. Hence, George argued, the private owner had not earned the increment, and the community should receive it. A tax taking the whole of this increase would supposedly destroy monopolies, distribute wealth more equally, and eliminate poverty. Single-tax societies sprang up in many cities, and in 1886 George, backed by labor and the Socialists, narrowly missed being elected mayor of New York.

Rivaling George in popularity was Edward Bellamy, whose *Looking Backward*, published in 1888, became a best seller within a few years and eventually topped the million mark. Bellamy's book was a novel, a romance of a socialist utopia. It described the experiences of a young Bostonian who in 1887 went into a hypnotic sleep from which he awakened in the year 2000. He found a new social order, based on collective ownership of property, where want, politics, and vice were unknown, and where people were incredibly happy. All this had come about through a peaceful and evolutionary process: trusts had gone on combining with one another until they formed one big trust, and the government had taken this over. Shortly, over 160 "Nationalist Clubs" sprang up to propagate Bellamy's ideas, and the author devoted the remainder of his life to championing his brand of socialism.

Thirty-eight similar novels appeared in the nineties, though none of them approached Bellamy's in success. It is not to be thought that the hundreds of thousands of Americans who read Bellamy and the other utopian authors wished to see a socialist system established in the United States. Nor were they merely seeking in literary fantasies an escape from the real problems of their times. The great majority were intrigued by the descriptions of societies that were prosperous and stable because government played a large role, and in their own troubled society they saw the need, not for a collective state, but for a larger place for government.

More realistic was the philosophy in Henry Demarest Lloyd's *Wealth Against Commonwealth*. Published in 1894, this book was a tremendous, although not always accurate, attack on the Standard Oil trust and the methods by which it had risen to dominance. Lloyd advocated strict governmental regulation of such monopolies.

Industrial Conflict

Very few industrial workers or labor leaders in late nineteenth-century America aimed to overthrow capitalism itself. What most of them wanted was a larger share of its benefits. Their efforts to get a larger share led to industrial conflicts that were often bitter and sometimes bloody.

LABOR ORGANIZES

As business became big, consolidated, and national, inevitably labor attempted to create its own organizations that would match the power of capital. The economic revolution changed the worker from an artisan who owned his own tools to a factory laborer who operated machines owned by his employer; it placed his wages, his tenure, his working environment at the pleasure of an impersonal corporation too powerful for the individual worker to bargain with. Between 1865 and 1897—a period of falling prices and a consequent decline in the cost of living—real wages increased, except for those workers who lost their jobs because of technological or cyclical unemployment. Nevertheless, at the turn of the century the income of the average worker was pitifully small: $400–$500 a year. Students of the standard of living estimated that, to maintain a decent level of comfort, a yearly income of $600 was the absolute minimum. According to one survey, 10 million Americans lived in poverty. The average workday in 1900 was ten hours, for a six-day week. Because employers paid little attention to safety devices or programs, the accident rate was appalling: 1 in every 26 railroad workers was injured, 1 in every 399 killed per year.

Against such conditions, labor fought back by forming unions to bargain collectively with employers. During the Civil War, twenty craft unions were formed, and by 1870 the industrial states counted thirty such organizations, nearly every one of which represented skilled workers. The first attempt to federate separate unions into a single national organization came in 1866, when, under the leadership of William H. Sylvis, the National Labor Union was founded. Claiming a membership of 640,000, it was a polyglot association that included, in addition to a number of unions, a variety of reform groups having little direct relationship with labor. After the Panic of 1873 the National Labor Union disintegrated and disappeared.

The trade unions experienced stormy times during the hard years of the 1870s. Their bargaining power weakened by depression conditions, they faced antagonistic employers eager to destroy them, and a hostile public that rejected labor's claim to job security. Several of the disputes with capital were unusually bitter and were marked by violence, some of it labor's fault and some not, but for all of which labor received the blame. Startling to most

Americans was the exposure of the activities of the "Molly Maguires" in the anthracite coal region of Pennsylvania. A terrorist group, the "Mollies" operated within the Ancient Order of Hibernians (that is, Irishmen) and intimidated the coal operators with such direct methods as murder. But excitement over this was nothing compared to the near hysteria that gripped the country during the railroad strikes of 1877. The trouble started when the principal Eastern railroads announced a 10-percent slash in wages. Immediately railroad workers, whether organized or not, went out on strike. Rail service was disrupted from Baltimore to St. Louis, equipment was destroyed, and rioting mobs roamed the streets of Pittsburgh and other cities.

The strikes were America's first big labor conflict and a flaming illustration of a new reality in the American economic system: with business becoming nationalized, disputes between labor and capital could no longer be localized but would affect the entire nation. State militia were employed against the strikers, and finally, and significantly, federal troops were called on to suppress the disorders. The power of the various railroad unions was seriously sapped by the failure of the strikes, and the prestige of unions in other industries was weakened by similar setbacks.

THE KNIGHTS AND THE AFL

Meanwhile, another national labor organization appeared on the scene, the Noble Order of the Knights of Labor, founded in 1869 under the leadership of Uriah S. Stephens. Instead of attempting to federate unions, as the National Labor Union had done, the Knights organized their association on the basis of the individual. Membership was open to all who "toiled," and the definition of a toiler was extremely liberal: the only excluded groups were lawyers, bankers, liquor dealers, and professional gamblers. The amorphous masses of members were arranged in local "assemblies" that might consist of the workers in a particular trade or a local union or simply all the members of the Knights in a city or district. Presiding laxly over the entire order was an agency known as the general assembly. Much of the program of the Knights was as vague as the organization. Although they championed an eight-hour day and the

abolition of child labor, the leaders were more interested in the long-range reform of the economy than in the immediate objectives of wages and hours which appealed to the trade unions.

Under the leadership of Terence V. Powderly, the order entered upon a spectacular period of expansion that culminated in 1886 with the total membership reaching 700,000. Important factors contributing to the increase in numerical strength were a business recession in 1884 that threw many workers out of jobs, and a renewal of industrial strife that impelled unorganized laborers as well as some trade unions to affiliate with the Knights. Not only was the membership enlarged, but the order now included many militant elements that could not always be controlled by the moderate leadership. Against Powderly's wishes, local unions or assemblies associated with the Knights proceeded to inaugurate a series of strikes. In 1885 striking railway workers forced the Missouri Pacific, a link in the Gould system, to restore wage cuts and recognize their union. Although this victory redounded to the credit of the Knights, it was an ephemeral triumph. In the following year a strike on another Gould road, the Texas and Pacific, was crushed and the power of the unions in the Gould system was broken. By 1890 the membership of the Knights had shrunk to 100,000, and within a few years the order would be a thing of the past.

Even before the Knights had entered on their period of decline, a rival organization, based on an entirely different organizational concept, had appeared. In 1881 representatives of a number of craft unions formed the Federation of Organized Trade and Labor Unions of the United States and Canada. Five years later this body took the name which it has borne ever since, the American Federation of Labor (AFL). Under the direction of its president and guiding spirit, Samuel Gompers, the Federation soon became the most important labor group in the country. As its name implies, it was a federation or association of national trade unions, each of which enjoyed essential autonomy within the larger organization. Rejecting completely the idea of individual membership and the corollary of one big union for everybody, the Federation was built on the principle of the organization of skilled workers into craft unions.

The Haymarket Tragedy
This is a contemporary artist's conception of the bomb exploding among the police.
(Library of Congress)

The program of the Federation differed as markedly from that of the Knights as did its organizational arrangements. Gompers and his associates accepted the basic concepts of capitalism; their purpose was to secure for labor a greater share of capitalism's material rewards. Repudiating all notions of fundamental alteration of the existing system or long-range reform measures or a separate labor party, the AFL concentrated on labor's immediate objectives: wages, hours, and working conditions. While it hoped to attain its ends by collective bargaining, the Federation was ready to employ the strike if necessary.

As one of its first objectives, the Federation called for a national eight-hour day, to be attained by May 1, 1886, and to be obtained, if necessary, by a general strike. On the target day, strikes and demonstrations for a shorter workday took place all over the country. Although the national officers of the Knights had refused to cooperate in the movement, some local units joined in the demonstrations. So did a few unions that were dominated by anarchists—European radicals who wanted to destroy "class government" by terroristic methods—and that were affiliated with the so-called Black International. The most sensational demonstrations occurred in Chicago, which was a labor stronghold and an anarchist center.

At the time, a strike was in progress at the McCormick Harvester Company; and when the police harassed the strikers, labor and anarchist leaders called a protest meeting at the Haymarket Square. During the meeting, the police appeared and commanded those present to disperse. Someone—his identity was never determined—threw a bomb that resulted in the death of seven policemen and injury to sixty-seven others. The police, who on the previous day had killed four strikers, fired into the crowd and killed four more people. The score was about even. News of the Haymarket affair struck cold fear into Chicago and the business community of the nation. Blinded by hysteria, conservative, property-conscious Americans demanded a victim or victims—to demonstrate to labor that it must cease its course of violence. Chicago officials finally rounded up eight anarchists and charged them with the murder of the policemen on the grounds that they had incited the individual who hurled the bomb. In one of the most injudicious trials in the record of American juridical history, all were found guilty. One was sentenced to prison and seven to death. Of the seven, one cheated his sentence by committing suicide, four were executed, and two had their penalty commuted to life imprisonment.

Although some of the blame for the Haymarket tragedy was unloaded on the AFL, at least as much fell on the Knights, who had had almost nothing to do with the May demonstrations. In the public mind the Knights were dominated by anarchists and Socialists. The Knights never managed to free themselves from the stigma of radicalism as the AFL did.

THE HOMESTEAD STRIKE

Some of the most violent strikes in American labor history occurred in the nineties. Two of the strikes, the one at the Homestead plant of the Carnegie Steel Company in Pennsylvania

The Homestead Riot
The scene at the Homestead plant of the Carnegie Steel Company in Pennsylvania after the Pinkerton strikebreakers had surrendered to the striking employees. Drawing by W. P. Snyder in Harper's Weekly, *July 16, 1892. (Library of Congress)*

and the one against the Pullman Palace Car Company in the Chicago area, took place in companies controlled by men who prided themselves on being among the most advanced of American employers: Andrew Carnegie, who had written magazine articles defending the rights of labor, and George M. Pullman, who had built a "model town" to house his employees.

The Amalgamated Association of Iron and Steel Workers, which was affiliated with the American Federation of Labor, was the most powerful trade union in the country. It had never been able, however, to organize all the plants of the Carnegie Steel Company, the largest corporation in the industry; of the three major steel mills in the Carnegie system, the union was a force only in one, the Homestead plant. In 1892, when the strike occurred, Carnegie was in Scotland, visiting at a castle that he maintained as a gesture of ancestral pride, and the direction of the company was in the hands of Henry Clay Frick, manager of Homestead and chairman of the Carnegie firm. Carnegie was, nevertheless, responsible for the company's course. Despite his earlier fine words about labor, he had decided with Frick before leaving to operate Homestead on a nonunion basis, even if this meant precipitating a clash with the union.

The trouble began when the management announced a new wage scale that would have meant cuts for a small minority of the workers. Frick abruptly shut down the plant, and asked the Pinkerton Detective Agency to furnish 300 guards to enable the company to resume operations on its own terms. (The Pinkerton Agency was really a strikebreaking concern.)

The hated Pinkertons, whose mere presence was enough to incite the workers to violence, approached the plant on barges in an adjacent river. Warned of their coming, the strikers met them at the docks with guns and dynamite, and a pitched battle ensued on July 6, 1892. After several hours of fighting, which brought death to three guards and ten strikers and severe injuries to many participants on both sides, the Pinkertons surrendered and were escorted roughly out of town. The company and local law officials then asked for militia protection from the Pennsylvania governor, who responded by sending the entire National Guard contingent, some 8,000 troops, to Home-

stead. Public opinion, at first sympathetic to the strikers, turned against them when an anarchist made an attempt to assassinate Frick. Slowly workers drifted back to their jobs.

THE PULLMAN STRIKE

A dispute of greater magnitude and equal bitterness, although involving less loss of life, was the Pullman strike in 1894. The Pullman Palace Car Company leased sleeping and parlor cars to most of the nation's railroads. At its plant near Chicago it manufactured and repaired cars. The company had built the 600-acre town of Pullman, containing dwellings that were rented to the employees. George M. Pullman, inventor of the sleeping car and owner of the company, liked to exhibit his town as a model solution of the industrial problem and to refer to the workers as his "children."

Nearly all of the workers were members of a union, a very militant one, the American Railway Union. This had recently been organized by Eugene V. Debs, a labor leader formerly active in the Railroad Brotherhoods. Becoming disgusted with the Brotherhoods' lack of interest in the lot of the unskilled workers, he had formed his own union, which soon attained a membership of 150,000, mainly in the Middle West.

The strike at Pullman began when the company during the winter of 1893–1894 slashed wages by an average of 25 percent. With revenues reduced by depression conditions, there was some reason for the company's action, but the cut was drastic, and several workers who served on a committee to protest to the management were discharged. At the same time, Pullman refused to reduce rentals in the model town, even though the charges were 20 to 25 percent higher than for comparable accommodations in surrounding areas. The strikers appealed to the Railway Union for support, and that organization voted to refuse to handle Pullman cars and equipment.

The General Managers' Association, representing twenty-four Chicago railroads, prepared to fight the boycott. Switchmen who refused to handle Pullman cars were summarily discharged. Whenever this happened, the union instructed its members to quit work. Within a few days thousands of railroad workers in twenty-seven states and territories were

Contrasting Opinions on the Pullman Strike [1894]

Eugene Debs issued this appeal for support of the boycott of Pullman cars:

To the Railway Employes of America: The struggle with the Pullman Company has developed into a contest between the producing classes and the money power of the country. We stand upon the ground that the workingmen are entitled to a just proportion of the proceeds of their labor. This the Pullman Company denied them. Reductions had been made from time to time until the employees earned barely sufficient wages to live, not enough to prevent them from sinking deeper and deeper into Pullman's debt, thereby mortgaging their bodies and souls, as well as their children's, to that heartless corporation.

One editor thus denounced the boycott:

The brigand who demands ransom for his prisoner, with mutilation or death as the alternative; the police captain who sells for money his power to arrest the dealers in vice and crime; the newsmonger who gathers scandal in order that he may be paid for suppressing it — these are the types of blackmailers whom all the world loathes. The boycott ordered by the railway union is morally no better than any of these acts. It is an attempt at blackmail on the largest scale.

---

on strike, and transportation from Chicago to the Pacific coast was paralyzed.

Ordinarily, state governors responded readily to appeals from strike-threatened business, but the governor of Illinois was different. John P. Altgeld had pardoned the Haymarket anarchists remaining in prison. Business was not likely to appeal to such an executive for aid, and Altgeld was not the man to employ militia to smash a strike.

By-passing Altgeld, the railroad operators besought the national government to send regular army troops to Illinois. At the same time federal postal officials and marshals were bombarding Washington with information that the strike was preventing the movement of mail on the trains. President Cleveland was inclined to gratify the companies, and so was his Attorney General, Richard Olney, a former railroad lawyer and a bitter foe of labor. Cleveland and Olney decided that the government could employ the army to keep the mails moving, and in July 1894 the President, over Altgeld's protest, ordered 2,000 troops to the Chicago area.

At Olney's suggestion, government lawyers obtained from a federal court an order restraining Debs and other union officials from interfering with the interstate transportation of the mails. This "blanket injunction" was so broad in scope that it practically forbade Debs and his associates to continue the strike. They ignored the injunction and were arrested, tried for contempt of court (without a jury trial), and sentenced to six months in prison. With federal troops protecting the hiring of new workers and with the union leaders in a federal jail, the strike quickly collapsed.

It left a bitter heritage. Labor was convinced that the government was not a neutral arbiter representing the common interest, but a supporter of one side alone. Debs emerged from prison a martyr in the eyes of workingmen, a convert to Marxian socialism, and a dedicated enemy of capital.

Despite all the organizations that were formed and all the strikes and demonstrations that were so hopefully launched, labor accomplished relatively little for its cause in the years between 1865 and 1900. Its leaders could point to a few legislative victories: the abolition by Congress in 1885 of the Contract Labor law; the establishment by Congress in 1868 of an eight-hour day on public works and in 1892 of the same work period for government employees; and a host of state laws governing hours of labor and safety standards, most of which were not enforced. But an overwhelming majority of employers still regarded labor as a force to be disregarded when possible and to be crushed when practicable, and the American public in overwhelming numbers considered unions to be alien and dangerous elements in the national economy.

Labor's greatest weakness was that only a small part of its vast strength was organized.

The AFL with its half million members, and the Railroad Brotherhoods (engineers, conductors, firemen, trainmen) represented the skilled workers, but the mass of laborers were not enrolled in any union. All told, only 868,500 workers were union members at the turn of the century. Big Business was firmly entrenched; Big Labor awaited the future.

Selected Readings

General Accounts
I. M. Tarbell, *The Nationalizing of Business, 1878–1898* (1936); S. P. Hays, *The Response to Industrialism, 1885–1914** (1957); E. C. Kirkland, *Industry Comes of Age: Business, Labor, and Public Policy, 1860–1897* (1961); Rendig Fels, *American Business Cycles, 1865–1897* (1959).

Inventions and Industries
Roger Burlingame, *Engines of Democracy: Inventions and Society in Mature America* (1940); Matthew Josephson, *Edison** (1959); R. N. Current, *The Typewriter and the Men Who Made It* (1954); H. C. Passer, *The Electrical Manufacturers, 1875–1900* (1953); R. A. Clemens, *The American Livestock and Meat Industry* (1932); C. B. Kuhlmann, *The Development of the Flour-Milling Industry in the United States* (1929).

The Railroads
G. R. Taylor and I. D. Neu, *The American Railroad Network, 1861–1900* (1956); E. G. Campbell, *The Reorganization of the American Railroad System, 1893–1900* (1938); J. F. Stover, *Railroads of the South, 1865–1900* (1955); R. E. Overton, *Burlington West: A Colonization History of the Burlington Railroad* (1941) and *Gulf to Rockies* (1953); James McCague, *Moguls and Iron Men* (1964), on the transcontinental lines.

Business Leaders
Matthew Josephson, *The Robber Barons** (1934); T. C. Cochran, *Railroad Leaders, 1845–1900* (1953); Allan Nevins, *Study in Power: John D. Rockefeller* (2 vols., 1953); B. J. Hendrick, *Andrew Carnegie* (2 vols., 1932); J. F. Wall, *Andrew Carnegie* (1971).

Capitalism, Pro and Con
E. C. Kirkland, *Dream and Thought in the Business Community, 1860–1900** (1956); Sidney Fine, *Laissez Faire and the General Welfare State: A Study of Conflict in American Thought, 1865–1901** (1956); Richard Hofstadter, *Social Darwinism in American Thought** (1944); I. G. Wyllie, *The Self-Made Man in America** (1954); A. E. Morgan, *Edward Bellamy* (1944); C. A. Barker, *Henry George* (1955); Samuel Churgerman, *Lester F. Ward, the American Aristotle* (1939); C. M. Destler, *Henry Demarest Lloyd and the Empire of Reform* (1963); H. H. Quint, *The Forging of American Socialism* (1953).

Immigration and Poverty
Oscar Handlin, *The Uprooted* (1951); John Higham, *Strangers in the Land* (1955); Barbara Solomon, *Ancestors and Immigrants** (1956); M. A. Jones, *American Immigration** (1960); R. H. Bremner, *From the Depths: The Discovery of Poverty in the United States* (1956); Jacob Riis, *How the Other Half Lives** (1890); C. D. Long, *Wages and Earnings in the United States, 1860–1890* (1960).

The Labor Movement
Henry Pelling, *American Labor** (1960); N. J. Ware, *The Labor Movement in the United States, 1860–1893** (1929); Philip Taft, *The A. F. of L. in the Time of Gompers* (1957); Bernard Mandel, *Samuel Gompers* (1963); S. B. Kaufman, *Samuel Gompers and the Origins of the American Federation of Labor* (1973); R. V. Bruce, *1877: Year of Violence* (1959); Henry David, *History of the Haymarket Affair* (1936); A. L. Lindsay, *The Pullman Strike** (1942); Harry Barnard, *"Eagle Forgotten": The Life of John Peter Altgeld** (1938); Ray Ginger, *Altgeld's America—Lincoln Ideal Versus Changing Realities** (1958).

Urban Development
A. M. Schlesinger, *The Rise of the City, 1878–1898* (1933); Blake McKelvey, *The Urbanization of America, 1860–1915* (1963); C. M. Green, *The Rise of Urban America* (1965); C. N. Glaab and A. T. Brown, *A His-*

*tory of Urban America** (1967); S. B. Warner, Jr., *Streetcar Suburbs: The Process of Growth in Boston, 1870–1900** (1962) and *The Urban Wilderness: A History of the American City** (1973); Stephan Thernstrom, *The Other Bostonians: Poverty and Progress in the American Metropolis, 1880–1970* (1973); David Ward, *Cities and Immigrants: A Geography of Change in Nineteenth Century America* (1971); C. W. Patton, *The Battle for Municipal Reform: Mobilization and Attack, 1875–1900* (1940).

*Titles available in paperback.

The End of the Old Frontier

Eighteen

The census report for 1890 noted that the unsettled area of the West had been "so broken into by isolated bodies of settlement" that a continuous frontier line could no longer be drawn. Three years later a young historian from the University of Wisconsin, Frederick Jackson Turner, startled the American Historical Association with a memorable paper, "The Significance of the Frontier in American History." The roots of the national character, Turner asserted, lay not so much in the East or in Europe as in the West. As he saw it, "the existence of an area of free land, its continuous recession, and the advance of settlement westward, explain American development." This experience, by stimulating individualism, nationalism, and democracy, had made Americans the distinctive people that they were. "Now," Turner concluded ominously, "four centuries from the discovery of America, at the end of a hundred years of life under the Constitution, the frontier has gone, and with its going has closed the first period of American history."

The foreboding of Professor Turner was, in one respect, a bit premature. A vast public domain still existed in 1890, and during the forty years thereafter the government was to give away many more acres than it had given as homesteads before that time. Nevertheless, most of the best farming land had already been taken up. Gone was the chance of acquiring a farm for little or nothing, of cultivating it at a relatively low cost, of selling it at a profit and moving on west to start all over again.

In the passing of the frontier, perhaps the greatest loss to the American people was a psychological one. So long as the country had remained open at one end, there had seemed to be constantly revitalizing opportunities in Americian life. Now there was a vague, premonitory sense of being hemmed in. The psychological loss was all the greater because of what Henry Nash Smith in *Virgin Land* (1950) has called the

Railroad Construction in the West
Railroads preceded settlement on much of the last frontier. Here workers are setting new speed records as they lay track across the bare plains from Minot, Dakota Territory, to Helena, Montana Territory, in 1887. This stretch later became part of the Great Northern Railway. (Burlington Northern photo)

"myth of the garden," the once widely held belief (to be found in many poems, novels, and other writings) that the West was a kind of potential Garden of Eden where life could be begun anew and all the ideals of democracy realized. The setting for utopia, once the New World as a whole, had shrunk to the West of the United States. To some extent Professor Turner himself reflected the myth in his "frontier interpretation" of American history.

Actually, long before 1890, the city had come to replace the "virgin land" as the symbol of opportunity in America. The great folk movement of the time was from the country to the city, not the other way around. But American values had long been shaped by the rural background in which most of the people were brought up. Only slowly and with considerable stress did these values change in response to the more and more pervasive influence of the urban environment. Change they nevertheless did, and in the last decades of the nineteenth century the culture of the city came to predominate in American civilization.

The Last West

In 1860 the frontier line, the western rim of settlement, conformed roughly to the western boundaries of the tier of states immediately beyond the Mississippi—Minnesota, Iowa, Missouri, Arkansas—jutting outward to include the eastern parts of Nebraska and Kansas and cutting across central Texas. West of this line was a huge expanse inhabited by roving Indians and wild animals, and peopled only thinly by whites until the settled districts of California and Oregon on the Pacific coast were reached. Within the confines of this vast West are three distinct natural, or physiographic, regions: the Great Plains, the Rocky Mountains, and the Basin and Plateau region between the Rockies on the east and the Sierra Nevada–Cascade mountain chain on the west.

DELAYED SETTLEMENT

When the westward-pushing pioneers entered upon the Great Plains, they saw a strange and even alien environment, utterly different from the fertile prairie lands behind them or the wooded areas of the Ohio Valley and the East. The physical features that in combination distinguish the Great Plains from earlier frontiers are a level surface, a dearth of timber, and a deficiency in rainfall. Early explorers had dubbed this region "the Great American Desert," and in the 1840s settlers had hastened through it on their way to California and Ore-gon. Its forbidding reputation was largely responsible for the curious fact that the frontier, after crossing the Mississippi, had jumped 1,500 miles to the Pacific coast.

By the 1860s, however, people had begun to head for the unsettled parts of the West. They were attracted by gold and silver deposits, by the short-grass pasture for cattle and sheep, and finally by the plains' sod and the mountain meadowland that seemed suitable for farming or ranching.

Settlement was encouraged by the great transcontinental railroad lines. These roads and their feeders moved settlers and supplies into the vast interior spaces and furnished access to outside markets; they provided what the region could not have had without them— the basis for a permanent population and a durable economy. In addition, they directly excited migration by disposing of their lands to settlers. All told, in national and state land grants, the railroads owned over 183 million acres. Although some companies attempted to reserve their lands or sell them at fancy prices, most of the lines realized that an increased population meant larger freight and passenger revenues. Consequently, they offered land for as little as $2.50 an acre, advertised the glories of the West in the East and in Europe, and transported prospective buyers at reduced rates.

Settlement was also encouraged by the land policy of the federal government, though

III. AFTER THE CIVIL WAR:
Academic Tradition and Its Challengers

Plate 1: Albert Bierstadt, THE ROCKY MOUNTAINS *(The Metropolitan Museum of Art, Rogers Fund, 1907)*

The post-Civil War period was characterized by a tremendous growth of industry, bringing with it a class of wealthy businessmen who turned to works of art to reflect both their nationalistic pride and their newfound status. Although American artists continued to look to European models for inspiration, in landscape painting the wonders of the newly explored far West generated an intense interest. With the same reverent feeling for the land that had earlier inspired the Hudson River painters, artists of the so-called Rocky Mountain School created grandiose panoramas of the Western wilderness, emphasizing the rugged terrain and unlimited horizons.

The most popular of these painters was Albert Bierstadt, born in Germany but brought to Massachusetts as a child. Bierstadt went to Europe for his training at the Düsseldorf Academy, but on his return to

America in 1857 he joined an expedition mapping an overland route across the Rocky Mountains to the Pacific Ocean. His firsthand observations of nature on this trip and many others are evident in the minute attention to topographical detail and the expressive textural quality to be found in Bierstadt's work. His paintings became increasingly popular and brought unprecedented prices from wealthy middle-class collectors. Although Bierstadt's huge canvases, such as "The Rocky Mountains," 1863 *(Plate 1)*, were painted inside the artist's studio, they were based on sketches made on location and provided an accurate if melodramatic sense of the expanding American frontier.

The large canvases of the Rocky Mountain School found adequate wall space in the high-ceilinged rooms of the Victorian period. The family portrait painted by Eastman Johnson in 1871 for the prominent New York

Plate 2: Eastman Johnson, THE HATCH FAMILY *(The Metropolitan Museum of Art, Gift of Frederic H. Hatch, 1926)*

stockbroker A. S. Hatch *(Plate 2)* shows a gilt-framed landscape panorama among the ornate furnishings and heavy wine-colored drapery of the drawing room.

Johnson, like Bierstadt, had acquired his technical facility at the Düsseldorf Academy, and his skill is evident in the informal arrangement of the large group of family members. In addition, his careful recording of specific detail in furniture and clothing provides an accurate picture of an upper-middle-class American home and family in the 1870s.

Although Americans traveled to other European academies for their artistic education, the Ecole des Beaux Arts in Paris remained throughout the nineteenth century by far the most important center of formal training. Augustus Saint-Gaudens, after his return from Parisian study in 1875, became the dominant figure in American sculpture during the last quarter of the century. He rejected the neoclassicism that had previously influenced American sculptors, such as Greenough, in favor of a greater naturalism that included more textured surfaces and

more realistic poses. Saint-Gaudens's innovations in the design of commemorative statuary are exemplified by his Sherman Monument in New York's Central Park, 1903 *(Plate 3)*. Unlike Greenough's stiffly posturing George Washington, Sherman is seated on horseback, and the rhythmically flowing robes of the winged allegorical figure beside him contribute to the general feeling of movement. Again in contrast to the Greenough, the sturdy, sculpturally conceived pedestal makes the whole statue appropriate for its outdoor setting.

Philadelphian Thomas Eakins also studied in Paris, where he learned the value of close observation and the precise technique which would characterize his painting throughout his long career.

Eakins's love for sports and the out-of-doors were combined in his 1871 painting of his boyhood friend Max Schmitt *(Plate 4)*. The artist's psychological insight, which is most evident in his portrayal of individual character, along with his life-long interest in anatomy and the scientific laws of perspective, enabled him to develop an objective style

Plate 3: Augustus Saint-Gaudens, SHERMAN MEMORIAL *(Photo by Sandak)*

Plate 4: Thomas Eakins, MAX SCHMITT IN A SINGLE SCULL
(The Metropolitan Museum of Art, Alfred N. Punnett Fund and gift of George D. Pratt, 1934; Photo by Sandak)

devoid of the sentimentality common to the period. In this remarkable portrait, the clarity of the composition and the brilliant technical handling of the light reinforce the honesty of the artist's perception.

Before the founding of the first architectural school in America after the Civil War, an individual interested in a career as a professional architect had two roads open to him. He might apprentice himself to an established architect and, after long years of diligent work, strike out on his own. Or he could sail to Europe, enroll at the Ecole des Beaux Arts in Paris and, after completing the course of study, return to America with the academic stamp of approval.

One of the first Americans to study architecture at the Ecole in Paris was Henry Hobson Richardson. He returned to Boston in 1865 and began his practice modestly in domestic design. But in 1872 he entered and won the competition for Trinity Church, Boston *(Plate 6)*. Richardson followed accepted nineteenth-century practice by cloaking his building in a style borrowed from the past, in this case the massive French Romanesque. The building, constructed between 1873 and 1877, features such medieval elements as arched portals, a central tower, turrets, and pinnacles. But despite its borrowings from the past, Trinity Church was no mere copy of an historic building; it was an original conception based on the needs of its congregation and the irregular site chosen for its location.

The success of Richardson's choice of the Romanesque had a profound impact on American architecture for the next quarter-century. Many designers began to utilize the dramatic masses and textural surfaces associated with the style in all types of structures, from libraries to railroad stations.

Equally influential was the interior of Trinity Church. Under the direction of the American artist John La Farge, the walls were covered with brightly painted murals. La Farge was also responsible for many of the stained-glass windows that grace the church. He had studied the medieval stained-glass technique while a student in France in

1856, and he developed a personal style characterized by the use of richly colored glass and of larger stained-glass sections that reduced the amount of metal framework required. His "Welcome" Window, 1909 *(Plate 5)* is characteristic of La Farge's stained-glass technique.

While many American artists continued to make their pilgrimage to Europe, others found inspiration closer to home. Boston-born painter Winslow Homer rejected the cold precision of French academic art in favor of a greater naturalism. Beginning his career as a free-lance illustrator for *Harper's Weekly*, Homer first came to public notice for his keenly observed illustrations of Civil War subjects. His later work, although continuing in the naturalistic tradition, showed figures on a more monumental scale and expressed a deep concern for humanity.

The conflict between man and nature was a common theme in Homer's painting. In his "Huntsman and Dogs," 1891 *(Plate 7)*, the figure of the young hunter stands silhouetted against the cloud-filled sky as his dogs circle around him. The deerskin and

Plate 5: John La Farge, WELCOME WINDOW *(The Metropolitan Museum of Art, Gift of Susan Dwight Bliss, 1944; Photo by Sandak)*

Plate 6: Henry Hobson Richardson, TRINITY CHURCH, BOSTON, MASSACHUSETTS *(Photo by Sandak)*

Plate 7: Winslow Homer, HUNTSMAN AND DOGS *(Philadelphia Museum of Art: The William L. Elkins Collection)*

felled tree stump symbolize man's triumph over the wilderness.

Although most Americans who traveled to Paris studied at the Ecole des Beaux Arts, some were more sympathetic with the new avant-garde French painting. The Impressionists, who had challenged the Academy in the 1870s with freer brushwork and greater interest in naturalistic conditions of light, inspired a number of American artists, including John Singer Sargent. In one of his most famous portraits, "The Daughters of Edward D. Boit," 1882 *(Plate 8)*, Sargent places his subjects in an interior of strongly contrasting lights and darks. The informal composition gives a feeling of spontaneity, as though the four young girls were surprised in a moment of play.

Like two of his notable contemporaries, James McNeill Whistler and Mary Cassatt, Sargent became an expatriate, choosing to live and work in Europe because he felt that the center of artistic life was still to be found there rather than in this country.

In architecture, the last years of the nineteenth century were characterized by an increased interest in eclectic design. French chateaux and Italian Renaissance palaces

began to rise on the Cliff Walk of Newport, Rhode Island as the summer "cottages" of the new millionaires. Paris-trained Richard Morris Hunt was the most sought-after architect of this exuberant and often extravagant pursuit of elegance. In his design for the Vanderbilts' "Marble House," 1892 *(Plate 9)*, Hunt achieved a lavish display of grandeur by his use of expensive imported materials and unrestrained ornamental decoration.

Another architect who studied in Paris was Louis Sullivan; but Sullivan rejected the academic precepts of eclectism in favor of an architecture based on experimentation and innovation. Sullivan's major contribution was in his design of the skyscraper, which he conceived of as a "proud and soaring thing." The skyscraper had been made possible by the newly developed technology of steel frame construction and the invention of the elevator; the increased price of land was creating a need for taller buildings. Sullivan executed a number of important tall buildings in cities from Chicago, where he began his career, to New York. In Buffalo he designed the Prudential Building, 1895 *(Plate 10)*, in which he stressed the height of the structure by

Plate 8: John Singer Sargent, THE DAUGHTERS OF EDWARD D. BOIT *(Courtesy Museum of Fine Arts, Boston)*

Plate 9: Richard Morris Hunt, MARBLE HOUSE:
DINING ROOM *(The Preservation Society of Newport County Photo)*

accenting the vertical supports from the base
to the cornice. Although Sullivan continued to
use ornamental motifs on his buildings, they
were not derived from historical sources but
were products of his own imagination.

Although the influence of the academic
tradition continued into the twentieth
century, many American artists began to
reject the fashionable Beaux Arts style.
Following the lead of such innovative
designers as Sullivan, they sought to create
an art more expressive of the realities of an
increasingly industrial and urban America.

Plate 10: Louis Sullivan,
PRUDENTIAL BUILDING,
BUFFALO, NEW YORK
(Photo by Sandak)

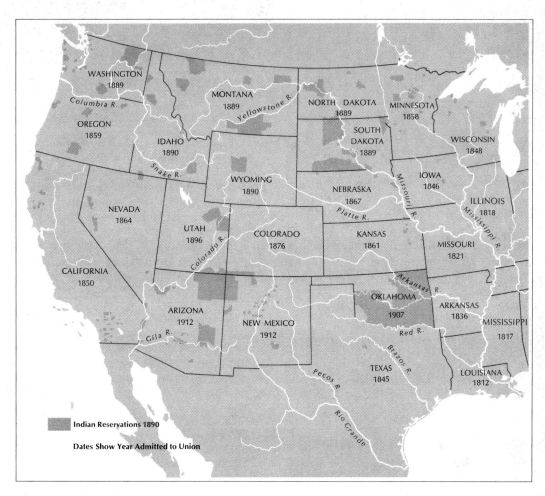

The Last Frontier

this had less effect than had been intended. According to the Homestead Act of 1862, for a small fee a settler could obtain a plot of 160 acres if he occupied and improved it for five years. (A similar acreage could be secured, ordinarily for $1.25 per acre, by the terms of the Preemption Act of 1841.) A good deal of idealism had gone into the framing of the Homestead Act. It was intended to be a democratic measure, the bestowal of a free farm on any American who needed one, a form of government relief to raise the living standards of the masses. But in practice the act proved a disappointment. Some 400,000 homesteaders became landowners, but a much larger number abandoned the attempt to stake out a farm on the windswept plains.

The Homestead Act was defective. It assumed that mere possession of land was enough to sustain farm life, but this ignored the increasing mechanization of agriculture and the rising costs of operation. Even worse, it was based on Eastern agricultural experiences that were inapplicable to the region west of the Mississippi. A unit of 160 acres was too small for the grazing and grain farming that came to be carried on in the Great Plains.

Responding to Western pressures, Congress acted to increase allotments. The Timber Culture Act (1873) permitted a homesteader to

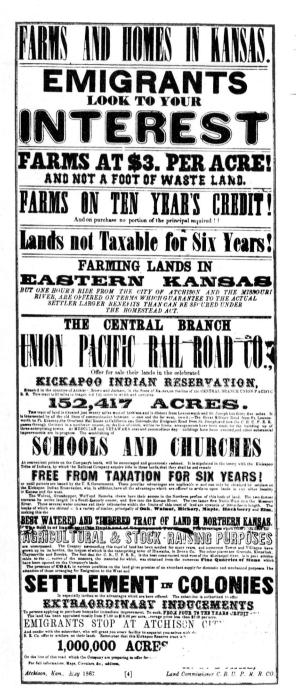

Railroad Land Promotion
*Railroads were eager to hasten the settlement of the
West. They stood to profit from the transportation of
migrants, the sale of land to them, and the freight
business from settled farmers. This 1867 poster
of the Union Pacific is fairly typical of Western
railroad advertisements from the 1860s to the 1890s.
(Union Pacific Railroad Museum Collection)*

receive a grant of 160 additional acres if he
planted on it 40 acres of trees. The Desert Land
Act (1877) provided that a claimant could buy
640 acres at $1.25 an acre provided he irrigated
part of his holding within three years. The
Timber and Stone Act (1878), presumably
applying to nonarable land, authorized sales of
quarter sections at $2.50 an acre.

Through the operation of the various laws,
it was possible for an individual to acquire at little cost 1,280 acres. Some enterprising persons
got much more. Fraud ran rampant in the administration of the acts. Lumber, mining, and
cattle companies, by employing "dummy" reg-
istrants and using other tricky devices, grasped
millions of acres of the public domain.

Settlement was made possible by the readiness of the federal government to police the
vast and desolate region and to subdue the red
men who resisted the white advance.

Political organization followed on the heels
of settlement. After the admission of Kansas as
a state in 1861, the remaining territories of
Washington, New Mexico, Utah, and Nebraska
were divided into smaller and more convenient
units. By the close of the sixties territorial governments were in operation in the new provinces of Nevada, Colorado, Dakota, Arizona,
Idaho, Montana, and Wyoming. Statehood rapidly followed. Nevada became a state in 1864,
Nebraska in 1867, and Colorado, attracting attention as the centennial state, in 1876. In 1889
the "omnibus states," North and South Dakota,
Montana, and Washington, won admission;
Wyoming and Idaho entered the next year.
Utah was denied statehood until its Mormon
leaders convinced the government in 1896 that
polygamy had been abandoned. At the turn of
the century only three territories remained
outside the fold: Arizona and New Mexico, excluded because of their scanty population and
wrong politics (they were predominantly Democratic) and their refusal to accept admission as
a single state, and Oklahoma, which was
opened to white settlement and granted territorial status in 1889–1890.

THE MINERS ARRIVE

The first colonists of the last frontier were miners, and the first part of the area to be settled
was the mineral-rich region of mountains and

plateaus. The life span of the mining frontier was brief. It burst into being around 1860, flourished brilliantly until the 1890s, and then abruptly declined.

News of a gold or silver strike would start a stampede reminiscent of the California gold rush of 1849. Settlement usually followed a pattern of successive stages: (1) individual prospectors exploited the first ores with pan and placer mining; (2) after the shallower deposits were depleted, corporations moved in to engage in lode or quartz mining; (3) commercial mining either disappeared eventually or continued on a restricted basis, and ranchers and farmers appeared on the scene to establish a more permanent economy.

The first great strikes occurred just before the Civil War. In 1858 gold was discovered in the Pike's Peak district of what would soon be the territory of Colorado, and the following year a mob of 50,000 prospectors stormed in from California and the Mississippi Valley and the East. Denver and other mining camps blossomed into "cities" overnight. Almost as rapid-

A Sod House on the Plains
Many settlers on the treeless Great Plains lived their first years in sod houses. They made these by cutting strips of the tough turf into pieces and laying them on top of one another to form walls. In some cases they first excavated and then erected the walls around the partial dugout. This photograph shows a combined dugout and sod house under construction in Nebraska in 1892. The wagon is bringing a fresh load of turf. (Solomon D. Butcher Collection, The Nebraska State Historical Society)

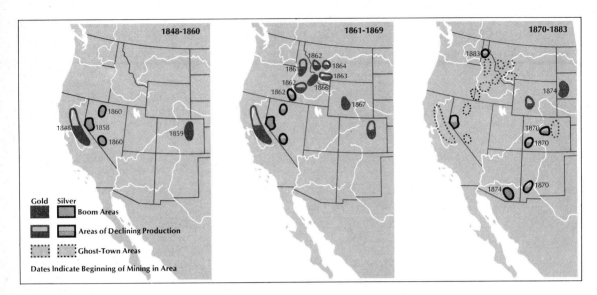

Mining Towns

ly as it developed, the boom ended. Eventually corporations, notably the Guggenheim interests, revived some of the glories and profits of the gold boom, and the discovery of silver near Leadville supplied a new source of mineral wealth.

While the Colorado rush of 1859 was in progress, news of another strike drew miners to Nevada, then a part of Utah Territory. Gold had been found in the Washoe district, but the most valuable ore in the great Comstock Lode and other veins was silver. The first prospectors to reach the Washoe fields came from California (here the frontier movement was from west to east), and from the beginning Californians dominated the settlement and development of Nevada. In a remote desert without railroad transportation, the territory produced no supplies of its own, and everything, from food and machinery to whiskey and prostitutes, had to be freighted in from California to Virginia City, Carson City, and other roaring camp towns. When the placer deposits ran out, California capital bought the claims of the pioneer prospectors and installed quartz mining. For a brief span the outside owners reaped tremendous profits; from 1860 to 1880 the Nevada lodes yielded bullion worth $306 million.

No new discoveries agitated the mining frontier until 1874, when gold was found in the Black Hills of southwestern Dakota Territory. Prospectors swarmed into the area, which was then and for years later served only by stagecoach transportation. Deadwood burst into life as a center of supplies and sin for other camps. For a short time the boom flared, and then came the inevitable fading of resources. Corporations took over from the miners, and one gigantic company, the Homestake, came to dominate the fields. The population declined, and the Dakotas, like other boom areas of the mineral empire, waited for the approach of the agricultural frontier.

Life in the camp towns of the mineral empire had a hectic tempo and a gaudy flavor not to be found in any other part of the last frontier. The speculative spirit, a mood of incredible optimism, a get-rich-quick philosophy gripped everybody and dominated every phase of community activity. The conditions of mine life—the presence of precious minerals, the vagueness of claim boundaries, the cargoes of gold being shipped out—tempted outlaws and "bad men," operating as individuals or gangs, to ply their trade. When the situation became intolerable in a community, those members interested in order set up their own law and enforced it through a vigilance committee, an agency used earlier in California. Sometimes criminals themselves secured control of the committee and sometimes the vigilantes continued to operate as private "law" enforcers after the creation of regular governments.

THE DAY OF THE COWBOY

The open range—that is, the unclaimed grasslands of the public domain—provided a huge area on the Great Plains where cattlemen could graze their herds free of charge and unrestricted by the boundaries that would have existed in a farming economy. The railroads gave the range-cattle industry access to markets and thus brought it into being; then they destroyed it by bringing the farmers' frontier to the plains.

In ancestry the cattle industry was Mexican and Texan. Long before the Americans invaded the Southwest, Mexican ranchers and vaqueros had developed the techniques and tools employed later by the cattlemen and cowboys of the Great Plains: branding (a device known in all frontier areas where stock was common), roundups, roping, and the equipment of the herder—his lariat, saddle, leather chaps, and spurs. All these things and others were taken over by the Americans in Texas and by them transmitted to the northernmost ranges of the cattle kingdom. Also in Texas were found the largest herds of cattle in the country, the animals descended from imported Spanish stock—the famous wiry, hardy longhorns—and allowed to run wild or semiwild. Here too were the horses that enabled the caretakers of the herds to control them—the small, muscular broncos or mustangs—sprung from blooded progenitors brought in by the Spanish and ideally adapted to the requirements of the cow country.

At the end of the Civil War an estimated 5 million cattle roamed the Texas ranges, and Northern markets were offering fat prices for steers in any condition. Early in 1866 some

Cowboys Branding Calves

To identify his own herd (which mingled with other herds on the open range) each cattleman had his calves branded with his distinctive mark of ownership. At the spring roundup, cowboys caught the calves, "wrassled" them to the ground, and applied searing hot branding irons. (Western History Research Center, University of Wyoming)

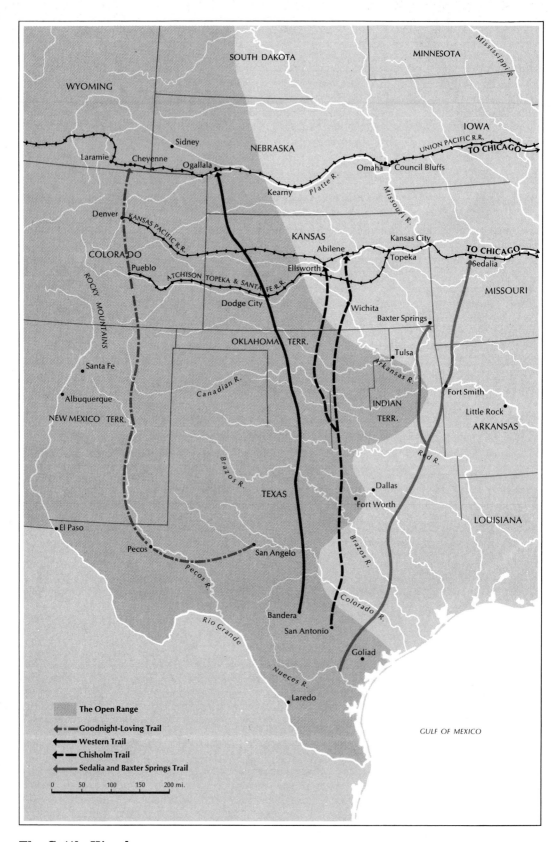

The Cattle Kingdom

Texas cattlemen started their combined herds, some 260,000 head, north for Sedalia, Missouri, on the Missouri Pacific Railroad. Traveling over rough country and beset by outlaws, Indians, and property-conscious farmers, the caravan suffered heavy losses, and only a fraction of the animals were delivered to the railroad. But a great experiment had been successfully tested — cattle could be driven to distant markets and pastured along the trail and would gain weight during the journey. The first of the "long drives" prepared the way for the cattle kingdom.

With the precedent established, the next step was to find an easier route leading through more accessible country. Special market facilities were provided at Abilene, Kansas, on the Kansas Pacific Railroad, and for years this town reigned as the railhead of the cattle kingdom. Between 1867 and 1871, 1,460,000 cattle were moved up the Chisholm Trail to Abilene, a town that when filled with rampaging cowboys at the end of a drive rivaled the mining towns in robust wickedness. But as the farming frontier pushed farther west in Kansas and as the supply of animals increased, the cattlemen had to develop other market outlets and trails. Railroad towns that flourished after Abilene were Dodge City and Wichita in Kansas, Ogallala and Sidney in Nebraska, Cheyenne and Laramie in Wyoming, and Miles City and Glendive in Montana.

From first to last, a long drive was a spectacular episode. It began with the spring, or calf, roundup. The cattlemen of a district met with their cowboys at a specified place to round up the stock of the owners from the open range. As the cattle were driven in, the calves were branded with the marks of their mothers. Stray calves with no identifying symbols, "mavericks," were divided on a pro-rata basis. Then the cows and calves were turned loose to pasture, while the yearling steers were readied for the drive to the north. The combined herds, usually numbering from 2,000 to 5,000 head, moved out, attended by the cowboys of each outfit.

Among the cowboys the majority (in the early years) were veterans of the Confederate army. Outnumbering all the rest — white Northerners, Mexicans, and other foreigners — were the Negroes, who usually were assigned the humbler jobs on the trail crew, such as those of wrangler or cook. (In the Wild West black men played a role not only as cowboys but also as explorers, trappers, miners, outlaws, and cavalrymen.) The cowboy was glorified as a Nordic superman in Owen Wister's novel *The Virginian* (1902) and in countless later "Westerns" that followed the Wister pattern. Actually the life of the cowboy, whatever his color, was dull, dirty, and rather brutish. He was at best only a hired hand who made little money and kept still less. The big profits went to his employer, the cattleman.

All cattlemen had to have a permanent base from which to operate, and so the ranch emerged. A ranch consisted of the employer's dwelling, quarters for employees, and a tract of grazing land. It might be fenced in or open, owned or leased or held by some quasi-legal claim, but it was definite and durable. Possession of a ranch meant unquestioned access to precious water. As farmers and sheepmen encroached on the open plains, the ranch began to replace the range.

There had always been an element of risk and speculation in the open-range cattle business. At any time the "Texas fever," transmitted by a parasite carried by ticks, might decimate a herd. Rustlers and Indians frequently drove off large numbers of animals. Sheepmen from California and Oregon brought their flocks onto the range to compete for grass and force cattle out (cattle will not graze after sheep); bitter "wars" followed between cattlemen and sheepherders in which men and stock were killed and equipment destroyed. Farmers, "nesters," threw fences around their claims, blocking trails and breaking up the open range. More wars were fought bringing losses to both sides.

Accounts of the lofty profits to be made in the cattle business — it was said that an investment of $5,000 would return $45,000 in four years — tempted Eastern, English, and Scottish capital to the plains. Increasingly the structure of the cattle economy became corporate in form; in one year twenty corporations with a combined capital of $12 million were chartered in Wyoming. The inevitable result of this frenzied extension was that the ranges, already severed and shrunk by the railroads and the farmers, were overstocked. There was not enough grass to support the crowding herds or sustain the long drives. Overstocking tumbled prices downward, and then nature intervened with a destructive finishing blow. Two severe winters, in 1885–1886 and 1886–1887, with a searing summer between them, stung and scorched the plains. Hundreds of thousands of cattle died, streams and grass dried up, princely ranches and costly investments disappeared in a season.

The open-range industry never recovered; the long drive disappeared for good. But the cattle ranches—with fenced-in grazing land and stocks of hay for winter feed—survived and grew and prospered, eventually producing more beef than ever.

The Dispersal of the Tribes

When the miners and cowmen sifted into the last frontier, they came face to face with its Indian inhabitants, and they had to advance against more determined and sustained resistance than whites had met anywhere else in the sweep across the continent. In the end the invaders triumphed. The Indian tribes were broken and their members were forced to adapt themselves to an approximation of the white man's culture.

THE PLAINS INDIANS

On the rolling, semiarid, treeless plains, the Indians followed a nomadic life. Riding their small but powerful horses, which were descendants of Spanish stock, the tribes roamed the spacious expanses of the grasslands. Permanent abodes were rare; when a band halted, tepees carried on the journey were quickly pitched as temporary dwellings.

The magnet that drew the wanderers and guided their routes was the buffalo, or bison. This huge grazing animal provided the economic basis for the plains Indians' way of life. Its flesh was their principal source of food, and the skin supplied materials for clothing, shoes, tepees, blankets, robes, and utensils. To the Indians, the buffalo was, as someone had said, "a galloping department store." They trailed the herds, estimated to number at least 15 million head in 1865, all over the plains.

The plains Indians were almost uniformly martial, proud, and aggressive. Mounted on their horses, they were a formidable foe, whether armed with bow, spear, or rifle. They possessed a mobility enjoyed by no previous Indians, and students of war have ranked them among the best light cavalry in military history.

It was the traditional policy of the federal government to regard the tribes as independent nations (but also as wards of the Great White Father in Washington) and to negotiate agreements with them in the shape of treaties that were solemnly ratified by the Senate. This concept of Indian sovereignty was responsible for the attempt of the government before 1860 to erect a permanent frontier between whites and red men, to reserve the region west of the bend of the Missouri as permanent Indian country. But by the sixties the related principles of tribal independence and a perpetual line of division were breaking down before harsh realities. Administration of Indian matters was divided between the Bureau of Indian Affairs, located in the Department of the Interior, and the army. The bureau was vested with general powers to supervise the disposition of Indian lands, disburse annuities, and, through its agents in Western posts, distribute needed supplies. From top to bottom, the personnel was shot through with the spoils system. Although some agents were conscientious and able men, more were dishonest and incompetent.

The army came into the picture only when trouble developed—when bands of Indians attacked homes or stagecoach lines or when a tribe went on the warpath. In short, its principal function was to punish, not to police. The army of the frontier was an effective fighting body, and it was led by some able officers. Still, in its "wars" with the Indians the army frequently experienced rugged going. The mobile plains tribesmen were fully a match for cavalrymen armed with carbines. But soon the superior technology of the whites shifted the balance. The Colt repeating revolver gave the army increased fire power, the railroads facilitated quick troop concentrations, and the telegraph reported almost immediately the movements of hostile bands. Even so, the business of suppressing Indians was frightfully expensive.

The Slaughter of the Buffalo

This sketch, sardonically entitled "Sport on the Plains," shows the way in which the buffalo was often hunted. A wealthy hunter has employed a guide and a driver and carriage to take him out to get a trophy. (Culver)

Three wars in the sixties cost the government $100 million, and one official estimated that the cost per Indian killed was $1,000.

The subjection of the fierce plains Indians was accomplished by economic as well as orthodox warfare—by the slaughter of the buffalo herds that supported their way of life. After the Civil War the demand for buffalo hides became a national phenomenon. It was partly based on economics—a commercial demand for the hides developing in the East; and it was partly a fad—suddenly everyone east of the Missouri seemed to require a buffalo robe from the romantic West. Gangs of professional hunters swarmed over the plains to shoot the huge animals, divided by the Union Pacific Railroad into southern and northern herds. Some hunters killed merely for the sport of the chase, though the lumbering victims did not present much of a challenge. The southern herd was virtually exterminated by 1875, and within a few years the smaller northern herd

met the same fate. Fewer than a thousand of the magnificent beasts survived. The army and the Indian agents condoned and even encouraged the killing. With the buffalo went the Indians' source of food and supplies and their will and ability to resist the white advance.

THE WARRIORS' LAST STAND

There was almost incessant Indian fighting on the frontier from the sixties to the eighties. During the Civil War the eastern Sioux in Minnesota, cramped on an inadequate reserve and exploited by agents, suddenly took to the warpath. Led by Little Crow, they killed over 700 whites before being subdued by a force of regulars and militia. Thirty-eight of the Indians were hanged, and the tribe was exiled to the Dakotas.

At the same time trouble flared in Colorado, where the Arapaho and Cheyenne had

Apache Warrior
*Geronimo (left, mounted) was not a chief, but he assumed the leadership of one of
the Apache bands when, in 1876, the United States government attempted to confine
the Apaches on a reservation in Arizona. He established a base in the mountains
of Mexico, and from there he led his warriors on raids across the border to
terrorize the American countryside. He kept this up for more than ten years.
(Culver Pictures)*

been restricted to the Sand Creek reserve.
Bands of braves attacked stagecoach lines and
settlements, provoking a concentration of territorial militia and threats from the army. The
governor urged all friendly Indians to congregate at army posts before retribution fell on the
hostiles. One Arapaho and Cheyenne band
under Black Kettle came into Fort Lyon on
Sand Creek and encamped nearby. Although
some braves just off the warpath were undoubtedly members of the party, Black Kettle understood he was under official protection. Nevertheless, Colonel J. M. Chivington, apparently
encouraged by the army commander of the
district, led a militia force to the unsuspecting
camp and massacred a disputed (but large)
number of men, women, and children. The

government then forced the Arapaho and
Cheyenne to accept an even less desirable
reservation, but the Senate neglected to ratify
the treaty.

At the end of the war against the southern
rebels, wars against the western Indians flared
up on several fronts. The most serious and sustained conflict was in Montana, where the
army attempted to build a road, the Bozeman
Trail, from Fort Laramie, Wyoming, to the mining centers. The western Sioux resented this
intrusion into the heart of their buffalo range,
and led by one of their great chiefs, Red Cloud,
they so harried the soldiers and the construction party that the road could not be completed.

Meanwhile, Congress, shocked by the
Chivington massacre and the continued hostili-

ties, appointed a committee to investigate the situation on the scene, and after studying its report created an Indian Peace Commission, composed of soldiers and civilians, to recommend a permanent Indian policy. The commission called the southern tribes to council at Medicine Lodge Creek in 1867, and the following year it met with the northern tribes at Fort Laramie. At Medicine Lodge the Arapaho and Cheyenne and other tribes agreed to accept reserves in the Indian Territory. At Laramie the Sioux accepted a reserve in southwestern Dakota, with rights to hunt as far as the Big Horn Mountains in Wyoming; they insisted, however, that the government abandon the Bozeman road, marking probably the only instance in which whites formally yielded to Indians. The minor plains tribes and the mountain tribes consented to smaller reserves. For its part, the government pledged annuity payments and regular supplies. Some of the Arapaho and Cheyenne had another bad experience before being finally settled on their reserve. Black Kettle, who had escaped the Chivington massacre, and his Cheyennes, some of whom had taken the warpath, were caught on the Washita River, near the Texas border, by Colonel George A. Custer, and the chief was killed and his people slaughtered.

After 1870 the broad outlines of a new Indian policy began to take shape. The tribes were now concentrated in two large reserves, one in Dakota and the other in the Indian Territory. Thus restricted, they found their powers to wage war severely limited. An advisory civilian Board of Indian Commissioners counseled the

---

A White Defender of the Indians

Among the few voices raised to defend the Indians and criticize the government's policy toward them was that of Helen Hunt Jackson, a writer who lived in Colorado Springs, Colorado. She presented her views in *A Century of Dishonor* (1881):

There is not among these three hundred bands of Indians [in the United States] one which has not suffered cruelly at the hands either of the Government or of white settlers. The poorer, the more insignificant, the more helpless the band, the more certain the cruelty and outrage to which they have been subjected. This is especially true of the bands on the Pacific slope. These Indians found themselves of a sudden surrounded by and caught up in the great influx of gold-seeking settlers, as helpless creatures on a shore are caught up in a tidal wave. There was not time for the Government to make treaties; not even time for communities to make laws. The tale of the wrongs, the oppressions, the murders of the Pacific-slope Indians in the last thirty years would be a volume by itself, and is too monstrous to be believed.

It makes little difference, however, where one opens the record of the history of the Indians; every page and every year has its dark stain. The story of one tribe is the story of all, varied only by differences of time and place; but neither time nor place makes any difference in the main facts. Colorado is as greedy and unjust in 1880 as was Georgia in 1830, and Ohio in 1795; and the United States Government breaks promises now as deftly as then, and with added ingenuity from long practice.

One of its strongest supports in so doing is the wide-spread sentiment among the people of dislike to the Indian, of impatience with his presence as a "barrier to civilization," and distrust of it as a possible danger. The old tales of the frontier life, with its horrors of Indian warfare, have gradually, by two or three generations' telling, produced in the average mind something like an hereditary instinct of unquestioning and unreasoning aversion which it is almost impossible to dislodge or soften.

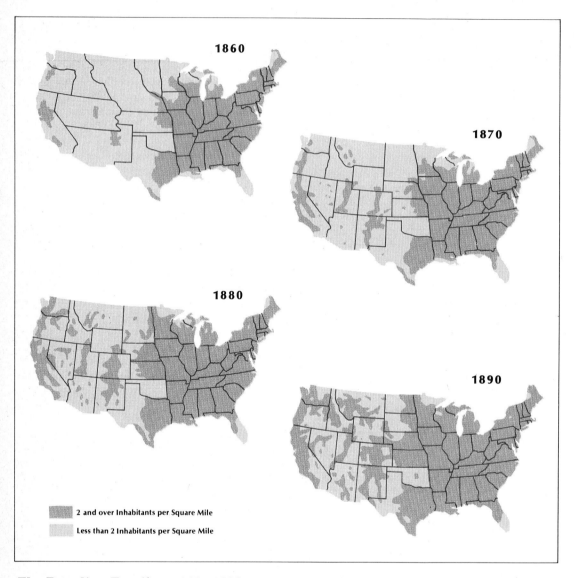

The Receding Frontier, 1860–1890
The term "frontier" refers to the line — and also to the area bordering the line — that divides the settled part of the country (population two or more per square mile) from the unsettled part (population less than two per square mile).

government to continue the reservation program and to break down the tribal structure with a view to assimilating the Indians to white culture. Congress responded in 1871 by abolishing the practice of treating the tribes as sov-

ereignties, a step calculated to undermine the collective nature of Indian life.

But Indian resistance was far from ended. A source of potential conflict smouldered on the northern plains, where the Sioux roamed from Dakota to Wyoming. It burst into flame in 1875 when many of the tribesmen, angered by the dealings of crooked agents and alarmed by the entrance of miners into the Black Hills, suddenly left the reserve. Commanded to return, they gathered in Montana under Crazy Horse, probably the greatest leader of the plains Indians, and Sitting Bull. Three army columns were sent to round them up. With the expedition as colonel of the famous Seventh Cavalry was the colorful and controversial George A. Custer, golden-haired romantic and alleged glory seeker. At the Battle of the Little Bighorn (1876) the Indians surprised Custer with part of his regiment and killed every man. Custer has been accused of rashness, but he seems to have ridden into something that no white man would have believed possible. On this occasion the chiefs had concentrated at least 2,500 warriors, perhaps 4,000, the largest Indian army ever assembled at one time in the United States.

But the Indians did not have the political organization or the commissary to keep their troops united. Soon they drifted off in bands to elude pursuit or search for food, and the army ran them down singly and returned them to Dakota. The power of the Sioux was now broken. The proud leaders, Crazy Horse and Sitting Bull, accepted defeat and the monotony of agency existence, and both were later killed by reservation police after being tricked or taunted into a last pathetic show of resistance.

In 1877 one of the most dramatic episodes in Indian history occurred in Idaho. Here the Nez Percé, a small and relatively pacific and civilized tribe, refused to accept a smaller reservation and were, in effect, forced into resistance. When troops converged on them, their able leader, Chief Joseph, attempted to conduct the band to Canada. A remarkable chase ensued. Joseph moved with 200 warriors and 350 women, children, and old people. Pursued by four columns, he covered 1,321 miles in seventy-five days, but was caught just short of the Canadian border. Like so many other crushed tribes, the Nez Percé were shipped to the Indian Territory.

The last Indians to maintain organized resistance against the whites were the Apaches, who fought intermittently from the sixties to the late eighties. The two ablest chiefs of this fierce tribe were Mangas Colorados and Cochise. Mangas was murdered during the Civil War, and in 1872 Cochise agreed to peace and a reservation for his followers. But one leader, Geronimo, continued to carry on the fight. When he was finally captured in 1886, formal warfare between Indians and whites may be said to have ended.

A final, tragic encounter in 1890 was hardly a battle. As the Indians saw their culture and their glories fading, they turned to an emotional religion which emphasized the coming of a Messiah and featured the "ghost dance," which inspired visions. Agents on the Sioux reservation, fearing the frenzy might turn into an outbreak, called for troops, and some of the Indians fled to the Badlands. The soldiers caught and tried to disarm them, at Wounded Knee. In the shooting that followed, about 40 of the soldiers were killed and more than 200 of the Indians, including women and children.

In 1887 Congress had finally moved to destroy the tribal structure that was the cornerstone of Indian culture. Although the motivation was partially a humanitarian impulse to help the Indian, the action was frankly designed to force him to become a landowner and farmer, to abandon his collective society and culture, to become, in short, a white man. The Dawes Severalty Act provided for the gradual abrogation of tribal ownership of land and the allotment of tracts to individual owners: 160 acres to the head of a family, 80 acres to a single adult or orphan, 40 acres to each dependent child. Adult owners were accorded the status of citizenship but, unlike other citizens, they could not alienate their property for twenty-five years. The act was hardly a success. The Indians were not ready for a wrenching change from a collective society to individualism. Congress attempted to facilitate the transition with the Burke Act of 1906. Citizenship was deferred until after the completion of the twenty-five-year period contemplated in the Dawes Act, but Indians who proved their adaptability could secure both citizenship and land ownership in a shorter period. Full rights of citizenship were conferred on all Indians in 1924. Even then many resisted white ways, and in the 1930s the government would make a notable attempt to restore some of the institutions of tribal culture.

Decline of the Farmer

The development of an industrial and urban civilization would have been impossible without a great increase in the productivity of agriculture. Yet on the whole the nation's farmers, while producing more than ever, were getting less and less in both pecuniary and psychological reward for their effort. Those who tried farming on the last frontier soon discovered that the West no longer provided much of a way out for them.

FARMING ON THE PLAINS

Some farmers had drifted into the Great Plains during its first stages of development, following the miners and cattlemen, but the great rush of settlement came in the late seventies. In the next decade the relentless advance of the farming frontier would gradually convert the plains country to an agricultural economy. The surge of migration came at a time when for years in succession the rainfall was well above the average. People scoffed at the idea that the plains were the Great American Desert, and they looked forward to an indefinite era of prosperity. They scoffed too at the old cowmen who warned that the light soil of the plains should not be deprived of its protecting turf by cultivation.

But even under the most favorable conditions, farming on the plains presented problems not encountered in any previous region.

Threshing Wheat on the Great Plains
This print of a Dakota field shows the magnitude of operations on a large landed unit and gives an idea of the high cost of farming on the plains. Here several steam-driven machines are in use. The average farmer could not afford even one thresher. In some areas owners of the machines went from farm to farm with hired crews during the harvest season. According to Raymond M. Wik in Steam Power on the American Farm, *the total horsepower of these engines increased from 1,200,000 in 1880 to 3,600,000 by 1910. (The Bettmann Archive)*

First and most critical was the problem of fencing. The farmer had to enclose his land, if for no other reason than to protect it from the herds of the cattlemen. But the traditional wood or stone fences were impossible on the plains. The cost of importing the material was prohibitive, and besides, such barriers were ineffective against range cattle. In the mid-seventies two Illinois farmers, Joseph H. Glidden and I. L. Ellwood, solved this problem by developing and putting on the market barbed wire. Produced in mass quantities — 40,000 tons a year — it sold cheaply, became standard equipment on the plains, and revolutionized fencing practices all over the country.

The second problem, present even when the rainfall was above average, was water. It became particularly acute after 1887, when a series of dry seasons began. One expedient resorted to was the use of deep wells and steel windmills, which assured a steady water supply for stock. Another was dry farming — a system of tillage designed to conserve moisture in the soil by covering it with a dust blanket — and the utilization of drought-enduring crops. In many areas of the plains, agriculture could not exist without irrigation. Large-scale irrigation, the only practicable kind, would have to be planned and supported by the government. The national government tried to hand the issue to the states, turning over to them in the Carey Act (1894) several million acres of public land to be reclaimed. The states made little progress, largely because the problems of reclamation cut across state boundaries.

Farming on the plains was always expensive and often risky. The uncertainty of rainfall and the danger of grasshopper plagues and tornadoes made every farm year a speculative experiment. Costs of operation ran high, partly because many supplies had to be imported into the region from distant points, but mainly because of the nature of plains farming. In all the farm areas of the country, machines were playing a larger part in the agricultural process, and they were especially vital on the plains, where grain farming was conducted on large land units.

The last West was not, as has so often been claimed, a refuge for the urban poor or a safety valve for proletarian unrest. The people who settled this area were mostly farmers, and they came from farms in the Middle West, the East, or Europe. In the booming eighties, with land values rising, credit was easy, and the farmers confidently expected to retire their obligations. With the advent of the arid years of the late eighties, the prospect changed with grim suddenness. There followed a reversal of the frontier movement, as many settlers retreated from the Great Plains. Those who remained gave an unintentional boost to the overproduction that caused farm prices to fall (wheat, which had sold for $1.60 a bushel at the end of the Civil War, dropped to 49 cents in the 1890s) and added to the distress of farmers elsewhere in the country.

CHANGES IN AGRICULTURE

Americans had always liked to talk about the wonderful life of the farmer. According to the popular myth, he was a sturdy yeoman, a simple, honest, happy man who dwelt close to nature and embodied all the virtues. Producing most of the things he and his family required, he was independent, subsisting on his own labor, depending not on the marketplace, and owing no man. The myth may have had some basis in Jefferson's time, but its reality was being destroyed by one of the great agricultural changes of the nineteenth century, the shift from subsistence, or self-sufficient, farming to commercial farming.

In commercial husbandry, the farmer specialized in a cash crop, sold it in a national or world market, ceased making his household supplies and bought them at the town or village store. This kind of farming, when it was successful, raised the farmer's living standards. But now he was dependent on other people and on impersonal factors he could not control: bankers and interest rates, railroads and freight rates, national and European depressions, world supply and demand. In short, he had become a businessman — but with a difference. Unlike the capitalists of the industrial order, he could not regulate his production or influence the prices of what he sold.

Machines came to the aid of the farmer as to the manufacturer. The mechanization of agriculture had accelerated during the Civil War, when the government called thousands of laborers into military service and forced farmers to employ labor-saving devices. For example, approximately 100,000 reapers were in use at the beginning of the war but 250,000 at its close.

In the years after 1860 a host of new machines — and improved models of old ones — were unveiled. Among these were the chilled steel plow, perfected by James Oliver; the sulky, or riding, plow; the disc and gang plows; various improvements of the reaper, notably the twine binder, introduced by John F. Appleby, which cut and bound grain; the grain drill, the seed planter, the corn binder, the corn lister, the potato planter, the cream separator, and the poultry incubator. The effect of the machines on production and labor was revolutionary.

Before 1900 farmers were generally hostile to the theories and teachings of scientific agriculture, to what they scornfully termed "book learning." In 1887 Congress passed the Hatch Act, providing for a system of agricultural experiment stations; this was the only major agricultural legislation passed by Congress between 1865 and 1900. But farmers generally spurned the new information because they felt no need for its aid and could see no benefits for themselves in its lessons. American agriculture before 1900 was, as it always had been, extensive and wasteful.

The period between 1865 and 1900 witnessed a tremendous expansion of agricultural facilities, not only in the United States but all over the world: in Brazil and the Argentine in South America, in Canada, in Australia and New Zealand, and in Russia. World production increased at the same time that modern means of communication and transportation — the telephone, telegraph, cable, steam navigation, railroads — were welding the producing nations into one international market. The American commercial farmer, always augmenting his production, produced more than the domestic market could absorb and disposed of his surplus in the world market. Cotton farmers depended on export sales for 70 percent of their annual income, and wheat farmers for 30 to 40 percent; other producers relied on a smaller percentage — it might be 10 to 25 — but it was large enough to make the difference between a year of profit and one of loss.

In the forty years after 1860 huge new areas of land were put under cultivation in America, machines became standard equipment on most farms, land values boomed, and production soared to ever higher levels. But while costs of operation increased, prices dropped after 1870. Meanwhile, though the proportion of people living on farms declined in relation to the total population, farm population increased by absolute standards. From 1860 to 1910 the number of farm families rose from 1.5 million to over 6 million. In 1860 agriculture represented 50 percent of the total wealth of the country, in the early 1900s only 20 percent. The farmer received 30 percent of the national income in 1860 and 18 percent in 1910. By the decade of the nineties, 27 percent of the owned farms in the country were under mortgages, and by 1910, 33 percent. In 1880, 25 percent of all farms were operated by tenants; in 1910, 37 percent. The agrarian scene as it presented itself in the 1890s hardly realized Jefferson's dream of sturdy and independent yeomen owning the land they tilled.

THE FARMERS' GRIEVANCES

The farmers were painfully aware that something was wrong. They did not recognize — and it would have been strange if they had recognized — the intricate implications of national and world overproduction. Instead, they concentrated their attention and anger on more immediate and easily understood problems, problems that were in truth real and important to them, such as freight rates, interest charges, and an adequate currency.

The farmers' first and most burning grievance was that against the railroads. In all sections, and especially in the states west of the Mississippi, farmers depended on the railroads to carry crops to the markets. In many cases the roads charged higher rates for farm than for other shipments and higher rates in the South and West than in the Northeast. Freight rates sometimes consumed so much of the current price that farmers refused to ship their crops and either let them rot or used them as fuel. Railroads controlled elevator and warehouse facilities in buying centers and charged arbitrary storage rates.

In the farmers' list of villains the sources that controlled credit — banks, loan companies, insurance corporations — ranked second to the railroads. Commercial farming was by its nature expensive, and ambitious producers needed credit to purchase machines or enlarge holdings. Though eager to advance loans during the boom period of rising land values, the lenders insisted on high interest rates. The farmers were in no position to resist, and in the West and the South they had to submit to charges running from 10 to 25 percent. Usually they borrowed money when it was cheap, or abundant, and then had to retire their debts when money had become dear, or scarce. According to one estimate, 1,200 bushels of grain would buy a $1,000 mortgage in the 1860s; twenty years later it took 2,300 bushels to repay the mortgage. With good reason, the farmers fought for an increase in the volume of currency.

A third grievance of the farmer concerned prices, both the prices he received for his products and the prices he paid for goods he bought. He disposed of his products as an individual in competition with countless other individuals in this and other countries. He possessed little or no advance information on the state of the market and probable price changes; he did not have storage facilities to hold his crop for a favorable price; and he was powerless to regulate his production. Instead of changing his marketing procedures, the farmer blamed his woes on personal villains—grain speculators in distant cities, international bankers, or regional and local middlemen. These operators, he became convinced (sometimes with justice), were combining to fix prices so as to benefit themselves while hurting him.

The farmer was also convinced that there was something of a conspiracy against him in the prices of the goods he purchased. He sold his crops in a competitive market but bought in a domestic market protected by tariffs and dominated by trusts and corporations. According to government reports, over one hundred articles purchased by farmers—farm machinery, tools, sewing machines, blankets, staple foods, clothing, plowshares, and others—were protected. On these necessary items the tariff added from 33 to 60 percent to the purchase price.

Last on the agrarian catalog of grievances was a vague yet tremendous resentment. In part, this was an outgrowth of the isolation of farm life before the days of paved roads, automobiles, telephones, and radios. Farm families in some parts of the country, particularly in the prairie and plains region where large farms were scattered over vast areas, were virtually cut off from the outside world and from other human companionship during the winter months or protracted spells of bad weather. This enforced seclusion was only partially alleviated when the national government established rural free delivery of mail in 1896. The drabness and the dullness of farm existence, the lack of adequate educational, recreational, and medical facilities, and the absence of community culture and action—these things helped to account for the tremendous migration of young people from the farms to the cities. The farmer, once eulogized as the surest support of American democracy, was now ridiculed as a "hayseed." He was losing status, and he knew it.

Knowledge for a New Society

While the farmer's ways declined in prestige, the urban environment increasingly made its influence felt upon the mind of the entire nation, despite the persistence of stereotypes from the rural past. The city's influence was spread through the educational system, which was being broadened and extended, and through the publishing industry, which centered in New York and reached out for a wider and wider readership.

THE PRAGMATIC APPROACH

Along with the economic and social changes of the time, there was a change in the philosophical assumptions of thinking Americans. This came about largely in response to the doctrine of evolution—the thesis that all living things had evolved from earlier forms and that the various species had resulted from a process of natural selection.

Christian Science

One of the new religions that came into being in the 1870s was Christian Science, founded by a woman, Mary Baker G. Eddy. She explained the essence of her belief as follows:

The Scriptures name God as good, and the Saxon term for God is also good. From this premise comes the logical conclusion that God is naturally and divinely infinite good. How, then, can this conclusion change, or be changed, to mean that good is evil, or the creator of evil? What can there be besides infinity? Nothing! Therefore the Science of good calls evil nothing. In divine Science the terms God and good, as Spirit, are synonymous. That God, good, creates evil, or aught that can result in evil,—or that Spirit creates its opposite, named matter,—are conclusions that destroy their premise and prove themselves invalid. Here is where Christian Science sticks to its text, and other systems of religion abandon their own logic. Here also is found the pith of the basal statement, the cardinal point in Christian Science, that matter and evil (including all inharmony, sin, disease, death) are unreal.

Here was a doctrine that challenged almost every tenet of the American faith. If Darwin and the scientists were right, man was not endowed with a higher nature, but was only a biological organism, another form of animal life—the highest form, it was true, but still like the other animals that had had their day in past ages. Instead of history's being the working out of a divine plan, it was a random process dominated by the fiercest or luckiest competitors.

All over the United States Darwinism became a subject of popular interest and an issue of debate. By 1900 the evolutionists had carried the day, except in the South and parts of the rural Midwest. Many Protestant ministers, especially those in urban centers, had managed a reconciliation between religion and science. Particularly in the cities and larger towns, more and more people accepted the basic principles of evolution. Science was enshrined in the university and college curriculums.

Out of the controversy over Darwinism there arose finally a new philosophy which was peculiarly American and peculiarly suited to America's changing material civilization. The name of the philosophy was pragmatism, and its principal formulators were Charles Peirce and William James in the period before 1900, and John Dewey later.

Pragmatism is difficult to define, partly because its advocates differed as to its meaning, but mainly because it avoided absolutes and dealt with relative standards. According to the pragmatists, who accepted the idea of organic evolution, the validity of human institutions and actions should be determined by their consequences. If the ends of an institution or the techniques of a group did not satisfy social needs, then a change was in order. In blunt terms, the pragmatists applied their one standard: Does it work? They subjected truth to the same test. There were no final truths or answers, they contended, but a series of truths for each generation and each society. Truth, like institutions, had to be validated by consequences. Said James: "The ultimate test for us of what a truth means is the conduct it dictates or inspires."

TOWARD UNIVERSAL SCHOOLING

Mary Antin, a Russian girl who came as an immigrant to the United States, had heard that in America everything was free. Best of all: "Education was free. That subject my father had written about repeatedly, as comprising his chief hope for us children, the essence of American opportunity, the treasure that no thief could touch, not even misfortune or poverty." Education in America after the Civil War was indeed free or in the process of becoming so—free, public, and almost universal.

In 1860 there were only 100 public high schools in the country, but by 1900 the number had reached 6,000; their total enrollment, however, was not more than 200,000. The most spectacular expansion occurred at the elementary or grade school level. Below the elementary level appeared the kindergartens, the first of which was established in St. Louis in 1873. By 1900 compulsory school attendance laws were in effect, although not always enforced, in thirty-one states and territories. In the expansion of school facilities, the Northeast led, the Middle West followed, and the South trailed behind.

Most of the elementary schools and many of the high schools in all sections were, by modern standards, small, inadequate, and unattractive. Dominating the curriculum were the traditional three Rs—reading, writing, and arithmetic—with history and a few other subjects holding a secondary place. Also traditional were the textbooks used, among them the Webster Spellers and the McGuffey Readers.

Teaching was not yet regarded as a profession. In 1900 the average annual salary was a mere $325, less than the average wage of unskilled workers. Thousands of teachers, with only a high school or elementary education, knew little more than their pupils. Nevertheless, real progress was achieved in establishing the idea that teaching was a profession and education a science. In 1865 there were only twelve teacher-training institutions, or normal schools, as they were called, in the country. By 1900 every state supported at least one such school, and in some of the leading universities, Chicago, Harvard, Columbia, Stanford, and others, schools of education had been set up. The states created boards or commissions of education to raise standards, and in 1867 the national government manifested its interest by establishing the office of Commissioner of Education to collect and disseminate educational information. By the turn of the century one in every five of the elementary teachers was a graduate of a professional school.

In the 1880s a number of innovations in educational methods began to make their influence felt. New, more up-to-date textbooks were introduced, and the curriculum was expanded to include more science and practical or vocational courses. At the same time German educational doctrines, stressing the necessity of arousing the student's desire to learn, stirred the attention of American educators. Among those impressed by the German theories was John Dewey, one of the pragmatic philosophers and a member of the faculty of the school of education of the University of Chicago. In lectures and essays in the 1890s, Dewey proposed that education should be considered as a part of the social process, that its purpose should be to prepare students to live in modern society, and that pupils should learn by doing instead of by the traditional rote or drill method. His program of progressive education had its greatest impact after 1900.

EXPANDING HIGHER EDUCATION

Powerfully stimulating the expansion of higher learning were huge new financial resources made available by the national government and private benefactors. The national government, by the Morrill Land Grant Act of the Civil War period, donated land to states for the establishment of colleges to teach, among other subjects, agriculture and mechanical arts. After 1865, particularly in the West and the South, states began to exploit the possibilities of the act to strengthen existing institutions or to found new ones. In some cases the proceeds went to a single state university with an agricultural and mechanical division, and in other cases to a separate college for the practical arts. In all, sixty-nine "land grant" institutions came into existence, among them the universities of Wisconsin, California, Minnesota, and Illinois.

Supplementing the resources of the government were the millions of dollars contributed by business and financial tycoons, who endowed private institutions. The motives of the magnates were various: they were influenced by the gospel of wealth; they thought that education would blunt class differences; they realized that the demands of an industrial society called for specialized knowledge—or they were simply vain. Men like Rockefeller and Carnegie gave generously to such schools as Harvard, Chicago, Northwestern, Syracuse, Yale, and Columbia. Other philanthropists founded new universities and thereby perpetuated their family names—Vanderbilt, Johns Hopkins, Cornell, Tulane, and Stanford.

Booker T. Washington on Negro Education [1895]

Washington rose from slavery to the leadership of his people. Founding Tuskegee Institute in Alabama, he advocated that the Negro improve his economic status before reaching for political rights. To that end Washington, in a speech in 1895, advocated a vocational type of education, which prompted some Negroes to accuse him of subordinating the race's struggle for equal rights:

Our greatest danger is that in the great leap from slavery to freedom we may overlook the fact that the masses of us are to live by the productions of our hands, and fail to keep in mind that we shall prosper in proportion as we learn to dignify and glorify common labour and put brains and skill into the common occupations of life; shall prosper in proportion as we learn to draw the line between the superficial and the substantial, the ornamental gewgaws of life and the useful. No race can prosper till it learns that there is as much dignity in tilling a field as in writing a poem. It is at the bottom of life we must begin, and not at the top. Nor should we permit our grievances to overshadow our opportunities.

Taking over as president of Harvard in 1869 at the age of thirty-five, Charles W. Eliot pioneered a break with the traditional curriculum. The usual course of studies at American universities emphasized classical and humanistic courses: ancient languages, mathematics, ethics, and rhetoric; and each institution prescribed a rigid program of required courses. Under Eliot's leadership, Harvard dropped most of its required courses in favor of an elective system and increased its course offerings to stress the physical and social sciences, the fine arts, and modern languages. Soon other institutions in all sections of the country were following Harvard's lead.

Eliot also renovated the Harvard medical and law schools, raising the requirements and lengthening the residence period, and again the Harvard model affected other schools. Improved technical training in other professions accompanied the advances in medicine and law. Both state and private universities hastened to establish schools of architecture, engineering, education, journalism, and business. The leading center for graduate study, based on the German system with the Ph.D. degree as its highest award, was the Johns Hopkins University (founded in 1876). In 1875 there were only 399 graduate students in the United States, but by 1900 the number had risen to more than 5,000.

Two groups in American society – women and Negroes – did not receive the full benefits of higher education. Before the Civil War, girls had been generally admitted on an equal basis to elementary and secondary schools, but the doors of most colleges were closed to them. A few private colleges for women had been founded, and a very few schools (three, to be exact) admitted girls to study with boys. After the war a number of additional women's colleges came into existence, generally as the result of donations from philanthropists: Vassar, Wellesley, Smith, Bryn Mawr, and Goucher. In addition, some the largest private universities established on their campuses separate colleges for women. But the greatest educational opportunities for women opened in the Middle West, where the state universities began to admit women along with men.

Negroes reaped the fewest advantages from the educational renaissance. In the South, and also in most parts of the North, they attended segregated elementary and secondary schools that were nearly always poorer than the white schools. Negroes desiring a higher education were almost universally barred from white institutions and had to attend one of the colleges established for their race by Northern philanthropy: Howard University, in Washington; Fisk University, in Nashville; Straight University, in New Orleans; or Shaw University, in Raleigh. Some Negro leaders were disturbed by the tendency of their people to seek a "classical" education that did not fit them for the economic position they occupied in the South. For the transitional period after emancipation, these leaders believed, an industrial education, stressing vocational training and the dignity of labor, was preferable. The result of their thinking was the establishment, with aid from private sources, of the Hampton Normal and Industrial Institute in Virginia and the Tuskegee Institute in Alabama, the latter presided over by Booker T. Washington, the most influential Negro leader of his times.

Many adults sought learning through agencies other than colleges. Summer after summer, thousands flocked to the Chautauqua Institution in western New York to hear lectures on a variety of subjects. Chautauqua offered a concentrated short course for teachers and others in residence; it also provided extension courses and a four-year home reading program for nonresident clients. In addition Chautauqua companies toured rural America bringing music and lectures to people who received no other exposure to such culture.

Public libraries appeared in increasing numbers, especially in the cities and larger towns. Andrew Carnegie gave $45 million of his steel fortune for the construction of public libraries, wisely stipulating that communities taking his money had to maintain the institutions. Through the benefactions of men like Carnegie and through public support, over 9,000 free libraries had come into being by 1900.

THE PUBLISHING BUSINESS

Newspapers and magazines provided the reading matter for most Americans. During the period 1870–1910 the circulation of daily newspapers had a nearly ninefold increase (from less than 3 million to more than 24 million), which was over three times as great as the increase in population.

Meanwhile, journalism changed in various ways: (1) Newspapers became predominantly news organs, while editorial opinion and the editorial page declined in importance. (2) The nature of news changed. Politics received less attention, and there was an increasing emphasis on what was called the "human-interest" story. (3) Journalism became a recognized and respected profession. Salaries of reporters doubled. Able and educated men were attracted to the profession, and schools of journalism

were begun on university campuses. (4) With the passing of personal journalism, newspapers became corporations, impersonal business organizations similar to those emerging in industry, their worth often reckoned in millions of dollars. At the same time, they tended to become standardized. The press services furnished the same news to all their subscribing papers, and syndicates came into existence to provide their customers with identical features, columns, editorials, and pictures. By the turn of the century there were several newspaper chains, harbingers of a development that would become stronger in the future. Thus the newspapers conformed to and reinforced the trend toward uniformity that characterized American society as a whole. (5) There was a distinct improvement in the physical appearance of newspapers. The traditional pages of poorly and closely printed columns, each with its own headlines, disappeared; in their place came something resembling the modern paper, complete with varied make-up, pictures, cartoons, and imaginative advertising.

For almost twenty years after the Civil War, the principal magazines in the country were monthlies and weeklies that reached only a limited number of readers. Essentially, they were literary journals run by literary men. They were always genteel and in good (but often dull) taste; they sold for 35 cents a copy (a high price for those times); and the circulation of the largest did not exceed 130,000. The leading monthlies were *Harper's Magazine* and the *Atlantic Monthly*, both of which antedated the war, *Scribner's Monthly*, which was founded in 1870 and became the *Century* in 1881, and *Scribner's Magazine*, established in 1887. Somewhat similar were the weeklies: the *Nation*, the *Independent*, and *Harper's Weekly*, all published in New York.

During the decade of the eighties, a new type of magazine appeared—the popular magazine, designed to appeal to the masses and to achieve a mass circulation. One of the important pioneers of the popular journal was Edward W. Bok, who took over the *Ladies' Home Journal* in 1889 and, by employing writers who produced material to appeal to female readers, built the circulation of the magazine to over 700,000. Following Bok was Frank A. Munsey, the greatest of the popular publishers, who utilized the techniques of mass production and technology—cheap but attractive printing, low prices, and lavish advertising—to make *Munsey's Magazine* one of the most widely read organs in the country. The older *Saturday Evening Post* adopted many of the new methods and, by catering to the standards of the middle class, it led all other journals in circulation. Popular magazines, priced at 5 to 15 cents, had circulations of up to a million.

Book publishing became a business, and, in line with the trend in industry, a big business. The corporation replaced the individual publisher, and publishing became more impersonal and increasingly commercial. For approximately twenty years after the war most publishing houses, of whom the American Pub-

lishing Company of Hartford, Connecticut, was a leading example, sold books only by subscription. But gradually this type of organization was supplanted by the large firm that sold its products to book stores and reached the public through advertising techniques. By 1900 most of the big publishing houses were centered in New York City, the recognized publishing capital of the country and also the largest literary market. The passage by Congress in 1891 of an International Copyright Law prevented American publishers from pirating foreign books without payment (and also prevented foreign pirating of American books). The result was that publishers had to rely more on American authors and pay them better.

Culture in the Gilded Age

In a novel, *The Gilded Age* (1873), Mark Twain and Charles Dudley Warner satirized the men and manners of industrial society and thus provided a name that is sometimes applied to the last decades of the nineteenth century. The novel deals with greedy men and their get-rich-quick schemes. It suggests that American life, though showy on the surface, was essentially acquisitive and corrupt. Its authors thus reflected the economic and social changes of the time. Different writers responded to these changes in a variety of ways. Some faced up to the realities of the industrializing and urbanizing trend; others sought a vicarious escape for themselves and for their readers.

REFLECTIONS IN LITERATURE

Though New York City was the publishing center, the production of literature—the actual writing—was done all over the country. A literary renaissance began in the West and the South as well as the East. Writers in each section, describing their home scenes in local-color stories, found a national market for their wares.

Writers of the local-color school thought of themselves as realists. Rebelling against the sentimentality of the tear-jerking popular novelists like Mary Jane Holmes (whose thirty-nine

novels sold more than 2 million copies), they insisted on careful reporting, real people and real plots, and an honest rendition of such things as dialect, dress, food, and manners. Usually, however, they were content with an accurate surface description that did not come to grips with fundamental problems, and on occasion some of them wrote sentimental nonsense.

In New England, Sarah Orne Jewett and Mary E. Wilkins Freeman portrayed the disappearing social order of their section: its rural scenes and ways, its isolated farms, and its decaying seaport towns. Of the two, Miss Jewett was the finer artist; her *The Country of the Pointed Firs* (1896) was far above the reportorial level of the average local-color author. In the South, George Washington Cable affectionately described the antebellum Creole life of Louisiana but was so outspoken on the race question that he had to take refuge in the North. Most famous of the Southern writers was Joel Chandler Harris, who recorded Georgia folk tales and Negro life in *Uncle Remus* (1880). Thomas Nelson Page extolled in fiction the old Virginia aristocracy. In the Middle West, Edward Eggleston presented an honest account of early Indiana life in *The Hoosier Schoolmaster* (1871), and James Whitcomb Riley gave a folksy view of contemporary Indiana life in his popular verse. In the Far West, Bret Harte

Mark Twain with His Friends
The author sat regally at the head of the table at a dinner given him on his seventieth birthday in the famous and garish Delmonico's restaurant in New York City. (Library of Congress)

wrote sentimental stories of the mining frontier. Mark Twain, while living in California, burst into national prominence with a humorous sketch, "The Celebrated Frog of Calaveras County," and he portrayed aspects of the last frontier in *Roughing It* (1872).

Mark Twain (born Samuel Clemens) began his career on a newspaper, and he long considered himself to be a journalist. The public long insisted on regarding him as merely a humorist, but he was probably the greatest American novelist in the era between 1865 and 1900. His first important success, *The Innocents Abroad* (1869), a tale of American tourists in Europe, was a loud and scornful laugh at Old World decay and hypocrisy — and also at American worship of European institutions. His literary fame, however, rests primarily on *The Adventures of Tom Sawyer* (1876) and *The Adventures of Huckleberry Finn* (1885), sensi-

tive and sympathetic accounts of life in rural mid-America.

Not all the writers were concerned with depicting departing cultures. Some viewed with misgiving the culture of their own times, and deplored its materialism and economic inequalities. Gradually there developed a literature of protest, expressed chiefly in the medium of the problem novel. The dissenters attacked their targets from many and varied angles. A few, like Henry Adams in *Democracy* (1880) and John Hay in *The Breadwinners* (1884), spoke for the old aristocracy, the former ruling class; in criticizing the crassness of the new rich, they merely expressed the resentment of their group at being dethroned. No novelist of stature voiced the aspirations of labor, although Stephen Crane in *Maggie: A Girl of the Streets* (1893) described slum conditions and urban poverty with somber realism. For rural America and its small towns, Hamlin Garland and Edgar W. Howe grimly performed a similar descriptive job. Garland, smashing the traditional idyllic picture of pastoral culture, exposed in *Main-Travelled Roads* (1891) the ugliness, isolation, and drudgery of farm life, and Howe in *The Story of a Country Town* (1883) starkly painted the narrow, provincial nature of the American village.

A few literary critics of the American scene retreated from its vigor and materialism and found refuge in Europe. Preeminent among them was Henry James, who studied and described his country from England. In such novels as *The American* (1876), *An International Episode* (1878), and *Daisy Miller* (1879), he detailed the impact of Europe's ancient culture upon visiting Americans. In his coldly realistic volumes, the Americans are usually frustrated or defeated by Europe, but nearly always they appear more virile than the civilization they cannot understand. During his later years, James confessed he wished he had remained in America.

The greatest realistic novelist of the period, ranking second only to Twain in the hierarchy of letters, was William Dean Howells. His realism was confined to the common and the average; shunning the abnormal, he was the most painstaking literary historian of what was normal in the America of his age. In *The Rise of Silas Lapham* (1884), he portrayed shrewdly and in not completely flattering terms the psychology of the self-made businessman. His later novels, written during the social upheaval and labor strife of the nineties, dealt with social problems and social injustices.

ART AND ARCHITECTURE

American attitudes toward the arts in the Gilded Age paralleled those manifested toward literature. Popular tastes, largely determined by the middle class, admired paintings that told a conventional story, pointed a moral, or photographically reproduced familiar people and scenes. The artists whose works were most widely viewed were the illustrators for the popular magazines and the weeklies.

But Americans also had opportunities to see the best painting and sculpture of Europe's past. The newly rich business magnates set out with vigorous determination to patronize art and artists and to acquire, as part of their process of acquiring culture, the finest collections their money would buy. They purchased, regardless of cost, many of the art treasures of Europe, which possessed, their agents taught them, the only art worthy of the name, and installed them in their palace homes. Sometimes they did more—they established public art galleries or museums of fine arts, and eventually nearly all of the private collections found their way into public depositories. At the close of the Civil War not a single American city could boast of a good art gallery, but by 1900 there was a gallery or museum of at least adequate status in every metropolitan center. Thousands of Americans could and did see the best paintings and sculpture of Europe's past.

In the years after the Civil War most American painters received their training in Europe. Some remained there as expatriates (like the writer Henry James), among them James McNeill Whistler and John Singer Sargent. Whistler, who is often ranked as the greatest genius in the history of American art, was equally proficient in several media—oil, watercolor, etching—and with several themes—portraits and his so-called nocturnes, impressionistic sketches of moonlight on water and other scenes. He was one of the first to appreciate the beauty of Japanese color prints and to introduce Oriental concepts into Western art. Equally versatile but not as talented was Sargent, who built his international reputation on his portraits.

Breaking away from European influences was a small group of artists, of whom the ablest were John La Farge, Winslow Homer, and Thomas Eakins. La Farge's experiments with light and color anticipated the Impressionists. He worked with both landscapes and portraits, was our first important muralist, and probably is still America's most distinguished stained-glass artist. Homer, who began as a magazine illustrator, was vigorously and almost blatantly American. All of his powerful and rugged paintings dealt with native scenes and people; his best pictures were of the sea and maritime life on the New England coast.

American sculpture in the years immediately following the Civil War was dominated by Italian influences and the neoclassical tradition. When American sculptors made statues of

American leaders, they produced figures that resembled Roman senators and indeed were often clothed in flowing robes or togas. But gradually France supplanted Italy as an influence, and American sculptors, many of whom were trained in Paris, began to work out an art form distinctively American. One of the first to break from the Italian tradition was John Quincy Adams Ward with his statues of Indians and Negroes. Another was Daniel Chester French, who produced a number of realistic statues of great Americans, the most famous being the imposing Lincoln in the Lincoln Memorial at Washington. Incomparably the greatest American sculptor of the period was Augustus Saint-Gaudens, an Irish shoemaker's son who did more than any native artist to free American sculpture from its European bonds. His statues of Generals Grant and Sherman and of Admiral Farragut and, above all, his Lincoln in Lincoln Park, Chicago, were authentically American and impressively beautiful.

Before the Civil War the dominant influence in American architecture had been the classic Greek. Public buildings and dwellings throughout the country copied the lines of ancient Greek edifices. By 1860, however, the so-called Greek revival had spent its force, and another style, also a revival, had appeared. It became the rage of the Gilded Age. This was Gothic or, more accurately, an American version of the Gothic, with generous borrowings from other styles and some original native techniques added.

One of the first Americans to break with the Gothic tradition was Richard Morris Hunt, who designed dozens of homes for the business tycoons and became known as the architect of fashionable society. Although his houses were as large and elaborate as the Gothic edifices, they sprang from a different influence and reproduced a different mood—the light and lavish spirit of the French Renaissance. French chateaux and townhouses by Hunt dotted the rural resort areas of the East and its cities. Another rebel against the Gothic was Henry Hobson Richardson, the best-known architect of the period, who attempted to adapt the Romanesque form of France and Spain to the American scene. His public buildings, of which his churches are the most famous, and his houses were marked by solid but often graceful arches, heavy, short pillars, and simple carving; in their low-lying strength they resembled nothing so much as forts. Still another dissenting note was sounded by C. F. McKim, of the New York firm of McKim, Mead, and White, who endeavored to revive the Renaissance style by fitting it to American needs.

These men, however large their talents, were essentially imitative and derivative. They copied and adapted European forms, and their designs had little relevance to the facts of American life and little utility for the needs of the American scene, especially for the growing urban centers. Both the virtues and the faults of American architecture were demonstrated at the Chicago World's Fair of 1893. Most of the buildings shown were in the classical style; although they possessed a certain stately beauty, they revealed fully the unimaginative character of American architecture and the strength of the European bonds holding it. But there also emerged from the Fair an authentic genius, the first great original American architect— Louis Sullivan. Sullivan, who designed the Transportation Building for the Fair, denounced the work done there by most of his colleagues as mere copies rather than creations, "a naked exhibition of charlatanry . . . conjoined with expert salesmanship of the materials of decay."

NEW USES OF LEISURE

Many Americans, especially those of the urban middle and professional classes, found that they had more leisure at their command, and they had incomes sufficient to gratify their demands for pleasure. Even the workers had more free time, and they too sought satisfactory forms of recreation. The late nineteenth century witnessed the rise of organized spectator sports, the presentation of athletic events as entertainment for large audiences, and the organization of sports as a business.

Most popular of all the organized sports and well on its way to becoming the national game was baseball. Its origins probably stretched back to 1839, when Abner Doubleday, a civil engineering student, laid out a diamond-shaped field at Cooperstown, New York, and attempted to standardize the rules governing the playing of such games as town ball and four old cat, the ancestors of baseball. By the

An Early Football Game
*Here, in an 1899 contest between Cornell and Rochester, the ball is being put into
play by a "scrum," similar to that of rugby. The ball was placed on the ground,
and a circle of players tried to kick it out to their respective teammates. The
"father of American football," one-time Yale star Walter Camp, led in modernizing
the game. He persuaded the rulemakers to reduce the number of players to eleven
on each side, to permit the offensive team to put the ball into play from a line of
scrimmage, with a quarterback, and to require the team to advance the ball five
yards in three plays (and then, later, ten yards in four plays) or give it up to the
opposing team. Camp also helped to eliminate excessive roughness from what had
been a remarkably brutal sport. He selected the first "All-American" eleven.
(Library of Congress)*

end of the Civil War, interest in the game had grown rapidly. Over 200 teams or clubs existed, some of which toured the country playing rivals; they belonged to a national association of "Baseball Players" that had proclaimed a set of standard rules. These teams were amateurs or semiprofessionals, but as the game waxed in popularity, it offered opportunities for profit, and the first professional team, the Cincinnati Red Stockings, appeared in 1869. Other cities soon fielded professional teams, and in 1876 the present National League was organized, chiefly by Albert Spalding. Soon a rival league appeared, the American Association. Competition between the two was intense, and in 1883 they played a postseason contest, the first "world's series." The American Association eventually collapsed, but in 1900 the American League was organized.

The second most popular game, football, arose in the colleges and universities. At first football had been played by rival student groups at the same school. Then in 1869 occurred the first intercollegiate game in this country, between Princeton and Rutgers, with twenty-five men on each side. Soon other Eastern schools fielded teams, organized a conference, the American Intercollegiate Football Association, and attempted to standardize the rules.

As football grew in popularity, it spread to other sections, notably to the Middle Western state universities, soon destined to overthrow the Eastern schools as the powers of the game. It also began to exhibit those taints of professionalism that have marked it ever since. Some schools employed as players "ringers," tramp athletes who were not even registered as students. In an effort to eliminate such abuses, Amos A. Stagg, athletic director and coach at the University of Chicago, led in forming the Western Conference, or Big Ten, in 1896.

A game that would eventually become one of the great spectator sports, basketball, was invented in 1891 at Springfield, Massachusetts, by Dr. James A. Naismith. It is the only major sport that is completely American in origin.

Boxing did not become a respectable sport until the 1880s. Before that time prize fights were illegal in practically every state, and bouts had to be conducted in isolated places beyond the reach of law officials. The existing rules were few and encouraged brutality. Contestants fought without gloves; a round ended when one man was knocked down; and a fight continued until one of the participants was unwilling or unable to go on. In the 1870s the Marquis-of-Queensberry rules were introduced in England and later in the United States. By these regulations, fighters were required to wear padded gloves, a round was limited to three minutes, and certain rough practices and types of blows were ruled out. The first American boxer to adopt the new rules was John L. Sullivan, who had become heavyweight champion of the world in 1882. Although Sullivan occasionally returned to bare-knuckle fighting, he invested the sport with a respectability it had never known. It was raised to a higher plane by James J. Corbett, "Gentleman Jim," who dethroned Sullivan in 1892. Five years later Corbett dropped the title to Bob Fitzsimmons, who in turn was knocked out by James J. Jeffries in 1899.

Before 1900 golf and tennis were almost completely participant rather than spectator sports. The first modern golf course in the United States was laid out at Yonkers, New York, in 1888, and the first golf tournament in the country was played at Newport, Rhode Island, six years later. The only courses were at exclusive private clubs, and until after 1900 the game was restricted to the rich. Much the same was true of tennis, first played at Eastern resorts frequented by the wealthy. The United States Lawn Tennis Association was organized in 1881 to standardize the rules and encourage the game, and in 1897 American tennis players engaged an English team in the first international match.

In the small towns and villages of rural America, recreation continued to follow more traditional patterns. People came together for entertainment at county fairs, political rallies, and court sessions. Always a big event in a rural community was the arrival of a Chautauqua company with its tent and array of lecturers, musicians, and other luminaries. Even more colorful was the circus with its display of exotic wonders, amazing to rural people who had never traveled far from their birthplace. To send a circus across the country was expensive, and many smaller companies could not stand the cost. By 1900 the circus industry was dominated by two large firms, Barnum and Bailey, and Ringling Brothers.

The nineties saw the birth of the bicycle craze. Bicycling was both a recreation and, for many people in urban areas, a convenient method of transportation. The bicycle in the 1880s, with a high wheel in front, often pitched the rider over the handlebars for a "header" in the dirt. It was too dangerous for practically everyone except the most daring young men. The "safety" bicycle of the 1890s, with two wheels of equal size and with pneumatic tires, invited riders of both sexes and all ages. By 1900 an estimated 10 million Americans, mostly adults, were riding bicycles. While it lasted, the mania had some influence on American life. It brought into being a new industry for the manufacture of the vehicles. The cyclists, organized in the League of American Wheelmen, spurred local governments to improve highways. And cycling changed clothing styles as many young women put on blouses and moderate-length skirts in place of the former dragging street dresses, which got in the rider's way.

The bicycle prepared the way for the coming of the automobile. The two-wheeler not only brought some good roads for the first cars to run on; it also provided essential components of the early models, such as tubular steel, wire wheels, pneumatic tires, and the chain-and-sprocket drive. Many of the pioneers among American automobile builders, such as Henry Ford, once had been bicycle mechanics.

Selected Readings

Frontier Interpretations and Miscellany

F. J. Turner, *The Frontier in American History**
(1920); R. A. Billington, *Frederick Jackson Turner*
(1973); H. N. Smith, *Virgin Land: The American West
as Symbol and Myth** (1950); W. P. Webb, *The Great
Plains** (1931); J. C. Malin, *The Grassland of North
America* (1947); H. R. Lamar, *The Far Southwest,
1846–1912* (1966); R. M. Robbins, *Our Landed Heritage: The Public Domain, 1776–1936** (1942); E. S.
Pomeroy, *The Territories and the United States,
1864–1890* (1947); Wayne Gard, *The Great Buffalo
Hunt* (1959).

Mining

W. S. Greever, *The Bonanza West: The Story of the
Western Mining Rushes, 1848–1900* (1963); R. W.
Paul, *Mining Frontiers of the Far West, 1848–1880*
(1963); C. H. Shinn, *Mining Camps: A Study in American Frontier Government** (1885); Wayne Gard,
Frontier Justice (1949).

Cattle and Sheep Raising

E. S. Osgood, *The Day of the Cattleman** (1929); E. E.
Dale, *The Range Cattle Industry* (1930); Lewis Atherton, *The Cattle Kings* (1961); J. B. Frantz and J. E.
Choate, Jr., *The American Cowboy: The Myth and the
Reality* (1955); Philip Durham and E. L. Jones, *The
Negro Cowboy* (1965); E. N. Wentworth, *Shepherd's
Empire* (1945).

Farming

F. A. Shannon, *The Farmer's Last Frontier, 1860–
1897* (1945); G. C. Fite, *The Farmer's Frontier, 1865–
1900* (1966); Everett Dick, *The Sod-House Frontier,
1854–1890* (1937).

The Indians

F. G. Roe, *The Indian and the Horse* (1955); H. H.
Jackson, *A Century of Dishonor** (1881); L. G. Priest,
*Uncle Sam's Stepchildren: The Reformation of the
United States Indian Policy, 1865–1887* (1942); H. E.
Fritz, *The Movement for Indian Assimilation, 1860–*

1890 (1963); C. M. Oehler, *The Great Sioux Uprising*
(1959); Robert Utley, *Last Days of the Sioux Nation**
(1963); J. C. Olson, *Red Cloud and the Sioux Problem*
(1965); Stanley Vestal, *Warpath and Council Fire*
(1948) and *Sitting Bull* (1957); F. F. Van de Water,
Glory Hunter (1934), on Custer; Jay Monaghan,
Custer (1959); Stan Hoig, *The Sand Creek Massacre*
(1961); O. B. Faulk, *The Geronimo Campaign* (1969);
R. K. Andrist, *The Long Death: The Last Days of the
Plains Indians* (1964); Dee A. Brown, *Bury My Heart
at Wounded Knee: An Indian History of the American
West* (1971); M. D. Beal, *"I Will Fight No More"*
(1963), on Chief Joseph.

Education

Frederick Rudolph, *The American College and University: A History** (1962); L. R. Veysey, *The Emergence of the American University* (1965); Richard
Hofstadter and Walter Metzger, *The Development of
Academic Freedom in the United States* (1955); L. A.
Cremin, *The Transformation of the School: Progressivism in American Education, 1876–1957** (1961);
L. R. Harlan, *Booker T. Washington: The Making of a
Black Leader, 1856–1901* (1972).

Religion

C. H. Hopkins, *The Rise of the Social Gospel in American Protestantism, 1865–1915* (1940); A. I. Abell,
*The Urban Impact on American Protestantism, 1865–
1900* (1943); H. F. May, *Protestant Churches and Industrial America* (1949).

Literature

Van Wyck Brooks, *New England: Indian Summer,
1865–1915** (1940); Larzer Ziff, *The American 1890's:
Life and Times of a Lost Generation* (1966); Everett
Carter, *Howells and the Age of Realism* (1954); Bernard De Voto, *Mark Twain's America** (1932); Justin
Kaplan, *Mr. Clemens and Mark Twain* (1966); Elizabeth Stevenson, *Henry Adams** (1955); R. B. Perry,
The Thought and Character of William James (2 vols.,
1935); F. O. Matthiessen, *The James Family* (1947);
Stow Persons, *The Decline of American Gentility*
(1973).

Architecture

W. A. Starrett, *Skyscrapers and the Men Who Built Them* (1928); John Szarkowski, *The Idea of Louis Sullivan* (1957).

Popular Culture

Ray Ginger, *The Age of Excess: The United States from 1877 to 1914* (1965); R. O. and Victoria Case, *We Called It Culture: The Story of Chautauqua* (1958); J. D. Hart, *The Popular Book** (1950); F. L. Mott, *A History of American Magazines*, vol. 3, *1865–1885* (1938), and vol. 4, *1885–1905* (1957); D. C. Seitz, *Joseph Pulitzer* (1924); J. K. Winkler, *W. R. Hearst* (1928); F. R. Dulles, *America Learns to Play* (1940); J. A. Krout, *Annals of American Sport* (1924).

*Titles available in paperback.

The Swell of Agrarian Protest

Nineteen

In the 1880s the major parties in the United States were like two bottles that had different labels but otherwise were identical—and both were empty. So it seemed to the Englishman James Bryce, the most perspicacious of all foreign commentators on American institutions next to the Frenchman Alexis de Tocqueville. "Tenets and policies, points of political doctrine and points of political practice, have all but vanished," Bryce wrote in *The American Commonwealth* (1888). "All has been lost, except office or the hope of it."

In American society there were serious problems arising out of the development of big business and monopoly, the organization of labor and the resulting industrial conflict, the decline of agricultural prices and the worsening position of the farmer, and the defects in the economic system that caused it to collapse every twenty years or so (in 1873 and again in 1893). But the leaders of the major parties evaded these problems as best they could.

Politics was more highly professionalized than ever, and the politicians played it like a game that had little to do with economic and social realities. With the politicians the object was to win power and jobs. In many cities or entire states a political boss headed a machine (organization) that operated as an "invisible government" controlling the official government of the city or state. The machine bought votes and sold governmental favors. The national parties looked to the boss and the machine to provide the votes with which to win elections.

The parties depended for support not only on the patronage of government but also on contributions from business. It took the assassination of a President to shock the politicians into accepting a partial reform of the spoils system. After that, the parties had to depend more and more on corporation gifts. The president of the sugar trust testified before a congressional investigating committee that during the 1892 campaign

---

"Division of Labor"
The farmer turns the grindstone of "war taxes" while the monopolist sharpens the ax of "high protection." The feeling that big business—with the aid of government taxes and tariffs—exploited the common people led to late-nineteenth-century protests such as Populism. From Puck, *February 1, 1888. (Culver Pictures)*

his company had contributed money to both the Republicans and the Democrats. "The American Sugar Refining Company has no politics of any kind," he concluded."Only the politics of business?" he was asked. "Only the politics of business," he replied.

Already, in the early 1890s, a tide of protest was swelling and dashing against the politics of business. It was headed by discontented farmers, but it included other dissatisfied groups whose numbers were increased by the onset of the depression. It encountered

the forces of conservatism and partially recoiled before them but recovered to reach a roaring climax in the election of 1896. Thereafter the protest movement receded, as the economic system demonstrated its capacity to enlarge the general well-being, and the political system showed its ability to absorb dissenters into the traditional two parties. Meanwhile, the protesters had displayed a moral fervor and a class bitterness that frightened and appalled the more secure and sober elements of society. "It was a fanaticism like the crusades," wrote the Kansas editor William Allen White.

The Politics of Complacency

It has sometimes been thought that political parties ought to define and discuss issues as sharply as do debating clubs. But the major parties in the United States have seldom divided on fundamental principles except in times of crisis (as during the 1850s and the 1890s). More commonly the parties have been concerned with confusing issues rather than clarifying them, with harmonizing interests rather than antagonizing them. The politics of the years from 1877 to 1888 illustrate in extreme form this function of the parties.

REPUBLICANS AND DEMOCRATS

Republicanism was almost a religion in the North. The Republican party, the Grand Old Party of Abraham Lincoln and the boys in blue, had saved the Union and freed the slaves. In election after election, long after Appomattox, Republican campaigners continued to recall the war record of their own party and attack the opposition as the party of treason and slavery. Related to this, as another reminder of the war, was the practice, every four years (except in 1884), of nominating as the Republican presidential candidate a veteran officer of the Union army.

Flights of campaign oratory thinly masked the economic composition and goals of the dominant party. Even more powerful in the party's councils than in the prewar era was the

business element, composed of manufacturers, bankers, investors, and government bondholders — more powerful because business was forging ahead of agriculture in the indices of national wealth and because industry was reaching out into every area and raising up champions in the West and South, which had been solidly agricultural. But still influential in the party was the farming wing, particularly because the farmers had more votes than businessmen. Other important elements of the party were the veterans of the Union armies, numbering perhaps a million and organized in potent pressure groups such as the Grand Army of the Republic, which found the Republicans cordial to the idea of soldier pensions, and which served as an auxiliary of the party.

In its economic composition the Democratic organization was, much as it had been in Jackson's time, largely a party of farmers and laborers — of small property holders. But it was a party without clear direction or goals, and here probably is the principal reason for its minority condition. The important Eastern wing, representing importing interests, was willing to accept the traditional Democratic low-tariff policy, but on other issues, and particularly on the question of a "sound" currency, it was as conservative as the Republicans. Any Democratic move to challenge the Republicans on economic issues was certain to scare off the Easterners. Even on the tariff, the Democrats

The Stalwart Boss of the Republicans
Handsome Roscoe Conkling, senator from New York, led the Stalwart faction of the Republicans. Blaine, who despised him, described Conkling as a "majestic, supereminent, overpowering, turkey-gobbler strut." In this cartoon Conkling is casting covetous eyes at the Republican presidential nomination for 1880, represented by the eagle. The smaller bird looking doubtfully at the boss is the independent vote. From Harper's Weekly *(1879).*

failed to demonstrate unity or take a firm position. As industry moved into the West and South, islands of protection appeared in these once free-trade regions to divide a once cohesive public opinion. In many elections the Democrats adopted an ambiguous tariff plank that hardly differed from that of their opponents, causing wags to quip that the party of Jefferson and Jackson stood for "a protective tariff for revenue only." In short, the party failed to devise a program that distinguished it from the Republicans, failed to offer a set of issues to those groups who were alarmed by the rise of big business, failed, above all, to be a party of opposition. It was a "me too" party asking for votes on the grounds that it could do what the Republicans were doing—only better and with less corruption.

Although the Republicans in a general sense represented the upper- and middle-income groups and the Democrats the average and lower groups, neither spoke for a precise economic interest. Both included people from all economic levels, and both embraced business and agricultural elements. When economic legislation was considered in Congress, the votes usually followed sectional rather than party lines; Western Republicans and Southern Democrats, for example, were likely to unite behind a measure of benefit to the agricultural interests.

Although the Republicans usually dominated the presidency, they did not always control Congress. The Democrats, with the solid South behind them and with the support of highly organized machines in Northern cities and states, sometimes managed to secure a majority in one or both houses of the legislative branch and thereby block Republican programs. When a Democrat sat in the White House, the converse was often true: the Republicans ruled at least one house and voted down Democratic measures. The failure of either party to control consistently all branches of the government is, of course, another reason for the absence of firm issues and the relative paucity of positive legislation.

Of the three branches of government, Congress was predominant. Retaining most of the powers and prerogatives it had seized in the struggle with Andrew Johnson, it easily overshadowed the presidency and the judiciary. Nor did it encounter any serious challenge from its traditional rival, the executive arm. None of the Presidents elected between 1868 and 1888, with the possible exception of Grover Cleveland, was a strong political leader.

The Republicans Matt Quay in Pennsylvania and Roscoe Conkling in New York were outstanding examples of the boss type. Tall, handsome, and flamboyant, Conkling ruled the Republican party in New York and swayed its councils in the United States Senate. To him politics was a game for professionals, not for amateur "carpet knights," and it was a rough game: "Parties are not built by deportment, or by ladies' magazines, or gush."

When Benjamin Harrison won the presidency in 1888, he ascribed his victory to Providence. Matt Quay knew better. "Providence hadn't a damn thing to do with it," he announced. He wondered if the candidate knew how many men had approached the gates of the penitentiary to make him President. Harrison soon learned the facts of political life. "When I came into power," he said later, "I found that the party managers had taken it all to themselves. I could not name my own Cabinet. They had sold out every place to pay the election expenses." The machines sustained their position by various techniques: making alliances with business interests and securing campaign contributions and other subsidies, assessing officeholders a share of their salaries, and employing gangs of vote "repeaters" or "floaters" or using other fraudulent methods to carry elections.

HAYES AND THE PATRONAGE

Before the end of Rutherford B. Hayes' administration two groups—the Stalwarts, led by Conkling of New York, and the Half-Breeds, captained by James G. Blaine of Maine—were competing for control of the Republican party, and threatening to split it. Only a subtle difference separated the factions. The Stalwarts, consisting of state bosses like Conkling and Oliver P. Morton of Indiana and Zachariah Chandler of Michigan, stood for machine politics and the allocation of political and material spoils to the victor. They were professional operators who believed in politics for its own sake. The Half-Breeds had practically the same concept of the functions of parties, but circumstances—specifically, the fact that the Stalwarts at first were stronger—forced them to adopt a more circumspect and sanctimonious role. They rendered lip service to such issues as civil service and governmental efficiency, although most of them were no more interested in reform than the Stalwarts.

Although Hayes awarded some offices to the machine elements of his party, he consis-

tently held up merit as the primary standard of appointment. His cabinet, headed by William M. Evarts as secretary of state, John Sherman as secretary of the treasury, and Carl Schurz as secretary of the interior, was an exceptionally able one; but four of the members had bolted the party in the Liberal defection of 1872 and one was a Southern Democrat. Hayes' patronage policy horrified the Stalwarts and hardly pleased the Half-Breeds; at the same time, it was sufficiently political to raise doubts among the civil-service reformers. The President yielded much of his power to influence any faction of his party when he announced early in his administration that he would not be a candidate for reelection. To complete Hayes' handicaps, the Democrats controlled the House

President and Mrs. Hayes
This photograph catches the dignity and sincerity that were the hallmarks of Hayes' character. His wife was strongly opposed to the drinking of intoxicating liquors and did not permit any to be served at White House functions. Critics dubbed her "Lemonade Lucy." (Library of Congress)

when he entered office, and two years later they captured the Senate too.

After settling the Reconstruction issue to his satisfaction, Hayes turned to the problem of governmental reform. Long an advocate of civil service, he instructed his executive deputies that he wished appointments awarded on the basis of merit, that assessments of salaries of employees for political purposes must stop, and that the party activities of officials should be limited. Schurz placed the Interior Department on a merit basis, and Treasury Secretary Sherman and a few other department heads also made some effort to comply with their chief's wishes. Others ignored or evaded them. The strength of the spoils system was so great that Hayes could not force the executive branch to accept his policy. He had even less luck with Congress. Despite repeated appeals by the President, the legislators refused to appropriate money to renew the civil-service commission created under Grant.

Hayes' persistent advocacy of civil service precipitated his biggest fight with Congress. As part of his campaign to reform the spoils-ridden Treasury bureaucracy, he removed from office two prominent officials in the New York custom house, Chester A. Arthur and Alonzo B. Cornell. Both men were leaders in Roscoe Conkling's organization, and the senator interpreted their removal as an attempt to undermine his machine. Striking back with the arrogance of a great state boss, he persuaded the Senate to deny confirmation of the men Hayes had named to replace Arthur and Cornell. Stubbornly the President refused to retreat, and kept on transmitting new appointments until finally the Senate ratified his choices. Hayes was the first President since 1865 to resist successfully the constant attempts of Congress to encroach on executive prerogatives.

THE MARTYRDOM OF GARFIELD

Fortunately for the faction-rent Republicans, prosperity had returned by the time of the election of 1880. An increased export trade and an upward spurt in industrial and agricultural production signaled the end of the depression and the beginning of another boom period. But the Republican leaders knew that not even prosperity could guarantee victory: they had to patch up their dissensions and settle on a nominee who could unite the party for another contest. Grant, backed by Conkling and the Stalwarts, was again a candidate, while the Half-Breeds were divided between Blaine and Sherman. At the Republican convention Grant led for thirty-five ballots but could not reach a majority. Then the anti-Grant forces united to nominate a "dark horse," James A. Garfield, a veteran member of the House of Representatives from Ohio. As Garfield was known as a Half-Breed, the convention, to conciliate the Stalwarts, gave the second place on the ticket to Chester A. Arthur, the Conkling henchman just dismissed from office by Hayes.

With the ancient and ill Tilden unavailable, the Democrats were without a leader. They acted as though they were also without hope of victory. As their candidate, they selected General Winfield Scott Hancock, who had won some fame as a corps commander in the Union army but was hardly a commanding national figure. Their apparent purpose was to refute the usual Republican charges of Democratic disloyalty in the Civil War. Also, having witnessed the success of the Republicans in running generals, they wanted to try their luck with a Democratic officer against Garfield, who had been a volunteer general. Although the platform called for a revenue tariff, it emphasized the "great fraud" of the election of 1876 as the paramount issue. As usual, the Democrats were harking back to the past instead of looking to the future.

During the bitter campaign, which revolved around such questions as Garfield's complicity in the Crédit Mobilier scandal and alleged errors committed by Hancock in the war, the Democratic candidate was pressed for a statement on the tariff. He replied that it was entirely a "local issue." As a description of how tariff schedules were arrived at in Congress, his phrase was reasonably accurate, but it constituted a virtual repudiation of the platform and removed the tariff as a campaign issue. In November Garfield piled up a decisive electoral majority of 214 to 155. But his popular vote was only about 10,000 more than his rival's: 4,454,000 to 4,444,000. The Republicans also captured both houses of Congress.

Up to the time of his accession to the presidency, the career of James A. Garfield had been a perfect example of the American success legend. Born in humble Ohio surroundings, in fact, in a log cabin, he worked from boyhood up, once laboring as a mule-driver on the Ohio Canal—"from the tow-path to the White House" was a theme the Republicans emphasized in the 1880 election. He worked his way through college, became a teacher, studied law and was admitted to the bar. In 1863 he was elected to the House of Representatives, where he served with increasing distinction until he became the Republican standard-bearer.

During his brief tenure of office, Garfield gave evidence that he intended to conduct a moderate Half-Breed administration. He appointed Blaine as secretary of state, and as postmaster general (the cabinet official having the most to do with patronage) Thomas L. James, a civil-service champion. Almost immediately James exposed a scandal in his department—the so-called star-route frauds. In many areas of the West mail was carried by stages or riders and assigned to contractors; on the postal list these routes were designated by stars. If a contractor could demonstrate that his costs had increased, his compensation could be raised without reopening the agreement. Investigation disclosed that collusive contracts had been awarded to certain Republican politicians, who then had secured increased payments for their services. Despite protests from some leading Republicans, Garfield backed up James in his inquiry. In dispensing patronage, Garfield gave the important jobs to Half-Breeds. He provoked a fight with Conkling by naming his own followers to federal positions in New York. When the President appointed a bitter Conkling foe as collector of the port of New York, the senator tried to prevent Senate confirmation. Failing this, he and his colleague, Platt, resigned and asked the New York legislature to reelect them. Their purpose was to awe Garfield into submission, but the legislators, in a fine display of perversity, chose two other men.

While the unseemly quarrel was dragging on, the evils of the spoils system were dramatically brought home to the American people. On July 2, 1881, after only four months in office, President Garfield was in the Washington railroad station, about to leave for a holiday trip, when a man in the crowd fired two pistol shots at him. As Garfield fell, the man with the gun shouted: "I am a Stalwart and Arthur is President now!" The assassin, Charles J. Guiteau, held a grudge because Garfield had refused to give him a government job (though evidently insane, Guiteau was hanged). Actually, Arthur was not yet President; Garfield lingered for nearly three months before dying. At his death, people concerned about the menace of machine politics were doubly grieved. Even some Republicans echoed the sentiment of the man who groaned: "Chet Arthur President of the United States! Good God!"

ARTHUR AND REFORM

For all of his political lifetime Chester A. Arthur had been a devoted, skilled, and open spoilsman. Before the assassination of Garfield, he had gone to Albany to lobby for the reelection of his benefactor and mentor, Conkling. But on becoming President, he pursued an independent course between the Republican factions, affiliating with neither and being dominated by neither, and he worked zealously and with partial success for the cause of reform. Undoubtedly he had been deeply affected by the grisly circumstances that brought him to the presidency. It may be that realizing he now stood in the spotlight of history, he guided his actions accordingly.

The revelation of the "new" Arthur dismayed most of the party bosses. Although the President reorganized the cabinet, he left the majority of Garfield's appointees in office. He vigorously pushed the prosecution of the star-route Republicans, who managed, however, to escape punishment. He vetoed a huge river and harbors bill on the grounds it was "pork-barrel" legislation, but Congress overrode him. In his first message to Congress he recommended a civil-service law, and he kept prodding the legislators to act. Although the spectacle of the great spoilsman championing reform seemed incongruous, Arthur was undoubtedly sincere, and his course was smart politics. With the public shocked by Garfield's assassination and disgusted by the postal frauds, sentiment for civil service was running high, and some kind of legislation would have been enacted whether Arthur had intervened or not.

Responding to popular as well as presidential pressure, Congress passed in 1883 the first national civil-service measure, the Pendleton

Act. By its terms a limited number of federal jobs were to be "classified": applicants for them were to be chosen on the basis of competitive written examinations. The law also forbade assessment of officeholders for political purposes. To administer the act, a bipartisan Civil Service Commission, headed by reformer Dorman B. Eaton, was established. At first only about 14,000 of some 100,000 offices were placed on the classified list. But the act provided that future Presidents might by executive order enlarge the number of positions subject to civil service. Every chief executive thereafter extended the list, primarily to "blanket" his appointees into office and prevent their removal by his successor. By this piecemeal and partisan process, the government finally achieved by the 1940s a system in which the majority of the people working for it were under the merit system.

RETURN OF THE DEMOCRATS

The election of 1884, with its absence of issues and its emphasis on the personal qualities of the candidates, epitomized the politics of the era of complacency. Arthur would have accepted the Republican nomination, but his independent course had pleased neither Half-Breeds nor Stalwarts. Ignoring him and other aspirants, the Republican convention nominated its most popular man and most vulnerable candidate, James G. Blaine, known to his adoring admirers as "the plumed knight" but to thousands of other Americans as "Old Mulligan Letters." His selection split the party badly. To the Stalwarts he was anathema; Conkling, asked if he intended to campaign for Blaine, snapped that he did not engage in criminal practice. The independent reform faction, now called the Mugwumps, announced they were prepared to bolt the party and support an honest Democrat. Rising to the bait, the Democrats nominated Grover Cleveland, the reform governor of New York. The platforms of the two parties were almost identical. Both endorsed revision of the tariff without endangering domestic industries, both approved and claimed credit for civil service, and both, taking account of popular rumblings against big business, spoke vaguely about subjecting corporations to some kind of national regulation.

With no real issues between the parties, the election was essentially a struggle for office, and the campaign developed into a mud-slinging contest involving the personal fitness, or more accurately, unfitness of the candidates. Eagerly the Democrats went to work on the plumed knight's unsavory record, reprinting the Mulligan correspondence and uncovering new damning letters. At torchlit rallies the Democrats chanted:

Blaine! Blaine! James G. Blaine!
Continental liar from the state of Maine!

Frantically the Republicans researched Cleveland's brief political career as mayor of Buffalo and governor of New York for evidence of corruption—a politician had to be corrupt, they seemed to assume—but found nothing. They did discover a juicy personal item. As a young man Cleveland had been accused of fathering an illegitimate child, and whether guilty or not, he had agreed to support the infant. He did not specifically deny the imputation when the Republicans brought it into the campaign. Thereafter at their rallies the Republicans roared out:

Ma! Ma! where's my Pa?
Going to the White House. Ha! Ha! Ha!

In addition to sex, the canvass featured the bloody shirt, waved vigorously by Blaine; freedom for Ireland from the British rule, held out to the Irish voters by Republican orators; and religion, a last-minute issue that may have decided the election. In the closing days of the campaign a delegation of Protestant ministers called on Blaine in New York City; their spokesman, Dr. Samuel Burchard, in the course of his remarks referred to the Democrats as the party of "Rum, Romanism, and Rebellion." Apparently Blaine, whose mother was a Catholic, did not catch the statement or notice its linking of elements. Soon the Democrats were spreading the news through New York and other Eastern cities that Blaine had countenanced a slander on the Catholic Church, and his denial came too late to counteract the charge. The so-called Burchard incident may have swung New York State to the Democrats, and New York was the pivotal state in what turned out to be an extremely close election. Cleveland had 219 electoral votes to Blaine's 182; the popular vote showed

James G. Blaine
*Blaine had an enthusiastic following among Republicans and was continually a
presidential hopeful from the 1870s to the 1890s, but he was handicapped by a
reputation for public dishonesty. This cartoon shows him as Narcissus—recalling
the Greek myth of the boy who fell in love with his own reflection and was
transformed into a flower. Blaine, covered with tattoos such as "corrupt lobby,"
here says to himself: "The remarkable resemblance to George Washington is what
strikes me!" (Culver Pictures)*

4,875,000 for Cleveland and 4,852,000 for
Blaine, a Democratic plurality of only 23,000.

Grover Cleveland was the ablest President
between Lincoln and Theodore Roosevelt.
Short and corpulent, brusque in manner, boldly beardless in a hirsute age, he was far from
being an appealing figure. He did possess character, courage, and integrity. In his brief career
in prominent offices—he had been elected
mayor of Buffalo in 1881 and governor of New
York in 1882—he had fought politicians, graft-
ers, pressure groups, and Tammany Hall. He
had become famous as the "veto mayor" and
the "veto governor," as an official who was not
afraid to say "No." This ability to be honestly
negative was the most positive feature of his

political personality; it was at once his greatest
strength and his most distressing weakness as a
political leader. It enabled him to withstand
pressure from any quarter, to oppose the
spoilsmen, and to uphold high standards of
official probity. It also rendered him tragically
incapable of understanding the problems of an
industrial society or the role of government in a
changing economic order.

CLEVELAND FINDS AN ISSUE

When Cleveland became President, he was
absorbed with plans to improve the administrative machinery of the government, to install

business standards in its operations, and to purify its processes. Issues such as the currency and the tariff did not greatly interest him, nor was he concerned with the problems of the farmer and the laborer. His knowledge of economics was slender and his economic philosophy almost primitively simple. He was sincerely opposed to a paternalistic and positive government that extended special favors to any group. Let all stand equal, the giant corporation and the worker, he proclaimed, never comprehending that there were vital power differences among contesting economic interests. He summed up his faith in a veto of an appropriation of $10,000 for drought-stricken farmers. The lesson must never be forgotten, he moralized, that "though the people support the Government, the Government should not support the people."

Although Cleveland was known as a civil-service reformer, in dealing with patronage he had to proceed with due partisan caution. After years of wandering in the political wilderness, the Democrats were hungry for offices, and they expected the President to throw the Republican "rascals" out—immediately and in wholesale lots. Instead, the President compromised in a manner that did not completely satisfy either his own party or his Mugwump followers. He added approximately 12,000 offices to the classified list, but of the jobs not under civil service he removed two-thirds of the incumbents and replaced them with deserving Democrats. Determined to check extravagance and congressional raids on the surplus, Cleveland vetoed a river and harbors bill, and attempted to introduce principles of economy and honesty into the awarding of soldier pensions.

On the pension issue, he stirred up a hornet's nest. For years real or alleged veterans of the Union army—who could not qualify under the existing general pension laws—had had no difficulty in getting Congress to enact private pension bills for their benefit. Many of the claims were fraudulent, but nobody ever examined them. Cleveland actually took the trouble to read them, and, outraged by what he found, vetoed over 200 such measures. When Congress, responding to pressure from the powerful Grand Army of the Republic (GAR), passed a Dependent Pension Bill to grant pensions to all veterans suffering from disabilities, no mat-

ter when or how contracted, he killed it with a veto. In reality, Cleveland was sympathetic to the claims of genuine veterans, and the total appropriation for pensions increased during his administration. But his vetoes enabled Republican and GAR orators to remind the voters of the peril of placing a Southern-dominated Democrat in the White House.

On another front of battle against corruption, Cleveland instructed his secretary of the interior to inspect past grants of public lands in the West to railroad, lumber, and cattle interests, and where the lands had been obtained on fraudulent or false ground to institute suits to recover them. Eventually some 81 million acres were restored to the government. Although businessmen bellowed that the President was acting like a radical, he was only being consistently conservative: no special favors to any group.

Cleveland himself precipitated one economic issue into the political arena. Always mildly dubious of the high tariff, he concluded after thorough study that the existing rates were responsible for the annual surplus that tempted Congress to reckless legislation. Once convinced, he acted with sudden and startling vigor. In December 1887 he devoted almost all of his annual message to the lawmakers to discussing the tariff and demanding its downward revision. Although he spoke bitingly of the great fortunes that had been built on protective duties and of the inflated living costs of the poor, he rested his case on immediate and practical considerations: the tariff was bringing in an unneeded surplus and the piling up of this surplus would eventually depress the economy. In a phrase that intrigued the public, he said: "It is a *condition* that confronts us, not a theory." Characteristically, he assured Congress that reductions could be made without endangering the interests of American manufacturers.

Immediately, the Southern and Western Democrats, who had been moving rapidly to a low-tariff position, responded to the President's leadership. They pushed the Mills Bill through the House, incorporating Cleveland's recommendations and providing for moderate reductions. Only four Democrats voted against it, and doubtless some of the Easterners went along in the knowledge that the Republican Senate would kill the measure. In the Senate

Grover Cleveland
*Cleveland was the first Democrat to be
elected President since the Civil War.
Honest, courageous, and stubborn, he was
extremely conservative and unable to
understand some of the new economic
problems emerging in his administration.
A bachelor when elected, he married while
in the White House. (Library of Congress)*

preferred another candidate. The platform emphasized the tariff question and pledged support to the President's policy of moderate revision. The Republicans had in protection what they were certain was a winning issue, but they were hard put to find an acceptable and available nominee. They finally decided on Benjamin Harrison of Indiana, who was relatively obscure and formidably respectable, and in their platform endorsed protection for American producers and generous pensions for Union veterans.

The campaign of 1888 was the first since the Civil War that was fought out on a definite issue, the first that involved a question of economic difference between the parties. It was also one of the most corrupt campaigns in American political history. Both parties employed the usual fraudulent methods of the day, but the Republicans, with a campaign fund contributed by apprehensive business interests and amounting to several million dollars, were the worse offenders.

When the votes were counted, it was obvious that the people had not registered a clear decision or authorized a definite mandate. Harrison had an electoral majority of 233 to 168, but Cleveland's popular vote exceeded Harrison's, 5,540,000 to 5,440,000.

the Republican leaders, believing that they could sell the tariff to the voters, met the issue head-on. As an alternative to the Mills Bill they enacted a protective measure. Action was deadlocked for the moment, and the tariff was squarely before the people as an issue in the election of 1888.

As the tariff fight swirled to a climax, the Democrats again named Cleveland as their standard-bearer, although some machine bosses and some Easterners, disgusted by his stand on civil service and lower duties, would have

The Farmers Organize

GRANGERS AND RAILROADS

Most farmers had always been strong individualists. But many of them eventually concluded that they could solve their problems – high costs, increasing debts, falling prices, declining status – only by overcoming their traditional individualism. They would have to organize and act in politics as a group.

The first farm organization to appear after the Civil War was established in boom times as a social association and was turned into an agency of agrarian protest at the onset of the 1873 depression.

On a tour through the South, Oliver H. Kelley, a clerk in the Department of Agriculture at Washington, became impressed with the isolation and drabness of rural life. In 1867 he and other department employees founded the National Grange of the Patrons of Husbandry, to which Kelley devoted years of labor as secretary. Local lodges of the order were called granges, and the organization is commonly known as the Grange. Its announced purposes were social, cultural, and educational. By bringing farm men and women together in groups, it aimed to diffuse knowledge of scientific agriculture, machines, and markets, to furnish a community feeling hitherto absent in rural society, and to keep agriculture in "step with the music of the age." Recognizing that human nature is intrigued by secrecy and ceremony, the founders provided for an elaborate system of initiation and ritual.

At first the Grange grew slowly. It filled an obvious rural need, but farmers were not attracted to it in large numbers while times were good. Then the depression of 1873 struck, and suddenly the farmers saw benefits to be achieved through organization. By 1875 the Grange claimed over 800,000 members and 20,000 local lodges. These appeared in almost every state but were most numerous in the staple-producing sections of the Middle West and the South.

As membership increased, the lodges in the Middle West turned to economic issues. They stressed the necessity of collective action by farmers to eliminate the middleman — through the organization of cooperatives — and the urgency of political action to curb the monopolistic practices of the railroads and warehouses. All over the midlands on Independence Day 1873, the "Farmers' Fourth of July," embittered yeomen assembled to hear Granger orators read "The Farmers' Declaration of Independence." The resolutions proclaimed that the time had come for farmers, "suffering from long continued systems of oppression and abuse, to rouse themselves from an apathetic indifference to their own interests." The declaration also vowed that the farmers would use "all lawful and peaceful means to free [themselves] from the tyranny of monopoly."

The Grangers launched the first major cooperative movement in the United States, though successful collective societies had exist-

ed earlier in England and other countries. The Grangers set up cooperative stores, creameries, elevators, warehouses, insurance companies, and factories that turned out machines, stoves, and other items. Some 400 enterprises were in operation at the height of the movement, but eventually most of them failed because of the inexperience of the operators and the opposition of middleman interests. Not all business groups fought the cooperatives; some sought their trade, and one corporation was formed specifically in 1872 to meet the wants of the Grangers, Montgomery Ward and Company, which brought the mail-order business into existence.

In political action the Grangers labored to elect to state legislatures candidates pledged to their program. Usually they operated through the existing Republican and Democratic parties, only occasionally putting up nominees under such party labels as "Antimonopoly" or "Reform." Marshaling their votes in the local lodges, they were able to gain control of the legislatures in most of the Middle Western states. Their purpose, openly and angrily announced, was to subject the railroads to social controls.

Between 1870 and 1874 the legislatures of Illinois, Iowa, Minnesota, and Wisconsin enacted laws to regulate railroads and warehouse and elevator facilities. These "Granger laws" authorized maximum rates for passenger and freight traffic, provided rules and rates for the storing of grain, and prohibited a number of alleged discriminatory practices. They were to be administered and enforced by special state commissions.

The railroads contested the legality of the laws, and eventually fought them from the state courts up to the United States Supreme Court. In 1877 the highest tribunal handed down a decision in the first of the "Granger cases," the case of *Munn* v. *Illinois*, involving the right of a state to fix storage rates for warehouses. Other cases concerned state laws establishing maximum rates for railroads.

Chief Justice Morrison R. Waite spoke for the Court in the Munn case, and his opinion formed the basis for the decisions on the railroad laws. The complainants, the warehouses and railroads, had rested their cause on two points: (1) the laws infringed the power of Congress to regulate interstate commerce; and

(2) they violated the due-process clause of the Fourteenth Amendment, namely, that a state could not deprive a "person" of property without due process of law. The plaintiffs were contending not only that a corporation was a person within the meaning of the Fourteenth Amendment, but also that expected income was property and that any regulation reducing income was deprivation of property within the meaning of the amendment. The Court rejected their arguments and validated the Granger laws. It held that a state in the exercise of its police power could regulate private property devoted to public use and affecting the general community; it conceded the right of a state to regulate interstate commerce in the absence of national regulation; and it dismissed "due process" with the observation that it was not intended to restrict the police power.

The Grange soon lost its position as a major force in the agricultural scene. By 1880 its membership had shrunk to 100,000. The collapse of its cooperative experiments and the ineffectiveness of its railroad laws drove some members away. Above all, it was weakened by a return of prosperity in the late seventies. The embattled farmers, who once had shouted for collective action, soon left the fold and resumed their old and familiar individualistic ways.

THE FARMERS' ALLIANCES

In the 1880s the prices of the great staples again declined, hard times returned to the South and the West, and the farmers of those regions, more embittered and frustrated than the Grangers, turned to more militant forms of organization. From the Carolinas to the Dakotas a multitude of farm societies bearing a variety of names mushroomed into existence, but by the end of the decade they had been combined into two major organizations: the National Farmers' Alliance, centering in the prairie states west of the Mississippi, and the Farmers' Alliance and Industrial Union, largely restricted to the South and known as the Southern Alliance. Loosely affiliated with the Southern order was a Negro branch, the Colored Farmers' Alliance. Of the two main alliances, the Southern was the more tightly knit and the larger, numbering over a million members.

At their beginning both alliances toyed with the same kind of objectives that had intrigued the Grange: social and educational activities and cooperative enterprises. But almost immediately they shifted their emphasis to politics—and to a program designed to save the farmer by state and national legislation rather than improved business techniques. The Northern leaders decided that farmers could expect nothing from the Democrats or Republicans and would have to create their own political organization. In the elections of 1890 they ran candidates for national and state office under diverse party labels in all the prairie states. The Southern Alliance turned to politics more reluctantly, but by 1890 it too was ready for action, though not in the form of a third party. Fearful that a new party would split the solidity of the one-party South and endanger white supremacy, the Southerners, heeding the counsel of such farm leaders as Benjamin F. Tillman of South Carolina, set their sights on capturing control of the Democratic party from its conservative Bourbon rulers. In 1890 Alliance-backed candidates competed with Bourbon aristocrats in every corner of the former Confederacy.

The farmers startled conservatives and surprised themselves with their success in 1890. The farm forces won partial or complete control of the legislatures in twelve states, eight in the South and four in the West, and elected six governors, three senators, and approximately fifty congressmen. The magnitude of the agrarian sweep was not, however, as great as it seemed. In the South, where the triumph was most complete, the farmers had stuck fast to the Democratic party. Over forty of the farm congressmen were Southern Alliance-endorsed Democrats; the one Southern representative to admit a third-party affiliation was Georgia's Thomas E. Watson.

THE PEOPLE'S PARTY

After the elections of 1890, the leaders of the Northern Alliance were certain that the time was ripe for the formation of a national farmer-labor party. Some of the Southern leaders—the fiery Watson, consumed with an emotional hatred for monopoly, and Leonidas L. Polk of

The Meaning of Populism

The historical literature on Populism is of comparatively recent origin. The first scholarly study of the movement appeared in 1931, when J. D. Hicks published *The Populist Revolt*. It is still the only general treatment of Populism, and as a full and factual account it remains the standard work. Its viewpoint has, however, in recent years been subjected to question and possible modification.

That viewpoint is summarized in Hicks' statement that Populism represented "the last phase of a long and perhaps a losing struggle – the struggle to save agricultural America from the devouring jaws of industrial America." Hicks wrote at a time when scholars tended to see certain evils in American industrial society and definite virtues in the older agrarian America of the previous century; inherent in his pages was an assumption that the reforms proposed by the Populists were good. He seemed to lament the failure of the Populist dream, and yet he conceded that parts of the dream eventually became reality when, in later years, many Populist proposals were enacted into law.

This favorable view of the Populists prevailed for over twenty years. Then, in 1955, Richard Hofstadter put forth a different thesis and unleashed an attack on the Populists in *The Age of Reform*. Hofstadter represented a new school of history, one having its roots in an urban society and having certain doubts about the older rural order. He argued that important aspects of Populism had been overlooked by Hicks and previous writers. According to Hofstadter, Populism had a "soft side." It was essentially romantic and did not face up to the hard problems of a modern society. It proposed simple solutions and favored returning to an older and simpler America. Moreover, it had a dark side. Many Populists denounced international bankers, some of whom were Jewish, and therefore the movement displayed anti-Semitic tendencies. Other writers expanded this charge to say that Populism possibly reflected a fascist psychology.

While some historians adopted and elaborated on the Hofstadter view, others undertook to refute it. C. Vann Woodward, author of *Tom Watson, Agrarian Rebel* (1938), now reminded the anti-Populist historians that Watson and other Southern party leaders had encouraged political cooperation between whites and blacks. In *The Populist Response to Industrialism* (1962) Norman Pollack argued that the Populists had a sophisticated conception of society, accepted the modern world, and proposed sensible solutions to economic problems. In *The Tolerant Populists* (1963) W. T. K. Nugent maintained that, at least in Kansas, the Populists were the very reverse of what Hofstadter had called them. They welcomed Jews and other immigrants to the party, and they offered a practical, up-to-date program.

Nowadays some journalists and political scientists as well as historians apply the terms "populism" and "populist" to a great variety of recent movements and public figures – to men as different as, for example, the late Senator Joseph McCarthy of Wisconsin and Senator George McGovern of South Dakota. Such loose handling of the terms makes them practically meaningless.

North Carolina, perhaps the ablest mind in the agrarian movement—were coming to the same conclusion. Reluctantly the Southerners recognized that their local successes would have no weight whatsoever in determining the course of the national Democratic party.

Plans for a third party were laid at meetings in Cincinnati (May 1891) and in St. Louis (February 1892), attended by many representatives of the Northern Alliance, some Southerners, and spokesmen of the fading Knights of Labor. Then in July 1892, 1,300 excited and exultant delegates poured into Omaha, Ne-

braska, in the heart of the plains country, to proclaim the new party, approve an official set of principles, and nominate candidates for the presidency and vice presidency. By common consent the party already had a name, one first used by the Kansas agrarians—the People's party—from which, by way of Latin, were derived the terms Populist and Populism.

In a spirit of dedicated idealism reminiscent of the antislavery crusade, the delegates at Omaha adopted a platform. To achieve their ends, they were willing to invest government with powers that would horrify business con-

A Populist Orator
The outstanding Kansas Populist, "Sockless" Jerry Simpson, also known as the "Socrates of the Prairies," is photographed while engaging in an outdoor debate in a small Kansas town during the campaign of 1892. (Kansas State Historical Society, Topeka)

servatives: "We believe that the power of government—in other words, of the people—should be expanded . . . as rapidly and as far as the good sense of an intelligent people and the teachings of experience shall justify, to the end that oppression, injustice, and poverty shall eventually cease in the land."

The Populist platform demanded national government ownership and operation of the railroad, telephone, and telegraph systems (a significant advance on the state regulation urged by the Grangers); a flexible national currency issued by the government and not by the banks; the free and unlimited coinage of silver; government-operated postal savings banks; a graduated income tax; the subtreasury plan, an arrangement whereby farmers could deposit nonperishable produce in government warehouses and borrow in United States treasury notes up to 80 percent of the current value of their commodities (thus enabling farmers to withhold crops from sale until the price was right); prohibition of alien land ownership; and reclamation of lands held by railroads and other corporations "in excess of their actual needs." Bidding for the support of labor, the platform also demanded shorter hours for workers and restrictions on immigration, and denounced the employment of private detective agencies as strikebreakers in labor disputes. Other planks called for new political techniques to place government more directly under democratic control: the Australian, or secret, ballot; the popular election of United States senators; the initiative, a device whereby state legislation could be introduced or enacted by the voters; and the referendum, a method whereby the voters could veto actions of state legislatures.

"It is a struggle," cried one Populist orator, "between the robbers and the robbed."

Populism was strong in only three geographic centers: the South, the plains and prairie region (but chiefly Kansas, Nebraska, and North and South Dakota), and the Rocky Mountain states. The Populists evoked little response in the old Granger states of the Middle West. In this previous center of protest, diversified techniques, emphasizing dairying and a corn-hog complex, had brought a new prosperity and induced a new conservatism. Even in the South the hold of Populism was tenuous and temporary. Populist leaders, seeking to

unite poor white and black people in politics, encountered the unyielding barriers of race. They could not, except for short periods and in a few states, persuade the white masses that class was paramount to color, and they could not overcome the traditional white loyalty to the Democractic party.

The Populists also failed to unite under their standard the forces of urban protest. Despite the brave platform talk about the common interests of rural and city workers, the Populists had no real interest in effecting such a combination. In any event, no realistic basis for an alliance between Populist farmers and urban dissenters existed. The Knights of Labor endorsed the new party, but the Knights were a dying organization.

Hardly any of the party leaders were dirt farmers. The great majority were of the rural middle class; they were professional men, editors and lawyers, or professional politicians and agitators. Only a handful had held office or exercised the responsibility of power. James B. Weaver, the party's presidential nominee in 1892, had run the political gamut. He had begun as a Democrat and deserted that party because it was controlled by the slavocracy, had joined the Republicans and left them because they were dominated by the business plutocracy, and had then become successively a Greenbacker and a Populist. Despite his seemingly erratic course, Weaver was a man with balance and ability and a fine sense of justice.

Many Populist leaders gave an impression of personal failure, of brilliant instability, of brooding communion with mystic forces. The matchless orator, Ignatius Donnelly of Minnesota, wrote one book locating the lost isle of Atlantis, another proving that Bacon wrote Shakespeare's plays, and a novel purporting to describe a Populist utopia. Georgia's Tom Watson, author of biographies of Jefferson and Napoleon (he referred curiously to the latter as a "great Democratic despot"), once championed political union across racial lines but ended his career baiting Negroes and Jews. Jerry Simpson of Kansas ridiculed a rival candidate for wearing silk socks and won the undying title of "Sockless Jerry, the Socrates of the prairies."

Despite the weaknesses of the People's party, its leaders and adherents looked forward enthusiastically to the election of 1892.

A Negative Response

At first the regular politicians gave a rather negative response to the demands of the organizing farmers. Although, yielding to pressure, Congress provided for the federal regulation of railroads, for the time being the government was given little real power to control rates. Then Congress passed an act to prohibit monopolies, but the government made no more than a half-hearted effort to enforce this law. And when Congress got around to acting on the tariff—that "mother of trusts"—it finally revised the rates, but it revised them in more an upward than a downward direction.

REGULATING THE RAILROADS

After the Supreme Court had upheld the Granger laws—by which some of the states were attempting to regulate railroad rates—the railroad companies continued to test the validity of these laws in the courts. Eventually the railroads won out. The undoing of the statutes came after new justices friendly to an expanded notion of property rights and willing to strike down state powers ascended to the Supreme Court.

The first step came in 1886 in the so-called Wabash case *(Wabash, St. Louis, and Pacific Railway Co.* v. *Illinois).* Involved was a statute prohibiting higher rates for a "short haul" than a "long haul" between points in Illinois and New York City. The Court held that the statute attempted to regulate interstate commerce and infringed on the exclusive power of Congress. Interstate rates were thus removed from state control, but within its own limits a state could still regulate railroads if the regulations did not directly affect interstate commerce. Later the roads eliminated even this regulatory power of the states by persuading the Court to accept the due-process clause as a "substantive" restriction on state authority. That is, due process, previously conceived of as guaranteeing the accused certain procedural rights, came to be defined as a limitation on the power of states to regulate private property or vested rights—with the judiciary acting as the guardian of property and reviewing the acts of legislatures. The Court arrived at this position gradually and with some indirection. It affirmed it in es-

sence, although not explicitly, in *Chicago, Milwaukee and St. Paul Railroad* v. *Minnesota* (1890) and thereafter in starkly specific terms. Constant judicial review of state decrees meant, of course, that state regulation had become a mockery.

The only solution to the problem was national regulation. Since the 1870s demands had been voiced in and out of Congress for some kind of supervisory legislation, and revelations of such railroad practices as pooling, rebates, and other discriminatory devices stirred public support for action. Even some railway operators, alarmed by the fierce competition in their industry, were willing to accept regulation. Sentiment became so strong that Congress was finally forced to act. In 1887 it passed the Interstate Commerce Act, a measure described by its sponsor, Senator Shelby M. Cullom, as "conservative legislation."

The Interstate Commerce Act prohibited rebates, pools, long-short haul discriminations, and drawbacks. It required railroads to publish their rate schedules and file them with the government. It provided that all charges in interstate rail transportation should be "reasonable and just," but failed to furnish a standard or method to determine the justness of a rate. To administer the act, a five-man agency, the Interstate Commerce Commission, was created, with powers to hear complaints from shippers, examine witnesses, and inquire into the books and accounts of railroads. The law did not clearly authorize the commission to fix rates. After investigating a complaint, the commission could issue a cease-and-desist order to a carrier to lower its charges. If the road refused, the commission had to take its case to the courts and justify its decree, a cumbersome procedure that militated against effective regulation.

For almost twenty years after its passage, the Interstate Commerce Act was without practical effect; it did not accomplish widespread rate reduction or eliminate discrimination. No wonder an attorney general of the United States advised a railroad president not to ask for repeal of the act: "It satisfies the popular clamor for government supervision of the railroads at the same time that that supervision is almost entirely nominal."

DISPOSING OF THE TRUSTS

Benjamin Harrison, the victor in the close and corrupt election of 1888, assumed the presidency the following year in the nation's centennial inauguration. Just forty-eight years before, his grandfather, William Henry Harrison, had entered the same office and died almost immediately, leaving no trace of his influence on the presidency. Benjamin Harrison served out his term, but he left behind a record of negative accomplishment. Intelligent and honest, he was colorless in personality, cold in manner, and singularly aloof—from people, from the new currents of social change, and from the more sordid realities of politics. In White House annals his administration is notable for the wiring of the executive mansion for electricity.

Harrison's cabinet was, like himself, competent but drab. Secretary of State Blaine was the only member who rose above the level of average ability. Though known as a moderate civil-service supporter, Harrison extended the classified list but slightly. He permitted his Postmaster General, John Wanamaker, a hefty contributor to his campaign fund, to sweep 30,000 postmasters out of office in a year. One of his worst appointments was that of "Corporal" James Tanner as commissioner of pensions. While his actions wrung from some people the prayer, "God help the surplus," Tanner replaced Cleveland's policy of careful examination of pension claims with a reckless generosity that delighted politicians and veterans alike.

Harrison exerted little effort to influence legislation. With slender majorities in both houses, the Republicans could carry through a program only by submitting to rigid leadership and acting as a disciplined unit. The leadership came from Maine's Thomas B. Reed, Speaker of the House and a master of parliamentary law and savage wit. Some fruits of his control were a Dependent Pensions Act that almost doubled the number of pensioners and even stunned the GAR, and a flood of appropriations bills for internal improvements, subsidies to steamship lines, and naval expansion.

Public opinion forced the Reed Congress to consider legislation affecting broad areas of the economy, and in 1890 important measures dealing with big business and the tariff were enacted. Some fifteen Western and Southern states had adopted laws prohibiting combinations that restrained competition. But corpora-

tions found it easy to escape limitations by incorporating in states that offered special privileges (New Jersey and Delaware were notorious examples). Acceptance by the Supreme Court of the argument that a corporation was a "person" before the law and entitled to the protection of the due-process clause of the Fourteenth Amendment in *Santa Clara County* v. *Southern Pacific Railroad* (1886) meant that any form of state control was subject to judicial negation. If antitrust legislation was to be effective, it would obviously have to come from the national government. In 1888 both parties promised to curb monopolies.

With little debate and by almost unanimous votes in both houses of Congress, the Sherman Antitrust Act became law in July 1890. Its provisions and phraseology were determined by the fact that the only basis for national action against trust derived from the power of Congress to regulate interstate commerce. The heart of the measure was in the first two sections: (1) "Every contract, combination in the form of trust or otherwise, or conspiracy, in restraint of trade or commerce among the several States, or with foreign nations, is hereby declared to be illegal"; (2) "Every person who shall monopolize, or attempt to monopolize . . . any part of the trade or commerce among the several States, or with foreign nations, shall be deemed guilty of a misdemeanor. . . ."

Even though the law on paper prohibited all combinations "in restraint of trade," Congress in passing it was making no very serious effort to break up monopolies. As one senator explained, his colleagues merely wanted to get up "some bill headed 'A bill to Punish Trusts' with which to go to the country" and get themselves reelected. Congress was making a gesture to appease popular discontent without changing the realities of contemporary economic life. The antitrust people now had their law, and business continued to have its trusts.

For over a decade after its passage there was little attempt to enforce the Sherman Act. Before 1901 the Justice Department instituted only fourteen suits under the law against business combinations, and failed to obtain convictions in almost every one. The courts, uniformly hostile to the law, proceeded to emasculate it. The crowning decision came in *United States* v. *E. C. Knight Co.* (1895), a case in which the government charged that the defendants controlled 98 percent of the manufacture of refined sugar in the country Chief Justice Melville W. Fuller, speaking for the Supreme Court, threw out the government's case with a curious distinction between manufacturing and commerce. He admitted that the present combination was a trust to monopolize the refining of sugar but denied that it was therefore illegal: the trust was not in interstate commerce but in manufacturing. The Knight decision created a "twilight zone" between state and national powers, an area of economic life outside the authority of any agency of government.

REVISING THE TARIFF

Having made an effort to dispose of the trust question, the Republicans turned with anticipation to the subject that most interested them and their business backers and that had been the paramount issue in the campaign of 1888, the tariff. William McKinley of Ohio, a rising party luminary and chairman of the House Ways and Means Committee, and Senator Nel-

son W. Aldrich of Rhode Island framed, with the assistance of the tariff lobbies, the highest protective measure yet offered to a Congress. It became law in October 1890 as the McKinley Tariff Act.

Seldom in American political history has a party in power suffered such a stunning reverse as befell the Republicans in the mid-term elections of 1890 Their majority in the Senate was slashed to 8, and in the House they could count only 88 seats to 235 for the Democrats and 9 for the Alliance-Populists. Popular revulsion against the McKinley duties, pictured by the Democrats as raising the living costs of the masses, was an undoubted factor in causing the Republican debacle; McKinley himself was among those going down to defeat. But the elections registered more than condemnation of a tariff. They reflected the deep anxieties of millions of Americans who were beginning to question the fundamental justice of the economic order.

In the presidential election of 1892 Benjamin Harrison was again the Republican nomi-

Populist Strength 1892

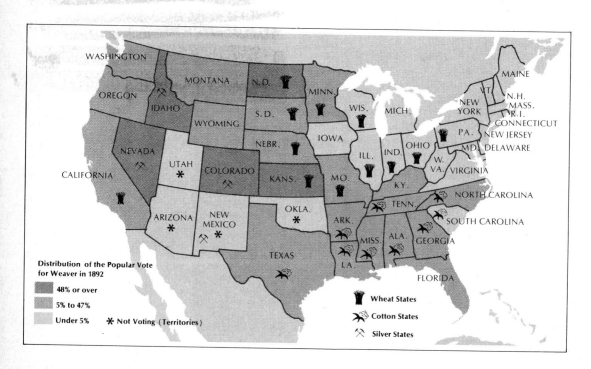

Distribution of the Popular Vote for Weaver in 1892

- 48% or over
- 5% to 47%
- Under 5%   ✱ Not Voting (Territories)

🌾 Wheat States
🐾 Cotton States
⚒ Silver States

To Arms Against the Populists
In no state did the Populists have greater support than in Kansas. In 1893, however, the Republicans disputed the results of a state election and claimed control of the legislature. For a time the Populists occupied and held the state house. Finally the Republicans armed themselves, drove out the Populists, and took control. (Kansas State Historical Society, Topeka)

nee and Grover Cleveland the Democratic. Once more the platforms of the two parties were almost identical except for the tariff, with the Republicans upholding protection and the Democrats pledging reduction. Both parties in their official pronouncements ignored the pulsing currents of unrest in the country. Only the Populists, with James B. Weaver as their candidate, advocated economic reform. Cleveland amassed 277 electoral and 5,557,000 popular votes as compared to Harrison's 145 and 5,176,000 votes. For the first time since the Civil War the Democrats won a majority of both houses of Congress. Weaver polled 22 electoral votes from six mountain and plains states and over a million popular votes and the Populists elected at least a dozen senators and congressmen.

Despite Cleveland's negative record, a large proportion of the people who had voted for him expected him to devise some original approach to the new problems troubling America. His inaugural address rudely disillusioned them, as he reaffirmed his devotion to laissez faire: "The lessons of paternalism ought to be unlearned and the better lesson taught that while the people should . . . support their Government its functions do not include the support of the people."

Cleveland called on his party to redeem its pledge to lower the existing tariff rates. In the House William L. Wilson of West Virginia introduced a bill in 1894 designed to accomplish moderate downward revision and yet provide adequate protection for domestic producers. To get Populist support and to compensate for an anticipated loss in revenues, the bill provided for an income tax with a 2-percent levy on incomes over $4,000. When the Wilson bill reached the Senate, the customary lobbying

The Supreme Court Denounces Protest

When the Pollock case was argued before the Court, the lawyers appearing against the income tax passionately appealed to the Court to preserve the sanctity of property and halt the onward march of radicalism. Some of the justices responded with opinions more sociological than legal. One wrote:

The present assault upon capital is but the beginning. It will be but the stepping stone to others, larger and more sweeping, till our political contests will become a war of the poor against the rich; a war constantly growing in intensity and bitterness.

and logrolling began Eastern Democrats, directed by Maryland's Arthur P. Gorman and abetted by Republicans, added 634 amendments, most of them altering Wilson's duties upward. Strong pressure from the Democratic leadership induced the House to accept the Senate version. Cleveland denounced it as a violation of the party's platform but allowed it to become law without his signature.

The Wilson-Gorman Tariff reduced the general scale of duties only 10 percent, and its duties on raw and refined sugar and other items afforded ample protection to the sugar trust and every other trust. Far from the kind of tariff the Democrats had promised the country, the act seemed to confirm the Populist contention that tariff-making was a sham battle between the major parties.

Even the one crust thrown to the Populists, the income tax, was shortly snatched away by the courts. In a case testing the right of the government to levy an income tax (*Pollock* v. *The Farmer's Loan and Trust Co.*, 1895), the Supreme Court declared in a 5-to-4 decision that a tax on incomes was a "direct" tax and hence had to be apportioned among the states according to population. Since an income tax, by its very nature, would be effective only if applied on a basis of individual wealth and would have no reality if reckoned on the distribution of population, the Court had made it impossible to levy such a tax.

"Battle of the Standards"

The Populists had done fairly well in 1892, and they were encouraged by the events that soon followed—the depression, the Pullman strike, and the growing bitterness of workers as well as farmers. In the state and local elections of 1894 the Populists added to their earlier victories. Then they looked hopefully toward the election of 1896.

But that year one of the major parties, the Democratic, adopted the most appealing of the Populist programs, free silver. Even so, the Democrats went down in defeat, and the People's party soon disappeared.

This short-lived party nevertheless left its mark on American history. One or both of the major parties sooner or later adopted other measures, besides free silver, that the Populists

had stood for. Some of these, in one form or another, became accepted features of American government—notably the income tax, a flexible (managed) currency, crop loans to farmers, the secret ballot, and the direct election of United States senators.

THE PANIC OF 1893

The Cleveland administration was hardly settled in office when the Panic of 1893 struck the country. There followed one of the most severe depressions up to that time. Its causes were various and complicated. The eighties had been a typical boom period, featuring overexpansion and overinvestment in railroads and industrial combinations. Depressed prices in agriculture since 1887 had weakened the purchasing power of a substantial section of the population. Depression conditions that had begun earlier in Europe were resulting in a loss of American markets abroad, a decline in the export trade, and a withdrawal by foreign investors of gold invested in this country. Whatever the causes of the depression, over 8,000 business concerns failed in a period of six months, 156 railroads went into receivership, and 400 banks suspended operations. Agricultural prices tumbled to new lows, and perhaps as many as a million workers, 20 percent of the laboring force, were thrown out of jobs.

Jacob S. Coxey, a Massillon, Ohio, businessman and Populist, proposed two lines of action: (1) Congress should issue $500 million in legal-tender notes to be used in the construction of roads throughout the country; and (2) local governments wishing to undertake public improvements should be authorized to issue noninterest-bearing bonds which could be exchanged at the federal Treasury for legal-tender notes. Coxey's ideas were hooted at in conservative circles. (But the notion of creating jobs by a building program would appeal to a later generation afflicted by depression. At the onset of the next great depression in the 1930s the government would inaugurate a public

works program. Coxey, who lived until 1951, thus saw his scheme finally put into effect.)

Seeking to dramatize his program, Coxey organized a march of the unemployed on Washington to present a petition for work relief to Congress. Only 500 of "Coxey's army" were able to make their way to Washington, and they were barred from the Capitol by armed police. Coxey was arrested on a trumped-up charge of walking on the grass, and the marchers were herded into camps because their presence supposedly endangered public health.

THE SILVER QUESTION

The financial panic deranged the government's monetary system, and in the minds of people like Cleveland the silver policy became the primary cause of the depression. This money question had a long history.

Since the beginning of the republic the country had been on a bimetallic standard: the government purchased and coined all the gold and silver offered to it for sale. At first the relative value of the two metals had been set by commercial demand for them, but eventually the government fixed a legal ratio. Back in Andrew Jackson's period the ratio had been

---

The Currency Issue

The Republican Platform: *The Republican party is unreservedly for sound money. It caused the enactment of a law providing for the redemption [resumption] of specie payments in 1879. Since then every dollar has been as good as gold. We are unalterably opposed to every measure calculated to debase our currency or impair the credit of our country. We are therefore opposed to the free coinage of silver, except by international agreement with the leading commercial nations of the earth, which agreement we pledge ourselves to promote, and until such agreement can be obtained the existing gold standard must be maintained.*

The Democratic Platform: *We demand the free and unlimited coinage of both silver and gold at the present legal ratio of 16 to 1 without waiting for the aid or consent of any other nation. We demand that the standard silver dollar shall be a full legal tender, equally with gold, for all debts, public and private, and we favor such legislation as will prevent for the future the demonetization of any kind of legal-tender money by private contract.*

placed at sixteen to one, meaning that the silver dollar had sixteen times as much silver as the gold dollar did gold. For sound economic reasons, hardly any silver dollars were coined. Because of the relative scarcity of silver bullion, the price of gold in the open market was almost never sixteen times the price of silver, so that what silver was mined was sold for commercial purposes. Nobody objected when in 1873 Congress enacted a measure that, while keeping existing silver money in circulation, removed the silver dollar from the coinage list. Soon the inflationists, charging a banker conspiracy, would be calling this act the "Crime of '73."

Almost immediately there occurred a drastic change in the supply of silver. The discovery of huge new deposits of the metal in the Far West, notably in Nevada, increased the amount in the domestic market; at the same time, several European countries went on the gold standard, melting their silver coins and swelling the world supply. The inevitable result was that the price of silver plunged downward and fell far below the legal ratio. Silver-mine owners, pinched by the dropping price, joined the discontented farmers in demanding that the government return to the bimetallic system, that it purchase all the silver brought to the mint—"the free and unlimited coinage of silver."

In 1878 the inflationists, a coalition of Democrats and Republicans from the Middle West, South, and Far West, attempted to pass a free-silver measure through Congress. They were forced, however, to accept a compromise, the Bland-Allison Act, which provided that each month the government must purchase not less than $2 million and not more than $4 million worth of silver and convert it into dollars at the ratio of sixteen to one. The inflation forces had won only a partial victory.

Later, in 1890, the Sherman Silver Purchase Act directed the Treasury to buy 4.5 million ounces of silver each month, an amount estimated to be the maximum domestic production, and to pay for the purchased bullion in treasury notes. The purchased silver was not to be coined. The amount of money in circulation did not increase materially, and the price of silver continued to drop. Creditors and conservatives still argued for the adoption of a single metallic standard; debtors and inflationists still

agitated for the unlimited coinage of silver at the rate of sixteen to one.

The Populists at first did not emphasize silver. But as the party developed strength, the money question came to overshadow all other issues. Currency reform was already a popular issue with debtor farmers, who with some reason believed that inflation would ameliorate their ills. Besides, the Populists desperately needed money to finance their campaigns, and the only source of help was the silver-mine owners who insisted on an elevation of the money plank and the subordination of other proposals.

The influence of silver on the thinking of Populists, agrarian Democrats, and farmers was graphically illustrated by the enormous popularity of a small and not particularly profound book, *Coin's Financial School*, written by William H. Harvey and published in 1894. "Professor Coin" ran a school, an imaginary institution specializing in finance, and the book reproduced his lectures and his dialogues with his students. The professor clearly indicated the marvelous restorative qualities of free silver: "It means the reopening of closed factories, the relighting of fires in darkened furnaces; it means hope instead of despair; comfort in place of suffering; life instead of death."

Ever since the Resumption Act of 1875 the Treasury had aimed to maintain a minimum gold reserve of $100 million to redeem its paper and silver dollars. During the prosperous eighties the reserve increased, and it reached the figure of $190 million by 1890. But in the last two years of the Harrison administration it fell off sharply. The prohibitive duties of the McKinley Tariff reduced imports and hence revenue; the pension and internal improvements appropriations ate up the surplus; and the Sherman Silver Purchase Act forced the government to buy increased amounts of silver and issue new treasury notes that the Treasury insisted on redeeming in gold. Holders of greenbacks and silver certificates, jittery at rumors the government might be swept off the gold standard, demanded gold, and when Cleveland assumed office in 1893, the reserve had shrunk to a little over $100 million.

The panic intensified the rush for gold, and soon the reserve sank below the minimum deemed necessary to sustain the gold standard.

Cleveland had always disliked the Sherman Silver Purchase Act, and now he was convinced that it was the chief factor draining gold from the Treasury and that, if allowed to stand, it would force the country off the gold standard and impair the government's financial honor. In one of his rare moods of leadership, the President summoned Congress into special session and demanded the repeal of the Sherman Act. He worked his will, but only by swinging the patronage lash hard on recalcitrant Democrats and enlisting the support of Eastern Republicans. Western and Southern Democrats fought repeal to the last, and in defeat were incredibly bitter. A historic party split was in the making.

The President had his victory, but the financial crisis deepened. In 1895, Cleveland approached the big New York bankers for help. A banking syndicate headed by J. P. Morgan agreed to take up a $65 million bond issue and to use the influence of the financial community to check the flow of gold to Europe. As a result, public faith that the government would maintain the gold standard was strengthened. The stampede to redeem notes eased. To agrarian Democrats and Populists, however, it seemed that Cleveland had sold out to Wall Street and concluded a crooked deal with the money lenders. Actually, there had been no deal and no corruption, though the bankers undoubtedly turned an excessive profit.

The Cleveland administration ended amidst flaming portents of social unrest. The Democratic party was bitterly divided. The President's gold policy had aligned the Southern and Western Democrats in a solid phalanx against him and his Eastern followers.

"A CROSS OF GOLD"

As the election of 1896 approached, Republicans were confident of victory.

Marcus A. Hanna, boss of the Ohio machine and soon to be national boss of the party, was a wealthy industrialist who aspired to be a President maker. He represented a new type in politics, the businessman who held office and actively manipulated parties instead of remaining in the background and paying out money for services rendered. He had picked out his man and had been grooming him carefully

since 1890. The man was William McKinley, governor of Ohio, who as a congressman had been the author of the tariff act of 1890. Hanna's support of McKinley included providing him with generous campaign contributions, bailing him out of a threatened bankruptcy, and advertising his availability to Republican bosses in other states.

By the time the convention met, Hanna had lined up enough Middle Western and Southern delegations to nominate McKinley. Everywhere and on every occasion he presented his candidate as "Bill McKinley, the advance agent of prosperity" and the champion of protection for American producers.

The platform as finally framed endorsed the protective tariff, ignored completely such questions as the income tax, railroad and trust abuses, and labor injunctions, and opposed the free coinage of silver except by international agreement with the leading commercial nations. As other countries, and particularly Great Britain, were unlikely to abandon the gold standard, the Republicans were supporting gold. Thirty-four delegates from the mountain and plains states walked out when the currency plank was adopted. Their obvious destination was the Democratic party.

The Democrats met amid scenes of drama seldom equaled in American politics. The Southern and Western delegates came to the convention determined to seize control of the party from the Easterners. Alarmed by the rise of Populist strength in their sections, they intended to write free silver and other planks of the third party into the platform and to nominate a silver candidate.

The resolutions committee presented to the convention two reports. The majority platform demanded tariff reduction, endorsed the principle of the income tax, denounced the issue of currency notes by the national banks, condemned the use of injunctions in industrial disputes, pledged a "stricter control" of trusts and railroads, and—this was the issue that headlined the platform—called for free silver: "We demand the free and unlimited coinage of both silver and gold at the present legal ratio of 16 to 1, without waiting for the aid or consent of any other nation." The minority resolution opposed the free coinage of silver except by international agreement, a stand identical to that of the Republicans.

William Jennings Bryan
*The United States has produced many orators who could sway crowds with the
magic of their voice, but it is generally agreed that Bryan had no superior in
power and persuasiveness. Here he is speaking at a later date than 1896. The
poster on the platform, in the lower left-hand corner of the picture, shows him as
he appeared when he was the Boy Orator of the Platte engaged in the silver
crusade. (Library of Congress)*

Six speakers debated the resolution, three
for gold and three for silver. The defenders of
gold had the better of the oratorical tournament — up to the final address. Then from the
Nebraska delegation a strikingly handsome
young man walked to the platform to close the
debate. He was William Jennings Bryan, thirty-
six years of age. His political experience was
limited to two terms in the House of Representatives, but he was widely known in the plains
country as a magnetic orator, and he eagerly
hoped for the presidential nomination.
Through the farthest reaches of the vast hall
now rang his magnificent organ-like voice.

He ended with a peroration that brought
the delegates and the spectators to their feet in
a frenzied tumult of passion and that was declaimed by later generations of schoolboys all
over rural America: "If they dare to come out

in the open and defend the gold standard as a
good thing, we will fight them to the uttermost.
Having behind us the producing masses of this
nation and the world, supported by the commercial interests, the laboring interests and the
toilers everywhere, we will answer their demand for a gold standard by saying to them:
'You shall not press down upon the brow of
labor this crown of thorns; you shall not crucify
mankind upon a cross of gold.' "

The majority platform was adopted. The
agrarians had found their leader, and the following day Bryan was nominated on the fifth
ballot. It is doubtful if he understood the technical implications of the money problem that he
discussed so eloquently before the convention.
It is even more dubious if he realized the full
import of the protest movement or the Populist
program. He seized on one Populist plank, free

silver, the most superficial of the various protest proposals, and erected it into a personal and political obsession.

One Republican (Joseph Foraker), when asked if he thought Bryan's title, the Boy Orator of the Platte, was an accurate phrase, replied that it was, because the Platte River was six inches deep and six miles wide at the mouth. More descriptive was another designation applied to Bryan: the Great Commoner. Born in Illinois of typical middle-class stock, he had attended a small sectarian college, had practiced law with only average success, and then, repeating a normal American pattern, had moved to Nebraska, a frontier area, to try his fortunes. Almost completely he represented the feelings and emotions of rural, middle-class America.

The choice of Bryan and the nature of the Democratic platform placed the Populists in a cruel quandary. They had expected both of the major parties to adopt conservative programs and nominate conservative candidates, leaving the Populists to represent the growing forces of protest. But now the Democrats had stolen much of the Populists' thunder. The Populists faced the choice of naming their own candidate and splitting the protest vote, or endorsing Bryan and losing their identity as a party. When the party assembled, the convention voted to approve Bryan but nominated its own vice-presidential candidate, Tom Watson, whom the Democrats were expected to adopt but whom they ignored.

BRYAN IS BEATEN

There has never been another campaign quite like the one of 1896. It had unequaled drama, intense excitement, a clean-cut issue, and a David-and-Goliath theme: the boy orator Bryan contending against the powerful boss Hanna. The boss had the great advantage of ample funds to spend on organization. The business and financial community, frightened beyond reason at the prospect of Bryan's sitting in the White House and taking advice from John P. Altgeld and Ignatius Donnelly, pressed contributions upon Hanna. Just how much money Hanna had to dispense has been disputed, but the lowest estimate is $3.5 million and the highest is $7 million. The Democrats, by contrast, reported expenditures of only

Election of 1896

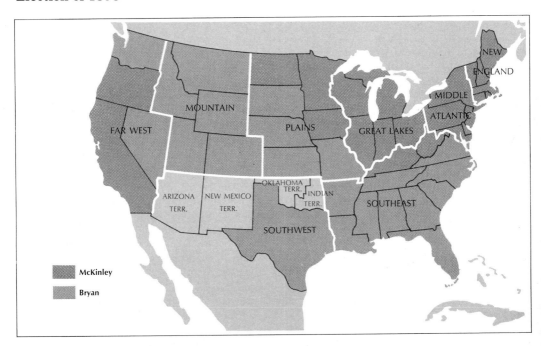

$300,000, a sum only slightly larger than the contribution of one firm, Standard Oil, to the Republican war chest. With his almost inexhaustible resources, Hanna organized the most lavish propaganda machine yet to operate in American politics.

Shrewdly, Hanna kept McKinley off the hustings, knowing better than to pit his solemn candidate against the matchless Bryan. From his home at Canton, Ohio, McKinley conducted a dignified "front-porch" campaign. To Canton came pilgrimages of the Republican faithful, organized and paid for by Hanna, to offer tribute to the standard-bearer. They came every day but McKinley always had a speech ready for them, and always he stressed one theme: the Republican party was the only agency that could bring prosperity to the country.

No such decorous restraint marked the campaigning of the young and vital Bryan. Joyously bearing the brunt of the battle for his party, he inaugurated techniques never before witnessed in American political contests. Previous candidates had addressed audiences in campaigns and had even toured the country to speak at a few selected points. But Bryan was the first to stump systematically every section, to appear in villages and hamlets, the first, really, to say frankly to the voters that he wanted to be President. He traveled 18,000 miles, speaking several times a day, and addressed an estimated 5 million people.

As Bryan's campaign mounted in intensity, cold fear gripped the East. Employers told their workers not to report for work in case of a Democratic victory: industry would have to close down in anticipation of being taken over by the government. Some employers threatened to dismiss workers who voted for Bryan. The banks let it be known that farmers supporting the Democratic candidate probably would have their mortgages foreclosed or at least not renewed.

Everything broke right for the Republicans in the closing weeks of the election. Crop failures abroad brought an increased demand for American products, and on the eve of the election the price of wheat almost doubled.

On Election Day, McKinley polled 271 electoral votes to Bryan's 176. The popular vote was 7,105,000 to 6,503,000. Bryan won the Confederate South plus Missouri, swept the plains and mountain states with the exception of North Dakota, but lost California and Oregon on the Pacific coast. In short, he carried only the mining regions and the areas where staple farming was predominant and agricultural prices were lowest. He went down to defeat in all the Granger states in the Middle West. The Democratic program, like that of the Populists, had been designed to serve the needs of one segment of one class, the most depressed fraction of agriculture, and this was too narrow an appeal to win a national election.

McKINLEY AND PROSPERITY

William McKinley, a shrewd political operator, was the last of a long list of officer veterans of the Union army (beginning with Grant) to sit in the White House. Friendly, kindly, and lovable, he was inclined to defer to stronger characters like Hanna and to act in harmony with his party's leaders. He and they realized the dangers inherent in the currency issue. Silver had many adherents, as evidenced by Bryan's huge popular vote, and the Republican party numbered many silverites in its Western wing. Impulsive action might divide the party in its hour of victory.

Postponing action on the money problem until a more propitious time, the administration turned to an issue on which Republicans were agreed, the necessity for higher tariff rates. Immediately after assuming office, McKinley summoned Congress into special session to consider tariff revision. With record brevity the Republican majority whipped into shape and passed the Dingley Tariff, raising the duties to an average of 57 percent, the highest in history.

On the currency question the administration proceeded in accordance with the party's platform pronouncement that bimetallism could not be established except by international action. McKinley sent a commission to Europe to explore the possibility of a silver agreement with Great Britain and France. As he and everyone else anticipated, Britain refused to abandon her gold standard, thus effectively ending any hopes for international bimetallism. The administration could now argue that if the United States embarked on a silver program alone it would be economically isolated from the rest of the world, and the argument was hard to refute. Believing that their position was unassailable, the Republicans finally moved to enact currency legislation. The Currency, or Gold Standard, Act of 1900 legalized the gold standard and enlarged the redemption fund, which was to be maintained as a separate and special charge to protect the supply of gold from depletion.

And so the "battle of the standards" ended in victory for the forces of conservatism. Economic developments seemed to prove that the conservatives had been right in the struggle. In 1898 prosperity returned to America. Foreign crop failures enlarged the farmer's market and sent farm prices surging upward. At the same time business entered another cycle of booming expansion. Prosperity and gold had come hand in hand – the lesson seemed obvious.

But it was not quite that simple. Bryan and the silverites were essentially right in demanding currency inflation. In the quarter century before 1900 the countries of Western civilization had experienced a spectacular augmentation of productive facilities and population. Yet the supply of money had not kept pace with economic progress, because the supply was tied to gold and the amount of gold remained practically constant. A committee of the British

House of Lords, hardly a radical agency, reported after a careful investigation that the world's economy required a larger money supply.

It so happened that the supply was vastly increased soon after the Republicans took over the government in 1897. A new technique for extracting gold from low-content ores, the cyanide process, made it possible to work mines previously considered marginal or unprofitable. At the same time huge new gold deposits were discovered in Alaska, South Africa, and Australia. In 1898 two and a half times as much gold was produced as in 1890, and the currency supply soon was inflated far beyond anything proposed by Bryan. The price level, which had been declining since 1865, started on an upward swing.

With McKinley, then, there came a tariff increase, the gold standard, and prosperity. There also came a new departure in foreign policy, as the nation entered upon the path of overseas imperialism and took its place among the "great powers" of the world.

Selected Readings

Overviews

W. A. White, *Masks in a Pageant* (1928); Matthew Josephson, *The Politicos, 1865–1896** (1938); D. J. Rothman, *Politics and Power: The United States Senate, 1869–1901** (1966).

Republican Politics

Harry Barnard, *Rutherford B. Hayes and His America* (1954); R. G. Caldwell, *James A. Garfield, Party Chieftain* (1931); D. S. Muzzey, *James G. Blaine, a Political Idol of Other Days* (1934); D. B. Chidsey, *The Gentleman from New York: A Life of Roscoe Conkling* (1935); G. F. Howe, *Chester A. Arthur* (1934); A. B. Sageser, *The First Two Decades of the Pendleton Act* (1935); H. J. Sievers, *Benjamin Harrison, Hoosier Statesman* (1959).

Cleveland and the Democrats

Allan Nevins, *Grover Cleveland: A Study in Courage* (1932); H. S. Merrill, *Bourbon Leader: Grover Cleveland and the Democratic Party* (1957) and *Bourbon Democracy of the Middle West, 1865–1896* (1953); J. R. Hollingsworth, *The Whirligig of Politics: The Democracy of Cleveland and Bryan* (1963); G. H. Knowles, *The Presidential Campaign and Election of 1892* (1942); J. A. Barnes, *John G. Carlisle* (1931), Cleveland's Secretary of the Treasury.

Agrarian Protest

S. J. Buck, *The Granger Movement** (1913); J. D. Hicks, *The Populist Revolt** (1931); Norman Pollack,

The Populist Response to Industrial America* (1962); W. T. K. Nugent, *The Tolerant Populists* (1963); R. F. Durden, *The Climax of Populism** (1965); Theodore Saloutos, *Farmer Movements in the South, 1865–1933** (1960); R. B. Nye, *Midwestern Progressive Politics: A Historical Study of Its Origins and Development, 1870–1958** (1958); C. V. Woodward, *Tom Watson, Agrarian Radical** (1938); F. B. Simkins, *Pitchfork Ben Tillman* (1944); Stuart Noblin, *Leonidas Lafayette Polk* (1949); Martin Ridge, *Ignatius Donnelly* (1962).

Economic Policies

F. W. Taussig, *The Tariff History of the United States* (1931); Milton Friedman and A. J. Schwartz, *Monetary History of the United States, 1867–1900* (1963); D. R. Dewey, *Financial History of the United States* (1934); F. B. Weberg, *The Background of the Panic of 1893* (1929); D. L. McMurry, *Coxey's Army* (1929).

Bryan and McKinley

S. L. Jones, *The Presidential Election of 1896* (1964); P. W. Glad, *The Trumpet Soundeth* (1960) and *McKinley, Bryan, and the People** (1964); P. E. Coletta, *William Jennings Bryan, Political Evangelist, 1860–1908* (1964); H. W. Morgan, *William McKinley and His America* (1963); Margaret Leech, *In the Days of McKinley* (1959); Herbert Croly, *Marcus Alonzo Hanna* (1912).

*Titles available in paperback.

Emergence of a World Power

Twenty

In the 1890s the United States took what seemed like a startling new departure in foreign affairs when it began to acquire possessions overseas. From the very beginning, however, the republic had been expansionist. As the American people moved relentlessly westward across the continent, their government from time to time acquired new lands for them to occupy: the trans-Appalachian region (in the treaty ending the Revolutionary War), the Louisiana Territory, Florida, Texas, a part of the Oregon country, California and New Mexico, Alaska.

Almost all these acquisitions — the fruits of what might be called the old Manifest Destiny — were contiguous with existing territories of the United States. Desired mainly as places for settlement by Americans seeking farms, these acquisitions represented a kind of agricultural imperialism. And they were expected to be organized as territories and ultimately as states, the equals of all the rest.

The expansionism of the 1890s, the new Manifest Destiny, was in some respects different. It meant acquiring island possessions — some of which were already thickly populated, were not suitable for settlement by migrants from the United States, and were expected to be held indefinitely as colonies — not as states or even territories. The new expansion was motivated largely (though not entirely) by considerations of trade. Thus it represented a kind of commercial imperialism.

Some Americans had begun to interest themselves in overseas acquisitions — Cuba, the Hawaiian Islands — as early as the 1850s, but the sectional controversy had intervened to frustrate that expansionist movement. In 1867 the United States annexed tiny Midway Island in the Pacific, and a few years later President Grant tried in vain to annex Santo Domingo in the Caribbean. The nation was not yet ready for the new imperialism.

The Expansion Rooster
As the twentieth century opened, the prevailing spirit of Americans was cockiness, as illustrated by this 1900 cartoon. At home, the country was prosperous; abroad, it was launching upon imperialism. The victorious Republicans were crowing. The anti-expansionist opposition, here labeled "Bryanism," was a dead bird. (The Bettmann Archive)

By 1900 the United States had finally become an empire. It was now recognized as a "world power," though in fact it had been one of the great nations of the world for some time. As such, it pursued three basic and long-standing foreign policies – one for each of three broad areas of the globe. With respect to Europe, the aim (often inaccurately called "isolation") was to promote commerce while avoiding diplomatic involvements. With respect to the Americas, the purpose was expressed in the Monroe Doctrine, as supplemented by the idea of Pan-Americanism. With respect to Asia, the slogan came to be the Open Door, signifying opportunity for American commercial interests in China. The Monroe Doctrine and the Open Door were reaffirmed and strengthened by events of the late nineteenth century. The policy of "isolation" began to be questioned, however, on the grounds that it was inconsistent with imperial obligations, with the responsibilities of "world leadership," and with the spirit of Anglo-American friendship which, by the end of the century, was about to prevail.

Imperialist Stirrings

In the two decades after 1870 the American people seemed to have forgotten the expansionist impulse of the prewar years. They were occupied with things closer to home – reconstructing the South, settling the last frontier, building a network of railroads, and expanding their great industrial system. By the 1890s they were ready – indeed, eager – to try imperialism, to resume the course of Manifest Destiny that had impelled their forebears to wrest an empire from Mexico in the expansionist forties.

THE NEW MANIFEST DESTINY

Various developments subtly played a part in shifting the attention of Americans from their own country to lands across the seas. The passing of the frontier gave rise to a feeling that resources would soon become scarce and that they must be sought abroad. The depression beginning in 1893 seemed to confirm the fear of certain businessmen that industry had been overbuilt and was producing more goods than customers at home could buy. The bitter class protests of the time – the Populist movement, the free-silver crusade, the bloody labor disputes – led many people to believe that the nation was threatened with internal collapse. Some politicians advocated a more aggressive foreign policy to divert the popular mind from dissensions at home.

The swelling volume of American exports to other countries altered the nature of our trade relations and directed the attention of political leaders to the importance of foreign markets – and to the possible necessity of securing foreign colonies. The value of American exports in 1870 was approximately $392 million; in 1890 the figure was $857 million, and by 1900 it had leaped to $1,394,000,000. "But today," Senator Albert J. Beveridge of Indiana cried in 1899, "we are raising more than we can consume. Today, we are making more than we can use. Therefore, we must find new markets for our produce, new occupation for our capital, new work for our labor."

In the century's closing years the powers of Europe partitioned most of Africa among themselves and then turned eager eyes on the Far East and the feeble Chinese empire. Imperialism was in the air, and a leading American expansionist, Senator Henry Cabot Lodge of Massachusetts, warned that the United States "must not fall out of the line of march."

A philosophic justification for expansionism was provided by historians, professors, clergymen, and other intellectuals, who found a basis for imperialism in Charles Darwin's theories. These thinkers contended that, among nations, or "races," as well as biological species, there was a struggle for existence and only the fittest could survive. If the strong dominated the weak, that was in accordance with the law of nature.

One of the first to argue this proposition was the popular writer John Fiske, who predicted in an article in *Harper's Magazine* (1885)

Defeat of the Anti-Imperialists
This 1899 lithograph, reproduced from Puck *magazine, pictures Bryan and other members of the "Anti-Expansion Band" leaving Washington in defeat and humiliation, while McKinley smilingly rides the "Expansion Train" toward continued political success. (Culver Pictures)*

that the English-speaking peoples would eventually control every land that was not already the seat of an established civilization. Support for Fiske's position came from Josiah Strong, a Congregational clergyman and champion of overseas missionary work. In a book entitled *Our Country: Its Possible Future and Its Present Crisis* (1885), Strong declared that the Anglo-Saxon "race," and especially its American branch, represented the great ideas of civil liberty and pure Christianity and was "divinely commissioned" to spread its institutions over the earth. John W. Burgess, founder of Columbia University's School of Political Science, gave the stamp of scholarly approval to imperialism. In his *Political Science and Comparative Law* (1890), he flatly stated that the Anglo-Saxon and Teutonic nations possessed the highest political talents. It was the duty of these nations, he said, to uplift less fortunate peoples, even to force superior institutions upon them if necessary: "There is no human right to the status of barbarism."

The ablest and probably the most effective apostle of imperialism was Alfred Thayer Mahan, an officer in the navy. Mahan presented his philosophy in three major works: *The Influence of Sea Power upon History, 1660–1783* (1890); *The Influence of Sea Power upon the French Revolution and Empire, 1793–1812* (1892); and *The Interest of America in Sea Power* (1897). His thesis may be briefly stated. The sea-power nations were the great nations of history, and the United States, a huge island, had to build its greatness on sea power. The essential links in sea power were a productive domestic economy, foreign commerce, a merchant marine to monopolize national trade, a navy to defend the trade routes and national interests, and colonies to provide raw materials and markets and to serve as bases for the navy. Specifically, Mahan advocated that the United States construct a canal across the isthmus of Central America to join the oceans, acquire defensive bases on both sides of the canal in the Caribbean and the Pacific, and take possession of Hawaii and other Pacific islands. "Whether they will or no," he proclaimed, "Americans must now begin to look outward."

Mahan doubted that the United States would achieve its destiny, because its navy was not large enough to play the role he envisioned for it. But he did not accurately gauge the progress of the naval construction program launched in the Garfield-Arthur administration and continued by every succeeding administration. By 1898 the United States had advanced to fifth among the world's naval powers, and by 1900 to third.

HEMISPHERIC HEGEMONY

The most ardent practitioner of the new, assertive diplomacy was Harrison's Secretary of State, James G. Blaine, who in 1889 was beginning his second tour of duty in the foreign office. He believed that his country was destined to dominate the Caribbean and the Pacific. His expansionist policy was based largely on his conviction that the United States had to find enlarged foreign markets for its surplus goods. The most likely foreign outlet, he believed, was Latin America, with whose countries he wanted friendly commercial relations.

During his first term of office (1881), Blaine had invited the Latin nations to a Pan-American conference at Washington to discuss trade matters and arbitration of disputes. But after Garfield's death Blaine left office, and his cautious successor withdrew the invitations. Shortly before the Harrison administration took office, however, Congress authorized the convoking of a conference, and the State Department issued the invitations. With delegates from nineteen American nations in attendance, the first Pan-American Congress assembled in 1889. Blaine tried to persuade the conference to endorse his two principal objectives: (1) to draw the United States and Latin America into a customs union and (2) to create machinery to arbitrate controversies among the hemispheric nations. The Latin delegates rejected both proposals. They preferred to buy in the cheaper European market, and they feared the dominance of the United States in arbitration. Still, the meeting was not entirely a failure. Out of it arose the Pan-American Union, an agency in Washington that became a clearing house for

distributing information to the member nations, and other congresses would meet in the future to discuss common hemispheric matters.

When, after the election of 1892, the Democrats took over, the change in personnel meant no break in the new self-assertive diplomacy. Indeed, in 1895 President Cleveland and his Secretary of State, Richard Olney, in a dispute with Great Britain over the boundary of Venezuela, carried the country close to the brink of war.

For years Britain and Venezuela had argued about the boundary between Venezuela and British Guiana, the dispute assuming new importance when gold was discovered in the disputed area. Both Cleveland and Olney, as well as the American public, were disposed to sympathize with Venezuela as the little, underdog country confronting the great power. The President and Congress publicly expressed hopes that Britain would see fit to arbitrate the matter. When the English government took no action, Olney drafted a note to Lord Salisbury of the foreign office protesting that Britain was violating the Monroe Doctrine. Any European interference with hemispheric affairs – and a boundary dispute constituted interference – came within the scope of the famous doctrine, said the secretary. In bellicose language designed to make England sit up and listen, he declared: "Today the United States is practically sovereign on this continent, and its fiat is law upon the subjects to which it confines its interposition."

After months of delay Salisbury replied to Olney. With firm finality and a touch of condescension, he informed the secretary that the Monroe Doctrine did not apply to boundary disputes or the present situation and was not recognized as international law anyway. Britain was not going to arbitrate. Cleveland was enraged. In December 1895 he sent a special message to Congress reviewing the controversy. He asked for authority to create a special commission to determine the boundary line, and declared that if Britain resisted the commission's decision the United States should fight.

Enthusiastically Congress voted support for Cleveland's plan, and war talk flamed all over the country. Belatedly the British government realized that it had stumbled into a genuine diplomatic crisis. The last thing in the world that England wanted or could afford was a war with the United States. Suddenly the British backed down and agreed to arbitration.

However clumsy the Cleveland-Olney techniques had been, they had produced the desired results. The prestige of the United States was enhanced, the Monroe Doctrine was vitalized, and the bonds of friendship between the two great English-speaking nations were actually strengthened by strain.

HAWAII AND SAMOA

The first area into which the United States directed its expansionist impulse after the Civil War was the vast Pacific Ocean region.

The islands of Hawaii in the mid-Pacific had been an important stopover station for American ships in the China trade since the early 1800s. The first American settlers to reach Hawaii were New England missionaries, who, like their fellows in Oregon at approximately the same time, advertised the economic possibilities of the islands in the religious press. Soon other Americans arrived to become sugar planters and to found a profitable new industry. Eventually, officers of the growing navy looked longingly on the magnificent natural base of Pearl Harbor on the island of Oahu.

The American residents of Hawaii came to dominate the economic life of the islands and also the political policies of the native ruler. Commercial relations were inexorably pushing Hawaii into the American orbit and making it, as Blaine accurately contended, a part of the American system. A treaty signed in 1875 permitted Hawaiian sugar to enter the United States duty-free and bound the Hawaiian kingdom to make no territorial or economic concessions to other powers. The trade arrangement tied the islands to the American economy, and the political clauses meant that, in effect, the United States was guaranteeing Hawaii's independence, and hence was making the islands a protectorate. In 1887 a new treaty renewed the existing arrangements and granted the United States exclusive use of Pearl Harbor as a naval station. The course of events was rendering outright political union almost inevitable.

Sugar production in Hawaii boomed, and prosperity burgeoned for the American planters. Then the McKinley Tariff of 1890 dealt the planters a bad blow; by removing the duty on foreign raw sugar and giving domestic producers a bounty, it deprived Hawaii of its privileged position in the American sugar market. Annexation seemed the only alternative to economic strangulation. At the same time there ascended to the throne a new ruler, Queen Liliuokalani, who was determined to eliminate American influence in the government.

The American residents decided to act at once. They started a revolution (1893) and called on the United States for protection. At a critical moment the American minister, John L. Stevens, an ardent annexationist and friend of Blaine, ordered 160 marines from a warship in Honolulu harbor to go ashore to aid the rebels. The Queen yielded her authority, and a delegation representing the triumphant provisional government set out for Washington to negotiate a treaty of annexation. They found President Harrison highly receptive, but before the resulting treaty could be acted on by the Senate he was succeeded by Cleveland.

However disposed Cleveland was to upholding American rights under the Monroe Doctrine, he had old-fashioned ideas about taking other people's property. Suspicious of what had happened in Hawaii, he withdrew the treaty and sent a special representative to the islands to investigate. When this agent reported that Americans had engineered the revolution, Cleveland endeavored to restore the Queen to her throne. But the Americans were in control of the kingdom and refused to budge. Reluctantly the President had to accord recognition to their government as representing the "republic" of Hawaii. Cleveland, actuated by honorable motives but opposing the course of history, had only delayed the inevitable. In 1898, with the Republicans again in power and with the United States, as we shall see, constructing a colonial empire in both oceans, Hawaii was annexed by joint resolution of both houses of Congress.

Three thousand miles to the south of Hawaii, the Samoan Islands dominated the sea lanes of the south Pacific and had long served as a way station for American ships in the Pacific trade. As American commerce with Asia increased after the completion of the first transcontinental railroad in 1869 and the extension of a steamship line from San Francisco to New Zealand, certain business groups regarded

Samoa with new interest, and the navy eyed the harbor of Pago Pago on the island of Tutuila. In 1872 a naval officer visited the islands and negotiated a treaty granting the United States the use of Pago Pago, but the Senate rejected it. President Grant nevertheless dispatched a special representative to Samoa to encourage American trading and business interests. The familiar chain of events leading to involvement was being set in motion. In 1878 a native prince was brought to Washington, where he signed a treaty, which was approved by the Senate, providing for an American naval station at Pago Pago and binding the United States to employ its "good offices" to adjust any differences between a foreign power and Samoa. This indicated that the American government meant to have a voice in Samoan affairs.

The opportunity for expressing that voice soon came. Great Britain and Germany were also interested in the islands, and they hastened to secure treaty rights from the native princes. For the next ten years the three powers scrambled and intrigued for dominance in Samoa, playing off one ruler against another

and coming dangerously close to war. In 1889 warships of the contending nations appeared in one Samoan harbor, and a clash seemed imminent. But a tropical hurricane dispersed the vessels, and the German government, not wishing to antagonize the United States, suggested a conference of the interested powers in Berlin to settle the dispute. Germany and Britain would have preferred a division of the islands, but Secretary Blaine insisted on preserving native Samoan rule. The result was that the conferees agreed on a tripartite protectorate over Samoa, with the native chiefs exercising only nominal authority.

The three-way arrangement proved unsatisfactory, failing altogether to halt the intrigues and rivalries of the signatory members. It was abrogated in 1899 when the United States and Germany divided the islands between them, with Britain being compensated elsewhere in the Pacific. Germany obtained the two largest islands, but the United States retained Tutuila with its incomparable harbor of Pago Pago. Everyone was satisfied — with the possible exception of the Samoans.

War with Spain

Though imperialist ambitions had begun to stir the United States, American imperialism did not flower until the coming of the war with Spain in 1898.

CONTROVERSY OVER CUBA

The immediate background of the Spanish-American War lay in the Caribbean island of Cuba, which with nearby Puerto Rico comprised nearly all that was left of Spain's once extensive Latin American empire. The Cubans had long resented Spanish rule, and they had engaged in a notable attempt to overthrow it between 1868 and 1878 (the Ten Years' War). During that revolt the American people were strongly sympathetic to the Cuban cause, but their feelings did not go beyond expressions of support. The government maintained a position of strict neutrality, despite the provocation offered by Spain. In 1873 the Spanish authori-

ties captured a Cuban-owned, arms-running ship, the *Virginius,* and executed fifty-three of her crew. Because the vessel had flown an American flag and some of her seamen were Americans, popular indignation was intense. But Secretary of State Hamilton Fish avoided a crisis by inducing the Spanish government to return the *Virginius* and pay an indemnity to the families of the executed men.

In 1895 the Cubans rose up again. Not only the continuing Spanish misrule but also the American tariff policy created conditions of misery that prepared the way for revolt. Cuba's principal export was sugar, and the bulk of the crop went to the United States. The Wilson-Gorman Tariff in 1894, with its high duties on raw sugar, shut off the island's chief source of wealth and prostrated its economy.

From the beginning the struggle took on aspects of ferocity that horrified Americans. The Cubans deliberately devastated the island to force the Spaniards to leave. To put down the insurrection, the Spanish resorted to methods equally extreme. General Valeriano Weyler—or "Butcher" Weyler, as he soon came to be known in the American press—confined the entire civilian population of certain areas to hastily prepared concentration camps, where they died by the thousands, victims of disease and malnutrition.

Many of the same savage techniques had been employed earlier in the Ten Years' War without shocking American sensibilities. But in the nineties a wave of anger ran through the American public. The revolt of 1895 was reported more fully and floridly by the American press than the former outbreak—and so reported as to give the impression that all the cruelties were being perpetrated by the Spaniards.

At this time Joseph Pulitzer with his New York *World* and William Randolph Hearst with his New York *Journal* were revolutionizing American journalism. The new "yellow press" specialized in lurid and sensational news; when such news did not exist, editors were not above creating it. To Hearst and Pulitzer, engaged in a ruthless circulation war, the struggle in Cuba was a journalist's dream. Both sent batteries of reporters and illustrators to Cuba with orders to provide accounts of Spanish atrocities. "You furnish the pictures," Hearst supposedly told a too scrupulous artist, "and I'll furnish the war."

The mounting storm of indignation against Spain left President Cleveland unmoved. Convinced that both sides in Cuba were guilty of atrocities and that the United States had no interests justifying involvement in the struggle, he issued a proclamation of neutrality and attempted to arrest the numerous filibustering expeditions being organized by a "junta" of Cuban refugees in New York City. When Congress, in a state of excitement, passed a resolution favoring recognition of Cuban belligerency, he ignored the action. His only concession to the demands for intervention was to offer America's good offices to mediate the conflict, a proposal that Spain declined.

When McKinley took over the presidency in 1897, he renewed the American mediation offer, which was again refused. Taking a stronger line than his predecessor, he protested to Spain against her "uncivilized and inhuman" conduct. The Spanish government,

alarmed that McKinley's course might forebode American intervention in Cuba, recalled Weyler, modified the concentration policy, and took steps to grant the island a qualified autonomy. At the end of 1897, with the insurrection losing ground, it seemed that war might be averted.

If there was any chance of a peaceful settlement, it was extinguished by two dramatic incidents in February 1898.

A Cuban agent in Havana stole a private letter written by Dupuy de Lôme, the Spanish minister in Washington, and thoughtfully turned it over to the American press. First published in Hearst's New York *Journal*, the minister's letter described McKinley as a weak man and "a bidder for the admiration of the crowd." This was no more than many Americans, including some Republicans, were saying about their President—Theodore Roosevelt described McKinley as having "no more backbone than a chocolate éclair"—but when a foreigner made such a remark it was a national insult. Popular anger was intense, and Dupuy de Lôme resigned before the outraged McKinley could demand his recall.

While the excitement was still at fever pitch, even more sensational news hit the front pages: the battleship *Maine* had been blown up in Havana harbor with a loss of over 260 lives. This vessel had been ordered to Cuban waters in January on a "friendly" visit, but the real reason for its presence was to protect American lives and property against possible attacks by Spanish loyalists. Many Americans jumped to the conclusion that the Spanish had sunk the ship—"an act of dirty treachery," Theodore Roosevelt announced—and the imperialists and the jingoists screamed for war. This opinion seemed confirmed when a naval court of inquiry reported that an external explosion by a submarine mine had caused the disaster. As war hysteria swept the country, Congress unanimously appropriated $50 million for military preparations. "Remember the *Maine*" became a national chant for revenge.

After the *Maine* incident there was little chance that the government could keep the people from war, although McKinley did not wish to resort to force. In March 1898, he asked Spain to agree to an armistice, with negotiations for a permanent peace to follow, and an immediate ending of the concentration system.

Wreck of the Maine
During the night after the explosion, the Maine *settled down into the mud on the harbor bottom, so that only the wrecked superstructure remained visible, as shown here. Soon afterward, divers examined the hull. From their findings and from other evidence a naval court of inquiry concluded that an underwater mine had exploded, setting off explosions in the ship's powder magazines. Years later, in 1911, the wreck was raised so that it could be examined for a second court of inquiry. This court agreed with the first one on the essential point—that there had been both external and internal explosions—but disagreed on certain significant details. Finally, the hulk was towed out to sea and sunk in water too deep to permit another examination. (National Archives)*

After a slight delay, Spain essentially accepted the American demands on April 9. Two days later McKinley asked Congress for authority to use military force to end the hostilities in Cuba—in short, for a declaration of war. After reviewing the reasons that impelled him to recommend war ("in the name of humanity, in the name of civilization, in behalf of endangered American interests"), he mentioned only casually, at the end of the message, that Spain was already capitulating to his requests.

By huge majorities Congress on April 19 passed a joint resolution declaring Cuba free and authorizing the President to employ force to expel the Spanish from the island. Added to the resolution was the Teller Amendment, disclaiming any intention on the part of the United States to annex Cuba.

"A SPLENDID LITTLE WAR"

The Spanish-American War was, in the words of Roosevelt's friend John Hay, "a splendid little war." Indeed, to all Americans, with the possible exception of the enlisted men who fought it, it was almost an ideal conflict. It was the last small, short, individualistic war before the huge, protracted, impersonal struggles of the twentieth century. Declared in April, it was over in August. Newspaper readers easily and eagerly followed the campaigns and the heroic exploits of American soldiers and sailors. Only 460 Americans were killed in battle or died of wounds, but some 5,200 perished of disease: malaria, dysentery, typhoid, and other ills.

Blithely and confidently the United States embarked on a war it was not prepared to fight. The regular army, numbering only 28,000 troops and officers scattered around the country at various posts, was a tough little force, skilled at quelling Indian outbreaks, but with no experience in large-scale warfare. Hastily Congress directed the President to increase the army to 62,000 and to call for 125,000 volunteers. It was expected that the National Guard, the state militia, would furnish the bulk of the volunteers, and in addition the President was authorized to accept directly into the national service three volunteer cavalry regiments. By far the most colorful of the cavalrymen were the Rough Riders, nominally commanded by Leonard Wood but actually by Theodore Roosevelt, who was about to burst onto the front pages as a war hero. The services of supply,

The Spanish-American War: Pacific Front

manned by elderly bureaucratic officers, proved incapable of meeting the modest wants of the forces raised during the war. On hand were enough Krag-Jorgensen repeating rifles, using smokeless powder, for the regulars, but the volunteers had to make do with the old black-powder, single-shot Springfields. American soldiers campaigning in tropical regions were clothed in the traditional heavy blue uniforms and fed canned rations that they called "embalmed beef."

The Spanish army numbered almost 130,000 troops, of whom 80,000 were already in Cuba at the beginning of the war. Despite its imposing size, it was not an efficient force; its commanders seemed to be paralyzed by a conviction of certain defeat. The American navy, fifth largest in the world, was far superior to the Spanish in ships, gunnery, and personnel.

The greatest weakness in the American military system was that no agency in it, either in the army or the navy, was charged with strategic planning. Only the navy had worked out an objective, and its objective had little to do with freeing Cuba.

The Assistant Secretary of the Navy in the McKinley administration was Theodore Roosevelt, ardent imperialist and proponent of war. In consultations with naval officers, Roosevelt prepared to seize Spain's Philippine Islands in the far Pacific. He strengthened the Asiatic squadron and instructed its commander, Commodore George Dewey, in event of war to attack the Philippines. Immediately after war was declared, Dewey left the China coast and headed for Manila, where a venerable Spanish fleet was stationed. On May 1 he steamed into Manila Bay, and as his ships prepared to pass down the line of anchored enemy vessels he uttered the first slogan of the war: "You may fire when ready, Gridley." When the firing was finished, the Spanish fleet was completely destroyed, one American sailor lay dead—of a heat stroke—and George Dewey, immediately promoted to admiral, had become the first hero of the war.

The Spaniards still held Manila city, and Dewey had no troops with which to attack them. While he waited nervously, the government assembled an expeditionary force to relieve him and take the city. Not until August 13 did the Americans receive the surrender of Manila.

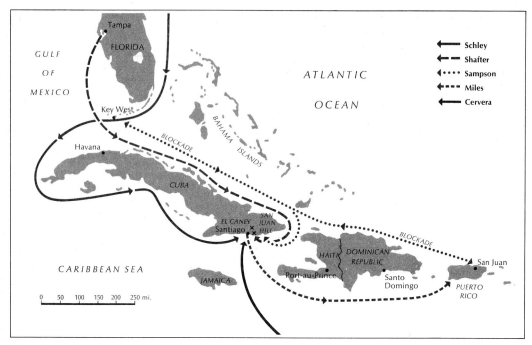

The Spanish-American War: Caribbean Front

In the rejoicing over Dewey's victory, few Americans paused to note that the character of the war was being subtly altered. What had begun as a war to free Cuba was becoming a war to acquire colonies.

But Cuba was not to be left out of the war picture. Late in April it was known in the United States that a Spanish fleet under Admiral Pascual Cervera had sailed for the west, presumably for a Cuban harbor. Cervera's antique armada was no match for the powerful American Atlantic squadron, as the Spanish government well knew. The Atlantic squadron, commanded by Admiral William T. Sampson, with Commodore W. S. Schley second in command, was expected to intercept and destroy Cervera before he reached his destination. (The squadron was "as strong as Sampson and as Schley as a fox," newspapers happily assured their readers.) But the Spaniard turned out to be the fox. Easily eluding his pursuers, he slipped into Santiago harbor on the southern coast of Cuba, where he was not discovered by the Americans until ten days after his arrival. Immediately the Atlantic fleet moved to bottle him up.

While the navy was monopolizing the first phases of the war, the War Department was trying to mobilize and train an army. The volunteer and National Guard units were collected near Chattanooga, Tennessee, while the regulars, plus the Rough Riders, were assembled at Tampa, Florida, under the command of General William R. Shafter. The entire mobilization process was conducted with remarkable inefficiency. There were appalling shortages of arms, ammunition, food, clothing, and medical supplies.

The army's commanding general, Nelson A. Miles, veteran of the Civil War, had planned to train the troops until autumn, then to occupy Puerto Rico and in conjunction with the Cuban rebels attack Havana. But with a Spanish naval force at Santiago, plans were hastily changed. It was decided to send Shafter with his force of 17,000 to take Santiago. So in June the expedition left Tampa, the Rough Riders, for want of transport space, having to leave their horses behind. The embarkation was accomplished amidst scenes of fantastic incompetence, but it was efficiency itself compared to the landing. Five days were required to put the army ashore, and this with the enemy offering no opposition.

Once landed, Shafter moved his army toward Santiago, planning to surround and capture it. On the way he fought and defeated the Spaniards at two battles, El Caney and San Juan Hill. In both engagements the Rough Riders were in the middle of the fighting and on the front pages of the newspapers. Colonel Roosevelt rapidly emerged as a hero of the war. Shafter was now before Santiago, but his army was so weakened by sickness that he feared he might have to abandon his position. When he besought Sampson to unite with him in a joint attack on the city, the admiral answered that mines in the harbor made it too dangerous to take his big ships in.

At this point disaster seemingly confronted the Americans, but unknown to them the Spanish government had decided that Santiago was lost. On July 3 Cervera, acting under orders from home, broke from the harbor to attempt an escape that he knew was hopeless. The waiting American squadron destroyed his entire fleet. Shafter then pressed the Spanish army commander to surrender, and that official, after bargaining for generous terms, including free transportation back to Spain for his troops, turned over Santiago on July 16. While the Santiago campaign was in its last stages, an American army landed in Puerto Rico and occupied it against virtually no opposition.

Spain was whipped and knew it. Through the medium of the French ambassador in Washington she asked for peace, and on August 12 an armistice ended the war.

DECISION FOR IMPERIALISM

In agreeing to a preliminary peace, the United States had laid down terms on which a permanent settlement must be based: Spain was to relinquish Cuba, cede Puerto Rico to the United States, cede also to the victor an island in the Ladrones, midway between Hawaii and the Philippines (this turned out to be Guam), and permit the Americans to hold Manila pending the final disposition of the Philippines. The last clause reflected the confusion in the McKinley administration as to what to do about the islands where its forces had won a foothold. The demands for Puerto Rico and Guam

showed how quickly the war to free Cuba had assumed an imperialist character. Aroused by the excitement of military victory and a heady sense of mastery, the American government and people were disposed to keep what American arms had won.

In October 1898, commissioners from the United States and Spain met in Paris, to determine a permanent peace. With little protest Spain agreed to recognize Cuba's independence, to assume the Cuban debt, and to cede Puerto Rico and Guam to the victor. Then the American commissioners acting under instruction from McKinley, startled the conference by demanding the cession of all the Philippines. The President later said that he had arrived at his decision as a result of divine guidance. Probably such mundane factors as the swelling sentiment for annexation in the country and the pressure of the imperialist leaders of his party influenced his thinking more. Stubbornly the Spanish resisted the American demand, although they realized they could retain the islands only by resuming the war. They yielded to the inevitable when the United States offered a money payment of $20 million. The Treaty of Paris was signed on December 10, 1898, and sent to the United States for ratification by the Senate.

When the treaty was submitted to the Senate, it encountered immediate and fierce criticism and occasioned in that body and throughout the country one of those "great debates" that frequently precede a departure in American foreign policy. The chief point at issue was the acquisition of the Philippines, denounced by many, including prominent Republicans, as a repudiation of America's high moral position in the war and a shameful occupation of a land that wanted to be free. Favoring ratification were the imperialists, the big navy lobby, the Protestant clergy, who saw in a colonial empire enlarged fields for missionary enterprise, and most Republicans. Business, which had opposed the war, swung over to support the treaty, converted by the notion that possession of the Philippines would enable American interests to dominate the Oriental trade. In the forces opposing the treaty were old-fashioned Americans who objected to their country's annexing other people against their will, traditionalists who feared that a colonial empire would necessitate large armaments and foreign alliances, a majority of the intellectuals, eco-

An Argument Against Imperialism [1899]

The anti-imperialists included both Democrats and Republicans and men as different as Andrew Carnegie and William Jennings Bryan. Most of them had long supported various political and social reforms. They organized the American Anti-Imperialist League, which in October 1899, in the midst of the Philippine insurrection, drew up a platform. This denied the obligation of Americans to support an unjust, undeclared war such as the one the United States was carrying on against the Filipinos. The platform also included the following statements:

We hold that the policy known as imperialism is hostile to liberty and tends toward militarism, an evil from which it has been our glory to be free. We regret that it has become necessary in the land of Washington and Lincoln to reaffirm that all men, of whatever race or color, are entitled to life, liberty, and the pursuit of happiness. We maintain that governments derive their just powers from the consent of the governed. We insist that the subjugation of any people is "criminal aggression" and open disloyalty to the distinctive principles of our Government. . . .

We hold, with Abraham Lincoln, that "no man is good enough to govern another man without that man's consent. When the white man governs himself, that is self-government, but when he governs himself and also governs another man, that is more than self-government—that is despotism. . . . Our reliance is in the love of liberty which God has planted in us. Our defense is in the spirit which prizes liberty as the heritage of all men in all lands. Those who deny freedom to others deserve it not for themselves, and under a just God cannot long retain it."

---

nomic interests like the sugar growers who foresaw colonial competition, and most Democrats.

After weeks of bitter wrangling, the treaty was ratified, February 6, 1899, but only because it received an unexpected assist from William Jennings Bryan, who expected to be his party's candidate again in the election of 1900. Bryan persuaded a number of Democratic senators to vote for ratification. It has been charged that he was looking for a campaign issue, and in his defense it has been said that he thought the question of the Philippines should be decided by a national referendum: if the

Democrats won in 1900, they would free the islands.

In 1900 Bryan ran against McKinley again, and this time Bryan went down to a crushing defeat. Although the Republicans claimed a popular mandate for imperialism, other factors had helped to determine the outcome. The victors had again exploited the money and tariff issues; they had harped on the continuing prosperity in the country under a Republican administration; and they had displayed to the voters the colorful personality of their vice-presidential candidate, the hero of San Juan Hill, Colonel Theodore Roosevelt.

The Republic as an Empire

The new colonial empire was extensive enough to warm the heart of the most ardent imperialist. Stretching from the Caribbean to the far reaches of the Pacific, it embraced Puerto Rico, Alaska, Hawaii, a part of Samoa, Guam,

the Philippines, and a chain of minor Pacific islands.

With the empire came new problems. Many of the predictions of the anti-imperialists proved accurate. Ultimately, as a colonial

An Argument for Imperialism [1900]

Senator Albert J. Beveridge of Indiana addressed the Senate on January 9, 1900, after visiting the Philippines, where American troops were fighting to put down the struggle of the Filipinos for independence. He began by saying that the "hurtful" resolutions and speeches of the anti-imperialists were "costing the lives of American soldiers." He continued:

> The Philippines are ours forever, "territory belonging to the United States," as the Constitution calls them. And just beyond the Philippines are China's illimitable markets. We will not retreat from either. We will not repudiate our duty in the archipelago. We will not abandon our opportunity in the Orient. We will not renounce our part in the mission of our race, trustee, under God, of the civilization of the world. . . .
>
> Mr. President, this question is deeper than any question of party politics; deeper than any question of the isolated policy of our country even; deeper even than any question of constitutional power. It is elemental. It is racial. God has not been preparing the English-speaking and Teutonic peoples for a thousand years for nothing but vain and idle self-contemplation and self-admiration. No! He has made us the master organizers of the world to establish system where chaos reigns. He has given us the spirit of progress to overwhelm the forces of reaction throughout the earth. He has made us adepts in government that we may administer government among savage and senile peoples. Were it not for such a force as this the world would relapse into barbarism and night. And of all our race He has marked the American people as His chosen nation to finally lead in the regeneration of the world.

power, the United States had to maintain large armaments, concern itself with the complexities of Far Eastern international politics, and modify its traditional policy of holding aloof from alliances.

GOVERNING THE COLONIES

Immediately, the nation faced the problem of how it was to govern its dependencies, and here a host of perplexing questions arose. Did Congress have to administer the colonies in accordance with the Constitution? Did the inhabitants of the new possessions have the rights of American citizens? Could Congress levy tariff duties on colonial imports? Or, in a phrase that pleased the public fancy, did the Constitution follow the flag? The Supreme Court pointed to a solution in the Insular Cases (*De Lima* v. *Bidwell, Downes* v. *Bidwell*, and others, 1900–1904), involving duties on colonial trade. In a series of decisions the Court distinguished, in extremely technical language, between "incorporated" and "unincorporated"

territories. In legislating for the latter – the insular possessions – Congress was not bound by all the limitations in the Constitution applicable to incorporated territories, although some restrictions did apply. What the Court was saying was that the Constitution followed the flag only if Congress so decided and that the government could administer its colonies in almost any way it saw fit.

Three of the dependencies – Hawaii, Alaska, and Puerto Rico – were given territorial status as quickly as Congress considered them ready for it. For Hawaii, with its large American population and close economic ties with the United States, a basis for government was provided by an act of 1900. This measure granted American citizenship to all persons who were citizens of the Hawaiian republic, authorized an elective two-house legislature, and vested executive authority in a governor appointed from Washington.

Alaska was being governed by appointed civil officials. The discovery of gold there in 1896 caused the first substantial influx of Americans, and in 1912 Alaska received territorial status and a legislature, and its inhabitants were given the rights of citizenship. In Puerto Rico the people readily accepted American rule. Military occupation of the island was ended and civil government was established by the Foraker Act in 1900. The governor and upper house of the legislature were to be appointed from Washington, while only the lower house was to be elected. The act did not declare the Puerto Ricans to be American citizens, this privilege being deferred until 1917.

Smaller possessions in the empire were dealt with more arbitrarily. Such places as Guam and Tutuila were placed under control of naval officials, and many of the small islands, containing only a handful of inhabitants, experienced no form of American government at all.

American military forces, commanded by General Leonard Wood, remained in Cuba until 1902, the occupation being protracted to enable American administrators to prepare the island for the independence promised in the peace treaty of 1898. The vigorous occupiers built roads, schools, and hospitals, reorganized the legal, financial, and administrative systems, and introduced far-reaching sanitary reforms.

At Wood's urging a convention assembled to draft a constitution for independent Cuba. This document contained no provisions concerning relations with the nation responsible for Cuba's freedom. The United States, with its expanding interests in the Caribbean, expected to exercise some kind of control over the island republic. Therefore, in 1901, Congress passed the Platt Amendment, as a rider to an army appropriation bill, and pressured Cuba into incorporating the terms of the amendment into her constitution. The Platt Amendment stated that Cuba should never impair her independence by treaty with a foreign power (this was equivalent to giving the United States a veto over Cuba's diplomatic policy); that the United States had the right to intervene in Cuba to preserve its independence, life, and property; and that Cuba must sell or lease to the United States lands for naval stations. The amendment left Cuba only nominally independent. With American capital taking over the island's economy—investments jumped from $50 million in 1898 to $220 million by 1914—Cuba was in fact, if not in name, an American appendage.

Among the possessions in the imperial system, only the Philippines offered resistance to American rule. The Filipinos, rebellious against Spain before 1898, had hailed Dewey and the expeditionary force sent to Manila as their deliverers from tyranny. When the hard fact sank in that the Americans had come to stay, the Filipinos resolved to expel the new invaders. In 1899 they resorted to war (rebellion, by the American definition) and, ably led by Emilio Aguinaldo, they fought the army of occupation from island to island until 1901. In the end the Americans repressed the uprising, but only after employing methods unpleasantly reminiscent of Weyler's tenure in Cuba, including the use of concentration camps, and at a cost of $170 million and 4,300 American lives. Civil government began taking over from the military in 1901, and the Filipinos, with great adaptability, began the process of adjusting to American culture. Thus they started on the long road that would lead, in 1946, to the independence they so ardently desired.

THE OPEN DOOR

The acquisition of the Philippines made the United States an Asian power. American interest in the Far East, already aroused by our growing trade with China, reached a new intensity immediately after 1898. Other nations more experienced in the ways of empire were casting covetous eyes on China, ancient, enfeebled, and seemingly open to exploitation by stronger countries. By the turn of the century the great European imperialistic powers—England, France, Germany, and Russia—and one Asian power, Japan, were beginning to partition China into "spheres of influence." One nation would force the Chinese government to grant it "concessions" to develop a particular area; another would use pressure to secure a long-term lease to a region. In some cases the outside powers even asserted ownership of territory. The process, if continued, threatened to destroy American hopes for a vast trade with China.

The situation posed a delicate problem for the men directing American foreign policy. Knowing that public opinion would not support any use of force, they had to find a way to protect American interests in China without risking war. McKinley's Secretary of State, John Hay, attempted an audacious solution. In September 1899 he addressed identical notes to

The Open Door in China
*"Uncle Sam has distanced all competitors in gaining access to the Flowery
Kingdom," says the caption of this cartoon. He holds the key to the door while
the other powers look on. Obviously, Secretary of State John Hay has aroused
much popular enthusiasm by his Open Door notes, though in fact they represented
no great diplomatic triumph for the United States. From the Utica, New York,
Saturday Globe, March 3, 1900. (Culver Pictures)*

England, Germany, and Russia, and later to
France, Japan, and Italy, asking them to approve a formula that became known as the
"Open Door." It embodied three principles: (1)
each nation with a sphere of influence was to
respect the rights and privileges of other nations in its sphere; (2) Chinese officials were to
continue to collect tariff duties in all spheres
(the existing tariff favored the United States);
and (3) each nation with a sphere was not to
discriminate against other nations in levying
port dues and railroad rates.

Hay could hardly have expected an enthusiastic response to his notes, and he got none.
Russia declined to approve the Open Door, and
the remaining powers gave evasive replies.

Each one stated in effect that it approved Hay's
ideas in principle but could make no commitment until the others had acted. Apparently the
United States had met a humiliating rebuff, but
Hay boldly announced that since all the powers
had accepted the principle of the Open Door,
his government considered their assent to be
"final and definitive." Although the American
public applauded his diplomacy, Hay had won
little more than a theoretical victory. The
United States could not prevent any nation that
wanted to violate the Open Door from doing
so—unless it was willing to resort to war.

Almost immediately after the diplomatic
maneuvering over the Open Door ended, a
secret Chinese society known as the Boxers

instigated an uprising against foreigners in China. The movement came to a blazing climax when the Boxers and their supporters besieged the entire foreign diplomatic corps in the British embassy in Peking. At this point the powers with interests in China decided to send an international expeditionary force to rescue the diplomats. The situation seemed to offer a perfect excuse to those nations with ambitions to dismember China.

The United States contributed 2,500 troops to the rescue force, which in August 1900 fought its way into Peking and broke the siege. McKinley and Hay had decided on American participation in order to secure a voice in the settlement of the uprising and to prevent the partition of China. Again Hay sent a note to the world powers. This time he called for the Open Door not only in the spheres of influence but in "all parts of the Chinese Empire." He also called for the maintenance of China's "territorial and administrative integrity." This—the integrity, or independence, of China—thus became a corollary of the Open Door policy. He persuaded England and Germany to approve his views, and then with their support he induced the participating powers to accept a money indemnity as satisfaction. The sum allotted to the United States amounted to almost $25 million, which greatly exceeded damages, but later the American government reduced the obligation and even remitted the unpaid balance. China gratefully used part of this money to educate Chinese students in the United States.

A MODERN MILITARY SYSTEM

The war with Spain had revealed glaring deficiencies in the military system. The greatest weakness had appeared in the army, but there had been an absence of coordination in the entire military organization that might have resulted in disaster had the United States been fighting a first-rate power. The army, now being called upon to police the new colonial possessions, obviously needed a thorough overhauling. To do the job McKinley appointed Elihu Root, an extremely able administrator, as secretary of war in 1899. Between 1900 and 1903 Root put into effect, by congressional authorization or by executive order, a series of reforms that gave the United States what amounted to a new military system.

The Root reforms may be conveniently listed in summary form:

1. An enlarged regular army, with a maximum size of 100,000.
2. Federal supervision of the National Guard, provided by the Dick Act of 1903.
3. The creation of a system of officer-training schools, crowned by the Army Staff College (later the Command and General Staff School) at Fort Leavenworth, Kansas, and the Army War College at Washington.
4. The establishment in 1903 of a General Staff headed by a Chief of Staff, who would replace the former commanding general of the army and act as military adviser to the Secretary of War.

While Root was intent on improving the professional quality and the efficiency of all segments of the army, his primary concern was to provide it with a central planning agency modeled on the example of European staffs. The General Staff was charged with many functions (it was to "supervise" and "coordinate" the entire army establishment), but one of its most important branches was to devote its whole work to planning for possible wars. To ensure interservice strategic cooperation, an Army and Navy Board, representing both services, was created.

Whatever the shortcomings of the Root reforms, they invested the army with a new and needed competence. The United States entered the twentieth century with something resembling a modern military system.

Life in the Imperial Republic

The acquisition of a far-flung empire did not noticeably affect the daily lives of the American people, who numbered nearly 76 million according to the census of 1900. But the lives of the people were being profoundly affected by other developments—in technology, culture, and economics—that went on contemporaneously with overseas expansion.

AUTOMOBILES AND AIRPLANES

As the twentieth century opened, great changes were under way in communication and transportation, changes that were to make the new century very different from the preceding one. The telephone was becoming a familiar feature of the home as well as the office. In 1900 the Bell system operated 677,000 telephones; by 1915 the number was nearly 6 million, and coast-to-coast lines were in operation. Radio was in its infancy. In 1901 the Italian inventor, Guglielmo Marconi, flying a kite aerial in Newfoundland, caught signals from Cornwall, England. The next year the Marconi Wireless Telegraph Company of America was established, and by 1910 all large ships were equipped with radios.

At the beginning of the new century, the day of the radio as a familiar part of American life still lay a few decades in the future, and so did the day of the airplane. But the day of the automobile was already arriving. Since the introduction of railroads, men had been intrigued with the idea of installing some kind of engine in carriages or cars that would run on roads. Throughout the nineteenth century, inventors had experimented with engines driven by steam or electric power, but the vehicles thus propelled all demonstrated impossible mechanical drawbacks. In the 1870s designers in France, Germany, and Austria began to develop the internal-combustion engine using the expanding power of burning gas to drive pistons, and the gasoline engine soon prevailed over all other types. France seized the lead in the early automotive industry, introducing such terms as "garage," "chassis," and the word "automobile" itself.

Meanwhile, in the United States, inventors—the Duryea brothers (Charles E. and J. Frank), Elwood Haynes, Ransom Olds, and Henry Ford—were busily designing their own models. In 1893 the Duryeas built and operated the first gasoline-driven motor vehicle in the United States. Three years later Ford produced the first of the famous cars that would bear his name, a two-cylinder, four-horsepower affair. Other "firsts" followed in rapid succession. In 1898 the first automobile ad in the country appeared in the *Scientific American;* its headline read: "Dispense with a horse." The first automobile salesroom was opened in New York in 1899, and the next year the first auto-mobile show was held at Madison Square Garden. In 1901 Ransom Olds built 1,500 curved-dash Oldsmobiles, thus becoming the first mass-producer of automobiles.

The first automobiles were built in various Eastern cities, but gradually production came to center at Detroit, Michigan. Detroit offered several attractions: it had an established carriage industry that could construct automobile bodies, and it was close to supplies of iron ore and lumber. In 1900 the automobile companies turned out over 4,000 cars, but the big development of the industry had to wait more than a decade.

A number of factors held back production. For one thing, the country's roads were not adequate for automobile transportation. Only 150,000 miles, 7 percent of the total mileage, were improved with gravel, oil, shell, or other forms of surfacing; by contrast, there were over 2 million miles of dirt roads. The greatest deterring force was the expense involved in the manufacturing process, which resulted in a car priced too high for the mass market. The first builders had to order their parts from many sources, including sewing-machine and bicycle companies, and then begin the job of assembling; but soon they turned to assembly-line techniques and mass-production methods.

There had been only four automobiles on the American highways in 1895; by 1917 there were nearly 5 million, and the automobile was beginning to remake American life. Automobiles then had become commonplace among upper middle-class families, just as telephones were almost essential in middle-class homes.

In 1903 the Wright brothers made their first flight at Kitty Hawk, North Carolina. It lasted only twelve seconds and covered a distance less than the wing span of the largest airplanes of fifty years later. Soon the Wrights and other inventors and pilots, in the United States and Europe, were busy improving the airplane, making longer flights with it, and even putting it to a few practical uses. In 1909 the Wrights delivered the first military plane to the United States Army. World War I stimulated rapid developments in aircraft design, especially in Germany and France. As early as 1914 a plane had begun to carry passengers on daily flights in Florida, and in 1918 regular air-mail service was started between New York City and Washington, D.C. For the time being, however, flying remained in an essentially experimental stage.

Herald Square 1910
By the first decade of the century, both electric trolley cars and automobiles were beginning to take over from the horse-drawn vehicles. New York City had entered the electric age with arc lights and illuminated signs. (Museum of the City of New York)

The Wright Brothers Making Their First Flight

On December 17, 1903, on the side of Kill Devil Hill at Kitty Hawk, North Carolina, Orville and Wilbur Wright became the first men to fly in a motor-driven machine heavier than air. Their airplane had a wing span of 40 feet; its two propellers were driven by an engine producing about 12 horsepower. "After running the motor for a few minutes to heat it up," Orville Wright later wrote, "I released the wire that held the machine to the track, and the machine started forward into the wind. Wilbur ran at the side of the machine, holding the wing to balance it on the track. . . . Wilbur was able to stay with it till it lifted from the track after a forty-foot run. One of the Life Saving men snapped the camera for us, taking a picture just as the machine had reached the end of the track and had risen to a height of about two feet." It traveled a little over 120 feet. Later Wilbur Wright stayed aloft 59 seconds and flew 852 feet. Only three papers bothered to print the news the next morning. (Official U.S. Air Force photo)

MASS PRODUCTION

Middle-class Americans, as they self-consciously greeted the twentieth century, congratulated themselves upon the enormous technical achievements that had advanced the United States to a position of preeminence in the world. The steel furnaces of Pittsburgh outproduced those of England and Germany and functioned with such efficiency and low cost that Carnegie could have sold steel rails at a profit in Birmingham, England. New manufacturing marvels of every sort were giving Americans the highest average level of living in the world's history.

In the factories, the new era meant acceleration of the introduction of labor-saving machinery. There was, for example, a bottle-making machine patented in 1903 that virtually eliminated the hand blowing of glass bottles, and another that ended manual production of window glass. The invention of a rotating kiln in 1899 made possible the cheap, standardized production of Portland cement at about the time a demand for paved highways was gaining momentum. A shift toward electric power was already well advanced. The first 5,000-horsepower alternating-current generator had been installed at Niagara Falls in 1895; within a few years steam generators of 100,000 horsepower

The Ford Assembly Line
In August 1913, at the main Ford plant in the Detroit suburb of Highland Park, it took twelve and one-half man-hours of labor to assemble every Model T chassis. Then the world's first moving assembly line for automobiles was installed; instead of the workers moving to the stationary work, the moving work came to the workers. Within six months, each chassis was being assembled in only one hour and thirty-three minutes. This picture, taken in 1914, shows a portion of the final assembly line where the radiator and the wheels were placed on the Model T chassis. At this time the company employed about 12,000 men in making cars, and another 1,000 men in making better tools to use in making cars—a fact that shows how the technical revolution in modern industry had been institutionalized and made continuous. (Ford Motor Company)

were commonplace. Electricity was entering the home, but even more important, it was becoming a great new source of efficient industrial motive power. In 1899 it ran only 5 percent of the machinery; by 1919, 55 percent; by 1925, 73 percent. Large-scale electric power also made possible electrolytic processes in the rapidly developing heavy chemical industry.

In the automobile and other industries, new principles of scientific management found spectacular application. Scientific management began with the work of an engineer, Frederick Winslow Taylor, who helped revolutionize the machine-tool industry with carbon steel high-speed cutting edges. As soon as Taylor learned

how to manufacture tools that could cut efficiently while running white hot, he began to insist that machinists operate their lathes at correspondingly fast speeds. Taylor was beginning to apply the same sort of scientific techniques to management as to machinery. At first he looked upon workmen much as he did at machines. Fewer and fewer men could perform simpler tasks at infinitely greater speed; if not, Taylor would discard them as unhesitatingly as he had discarded the poorer cutting steel.

The new system, "Taylorism," meant less need for skills among workmen and more monotonous tasks for them. At first organized labor rebelled, and won at least a minor victory when it persuaded Congress in 1915 to forbid the introduction of efficiency systems into government arsenals or navy yards. But Taylor and his followers regarded themselves as scientific seekers after higher production and thus a higher living standard. He talked of the greatest good for the greatest number, including the workers. Indeed, if Taylorism were used to eliminate the intolerable inefficiencies in many industries, it could mean not only lower prices for consumers but also higher wages for employees. By the 1920s some unions recognized this and were cooperative.

American industrialists, usually ready to try new techniques, increasingly undertook Taylor "scientific management" studies of workers' motions. They also brought scientists and engineers into their plants to engage in research for new tools and products. A few years earlier any industrialist who established a laboratory would have been looked upon as a crackpot. Now laboratories became accepted, partly because of the phenomenal success of some of the pioneering ones. There was, as every schoolboy could proudly cite, the industrial laboratory of Thomas A. Edison at Menlo Park, New Jersey, out of which had come the incandescent lamp, the phonograph, the motion picture, and scores of other devices. By 1913 Bell Telephone, Du Pont, General Electric, Eastman Kodak, and about fifty other companies had established laboratories with budgets totaling hundreds of thousands of dollars per year.

Out of these new methods and machines came mass production. It required the technology, raw materials, transportation, and markets that the United States could supply in the twentieth century. Precision manufacturing made possible interchangeability of parts even in assembling a machine as complicated as the automobile. Ford began with stationary assembly, earlier used in manufacturing guns, clocks, and the like, then gradually changed by 1914 to the moving assembly line. This revolutionary technique cut the time for assembling a chassis from twelve and a half hours to an hour and a half. While Ford raised the wages and lowered the hours of his workers, he cut the base price of his Model T car from $950 to $290. Other industrialists, following his example, soon took over the assembly line and mass production for their plants also.

By 1914 American manufacturers were producing 76 percent more goods than in 1899. They were doing so with only 36 percent more workers and 13 percent more establishments. The greater output of goods reflected the rising living standards and the growth of population at home as well as the growth of the foreign market.

SOCIAL AND CULTURAL ADVANCES

In other ways, too, the United States took giant strides into the twentieth century. Medical advances helped bring about marked improvement in public health. The Caribbean adventures of the United States led to great discoveries in tropical medicine. In 1900 Dr. Walter Reed and his associates proved conclusively the hypothesis of a Cuban doctor that a striped variety of mosquito transmitted yellow fever. During the digging of the Panama Canal (1904–1914), Major William C. Gorgas applied the new knowledge so thoroughly that not one case of yellow fever originated there, and malaria was virtually eradicated. In Puerto Rico, Major Bailey K. Ashford discovered that the cause of the widespread anemia was hookworm and developed an inexpensive cure.

All this knowledge was valuable in the southern United States. In 1909 Rockefeller gave $1 million for the eradication of hookworm in the South, where almost 60 percent of the schoolchildren had some infestation. With chemicals and vaccines, some of which were important European developments, the nation made encouraging progress in combating venereal diseases, typhus, typhoid, and diphtheria. Sanitariums and a national association successfully combated tuberculosis. Campaigns against mosquitoes and flies, improvements in sanitation, the inspection of milk, and, beginning in 1908, the chlorination of water supplies reflected the new vigor of the state and municipal boards of health. To cap the entire program, the old marine hospital service was expanded in 1902, and in 1912 became the United States Public Health Service. The death rate dropped from 17 per thousand in 1900 to 13.2 in 1920; life expectancy increased from 49 years in 1901 to 56 in 1920.

The number of public high schools nearly doubled between 1900 and 1914; the number of students increased two and a half times. In higher education, enrollment more than doubled (to 216,493), while professional and graduate schools were greatly strengthened. In many fields, American universities at last rivaled those of Europe. Nevertheless, much remained to be accomplished in education. In 1900 the average child in elementary school attended a one-room school about half the time during a 143-day school year, to be taught by rote by an untrained young woman who received $38 per month. By 1914, he might attend 86 days out of 158, and be taught rather better by a woman receiving $66. American children went to school an average of only 6.16 years.

In increasing numbers people purchased the new popular newspapers, sending their circulation soaring, making them also big business. Several newspaper chains developed; the most powerful, that of William Randolph Hearst, by 1914 already numbered nine newspapers and two magazines. Most of the papers used their new wealth for greatly improved reporting, sprightly features and cartoons, and increased pictures. As papers drew more of their news from the Associated Press and the new United Press, founded in 1907, they became more standardized.

Before 1898 few American novels had sold 100,000 copies; by 1901 a number were doing

The Duryea Car
J. Frank Duryea sits at the tiller of his automobile after winning the first motor vehicle race in America in 1895. With him is one of his umpires. (Motor Vehicle Manufacturers Association of the United States, Inc.)

so. Edwin Westcott's homespun *David Harum* (1898) eventually sold more than a million copies, and two historical novels by the American Winston Churchill, *Richard Carvel* and *The Crisis*, 420,000 and 320,000 respectively. By 1904 the craze for historical fiction gave way to a vogue for the adventure stories of Jack London and Rex Beach, the sentimentalism of Kate Douglas Wiggin and Alice Hegan Rice, and the shrewd portrayal of American life, whether middle class or genteel, of Booth Tarkington and Edith Wharton. Popular fiction was for the most part American in theme, and some of it became progressive in overtone. London lost much of his audience when he turned from adventure to socialism, but Churchill kept his when he attacked the railroads in *Mr. Crewe's Career* (1908). Tarkington's first best seller, *The Gentleman from Indiana* (1899) portrayed an idealistic small-town editor, almost the progressive prototype.

The literary pioneers of the period, the so-called naturalists, drew for inspiration upon the French writer Emile Zola and European literary movements, but presented American realities harshly, in the spirit of rural and urban revolt. Theodore Dreiser's blunt, powerful *Sister Carrie* (1900) dealt so frankly with sex that it was suppressed by its publisher; it was not until 1911 when the public attitude had changed that his next novel appeared. Then in *The Financier* (1912) and *The Titan* (1914) he portrayed a ruthless Chicagoan who destroyed his business competitors. Frank Norris also wrote of unscrupulous businessmen, California railroad barons in *The Octopus* (1901) and Chicago grain speculators in *The Pit* (1903).

The new poets either extolled the common man or wrote about him with realism. Carl Sandburg, in free verse, applied the themes of Whitman to Chicago; Vachel Lindsay wrote chants like *The Congo*, full of mysticism and rhythm. In Chicago, Harriet Monroe founded *Poetry* magazine in 1912. In New England, Edwin Arlington Robinson seemed to represent a fading afterglow of Puritanism and transcendentalism; his verses in the *Outlook* received the praises of President Roosevelt. Robert Frost, writing in a quiet, almost vernacular way about the rural folk and nature of New England, failed at first to find an audience. In 1915 he returned from England, where he had published two books, to take his place as an accepted poet. Closer to European movements than American, Ezra Pound, an expatriate from Idaho, proclaimed the techniques of the Imagists. Among them were Amy Lowell of Boston and later T. S. Eliot of St. Louis, who in 1914 moved permanently to London. The Imagists discarded rhyme from their work as an obstacle in the way of creating a pure image of everyday life.

A similar ferment stirred other branches of the arts. In 1908 a group of eight young American painters—including John Sloan, George Luks, and George W. Bellows—rebelled against conventional academicians and painted urban life as Dreiser wrote about it. Conservatives dismissed these realists as the "Ash Can School," but were even more shocked by the Armory Show of 1913 which exhibited the American moderns and brought French Post-Impressionism to America. Modernistic architecture began with the low-lying "prairie houses" of Frank Lloyd Wright, whose designs influenced Europe more than the United States until the late 1920s. Well-to-do Americans did not accept Wright but reverted to graceful colonial styles for their homes.

The expanding theatrical business was dominated by a syndicate which nationally booked romantic plays and popular vaudeville. It was the heyday of the matinee idol. Experimental realism began, but only in the realm of little-theater groups like the Provincetown Players and in the "47 Workshop" of Professor George P. Baker of Harvard. These could hardly appeal to wide audiences. The real threat to the great theatrical producers like David Belasco and the mediocre playwrights who served them came from the motion picture. At first the idea of movies competing with the stage was ludicrous. The first film telling a continuous story was a melodrama, *The Great Train Robbery*, produced in 1903. By 1905 stores were being converted into "nickelodeons," which still seemed no threat to the stage, but by 1915 the lengthy, impressive feature film had arrived with *The Birth of a Nation*. This motion picture was as significant in marking the coming of age of a new art form as it was deplorable in its glorification of the Ku Klux Klan. A motion-picture monopoly movement began in 1909 and was smashed by the government in 1914, but the cinema was becoming a multimillion-dollar industry, and movies were being shown in large and impressive theaters.

HIGH NOON OF MONOPOLY

Twentieth-century industrialism brought evil as well as good. Populists, socialists, and the relative few who had followed reform theoreticians like the single-taxer Henry George and the utopian Bellamy no longer were alone in proclaiming that the American economic system was in need of reform. Even the thoroughly conservative Judge Peter S. Grosscup, who had issued the injunction to help break the Pullman strike, proclaimed in 1905 that the modern corporation was destroying the opportunity for the individual to participate in the proprietorship of the country. This was the recurring complaint of the middle class.

Monopolies could lead to higher prices and higher profits, which were often the basic reasons for the creation of combinations. (Their promoters argued the reverse, that they led to greater efficiency, lower prices, and a higher living standard.) Furthermore, the monopolists could use their great economic strength to wield proportionately great political power.

Despite all the agitation against "trusts," American industry moved toward greater consolidation and monopoly. From 1887 to 1897 there had been only 86 industrial combinations, and the capitalization of all of these combined had been less than $1.5 billion. By 1904 there were 318 so-called trusts with a capitalization of over $7 billion. These combinations included basic industries like copper, oil, and steel, and industries directly affecting the consumer like sugar and tobacco. Six financial groups controlled 95 percent of the nation's railway mileage. In the highly competitive steel industry, twenty-one significant mergers between 1898 and 1901 prepared the way for a large-scale struggle between Carnegie and Morgan. When Carnegie announced plans for plants that might be ruinous to Morgan and his associates, they chose to buy him out at his own inflated figure of $447 million and they then established the nation's first billion-dollar corporation, United States Steel. It was able to set standard prices for steel everywhere in the United States — prices from which none of the smaller steel companies dared to deviate.

Whatever pride Americans might have felt over the emergence of these industrial giants was mingled with serious misgivings. The United States Industrial Commission reported in 1902: "In most cases the combination has exerted an appreciable power over prices, and in practically all cases it has increased the margin between raw materials and finished products. Since there is reason to believe that the cost of production over a period of years has lessened, the conclusion is inevitable that the combinations have been able to increase their profits." Whether or not monopolies were to blame, prices were rising so rapidly between 1897 and 1913 that the cost of living went up about 35 percent.

THE RICH AND THE POOR

For millions of Americans the economic system meant personal poverty and misery. There was a vast disparity between the incomes of the wealthy few and those of the poor multitudes. One percent of the families owned nearly seven-eighths of the wealth; seven-eighths of the families owned only one-eighth of the wealth. While a fifth of the families were comfortable or even rich, four-fifths lived precariously. A careful estimate in 1904 indicated that about one-eighth of the people, or a total of 10 million, lived in poverty.

At the top, Carnegie had earned an estimated $23 million from his steel company alone in the one year 1900. It had paid him an average of $10 million a year during the previous five years. On none of this did he have to pay a cent of income tax. Carnegie lived comparatively modestly and devoted his millions to worthy causes, but many of the very rich created sensational headlines through their ostentatious living. The Vanderbilts, like a clan of feudal barons, maintained, in addition to their many country estates, seven mansions in seven blocks on Fifth Avenue in New York City.

These wealthy few often spent incredible sums on parties, accounts of which fascinated but also angered readers of yellow journals. The most notorious was the ball upon which Mrs. Martin Bradley spent $250,000; it created such a furor that she and her husband fled to exile in England. A less exceptional dinner, served on gold plates at the old Waldorf-Astoria in 1899, cost $10,000 for forty people, or $250 apiece. At this time, $250 was six months' wages for the average workingman. In part the millionaires were able to get their huge in-

Child Labor and Child Luxury

In the early 1900s, "breaker boys" worked long hours picking slate from coal at Pennsylvania mines. Often the coal dust was so thick that the boys could hardly be seen. (Photograph by Lewis Hine, International Museum of Photography, George Eastman House, Rochester, N. Y.) At the same time, the children of the rich enjoyed everything that money could buy. Here the children of the American multimillionaire George Jay Gould ride the streets of Paris in "voiturettes," French-made miniature electric automobiles. (Culver Pictures)

comes because of the low cost of labor in their factories, and to afford their huge estates and townhouses because of the low cost of servants. Middle-class families also benefited from cheap labor. While they did not enjoy the great variety of household appliances of later generations, they were able with the aid of servants to maintain large homes.

Servants at least were entitled to meals and garret rooms. Working girls could not count upon even these. One woman in five worked, and often for wages as low as $6 or $8 per week. Unless a girl lived at home, it was almost impossible for her to exist upon these wages. The popular magazine writer O. Henry (William Sidney Porter) was reflecting the widespread indignation of contemporary Americans when he described in his short stories how strong the temptation was for these nearly starving girls to succumb to predatory men. Advocates of a minimum wage law to protect women created a sensation in Chicago by bringing several women to a hearing to testify that low pay and poverty had driven them to prostitution. Nevertheless, the Illinois legislature failed to enact the desired law.

Child labor, which had always existed in the United States, was becoming an increasingly serious problem by the early 1900s. At least 1.7 million children under sixteen were employed in factories and fields. Ten percent of the girls between ten and fifteen, and 20 percent of the boys, were gainfully employed. At least thirty-eight states had laws to protect chil-

dren, but these typically applied only to children employed in factories, and set a minimum age of twelve years and a maximum workday of ten hours. Sixty percent of the child workers were employed in agriculture, which could mean a twelve-hour day picking or hoeing in the fields. In the cotton mills of the South, children working at the looms all night were kept awake by having cold water thrown in their faces. In canneries, little girls cut fruits and vegetables sixteen hours a day. Some children worked at dangerous machines without safety devices. As these young workers became exhausted at the end of a long day, or night, they might become careless as they leaned over a loom to retie broken threads, have their hair caught in machinery, and be scalped as it suddenly started up again.

Industrial accidents were commonplace. For most laborers, whether children, women, or men, working conditions were far from ideal. Many women labored in dark, cold, dirty factories or sweatshops without restrooms or fire escapes. For men, working conditions were even worse. As early as 1877 Massachusetts had required safety devices on elevators and machinery; some states also required mine inspection. But there was little effective enforcement of the laws, if indeed personnel for enforcement existed. In American factories and mines, and on the railroads, the accident rate was higher than in any other industrial nation in the world. As late as 1907 an average of twelve railroad men a week were killed. In fac-

---

"The Steerage" by Alfred Stieglitz
When Stieglitz (1864–1946), crossing the Atlantic in 1907, took this photograph of immigrants crowded in the cheapest quarters, his intent was not documentary, nor was his object to publicize the misery of these passengers. Rather, he was trying to utilize photography as a form of creative expression—an art in itself rather than an imitation of other arts. Picasso remarked of "The Steerage," "This is exactly what I have been trying to say in paint."

Stieglitz demonstrated the way in which an art form could take advantage of technical advances (in this instance, photographic emulsions) by taking unparalleled night photographs and capturing the feeling of rainstorms and snow. He also helped change American taste in painting. Between 1905 and 1917 at his New York gallery he displayed, in addition to photographic art, the paintings of French impressionists and their successors, at that time unknown in the United States, from Cézanne through Picasso. He became associated with an equally advanced group of American artists, including John Marin, Max Weber—and Georgia O'Keeffe, whom he married. (Collection Museum of Modern Art)

tories, not much had been done to prevent occupational diseases such as phosphorus and lead poisoning.

Nor was there economic incentive for employers to improve working conditions. Under the common law, if an accident was due, even in part, to the negligence of an employee himself or a fellow employee, the employer bore no responsibility. Even if the employer was liable under the common law, the courts were slow, and often too expensive for the maimed worker or his widow. Until 1911 there were almost no state workmen's compensation laws.

Cheap labor was one of the reasons for high profits; unrestricted immigration was one of the reasons for cheap labor. At the same time that the big industrialists fought against a lowering of the tariff bars, they welcomed and even recruited the low-paid workers of Europe. While the flow of the "old immigrants" from northern and western Europe continued, a new flood, comprising about 72 percent of the total immigration between 1900 and 1910, poured in from southern and eastern Europe. For the most part they were Italians, Slavs, and Jews. In the single year 1905, over 1.2 million arrived. In most big cities of the North, immigrants and their children outnumbered the native-born. Bewildered at being thrust into an alien culture, living under conditions far below the level of native Americans (except Negroes), they filled most of the backbreaking unskilled jobs in the new heavy industries, on the railroads, and around the cities. The Jews, many of whom brought their skill with the needle, went into the garment trade, but under just as wretched circumstances.

The American Federation of Labor (whose president, Samuel Gompers, was himself an immigrant) fought to cut off this flood of cheap, unskilled foreign labor, which was said to keep wages down and hamper unionization. Many Americans, both conservative and progressive, were susceptible to the popular dogma of Anglo-Saxon superiority and joined in the anti-immigration movement. They feared the high birth rate among immigrants as compared with the low birth rate among natives in the higher income groups; Theodore Roosevelt warned darkly against "race suicide." They blamed the squalor of the slums and the power of the political bosses largely upon the immigrants, and felt that through restriction could come improvement. In 1907 they succeeded in stopping the immigration of Japanese to the agricultural lands of the Pacific Coast through the "gentleman's agreement" that Roosevelt negotiated with the Japanese government. A series of restrictive laws prohibited various undesirables, ranging from ex-convicts to alcoholics, from entering the United States. In 1917, over the veto of President Wilson, Congress passed a law setting up a literacy test as a means of reducing the number of immigrants.

For all those, immigrants or natives, who were crowded into city tenements, life was far from enviable. Jacob Riis, the crusading journalist, thought that by 1900 the worst of the New York slums were gone. In their place were a scattering of parks and playgrounds; in some of the worst remaining areas there were privately financed settlement houses to aid the poor. Nevertheless, for millions of city dwellers, housing was barely tolerable. In New York City, two-thirds of the 3.5 million people lived in tenement houses. A typical tenement had direct light and air in only four rooms of the fourteen on each floor.

Selected Readings

The New Great Power

E. R. May, *Imperial Democracy: The Emergence of America as a Great Power* (1961); Walter LaFeber, *The New Empire: An Interpretation of American Expansion, 1860–1898** (1963); J. A. S. Grenville and G. B. Young, *Politics, Strategy, and American Diplomacy: Studies in Foreign Policy, 1873–1917* (1966); Dexter Perkins, *The Monroe Doctrine, 1867–1907* (1937).

Imperialist Stirrings

A. F. Tyler, *The Foreign Policy of James G. Blaine* (1927); D. M. Pletcher, *The Awkward Years: American Foreign Relations Under Garfield and Arthur* (1962); G. R. Dulebohn, *Principles of Foreign Policy Under the Cleveland Administration* (1941); S. K. Stevens, *American Expansion in Hawaii, 1842–1898* (1945); W. E. Russ, Jr., *The Hawaiian Revolution* (1959) and *The Hawaiian Republic* (1961); G. H. Ryden, *Foreign Policy of the United States in Relation to Samoa* (1933).

War with Spain
J. W. Pratt, *Expansionists of 1898** (1936); Walter Millis, *The Martial Spirit** (1931); Frank Freidel, *The Splendid Little War* (1958), a pictorial history; F. E. Chadwick, *The Relations of the United States and Spain: The Spanish-American War* (2 vols., 1911); Orestes Ferrara, *The Last Spanish War* (1937), a Spanish view; Theodore Roosevelt, *The Rough Riders* (1899).

The Colonies
J. W. Pratt, *America's Colonial Experiment* (1950); G. A. Grunder and W. E. Livezey, *The Philippines and the United States* (1951); J. F. Guggenheim, *The United States and Cuba* (1934).

The Open Door
Tyler Dennett, *John Hay, from Poetry to Politics* (1933); C. S. Campbell, Jr., *Special Business Interests and the Open Door Policy* (1951) and *Anglo-American Understanding, 1898–1903* (1957); L. M. Gelber, *The Rise of Anglo-American Friendship* (1938).

The Army and the Navy
P. C. Jessup, *Elihu Root* (2 vols., 1938); J. D. Hittle, *The Military Staff* (1949); Harold and Margaret Sprout, *The Rise of American Naval Power, 1776–1918** (1939); R. S. West, Jr., *Admirals of the American Empire* (1948); W. R. Herrick, *The American Naval Revolution* (1966); G. A. Cosmas, *An Army for Empire: The United States Army in the Spanish-American War* (1972).

Automobiles and Airplanes
J. B. Rae, *The American Automobile* (1965); D. L. Cohn, *Combustion on Wheels* (1944); Allan Nevins and F. E. Hill, *Ford: The Times, the Man, the Company* (1954); Douglas Rolfe, *Airplanes of the World from Pusher to Jet, 1490–1954* (1955); C. H. Gibbs-Smith, *The Aeroplane: An Historical Survey* (1960) and *The Invention of the Aeroplane* (1965).

Technology
Siegfried Giedion, *Mechanization Takes Command* (1948); Samuel Haber, *Efficiency and Uplift: Scientific Management in the Progressive Era, 1890–1920* (1964); M. J. Nadworny, *Scientific Management and the Unions, 1900–1932* (1955); H. G. J. Aitken, *Taylorism at Watertown Arsenal* (1960); Kendall Birr, *Pioneering in Industrial Research: The Story of the General Electric Research Laboratory* (1957).

Society and Culture
Mark Sullivan, *Our Times* (6 vols., 1926–1935); F. L. Allen, *The Big Change** (1952); H. F. May, *The End of American Innocence* (1959); Van Wyck Brooks, *The Confident Years: 1885–1915* (1952); W. L. O'Neill, *Divorce in the Progressive Era* (1968); Albert Rees, *Real Wages in Manufacturing, 1890–1914* (1961).

*Titles available in paperback.

The Progressive Movement

Twenty-one

In the opening years of the twentieth century a new political impulse – which came to be known as "progressivism" – aroused a large number of Americans. Those who thought of themselves as "progressives" saw with great concern the nation's rapid technological development and growing involvement in international affairs. They wanted to make sure that the United States, as an industrial giant and a world power, held on to the democratic ideals that it had inherited from the past.

There were many wrongs to be righted, and the progressives differed among themselves in both their aims and their methods. To some, the main evil was monopoly; to others, corruption in city government; to still others, the unequal status of women. And so it went. Various groups combined and cooperated, or they divided and worked against one another, on certain issues. For example, some favored and others opposed imperialism. Thus progressivism may be considered as an aggregate of causes rather than a single movement. Still, most progressives had in common the following convictions: (1) "the people" ought to have much more influence in government, and the "special interests" much less, and (2) government ought to be stronger, more active, and more efficient in serving the public welfare.

In certain respects, progressivism was a continuation of Populism. Progressives advocated some (though not all) of the reforms that the Populists had proposed, and some of the former Populists joined the progressive movement. But progressivism and Populism differed in important respects. The People's party members had been mostly distressed farmers of the Southern and the Great Plains and Rocky Mountain states. The progressive ranks included men and women from all parts of the country, but especially from the Northeast and the Midwest, and prominent among the progressives were persons of the urban middle class. The progressives had a broader concept of both "the people" and the public welfare than the Populists had had.

Suffragettes in Action
In the early 1900s, many young women became political activists seeking the right to vote, but their efforts were not realized until 1920 when the Nineteenth Amendment was passed. (Culver Pictures)

A third party took the name "Progressive," but the movement was too broad to be confined by party lines. Active in it were both Republicans and Democrats, though the Republicans were the more numerous. For most of them, regardless of party, the path of reform led from the city hall to the state capitol to the chambers of Congress and the White House. Many conspicuous evils of the time, incapable of cure by local or state authorities, required action by the federal government. Prominent figures of both major parties brought progressivism into national politics. Among the leading Republicans were Robert M. La Follette, Theodore Roosevelt, and William Howard Taft; among the Democrats, William Jennings Bryan and Woodrow Wilson. From 1901 to 1916, politics and government largely reflected the opinions and ambitions of these men—especially Roosevelt and Wilson—and their respective followings.

Local and State Beginnings

Progressivism in some of its phases got its start in the cities. Here it took two main forms: a movement for "social justice" and another for governmental reform. The proponents of governmental reform soon directed their attention also to the evils of statewide politics.

THE URBAN PROGRESSIVE

Progressive leaders were largely members of the urban middle class and were to a remarkable extent college-educated and self-employed professional men or small businessmen, of native-born Protestant background. For the most part they were about forty years old, financially secure civic leaders who had earlier been McKinley Republicans.

Following these leaders was a middle class, like them still clinging to the traditional agrarian values, but caught up in the social whirlpool of the new industrial age. The older segment of the middle class—the independent professional men and businessmen from which such a high proportion of progressive leaders came—somewhat more than doubled between 1870 and 1910. This meant it grew as rapidly as the population as a whole, which increased about two and a third times. The working class (including farm laborers) trebled; farmers and farm tenants doubled. But there was another group, a new middle class of white-collar workers—the clerks, sales people, and technicians who worked for corporations or service enterprises. This group increased almost eight times, from 756,000 to 5,609,000 people, thus reaching a number almost double the size of the older middle class.

While members of this new white-collar class did not provide leadership for the progressive movement, they did help to provide it with voting strength. Political action was their only outlet for economic protest, since they did not belong to unions or trade associations. Often it was they, on their fixed salaries, who were worst caught by rising prices. And basically, like the older middle class, they were urbanites who still expressed the emotions of their rural backgrounds. These two groups, the white-collar class and the older middle class, combined to form the respectable element of the towns and cities who, along with many of the more successful farmers and some of the laborers, were ready to accept the new progressive creed.

Middle-class people were frightened by urban political bosses, not only because of their corrupt ties with the industrial moguls but also because of their hold over the ignorant laboring masses (often largely immigrants) of the cities. Moreover, these middle-class people had some fear of the new rising labor unions. Populist farmers had shared these suspicions of the moguls and the masses. One of the Populist papers had said the purpose of the party was to serve as a "bulwark against the anarchy of the upper and lower scums of society." Progressives continued the same prejudices.

Theodore Roosevelt in his *Autobiography* has stated clearly the reasoning that led him, a conservative young plutocrat of the upper middle-class gentry, to enter politics. The men

Roosevelt knew best, cultivated clubmen, warned him that politics was a cheap affair of saloon keepers and horsecar conductors, which gentlemen should shun. "I answered," Roosevelt wrote, "that if this were so it merely meant that the people I knew did not belong to the governing class, and that the other people did – and that I intended to be one of the governing class."

Many progressives were converted to the cause by the writings of the so-called muckrakers. The muckrakers were the many journalists who dramatized the need for reform by writing exposés of the unsavory in business and government. They began to attract attention toward the end of 1902 and were at their peak of popularity in 1906. There long had been a literature of exposure, from the *Harper's Weekly* crusade against the Tweed Ring through Henry Demarest Lloyd's denunciation of Standard Oil in *Wealth Against Commonwealth* (1894). What was new was the scale of the revelations and the rapid attraction of a wide audience. Muckraking began almost by accident in about ten of the new popular magazines, selling for 10 or 15 cents, which were then building mass circulation. *McClure's*, already a magazine of broad appeal, began publishing Ida Tarbell's series on Standard Oil. The publisher, S. S. McClure, sent a new editor, Lincoln Steffens, out to see the country first-hand; this experience led Steffens to begin a series on municipal corruption. At the same time, Ray Stannard Baker contributed an article denouncing a union for wrongdoing during a coal strike.

At the height of the muckraking movement, ten journals with a combined circulation of about 3 million were devoting considerable space to the literature of exposure. In addition, some books like Upton Sinclair's *Jungle* (1906), an exposure of the meat-packing industry, sold over 100,000 copies. Many newspapers, most notably the New York *World* and the Kansas City *Star*, printed articles by muckrakers. It was exciting for a while, but by 1912 it was over. This was due partly to the hostility of business, which at times withheld credit and advertising from the muckraking magazines.

SOCIAL JUSTICE

The social-justice movement was already well advanced by the turn of the century. It had its roots in European, especially English, reform movements. Almost every prominent English reformer visited the United States, and conversely almost every American progressive leader fell under the influence of the British. Young Jane Addams had worked at the newly established Toynbee Hall in the Limehouse section of London; in 1889 she returned to the United States to establish Hull House, a slum relief center, in Chicago. Settlement houses, slum clearance agitation, and a great variety of other English reforms quickly had their counterpart in the United States.

The Salvation Army, which had recently come to the United States from England, by 1900 boasted a corps of 3,000 officers and 20,000 privates. It offered aid as well as religion to the dregs of the cities. So did ministers, priests, and rabbis who by the nineties were working in the slums. These men were united in their determination to improve the existence of the miserable people around them in addition to saving their souls. "One could hear human virtue cracking and crushing all around," Walter Rauschenbusch wrote of Hell's Kitchen (a slum section) in New York City. To him the way of salvation for these human souls seemed to be a Christian reform of the social and economic system. Thus many an American Protestant minister arrived at the "social gospel." Catholics like Father John Augustine Ryan joined in the fight for social justice under the authority they found in Pope Leo XIII's encyclical *Rerum Novarum*. This declared that "a smaller number of very rich men have been able to lay upon the masses of the poor a yoke little better than slavery itself. . . . No practical solution of this question will ever be found without the assistance of religion and the church."

Close behind the ministry were middle-class and upper-class women. In the 1890s many of them had seemed restless and discontented, reading more widely than their husbands or brothers, joining literary circles and women's clubs. By the early 1900s these clubs were beginning to display a remarkable growth. The General Federation of Women's clubs, from a membership of 50,000 in 1898, grew to over 1 million by 1914. In the new era, the members of the clubs were quick to take up the fight for the ballot and legal equality for themselves, and for a wide array of reforms on behalf of children and working women.

Another small but mighty social-justice group consisted of those who gathered careful

Chicago's "Ghetto": Jefferson and 12th Streets   1906
Typical of the residents in this area were a Russian man and his wife who earned
$2 a day finishing coats. Their household was thus described: "Three small
children and the grandmother constitute the family, the latter dying of a cancer
without medical attendance or nursing. Man has been 18 years in this country and
owns a populous frame tenement house. He also owns the wretched rear cottage, on
the second floor of which his family lives. His work room contains a bed, an
upright piano, dining table, sewing machine and the couch on which his mother
lies dying. The filth and smell are intolerable. He does only the finest custom work
and was making a valuable coat. Most of the year he has been making police
uniforms." (Top left, Courtesy Chicago Historical Society)

Life in an Immigrant Slum
An Italian mother holds her baby in what appears to be a basement room in a New
York City tenement. This photograph was taken around 1900 by the Danish
immigrant, newspaperman, and crusader for housing reform, Jacob A. Riis.
(Bottom left, The Jacob A. Riis Collection, Museum of the City of New York)

---

data and statistics on the need for reform. They were often social-welfare workers who prepared articles for *Survey* magazine, or they were frustrated crusaders working for federal or state agencies. In many states before 1900 there were bureaus of labor which compiled great quantities of data on deplorable working and living conditions.

MUNICIPAL REFORM

The Shame of the Cities was the title Lincoln Steffens gave to his notable series of exposés which first appeared in *McClure's*, and shame was what civic-minded progressives felt. They tried to wrest control of their city governments away from the machines, reorganize the governments scientifically, and use them as instruments of economic and social reform.

Arrayed in opposition were the bosses, and behind them those interests so abhorrent to the progressives, the saloons, brothels, and various businesses that could gain more from the bosses than from clean government. Allied with the bosses were some newspapers, which ridiculed the progressives as either kill-joys or scoundrels. Finally, there was the great constituency of city working people, mostly of immigrant origins. To them the bosses were friends who could be counted upon to help them when they violated the law in some minor way, or were in need of jobs or food. Progressives, on the other hand, seemed to be do-gooders who were trying to take away the saloon — the poor man's club — and to deprive him of his amusements from prize fighting to Sunday baseball.

Many progressives, finding it difficult to grasp the relationship between the bosses and their constituents, saw the problem in simple moral and legal terms. Bad government, they thought, came from bad charters. Reformers should seize the municipal governments and, by remaking the charters, usher in the urban millennium.

Municipal reform began in response to a tragedy in Galveston, Texas, where the old, ineffective government broke down in the wake of a tidal wave. The citizens replaced it with a commission of five, whose members were jointly enacting ordinances and singly running the main city departments by 1908. In 1907 Des Moines adopted the commission plan with modifications to make it more democratic, and other cities followed. Another variation was the city-manager plan which placed a trained expert, similar to the manager of a business, in charge of the city, and made him responsible to the commission or the mayor and council. Staunton, Virginia, hired a city manager in 1908, and the new device attracted national attention when Dayton, Ohio, adopted it in 1913 to speed rehabilitation from a serious flood. By the end of the progressive era approximately 400 cities were operating under commissions, and another 45 under city managers.

Whether through old or new city machinery, progressives fought to destroy economic privilege on the municipal level. This meant primarily trying to prevent the sale of streetcar franchises, or to force exorbitantly high fares downward. The most notable of the reform mayors was Tom Johnson of Cleveland, who had invented the streetcar fare box. He was a "traction magnate" (a street-railway entrepreneur) converted to the ideas of Henry George. As mayor, Johnson fought to raise the ridiculously low assessments upon railroad and utility property, introduce city planning, and above all, lower streetcar fares to 3 cents. After his defeat and death, his brilliant aide, Newton D. Baker, was elected mayor and helped maintain Cleveland's position as the best-governed American city.

Many of the urban gains of progressivism were permanent, but in some cities, as soon as progressives relaxed, the old forces recaptured the city hall. In other municipalities, state control over city government made reform almost impossible. Cities derived all of their powers from the state, and many state legislatures granted new charters only reluctantly or controlled a large city within the state through special legislation. In the state of New York, which functioned this way, the reform mayor of Schenectady complained: "Whenever we try to do anything, we run up against the charter. It is an oak charter, fixed and immovable." Consequently, a municipal home-rule movement spread, to try to obtain state laws allowing cities to write their own charters. Much of the difficulty with state legislatures was even more serious. Many a reformer, like Johnson in Cleveland, or Joseph W. Folk in St. Louis, found himself helpless in the cities because the trail of corruption led back to the legislature.

IN THE STATEHOUSE

Hiram Johnson in California, Folk in Missouri, and other progressives moved on from cities, where they had been crusading district attorneys, to become progressive governors. Only by taking this step could Folk, for example, break the bosses. Johnson's avowed purpose as governor of California was to end the political hold of the Southern Pacific Railroad upon the state.

At the state level, progressives enacted a wide array of legislation to increase the power of crusading governors, give the people more direct control over the government, and decrease the functions of legislators. These ill-paid, relatively inconspicuous men were being exposed by muckrakers as the villains in many states. William Allen White in *McClure's*, December 1905, wrote of Missouri: "The legislature met biennially, and enacted such laws as the corporations paid for, and such others as were necessary to fool the people, and only such laws were enforced as party expediency demanded." This view of the legislatures led progressives to circumscribe and circumvent them in almost every conceivable way. The most important of the devices, the initiative and the referendum, were first enacted in Oregon in 1902 as a result of the quiet but persistent advocacy of the secretary of several voters' organizations, William S. U'Ren. The initiative enabled voters to short-circuit the legislature and vote upon measures at general elections; the referendum forced the return of laws from the legislature to the electorate. By 1918 twenty states had adopted these schemes.

Progressives also tried to obtain better officials. They tried to eliminate machine choice of candidates through the direct primary, first instituted in Mississippi in 1902 and adopted in some form by every state by 1915. Unfortunately, machines often dominated the primaries.

One device for improving officials was the recall, which made possible their removal at a special election to be called after sufficient numbers of the electorate had signed petitions. This became a national issue when President Taft vetoed a bill admitting Arizona as a state because its constitution authorized recall of judges. Horrified conservatives approved of the veto, but soon after Arizona entered the Union without the offensive provision, the state's voters restored it.

Undoubtedly all these devices did bring about a greater degree of democratization. Progressives used them to obtain control of states, and then eradicated corruption and passed reform legislation. Robert M. La Follette in Wisconsin obtained firm regulation of railroads, compensation for workmen injured in industrial accidents, and graduated taxation of inheritances. Charles Evans Hughes in New York obtained a commission to regulate public utilities. In New Jersey, when Woodrow Wilson, fresh from the presidency of Princeton University, became governor in 1911, he obtained from the legislature a substantial array of measures to transform the state from the backward "mother of trusts" into a model of progressivism.

Until the 1940s, historians generally took progressives at their word and treated progressivism as a protest of "the people" against "special interests," as a broadly based campaign against abuses in both business and government, as a great popular surge toward the fuller realization of political, economic, and social democracy.

Then, in *The California Progressives* (1951), George Mowry described the California participants in the movement not as the mass of the people but as a comparatively small group of business- and professional men. According to Mowry, these men found themselves caught between big corporations and labor unions. They wanted to restore individual enterprise and their own social importance and self-esteem. Richard Hofstadter expanded this idea and applied it to progressives throughout the country in *The Age of Reform* (1955). Hofstadter saw them as middle-class people who, in the prosperous years of the progressive period, were suffering from "status anxiety" and responding to psychological rather than economic discontent.

Most historians accepted the Mowry-Hofstadter thesis, but some questioned it. Samuel P. Hays, in *The Response to Industrialism, 1885–1914* (1957) and in other writings, contended that the progressives were upper-class businessmen who desired to bring efficiency to government and order to economic life. J. Joseph Huthmacher disagreed, pointing out in an article (1962) that members of the working class, especially immigrants, pressed for a number of progressive reforms, such as workmen's compensation and wage and hour laws. The New Left historian Gabriel Kolko, however, went so far as to say, in *The Triumph of Conservatism* (1963), that the "progressive era" was really an "era of conservatism." True, a major aim was the regulation of business. "But the regulation itself was invariably controlled by the leaders of the regulated industry, and directed toward ends they deemed acceptable or desirable."

Dissenting from both the "status anxiety" and the "age of conservatism" views, David P. Thelen showed that, at least in Wisconsin, the progressive movement actually corresponded quite closely to the progressive rhetoric of the time. In *The New Citizenship: Origins of Progressivism in Wisconsin, 1885–1900* (1972) Thelen found a real clash between the "public interest" and "corporate privilege" in that state. The depression of the 1890s, he indicated, brought people of widely varying backgrounds together, as citizens and consumers, to try and make both business and government more responsible.

The foregoing and other writers used the term "progressive" to describe leaders as different as Theodore Roosevelt and Robert M. La Follette and to designate a great variety of demands for reform or change. Perhaps the phrase "progressive movement" (like "Jacksonian Democracy") was more confusing than helpful. "It is time to tear off the familiar label," Peter G. Filene suggested in 1970, "and, thus liberated from its prejudice, see the history between 1890 and 1920 for what it was—ambiguous, inconsistent, moved by agents and forces more complex than a [single, uniform] progressive movement."

Much of the sorely needed legislation came only late and after a hard struggle. New York, for example, adopted factory safety laws only when shocked into action by the Triangle Shirtwaist Factory fire (1911), which trapped and killed 148 persons, most of them young women, in New York City.

Progressive legislators in the states ran the risk that the Supreme Court would invalidate their handiwork. The Court made one great, although temporary, shift toward progressivism. This came in 1908 when Louis D. Brandeis argued in support of an Oregon law to limit women workers to a ten-hour day. He presented a brief in which he devoted only 2 of 104 pages to the legal precedents and the remainder to proofs that Oregon's police power was necessary to protect the health and general welfare of the mothers, and thus of all mankind. The Supreme Court accepted this argument and thus moved toward the "sociological jurisprudence" which Dean Roscoe Pound of the Harvard Law School had been developing. This, Pound explained, was intended to adjust "principles and doctrines to human conditions they are to govern rather than to assumed first principles."

Progressives seeking state reforms looked not only to the Supreme Court but also to Congress and the White House. Here obviously rested the ultimate power for the control of the many problems that crossed state lines. Reformers obtained from Congress in 1910 several laws to reinforce state legislation. The Webb-Kenyon Act, passed over Taft's veto, prohibited the interstate shipment of liquor into dry areas. The Mann Act outlawed the interstate transportation of "white slaves" and thus helped in the fight to break up prostitution syndicates, one of the main sources of underworld income.

At the state level, progressives fought to liberalize the United States Senate through the direct election of senators. State legislatures were occasionally open to bribery, and much too often they elected conservatives who did not represent the public choice. David Graham Phillips in his senatorial articles, "The Treason of the Senate," scourged the body as a rich men's club; a California senator replied that there were only ten millionaires in the Senate.

By 1902 the House of Representatives had already passed resolutions five times for a constitutional amendment for direct election of senators; each time the Senate blocked the amendment. Impatient progressives in various states provided in effect for direct election by means of preferential votes for senators; the legislatures were obligated to choose the candidate whom the voters preferred. By 1912 twenty-nine states had adopted these devices. In 1911 Governor Wilson of New Jersey gained renown by blocking the legislative election of a party boss. At the same time, in New York, Franklin D. Roosevelt, just twenty-nine, won his political spurs by leading legislative insurgents against Tammany's hand-picked candidate, a Buffalo traction magnate. That same year, the Senate ousted one of its members, Boss William E. Lorimer of Chicago, for vote-buying. In the wake of the public indignation that followed, the Senate in 1912 passed the Seventeenth Amendment, for the direct election of senators, and by 1913 the requisite number of states had ratified it. The new amendment did not startlingly modify the nature of the Senate, since most progressive states had already elected senators of a new mettle.

Neither did another progressive reform measure, the preferential presidential primary, have much consequence. This was begun in Oregon in 1910 and spread to twenty states by 1920, but it by no means eliminated the maneuvering in conventions. Its main effect was to provide a series of statewide popularity contests among leading candidates in the months before the convention.

WOMEN'S CAUSES

Women took an active part in many of the progressive reforms, such as those for the protection of female employees, who by 1910 included approximately 25 percent of all women over the age of fifteen. Women were especially important in the furthering of two causes that long antedated the progressive period but received new impetus from the reform spirit of the time. These two were temperance and woman suffrage.

Since 1874 the Woman's Christian Temperance Union, whose greatest leader was Frances E. Willard, had worked through schools and churches to arouse public opinion against strong drink. The Anti-Saloon League, containing both men and women, joined the crusade in 1893. For many years the cause

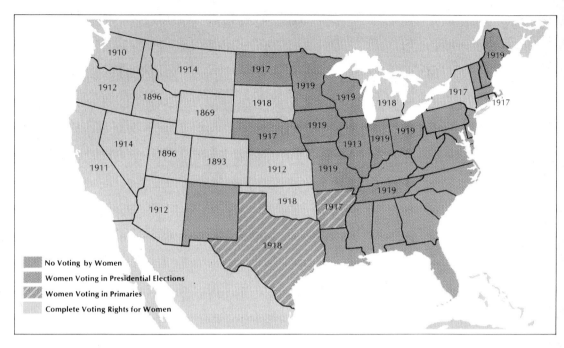

Woman Suffrage Before the Nineteenth Amendment

gained publicity from the one-woman campaign of Carry Nation, who took out after the saloons in her home state of Kansas with a hatchet.

Since 1880 Kansas had had an antiliquor law, but it was poorly enforced. The temperance crusaders undertook to get antiliquor legislation in other states and also to obtain a national prohibition amendment. By 1917 more than half of the states had banned liquor sales, and several others had permitted counties or municipalities to do so (through "local option"). In 1917 Congress approved an amendment prohibiting the manufacture, sale, or transportation of intoxicating beverages throughout the country. This, the Eighteenth Amendment, went into effect in 1920.

Of all the rights that women sought, the most important was the right to vote, for this would enable them to secure their other rights. So it seemed, at least, to feminist leaders of the late nineteenth and early twentieth centuries. A great many women contributed to the suffrage movement, but the two who had the most to do with its ultimate success were Susan B. Anthony (born in North Adams, Massachu-

setts, in 1820) and Carrie Chapman Catt (born in Ripon, Wisconsin, in 1859).

As early as 1868, Miss Anthony and her friend Elizabeth Cady Stanton had persuaded a congressman to introduce an amendment to enfranchise women, but nothing came of it. At that time the demand for woman suffrage was a response to the proposal of Negro suffrage. Miss Anthony and like-minded feminists called for "educated suffrage irrespective of sex and color." They objected to the Fifteenth Amendment, since it removed only race and not sex as a bar to voting. When black men began to vote, Miss Anthony voted and was arrested for doing so. In 1878 the suffragists got another amendment introduced in Congress, and they got it reintroduced in every session after that.

While urging the federal government to act, Miss Anthony also carried her campaign to the state legislatures. After taking over the leadership of the movement in the 1890s, Mrs. Catt decided to concentrate on state action, so as to produce enough "suffrage states" to compel the federal government to go along. When Wyoming entered the Union, in 1890, it was the only state with equal suffrage, having adopted

Are Women Human Beings? [1912]

Charlotte Perkins Gilman was probably the greatest intellect among the American feminists of her time. She gained international fame from her book *Women and Economics* (1898), in which she analyzed the effects of industrialization on women and argued for their economic independence. In a subsequent magazine article (1912) she raised the question "Are Women Human Beings?" She answered in part:

As social evolution has never waited for the complete enlightenment of mankind, we find the enfranchisement of women going on in all civilized countries; but since the opposition to it is strong enough to cause years of delay and a continuous outlay of organized effort, it seems worthwhile to point out the main error actuating that opposition. . . .

This error is due to a certain arrested development of thought. It consists in seeing in women only feminine characteristics; and, conversely, seeing in all the complex functions of civilization only masculine characteristics.

Under this conception it is held, quite naturally, that women need do nothing more than fulfill their "womanly duties," i.e., to be wives, mothers, and houseworkers; that for them to desire any other activities in life is to be unwomanly, unnatural, to become some sort of pervert or monster. They are spoken of as "denatured women," as "epicene," as "unsexed," as "seeking to become men." Miss Ida Tarbell in a recent magazine article describes women's professional and industrial advance as "making a Man of Herself. . . ."

As animals, we share in the universal distinction of sex; but as human beings, we alone possess a whole new range of faculties, vitally essential and common to both sexes. . . .

This universal, glaring fact is what these sex-obsessed opponents of the normal progress of women cannot see. They see only the feminine characteristics of women, and fail to see the human ones. . . .

The women of our age in most countries of the same degree of development are outgrowing the artificial restrictions so long placed upon them, and following natural lines of human advance. They are specializing, because they are human. They are organizing, because they are human. They are seeking economic and political independence, because they are human. They are demanding the vote, because they are human.

---

it as a territory in 1869. During the 1890s the neighboring states of Colorado, Utah, and Idaho followed the example of Wyoming. By 1914 a total of eleven states, all but one of them west of the Mississippi River, allowed women the same voting privileges as men. In 1916 the women voters of Montana helped to elect the first woman ever to serve as a member of Congress, Jeannette Rankin.

Progress with state action was so slow that, in the meantime, Mrs. Catt and most of the feminists had returned to the earlier emphasis on federal action. They disagreed, however, on the methods they should use. One leader, Alice Paul, favored imitating the "nuisance tactics" of radical English suffragettes who smashed windows, destroyed mailboxes, and disrupted public meetings to get attention for the cause. American suffragettes did march in parades and picket the White House, but Mrs. Catt and the majority of the leaders in the United States preferred the more conventional methods of persuasion and political pressure.

Resistance was strong. Antifeminists formed the Association Opposed to Woman Suffrage and chose a woman to head it. They had the support of the "liquor interests," who feared that women with the vote would hasten the day of national prohibition. The opponents also had the support of "preparedness" advocates, who argued that woman suffrage would weaken the nation in the face of possible war.

One male opponent (Henry L. Stimson) declared: "Participation in the decision of such questions by woman, who is not only wholly ignorant of the methods of force, but whose very nature shrinks from the thought of it, cannot but be a source of peril to the government which permits it."

Congresswoman Rankin did, indeed, oppose the declaration of war in 1917 (and she was to be the only member of Congress to vote against it in 1941). But Mrs. Catt, though herself a pacifist, believed that the cooperation of women in the war effort would help them to gain the vote. She was right. Women, suffragettes among them, contributed to victory in World War I by working on farms and in factories, assisting in the sale of war bonds, and joining in other patriotic activities on the home front. In 1919, more than half a century after the introduction of the first woman suffrage proposal, Congress finally endorsed the Nineteenth Amendment, which made it unconstitutional to deny or abridge "on account of sex" the right to vote. This was ratified in time for the election of 1920.

THE NEGLECTED NEGRO

The Negro was the forgotten man of the progressive era. He made few gains except in literacy—between 1900 and 1910 the percentage of Negroes who could read and write increased from about 65 to 70. In the South, despite the "separate but equal" theory, Negro schools were far inferior to those of the whites. In the nation as a whole there were, as late as 1910, only 8,251 Negroes attending high school.

In some respects the plight of black Americans worsened, and progressives themselves

---

The Souls of Black Folk [1903]

William E. Burghardt Du Bois, born in Great Barrington, Massachusetts (1868), was teaching at Atlanta University when he wrote *The Souls of Black Folk* (1903). At that time the problem of race relationships was largely, though by no means entirely, a regional one, since the vast majority of Negro Americans were still concentrated in the South. Of their position, Du Bois observed:

The dangerously clear logic of the Negro's position will more and more loudly assert itself in that day when increasing wealth and more intricate social organization preclude the South from being, as it so largely is, simply an armed camp for intimidating black folk. Such waste of energy cannot be spared if the South is to catch up with civilization. And as the black third of the land grows in thrift and skill, unless skilfully guided in its larger philosophy, it must more and more brood over the red past and the creeping, crooked present, until it grasps a gospel of revolt and revenge and throws its new-found energies athwart the current of advance. Even to-day the masses of the Negroes see all too clearly the anomalies of their position and the moral crookedness of yours. You may marshal strong indictments against them, but their counter-cries, lacking though they may be in formal logic, have burning truths within them which you may not wholly ignore, O Southern Gentlemen! If you deplore their presence here, they ask, Who brought us? When you cry, Deliver us from the vision of intermarriage, they answer that legal marriage is infinitely better than systematic concubinage and prostitution. And if in just fury you accuse their vagabonds of violating women, they also in fury quite as just may reply: The wrong which your gentlemen have done against helpless black women in defiance of your own laws is written on the foreheads of two millions of mulattoes, and written in ineffaceable blood. And finally, when you fasten crime upon this race as its peculiar trait, they answer that slavery was the arch-crime, and lynching and lawlessness its twin abortion; that color and race are not crimes, and yet they it is which in this land receive most unceasing condemnation, North, East, South, and West.

were largely to blame for this in the Southern states. Progressive leaders there concluded that political reform was hopeless so long as the Negro remained a potential voter, for their opponents could argue that the progressive movement, by dividing the whites and disrupting the solid South, would lead to "Negro domination." Hence progressives joined in the popular demand to remove the Negro, finally and completely, from politics.

Meanwhile Negroes suffered more and more at the hands of lynching mobs in the South and rioters in both the South and the North. In 1908, while the city's leaders were planning a 1909 celebration of the centennial of Abraham Lincoln's birth, a bloody race riot broke out in Springfield, Illinois, Lincoln's hometown. This event led directly to the rise of the first effective nationwide organization for Negro rights.

The emerging leader in the cause was William E. Burghardt Du Bois, a Negro historian and sociologist with a Harvard Ph.D. Du Bois openly challenged Booker T. Washington as the spokesman for their race. Washington taught Negroes that they must be patient and submissive until they had proved their worth, and thus he "tended to make the whites, North and South, shift the burden of the Negro problem to the Negro's shoulders and stand aside as critical and rather pessimistic spectators," Du Bois charged; "when in fact the burden belongs to the nation, and the hands of none of us are clean if we bend not our energies to righting these great wrongs."

At first Du Bois and a group of like-minded reformers, black and white, met from time to time in a fellowship known as the Niagara Movement. Then, on Lincoln's Birthday in 1909, they organized the National Association for the Advancement of Colored People. White men were named to most of the offices of the NAACP, but Du Bois as its director of publicity and research remained the guiding spirit. From 1909 on, the NAACP worked slowly but steadily for equal rights, mainly through legal strategy, through filing and winning one lawsuit after another in the federal courts.

The Square Deal

After intervening on behalf of striking coal miners (in 1902), President Roosevelt said he had tried to give them a "square deal." He also used this expression in reference to other reforms he sponsored, and it came to be a catch phrase for the domestic policies of his administration.

THE FIRST ROOSEVELT

Theodore Roosevelt gave the muckraking movement its name. At a banquet shortly after the appearance of David Graham Phillip's shocking articles on "The Treason of the Senate," Roosevelt arose to liken the writer to the man in *Pilgrim's Progress* who was so busy raking the muck at his feet that he could not see the heavenly crown that was offered him from above. The cynical, conservative Speaker of the House, "Uncle Joe" Cannon, is supposed to have replied to Roosevelt: "Yes, you're the chief muckraker." This was true. The great role of the muckraker was to publicize the need for reform. No one succeeded better than Roosevelt in dramatically arousing the indignation of the progressives and leading them toward political action on a national scale.

Roosevelt was an "accidental" occupant of the White House. As Vice President, he had taken over the presidency after McKinley's assassination in September 1901. The assassin, who shot McKinley at an exposition in Buffalo, New York, was a young drifter named Leon F. Czolgosz, who proclaimed himself an anarchist and said he had had an urge to kill a "great leader." He was electrocuted.

At the news of McKinley's death, his friend and mentor Mark Hanna exclaimed: "Now look, that damned cowboy is President of the United States!" Actually, as a rather uncertain fledgling President, only forty-two years old when he took office, Roosevelt had little inclination to put a vigorous progressive program into operation. He later admitted: "I cannot say that I entered the presidency with any deliber-

President Theodore Roosevelt in Yosemite Valley

Seen here with John Muir, the naturalist, Roosevelt dramatized his interest in conservation when he visited Yosemite and later succeeded in bringing it under federal administration. It became a national park in 1906. (The Bettmann Archive)

ately planned and far reaching scheme of social betterment." His greatest ambition obviously was to be elected President in his own right.

Even had Roosevelt possessed a detailed plan of legislation, he could have done little to forward it in the fall of 1901. Congress, like most of the governmental machinery in the United States from the municipalities up, was under the control of old-style politicians. "Uncle Joe" Cannon, as Speaker of the House, operated under the autocratic powers "Czar" Reed had

seized in 1890. Though genial, Cannon so firmly controlled appointments to committees and debates on legislation that the few progressives beginning to appear in the House were obliged either to cooperate or to sit as impotent witnesses to Cannon's dictatorship. The Senate was under the domination of an intelligent and competent oligarchy of conservatives. The most commanding of them was tall, austere Nelson Wilmarth Aldrich, a wealthy banker of Rhode Island.

Roosevelt realized how futile it would be to thrust his spear single-handedly against the conservatives in Congress. For the time being, therefore, he was cautious and conciliatory toward their leaders. As he planned his first annual message to Congress, his strategy obviously was to try to attract a wide following without alienating these powerful men. "Before I write my message," he wrote Aldrich in 1901, "I should like to have a chance to go over certain subjects with you." Roosevelt wrote to Senator Chauncey Depew of the New York Central Railroad: "*How* I wish I *wasn't* a reformer, oh, Senator! But I suppose I must live up to my part, like the Negro minstrel who blacked himself all over!"

Roosevelt dispensed patronage throughout the Middle West in a manner calculated to break Hanna's control over the party, although the policies of the two men were in reality basically similar. It made little difference whether these appointments took Roosevelt to the left or right. In Kansas he backed a former Populist against Hanna's GAR supporter. From Wisconsin, to the chagrin of La Follette, he chose Henry Clay Payne of the Old Guard to be postmaster general. Payne, through his wide distribution of spoils, helped rally right-wing Republicans and Democrats behind Roosevelt. Finally, Roosevelt cemented alliances with businessmen in the North and reshuffled the unstable Republican organizations in the South. In the South, he reversed Hanna's "lily-white" policy, to appoint some qualified Negroes to office. Indeed, it was to discuss appointments that Roosevelt took the sensational step of inviting Booker T. Washington to the White House in the fall of 1901.

While playing the game of political patronage, Roosevelt markedly improved the quality of officeholders. Gradually he was able to pull into public service a group of distinguished men, both old and young, of a sort that previously had shunned government work. Henry L. Stimson, who had been earning enormous fees as a corporation lawyer, became United States attorney for the New York City area and brought into his office a group of brilliant and idealistic young lawyers, including Felix Frankfurter.

Partly because Roosevelt had attracted into the government progressives of stature, bound to him by strong ties of personal loyalty, and even more because he had won over or neutralized the Republican machines, he was in firm control of the party by 1904. He had not made it progressive, but he had made it answerable to him. Hanna died early in the year; had he lived and felt the inclination, he could have mustered little strength against Roosevelt at the convention.

In 1904 the Democrats abandoned Bryan to nominate Cleveland's former law partner, Alton B. Parker. When Roosevelt, fearing that Wall Street was putting $5 million behind Parker, allowed his campaign manager to tap the trusts, the money came pouring in. Businessmen might call Roosevelt the "mad messiah," but they were not really afraid of him. E. H. Harriman personally contributed $50,000 and J. P. Morgan, $150,000; far more came from their associates. The steel, beef, oil, and insurance trusts, and the railroads all aided. Roosevelt was not aware of the source of all the donations, nor did he feel he was putting himself under obligation.

After a dull campaign, he won by a popular majority of 2.5 million votes. While businessmen were convinced he was safe, progressives were confident he would lead in reform. In state elections throughout the nation, progressives were generally victorious. As a sidelight, the Socialists under Eugene V. Debs (often regarded as a left-wing offshoot of the progressives), received 400,000 votes, four times as many as in 1900. The growth of Socialist feeling gave Roosevelt a convincing argument that sane and slow reform was essential to forestall a violent upheaval.

TRUST BUSTING

While Roosevelt was quietly taking over the Republican machinery, he was spectacularly building an excited national following. He launched a series of attacks upon the corporate plutocracy—attacks that were vigorous but at the same time moderate.

In his first annual message to Congress, December 3, 1901, he set forth his basic policy toward trusts: "There is a widespread conviction in the minds of the American people that . . . trusts are in certain of their features and tendencies hurtful to the general welfare. This . . . is based upon sincere conviction that combination and concentration should be, not prohibited, but supervised and within reasonable limits controlled; and in my judgment this conviction is right." Roosevelt's position on trusts was ready-made for burlesque by Finley Peter Dunne's character, Mr. Dooley: "Th' trusts, says he, are heejoous monsthers built up be th' enlightened intherprise iv th' men that have done so much to advance progress in our beloved country, he says. On wan hand I wud stamp thim undher fut; on th' other hand not so fast."

Specifically, Roosevelt asked for legislation to give the government the right to inspect and examine the workings of great corporations, and subsequently to supervise them in a mild fashion. What he desired first was the power to investigate them and publicize their activities; on the basis of these data, Congress could later frame legislation to regulate or tax the trusts. Consequently he requested the establishment of a Department of Commerce and Labor, containing a Bureau of Corporations to carry on investigations. Congress set up such a department in 1903.

The establishment of a great railroad monopoly in the Northwest, after a bitter and spectacular stock-market battle in 1901, gave Roosevelt an opportunity to begin prosecution under the Sherman Antitrust Act. And so he did, even though his avowed purpose had been to regulate, not destroy, and to stamp underfoot only "malefactors of great wealth," while sparing large corporations that were benign. The new Northern Securities Company had emerged out of the struggle for control of the Northern Pacific between E. H. Harriman of the Union Pacific on the one side and James J. Hill of the Great Northern and J. P. Morgan on the other. In the eyes of progressives, these men were malefactors.

Morgan, feeling his position challenged, hastened to the White House, accompanied by Senators Hanna and Depew. According to Roosevelt, Morgan declared: "If we have done anything wrong, send your man to my man and they can fix it up." Morgan, Roosevelt later remarked, "could not help regarding me as a big rival operator, who either intended to ruin all his interests or else could be induced to come to an agreement to ruin none." Roosevelt was not set upon ruining Morgan, but to the joy of progressives, he was using his power as President to discipline industry.

When, in 1904, Roosevelt won the case and the Supreme Court dissolved the Northern Securities combine, it in no material way injured Harriman, Hill, or Morgan. But it convinced progressives that Roosevelt, however cautious his avowed policies might be, was a heroic "trust buster."

Trust busting was popular and proceeded rapidly. Roosevelt's attorneys obtained twenty-five indictments altogether and instituted suits against the beef, oil, and tobacco combinations. In these, the government was ultimately successful, but the Supreme Court instituted a "rule of reason," declaring in effect that the Sherman Act prohibited only unreasonable restraints upon trade. Even though President Taft initiated ninety more suits and obtained forty-three additional indictments, the results of trust busting were disappointing.

Although Roosevelt's followers believed he was leading them into the millennium, the panic of 1907 illustrated the serious flaws still present in the American economic structure—and the President's unwillingness to go very far in trying to remedy them. Speculation and mismanagement during the boom years since the Spanish-American War led to a sharp break in prosperity in 1907. Roosevelt was quick to conciliate Wall Street. Judge Elbert H. Gary and Henry C. Frick called upon him one morning to tell him that unless United States Steel took over shares of the Tennessee Coal and Iron Company, this company would fail and its failure would threaten a widespread industrial smash-up. Gary and Frick desired assurance that the government would not consider the purchase a violation of the Sherman Act. Roosevelt tacitly agreed. United States Steel was thus able to buy out a vigorous competitor at a bargain price, thus reducing competition and holding back the development of the iron and steel industry in the South.

GOVERNMENT AND LABOR

Presidential intervention in labor disputes was nothing new—there had been, for example, the Pullman strike—but the government had usually acted as a strikebreaker for the employers. Now Roosevelt was ready to make the government an impartial arbiter instead. Here again, as in dealing with capitalists, he wished the government to be paramount over the conflicting economic forces and neutral in dealing with them. Organized labor, as long as it was well

Strikers Confront Militia   1912

*In January 1912, mill workers in Lawrence, Massachusetts, struck in protest
against a wage cut. Organizers from the radical IWW arrived to assist the
strikers and win recruits to the union. The mayor called in state militia, who
threatened the workers with guns. Before the strike ended, a woman was killed in
a clash between strikers and policemen. (Library of Congress)*

behaved, did not frighten the progressives
nearly as much as did organized capital. The
unions were comparatively weak; despite the
great upsurge of the American Federation of
Labor in the 1890s, by 1900 only about 4 percent
of the working force, even excluding agricultural laborers, was organized.

Injustice toward workers was most extreme in anthracite coal mining. Eight coal railroads under Morgan's domination held a virtual monopoly over the industry. Wages were
substandard, hours long, and the accident rate
shockingly high. The workers, under John
Mitchell, struck in May 1902, for an eight-hour
day, a 20-percent wage increase, and recognition of the union. Mitchell so effectively presented the miners' claims, and George F. Baer,
spokesman for the operators, was so truculent,

that public sympathy was aligned with the
strikers. Baer foolishly asserted the divine right
of the operators to deal with miners as they saw
best. He remained adamant when Roosevelt
called operators and miners to the White
House early in October to ask them to accept
arbitration. In contrast, Mitchell was quite willing to accept. Roosevelt eventually persuaded
Morgan to force arbitration upon the operators.
Even so, the miners after their long strike failed
to gain union recognition and obtained only a
10-percent wage increase.

The coal strike and its settlement were
evidence of "a honeymoon period of capital
and labor," stretching from McKinley's inauguration through Roosevelt's first term. Union
membership jumped from less than a half million to over 2 million. Monopolistic companies

could well afford to deal liberally with unions, since the companies could thus avoid work stoppages in prosperous periods and pass on increased labor costs to the consumers. It was altogether fitting that Hanna, the high priest of modern big business, should assume the presidency of the National Civic Federation, which was founded in 1901 to bring about friendly relations between capital and labor, and that Samuel Gompers should become vice president.

Not all laborers were ready to accept the assumption of leaders like Gompers and Mitchell that differences with capitalists could easily be adjusted around a conference table. The Socialist minority within the American Federation of Labor succeeded in capturing unions of machinists and miners. Socialists won municipal elections in Milwaukee, Schenectady, and Berkeley. Militant western miners in 1905 founded the Industrial Workers of the World, which tried to organize the great masses of unskilled workers, mostly immigrants, whom the AFL ignored. The IWW, a syndicalist organization, aimed ultimately to form "one big union" including all workers, hold one big strike, and thus paralyze and then take over the government. Its members, popularly known as "Wobblies," were accused of responsibility for acts of violence. Employers and state and local authorities certainly did not hesitate to use violence against the Wobblies. Two episodes, neither the work of the IWW, especially outraged orderly progressives. These were the murder of a former governor of Idaho and the dynamiting of the plant of the Los Angeles *Times*, which was militantly antiunion.

Such episodes prompted many progressives to listen to the antiunion slogans of the National Association of Manufacturers and kindred organizations. The NAM, which proclaimed itself against union recognition in 1903, was predominantly made up of men who ran small plants and were dependent upon low labor costs to survive in highly competitive markets. It called the open shop the "American Plan," and the independent workman (strikebreaker) the "American hero." President Charles W. Eliot of Harvard gave formidable support by asserting that nothing was "more essential to the preservation of individual liberty" than protection of the independent workman.

The manufacturers had the backing of federal judges. The most spectacular court blow against collective bargaining grew out of the Danbury Hatters' strike of 1902. The courts held that the union's efforts to obtain a nationwide boycott of Loewe hats was a violation of the Sherman Act and assessed triple damages of $240,000 against the union. In another boycott case, involving the Buck's Stove and Range Company of St. Louis, a federal court issued a sweeping injunction that forbade the AFL to carry on the boycott, to include the company in a "We Don't Patronize" list in its newspaper, or even to mention the dispute orally or in writing. When Gompers and other AFL officials defied the injunction by mentioning the dispute, they were sentenced to prison for contempt of court. The sentences were never served, but the principle of the injunction stood. Union officials began a concerted and vigorous campaign to exempt labor organizations from the Antitrust Act and to outlaw antilabor injunctions.

Gompers and his followers demanded an end to governmental discrimination against them; they were not asking for welfare laws. To some extent Roosevelt sympathized with them. He denounced the Buck's Stove decision and inveighed against court abuse of injunctions. But he was more interested in paternalistic legislation for labor, similar to that being proposed in many state legislatures. He asked Congress for laws to regulate the hours and working conditions of women and children, establish employers' liability for accident compensation, and improve railroad safety measures. For the moment he made no headway.

REGULATION AND CONSERVATION

Roosevelt accepted his 1904 victory as a mandate for progressive reform. He was now free from his earlier preoccupation with winning reelection, having announced that he would not seek another term. He continued to operate from the political center, offending big businessmen who had contributed to his campaign, and at the same time offending Midwestern progressives who took up what he called "the La Follette type of fool radicalism."

While leaving the tariff alone, Roosevelt now exercised his presidential leadership to obtain more effective railroad-rate regulation. The courts had practically nullified the Interstate Commerce Act of 1887. By a series of intricate maneuvers, Roosevelt managed to force a new regulatory law through Congress. At one point he seemed to join Senator Robert M. La Follette, the recent reform governor of Wisconsin, in demands for really drastic regulation of railroads. La Follette wished to give the ICC power to evaluate railroad property as a base

Robert M. La Follette Campaigning in Wisconsin
"Battling Bob" La Follette (1855–1925) in the 1880s was a Republican congressman sufficiently regular to help prepare the McKinley tariff. Although he remained in the party during the 1890s, he began to champion reforms of a Populist nature. In 1901, pledged to fight for a direct primary, tax reform, and railroad control, he was elected governor of Wisconsin. His advice came from experts at the University of Wisconsin, his votes largely from a rural constituency. In 1905, he finally obtained a legislature that would enact his program. Although he had already been elected United States Senator, he remained governor until the end of the year when his proposals had become law. In Washington he advocated a similar national program, especially rigorous regulation of railroads. It brought him into conflict with both the Old Guard and President Roosevelt; he entitled a chapter of his autobiography "Alone in the Senate." Roosevelt, La Follette wrote, "acted upon the maxim that half a loaf is better than no bread. I believe that half a loaf is fatal whenever it is accepted at the sacrifice of the basic principle sought to be attained." Although nationally La Follette was at times isolated in his advanced agrarian progressive position, in Wisconsin he and his sons commanded so loyal a following that they dominated the state politically for nearly forty years. (State Historical Society of Wisconsin)

The Sausages
[1906]

There was never the least attention paid to what was cut up for sausage; there would come all the way back from Europe old sausage that had been rejected, and that was mouldy and white—it would be dosed with borax and glycerine, and dumped into the hoppers, and made over again for home consumption. There would be meat that had tumbled out on the floor, in the dirt and sawdust, where the workers had tramped and spit uncounted billions of [tuberculosis] germs. There would be meat stored in great piles in rooms; and the water from leaky roofs would drip over it, and thousands of rats would race about on it. It was too dark in these storage places to see well, but a man could run his hand over these piles of meat and sweep off handfuls of the dried dung of rats. These rats were nuisances, and the packers would put poisoned bread out for them; they would die, and then rats, bread, and meat would go into the hoppers together.—Upton Sinclair, The Jungle (Garden City, N.Y.: Doubleday, 1906).

for determining rates. He felt betrayed when Roosevelt abandoned him. Although the Hepburn Act of June 1906 was in La Follette's eyes only half a loaf, it was at least the beginning of effective railroad regulation. It empowered the ICC to put into effect reasonable rates, subject to later court review; extended its jurisdiction to cover express, sleeping-car, and pipeline companies; separated railroad management from other enterprises such as mining; prescribed uniform bookkeeping; and forbade passes and rebates.

It was a large half-loaf, and La Follette and his supporters in Congress soon were able to obtain the remaining part. In 1910 insurgent Republicans and Democrats passed the Mann-Elkins Act, prohibiting discriminatory freight rates, further extending the jurisdiction of the ICC, and strengthening other features of the Hepburn Act. The ICC could now suspend proposed new rates up to ten months, and could demand proof from the railroads that they would be reasonable. Finally, in 1913, La Follette's long agitation resulted in passage of a law authorizing the ICC to evaluate railroads and to set rates that would give a fair return of profit.

One of the many reasons for the clamor for lower freight rates had been to lower the rising cost of lumber. The forests of the Great Lakes area were depleted, and the increasing amounts of lumber coming from the Pacific Northwest had to bear the heavy cost of transportation eastward. Furthermore, trees were being felled faster than they were being grown. At this point, conflict developed between pro-

gressives in the West and those in the East. Westerners wanted the government to aid in the rapid development of their resources. Easterners were more interested in preserving the remaining wilderness; their concern was aesthetic and recreational.

Roosevelt, ardent sportsman and naturalist that he was, along with his Chief Forester, Gifford Pinchot, and most Eastern progressives, felt that the United States must develop great national forests like those of the European countries. For years Major John Wesley Powell, explorer of the Grand Canyon, and other experts had been advocating new policies for husbanding the public domain.

A beginning had come with the passage of the Forest Reserve Act of 1891; under its provisions 47 million acres had been set aside as national forests. Roosevelt, clothing his actions with the terminology of the progressive struggle against the vested interests, rapidly extended the government reserves. In 1907 Western congressmen succeeded in attaching a rider (unrelated amendment) to an appropriation bill, prohibiting him from withdrawing further lands. Roosevelt could not veto the appropriations bill without calamitous effects. So he quickly withdrew practically all remaining forests in the public domain and then signed the bill. Altogether he added about 125 million acres to the national forests, and reserved 4.7 million acres of phosphate beds and 68 million acres of coal lands—all the known coal deposits in the public domain.

At the same time, Roosevelt prepared the way for a new government policy on electric power by reserving 2,565 water-power sites, which expanding private utility companies were interested in obtaining. Further, he vetoed a bill to permit private exploitation of the power at Muscle Shoals on the Tennessee River, which a generation later became the heart of the Tennessee Valley Authority (TVA). The way was open for government development of huge power projects, a program as popular in the West as the withdrawal of other land was unpopular.

It was not the President but a Democratic senator from Nevada, Francis G. Newlands, who proposed an extensive federal reclamation program for the West. Roosevelt endorsed it and was able to win much of the credit for the Newlands Reclamation Act of 1902. This provided that money from the sale of Western lands should go into a revolving fund to undertake irrigation projects too large for private capital or state resources. Eventually, the government built huge dams for the development of power and storage of water, and extensive systems of canals to carry the water to arid lands. By 1915 the government had invested $80 million in twenty-five projects, of which the largest was the Roosevelt Dam on the Salt River of Arizona. The principle of government aid

in irrigation and power development in the West had become firmly established.

Progressives undertook to legislate the nation into better health after muckrakers had made the public aware of the disgusting and dangerous substances that were being sold and eaten as food. None created a more shocked reaction than Upton Sinclair, who wrote a powerful novel of protest against exploitation of immigrant labor in the stockyards, and incidentally included nauseating descriptions of the preparation of meats. When *The Jungle* appeared in 1906, it hit Americans' stomachs as much as their consciences.

Roosevelt himself was horrified, and when a commission verified the descriptions in *The Jungle,* he sought reform. Two pieces of legislation were passed in June 1906. One was the Meat Inspection Act, which eventually did much to bring about the eradication of some animal diseases, especially tuberculosis. The other was the Pure Food and Drug Act, which bore the impressive descriptive title: "An Act for preventing the manufacture, sale, or transportation of adulterated or misbranded or poisonous or deleterious foods, drugs, medicines, and liquors, and for regulating traffic therein, and for other purposes."

A Rift in Republican Ranks

As early as 1904 Roosevelt had tentatively decided that his good friend William Howard Taft, then secretary of war, would make an excellent successor as President. But after Taft's election the two were to fall out and, in doing so, were to split the Republican party.

TAFT AND THE TARIFF

Taft was known for his achievements as one of the first viceroys of the new American empire. Between 1900 and 1908, he traveled over 100,000 miles on assignment to Manila, Rome, Panama, Cuba, and within the United States. His achievements were almost all in the realm of colonial or foreign policy; he had little to do with Roosevelt's domestic policies, although privately he subscribed to almost every one of them. If he was to the right of Roosevelt, it was

only by a hairline. The great distinction was that while he regarded Roosevelt's objectives as justifiable, he felt, as he commented in 1910, that Roosevelt "ought more often to have admitted the legal way of reaching the same ends." This colorless way of saying things marked another contrast between Taft and Roosevelt.

In 1908 Roosevelt had no difficulty in securing the nomination of Taft. The smooth-running Republican machinery followed Roosevelt's bidding and gathered the votes of the delegates: organization men, officeholders, and Southern Republicans.

Business moguls preferred the gingerly progressive Republican candidate to the more forthright William Jennings Bryan, running forlornly for a third time. Rockefeller wired Taft congratulations on the nomination; Morgan remarked, "Good! good!" Carnegie sent a campaign contribution of $20,000. This did not mean that Taft had capitulated to Wall Street; indeed he was more careful about accepting corporate campaign contributions than Roosevelt had been in 1904.

Taft campaigned as the champion of smaller business interests. In his acceptance address he promised that he would perfect the machinery for restraining lawbreakers and at the same time interfere with legitimate business as little as possible. Most important, he appealed to small-business and middle-class concern over the rising cost of living by firmly promising a reduction in the tariff.

The election result was a foregone conclusion, a sweep for Taft. The electoral vote was 321 to 162, but there were portents of national unrest in the victory. Taft's lead over Bryan was only half the size of Roosevelt's plurality in 1904; several Western states shifted to Bryan, and several others in the Middle West elected Democratic governors even though they gave their electoral votes to Taft. Republican progressives, pleased at the outcome, proclaimed: "Roosevelt has cut enough hay; Taft is the man to put it into the barn." Republican conservatives rejoiced that they were rid of the "mad messiah."

Certainly Taft's intention was to load Roosevelt's hay into the barn, but the hay soon was drenched by violent political storms. Taft seemed incapable of negotiating with the Old Guard, as Roosevelt had done, without giving the impression that he had joined them. To the progressives Taft seemed guilty of betrayal.

The first of his betrayals in the eyes of progressives was the fiasco that occurred when Taft called Congress into special session to

"The Easy Umpire"
"He slugs me every chance he gets, and you can't or won't see it," the tiny player labeled "The Plain People" protests to the umpire, President Taft, while pointing at the bully, Senator Aldrich. For years the dominant figure in the Senate, Aldrich furthered the interests of big business. From Puck, *November 10, 1909. (Culver Pictures)*

enact a lower tariff. "I believe the people are with me," he had written, "and before I get through I think I will have downed Cannon and Aldrich too." But having proclaimed a tariff crusade, he remained behind while Middle Westerners carried their lances into battle. They were not "free traders" like some Southern Democrats, but they did want to weaken trusts by exposing them to foreign competition. The way to do this, they thought, was to lower tariff rates substantially. They thought the President was behind them, but he failed to send Congress a fighting message or to intervene with his patronage powers when congressmen began to succumb to the blandishments of lobbyists and logrollers.

The Payne-Aldrich tariff passed Congress over the votes of Midwest Republicans and was signed by Taft on August 5, 1909. He said it was not a perfect bill but represented "a sincere effort on the part of the Republican party to make a downward revision." Also it provided for a Tariff Commission which was to make scientific studies of rates — an appealing idea to some progressives, who felt that the tariff, like most problems, should be determined scientifically and taken out of politics.

Nevertheless, the Payne-Aldrich tariff seemed to favor Senator Aldrich's New England at the expense of the rest of the country. On a tour around the country in the fall of 1909, Taft tried to defend the new tariff in a hastily prepared speech delivered in the heart of the area of resentment, Winona, Minnesota. One line from that speech made damaging headlines against the President. He said: "On the whole . . . the Payne bill is the best bill that the Republican party ever passed." The remainder of the trip through the Midwest, wrote a reporter, was "a polar dash through a world of ice."

In 1911 Taft further alienated Middle Westerners when he submitted to the Senate a reciprocal trade agreement with Canada, an agreement that would have lowered tariffs on both sides and in effect would have brought the two countries into an economic union. Many Eastern manufacturers, seeing larger Canadian markets for their goods, were enthusiastic, but the Middle Westerners, fearing a flood of competing Canadian farm products and raw materials, were bitterly hostile. La Follette complained: "It singles out the farmer and

forces free trade upon him, but it confers even greater benefits upon a few of the great combinations sheltered behind the high rates found in the Payne-Aldrich tariff." He and his cohorts formed a strange alliance with die-hard members of the Old Guard but were defeated by Eastern Republicans and Southern free-trade Democrats. The Senate approved the reciprocity arrangement, 55 to 27. But the Canadian parliament refused to act, for many Canadians feared that tariff reductions might somehow lead to Canada's being annexed by the United States.

T. R. AGAINST TAFT

The progressive Republicans of the Midwest had cut loose from Taft. They blamed him, unjustly, for their failure to oust Speaker Cannon in 1909. By 1910, without the presidential blessing, they were strong enough to resume the effort. Under the leadership of George W. Norris they breached Cannon's formidable parliamentary defenses and opened a fierce debate that raged for nearly thirty hours. It ended with Cannon's removal from the Rules Committee, which henceforth was to be elected by the House. He remained as House Speaker, but he was no longer the obstacle he had been to progressive legislation.

Meanwhile, through the sensational Ballinger-Pinchot controversy, Taft lost the sympathy of most of Theodore Roosevelt's following in the urban East and the Far West. Taft had replaced Roosevelt's secretary of the interior with a man who wished to distribute to private interests the natural resources in the public domain. The viewpoint of the new secretary, Richard Ballinger, was dominant among businessmen of the West, who wished themselves to prosper and to see their region grow. But Taft had left in charge of the Forestry Service in the Department of Agriculture Roosevelt's ardent admirer, Gifford Pinchot of Pennsylvania, who, like most Eastern nature lovers and sportsmen, was zealous to preserve the public domain unspoiled, as a part of the nation's heritage. A violent clash between these two men was almost inevitable.

The occasion was the spectacular charge that Ballinger was conniving to turn over valu-

"Revising the Tariff Downward (?)"
(J. N. "Ding" Darling in the Des Moines Register)

able coal lands in Alaska to a Morgan-Guggenheim syndicate. Taft, accepting Ballinger's rebuttal, publicly exonerated him. Immediately Roosevelt progressives throughout the country championed Pinchot as the defender of the national domain against the corrupt onslaught of big business. Pinchot, by going over the President's head directly to Congress, provoked Taft to discharge him for insubordination. A congressional committee investigated and, since the Old Guard dominated it, reported in favor of Ballinger. To the end, Taft stood by his Secretary of the Interior, whom he correctly considered to be an honorable man. But in refusing to dismiss Ballinger as an anticonservationist, Taft opened a rift between himself and the Roosevelt following that was as wide and deep as the one separating him from the La Follette supporters.

As early as the tariff fiasco in 1909, progressives had begun to look to the African jungle for their next presidential candidate. In the middle of June 1910, loaded with trophies from Africa and fresh impressions of reform from Europe, Roosevelt returned. Observers noted that his first hello was to Pinchot and that he

turned down Taft's invitation to the White House. Indeed, he had already met Pinchot in Europe, bearing messages from progressives, and had come to the conclusion that Taft had "completely twisted around the policies I advocated and acted upon."

Furious with Taft for helping bring about the split in the party, Roosevelt determined to do all he could to reunify it. He told reporters he was seeing all Republicans — "regulars and insurgents, party men and independents." But at Osawatomie, Kansas, on September 1, he delivered a speech that returned him to command of the progressives. At Osawatomie, he proclaimed the doctrines of the New Nationalism, emphasizing that social justice could be attained in the nation only through strengthening the power of the federal government so that the executive could be the "steward of public welfare." Men thinking primarily of property rights and personal profits "must now give way to the advocate of human welfare, who rightly maintains that every man holds his property subject to the general right of·the community to regulate its use to whatever degree the public welfare may require it." Going beyond these generalizations, frightening enough to the Old Guard, Roosevelt listed some specific proposals: graduated income and inheritance taxes, workmen's accident compensation, regulation of the labor of women and children, tariff revision, and firm regulation of corporations through a more powerful Bureau of Corporations and Interstate Commerce Commission. From the Mississippi westward, progressives were ready to acclaim him as the next presidential candidate, but among his right-wing enemies, Lodge warned him, he was regarded as "little short of a revolutionist."

Progressive Republicans of the Middle West hoped they could wrest the presidential nomination from Taft in 1912. In January 1911, a group of them formed the National Progressive Republican League to work for the nomination of La Follette. But a great majority of the progressive Republicans continued to hope that Roosevelt could be persuaded to run.

With Roosevelt receptive, many of La Follette's supporters switched to him with indecent haste after La Follette on February 2, 1912, exhausted and worried, delivered a rambling, repetitious talk. Roosevelt thus acquired new recruits, but he also won the undying hatred of La Follette and his loyal Middle Western progressive following. Nevertheless, in the primaries Roosevelt demonstrated that he was overwhelmingly the presidential choice of Republican voters.

The nomination at the Republican convention would depend upon the seating of the delegates; more than a third of the seats were contested. The Republican National Committee, made up almost entirely of loyal Taft supporters, allowed Roosevelt only 19 out of 254 contested seats, and thus in advance counted him out of the nomination.

Roosevelt had come in person to the convention to direct his forces, and the night before it opened, he told a hysterically cheering throng of 5,000 that he would not be bound by the convention if it failed to seat his contested delegates. He concluded thunderously: "We stand at Armageddon, and we battle for the Lord." As good as his word, he bolted, leaving the conservatives in complete command at the Republican convention. With Roosevelt's onetime friend Elihu Root presiding, Warren G. Harding, one of the most regular of the regulars, mellifluously nominated Taft, who was chosen on the first ballot.

During the Republican convention, Roosevelt had agreed to the formation of a new, Progressive party when Frank Munsey, the newspaper magnate, and George W. Perkins, of United States Steel and International Harvester, promised him financing. Announcing his willingness to run, Roosevelt said he was as fit as a bull moose, giving the party a symbol as well as a name. When the Progressives met at Chicago in August to nominate Roosevelt formally, the conclave was far more symbolic of progressivism than of ordinary American politics. Missing were La Follette and his following, five of seven governors who had signed a call for Roosevelt in January, and such notable Republican insurgents as Norris of Nebraska and William E. Borah of Idaho.

The convention was more like a camp meeting than the gatherings to which Roosevelt was accustomed. The delegates sang "Onward Christian Soldiers" and closed the convention with the "Doxology." Roosevelt seemed bewildered as he acknowledged their almost fanatical, hymn-singing welcome, for "they were crusaders; he was not."

Roosevelt's program would accept big business but would regulate it through a national industrial commission. And a Federal Securities Commission would police stocks and bonds. In the program there was much to appeal to the progressives of the cities, whether reformers or businessmen, but little of interest to farmers, and much paternalism but no guarantee of collective bargaining for organized labor. In an effort to win disgruntled Southern businessmen away from the Democratic party, Roosevelt endorsed a lily-white (excluding Negroes) Progressive party for the South.

The New Freedom

Between the time Roosevelt bolted the Republican convention and the time he received the Progressive nomination, the Democrats met in Baltimore and exulted in the knowledge that, though theirs was a minority party, they were almost certainly choosing the next President.

Woodrow Wilson and Champ Clark

Speaker Clark seemed an almost certain nominee at the 1912 Democratic convention, at one point receiving well over a majority of the delegates' votes, 556 to 350½, but it took two-thirds to nominate. When finally he lost to Wilson he went to Sea Girt, New Jersey, where Wilson was spending the summer, to demonstrate his party support. (Culver Pictures)

WOODROW WILSON WINS

In Baltimore, Bryan, who long had dominated the party, stood aside while four contenders battled for the nomination. These were Governor Woodrow Wilson of New Jersey, Speaker Champ Clark of Missouri, the right-wing Governor Judson Harmon of Ohio, and Representative Oscar W. Underwood of Alabama, the champion of Southern conservatives and a low tariff. Wilson's spectacular reform achievements in New Jersey had made him the favorite of Democratic progressives in Eastern cities, and he took a quick lead for the nomination as he crisscrossed the nation to make hundreds of inspiring speeches denouncing special privilege and heralding the new progressive order. Yet, in 1912, he emerged from the primaries and state conventions with only 248 delegates to Clark's 436. Underwood swept most of the South.

It was little short of a miracle that Clark, who had the rural Democrats and most of the bosses behind him, and who obtained more than a majority of the votes on ballot after ballot, nevertheless failed to win the nomination. The main reason for the miracle was that the Wilson and Underwood forces stood firm, blocking Clark's nomination, while Wilson's managers negotiated deals with the machines and with Underwood's following. To some extent Clark's defeat may have been due to Bryan, who threw his support to Wilson at a critical moment in the convention struggle.

A crusade requires a crusader, and the Democrats obtained one at last on the forty-sixth ballot when they nominated Wilson. This lean, lantern-jawed son of a Southern Presbyterian preacher looked as well as acted the part. His aspiration had always been to become a political leader, but when he found the road rough as a beginning lawyer in Atlanta, he took a Ph.D. degree at Johns Hopkins, became a professor of political economy, and then served as president of Princeton University.

Both as president of Princeton and as governor of New Jersey, Wilson demonstrated the courageous strength and alarming weaknesses that would characterize his presidency. He had the vision to inspire multitudes but was dogmatic and distant with individuals. He could lecture an opponent in high moral terms, but his sense that he and he alone was absolutely right prevented him from stooping to necessary political negotiations.

Wilson had won the nomination without badly splitting the party. Backed by a progres-

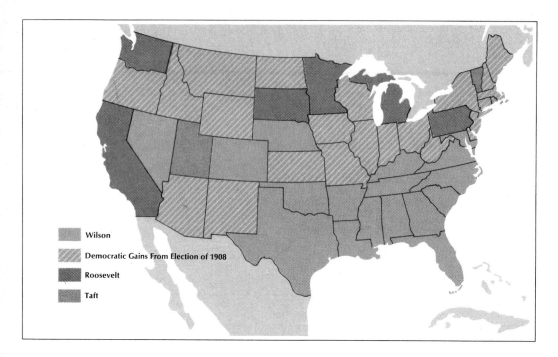

Wilson

Democratic Gains From Election of 1908

Roosevelt

Taft

Election of 1912

sive platform, he appeared before the electorate in armor at least as brightly shining as Roosevelt's. The distance between the positions of the Democratic party and the new Progressive party was not as great as campaign oratory made it out to be, just as personality more than principles separated Wilson from Roosevelt. Nevertheless, the differences in platform were significant in the campaign and in Wilson's future program as President.

Wilson's program, called the New Freedom, emerged as the campaign unfolded. His conversion to progressivism had come only two or three years before, and he had continued to cling to the state-rights position that the task of the federal government was the purely negative one of destroying privilege. Thus Wilson hoped to restore the good old days, which in reality had never existed, by recreating full opportunity for the small enterpriser. Roosevelt's New Nationalism, Wilson charged, would mean the federal licensing of the juggernauts of big business to crush the American people. In contrast, Wilson proclaimed his New Freedom as the fight for emancipation of the small businessman, the "man on the make." He pro-

claimed: "If America is not to have free enterprise, then she can have freedom of no sort whatever."

Wilson was able to win over Bryan's rural and small-town following with the same religious appeal, the same denunciation of the Wall Street money trust, that the "Great Commoner" had always used. Some well-educated people who had always scorned Bryan as a fool came to worship Wilson as a saint.

Thus Wilson was able to hold Democratic progressives, while Roosevelt was able only to pull progressives out of the Republican party. As for Taft, after several sad speeches, so conservative that they might have been written by Aldrich, he lapsed into silence. The Socialists, at the peak of their strength under Eugene V. Debs, criticized all three major candidates as defenders of capitalism. The main effect of the Socialists was to serve as a bugaboo for progressive leaders, who could warn that the only alternative to their own safe, moderate programs would be the drastic remedies of Socialism. Even in 1912, their heyday, the Socialists attracted only 901,000 votes, 6 percent of the total votes cast.

Because of the three-cornered contest, Wilson carried the electoral college overwhelmingly, with 435 votes to 88 for Roosevelt and only 8 for Taft. Wilson had received less than 42 percent of the popular vote, fewer votes than Bryan in any of his three campaigns. Yet, considering the combined Democratic and Bull Moose totals, the newly elected President had an overwhelming progressive mandate.

PRESIDENTIAL LEADERSHIP

Few Presidents have taken more seriously their electoral mandate or worked more effectively to transform it into law than did Wilson. He brought back into the White House a strong belief in firm, positive presidential leadership.

The closest of Wilson's advisers was the shrewd and ubiquitous Colonel Edward M. House, who virtually shared presidential powers as Wilson's alter ego until 1919. House served as an agent for Wilson in negotiations first with the men of economic power in America, and later with those of political power in Europe. His discretion and anonymity were so consumate that one contemporary remarked: "He can walk on dead leaves and make no more noise than a tiger."

Wilson's official advisers, the members of his cabinet, were less influential. Bryan had to be offered the post of Secretary of State in recognition of his long leadership of the party. Representative William B. Wilson, former secretary-treasurer of the United Mine Workers, became the first Secretary of Labor, establishing a twenty-year precedent that the office should be filled by a labor leader. It was the most Southern cabinet since the Civil War; half of its members were Southerners, at least by birth.

Wilson promptly undertook what Roosevelt had avoided and Taft had failed to achieve—a substantial lowering of the tariff. On the day he took office he called a special session of Congress. When it met, he did what no other President since Jefferson had done: he appeared before Congress in person. His short graphic message was aimed less at congressmen than at their constituents. It brought to a blaze the sentiment for real tariff reform. With the President's active support, Underwood introduced a bill in the House providing for tariff cuts substantial enough to bring European manufacturers into competition with Americans.

To make up for the loss of revenue under the new tariff, Representative Cordell Hull drafted a section for the bill, providing for a graduated income tax under the Sixteenth Amendment. Hull cautiously set the rates exceedingly low. Then, to his delight, progressive Republican and Democratic senators forced substantially higher rates upon the conservatives and the administration. This first modern income tax imposed a 1-percent tax upon individuals and corporations earning over $4,000, and an additional 1-percent tax on income over $20,000, ranging up to a maximum of 6 percent on income over $500,000. This income tax was the beginning of a great change in the American tax structure. Although more slowly than England and some other nations, the United States was beginning to place a proportionately greater share of the cost of government upon the rich. In so doing, it was beginning to chip away at the enormous disparity in incomes in the United States.

THE TRUSTS AGAIN

Rather than lose momentum, President Wilson held Congress in session through the sweltering summer to begin work on banking reform. In 1911 he had declared: "The great monopoly in this country is the money monopoly. So long as that exists, our old variety and freedom and individual energy of development are out of the question." Early in 1913, a House investigating committee headed by a Democrat, Arsene Pujo, published frightening statistics to back Wilson's accusation. These figures, to which Louis D. Brandeis gave wide circulation in a series of articles entitled "Other People's Money," indicated that small banks were depositing their surpluses with larger ones, which in turn deposited with a few great investment bankers concentrated on Wall Street. These bankers with their enormous capital, representing the aggregate savings of millions of people, were able to demand control over corporations in return for granting them financing, "the life blood of business." The Morgan-Rockefeller empire held "in all, 341 directorships in 112 corporations having aggregate

The Credit Monopoly [1913]

Far more dangerous than all that has happened to us in the past in the way of elimination of competition in industry is the control of credit through the domination of these groups over our banks and industries. . . .

Whether under a different currency system the resources in our banks would be greater or less is comparatively immaterial if they continued to be controlled by a small group. . . .

If the arteries of credit now clogged well-nigh to choking by the obstructions created through the control of these groups are opened so that they may be permitted freely to play their important part in the financial system, competition in large enterprises will become possible and business can be conducted on its merits instead of being subject to the tribute and the good will of this handful of self-constituted trustees of the national prosperity. — Report of the Pujo Committee, *February 28, 1913.*

---

resources or capitalization of $22,245,000,000." This was in 1913, when the entire national wealth was less than ten times this figure.

To Wilson, there was clearly a need to break the money trust. At the same time, paradoxically, one of the serious ills of the American banking system was its decentralization and independence, except for the loose tie of urban clearing houses. This, and the defective functioning of the national banking system, meant that in time of financial crisis and deflation it was hard for banks to draw upon their reserves or to expand their currency. With Wilson's encouragement, Congress responded to the need for banking reform.

The Federal Reserve Act (1913) created twelve regional banks. Each was to serve and be owned by the banks of its district. The Federal Reserve Bank would rediscount their notes, issue a new type of paper currency — Federal Reserve notes — and fulfill other banking functions for member banks and for the government. The act required national banks to become members and encouraged other banks to do so. Nearly half the nation's banking resources were represented in the system within its first year of operation, and four-fifths by the late 1920s. Bankers had no cause to fear the Federal Reserve Board, which governed the system, and to which Wilson appointed conservative, sympathetic men. The system was a notable advance in banking regulation, providing as it did for a more elastic currency, though it did not destroy the "money trust."

There remained the problem of the great business combinations. As several antitrust bills began to move through Congress in 1914, Wilson gave his support to one bill prohibiting unfair trade practices and establishing a Federal Trade Commission to watch out for them. He accepted the Clayton Antitrust Act, though it was not quite as strong a measure as he had desired. Conservatives in Congress put qualifying clauses around the sections outlawing interlocking directorates or stockholdings and exclusive selling contracts, so that the clauses, as a progressive Republican senator complained, did not have enough teeth to masticate milk toast. Labor gained nothing of practical importance from the bill, which did, however, contain a platitude that labor was not a commodity and declared that unions were not conspiracies in restraint of trade. President Gompers of the AFL chose to hail the Clayton Act as "Labor's Magna Carta" and to insist that organized labor was now exempted from antitrust prosecution. This assumption served merely to make bitterness and resentment greater when courts continued in the twenties to follow their earlier inclinations. The Sherman and Clayton acts, though ineffective for breaking up business monopolies, were stout clubs for disciplining boycotters and strikers.

The debate over antitrust legislation during the first half of 1914 coincided with a decline in prosperity. This came because the United States, still a debtor nation easily affected by European money markets, suffered from credit restrictions growing out of European pessimism over the Balkan wars and the likelihood of a bigger war. Within this country, businessmen blamed the recession upon the Underwood tariff, and the other legislation of the New Freedom. Wilson tried to placate business titans through friendly conferences and mild administration of his new reform legislation. He assured the leaders that he only opposed businesses that expanded "by methods which unrighteously crushed those who were smaller."

RETREAT AND ADVANCE

Through 1914 and 1915, to the disappointment of many advanced progressives, Wilson again and again applied the brakes to reforms. With a state-rights answer he turned aside the plea for female suffrage. He condoned the actions of his Southern cabinet members when they introduced Jim Crow practices (discriminating against Negroes) into the administration to an unprecedented degree. Only the angry protests of Northern liberals brought some reversal. He opposed a bill to establish federally backed land banks to ease credit to farmers, declaring it went beyond the proper scope of the government. He gave no aid to a child-labor bill because he thought it unconstitutional. Only with reluctance did he sign the La Follette Seamen's bill of 1915, the work of the eloquent president of the Seamen's Union, Andrew Furuseth, which improved safety regulations and working conditions for men in the merchant marine.

For Wilson, the New Freedom might be complete, but not for the progressive Democrats in Congress. At times they expressed their sharp dismay, though they did not have to engage in warfare with him as the Republican insurgents had done with Taft. When the election year 1916 opened, two things were apparent. The Progressive party, which had never been much more than a Roosevelt vehicle, was disintegrating. Unless the Democrats, who were normally a minority, presented a new, strong progressive program, they would be swamped at the polls by the reunited Republicans. Wilson saw this danger and again became an enthusiastic reformer, going beyond the New Freedom and allying himself with the progressives, farmers, and laborers to accept a series of laws that in many respects enacted the Progressive party program of 1912. From a negative policy of restriction he moved to a positive one of vigorous federal economic and social intervention. Curiously, this came at a time when Roosevelt had moved to the far right and no longer supported his 1912 proposals.

In January 1916, Wilson named Louis D. Brandeis to the Supreme Court and weathered the conservative storm in order to obtain Senate confirmation. Brandeis was both liberal and Jewish, the first man of his faith to serve on the highest bench.

In May the President accepted a farm-loan bank system in the Federal Farm Loan Act. At the urging of progressives, he applied pressure upon the Democratic leaders in the Senate to obtain a workmen's compensation system for federal employees and the first federal child-labor law. The child-labor law, the Keating-Owen Act of 1916, prohibited the shipment in interstate commerce of products manufactured by children. It marked not only a significant reversal on the part of Wilson but also a new assumption of federal control over manufacturing through the commerce clause. When the Supreme Court invalidated the law by a 5-to-4 decision in 1918, Congress passed an act levying a heavy tax on the products of child labor. This too President Wilson signed, and the Supreme Court ultimately invalidated, with Chief Justice Taft writing the decision.

Despite the setback in regard to child labor, this second wave of legislation of the Wilson administration significantly restored and enlarged the regulatory function of the federal government. After Wilson had failed to mediate a dispute between the railroad brotherhoods and the railroads, he signed an emergency measure, the Adamson Act, to prevent a nationwide railroad strike that would have paralyzed commerce. The measure provided for an eight-hour day at the previous ten-hours' pay for all railroad workers.

Other lesser-known pieces of legislation brought about even greater changes. Without attracting much attention, they undermined state rights by granting subsidies on a dollar-matching basis for states to undertake various types of programs. These laws, in combination with the new income tax, took money out of the wealthier Northeastern areas and redistributed it in the South and West. The first such law was the Smith-Lever Act of 1914, which provided money for states to establish extension work in agricultural education. This formalized and nationalized the new system of county agents to advise farmers, and facilitated the rise of the powerful American Farm Bureau Federation. It was followed by the Smith-Hughes Act of 1917 which subsidized vocational courses in

secondary schools. Most important of all, the Federal Highway Act of 1916 appropriated $75 million to be spent for road-building over a period of five years.

Wilson was justified in his boast that the Democrats had come close to carrying out the Progressive party's platform as well as their own.

Selected Readings

Synthesis and Interpretations
Richard Hofstadter, *The Age of Reform** (1955); Eric Goldman, *Rendezvous with Destiny: A History of Modern American Reform** (1952); R. H. Wiebe, *Businessmen and Reform* (1962) and *The Search for Order, 1877–1920** (1967); Christopher Lasch, *The New Radicalism in America, 1889–1963* (1965); Gabriel Kolko, *The Triumph of Conservatism* (1963); J. R. Chamberlain, *Farewell to Reform** (1932).

Progressive Journalism
C. C. Regier, *The Era of the Muckrakers* (1932); Walter Johnson, *William Allen White's America* (1947); Charles Forcey, *The Crossroads of Liberalism: Croly, Weyl, Lippmann, and the Progressive Era, 1900–1925** (1961); Herbert Croly, *The Promise of American Life** (1909); Lincoln Steffens, *Autobiography* (2 vols., 1931).

States and Cities
G. E. Mowry, *California Progressives** (1951); R. S. Maxwell, *La Follette and the Rise of Progressivism in Wisconsin* (1944); D. P. Thelen, *The New Citizenship: Origins of Progressivism in Wisconsin, 1885–1900* (1972); H. L. Warner, *Progressivism in Ohio, 1897–1917* (1964); R. M. Abrams, *Conservatism in a Progressive Era: Massachusetts Politics, 1900–1912* (1946); Jane Addams, *Forty Years at Hull House** (1935); A. F. Davis, *Spearheads of Reform: The Social Settlements and the Progressive Movement, 1890–1914* (1968); Ray Lubove, *The Progressives and the Slums: Tenement House Reform in New York City, 1890–1917* (1962); J. D. Buenker, *Urban Liberalism and Progressive Reform* (1973).

Roosevelt
G. E. Mowry, *The Era of Theodore Roosevelt** (1958) and *Theodore Roosevelt and the Progressive Movement** (1946); H. F. Pringle, *Theodore Roosevelt* (1931); W. H. Harbaugh, *Power and Responsibility** (1961); J. M. Blum, *The Republican Roosevelt** (1954); J. A. Garraty, *Right Hand Man: The Life of George W. Perkins* (1960), a leading Bull Mooser.

Taft and the Insurgents
H. F. Pringle, *The Life and Times of William Howard Taft* (2 vols., 1939); Kenneth Hechler, *Insurgency: Personalities and Policies of the Taft Era* (1940); James Holt, *Congressional Insurgents and the Party System, 1909–1916* (1967); D. F. Anderson, *William Howard Taft: A Conservative's Conception of the Presidency* (1973).

Wilson
A. S. Link, *Wilson: The Road to the White House* (1947), *Wilson: The New Freedom* (1956), and *Woodrow Wilson and the Progressive Era, 1910–1917** (1954); A. C. Walworth, *Woodrow Wilson* (2 vols., 1958); J. M. Blum, *Woodrow Wilson and the Politics of Morality** (1956) and *Joe Tumulty and the Wilson Era* (1951); W. E. Leuchtenberg, ed., *Wilson: The New Freedom** (1961), containing selections from Wilson's writings.

Progressives and Conservatives
Belle and Fola La Follette, *Robert M. La Follette* (2 vols., 1953); R. M. La Follette, *Autobiography** (1913); Richard Lowitt, *George W. Norris: The Making of a Progressive, 1861–1912* (1963) and *The Persistence of a Progressive, 1913–1933* (1971); C. G. Bowers, *Beveridge and the Progressive Era* (1932); A. T. Mason, *Brandeis: A Free Man's Life* (1946); F. L. Allen, *The Great Pierpont Morgan* (1949); N. W. Stephenson, *Nelson W. Aldrich* (1920); Richard Leopold, *Elihu Root and the Conservative Tradition** (1954).

Progressive Policies
S. P. Hays, *The Gospel of Efficiency: The Progressive Conservation Movement, 1890–1920** (1959); E. R. Richardson, *The Politics of Conservation: Crusade and Controversies, 1897–1913** (1962); O. E. Anderson, *The Health of a Nation: Harvey W. Wiley and the Fight for Pure Food* (1958); A. Martin, *Enterprise Denied: Origins of the Decline of the American Railroads, 1897–1917* (1971).

Socialists and Unions

Ray Ginger, *The Bending Cross: A Biography of Eugene Victor Debs* (1949); Ira Kipnis, *The American Socialist Movement, 1897–1912* (1952); D. A. Shannon, *The Socialist Party of America* (1955); J. R. Conlin, *Bread and Roses Too: Studies of the Wobblies* (1971); Marc Karson, *American Labor Unions and Politics, 1900–1918* (1958); R. J. Cornell, *The Anthracite Coal Strike of 1902* (1957).

The Negro

I. A. Newby, *Jim Crow's Defense: Anti-Negro Thought in America, 1900–1930* (1965); E. M. Rudwick, *W. E. B. DuBois: A Study of Minority Group Leadership** (1960); R. S. Baker, *Following the Color Line** (1908); E. S. Redkey, *Black Exodus: Black Nationalism and Back-to-Africa Movements, 1890–1910** (1969).

*Titles available in paperback.

The War to End War

Twenty-two

While Americans clung to the old idea of keeping out of Europe's quarrels, the nation drifted toward the twentieth-century maelstrom of world conflict. The industrial developments in Europe had brought, along with increased material abundance, a heightened competition for markets, sources of raw materials, places for investment, and sheer national prestige. To the great powers came not only social gains but also military ambitions, with an arms race that grew more and more frightening as Europe divided into two hostile alliances.

As the foremost of all industrial nations, the United States could scarcely remain unaffected by world events for long. Its emergence from the Spanish-American War with Pacific and Caribbean colonies intensified the risks of involvement. So did certain phases of the progressive spirit itself, which stimulated increased activity in foreign affairs. Some progressives aspired not only to revitalize democracy at home but also to extend it abroad. Finally, World War I brought the greatest challenge in a hundred years to the time-honored policy of neutrality and diplomatic independence.

For three years, from 1914 to 1917, the United States remained at peace, and then it joined in the hostilities. Its entrance hardly meant that the traditional policy had failed, for strict neutrality had not been tried. The American people had closer ties of kinship and commerce with one set of European belligerents than with the other. The prosperity of this country had come to depend on swollen wartime trade with the one side, which needed supplies in order to continue the war. Both groups of warring countries attempted to cut off the other's imports, and both used methods that were contrary to international law as the United States had long interpreted it. But now the American government drew a sharp distinction between the violations of neutral rights on the one side and on the other. In the one case this government protested long-windedly and

Signing the Peace Treaty 1919
On June 28, 1919, in the resplendent Hall of Mirrors in the Versailles Palace, the Allies and Germany signed a treaty to end World War I. In this painting by Sir William Orpen, the Big Three among the Allied peacemakers — Wilson, Clemenceau, and Lloyd George — are sitting at the front, center. (Courtesy, Trustees of the Imperial War Museum)

perfunctorily; in the other, it took a stern and threatening stand, demanding a "strict accountability."

According to this country's constitutional system, one man has the ultimate responsibility for war or peace—the President. In 1917 President Wilson made the decision for war. He saw it as a war to end war, to bring about an international organization for keeping the future peace, and thus to "make the world safe for democracy." After the military victory had been won, however, the Senate refused to accept his plan for a League of Nations, despite his pleas that the United States must join the League if a second world war were to be prevented. At the height of his struggle for the League, he suffered a stroke that left him a partially paralyzed as well as a deeply embittered man.

Progressivism by the Sword

Progressive foreign policy, as practiced by Roosevelt, Taft, and Wilson, from 1901 to 1917, was rather aggressive, particularly in dealings with Latin America and the Far East.

T. R. AND WORLD POLITICS

As much as any other progressive, Theodore Roosevelt liked to engage in moralizing about the position of the United States in the world. His most often repeated theme was, as he once put it: "The just war is a war for the integrity of high ideals. The only safe motto for the individual citizen of a democracy fit to play a great part in the world is service—service by work and help in peace, service through the high gallantry of entire indifference to life, if war comes on land." This kind of talk rallied the support of many progressives, even those who were revolted by Roosevelt's blatant militarism—his equally incessant extolling of the soldierly virtues as "the most valuable of all qualities." Despite his bombast, he conducted foreign affairs with a sure hand.

Roosevelt's concept of the role of the United States in world politics emphasized sea power. Now that the United States had colonies, it needed to build a navy powerful enough to keep the sea lanes open to them. It also needed to build an Isthmian canal so that naval units could sail quickly from one ocean to another, and not have to make a long and difficult voyage around Cape Horn, as the *Oregon* had done during the Spanish-American War. In addition it needed to protect the Caribbean approaches to the canal from encroachment. All this predicated a strong naval policy at a time when the key to strength in the world was a powerful fleet. This meant a navy second only to that of Great Britain.

Such were the views of President Roosevelt at the time when Kaiser Wilhelm II was launching Germany upon a gigantic naval race with Great Britain. As Britain began construction of the first dreadnought (large modern battleship) in 1905, both Germany and the United States were building more and larger warships, amid growing alarums of war. Urged on by Roosevelt, the most effective of naval lobbyists, Congress voted appropriations for ten battleships and four armored cruisers between 1902 and 1904. These were more powerful and more widely ranging than the relatively light vessels of the nineties, which had been designed primarily to defend the American coast. By 1906 the American navy was second only to the British, but in the next few years was surpassed by the German navy.

Roosevelt liked to quote an African proverb: "Speak softly and carry a big stick." This certainly characterized his action in the Far East, as well as in the Caribbean. He hoped to make the Open Door policy effective against Russian expansion in Manchuria. For a moment in 1903 he expressed such indignation over the "treachery" and "mendacity" of Russia that he toyed with the idea of going to "extremes" with her. His practical policy, however, was to encourage Japanese efforts to check the Russian drive. When the Japanese made a surprise attack upon the Russian fleet at Port Arthur, Manchuria, in 1904, he was inclined to cheer, as were most Americans. He warned the French and Germans against aiding Russia, but he did not wish to see the Japanese totally victorious, since this might "possibly mean a struggle between them and us in the future."

Roosevelt pursued this same policy in the peace negotiations. Though the Japanese won a series of spectacular victories, they faced such serious financial difficulties that they asked Roosevelt to mediate. He agreed and called a peace conference at Portsmouth, New Hampshire, in the summer of 1905. But he soon offended the Japanese by opposing their demands for an enormous indemnity. He lost their good will even though he approved their territorial gains at the conference—control over Korea and South Manchuria and annexation of the southern half of Sakhalin Island, which had belonged to Russia.

Japanese-American relations, thus suddenly made worse, were not much improved by a secret Japanese-American agreement which was effected at the time of the Portsmouth conference. President Roosevelt had dispatched Secretary of War Taft from Manila to Tokyo to reach a Far Eastern understanding with the Japanese. In the resulting Taft-Katsura memorandum of July 1905, the Japanese prime minister acknowledged American sovereignty in the Philippines, and the American President recognized the suzerainty of Japan over Korea.

Roosevelt's role in helping to negotiate the 1905 Treaty of Portsmouth won for him the Nobel Peace Prize. His actions did indeed contribute to preservation of the peace by maintaining a power balance between Russia and Japan on the Asian mainland. But in Asian waters, Japan had risen to a new ascendancy through its destruction of the Russian fleets. Japan repaired and refloated many of the vessels and rapidly built new ships in the following years. Japan undoubtedly had become powerful enough to seize the Philippines (which Roosevelt came to regard as an Achilles heel) because the American fleet would have had trouble fighting effectively so far from home. Unfortunately, at this same time, the people of Japan and the United States became angry with each other.

In October 1906, within a year after Japan's victory over a great European power, the San Francisco school board ordered the segregation of Oriental schoolchildren. This step was taken in response to the feelings of Californians against the 500 to 1,000 Japanese immigrants coming in each year, feelings which were intensified by lurid "Yellow Peril" articles in the Hearst and other newspapers. Resentment in Japan flared high, and jingoes in each country fanned the flames still higher.

Roosevelt worked skillfully to douse the flames. He persuaded San Francisco to desegregate its schools, and in return in 1907 he negotiated a "Gentlemen's Agreement" with Japan to keep out agricultural laborers. Then, lest the Japanese government think he had acted through fear, he launched a spectacular naval demonstration. He sent sixteen battleships of the new navy, "the Great White Fleet," on an unprecedented 45,000-mile voyage around the world. It gave the navy invaluable experience in sailing in formation while demonstrating the danger of dependence on foreign-owned coaling stations. The Japanese invited this formidable armada to visit Yokohama and gave it a clamorous welcome. Thus Roosevelt came to feel that through brandishing the big stick he had helped the cause of peace.

For the moment, the United States had demonstrated sufficient naval strength to restore an unsteady balance in Asian waters. In 1908, before the fleet had returned home, Japan and the United States negotiated the comprehensive Root-Takahira Agreement. Both countries agreed to support the Open Door in China. The United States tacitly seemed to give Japan a free hand in Manchuria (where rivalry with Russia continued) in return for an explicit guarantee of the status quo in the Pacific. This precarious equilibrium might be destroyed by any future upset in the naval ratios.

At the same time that he was directly engaged in balancing the powers in the Pacific, Roosevelt was participating somewhat less directly in trying to maintain a balance in Europe. American relations with Great Britain were increasingly cordial. In 1903, the British agreed to refer a troublesome dispute over the boundary between Alaska and Canada to a tribunal of three Americans, two Canadians, and one Englishman. To cultivate the friendship of the United States, the English member of the tribunal voted against the Canadians and in favor of the American claim. Then the British government made another concession by pulling its naval units out of the Caribbean and leaving it as virtually an American lake.

When Germany and France quarreled over Morocco, Roosevelt was reluctant to involve the United States. "We have other fish to fry," he told Taft in 1905. Nevertheless, he resolved to try "to keep matters on an even keel in Europe." Consequently he intervened on behalf of the German Kaiser to persuade France and England to attend an international conference for establishing the status of Morocco. Germany was protesting because the French had set up a protectorate there. At the conference, which met in Algeciras, Spain, in 1906, the American delegates sided with the British and the French to keep France dominant in Morocco while making some concessions to appease Germany. For the moment the United States had helped avert, or at least postpone, a war into which it might ultimately be dragged.

THE IRON-FISTED NEIGHBOR

Roosevelt's preoccupation with the American strategy of defense in the Caribbean—especially his almost obsessive fear of German penetration—betrayed him into acting like an iron-fisted neighbor toward small countries to the south. He first used his might impetuously to start work on a canal in Panama.

Before Roosevelt became President, the McKinley administration was negotiating with England to remove an old obstacle, the 1850 treaty agreeing that the two countries would jointly construct, operate, and defend any canal to be built in Central America. In 1901 the British, eager to court American friendship, consented in the Hay-Pauncefote treaty to exclusive American construction, operation, and fortification of a canal.

The next question was where to locate the canal. There were two possible routes. The

T. R. at the Panama Canal
Visiting Panama in 1906, while the canal was under construction, President Roosevelt posed at the controls of a gigantic steam shovel, which was being used for excavation at Culebra Cut. (Library of Congress)

Theodore Roosevelt's Latin American Policy [1905]

It cannot be too often and too emphatically asserted that the United States has not the slightest desire for territorial aggrandizement at the expense of any of its southern neighbors, and will not treat the Monroe Doctrine as an excuse for such aggrandizement on its part. . . . Moreover . . . we do not intend to permit the Monroe Doctrine to be used by any nation on this Continent as a shield to protect it from the consequences of its own misdeeds against foreign nations. . . . On the one hand, this country would certainly decline to go to war to prevent a foreign government from collecting a just debt; on the other hand, it is very inadvisable to permit any foreign power to take possession, even temporarily, of the custom houses of an American Republic in order to enforce the payment of its obligations; for such temporary occupation might turn into a permanent occupation. The only escape from these alternatives may at any time be that we must ourselves undertake to bring about some arrangement by which so much as possible of a just obligation shall be paid. . . . The justification for the United States taking this burden and incurring this responsibility is to be found in the fact that it is incompatible with international equity for the United States to refuse to allow other powers to take the only means at their disposal of satisfying the claims of their creditors and yet to refuse, itself, to take any such steps. — Annual Message to Congress, December 5, 1905.

---

shortest one would be across the Isthmus of Panama, but the rights there were owned by a French company, the successor of an earlier company that had tried and failed to dig a canal. For its franchise, the French company wanted $109 million, which would make a Panama canal more expensive than a Nicaraguan one. Consequently, both Congress and President Roosevelt favored the Nicaraguan route. But the French company had expert agents — Philippe Bunau-Varilla, its chief engineer, and William Nelson Cromwell, an attorney who had contributed heavily to the Republican campaign fund in 1900 — who hastily cut the price of their rights to $40 million. Unless sold to the United States and sold quickly, the rights would be worthless, for they would expire in 1904. This price cut and able lobbying caused Congress and the President to change their minds.

Impatient to begin construction, Roosevelt put pressure upon Colombia, which owned Panama, to conclude a treaty authorizing the United States to dig a canal there. In January 1903, Secretary of State Hay and the Colombian chargé d'affaires Tomas Herrán signed a treaty that was most unfavorable to Colombia. It authorized the United States to construct a canal in return for a payment of only $10 million and an annual rental of $250,000, as com-

pared with the $40 million the French company was to receive. The Colombian Senate, as it had every right to do, rejected the treaty.

Roosevelt was too furious to give thought to niceties or to the value of a friendly policy toward Latin America. Fuming that the Colombians were "inefficient bandits," he considered seizing Panama through twisting a technicality in an 1846 treaty with Colombia (then New Granada) guaranteeing the neutrality and free transit of the Isthmus. Roosevelt's intended seizure became unnecessary, because Bunau-Varilla helped organize a Panamanian revolution. There had been many previous revolts, all failures. But at the outset of this one, the United States landed troops from the U.S.S. *Nashville*, and, invoking the 1846 treaty obligation to maintain order, prevented Colombian forces from putting down the rebellion. Three days later the United States recognized the new republic of Panama and, soon after that, negotiated a treaty paying Panama the sum Colombia had rejected, in return for the grant of a zone ten miles wide. The minister from Panama who arranged the treaty was Bunau-Varilla.

Work on the canal proceeded smoothly and efficiently. The elimination of tropical diseases in the area, the digging of the tremendous cuts, and the installation of huge locks at a total cost $375 million filled Americans with patriotic enthusiasm, though some were ashamed of Roosevelt's ruthlessness. In 1911 he boasted: "I took the Canal Zone and let Congress debate; and while the debate goes on, the Canal does also." It opened in 1914.

Meanwhile Roosevelt was enlarging the Monroe Doctrine. In 1902 he had written to a German friend: "If any South American country misbehaves toward any European country, let the European country spank it." Germany, along with Italy and Great Britain, proceeded to spank Venezuela by blockading her coast. The object was to force the Venezuelan dictator to pay his country's debts to European bankers.

By 1903 Roosevelt had changed his mind. Americans were angered at the news of the German bombardment of a Venezuelan port, and he himself was beginning to fear that the Germans planned to establish a permanent base in Venezuela. He warned the Germans (according to his own later account) that Admiral Dewey had his fleet in the Caribbean and was ready to act in case they tried to acquire any territory. The Germans finally withdrew— as the British and Italians already had done— and agreed to submit the debt question to arbitration.

The Venezuela incident led to a new Caribbean policy usually called the "Roosevelt Corollary" of the Monroe Doctrine. The Hague Court declared that the powers that had threatened Venezuela had prior claim on payment of their debts; this increased the likelihood of future European intervention in the Western Hemisphere. For Roosevelt, who still believed that small nations must pay their just debts, the only way out seemed a drastic new device. If these little countries could not behave themselves, the United States reluctantly would police them and collect debt payments from them in order to forestall European intervention. Uncle Sam would act as a bill collector for European bankers. Roosevelt declared to Congress in 1904 that the United States might be forced, "however reluctantly, in flagrant cases of . . . wrongdoing or impotence, to the exercise of an international police power."

The occasion for putting the Roosevelt Corollary into operation was the defaulting of Santo Domingo on about $22 million of its debt to European nations. France and Italy threatened to intervene. In effect, the United States established a receivership, taking over Dominican customs, paying 45 percent of the receipts to the Dominican government, and paying the rest to foreign creditors.

As a part of an American strategy of Canal defense, Roosevelt's Caribbean policy was doubtless successful. As a means of securing the support and cooperation of nations to the south, it left much to be desired. Roosevelt's tactics inspired fear rather than friendship.

TAFT AND DOLLAR DIPLOMACY

President Taft was no readier in foreign affairs than at home to exert strong personal leadership as Roosevelt had done. For the most part he left the State Department to his Secretary of State, a former corporation lawyer, Philander C. Knox. Taft and Knox made no real effort to maintain a balance of power in either Europe or Asia. Instead, they concentrated upon promoting American banking and business interests overseas.

In Far Eastern relations, this policy brought to the forefront young Willard Straight, an agent of American bankers, formerly consul general at Mukden, Manchuria. He argued that dollar diplomacy was the financial expression of the Open Door policy, that it would make "a guaranty for the preservation, rather than the destruction of China's integrity." Taft, therefore, was ready to ignore Roosevelt's tacit arrangement with Japan that the United States would stay out of Manchuria, and to support the right of Americans to invest both there and in China. When British, French, and German bankers formed a consortium to finance railroads in China, Secretary Knox insisted that Americans should also participate. In 1911 they were admitted. Then Knox proposed that an international syndicate purchase the South Manchurian Railroad in order to neutralize it. This led the rivals Russia and Japan to sign a treaty of amity in 1910, thus closing the Manchurian door in Taft's face.

In the Caribbean there were no other great powers to block the amateurish American operations. As a result, a new pattern emerged there of interventions going far beyond Roosevelt's limited ones, to establish firm military, political, and, above all, economic control over several unstable republics to the south. Advocates of this program argued that

American investors must be invited in to re-place European investors, who otherwise might eventually bring about European inter-vention. This was a logical step beyond the Roosevelt Corollary.

The new policy began in 1909 when Knox tried to arrange for American bankers to estab-lish a financial receivership in Honduras. He persuaded New York bankers to invest in the National Bank of Haiti. Then he sent marines to Nicaragua to protect revolutionaries, spon-sored by an American mining company, who were fighting to overthrow a hostile dictator. Knox negotiated a treaty with the new friendly government giving the United States financial control, but the United States Senate failed to approve it. American bankers, less reluctant, accepted Knox's invitation to move in. By 1912 the new pro-American government was so unpopular that a revolt broke out. Taft sent marines to crush the uprising, and some of them remained as late as 1925.

Even more than Roosevelt's policies, those of Taft alienated the neighboring countries to the south.

WILSONIAN INTERVENTION

President Wilson brought to the determination of foreign policy a flair for idealistic pronounce-ments. He was never unsure of his moral posi-tion but was often uncertain how to reach it. He and his Secretaries of State and the Navy, Wil-liam Jennings Bryan and Josephus Daniels, were all devoutly religious, war-hating men of good will, who disapproved of the exorbitant moneymaking sometimes connected with dol-lar diplomacy. But the temptation to make use of the force at their disposal to uplift their brothers to the south was too great to resist. The need to do so seemed compelling to them, because like their predecessors they felt that they must maintain an American-sponsored stability in the Caribbean as a vital part of na-tional defense.

Wilson expounded his new policies in a speech at Mobile, Alabama, in the fall of 1913. He disavowed imperialist intent. "The United States will never again seek one additional foot of territory by conquest," he declared. Rather, he sought "the development of constitutional liberty in the world."

The Wilson administration not only regu-larized through treaty the continuing occupa-tion of Nicaragua, but also initiated new inter-ventions in Santo Domingo and Haiti—to head off a supposed threat of German intervention. In spite of American customs control, revolu-tion after revolution had swept through and impoverished Santo Domingo. The United States took over all Dominican finances and the police force, but the Dominicans would not agree to a treaty establishing a virtual protec-torate. In 1916 Wilson established a military government. During the eight years that this government continued, the United States forci-bly maintained order, trained a native constab-ulary, and promoted education, sanitation, and public works.

On the other end of the island of Hispanio-la, the Negro republic of Haiti was even more revolution-wracked, the violence culminating in 1915 when a mob tore an unpopular presi-dent limb from limb. Wilson again sent in the marines, established another military govern-ment, and began the task of improving living conditions in Haiti. The marines demonstrated their efficiency in 1918 when they supervised an election to ratify a new American-sponsored constitution. The vote for it was 69,377 to 355. Nevertheless, that year they had to put down a serious revolt, killing some hundreds of Hai-tians in the process.

There was a persistent fear that the Ger-mans might try to acquire the Danish West In-dies. In 1902 the Senate ratified a treaty for their purchase, but the Danish parliament re-jected it. Finally in 1917 the United States ac-quired the poverty-stricken islets, which were then renamed the Virgin Islands, for an exorbi-tant $25 million. Their value was negative: the United States wanted to make sure they were not in the possession of any potentially hostile power.

MAKING MEXICO BEHAVE

American business interests had invested about $1 billion in Mexico during the regime of a friendly dictator, Porfirio Díaz. They owned over half the oil, two-thirds of the railroads, and three-fourths of the mines and smelters. Popu-lar though Díaz was in the United States, he came to be hated in Mexico because, while he encouraged foreigners to amass huge profits, he suppressed civil liberties and kept the masses in peonage. For the average Mexican, there was little of the progress toward democracy or economic security that President Wilson desired. In 1910 the aged Díaz was overthrown by a democratic reform leader, who in turn was murdered and succeeded by the reactionary Victoriano Huerta just before Wilson took office. Wilson turned a deaf ear to American investors who saw in Huerta's presidency an opportunity to return to the "good old days." Rather, he refused to recognize "the government of butchers."

Years of tedious complications followed. Wilson hoped that, by refusing recognition to Huerta's government, he could bring about its collapse and the development of constitutionalism in Mexico. He offered in June 1913 to mediate between Huerta and the opposing Constitutionalists of Venustiano Carranza. Both sides refused.

For several months Wilson pursued a policy of "watchful waiting," but when Huerta established a full military dictatorship in October 1913, Wilson began to bring increasing pressure against him. First he persuaded the British (who were obtaining most of their naval oil from Mexico) to stop supporting Huerta. Next he offered to send American troops to the aid of Carranza, but again he was rebuffed, since all Carranza wanted was the right to buy arms in the United States. Wilson granted this in February 1914 by lifting President Taft's arms embargo, but still the Carranzists did not win.

Wilson was in a dilemma: he might have to choose between recognizing Huerta, stronger than ever, or intervening with armed force, which could mean war against all the Mexican factions. Off the coast of Mexico, the commanders of American fleet units, engaged in watchful waiting, became increasingly restless. The precipitate action of one of them gave Wilson a way out. In April 1914 one of Huerta's officers arrested several sailors of the U.S.S. *Dolphin* who had gone ashore at Tampico; a superior officer quickly released them and apologized. But the American admiral demanded a twenty-one gun salute to the United States flag in addition. At this Huerta balked. Wilson, deciding to back the admiral, sent all available warships to Mexican waters and asked Congress for authority to take drastic action. Then, anxious to prevent a German ship loaded with munitions from reaching Huerta's forces, Wilson, without

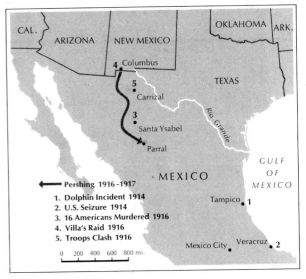

The U.S. in Mexico   1914–1917

waiting for Congress to act, ordered the navy to seize Veracruz. It did so, on April 21 and 22, 1914, but not in the bloodless way that Wilson had anticipated. The Mexicans suffered 126 killed and 195 wounded; the Americans, 19 killed and 71 wounded.

At this difficult point, Argentina, Brazil, and Chile offered to mediate. With relief, Wilson accepted, and sent his delegates to confer with Huerta's at Niagara Falls, Canada, from May to July 1914. As the negotiations went on and on, the Carranzists advanced on Mexico City, finally bringing the result Wilson wished, the abdication of Huerta.

Under Carranza's presidency, the Mexican muddle did not clear up but got worse. By September 1914 civil war was again devastating Mexico, as a former general of Carranza's, Francisco ("Pancho") Villa, tried to overthrow him. In October 1915 the United States gave de facto recognition to Carranza's government.

This antagonized Villa, who was still roaming northern Mexico. He tried to bring about a war between the United States and Mexico by shooting sixteen Americans he seized from a train in January 1916. When that failed, in March he raided Columbus, New Mexico, just across the border, killing nineteen more Americans. Wilson retaliated by ordering a punitive expedition under Brigadier General John J.

IV. THE NEW CENTURY:
The Avant Garde and Isolationism

Plate 1: Cass Gilbert,
WOOLWORTH BUILDING, NEW YORK
(Photo by Sandak)

The beginning of the twentieth century was a turbulent time for the development of American art. The traditional flow of European influence continued to affect accepted taste, but, at the same time, energetic and inventive American artists, architects, and craftsmen began to challenge the artistic establishment and strive to create a truly American art.

The battle lines between progressive and conservative expression can best be observed in the evolution of that uniquely American structure, the skyscraper. Just as it seemed that Louis Sullivan and the Chicago school of architects had freed the tall building from the veneer of historical styles, a new wave of eclecticism spread across the country. The renewed interest in the Paris School of Beaux Arts gained impetus from the highly successful Chicago World's Fair of 1893, which emphasized historical and borrowed styles; and Sullivan's functionally inspired emphasis on the steel grid structure for the skyscraper gave way to a new variety of decorative shells.

The Woolworth Building *(Plate 1)*, erected in 1913 by Cass Gilbert, utilized a medieval vocabulary of gargoyles and intricate tracery to create a Gothic profile on the skyline of New York. The choice of historical style was influenced by a prevailing deification of business, reflected in the sentiments of the architect and his client, who called the building a "Cathedral of Commerce."

Not only the skyscraper but all forms of progressive architecture had been dealt a severe setback by the World's Fair of 1893. However, a new generation of designers in Chicago, led by Frank Lloyd Wright, arose to challenge the traditional approach. Wright, who was to become one of the century's most influential architects, began his long and creative career designing homes in suburban Chicago. As a young man Wright had worked

Plate 2: Frank Lloyd Wright, WARD WILLITS HOUSE, HIGHLAND PARK, ILLINOIS *(Photo by Sandak)*

as a draftsman for Sullivan, and he deeply respected the master's concern for functionalism. But Wright added to this a personal love of the natural environment. His domestic buildings of the period reflect in their low horizontal lines the flatness of the midwestern prairie on which they were built. In Wright's design for the Ward Willits house, built in Highland Park, Illinois, in 1902 *(Plate 2)*, the dominant feature is the roof, which spreads out over the structure and anchors it visually to its site. Wright's use of the massive roof, as well as the openness and freedom of the interior plan, were derived in part from Japanese architectural sources.

In painting as in architecture the traditional Beaux Arts approach was challenged by a new generation of young artists. They were led by Robert Henri, who, although he had studied in Paris, rejected the idealism and sentimentality associated with

academic painting in favor of an unflinching objectivity and an emphasis on momentary effects. This new school of American painters, known simply as "The Eight," derived their subjects from the teeming life of the cities and depicted them with vigor and immediacy.

Henri's portrait of a "Laughing Girl," ca. 1907 *(Plate 3)*, is boldly painted in a technique reminiscent of the seventeenth century Dutch master Franz Hals. The dynamic personality of the sitter is captured in the explosive brushwork.

Another of the painters of The Eight was John Sloan. Sloan's early training as a newspaper illustrator in Philadelphia was excellent preparation for his painting of the urban environment. His depiction of common, everyday people and events, as in his "Backyards, Greenwich Village," 1914 *(Plate 4)*, transformed the poor overcrowded immigrant section of New York into a vibrant

Plate 3: Robert Henri, LAUGHING GIRL
(The University of Kansas Museum of Art)

document of city life at the turn of the century.

The Eight — or the "Ashcan School" as they were derisively called by the establishment — had an immediate impact on American painting, and their exhibition at the Macbeth Galleries in 1908 focused attention on the innovative direction in American art. But just as these young painters were establishing a new American school another wave of European influence made itself felt. This time the imported style was that of the avant-garde Fauves and Cubists, whose work was first shown to the American public at the famous Armory Show of 1913 in New York.

This exhibition of the experimental European styles had a profound effect on many American painters. One of these was Joseph Stella, who, under the influence of the Italian Futurists, adopted the cubist technique of viewing an object simultaneously from a number of points of view. He utilized this technique in order to capture the dynamic rhythms of the new industrial age. In Stella's

Plate 4: John Sloan, BACKYARDS, GREENWICH VILLAGE *(Collection of the Whitney Museum of American Art)*

canvas of "The Bridge," 1922 *(Plate 5)*, the structural elements of the towers and cables frame the cubist fragments of the city skyline. Like the painters of The Eight, Stella's theme was the American city; but he attempted to recreate the abstract qualities of movement and dynamics rather than the visual facts of appearance.

Although the Armory Show represents one of the earliest appearances of abstract art in this country, some American artists learned about the new styles through their own travels in Europe. Edward Hopper, who at the turn of the century studied with Henri, went to Paris in 1906 where he saw the experimental painting of Matisse and Picasso. Hopper, however, rejected the abstract subjectivity of contemporary European art, preferring an objectivity based on the reality he saw around him. He was fascinated by the theme of the city, but unlike his teacher Henri, whose interest was the outward drama of urban America, Hopper invests his painting with a mood of reflective introspection. In his canvas of 1939 entitled "New York Movie" *(Plate 6)*, the subject is the ornate interior of a motion picture theatre. In subdued light, the diffused image of the black-and-white screen is contrasted with the yellowish glow behind the usher. The power of Hopper's painting is

Plate 5: Joseph Stella, THE BRIDGE
(Collection of the Newark Museum)

Plate 6: Edward Hopper, NEW YORK MOVIE *(Collection, The Museum of Modern Art, New York)*

derived from its bold simplification of forms sensitively rendered in a haunting quality of light.

American sculpture in the first quarter of the twentieth century was largely unaffected by the avant-garde styles introduced by the Armory Show. Many Americans followed in the tradition of the French realist sculptor Auguste Rodin, working in a technique of roughly modeled surfaces. But in the nineteen-twenties an interest in primitive sculpture brought about a new style. One of the leaders of this new direction was Paul Manship, who was inspired by the archaic art of Greece and the simplified forms of oriental sculpture. His rhythmic compositions often depicted human figures with stylized anatomy and flowing decorative drapery. Manship's greatest success was in large-scale figures such as the statue of Prometheus for the Lower Plaza of Rockefeller Center, 1934 *(Plate 7).* Here the

carefully balanced, streamlined figure floats elegantly above a dramatic fountain display. Although Manship's decorative treatment is sometimes overly refined, he was the most popular sculptor of the period.

The years between the World Wars produced a number of innovations in American architecture. Once again Frank Lloyd Wright led the way in inventive design. In his 1936 Administration Building for the S. C. Johnson & Son Co. in Racine, Wisconsin *(Plate 8),* Wright introduced a new technological advance in the use of reinforced concrete columns. These cone-shaped supports widen from their narrow base into Wright's famous "lily pad" capitols which support the ceiling. The ceiling also represents an innovative design in its use of bands of glass tubing which provide an even and diffused light into the interior. In both his inventive approach to structural problems and his imaginative use of materials, Wright represents one of the major shapers of twentieth-century architecture.

In the 1930s, with the onset of the Great Depression, American painting, like American politics, moved away from European influence toward a greater isolationism. Many painters rejected avant-garde modernism, especially abstraction, in favor of a realistic narrative style. One such group of painters, known as Regionalists, took their subject matter from the folk legends of the Midwest. Their desire to create an American idiom was shared by writers and musicians of the period – among them William Faulkner and Aaron Copland – and supported by government-sponsored programs.

One of the artists associated with the

Plate 7: Paul Manship, PROMETHEUS *(Courtesy of Rockefeller Center, Inc.)*

Plate 8: Frank Lloyd Wright,
JOHNSON WAX ADMINISTRATION BUILDING:
LOBBY *(Photo Courtesy of Johnson Wax)*

Plate 9: John Steuart Curry, BAPTISM IN
KANSAS *(Collection of the Whitney Museum of
American Art)*

Plate 10: Jack Levine, WELCOME HOME *(The Brooklyn Museum, J. B. Woodward Memorial Fund)*

Regionalist movement was John Steuart Curry. In his 1928 painting "Baptism in Kansas" *(Plate 9)*, Curry captures the image of the American "Bible Belt" heartland. The melodramatic event is realistically and vigorously rendered. At best Curry and the Regionalists were the expression of a search for a national style, but often their art degenerated into a narrow chauvinism, defensively rejecting urbanism and the new directions in modern art.

Whereas the Regionalists tried to rediscover America in picturesque depictions of grass-roots culture, another group of artists, more urban-oriented, derived their subjects from the social upheavals caused by the Great Depression. The style of the Social Commentators, as they were called, drew its inspiration from journalistic caricature, and their themes were often expressed as protests against inequality in American society. Whether depicting the conflict of racial exploitation, or dramatizing the plight of the dispossessed, these artists became propagandists in the struggle for social justice.

One of the leading figures of the movement was Jack Levine. Although his style was strongly influenced by such satiric painters as Goya and Daumier, his technique was extremely original. In his painting "Welcome Home" *(Plate 10)*, executed in 1946 at the end of World War II, Levine caricatures through distortion and color intensity his feelings of disdain for those who profited from the war. His visual criticism, like that of his fellow Social Commentators, attacked corruption and used the painting medium to express his personal point of view.

Pershing to hunt down Villa. For this, Wilson had the permission of Carranza, but as Villa drew the American forces 300 miles into Mexico, two skirmishes with Carranza's army almost led to war. Again the peace forces outweighed the jingoes in the United States, and again Wilson accepted compromise. On July 4, 1916, Carranza suggested the appointment of a Joint High Commission to consider the problem. The commission debated into January 1917, when it broke up without establishing a basis for the withdrawal of American troops. By then the United States was so close to war with Germany that Wilson nevertheless withdrew the troops and in March 1917 gave recognition to Carranza's government.

Wilson had been elected President on a program of domestic reform, the New Freedom. Shortly before his inauguration he remarked: "It would be the irony of fate if my administration had to deal chiefly with foreign affairs." But so it was to be.

WAR IN EUROPE

Bryan, before he took office as secretary of state, suggested to Wilson a scheme for "cooling off" treaties with all the nations of the world. These would provide that disputes should go to permanent commissions for a one-year investigation before either party could strengthen its armaments or go to war. This proposal was in keeping with the progressive theory that war was unthinkable and that all disputes could be settled through reasonable discussion. Bryan negotiated thirty such treaties with large and small nations—but none with Germany.

The problem of the European balance gave Wilson at least slight concern in May 1914 when he authorized Colonel House to sail abroad to try to bring an end to the arms race. Within a few months, Europe became Wilson's greatest cause for anxiety, as fate directed his administration toward an overwhelming concern with foreign affairs.

Nothing but trouble had come out of Wilson's long and muddled intervention in Mexico. His bad tactics had aroused a hostility among the Mexican people which did not dissipate for years.

In other respects Wilson and his Secretary of State were slightly more successful in improving relations between the United States and Latin America. During 1913 and 1914 they negotiated a treaty with Colombia expressing "sincere regrets" for the Panama incident and paying an indemnity of $25 million. Roosevelt thundered that it was a "blackmail treaty," and his Republican friends in the Senate blocked it until after his death. In 1921 Congress voted to pay the indemnity but omit the apology.

Unneutral Neutrality

Americans paid little attention to the minor alarms that followed the assassination of the Austrian Archduke in Sarajevo, Bosnia, at the end of June. Balkan crises were familiar and boring news; events in Mexico where Carranza was driving out Huerta seemed more sensational. Even when Austria-Hungary declared war on Serbia on July 28, Americans were not shocked, but the week that followed left them stunned. The declaration of war against Serbia triggered a chain reaction of threats and counterthreats, commitments and countercommitments among the alliances. It detonated an explosion no one seemed really to want, but no one seemed able to avoid. By August 5, England, France, and Russia were at war with Germany and Austria-Hungary. The explosion had blown to bits the comfortable, optimistic Europe that had seemed so safe and stable.

Bewildered Americans congratulated themselves that at least the explosion could not extend to their shores; the New World was still secure. A sizable number, who were of German ancestry or had been educated in German universities, automatically saw the war as a valiant German struggle against the cruel despotism of Tsarist Russia. And most Irish-Americans sympathized with Germany as the foe of their ancient oppressor, England. But the vast majority of the people, with greater educational, economic, or sentimental ties to England

and France, were shocked by the German invasion of Belgium in defiance of a treaty. They were pro-Allied without being at all sure what the war was about. None of them in August 1914 envisaged American entrance into the war. There was no clear call for an American democratic crusade.

With the outbreak of war in Europe, Wilson feared that Japan would take advantage of the preoccupation of the Western powers to expand in the Orient. He reverted to a balance-of-power policy to try to stem the Japanese tide as much as possible. Japan declared war upon Germany and seized the German holdings on the Shantung peninsula of China; this the United States could not criticize. Next Japan tried to impose upon the Chinese a treaty embodying twenty-one demands that would have made China virtually a protectorate. At this point (in 1915), the American government with the aid of the British, exerted such strong pressure that Japan abandoned the treaty.

But the United States appeased Japan in the Lansing-Ishii Agreement of November 2, 1917. This recognized that Japan had "special interests in China, particularly in the part to which her possessions are contiguous." The Japanese were pleased, because in translating the ambiguous document into Chinese they could give the impression that the United States approved their policy. Secretary of State Lansing was satisfied because he felt he had protected China for at least the duration of the European war. For both nations, if they held to their policies, there was trouble ahead.

BLOCKADE AND SUBMARINES

In 1914 President Wilson had proclaimed neutrality and, going beyond that, had called upon the American people to remain impartial in thought as well as in action. Yet from the beginning he himself took one attitude toward the Allies and quite a different attitude toward Germany.

The immediate problem for Wilson was domestic: to bolster the economy, which was staggering under the impact of war. As European nations sought to liquidate their investments in the United States, Wilson closed the stock exchange to prevent panic and discouraged loans to belligerents in order to preserve the gold reserve. (Secretary Bryan asserted

that such loans by banks would be unneutral.) Then war orders began to turn the panic into a boom.

Americans soon learned that the nation in control of the seas would countenance no neutral trade with the enemy. President Wilson acquiesced, though not without protests, as the British developed and tightened their system of control. The United States could have retaliated with an embargo, but this would have created serious economic distress among American farmers and it would have hurt industry. Besides, the basically pro-Allied sympathies of the administration and a great majority of the people made so drastic a step unthinkable. Hence, the United States accepted the British blockade of the Central Powers but was not so ready to accept a German counterblockade.

Blockade warfare became essential to the strategy of both the British and the Germans. The development of rapid-firing cannons and of machine guns made frontal assault prohibitively expensive, so the war in Europe settled down into an exhausting trench warfare between the combatants. The counterpart on the high seas was the blockade. From the outset, Great Britain made use of her superior navy to wage economic warfare against Germany. Gradually she extended the "contraband" list. She even seized American vessels carrying foodstuffs to neutral countries, on the grounds that such shipments might release supplies that could go to Germany. Americans complained that the British were using the controls to benefit British firms at the expense of American business.

On the whole, the British blockade proved to be no economic handicap for the United States, since by early 1915 heavy war orders were arriving which more than filled the trade gap it had created. While trade with the Central Powers almost came to an end, that with the Allies between 1914 and 1916 jumped from $824 million to $3,214 million—a staggering figure for that time. In March 1915 the government relaxed its regulations to allow the Allies to float huge loans in the United States for financing their purchases. In effect the United States, embarking upon the greatest boom in its history, was becoming the great arsenal for the Allies.

This the Germans could not permit. During the first weeks of the war they imposed no blockades but concentrated upon trying to win

According to official propaganda, the United States went to war in 1917 to preserve the "freedom of the seas" and to "make the world safe for democracy." Afterward many Americans were disillusioned by the rise of dictatorships in Europe and by the findings of a Senate committee headed by Gerald P. Nye, which from 1934 to 1936 looked into the role of bankers and munitions makers in bringing about American involvement. The disillusionment found expression and further encouragement in a number of books, of which the most widely read was *Road to War, 1914–1917* (1935) by Walter Millis, a leading journalist. Millis thought that the decision to intervene was foolish, a result of sentimental ties with Great Britain and France, the effectiveness of British propaganda, American loans to the Allies, and the profit-seeking of manufacturers of war materials. The international lawyers Edwin M. Borchard and William P. Lage, hoping to keep this country out of a second world war, argued further, in *Neutrality for the United States* (1937), that neutrality had not failed in 1917; it had not even been seriously attempted, the Wilson administration having been partial to the Allies from the beginning.

After World War II the career diplomat George F. Kennan, author of *American Dipomacy, 1900–1950* (1950), and the political scientist Hans J. Morgenthau, author of *In Defense of the National Interest* (1951), criticized the Wilson policy on other grounds. These writers accused Wilson of pursuing unrealistic goals, of mouthing high-sounding "legalistic-moralistic" phrases instead of concentrating on the true national interest. But another political scientist, Edward H. Buehrig, disagreed. In *Woodrow Wilson and the Balance of Power* (1955) Buehrig contended that Wilson and his advisers were concerned not only with legal and moral issues but also with the problem of restoring the world balance (which had been upset by Germany) and thus maintaining the security of the United States.

All along, Wilson also had defenders among historians. Charles Seymour, in *American Neutrality, 1914–1917* (1935), insisted that Wilson sincerely desired to avoid war but had no alternative when Germany began her unrestricted submarine operations in 1917. Thus, according to Seymour, the cause of American entry could be summarized in one word, "submarine." Wilson's foremost biographer, Arthur Link, in *Wilson the Diplomatist* (1957) and in other writings, agreed with Seymour that, by 1917, Wilson had few or no alternatives. So did Ernest E. May, in *The World War and American Isolation* (1959). May believed that "in nearly every case requiring a decision by the President [from 1914 to 1917], there were present considerations of law, morality, power, national prestige, and domestic politics, all of which had to be taken into account." The ultimate responsibility for war, May implied, was the German government's, not Wilson's.

In recent years, historians have been less concerned about the rights and wrongs of American involvement than about the hows and whys. It has become a subject about which they can be reasonably objective—like the causes of the Trojan War.

a decision in France. The German armies drove deep but were halted short of Paris in the Battle of the Marne in September 1914. While on the Russian front great armies continued to move back and forth for several years, in the west the war turned into the grinding attrition of trench combat along lines extending from the North Sea to Switzerland. As a stalemate developed along the Western Front, Germany turned toward the submarine as a possible means of breaking the British blockade. Submarines had the advantage of surprise but were so vulnerable to attack by an armed ship that they could scarcely follow the accepted rules of international law. These rules called for visit and search of enemy merchantmen and allowed sinking only if provision were made for the safety of passengers and crew. The sinking of merchant vessels without warning seemed to Americans to add a new and frightful dimension to warfare.

Beginning on February 4, 1915, Germany announced that she would sink enemy vessels in a broad zone around the British Isles. This policy, the Germans explained, was in retaliation for the British food blockade, which they claimed would starve women and children in Germany. President Wilson declared on February 10 that he would hold Germany to "strict accountability" for unlawful acts.

A serious crisis came when, on May 7, 1915, a submarine fired a torpedo without warning into the Cunard liner *Lusitania*. The ship went down in eighteen minutes, drowning 1,198 people, among them 128 Americans. "An act of piracy," Theodore Roosevelt called it.

A few days earlier, April 22, the Germans had launched against the Allied lines at Ypres a new weapon of frightfulness, poison gas. On May 13 American newspapers carried lengthy excerpts from an official British report on almost unprintable alleged German atrocities in

The Lusitania Sailing From New York City
On May 1, 1915, newspapers carried both the Cunard advertisement that the Lusitania was sailing that day and an unusual German warning: "Vessels flying the flag of Great Britain, or any of her allies, are liable to destruction ... and ... travelers sailing in the war zone on ships of Great Britain or her allies do so at their own risk." Passengers and crew discussed the announcement, but the Lusitania sailed on time, and by May 6 was proceeding along the coast of Ireland much as in peacetime, at a slow pace and not zigzagging. The commander of the German submarine U-20, seeing a large ship, fired a torpedo. Almost immediately the ship listed so sharply that few lifeboats could be launched; then it sank. As its bow went high in the air, the U-boat commander for the first time read on the ship the name Lusitania. (Brown Brothers)

Belgium. Although it bore the respected name of the former ambassador to the United States, Lord Bryce, this report contained fabrications. Yet few Americans questioned its authenticity, for by this time most people were ready to believe almost anything against Germany. Even in their revulsion, however, they were not ready to fight.

Wilson came close to the point of coercion over the *Lusitania* incident, in the ensuing exchange of notes with Germany. In his first note he virtually demanded that Germany end its submarine blockade. When the Germans sent an argumentative reply, he drafted an even stronger second note—so strong that the peace-minded Secretary Bryan resigned rather than sign it. Wilson appointed the Counselor of the State Department, Robert Lansing, an expert in international law, to be the new secretary. Lansing was ready to take an adamant position. Wilson had said: "There is such a thing as a man being too proud to fight." Yet he was ready to risk war rather than surrender to Germany what he considered to be American maritime rights.

New trouble developed in the early months of 1916 when the Allies began arming merchantmen and ordering them to attack submarines. On February 10, 1916, Germany gave notice that she would sink them without warning. Wilson reiterated his doctrine of "strict accountability," and on March 24, when the channel steamer *Sussex* was torpedoed, he threatened to break off diplomatic relations if Germany did not abandon her unrestricted submarine campaign. He made the threat at a time when Germany still lacked sufficient submarines to maintain a tight blockade and did not wish to bring the United States into the war. Consequently, on May 4, the German foreign office pledged that submarine commanders would observe rules of visit and search. The President had won a diplomatic victory, and relations with Germany became less tense during the eight months that followed.

PREPAREDNESS—OR PACIFISM?

With the outbreak of war, generals and admirals, who in peacetime attracted little attention, began to gather followings as they raised a hue and cry for increased defenses. President Wilson through his pacifist Secretary of the Navy,

Josephus Daniels, was able to muzzle the navy rather effectively. Its demands for a huge fleet-building program and its warnings of the catastrophe that faced America if the British Grand Fleet collapsed appeared for the most part indirectly through friendly politicians and publicists. Roosevelt's close friend, Major General Leonard Wood, who had just finished a term as Chief of Staff, was not so easy to silence. The Secretary of War, Lindley M. Garrison, was a zealous advocate of preparedness, and several influential civilians like Roosevelt constantly made the headlines with their warnings.

The army was much less ready than the navy to fight a major war. The establishment of the General Staff and other administrative reforms had come into effect in the Roosevelt administration, but the older officers were still antagonistic toward such changes. The Quartermaster Corps in 1913 was thinking about using trucks, but as yet not seriously testing them. The air force, consisting of seventeen planes, was part of the Signal Corps; its 1913 appropriation was $125,000. The army numbered less than 80,000 men, a large part of whom were required to maintain the posts within the United States. The National Guard was somewhat larger, but was scarcely professional.

Wilson opposed new armaments, and so did public opinion, until the crisis over submarine sinkings frightened the nation into preparedness. In November 1915 the President proposed a long-range program which by 1925 would give the United States a navy second to none and would reorganize the army and provide a reserve force of 400,000 men. This proposal touched off a hot debate in Congress and throughout the country. Large numbers of those who had been agrarian progressives of the West and South rallied behind the House majority leader, Claude Kitchin of North Carolina, to block the army program. Throughout the country, the pleas of Bryan and peace organizations strongly appealed to farmers and workingmen. Wilson took the issue to the country in speeches in January and early February 1916, but the House would not budge.

Wilson had to compromise. He accepted the resignation of Secretary of War Garrison, and appointed in his place Newton D. Baker, an able Ohio progressive who had opposed preparedness only a few weeks earlier. Ultimately Congress passed legislation providing

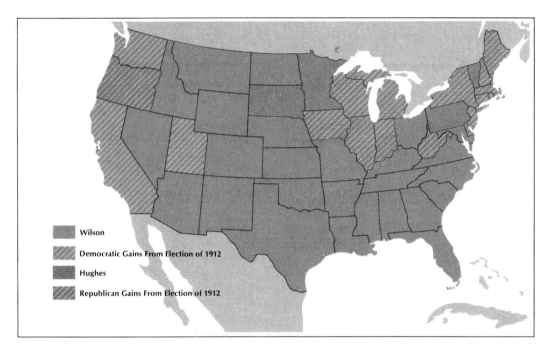

Wilson

Democratic Gains From Election of 1912

Hughes

Republican Gains From Election of 1912

Election of 1916

for substantial increases in the army, the navy, and merchant shipping. The Merchant Marine Act of 1916 established the United States Shipping Board, which was empowered to own and operate vessels and regulate shipping.

Conservatives wished to finance the defense expenditures through bonds, but the administration proposed new, heavier taxes. Progressives denounced the tax proposals as falling too heavily upon the masses. In Congress the progressives fought through a tax measure frankly aimed at making the wealthy, whom they blamed for preparedness demands, pay the bill. The Revenue Act of 1916 levied income and inheritance taxes heavily upon the rich for the first time in American history.

In 1916 Democrats and Republicans fought the presidential campaign over the issue of foreign policy before a seriously divided people. At the Democratic convention, the keynoter began citing Wilson's interchanges with Germany, and the crowd whooped with enthusiasm. "What did we do? What did we do?" the

delegates chanted, and the keynoter responded: "We didn't go to war, we didn't go to war." Out of the convention came the slogan (which Wilson himself never used): "He kept us out of war." The Democrats went into the campaign far stronger than had been expected of a minority party battling against the reunited Republicans. Many of the former Bull Moosers, Republican farmers in the Midwest, and workers who had once voted for a full dinner pail now favored the Democrats. In part they did so because of Wilson's progressive domestic policy but still more because of their hope that the President could continue to keep the country out of the war.

As for the Republicans, they persuaded Charles Evans Hughes, who had an impeccable progressive record, to resign from the Supreme Court and accept the nomination. Primarily because of the whooping of Roosevelt and others on the sidelines, the Republicans gradually began to look like the war party. Hughes, under pressure from militant Republicans, wired Roosevelt congratulations on war-like speeches. This and Hughes' own remarks led voters to believe that he was more likely than Wilson to adopt a militant policy.

Wilson warned that a Republican victory would mean intervention in Mexico and war in Europe. The lure of progressivism and peace were still so irresistible in 1916 that the Democratic party, though normally a minority, squeezed through to victory. On election night returns from the East were almost solidly for Hughes; he appeared elected. Then, as returns from the West came in, the picture began to change, though it was not until Friday that Wilson's election was certain. The Democrats also retained a precarious control over both houses of Congress.

"A FEARFUL THING"

So far as elections can be regarded as national plebiscites, Wilson had received a narrow mandate to continue along the path of progressivism and peace. Undoubtedly he intended to follow such a course. Since the outbreak of the war he had repeatedly sought means to bring the warring nations into a peace conference. But both sides had invested too heavily in the conflict, and were still too hopeful of gaining from their investment, to talk of a negotiated peace.

Immediately after the election, in November 1916, Wilson renewed negotiations looking toward a settlement. The Germans, successful on the Russian front, for a while appeared to be willing. But the top German generals did not want any conference at all. Nevertheless, on January 22, 1917, Wilson spread his plan before the Senate, calling for a lasting peace that the American people would help maintain through a league of nations. It would be a peace with freedom of the seas, disarmament, national self-determination for subject peoples, and equality among nations. "Peace among equals" — a lasting peace — could come only through "peace without victory."

On January 9 the military leaders of Germany had decided upon one final cast of the iron dice. They had resolved to return to unrestricted submarine warfare even though it would bring the United States into the war.

They hoped that they could crush France on land and starve Britain from the sea before America could make her weight felt. On January 31 the German ambassador announced that, beginning the following day, submarines would sink all ships, enemy or neutral, in a broad zone around the British Isles.

President Wilson now faced a dilemma of his own making. He had in effect during the previous eighteen months drawn a narrow line — the right of American citizens and vessels to travel on the high seas in time of war — and threatened Germany with war if she transgressed it. How could Wilson take the United States into a war against Germany for such a limited end, and still bring about the sort of peace he wanted, a just peace among equals, a peace without the victor dictating to the vanquished?

Gradually events carried Wilson toward war. On February 25 the British turned over to him an intercepted note from the German foreign secretary, Arthur Zimmerman, proposing that in the event of war, Mexico should attack the United States and receive in return her lost provinces north of the border. Americans were infuriated. At about the same time, the Russian revolution eliminated one of the moral problems in Wilson's mind by replacing a despotism among the Allies with a constitutional monarchy. (This government lasted only until November 1917, when Lenin and the Communists came into power.)

On March 18, 1917, news came that submarines had torpedoed three American ships. On March 20 the cabinet unanimously advised the President to ask Congress for a declaration of war. On the evening of April 2, 1917, President Wilson delivered his war message to Congress. After enumerating the German transgressions of American neutral rights, he declared: "It is a fearful thing to lead this great peaceful people into war, into the most terrible . . . of all wars. . . . But the right is more precious than peace, and we shall fight for the things which we have always carried nearest our hearts — for democracy, . . . for the rights and liberties of small nations, for a universal dominion of right by such a concert of free peoples as shall bring peace and safety to all nations and make the world itself at last free." Four days later, Congress passed the war declaration and the President signed it.

War Without Stint

President Wilson had called for war "without stint or limit." In this spirit the American government proceeded to mobilize economic resources on a grand scale, to launch massive campaigns against German submarines in the Atlantic and against German armies in France, and to indoctrinate the American people for enduring the burdens and the sacrifices of the total war.

CONTROLLING THE ECONOMY

Clumsily at first, but steadily and impressively, the unprepared nation built a gigantic war machine. Nearly 5,000 government agencies were set up to see that men, money, and materials were directed toward the war effort. These agencies brought an unprecedented degree of regulation and control to American economic life.

Troops had to be raised, the army enormously enlarged. Theodore Roosevelt, elderly and ill, still seemed to think in terms of the Spanish-American War; backed by a clique of Republican senators, he fought for permission to take a volunteer division to the Western Front. Speaker Champ Clark was so incensed at the prospect of a draft that he asserted from the floor of the House during debate: "In the estimation of Missourians there is precious little difference between a conscript and a convict." For weeks the debate went on, but in the end Roosevelt was turned down, and the Selective Service Act was passed.

During the debate it had become clear what a large figure in both money and men the President must write into the blank check that Congress (and the American people) had signed. In April British and French missions arrived and made clear for the first time their desperate need for money, men, and ships if they were to stave off imminent defeat. Congress soon authorized the Treasury Department to borrow $7 billion, of which $3 billion were to go as loans to the Allies.

In financing the war, Secretary of the Treasury William G. McAdoo raised about one-third of a $32 billion total through taxation. He felt that additional taxes would put too heavy a burden on low-income groups. The War Rev-

enue Act of 1917 imposed a great variety of excise taxes and income taxes steeper than any before—so steep as to take two-thirds of a $2 million income. Altogether, the taxes on individual and corporate incomes, excess profits, and inheritances provided 74 percent of the war tax revenues. There was one conspicuous loophole: many corporations distributed to their stockholders stock exempt from taxes, rather than giving them dividends.

In his borrowing policy, McAdoo tried, again, to keep the burden of the war from falling too heavily upon the poorer people. He sought to sell as many Liberty Bonds as possible to them so that they, not richer people, would reap the ultimate profit. Despite McAdoo's efforts, those with moderate incomes (under $2,000 a year) probably purchased no more than 30 percent of the $23 billion worth of bonds sold.

During the preparedness period, in August 1916, Congress had approved the establishment of a Council of National Defense, consisting of six cabinet members, and an Advisory Commission made up of representatives of industry, transportation, business, and labor. In July 1917 the council set up a centralized War Industries Board to coordinate government purchases. Wilson reorganized this board, conferred upon it sweeping powers over industry, and appointed as chairman a Wall Street broker, Bernard Baruch.

Food was almost as vital as munitions for the Allies. At the suggestion of the Council for National Defense, a Food Administration was set up by the President. After vigorous debate, it was later authorized by Congress, in the Lever Act of August 10, 1917. Its administrator was one of the most spectacular civilian heroes of the war, an American mining engineer, Herbert Hoover, who had supervised the relief feeding of Belgium. His task was to increase food production, cut waste, substitute plentiful for scarce foods, and protect consumers from speculators. Hoover, in keeping with his experience in Belgium, wished to be an administrator, not a dictator, and to run his program on a voluntary basis as far as possible. To a remarkable degree he was able to enlist the patriotic support of the public in conserving food and observing meatless and wheatless days. His slogan, seen on widely distributed posters, was "Food will win the war."

The shortage of wheat was especially critical because 1916 had been a bad crop year. Hoover encouraged wheat production by guaranteeing the purchase of the entire 1917 crop at $2.20 per bushel, a figure high enough to assure farmers a substantial profit. Wheat acreage jumped from 45 million in 1917 to 75 million in 1919, and the land produced bumper crops.

Hoover opposed retail price fixing, which he thought would lead to black markets, but he did protect consumers from speculation. Food prices went up gradually.

The Lever Act which established the Food Administration also authorized a Fuel Administration, which fixed the price of coal high enough to bring submarginal coal mines into operation and increase bituminous coal production by about 50 percent. In spite of this increase, the fuel shortage became so acute that the Fuel Administration had to order a series of coal holidays for Eastern industries in the early months of 1918.

In order to guarantee war production in German-owned factories in this country, especially those producing chemicals, these and all other German assets came under the custody of an Alien Property Custodian, A. Mitchell Palmer. The Trading-with-the-Enemy Act of October 1917, provided for their seizure and administration. Palmer obtained additional authority to sell German property, which he utilized especially to license dye and chemical patents to American industry. This was punitive toward the Germans, immensely profitable for some American businessmen, and helpful for the development of a strong chemical industry in the United States.

The Aircraft Production Board failed to produce a promised 22,000 airplanes by July 1918 — a ridiculous figure, since neither side on

Fourth Liberty Loan Parade, New Orleans

Coming shortly before the armistice, in October 1918, the Fourth Liberty Loan drive set out to raise $6 billion. American heroes, celebrities, and volunteer workers all did their bit; the news from the Western Front was exciting. Again the loan was oversubscribed. (National Archives)

the Western Front ever had as many as 2,500 planes at one time. The failure to fulfill this overoptimistic promise led to harsh criticism. By the time the armistice was signed, the United States had delivered to France 1,185 De Haviland bombers and 5,460 Liberty motors.

In April 1918 President Wilson established the National War Labor Board to serve as a sort of supreme court for labor disputes. Labor and industry each provided five representatives for the board; the two chairmen represented the public. The War Labor Board would not countenance strikes or lockouts, but recognized the right of unions to organize and bargain collectively. It favored the eight-hour day, the establishment in any given area of the wages prevailing in it, the maintenance of a basic living standard for workers, and equal pay for women who did equal work. Like some other war agencies, it had to function through persuasion or use of the President's war powers.

President Gompers of the AFL did much during the war to enhance the prestige of organized labor. He sat with industrialists on the Council of National Defense and pledged to see that there would be no strikes, in return for recognition of unionism and wage increases. He also cooperated in the government onslaught against labor radicals, which meant the Industrial Workers of the World, who were engaging in sabotage in the West. The IWW almost disappeared, while membership in other unions jumped from 2,716,900 in 1914 to 3,104,600 in 1917 and 4,169,100 in 1919. Still, this was no more than one-eighth of all wage earners.

DELIVERING THE GOODS

Increased production and stringent economy within the United States would be of no avail unless supplies could be delivered to Europe. Into the winter of 1917–1918, transportation difficulties plagued the nation. Railroads could not get raw materials to Eastern factories or munitions to ports, even through cooperation with a voluntary Railroad War Board. On December 28, 1917, Wilson put the railroads under a Railroad Administration headed by Secretary of the Treasury McAdoo. He utilized expert railroad men to run the lines as one unified system. Railroads could draw upon a half-billion-dollar revolving fund for improvements, and received rent equivalent to their average earnings in 1914–1917. The transportation snarl was so effectively untangled that a freight-car shortage of 150,000 in 1917 was transformed into a surplus of 300,000 by the end of 1918.

Shipping was a still greater and more persistent problem. By the summer of 1917, submarines had sunk nearly a quarter of the British merchant fleet; that of the United States was relatively small, and mainly committed to coastal trade. The Emergency Fleet Corporation under the Shipping Board eventually began to make remarkable progress in building new shipyards to turn out 1,700 ships of steel and 1,000 of wood.

War vessels escorted fleets of transports and supply ships across the Atlantic to protect them from submarine attacks. At first, the British admiralty had opposed the use of such convoys and kept most of its destroyers as a curtain to protect the Grand Fleet and the channel ferries. Eventually, however, United States Admiral William S. Sims broke down the resistance of the admiralty, so that a convoying system was well established by August 1917.

Sinkings, which had totaled nearly 900,000 tons in April 1917, dropped to 350,000 tons by December 1917, and to only 112,000 tons by October 1918. This was primarily a British achievement, but the United States contributed to it substantially. The British provided 70 percent of the escorting ships, the French 3 percent, and the Americans 27 percent.

The American navy grew enormously in size and efficiency. By the time the armistice was signed, it had 200,000 men and 834 vessels convoying across the Atlantic or serving in European waters. It had grown in overall size to 533,000 men and 2,000 ships. It performed great feats in moving men and supplies across the Atlantic.

PEACE IDEALS AND WAR HATREDS

Ever since the hesitant entrance of the United States into the war, official agencies and private groups, from President Wilson and the Committee on Public Information to the yellow press, had sought to mold the minds of Americans. In conflicting ways they tried to explain the significance of the war, encourage Ameri-

**The Sedition
Act
[1918]**

*Be it enacted. . . . Whoever, when the United States is at war, shall
wilfully make or convey false reports or false statements with intent to
interfere with the operation or success of the military or naval forces of
the United States . . . or . . . obstruct the sale by the United States of
bonds . . . or incite . . . insubordination, disloyalty, mutiny, or refusal of
duty in the military or naval forces of the United States, or shall wilfully
obstruct . . . the recruiting or enlistment service . . . [or] wilfully utter,
print, write, or publish any disloyal, profane, scurrilous, or abusive
language about the form of government of the United States, or the
Constitution of the United States, or the military or naval forces of the
United States, or the flag . . . or the uniform of the Army or Navy of
the United States . . . or shall wilfully . . . urge, incite, or advocate any
curtailment of production in this country of any thing or things . . .
necessary or essential to the prosecution of the war . . . and whoever
shall wilfully advocate, teach, defend, or suggest the doing of any of the
acts or things . . . enumerated . . . shall be punished by a fine of not
more than $10,000 or imprisonment for not more than twenty years, or
both. . . .*

---

cans in its vigorous pursuit, and prepare them
for the peace to follow. As is all too easy in such
circumstances, Americans learned readily to
hate the Germans and German sympathizers
but prepared themselves less well to assume a
commanding role in maintaining a just peace in
the postwar world. This in the end was to be
the tragedy of President Wilson, of the American people, and consequently of all mankind.

Even before America entered the war,
President Wilson had begun a series of idealistic addresses outlining the nature of the postwar world he wished to see emerge. He talked
then of "peace without victory" and the right of
the several submerged nationalities in Europe
to organize governments of their own choosing.
He asserted too that the American people
would be willing to join a postwar association of
nations. Many Americans of good will, like the
members of the League to Enforce Peace,
thrilled to Wilson's words. But his speeches remained merely words, since Wilson had not
bound the Allies to his conditions as a basis for
American intervention. And he seemed to reinforce the distinction between the United States
and the Allies through the fiction that we were
fighting Germany separately as an "associated
power."

After American entrance Wilson had discovered that the Allies had made secret treaties among themselves. These treaties divided
among the Allies the enemy's colonies as spoils
of the war. The new Bolshevik government of

Russia publicized some of the treaties; their
terms seemed to run counter to the idealism for
which Wilson was exhorting Americans to
fight. Wilson was sure that in time he could
counteract the treaties and force the British
and French to accept a just peace. On January
8, 1918, he expounded his own war aims, under
fourteen headings, in a speech before a joint
session of Congress.

His Fourteen Points, coming at a time
when all the belligerent peoples were overwhelmingly weary of the war, met with an
enthusiastic response among liberals and
working people in the United States, in the Allied nations, and throughout the world. Even
many Germans welcomed them and a later
clarification of them, "the five particulars," as
the promise of a democratic Germany that
could assume a position of equality among nations. They were the most stirring and effective
piece of propaganda the war produced.

It was not clear that Wilson had the American people behind him, even though his Committee on Public Information had been engaged in a large-scale effort to sell the war.
George Creel, a progressive newspaperman
who had worked in the 1916 presidential campaign, headed the committee. He persuaded
newspapers to engage in voluntary self-
censorship, an idea not entirely palatable to
them. The committee disseminated countless
tons of propaganda, and enlisted the services
of 150,000 writers, lecturers, actors, and artists.

Throughout the country, 75,000 such volunteers arose to speak on almost every conceivable occasion. Throughout the United States and the world, 75 million pieces of printed matter carried the American view of the war. Much of what the Creel Committee disseminated was idealistic, in keeping with Wilson's speeches and the Fourteen Points, depicting the war as a great crusade for humanity. Much also, unfortunately, appealed more to fear and hate than to a spirit of altruistic sacrifice.

Throughout the country spread a hysterical hatred of all that seemed unpatriotic. Congress reflected and encouraged the hysteria by passing stern laws for the suppression of dissent. The Espionage Act of June 15, 1917, provided penalties running up to a $10,000 fine and twenty years' imprisonment, not only for those engaged in espionage, sabotage, and obstruction of the war effort, but even for those who should "willfully cause or attempt to cause insubordination, mutiny, or refusal of duty" or "willfully obstruct the recruiting or enlistment service." The law also empowered the postmaster general to ban from the mails any matter that in his opinion was seditious. The Trading-with-the-Enemy Act of October 1917 established censorship over international communications and the foreign-language press (in addition to authorizing various types of economic warfare against the Germans).

These measures were vigorously, and at times capriciously, enforced, but the administration sought still greater punitive powers to discipline the disloyal. Congress responded with the Sabotage Act of April 20, 1918, aimed primarily at the IWW, and the Sedition Act of May 16, 1918. The Sedition Act, modeled after a Montana statute for suppressing the IWW, was harsh beyond any previous legislation in American history. The enforcement of these laws was almost as stern as any lynch mob could desire. Over 1,500 were arrested for seditious utterances, though only 10 were taken into custody for sabotage. The force of the laws continued unabated after the armistice. In the fall of 1918, after a four-day trial, the Socialist leader, Eugene V. Debs, who had been pacifist, not pro-German, was sentenced to ten years in a federal penitentiary under the Espionage Act; in March 1919 the Supreme Court upheld his conviction.

Whatever pacifist or pro-German offenders escaped the federal net were likely to be caught in the meshes of state sedition laws, or to suffer the wrath of vigilantes. The furor was rather ludicrous in some ways, as sauerkraut became "liberty cabbage," and hamburger, "liberty sausage." It was a bit less funny to ban all German music, the teaching of the German language, or the keeping of German books in public libraries, as was done in many places. And it was frightening when a vigilance committee in Minnesota, having forbidden a pastor to speak German, caught him praying at the bedside of a dying woman who spoke only German, tarred and feathered him and rode him out of town on a rail.

THE AEF IN FRANCE

American strategic plans were drawn up after the country entered the war, and essentially these plans were developed in France at the headquarters of the commanding general of the American Expeditionary Force (AEF), John J. Pershing, a highly intelligent officer and a driving personality.

Pershing's goal was to build an American force in France numbering 1 million men by June 1, 1918. Many obstacles stood between him and his objective, as he came to realize after he arrived in Paris on June 14, 1917. The dispirited Allies stood on the defensive against the desperately aggressive enemy; they needed fresh American troops but wished to use them piecemeal as reinforcements along their own weary lines. They did not like Pershing's insistence that the Americans should operate as a separate army; they had no reason to trust the untried American soldiers or officers. In truth, there had been nothing in American military activities during the Spanish-American War and the Mexican intervention to warrant confidence. But General Pershing stood firm, with President Wilson behind him.

In the winter of 1917–1918 the Germans knocked the Russians out of the war. Lenin and his followers in Russia overthrew the constitutional government of Kerensky and opened peace negotiations. Meanwhile, the Germans along with the Austrians delivered a near fatal blow to the Italians at Caporetto. The stunned Allies organized a Supreme War Council and looked desperately to the United States for manpower. Pershing gradually had been building port facilities, running railroads

Captain Edward V. Rickenbacker and Other Pilots of the 94th Pursuit Squadron

The "hat-in-the-ring" squadron, as it was popularly known, was the first American-trained squadron to engage in combat. It began operations on April 3, 1918. The overall record of the Americans, who engaged for the most part in individual combat against German aviators flying the superior Fokker planes, was not impressive. At the armistice they constituted only 10 percent of the Allied air power. Individually they were brave to the point of foolhardiness—they refused to wear parachutes. The exploits of the seventy-one American aces (those who shot down five or more enemy airplanes) were followed eagerly at home by newspaper readers hungry for heroes. Captain Rickenbacker (center), who shot down at least twenty-six German planes, became more famous than most generals. (National Archives)

across France, and constructing training camps and supply dumps. As a trickle of troops began to arrive, he tried to give them three months' training before putting them into combat. While the number was small, he was willing to brigade his units temporarily among the Allies to give them experience and to meet emergencies. Thus the First Division went into action with the French in Lorraine in October 1917 and took over a quiet sector of its own near Toul in January 1918.

In the early months of 1918 Germany moved troops from the east and slammed them against the Allies in a series of great offensives designed to end the war before a significant number of Americans could arrive. The Ger-

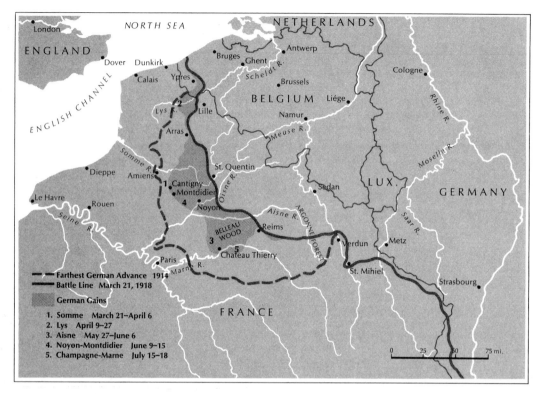

Major German Offensives   1918

mans had not succeeded by July 1, when Pershing had his million soldiers in France.

On May 30 the Germans had crossed the Marne River at Château-Thierry and threatened Paris fifty miles away. American and French troops, under the French command, fought to blunt the German drive. After a week of bitter counterattacking, the Americans recaptured Belleau Wood and thus helped stabilize the line. A little farther south at Reims, in the great bulge toward Paris, the Germans tried on July 15, the morning after Bastille Day, to crash through the French lines. Some 85,000 American troops helped repel the German thrust. By July 18 the German offensive was over; and the Allies began a counteroffensive, with American divisions participating, to liquidate the Marne salient (outward projection in the battle line). By August 6 it was gone.

In the months that followed, as American troops disembarked at a rate averaging 263,000 per month, the reinvigorated Allies pressed the exhausted Germans from Lorraine to the North Sea. On August 12 Pershing for the first time launched an offensive under his own command. He directed the First Army, consisting of 550,000 American troops, against the St. Mihiel salient protruding south of Verdun. Within thirty-six hours the drive had succeeded.

On September 26, 1918, the Americans began to advance along a 24-mile front in the Argonne Forest, as part of a grand, 200-mile-wide offensive, which was to continue for a total of forty-seven days. The American troops fought through what Pershing described as a "vast network of uncut barbwire, the deep ravines, dense woods, myriads of shell craters, and a heavy fog." The Allied high command had not imagined the Americans could make much progress against these obstacles, but after October 4 the regrouped army advanced. By the end of the month it had overrun almost all of the enemy's fixed positions, was beyond the Argonne Forest, and was driving toward vital German communications. On November 7 the Americans established bridgeheads across the

Meuse River, planted their guns looking down on the famous fortress of Sedan, and cut the railroad that carried German supplies to the front. It had been the greatest battle in which American troops had ever fought. The 1.2 million soldiers had used a greater weight of ammunition than had all of the Union forces through the four years of the Civil War.

During the Argonne fighting, other American divisions were deployed elsewhere along the front. All together, Americans participated in thirteen major operations, of which only two were under Pershing's command. By early November the weight of American troops was becoming irresistible; 2 million of them were serving in France.

All along the line, millions of Allied troops had pushed back the Germans, whose reserves were gone, regiments weakened, and communications threatened. They faced an invasion of their own country. They began to seek an armistice, a temporary cease-fire. Pershing, convinced that the Allies should demand a sur-render instead, would have liked to push on to Berlin, to make the Germans really feel the war. The day after the Americans reached Sedan, German envoys crossed the lines to meet the Allied Commander in Chief, the French General Ferdinand Foch, and receive armistice terms from him—terms so stiff that a resumption of hostilities would be impossible. The Germans accepted, and on November 11, 1918, the armistice went into effect.

Rejoicing Americans credited their armies with winning the decisive battles—"We won the war." Beyond question they had supplied the margin of victory. Still, the really crushing burden of the war had not fallen upon the American troops or the American people. The United States lost 112,000 men from enemy action or disease; 237,000 more were wounded. By comparison 1,385,000 French and 900,000 British died. Only 7 percent of the soldiers from the United States were casualties, compared with 73 percent of those from France and 36 percent of those from the British Empire.

U.S. Participation in Allied Offensives 1918

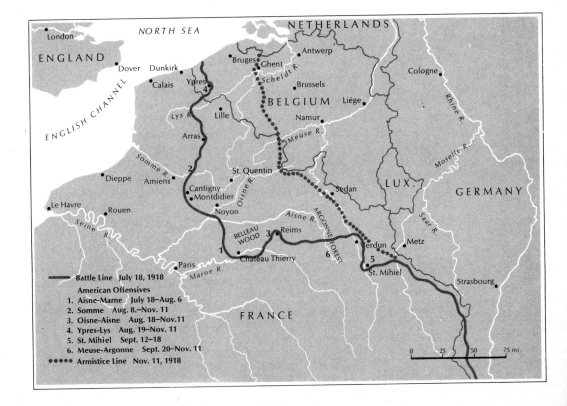

Battle Line July 18, 1918

American Offensives
1. Aisne-Marne   July 18–Aug. 6
2. Somme   Aug. 8.–Nov. 11
3. Oisne-Aisne   Aug. 18–Nov.11
4. Ypres-Lys   Aug. 19–Nov. 11
5. St. Mihiel   Sept. 12–18
6. Meuse-Argonne   Sept. 20–Nov. 11

•••• Armistice Line Nov. 11, 1918

A Frustrated Peace

Wilson planned to attend the peace conference in person, and there he hoped to represent the masses of the world. Before the conference began, however, he had cause to wonder whether he would have even the people of the United States behind him.

REPUDIATION AT THE POLLS

Though the war had raised the income of millions of previously low-paid Americans, the Wilson administration failed to get the approval of a majority of the voters in the congressional elections of 1918. Throughout the war, Wilson had faced dissension within his own party as some of his congressional leaders of agrarian progressive background fought drastic war measures, helped impose heavy taxation on the more well-to-do, and hurried through wartime prohibition and a prohibition amendment to the Constitution. City Democrats were particularly unhappy over losing their beer. Southern Democrats prevented the limiting of the price of cotton while the price of wheat was controlled. The Midwestern grain belt, as a result, reacted angrily against all Democrats.

Even before the 1918 elections, it seemed likely that conditions at home would influence voters more than policies abroad. Nevertheless, with the war obviously almost over, the President put the election on the basis of high international policy. On October 24 he declared: "The return of a Republican majority to either house of the Congress would . . . be interpreted on the other side of the water as a repudiation of my leadership." This outraged those Republicans who had supported him in his foreign policy, since he had earlier declared "politics is adjourned" for the duration of the war. The fact that the Republicans captured both houses of Congress in 1918 would itself have a serious effect on foreign policy; the effect was exaggerated by Wilson's ill-considered appeal.

THE ARMISTICE

Repudiation at the polls created a sad atmosphere for Wilson's assumption of peace negotiations. The President, like the nation, was tense and tired, but he was ready to drive ahead. He strove to pull his own country and the reluctant Allies with him in his determination to make the Fourteen Points and especially the fourteenth—the League of Nations—a reality.

The pulling and hauling with the Allies went on through most of October 1918, during the negotiations that led to the armistice. The Germans sought through Wilson an armistice based on the Fourteen Points. The Allies denied even knowing what these points were, for the Allies were by no means ready to give up their claims for reparations and annexations. Only after Wilson had twice threatened to negotiate a separate peace were they willing to present a united façade. The Allies seemed to agree to the Fourteen Points in entirety, except for explicit reservations on reparations and freedom of the seas, and this apparent agreement led the Germans to expect generous treatment. Further misunderstanding developed because, while the Allies laid down military and naval terms that would make it impossible for the Germans to resume warfare, they used the term "armistice," which meant a negotiated pause in hostilities, rather than the word "surrender." What followed at Versailles was a conclave of victors dictating to a vanquished country, not a negotiated peace or the peace without victory that Wilson had once recommended.

The armistice that went into effect on November 11, 1918, provided that the Allies would negotiate peace on the basis of the Fourteen Points. The Germans agreed to withdraw their forces from France and Belgium and to surrender huge quantities of matériel. They accepted what was virtually the unconditional surrender of their fleet. While the peace was being drafted, the Allied blockade continued.

To the Allies as they assembled in Paris, there seemed no need to consult Germany on the nature of the peace. Indeed, the only obstacle to the kind of postwar world they had planned in their secret treaties was President Wilson. He made the unprecedented decision to leave the United States and attend the peace conference in person. Colonel House and other advisers urged him not to go.

**Summary
of the
Fourteen
Points
[1918]**

I. Open covenants of peace, openly arrived at. . . .

II. Absolute freedom of navigation upon the seas. . . .

III. The removal, so far as possible, of all economic barriers, and the establishment of an equality of trade conditions among all the nations consenting to the peace and associating themselves for its maintenance.

IV. Adequate guarantees given and taken that national armaments will be reduced to the lowest point consistent with domestic safety.

V. A free, open-minded, and absolutely impartial adjustment of all colonial claims. . . .

VI. The evacuation of all Russian territory. . . .

VII. Belgium, the whole world will agree, must be evacuated and restored. . . .

VIII. All French territory should be freed and the invaded portions . . . and . . . Alsace-Lorraine . . . [restored].

IX. A readjustment of the frontiers of Italy should be effected along clearly recognizable lines of nationality.

X. The peoples of Austria-Hungary . . . should be accorded the freest opportunity of autonomous development.

XI. Rumania, Serbia, and Montenegro should be evacuated . . . Serbia accorded free and secure access to the sea. . . .

XII. The Turkish portions of the present Ottoman Empire should be assured a secure sovereignty, but the other nationalities . . . should be assured . . . autonomous development, and the Dardanelles should be permanently opened. . . .

XIII. An independent Polish state should be erected . . . which should be assured free and secure access to the sea. . . .

XIV. A general association of nations must be formed. . . .

Wilson seriously miscalculated in refusing to take with him as one of the peace commissioners a leading Republican like Elihu Root or William Howard Taft. He would have done well, too, to include one of the powerful Republican senators, since it would take many Republican votes to muster the requisite two-thirds majority for the treaty in the Senate. Nevertheless, Wilson took only a nonpolitical Republican diplomat, Henry White, and relied neither upon him nor upon the other commissioners.

Arriving in Europe in December 1918, before the other European leaders were ready to confer, Wilson toured France, Italy, and England. Wherever he went hysterically cheering crowds greeted him; everywhere boulevards and plazas were renamed for him. The cheering millions reinforced his feeling that he was the spokesman for humanity. He was not aware that in each nation these masses looked to him to obtain for them much that ran contrary to the Fourteen Points. A little later, when he fought against some of their national claims, their adulation evaporated into disillusion.

WILSON AT VERSAILLES

The sessions at Paris began January 12, 1919, in an atmosphere of idealism tinctured with national aggrandizement, amidst glittering scenes reminiscent of the Congress of Vienna. To the east, however, there was an urgency born of imminent starvation and the threatening spread of Communism. Hoover, trying to get food into central Europe to fend off both threats, declared: "The wolf is at the door of the world." One of the greatest difficulties was that Russia, where Red Bolsheviks were still fighting White counterrevolutionaries, was entirely unrepresented.

At the outset Wilson had to struggle to prevent a division of spoils under the secret treaties. He tried to block the Japanese from obtaining permanently the German treaty rights in the Shantung peninsula of China and the former German islands north of the Equator in the Pacific, which could be Japanese strongholds. He had to give way, however, to the insistence of the British that they honor the treaty promises with which they had lured the

Japanese into the war. Wilson with more success persuaded the Allies to hold former German colonies and Turkish territories on a basis of trusteeship responsible to the League of Nations. This was the new and unprecedented "mandate" system.

Simultaneously, Wilson worked on the drafting of the League Covenant. He insisted that it form the first part of the treaty and be inseparable from it, and he labored long and hard to draft it in meticulous detail. In the League Covenant he saw the one possible way of overriding the vengeful selfishness that seemed dominant among the victorious nations. Whatever imperfections and inequities there were in the treaty he thought could be rectified through the League: through it and it alone, the world could avoid future wars. In the League he envisaged a potentially powerful (but not armed) international organization through which the nations of the world could share responsibility in maintaining the security of all against any aggressor.

At the end of February 1919, as Congress prepared to adjourn, Wilson came home to sign bills. He brought with him the League Covenant, determined that he would force the Senate to accept it without compromise. The acclaim with which Bostonians greeted him, the friendliness of editorials in most newspapers, and the energy with which large and influential organizations advocated the League, all encouraged him to think public sentiment was overwhelmingly behind him. When Colonel House warned him he must be prepared to compromise with the Senate, he retorted: "I have found that you get nothing in this world that is worth-while without fighting for it."

A stiff fight was taking form. In the Senate, on March 4, 1919, Henry Cabot Lodge produced a round robin signed by thirty-nine senators, a number sufficient to block the treaty, announcing that they would not accept the Covenant in its existing form. Wilson, about to reembark for Paris, retorted angrily. But back at the conference he did obtain some of the amendments upon which the Senate would obviously insist. These provided that a nation need not accept a mandate against its will, that a member could withdraw with two years' notice, that the League would not regulate immigration and other internal matters, and that it would not infringe upon the Monroe Doctrine. The Republican senators, however, were not

appeased. Many of them saw in the struggle over the Covenant a means of embarrassing Wilson, stripping him of some of his glory, and developing a winning issue for the campaign of 1920.

While Wilson was obtaining revisions to the Covenant, the conference was also grappling with the critical problem of Germany and the remaking of the European map. Together with the British prime minister, Lloyd George, Wilson resisted the French proposal to break up western Germany into buffer states. He did sanction the return of Alsace-Lorraine to France, and the establishment of a strong Poland and Czechoslovakia on Germany's borders, all in keeping with the national self-determination clauses of the Fourteen Points. He also supported German demilitarization, long-term Allied occupation of the west bank of the Rhine, and an Anglo-French-American mutual defense pact (which was never ratified). If maintained, these security provisions should have prevented the resurgence of Germany as a military menace to the West.

Elsewhere the remapping of Europe proceeded rather fitfully. Italy obtained the Brenner Pass area, in which 200,000 Austrians lived, then was outraged at not also receiving Fiume, which Wilson felt must be a port for the new nation of Yugoslavia. In this region and others, the economic needs of nations conflicted with the principle of national self-determination of peoples. Back in the United States, ethnic groups were ready to clamor for more for their native countries. The Irish in the United States insisted that Wilson should fight for national self-determination for Ireland, wracked by civil war. Wilson took up the matter privately with Lloyd George but did not make a public stand.

Wilson's most important departure from the Fourteen Points was his acceptance of British and French demands for heavy reparations from the Germans. Even before the armistice, he had partly accepted the demands that Germany pay for civilian damages. At the conference, he permitted these demands to cover even pensions for veterans; the astronomical sum was to be set later by a reparations commission. Meanwhile, though Wilson himself for years had taken an economic-determinism view of the origins of the war, the other powers insisted that Germany must accept sole responsibility for starting it. The "war-guilt" clause and the reparations bill embittered the German people. Even in the United States, the harsh peace meted out against Germany disillusioned many liberals and alienated them from Wilson. They regarded the treaty as a "hell's brew" which would ultimately lead to another war.

THE LEAGUE REJECTED

Wilson returned to the United States confident that the Senate, despite the difficulties Lodge was stirring up, would ratify the treaty. On July 10, 1919, when he presented it to the Senate, he asked rhetorically: "Dare we reject it and break the heart of the world?"

Through a combination of coercion and compromise he might have brought about ratification. But he was suffering from hardening of the arteries and, while in Paris, had been so ill that he may have been close to a stroke. His physical condition robbed him of political suppleness; instead of using patience and tact, he was more likely to shower his opponents with self-righteous anger.

Wilson's opponents in the Senate were moved by both principle and partisanship. The fourteen "irreconcilables" were men of conscience, of Middle Western or Far Western progressive tradition, like Republicans William E. Borah of Idaho, Hiram Johnson of California, and Robert M. La Follette of Wisconsin, and Democrat James Reed of Missouri. They acted from a deep conviction that their nation could best be served by staying out of the League. Other opponents with less conviction were more concerned with constructing a winning issue for the Republicans in the 1920 election than they were with assuring the future of the world. Senator Lodge, applying all his brilliant intellect to his loathing for Wilson, was ready, as chairman of the Senate Foreign Relations Committee, to use every possible tactic to obstruct, delay, and defeat the treaty. Public sentiment seemed to favor ratification, and Lodge needed time to marshal forces against it. Consequently, he spent the first two weeks after it reached the committee reading aloud every word on its nearly 300 pages. Next, he held a full six weeks of public hearings, listening to the complaints of every disgruntled minority.

From the White House, Wilson did some conferring with Republican senators. He explained to them that he considered the collec-

tive-security provision of Article X (according to which League members guaranteed one another's territorial integrity) to be more of a moral obligation upon the United States than a legal one — but to Wilson moral obligations were the more important. The senators were not impressed; it began to appear that Wilson would have to accept some of Lodge's reservations if he wished to obtain ratification. When one senator told him this, he retorted: "Never! Never! . . . I'll appeal to the country!"

So Wilson, at the end of his physical resources, against the stern warnings of his physician, undertook a cross-country speaking tour, writing his speeches as he went along, delivering them night after night. In twenty-two days he traveled over 8,000 miles, giving thirty-six addresses averaging an hour in length. At first the halls were not entirely filled nor were his speeches always well polished. As the tour proceeded, he gained larger and more enthusiastic audiences and grew more eloquent in his moral fervor. Had it been possible to sway the United States Senate through public opinion, the tour might have been a success. But Wilson became more and more frail. Finally after speaking at Pueblo, Colorado, September 25, he suffered such acute headaches that he had to cancel the tour and return to Washington.

Then he suffered an acute stroke which partially paralyzed his left side. For two weeks he was close to death, and for six more weeks so seriously ill that he could attend only to what little business his devoted wife and doctor thought would not unduly upset or fatigue him. When some officials tried to see the President on vital matters, Mrs. Wilson turned them away, saying: "I am not interested in the President of the United States. I am interested in my husband and his health."

At this critical juncture the Senate Foreign Relations Committee finally reported the treaty, recommending forty-five amendments and three reservations. Lodge managed to marshal the Republican senators so well that in November he obtained adoption of fourteen reservations. By this time Wilson had recovered sufficiently to give stern directions to the Democratic minority: they must vote only for the treaty without any reservations whatsoever. Although none of the Lodge reservations would have devitalized the League, Wilson preferred no ratification of the treaty to ratification with reservations. While he was by no means his old self, he was able to exert power enough to maintain discipline over the loyal Democrats. When the vote came on November 19, 1919, forty-two Democrats joined with the thirteen Republican irreconcilables to vote down the treaty with reservations. Next, the Senate voted on ratification of the treaty without reservations. There were thirty-eight sena-

tors, all but one of them a Democrat, who voted for it; fifty-five voted against it.

On the day of the final vote, March 19, 1920, when the Senate considered the treaty with fifteen reservations, it came within 7 votes of receiving the requisite two-thirds majority. By this time, President Wilson was looking to the election of 1920 as a "solemn referendum" on the League issue.

Selected Readings

T. R. and the Far East
H. K. Beale, *Theodore Roosevelt and the Rise of America to World Power** (1956); C. E. Neu, *An Uncertain Friendship: Theodore Roosevelt and Japan, 1906–1909* (1967); R. A. Esthus, *Theodore Roosevelt and Japan* (1966); T. A. Bailey, *Theodore Roosevelt and the Japanese-American Crisis* (1934); Tyler Dennett, *Roosevelt and the Russo-Japanese War* (1924); P. J. Treat, *Diplomatic Relations Between the United States and Japan, 1895–1905* (1938); E. H. Zabriskie, *American-Russian Rivalry in the Far East, 1895–1914* (1946); W. R. Braisted, *The United States Navy in the Pacific, 1897–1909* (1958); M. H. Hunt, *Frontier Defense and the Open Door: Manchuria in Chinese-American Relations, 1895–1911* (1973).

Caribbean Policy
Dexter Perkins, *The United States and the Caribbean* (1947); D. G. Munro, *Intervention and Dollar Diplomacy in the Caribbean, 1900–1921* (1964); W. H. Callcott, *The Caribbean Policy of the United States, 1890–1920* (1942); Gerstle Mack, *The Land Divided: A History of the Panama Canal and Other Canal Projects* (1944); D. C. Miner, *The Fight for the Panama Route* (1940); D. F. Healy, *The United States in Cuba, 1898–1902* (1963); G. K. Lewis, *Puerto Rico: Freedom and Power in the Caribbean** (1967).

Mexican Relations
D. M. Pletcher, *Rails, Mines, and Progress: Seven American Promoters in Mexico, 1867–1911* (1959); C. C. Clendenen, *The United States and Pancho Villa: A Study in Unconventional Diplomacy* (1961); R. E. Quirk, *An Affair of Honor: Woodrow Wilson and the Occupation of Vera Cruz* (1962).

Wilsonian Diplomacy
Harley Notter, *The Origins of the Foreign Policy of Woodrow Wilson* (1937); A. S. Link, *Wilson the Diplomatist** (1957); N. G. Levin, Jr., *Woodrow Wilson and World Politics: America's Response to War and Revolution* (1968); R. E. Osgood, *Ideals and Self-Interest in America's Foreign Relations* (1953).

Going to War
E. R. May, *The World War and American Isolation, 1914–1917** (1959); E. H. Buehrig, *Woodrow Wilson and the Balance of Power* (1955); Charles Seymour, *American Diplomacy During the World War* (1934) and *American Neutrality, 1914–1917* (1935); Walter Millis, *Road to War: America, 1914–1917* (1935); E. M. Borchard and W. P. Lage, *Neutrality for the United States* (1937); C. C. Tansill, *America Goes to War* (1938); Armin Rappaport, *The Navy League of the United States* (1962); R. H. Heindel, *The American Impact on Great Britain, 1898–1914* (1940); Bradford Perkins, *The Great Rapprochement: England and the United States, 1895–1914* (1968).

Combat
E. M. Coffman, *The War to End All Wars: The American Military Experience in World War I* (1969); H. A. De Weerd, *President Wilson Fights His War: World War I and the American Intervention* (1968); D. F. Trask, *The United States in the Supreme War Council: American War Aims and Inter-Allied Strategy, 1917–1918* (1961); J. G. Harbord, *The American Army in France, 1917–1919* (1936); Frank Freidel, *Over There: The Story of America's First Great Overseas Crusade* (1964), a pictorial history; E. E. Morison, *Admiral Sims and the Modern American Navy* (1942); J. J. Hudson, *Hostile Skies: A Combat History of the American Air Service in World War I* (1968).

The Home Front
F. L. Paxson, *American Democracy and the World War* (3 vols., 1936–1948); S. W. Livermore, *Politics Is Adjourned: Woodrow Wilson and the War Congress, 1916–1918* (1966); D. R. Beaver, *Newton D. Baker and the American War Effort, 1917–1919* (1966); Margaret Coit, *Mr. Baruch* (1957); B. M. Baruch, *American Industry in the War* (1941); H. N. Scheiber, *The Wilson Administration and Civil Liberties, 1917–1921* (1960); H. C. Peterson and G. C. Fite, *Opponents of War, 1917–1918* (1957); J. R. Mock and Cedric Larson, *Words That Won the War* (1939); H. C. Peterson, *Propaganda for War* (1939).

Peacemaking

R. J. Bartlett, *The League to Enforce Peace* (1944); H. R. Rudin, *Armistice, 1918* (1944); L. E. Gelfand, *The Inquiry: American Preparations for Peace, 1917–1919* (1963); T. A. Bailey, *Woodrow Wilson and the Lost Peace** (1944) and *Woodrow Wilson and the Great Betrayal** (1945); L W. Martin, *Peace Without Victory: Woodrow Wilson and the British Liberals* (1958); D. F. Fleming, *The United States and the League of Nations, 1918–1920* (1932); J. M. Keynes, *Economic Consequences of the Peace* (1919); Herbert Hoover, *The Ordeal of Woodrow Wilson* (1958); J. A Garraty, *Henry Cabot Lodge* (1953).

*Titles available in paperback.

The Illusion of Normalcy

VOL. LXXVI...No. 25,319.   • • •   NEW YORK, SATURDAY, MAY 21, 1927.

LINDBERGH SPEEDS ACROSS NO[
KEEPING TO SCHEDULE OF 100 [
SIGHTED PASSING ST. JOHN'S,

LOWMAN GETS POST AS ANDREWS QUITS IN BIG DRY SHIFT

Mellon, in Same Stroke, Names Chief Chemist Doran Commissioner in Place of Haynes.

STEP TO CHECK FRICTION

Andrews Will Retire Aug. 1 With Work Completed—Haynes Is Forced Out in Shake-Up.

MOVE SATISFIES ALL SIDES

Both Nominees Are on Record as Prohibition Advocates and Are Acceptable to Dry League.

Special to The New York Times.

WASHINGTON, May 20.—In the most drastic overturn in the history of dry enforcement, which is expected to lead to further changes in the Washington headquarters as well as in the field, Secretary Mellon at one stroke today accepted the resignation of General Lincoln C. Andrews of New York, as Assistant Secretary of the Treasury in charge of prohibition enforcement, and appointed a successor to Major Roy A. Haynes of Ohio, the Acting Commissioner of Prohibition.

Mr. Mellon designated Seymour W. Lowman, former Lieutenant Governor of New York, for Presidential appointment to the post of General Andrews and named Dr. James M. Doran of North Dakota, now Chief Chemist of the Prohibition Unit, to be Prohibition Commissioner in place of Major Haynes.

Mr. Lowman is expected to enter upon his duties as Assistant Secretary on Aug. 1, assuming jurisdiction over the Customs and Prohibition Bureaus and the Coast Guard. Dr. Doran will take charge of the Prohibition Bureau at once.

End of Factionalism Expected.

Hope was expressed today by Administration officials that the retirement of General Andrews and Major Haynes would end the factionalism in the Prohibition Bureau, which, in their opinion, has tended to lessen the efficiency of enforcement. Major Haynes, a former officer of the Anti-Saloon League, has been at swords' points with his Treasury superiors for years and the law enforcement work of General Andrews has been frequently criticized by Wayne B. Wheeler and others associated with the Anti-Saloon League.

Major Haynes's failure to land the Prohibition Commissionership is regarded here as a defeat for the Anti-Saloon League and a victory for dry leaders who do not train with the Wheeler organization. At the same time league officials take comfort from the prospective retirement of General Andrews, whom they have long regarded as "unfriendly" to their purposes.

Party Chiefs Sponsored Lowman.

Mr. Lowman was endorsed for the assistant secretaryship by National Committeeman Hilles and Ogden L. Mills, Under Secretary of the Treasury. He was the running mate of Mr. Mills on the Republican gubernatorial ticket in New York last year, and has a record as a dry that makes him acceptable to most of the dry leaders. He was originally considered for Commissioner of Prohibition, but a switch was made when General Andrews gave notice of his resignation.

It is assumed here that Secretary Mellon consulted with the President before he announced his designation of Mr. Lowman. Mr. Lowman will come to Washington on June 1 to familiarize himself with the duties of his new office, but he does not expect to be sworn in until General Andrews quits on Aug. 1.

No provision has been made for Major Haynes to remain in the dry service and he is expected to resign forthwith. He is now functioning as "Acting Commissioner" under a temporary arrangement that became effective under the reorganization law on April 1.

Major Herbert D. White, special investigator, probably will be named Assistant Commissioner. James E. Jones and L. G. Nutt, who were appointed Deputy Commissioners in April, will remain in those positions at least for the present.

Mellon Stresses Promotion System.

In announcing the appointment of Dr. Doran, Secretary Mellon stated that because of his long service and intimate knowledge of the work, Dr. Doran was well qualified for the post

'Too Old,' Says Hughes at 65, To Ran for the Presidency

Declaring that he was "too old to run for President," Charles Evans Hughes, after reading in the morning papers yesterday of a movement to start a Hughes boom in the event that President Coolidge should decide not to become a candidate for re-election, issued a statement declaring he would not accept a nomination. He was 65 years old April 11.

"I know nothing of the movement to which reference is made," Mr. Hughes said. "There should be no doubt as to my own attitude. I am for President Coolidge, first, last and all the time, and I believe that he will be renominated and re-elected. I do not wish my name to be used in any contingency. I am too old to run for President and I would neither seek nor accept the nomination."

SINCLAIR SENTENCED TO 3 MONTHS IN JAIL

Oil Man Is Also Ordered to Pay $500 Fine for Refusing to Reply to Senators.

APPEALS AND GIVES BOND

Littleton Argues in Vain That His Client Exercised His Constitutional Rights.

Special to The New York Times.

WASHINGTON, May 20.—Harry F. Sinclair, oil operator, under indictment with former Secretary Fall for conspiracy to defraud the Government, was sentenced today to pay a fine of $500 on a charge of contempt of the Senate committee which investigates the naval reserve oil leases. Immediately after Justice William Hitz pronounced the sentence in the District of Columbia Supreme Court, Sinclair gave bond in the sum of $5,000 pending appeal to the Appellate Court.

The penalty was imposed notwithstanding the plea by Martin W. Littleton, Sinclair's counsel, that the Court do nothing which would humiliate, shame, disgrace, mortify or worry his client, and despite Mr. Littleton's argument that the entire proceedings, beginning with Mr. Sinclair's appearance before the Senate committee March 22, 1924, and ending with the sentence, were "irregular."

Mr. Sinclair was originally charged with refusing to answer nine questions by the Senate committee regarding the lease of the Teapot Dome reserve in Wyoming by his Mammoth Oil Company. Sinclair's counsel filed a demurrer, and the number of questions was reduced to six.

A special appeal was then allowed, but the progress of this was blocked by the Walsh bill, initiated by Senator Walsh of Montana, "prosecutor" for the Senate committee, and designed to prevent appeals from interlocutory orders of the criminal courts. Following the passage by Congress of the Walsh bill, Sinclair was tried in April and was convicted. The number of questions involved was reduced at the trial to four.

No Crime, Says Littleton.

When Sinclair stood up for sentence, he declared that he had nothing to say. Mr. Littleton, however, related the history of similar cases, and stated that when he advised Mr. Sinclair to refuse to answer the Senate committee's questions he was not giving his client a "horseback opinion," but an opinion which was founded on substantial law.

"My client has done nothing to warrant this procedure," Mr. Littleton declared. "The question of the right of either house of Congress, acting separately or together, to compel a citizen to testify has never been definitely decided and, in fact, the United States Supreme Court in the case of Kilbourne versus Thompson deliberately refused to decide that question.

"The committee which summoned Mr. Sinclair was denied nothing, nor did he impose a single obstruction in the path of the committee. There is no crime committed here, no offense involving moral turpitude—merely a citizen of the United States who had and exercised a right which belongs to every American gentleman."

The Four Questions Asked.

The four questions which Mr. Sinclair declined to answer, on advice from Mr. Littleton, and which were included in the indictment, follow:

By Senator Walsh—Mr. Sinclair

LINDBERGH LEAVES NEW YORK AT 7:52 A. M.

With Cool Determination He Braves Death to Get Off in the Misty Dawn, Winning Out by Luck and Skill.

PLANE FALTERS AND THEN RISES AND IS OFF

Hundreds Gasp as Unconquerable Youth by Sheer Wizardry Lifts Machine Carrying 5,200-Pound Load, With Failure a Few Yards Off.

By RUSSELL OWEN.

Staff Correspondent of The Times, Who Reported the Polar Flights of Byrd and Amundsen.

Copyright, 1927, by The New York Times Company.

A sluggish, gray monoplane lurched its way down Roosevelt Field yesterday morning, slowly gathering momentum. Inside sat a tall youngster, eyes glued to an instrument board or darting ahead for swift glances at the runway, his face drawn with the intensity of his purpose.

Death lay but a few seconds ahead of him if his skill failed or his courage faltered. For moments, as the heavy plane rose from the ground, dropped down, staggered again into the air and fell, he gambled for his life against a hazard which had already killed four men.

And then slowly, so slowly that those watching it stood fascinated, as if by his indomitable will alone, the young pilot lifted his plane. It dipped and then rose with renewed speed, climbing heavily but steadily toward the distant trees.

The spirit of unconquerable youth had won, and "Slim" Lindbergh was on his way to Paris.

All the romance which had surrounded this boy since his meteoric flight here from the Pacific Coast a week ago reached its climax in that take-off. The uncertainty of it, the frightful disaster which threatened him, the quick recoveries which showed a cool, keen mind fighting for mastery, made veteran pilots gaze in fascination.

"God be with him!" exclaimed Commander Byrd fervently, when at last it seemed that Lindbergh was safely on his way.

The boyish, smiling lad, with the quiet confidence of bravery and belief in his own ability, has won the hearts of every one who came near him. Until two weeks ago he was hardly considered a factor in the race to be first through the air to Paris, that long, treacherous flight of 3,600 miles. And then he came on with speed of the wind, making only one stop between the Pacific Coast and New York, and while rival camps squabbled over money or worked through long, tedious tests, Lindbergh rolled his plane out in the gray dawn and got away, all alone.

Youth Breaks All Barriers.

It may not have been the safest kind of flying; perhaps it was only a daring gesture, but it was magnificent. It was youth refusing to admit obstacles, breaking down barriers, and it brought him luck. For even as Lindbergh prepared his plane the fog that had choked his path to Newfoundland rolled back, and all the way from New York to Europe stretched a clear path of fair weather, with gentle favoring winds. The sun came out as he started, and it seemed that the fates which deal with brave men's lives were smiling at the youth who had defied them.

When Lindbergh made his decision to start just before midnight on Thursday, it seemed the height of folly. Heavy fog settled over Roosevelt Field under inky black skies which dripped slow drops of rain. It was dismal and threatening. But the young pilot, who has guided his temerity with a keen and thoughtful mind, saw in the late weather reports the possibility that the skies might clear to the north. All he needed was one look at Newfoundland before he left the land for his long, weary flight across the sea which had already claimed Nungesser and Coli.

The huge hangar in which his plane was housed was closed to every one except the mechanics, who went over the plane with zealous care and partly filled the gasoline tank. Lindbergh, after a parting word with them, went to the Garden City Hotel at midnight for a brief sleep. He lay down with orders that he be called at 2:15 o'clock in the morning, but before 2 o'clock he was downstairs.

While he had been resting weather reports indicated that the fog was lifting all along the coast, although it was depressingly wet at the field. The clouds had opened and poured down a short deluge, which left puddles in which shone the glare of many lights. Through a small opening in the hangar door the silver nose of Lindbergh's plane gleamed through the glancing rain drops.

Hundreds of people had gathered at midnight, but the rain drove many of them away. There were still about 500 stand-

CAPTAIN CHARLES A. LI[
The First American Flyer to Start on th[York and Paris.

LINDBERGH'S STORY FOR

When next heard from, Lindbergh will u[exploit especially for readers of The Times and[newspapers. It will appear in New York a[

BELLANCA FLIGHT HELD BACK BY WIND

Hop, Set for Dawn, Is Called Off After All Preparations— Bertaud Writ Thown Out.

With Captain Lindbergh well on his way to Paris last night, those connected with the Columbia Aircraft Company's Bellanca monoplane Columbia made arrangements for a hop-off from Roosevelt Field at 4 o'clock this morning. Before midnight Charles A. Levine, backer of the company, made a definite statement that the Bellanca plane would start at daylight.

At 1:30 A. M., however, Clarence Chamberlin, senior pilot of the monoplane, announced that there would be no start today.

"The weather report shows northwest winds, which would give us a head wind all the way to Newfoundland," he said. "We will not make the attempt today."

Levine's statement earlier in the evening was supplemented by additional information from a spokesman for him.

"After a conference at the Hotel Biltmore tonight between Charles A. Levine, Chairman of the Board of Directors of the Columbia Aircraft Corporation, and ex-Senator Charles Lockwood, representing Clarence D. Chamberlin, Mr. Levine decided that as a purely sporting proposition the flight should be made at once," the spokesman said.

He refused to reveal the name of the navigator who had been selected to replace Lloyd Bertaud and accompany Chamberlin on the flight.

"The navigator," he said, "will not be announced until just before the flight."

Lloyd Bertaud was definitely grounded and eliminated from the flight by the decision of Supreme

LONE FRENC[

Lindber[to Pa[Co[

Copyright, 192[Special [

PARIS, Lindbergh[the Atlant[the Frenc[have done.[has tonig[prayers fo[His air and efficie[panied by[French m[real. Amer[the dough[Mihiel an[for sundry[since.

To welco[so huge a[greeted Ca[Coli in he[of all Fran[ica's anxie[arrow fro[denied the[which Cap[makes so g[

As fully[chanic's hav[Lindbergh'[ly, the we[is not so ov[been for so[is not onl[the predic[clouds foll[rising tem[stay in th[help to the[

Twenty-three

ATLANTIC,
ES AN HOUR;
., AT 7:15 P.M.

GETS HIS BEARINGS IN NEWFOUNDLAND

With the First Leg of His Flight to Paris Over, He Puts to Sea and Heads for Ireland

ALL OF THE "BREAKS" ARE IN HIS FAVOR

Fog Disperses, Weather Clears and Gentle Following Winds Help to Speed Him Along on His Hazardous Venture.

Copyright, 1927, by The New York Times Company.
Special Cable to The New York Times.

ST. JOHN'S, N. F., May 20.—Captain Lindbergh's airplane passed over St. John's at 8:15 o'clock tonight [7:15 New York Daylight Saving Time]. It was seen by hundreds and disappeared seaward, heading for Ireland. It is assumed that it passed over Cape Race and places south of this in the dense fog which prevailed there all day.

It was flying quite low between the hills near St. John's and went east over the Signal Hill Station, following the track of Hawker and Greeve and also of Alcock and Brown on the first transatlantic flights eight years ago.

There was intense excitement during the passage of Lindbergh's plane, and citizens motoring in the suburbs or strolling on the country roads are coming back with tales of its transit. Many noted the fact that the flier seemed to be getting his bearing before setting out on the second leg of his flight.

Michael Sullivan, member of the Newfoundland Cabinet, saw the plane while motoring and followed its progress in his car on the road that leads to the signal station, keeping it in sight for several minutes, but when he reached the summit it had passed from sight, so great was its speed.

Robert Job, principal of the firm of Job Brothers, shipping merchants, also saw it and watched its course over the city. He could see it so distinctly as to notice that it had some letters on its side, though he could not make out words.

Strong Wind Is in His Favor.
By The Associated Press.

ST. JOHN'S N. S., Saturday, May 21.—Strong westerly breezes, approaching gale force, were blowing here early tonight and marine authorities declared that they should be of great assistance to Captain Lindbergh in his transatlantic crossing.

It was estimated here that he might reach the Irish coast by daylight.

Leaves American Continent.
Copyright, 1927, by The New York Times Company.
Special to The New York Times.

SYDNEY, N. S., May 20.—Captain Lindbergh got his last sight of the American continent at 5 o'clock [4 o'clock Eastern Daylight Time] this afternoon when he passed out into the Atlantic over Main-a-dieu, Cape Breton. The plane was flying low and at great speed, and her number, 211, was plainly visible to watchers with powerful glasses.

Should Lindbergh succeed in navigating through a fairly dense curtain over the Newfoundland banks he will have fair weather across the North Atlantic, ships at sea reporting good visibility with no indications of a storm within the next twenty-four hours.

By The Associated Press.

HALIFAX, N. S., May 20.—Captain Lindbergh passed over Mulgrave on the Strait of Canso, which separates the mainland of Nova Scotia from Cape Breton Island, at 4:05 P. M. Atlantic Day Time [3:05 o'clock Eastern Daylight Saving Time]. He was flying high and the markings on his gray monoplane could not be seen.

Reaches Nova Scotia Coast.
Copyright, 1927, by The New York Times Company.
Special to The New York Times.

YARMOUTH, N. S., May 20.—Captain Lindbergh passed over New Tusket, about forty miles from here, at 12:45 o'clock this afternoon (11:45 Eastern Daylight Time). He was flying low, but traveling very fast.

By The Associated Press.

MIDDLEBORO, Mass., May 20.—A monoplane, believed to be that of Captain Lindbergh, was seen over West Middleboro about 9:15 this morning flying northeasterly.

Chester Rice, clerk at the Middleboro police station, could not make out the letters on the wings, but is sure the numbers were 211.

Lindbergh Keeps to Schedule.

"America's present need is not heroics, but healing; not nostrums, but normalcy." The year was 1920, and the speaker, with a fine sense of alliteration as well as a feeling for the spirit of the time, was Warren G. Harding, soon to be President of the United States. "The world needs to be reminded that all human ills are not curable by legislation."

Harding's remarks provided a catch phrase for the period following World War I. The American people, or at least the majority of them, were tired of legislation, tired of wartime restrictions, tired of progressive reforms. They wanted a return to "normalcy," to the good old days, to the days that never had existed except in nostalgic reverie.

The days that were to come in the 1920s were old in some respects but new in others. They were old—like those of the late nineteenth century—in respect to the position of big business, which again dominated both government and society. Indeed, business was more sanctified than ever. "The business of America is business," said Calvin Coolidge, who succeeded Harding in the presidency. In *The Man Nobody Knows* (1925), a best seller of the period, Bruce Barton described Jesus Christ as "a startling example of business success," the author of "the most powerful advertisements of all time," and "the founder of modern business."

But much was new in the decade of the twenties. This was the time when the automobile came into its own, with production increasing from 1.5 million cars in 1921 to 4.75 million in 1929, by which year the automotive industry was responsible, directly or indirectly, for the employment of more than 3 million persons. It was the time of the coming of numerous household gadgets: the radio, the refrigerator, the vacuum cleaner, and many others. It was an age when the federal government sought to impose a species of morality by prohibiting the manufacture, sale, or transportation of intoxicating

---

"Lindbergh Speeds Across North Atlantic"
On May 20, 1927, Charles Lindbergh began the first solo nonstop flight from New York to Paris. The trip, which took almost thirty-three and a half hours, made Lindbergh a national hero. (© 1927 by The New York Times Company. Reprinted by permission.)

beverages—and an age of what seemed to many like unprecedented license in speech and behavior, the age of "flaming youth" and of unrestrained dances like the "bunny hug" and the "Charleston."

From 1923 to 1929 it was also a time of remarkable prosperity (for most but by no means all Americans). The people generally assumed—and experts in business, economics, and government told them—that this was veritably a new era in human history. The country had reached a "permanent plateau" of prosperity and need never worry again about the possibility of a serious slump. But prosperity, like "normalcy," proved to be an illusion. Eventually the country fell into much the worst economic depression it had ever known.

The Postwar Reaction

In the immediate postwar years, prices rose and people complained of the "h. c. l.," the high cost of living. Suddenly, in 1921, prices dropped and a brief recession followed, giving way to full recovery by 1923. Meanwhile, fears of radicalism, heightened by the spread of Communism in Russia and elsewhere in Europe, provoked a hysterical spirit of reaction in America.

THE RED SCARE

Union workers tried to preserve their wartime economic gains by striking for higher wages as living costs went upward. In 1919 a great wave of strikes spread across the country, involving about 4 million workers. In many of these strikes—such as those conducted by longshoremen, printers, and laborers in the clothing, textile, telephone, and other industries—the strikers succeeded in raising their living standards. In the process they alienated much of the public, which was quick to accept the industrialists' explanations that higher wages were responsible for higher prices, and that the strike leaders were radicals.

The outbreak of a steel strike in September 1919 brought antilabor feelings to a boil. The grievances of the workers were serious. They were working an average of nearly sixty-nine hours per week for bare subsistence wages and were becoming so discontented that the AFL's organizing committee made rapid headway among them. United States Steel discharged all union men and refused to negotiate with Gompers or any other union official. Some

343,000 men struck in the Chicago area, and additional workers left their jobs in other areas. Despite the workers' valid claims, United States Steel was able to swing public sentiment away from the strikers by claiming that the leaders were Communists. The chief organizer, William Z. Foster, once a follower of Bryan, was to emerge in 1924 as the presidential candidate of the Communist party. The company brought in Negro strikebreakers, and state and federal troops prevented picketing. In rioting at Gary, Indiana, eighteen strikers were killed. Within a few weeks tens of thousands of strikebreakers under armed protection were operating the plants at three-quarters capacity, and by January the workers were starved out.

Public opinion turned even more firmly against organized labor when a police strike broke out in Boston. The policemen were working long hours on prewar salaries under unpleasant conditions. After their organization, the Boston Social Club, obtained an AFL charter and threatened to strike, a Mayor's Citizens Committee prepared to meet their demands except for recognition of their union. The police commissioner, responsible only to the governor, refused and dismissed nineteen leaders. In response, the police struck. As mischief-makers and rowdies took over, horrified citizens put on their military uniforms and, armed with rifles and shotguns, began patrolling the streets. The mayor mobilized state troops and restored order. The following day Governor Calvin Coolidge, who had done nothing to prevent the strike or preserve the peace, suddenly acted. He ordered in troops and backed the decision of the police commissioner never to reemploy any of the strikers. When President Gompers of the AFL appealed to Coolidge, the governor wired back: "There is no right to strike against the public safety, anywhere, anytime." This one telegram made Coolidge a formidable contender for the Republican presidential nomination in 1920.

In Washington Attorney General A. Mitchell Palmer was becoming prominent through his war on both labor and radicals. When the new president of the United Mine Workers, John L. Lewis, took the bituminous coal workers out on strike in November 1919, Palmer smashed the strike with federal court injunctions.

Sacco and Vanzetti Being Taken into Court   1927

When Sacco and Vanzetti were brought before Judge Webster Thayer on April 9, 1927, they were allowed to speak. Sacco said: "I never knew, never heard, even read in history anything so cruel as this Court. . . . I know the sentence will be between two classes, the oppressed class and the rich class, and there will always be collision between one and the other." Vanzetti said: "I am suffering because I am a radical and indeed I am a radical; I have suffered because I was an Italian, and indeed I am an Italian. . . . but I am so convinced to be right that you can only kill me once but if you could execute me two times, and if I could be reborn two other times, I would live again to do what I have done already." Judge Thayer then sentenced them to death. One of the counsel for the two men who did not "belong even remotely to [their] school of thoughts," warned after the execution of "minds that are closed by deep prejudice or transient passion." "If," he declared, "the local hostility was inflamed by foolish words of their sympathizers or wicked deeds of their exploiters, this also is a fact to be recollected." The publisher of the conservative Boston Herald, which had called for an impartial commission to review the case, asserted: "The momentum of the established order required the execution of Sacco and Vanzetti, and never in your life or mine, has that momentum acquired such tremendous force." (Brown Brothers)

Palmer attracted even more attention with his crusade against Reds. Throughout the country the violent suppression of alleged pro-German activities during the war had been continued in the persecution of the Industrial Workers of the World (IWW), the Socialists, and all other left-wingers. Both Congress and the New York state legislature denied seats to Socialists. By 1920 one-third of the states had enacted criminal syndicalist laws to punish radicals. The New York law prohibited "advocating, teaching, or aiding and abetting the commission of crime and sabotage, or unlawful acts of force and violence or unlawful methods of terrorism as a means of accomplishing a change in industrial ownership or control, or affecting any political change."

Bombings and attempted bombings captured the headlines. A bomb damaged the front of Palmer's home in June 1919; bombs addressed to a number of government leaders were discovered in the mails; a year later an explosion on Wall Street killed thirty-eight people. Four members of the newly founded American Legion were killed in an attack on IWW headquarters in Centralia, Washington, on Armistice Day 1919. These incidents furnished the material out of which the newspapers, with some aid from Palmer, built a great national panic. Within the country there were very few radicals to undertake a revolution: IWW membership was down to 35,000 and continued to decline; the Socialist party numbered 39,000 and was not revolutionary anyway; the Communist-Labor party (left-wing Socialists) had 10,000 to 30,000 members; and the Communist party, organized September 1, 1919, had 30,000 to 60,000.

Palmer's goal was to ferret out and eliminate the Communists. He proposed a sedition bill so drastic that Congress would not enact it, then he proceeded anyway without it. The Labor Department had already arrested and deported to Finland 249 Russian Communists. Nevertheless, Palmer, without advance notice to the Labor Department, conducted a great Red roundup on January 1, 1920, jailing some 6,000 suspects. Communists who were United States citizens he turned over to states for prosecution. The aliens came under the jurisdiction of the Labor Department, which gave them fair treatment. Only 556 proved Communists were deported.

In Massachusetts, a payroll robbery and murder in April 1920 led to the trial and conviction of two anarchists, Nicola Sacco and Bartolomeo Vanzetti. Many believers in civil liberties felt that the two men were being prosecuted more on the basis of their radicalism than on the criminal evidence. Ultimately throughout the country and even in western Europe, outraged liberals and radicals demanded the release of the two men, but in August 1927 they were executed. The Sacco and Vanzetti case was a *cause célèbre* of the 1920s.

XENOPHOBIA AND NEGROPHOBIA

War propaganda had stimulated a demand for "one hundred percent Americanism" and had aroused a feeling of hatred against the enemy, the "Hun." After the war, defeated Germany no longer served as an object of hate, yet the wartime emotion could not be immediately turned off. Much of it was redirected against radicals, racial and ethnic minorities, and other allegedly "un-American" groups within the United States.

On the part of rural Americans, especially native white Protestants, there had long been a suspicion of big cities, crowded as these were with immigrants, many of whom were Roman Catholics. Now, as the census of 1920 revealed, the urban population had come to outnumber the rural. This was seen as a menace to the traditional values of the small town and the farm.

The danger seemed likely to increase with the arrival of a new flood of immigrants, refugees from war-torn Europe. During the war, immigration had been cut off, but afterward it began to surge, rising from 111,000 in 1919 to 430,000 in 1920 and 805,000 in 1921. The Red scare, with the arrest of foreign-born radicals, led to fears that immigrants would bring a continuing infection of Communism from Europe to America. For a time it was thought that even returning American soldiers might carry the Communist germ. While still in Paris, in 1918, a group of army officers had founded the American Legion with the aim of organizing the veterans and instilling in them patriotism as an antidote to radicalism.

The Eighteenth Amendment, bringing nationwide prohibition in 1920, represented a victory for native Protestantism as well as for

The Ku Klux Klan Parading in Washington, D.C.
In 1926 the Ku Klux Klan was still so powerful that it could march down Pennsylvania Avenue with the Capitol in the background. It professed to be a patriotic organization, but was openly anti-Negro, anti-Catholic, anti-Semitic, anti-foreigner, and anti-Union. (Culver)

women's rights. It got its strongest support from Methodists and Baptists, particularly in the rural areas of the South and West. It met its greatest opposition among Roman Catholics, especially in the cities of the Northeast.

The spirit of the time was also reflected in the postwar revival of the fundamentalist movement, which made its greatest headway within the Protestant churches of the South. Fundamentalists believed in the literal truth of every statement in the Bible. To them, the Darwinian theory of evolution was irreligious and wrong, since it conflicted with the account of Creation given in the book of Genesis. The fundamentalists campaigned for and succeeded in establishing state laws to prevent the teaching of evolution in public schools in Tennessee and a few other Southern states.

In 1925 a Tennessee schoolteacher, John T. Scopes, was brought to trial for violating the antievolution law. Defending him was the country's best-known criminal lawyer, Clarence Darrow, and assisting in the prosecution was the famous politician and orator William Jennings Bryan. The trial reached a spectacu-

lar climax when Bryan took the stand as a Bible expert and allowed Darrow to cross-examine him. At first, Bryan insisted that God had created the earth in exactly six days, just as the Bible said, but later he admitted that a "day" in Biblical terms might mean many thousands of years. Thus he gave away the main point of the fundamentalist argument, though the prosecution won the case. Scopes, after being convicted, was freed on a technicality.

Intolerance and nativism took their most extreme form in the new Ku Klux Klan. Revived in 1915 in Atlanta, Georgia, the Klan spread throughout the country, but it, too, drew its main strength from the rural areas of the South and West. At its height, in the mid-1920s, the Klan claimed 5 million members. They professed to stand for Christianity, morality, and Americanism. White-robed, hooded, often masked, Klansmen used fiery crosses, threats, torture, and even murder to intimidate people they considered immoral or un-American. The targets and victims were mostly members of minority groups, especially Roman Catholics and blacks.

The Klan became a political power in many states, most notably in Indiana, where a Klansman made himself governor and virtually dictator for a time. In national politics the Klan was strong enough to prevent the Democrats from nominating a Roman Catholic, Al Smith, for President in 1924 and to help defeat Smith after his nomination in 1928. Meanwhile, weakened by exposures of crime and vice among its leaders, the Klan had begun to decline in membership and influence.

No other group suffered so much from the postwar wave of intolerance as did the Negroes. For many of them the war had seemed to offer an opportunity to break out of the oppressive caste system of the South. Hundreds of thousands moved to the industrial centers of the North to get employment in the booming war industries and, they hoped, to find a less discriminatory society. In the North, however, they usually had to take jobs with the lowest pay, live in the worst slums, and contend with the animosity of unskilled white workers who feared black competition.

Some 400,000 blacks served in the army, half of them in Europe, where the local people usually drew no color line. Black veterans returned with a new-found sense of respect and dignity and with a determination to improve their status at home. They had fought in a war to "make the world safe for democracy," and some of them now applied the slogan to the United States. Speaking for the returning blacks, the NAACP magazine *The Crisis* proclaimed in 1919: "Make way for Democracy! We saved it in France, and by the Great Jehovah, we'll save it in the U.S.A., or know the reason why." They were soon disillusioned.

In both North and South, Negroes faced explosive resentment against them. In order to intimidate them back into their former subservience, Southerners resorted to the terrorism of the Klan and to lynchings, which increased from thirty-four in 1917 to more than seventy in 1919. Terrible race riots broke out, beginning in July 1919, in twenty-six towns and cities, mostly in the North. Hundreds of persons were killed or wounded, and millions of dollars' worth of property was destroyed. The worst of the outbursts began on a Chicago bathing beach and continued through thirteen days of pillaging and burning in the Negro district; 23 blacks and 15 whites were killed, 500 were injured, and

1,000 families, mostly Negro, were left homeless.

These terrors led millions of Negroes to follow a persuasive charlatan, Marcus Garvey, founder of the Universal Negro Improvement Association. In return for their contributions, he promised to take them home to an African empire. In 1923 Garvey was convicted of swindling and sentenced to federal prison, but Negro nationalism nevertheless persisted.

PERSISTING PROGRESSIVISM

Some Americans — not radicals but old progressives — would have liked to see the continuation of wartime government regulation or even ownership. At the close of the war the government owned most of the nation's commercial radio facilities (used as yet only for sending messages), commanded a vast merchant fleet, and controlled the railroads.

The call for nationalization, which frightened many Americans, went beyond the old progressive bounds. Congress was not willing to go so far but did pass the Esch-Cummins Transportation Act of 1920, establishing as tight federal control over railroad rates and securities as any progressive had ever visualized. Railroads suffered from the new rigorous competition of motor vehicles and other carriers and were seldom able to earn the 6-percent return the Interstate Commerce Commission allowed.

Shipping remained partly under direct government ownership, because private operation had to be heavily subsidized one way or another in order for American companies to compete successfully with those of other countries. These companies were subsidized by low prices and easy terms in buying government-owned ships and by generous mail contracts under the Merchant Marine Act of 1920. Congress refused to allow the navy to continue operating commercial radio communications, and so the navy reluctantly sold its stations to the newly established Radio Corporation of America.

Western progressives obtained two measures to stave off corporate onslaughts. One, the General Leasing Act, was intended to protect the naval oil reserves from oil companies that for some years had been trying to obtain them. It also authorized the leasing of other mineral and oil lands on terms favorable to the government. The other measure, the Water Power Act of 1920, was a first tentative step toward federal regulation of power. It established a Federal Power Commission (con-sisting of the secretaries of war, the interior, and agriculture) to license the construction and operation of hydroelectric plants on public lands and to regulate rates on power from these plants when it passed across state bound-aries.

Republican Prosperity

Though progressivism persisted, it had to yield to conservatism during the boom years of the 1920s. The wartime production miracles and the postwar writings of public relations experts and advertising men gave most Americans a renewed faith in business. The heroes of the time were the leaders of the great industries, and their interests were reflected by the domi-nant Republicans in politics.

THE HARDING TRAGEDY

In 1920 domestic politics made impossible a sol-emn referendum on a League of Nations; only an ill man sequestered from the flow of events, as President Wilson was, could have expected such a thing. A Democratic victory was so im-probable that Republican leaders felt no com-pulsion to put forth any of their strong candi-dates.

The two leading contenders were Leonard Wood and Frank O. Lowden. General Wood, an ardent conservative nationalist, command-ed most of Roosevelt's former following and collected a campaign chest of startling propor-tions ($1,773,000), with which he battled Low-den for delegates. Lowden, favorably known as an efficient governor of Illinois, also com-manded large campaign funds, totaling $414,000. Progressive Republican charges that both contenders were deeply indebted to big business helped induce party managers to ignore them when the two deadlocked at the convention. Late one night in a smoke-filled hotel room a cabal of senators led by Henry Cabot Lodge turned to one of the most regular and pliable of their colleagues, Warren G. Harding of Ohio. The convention nominated Harding on the tenth ballot and chose as his running mate the Massachusetts governor, Calvin Coolidge. These two were thoroughly conservative candidates running on a thoroughly conservative platform.

The Democrats, assembling at San Fran-cisco, were rather confused because President Wilson, who could have easily designated a candidate, seemed to be waiting with pathetic coyness to be renominated for a third term. This was out of the question. For thirty-eight ballots, two of Wilson's cabinet members, his efficient son-in-law William G. McAdoo and his superpatriotic Attorney General, A. Mitchell Palmer, battled for the nomination. In the end the urban bosses stepped in and secured the nomination of an antiprohibition candidate who might salvage their city tickets for them. This was the former progressive governor of Ohio, James M. Cox. As a gesture toward the Wilsonians, Assistant Secretary of the Navy Franklin D. Roosevelt was nominated for Vice President.

Cox and Roosevelt campaigned arduously to make the election the League referendum that Wilson wished it to be. Harding, following the advice of his managers, made few speeches and took few positions on the issues of the day except to promise a return to what he earlier had called "normalcy." He displayed an ambiv-alence that was politically most successful. On the League he at first gave the impression that he favored adherence, then as city resentment against it flared, gave the impression he was against it. Lest Cox's crusade win away Repub-lican votes, thirty-one distinguished Republi-cans signed a statement declaring that a vote for Harding was a vote for American entrance into the League with reservations.

The landslide exceeded even the expecta-tions of the Republicans. Harding received 16,152,000 popular votes, 61 percent of the total, and carried every state outside of the solid

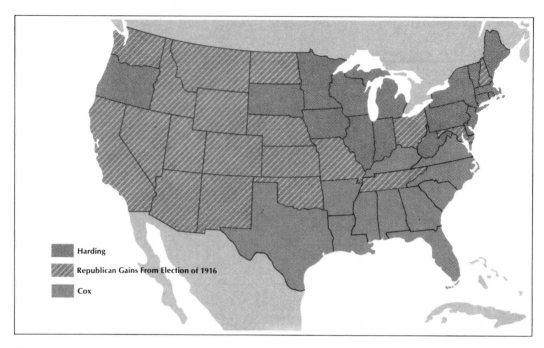

Harding

Republican Gains From Election of 1916

Cox

Election of 1920

South. He even won Tennessee. Cox received only 9,147,000 popular votes. Eugene V. Debs, running on the Socialist ticket while in the Atlanta penitentiary, received 920,000 votes. The sweep brought a Republican majority of 22 in the Senate and 167 in the House.

In voting against Wilsonianism, the electorate brought into power a weak, amiable conservative. Alice Roosevelt Longworth, daughter of a President and wife of the Speaker of the House, reared in the genteel tradition of Republican politics, could not forget the sight of a poker session in the President's study. "Harding was not a bad man," she reminisced. "He was just a slob."

President Harding wished to surround himself with the best-qualified men, and in part he succeeded. When he was persuaded that his friend Albert B. Fall was not of a caliber to be secretary of state, he placed Fall, a notorious anticonservationist, in charge of the Interior Department. He then appointed the brilliant and distinguished Charles Evans Hughes to be secretary of state. He placed Herbert Hoover, the friend of small enterprise and expert on efficiency, in charge of the Commerce Depart-

ment, and made Henry C. Wallace, spokesman for the Midwest farmers, secretary of agriculture. Andrew W. Mellon represented big business as secretary of the treasury. These able men, pulling in several directions, together with the congressional leaders, developed government policies.

The President seemed to be carrying out his campaign slogan: "Less government in business and more business in government." The Democrats made strong gains in the 1922 elections, reflecting the hard times that followed the war, but the return of prosperity soon afterward heightened Harding's popularity. He occasionally was even vigorous in his humanity. He took a step Wilson had curtly declined; on Christmas Day, 1921, he pardoned the Socialist Debs. At the urging of Hoover, he pressured the steel companies into granting an eight-hour day to their workers. The press of the country, overwhelmingly Republican, created the illusion that Harding was an exceptionally fine President.

Behind the façade, rot had set in. With singularly bad judgment, Harding had placed a number of his poker-playing and drinking companions into positions of trust, where they betrayed him and the American people. Probably Harding never knew in detail how shockingly they were looting the government, but he knew enough to be heartsick. One of the "Ohio Gang," Attorney General Harry Daugherty's friend Jesse Smith, had been engaging in large-scale "fixing" in the Department of Justice. After Harding ordered him out of Washington, Smith committed suicide. The director of the Veterans' Bureau, Charles R. Forbes, engaged in such colossal thievery that the total loss ran to nearly $250 million. When Harding received intimations of the corruption, he allowed Forbes to flee the country and resign. Ultimately Forbes served a two-year penitentiary sentence for defrauding the government.

The most spectacular fraud involved the rich naval oil reserves at Teapot Dome, Wyoming, and Elk Hills, California. Secretary of the Interior Fall persuaded Harding to transfer the oil reserves to his department, then secretly leased them to Harry F. Sinclair and Edward L. Doheny. Fall, who had been in financial straits, suddenly became affluent. An investigation headed by Senator Thomas J. Walsh of Montana during the fall and winter of 1923 and 1924 uncovered the reason. Sinclair had loaned Fall $308,000 in cash and government bonds and a herd of cattle for his ranch; Doheny had loaned him $100,000 more. In 1929 Fall was convicted of bribery, fined $100,000, and sentenced to a year in a federal penitentiary.

In the summer of 1923 Harding journeyed to Alaska. Tired and depressed, he responded wanly to the cheering throngs, who had no inkling of the mess in Washington. He never had to face the exposure of the mess because upon his return to Seattle he became ill. It was reported that he had been poisoned by seafood, but actually he had suffered a serious heart attack. He seemed to improve, so he continued to San Francisco. There he had a second attack and suddenly died. In the months that followed, as exposure after exposure crowded the headlines, his reputation collapsed.

KEEPING COOL WITH COOLIDGE

It was the singular good fortune of Calvin Coolidge to become President of the United States at a time when his largely negative custodial approach to the presidency could bring him popularity rather than disaster. He had reached the office through a curious mixture of luck, political regularity, and Yankee shrewdness. Unlike Harding, he had a clear-cut conservative philosophy. He always cooperated wholeheartedly with the big interests because he believed in them.

To the older circle in Washington, Coolidge's personality was not especially appealing. To the American public, however, there was an infinite appeal and security in his folksy virtues, so lavishly detailed and praised in the nation's press. Coolidge reinforced this appeal with little homilies drawn from his Vermont boyhood—exhortations (in which he fervently believed) to thrift, hard work, and respect for business.

Under this comforting moral leadership, the men of power in the United States could take a calm and even incredulous view of the Harding scandals as they came to light one by one in the winter of 1923–1924. Indeed, the respectable press showered indignation less upon the corrupt officials than upon those pressing the investigations. The two progressive Democratic senators, Thomas J. Walsh and Burton K. Wheeler, appeared to *The New York Times* to be "assassins of character."

Under Coolidge the Republicans seemed so patently incorruptible that the exposures appeared if anything to backfire against the exposing Democrats. Ultimately Coolidge forced Attorney General Daugherty to resign and helped clean up the scandals. As the election of 1924 approached, the revelations seemed to be doing no appreciable harm to the Republican party. The nation appeared ready to heed the party's campaign slogan: "Keep cool with Coolidge."

In 1924 the Democratic party was badly split between its rural and urban wings. Rural Democrats were backing as their candidate William Gibbs McAdoo, the competent heir to Wilsonianism. Strangely, the Teapot Dome scandal, which did no harm to the Republicans, tarnished McAdoo's reputation because he had served as a lawyer for Doheny, the California oil magnate. As for the urban wing of the party, it was advancing the candidacy of the equally competent liberal governor of New York, Alfred E. Smith, who was the son of Irish immigrants and had made his way upward from the Lower East Side of New York. Because of his background, and because he was a Catholic and a "wet" (an opponent of prohibition), he was the idol of many new Americans but an anathema to rural Democrats.

Finally both contenders withdrew, and on the 103rd ballot at the convention in Madison Square Garden the exhausted delegates nominated a compromise candidate, John W. Davis. Originally a West Virginian, Davis as solicitor general under Wilson had ably defended the legislation of the New Freedom before the Supreme Court. In the years since, he had become a lawyer for J. P. Morgan and some of the great corporations and had amassed a fortune.

While the Democratic convention dragged on, insurgent Republicans and allied representatives of labor held a third convention to organize a Progressive party and nominate Robert M. La Follette and Burton K. Wheeler. Their platform took an advanced progressive position, attacking monopoly and promising reforms for the farmers and workingmen. The party's support came from farmers, chiefly on the Great Plains, who had earlier formed the Nonpartisan League and the Farmer-Labor party, and from the Railroad Brotherhoods and the AFL.

This third party apparently was a real contrast to the Republican and Democratic tickets, and it served as a made-to-order target for the Republicans. They campaigned to frighten the electorate into choosing Coolidge as the only alternative to the "red radicalism" of La Follette. Before Election Day, labor became lukewarm toward La Follette; Republican farmers, as crop prices rose, decided to stay within the party. In its last thrust, the old Midwestern insurgency carried only Wisconsin and secured but 16.5 percent of the popular vote throughout the country. Coolidge polled 54 percent, and Davis only 28.8 percent.

In his inaugural, March 4, 1925, President Coolidge, declaring that the nation had achieved "a state of contentment seldom before seen," pledged himself to the maintenance of things as they were. During the prosperous years of the Coolidge era, as revenues came pouring in, the federal government did not greatly enlarge its services. It spent nothing in such areas as public housing, and little for farm relief or public works. Arms expenditures were a relative pittance. Consequently, the budget varied little between 1923 and 1929. Meanwhile, the national debt dropped by nearly a quarter.

FAVORED BUSINESS

Big business had a special friend in the government during the 1920s. Andrew Mellon, the Pittsburgh aluminum baron who served as secretary of the treasury from Harding's inauguration into the Hoover administration, was widely hailed as the greatest secretary of the treasury since Alexander Hamilton. His main function seemed to be to preside over tax cuts; cartoonists routinely pictured Mellon slicing a tax melon. So far as he could do so, as a matter of principle, he divided these cuts among the wealthy to give them the incentive to earn more money.

Smaller businessmen also had a strong champion in the government, Secretary of Commerce Hoover. In his own spectacular rise as an international mining engineer, Hoover epitomized the self-made businessman. Denouncing both the radicalism and reaction he had seen in Europe, Hoover set forth his own credo in 1922 in a small book entitled *American Individualism*. It extolled the equality of opportunity that enabled Americans to succeed on their own merits, and the "rising vision of service" that led them to develop community responsibility rather than merely to seek "the acquisition and preservation of private property." This had been Hoover's own way of life.

Hoover made Commerce the most active of the departments, as he sought to help small business become as efficient and profitable as big business. Through commercial attachés whom he sent to American embassies, he solicited foreign orders for American industry at the same time that he favored the tariff to protect it from overseas competition. Through the National Bureau of Standards, he performed innumerable other services for industry, such as standardizing products and eliminating waste.

The most significant of the ways to help small business was the sponsorship of voluntary trade associations similar to the committees of the War Industries Board. By 1921 some 2,000 were in operation. These associations, free from government regulation, could establish codes of ethics, standardize production, establish efficiency, and make substantial savings. They could serve even better than government prohibition of evil practices, Hoover had pointed out, to secure "cooperation in the business community to cure its own abuses." They could also arrive indirectly at higher standard prices which would bring them good profits. Their real value to highly competitive smaller businesses was to eliminate competition through setting up standardized schedules of quality and prices.

Voluntarism was at the heart of all of Hoover's projects. As the new field of commercial radio broadcasting began to develop, Hoover fostered voluntary self-regulation for it. When the efforts to keep stations off each other's wave lengths completely broke down, he moved toward compulsory government regulation through the Federal Radio Commission, established in 1927. In the same way, the Department of Commerce finally took over regulation of commercial aeronautics through the Air Commerce Act in 1926.

On the whole, business thrived from 1923 to 1929. In part this was due to benign governmental policies. Hoover's laudable efforts to bring about increased standardization and efficiency took the economy further away from free competition and contributed to the increased profits of business and consequently to the concentration of wealth. Secretary Mellon's tax policies helped the rich to become richer, while incomes of poorer people advanced little if at all. The tendency of the courts to frown upon trade-association price schedules helped stimulate mergers. And mergers helped to sustain the trend toward concentration of business which had begun after the Civil War. During the twenties, 8,000 mining and manufacturing companies disappeared into combinations, and 5,000 public utilities were swallowed, mostly by holding companies. By 1929 chain stores were selling more than a quarter of the nation's food, apparel, and general merchandise. The 200 largest nonfinancial corporations owned nearly half of all corporate wealth, and 22 percent of all national wealth. The 503 persons with the highest incomes received as much money as the total wages of 615,000 automobile workers.

THE DECLINE OF UNIONS

The onslaught against all Americans who did not conform, against any who might disturb the status quo, reacted strongly to the advantage of business leaders, who already basked in the public favor. These leaders were able to reestablish in the minds of many people the feeling that unionism was somehow un-American. In 1920 they began a great open-shop movement to break unions and reduce wages, under the alluring title, "The American Plan."

The paternalistic policies of welfare capitalism, together with the antiunion campaign, led to a decline in union membership during the 1920s. Many companies greatly improved working conditions by installing safety devices and improving sanitation. They raised their workers' morale by building attractive cafeterias and promoting athletic teams. Company welfare workers looked into the workers' family problems. By 1926 nearly 3 million workers could look forward to pensions upon retirement. In some companies they could buy stock below market value. Altogether they owned less than 1 percent, but even this did much to change some workers' attitudes. Further, they could voice their grievances through company unions or workers' councils, which were often effective safety valves for the employer. Through devices like these, companies helped fend off unionism from the new mass-production industries such as automobile manufacturing.

Within the skilled crafts, the AFL continued quietly and conservatively under the presidency of William Green. Its leaders seemed more interested in maintaining labor monopolies, especially in the building trades, than in organizing industrial workers. Membership in the United Mine Workers dwindled after unsuccessful strikes in 1922. Union membership declined from over 5 million in 1920 to around 4.3 million in 1929.

In some industries, like coal mining and textiles in the South, hours were long and wages were pitiful. At Elizabethton, Tennessee, in 1929, mill girls were working fifty-six hours a week for 16 to 18 cents an hour. Behind the harried workers was always the threat of legal action if they sought to help themselves through unions. Federal courts were granting injunctions to break boycotts or to enforce antiunion ("yellow dog") contracts. For most workingmen, however, conditions of labor had improved and living standards were up. Real wages increased about 26 percent between 1919 and 1929. They still were far from adequate. The average was less than $1,500 a year at a time when it was estimated that $1,800 was required to maintain a minimum decent living standard.

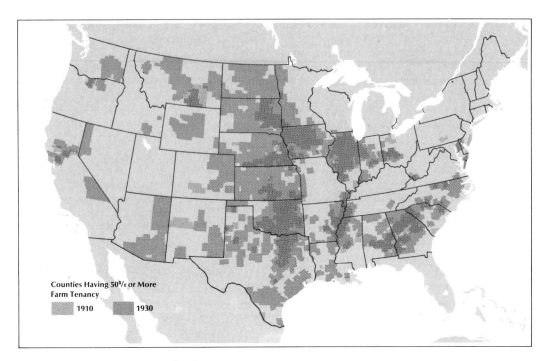

Farm Tenancy: 1910 and 1930

NO PARITY FOR FARMERS

While the income of most Americans advanced during the 1920s, that of the farmers drastically declined. In 1920 they lost their price supports at the same time that the bloated wartime European market contracted. At home, as machines released men from heavy manual labor, consumption of starches sharply dropped.

Within agriculture there were great variations. Truck gardening more than doubled, and dairying and citrus growing increased a third, reflecting the shifts in eating habits. Many such farmers enjoyed satisfactory incomes. At the same time, those on marginal or submarginal lands suffered so acutely that in the five years after 1919 13 million acres were abandoned. Poor farmers were unable to compete with large landowners using new, expensive machinery, which especially helped contribute to the glut of wheat. The number of tractors in use increased from 230,000 in 1920 to 920,000 in 1930, displacing 7,450,000 horses and releasing an additional 35 million acres of land for crops. On the Great Plains, speculators bought the lands of bankrupt farmers, and grew wheat on it with improved tractors and combines. In the Texas Panhandle alone, nearly 3 million new acres were ploughed.

The success of the big operators made the desperation of small farmers even more acute. In the year ending June 30, 1927, the average income of all the 6.3 million farmers was only $548, and out of this farmers had to meet a variety of pressing obligations. Farm income in 1920 was 15 percent of the national total; by 1929 it was only 9 percent. The agricultural population dropped 3 million between 1921 and 1928. Many of those who remained on the farms ceased to own them and became tenants. Distressed farmers, both owners and renters, began to agitate militantly for relief.

Even during the bonanza years of the war, agrarian agitation had stirred the Great Plains. In 1915 wheat growers of North Dakota had organized the Nonpartisan League, pledged to strict regulation of railroads and banks, and state ownership of grain elevators and farm credit agencies. The league won control of the North Dakota government in 1916, then began to organize in adjacent states, and in 1920 joined with other radical groups to form the Farmer-Labor party. The new party had some success in the congressional election of 1922, but by 1924 even La Follette would not accept its support. It was too radical for farmers who were earning $1,000 to $4,000 a year.

These men, the middle 40 percent of the farmers in terms of income, produced 46 percent of the farm products, and were solid citizens in their communities. Often acting through the Farm Bureau Federation or the Grange, they sought government price supports. From the outset they had powerful strength in the Congress. During the special session of Congress in the spring of 1921, Midwestern congressional leaders from both parties, meeting in the offices of the Farm Bureau Federation, organized a farm bloc.

One price-raising scheme came to dominate the farmers' thinking. Behind the tariff barrier, the American-protected price for crops should be raised to a "fair exchange value" based on the price of the crop during ten prewar years as compared with the general average of all prices during the same period. This was the "parity" price. The means of obtaining parity for farmers would be for the government to buy up the surplus at the high American price and sell it abroad at whatever it would bring on the world market. In order to make up for the loss, an equalization fee or tax would be charged the farmers on their entire crop.

Between 1924 and 1928 Senator Charles L. McNary of Oregon and Representative Gilbert Haugen of Iowa promoted this scheme in Congress. In 1924 the McNary-Haugen bill covered only grain, and was defeated in the House, but in 1926 the addition of cotton, tobacco, and rice brought Southern support. In 1927 Congress passed it, but President Coolidge coldly vetoed it as being preferential legislation contrary to the principles of laissez faire. (On the same day he signed an order raising the tariff on pig iron 50 percent.) A year later Congress again passed the McNary-Haugen bill, and Coolidge again vetoed it.

The Resurgence of Isolationism

The task of developing Republican alternatives to Wilsonian foreign policy fell largely on the shoulders of Secretaries of State Charles Evans Hughes (1921–1925) and Frank B. Kellogg (1925–1929).

STEPS TOWARD PEACE

Hughes' policy involved first of all ending the war with Germany by an act of Congress, which was signed July 2, 1921. Hughes then negotiated separate peace treaties with the former Central Powers, to secure for the United States the benefits without the responsibilities of the Paris treaties. In time, Hughes permitted American delegations to participate in League conferences on minor matters as long as they did not make commitments. Throughout his years as secretary of state he was chilly toward every European proposal for collective security. He did, in February 1923, persuade President Harding to recommend that the United States join with reservations the World Court, an almost completely powerless body. But the World Court was an instrument of the League, and while internationally minded Americans ardently favored joining, the irreconcilables in the Senate violently fought it. Each succeeding President through Franklin D. Roosevelt advocated American adherence to the League; each time, through 1935, the Senate blocked it.

Through the Washington Arms Conference, Republicans made it appear that they were taking positive steps to preserve the peace. This was in effect a Republican substitute for entrance into the League. In May 1921 Senator Borah had introduced a resolution calling for a conference to reduce armaments, but the basic impetus for the meeting came from the British, who feared a three-way naval race with the Americans and the Japanese. Japan had emerged from the war stronger than before in China and with troops still stationed in Siberia. She threatened to expand still further, to shut the "Open Door" in China, and to arm her new island possessions in the Pacific. American public opinion saw an even more serious threat in the Anglo-Japanese alliance. Hence the British, wishing to strengthen their amicable relations with the United States, proposed the conference. Hughes seized the initiative and President Harding issued invitations.

The arms conference opened on November 12, 1921, the day after burial rites for the Unknown Soldier at the Arlington Cemetery. Hughes in his opening speech startled the delegates and won enormous acclaim by dramatically presenting a concrete plan for the reduction in size of the fleets of the United States, Great Britain, and Japan. He proposed a ten-year moratorium on capital-ship construction (battleships, cruisers, and carriers) and the scrapping by the three powers of nearly 1.9 million tons of ships already built or under construction. A British observer declared: "Secretary Hughes sank in thirty-five minutes more ships than all the admirals of the world have sunk in a cycle of centuries."

In the negotiations that followed, Japan agreed to limit her capital ships to a total of approximately 300,000 tons compared with 500,000 tons each for the United States and Great Britain. In addition the United States pledged itself not to increase its fortifications in Guam and the Philippines. Japan and Great Britain made similar pledges. Thus the Five Power Pact of 1922 provided a ratio of 5:5:3 for the United States, Great Britain, and Japan, and 1.75:1.75 for France and Italy, stopping what otherwise could have become a disastrous armaments race. Two other treaties aimed at guaranteeing the status quo in the Far East. The Nine Power Pact pledged a continuation of the Open Door policy in China. Afterward Japan restored full sovereign rights to China in the Shantung peninsula and promised to withdraw the Japanese troops from Siberia. The Four Power Pact—among the United States, Great Britain, France, and Japan—represented a mutual recognition of insular rights in the Pacific. Upon its ratification, Japan relinquished her alliance with Great Britain.

These Washington treaties lowered the tension between the United States and Japan for nearly a decade. Their one unfortunate result was that the United States relinquished the physical force with which to impose its will in the Far East but retained its moral, economic, and political objectives in that area. The Senate came close to rejecting the Four Power Pact for fear it would commit the United States to some collective security arrangement in the Orient. On the other hand, the popularity of the Naval Limitation Treaty (Five Power Pact) is shown by the fact that only one senator voted against its ratification.

During the Coolidge administration millions of Americans signed petitions urging the United States to promote a multilateral treaty outlawing war. The French foreign minister, Aristide Briand, proposed a treaty of this sort between France and the United States. Secretary Kellogg responded by suggesting that other countries be invited to join. So, at Paris in 1928, most of the great nations, including the United States, signed a treaty solemnly renouncing war as an instrument of national policy, but providing no machinery whatever for enforcement. The treaty evoked much enthusiasm in the United States, for it seemed to offer collective security without any risks.

Hughes tried to extend the good will of the United States toward Latin America. During his first months in office, he was decidedly influenced by Sumner Welles, later one of the chief molders of the Good Neighbor policy. By 1924 Hughes had ended the marine occupation of Santo Domingo and prepared for its end in Nicaragua. He felt that the occupation was still necessary in Haiti.

Hughes moved away from the progressive policy of intervention and tried wherever possible to substitute the nonrecognition of undesirable governments for the landing of the marines. Neither he nor his successor in the Coolidge administration was ready to give up intervention entirely. For a time during the Coolidge administration, trouble with Mexico over the rights of American oil companies and renewed marine intervention in Nicaragua seemed to indicate a retreat to the old policies.

ECONOMIC NATIONALISM

In European affairs a persisting and troublesome issue was that of reparations and war debts. The failure of the United States to join the League of Nations had most serious repercussions on this problem, since the League's Reparations Commission, which was not under the chairmanship of an American as had been expected, set astronomically high sums for Germany to pay. Reparations payments depended to a considerable degree upon American private loans to Germany; war-debt payments from the Allies to the United States depended, in turn, almost entirely upon reparations. The American public insisted that the Allies should repay the $10 billion the

United States had loaned during the war. Coolidge later epitomized the popular view when he remarked simply: "They hired the money, didn't they?"

The United States pressured the former Allies, through a World War Foreign Debt Commission, to negotiate long-term schedules of debt payments. Between 1923 and 1926 the commission reached agreements with the Allies in regard to their debts (which the United States government insisted bore no relationship to German reparations payments). The administration did not worry as to how Germany, France, Italy, and the other debtors could make payments over the high tariff wall that the United States was raising against their exports.

What kept the payments going during the twenties was the huge total of private American loans pouring into German governmental units or corporations—about $2.5 billion between 1923 and 1930. Germany paid about $2 billion in reparations, and the former Allies about $2.6 billion in war-debt payments. Thus the Germans were paying the Allies, and the Allies paying the United States, with dollars that Americans were lending to the Germans.

As soon as the Republicans had come into power in 1921, they enacted an emergency tariff measure to raise the low Underwood rates. In 1922 they passed the Fordney-McCumber Act providing protection especially for agriculture, the chemical industry, and manufacturers threatened by Japanese and German competition. The tariff gave agriculture little real protection, but it provided industrialists with several benefits. It accepted the principle that, when foreign firms had costs of production lower than their American competitors, the tariff should be high enough to offset the differential. It prohibited most competing imports and led to higher prices at home. Other nations followed the American lead in economic nationalism; by 1928 some sixty countries had raised their tariffs.

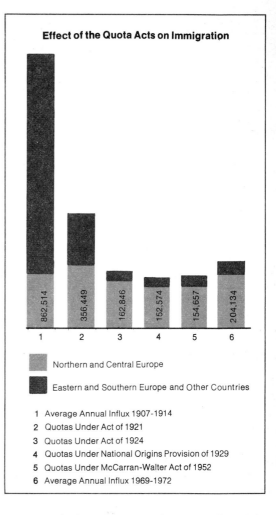

Effect of the Quota Acts on Immigration

862,514   356,449   162,846   152,574   154,657   204,134

1   2   3   4   5   6

▢ Northern and Central Europe

■ Eastern and Southern Europe and Other Countries

1 Average Annual Influx 1907-1914
2 Quotas Under Act of 1921
3 Quotas Under Act of 1924
4 Quotas Under National Origins Provision of 1929
5 Quotas Under McCarran-Walter Act of 1952
6 Average Annual Influx 1969-1972

The bars above show the drastic effect of the laws of the 1920s in restricting immigration from Old World countries except those of Northern and Central Europe. The act of 1952 made little change, but the act of 1965 (taking effect in 1969) led to a considerable shift in Old World sources of immigration. The chart omits immigration from the Western Hemisphere. This was not restricted until the 1965 law put a ceiling of 120,000 a year on it.

IMMIGRATION RESTRICTION

Along with high walls against competing goods, Congress finally succeeded in erecting barriers against incoming foreigners. Racist objections to the "new immigrants," and the unionists' fear that the newcomers were perpetuating a pool of cheap labor in the United States, were reinforced by the allegation that some of them were radicals. This led employers who had previously favored immigration to switch to the restrictive side.

In 1921 Congress passed an emergency

immigration act, setting up a quota system: immigrants from any country could not exceed 3 percent of the number of persons of their nationality who had been in the United States in 1910. This cut the number of immigrants from 800,000 in the year ending June 30, 1921, to about 300,000 in the following twelve months. Racists still were not satisfied, so Congress in 1924 enacted the National Origins Act. This measure not only banned the people of East Asia entirely, but set a quota of 2 percent for Europeans, and this on the basis of the 1890 census. It cut the yearly total to 164,000, heavily weighted in favor of those from northwestern Europe. On July 1, 1929, an overall limit of about 150,000 immigrants a year went into ef-

fect, but during the entire depression decade of the thirties the total net immigration was less than 70,000. The great flood of so many decades had been cut to a few drops.

Excluding all aliens ineligible to become citizens meant excluding the Japanese in particular. It was an unnecessary insult to the Japanese, since the Gentlemen's Agreement had worked well, and the application of a quota system to Japan would have allowed only a tiny trickle of immigrants. Indignation in Japan against the act of 1924 was so extreme that Hughes lamented privately: "It has undone the work of the Washington Conference and implanted the seeds of an antagonism which are sure to bear fruit in the future."

Life in the Twenties

For those who shared in the prosperity, the decade of the twenties was a wonderful era. The wealth of the United States, as newspapers never tired of reminding their readers, was almost as great as that of all Europe. "My God, how the money rolls in!" went the words of a popular song. And some of the money was spent in remarkable ways.

THE JAZZ AGE

It was the era when Florida real-estate salesmen hired the famous orator William Jennings Bryan to lecture on the climate. Even though only an infinitesimal portion of Americans bought real estate in Florida during the land boom of 1924–1925, the impression was that most people were dabbling in the speculation. So too with the stock market later in the decade. Millions shared in the national frenzies, but most of them did so only vicariously while living sober, quiet lives.

The average middle-class American family owned an automobile. There were 23 million cars in use by 1929, and on Sundays it seemed as though they were all out on the new concrete highways. At home, people listened to the radio. The first commercial station, KDKA, broadcast the news of Harding's election in November 1920. By 1924 the National Broadcasting Company had organized a nationwide

network of stations, and by 1930 over 12 million American families had radios. Millions also had electric vacuum cleaners and washing machines; many were beginning to buy electric refrigerators. Household appliances were supplanting the housemaid and the hired girl. Food and clothing accounted for only 44 percent of the family expenditures, compared with 58 percent in 1899 – a clear indication of the rising living standards.

The prosperity of the twenties spilled over into the educational system. The per-pupil expenditure jumped from $24 in 1910 to $90 in 1930. Free elementary education had become established throughout the nation; illiteracy dropped from 7.7 percent to 4.3 percent. Enrollment in high schools increased 400 percent, and enrollment in colleges and universities grew almost as fast.

Much money went to bootleggers, the dealers in illicit liquor, a new multimillion-dollar business. This was a response to the Eighteenth Amendment, which prohibited intoxicating beverages, and to the Volstead Act (1919), which defined them as all beverages containing more than one-half of 1 percent of alcohol, thus ruling out beer and light wines as well as hard liquor. The first prohibition commissioner had optimistically announced his determination to see that alcoholic beverages were "not manufactured, nor sold, nor given away, nor hauled in anything on the surface of the earth or under

Disposing of Illegal Booze

During the 1920s federal prohibition agents—like those emptying bottles down a sewer in this photograph—were assigned to confiscate and get rid of bootleg liquor. But the agents could not keep up with the bootleggers. The head of the Prohibition Bureau once estimated that law enforcement agencies were catching only one-twentieth of the liquor that was being smuggled in from Canada and other countries, to say nothing of the tremendous quantities that were being produced illegally in the United States. (Culver Pictures)

the earth or in the air." But with an insufficient budget and only a few thousand poorly paid agents—and with little or no cooperation from state and local authorities—the commissioner had an almost impossible task in patrolling 18,000 miles of coastline, guarding against the diversion of any of the 57 million gallons of industrial alcohol, overseeing hundreds of millions of medical prescriptions, and checking on 20 million homes to prevent the concoction of home brew, wine, or "bathtub gin."

Gangsters turned to the large-scale smuggling or manufacture and distribution of liquor. In Chicago, "Scarface" Al Capone built an underworld empire that was based on beer and extended out into slot machines, laundries, and labor unions; it grossed about $60 million per year. He guarded it against interlopers

with an army of 700 to 1,000 gunmen. Between 1920 and 1927 over 250 men were killed in Chicago gang warfare. Capone miraculously survived both his rivals and the forces of the law, until finally in 1931 he was convicted of federal income-tax evasion.

New ways of life, alarming to the older generation, swept America. Men wore wrist watches and smoked cigarettes, both of which had seemed rather effeminate before the war. Women seemed to have lost their modesty as they bobbed their hair, applied lipstick, donned short skirts and silk stockings, and unblushingly began using words previously reserved for males.

Young people talked openly and frankly about sex. Often their talk reflected the remote influence of Sigmund Freud, the Austrian founder of psychoanalysis, who had visited the United States before the war but had gotten little public attention at that time. During the 1920s, though few Americans read his works, many received a simplified and distorted version of his theories from popular magazines. The impression spread, erroneous though it was, that Freud had given a scientific justification for promiscuity. Mouthing Freudian terms such as "libido" and "inhibition," youthful Americans often were quite willing to believe that any repression of the sex urge was psychologically unhealthful.

The sex talk of the young, which frightened their elders, was made doubly frightening by the disappearance of chaperons and the availability of automobiles. Compounding the evil in the eyes of elders were the many new roadhouses and speakeasies, where young people flouted prohibition by drinking beer or cocktails. There too they listened to jazz and danced the new steps like the Charleston, which some preachers denounced to their flocks as lascivious. It seemed to many critics that Gertrude Stein had correctly labeled this the "lost generation"; these people could not believe that in time the "flaming youth" would mature into censorious middle age.

Motion pictures flamboyantly heralded the new moral code and together with tabloid papers helped fabricate false stereotypes of the period. An estimated 50 million people a week went to theaters to see the "it" girl, Clara Bow, the glamorous Rudolph Valentino, the comedian Charlie Chaplin, gangster pictures, Westerns, and great spectacles like the first film version of *The Ten Commandments*. These helped standardize American habits, and not always in the most edifying way. Further, since nine-tenths of the world's motion pictures were made in the United States, they brought curiously distorted notions of American culture to other countries. In 1927 a revolution struck the motion-picture industry when the first important all-talking picture, *The Jazz Singer*, starring Al Jolson, was a phenomenal success. Motion pictures also began to carry American speech around the world.

In journalism, the twenties brought an even greater sensationalism than the nineties in some mass-circulation city papers. From England came the idea of the half-sized tabloid, which led to the founding of the *News*, *Mirror*, and *Graphic* in New York City, and similar papers throughout the country. Tabloid journalism came to mean what "yellow journalism" had meant earlier, with the addition of a strong emphasis upon serial comic strips and sensational photographs. Millions of readers followed the gang wars in Chicago and murder trials in New York and elsewhere. Even *The New York Times* had to capitulate its dignity to reader demands and lavish front-page space upon one spectacular murder trial, the Hall-Mills case, concerning the murder of a minister and a choir singer.

Among magazines, the *Saturday Evening Post*, with its conservative editorials and well-written stories, mirrored the era as faithfully as did President Coolidge. Close behind it in capturing the popular spirit was a reprint magazine founded in 1921, *Reader's Digest*, which filled its readers with inspiration and optimism, and guided them effortlessly through what they might consider difficult, serious subjects. It was the beginning of predigested reading. Much the same formula went into *Time*, the first of the news magazines, founded in 1925. In its cleverness, *Time* was one of the magazines tailored for the college graduates of the twenties. Another was the gay, sophisticated *New Yorker*, founded in 1925, which, with its clever cartoons and polished articles and stories, soon eclipsed the older *Life* and *Judge*. But the magazines that best typified the iconoclastic spirit of the intelligentsia and its rejection of middle-class values were *Smart Set* and the *American Mercury*. Their editors, Henry L. Mencken and George Jean Nathan, ridiculed the shibboleths of the decade, but more than that introduced to their readers many of the most vigorous writers of the era.

WRITERS, ARTISTS, MUSICIANS

Seldom before in American history has such a remarkable galaxy of new writers appeared at one time. There was as much negativism from the expatriates in Paris as there had been before the war from Greenwich Village; many took perverse delight in damning the United States as a dollar-grubbing philistine civilization. Despite this spirit, it was not a generation lost to letters, nor were the voices of protest ignored.

Sherwood Anderson, giving up his paint factory, wrote tart Freudian sketches of small-town America in *Winesburg, Ohio* (1919). Sin-

The Sinclair Lewises Go Camping

*In 1916 Lewis bought a Model T Ford, and with his wife, Grace Hegger Lewis,
embarked on a four-month trip from Sauk Center, Minnesota, to San Francisco.
Lewis wanted to see firsthand more of the small-town life about which he wished
to write a novel. This photograph was taken in Duluth. (Brown Brothers)*

clair Lewis more spectacularly exploited the same vein in his satiric *Main Street* (1920) and *Babbitt* (1922). His onslaught against business philistinism, in a long series of novels, at times verged close to caricature, but in time brought Lewis a Nobel Prize. With far more pessimism, utilizing experimental episodic techniques, John Dos Passos dissected the life of the metropolis in *Manhattan Transfer* (1925). Theodore Dreiser came into his own in 1925 with *An American Tragedy*, which analyzed with compassion both the psychological and environmental factors that led a young man to consider drowning his mistress.

The novelist who best embodied the jazz age in both his personal life and his writing was F. Scott Fitzgerald, catapulted to success with *This Side of Paradise* (1920). Young novelists who helped set patterns for later decades were Ernest Hemingway and William Faulkner. Hemingway stated the reaction against war most vigorously in his novel of disillusion, *A Farewell to Arms* (1929), which also helped set a new literary style. Faulkner, analyzing the

South with morbid intensity in novels like *The Sound and the Fury* (1929) and *Sanctuary* (1931), developed an abstruse stream-of-consciousness technique which profoundly influenced other writers.

In drama these were the golden years of Eugene O'Neill, who drew from Ibsen, Strindberg, and Freud to develop American plays that were both critical and popular successes. *The Emperor Jones* (1920), *Anna Christie* (1922), *Strange Interlude* (1928), and other plays won O'Neill three Pulitzer Prizes in the decade, and helped maintain him in the forefront of American dramatists a decade later. A number of other young playwrights wrote for the experimental stage, which flourished at scores of colleges and cities, even while motion pictures were superseding the old legitimate theater circuits.

In poetry, two of the most significant writers were expatriates from the United States. These were T. S. Eliot in London, whose *The Waste Land* appeared in 1922, and Ezra Pound, who settled in Italy where he wrote *Cantos* and

T. S. Eliot on Expatriates of the Twenties

The situation is different for the young men of today compared with the earlier part of this century. I don't know what Prohibition had to do with it. Certainly it was easier then for youngsters to earn a living overseas. And the American literary scene didn't offer them much encouragement. That was a very dull period.

In Europe there was a desire to aid younger people. Pound introduced me to Yeats. I got to know Virginia Woolf. People were interested in my poetry. I had never experienced such interest at home. But now the trend seems to be in the other direction. Young Americans go back and find they can make a living teaching in colleges, that there is genuine interest in them. A young writer needs the society of other writers, both his contemporaries and benevolent older writers whom he can respect. There are more of these now in the United States. — The New York Times, *March 30, 1959.*

---

embraced Fascism. At home, Edna St. Vincent Millay typified the twenties with her hedonistic love poetry, while Robinson Jeffers turned to dark naturalistic themes. Older poets like Edwin Arlington Robinson and Robert Frost continued to write in established veins, and numerous young poets experimented with innovations in techniques and topics.

American artists continued to produce along lines that in many cases had been pioneered before the war. Architects filled the great cities with skyscrapers and were active in city planning. Some of the surplus wealth of the twenties poured into European painting; Mellon matched his ingenuity in keeping taxes down with his lavish purchases of old masters, some of them from the dollar-hungry Soviet Union. By 1930 American art galleries owned $2 billion worth of paintings. Along with this went a rapidly widening popular appreciation of fine art.

In music the twenties were notable for the rise of jazz, "the most important musical expression that America has achieved." It had originated among Negro musicians in the South, particularly in New Orleans, who drew upon their African heritage in composing and playing tunes with improvised harmonies and a syncopated beat. Among the outstanding black creators of jazz were the guitar-playing singer Huddie Ledbetter ("Leadbelly") and the band conductor William C. Handy, the "father of the blues," whose compositions include *St. Louis Blues* (1914). The new music first became widely known when jazzmen moved with the

general black migration northward during and after World War I. The great trumpet-player Louis ("Satchmo") Armstrong, for example, went from New Orleans to Chicago in 1922 to join a band that helped spread jazz through phonograph recordings. Meanwhile, white musicians had begun to take up the new form, modify it, and make it increasingly popular and even respectable by treating it as serious music. Prominent among them were the composer George Gershwin, who incorporated jazz elements in his *Rhapsody in Blue,* and the conductor Paul Whiteman, whose band presented a pioneering jazz concert in New York City in 1922.

"It was the period when the Negro was in vogue," Langston Hughes recalled of the 1920s. Certainly it was a time when Hughes and other black writers, as well as black musicians, gained recognition for contributing to American culture. So many excellent poets, novelists, and playwrights flourished in Harlem — Hughes, Claude McKay, and James Weldon Johnson outstanding among them — that the black literary revival came to be known as the Harlem Renaissance. It produced an eloquent and often bitter literature of protest. Though quite race-conscious, expressing a new pride in their blackness, the authors seldom repudiated the values of white society. They protested not so much against the country's democratic ideals as against its failure to live up to them. "In this approach," as John Hope Franklin has observed, "they proved to be as characteristically American as any writers of the period."

The Negro Artist [1926]

Born in Missouri in 1902, Langston Hughes traveled in Mexico, Africa, and Europe before settling in New York City, where he became the most prolific and versatile of the black writers, earning for himself the reputation of "Shakespeare in Harlem." In an article "The Negro Artist and the Racial Mountain," in *The Nation*, June 23, 1926, he wrote:

One of the most promising of the young Negro poets said to me once, "I want to be a poet—not a Negro poet," meaning, I believe, "I want to write like a white poet"; meaning subconsciously, "I would like to be a white poet"; meaning behind that, "I would like to be white." And I was sorry the young man said that, for no great poet has ever been afraid of being himself. And I doubted then that, with his desire to run away spiritually from his race, this boy would ever be a great poet. But this is the mountain standing in the way of any true Negro art in America—this urge within the race toward whiteness, the desire to pour racial individuality into the mold of American standardization, and to be as little Negro and as much American as possible.

. . . We younger Negro artists who create now intend to express our individual dark-skinned selves without fear or shame. If white people are pleased we are glad. If they are not, it doesn't matter. We know we are beautiful. And ugly too. The tom-tom cries and the tom-tom laughs. If colored people are pleased we are glad. If they are not, their dispeasure doesn't matter either. We build our temples for tomorrow, strong as we know how, and we stand on top of the mountain, free within ourselves.

A SEARCH FOR VALUES

In letters, the arts, and learning, there was a seeking for values that would be something more than the advertising man's paeans to mass-production cultures, as expressed in Bruce Barton's *The Man Nobody Knows*. This seeking is the reason so many of the younger writers were rejecting the popular values of the United States for those of Europe, which did not seem to them as yet caught in the new commercial maelstrom. Others were trying to interpret the new society with the psychoanalytical approach suggested by Sigmund Freud, or the economic determinism stemming from Karl Marx.

Among ministers, publicists, philosophers, and economists seeking to interpret the new order, there was some confusion. The fundamentalist ministers went on much as before, although in some quarters they were subjected to ridicule after 1925 when their champion, William Jennings Bryan, matched wits with the agnostic Clarence Darrow in the famous Scopes trial. Ministers to the middle class who earlier had so exuberantly preached the social gospel or the great crusade in Europe had been beaten down in 1919 when they took up the cause of the striking steelworkers. Many businessmen were ready to adopt paternalistic policies and label them "Christian industrialism," but they denounced the militant social gospel as Bolshevism. Ministers further lost their hold on their following as middle-class reaction spread against two of the causes in which they had been so deeply involved—the war in Europe and prohibition. Many ministers tended, consequently, to concentrate upon the building of fine churches and the development of a sophisticated theology embracing the new psychological concepts.

Many of the most popular publicists were negative in their view of government. Henry L. Mencken and Irving Babbitt launched some of their most scathing attacks against the American democratic system. Walter Lippmann, who had been deeply involved in the New Nationalism and the New Freedom, became aloof and brilliantly analytical in his observation of American society. The Socialist candidate for President in 1928, Norman Thomas, remarked: "The old reformer has become the Tired Radical and his sons and daughters drink at the fountain of the *American Mercury*."

H. L. Mencken
[1933]

As columnist for the Baltimore *Sun,* and especially as editor of the *Smart Set* and the *American Mercury,* Mencken exercised great influence for the fifteen years following World War I. Often regarded as an iconoclast whose value was purely negative, Mencken actually used the grace and taste of the eighteenth-century aristocracy as a standard to condemn the "booboisie" he saw around him. Outstanding for his pioneering studies of the American language, for his opposition to censorship and prohibition, and for his championing of such writers as Joseph Conrad, Theodore Dreiser, and Ring Lardner, he wrote a virile and sinewy prose. His wit (and his scorn for American politicians) shows in his obituary for Calvin Coolidge, published in April 1933:

In what manner he would have performed himself if the holy angels had shoved the Depression forward a couple of years—this we can only guess, and one man's hazard is as good as another's. My own is that he would have responded to bad times precisely as he responded to good ones—that is, by pulling down the blinds, stretching his legs upon his desk, and snoozing away the lazy afternoons. . . . He slept more than any other President, whether by day or by night. Nero fiddled, but Coolidge only snored. . . . Counting out Harding as a cipher only, Dr. Coolidge was preceded by one World Saver and followed by two more. What enlightened American, having to choose between any of them and another Coolidge, would hesitate for an instant? There were no thrills while he reigned, but neither were there any headaches. He had no ideas, and he was not a nuisance.

Nevertheless, some of the most influential philosophers and social scientists continued to write in modified progressive terms. John Dewey, at the peak of his influence, was expounding a socialized pragmatism: man through science and technology could develop an organized social intelligence which could plan a rational and fruitful future society. The aged Thorstein Veblen was placing a similar faith in science: the engineers in contrast to the businessmen could bring forth an economic utopia. This doctrine, carried to its ultimate conclusion, engendered the technocracy movement of the early thirties. Other economists would not go this far, but some of them accepted Veblen's emphasis upon craftsmen and technicians, who, unlike businessmen, would not raise prices and restrict markets. Around them could develop an economy of still greater abundance. Agricultural economists, who were thinking in opposite terms of restriction, also looked forward to an age of social and economic planning.

Charles A. Beard was disseminating some of these ideas among a wider group of readers. In his and Mary Beard's *Rise of American Civilization* (1927), expressing mild economic determinism and emphasizing social and cultural factors, he did much to perpetuate progressive thinking among the new generation of intellectuals. Vernon L. Parrington's *Main Currents of American Thought* (1927), tracing the same themes in literature, helped create a Jeffersonian cult. Writing on a popular level, Claude Bowers developed similar ideas. Franklin D. Roosevelt, reviewing Bowers' *Jefferson and Hamilton* in 1925, commented: "Hamiltons we have today. Is a Jefferson on the horizon?"

The Great Depression

"I do not choose to run in 1928," President Coolidge had announced. The way to perpetuate Coolidge prosperity, it seemed to Republicans, was to elect Herbert Hoover, the "Great Engineer," whose policies as secretary of commerce promised a continuation of businessmen's government. The Republicans nominated him on the first ballot. In accepting the nomination, he proclaimed: "Given a chance to go forward with the policies of the last eight years, we shall soon with the help of God be in sight of the day when poverty will be banished from the nation."

ELECTION OF 1928

Among Democrats, the experienced politicians were still almost as badly divided as in 1924, but they saw no reason to turn their convention into another brawl when their candidate had no chance of winning against Republican prosperity. Even those who were ardently dry and Protestant raised no barrier against the wet, Roman Catholic governor of New York, Alfred E. Smith. He was nominated to run on a platform not much more positive than that of the Republicans. It did, however, include a plank offering farmers the McNary-Haugen plan. More important, Smith promised to relax the Volstead Act for enforcing the Eighteenth Amendment. This brought prohibition to the forefront of the campaign. There was little except that and religion to campaign about.

Both Hoover and Smith were self-made men and proud of it. Hoover's path, from an Iowa farm through Stanford University, had been marked by a phenomenally successful rise as a business and government executive. Smith's path led from the East Side of New York through the Fulton Fish Market and the Tammany hierarchy to the governorship of New York. There he had demonstrated a consummate political and administrative skill. He had reorganized the state government, fought to build schools, parks, and parkways, and struggled for public development of the great power sites.

In the campaign, Hoover stressed prosperity, which was popularly translated into the notion of a chicken in every pot and two cars in every garage. Smith evoked more enthusiastic loyalty and venomous hatred than any candidate since Bryan. Millions of the urban masses, mostly of immigrant and Catholic background themselves, saw in Smith their spokesman, their great hero. Millions of Protestants in the rural South, where belief in prohibition was strong and the Ku Klux Klan boisterous in its anti-Catholicism, looked upon him as a threat

Election of 1928

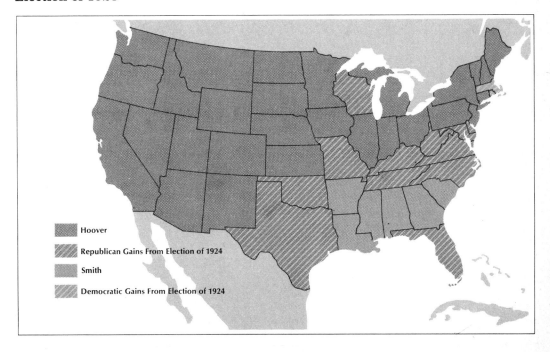

Hoover

Republican Gains From Election of 1924

Smith

Democratic Gains From Election of 1924

to their way of life. Fiery crosses greeted him near Oklahoma City, where he courageously denounced the Klan. But his cause was hopeless. The Republican landslide exceeded expectations, as Hoover received a popular vote of 21 million to 15 million for Smith.

THE WALL STREET CRASH

President Hoover, the prophet of permanent prosperity, had been in office scarcely six months when the Great Depression began. It was touched off by a collapse of the stock mar-ket. For several years stock prices had been rising so rapidly that they ceased to have much relation to the actual earning power of corporations. The New York Stock Exchange had become for many speculators a great national gambling casino, where everyone won almost all the time. By the summer of 1929, however, there were many disquieting signs that the prosperity, so long gone for the farmers, was coming to an end for businessmen also. Construction had passed its peak and was declining rapidly; automobiles were filling dealers' garages; business inventories of all sorts were three times larger than a year before; freight

The stock market crash marked only the beginning of the price decline. Stocks stayed low in 1930s and even relatively low in the 1940s. By the Korean War the great bull market was underway and continued with only brief interruption until the 1960s. The stock prices shown above are based on the Dow-Jones stock averages.

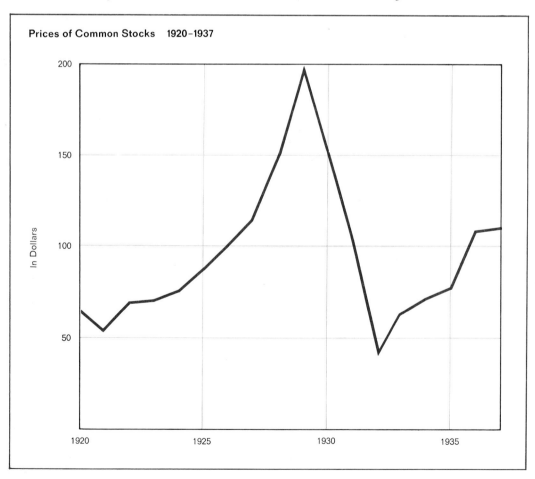

Prices of Common Stocks   1920–1937

carloadings, industrial production, and whole-sale prices were all slipping downward.

On October 21, 1929, the stock market dropped sharply, and two days later the big crash began. Temporarily, J. P. Morgan and Company and other big bankers managed to stave off disaster, but on October 29 their efforts failed. That day 16 million shares were sold. Total losses for the month reached $16 billion. For two weeks more the market continued to drop, until stocks had lost over 40 percent in value.

The stock market collapse, though not the cause of the depression, precipitated it by replacing the inflationary spiral with a deflationary one even harder to stop. It brought to an end a decade of business optimism and opened one of almost unquenchable pessimism. Bewildered businessmen saw their only hope in retrenchment, and the more they retrenched, the worse conditions became.

For years afterward, economists, businessmen, and political leaders debated the causes of the depression. Certainly there had been serious defects in the economy of the 1920s. As production rose, too little of the profits went to farmers, other producers of raw materials, or workers. Too much went into the building of new industrial plants. So long as the expansion of capital facilities continued, new investments stimulated the economy, but the investments created more plant space than could be profitably used. By 1929, factories were pouring out more goods than consumers could purchase. This did not mean that Americans would not have consumed more had they had more income, for even in 1929 only one family in six had an automobile, only one in five a fixed bathtub or electricity, and only one in ten a telephone.

Government had played the wrong role in the economic system during the twenties. Taxes, by sparing the rich, had added to the inequality of incomes. High tariffs had discouraged foreign trade; large exports could have continued only so long as Americans kept on lending abroad. Failure to break up or regulate big business had encouraged concentration and resulted in rigidly high prices. Nothing had been done to check speculation or supervise the securities market, and nothing effective had been done to restore the buying power of farmers.

THE HOOVER PROGRAM

In the view of critics a generation later, the government continued to do the wrong things in facing the depression. It concentrated upon balancing the budget and maintaining the gold standard, both of which were deflationary, at a time when the country was already suffering from too much deflation. Blame for these policies should not fall solely upon President Hoover. They were the ancient formulas for the conduct of government during a depression; they were urged upon the President by leaders of both parties and of business and by experts in economics.

Actually, President Hoover was far more energetic and imaginative than any previous American President in trying to combat the depression. His Secretary of the Treasury, Mellon, was a "leave-it-alone liquidationist" who thought a thoroughgoing cycle of bankruptcy and deflation would be healthful. Hoover did not agree. He determined that the government should intervene positively but in a very limited way, seeking the voluntary cooperation of business and labor.

First, to restore confidence, Hoover declared: "The fundamental business of this country, that is, production and distribution of commodities, is on a sound and prosperous basis." Most of the business leaders echoed him. Next, he held a number of highly publicized meetings of business, farm, and labor leaders in an effort to rally the country to adopt a voluntary program. Businessmen pledged themselves not to cut payrolls or production; labor leaders, not to ask for better wages or hours. Hoover also announced a significant tax cut and arranged for the Federal Reserve to provide increased bank credit. He asked Congress for an increase of $423 million in public works—a huge sum for the period—and called upon mayors and governors to engage in the "energetic yet prudent pursuit" of public construction.

Already, in April 1929, Hoover had called Congress into special session to provide farm relief and raise the tariff. His farm program, embodied in the Agricultural Marketing Act of 1929, set up large-scale government machinery to aid the farmer. The program, as Hoover insisted, was voluntary and did not include any of the price-fixing schemes for which farm or-

Hoover Dam
Conservationists for years urged the construction of a huge dam on the Colorado River to utilize its large flow for irrigation and power production and to prevent disastrous flooding of the Imperial Valley in California. Only the federal government was large enough to provide sufficient funds for the project. Through the 1920s, Hoover worked as chairman of the Colorado River Commission to reconcile conflicting claims of the seven states in the Colorado basin and to obtain President Coolidge's reluctant approval of preliminary surveys. Hoover himself insisted that the power be sold as falling water to keep the government even out of the business of generating electricity. Work on the dam began in the Hoover administration. It was the first of the great self-liquidating public works to be constructed during the depression, directly employing 4,000 workers, and indirectly aiding thousands more. The dam and power houses cost $108 million; in addition, the cities of southern California constructed a $220 million aqueduct to carry part of the water 259 miles to the Pacific coast. The dam, 726 feet high, created an artificial lake stretching 115 miles up the river, holding enough water to cover the state of Connecticut to a depth of 10 feet. When the dam was finished in 1935, two years ahead of the contract date, it was dedicated by President Franklin D. Roosevelt. (National Archives)

ganizations were lobbying. It encouraged the voluntary combination of farmers to help themselves under government auspices. A Farm Board of eight members administered a revolving fund of $500 million, from which the board could make loans to national marketing cooperatives or establish corporations to buy surpluses and thus raise prices.

Within six months the depression precipitated farm prices toward new lows. Until the summer of 1931, the Wheat Stabilization Corporation and the Cotton Stabilization Corporation were able to keep prices a bit above world levels. By 1932 their funds were spent, their warehouses full, and grain prices at the lowest point since the founding of the American colonies. The Farm Board had operated on too small a scale, and it had lacked power to limit production. When President Hoover later called for voluntary reduction of the wheat crop, acreage dropped only 1 percent in Kansas. The Farm Board experiment thus underscored the futility of a voluntary crop-control program and prepared the way for a more drastic measure.

Congress, taking President Hoover's advice to raise agricultural tariffs, prepared an overall measure, the Hawley-Smoot bill, which contained 75 increases on farm products, and 925 on manufactured goods. It raised the average duty from the 26 percent of the Fordney-McCumber Act to a new high of 50 percent. By the time it was ready for the President's signature in the spring of 1930, a thousand members of the American Economic Association had signed a petition urging him to veto it as an unwise piece of economic nationalism. He ignored such warnings and signed the measure. Other nations in reprisal placed new restrictions on American goods. In a time of world depression, rampant economic nationalism was perhaps inevitable, but it was unfortunate that the United States led the way.

The worsening depression gave Democrats a political issue. In the fall of 1930 they won a bare majority in the House of Representatives and, with the aid of Republican progressives, took effective control of the Senate. From this point on, Congress began seriously to harass Hoover, demanding that he move from voluntary measures to large-scale federal relief and spending. He refused to budge. By the spring of 1931 conditions seemed to be improving, and Hoover and others thought the worst was over. But the American economy took another downturn in consequence of a European financial panic. By May 1931 the largest bank in Austria had collapsed, and the disaster threatened to wreck the banking and monetary systems of Germany and other nations of Europe.

To avert this, President Hoover proposed a one-year moratorium on reparations and war-debt payments, but France destroyed much of the good effect through her delay in accepting the plan. By September, England and most other nations of the world had gone off the gold standard. The crisis in western Europe caused European gold to be withdrawn from American banks, and European holdings of American securities to be dumped on the market. As other nations devalued their currency in going off the gold standard, American trade with them declined disastrously.

By December 1931, when Congress met, conditions were so frightening that President Hoover abandoned his reliance upon voluntary measures and proposed direct governmental action of an unprecedented sort to combat the depression. In January 1932 Congress created a giant loan agency, the Reconstruction Finance Corporation, which during 1932 loaned $1.5 billion, mostly to banks, railroads, and other businesses. Hoover, trying to parry criticism that he had set up a bread line for big business, asserted that his purpose was to stop deflation and thus increase employment, mainly by helping relatively small companies. Congress also provided for banks, together with further capital for existing loan banks, to help prevent mortgage foreclosures.

On the issues of very large-scale public works and direct relief for the unemployed, the President clashed bitterly with Republican progressives and Democrats in Congress. In July 1932 he vetoed their bill as being impractical and dangerous; he felt that direct relief was a state and local responsibility. Subsequently, he signed a bill he himself had recommended, authorizing the RFC to lend $300 million for relief, and another $1.5 billion for self-liquidating public works.

Hoover believed that, while people must not go cold and hungry, feeding them was a voluntary and local responsibility. "If we start appropriations of this character," he had declared, "we have not only impaired something infinitely valuable in the life of the American people but have struck at the roots of self-government." It was hard for desperate people to appreciate such niceties of thought. Hoover, who had been one of the most popular of American heroes, became the scapegoat for the depression.

To some observers the 1928 election had seemed to be a great national referendum in favor of prohibition, yet prohibition was not to last much longer than prosperity. Though Hoover had referred to it as a "noble experiment," enforcement was breaking down so badly that Congress stiffened the penalties for violating the Volstead Act and authorized the new President to appoint a National Law Enforcement Commission. This commission, headed by a former Attorney General, George Wickersham, ultimately reported in 1931 that prohibition was not only unenforced but virtually unenforceable.

Rampant gangsterism and the open flouting of the law by millions of otherwise respectable citizens convinced many thoughtful Americans that prohibition was not worth its price in lawlessness. With the coming of the depression, some well-to-do people, already banded into antiprohibition organizations, redoubled their efforts in the hope that repeal would bring lower income taxes and greater prosperity. In February 1933 Congress submitted to the states the Twenty-first Amendment, repealing prohibition; by December it had been ratified, and the experiment was at an end.

DEEPENING DESPAIR

As the depression deepened, there were surprisingly few signs of social disorder or outbursts of violence within the United States. Communists agitated, won a few converts among intellectual leaders, but made almost no impact upon the masses.

The chain reaction of unemployment slowly spread from 1930 into 1933. At first those in marginal or poorer jobs were hit hardest, as those who had been in better jobs moved downward. In time millions who had never been unemployed for any length of time were jobless and unable to find work of any sort. They were bewildered, for they had been brought up in the sturdy tradition of self-reliance and had accepted the doctrine of rugged individualism—that opportunities were limitless if only one had the ambition and energy to take advantage of them. Now these people were humiliated and baffled at not being able to provide for themselves and their families. As they remained idle for months and then years, they were in danger of losing their skills as well as their morale. Physical and moral erosion threatened.

Care of the unemployed had always been a responsibility primarily of private charity, and for several years the President and governors exhorted citizens to contribute to the Red Cross or to emergency funds. But the task soon became far too great for private charity to handle. By 1931, the Red Cross could provide only 75 cents a week to feed each hungry family in southern Illinois.

Although several European nations had maintained unemployment insurance programs for decades, not a single state in the United States enacted such a law until January 1932, when Wisconsin passed one. Even as the distress grew, many magazines and newspapers proclaimed that any permanent system of direct unemployment relief like the British dole would bankrupt the government and undermine the moral fiber of the recipients. Not until September 1931 did the New York legislature at the insistence of Governor Franklin D. Roosevelt establish the first relief organization of any state, the Temporary Emergency Relief Administration, which became the model for other states and the prototype of the later federal relief agency.

To some of the unemployed who had recently moved to cities, the solution seemed to be to return to the farm; the migration away

---

Shacks of the Unemployed, New York City   1932

Robert Bendiner has written: "To a New Yorker . . . the signs of collapse were aggressive. Along the Hudson, below Riverside Drive, I daily passed the tarpaper huts of a Hooverville, where scores of families lived the lives of reluctant gypsies, cooking whatever they had to cook over open fires within sight of passengers on the double-decker Fifth Avenue buses. Dozens of such colonies had sprung up in the city . . . but not nearly enough to accommodate the swelling army of the jobless and dispossessed." (Top right, Culver)

An Apple Seller in New York City

In the fall of 1931 and 1932, a number of unemployed tried to gain a pittance for themselves by selling apples. President Hoover later wrote: "One incident of these times has persisted as the eternal damnation of Hoover. Some Oregon or Washington apple growers' association shrewdly appraised the sympathy of the public for the unemployed. They set up a system of selling apples on the street corners in many cities, thus selling their crop and raising their prices. Many persons left their jobs for the more profitable one of selling apples. When any left-winger wishes to indulge in scathing oratory, he demands, 'Do you want to return to selling apples?' " (Bottom right, Culver)

from farms was now reversed. But farm prices fell so low that once again, on parts of the plains, farmers burned corn to keep warm. A rancher sold seven lambs in the Denver livestock market and, after paying commissions and fees, received a check for 75 cents. In a railroad diner, two lamb chops cost the same amount. Prices of manufactured goods were relatively so high that it took ten bushels of wheat to buy a cheap pair of shoes. In drought areas farmers lacked even sufficient food.

Some bewildered farmers around Sioux City, Iowa, in 1932 embargoed milk bound for the city because they were receiving 2 cents a quart and it retailed for 8 cents. Many more Iowa farmers participated in Milo Reno's militant Farmers' Holiday Association to block all farm products from the market until prices rose.

Through the summer of 1932, some 12,000 to 14,000 unemployed veterans congregated in Washington to demonstrate for the immediate payments of their bonus for wartime service, not due until 1945. For weeks they lived in squalor in abandoned tenements and in shanties on the mud flats of the Anacostia River. After Congress failed to pass a bonus bill, about half of them, discouraged, went home. The continued presence of the rest alarmed Hoover and many Washingtonians. After a riot, the President called upon the army to oust the veterans. Under the personal command of General Douglas MacArthur, with tanks, gas masks, and fixed bayonets, the army did so. "That was a bad looking mob," MacArthur declared, expressing the alarm of conservatives. "It was animated by the essence of revolution."

Selected Readings

Surveys and Interpretations
J. D. Hicks, *Republican Ascendancy, 1921–1933**
(1960); W. E. Leuchtenberg, *The Perils of Prosperity, 1914–32** (1958); George Soule, *Prosperity Decade: From War to Depression, 1917–1929* (1947); A. M. Schlesinger, Jr., *The Crisis of the Old Order** (1957).

Aspects of Life
G. H. Knoles, *The Jazz Age Revisited* (1955); F. L. Allen, *Only Yesterday** (1931); R. S. and H. M. Lind, *Middletown** (1929); N. F. Furniss, *The Fundamentalist Controversy, 1918–1931* (1954); Ray Ginger, *Six Days or Forever?** (1958), about the Scopes trial; Erik Barnouw, *A Tower in Babel: A History of Broadcasting in the United States*, vol. 1: to 1933 (1966); W. R. Ross, *The Last Hero: Charles A. Lindbergh* (1967).

Radicalism and Reaction
W. Preston, Jr., *Aliens and Dissenters: Federal Suppression of Radicals, 1903–1933* (1963); R. K. Murray, *The Red Scare** (1955); Zechariah Chafee, Jr., *Free Speech in the United States* (1941); S. Coben, *A. Mitchell Palmer, Politician* (1963); G. L. Joughin and E. M. Morgan, *The Legacy of Sacco and Vanzetti** (1948); David Brody, *Labor in Crisis: The Steel Strike of 1919** (1965); Irving Bernstein, *The Lean Years: A History of the American Worker, 1920–1933** (1960); David Chalmers, *Hooded Americanism** (1965), on the Klan; E. D. Cronon, *Black Moses: The Story of Marcus Garvey** (1955).

The Eighteenth and Nineteenth Amendments
J. H. Timberlake, *Prohibition and the Progressive Movement, 1900–1920* (1963); Andrew Sinclair, *Prohibition: The Era of Excess** (1962); Charles Merz, *Dry Decade* (1931); Virginius Dabney, *Dry Messiah: The Life of Bishop Cannon* (1949); A. S. Kraditor, *The Ideas of the Woman Suffrage Movement, 1890–1920* (1965); David Morgan, *Suffragists and Democrats: The Politics of Woman Suffrage in America* (1972); J. S. Lemons, *The Woman Citizen: Social Feminism in the 1920's* (1973); A. F. Scott, *The Southern Lady: From Pedestal to Politics, 1830–1930* (1970).

Literature
Alfred Kazin, *On Native Grounds: An Interpretation of Modern American Prose Literature** (1942); Edmund Wilson, *The Shores of Light** (1952) and *The American Earthquake** (1958); Frederick Hoffman, *Freudianism and the Literary Mind** (1947); Mark Schorer, *Sinclair Lewis** (1961); M. K. Singleton, *H. L. Mencken and the American Mercury Adventure* (1962).

Harding and Coolidge
S. H. Adams, *Incredible Era: The Life and Times of Warren G. Harding** (1939); Andrew Sinclair, *The Available Man* (1965), on Harding; Burl Noggle, *Teapot Dome: Oil and Politics in the 1920's* (1962); J. L. Bates, *The Origins of Teapot Dome: Progressives,*

Parties, and Petroleum, 1909–1921 (1963); W. A. White, *A Puritan in Babylon** (1938), on Coolidge; D. R. McCoy, *Calvin Coolidge, the Quiet President* (1967); H. H. Quint and R. H. Ferrell, eds., *The Talkative President: The Off-the-Record Press Conferences of Calvin Coolidge* (1964).

Foreign Affairs
J. C. Vinson, *The Parchment Peace* (1955); M. J. Pusey, *Charles Evans Hughes* (2 vols., 1951); Dexter Perkins, *Charles Evans Hughes and American Democratic Statesmanship* (1953); R. H. Ferrell, *Peace in Their Time* (1952); R. J. Maddox, *William E. Borah and American Foreign Policy* (1969).

Political Opposition
K. C. Mackay, *The Progressive Movement of 1924* (1947); J. J. Huthmacher, *Massachusetts People and Politics, 1919–1933** (1959); Frank Freidel, *Franklin D. Roosevelt: The Ordeal* (1954); Oscar Handlin, *Al Smith and His America** (1958); E. A. Moore, *A Catholic Runs for President* (1956); R. C. Silva, *Rum, Religion, and Votes: 1928 Re-examined* (1962).

Hoover and the Depression
A. U. Romasco, *The Poverty of Abundance: Hoover, the Nation, the Depression** (1965); H. G. Warren, *Herbert Hoover and the Great Depression* (1959); Herbert Hoover, *Memoirs: The Great Depression, 1929–1941* (1952); J. H. Shideler, *Farm Crisis, 1919–1923* (1957); Theodore Saloutos and J. D. Hicks, *Twentieth Century Populism: Agricultural Discontent in the Middle West, 1900–1939** (1951); J. K. Galbraith, *The Great Crash** (1955); Milton Friedman and A. J. Schwartz, *The Great Contraction, 1929–1933** (1965); R. Daniels, *The Bonus March: An Episode of the Great Depression* (1971).

*Titles available in paperback.

Twenty-four

During 1917 and 1918 the government of the United States, in order to win a war, had undertaken to control nearly all aspects of the economy. But never before the 1930s had the government intervened in so many ways in order to overcome a depression. Between 1933 and 1938, under the leadership of President Franklin D. Roosevelt, the government launched a bewildering variety of programs and set up a jumble of "alphabetical agencies"—AAA, NRA, TVA, and so on—to administer them. Some of these were intended to provide immediate relief for people facing a loss of income or property. Others were expected to stimulate economic activity and bring about recovery from the depression. Still others were designed to reform the economic system in order to reduce poverty and insecurity and avoid future depressions. Some of the programs served two or all three of these aims. All together, the series of measures constituted the New Deal.

The "three Rs" of the New Deal, then, were Relief, Recovery, and Reform. Its conservative critics, among them former President Hoover, contended that it involved also a "fourth R," namely, Revolution. Certainly the New Deal, which at first was rather cautious, emphasizing short-term measures of relief and recovery, gradually became somewhat more daring and placed greater emphasis on lasting reforms. All along, however, the programs were directed toward patching up and preserving, not destroying, the political and economic institutions that President Roosevelt and the American people had inherited. The programs were mostly improvisations that were drawn up to meet the needs of the moment. They were based on previous American experience. A precedent for practically every one of them can be found in something that had been proposed or tried out earlier. The New Deal was revolutionary only in the sense that it embodied a larger number of undertakings at one time and carried them to greater lengths than other

Rallying for the NRA 1933
The NRA emblem was a blue eagle clutching a cogwheel and a thunderbolt. To foster compliance with the NRA codes of fair competition, merchants and householders displayed the emblem on posters and communities staged rallies. Here, at a San Francisco rally, 8,000 children form a giant eagle on a baseball field. (UPI)

comparable movements, such as the New Freedom, had done.

The New Deal failed to bring about full recovery; not until after 1941 did war, the greatest of public works, take up the slack in the employment of human and other resources. But the relief measures enabled both the people and the economic system to survive the depression, and the reform measures made significant and enduring changes in the system itself. The role of government in economic life was vastly increased (and was to be increased still further by the ensuing war). The nation had become a welfare state. Henceforth the principle was to be generally accepted — though not always completely realized — that it was the government's duty to "provide for the general welfare" by controlling business and agriculture, maintaining full employment, and assuring at least a basic economic security to all members of society.

A Change of Leadership

In 1932 Republicans meeting in Chicago renominated Hoover in a spirit far from jubilant; they had little illusion about the outcome of the election. The Democrats, assembling later in an excited, expectant mood, saw almost certain victory after twelve years out of power. Almost anyone they nominated was sure to be elected.

THE INTERREGNUM OF 1932–1933

Well over a majority of the delegates came pledged to vote for Governor Franklin D. Roosevelt of New York. Roosevelt had been working astutely for the nomination for years. To a considerable degree he bridged the gulf between the urban and rural Democrats. He was ready to emphasize economic issues and ignore the earlier divisions over prohibition and religion.

Breaking precedent, Roosevelt flew immediately to Chicago to deliver his acceptance address before the convention. He endorsed the Democratic platform, which except for a promise of prohibition repeal was not much bolder than that of the Republicans. He declared: "I pledge you, I pledge myself, to a new deal for the American people." Thus the Roosevelt program acquired a name before the electorate had more than the haziest notion what it might embody.

Nor did the voters learn much during the campaign, for Roosevelt shrewdly confined himself to warm generalities which would offend few and yet would bring him the enormous vote of protest against Hoover. Through Roosevelt's speeches ran many of the old progressive themes, together with new suggestions of economic planning. An able team, largely of university professors under the leadership of Raymond Moley, helped devise policies and draft speeches for him. Newspapermen dubbed his group of advisers the "brain trust." At the Commonwealth Club in San Francisco, Roosevelt broke furthest from the past by insisting that the government must assist business in developing a well-regulated economic system. Everyone, he said, had a right to a comfortable living; the nation's industrial and agricultural mechanism could produce more than enough. If need be, to achieve this end, government must police irresponsible economic power. Roosevelt felt he was doing no more than restating the objectives of Jefferson and Wilson in terms of the complexities of the thirties when he proposed that the government should act as a regulator for the common good within the existing economic system. So far as Roosevelt explained the New Deal during the campaign, this was its essence.

President Hoover, tired and grim, took to the road in October to warn the populace that without his program things might be infinitely worse. His speeches, though earnest, were dull and dreary in both style and delivery compared with Roosevelt's breezy, optimistic performances. Hoover was the last of the Presidents to scorn the aid of speech writers.

Some voters, disappointed because they could detect little difference between Roosevelt's program and Hoover's, turned to Norman Thomas and the Socialists or to William Z. Foster and the Communists. Yet, even in this year

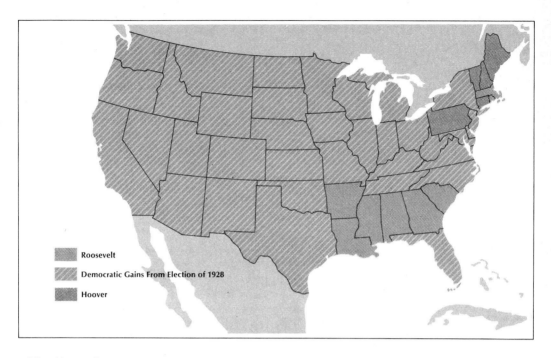

Election of 1932

of despair, the Socialists polled only 882,000 votes, and the Communists only 103,000. Roosevelt received 22,822,000 popular votes (57.4 percent), Hoover 15,762,000 (39.7 percent). The Democrats carried both houses of Congress by top-heavy majorities. Roosevelt had won an overwhelming mandate — but for what?

Actually, there had been discernible differences between the two candidates and their programs — besides the obvious difference that Hoover was a worn, discredited President, and Roosevelt a buoyant candidate. Hoover had seen the depression as world-wide in origin and development; rather inconsistently he was ready to combat it internationally through currency stabilization, and nationally, through raising the tariff still higher if need be. Roosevelt chose to regard the depression as domestic, specifically Republican, in origin. During the campaign Hoover had forced him to equivocate on the old Democratic low-tariff position. Roosevelt was ready (as both his record as governor and his speeches indicated) to move toward economic nationalism. But he agreed with Hoover on the need for government thrift and a balanced budget.

President Hoover faced an agonizing four months before Roosevelt would take office on March 4: the Twentieth ("lame duck") Amendment to end this long carry-over of a defeated President and Congress was not ratified until February 1933. There had been a brief economic upswing in the spring months of 1932, reaching a peak in July. (Economists later ascribed this to Hoover's own brief plunge into deficit financing through public works spending and Reconstruction Finance Corporation loans.) Hoover felt he was bringing an end to the depression and that only the threat of unsettling measures from Roosevelt was preventing continued recovery. Hence, in a series of interchanges with Roosevelt during the winter of 1932–1933, he tried to bind the President-elect to economic orthodoxy.

Hoover favored the reestablishment of an international gold standard. He hoped that the United States and other nations would agree to this at an economic and monetary conference that was scheduled to meet in London after Roosevelt's inauguration. But Roosevelt would make no commitment.

By February 1933 an acute banking crisis had developed. Bank resources and deposits had been declining at an alarming rate. In the previous three years, 5,000 banks had failed, and now one after another was collapsing as depositors lined up to withdraw their deposits. To stop the run on the banks, governors began proclaiming banking holidays in their states. By March 4 banking was at a halt or drastically restricted in all states but one.

President Hoover wrote a letter to Roosevelt, charging that the crisis was caused by "steadily degenerating confidence" in the President-elect, and calling upon him to give prompt public assurance that there would be no tinkering with the currency, no heavy borrowing, no unbalancing of the budget. Roosevelt had not the slightest intention of adopting Hoover's views.

F. D. R. TAKES COMMAND

When Roosevelt was inaugurated, on March 4, 1933, most of the nation's banks were closed. At least 13 million people were unemployed, some of them so close to starvation that they were scrabbling for food scraps in garbage dumps. Millions of farmers were on the brink of foreclosure; many others had fallen over the brink.

In his inaugural address, President Roosevelt spoke with vigor and confidence. "This great Nation will endure as it has endured, will revive and will prosper," he declared. "So, first of all, let me assert my firm belief that the only thing we have to fear is fear itself." Somehow these words, although they said nothing new, helped inspire the American people. From their depths of helplessness they were ready for the moment to be commanded, and in Roosevelt they saw someone ready to take strong leadership. Such leadership he promised. If Congress did not act, he announced, he would ask for "broad executive power to wage a war against the emergency, as great as the power that would be given to me if we were in fact invaded by a foreign foe."

Few Presidents have been better trained for the White House. Roosevelt had served in the New York state senate, been wartime assistant secretary of the navy, and had been twice elected governor of New York. He was skilled in both legislative and administrative techniques as well as in practical politics. As a youth he had spent much time in Europe, and maintained a continuing interest in foreign affairs. Roosevelt's ideology was progressive, influenced by his wife's uncle, Theodore Roosevelt, whom he admired, and his former chief, Woodrow Wilson, whom he revered.

Neither the new President nor his advisers were clear-cut in their thinking. What was important was that Roosevelt, while basically rooted in the older economics and the social-justice tradition of the progressives, was ready to experiment. His program would be flexible, not doctrinaire; the new economic theories would grow from it, not it from the theories. When one of the brain trusters warned of perils ahead, Roosevelt declared: "There is nothing to do but meet every day's troubles as they come." This was his political pragmatism, and out of it grew the New Deal economic policies.

With the banking crisis at its height, he might well have taken drastic steps such as nationalization of the banks. But he seemed bent above all upon restoring the confidence of businessmen. His initial program differed little from what they had been advocating. He met the banking crisis in a manner pleasing to the banking community. He issued a proclamation on March 6, 1933, closing all banks and stopping transactions or exports in gold for four days until Congress could meet in special session. On March 9 he sent in a conservative bill which would bolster the stronger banks. It authorized the Federal Reserve System to issue notes against their assets, and the Reconstruction Finance Corporation to make them loans. The bill dealt a death blow to weaker banks; inspectors would deny them licenses to reopen. It stopped the ebb of gold from the Treasury and the country through prohibiting hoarding and exportation. In effect, the country went off the gold standard (officially it did so April 19, 1933). Congress passed the bill within four hours of its introduction. In the House, a rolled-up newspaper substituted for it, since there had not been time to print copies.

On March 12, in the first of his "fireside chats" over the radio, the President, speaking in a warm, intimate manner, told the American people that the crisis was over. "I can assure you," he declared, "that it is safer to keep your money in a reopened bank than under the mattress." And so indeed it was; by his legislation and his confident leadership, Roosevelt had averted the threat to banks and the capitalist system. Three-fourths of the banks in the Federal Reserve System reopened within the next three days, and a billion dollars in hoarded currency and gold flowed back into them within a month. Practically all unsafe banks were now out of business; there were very few new failures in the years that followed.

On the morning after the passage of the Emergency Banking Act, Roosevelt further reassured business by sending Congress an economy bill, to balance the budget by cutting

---

**Roosevelt and Hoover en Route to Roosevelt's Inauguration
March 4, 1933**

Roosevelt never forgot the awkwardness of his ride to the Capitol with the grim, unresponsive Hoover, exhausted from grappling with the banking crisis. No one would have guessed in the black days before March 4, 1933, that the incoming President would set his mark on the age as have few Chief Executives. He alarmed even those closest to him with his amiability, his ready acceptance of suggestions, his quick "Fine, fine, fine." New Yorkers, fearful that his jaunty buoyancy, his facility at compromise, and his skill at political maneuver were a façade for weakness, had sometimes referred to him as "the Grin" or the "Boy Scout Governor." They did not as yet see the energy and persistence with which he applied himself, or the cold iron sometimes not far beneath the charm. His physical courage they realized, for after his polio attack in 1921 he had indomitably stayed in politics, refusing to surrender to his infirmity. He had subordinated it so thoroughly that most people regarded him only as somewhat lame and never thought of him as using a wheelchair. Again he demonstrated his self-possession at Miami in February 1933, by remaining astoundingly calm when an insane assassin missed him but mortally wounded the mayor of Chicago sitting beside him. Somehow Roosevelt was able to transmit some of his courage to the nation in March 1933. (United Press International)

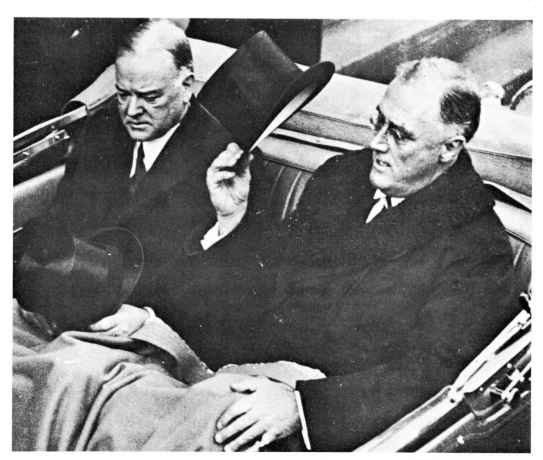

salaries of government employees and pensions of veterans as much as 15 percent. This, Roosevelt declared, was the only way to avoid a billion-dollar deficit. This bill too passed almost instantly, although with such fierce opposition from veterans' organizations that it carried the House only with Republican votes. Pressure from veterans soon led Congress to rescind the pension cuts over Roosevelt's veto, but the President drastically slashed the regular expenditures of the government.

On March 13, 1933, Roosevelt proposed legalizing beer that had a 3.2 percent alcoholic content, pending repeal of the prohibition amendment. This, he felt, would stimulate recovery and bring in needed taxes. (It would also, as it turned out, rescue millions of law violators from the rigors of home brew and gangster-made beer.)

Thus far, except for the gold clause in the Emergency Banking Act, the program of the new administration might have been that of a Hoover with a smile. It restored the confidence of bankers and businessmen, the stock market going up 15 percent. But this was anticipatory of the real recovery to follow; for the moment nothing had been improved but the confidence of the American nation.

Tentative Beginnings

During his first hundred days in office, keeping Congress in special session, Roosevelt put through a series of laws and began to take steps that led him away from the "sound" position—so reassuring to bankers and other businessmen—that he originally had assumed.

EMERGENCY RELIEF

The first step was to feed the millions of hungry unemployed. While Roosevelt subscribed to his predecessor's maxim that relief was primarily the task of states and communities, he proposed that the federal government provide grants rather than loans to states. Congress established the Federal Emergency Relief Administration, and appropriated an initial half-billion dollars for it. Roosevelt appointed the director of the New York state relief agency, Harry Hopkins, whom he hardly knew as yet, to run the federal program. Hopkins was a dedicated social worker with a lively tongue and a keen sense of professional ethics. He ardently believed in work relief rather than direct relief, but in the spring of 1933 everyone hoped recovery was at hand so that relief would be needed only for a few months.

But recovery lagged, and some new way had to be found to care for the unemployed through the winter of 1933–1934. Relief administrator Hopkins persuaded the President to establish a temporary work relief program, the Civil Works Administration. Between November and April it put 4 million people to work at emergency projects. Sometimes it was madework like leaf raking, to which critics applied an old Texas term, "boondoggling." Some of the projects, despite lack of funds for materials and tools, made substantial improvements. The output was of secondary importance; the work raised the morale of the unemployed and increased their buying power by $950 million. The purchasing power thus injected into the economy was probably responsible for the wavering recovery, as the index of production rose from 71 in November 1933 to 86 in May 1934. But soon Roosevelt capitulated to fierce conservative criticism and liquidated the program.

Congress also created an organization that reflected Roosevelt's keen interest in preserving natural as well as human resources, the Civilian Conservation Corps. It received a grant of $300 million to enroll 250,000 young men from relief families and 50,000 veterans and woodsmen, to work at reforestation and flood control. Ultimately the CCC enrolled 500,000 young men, but this was only a fraction of the unemployed youths in the nation.

Mortgage relief was a pressing need of millions of farm owners and home owners. Roosevelt quickly consolidated all farm credit organizations into a new Farm Credit Administration. Congress voted such large additional funds for it that within two years it had refinanced a fifth of all farm mortgages in the

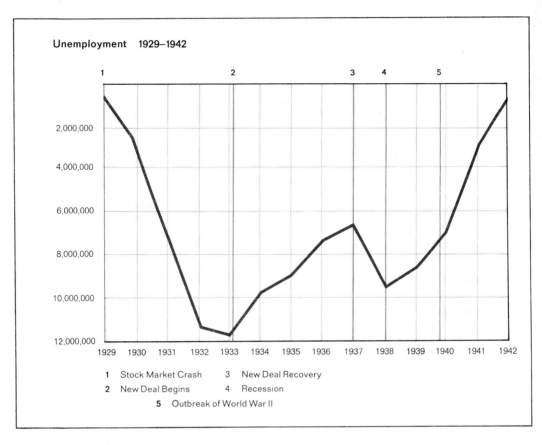

Unemployment 1929–1942

| | 1 | | | | 2 | | | | 3 | 4 | | 5 | |

2,000,000

4,000,000

6,000,000

8,000,000

10,000,000

12,000,000

1929 1930 1931 1932 1933 1934 1935 1936 1937 1938 1939 1940 1941 1942

1 Stock Market Crash   3 New Deal Recovery
2 New Deal Begins   4 Recession
            5 Outbreak of World War II

Unemployment was especially high among young people, those who lived in areas where the textile mills and coal mines had been closed, and among the minority groups. The rate of unemployment changed drastically with the acute shortage of labor during the war years. Although the 1942 employment figures were up to the 1929 high, this chart does not reflect the proportionate population growth.

United States. The Frazier-Lemke Farm-Bankruptcy Act of 1933 enabled some farmers to regain their farms even after the foreclosure of mortgages. Unfortunately, these measures came too late to save all farmers; by 1934 a quarter of them for one reason or another had lost their property. A comparable Home Owners' Loan Corporation, established in June 1933, in a three-year period loaned $3 billion to refinance the mortgages of over a million distressed householders. Altogether it carried about a sixth of the nation's urban mortgage burden. A year later Congress established a Federal Housing Administration to insure mortgages for new construction and home repairs—more properly a recovery than a relief agency. All these mortgage agencies not only

rescued mortgage holders, but also eased the burden on banks and insurance companies, thus filling a recovery function.

Under the New Deal, the Reconstruction Finance Corporation continued to function as the key loan agency for relief to business. The Democratic Congress inveighed against the RFC policy of making large loans only to big businesses and not to individuals. Congress therefore broadened the RFC's lending power so that it could, and indeed did, also lend to small businessmen. Under the conservative management of a shrewd Texan, Jesse Jones, it continued to make most of its loans to large enterprises, including banks, and to governmental units, on sound security and with a high percentage of ultimate repayment.

THE FIRST AAA

The Agricultural Adjustment Administration, created in May 1933, marked the triumphant conclusion of the farmers' long struggle to get government aid for raising farm prices. Henceforth the farmers, who continued to be a declining fraction of the whole population, received preferential treatment from the government.

Roosevelt was mainly interested in the relatively substantial farmers, such as the 300,000 who even in 1933 were paying dues of $10 a year or more to the Farm Bureau Federation. These and the Grange members desired a program to limit crops. Poorer members of other farm organizations like the Farmers' Union and the National Farmers' Holiday Association opposed production cuts, seeking instead direct relief and, above all, inflation. Roosevelt hoped to develop a program that would fit the Farm Bureau formula and yet would not drive poorer farmers into new revolt. He let the various farm organization leaders devise their own plan. Fifty of them met in Washington early in March 1933 and drafted an omnibus bill that contained scraps and reworkings of most of the old schemes. It provided for a "domestic-allotment" system. Producers of seven basic commodities (wheat, cotton, corn, hogs, rice, tobacco, and milk and other dairy products) were to receive benefit payments if they cut acreage or production. Funds for these payments would come from a tax upon the processing of commodities—for example, a tax on the milling of wheat. The tax would be added to the price of the flour or other product, and so it would be passed on to the consumer, who would thus indirectly pay the farmer for growing less. Farm prices were to be brought up to "parity," that is, a level that would provide the same

Drought Refugees Stalled on the Highway
Between 1935 and 1939, drought and depression impelled some 350,000 people to leave their farms in the Dust Bowl states, especially Oklahoma, and to seek precarious employment in the fields and orchards of California. In his novel The Grapes of Wrath *(1939) John Steinbeck gave a heart-rending account of an Oklahoma family's journey on Highway 66 across plains, deserts, and mountains. Breakdowns along the way were frequent—like this one photographed in New Mexico in 1937 by Dorothy Lange for the Farm Security Administration. (Library of Congress)*

Denouncing the New Dealers, former President Herbert Hoover once said they professed the "three Rs" of Relief, Recovery, and Reform but secretly espoused the "fourth R" of Revolution. How revolutionary was the New Deal in fact? To what extent did it break with the American past? Historians have given a wide variety of answers to these questions.

Some authors maintained that the New Deal was more evolutionary than revolutionary, that in essence it was an extension of the progressive movement. In *The History of the New Deal* (1944) Basil Rauch made a distinction between a "first" and a "second" New Deal. The first (1933–1935), rather conservative, concentrated on recovery as the chief aim and gave aid mostly to big business and big agriculture. The second (1935–1938), relatively liberal, paid more attention to reform and provided more benefits to industrial workers and small farmers. In *Rendezvous with Destiny* (1952) Eric F. Goldman saw the first phase as similar to Theodore Roosevelt's New Nationalism, the second as reminiscent of Woodrow Wilson's New Freedom, though Goldman thought "there was something more to New Deal liberalism," since it included such unprecedented measures as social security. But William E. Leuchtenburg, in *Franklin D. Roosevelt and the New Deal, 1932–1940* (1963), felt that the extent of the leftward shift had been exaggerated.

Other writers emphasized the elements of change rather than those of continuity. Richard Hofstadter, *The Age of Reform* (1955), conceded that there were continuities from progressivism but insisted that, as a whole, the Franklin D. Roosevelt program was a "drastic new departure" and was "different from anything that had yet happened in the United States." Hofstadter pointed out that many old progressives, still living in the 1930s, opposed the New Deal. Carl N. Degler, *Out of Our Past* (1959), called the New Deal the "Third American Revolution" (the first two being the Revolution of 1776 and the Civil War) and said it "marked the crossing of a divide from which, it would seem, there could be no turning back."

All the foregoing historians thought of themselves as liberals and, though in some respects critical, were basically sympathetic with Roosevelt and his program. A conservative, anti-Roosevelt historian, Edgar E. Robinson, considered the New Deal a sharp break with the past but deplored it. In *The Roosevelt Leadership, 1933–1945* (1955) Robinson complained that Roosevelt, "an eloquent proponent of revolutionary change," moved the country toward "many of the primary leveling objectives of communism."

Young radicals of the 1960s took just the opposite view. Concerned about the unsolved problems of their own generation, they criticized the New Deal for having preserved too many of the evils of capitalism. "Many millions—businessmen, professionals, unionized workingmen, commercial farmers—had been given substantial help," the New Left historian Howard Zinn wrote in his introduction to *New Deal Thought* (1966). "Many millions more—sharecroppers, slum-dwellers, Negroes of North and South, the unemployed—still awaited a genuine 'new deal.'"

price relationship of farm products to manufactured goods as during the period 1909–1914.

Because the 1933 farm season was well under way when the AAA began operations, large-scale destruction was necessary to cut surpluses. Six million pigs and 220,000 sows about to farrow were slaughtered. Nine-tenths of their weight was inedible and processed into fertilizer, but they nevertheless provided 100 million pounds of pork for needy families. Bad weather so drastically cut the wheat crop that the AAA did not have to intervene to reduce it. Cotton farmers ploughed under a quarter of their crop—but it was the poorest quarter and they so intensively cultivated the rest that 30 million acres produced more than 36 million had done the previous year.

Despite continued high cotton production, a short textile boom sent the price up from 5.5 cents per pound to 10.6 cents in the summer. Then the price began to sag again and was held to 9.6 cents only through another device. A subsidiary of the AAA, the Commodity Credit Corporation, loaned 10 cents per pound to cotton farmers who would agree to take additional land out of production the next year. Since the loan was in excess of the market value of cotton, the government in effect was buying the crop at a premium price in return for the promise of drastic cuts in production. In this way cotton farmers received double the cash in 1933 that they had in 1931.

Farmers in other crop-reduction programs did not fare as well, although corn producers too could obtain commodity loans in the fall of 1933. Drought more than crop limitations reduced the output of wheat, corn, and hogs. Rising prices of manufactured goods canceled out most of the farmer's gain in real income. Yet on the whole his relative position improved somewhat.

The AAA actually hurt many of the farmers on the least productive farms, especially in the cotton belt. At times the AAA indirectly dispossessed them because planters, in reducing their acreage, sometimes evicted tenants and fired field hands. Unintentionally the AAA stimulated the great migration away from sharecropper cabins, at a time when city jobs no longer awaited the migrants. Rapid mechanization of farms and destructive wind storms on the Great Plains gave the great migration its impetus.

THE NRA

Hard-pressed businessmen sought measures providing for government stabilization of business. Since 1931 leaders of the United States Chamber of Commerce and others had been urging an antideflation scheme that involved price fixing through trade associations. This plan would have necessitated suspension of the antitrust laws. President Hoover, who earlier had given strong support to the trade association movement, indignantly opposed price-fixing schemes. His attorney general forced five leading trade associations to dissolve, and the Federal Trade Commission compelled revision of the trade association codes for sixty-two industries.

In the spring of 1933, businessmen sought from Roosevelt what Hoover had refused them. Many of them also demanded government enforcement of their agreements in order to raise prices and stabilize production. The New Deal was ready to give them what they wanted if they would accept wages-and-hours regulation and other concessions for labor. As a consequence of such an arrangement, prices and wages would go up. Consumers' buying power might lag and thus defeat the scheme. Therefore the New Dealers drafting the great recovery bill added another ingredient for which there was much pressure: a large-scale public works spending program to prime the economic pump. This was the genesis of the National Industrial Recovery Act, which passed Congress in June 1933.

A new era of government alliance with business for the common good seemed to be opening. Roosevelt as he signed the act called it "the most important and far-reaching legislation ever enacted by the American Congress." On the same day, the President appointed as administrator the volatile, colorful General Hugh S. Johnson, who pictured himself as a sort of benign dictator presiding over the economy.

The President turned over the $3.3 billion for public works to Secretary of the Interior Harold L. Ickes, who slowly and methodically began to gather plans for projects, checking each carefully to make sure it would be really worthwhile. The need was for heavy spending in the next few months, but it was four years before Ickes' Public Works Administration pumped appreciable amounts of money into the economy.

President Roosevelt and NRA administrator Johnson called upon an excited nation to accept an interim blanket code, providing minimum wages of 30 cents or 40 cents an hour, maximum working hours of thirty-five or forty per week, and the abolition of child labor. Employers who agreed with the code were to display the NRA blue-eagle symbol; consumers who cooperated were to sign pledges that they would buy only from blue-eagle establishments. In much the spirit of 1917, the nation participated in NRA parades and rallies. As Johnson began negotiating codes with big industries, recovery seemed really imminent.

By the beginning of September 1933, specific codes for most of the big industries were in operation. In the drafting of the codes, Johnson had tried to serve as arbiter to balance the conflicting interests of business, labor, and the consumer. All three were represented at the bargaining table and received some degree of protection. Nevertheless, the real power in drawing up the regulations went to the businessmen themselves, to the leaders within each industry. They flocked to Washington and in the urgency of the moment rewrote their old trade association agreements into new NRA codes. These codes often contained provisions that were difficult for small units in the industry to maintain. Most of them provided for limiting production and, though often in disguised form, for price fixing.

Production, after a sharp rise, skidded downward during the fall of 1933, from an index figure of 101 in July to 71 in November, even as prices began to creep upward. The brave words and great NRA demonstrations of the spring and summer had not brought recovery. The New Deal honeymoon was over, and as General Johnson had predicted, the dead cats began to fly.

In the spring of 1934 a National Recovery Review Board under the famous iconoclastic lawyer, Clarence Darrow, reported that the NRA was dominated by big business; he hinted that what was needed was socialism. In the ensuing storm of vituperation between Johnson and Darrow, the NRA lost still more prestige.

A case involving the National Recovery Administration finally reached the Supreme Court. The Constitutional basis for the NRA was the power of Congress to regulate commerce among the states, but the test case involved alleged code violations by the Schechter brothers, who were operating a wholesale poultry business confined to one locality, Brooklyn. Among the charges against them were the selling of poultry in poor condition and the unfair treatment of employees. The Court (1935) unanimously held that the Schechters were not engaged in interstate commerce, and that Congress had unconstitutionally delegated legislative power to the President to draft the codes.

The "sick chicken" decision outraged Roosevelt. Seeing in it a threat to the whole New Deal, he lashed out at the judges for thinking in terms of the horse-and-buggy era. Actually, the decision proved to be more a blessing than a catastrophe for the New Deal, since it ended the decrepit NRA code system with its tacit suspension of the antitrust laws. "It has been an awful headache," Roosevelt confessed privately.

TVA AND CONSERVATION

Increasingly New Dealers turned their attention to measures that would remedy conditions they felt had helped bring on the depression. Their indignation burned expecially hot against the private power interests, which they felt had gulled investors and overcharged consumers. The spectacular collapse of the great Insull utility empire in the Middle West lent credence to their charges. Hence the first and most far-reaching of the New Deal reform measures was the creation of the Tennessee Valley Authority.

Through the twenties, millions of progressive Americans of both parties had shared the dream of Senator George Norris of Nebraska that the government might develop the nation's great water resources to provide cheap electric power. Millions of others accepted the educational program of the utilities companies, which spent $28 million to $35 million per year combating the idea of a national power program. The battle centered on the great dam that had been started at Muscle Shoals on the Tennessee River but had not been finished in time to provide nitrates during the war. Coolidge and

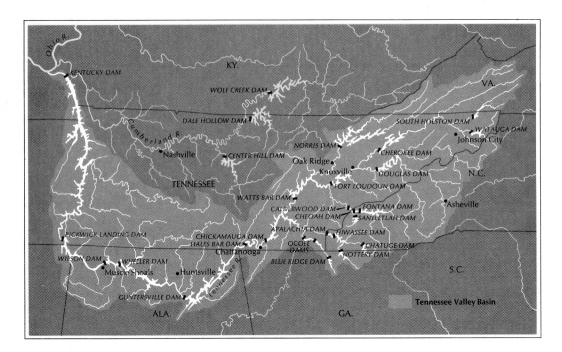

The Tennessee Valley Authority

the conservatives wished to sell it to Henry Ford for private development. Norris and his cohorts in Congress blocked them. Norris wished to make Muscle Shoals the center for developing the resources of the area and bringing abundance to millions of people living in poverty. His bill was vetoed by Coolidge and again by Hoover but was approved by Roosevelt in May 1933.

Basically, the TVA aimed to prevent the devastating floods that all too frequently had rolled down the rivers of the area, and to provide cheap, plentiful electricity as a yardstick for the measurement of private rates. More than this, the project became a great experiment in regional planning and rehabilitation.

Under a three-man board of directors with wide powers, the TVA in the next twenty years improved five existing dams and constructed twenty new ones. It stopped floods in the largest heavy-rainfall region in the nation and, by holding back the water, provided an inland waterway system with a nine-foot channel 652 miles long, soon heavy with traffic. From water power, and increasingly from steam plants, the TVA became the greatest producer of electricity in the United States. It also manufactured low-cost phosphate fertilizers. It taught farmers how to use them, how to restore the fertility of their soil, and how to end erosion by means of contour plowing and reforestation. TVA worked no miracles, but it did bring a higher living standard to the farmers of the area. It brought new light industry and increased business. When World War II came, the new power plants provided indispensable electricity for the production of munitions, aluminum, and plutonium.

In its "yardstick" function, TVA drove down the price of power in the area from 10 cents a kilowatt hour to 3 cents. Throughout the country, because of TVA and other pressures, the average residential rate dropped from 5.52 cents in 1933 to 3.67 cents in 1942. To private power companies the "yardstick" seemed grossly unfair, and they claimed that the TVA did not set its rates on the basis of true costs, including taxes. Its officials replied that its payments to local and state governments were comparable to the taxes assessed against private power companies.

Other great public power and irrigation developments were under way in the West during the same years. On the Colorado River, the Hoover Dam (begun during the Hoover administration) was finished in 1936, and on the Columbia River the Bonneville Dam was constructed in 1937 and the Grand Coulee Dam in 1942. In 1937 Norris proposed the creation of six additional regional authorities like the TVA; Congress failed to act, and the debate over public versus private development of power continued.

To combat drought conditions in the West, Roosevelt in 1934 by executive order set aside $15 million to build a "shelter belt" of trees on the Great Plains, to break the wind, collect moisture, and harbor wildlife. Critics scoffed, but somehow the trees grew where no one had believed they would. A Soil Erosion Service (later Soil Conservation Service), using much Civilian Conservation Corps manpower, was active, especially in the West. Homesteading on the range, which meant dry farming under almost insuperable difficulties, came to an end with the passage of the Taylor Grazing Act of 1934, which withdrew overgrazed land and set regulations for the use of public rangeland. Spoliation of Indian lands came to at least a temporary halt with the passage of the Indian Reorganization Act of 1934, intended to preserve the tribal domain, customs, and civil liberties of the Indians.

MONEY AND BANKING

Much of the New Deal was aimed at raising prices as a means of stimulating recovery. One way was to cut down production, as the AAA tried to do for agriculture and the NRA for industry. Another way was to put money into circulation through government spending, as was done in the relief programs (though recovery was not the primary aim of these). Still another way — at least in theory — was to manipulate the currency so as to increase the money supply.

By the summer of 1933, Roosevelt was ready to follow the reasoning of two Cornell University agricultural economists, who contended that if the price of gold were raised, the prices of other commodities would rise in rough proportion. The government needed only to purchase quantities of gold and cut the gold content of the dollar (as authorized by Congress). When financially orthodox Treasury officials refused to make the purchases, Roosevelt turned to the head of the Farm Credit

Administration, Henry Morgenthau, Jr., who began buying gold every day along with wheat, corn, and oats. Soon Morgenthau was made secretary of the treasury.

The silver-purchase program had much the same object as the gold-purchase program. From the seven silver-producing states with their fourteen senators came strong pressure, reminiscent of that of the Populist era, culminating in the Silver Purchase Act of 1934. This measure nearly tripled the price of silver at home. It also sent up the world silver price and wrought havoc in nations whose currency was on a silver standard. It did little or nothing to raise prices in the United States.

Roosevelt explained to a critical congressman: "I have always favored sound money, and do now, but it is 'too darned sound' when it takes so much of farm products to buy a dollar." In January 1934 he fixed the gold content of the dollar at 59.06 percent of the former amount. The resort to managed currency created new precedents for government action and thus, like the income tax a generation earlier, helped bring about an important change in the relationship of government and the economy. But it had little immediate effect upon recovery.

Through other legislation the government acquired new powers over the banks, including the power to manage the supply of bank credit through increased control over the Federal Reserve System. In June 1933 Roosevelt signed the Glass-Steagall Act aimed at curbing speculation by banks. This also established the Federal Deposit Insurance Corporation, which he had not favored. The FDIC guaranteed small deposits up to $2,500 and functioned so successfully that the guarantee was raised by successive stages, eventually reaching $15,000. It was a longer task to work out a comprehensive overhauling and strengthening of the Federal Reserve System to remedy the defects that had appeared during the depression. This was accomplished through the Banking Act of 1935, which established a seven-man board of governors with direct power over interest rates. By lowering the rates, the board could encourage borrowing from banks, and this would ordinarily have an inflationary (price-raising) effect.

To protect investors further, Congress passed the so-called Truth in Securities Act of 1933, requiring corporations floating new securities to register them with the Federal

Trade Commission, and provide full and accurate information on them. In June 1934 Congress went further and established the Securities and Exchange Commission to police the stock markets. Wall Streeters protested, but their complaints lost some of their effect when a former head of the New York Stock Exchange was sentenced to Sing Sing for larceny.

A Shift to the Left

Though President Roosevelt originally wished to provide for the welfare of each of the main economic and political groups in the nation, realities forced him to become the champion of the new political coalition of farmers, laborers, and the underprivileged in general. Roosevelt shifted partly because he felt that large business had defected, that it had betrayed his recovery program and was fighting politically to destroy the New Deal. Aligned against him were about 70 percent of the newspaper publishers and most of the large contributors of campaign funds.

Far more important was the threat from the left; this was mainly responsible for the gradual change in emphasis of the New Deal. In undermining this threat, Roosevelt's political pragmatism combined with his humanitarian inclinations to carry him even further than the progressives had dared venture toward positive government action for the general welfare.

THE PRESSURE OF POLITICS

Through 1934 the President was still trying to hold the support of businessmen and bankers. As late as October he told the American Bankers' Association: "The time is ripe for an alliance of all forces intent upon the business of recovery. In such an alliance will be found business and banking, agriculture and industry, and labor and capital. What an all-American team that would be!" There was little chance of it. In August 1934 conservative businessmen and self-styled Jeffersonian Democrats founded the American Liberty League to fight for free enterprise, state rights, the open shop, and an end to New Deal bureaucracy.

As the congressional elections of 1934 approached, conservatives within the Liberty League and without campaigned against the New Deal on the grounds that it was destroying the Constitution and driving the country to-

ward bankruptcy. All they succeeded in doing was to drive the dispossessed millions closer to the New Deal. Instead of losing ground to the Republican party—which would have been normal in a midterm election—the Democrats gained an additional ten seats in the Senate and also in the House.

Throughout the nation leaders arose who promised much to those despairing people whom the New Deal had not yet rescued. An elderly physician in California, Dr. Francis E. Townsend, attracted a following of 5 million destitute old people with his plan to obtain a federal pension of $200 per month for everyone over sixty. This would have cost nearly half the national income. The Townsendites claimed, however, that since the pensions would have had to be spent within the month, "the velocity of money" would have ended the depression. The immediate realities of the movement were that its promoters raised nearly a million dollars in two years and commanded a formidable bloc of votes.

Among restless people in Northern cities, Father Charles Coughlin's politico-religious broadcasts attracted a wide following. Starting with a mixture of papal encyclicals and Populism, he at first supported, then went far beyond, Roosevelt. Coughlin advocated silver inflation and nationalization of banks, utilities, and natural resources. Ultimately in 1938 he founded the antidemocratic, anti-Semitic Christian Front. In January 1935 he was able to demonstrate his power by inspiring an avalanche of letters and telegrams to senators protesting against the World Court. His program was vague, but the discontent he was able to tap was concrete.

From the South, Senator Huey P. Long of Louisiana succeeded in launching a far more telling assault upon the New Deal. A skillful politician, he built a powerful organization in Louisiana and a rapidly growing following that spilled out first into neighboring states, then by

1935 into the Middle West, the Pacific Coast, and indeed every part of the country. Within Louisiana, he had delighted his poverty-stricken supporters by immobilizing their traditional enemies through his strong-armed techniques. Within the state, he built bridges, roads, hospitals, and a modern educational system. It was an era of dictators in Europe, and it was easy to assail the self-styled Louisiana Kingfish with ambitions to be a Fuehrer, although his techniques were the time-honored ones of the American political boss. Ambitious to become President, he lured the masses by offering them more than Roosevelt. His "Share Our Wealth" program promised through confiscatory taxes on great fortunes to provide every family with what in those depression years seemed in itself a fortune: an income of $2,500 per year and a homestead worth $5,000. Even in Iowa, farmers guffawed when he called the Secretary of Agriculture "Lord Corn Wallace." The New Dealers' political tactician, Postmaster General James A. Farley, estimated in the spring of 1935 that Long could poll 3 or 4 million votes on a third-party ticket and possibly could throw the 1936 election to the Republicans.

The "thunder from the left" was so ominous early in 1935 that many despairing New Dealers, chafing at Roosevelt's apparent inertia, predicted defeat in 1936. Roosevelt, who never liked to explain his tactics, remarked confidentially that he had no intention of engaging in public debate with the leaders of the "lunatic fringe." Rather, he quietly went about stealing their thunder with the reform programs the New Dealers had long been planning.

THE WORKERS' WELFARE

Frances Perkins, the first woman cabinet member, had accepted the office of labor secretary only with Roosevelt's pledge that he would support a social-security program. For several years, she and a group of New Dealers sought to win converts in the cabinet, in Congress, and throughout the country to their view that social insurance would not only aid the unemployed but also help prevent future depressions.

The Social Security Act of 1935 provided two types of assistance for the aged. Those who were destitute could receive federal aid up to $15 per month, depending upon the matching sums that the states provided. Those who were working could receive upon retirement annuities provided from taxes upon their earnings and their employer's payroll. The 1935 law specified payments, to begin in 1942, ranging from $10 to $85 per month, and excluded wide categories of workers from the program — but it was a beginning. The act also provided for unemployment insurance, aid for the blind and crippled, and assistance for dependent mothers and children, all such funds to be administered by the states in keeping with minimum federal standards. A Social Security Board supervised the entire system.

Social security could not immediately help those already unemployed in 1935; to aid them, Congress in April voted $5 billion to supplant direct relief with the Works Progress Administration. Work relief was more expensive but was essential to prevent the moral erosion, and if possible to save the skills, of the unemployed.

The WPA under Harry Hopkins did much to "help men keep their chins up and their hands in." It enrolled an average of 2.1 million workers between 1935 and 1941 on a wide variety of projects. Since the WPA workers were, theoretically at least, the least employable segment of the working force, and since almost all WPA money went for wages rather than tools and materials, its undertakings could not compare in efficiency with private construction projects. Many people tended to forget this and regard WPA as a politically inspired paradise for loafers. Nevertheless, WPA built nearly 600 airports and built or rebuilt 110,000 public buildings, more than a half-million miles of roads and streets, over 100,000 bridges, a half-million sewers, and over a million privies. In the realm of art, music, and the theater it gave opportunities to a remarkable proportion of the nation's talented people: its writers, for example, produced a useful set of state guidebooks.

The National Youth Administration, established in June 1935, as a sort of "junior WPA," aided young people between sixteen and twenty-five, seven-eighths of whom received student aid in schools and colleges.

Meanwhile, improved living quarters were being provided for working-class families. From the outset in June 1933, the Public Works Administration (PWA — not the same as WPA), through an Emergency Housing Division, began federal sponsorship of public housing. It cleared some of the nation's most notorious slum blocks, replacing them with about fifty developments containing almost 22,000 family units. The rent was an average of $26 per month, too high during these years for many previous slum dwellers to meet. Congress in 1937 finally passed Senator Wagner's bill creating the United States Housing Authority, which with $500 million (later in 1941 increased to $1.6 billion) took over and expanded the housing program to 511 projects with 161,000 units intended for the truly poor. Almost one-third of the units went to Negroes – one of the largest pieces of federal aid they had ever received.

ENCOURAGING UNIONS

For those fortunate enough to be employed, Roosevelt preferred a paternalistic program of wages-and-hours guarantees and social security benefits. Union leaders wanted to use collective bargaining to gain these advantages for their workers, so they would look to the unions, not to the government.

Labor leaders had gained much of what they wanted just before the advent of the New Deal, with the passage in 1932 of the Norris-La Guardia Act. This prohibited the courts from issuing injunctions against most ordinary collective-bargaining practices, and it made unenforceable any "yellow-dog contracts" – pledges from employees that they would not join unions. The Norris-La Guardia Act stopped federal courts from interfering on behalf of employers in struggles with employees. It left management and the unions free to bring economic pressure upon each other as best they could in collective-bargaining procedures.

In the depression years, however, employers were usually stronger than unions. Besides, strikes could interfere with economic recovery. Hence in 1933 Section 7a of the National Industrial Recovery Act affirmed the right of labor to bargain collectively, and led to the establishment of a government agency – the National Labor Board – to settle disputes arising under Section 7a. The relatively weak board was at first favorable to employers.

While Roosevelt had always maintained cordial relations with labor leaders, he was little inclined to give them firm collective-bargaining guarantees in place of the weak Section 7a in the National Industrial Recovery Act. Congress, under the leadership of Senator Robert F. Wagner, felt differently. In May 1935 the Senate passed Wagner's bill providing strong government protection for the unions. Roosevelt, bowing to the inevitable, signed the measure. What he had reluctantly accepted became one of the mainstays of the New Deal. The Wagner Act, passed at a time when unions were relatively weak, outlawed a number of the "unfair practices" by which management had been bludgeoning them, and created a powerful National Labor Relations Board to police the employers. Militant labor thus obtained the governmental backing essential to a

---

The Wagner Act [1935] The National Labor Relations Act made it unlawful for employers to engage in the following unfair labor practices:

1. To interfere with employees in their right to self-organization, to form, join, or assist labor organizations, to bargain collectively through representatives of their own choosing, and to engage in concerted activities, for the purpose of collective bargaining or other mutual aid or protection.

2. To dominate or interfere with the formation or administration of any labor organization or contribute financial or other support to it.

3. By discrimination in regard to hire or tenure of employment or any term or condition of employment to encourage or discourage membership in any labor organization.

4. To discharge or otherwise discriminate against any employee because he has filed charges or given testimony under this Act.

5. To refuse to bargain collectively with the representatives of his employees duly chosen pursuant to other provisions in the Act.

Police Battling Strikers 1937
A newsreel photographer took pictures of the "Memorial Day Massacre," in which policemen wielding guns and billy clubs attacked strikers at the Republic Steel plant in South Chicago. The police killed ten C.I.O. pickets and seriously injured many other demonstrators. (Wide World)

drive to unionize the great mass-production industries.

Even before the adoption of the Wagner Act, union membership had risen from a depression low of less than 3 million to 4.2 million. A group of leaders of industrial unions (which offered membership to everyone within an industry) had chafed over the conservatism of the craft unions (which took in only those working at a given trade). In 1934 men like the head of the United Mine Workers, John L. Lewis, and the leaders of the two great garment unions, Sidney Hillman of the Amalgamated Clothing Workers and David Dubinsky of the International Ladies' Garment Workers, had forced President William Green of the AFL and the craft unionists to agree to charter new industrial unions in the big unorganized industries.

In 1935 organization of these industries began. It led to violent opposition not only from the corporations but also from the AFL craft unions, which feared they would be submerged by the new giant unions. Jurisdictional fights led to a schism between the AFL leadership and the industrial unionists, who formed a Committee for Industrial Organization (within the AFL) in November 1935. Industrial warfare followed, as both the AFL and the CIO mounted great rival organizational drives.

President Roosevelt and a few industrial leaders favored industrial unionism. Gerald Swope of General Electric told Roosevelt that his company could not conceivably negotiate with a large number of craft unions but might find advantages in contracting with a single industrial union. Generally, however, in the spring of 1936 the point was still far off when big business could see advantages in big labor. Vigorous young organizers had to battle it out, often by physical force, with "loyal" strong-arm squads, occasionally with the police, and sometimes with rival organizers. The great difference between this and earlier periods of labor warfare was the aid the federal government provided unions through the National Labor Relations Board.

Through 1936 the United Automobile Workers gained recruits despite vigorous company opposition. There was good reason, for in 1934, at about the time the organizing drive began, nearly half of the auto workers were receiving less than $1,000 per year. General Motors alone, in an effort to keep down union organization, spent almost $1 million on private detectives between 1934 and 1936. In the first two months of 1937, workers closed seventeen General Motors plants through the new device of the sit-down strike, the workers staying by their machinery inside the plants. General Motors soon recognized the UAW, and other automobile companies gradually did the same. Rubber and other industries were similarly organized. Newspapers saw in the sit-down strikes a menace to private property, and much of the public became thoroughly alarmed.

Bloody warfare in the steel industry heightened the alarm. In 1936 the CIO voted a $500,000 fund to organize the industry and began its great onslaught, winning tens of thousands of workers from company unions. United States Steel chose to capitulate rather than face a long strike just as prosperity seemed to be returning. In March 1937, to the amazement of the nation, one of the company's subsidiaries signed a contract with the Steel Workers' Organizing Committee. For the first time, "Big Steel" was unionized. But three of the "Little Steel" companies, under the leadership of Tom Girdler of Republic Steel, resisted furiously. At the Republic plant in South Chicago on Memorial Day 1937, the police killed ten strikers. Republic Steel, according to the prolabor La Follette committee, was the largest purchaser of tear gas and sickening gas in the United States: Youngstown Sheet and Tube Company owned an arsenal of over a thousand weapons. The Republic strikers lost completely, to the relief of middle-class Americans who, like the newspapers they read, blamed the strife upon the unions and the New Deal.

Yet organized labor continued to grow. By 1941 union membership totaled about 9.5 million.

MORE FOR FARMERS

In January 1936 the Supreme Court held that it was unconstitutional for the AAA to regulate farm production or to impose a tax for such a purpose. Congress hastily passed a law (the Soil Conservation and Domestic Allotment Act) to meet the Court's objections and yet continue the crop-reduction effort. Under the new law, Congress appropriated money to pay farmers for conserving the soil by leaving part of their land uncultivated. The law provided that landlords must share with their tenants and sharecroppers the payments for withdrawing land from production. Nevertheless, in 1937, while the average plantation operator was grossing $8,328, of which $833 came from the soil conservation program, the average tenant family received only $385, of which $27 came from the government.

Agricultural interests pressed for a new AAA to cope with an enormous threatened surplus. The end of the drought, increased mechanization, and other improvements like the rapid spread of hybrid corn in the Middle West outmoded the crop controls of the 1936 legislation. The Agricultural Adjustment Act of 1938 – the "second AAA" – provided a number of devices to cut back production: soil conservation payments, marketing quotas, export subsidies, and crop loans. Surpluses of five nonperishable commodities upon which farmers received federal loans would be stored under government seal until needed in lean years, thus creating what Secretary Wallace termed an "ever normal granary." The surpluses so stored were to be of vital aid in feeding allies during the war years. The 1938 act also established a Surplus Marketing Administration to channel surpluses to needy persons and provide food for school lunches.

To improve the condition of the poorer farmers, those on submarginal soil, the government undertook to resettle them on better land. The Resettlement Administration (1935) and its successor, the Farm Security Administration (1937), made short-term loans for rehabilitation and long-term loans for purchasing farms but

Father and Sons Walking in the Face of a Dust Storm, Cimarron County, Oklahoma

Beginning late in 1933, years of extreme drought and high winds further afflicted the depression-plagued farmers of the Great Plains. The worst-hit area, centering on the panhandles of Texas and Oklahoma, eastern Colorado and New Mexico, and western Kansas, came to be known as the "Dust Bowl." "Only those who have been caught out in a 'black blizzard' can have more than a faint conception of its terrors," Lawrence Svobida, a Kansas wheat farmer, has written. "The dust begins to blow with only a slight breeze. . . . The wind increases its velocity until it is blowing at forty to fifty miles an hour. Soon everything is moving—the land is blowing, both farm land and pasture alike. The fine dirt is sweeping along at express-train speed, and when the very sun is blotted out, visibility is reduced to some fifty feet; or perhaps you cannot see at all, because the dust has blinded you and even goggles are useless to prevent the fine particles from sifting into your eyes."—Lawrence Svobida, An Empire of Dust (Caldwell, Idaho: The Caxton Printers, 1940). (Library of Congress)

succeeded in moving only a few thousand farm families.

The more fortunate farmers were benefited by the Rural Electrification Administration, which was established in 1935 to extend power lines to farms through cooperatives. Since its activities also stimulated private power companies to extend into the country, it was effective both directly and indirectly. Power lines had reached only 4 percent of the farms in 1925; they reached 25 percent by 1940.

LESS FOR BIG BUSINESS

After the NRA had been declared unconstitutional, parts of the law were reenacted piecemeal and with alterations to form a "little NRA." As early as February 1935, in response to the Supreme Court invalidation of legislation to prevent the overproduction of oil, Congress passed the Connally Act prohibiting the shipment of "hot oil" (oil produced in excess of state limitations) in interstate commerce. The

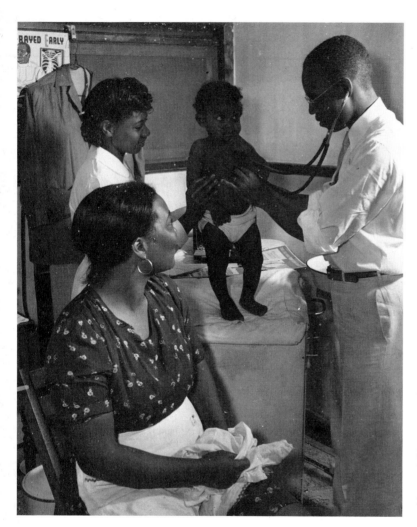

Caring for Farm Workers
The Farm Security Administration tried to relocate and rehabilitate displaced farmers and migrant workers. Here a camp doctor examines a patient at an FSA agricultural camp, Bridgeton, New Jersey, in 1942. From an FSA photograph. (Library of Congress)

Guffey Act of August 1935 virtually reenacted the NRA bituminous-coal code, fixing prices, limiting production, and protecting labor. When the Supreme Court threw out the new coal-control law in 1936, Congress passed the second Guffey Act of 1937. Roosevelt feared a wages-and-hours law would be unconstitutional, but he signed the Walsh-Healey Act of August 1936, setting minimum wages and maximum hours for work done on federal contracts. In order to protect small retailers, the Robinson-Patman Act of 1936 prohibited wholesalers or manufacturers from giving preferential discounts or rebates to chain stores or other large buyers; the Miller-Tydings Act of 1937 fortified state "fair trade" price-fixing laws.

As yet, Roosevelt did not resort to vigorous use of the antitrust laws, but he advocated tightening the regulation of big business. In March 1935 he recommended passage of an act to prohibit after five years the pyramiding of utility holding companies, which had led to flagrant abuses in the 1920s. In the 1930s thirteen companies still controlled three-fourths of the nation's electric power. They fought desperately through the summer of 1935 against what they viewed as a threatened "death sentence." One company alone spent $700,000 lobbying against the measure. In the Holding Company Act of 1935, the companies gained a partial victory; it permitted two strata of holding companies above the operating companies.

Between 1935 and 1940 Congress passed a series of other laws stiffening federal regulation. These strengthened the Federal Power Commission, brought trucks and carriers on inland waterways under the supervision of the Interstate Commerce Commission, created a new Maritime Commission to subsidize and regulate a merchant fleet, and set up a Civil Aeronautics Authority (later Board) to regulate airlines.

One of the most effective ways to regulate was to tax, and in 1935 Roosevelt proposed democratizing the federal tax structure by placing far higher levies upon big corporations and wealthy people. He pointed out that a person receiving $6,000 per year paid twice as high a tax as one receiving $4,000, yet the tax upon a $5 million income was only about five times as high as on $1 million. Conservative newspapers immediately attacked this proposal as a "soak the rich" tax scheme, but it passed Congress. It wiped away the last vestiges of Secretary Mellon's influence on tax policy, as it established the highest peacetime rates in history at the top: a maximum 75 percent income tax, 70 percent estate tax, and 15 percent corporate income tax. It was an important step toward the redistribution of American income.

Big business seemed to have grown bigger through New Deal inadvertence. The NRA relaxation of the antitrust laws had given it an opportunity to thrive at the expense of smaller business. In the two years after the end of the codes, the Attorney General initiated even fewer antitrust suits than during the NRA period.

Then, in April 1938, the President sent Congress a message vehemently denouncing the unjustifiable concentration of economic power. Less than 5 percent of all corporations in 1935 owned 87 percent of all the assets, he declared. This was leading to such a serious maldistribution of income, he pointed out, that in 1935–1936 the upper 1.5 percent of the population had a share of the national income as great as the 47 percent at the bottom—and these had less than $1,000 per year per family. The remedy, Roosevelt proposed, was to study economic concentration and enact more modern antitrust laws to cope with the newer techniques of monopoly. In response, Congress established the Temporary National Economic Committee under the chairmanship of Senator O'Mahoney. It conducted lengthy public hearings and published thirty-nine volumes of reports and forty-three scientific monographs by the end of 1941. By that time the national attention was entirely engrossed elsewhere; legislation never followed.

Meanwhile, Roosevelt launched an immediate trust-busting program through Thurman Arnold, whom he appointed head of the Antitrust Division of the Department of Justice. Arnold, who felt there was nothing wrong with existing legislation, made new and sophisticated use of the Sherman and Clayton acts as he undertook 215 major investigations and 92 test cases.

The Limits of Reform

In 1936 Roosevelt was at the zenith of his popularity and power. But soon he was to run into stronger political opposition than ever, and by 1938 he was to turn his attention from domestic reform to foreign policy and military defense.

MANDATE FROM THE PEOPLE

Roosevelt's vigorous reform program, enacted in its main outlines by 1936, made him a sure winner in the election of that year. Many millions felt that their personal lot had been improved by the New Deal. The violent attacks upon it from the right, and the cries of anguish

over such measures as the "soak the rich" taxes, convinced them even more that Roosevelt was their friend. Despite the misgivings of many conservatives within the party, the Democratic convention in 1936 renominated him by acclamation. His control was so complete that he even obtained abrogation of the two-thirds rule through which minorities had often hamstrung conventions.

As for the Republicans, they nominated their strongest candidate. Ignoring former President Hoover and the right wing, which was crying calamity, they chose a one-time Bull Mooser who had never strayed far from the 1912 Progressive position. This was the compe-

**President
Roosevelt's
Second
Inaugural
Address
[January 20,
1937]**

*I see a great nation, upon a great continent, blessed with a great wealth
of natural resources. . . . I see a United States which can demonstrate
that, under democratic methods of government, national wealth can be
translated into a spreading volume of human comforts hitherto
unknown, and the lowest standard of living can be raised far above the
level of mere subsistence.*

*But here is the challenge to our democracy: In this nation I see tens of
millions of its citizens—a substantial part of its whole population—who at
this very moment are denied the greater part of what the lowest
standards of today call the necessities of life.*

*I see millions of families trying to live on incomes so meager that the
pall of family disaster hangs over them day by day.*

*I see millions whose daily lives in city and on farm continue under
conditions labeled indecent by a so-called polite society half a century
ago.*

*I see millions denied education, recreation, and the opportunity to
better their lot and the lot of their children.*

*I see millions lacking the means to buy the products of farm and factory
and by their poverty denying work and productiveness to many other
millions.*

I see one-third of a nation ill-housed, ill-clad, ill-nourished.

---

tent governor of Kansas, Alf M. Landon. His
running mate was another Bull Mooser who
had moved well to the right, the Chicago publisher Frank Knox. The Republican platform
promised to do most of what the New Deal was
undertaking—but more competently, constitutionally, and without running a deficit. Landon's dry voice could not match Roosevelt's
radio eloquence, and Landon was further
handicapped because, though he was a moderate, he had to try to hold the militant Republican right.

The election demonstrated the extent to
which the New Deal depended upon a coalition
of farmers, union men, and the poor. The
unions were the heaviest Democratic campaign
contributors, providing $1 million. Negroes
switched en masse from the party of Lincoln to
that of Roosevelt. The "lunatic fringe" coalition
against Roosevelt stirred hardly a ripple. Huey
Long had been assassinated the year before;
the Union party candidate was "Liberty Bell"
William Lemke—who was "cracked," said
wiseacres. His ticket polled only 890,000 votes;
the Socialists, 190,000; the Communists, under
80,000.

A preelection postal card poll by the *Literary Digest* had indicated that Landon would
win by a big margin. How could it be so wrong?
The names and addresses of those polled were

taken from old telephone directories. A majority of people who could afford telephones and
had not been forced to move favored Landon.
In the election he received 16,680,000 popular
votes, compared with 27,477,000 for Roosevelt,
and got the electoral votes of only Maine and
Vermont.

In the campaign Roosevelt had challenged
his right-wing opponents—"economic royalists," he called them—and now he had not only
received an overwhelming endorsement for
himself, but he had carried with him many
congressmen pledged to his support. Nevertheless, those economic royalists would still have
the upper hand so long as the Supreme Court
continued to check New Deal laws. He felt he
had a mandate from the people to do something about the obstructionist Court.

STORM OVER THE COURT

Foes of the Coal Act, the Holding Company
Act, the National Labor Relations Act, and the
Social Security Act were openly flouting these
laws, confident that the Supreme Court would
disallow them as it had already done the NRA
and the first AAA. The Court, through its narrow interpretation of the federal power over
commerce and taxation, and its broad interpre-

tation of freedom of contract in the Fourteenth Amendment, seemed to have created an economic no man's land within which neither the federal nor the state governments could act.

Critics of the Court had been urging passage of some sort of constitutional amendment to provide the federal government with more extensive economic powers. Roosevelt's opinion (which subsequent Supreme Court decisions were to sustain) was that the Constitution granted adequate powers. All that was wrong was the Court's antiquated interpretation, he felt, but the four or five justices firmly opposed to the New Deal enjoyed excellent health and showed no signs of resigning. Consequently Roosevelt decided to propose adding to the Supreme Court—and to lower federal courts— new justices (presumably sharing his viewpoint) to match superannuated ones.

At this point Roosevelt's political sixth sense deserted him and, instead of presenting his proposal frankly and firmly in terms of its economic implications, he enclosed it in a larger scheme. Without informing congressional leaders in advance, in February 1937 he sent a surprise message proposing a needed general overhauling of the federal court system and the appointment of as many as six new Supreme Court justices. His nearest approach to frankness was a statement that the addition of younger blood would revitalize the courts and help them meet the needs and facts of an ever-changing world.

There was no real question about the constitutionality of Roosevelt's proposal, since Congress had from time to time changed the number of justices on the Supreme Court. Nevertheless, the plan aroused a great furor throughout the country. Many thoughtful people who had supported Roosevelt in 1936 heeded the warning of conservatives that, through such constitutional shortcuts, dictators came into power. Within Congress, the controversy cut across party lines. Some Democrats fought against the "packing" of the Court, while the Republican progressive Senator Robert M. La Follette, Jr., supported the President. La Follette declared that the Court had already been "packed" for years "in the cause of Reaction and Laissez-Faire."

Some of the old-line Democratic leaders, especially from the South, had gone along with the New Deal mainly because of party loyalty and pressure from their constituents. Now that

Election of 1936

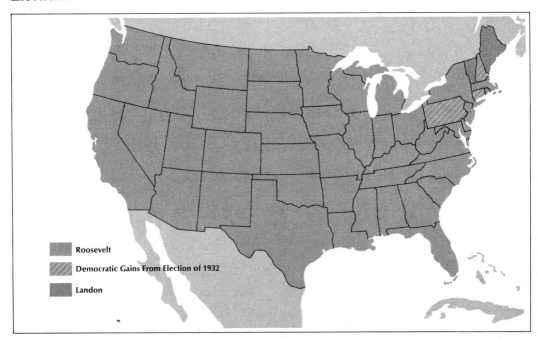

Roosevelt

Democratic Gains From Election of 1932

Landon

"Nine Old Men"

*President Roosevelt justified his plan to enlarge the Supreme Court on the ground
that too many of its members were old men who resisted progress and acted as if
they were still living in the "horse-and-buggy days." This cartoon endorsing
Roosevelt's view appeared in the radical magazine* New Masses *in March 1937.
(Brown Brothers)*

much of the electorate was turning against the administration, these conservatives broke loose. They joined with the bulk of the Republicans to form a new conservative coalition in Congress. Roosevelt fought back by using every device of party discipline to round up votes in Congress. He might have succeeded in obtaining at least a compromise measure, had not the Supreme Court itself eliminated the necessity for one.

The justices — including Louis D. Brandeis, the oldest and most liberal — had been indignant over charges that they were too old to handle the business of the Court. Chief Justice Charles Evans Hughes even wrote a letter insisting that they were not falling behind in their work. Four of them, far to the right, were of no disposition to take a broader view of the Constitution. Three of them took a more progressive if not a New Deal view. Chief Justice Hughes on occasion voted with them, while Justice Owen J. Roberts more often voted with the conservative four.

Just before the President sent his court plan to Congress, Roberts joined with Hughes

and the three more liberal justices in the case of *West Coast Hotel* v. *Parrish* to validate, by a 5-to-4 decision, a state minimum-wage law. This reversed a 5-to-4 decision of the previous year invalidating a similar law. "You may have saved the country," Hughes jubilantly told Roberts. The decision was announced on March 29, 1937. Two weeks later, the Court, again 5-to-4, upheld the Wagner Act, and in May, the Social Security Act. Since there no longer seemed to be any pressing need for judicial reform, the new conservative alliance in Congress easily dealt Roosevelt a personal defeat by voting down his court plan. At the same time, the shift of the Supreme Court's interpretation of the Constitution was a significant victory for Roosevelt and the New Deal.

Almost at once the older justices began retiring, and Roosevelt replaced them one by one with his appointees. In the next decade the Roosevelt Court rewrote large sections of constitutional law. The new justices sharply divided among themselves, but usually upon technical matters. In the main they interpreted the commerce and tax clauses so broadly and

The New Deal: Relief, Recovery, and Reform [1933–1938]

In their New Deal program, President Roosevelt and his advisers sought to achieve three objectives at once: to provide relief for those suffering from the depression, to bring about the recovery of business and agriculture, and to make reforms in the economic system. Not all the measures can be separated and put in neat categories according to the immediate objectives of relief and recovery and the long-range objective of reform; some measures were intended to accomplish more than one of these aims. Nevertheless, the following lists may facilitate an understanding of the complex and multifarious legislation of the period:

Relief and Recovery	Reform
Emergency Banking Act, 1933	Tennessee Valley Authority, 1933
Economy Act, 1933	Federal Securities Act, 1933
Civilian Conservation Corps, 1933	Glass-Steagall Act, 1933
Federal Emergency Relief Administration, 1933	Gold Reserve Act, 1934
Civil Works Administration, 1933	Reciprocal Trade Agreements Act, 1934
Public Works Administration, 1933	Public Utilities Holding Company Act, 1935
National Recovery Administration, 1933	Social Security Act, 1935
Agricultural Adjustment Administration, 1933	National Labor Relations Act, 1935
Farm Credit Administration, 1933	Soil Conservation and Domestic Allotment Act, 1936
Federal Housing Administration, 1934	National Housing Act, 1937
Works Progress Administration, 1935	Farm Security Administration, 1937
	Fair Labor Standards Act, 1938

the Fourteenth Amendment so narrowly that there remained few restrictions upon economic regulation by either the federal or the state governments. For several years the judges tended to restrict governments in their interference with organized labor, but by the end of a decade, labor too was subject to firm restraints. Thus almost all constitutional impediments to government regulation of the economic system were removed.

RECOVERY AND RECESSION

A sharp recession developed in the fall of 1937. It came just as many economists were fearing that an inflationary boom might get out of hand. There had been a remarkable recovery. The national income, which had dropped from $82 billion in 1929 to $40 billion in 1932, was back up to nearly $72 billion. Yet there were still 7.5 million unemployed and nearly 4.5 million families on relief. And there had been no upsurge of capital investment and business expansion as in the 1920s.

Recovery had come because of the enor-mous sums spent on work relief, the gradual momentum of the public works program, the loans to farmers, and the payment in 1936 (over Roosevelt's veto) of the veterans' bonus. All this government spending had powerfully stimulated the economy. Out of this experience emerged new economic theories, centering upon the concept that the government could help pull the nation out of a depression by liberal expenditures. As a corollary, the government could help curb inflationary booms by means of restrictive policies. These new economic theories came to be known as Keynesianism, after the famed British economist John Maynard Keynes.

In 1937 Roosevelt as much as his Republican opponents abhorred a deficit and worried about the mounting national debt, which had risen to $30 billion. He actually feared another disastrous crash like that of 1929. Acting in terms of the older economics, he had the Federal Reserve tighten credit even though the upswing had been sound rather than speculative. More important, he tried to balance the budget by drastically reducing government spending. Between January and August, 1937, he cut the WPA in half, sending 1.5 million workers on unpaid "vacation."

And since, with the ending of the drought, a huge farm surplus was again imminent, produce prices fell sharply. The fragile new boom collapsed and sent the economy plummeting. The index of production dropped from 117 in August 1937 to 76 in May 1938; 4 million additional workers were thrown out of employment. It seemed like 1932 all over again.

In October 1937 the President called Congress into special session to renew heavy public spending and to reform the "selfish interests" he blamed for the recession. Congress passed an emergency appropriation of $5 billion; the public works and work relief programs once again poured these large sums into the economy, and by June 1938 recovery was under way. The "spending school" had scored a point, and the government seemed to have assumed a new role in warding off threatened economic disaster.

Thus the New Deal entered into its final stage of reform, combining what was as new as Keynesianism with what was as old as progressivism. The trend had been toward big business, and now big government had come with the active intervention of the New Deal in so many aspects of the economy. The number of civilian government employees swelled from 588,000 in 1931 to 1,370,000 in 1941.

Since questions of constitutionality no longer seriously interfered after the changes in the Supreme Court, New Dealers fought the Fair Labor Standards Act through Congress in 1938. This established a minimum wage of 25 cents an hour (to be raised gradually to 40 cents by 1945) and a maximum work week of forty-four hours (to be lowered to forty) for most laborers, excepting agricultural, domestic, and maritime workers. It also forbade employment of children under sixteen in most areas except agriculture. Low though these standards were, they raised the pay of 300,000 workers and shortened the work week for 1.3 million. In subsequent years the standards were raised repeatedly, and the scope of the law was broadened to include additional categories of workers.

Roosevelt worried about the strong negative power the conservative coalition was developing in Congress. In many states, the Democratic party was under the leadership of conservatives. Postmaster General Farley, in charge of patronage, had done little to aid New Dealers who tried to challenge this leadership. In 1938 Roosevelt intervened in several primaries, mostly in the South, to try to defeat powerful conservative Democrats who headed congressional committees. Since these men had strong organizations behind them, and the New Deal candidates were relatively unknown, the conservatives won in almost every contest. The 1938 elections reflected the degree to which the prestige of Roosevelt and the New Deal were waning. The Republicans gained eighty seats in the House and seven in the Senate. Together with the conservative Democrats, the Republicans could dominate Congress.

By the end of 1938 the New Deal was close to its limits. The threat of a second world war was beginning to overshadow even the most critical domestic problems. The President could drive Congress with its Southern committee chairmen in the direction of strong defense legislation and a vigorous foreign policy only if he conciliated them by abandoning reform.

Culture in the Depression

EXPRESSION AND ESCAPE

Both the depression and the government's efforts to combat it left a mark on the cultural life of the time. Unemployment left many people with unaccustomed leisure, which they used either to protest against or to escape from unpleasant realities. The federal government became a patron and promoter of culture on a scale it had never attempted before.

Even before the establishment of the Federal Art Project, which eventually enrolled 5,000 persons, the government had aided artists through an earlier relief project and the commissioning of extensive murals for new public buildings. Some of these artists expressed leftist themes comparable to those of the highly popular Mexican muralists. Many turned their attention, sometimes satirically, to the American scene. This was the heyday of Grant Wood, with his patterned Iowa landscapes and austere rural portraits, and of Thomas Hart Benton, who with dramatic sympathy portrayed sharecroppers and Negroes. In sculpture, responding to the new government aid and the resurgent nationalism, Gutzon Borglum finished the enormous heads of Washington, Jefferson, Lincoln, and Theodore Roosevelt which were carved on a rocky mountainside in the Black Hills. Altogether, thousands of artists and sculptors worked during the depression years; never before had America possessed so many who were competent and promising.

Appreciation of the arts took a strong upturn, partly through art classes sponsored by the Federal Art Project, partly through the opening of new art museums. In 1941, the National Art Gallery in Washington opened, displaying collections of European art valued at $35 million, the gift of Andrew W. Mellon. Samuel H. Kress added 400 Italian paintings. More people than ever before visited galleries and bought reproductions of the old masters and of the French impressionists, especially Vincent Van Gogh.

Although jazz more than held its own, interest in classical music increased. The Federal Music Project employed 15,000 persons. They brought concerts to 100 million people and gave free music lessons to over a half-million pupils, most of whom could have afforded neither concerts nor lessons. Much of the music they played was that of American composers, such as Roy Harris' Third Symphony, and Aaron Copland's *Music for the Theatre*. Through new high-quality radio receivers and recordings, many additional millions listened to fine music, especially the symphony broadcasts conducted by Arturo Toscanini and the Metropolitan Opera performances. In 1940 listeners contributed over $300,000 to help "save the Met." Many millions more mourned the death in 1937 of young George Gershwin, composer of *Porgy and Bess* and *Rhapsody in Blue*. To the great mass of Americans, music still meant either sweet popular songs played by bands like Guy Lombardo's, or jazz like Benny Goodman's which came surging back into favor in 1934.

After depression and competition from motion pictures had thrown most actors and old vaudeville performers out of employment, the Federal Theater Project found employment for 12,500 of them. It brought performances to millions who had never previously seen a stage production. Some of these were highly successful as entertainment, some were of an advanced experimental nature, and some were so far to the left that they kindled the wrath of Congress, which killed the project in 1939. Many of the Broadway playwrights, impervious to congressional hostility, also took a critical look at social problems, as did Lillian Hellman in *The Little Foxes*. Robert E. Sherwood, who illustrated another trend, stopped writing light comedies and dramatized the impotence of the intellectual *(The Petrified Forest*, 1936) and the menace of war *(Idiot's Delight*, 1936). Later, in the pressure of world events, he reversed themes, and glorified the intellectual fighting totalitarian aggression *(There Shall Be No Night*, 1940). Meanwhile, Thornton Wilder wrote *Our Town* (1938) and Eugene O'Neill, who in 1936 won a Nobel Prize, labored quietly on a long-continuing cycle of plays.

Novelists likewise divided into those who, like William Faulkner, seemed to be largely unaffected by the era, and others like Ernest Hemingway, who paralleled Sherwood's cycle from 1929 *(A Farewell to Arms)* to 1940 *(For Whom the Bell Tolls)*. Thomas Wolfe richly and poetically portrayed the world swirling around him, in his *Of Time and the River* (1935) and his posthumous *You Can't Go Home Again* (1940). Many other novelists turned out proletarian themes from Marxist molds. John Steinbeck sentimentalized his suffering protagonists in his best-selling novel about the Oklahoman trek to California, *The Grapes of Wrath* (1939). The lure of romantic escape and the bargain of the sheer bulk helped make best sellers of Hervey Allen's *Anthony Adverse* (1933) and Margaret Mitchell's *Gone with the Wind* (1936).

Reading was one of the most inexpensive pursuits of the depression years, and although libraries suffered from slashed funds, book circulation increased considerably. Depression likewise cut the cost of radios and enlarged the size of audiences. In 1929 12 million families owned radios; by 1940 28 million families, comprising 86 percent of the population, owned them. This in part explains why Roosevelt, the master of the radio "fireside chat," campaigned so successfully with at least 70 percent of the metropolitan newspaper circulation opposing him. A radio serial, *Amos and Andy*, was so popular that Huey Long took the name of one of its characters, the Kingfish, as his sobriquet. Motion-picture audiences dropped one-third early in the depression, then by 1939 boomed to a yearly box-office average of $25 per family. Like radio serials, motion pictures dispensed mostly escapist themes—because of the vigor of the Catholic-led Legion of Decency, founded in 1934, it was a less sexy escape than in the twenties. Theaters also dispensed two movies rather than one and offered give-aways of a wide variety in order to bolster the box office. As yet, the coming threat to the movies, television, was still in the engineering laboratory—a curiosity exhibited at the New York World's Fair of 1939. It was too expensive for commercial development during the depression.

EDUCATION
AND THE PROFESSIONS

The two depression factors of lack of funds and excess of leisure also operated in education. It was estimated in 1935 that one-third of the unemployed were young people. Many went to school for lack of an alternative, and high school enrollment increased by one-third between 1929 and 1935. In spite of this, economy-minded chambers of commerce and citizens' committees led a drive for cuts so deep that they carved out educational sinew along with the fat. Colleges and universities dropped in enrollment until 1935, then more than recuperated but continued to suffer budgetary crises. Vocational education was strongly emphasized on both the high school and the college levels. Serious students explored social and economic questions so energetically that frightened civic and patriotic organizations warned that "pinks" were taking over the educational systems.

Alarmists feared pinks were taking over the churches also, for ministers responded as enthusiastically to the new demands for human welfare as they once had responded to the "social gospel." Of 20,000 ministers polled in 1934, nearly one-third favored socialism, and three-fifths, a "drastically reformed capitalism." The main intellectual current among ministers was toward neoorthodoxy. Reinhold Niebuhr, without disavowing political and social liberalism, found powerful psychological pressures driving man toward sin, from which man could be rescued only by faith, that is, submission to God.

Though the depression seriously cut funds for medical research, the thirties were another decade of advance in medical knowledge. Ironically, by 1935, when the American Medical Association was warning that 20 million people were suffering malnutrition or were close to it, highly publicized discoveries in vitamin research were leading the well-fed to consume a variety of vitamin-fortified foods and to swallow vitamin pills in quantities second only to laxatives. Sulfa drugs, typhus vaccine, blood plasma, and the "artificial lung" all came into use. Life expectancy increased from fifty-six years in 1920 to sixty-four in 1940, but malnutrition, illness, and sometimes lack of good medical care wrought a heavy toll during the depression. Army medical examiners rejected almost half of the first 2 million young men Selective Service called up in 1940–1941.

Yet doctors were ill-paid (even in 1929 half of them netted less than $3,000) and were idle much of the time. When some relief units and the Farm Security Administration offered medical aid to the destitute, the demand was overwhelming. Senator Wagner in 1938 introduced a national health bill, but it met stern opposition from the American Medical Association. Voluntary group health and hospitalization plans spread rapidly in some sixty cities and gained 3 million or more subscribers.

While scientists suffered temporary cuts in research funds, university budgets and industrial resources for research were back at a peak level by 1936; federal expenditures, by 1940. Thus the decade was one of increasing scientific investigation. The need for reorganization and reinvigoration of some of the government's scientific agencies led to the creation in 1933 of a Science Advisory Board, which futilely tried to obtain a New Deal for science. In 1935 the National Resources Committee (succeeding several similar planning agencies) took over the problem and prepared a study, *Research—A National Resource* (1940). The way was being prepared for centralized scientific planning in the future.

The thirties were years of marked scientific achievement in both basic and applied research in many fields. A series of discoveries by men of many nationalities opened the way to the possibility of nuclear fission. In 1931 Harold C. Urey of Columbia discovered a heavy isotope of hydrogen—deuterium—which, combined with oxygen atoms, formed heavy water. Bombardment of deuterium atoms by various types of atom smashers brought new knowledge about the nature of the atom, knowledge that could lead to revolutionary applications. Science, a neglected stepchild of the New Deal, was to become the nation's savior in time of war.

Selected Readings

Roosevelt and the New Deal
Basil Rauch, *History of the New Deal** (1944); A. M. Schlesinger, Jr., *The Age of Roosevelt: The Coming of the New Deal** (1959) and *The Politics of Upheaval** (1960); W. E. Leuchtenberg, *Franklin D. Roosevelt and the New Deal, 1932–1940** (1963); Frank Freidel, *Franklin D. Roosevelt: The Triumph* (1956); J. M. Burns, *Roosevelt: The Lion and the Fox** (1956); R. G. Tugwell, *The Democratic Roosevelt* (1957); Frances Perkins, *The Roosevelt I Knew** (1946).

Some New Dealers
J. R. Kearney, *Anna Eleanor Roosevelt: The Evolution of a Reformer* (1968); H. L. Ickes, *The New Democracy* (1934); Thurman Arnold, *The Folklore of Capitalism** (1937); Raymond Moley, *After Seven Years* (1939); J. M. Blum, *From the Morgenthau Diaries: Years of Crisis, 1928–1938* (1959); J. J. Huthmacher, *Senator Robert F. Wagner and the Rise of Urban Liberalism* (1968); O. L. Graham, *An Encore for Reform** (1967).

Relief, Recovery, Reform
S. F. Charles, *Minister of Relief: Harry Hopkins and the Depression* (1963); J. A. Salmond, *The Civilian Conservation Corps, 1933–1942* (1967); Roy Lubove, *The Struggle for Social Security, 1900–1935* (1968); Jesse Jones, *Fifty Billion Dollars* (1951), on the RFC; M. L. Eccles, *Economic Balance and a Balanced Budget* (1940), on spending for recovery; H. S. Johnson, *The Blue Eagle from Egg to Earth* (1935); E. W. Hawley, *The New Deal and the Problem of Monopoly* (1966); D. E. Lilienthal, *TVA: Democracy on the March** (1953); T. K. McGraw, *TVA and the Power Fight, 1933–1939* (1971); R. F. de Bedts, *The New Deal's SEC: The Formative Years* (1964); P. K. Conkin, *Tomorrow a New World: The New Deal Community Program* (1959); Richard Polenberg, *Reorganizing Roosevelt's Government* (1966).

The Farmers
H. A. Wallace, *New Frontiers* (1934); J. L. Shover, *Cornbelt Rebellion: The Farmers' Holiday Association* (1965); C. M. Campbell, *The Farm Bureau and the New Deal* (1962); R. S. Kirkendall, *Social Scientists and Farm Politics in the Age of Roosevelt* (1966); D. E. Conrad, *The Forgotten Farmers: The Story of Sharecroppers in the New Deal* (1965); Sidney Baldwin, *Poverty and Politics: The Rise and Decline of the Farm Security Administration* (1968).

The Unions
Irving Bernstein, *New Deal Collective Bargaining Policy* (1950); H. A. Millis and E. C. Brown, *From the Wagner Act to Taft-Hartley* (1950); Herbert Harris, *Labor's Civil War* (1940); Walter Galenson, *The CIO Challenge to the AFL* (1960); J. S. Auerbach, *Labor and Liberty: The La Follette Committee and the New Deal* (1966).

Opposition from Left and Right
D. R. McCoy, *Angry Voices: Left-of-Center Politics in the New Deal Era* (1958) and *Landon of Kansas* (1966); T. H. Williams, *Huey Long* (1969); C. J. Tull, *Father Coughlin and the New Deal* (1965); Abraham Holtzman, *The Townsend Movement* (1963); F. A. Warren, *Liberals and Communism: The "Red Decade" Revisited* (1966); George Wolfskill, *Revolt of the Conservatives* (1962), on the Liberty League; J. T. Patterson, *Congressional Conservatism and the New Deal: The Growth of the Conservative Coalition in Congress, 1933–1939* (1967).

The Supreme Court
E. S. Corwin, *Court over Constitution* (1938); R. H. Jackson, *The Struggle for Judicial Supremacy* (1941); C. H. Pritchett, *The Roosevelt Court* (1948).

Aspects of Life
F. L. Allen, *Since Yesterday* (1940); R. S. and H. M. Lind, *Middletown in Transition* (1935); Leo Gurko, *Angry Decade* (1947); Dorothea Lange and P. S. Taylor, *An American Exodus: A Record of Human Erosion in the Thirties* (1969); G. B. Tindall, *The Emergence of the New South, 1913–1945* (1967); D. T. Carter, *Scottsboro: A Tragedy of the American South* (1969).

Cultural Expression
Harvey Swados, ed., *The American Writer and the Great Depression** (1966); Daniel Aaron, *Writers on the Left** (1961); J. D. Mathew, *The Federal Theatre, 1935–1939* (1967); R. D. McKinzie, *The New Deal for Artists* (1972).

*Titles available in paperback.

The Abandonment of Isolation

PEACE WITHOUT VICTORY

VERSAILLES

Twenty-five

Having fought a war to end war and make the world safe for democracy, Americans of the 1920s were generally optimistic about the prospects whenever they gave thought to international affairs. True, the United States had failed to join the League of Nations, the organization that was intended to keep the peace. But this country took the lead in bringing the nations of the world to renounce war in the Kellogg Pact (1928), which many people hailed as the sign of a warless future. Henceforth, said admirers of the pact, aggressive war was illegal.

Optimism faded after the great depression struck. During the 1930s, Japan under fanatical militarists, Germany under Hitler and the Nazis, and Italy under Mussolini and the Fascists each launched programs of domestic tyranny and foreign conquest. Opposed to these aggressive nations were the contented powers of Europe – Great Britain, France, and the Soviet Union – which disagreed on many things but had a common interest in maintaining the status quo.

The American government faced a choice between two broad lines of policy. On the one hand, the United States might back Great Britain, France, and the Soviet Union (if they could manage to get together themselves) in the hope that all somehow could and would provide for their "collective security," enforce the Kellogg Pact, prevent aggression, and maintain peace – though in this there was the real risk of hastening a general war. On the other hand, the United States might follow a policy of so-called isolation. That is, this country might strengthen its position in the Western Hemisphere and concentrate on keeping out of war instead of preventing it.

Most of the American people favored the second of these alternatives. They were preoccupied with the depression and were determined to set their own country to rights, regardless of what might go on in the rest of the world. They were disillusioned about their

"Lest We Forget———"
As Americans faced the question of involvement in World War II, they were reminded of their disillusionment with World War I, which they had joined in order, supposedly; to "end war" and "make the world safe for democracy." This cartoon by Daniel R. Fitzpatrick of the St. Louis Post-Dispatch *was published on August 25, 1940.*

earlier effort to bring peace through war—more than 70 percent of them, according to an opinion poll in 1937, thought it had been a mistake to go to war in 1917—and they were in no mood to go on a second crusade. Ever regardful of public opinion, President Roosevelt hesitated to come out openly and clearly in favor of collective security even after the long-expected war had broken out in Europe in 1939. He continued to talk the language of isolationism, representing his policy as one of keeping out of war, while he committed the country to greater and greater support of Great Britain and her allies. The issues became more and more confused as the debate between "interventionists" and "isolationists" grew hotter. Suddenly, on December 7, 1941, the debate was stilled.

Depression Diplomacy

Herbert Hoover—a Quaker, an engineer, and a man of wide experience in international affairs—was impressed by the wastefulness of war as a human enterprise. As President, he held the United States to a rather modest and cautious role in world politics. Franklin D. Roosevelt, an admirer of his cousin Theodore Roosevelt's bold and vigorous approach, favored an active role for the United States, but during his first term he was restrained by his preoccupation with the New Deal as well as by his concern for public opinion.

HOOVER-STIMSON POLICIES

With regard to Latin America, Hoover continued the movement that under his successor became the Good Neighbor policy. Before his inauguration he toured much of the hemisphere, promoting good will; during his administration he prepared for the removal of marines from Haiti and finally withdrew them from Nicaragua. He refused to intervene in Cuba, which was restless under a dictatorship. Throughout Latin America, as depression toppled about half the regimes, he recognized de facto rulers without questioning the means by which they had come into power. Even when several countries defaulted on their obligations in October 1931, he did not press them to pay or threaten to seize their customs houses.

With reference to Europe, policy became increasingly concerned with economic conditions as the depression deepened. The moratorium on war-debt and reparations payments, begun in June 1931, aided Europe temporarily. Secretary of State Henry L. Stimson wished it to lead to a general cancellation of these obligations but could not convince the President, who considered them sacred. Soon Germany ceased reparations payments, and nations owing money to the United States, except for Finland, began to default or make mere token payments.

With regard to the Far East, policies were aimed at safeguarding American rights while preserving peace. As unstable conditions in China continued throughout the 1920s, the United States could do little to protect China from the encroachments of strong nations. As Russia became stronger, she built up her forces in eastern Siberia, and in 1929, when China tried to oust her from northern Manchuria, Russia fought an undeclared war to retain her foothold. Stimson tried to invoke the Kellogg-Briand Pact, which outlawed war, and to bring about mediation; he failed, demonstrating the weakness of the pact.

Japanese military leaders, feeling that their treaty rights in southern Manchuria were being threatened both by the Russians and by the Chinese Nationalists under Chiang Kai-shek, wrested the initiative from the Japanese foreign office in a manner little short of mutiny. In September 1931 they launched a large-scale military campaign in Manchuria at a time when the United States and Great Britain were preoccupied with the monetary crisis. For several weeks Stimson was moderate, in the hope that the civilians in the Japanese cabinet could regain control; the British were even less disposed to pursue a strong policy. The Japanese foreign office engaged in conciliatory talk but was unable to alter events as the army plunged deeper into Manchuria. By January 2, 1932, the conquest was complete.

The Stimson Doctrine [1932]

The American Government . . . can not admit the legality of any situation de facto nor does it intend to recognize any treaty or agreement entered into between those governments, or agents thereof, which may impair the treaty rights of the United States or its citizens in China, including those which relate to the sovereignty, the independence, or the territorial and administrative integrity of the Republic of China, or to the international policy relative to China, commonly known as the open-door policy; and . . . it does not intend to recognize any situation, treaty, or agreement which may be brought about by means contrary to the covenants and obligations of the pact of Paris of August 27, 1928, to which treaty both China and Japan as well as the United States, are parties.

Identical notes were sent to Japan and China, January 7, 1932.

As early as October 1931, Stimson had felt the United States might have to cooperate with the League of Nations in imposing economic sanctions against Japan even though these might lead to war. Hoover strongly opposed such action and, in cabinet meetings, discouraged Stimson by referring to the Washington treaties and the Kellogg-Briand Pact as scraps of paper. He learned from the British that they too opposed sanctions. Hoover was willing to allow Stimson to exert moral suasion against the Japanese, and suggested that he apply the doctrine of nonrecognition against territorial changes brought by force of arms. Stimson did so on January 7, 1932.

The American people were eager to see the United States assume moral leadership — and nothing more — against aggression. Their ideal was international disarmament, not policing. Hoover himself took the same view.

After the Geneva Conference of 1927 had failed to extend quotas to destroyers, cruisers, and submarines, the United States had threatened to begin a substantial building program. Hoover, fearing a naval race, called a conference which opened in London in January 1930. There the United States, Great Britain, and Japan agreed not to build the capital ships authorized under the Washington treaty, and even to scrap some existing ships. They also agreed to ratios on smaller ships, to continue until 1936.

The United States participated vigorously in the World Disarmament Conference that opened under League sponsorship at Geneva in February 1932. With the Japanese attacking Shanghai, and Hitler daily winning new converts to his militaristic Nazi movement in Ger-

many, the French firmly demanded an international army and compulsory arbitration rather than disarmament. In June 1932 Hoover tried to break the deadlock with a proposal to abolish immediately all offensive weapons, such as bombing planes and tanks, and to cut all land and naval forces approximately 30 percent. Despite much enthusiasm for the proposal, nothing came of it.

SEEKING FRIENDS AND CUSTOMERS

President Roosevelt inherited from the Hoover administration the questions of war-debt settlements, disarmament, and currency stabilization. He did not share Hoover's view that the proper settlement of these was a key to recovery. In April 1934 he signed an act sponsored by Senator Hiram Johnson, forbidding private loans to any defaulting nations; from then on all war-debt payments, except those from Finland, stopped altogether. Meanwhile, the United States continued to assert a strong moral position to try to bring about substantial disarmament. But Hitler was bent upon rearming, not disarming, and in October he withdrew from both the Geneva Conference and the League of Nations. A new arms race was under way.

In the same months that hopes for an arms settlement collapsed, so did those for international economic stabilization, and the blame this time was assessed against Roosevelt. He had agreed to cooperate in the World Economic Conference which President Hoover had called to meet in London in June 1933. He

Secretary of State Cordell Hull
Secretary Hull (1871–1955), born in a log cabin in backwoods Tennessee, was first elected to Congress in 1907. Except for two years as chairman of the Democratic National Committee, he served in one or the other house of Congress until 1933, strongly advocating lower tariffs. William L. Langer and S. Everett Gleason in The Challenge to Isolation *have analyzed his policies this way: "Even earlier than Mr. Roosevelt, he had sensed the dangers in the world situation and had warned the country of them. As a man of great integrity and high principle he was especially disturbed by the rapidly progressing breakdown of international law and morality. His prescription against this menace was reaffirmation of traditional standards of justice and fair dealing, insistence on the value of peaceful methods to settle international differences, and return to more liberal trade relations as the only way to alleviate the existing world tension. His was a somewhat rigid, doctrinaire approach, criticized by those who felt that his constant harping on general principles revealed a disinclination to come to grips with concrete, practical problems. Mr. Hull was a man of the people and as such easily moved to that moral indignation characteristic of the American people when confronted by the iniquities of foreigners." (New York: Harper & Row, 1952.) (Karsh, Ottawa)*

gave vague assurances to the representatives of eleven countries who visited him in advance that he favored currency stabilization, which he announced on May 16 was essential to "establish order in place of the present chaos." This was the policy under which Secretary of State Cordell Hull, a firm believer in international economic cooperation, and the American delegation went to London. After their arrival, President Roosevelt changed his mind, deciding that currency stabilization would be disadvantageous until the dollar had fallen to a competitive position on the world market. Whatever chance of agreement there had been disappeared when Roosevelt on July 3, 1933, cabled Hull a "bombshell message" disavowing currency stabilization.

The hope of stimulating foreign trade led Roosevelt to recognize Soviet Russia in November 1933. Since the revolution of November 1917, the Russian government had gone unrecognized while a number of irritating questions between the two nations continued to fester. Americans, hungry for what they unrealistically dreamed would be a substantial Russian trade, were eager for recognition. The Russians had even stronger motives for obtaining recognition, for they were afraid of being attacked by Japan. Maxim Litvinov, the Russian foreign minister, after discussions with Roosevelt at the White House, agreed that Russia would end its propaganda activities in the United States, guarantee religious freedom and protection in the courts to Americans resident in Russia, and negotiate a settlement of debts and claims.

By January 1934 Roosevelt was ready to listen seriously to Hull's homilies on the necessity of lowering tariff barriers in order to improve foreign trade. With Roosevelt's support, Congress (in June 1934) passed Hull's cherished program, the Reciprocal Trade Agreements Act. It authorized the administration to negotiate agreements, lowering tariffs by as much as 50 percent on specified goods coming in from individual nations in return for their reducing tariffs on American goods.

The immediate effect of the reciprocal trade agreements is difficult to estimate. During the depression years they were drafted carefully to admit only products not competitive with American industry and agriculture. By 1939 Hull had negotiated agreements with twenty-one countries, ranging from Cuba to the United Kingdom. These lowered the tariff an estimated 29 percent, at the same time that they gained concessions for American exporters, especially growers of cotton and tobacco. By the end of 1938 American exports to the sixteen nations with which it then had trade agreements had increased nearly 40 percent.

At the Inter-American Conference at Montevideo in December 1933, Hull won such acclaim with his proposals for reciprocity that President Roosevelt gave him full support upon his return home. To small nations like Cuba, dependent upon exports to the United States, reciprocity seemed a way out of the depression. While Hull offered economic succor, he reiterated to the people of Latin America at Montevideo (and Roosevelt said the same thing in Washington), that the United States was opposed to armed intervention in Latin America. Hull even signed a convention declaring: "No state has the right to intervene in the internal or external affairs of another."

Thus Hull took the United States a step further than the Hoover administration, which had unofficially disavowed the Theodore Roosevelt Corollary to the Monroe Doctrine but had reserved the right to intervene in self-defense. This seemed to be the American policy, as late as the summer of 1933, when revolution exploded in Cuba. Sumner Welles, one of the chief draftsmen of the new Latin American policy, was sent into Cuba to offer the "good offices" of the United States. Welles helped bring pacification without calling in the marines. In 1934, when a more conservative government came into power in Cuba, the United States gave up its right of intervention under the Platt Amendment. It also withdrew the last marines from Haiti and negotiated a treaty (not ratified until 1939) relaxing the restrictions upon Panama.

The new Good Neighbor policy of nonintervention received a severe testing in 1938 when Mexico expropriated all foreign oil holdings, including property valued by its American owners at $200 million. The United States conceded the right of expropriation but at first contended that the price the Mexicans wished to pay was so trivial as to be confiscation. In 1942, after years of involved controversy, a commission evaluated the property at $24 million, and the State Department then told the protesting oil companies that they must accept the settlement or receive nothing. This renunciation of the right to intervene for the purpose of protecting American property in Latin America was a reversal of dollar diplomacy. In encouraging trade, the new policy was of immediate benefit. It came to be even more valuable in promoting mutual defense, as the threat of war in Europe increased.

As for the Philippines, primarily the depression and secondarily isolationism brought them the long-sought but economically dubious blessing of independence. American producers of sugar, fats, and oils were determined to push their Filipino competitors outside the tariff wall. Isolationists were also eager to drop this dangerous Far Eastern military commitment. The Tydings-McDuffie Act of 1934 thrust upon the Philippines complete independence rather than the dominion status they sought. In 1935 the Philippines entered upon a transitional commonwealth period; on July 4, 1946, they became a fully independent republic. The United States was demonstrating that it was trying to rid itself of possessions rather than seize new ones.

At the London Naval Conference of 1935, the Japanese withdrew after they failed to obtain equality with the Americans and British in place of the 5:5:3 ratio, and thus the way was opened for competitive naval building. The United States soon turned to building the fleet with which it was later to fight the opening battles of a Pacific war.

LEGISLATING NEUTRALITY

With the breakdown of the naval status quo and the threatened aggressions in both Asia and Europe, most Americans felt that at all costs they must stay out of impending wars. Many leaders of the peace movement – dedicated Wilsonians and advocates of the League – had become disgusted with the League's inability to stop Japanese aggression. They reasoned that internationalism had failed to maintain the peace. Others, taking an economic-determinist view of wars, concluded that Wall Streeters and munitions makers, along with Wilson's legalistic insistence upon outmoded neutral rights on the high seas, had trapped the nation into World War I. Senate investigators, under the progressive Republican Gerald P. Nye of North Dakota, revealed exorbitant wartime profits and tax evasion and claimed that bankers had sought war to rescue their loans to the Allies. President Roosevelt, himself impressed by the Nye investigation, privately wrote his regret that Bryan had left the State Department in 1915.

The Nye Committee findings and similar sensational popular writings convinced a large part of the public that entrance into World War I had been a frightful mistake. The way to avoid its repetition seemed to be to legislate against the supposed causes. As Mussolini openly prepared to conquer Ethiopia in 1935, Americans feared that a general European war might develop. They felt that the way to avoid involvement was not to participate in strong deterring pressure against Italy, since Mussolini might strike back. Rather it was to isolate the nation by means of neutrality laws.

President Roosevelt also favored legislation, but he desired, as Hull had proposed in 1933, a law that would enable the President to embargo war supplies to the aggressor and allow their sale to the victim. But Congress passed a neutrality act providing a mandatory embargo against both aggressor and victim and empowering the President to warn American citizens that they might travel on vessels of belligerents only at their own risk. This first Neutrality Act of 1935, a temporary measure, was renewed in 1936 and again, with even stronger provisions, in 1937.

When the attack upon Ethiopia came, in October 1935, the League branded Italy an aggressor and voted sanctions against her. England and France made gestures against Italy but showed no inclination toward determined action. Hull imposed a "moral embargo" upon oil. Mussolini easily conquered his African empire, and then withdrew from the League. In October 1936 he joined with Hitler to form a new Rome-Berlin axis.

All this seemed to strengthen the determination of the American people to stay out of war. The new public opinion polls (based on samplings of only 1,500 to 3,500 people, with a probable error of 4 to 6 percent) indicated top-heavy opinion against involvement. A typical poll in November 1935, after the attack on Ethiopia, queried: "If one foreign nation insists upon attacking another, should the United States join with other nations to compel it to stop?" The answer: yes, 28 percent; no, 67 percent; no opinion, 5 percent.

This anti-involvement sentiment continued to be the mood of the nation when a new danger arose in July 1936, as General Francisco Franco and the Falangists (modeled after the Fascists) revolted against the republican government in Spain. Hitler and Mussolini sided with Franco; Russia, France, and, to a lesser extent, Great Britain favored the Loyalists. To prevent the Spanish Civil War from spreading into a general European conflict, England and France agreed to send no aid to either side. Roosevelt, trying to cooperate with France and England, persuaded Congress to apply the existing Neutrality Act to civil as well as international wars. The result was that the United States and other Western nations denied assistance to republican Spain. The republican government came to depend increasingly upon Russia for what little help it received. As for Franco, he received massive aid from Mussolini and Hitler, and ultimately crushed the Loyalists.

American feelings became inflamed over the invasion of Ethiopia and the Spanish Civil War, but President Roosevelt voiced the majority attitude in August 1936, a month after the outbreak of the war in Spain, when he asserted: "We shun political commitments which might entangle us in foreign wars; we avoid connection with the political activities of the League of Nations. . . . We are not isolationists except in so far as we seek to isolate ourselves completely from war."

World War Again

A great Japanese drive into the five northern provinces of China began in the summer of 1937. At first the State Department pursued a middle-of-the-road policy, favoring neither

country. Japan avoided declaring war, and President Roosevelt did not invoke the Neutrality Act. Private American ships at their own risk could carry arms and munitions to both belligerents. The administration's purpose was to help the Chinese, who needed American supplies more than the Japanese did.

FACING JAPAN AND GERMANY

By October 1937 the administration was ready to take a firm position against Japan. The British proposed a joint arms embargo, which seemed to involve no great risk. At this time and during the next four years, the consensus of the experts was that Japan was a mediocre military power. Hull persuaded Roosevelt to make a statement to counteract isolationism. The President, speaking in Chicago, declared: "The peace-loving nations must make a concerted effort in opposition to those violations of treaties and those ignorings of humane instincts which today are creating a state of international anarchy, international instability from which there is no escape through mere isolation or neutrality." War, he asserted, was a contagion which must be quarantined by the international community.

There is evidence that Roosevelt had in mind nothing more drastic than a collective breaking off of diplomatic relations, that he did not favor economic or military sanctions. Immediate press reaction and White House mail was favorable, but within a few days, as the Chicago *Tribune* and Hearst press continued to draw sinister implications from the "quarantine" speech, it plunged the nation, as the *Tribune* reported, into a "hurricane of war fright." This set back Roosevelt in his thinking. In November 1937 he sent a delegate to an international conference in Brussels to consider the Japanese aggression—but instructed him neither to take the lead nor to be a tail to the British kite.

Japan had no need to fear economic or military reprisals from the United States. On December 12, 1937, young Japanese aviators bombed and sank the United States gunboat *Panay* on the Yangtze River. The aviators claimed they bombed it in error, but visibility was excellent and an American flag was painted on the deck. As at the sinking of the *Maine* in 1898, a wave of excitement swept the country, but this time it was fear that the nation might become involved in war. The United States quickly accepted the profuse Japanese apologies and offers of indemnity.

At the end of 1938, as the Japanese supplanted the Open Door with their so-called New Order in East Asia, they were making conditions almost untenable for Americans in China. But the threat of war in Europe overshadowed the Asian impasse.

The traditional American isolationism, as exemplified by Hearst editorials and the speeches of several senators, implied strict nonintervention in Europe but a considerably more active role in Asia—no sanctions, but an insistence upon the Open Door in China. Within the Western Hemisphere, these isolationists were ready to give the President almost a free hand toward both Canada and Latin America. Indeed there were no more devout exponents of the Monroe Doctrine than they.

Roosevelt took full advantage of these feelings to inaugurate, within the hemisphere, policies that he could later apply across the Atlantic and the Pacific. In December 1936 he traveled all the way to Buenos Aires to put his personal prestige behind a pact to enlarge the Monroe Doctrine into a mutual security agreement. Henceforth, if any outside power threatened the American republics, instead of the United States acting unilaterally they would all consult together for their own protection. The understanding covered disputes among the republics themselves but was specifically aimed at meeting the threat of the Axis. It provided that the members would consult "in the event of an international war outside America which might menace the peace of the American Republics." In December 1938, with war in Europe imminent, the republics, at a meeting in Lima, Peru, established a means of consultation. Roosevelt also extended hemispheric security to the north when he issued a declaration of solidarity with Canada in August 1938.

By 1938 Hitler had rebuilt such a strong German army and air force that he was ready to embark upon a course of intimidation and conquest. In March he proclaimed union with Austria and paraded triumphantly through Vienna. This union put western Czechoslovakia into the jaws of a German vise. Hitler began tightening it with demands on behalf of the minority of 3.5 million Germans in Czechoslovakia. In September 1938 he brought Europe to the brink of war with his demands for the cession of the Sudeten area in which the minority lived. The Czechs, who had a strong army, were ready to fight rather than submit, but the people of other Western nations, appalled at the threat of another world conflict, were eager for a settlement on almost any terms. Roosevelt joined in the pleas to Hitler for a peaceful solution. At Munich on September 29 the French and the British signed a pact with Hitler granting his demands in Czechoslovakia. "This is the last territorial claim I have to make in Europe," he declared.

Within a few weeks, the once strong Czechoslovakia was whittled down to impotence. In March 1939 Hitler took over the remaining areas as German protectorates, thus demonstrating the worthlessness of his Munich pledge. In April, he began harassing Poland. The British and French, seeing clearly that appeasement had failed, gave firm pledges to Poland and to other threatened nations. They made half-hearted gestures toward Russia, which had been left out of the Munich settlement, but Stalin signed a nonaggression pact with Hitler in August. This freed Hitler to attack Poland if he could not frighten that country into submission. Poland stood firm, and Germany invaded her territory on September 1, 1939. Great Britain and France, true to their pledges, declared war on Germany on September 3. World War II had begun.

AIDING THE ALLIES

With the outbreak of war, Roosevelt issued a neutrality proclamation pointedly different from Wilson's 1914 plea for Americans to be impartial in thought as well as action. "This nation will remain a neutral nation," Roosevelt stated, "but I cannot ask that every American remain neutral in thought as well."

Promptly, Roosevelt called Congress into special session and, despite a heated debate, was able to muster the votes for a revision of the Neutrality Act. The 1939 measure still prohibited American ships from entering the war zones, but it allowed belligerents to purchase arms on a "cash-and-carry" basis. Had England and France been able to defeat Hitler with this limited assistance, Roosevelt probably would have been satisfied with it. Indeed, after the quick Nazi overrunning of Poland, over-optimistic American publicists during the quiet winter of 1939–1940 asserted that the Allies were calling Hitler's bluff and, after a long and

boring blockade on sea and land, would triumph. During these months of the "phony war," American indignation flared hottest over the Russian invasion of Finland. The administration applied a tight "moral embargo" on shipments of munitions to Russia but went no further.

Optimistic illusions about Hitler's weakness turned into panic in the spring of 1940 when the Nazis invaded Denmark and Norway, then swept across Holland and Belgium deep into France. On May 16 Roosevelt asked Congress for an additional billion for defense expenditures and obtained it quickly. On the premise that the United States must build great air armadas to hold off the Nazis, he set a goal of at least 50,000 airplanes a year.

On June 10, 1940, Mussolini joined the Germans by attacking France. Roosevelt that evening asserted: "The hand that held the dagger has struck it into the back of its neighbor." And, with France tottering from the German onslaught, he proclaimed that the United States would "extend to the opponents of force the material resources of this nation." He was taking the United States from a status of neutrality to one of nonbelligerency on the side of the democracies.

Twelve days later France fell, and in all western Europe only the shattered remnants of the British army that had been retrieved from Dunkirk opposed the Nazis. Already the new prime minister, Winston Churchill, was showering Roosevelt with requests for destroyers and arms of all kinds to help the British man their bastion. The odds against the British were heavy, but Roosevelt made the bold and dangerous decision to "scrape the bottom of the barrel" and make it possible for the British to buy all available war materials. As the Germans, preparing for an invasion, began to bomb Britain from the air, Roosevelt gave Britain fifty overage destroyers in return for ninety-nine-year leases on eight bases to be located on British possessions ranging from Newfoundland to British Guiana in the Western Hemisphere. The "destroyer deal" was, as Churchill later wrote, "a decidedly unneutral act." Roosevelt also turned back to the factories government-purchased war planes to be resold to Britain. In September 1940 he gave an indication that aid would not be confined indefinitely to materials alone when he pushed through Congress the Burke-Wadsworth bill, which inaugurated the first peacetime conscription of men in American history.

Roosevelt threw the resources of the United States behind the British as completely as Congress would let him. He did so with the feeling that an Axis victory would mean disaster to the nation. A large part of the public suddenly seemed to agree. In March 1940 only 43 percent of those polled thought a German victory would be a threat to the United States; by July, 69 percent did. In May 1940 only 35 percent favored aid to Britain at the risk of American involvement; four months later, 60 percent did. Yet as late as November 1941 only 20 percent of those polled favored a declaration of war against Germany. Roosevelt and the American public seemed to share incompatible aims. They wished to bring about the defeat of the Axis without involving the United States in a shooting war. Sometime in the next eighteen months, Roosevelt probably came to feel that complete entrance into the war was desirable; the public never did.

"INTERVENTION" OR "ISOLATION"?

The whole country was drawn into a great debate on the issue of neutrality as against all-out aid to the Allies. With a rather careless use of words on both sides, the advocates of neutrality called their opponents "interventionists," and the advocates of all-out aid responded with the term "isolationists."

William Allen White, the Kansas editor, headed the Committee to Defend America by Aiding the Allies, often called the White Committee. White himself (like a large percentage of Americans) favored merely aid, but a minority wanted to go further and declare war. In April 1941 this group founded the Fight for Freedom Committee. On the anti-involvement side, a Yale student, R. Douglas Stuart, Jr., organized an America First Committee under the chairmanship of a leading Chicago businessman, General Robert E. Wood. It drew upon the oratorical talent of the aviation hero Charles Lindbergh, General Hugh Johnson, and Senators Nye and Wheeler. It won the editorial support of the Hearst and other large newspapers. It appealed to a considerable

segment of patriotic Americans, and inevitably it also attracted a small fringe of pro-Nazi, anti-Semitic, and American Fascist fanatics. The debate was bitter, and through the summer and fall of 1940 it was complicated by a presidential election.

The Republicans met at Philadelphia in June, at the time of the collapse of France. National defense suddenly became the most important issue. Roosevelt underscored this and stole headlines from the Republican convention by appointing to his cabinet two of the most distinguished Republicans. He made the elder statesman Henry L. Stimson, secretary of war, and the 1936 vice-presidential candidate and sharp critic of the New Deal, Frank Knox, secretary of the navy.

The chagrined Republicans at Philadelphia promptly read Stimson and Knox out of the party but could not ignore the defense issue. They succumbed to the grassroots pressure, which had been built up through a careful advertising campaign, and nominated a young internationalist, Wendell Willkie. This was a startling blow to the isolationist majority among the Republican politicians, but it provided them with a tousle-haired, personable candidate who could win hysterical devotion from the amateur party workers. Both the platform and the candidate pledged that the nation would be kept out of war but would aid peoples fighting for liberty.

By the time the Democrats met in mid-July, it was a foregone conclusion that they would renominate Roosevelt. He was even able to force the Democratic politicians to swallow his choice for Vice President, Secretary of Agriculture Henry A. Wallace, who was considered an advanced New Dealer.

Willkie embarked upon an appealing but slightly amateurish campaign, whistle-stopping so vigorously that he nearly lost his voice, denouncing the bad management of the New Deal rather than its basic program, and always referring to his opponent as "the third-term candidate" (no President had ever run for a third term before). Numerous right-wing Democrats and even some early New Dealers like Moley and General Johnson supported him. John L. Lewis threatened to resign as president of the CIO if Willkie were not elected—a possibility that did not seem to frighten organized labor.

Lindbergh's Isolationist Argument [1941]

I know I will be severely criticized by the interventionists in America when I say we should not enter a war unless we have a reasonable chance of winning. . . . But I do not believe that our American ideals, and our way of life, will gain through an unsuccessful war. And I know that the United States is not prepared to wage war in Europe successfully at this time. . . .

There is a policy open to this nation that will lead to success—a policy that leaves us free to follow our own way of life, and to develop our own civilization. It is not a new and untried idea. . . .

It is based upon the belief that the security of a nation lies in the strength and character of its own people. It recommends the maintenance of armed forces sufficient to defend this hemisphere from attack by any combination of foreign powers. It demands faith in an independent American destiny. This is the policy of the America First Committee today. It is a policy not of isolation, but of independence; not of defeat, but of courage.—The New York Times, *April 24, 1941.*

Roosevelt, a wily old campaigner, tried to give the appearance of not campaigning at all. Defense problems were so acute, he insisted, that he had to spend his time touring army bases, munitions plants, and shipyards. He followed routes that somehow took him through innumerable cities, where he cheerily greeted quantities of voters.

Foreign policy was paramount. On this, both Willkie and Roosevelt had much the same views. Willkie approved of the destroyers-bases agreement. Both made fervent antiwar

Election of 1940

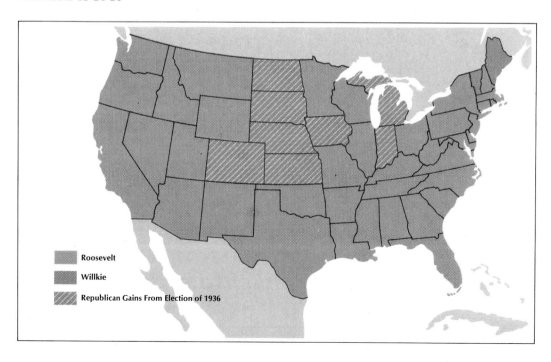

Roosevelt

Willkie

Republican Gains From Election of 1936

"Stop Hitler Now!" [1940]

We Americans have naturally wished to keep out of this war — to take no steps which might lead us in. But —

We now know that every step the French and British fall back brings war and world revolution closer to US — our country, our institutions, our homes, our hopes for peace.

Hitler is striking with all the terrible force at his command. His is a desperate gamble, and the stakes are nothing less than domination of the whole human race. . . .

WE CAN HELP — IF WE ACT NOW — before it is forever too late.

We can help by sending planes, guns, munitions, food. We can help to end the fear that American boys will fight and die in another Flanders, closer to home. . . .

The United States of America is still the most powerful nation on earth — and the United States of America is YOU!" — Advertisement written by Robert Sherwood for the Committee to Defend America by Aiding the Allies and widely published in June 1940.

---

statements to placate the isolationists. Willkie declared that if Roosevelt's promise to stay out of a foreign war was no better than his pledge to balance the budget, the boys were "already almost on the transports." This was an effective campaign issue which cut into Roosevelt's support. In Boston, Roosevelt (making the mental reservation that any attack upon the United States would not be a foreign war) picked up the challenge in words the isolationists were to mock incessantly: "I have said this before, but I shall say it again and again and again: Your boys are not going to be sent into any foreign wars."

A large part of the vote of those opposing aid to the Allies went to Willkie. Those favoring vigorous aid or even intervention (including many who fervently opposed New Deal domestic policies) voted for Roosevelt. They preferred Roosevelt's sure leadership to Willkie's inexperience. It was a relatively close vote: 27,244,000 for Roosevelt, and 22,305,000 for Willkie; 449 electoral votes to 82. The combined third-party vote was less than 200,000. Within a few weeks Willkie was on his way to England with a letter from Roosevelt to Churchill in his pocket.

ARSENAL OF DEMOCRACY

By mid-December, the British had so nearly exhausted their financial resources that they had practically stopped making new contracts,

yet Churchill warned Roosevelt that their needs would increase tenfold in the future. The Neutrality Act of 1939 and the Johnson Act of 1934 forbade American loans; a request for repeal would have reawakened the old ill feelings about unpaid war debts. Roosevelt, cruising in the Caribbean after the election, thought of a formula. The United States, "to eliminate the dollar sign," should lend goods rather than money, while serving as an "arsenal of democracy."

A "Lend-Lease" bill went into the congressional hopper at the right moment to bear a significant number: it became House Resolution No. 1776. After fierce debate, the bill went through Congress by a wide margin and was signed by the President in March 1941. It empowered him to spend an initial $7 billion — a sum as large as all the controversial loans of World War I.

Lend-Lease formally committed the United States to the policy the President had been following since the fall of France, the policy of pouring aid into Great Britain to help her withstand the German onslaught. Since Lend-Lease shipments had to cross the Atlantic to be of aid, the United States acquired a vital interest in keeping the Atlantic sea lanes open against the formidable wolf packs of German submarines, which in the spring of 1941 were destroying a half-million tons of shipping a month, twice as much as could be replaced. The President did not dare to convoy vessels openly to England as Secretary Stimson urged; isolationists in Congress were too powerful. Instead he fell back upon the device of "hemispheric defense." The American republics had proclaimed an Atlantic neutrality zone in 1939; in 1941 Roosevelt extended it far to the east, almost to Iceland, and ordered the navy to patrol the area and give warning of aggressors. This meant radioing to the British naval and air forces the location of Nazi submarines. The United States occupied Greenland in April 1941 and began escorting convoys as far as Iceland in July.

In secret, the United States had gone even further, for in the spring of 1941 American and British officers in Washington reached agreement on the strategy to be followed if the United States should enter the war. President Roosevelt demonstrated publicly in August 1941 how close he had come to carrying the United States from nonbelligerency to cobelligerency with England when he met with Prime Minister Churchill off the coast of Newfoundland. Roosevelt refused to make military commitments but did join Churchill in signing a press release on mutual war aims — the Atlantic Charter. As Churchill later pointed out, Roosevelt, representing a nation not at war, subscribed to a document that referred to "the final destruction of the Nazi tyranny" as a war aim.

In June 1941 Hitler unleashed against Russia a surprise attack so powerful that American military leaders predicted that Russia would collapse in a few weeks or months. The Russians fell back before the deep Nazi invasion but continued to fight, and in September Roosevelt, again gambling, extended Lend-Lease to them. This made it even more imperative to patrol the seas effectively.

The German answer was to strike back with submarines. In May 1941 they sank the American ship *Robin Moor* off the coast of Brazil. The Nazis replied to protests by saying: "Germany will continue to sink every ship with contraband for Britain whatever its name." In September a submarine attacked but failed to hit the destroyer *Greer*, which was radioing the submarine's position to the British. President Roosevelt, who did not know or at least did not reveal what the *Greer* was doing, issued orders to the navy to "shoot on sight." In October another destroyer was hit, and the *Reuben James*

was sunk. Congress voted legislation to arm merchantmen and allow them to sail to belligerent ports. Naval war with the Nazis was under way.

The Chief of Naval Operations, Admiral Harold R. Stark, wrote in his diary that Hitler "has every excuse in the world to declare war on us now, if he were of a mind to." But Hitler was not, and war came from the Pacific, not the Atlantic.

PEARL HARBOR

The Japanese saw in the European crisis an unparalleled opportunity to extend their empire. In the summer of 1939 they forced from Great Britain concessions that demonstrated their intentions. The United States promptly took a most serious step and gave the requisite six months' notice to terminate its 1911 commercial treaty with Japan. Beginning in January 1940, the United States was free to cut off its shipments of oil, scrap iron, and other raw materials.

The United States was determined to restrain Japan, even at the risk of a war. More was at stake than tin, rubber, and other vital raw materials. In September 1940 Japan signed a defensive alliance with Germany and Italy (the Tripartite Pact); any further Japanese thrusts would damage the world status quo to which the State Department was committed. The administration policy toward Japan was inseparably interrelated with and subordinate to that policy toward Germany.

Under the Export Control Act, by the fall of 1940 the United States had placed an embargo upon aviation gasoline and almost all raw materials with military potential, including scrap iron and steel. Already war was close. The Japanese government of Prince Konoye wished to conciliate the United States if it could do so without serious concessions. Negotiations began in the spring of 1941 and dragged on into December. At first the Japanese informally suggested rather generous proposals, but by May they were making formal ones that were unacceptable: the United States should ask Chiang Kai-shek to make peace on Japan's terms, should restore normal trade with Japan, and should help Japan procure natural resources in Southeast Asia.

The Background of Pearl Harbor

After the end of World War II a number of critics charged that the Roosevelt administration had deliberately brought the United States into the war by provoking the Japanese to attack Pearl Harbor. Charles A. Beard, for one, presented the case against the administration in his *President Roosevelt and the Coming of the War, 1941* (1948). According to Beard, the American government refused to compromise with Japan and allow her to buy the raw materials she needed for her military adventure in China. Hence Japan had little choice but to strike out in the southwest Pacific and take the necessary supplies by force, even at the risk of war with the United States. From decoded Japanese radio messages, Roosevelt and his advisers must have known, by late November, that Japan was about to begin hostilities. Indeed, as War Secretary Henry L. Stimson recorded in his diary, Roosevelt at a cabinet meeting "brought up the event that we were likely to be attacked" in the near future, for the Japanese were "notorious for making an attack without warning." Stimson added, significantly: "The question was how we should maneuver them into the position of firing the first shot."

In *Roosevelt from Munich to Pearl Harbor* (1950) Basil Rauch undertook to refute Beard's argument, yet Rauch conceded that the administration had had in mind a "maneuver" of sorts. "The question," he explained, "was whether the President should ask Congress for a declaration of war *prior* to a Japanese attack on the Philippines or Guam, in order to avoid giving Japan the advantage of a surprise attack, or wait until Japan attacked American territory, that is, 'maneuver' Japan into firing the first shot."

Disagreeing with both Beard and Rauch, R. N. Current contended in *Secretary Stimson: A Study in Statecraft* (1954) that Roosevelt and his advisers intended neither to provoke an attack on Pearl Harbor nor to await one on Guam or the Philippines. Stimson and the others were expecting the Japanese to move against Dutch or British but *not* American possessions. When Stimson said "we were likely to be attacked," he meant "we" in the sense of "our side," including the British and the Dutch. If he and his colleagues had really been anticipating a blow at Pearl Harbor, they obviously would not have had to worry about how to provoke the Japanese to attack there. The real question, as Stimson saw it, was how to make the Japanese *appear* to be firing on the United States—in the sense of threatening vital American interests—if and when they aggressed upon Dutch or British territory in the southwest Pacific. He assumed that such a "maneuver" as this would be necessary in order to persuade Congress to pass a war declaration, which he believed to be in the best interests of the United States.

The most thorough and scholarly study of the subject is *Pearl Harbor: Warning and Decision* (1962), by Roberta Wohlsetter, who on the whole is favorable to the Roosevelt policy. Today few if any historical experts hold to the Beard provocation thesis, but they continue to disagree among themselves in regard to the appropriateness of various American diplomatic and military measures preceding the attack.

The Magazine of the U.S.S. Shaw Exploding During the Japanese Raid on Pearl Harbor
The destroyer Shaw, *in a new floating drydock, went through the first attack unscathed. One of the second wave of bombers at 9:12* A.M. *hit her badly, and fire spread to her forward magazine, which about 9:30 went up spectacularly, blowing off her bow and sinking the dock. From the bridge aft the damage was so slight that the* Shaw *was refloated and a month later put in the same repaired dock to be fitted with a temporary bow. She steamed to the mainland to be rebuilt and later rejoined the fleet. (Official U.S. Navy photo)*

The German attack upon Russia relieved the Japanese of one of their greatest worries, since they thought they no longer needed to fear interference from Siberia. They decided to move into southern Indochina and Thailand. The United States had broken the Japanese code and, through intercepted messages, knew this was probably a prelude to attacks upon Singapore and the Dutch East Indies. At the end of July 1941, when the Japanese occupied southern Indochina, the United States, acting firmly with the British and the Dutch, froze Japanese assets in their respective countries, so that the Japanese could not convert these assets into cash. This put the Japanese into such a desperate plight that they would either have to abandon their aggressions or attack British or Dutch East Indian possessions to get needed supplies.

Since the Japanese naval leaders wished to avoid a war they feared they might lose, the Japanese cabinet sought a compromise. Prince Konoye requested a personal meeting with Roosevelt at which Konoye was ready to make some concessions. (Simultaneously Japan prepared for war in case agreement could not be reached.) Roosevelt was enthusiastic, since Konoye was ready to promise that Japan would not expand farther southward and would not attack the United States in the event of war with Germany. Hull was becoming discouraged because he feared Konoye could not bind the Supreme Command. On Hull's advice, Roosevelt refused to meet Konoye without specific advance commitments about China, and these Konoye would not give.

Roosevelt and Hull seemed to make the foolish error of thinking Japan was bluffing when she was not. Instead of granting limited concessions that would have strengthened the Japanese moderates and postponed or avoided a war that the United States was in no position to fight in 1941, the American policy makers took an adamant moralistic position which played into the hands of the Japanese extremists. The Japanese made an even more grievous miscalculation by provoking a war that few of their leaders were sure they could win.

Each nation refused to budge on the question of China. On November 20, 1941, Japan offered a modus vivendi (temporary settlement) highly favorable to herself. Hull rejected it and replied in the basic American terms, insisting that Japan get out of China. He not only knew Japan would not accept these terms but knew also, through intercepted Japanese messages, that she had made her last offer and that after November 29 things would happen automatically. "I have washed my hands of the Japanese situation," Hull told Stimson on November 27, "and it is now in the hands of you and Knox, the Army and Navy."

The United States knew that Japan was on the move and that war was imminent. A large Japanese convoy was moving southward through the China Sea. The administration thought an attack upon American territory unlikely. The commanders in Hawaii were routinely warned. Negligence there and in Washington, not diabolical plotting as was later charged, led to the disaster ahead. Meanwhile, on November 25, a Japanese naval task force had sailed eastward from the Kuriles.

At 7:55 on Sunday morning, December 7, 1941, the first wave of Japanese airplanes hit the United States naval base at Pearl Harbor, Hawaii; a second wave came an hour later. The attacks were successful beyond Japan's greatest expectations. Within two hours the planes destroyed or severely damaged 8 battleships, 3 light cruisers, 4 miscellaneous vessels, 188 airplanes, and important shore installations. There were 3,435 casualties. The Japanese task force withdrew without being detected, having lost 29 airplanes, 5 midget submarines, and fewer than 100 men. In the first strike, the United States was rendered almost impotent in the Pacific, but the bitterly wrangling nation was suddenly unified for the global war into which it had been precipitated.

The Battle for Production

"Yesterday, December 7, 1941 – a date which will live in infamy – the United States of America was suddenly and deliberately attacked by the naval and air forces of the Empire of Japan." Thus President Roosevelt addressed Congress on the Monday after the debacle at Pearl Harbor. Within four hours, the Senate unanimously, and the House 388 to 1, voted for a war resolution against Japan. Three days later Germany and Italy declared war against the United States, and on the same day, December 11, Congress reciprocated without a dissenting vote.

Total war made the planning of industrial production as vital as military strategy. "War is no longer simply a battle between armed forces in the field," the Industrial Mobilization Plan of 1939 had stated, "– it is a struggle in which each side strives to bring to bear against the enemy the coordinated power of every individual and of every material resource at its command. The conflict extends from the soldier in the front line to the citizen in the remotest hamlet in the rear."

MOBILIZING FOR DEFENSE

At the time of the Munich crisis in 1938, Roosevelt had ordered the armed forces to modernize their production plan. Just before the outbreak of war in Europe, he authorized the War and Navy departments to appoint a civilian advisory committee to survey the 1939 plan. This was the War Resources Board, made up of five leaders of big business together with the presidents of the Massachusetts Institute of Technology and the Brookings Institution, and an army colonel. At this point politics began. The unfortunate use of the word "war" rather than "defense" in the title frightened the public, especially after the invasion of Poland when even the existence of such a body seemed a move toward involvement. The firmly anti-New Deal attitude of the board pained Roosevelt. He speedily disbanded the War Resources Board and submitted to the pressures against substituting any new defense agencies.

With the collapse of France in the late spring of 1940, Roosevelt could delay no longer, even though he was embarking upon a new presidential campaign and wished to temper isolationist hostility. Rather than ask Congress to create defense agencies, he drew upon a 1916 statute for authority and reestablished the Advisory Commission of the Council of National Defense. This time he used the word "defense" rather than "war," and carefully balanced all of the major national interests. He headed it with William Knudsen, of General Motors.

Out of this prototype grew the many defense agencies with their shifting or nebulous lines of authority and often ill-defined powers. Out of it came many of the heads of subsequent war agencies. Out of it too came one clear fact amid the many uncertainties: whatever war agencies developed, Roosevelt was of no disposition to abdicate or share his presidential powers. At its first meeting, Chairman Knudsen asked Roosevelt: "Who's boss?" The President replied: "I am."

In January 1941, after the Advisory Commission had almost broken down and had lost its control over priorities to the military, Roosevelt set up a new Office of Production Management. After American entrance into the war, he replaced this with a War Production Board under Donald Nelson, of Sears, Roebuck and Company. Though personable and a good organizer, Nelson was not strong enough to force civilian control over priorities, or a more equitable distribution of contracts among smaller manufacturers, or a well-balanced production plan. He lost much of his power when President Roosevelt persuaded Justice James F. Byrnes to resign from the Supreme Court and act as a sort of assistant president in charge of war production. Brynes was at first head of the Office of Economic Stabilization, then (after May 1943) of the Office of War Mobilization, which developed into an effective agency.

MATERIALS FOR VICTORY

Meanwhile, with the awarding of the first large government contracts in the summer of 1940, industry began to boom.

Some manufacturers, still thinking in depression terms of an economy of scarcity, were at first reluctant to build new plants, which they feared would lead to overproduction after the war. Still others would not accept contracts until they were sure of an adequate profit. It was the initial task of Knudsen, the production genius of General Motors, to persuade manufacturers that it was their patriotic duty to take contracts. As for the new war plants, even if later they should prove to be excess capacity, manufacturers need not worry about paying for them; the Reconstruction Finance Corporation received authorization from Congress (June 1940) to finance the construction, expansion, and equipment of plants and to lease them to contractors. Or, if manufacturers put their own capital into defense construction, they would receive a fast five-year tax write-off. This meant that instead of deducting a normal 5 percent a year for depreciation from their taxes on wartime profits, they could deduct 20 percent of the cost of the plant. Manufacturers who turned to war production were not to suffer financially.

Neither were the war workers. The manufacturers, backed by the War and Navy departments, wished to abrogate New Deal restrictions on government contracts in order to lengthen the hours of workers without paying overtime. Labor leaders, wishing to increase employment, fought bitterly for double shifts. Ultimately the government decreed a forty-hour week with time-and-a-half for overtime. Contractors had to comply with New Deal labor legislation — the Walsh-Healey, Fair Labor Standards, and Wagner acts.

The Mushrooming of War Plants

These two pictures of a West Virginia valley taken from the same spot, the first in 1941 and the second in 1942, indicate the remarkable speed with which the Morgantown Ordnance Plant was built and went into production. This was typical of the mushrooming construction all over the nation. The plant was one of fifty-four built by Du Pont in thirty-two locations for the government at a total cost of $1,034,000,000. Du Pont received a total fee, after taxes and all applicable charges, of one-fifteenth of 1 per cent of the construction cost. (Du Pont)

At the time of Pearl Harbor, the United States still had little armament because so much had been shipped to Great Britain and because so many of the plants had only recently begun production. The new productive capacity was remarkably large. Despite errors and chaotic conditions, the United States was producing more combat munitions than any of the belligerents — indeed almost as much as Germany and Japan combined. Airplane production was up to a rate of almost 25,000 per year. The armed forces already had inducted and were training 2 million men. This mobilization was only a fraction of what was soon to come, for a large-scale construction of factories and training camps was under way. While the nation during the debate over neutrality had not built its defenses with the smoothness and speed that critics demanded, it had achieved a substantial degree of preparedness.

The Japanese attack on Pearl Harbor created almost as much chaos indirectly in American war production as it did directly in the fleet in the Pacific. The war agencies in Washington began ordering tremendous quantities — indeed far too much — of everything.

The problem of restoring some order to war production, then raising it to astronomical totals, was a joint one. The armed forces, the Maritime Commission, and other procurement agencies did the ordering. The War Production Board tried to control the size of the procurement program and to allocate materials between the armed forces and the civilians. The WPB was thus trying to control the entire economy and inevitably was coming into collision with the armed forces over the size and nature of war orders as opposed to what was to be reserved for civilians. Internecine conflict among the agencies and personality clashes among the administrators were unavoidable.

Out of the confusion a pattern gradually emerged. The first step, oddly enough, was to cut back the building of plants, although at times this created a furor throughout a region, as when the Higgins Shipyards in New Orleans were abandoned. After the middle of 1942, the amount of new construction being started declined sharply; in another six months, the larger part of the war plants and military facilities had been built.

The second step was to coordinate the various phases of the war-production program. As late as the summer of 1942, bottlenecks were halting some assembly lines. The vital shipbuilding program had to be cut back because of scarcities of raw materials like steel plate and glass, and of components like valves, turbines, and engines. The WPB eventually broke most of the bottlenecks through the Controlled Materials Plan, which established a balanced production of finished products and allocated precise quantities of raw materials to each manufacturer.

The shortage of rubber became so critical in 1942 that it required special attention. After the WPB failed to solve the problem, Roosevelt appointed a committee under Baruch to make a special report. This recommended sharp restrictions upon the use of motor vehicles, including a national speed limit of thirty-five miles per hour, and immediate construction of enormous synthetic rubber plants. Roosevelt ordered the restrictions, and appointed a Rubber Director in the WPB, William M. Jeffers, president of the Union Pacific Railroad, to construct the plants. By the end of 1943 the synthetic rubber industry was producing a third again as much rubber as the country had normally used before the war.

An indispensable adjunct of the war agencies was the Senate War Investigating Committee, headed by Harry S Truman, previously little known. The senators consciously patterned it after the Committee on the Conduct of the War of the Civil War period, but avoided the pitfalls of their predecessors by ruling out questions of military policy. Instead, they ferreted out incompetence and corruption in the war-production and military-construction programs: outrageous expense in building army camps, improper inspection of airplane engines, a quixotic scheme to build an Arctic pipeline, and the like. The Truman Committee uncovered and stopped hundreds of millions of dollars of waste. In the wartime expenditure of $400 billion there was amazingly little corruption.

By the beginning of 1944 factories had turned out what seemed to be needed to win the war. The output was double that of all Axis countries combined. Cutbacks began but were haphazard and ill-planned, and when the armed forces met reverses, some turned out to have been premature. With the cutbacks came pressure for a resumption of the manufacture of civilian durable goods. The military leaders staunchly opposed this.

War needs even at their peak took only about one-third of American production. While manufacture of such goods as automobiles, most electrical appliances, and nondefense housing had come to a halt in 1942, production of food, clothing, and repair and maintenance goods was continued or even slightly increased.

TRANSPORTING THE SUPPLIES

As war production grew, the problem of transporting the supplies within the country and overseas became acute. Inside the United States, the Office of Defense Transportation, established in December 1941, coordinated all forms of transport—railroads, trucking, airlines, inland waterways, and pipelines. In contrast to the system in World War I, railroads remained under private control, but functioned effectively, carrying double the traffic of 1939 with only 10 percent more locomotives and 20 percent more freight cars. Since they could not, however, transport sufficient oil to the East when German submarines began attacking coastal tankers in 1942, the government authorized construction of the Big Inch pipeline from Texas to eastern Pennsylvania.

Transporting troops and supplies overseas required one of the most spectacular construction programs of all. The Germans had sunk more than 12 million tons of shipping by 1942. To replace it, the United States Maritime Commission had to abandon its program of building fast, efficient ships requiring scarce turbines, valves, and electrical equipment. As early as July 1940, Admiral Emory S. Land, head of the commission, and Knudsen recommended to the President mass production of a freighter that, while slow (sailing only eleven knots), would be simple to construct and would not require scarce components. By using the existing designs for an old-fashioned British tramp steamer with a reciprocating engine and steam winches, they saved six months in starting production. This "ugly duckling" was the Liberty ship. After a slow beginning, builders substituted welding for riveting and applied prefabrication and subassembly techniques in constructing it. In 1941 construction of a Liberty ship required an average of 355 days; by the end of 1942 the time had been cut to 56 days, and one of Henry J. Kaiser's companies completed one in 14 days. During 1942 alone 8 million tons of shipping were built; by 1945 the United States had over 36 million tons of ships afloat.

SCIENTISTS AGAINST THE AXIS

The most revolutionary changes for the future came out of laboratories, as scientists pooled their skill in a race against those of the Axis—above all the Germans—to turn the basic knowledge that was available to all into decisive weapons of war. Between the two wars, while the United States had neglected military research and development, Germany had sprinted far ahead, except in the field of radar. In the 1920s the Naval Research Laboratory in Washington had discovered the principle of radar by bouncing back a radio beam directed at a ship on the Potomac. The British had developed radar most highly, and it was their salvation during the air blitz of 1940–1941.

Other potential weapons were in the offing which, if the Germans developed them first, could mean Nazi victory in the war. (This was one of the reasons why the armed forces had decided to concentrate upon defeating Germany first.) The only way in which American scientists could catch up seemed to be through teamwork. The German threat brought the creation of a government scientific agency such as the New Deal had failed to produce. A leading scientist, Vannevar Bush, persuaded President Roosevelt to create a committee for scientific research in June 1940. A year later, under the direction of Bush, it became the Office of Scientific Research and Development, which mobilized scientists with such effectiveness that in some areas they outstripped their German opponents.

The Americans and the British developed superior radar, which not only detected enemy airplanes and ships but helped direct shells against them. In these shells, by 1943, were radio-directed proximity fuses that detonated the shells as they neared their targets. American rocket research produced weapons that enormously increased the fire power of airplanes, ships, and tanks. But the Americans still lagged behind the Germans, who before the end of the war were blasting London with enormous V-1 and V-2 rockets. The Germans also built the first jet airplanes and snorkel submarines, which would have been an even more serious menace if they had come into full production.

There was a danger, little publicized, that Germany might develop an atomic weapon. In the summer of 1939, a physicist, Enrico Fermi, and a mathematician, Albert Einstein, got word to President Roosevelt that German physicists had achieved atomic fission in uranium; what had long been theoretically possible had been accomplished. Next might come a bomb. The President authorized a small research project, and a race in the dark against the Nazis began.

In December 1942 physicists produced a controlled chain reaction in an atomic pile at the University of Chicago. The problem then became the enormous technical one of achieving this release of power in a bomb. Through the Manhattan District of the Army Engineer Corps, the government secretly poured nearly $2 billion into one project for producing fissionable plutonium and into another, under the supervision of J. Robert Oppenheimer, for building a bomb. This was an enormous and frightening gamble, against the hazards that the thing might not work and that the enemy might succeed first. Only after the war did the United States discover that the Germans were far from developing a usable atomic device. On July 16, 1945, after the end of the war in Europe, the first A-bomb was exploded, on a tower in New Mexico, producing the most blinding flash of light ever seen on earth, and then a huge billowing mushroom cloud.

The Impact on Civilians

No American could escape the impact of the war effort. Everybody was affected—and most people very deeply—by war jobs, wages, prices, rationing and other controls, taxes, and propaganda.

MANPOWER AND WOMANPOWER

The nation, after grappling for years with the problem of millions of unemployed, found itself hard pressed for sufficient people to swell the

The Home Front [1942] *That was the spring when women took to wearing slacks in the streets (a great blow to the human race), old toothpaste tubes had to be turned in for new ones, men's trousers were commanded to be cuffless, and a radio comedian named Bob Hope began to play soldiers' camps around the country. . . . That was the spring we first heard about sugar rationing, with gasoline rationing to come. Ice cream was reduced to ten flavors, and civilian suffering really hit its stride when the War Production Board banned the use of metals for asparagus tongs, beer mugs, spittoons, bird cages, cocktail shakers, hair curlers, corn poppers, and lobster forks. New York blacked out, and for days we talked about how beautiful the great city looked stark and naked, silhouetted against the moon and the stars. . . . Sex reared its pretty head in factories as an occupational hazard. Girls were requested to quit wearing sweaters, peekaboo waists, halters, and other revealing garments. The boys were rubbernecking themselves into too many accidents.* — Paul Gallico in Jack Goodman, ed., *While You Were Gone* (New York: Simon and Schuster, 1946).

Women in War Work
"Rosie the Riveter" was the subject of a popular song during World War II. Here women riveters help with the production of planes for the army. (Library of Congress)

fighting forces, man the war plants, till the fields, and keep the domestic economy functioning. There were periodic demands for national service legislation or a labor draft, but unions were so vehemently opposed that no such measure ever passed the Senate. The relatively weak War Manpower Commission tried to coerce workers into remaining at defense jobs at the risk of being drafted, but the war came to an end without any tight allocation of manpower comparable to that of materials. The armed forces had first call upon men through Selective Service, which had been in operation since the fall of 1940. Altogether draft boards registered 31 million men. Including volunteers, over 15 million men and women served in the armed forces during the war. Nevertheless the working force jumped from 46.5 million to over 53 million as the 7 million unemployed and many previously considered unemployable, the very young and the elderly,

and several million women found jobs. The number of civilian employees of the federal government trebled.

This mobilization of manpower entailed the greatest reshuffling of population within such a short time in the entire history of the nation; altogether 27.3 million people moved during the war. It also meant a heavy weight of wartime tension on American families. With the return of prosperity and the impending departure of soldiers, both marriage and birth rates rose. In 1942 and 1943 about 3 million children were born each year, compared with 2 million a year before the war. But young wives and mothers fared badly in crowded housing near defense plants or army bases, or, after husbands had been shipped overseas, back home with parents. Draft boards deferred fathers as long as possible, but more than 1 million were ultimately inducted. More than 2.5 million wives were separated from their husbands because of the war. The divorce rate increased slowly. Because men in the armed forces could not be divorced without their consent, and many estranged wives stayed married in order to continue receiving allotment checks, a heavy backlog was built for postwar divorce courts.

When mothers were forced to work, children often suffered neglect, or were upset over the change. Court cases involving juvenile delinquency, especially among children from eight to fourteen, and among girls, the "bobby-soxers," increased 56 percent. Even among the nondelinquents, a serious price had to be paid at the time and later for the disruption of more American families for a longer period of time than ever before.

As adolescents found jobs, the percentage of those between fourteen and nineteen who attended school dropped from 62 in 1940 to 56 in 1944. Teachers also left for the armed forces or better-paying war jobs. Universities kept functioning through military research projects and training programs.

The great migration to war plants was stripping the agricultural South of underprivileged whites and blacks alike, as 5 million people moved within the South, and another 1.6 million left the area completely. In the South this exodus led to the false rumor among outraged white housewives that the departing Negro domestics had formed "Eleanor Clubs," named after Mrs. Roosevelt, to "get a white woman in every kitchen by 1943." In the North, it led to explosive tension when Negroes, enjoying their new freedom, were jostled in crowded streetcars against indignant whites newly migrated from the South. A serious riot, in which twenty-five blacks and nine whites were killed, shook Detroit in June 1943. New York narrowly averted a similar disaster. At the very time when the United States was fighting a war against the racist doctrines of Hitler, many whites became resentful over the rapid gains Negroes were making.

In June 1941, after the head of the Pullman porters' union, A. Philip Randolph, had threatened a march on Washington, President Roosevelt established the Fair Employment Practices Committee. It worked diligently throughout the war against discrimination in employment. By 1944 2 million Negroes were at work in war industry, and many previous barriers to economic opportunities for Negroes were permanently cracked.

Not everyone shared in the new prosperity. Government economists reported in 1943 that 10 million families still received less than the $1,675 per year requisite for a minimum standard of living. Most Americans, however, were relatively more affluent than they had been. The living standard of working people advanced rapidly. This was due less to wage increases than to payment of time-and-a-half for overtime beyond 40 hours. The average workweek lengthened from 40.6 hours in 1941 to 45.2 in 1944. As living costs rose (on a 1935–1939 base of 100) from 100.4 in 1940 to 128.4 in 1945, gross weekly wages went up from $25.20 to $43.39. Working women and children created social problems, but they also brought additional prosperity to millions of families.

RESTRAINING LABOR UNIONS

Labor unions rapidly grew in strength during the war, and their unpopularity among Americans of the middle and upper classes increased. Union membership rose with the rise in the working force, from about 10.5 million workers in 1941 to over 13 million in 1945. Keeping these workers satisfied was no easy matter. The administration was determined to prevent strikes and to restrain the formidable pressure of the labor unions from forcing wages, and thus all prices, upward. President Roosevelt followed the procedure of World War I by establishing a National Defense Mediation Board (March 1941) made up of representatives of management, labor, and the public. In November 1941 it broke down when the CIO members resigned over the refusal of the board to recommend a union shop (that is, one in which all new workers hired must join the union) in coal mines. In January 1942 Roosevelt replaced it with the National War Labor Board, similarly constituted but much stronger. This board could set wages, hours, and working conditions, and through the war powers of the President it could enforce these in a final extremity by government seizure and operation of plants.

On the union-shop question, which was creating much hostility between management and labor, the board arrived at a compromise, the "maintenance of membership" clause. Nonmembers hired into a war plant did not have to join a union, but members had to remain in it, and the union remained the bargaining agent for the duration of the contract. Pressure for wage increases, which might contribute to inflation, was more serious. The board hit upon a solution in ruling upon the Little Steel cases in July 1942. Taking January 1, 1941, as the base date when workers had received a standard wage, it recognized a 15-percent rise in the cost-of-living index since then. Consequently, it felt that a proportionate increase for steel workers would be equitable. The Little Steel formula, except for those receiving substandard wages (like some textile workers), served thereafter as a wage ceiling.

Despite the no-strike pledges of the major unions, there were nearly 15,000 work stoppages during the war, involving the loss of more than 36 million man-days. These stoppages involved only one-ninth of 1 percent of the working time (though they indirectly caused more damage than this). When John L. Lewis' United Mine Workers defied the government in their strike against the Little Steel formula in May 1943, Congress reacted by passing over Roosevelt's veto the Smith-Connally or War Labor Disputes Act (June 1943). This act required unions to wait thirty days before striking and empowered the President to seize a struck war plant.

PRICE CONTROLS, WAR FINANCE

At the beginning of the war, with a two-year supply of wheat, cotton, and corn stored in Secretary Wallace's ever-normal granary, there seemed no danger of food shortages in the United States. But within six months after Pearl Harbor, scarcities of many sorts began to develop. The United States felt the increased demand of the armed forces and its allies and the reduction of supplies due to the loss of fibers and oils from Southeast Asia. By 1942 meat production was half again that of depression years, but American consumers with their increased buying power were eager to buy even more. Consumer income in 1943 was 65 percent above depression levels, and much of it was in the pockets of people who had not eaten adequately for years.

A food administrator did exist, Chester Davis, but he resigned in protest when his views (and those of the American Farm Bureau Federation) did not prevail; his successor was Marvin Jones. Neither man had the dictatorial powers to provide the scarce supplies and manpower that the dominant farm bloc in Congress would have liked to bestow upon agricultural producers. Rather, farmers had to depend upon whatever the War Production Board would allocate to them, and upon a generous draft-exemption program they obtained from Congress. They also received legislation raising the ceiling on commodity prices to 110 percent of parity. Since this came into conflict with the anti-inflation efforts of the administration, a dogged struggle developed between the President and the congressional farm bloc over farm prices. Neither side won entirely.

Pressures from business, farmers, and labor, combined with the scarcity of consumer goods and the burgeoning of buying power, created an almost irresistible trend toward inflation. During the defense period, the Office of Price Administration (OPA), under a vigorous New Dealer, Leon Henderson, lacked real coercive power and failed to halt inflation. Between the invasion of Poland and the attack on Pearl Harbor, prices of twenty-eight basic commodities rose by nearly one-fourth. Immediately thereafter, pressures became so acute that prices went up 2 percent per month. Soon Congress hastily passed a bill authorizing only selective price fixing and setting ceilings with a preferential trap door for agriculture.

In April 1942 the OPA issued a General Maximum Price Regulation that froze prices of consumer goods, and of rents in defense areas only, at their March 1942 level. But the rise of uncontrolled farm prices toward 110 percent of parity forced an upward revision of food prices. This gave ammunition to the labor unions' barrage against fixed wages. In October 1942 Congress grudgingly responding to the President's demand, passed the Anti-inflation Act. Under its authority, Roosevelt immediately froze agricultural prices, wages, salaries, and rents throughout the country.

In July 1943 Roosevelt appointed a former advertising executive with remarkable administrative talents, Chester Bowles, to head the OPA. With a small enforcement staff, Bowles braved general unpopularity to hold the increase in living costs during the next two years to 1.4 percent. Altogether, the price level went up less than 29 percent from 1939 to the end of the war, compared with 63 percent between 1914 and the armistice.

Fuel Oil Ration Stamps
During and immediately after World War II, the Office of Price Administration not only set price ceilings but also issued rationing stamps, which entitled each consumer to buy certain amounts of rationed commodities. Rationing was intended to insure an equitable distribution of scarce goods and also to help hold prices down by limiting the demand. (Courtesy of G. Litton)

Consumers nonetheless suffered numerous irritations and discomforts. The OPA, through unpaid local volunteers manning 5,600 price and rationing boards, administered the rationing of canned goods, coffee, sugar, meat, butter and other fats, shoes, tires, gasoline, and fuel oil. The OPA could not, however, control deterioration of quality. Black-marketing and overcharging grew in proportions far beyond OPA policing capacity; in 1943 Congress slashed the funds of the enforcement division.

One of the most important inflationary controls was the sale of war bonds and stamps to channel off some of the excess purchasing power, which for the single year 1945 mounted to nearly $60 billion. Throughout most of the war, personal incomes were at least one-third greater than the available civilian goods and services. The Treasury Department, through eight war bond drives and its payroll deduction plans, but with few of the lurid or coercive touches of World War I, sold $40 billion worth of series "E" bonds to small investors, and $60 billion more to individuals and corporate entities other than banks.

Had this been the total of government loans, the effect would have been to quell inflation, but the Treasury had to borrow $87.5 billion more from Federal Reserve and commercial banks. Since in effect the banks created new credits which the government then spent, the result was to inflate bank credits and money in circulation by over $100 billion.

Taxes did much more to drain off surplus purchasing power. The government raised 41 percent of its war costs through taxation, compared with 33 percent during World War I. The Revenue Act of 1942, which Roosevelt hailed as "the greatest tax bill in American history," levied a 94-percent tax on the highest incomes; the President had suggested that no one should net more than $25,000 per year during the war. Also, for the first time, the income tax fell upon those in lower income brackets. To simplify payment for these new millions, Congress enacted a withholding system of payroll deductions in 1943. Corporation taxes reached a maximum of 40 percent on the largest incomes. In addition, excess profits were subject to a 90-percent tax, reclaiming for the government a large part of the return from war contracts. However, these taxes could be rebated to companies to aid them in reconversion (changing back to peacetime production), a provision of future significance. In effect, the government taxed away a large part of the profits of corporations, then returned it later when it was needed. Heavy excise taxes on transportation, communication, luxuries, and amusements completed the levies.

Between 1941 and 1945 the government raised $138 billion through taxation—nearly a $100 billion of it from income and excess profits taxes. Those in the top 5 percent of the income scale suffered a serious relative economic loss, as their share of disposable income dropped from 26 percent in 1940 to 16 percent in 1944. Few persons or corporations were able to make fortunes out of the war, and a considerable amount of economic leveling—upward more than downward—had taken place. Despite the heavy taxation, by the end of the war consumers possessed an estimated $129 billion in liquid savings.

From 1941 to 1945 the federal government spent twice as much as the total appropriations from the creation of the government to 1941, and ten times as much as the cost of World War I—a total of $321 billion. The national debt rose from $49 billion in 1941 to $259 billion in 1945, yet the black warnings of national bankruptcy that had punctuated the New Deal years all but disappeared.

INFORMATION AND MISINFORMATION

As an incentive for winning the war, advertisers presented a vision of a postwar America in which every husband would have a chrome-trimmed car and every wife a gleaming kitchen filled with wonder-working gadgets. President Roosevelt promised even more. "In the future

days, which we seek to make secure," he told the people (January 1941), "we look forward to a world founded upon four essential freedoms." These were freedom of speech and worship, and freedom from want and fear. They were for the postwar future, not necessarily for the wartime present.

From Pearl Harbor on, there was the suspicion that through the Office of Censorship, almost immediately established under a competent Associated Press executive, Byron Price, the government was withholding information not because it was vital to the enemy but because it would be damaging to public opinion of the armed forces. Diligent newspapermen, aided by Price, exerted pressure on the armed forces to make censorship an instrument for security, rather than for the concealing of incompetence. Newspapers following

Taken by itself, the growth of the national debt since the 1930s appears to have been tremendous. It seems less disturbing in comparison with the even more rapid growth of the economy, as measured by the increase in the Gross National Product. The GNP for a given year represents the total value, at current prices, of all goods and services produced in the country during that year. The growth of the GNP reflects a rising price level as well as an increasing output of goods and services. The actual increase in output has been much less, therefore, than the graph seems to indicate.

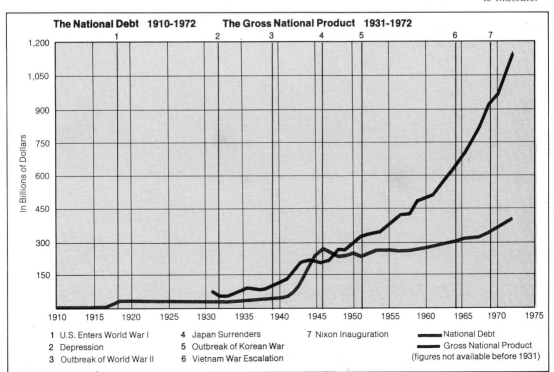

Office of Censorship rules censored themselves to withhold local news that might be of value to the enemy.

The overlapping and conflict among government information agencies led to the establishment in June 1942 of the Office of War Information under a shrewd news commentator, Elmer Davis. Although the OWI consolidated four previous organizations, it coordinated rather than assumed the information function of domestic war agencies.

The OWI aroused the misgivings of Congress, partly because of internal feuding and the mass resignation of the pamphlet writers, but mainly because conservatives objected to several of the OWI pamphlets: one on the dangers of inflation, another on Negroes in the war, and another on the need for high taxes. A fourth pamphlet, intended only for overseas distribution, a cartoon biography of Roosevelt, especially worried antiadministration congressmen. They feared that the OWI might promote New Dealish policies and the 1944 candidacy of Roosevelt. In 1943 Congress cut funds for the domestic branch of the OWI so drastically that it had to stop producing propaganda.

Overseas, the OWI carried on a program employing 8,400 persons by V-E Day. Through Voice of America broadcasts begun in 1941 and propaganda of many sorts, it presented an idealistic view of American war aims and aspirations for a peaceful postwar world. As the symbol of this idealism it dramatized President Roosevelt. By the end of the war, Roosevelt was more of a hero overseas than at home, and American aims appeared more idealistic abroad than in the United States.

The war produced less hatred and vindictiveness at home than had World War I. The energy that had gone into crude vigilantism in the earlier war now went into serving as air-raid wardens and doing similar duties for the Office of Civilian Defense. People continued to eat hamburgers and sauerkraut and listen to Wagner. They demonstrated little animosity toward Americans of German background and practically none toward Italians. A few Nazi agents and American Fascists were jailed, but the most ambitious effort to punish them, a sedition trial of twenty-eight, ended in a mistrial after the defendants' lawyers had engaged in long weeks of delaying tactics. A few papers like Father Coughlin's *Social Justice* were barred from the mails. But Socialists went unpunished, and religious conscientious objectors who were willing to register went to Civilian Public Service camps rather than to prison.

FATE OF JAPANESE-AMERICANS

In sad contrast to this moderation, the frenzy of public fury turned toward the Japanese. The fighting in the Pacific developed a fierce sav-

Relocation of Japanese-Americans
Americans of Japanese birth or ancestry living on the Pacific Coast were forced to leave their homes and move to camps in the interior of the country, where they were to stay for the duration of the war. The American Civil Liberties Union called the evacuation of these people "the worst single wholesale violation of civil liberties of American citizens in our history." In this news photo of September 21, 1942, members of the first group to depart from Los Angeles begin their trip to a camp in Arkansas. (ACM)

agery, reflected in the public anger within the United States. On the Pacific Coast, hatred of Americans of Japanese background became extreme. Wild stories circulated about sabotage at Pearl Harbor and plots to aid a Japanese landing on the California coast—later proved completely untrue. Under public pressure, Roosevelt, in February 1942, authorized the army to remove all people of Japanese ancestry from the West Coast. Some 117,000 people, two-thirds of them United States citizens, were abruptly herded behind barbed wire, and later shipped into ten relocation centers in wild and disagreeable areas. They suffered the financial loss of at least 40 percent of their possessions and for several years were barred from lucrative employment. Yet Japanese-Americans in Hawaii were left unmolested without incident throughout the war. There were 17,600 Japanese-Americans in the armed forces. Their units, especially in Italy, established outstanding records for bravery under fire.

The Supreme Court in 1944 validated the evacuation and, in other decisions as well, upheld military control over civilians. In time of war or national emergency, United States citizens apparently could expect no court protection of their civil rights from military or executive authority.

Selected Readings

Biographical Studies
E. E. Morison, *Turmoil and Tradition: A Study of the Life and Times of Henry L. Stimson* (1960); R. N. Current, *Secretary Stimson: A Study in Statecraft* (1954); R. E. Sherwood, *Roosevelt and Hopkins** (1948); J. W. Pratt, *Cordell Hull, 1933–44* (1964); W. S. Cole, *Senator Gerald P. Nye and American Foreign Relations* (1962); E. D. Cronon, *Josephus Daniels in Mexico** (1960).

Depression Diplomacy
R. H. Ferrell, *American Diplomacy in the Great Depression* (1957); S. F. Bemis, *The Latin American Policy of the United States* (1943); Alexander De Conde, *Herbert Hoover's Latin American Policy* (1951); E. O. Guerrant, *Roosevelt's Good Neighbor Policy* (1950); Bryce Wood, *The Making of the Good Neighbor Policy** (1961); A. W. Griswold, *The Far Eastern Policy of the United States* (1938); Dorothy Borg, *The United States and the Far Eastern Crisis of 1933–1938* (1964); R. P. Browder, *The Origins of Soviet-American Diplomacy* (1953); W. A. Williams, *American-Russian Relations, 1781–1947* (1952); R. P. Traina, *American Diplomacy and the Spanish Civil War* (1968); A. Guttmann, *The Wound in the Heart: America and the Spanish Civil War* (1962).

Interventionists Versus Isolationists
Alexander De Conde, ed., *Isolation and Security: Ideas and Interests in Twentieth-Century American Foreign Policy* (1957); R. A. Devine, *The Illusion of Neutrality* (1962); M. L. Chadwin, *The Hawks of World War II* (1968); J. K. Nelson, *The Peace Prophets: American Pacifist Thought, 1919–1941* (1967); Manfred Jonas, *Isolationism in America, 1935–1941** (1966); W. S. Cole, *America First* (1953); Walter Johnson, *Battle Against Isolation* (1944); Warren Moscow, *Roosevelt and Willkie* (1968).

Steps Toward War
W. L. Langer and S. E. Gleason, *The Challenge to Isolation, 1937–1940* (1952) and *The Undeclared War,* 1940–1941 (1953), comprehensive accounts; C. A. Beard, *American Foreign Policy in the Making, 1932–1940* (1946) and *President Roosevelt and the Coming of the War, 1941* (1948), highly critical of F. D. R.; Basil Rauch, *Roosevelt from Munich to Pearl Harbor** (1950), an attempt to refute Beard; Herbert Feis, *The Road to Pearl Harbor** (1950); Roberta Wohlsetter, *Pearl Harbor: Warning and Decision* (1962); R. J. C. Butow, *Tojo and the Coming of the War* (1961); P. W. Schroeder, *The Axis Alliance and Japanese-American Relations, 1941* (1958); W. F. Kimball, *The Most Unsordid Act: Lend-Lease, 1939–1941* (1969).

War Production
Bureau of the Budget, *The United States at War* (1946); D. M. Nelson, *Arsenal of Democracy* (1946); Bruce Catton, *War Lords of Washington* (1946); Eliot Janeway, *The Struggle for Survival* (1951); H. M. Somers, *Presidential Agency: OWMR* (1950); L. R. Groves, *Now It Can Be Told* (1962), on development of the A-bomb; J. P. Baxter III, *Scientists Against Time* (1946); W. W. Willcox, *The Farmer in the Second World War* (1947); W. A. Nielander, *Wartime Food Rationing in the United States* (1947).

Wartime Life
Jack Goodman, ed., *While You Were Gone: A Report on Wartime Life in the United States* (1946); W. F. Ogburn, ed., *American Society in Wartime* (1943); R. Polenberg, *War and Society: The United States, 1941–1945* (1972); Reuben Hill, *Families Under Stress* (1949); E. S. Corwin, *Total War and the Constitution* (1947); Morton Grodzins, *Americans Betrayed: Politics and the Japanese Evacuation* (1949); R. Daniels, *Concentration Camps, USA: Japanese Americans and World War II* (1971); M. Q. Sibley and P. E. Jacob, *Conscription of Conscience: The Conscientious Objector, 1940–1947* (1952).

*Titles available in paperback.

Victory Without Peace

Twenty-six

President Woodrow Wilson had turned from progressive reform to a foreign crusade, with disillusioning results. Similarly, President Franklin D. Roosevelt turned from the New Deal to national defense and then war abroad, but he hoped to escape the frustrations that had befallen his predecessor. In trying to avoid the "mistakes" that Wilson had made, Roosevelt pursued essentially the same objectives by almost exactly the opposite means, so that at times his policies appeared to be the very reverse of Wilson's.

Thus, during World War II, Roosevelt did not hold the United States somewhat aloof from its allies and call it merely an "associated" power, as Wilson had done during World War I. To the contrary, under Roosevelt this country took the initiative in drafting and signing a Declaration of the United Nations (January 1, 1942). The document set forth the war aims of the Atlantic Charter, committed the country's entire military and economic resources to the prosecution of the war, and pledged unlimited cooperation with the other signatories to fight on and make no separate peace. In effect, the United States was taking the lead in forming a grand alliance among the twenty-six original partners and the twenty more that signed before the war was over.

In peacemaking as in warmaking, Roosevelt followed a course quite different from Wilson's. True, the war aims he presented in the Atlantic Charter, which he cosigned with Prime Minister Winston Churchill, were vaguely reminiscent of those that Wilson had announced, unilaterally, in his Fourteen Points. But Roosevelt, with his slogan of "unconditional surrender," was determined to allow no armistice short of the enemy's utter defeat. And he was careful to keep from repeating the steps that had led the United States to a fiasco in relation to the Versailles Treaty and the League of Nations. This time

---

Mushroom Cloud, Nagasaki
When the atomic bomb exploded over Nagasaki, Japan, August 9, 1945, people in the city saw an "intense flash," heard a "tremendous roaring sound," and felt a "crushing blast wave and intense heat," according to an official Japanese report. The "whole city suffered damage such as would have resulted from direct hits everywhere by ordinary bombs." (Official U.S. Air Force photo)

there was to be no general peace conference comparable to the one at Versailles, and the new peacekeeping arrangement was to be kept quite separate from the political settlements to be made. The wartime alliance itself was to be converted into a peacekeeping body—the United Nations organization.

When, at the war's conclusion, the Senate approved American membership in the U. N. organization, many liberal Americans rejoiced that their country now was righting the wrong it presumably had done in rejecting the League. They assumed that, with the United States as a member, the League would have prevented a second world war; surely the U. N. would prevent a third. This optimism soon passed. For Americans the consequences of the Second World War were to prove even more disillusioning than those of the First, as the people came to realize that the victory of the grand alliance had brought no real peace to the world.

Fighting a Global War

In December 1941 neither the army nor the navy seemed very well prepared for the enormous tasks ahead, and the disaster at Pearl Harbor did not improve confidence in their commands. Enormous industrial production alone could not win the war. The military leaders must know what to order, and where and how to use it, on a scale they had not envisaged in their prewar establishments.

THE AMERICAN WAR MACHINE

At the outset the navy possessed only 300 combat ships, but at the close of the war it had 1,167 and was employing only one of the prewar vessels in the final attacks on Japan.

The army in 1939 had in theory nine infantry divisions but actually only the equivalent of about three and a half at half strength. Nor could it organize tactical units larger than a division. By mid-1941 it had twenty-nine infantry and cavalry divisions at nearly full strength, organized into four field armies—still less than half a million men. The army air force, nominally under the army but in practice almost independent, had only 22,000 officers and men and 2,400 aircraft in 1939.

There was little hint of what was to come. The most important of the war plans, "Orange," devised to go into effect in case of conflict with Japan, had presumed primarily a naval war, with the army mobilizing over a million men. By 1940 the more comprehensive "Rainbow" plans superseded these; by December 1941 a substantial mobilization was under way, though it was still far short of wartime totals.

Vast increases in personnel and equipment forced rapid changes in planning and organization. General George C. Marshall, Chief of Staff of the Army, reorganized the army high command in March 1942. That same month, Admiral Ernest J. King, a clear-headed hard driver, became Chief of Naval Operations. Together with General H. H. Arnold of the army air force, these men met with a personal representative of the President, Admiral William D. Leahy, to constitute the Joint Chiefs of Staff. They functioned as the overall command and represented the United States in combined planning with the British or occasional negotiations with the Russians.

Over the Joint Chiefs of Staff was the Commander in Chief, President Roosevelt, who bore responsibility for the conduct of the war. Personally, and through assistants like Harry Hopkins and cabinet members, he coordinated the war planning of the Joint Chiefs with war production and manpower and with foreign policy. The War Plans Division of the Army General Staff had pointed out that civilians should decide the "what" of national policies, and the professional soldiers the "how." Roosevelt, who had always zealously guarded civilian control even in the Navy Department and the War Department, followed this course throughout the war. He depended heavily

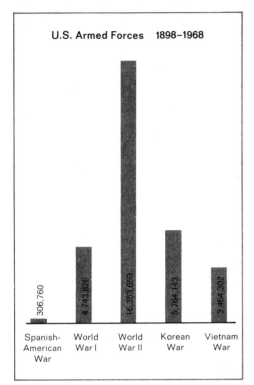

U.S. Armed Forces   1898–1968

306,760 — Spanish-American War
4,743,826 — World War I
16,353,659 — World War II
5,764,143 — Korean War
3,464,302 — Vietnam War

In the seventy years opening with the Spanish-American War, the United States was engaged in five major confrontations, yet the total deaths during this period were less than those in the Civil War. Much of the difference was due to improvements in military medicine and handling of casualties.

upon the advice of the Joint Chiefs of Staff and, once major policy had been decided, seldom interfered with their strategy.

The first of the great policy decisions had come in 1940 when the Americans decided that, even if Japan entered the war, their primary goal would be to defeat Germany with its superior military force, war production, and weapons development. The United States confirmed this priority in the initial wartime conference with the British at the end of December 1941. This decision did not mean neglecting the war against Japan. By August 1941, when the build-up, especially of airplanes, was under way in the Philippines, and later when General Douglas MacArthur received orders to fight, the strategy was shifting to a two-front war. The war against Germany was to be offensive, while that against Japan was to be defensive. It was difficult to hold to this policy as the Japanese tide in the Pacific swelled far beyond the bounds that the most pessimistic planners had anticipated. For the President, furious over Japanese treachery, and the navy, primarily responsible in the Pacific, it was not an easy decision to maintain. General MacArthur, the panic-stricken public on the Pacific Coast, and most Americans elsewhere clamored for prompt and stern action against the Japanese.

During the first chaotic months of shocking reverses, the armed forces allotted their men and supplies piecemeal to try to meet each new Axis threat. Top strategists emphatically warned that such dissipation of effort might lead to defeat. No one was more insistent than Dwight D. Eisenhower, who had been brought to Washington after Pearl Harbor as a Far Eastern expert, and who by the spring of 1942 was head of the Operations Planning Division under General Marshall. In emphatic memoranda, Eisenhower hammered away at the need to build up men and supplies in Europe for the invasion of North Africa that Roosevelt and Churchill had decided upon in their December 1941 meeting. Because of his vigor and his important role in developing an invasion plan, Eisenhower became the logical man to send to England (in June 1942) as commanding general in the European theater.

ON THE DEFENSIVE 1941–1942

While the United States was building and equipping its fighting forces, it had to depend upon the Russians and the British to hold back the Germans as best they could. During the discouraging first six months of American participation, the American forces had to stand perilously on the defensive in both the Atlantic and the Pacific. There even seemed danger of a breakthrough in Egypt and the Caucasus which might enable the Germans and Japanese to join forces in the Middle East or India.

Ten hours after the strike at Pearl Harbor, Japanese airplanes hit the airfields at Manila, destroying half the American bombers and two-thirds of the fighter planes. That same day the Japanese sank two British warships off Malaya, the only Allied warships in the Far

East. Three days later Guam fell; then, in the weeks that followed, Wake Island and Hong Kong. The great British fortress of Singapore in Malaya surrendered in February 1942, the Dutch East Indies in March, and Burma in April. In the Philippines on May 6 the exhausted Philippine and American troops, having made brave withdrawals to the Bataan peninsula and the Island of Corregidor in Manila Bay, ran down the last American flag in the Far East.

Only one weak outpost, Port Moresby in southern New Guinea, stood as a bulwark against the invasion of Australia. It seemed likely to fall, but there containment began through the efforts on land of Australian and American troops, and on the sea, of American aircraft carriers. In the Battle of Coral Sea on May 6–7, 1942, the Americans turned back Japanese invasion forces threatening Port Moresby. Under General MacArthur, who had escaped from the Philippines, American and Australian troops began clearing the Japanese from New Guinea.

After the Battle of Coral Sea, the navy, having intercepted Japanese messages, knew the next move and rushed every available plane and vessel into the central Pacific. Near Midway Island, June 3–6, 1942, these forces inflicted heavy damage on a Japanese invasion fleet and headed off a drive to capture the island and neutralize Hawaii. The United States had achieved its goal of containment in the Pacific, and as men and supplies could be spared from the operations against the Nazis, it could assume the offensive against Japan.

In the Atlantic during the early months of 1942, the Nazis tried by means of submarines to confine the Americans to the Western Hemisphere. By mid-January the Germans had moved so many submarines to the Atlantic coast, where at night they torpedoed tankers silhouetted against the lights of cities, that they created a critical oil shortage. Against convoys bound for Europe they made attacks with devastating success. In the first eleven months they sank over 8 million tons of shipping—1.2 million more than the Allies meanwhile built—and threatened to delay indefinitely the large-scale shipment of supplies and men to Europe. Gradually the United States countered by developing effective antisubmarine vessels, air patrols, detecting devices, and weapons.

The submarines made it difficult to send assistance to the British and Russians in the summer of 1942 when they needed it most. The German *Afrika Corps* raced to El Alamein, only seventy-five miles from Alexandria, Egypt, threatening the Suez Canal and the Middle East. At the same time, German armies in Russia were plunging toward the Caucasus. In May the Russian foreign minister, Vyacheslav Molotov, visited Washington to demand an immediate second front that would divert at least forty German divisions from Russia; the alternative might be Russian collapse. Roosevelt promised to do everything possible to divert the Germans by invading France. But Churchill arrived the next month, when the Gemans were threatening Egypt, and he strongly urged an invasion of North Africa instead.

THE MEDITERRANEAN OFFENSIVE

The overwhelming losses in the August 1942 raid on Dieppe, France, undertaken by experienced Canadian troops, indicated the wisdom of making the first American landing on a relatively unprotected flank. Through advance negotiations with officials of the Vichy government of defeated France, the Americans hoped to make a bloodless landing in French North Africa. At the end of October 1942 the British opened a counteroffensive at El Alamein which sent the *Afrika Corps* reeling back. On November 8, Anglo-American forces landed at Oran, Algiers, and Casablanca, Morocco, with some bungling and gratifyingly few losses. They met determined Vichy French resistance only at Casablanca.

Admiral Jean Darlan, earlier one of the most notorious collaborators with the Nazis, signed an armistice with the Allies on November 12. He ordered a cease-fire and promised the aid of 50,000 French colonial troops. Outraged American liberals protested against the deal with the Vichyites as opposed to the French resistance forces under General Charles de Gaulle. The critics quieted somewhat a few weeks later when Darlan was assassinated. Unsavory though it was to idealists, the Vichy gamble probably saved lives and speeded the liberation of North Africa.

The Germans tried to counter the invasion by ferrying troops from Sicily into Tunisia at

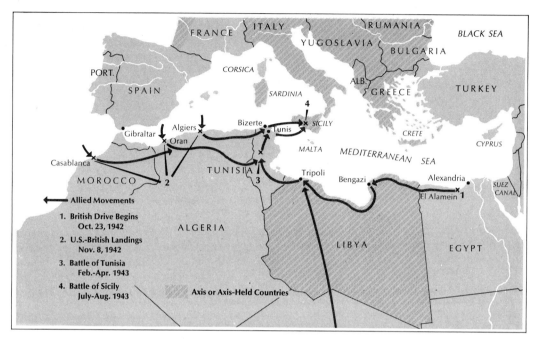

The North African and Sicilian Campaigns

the rate of a thousand a day. Early in 1943 the *Afrika Corps*, which had retreated westward across Tripoli, joined them and threw the full weight of its armor against the green American troops. The Americans lost heavily but with the aid of the British held onto their bases and gained in experience. Allied air power and the British navy so seriously harassed the Axis supply line from Sicily that Germany decided not to make a major stand in Tunisia. From March into May, the British army in the east and the armies in the west under Eisenhower gradually closed a vise on the German and Italian troops. On May 12, 1943, the last Axis troops in North Africa surrendered. The Mediterranean had been reopened, and the Americans had learned lessons that would be useful in the successful invasion of France.

That invasion, despite the continued clamoring of the Russians, was not to take place immediately. The fighting in Tunisia had tied up too large a part of the Allied combat resources for too long. Nazi submarines were still taking too heavy a toll of the Allies' inadequate shipping. Some of the ships and production had to be diverted to the antisubmarine war, and

others to the prosecution of the Pacific campaigns. Also, the planners in London had come to recognize that an enormous build-up was necessary for a successful cross-channel invasion. Fortunately for the Allies, the tide turned for the Russians also during the winter of 1942–1943, when they successfully held the Germans at Stalingrad in the Ukraine, eliminating an army of 250,000 men.

As early as mid-January 1943, Roosevelt and Churchill and their staffs, while conferring at Casablanca, looked ahead to the next move. This was to be an invasion of Sicily, even though General Marshall feared it might delay the invasion of France. Churchill argued persuasively that the operation in Sicily might knock Italy out of the war and lead the Germans to tie up many divisions in defense of Italy and the Balkans.

On the night of July 9, 1943, American and British armies landed in the extreme southeast of Sicily, where defenses were comparatively light. The Americans made grievous errors, the worst being to shoot down twenty-three planeloads of their own paratroops, but learned from their mistakes. In thirty-eight days the Allies conquered the island and looked toward the Italian mainland. Mussolini now fell from power, to be replaced by the pro-Allied Marshal Pietro Badoglio. At once Badoglio opened complicated negotiations to switch Italy to the side of the United Nations. As the negotiations went on, the Nazis moved eight strong divisions into northern Italy, concentrated other troops near Rome, and turned the country into an occupied defense bastion.

A limited but long and punishing campaign opened on the Italian peninsula on September 3, 1943. It started with the greatest optimism, for that same day the Italian government signed an armistice agreement, and the Allies quickly seized bases and airfields in southern Italy. But the Nazi defenders fought so fiercely from hillside fortifications that by early 1944 they had stopped the slow and deliberately moving Allies at Monte Cassino. When the Allies tried to break behind the line by landing at Anzio, south of Rome, they were almost thrown back into the sea. With relatively few divisions, the Nazis were tying down the Allies while concentrating their main effort upon Russia. Finally, in May 1944, the Allies captured Cassino, pressed on from the Anzio beachhead, and on June 4 captured Rome, just before the cross-channel invasion of France began.

THE LIBERATION OF EUROPE

In the fall of 1943 Germany was already reeling under the incessant blows from the growing Allied air power. Great Britain had begun its

The Invasion of Normandy
A coast guard combat photographer, climbing beyond the Nazi trench in the foreground to the top of the cliff, looked out at this panorama of channel waters crowded with ships while landing craft were putting ashore men and supplies. The barrage balloons floated overhead to protect the ships from low-flying enemy strafers. One of them is resting on the deck of an LST (landing barge). Long lines of trucks were heading inland, carrying reinforcements for the battle for the Cotentin peninsula. (Official U.S. Coast Guard photo)

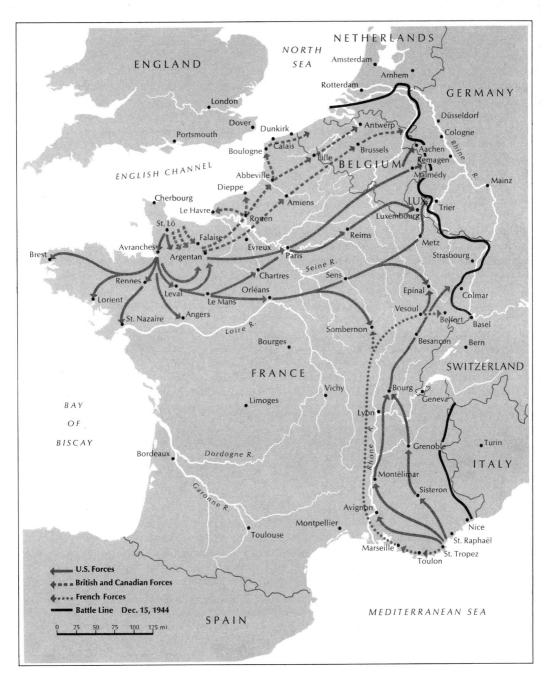

The Liberation of France

mass bombing of German industrial centers in the late spring of 1942 with a thousand-plane night raid on Cologne. In August the Americans made their first experimental daytime raids on the Continent. Bombing almost

around-the-clock began on a gigantic scale in February 1944. One of the objects of these bombing raids was to draw German fighter planes into battle. By the end of the war the Americans were flying over 7,000 bombers and

6,000 fighters in Europe, had dropped nearly a million and a half tons of bombs, and had lost nearly 10,000 bombers. British figures were similar. Especially in the last year of the war, the bombing drastically cut production and impeded transportation. As early as the winter of 1944 it had so seriously demoralized the German people that 77 percent of them already regarded the war as lost.

The bombing attacks, first upon the aviation industry, then upon transportation, did much to clear the way for the invasion in the late spring. By May 1944 the *Luftwaffe* was incapable of beating off the Allied air cover for an invasion. As D-Day (invasion day) approached, the invasion was postponed from the beginning of May until early June despite the likelihood of worsening weather, in order to obtain an additional month's production of special landing craft. A sudden storm delayed the operation for a day, but on the morning of June 6, 1944, the invasion came, not at the narrowest part of the English Channel, where the Nazis expected it, but along sixty miles of the Cotentin peninsula on the Normandy coast. While airplanes and battleships offshore incessantly bombarded the Nazi defenses, 4,000 vessels, stretching as far as the eye could see, brought in troops and supplies.

Within two weeks after the initial landings, the Allies had put ashore a million men and the equipment for them. They also had captured Cherbourg, only to find that the Germans had blocked its harbor so skillfully that it could not be used until August.

Well into July, the Allies fought mile by mile through the Normandy hedgerows. The breakthrough came on July 25, 1944, when General Omar Bradley's First Army, using its armor as cavalry had been used in earlier wars, smashed the German lines in an enormous sweep southward, then eastward. The invasion on the Mediterranean coast, beginning on August 15, quickly seized new ports (also seriously blocked) and opened new supply lines for the Allies. On August 25 French forces rode into Paris, jammed with cheering throngs. By mid-September the Allied armies had driven the Germans from almost all of France and Belgium, including the port of Antwerp, and had come to a halt against a firm line of German defenses.

Cold weather, rain, and floods aided the Germans. In December they struck with desperate fury along fifty miles of front in the Ardennes Forest, driving fifty-five miles toward Antwerp before they were stopped (in the "Battle of the Bulge") at Bastogne.

While the Allies were fighting their way through France to the Westwall (German defense line) and up the Italian peninsula, the Russian armies had been sweeping westward into central Europe and the Balkans. The Russian armies advanced more rapidly than had been expected and, in late January 1945, launched an offensive of over 150 divisions toward the Oder River, far inside Germany.

After liquidating the German thrust into the Ardennes, which had almost exhausted the Nazi fighting capacity, the Allied armies pushed on to the Rhine. The Americans captured Cologne on the west bank March 6, 1945, and on the next day, through remarkable luck, captured a bridge across the Rhine at Remagen. Troops poured across it. By the end of March the last great drives were under way as the British commander Montgomery with a million troops pushed across the north while Bradley's army, sweeping through central Germany, completed the encirclement and trapping of 300,000 German soldiers in the Ruhr. Russian troops were about to mount a spring offensive only 35 miles from Berlin.

There were fears that the Nazis were preparing for a last stand in an Alpine redoubt centering on Berchtesgaden on the Austrian border. In fact, however, the German western front had been demolished. The only real questions were where the Americans would drive next and where they would join the Russians. The Americans, capable of moving much farther eastward than had been anticipated, could have beaten the Russians to Berlin and Prague. This would have cost American lives but would have reaped political gain in Europe. General Eisenhower decided, instead, to send American troops to capture the Alpine redoubt and then halt along the Elbe River in central Germany to meet the Russians.

On May 8, 1945, the remaining German forces surrendered unconditionally. V-E (Victory in Europe) Day arrived amidst monster celebrations in western Europe and in the United States. The rejoicing was tempered only by the knowledge of the continuing war against Japan.

THE PACIFIC OFFENSIVE

The offensive strategy against the Japanese involved amphibious warfare of a type that the marine corps had been developing since the early 1920s. In the Pacific these new tactics came to be so perfected that troops were able to cross and seize vigorously defended beaches when the United States could not by-pass them and immobilize advanced Japanese strong points. The American strategy was, whenever feasible, "Hit 'em where they ain't."

The southern Solomon Islands to the east of New Guinea were being developed as a Japanese base for air raids against American communications with Australia. In August 1942 the navy and marines opened an offensive against three of these islands, Gavutu, Tulagi, and Guadalcanal. Around and on Guadalcanal

a struggle of unprecedented ferocity developed as the United States and Japanese navies battled for control in a series of large-scale engagements. By the time the struggle was over, the United States and its allies had lost heavily in cruisers, carriers, and destroyers, but had sunk forty-seven Japanese vessels. The Japanese navy had lost its offensive strength and thereafter concentrated upon defensive operations.

During the months when the great naval battles had been going against the United States, the Americans had gained control of the air and thus were able to sustain the marines, and subsequently the army, in their precarious jungle onslaught. By February 1943 Guadalcanal had been won. Through the year the island-hopping continued all around the enormous Japanese-held perimeter: in the South

The War in the Pacific

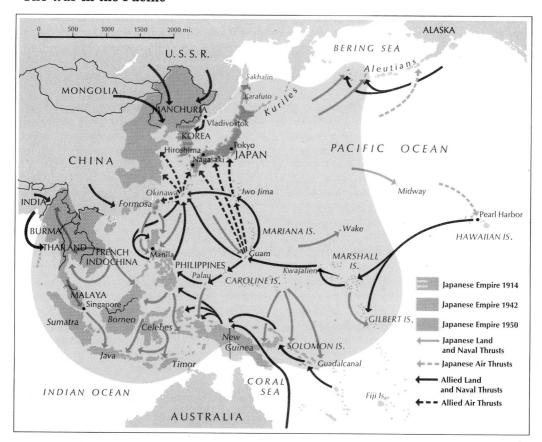

Pacific through the northern Solomons to New Georgia, and in November to Bougainville; in the central Pacific, also in November, the marine landing on Makin and the bloody assault on Tarawa in the Gilberts; in the northern Pacific, the inexpert reconquest of Kiska and Attu in the Aleutians.

Victories in the Marshall Islands in February 1944 cracked the Japanese outer perimeter, and before the month was out the navy had plunged far within it to wreck the bastion at Truk and raid Saipan in the Marianas. American submarines were increasingly harassing Japanese shipping, and thus hampering the economy. In 1943 the Americans sank 284 ships; in 1944 they sank 492—necessitating by summer a cut of nearly a quarter in skimpy Japanese food rations and creating a crucial gasoline shortage. The inner empire of Japan was coming under relentless siege.

Meanwhile, in 1942, the Japanese forced General Joseph H. Stilwell out of Burma and brought their troops as far west as the mountains bordering on India. China was so isolated that the United States could send in meager supplies only through an aerial ferry over the "hump" of the Himalayas. On the return trip, the planes brought Chinese troops for Stilwell to train and arm. Through 1943, Stilwell with Chinese, Indian, and a few American troops fought back through northern Burma, constructing a road and parallel pipeline across the rugged mountains into Yunnan province, China. The Ledo or Stilwell road was not open until the fall of 1944, but meanwhile the Air Transport Command managed to fly in sufficient supplies to enable the Fourteenth Air Force (before Pearl Harbor, the "Flying Tigers") to harass the Japanese. The Command undertook a still larger task when B-29 bombers struck the Yawata steel mills in Japan from Chinese bases (June 1944). The Japanese retaliated in the next few months by overrunning the bases from which the bombers operated, and clearing the coastal area so they could bring supplies northward from Southeast Asia by rail or road. The drove so far into the interior that they threatened the Chinese terminus of the Ledo Road, and perhaps even the center of government at Chungking.

The great Japanese offensive precipitated a long-simmering crisis in Chinese-American affairs, centering upon the relations between General Stilwell and Chiang Kai-shek. Stilwell was indignant because Chiang was using many of his troops to maintain an armed frontier against the Chinese Communists and would not deploy them against the Japanese. In order to have bolstered Chiang adequately, the United States would have had to send such substantial immediate support that the campaigns against Germany and directly against Japan might have had to be slowed down or postponed.

During 1944 Japan came under heavy blockade from the sea and bombardment from the air. American submarines firing torpedoes and laying mines continued to make heavy inroads in the dwindling Japanese merchant marine.

In mid-June an enormous American armada struck the heavily fortified Mariana Islands, quickly but expensively capturing Tinian, Guam, and Saipan, 1,350 miles from Tokyo. These were among the bloodiest operations of the war. In September the Americans landed on the western Carolines. The way was being prepared for the return to the Philippines. For weeks in advance navy craft swept the central Pacific, and airplanes ranged over the Philippines and Formosa. Finally, on October 20 General MacArthur's troops landed on Leyte Island in the Philippines. The Japanese, threatened with being fatally cut off from their new empire in Southeast Asia, threw their remaining fleets against the invaders in three major encounters—together comprising the decisive Battle of Leyte Gulf, the largest naval engagement in history—and lost almost all their remaining sea power.

ATOMIC TRIUMPH OVER JAPAN

With remarkable speed but grievous losses the American forces cut still deeper into the Japanese empire during the early months of 1945. While fighting continued in the Philippines, the marines landed in February on the tiny volcanic island of Iwo Jima, only 750 miles from Tokyo. The Americans needed Iwo Jima to provide fighter cover for Japan-bound bombers and a landing place for crippled ones. The Japanese defended the island so grimly that the marines suffered over 20,000 casualties. It was the bloodiest battle in the history of the marine corps.

The battle for Okinawa, an island sixty-five miles long, beginning on April 1, 1945, was even

Hiroshima, Japan, Looking Northeast   October 1945
"A single atomic bomb, the first weapon of its type ever used against a target, exploded over the city of Hiroshima at 0815 on the morning of 6 August 1945. Most of the industrial workers had already reported to work, but many workers were en route and nearly all of the school children and some industrial employees were at work in the open on the program of building removal. . . . The explosion came as an almost complete surprise, and the people had not taken shelter. Many were caught in the open, and most of the rest in flimsily constructed homes or commercial establishments. The bomb exploded slightly northwest of the center of the city. Because of this accuracy and the flat terrain and circular shape of the city, Hiroshima was uniformly and extensively devastated. Practically the entire densely or moderately built-up portion of the city was leveled by blast and swept by fire. . . . The surprise, the collapse of many buildings, and the conflagration contributed to an unprecedented casualty rate. Seventy to eighty thousand people were killed, or missing and presumed dead, and an equal number were injured."
— Report, United States Strategic Bombing Survey. (National Archives)

bloodier. This island lies 370 miles south of Japan, and its conquest clearly would be a prelude to an invasion of the main islands. On land and from the air, the Japanese fought with literally a suicidal fury. Week after week they sent *kamikaze* suicide planes against the American and British ships, losing 3,500 of them but inflicting great damage. Ashore at night, Japanese troops launched equally desperate attacks on the American lines. The United States and its allies suffered nearly 50,000 casualties on land and afloat before the battle came to an end in late June 1945. The Japanese lost 110,000 killed and 7,800 prisoners.

This same sort of bitter fighting seemed to await the Americans when they invaded Ja-

pan — if indeed they should ever have to invade. There were signs that the Japanese might surrender, for they had almost no ships and few airplanes with which to fight. In July 1945 American warships stood offshore with impunity and shelled industrial targets, most of which were already in ruins from the heavy bombing attacks. Long since, moderate Japanese leaders had regarded the war as lost. Upon the invasion of Okinawa, the Emperor appointed a new premier and instructed him to sue for peace. The premier could not persuade the army leaders to lay down their arms, but nevertheless he, and in early summer the Emperor himself, tried to obtain mediation through Russia.

Apparently the Russians were determined, at their own time, to enter the war. But the atomic bomb rather than Russian intervention was to be decisive in bringing the war to an end. At a meeting of Allied leaders in Potsdam, Germany, in mid-July 1945, President Harry S Truman (who had succeeded Roosevelt) received word that the first atomic test was successful. He and Prime Minister Clement Attlee (who had succeeded Churchill) issued the Potsdam Declaration urging the Japanese to surrender or face utter devastation. The Japanese premier wished to accept the ultimatum, but the army leaders would not surrender. President Truman had set August 3 as the deadline; when it passed and the Japanese continued to fight, he ordered an atomic bomb to be dropped on one of four previously selected Japanese cities.

On August 6, 1945, a B-29 dropped an atomic bomb on Hiroshima, destroying most of the hitherto undamaged city, and killing 80,000

people (according to American estimates) or 200,000 (according to the Japanese). Even after the horror of Hiroshima, the Japanese army remained adamant. Russia declared war on Japan as of August 9. That same day, the air force dropped a second atomic bomb, on Nagasaki. This was the final blow. After frantic negotiations, on August 14 the Japanese government agreed to give up. On September 2, 1945, aboard the battleship *Missouri* in Tokyo Bay, the articles of surrender were signed.

World War II was at an end. All together, some 14 million men under arms had been killed, and countless millions of civilians had died. In comparison, about 322,000 Americans had been killed or were missing; total United States casualties were about 1,120,000. Despite this frightful expenditure in lives and an astronomical cost in material resources, the American people faced a future made uncertain and perilous by the tensions with the Russians and the threat of future atomic wars.

Frustrations of Peacemaking

Only the imminent threat of Axis victory had forced an uneasy and unsatisfactory form of cooperation between Russia and its Western allies, Great Britain and the United States. As the threat began to lift in 1943, it became increasingly difficult to keep the alliance cemented and to plan for a postwar world in which a decent peace could be maintained.

THE DANGEROUS ALLIANCE

The difference between British and American strategy—the British opposing a cross-channel invasion and preferring campaigns in southern and eastern Europe—affected the two nations' dealings with the Russians. To a certain extent the United States seemed nearer to the Russians in insisting with them upon an early invasion of France. Roosevelt seemed at times to take a middle position between Stalin and Churchill.

As the Nazi tide receded, the postwar patterns began to emerge throughout eastern Europe, as they were already doing in Italy. Firm political agreements were necessary if

these areas were not to fall entirely under Russian hegemony, just as firm military plans were essential to the achievement of final victory.

At Casablanca, Morocco, in January 1943, after previous consultation with Churchill, Roosevelt announced the doctrine of unconditional surrender by the Axis. What Roosevelt seemed to desire was to avoid the sort of negotiations that had marred the 1918 armistice, causing bickerings among the Allies at the time and German misunderstandings afterward. As the war progressed, it became clear that "unconditional surrender" left the United Nations free to state to the Axis powers the peace terms the latter might expect. Roosevelt and Churchill both emphasized that the phrase did not mean, as the Nazi propagandists charged, that extremely severe terms would be imposed. Yet, after the war, some historians charged that the "unconditional surrender" doctrine seriously discouraged the anti-Nazi German underground movement, stiffened the Nazi will to fight, and thus lengthened the war.

In October 1943 Secretary Hull, although he was seventy-two and in precarious health, flew to Moscow to confer with the British and

Russian foreign ministers. His faith in Wilsonian idealism almost limitless, Hull returned from Moscow elated because the Russians had agreed to a Declaration of Four Nations on General Security. (China was the fourth nation.) This was a pledge to continue the united action of war "for the organization and maintenance of peace and security" and to create, as soon as practicable, a general international organization.

With an air of optimism Roosevelt and Churchill traveled eastward in November 1943 for a long-awaited meeting with Stalin at Teheran, Iran. On the way they stopped at Cairo to confer with Chiang Kai-shek and to prepare a statement (released after the Teheran conference) drawing a map for the postwar Far East. They proposed stripping Japan of her empire in order to restore Manchuria, the Pescadores, and Formosa to China, and to create in due course a free and independent Korea. Japan was to lose, in addition, all other territory she had acquired since 1914.

At Teheran, Roosevelt undertook to establish a friendly, intimate relationship with Stalin of the sort he enjoyed with Churchill. Stalin reaffirmed his intention to bring Russia into the Pacific war soon after hostilities had ended in

---

Stalin, Roosevelt, and Churchill at Teheran

"We—The President of the United States, the Prime Minister of Great Britain, and the Premier of the Soviet Union, have met these four days past, in this, the Capital of our Ally, Iran, and have shaped and confirmed our common policy.

"We express our determination that our nations shall work together in war and in the peace that will follow. . . .

"Emerging from these cordial conferences we look with confidence to the day when all peoples of the world may live free lives, untouched by tyranny, and according to their varying desires and their own consciences.

"We came here with hope and determination. We leave here, friends in fact, in spirit and in purpose."—From a joint statement issued December 1, 1943. (National Archives)

Europe, and expressed his satisfaction with the Cairo communiqué on Japan. In a cordial way the three leaders discussed the means, through an international organization, of keeping Germany from ever again becoming a menace. Stalin wished Russia to retain the areas she had seized in her period of collaboration with Germany, including eastern Poland as far as the so-called Curzon line proposed in 1919. Roosevelt and Churchill agreed to the Polish boundary.

Roosevelt and Churchill seem not to have recognized realistically the nature of the peace that was being foreshadowed at Teheran. In the general rejoicing over the apparent accord among the Big Three, and in their assumption that Russia would be content within its new boundaries, they overlooked the appraisal that one of the American participants at Teheran wrote a few days later: "The result would be that the Soviet Union would be the only important military and political force on the continent of Europe. The rest of Europe would be reduced to military and political impotence."

It was unrealistic to expect, as Roosevelt apparently did, that the Russians would forbear from exploiting the great European and Asian power vacuums that the defeat of Germany and Japan would create. This miscalculation led the United States into a tragic triumph—a victory without peace.

THE YALTA CONFERENCE

Churchill's mood fluctuated with the ebb and flow of Russian good will. Upon leaving Moscow, after a visit in the fall of 1944, he wrote Stalin: "This memorable meeting . . . has shown that there are no matters that cannot be adjusted between us when we meet together in frank and intimate discussion." By January 1945 he was so badly disillusioned that he wrote Roosevelt concerning the forthcoming Yalta meeting: "This may well be a fateful Conference, coming at a moment when the Great Allies are so divided and the shadow of the war lengthens out before us. At the present time I think the end of this war may well prove to be more disappointing than was the last." Such was the bleak and unpromising setting for the great conference at Yalta in the Crimea (February 1945).

At that time American forces were having to reduce Germany mile by mile; there seemed no reason to think Japan would be different. General MacArthur insisted on the necessity for Russian aid, taking the position that otherwise the United States would have to fight a series of difficult and expensive campaigns to overcome the Japanese in Manchuria. Consequently the Joint Chiefs did not revise their timetable calling for the defeat of Japan eighteen months after German surrender, and they continued to regard Russian aid as indispensable. Roosevelt expressed to Stalin his hope that Japan could be bombed into submission without invasion—but the Americans could not count upon it.

These were the limitations upon the Americans in their bargaining at Yalta. In return for Stalin's reiterated promise to enter the Far Eastern war two or three months after German surrender, Roosevelt and Churchill promised him the Kurile Islands north of Japan and the restoration of "the former rights of Russia" lost in the Russo-Japanese War. This meant the return of southern Sakhalin Island, the return of a lease on Port Arthur as a naval base and internationalizing of the port of Dairen, Manchuria (in both instances with recognition of Russia's preeminent interests), and joint operation with China of the Chinese Eastern and South Manchurian railroads feeding into the ports. China was to retain sovereignty over Manchuria, but Roosevelt did not clarify what "preeminent interests" meant. (For many months these clauses remained secret because Russia was still at peace with Japan.)

In its disposition of central European questions, the Yalta conference for the most part ratified previous decisions. Germany was to be divided into zones of occupation previously agreed upon. Since Berlin was to be deep in the Russian zone, the Americans and British proposed an accord providing freedom of transit into Berlin. The Russians held back, and in the general spirit of amity at Yalta, the matter was postponed. At the time, the Russian demands for heavy reparations in the form of German factories, goods, and labor seemed far more important. The British tried to scale down the Russian demand for $20 billion in such reparations, of which Russia was to obtain half. This would so strip and starve the Germans, Churchill pointed out, that the United States

Enlisting Russian Aid Against Japan at Yalta [1945]

I think there was the belief that Russia's entry into the war [against Japan] before we hit the islands would save hundreds of thousands of American casualties. . . . The disposition of Chinese territories, as you know, was subsequently embodied in the Soviet-Chinese Treaty of August 1945, which was almost universally hailed in this country, as well as, I believe, in China, as a great event, because this treaty involved the recognition by the Soviet Union of the sovereignty of the Chinese Nationalist Government over Manchuria. . . .

The first reaction from the Chinese was not one that they had been sold, as it were, down the river. Mr. T. V. Soong in his negotiations in Moscow found the Yalta agreement of considerable use to him as a backstop.

There are now, in retrospect, two valid criticisms of the agreement: First it was unnecessary, the war did not take the course predicted; and, secondly, it was done without the participation of the Chinese Government. — Testimony of Charles E. Bohlen (who had been an assistant to the Secretary of State and interpreter at Yalta), on his nomination as ambassador to Russia, before the Senate Committee on Foreign Relations, 1953.

---

and Great Britain would have to feed them. Consequently he and Roosevelt agreed to the Russian figure only as a basis for discussion by a reparations commission. Already, in the light of reality, the West had left far behind the Morgenthau plan (initialed by Roosevelt and Churchill at Quebec in October 1944) for the pastoralization of Germany.

One of the touchiest questions was what would constitute a democratic government for Poland, a matter over which Russia and the West had negotiated for months. The Russians did not wish to allow the Polish government in exile in London or the Polish underground to assume any substantial share of power with a government the Russians had established at Lublin. At the beginning of August 1944, as the Red army drove within ten miles of Warsaw, the underground in the city arose against the Germans. The Russians halted, ignored the revolt, and despite the strong pleas of the United States and Great Britain, stood by while the Polish patriots were annihilated in sixty-three days of fighting. The Russian explanation was military exigency, but the situation seemed to show the sort of government Stalin was determined to establish in Poland.

At Yalta the West managed to obtain Stalin's agreement that the Lublin (Communist) government should be broadened to include democratic leaders from Poland and abroad.

What the percentage should be was not specified. Subsequently the new government should hold "free and unfettered elections as soon as possible on the basis of universal suffrage and secret ballot." It would have been a satisfactory arrangement for the West if the terms had been interpreted in their Western meaning. As for the Polish boundary, it was to follow the Curzon line in the east, and the Poles were to receive territorial compensation in the north and west.

For the rest of liberated or defeated Europe, the Big Three agreed to establish interim governments "broadly representative of all democratic elements" and to provide for free elections that would create "governments responsible to the will of the people."

In years after the war, disappointed Americans harshly criticized the Yalta agreements, especially for their violations of the Atlantic Charter. The morality of the Far Eastern arrangements is open to challenge. Their purpose was to obtain Russian aid, which top military leaders thought would shorten the war against Japan and perhaps prevent a million American casualties. The terms promised nothing to Stalin that he could not have taken anyway. The morality of the European arrangements (except perhaps for the ethnic dislocations wrought by the new Polish boundaries) would have been defensible if the terms had received their customary Western interpretation. Roosevelt may be most severely criticized for not insisting at every point upon absolutely clear, sharply defined agreements that could receive only one interpretation in Russia—the interpretation as understood by the West. This was especially true of the question of entry into Berlin. Experience with the Russians long before Yalta had pointed to the need for precise understandings.

Roosevelt was careless in this respect because he pinned his hopes upon the good faith of the Russians and their willingness to enter into and actively participate in an international organization for the preservation of the peace.

THE U. N. ORGANIZATION

A few months before war broke out in Europe—and long before the attack at Pearl Harbor—Secretary Hull had taken the first step toward proposing a new international organization in which the United States would participate. In January 1940 he appointed an Advisory Committee on Problems of Foreign Relations. Its membership was composed of congressmen from both parties and distinguished experts from within and without the State Department. Several private organizations like the Council on Foreign Relations also prepared numerous studies for the State Department.

Signing the U.N. Charter
Delegates from fifty nations attended a conference that met in the San Francisco Opera House, April 25, 1945, to prepare a charter for the United Nations organization. The delegates signed the completed charter on June 26. In this photograph President Truman shakes hands with Secretary of State Edward R. Stettinius, Jr., chairman of the American delegation, after the signing by the Americans. (United Nations)

President Roosevelt, firmly determined to avoid Wilson's failure, encouraged Hull to include Republicans in the planning for the peace. However, Roosevelt did not consult Congress before making his most famous statements of war aims: Senator Robert A. Taft asserted in 1943 that he did not believe "we went to war to establish the 'four freedoms' or any other freedom throughout the world," nor "for the purposes set forth in the Atlantic Charter." The administration, to counter this sort of resentment, included prominent Republicans in at least sketchy briefings on wartime diplomacy and let them participate more fully in postwar planning of many kinds. In this way it won their support. In 1943 four senators, two Republican and two Democratic, none of whom were serving on the Foreign Relations Committee, introduced a resolution calling for American leadership in establishing a United Nations organization. Public opinion polls indicated a general enthusiasm for the resolution; the Senate passed a similar declaration 85 to 5. Senator Arthur H. Vandenberg of Michigan, previously one of the most forthright isolationists, assumed Republican leadership in helping mold a "bipartisan" foreign policy. He thus gained for himself and the Republican party new power and stature.

The Big Four powers, conferring in the summer and fall of 1944 at Dumbarton Oaks, a Harvard-owned estate in Washington, drafted tentative outlines for a new international organization. These were the starting points for the drafting of a United Nations charter at a conference of fifty nations in San Francisco, opening April 25, 1945. President Roosevelt had appointed a bipartisan delegation headed by his new Secretary of State, Edward R. Stettinius, Jr. One of its most effective members was Senator Vandenberg, who helped to wrest concessions from the Russians at San Francisco and to win the votes of reluctant Republicans for ratification in the Senate.

Basically the charter of the United Nations was a refurbishing of the old Wilsonian League covenant with the former American objections removed through giving a veto to each of the five main powers. The Americans and British, as well as the Russians, had insisted upon the veto as a seemingly necessary protection of their sovereignty. The American delegates, led by Vandenberg, succeeded in obtaining for the small nations in the General Assembly freedom to discuss and make recommendations—in effect creating "a town meeting of the world."

The Senate quickly ratified the charter (July 1945) by a vote of 80 to 2, in remarkable contrast to the slow and painful defeat it had administered to American membership in the League of Nations. But the great and growing gulf between Russia and the West destined the United Nations to be, like its predecessor, the League, a town meeting for international discussion or a sounding board for national views, rather than the forerunner of a world government.

A FOURTH TERM FOR F. D. R.

With "bipartisanship" prevailing, there had been no serious disagreement between Democrats and Republicans on the issues of peace planning. But in regard to domestic questions there had been politics as usual. Indeed, despite all the platitudinous pleas to put aside politics in the interest of national unity, the struggles became even more virulent during the war.

Conservatives saw in the war an opportunity to eradicate hated remnants of the New Deal; some liberals regarded it as an opportunity to bring Wilson's ideas to fruition, and even go beyond them to establish a global New Deal. Every one of the great pressure groups in the country fought to maintain or improve its relative position; spokesmen for large business and small, farmers and labor, jockeyed for position in Washington. The tenor of Congress continued to be conservative, and it was sensitive as always to the demands of organized constituents. Throughout the war, key committee chairmen who were leaders of the conservative coalition dominated Congress and forced their will upon President Roosevelt. Through the election of 1942, as the United States and its allies suffered unparalleled military disasters and the war administration in Washington seemed to compound confusion, the criticism rose to a crescendo. In the election, the Republicans gained forty-seven seats in the House and ten in the Senate. Within both parties the trend was to the right.

President Roosevelt, in order to get crucial congressional support in prosecuting the war and planning the peace, continued to accept the sacrifice of New Deal measures. At a press conference in 1943 he announced that "Dr. Win-the-War" had replaced "Dr. New Deal."

Dissatisfaction with wartime regimentation and smoldering resentments still glowing from the prewar debate over intervention seemed to give the Republicans an opportunity in 1944. They had seen auguries of a national shift toward the right in the congressional election of 1942. In their vigorous young candidate, Governor Thomas E. Dewey of New York, who ran with Governor John W. Bricker of Ohio, they seemed to have an answer to Roosevelt and the aging New Dealers.

As for President Roosevelt, it was a foregone conclusion that he would be nominated for a fourth term if he so desired. There was none of the suspense that had preceded the third-term nomination. Rather, since he was visibly aging, unwell, and thinning so that his clothes ill fit him, there was much speculation over his choice for the vice-presidential nominee. During the war, Vice President Wallace was the hero of most advanced New Dealers and much of the CIO membership. But he was sneered at by party bosses and some Southern Democrats as a visionary who wished to extend the New Deal to the entire globe, to bring "a quart of milk for every Hottentot." They rallied behind James M. Byrnes of South Carolina, who had been functioning ably as the unofficial assistant president—but Byrnes was unacceptable to organized labor. Out of the skirmishing among the rival factions within the Democratic party came Roosevelt's proposal of a compromise candidate acceptable to most of them, Senator Harry S Truman of Missouri. Truman had won newspaper approval as chairman of the Senate War Investigating Committee, was a consistent New Dealer in his voting record, and was from a border state. He was popular in the Senate.

In keeping with the bipartisan spirit, Republican and Democratic leaders had arranged for practically identical planks on foreign policy, thus eliminating it as an issue in the campaign. Dewey had a good chance to make it an issue when he got word that American intelligence had broken the Japanese code before Pearl Harbor. With this information, he could have charged that the Roosevelt administration knew—or should have known—of the coming Japanese attack. But an envoy from General Marshall dissuaded Dewey from using the information, which if made public would have caused the Japanese to change their code (American intelligence was still exploiting it) and thus would have disadvantaged United States forces fighting in the Pacific. Even without this issue, the election promised to be close—partly because the vote was likely to be small, and presumably a light vote would aid the Republicans.

The possibility was like an injection of adrenalin into Roosevelt. At the end of September 1944, addressing a raucously appreciative audience of Teamsters Union members, he was at his sardonic best. He followed this triumph with a strenuous campaign in Chicago and throughout the East. This he climaxed with a day-long drive in an open car through New York City in a soaking rain.

Roosevelt's seeming capacity to serve four more years, his international leadership, and his promise to return to the New Deal after the war were a winning combination. Organized labor, working through the CIO Political Action Committee, brought out the workers' votes. The President defeated Dewey by a margin of 432 electoral votes to 99, and a popular vote of 25,602,000 to 22,006,000. The Democrats lost one seat in the Senate, but gained twenty in the House. The Democratic victory seemed to mean a revival of the New Deal at home, and the campaign promises of both parties indicated that the United States would continue to take a lead in international affairs.

But President Roosevelt lived to see neither the triumph in war nor the tragedy of peace. Already his vigor was draining away, and he could ill afford the exertions of the campaign or those of the grueling trip to Yalta. Addressing Congress on his return, he was very tired and for the first time he made public reference to his paralyzed legs and his heavy steel braces as he remained seated and spoke optimistically of the Yalta agreement—which he said contained no secret provisions. Suddenly, on the afternoon of April 12, 1945, he died of a cerebral hemorrhage at his private retreat in Warm Springs, Georgia.

TRUMAN TAKES OVER

Through no fault of his own, President Harry S Truman was unbriefed and poorly prepared for the task of concluding the war and making the peace. No one doubted his sincerity when he remarked to reporters the day after he had suddenly taken his oath of office: "I felt like the moon, the stars, and all the planets had fallen on me. I've got the most terribly responsible job a man ever had."

During the first phase of his relations with the Russians, Truman was moderately firm but tried to give the Soviet government no cause for protest. He was chagrined when in May 1945 the Foreign Economic Administration enforced his order ending Lend-Lease so precipitately as to call back some ships at sea. The British were the most hard-hit, but Stalin complained most bitterly.

At the Potsdam conference (July 1945) Truman could secure few satisfactory agreements on questions involving occupied and liberated countries. Despite the failure at Potsdam, Truman's Secretary of State, James F. Byrnes, continued in a conciliatory fashion to seek accommodation with the Russians.

The Potsdam conferees provided for a Council of Foreign Ministers to draft treaties with Italy and the former Axis satellites. During a tedious and depressing round of meetings of the council in London, Moscow, Paris, and New York (between September 1945 and December 1946), relations between the West and Russia steadily deteriorated, though five treaties were concluded. The one with Italy reflected Western demands; those with Finland, Hungary, Rumania, and Bulgaria in effect incorporated Soviet armistice terms. By ratifying the three latter treaties, the United States acquiesced in the Russian domination of these nations.

In Berlin a four-power Allied Control Council began sessions marked by the same blocking and delaying tactics that made other joint conferences with the Russians so dismal. The Western nations had visualized unified controls for Germany to prevent its resurgence. But the Russians had no interest in a Germany reunified in a manner acceptable to the West. Germany was to remain split indefinitely.

Meanwhile in occupied Germany and Japan, the United States pursued firm but conflicting policies compounded of harshness and idealism. During the war the American people had come to hate the enemy leaders and were insistent that they be punished for their war crimes, especially those Nazis who were responsible for the maintenance of frightful con-

centration camps like Buchenwald and for the gas-chamber murder of millions of Jews. This led to the trials of thousands of Nazis and war criminals, capped by that of twenty-two key Nazi leaders before an International Military Tribunal at Nuremberg in 1945–1946. Eleven were sentenced to death.

There was also a sweeping purge of Japan, and a trial was held for twenty-five former top Japanese military and civil officials. Seven of them, including two premiers, were executed. The dangerous precedent seemed to be established, as Churchill pointed out, that "the leaders of a nation defeated in war shall be put to death by the victors."

At first the Americans seemed bent on the pastoralization as well as reform of conquered Germany. They banned all industry directly or indirectly contributing to German war potential, including even the construction of seagoing ships, drastically cut steel and chemical production, destroyed munition plants, and allowed the dismantling of some factories for shipment to the Russians. They disbanded cartels and encouraged only agriculture and peaceful domestic industries. Along with this, they wished to foster American-style democracy in place of the repudiated Nazism. These economic policies, coming at a time when so much of German housing and industry was rubble, and when several million exiles were making their way from eastern Germany and from Czechoslovakia, reduced western Germany to a living standard not much better than that of a giant relief camp. The army undertook to feed the German people between 1945 and 1948 at a subsistence level of 950–1,550 calories per day.

Even this near-starvation diet cost the British and Americans nearly half a billion dollars per year. The Russians were adding further to the economic burden by taking out of their zone (and from the western zones to the extent agreed at Potsdam) reparations totaling $1.5 to $3 billion dollars per year. They were siphoning out of Germany more than the Americans and British could pump in.

In Japan American occupation policy suffered fewer obstacles and profited from the initial errors in Germany. During the first critical weeks General MacArthur, the Supreme Commander for the Allied Powers (SCAP), set up an overwhelmingly American occupation, based on a directive radioed him from Washington on August 29, 1945. Truman refused Stalin's demand that Russians occupy part of the northern Japanese island, Hokkaido. The irritated Russians had a voice, but no real power, on an eleven-country Far Eastern Commission in Washington and on a four-power Allied Council to advise MacArthur in Tokyo.

The American occupation authorities in Japan acted rapidly to demilitarize and democratize the country. From the outset they recognized that Japan must be left with a healthy economy, but in practice—by limiting the nation's war potential—they reduced Japan like Germany to a relief state.

Postwar Readjustments

The glad new day that wartime propaganda had foretold was not to dawn when the fighting stopped. Somehow, Americans had to readjust to the troublesome realities of postwar life. The most serious political problems had to do with the adaptation of the military establishment and the economic system to the new conditions—which were themselves uncertain.

MILITARY REORGANIZATION

In the face of growing menaces in Europe and Asia, the United States speedily dismantled its army, air force, and navy. At the end of the war, there was a popular demand to "bring the boys back." In April 1946 President Truman announced that nearly 7 million men had been released from the army—"the most remarkable demobilization in the history of the world, or 'disintegration,' if you want to call it that." He proposed a system of universal military training, but Congress did no more between 1946 and 1948 than to pass limited Selective Service measures. The gradual whittling of the armed forces continued, until by the spring of 1950 the army was down to 600,000 men, and the ceiling on defense expenditures, to $13 billion. Lacking land armies, the United States sought to balance the Soviet power with atomic bombs and an air force that could deliver them.

Since September 1945 the administration had been ready to negotiate an agreement with Russia which would "control and limit the use of the atomic bomb as an instrument of war" and "direct and encourage the development of atomic power for peaceful and humanitarian purposes." Great Britain and Canada joined with the United States in proposing international control of atomic energy. The United Nations Assembly responded by creating the

United Nations Atomic Energy Commission (January 1946), to which the American member, Bernard Baruch, submitted a plan. This proposed a thoroughgoing system of control and inspection of atomic energy development through a United Nations agency. When the system became effective, the United States would liquidate its stockpile and join in an international ban on atomic bombs.

The Russians refused to accept the Baruch plan for international inspection and control of atomic development. They demanded that the United States first destroy its stockpile of atom bombs. Through their widespread propaganda the Russians tried to marshal world indignation against the United States while they rushed ahead with their own research on atomic weapons. American scientists and military leaders, not aware as yet of the successful Russian espionage, and underrating Russian scientific and technical proficiency, predicted that it would be many years before the Soviet Union could produce a successful bomb.

Meanwhile, Congress lengthily debated the domestic control of American atomic energy. Democrats wished to vest control in civilians; Senator Vandenberg and the Republicans urged giving it to the heads of the armed forces. A compromise was reached in the Atomic Energy Act of 1946. This created a five-man civilian Atomic Energy Commission with complete control over research and development of fissionable materials; linked to it was a Military Liaison Committee.

Under the protection of an atomic umbrella, military leaders indulged in the luxury of a vigorous and prolonged controversy over unification of the various armed forces. This measure, proposed to bring greater efficiency and effectiveness, led instead to heightened rivalry, as the generals pushed for it, and the admirals feared for the loss of the marine corps and the relative weakening of the navy. Both sides brought the utmost pressure upon Congress. Finally, the National Security Act (July 1947) provided for a secretary of defense to preside over separate Departments of the Army, Navy, and Air Force, with the Joint Chiefs of Staff serving as advisers to him and to the President. To coordinate diplomacy and military planning, the 1947 act also provided for a National Security Council to consist of the President, certain cabinet members, and other advisers on foreign and military policy. This control was to be served by two other new agencies, a National Security Resources Board and a Central Intelligence Agency.

Within the reorganized Pentagon Building the old rivalries continued. Indeed, through the creation of a separate air force there now appeared to be three separate services where there had been only two before. The first Secretary of Defense, James V. Forrestal, exhausted by the struggle to make unification effective, resigned in 1949 and committed suicide. His successor, Louis A. Johnson, became embroiled in a violent quarrel over cancellation of construction of a huge new aircraft carrier, a quarrel culminating in the resignation of the Secretary of the Navy and the replacement of the Chief of Naval Operations. This crisis led to amendments to the National Security Act, forcing greater unification, and formally establishing a Department of Defense.

RECONVERSION AND INFLATION

On September 6, 1945, only four days after the Japanese surrender ceremonies, the President sent to Congress a twenty-one-point domestic program outlining what he later termed the "Fair Deal." He called for the expansion of social security, the raising of the legal minimum wage from 40 to 65 cents an hour, a full employment bill, a permanent Fair Employment Practices Act, public housing and slum clearance, long-range planning for the protection of natural resources and building of public works (like TVA), and government promotion of scientific research. Within ten weeks he sent additional recommendations to Congress for federal aid to education, for health insurance and prepaid medical care, and for the St. Lawrence seaway project.

Congress acted upon several of the President's recommendations. The Maximum Employment Act became law in 1946. It established a three-man Council of Economic Advisers to aid the President and issue an annual economic report. Although the experts frequently disagreed, they became an integral part of the governmental machinery. They did much to accustom the public to the new economics that had been emerging during the New Deal and the war.

Congressional conservatives tried to steer Congress and the public away from the Fair Deal program by concentrating upon the reconversion of industry to peacetime production. Truman himself recommended, first, speedily removing all possible controls that would hamper reconversion and, second, preventing increases in prices, rents, and wages. The two aims could easily conflict.

Under the friendly Roosevelt administration, union membership soared during the New Deal and World War II. Note that CIO figures are not available for 1948–1950; from 1951 on, the chart indicates the combined AFL and CIO membership.

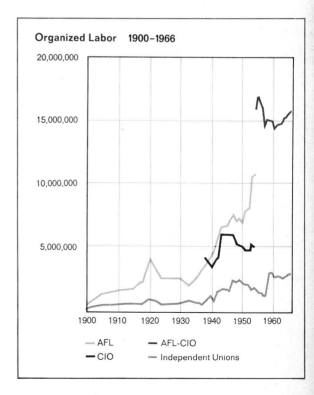

Organized Labor   1900–1966

After Germany surrendered, cutbacks in war orders began, and after Japan capitulated, $35 billion in contracts was suddenly cancelled. The War Production Board soon dropped controls, except on commodities that were still very scarce. Congress passed a new revenue bill cutting taxes nearly $6 billion. The War Assets Administration, established in January 1946, sold several hundred war plants, mostly to the corporations that had been operating them, and disposed of mountains of surplus, some of which enabled veterans with priorities to start small businesses. Members of the armed forces, who were being demobilized at an unparalleled pace, found their problems of readjustment to civilian life eased by the Servicemen's Readjustment Act of 1944 (the "G.I. Bill of Rights") which provided them with further education and training, or aid while unemployed or starting in business or farming.

Industry changed back to civilian production with more speed and less economic dislocation than had been expected. The gloomy forecasts of 8 million unemployed did not materialize. By the end of November 1945, peacetime employment was up to the end-of-the-war total, and 93 percent of the war plants had been reconverted.

The expected glut of surplus goods did not materialize either. Instead, acute problems of scarcity arose. Shortages ranged from automobiles and appliances to men's suits, nylon stockings, and beef. Consumers commanded some $129 billion or more in savings and billions more in credit with which to back their demands. Added to these were the needs of the rest of the world. Against such pressures, it was impossible for the Office of Price Administration to hold prices down to the 1941–1942 level.

If prices were to be checked, wages must be also, and if wages were to be held down, so must prices be. It was a vicious circle. By January 1946 workers had gone on strike in a number of the nation's critical industries—steel, automobiles, electrical manufacturing, and others. When Philip Murray demanded a 25-cents-an-hour increase for the United Steelworkers to bring them up to their wartime take-home pay, President Benjamin F. Fairless of United States Steel, acting as spokesman for the industry, refused unless the government would allow a $7-per-ton increase in the price of steel. President Truman announced that labor was entitled to the 33 percent that living costs had gone up since January 1941. The Wage Stabilization Board must approve the increase; but if it cut profits below the prewar level, the companies might obtain corresponding price increases. Ultimately there was a steel settlement allowing raises of 18-1/2 cents an hour and $5 per ton. Throughout industry, the "bulge" led to a round of similar raises in wages and prices.

In April 1946 John L. Lewis precipitated a fresh crisis. He demanded that the bituminous coal workers receive, even before wage increases, drastic improvement in safety rules and substantial contributions to a health and welfare fund. Refusing White House suggestions of compromise, he led out 400,000 miners. Within six weeks, as coal supplies dwindled, much of the nation's industrial production had to be cut back. In mid-May Lewis allowed his workers back for twelve days' mining; in the interim a railroad strike threatened. The President, by broadcasting a warning that the army would run the railroads, managed to avert a new walkout. The government took over the coal mines and provided the workers with most of what Lewis had demanded.

While unions were going on strike for higher wages, businessmen and farmers were exerting almost equal pressure upon Congress to obtain higher prices. Controls, they argued, were preventing full production, encouraging a black market, and robbing producers of a fair profit. After long debate, Congress passed a circumscribed price-control bill on June 27, 1946, just three days before the existing act was to expire. President Truman unexpectedly vetoed the bill as "a sure formula for inflation," and most price controls expired.

During the first sixteen days of July 1946, the index of prices of twenty-eight basic commodities jumped 25 percent, compared with 13 percent during the previous three years. On the first day of free trade at the Chicago stockyards, prime beef jumped from $18 to $22 per hundred weight. As prices soared, stock raisers, who had been holding back their cattle, rushed them to market. Congress quickly passed a new price-control bill only slightly stronger than the vetoed one, and on July 25 President Truman signed it. The decontrol board it created studied meat prices, decided they were unreasonable, and ordered prices rolled back to the old levels. Stockmen once again held back cattle until they could force abandonment of controls; angry consumers chafed in near-empty butcher shops.

For several weeks President Truman stood firm, but as public discontent focused on the Democratic party, politicians already fearful of the worst in the congressional elections of 1946 persuaded him to relent. On October 14 he announced the immediate ending of meat controls. Meat came back, but like many other commodities, with new price tags so high that the old black-market price seemed to have become the new legal standard. Millions of consumers on small, inflexible salaries or pensions were hurt. Real earnings dropped 12 percent below those of July 1945.

"HAD ENOUGH?"

All that the Republicans needed in the fall of 1946 was the slogan, "Had Enough? Vote Republican." They captured both houses of Congress, controlling the House 246 to 188, and the Senate, 51 to 45.

President Truman, accepting the returns as a mandate to liquidate regulations, dropped almost all remaining controls on wages and prices and on the channeling of construction into low-cost homes. Congress continued rent control to March 1, 1948, but allowed rents to go up 15 percent. Retail prices moved upward 3 percent per month, canceling the gains organized labor had won in the spring of 1946. Unions fought for and obtained a second round of in-

creases in 1947, and in 1948 as prices still went upward, a third round. The spiral of inflation was creeping upward relentlessly. Workers and others in modest circumstances began to notice that it was taking place under a Republican Congress whose spokesmen had asserted that laissez faire would cure the nation's ills.

The Chairman of the House Appropriations Committee, John Taber, proclaimed that he would apply a "meat-axe to government frills." He did so. Congress refused to appropriate funds for public housing, even of the moderate sort championed by Taft. It would not aid education, or extend social security; it slashed budget allowances for reclamation and power projects in the West. It passed a tax bill that, as President Truman pointed out in vetoing it, reduced the taxes of families receiving $2,400 or less by only 3 percent, but those of families receiving $100,000 or more, from 48 to 65 percent.

One of the few noncontroversial domestic achievements of this Congress was authorization of a commission on reorganization of the executive departments. President Truman appointed former President Hoover chairman of the commission. Congress already had voted to improve its own procedures and to reorganize its committees, cutting those in the House from forty-eight to nineteen, and in the Senate from thirty-three to fifteen.

The principal positive handiwork of the Eightieth Congress was a new basic labor law to supplant the pro-labor Wagner Act of 1935. The Taft-Hartley Labor-Management Rela-

---

Restrictions on Unions in the Taft-Hartley Act [1947]

Outlawed "closed shop" (which required that one must be a union member to be hired), but permitted "union shop" (which meant that if the contract so provided, one had to join the union after being hired).

Provided "cooling off" periods and empowered the President to issue injunctions to prevent strikes imperiling national safety or health.

Prohibited as "unfair" union practices: jurisdictional strikes, refusal to bargain in good faith, secondary boycotts, exaction of pay for work not performed, and union contributions to political campaign funds.

Prohibited certification of unions as bargaining agents with employers until officers had filed affidavits that they were not Communists.

Required unions to register with the Secretary of Labor and submit annual financial reports to him.

Allowed employers to present their side during organizational campaigns, petition the National Labor Relations Board for elections to determine bargaining agents, and sue unions for breach of contract.

tions Act loosened some of the previous restrictions upon employers and added several prohibitions against the unions. It also provided for "cooling-off" periods before unions could strike. President Truman stingingly vetoed it on June 20, 1947. That same day Republicans and Southern Democrats in the House overrode his veto; the Senate followed three days later. In practice, the Taft-Hartley Act did not cripple organized labor, partly because of the skill of labor leaders and because of President Truman's appointment to the National Labor Relations Board of members sympathetic toward labor. But the law did emphatically turn most of organized labor against the Republicans and back to the support of President Truman.

TRUMAN BEATS DEWEY

When the Republicans met in Philadelphia (June 1948) to nominate a presidential candidate, they rejected Senator Robert A. Taft, the vigorous leader of the Eightieth Congress. Though the idol of many businessmen, Taft was hampered by his prewar isolationism and his lack of glamor as a campaigner. The Republicans again nominated Governor Thomas E. Dewey, who favored the new role of the United States in world affairs, and whose stand on domestic issues came closer to the Fair Deal than to the Republican record in Congress. His running mate was Governor Earl Warren of California, who was even more liberal. Their platform was a promise to continue all the things the Democrats had established, but to do them more efficiently and cheaply.

It seemed a winning ticket and program, especially since the Democratic party suffered from two schisms. A faction to the left followed Henry A. Wallace out of the party. Wallace ran on a "Progressive" ticket to fight for thoroughgoing reform at home and more friendly relations with Communists overseas. Around him rallied a sprinkling of Americans who felt that the Truman domestic policies were too slow and ineffective and who feared that the foreign policies would lead to a third world war. Around him also rallied the American Communists and fellow travelers.

Despairing Democratic liberals organized as Americans for Democratic Action, sought

Election of 1948

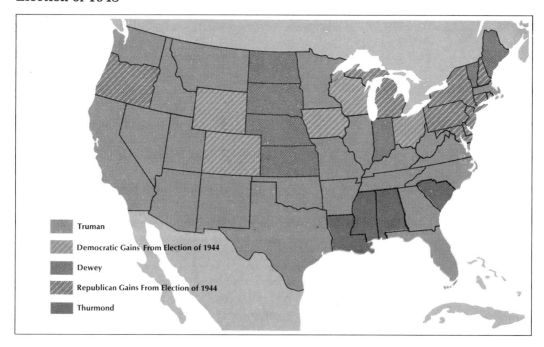

Truman
Democratic Gains From Election of 1944
Dewey
Republican Gains From Election of 1944
Thurmond

President Harry S Truman

As a campaigner, President Truman apparently had no chance in 1948, but he was remarkably successful in his extemporaneous speaking at whistle-stops, which together with his policies had rallied behind him much of the farm and labor vote. On the morning after the election, he gleefully displayed a newspaper that had underestimated him—as indeed had much of the American public. (United Press International)

some more glamorous candidate than President Truman. The one candidate they could be sure would win votes by the million, General Eisenhower, rejected their overtures. At their convention (July 1948) the Democrats gloomily accepted the inevitable, the nomination of President Truman. Certain of defeat, the liberals salvaged what they could by fighting through a platform containing a strong civil-rights plank that proposed federal legislation to prevent discrimination in employment, penalize lynching, and outlaw poll taxes. This platform was expected to help Northern and city Democrats in their local and state elections.

But it drove Southern Democrats, already angered by President Truman's espousal of a strong civil-rights program, into open revolt. Waving Confederate flags, a number of them met at Birmingham, Alabama (July 1948), to form the States' Rights Democratic party and nominate Governor J. Strom Thurmond of South Carolina. They captured the party organization in Alabama, Louisiana, Mississippi, and South Carolina.

The defections on both the left and the right seemed to leave President Truman in a pathetically hopeless position; all the public opinion polls showed him trailing far behind. Governor Dewey, campaigning in a cold and formal way, aroused as little animosity as possible, and seemed to be delivering previews of his inaugural. Instead of campaigning against the impeccable Dewey, who stood for much the same in domestic and foreign policy, Truman launched his attack at the Republican Congress. Because he felt the press was giving a hostile impression of his administration, Truman embarked upon a strenuous personal tour of the United States, traveling 31,700 miles to speak 356 times directly to the American people. In this "whistle stop" tour, he spoke only a few times from manuscripts, preferring his far more effective, rather blunt extemporaneous style. To all those groups who could be convinced they had a grievance against the Republican Congress, he appealed effectively, winning the strong support of organized labor, disgruntled farmers, and Northern Negroes.

On Election Day, to the amazement of everyone but himself, President Truman defeated Dewey, 24,106,000 to 21,969,000 in the popular vote, and 304 to 189 in the electoral vote. Thurmond's Dixiecrat ticket received 1,169,000 popular and 38 electoral votes. Wallace polled only 1,156,000. The Democrats also regained both houses of Congress by a margin of ninety-three seats in the House and twelve in the Senate.

Selected Readings

Military Operations
A. R. Buchanan, *The United States and World War II** (2 vols., 1962); Winston S. Churchill, *Second World War* (6 vols., 1948–1953); Fletcher Pratt, *War for the World* (1950), a brief account; K. R. Greenfield, *American Strategy in World War II* (1963); S. E. Morison, *Strategy and Compromise** (1958); M. S. Watson, *Chief of Staff: Prewar Plans and Preparations* (1950); R. S. Cline, *Washington Command Post* (1951); H. L. Stimson and McGeorge Bundy, *On Active Service in Peace and War* (1948); Forrest Pogue, *George C. Marshall* (2 vols., 1963–1966); D. D. Eisenhower, *Crusade in Europe** (1948); Chester Wilmot, *The Struggle for Europe** (1952), critical of Eisenhower; H. H. Arnold, *Global Mission* (1949); O. N. Bradley, *A Soldier's Story** (1951); S. E. Morison, *The Two Ocean War: A Short History of the United States Navy in the Second World War* (1963); E. J. King and W. M. Whitehill, *Fleet Admiral King* (1952).

Wartime Diplomacy
J. L. Snell, *Illusion and Necessity: The Diplomacy of Global War, 1939–1945* (1967); Gaddis Smith, *American Diplomacy During the Second World War, 1941–1945* (1965); W. L. Langer, *Our Vichy Gamble** (1947); W. R. Deane, *The Strange Alliance* (1947); H. W. Baldwin, *Great Mistakes of the War* (1950), critical of "unconditional surrender"; Anne Armstrong, *Unconditional Surrender* (1961); W. L. Neumann, *After Victory: Churchill, Roosevelt, Stalin, and the Making of the Peace* (1967); E. R. Stettinius, *Roosevelt and the Russians: The Yalta Conference* (1949); J. F. Byrnes, *Speaking Frankly* (1947); R. L. Walker and George Curry, *American Secretaries of State: E. R. Stettinius, Jr., James F. Byrnes* (1965); Herbert Feis, *Churchill, Roosevelt, Stalin** (1957), *Between War and Peace: The Potsdam Conference** (1960), *Japan Subdued* (1961), and *Contest over Japan* (1967); R. J. C. Butow, *Japan's Decision to Surrender** (1954); R. H.

Minear, *Victor's Justice: The Tokyo War Crimes Trial* (1973); John Hersey, *Hiroshima** (1946); Gar Alperovitz, *Atomic Diplomacy: Hiroshima and Potsdam* (1965); R. A. Divine, *Second Chance: The Triumph of Internationalism in America During World War II* (1967), on the U. N.; R. B. Russell, *A History of the United Nations Charter: The Role of the United States, 1940–1945* (1958).

Domestic Politics
A. H. Vandenberg, Jr., *The Private Papers of Senator Vandenberg* (1952); H. S Truman, *Memoirs** (2 vols., 1955–1956); Roland Young, *Congressional Politics in the Second World War* (1955); Jonathan Daniels, *Frontier on the Potomac* (1946); Joseph Gaer, *The First Round: The CIO Political Action Committee* (1944); R. A. Lee, *Truman and Taft-Hartley* (1967); E. C. Brown, *From the Wagner Act to Taft-Hartley* (1950); L. V. Chandler, *Inflation in the United States, 1940–1948* (1951); Jules Abels, *Out of the Jaws of Victory* (1959), on the 1948 election; Irwin Ross, *The Loneliest Campaign: The Truman Victory of 1948* (1968); K. M. Schmidt, *Wallace: Quixotic Crusade* (1960); C. W. Mills, *The New Men of Power* (1948); Samuel Lubell, *The Future of American Politics** (1952); E. F. Goldman, *The Crucial Decade: America, 1945–1955** (1956); John Gunther, *Inside U. S. A.* (1951); A. L. Hamby, *Beyond the New Deal: Harry S Truman and American Liberalism* (1973).

*Titles available in paperback.

A Balance of Terror

Twenty-seven

In 1942 the American geopolitical expert Nicholas J. Spykman wrote that the United States had found itself in World War II because the balance of power on the opposite shores of both the Atlantic and the Pacific had been upset. So the American war aim should be to restore the balance, Spykman said. It should not be to annihilate either Germany or Japan, lest this leave Europe and the Far East exposed to Soviet domination. As for Europe: "A Russian state from the Urals to the North Sea can be no great improvement over a German state from the North Sea to the Urals." As for the Far East: "The danger of another Japanese conquest of Asia must be removed, but this does not inevitably mean the elimination of the military strength of Japan and the surrender of the Western Pacific to China or Russia."

In fact, however, the war was fought for "unconditional surrender," for total victory over the Axis, not for a restoration of the balance. The upshot was that Germany and Japan were eliminated as military powers for the time being. A "power vacuum" was left in Europe, and another in Asia. Only two really great powers remained in the world—the Soviet Union and the United States. Into the voids left by the war, the influence of the Russian Communists and later that of the Chinese Communists began to flow. The United States undertook to resist the spread of Communist power and thus came into collision with its recent allies, the Russians and the Chinese. It now sought new alliances not only with old associates like Great Britain and France but also with former foes, Germany (or a part of that country) and Japan, which it began to help revive and rebuild as strong nations. Such, in essence, was the "cold war" that commenced within two years after the end of World War II.

At first the United States appeared to hold the upper hand, for it had a monopoly of atomic weapons. But within a short time, in 1949, the Russians exploded an

Nuclear Disarmament?
Limitation and control of nuclear weapons seemed desperately urgent after the U.S.A. and the U.S.S.R. had acquired the ability to destroy one another, but disarmament talks in 1957 made no progress. As this 1957 cartoon by Reg Manning illustrates, neither country was willing to let its guard down without assurances that the other would do the same. (McNaught Syndicate, Inc.)

A-bomb of their own. The Americans got ahead again, in 1952, with the vastly more destructive hydrogen bomb, but the Russians produced an H-bomb, too, the following year. By 1957, when the Russians put into orbit the first artificial satellite, they seemed to have taken the lead in the capacity to deliver missiles with nuclear warheads. In any event, each of the great contestants now had the capability, quite literally, of destroying the other. A wholly new era had arrived, in which another world war could wipe out mankind itself. Nobody really knew whether the old rules of power politics had relevance any longer. If humanity was spared an all-out war, the reason was perhaps that the world had reached what *The New York Times* (in 1958) called a new "balance of terror."

Start of the Cold War

As early as January 1946 President Truman, concerned over Russian delay in withdrawing troops from Iran and Russian threats against Turkey, had written his secretary of state: "Unless Russia is faced with an iron fist and strong language another war is in the making."

CONTAINMENT OF COMMUNISM

Truman faced a peculiarly difficult task in trying to convince the American public that a truly deep and serious rift was developing between Russia and the West. During the war years they had listened to publicists ranging from the advanced New Dealer Henry Wallace to the Republican president of the United States Chamber of Commerce, Eric Johnston, praising the Russians and picturing Stalin as a sympathetic figure. Many had come to imagine him as a benign, pipe-smoking sage, "good old Uncle Joe." Not even the revered Winston Churchill could shift American opinion. In March 1946, speaking at Westminster College in Fulton, Missouri, Churchill proclaimed a grim warning: "From Stettin in the Baltic to Trieste in the Adriatic an iron curtain has descended across the Continent."

A new Truman policy for countering Communist aggression began to unfold in the spring of 1947. This policy followed the line laid down by State Department expert George F. Kennan, who proposed "a long-term, patient but firm and vigilant containment of Russian expansive tendencies." Russian pressure on Turkey and support of Communist guerrilla forces in Greece emphasized the immediacy of the Soviet threat. The British had been aiding the Greek government, but could no longer carry the burden. Unless Stalin were checked, he might achieve the centuries-old Russian prize of the straits leading from the Black Sea into the Mediterranean. Russia already controlled Albania on the Adriatic.

On March 12, 1947, President Truman appeared before Congress to request $400 million to bolster the armed forces of Greece and Turkey, and to enunciate the doctrine that came to bear his name: "I believe that it must be the policy of the United States to support free peoples who are resisting attempted subjugation by armed minorities or by outside pressures." Senator Vandenberg again backed the President, and the Republican Congress voted the Greek-Turkish Aid Act. The initial military aid and subsequent appropriations eased Russian pressure upon Turkey, and by the fall of 1949 brought to an end the long civil war against Communists in Greece.

Military aid was not enough. The Truman Doctrine logically led to a program of economic reconstruction to bolster the stability of Europe and help eradicate the misery out of which the Communist parties in western European countries were gaining recruits. In April 1947 Secretary of State George C. Marshall returned from the Conference of Foreign Ministers in Moscow convinced that the Russians were interested only in profiting from the economic plight of Europe, not in ameliorating it. The solution, he and President Truman agreed, lay in State Department plans to aid European nations that were willing to cooperate with each other in rebuilding their economies. Speaking at the Harvard University commencement in June 1947, Secretary Marshall offered aid to all those European nations (including Russia) who would join in drafting a program for recovery.

Kennan on Containment [1947]

The Soviet pressure against the free institutions of the Western world is something that can be contained by the adroit and vigilant application of counterforce at a series of constantly shifting geographical and political points, corresponding to the shifts and maneuvers of Soviet policy, but which cannot be charmed or talked out of existence. The Russians look forward to a duel of infinite duration, and they see that already they have scored great successes. . . .

But in actuality the possibilities for American policy are by no means limited to holding the line and hoping for the best. It is entirely possible for the United States to influence by its actions the internal developments, both within Russia and throughout the international Communist movement, by which Russian policy is largely determined. . . . It is . . . a question of the degree to which the United States can create among the peoples of the world generally the impression of a country which knows what it wants, which is coping successfully with the problems of its internal life and with the responsibilities of a World Power, and which has a spiritual vitality capable of holding its own among the major ideological currents of the time. — "X" [George F. Kennan], Foreign Affairs, July 1947.

Russia denounced the Marshall Plan as American imperialism and intimidated the satellites and Finland and Czechoslovakia into staying away from the planning conference. Germany had no government, and Spain was not invited. Sixteen other nations of Europe joined a Committee of European Economic Cooperation, which in September 1947 presented specifications for reconstruction to create a self-sufficient Europe by 1951. Opposition formed in Congress, but it was embarrassed from the start by possessing as unwelcome allies the American Communists, and in February 1948 it was overwhelmed by a shocked and aroused public opinion when Czech Communists seized power in Prague. Congress in April established the Economic Cooperation Administration and voted an initial $4 billion for it.

Altogether over a three-year period the United States spent $12 billion through the ECA. This helped to stimulate a remarkable recovery in Europe. By the end of 1950 industrial production was up 64 percent, economic activity was well above prewar levels, and Communist strength among voters in most areas was dwindling.

THE NORTH ATLANTIC ALLIANCE

In his inaugural address, January 20, 1949, President Truman challenged the nation to come to the aid of the "more than half the people of the world" who were "living in condi-

tions approaching misery." Point Four of his foreign policy proposals was a plan for aiding them through technical assistance and the fostering of capital investment. The Point Four or Technical Cooperation program began in 1950 with an appropriation of only $35 million, but spent $400 million in the next three years.

Soviet leaders reacted vigorously against the American efforts for world economic recovery. They had organized their own Warsaw Alliance of nine satellite nations (September 1947) to combat "American imperialism." Through a new Cominform (Communist Information Bureau) they sought to eradicate traces of nonconformity throughout eastern Europe. Their successful coup in democratic Czechoslovakia in February 1948, as horrifying to western Europeans as to Americans, helped unify the Western world against the Communist countries. Later in the year, the pressure of Stalin and the Cominform on Marshal Tito provoked him to pull Communist Yugoslavia out of their orbit, and with American aid to embark upon an independent course between Russia and the West. In western Europe, Communist parties tried to thwart the Marshall Plan, especially by calling out on strike the unions they controlled in Italy and France. Despite the strikes, progress continued.

Meanwhile, the United States moved with the British and the rather reluctant French toward the creation of a self-governing, economically strong West Germany. The culmination came on June 7, 1948, when they announced plans for a new federal West German government with sovereignty over domestic matters and full membership in the European Recovery Program. They also reformed the currency to stop the inflationary flood of marks from the Soviet zone, which was hampering recovery.

The Russians retaliated. Taking advantage of a lack of a written guarantee of land transit across the Soviet zone, they clamped a tight blockade around the western sectors of Berlin. The object was to force the Western powers to abandon either Berlin or the proposed West German republic. President Truman, unwilling to risk war by sending in armed convoys by land, ordered the supplying of Berlin by air. Through the winter and into the spring of 1949, the airlift continued, carrying in more supplies than had previously been brought by train. Finally the Russians backed down and ended the blockade.

In October 1949 the German Federal Republic came into existence at Bonn in West Germany, and the Soviets established a German Democratic Republic for East Germany.

Meanwhile Russian intransigence was leading to the consolidation of the Western countries in a new grand alliance. The North Atlantic Treaty was signed April 4, 1949, by twelve nations, and subsequently also by Greece and Turkey. It declared that an armed attack against one would be considered an attack upon all, and provided for the creation of joint military forces. Under it, the signatory powers established the North Atlantic Treaty Organization to construct a defense force that, while not equal to that of the Russians, would be large enough to discourage an attack. The Mutual Defense Act of 1949 appropriated an initial billion dollars for armaments for the signatories.

The governing body of NATO, the North Atlantic Council, established military head-

Divided Germany and Austria

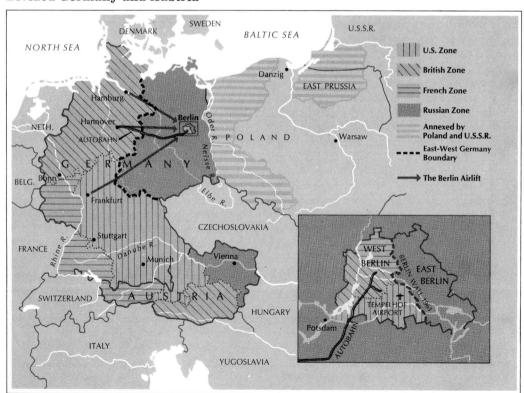

The Berlin Airlift
*"It was inspiring and somewhat heart-rending to witness the spontaneous visits of
the women and children of Berlin to Tempelhof airport to show their appreciation
of the airlift, bringing with them some precious last possession as a token of
gratitude to the members of the air crews," wrote General Lucius D. Clay,
military governor of the American zone. The pilots called the airlift "Operation
Vittles," and some of them informally instituted "Operation Little Vittles,"
dropping candy tied to handkerchief parachutes to the children. "Berlin had kept
its courage," Clay declared. Despite unemployment and an acute shortage of heat
and electricity through the winter, "the determination of the people did not falter.
They were proud to carry their burden as the price of their freedom." (United
Press International)*

quarters near Paris early in 1951 under the
supreme command of General Dwight Eisenhower. This was SHAPE (Supreme Headquarters, Allied Powers in Europe). The number of
divisions and airplanes under NATO command
began gradually to grow, but while its power
was still relatively feeble, its chief significance
was the commitment that the United States had
made with the nations of western Europe to
stand firm against Russian threats.

That these threats were not to be taken
lightly became even clearer on September 23,
1949, when President Truman issued a press
statement: "We have evidence that within re-

cent weeks an atomic explosion occurred in the
U.S.S.R." The years of relative safety for the
American people were already at an end.

CHINA TURNS RED

While the United States was struggling to contain Russia in Europe between 1947 and 1949,
the Chinese Communists were destroying the
armies of Chiang Kai-shek. To prevent civil
war and to effect a coalition government, the
Truman administration in December 1945 had
sent General George C. Marshall to China. At

first he obtained a cease-fire and encouraging signs of accommodation, but irreconcilable differences kept apart the two Chinese governments — the *Kuomintang* (Nationalists) and the Communists.

Full-scale war broke out. Although the Nationalist armies were larger and better equipped, they soon began to fall back before the better-trained, more vigorous Communist forces. As the inept Chiang Kai-shek government failed both on the fighting front and at home, where inflation and inefficiency were rampant, it was plunging toward defeat.

President Truman now sent General Wedemeyer, who had been Chiang's chief of staff, to investigate. Wedemeyer warned that Communist control of China would imperil American interests, since the Communists were in fact closely tied to the Soviet Union. He believed that the United States could rescue Chiang only by sending 10,000 army officers and other advisers to introduce reforms, together with massive material support.

President Truman did not request such large-scale aid for Chiang, but did ask Congress to provide $570 million; in April 1948 it voted $400 million. The administration had decided, as Secretary Marshall made clear, that there was no feasible way the United States could make the Nationalist government "capable of reestablishing and then maintaining its control throughout all of China." The collapse was rapid, and it came through lack of morale rather than shortages of arms and supplies. At the end of 1949, Chiang and the Nationalists fled to Formosa. Though Great Britain and some of the western European nations recognized the new People's Republic of China, the United States refused to do so and blocked its entry into the United Nations.

Beginning in 1947, the American government had introduced new policies in Japan to strengthen that nation in a manner similar to the rebuilding of Germany. The American occupation in Japan was bringing a democratization of the government, extension of rights to women and underprivileged groups, expansion of the educational system (from a starting point as high as the goal of educational reform in China), land reform that was as drastic as that in China, a curbing of the power of the monopolistic *zaibatsu* industrial system, and an improvement in the status of labor. In Japan, more than anywhere else in Asia, the United States helped develop a dynamic alternative to Communism. In 1949, to stimulate Japanese recovery, the United States ended its reparations and stopped the dismantling of industrial combinations.

Negotiation of a Japanese peace treaty began in 1950 through the skilled offices of a Republican, John Foster Dulles, whom President Truman appointed to undertake the task. Aside from the fact that it stripped Japan of all her recent conquests, it was a generous treaty, a "peace of reconciliation," as Dulles called it. By recognizing the right of the sovereign Japanese nation to self-defense, it opened the way to rearmament. Thanks partly to its negotiation by a Republican, the treaty easily received Senate ratification and went into effect in 1952. A security treaty, signed at the same time, permitted the United States to maintain armed forces in Japan. Two years later, a mutual-defense-assistance pact provided for Japanese rearmament with American aid, but the building of armed forces proceeded slowly. Disarmament had been one of MacArthur's most cherished reforms, and the American-imposed Japanese constitution had banned war forever. This encouraged such a strong pacifist sentiment that as late as 1957 only 100,000 Japanese had joined the armed forces. The task of defending Japan continued to rest largely with the United States.

Several nations to the south that had suffered either invasion or the threat of invasion during the war viewed with some concern the rebuilding of Japan as a military power. To reassure them, the United States in 1951 signed a security treaty with the Philippines, and the ANZUS pact with Australia and New Zealand.

While rebuilding Japan, the Truman administration refused to capitulate to the demands of the so-called China Lobby for military and naval aid to Chiang on Formosa which might lead the nation into a war against Red China. In January 1950 Secretary of State Dean Acheson publicly outlined a Pacific defense perimeter which did not include Formosa or Korea. If these areas were attacked, he declared, the people invaded must rely upon themselves to resist, "and then upon the commitments of the entire civilized world under the charter of the United Nations."

Within a few months, East Asia became the focal point of American foreign policy as the cold war turned hot in Korea.

Origins of the Cold War

According to spokesmen for the American government, the Soviet Union was entirely to blame for the cold war. Stalin violated the Yalta agreement, imposed Russian control upon eastern Europe, and schemed to spread Communism throughout the world. The United States, reacting defensively, tried to contain Soviet expansion by means of the Truman Doctrine, the Marshall Plan, and the North Atlantic Treaty Organization. At first, American historians with few exceptions agreed substantially with the official view.

As time passed, and especially after the Vietnam War disillusioned many Americans about the containment policy, an increasing number of historians undertook to "revise" the interpretation of the cold war, as earlier historians had done with previous wars. Most of the cold war revisionists belonged to the New Left. The pioneer among them was William A. Williams, who anticipated most of the revisionist themes in his *American-Russian Relations, 1781–1947* (1952) and *The Tragedy of American Diplomacy* (1959).

According to the New Left writers, the United States was mainly if not solely responsible for the cold war. At the close of World War II, the Soviet Union was exhausted and in no position to threaten the United States. But this country, with a monopoly of nuclear weapons, was in a position to threaten the Soviet Union. In the opinion of some revisionists, Franklin D. Roosevelt would have continued the wartime Soviet-American cooperation, but Harry S Truman abandoned the Roosevelt policy and adopted a hard line toward the Russians. In the opinion of other revisionists, the line would have been the same regardless of any change in the presidency, since American foreign policy was simply a response to the needs of American capitalism, which sought American-controlled markets throughout the world.

As early as 1948 a British physicist, P. M. S. Blackett, in *Fear, War, and the Bomb*, had written that the dropping of the atomic bombs on Hiroshima and Nagasaki was "not so much the last military act of the second World War as the first major operation of the cold diplomatic war with Russia." Taking up the idea, a New Left political economist at the University of Cambridge, England, Gar Alperovitz, suggested in his *Atomic Diplomacy* (1965) that the United States dropped the bombs on an already defeated Japan in order to impress the Russians and make them more "manageable." In *The Atomic Bomb and the End of World War II* (1966) a former official in the Roosevelt and Truman administrations, Herbert Feis, argued (as Truman himself had done) that the United States used the bombs simply to assure a quick and complete victory over Japan with a minimum loss of lives.

Reviewing the work of Williams, Alperovitz, and five other revisionist authors, Robert J. Maddox in *The New Left and the Origins of the Cold War* (1973) charged them with misusing source materials and drawing conclusions at variance with their own evidence. "There is every reason to be sharply critical of recent American foreign policy," Maddox said, "but the criticisms should rest on more substantial foundations."

In *The United States and the Origins of the Cold War, 1941–1947* (1972), John L. Gaddis maintained that a variety of preconceptions had influenced the policy makers in both Washington and Moscow. He concluded that "neither side can bear sole responsibility for the onset of the Cold War."

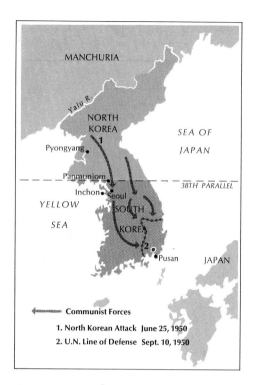

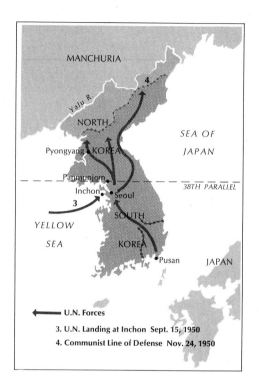

The Korean War   1950–1953

DEFENDING SOUTH KOREA

During the hectic days at the end of the war in the Pacific, the United States had hastily proposed that Americans accept the surrender of the Japanese in the lower half of Korea, up to the 38th parallel, and that the Russians do the same in the northern half. At the moment the arrangement was useful to the United States. Afterwards, however, the Russians were willing to accept a reunited Korea only if it were Communist-dominated.

The 38th parallel became more and more an impenetrable barrier. To the north of it, the Communists developed a "peoples' government" with a strong aggressive army. To the south, the United Nations held elections that led to a government under the ardently nationalistic Dr. Syngman Rhee, long an exile in the United States. Rhee would have liked to extend his government to the north, but the United States provided the South Korean army only with relatively light defensive weapons.

Consequently when the United States withdrew its forces from below the 38th parallel in June 1949, South Korea was left militarily weaker than its even more aggressive northern twin.

On June 24, 1950, the North Koreans acted swiftly, launching a full-scale invasion that caught the South Koreans and Americans completely by surprise. Almost immediately President Truman and Congress reversed the policy of withdrawal from the Asiatic mainland. The President brought the question of the invasion before the United Nations Security Council. It could act more quickly than the Assembly, and at the moment the Russians were boycotting it, and hence had no representative present to vote a paralyzing veto. The Council on June 25 passed an American resolution demanding that the North Koreans withdraw behind the 38th parallel, and two days later called upon members of the United Nations to "furnish such assistance to the Republic of Korea as may be necessary to repel

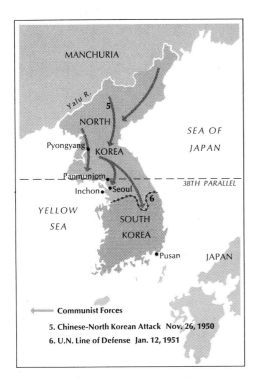

Communist Forces
5. Chinese-North Korean Attack Nov. 26, 1950
6. U.N. Line of Defense Jan. 12, 1951

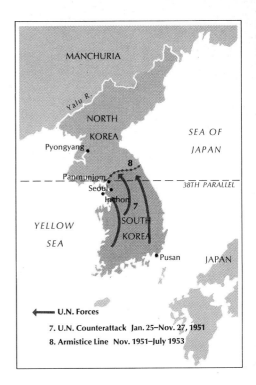

U.N. Forces
7. U.N. Counterattack Jan. 25–Nov. 27, 1951
8. Armistice Line Nov. 1951–July 1953

the armed attack." President Truman on June 27 sent United States air and sea forces to the aid of the South Koreans; on June 30 he ordered ground forces into Korea, and sent the Seventh Fleet to act as a barrier between the Chinese mainland and Formosa.

The Council of the United Nations on July 7, 1950, requested those nations providing troops to place them under a unified command headed by the United States. President Truman appointed General MacArthur commander in chief. Some fifteen nations besides the United States and the Republic of Korea provided troops, but these never comprised more than 9 percent of the total fighting force. The United States sent about 48 percent; South Korea mustered 43 percent. What was officially a United Nations "police action" came to most Americans to seem a war on the part of the United States.

General MacArthur, who at first could draw upon only four understrength divisions in Japan, rushed in troop units piecemeal to slow the rapidly advancing North Koreans as they pushed southward past Seoul, threatening to envelop the entire tip of the peninsula. By thus sacrificing themselves, these forces gave MacArthur an opportunity to build stable defenses around the port of Pusan in the extreme southeast. When the North Koreans struck there in force early in August, strong army and marine reinforcements fresh from the United States hurled them back at each point of assault. As men and supplies poured into Pusan, marine officers devised a bold plan of attack which General MacArthur reluctantly accepted. Rather than try to push the North Koreans back mile by mile, on September 15, 1950, while the United Nations troops around Pusan opened a sharp counteroffensive, he launched an amphibious assault far behind the North Korean lines at Inchon, near Seoul. It caught the Communists almost completely unprepared. The United Nations troops quickly recaptured Seoul; within two weeks the North Korean armies, disrupted and demoralized, were fleeing as best they could to north of the 38th parallel.

RETREAT FROM NORTH KOREA

Amid jubilation, the United States and the United Nations had to make new decisions. Should they capitalize upon their spectacular victory and move into North Korea? The premier of Red China on October 1 warned that the Chinese would "not allow seeing their neighbors being invaded by imperialists." A few days later, he announced the Chinese would send troops, and dispatched a warning to the United Nations through India. These threats worried American strategists, but there was a possibility that China was bluffing, and there was the probability that the North Koreans, unless pursued, would recoup their strength and strike new blows.

The Joint Chiefs of Staff on September 27, 1950, ordered MacArthur to destroy the North Korean armed forces, but under no circumstances to cross the borders of China or Russia. The United Nations Assembly gave its sanction to the project on October 7, reiterating its aim to create "a unified, independent and democratic Korea." Two days later, the United Nations forces poured across the 38th parallel toward the Yalu River, which marked the boundary with Manchuria.

For several weeks the advance into northern Korea went well. On October 19, the capital, Pyongyang, fell, and parachutists landed thirty miles beyond to trap much of the remaining North Korean army. Then, on October 26, a Chinese Communist soldier was captured; four days later, fourteen more were taken. By November 4, eight Chinese divisions had been identified, and Russian-made MIG fighter planes had briefly engaged the United Nations air force.

General MacArthur issued a special communiqué warning that "a new and fresh army now faces us," and he excoriated the Chinese for their international lawlessness in intervening without notice and "massing a great concentration of possible reinforcing divisions with adequate supply behind the privileged sanctuary of the adjacent Manchurian border." Both in his private communications to the Joint Chiefs of Staff and in the encouragement he gave to pressure groups in the United States, MacArthur engaged in a vigorous campaign for permission to bomb this "privileged sanctuary." President Truman refused to allow all-out military action against China, because, he later explained, "if for no other reason . . . it was a gigantic booby trap."

When the Chinese suddenly appeared in overwhelming numbers, they stalled MacArthur's offensive and hurled back advance units. Through December 1950, in bitter weather, the outnumbered Eighth Army and X Corps fought a heroic withdrawal from North Korea. The United Nations tried to negotiate peace with the Chinese, but the Communists, as they swept below the 38th parallel and recaptured Seoul, set impossibly stiff terms. In March 1951 the Eighth Army counterattacked, for a second and final time capturing Seoul and recrossing the 38th parallel. President Truman was ready again to seek a negotiated peace.

General MacArthur, far from ready to accept the position of his commander in chief, repeatedly made public his eagerness to win total victory in Korea at the risk of full involvement in war with China. On March 20, 1951, he communicated his views to the Republican minority leader in the House of Representatives, Joseph W. Martin, concluding: "There is no substitute for victory."

President Truman clung to his thesis that, in the great struggle against Communism, western Europe with its concentration of heavy industry, not industrially weak Asia, was the main potential battlefield. He could not have won the support of western European partners in the United Nations for a more militant policy in Asia. He would not accept the arguments of the Asia-firsters that the United States should undertake unilateral action—"go it alone."

General MacArthur thus emerged as a major figure in American politics, trying to reverse the administration policies. Five days after Representative Martin released MacArthur's letter to the press, President Truman, on April 11, 1951, relieved General MacArthur of his commands. A groundswell of outrage swept the United States; a Gallup poll reported that 69 percent of those interviewed favored the General, only 29 percent the President. MacArthur upon his return was greeted hysterically wherever he appeared; millions watched their television sets as he addressed Congress.

Truman's policy of fighting a limited war of containment continued to baffle and exasperate a considerable part of the American people. It went against the American tradition of total victory. It was hard to explain to the public or to the soldiers fighting endlessly through the rice paddies and over the hilltops of Korea.

In June 1951 the Russian delegate to the United Nations hinted that settlement was possible. Armistice negotiations began on July 10, 1951, near the 38th parallel, and continued for many weary months at Panmunjom. They came to revolve around the difficult questions of locating the cease-fire line, enforcing the armistice, and repatriating prisoners of war. By the spring of 1952, agreements had been reached upon all but the last question. Finally, in October 1952, the negotiations were recessed. By then the nation was in the midst of a presidential campaign, and though there was no large-scale fighting in Korea, the interminable negotiations, endless skirmishing, and ever-growing casualties had worn out the patience of the American people.

The Politics of Fright

In the disappointing months and years that followed World War II, as warm friendship toward Russia turned into apprehension and alarm, the American public became increasingly afraid that traitors within the government were betraying it to the Communists.

HYSTERICAL LOYALTY

During the period of the New Deal and the war there had been some Communists and Communist sympathizers in the government. At a time when the Russians and the United States were allies this seemed of little consequence, but in 1942 and 1943 President Roosevelt established loyalty checks. By 1946 Russia seemed more a potential enemy than an ally. The Canadian government discovered that at least twenty-three of its employees in positions of trust had turned over secrets, some of them concerning nuclear fission, to Russian spies. Several of the spy rings had operated across the boundary in the United States.

The federal government began extensive efforts to ferret out Communists. President Truman established a Temporary Commission on Employee Loyalty (November 1946) to recommend loyalty investigation systems and safeguards of fair hearings. This led to the establishment of loyalty boards (March 1947) to undertake a sweeping investigation of all federal employees. In August 1950 the President authorized the dismissal in sensitive departments of even those deemed no more than "bad security risks." By 1951 more than 3 million government employees had been cleared, over 2,000 had resigned, and 212 had been dismissed.

Against the recommendations of the Departments of Defense and Justice and of the Central Intelligence Agency, Congress overrode the President's veto and passed the Mc-Carran Internal Security Act (September 1950). This did not outlaw Communist organizations but required them to publish their records. It barred Communists from employment in defense plants and denied them passports.

Already, in 1948, the Attorney General had obtained indictments against eleven key Communist leaders for violation of the Smith Act of 1940, which prohibited conspiring to teach the violent overthrow of the government. During their nine-month trial in 1949, the Communists engaged in elaborate harassing tactics, which further aroused the public against them. They were convicted. In the 1951 case of Dennis v. United States, the Supreme Court in a 6-to-2 decision rejected their appeal. Chief Justice Fred Vinson held that advocating or teaching revolution in the existing state of the world, or even conspiring to do so, fell within Justice Holmes' earlier definition of what was punishable—that it constituted a "clear and present danger." In dissenting, Justice Hugo Black remarked: "There is hope that in calmer times, when the present pressures, passions, and fears subside, this or some later court will restore the First Amendment liberties to the high preferred place where they belong in a free society."

While the Supreme Court was solemnly deciding that civil liberties must be circumscribed to protect the modern state, some less careful politicians were capitalizing upon the growing public hysteria, among them Richard M. Nixon, of California. Nixon first gained national attention by helping to expose Alger Hiss. As a handsome and ambitious young man, Hiss had risen rapidly in the government during the 1930s to become a high-ranking official of the State Department. He was present as a clerk at the Yalta conference, but in no way influenced policy there. In 1947 he resigned to head the Carnegie Endowment for International Peace. Whittaker Chambers, a self-avowed former Communist agent, had denounced Hiss as early as 1939, but because he provided no details and no supporting evidence, Chambers was ignored. In 1948 he repeated his accusations before the House Un-American Activities Committee. When Hiss sued him for slander, Chambers produced microfilms of classified State Department documents that Hiss allegedly had given him in 1937 and 1938.

Hiss was brought to trial for perjury (the statute of limitations prevented indictment for espionage). He called upon a number of the nation's most distinguished liberals to bear witness to his character. The first trial ended with a hung jury (July 1949); the second ended with conviction (January 1950).

More important in convincing Americans that a real Communist menace existed was the revelation, in February 1950, that a young British scientist, Dr. Klaus Fuchs, had turned over to Russian agents full details on the manufacture of atomic bombs. His confession led to the trial and ultimate execution of Julius and Ethel Rosenberg, Americans who were alleged to have been his accomplices—and who were hailed as martyrs by Communists throughout the world.

A TROUBLED ELECTORATE

In 1950 the voters were disturbed by the charges of subversion, by the Communist victory in China, and by the Korean War. Many were led to believe that the events in China and Korea had resulted from a conspiracy in the State Department. Representative Nixon declared: "Traitors in the high councils of our own government have made sure that the deck is stacked on the Soviet side of the diplomatic tables." Bipartisanship in foreign policy disappeared as the Republicans pressed their issue. They did not capture Congress in November 1950, but they gained twenty-eight seats in the House and five in the Senate.

Meanwhile, President Truman made but little headway with his Fair Deal. Congress passed the Displaced Persons Act of 1950, liberalizing the 1948 legislation that the President had denounced as discriminatory against Catholics and Jews because its quotas were unfavorable to people from southern and eastern Europe. The new law increased the number of persons to be admitted from 205,000 to 415,000—but even this latter figure was a total for a three-year period, not a yearly number. Congress also implemented some of Truman's proposed reforms. The National Housing Act of 1949 provided for the construction over the succeeding six years of 810,000 housing units for lower-income families, together with a subsidy for forty years to bridge the gap between costs and the rents the tenants could afford to pay. It also provided grants for slum clearance and rural housing. Congress voted increased appropriations for power development and reclamation in the West, for TVA and for the Farmers' Home Administration (which carried on the rehabilitation work of the earlier Resettlement Administration and Farm Security Administration). In contrast, the Fair Deal health-insurance program went down to crashing defeat under the vigorous opposition of the American Medical Association, which raised a $3 million fund to combat it. Federal aid for education failed because of dissension over whether aid should go to parochial schools.

Republicans undermined the Truman administration with charges of favor-peddling and corruption, which implicated men in the White House though not the President himself. The President's military aide had received as a gift a $520 deep-freeze unit; the wife of an examiner of loans for the Reconstruction Finance Corporation had acquired a $9,540 mink coat. These became the symbols of a moral malaise in Washington. Apparently go-betweens, in return for a 5-percent fee, could obtain contracts, arrange RFC loans, and take care of tax difficulties in the Bureau of Internal Revenue. President Truman reorganized the RFC and reformed the Bureau of Internal Revenue and the Department of Justice, but much too slowly to satisfy his Republican critics.

As the election of 1952 approached, there was no indication that the majority of voters wished to reverse either Truman's foreign policy or his domestic program. They did want to "clean up the mess in Washington," and above all they wanted to see an end to the drawn-out, wearying Korean War.

EISENHOWER ELECTED

It was not surprising that in times so troubled the voters overwhelmingly turned to a successful and popular general who they felt could lead them to security in a frightening world. They turned not to MacArthur but to Dwight D. Eisenhower, who was closely linked to the military and foreign policies of the Roosevelt and Truman administrations.

The wing of the Republican party holding to the views of MacArthur was committed to Senator Robert A. Taft—but it was a minority with the party, even though it controlled the Republican National Committee. The majority looked to General Eisenhower—whom some liberal Democrats had sought to draft in 1948. In a violent struggle on the floor of the convention, the Eisenhower forces won contested delegations and, with them, the nomination on the first ballot. Senator Richard M. Nixon, who was acceptable to conservative Republicans, was nominated for the vice presidency. The platform was ambiguous enough to cover disagreements between the two wings of the party.

As for the Democrats, President Truman had announced that he would not run again. So the Northern leaders drafted Governor Adlai E. Stevenson of Illinois, who had earlier declared he would not run. His running mate was the liberal Senator John J. Sparkman of Alabama. The platform stated the positions of the Northern Democrats: endorsement of the Truman foreign policies, civil rights, repeal of the Taft-Hartley Act, and high price supports for farmers.

Governor Stevenson began delivering speeches brilliant in their eloquence, clever in their wit, and startling in their candor. As he promised to "talk sense to the American peo-

Election of 1952

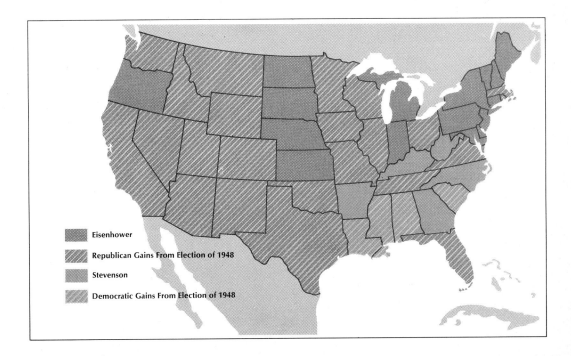

- Eisenhower
- Republican Gains From Election of 1948
- Stevenson
- Democratic Gains From Election of 1948

ple," he drew the hearty support of most intellectuals, whose critics derisively called them "eggheads." But General Eisenhower appealed much more effectively to businessmen and the masses by promising to end their various frustrations.

Republican campaigners played upon the triple theme of "Communism, corruption, and Korea." Speaking in Detroit on October 24, 1952, Eisenhower promised to bring the war to "an early and honorable end." To help do so, he promised he would make a personal trip to Korea. The response at the polls was overwhelming: Eisenhower getting 33,936,000 votes to 27,315,000 for Stevenson. Despite Eisenhower's victory, the Republicans failed to gain complete control of Congress. They won a majority of eight seats in the House and only an even split in the Senate. The Republican candidate was far more popular than his party.

New Hands at the Helm

John Foster Dulles, the Republican expert in foreign policy, had criticized the Democratic program of "containment" as a passive one that left the initiative to the Communist side. Dulles proposed, instead, a program of "liberation" that would lead to a "roll-back" of Communist expansion. As secretary of state in the Eisenhower administration, he continued to talk of new approaches. Yet the Eisenhower-Dulles policy was to be essentially a continuation of the Truman-Acheson policy.

A KOREAN ARMISTICE

Before his inauguration President-elect Eisenhower flew to Korea to talk to commanders about means of obtaining an honorable truce. In his inaugural he committed himself to a firm

Eisenhower in Korea
In the presidential campaign of 1952 General Eisenhower promised that, if elected, he would go to Korea, presumably to bring the war to an end. After his election and before his inauguration he did go to Korea. Here he is shown (left) at mess with American officers there. (U.S. Army photograph)

**Secretary of State John Foster Dulles Reporting
to President Eisenhower   May 17, 1955**
*The Eisenhower administration made extensive use of television
to dramatize its actions among the American people. For the first
time the President's press conferences were televised, and on several
occasions like this, Secretary Dulles reported to the President in
front of the television cameras. He had just returned from Europe,
where he had signed the treaty restoring sovereignty to Austria. (U.S.
Department of State)*

policy in Korea and elsewhere in the struggle against Communists.

Less than two months after President Eisenhower took office, Stalin died. This opened the possibility of an end to the Korean War and perhaps some moderation of the cold war. When the new Soviet Premier, Georgi Malenkov, seemed conciliatory, the President called upon the Russians to show their good faith by signing an Austrian peace treaty and supporting an armistice in Korea. On July 27, 1953, an agreement was finally signed at Panmunjom. It provided for a cease-fire and withdrawal of both armies about a mile and a half back of the existing battle line, which ran from coast to coast, from just below the 38th parallel in the west to thirty miles north of it in the east. A conference was to be held to seek peaceful reunification of Korea, but at the Geneva meeting

(1954) no agreement was reached. The armistice turned into an uneasy and indefinite armed truce.

The Korean War (officially only a "police action") had lasted more than three years and cost the United States alone 25,000 dead, 115,000 other casualties, and $22 billion. For Americans who liked to think in terms of total victory, it all seemed painfully inconclusive. The fighting had settled no problems in the Far East except to prevent the Communist conquest of South Korea.

"MASSIVE RETALIATION"

As secretary of state from 1953 to 1959, Dulles gave the impression of formulating policy decisions on his own. A sturdy moralist, a skilled and stubborn advocate, and a tireless worker, he seemed to feel that he must participate personally in innumerable top-level negotiations all over the globe. Since as secretary he flew 479,286 miles outside of the United States, his detractors liked to wisecrack that he was demonstrating an infinite capacity for taking planes. Assuming many of the normal functions of State Department officials, diplomats, and even the President, he dominated the making of foreign policy.

The Eisenhower administration had come into office firmly committed to existing collective-security arrangements and a Europe-first priority. Nevertheless, it maintained a tenuous compromise with the ardently nationalistic Asia-first wing of the party. This group was exploiting at home the thesis that setbacks in Asia were due to internal subversion in the Truman administration, that Communist aggression in Asia must be met with military force, and that economic aid to remove the grievances the Communists were exploiting was a waste of money. The hero of the Asia-firsters was Chiang Kai-shek, and their special villain, Red China, which they insisted must be curbed or destroyed at all costs. Concurring with this group at some points were the business leaders dominant in the Eisenhower administration, who were determined that defense expenditures must fit within a balanced budget.

The pressures of these groups helped lead to crucial decisions in 1953. Again, as before the Korean War, a movement began to reduce the military establishment. At the same time, the Eisenhower administration wished to meet the Communist challenge in Indochina and elsewhere. The solution seemed to lie in a "new look" in defense policy, equally pleasing to the secretaries of defense, the treasury, and state. This meant cutting the expensive army ground forces and basic scientific research. The United States would depend especially upon its thermonuclear weapons and their delivery by the air force. Popularized, this was the policy of "more bang for a buck."

A new diplomatic and strategic approach was necessary to make the "new look" in defense operate adequately. Secretary of the Treasury George M. Humphrey, looking at it from a standpoint of cost, asserted that the United States had "no business getting into little wars." If the nation had to intervene, he declared, "let's intervene decisively with all we have got or stay out." This was the economic basis for Secretary of State Dulles' proposal of "massive retaliation." The United States would depend less on local defense, he declared in an address on January 12, 1954, and depend more on "the deterrent of massive retaliatory power . . . a great capacity to retaliate instantly, by means and at times of our own choosing."

CHINA AND INDOCHINA

The Indochina crisis of 1954 offered the first test of the new approach. Under the leadership of Ho Chi Minh the people of Indochina, a French colony that had fallen to Japan in World War II, had been fighting for their independence—against the Japanese and then against the French. The end of the Korean War enabled the Chinese Reds to give indirect aid to the Indochinese nationalists, who were largely Communists, at a time when the French were tottering on the edge of military disaster. In 1954 the rebels besieged an army of 12,000 Frenchmen and friendly Indochinese in the frontier fortress of Dienbienphu. Already the United States was paying 70 percent of the French war costs, thus supporting colonialism as an alternative to Communism. Now, it appeared, the United States would also have to send direct military aid if Dienbienphu and all of Indochina were not to fall under Communist control.

At a press conference, President Eisenhower likened the nations in Southeast Asia to a row of dominoes. The moral was implicit; the first domino must not be allowed to fall. Many of the President's advisers favored at least bombing the besieging army with carrier-based planes, but Dulles failed to gain support among allied nations. Congressional leaders had no stomach for an intervention that might soon involve more ground troops than the Korean War, and in which the United States might have to fight alone. The United States did not intervene; there was no "massive retaliation." Dienbienphu fell on May 7, 1954. At a conference in Geneva, the United States, stripped of bargaining power (except for the threat of unilateral intervention), had to stand by, neither associating itself with negotiations with Red China, nor approving the agreements of July 1954, which provided for a cease-fire and the partitioning of Indochina into three independent nations.

After the Geneva conference, Secretary Dulles succeeded in building a Southeast Asia Treaty Organization (SEATO) to serve as a counterpart of NATO and help contain Communism. SEATO (established September 1954) was far less impressive, since the terms of the Geneva conference kept Nationalist China and nations of Indochina (Vietnam, Laos, and Cambodia) from participating. Several of the most important Asian states (India, Ceylon, Burma, and Indonesia) refused to join because they were committed to neutralism. This left only three nations of Southeast Asia—Pakistan, Thailand, and the Philippines—to join with the United States, Great Britain, France, Australia, and New Zealand. They drew up a pact, weaker than the North Atlantic Treaty, providing only that an attack upon one would be regarded as a threat to the others. SEATO opened the way for economic and military aid, but without the key nations of Southeast Asia participating, it remained a relatively ineffective organization.

The United States continued to function in Asia as best it could on a virtually unilateral basis. Trouble with Communist China developed over some offshore islands that Chiang continued to garrison—Quemoy and Matsu and Tachen Islands. Occasionally Chiang's air force attacked the Communists from them. Since the Mutual Defense Treaty with Chiang, signed at the end of 1954, did not include these islands, Red China in January 1955 began air attacks upon the Tachens and bombardment of Quemoy. Before invasion could follow, Congress granted President Eisenhower rather indefinite emergency powers to aid Chiang. These sufficed to maintain a precarious status quo.

Intermittently, the Chinese Communists renewed their pressure upon Quemoy and Matsu. In August 1958 they began another serious bombardment. Secretary Dulles, although not always clear in what he said, implied repeatedly that the United States would help Chiang defend the islands. But the United States could not count upon the support of other Western nations if a large-scale struggle with Red China developed. The militant Chinese Communists in 1959 pressed on other borders. After crushing a revolt in Tibet, they pushed troops across several ill-defined frontiers into areas claimed by India. Of much more

serious concern to the United States, they backed a Communist penetration deep into Laos, one of the nations of Indochina.

In the involved and unending struggle with Communist China, the American arsenal of atomic weapons was of relatively little effect even against a nation that as yet did not possess any. Against Russia, with its rapidly expanding nuclear strength, the threat of massive thermonuclear retaliation was still less effective.

OUR GERMAN ALLY

Fortunately, the United States and its allies did not depend upon nuclear power alone. The concept of the North Atlantic Treaty Organization was embodied in its emblem of a sword and a shield. The sword stood for atomic weapons, the striking force, and the shield for conventional ground forces, to deter or withstand attack. During the Korean War the United States began to rebuild its military establishment at home and gradually to pour funds into NATO, to strengthen its defenses in terms of ground forces as well as atomic weapons.

Europeans worried over the slowness of the United States to provide arms and men, its failure (partly because of constitutional limitations) to commit itself clearly in advance to resist any armed attack on western European nations, and its desire to rearm Germany.

While the French were still afraid of the Germans, the Germans themselves were so war-weary that it was difficult to persuade them to arm again. Between 1950 and 1954 they were able to win back step by step almost all their sovereignty in return for rearming.

To make the rearming of Germany acceptable to France, Great Britain promised in 1954 to keep four divisions and a tactical air force on the Continent as long as her allies wanted them. With this reassurance, France agreed to a treaty that same month restoring full sovereignty to Germany (except for the stationing of allied troops in West Berlin until Germany was reunified). The West German army was to be limited to twelve divisions, which would be supplied to NATO. Germany promised not to seek reunification or extension of her boundaries through force, and was prohibited from manufacturing nuclear, biological, or chemical weapons. Germany joined NATO and thus directly became a military ally of the United

States. In 1957 she contributed her first forces — five divisions totaling 120,000 men.

THE GENEVA SPIRIT

After the death of Stalin in 1953, there were increasing signs that new Russian policies might lead to some enlargement of freedom behind the Iron Curtain and some relaxation of tensions with the Western powers. Russia extended a peace overture to Tito of Yugoslavia, returned a key base to Finland, recognized the Federal Republic of West Germany, and signed a peace treaty with Japan. Above all, the Soviet Union joined with the Western powers in signing a peace treaty with Austria, making it a neutral state, and terminating the long military occupation.

The softening of Soviet policy and the increase in international exchanges led to demands from Europeans, Asians, and even Americans for a conference among the heads of state — a "summit conference" — to consider means of easing international tensions. But the greatest single motive for such a meeting was the knowledge that both the United States and Russia were manufacturing hydrogen bombs of staggering destructive power.

In August 1953 the Russians had set off a hydrogen explosive. President Eisenhower warned a few weeks later that the physical security of the United States had "almost totally disappeared before the long-range bomber and the destructive power of a single bomb." The meaning of this became dramatically clear in the spring of 1954 when the United States announced that it had exploded in the Pacific a bomb powerful enough to destroy or put out of commission all of New York City.

Against this background, the American people, after an initial wariness, became enthusiastic about the meeting of the heads of the United States, Great Britain, France, and Russia in Geneva (July 1955). President Eisenhower, hopeful that he could wage "a war for peace," proposed at the meetings that the Russians and the United States exchange blueprints of their armed forces and permit inspection of their military installations from the air. He declared to Premier Nicolai A. Bulganin: "The United States will never take part in an aggressive war." Bulganin replied: "Mr. President, we believe that statement."

The affability of the Russians at Geneva immensely relieved the American people, who were hopeful for the moment that a real change of policy had come about. This "Geneva spirit," as newspapermen called it, led to a general feeling on the part of most Western nations that a nuclear war between Russia and the United States would not develop. Secretary Dulles declared, however, that the conference had avoided "creating an illusion that all was now so well that we could safely relax our efforts to build individual and collective self-defense." All proposals from both sides had been referred to a future foreign ministers' conference. Even before it met, several nations began to scale down their NATO contributions.

President Eisenhower upon his return from Geneva warned: "We must never be deluded into believing that one week of friendly, even fruitful negotiations can wholly eliminate a problem arising out of the wide gulf that separates East and West." The American public, less inclined to caution, greeted the President with unrestrained acclaim.

The subsequent foreign ministers' conference failed dismally to agree upon German unification, disarmament, or lowering of trade barriers. Even before it adjourned, the "Geneva spirit" rapidly evaporated throughout the West.

MENACE IN THE MIDDLE EAST

Soon a new Russian drive was launched toward the Middle East, where the United States had long been deeply involved because of its conflicting interests in the people of the new state of Israel and in the oil of the Arab states.

During World War II, the British, in order not to offend the Arabs, had continued restrictions upon immigration to Palestine. Both political parties in the United States favored lifting these restrictions and creating a Jewish state. After the war, the British brought the problem to the United Nations, which recommended partitioning Palestine between Jews and Arabs. The Jews successfully fought off military attacks by the Arabs and, on the day the British mandate ended, May 14, 1948, proclaimed a new government. President Truman recognized it within a few minutes, thus ending United Nations proposals to put Palestine under a temporary trusteeship. The new nation, Israel, fought off armies from surrounding

Arab countries until the United Nations established an unstable truce in 1949. Although the United States tried to promote amity, relations between Israel and its neighbors continued close to the point of explosion, and other quarrels in the Middle East persisted.

Gradually the United States won over some of the Arab nations to the Western defense system. This country leased air bases from Saudi Arabia; and through the Baghdad Pact of 1955 Secretary Dulles managed to bring the northern bloc of Arab states — Iraq, Iran, and Pakistan — into the defense arrangement.

Dulles' diplomacy was less successful with Egypt, which for years had quarreled with the British over the Sudan and British bases along the Suez Canal. The United States tried to mediate; in 1954 the British agreed to remove their troops from the Suez area. After Gamal Abdel Nasser came to power, the State Department tried to woo him, although he proclaimed emphatic neutralist and Arab nationalist policies, and strove for leadership of the entire Arab world. Secretary Dulles tried to win him with offers of economic aid — even the sum needed to construct an enormous dam on the Nile. Meanwhile, the Russians concluded a deal, made public in September 1955, by which they gave Nasser large quantities of armaments in exchange for cotton.

With sufficient Communist arms Nasser might destroy Israel. He could also threaten the security system the United States was trying to build in the Middle East. With the arms that went to Nasser and his close ally, Syria, would also go Russian experts to show Egyptians how to use them. Secretary Dulles met the challenge. Instead of continuing to be conciliatory toward Egypt, in July 1956 he suddenly withdrew his promise to provide funds for a dam. A week later Nasser retaliated by seizing the Suez Canal, purportedly to obtain money for the Nile project. This action gave him a stranglehold on the main oil line to Europe, since two-thirds of the proved oil reserves of the world were in the Middle East, and four-fifths of the oil for western Europe flowed from there.

During the tedious months of negotiations with Nasser that followed, Great Britain, France, and Israel all came to feel that they were not obtaining as much support as they should from the United States. Meanwhile, the armed strength of Egypt was growing rapidly.

On October 29, 1956, Israeli forces struck a preventive blow at Egypt. The next day the British and French intervened to drive the Egyptian forces from the Suez Canal zone. They were militarily successful, but not before the Egyptians had thoroughly blocked the canal. The United States led the United Nations in denouncing the military intervention; the Western alliances seemed in danger of dissolving; Russia threatened to send "volunteers" to the aid of Egypt. Under these pressures, the British and French issued a cease-fire order on November 6. Another prolonged truce between Egypt and Israel began under the supervision of the United Nations.

The power vacuum in the Middle East in the weeks after the Suez cease-fire created new opportunities for the spread of Communism. Once again the American public was alarmed and incensed, since coincident with the Suez crisis came brutal Soviet suppression of an uprising in Hungary. Because of the nuclear stalemate, the United States could not intervene in Hungary. It limited itself to fostering United Nations resolutions of censure and to admitting tens of thousands of refugees.

In the Middle East more positive action afterward seemed possible. The public was receptive when the President appeared before Congress on January 5, 1957, to enunciate what came to be called the "Eisenhower Doctrine." He asked Congress to authorize military and economic aid "to secure and protect the territorial independence" of Middle Eastern nations "against overt armed aggression from any nation controlled by international communism." Congress authorized the President to use armed force as he deemed necessary, and to spend $200 million on economic aid in the area.

As an instrument of pressure upon Egypt, the Eisenhower Doctrine was of little effect. Nasser reopened the Suez Canal on his own terms. In April 1957 American policy seemed more successful when the United States rushed its Sixth Fleet to the eastern Mediterranean to bolster the government of Jordan. Three other states, Saudi Arabia, Iraq, and Lebanon, seemed to give at least tacit support to the Eisenhower Doctrine.

Soviet penetration in the next few months, both through feeding Arab nationalism and through providing arms to Egypt, Syria, and Yemen, effectively countered the American policy. In August 1957 the Russians negotiated a $500 million arms-and-aid pact with Syria. In its aftermath, a pro-Soviet army clique seized power. Since the clique of course did not ask for American aid, the Eisenhower Doctrine was inoperative in Syria, but the State Department, declaring that Syria's neighbors were alarmed, sent them weapons. The strong tone of the United States led to an unfavorable reaction among the Arab nations, and they reaffirmed their solidarity.

Egypt and Syria, combining to form the United Arab Republic, continued to exert pressure on their neighbors. When a pro-Nasser clique took over Iraq (July 1958), it appeared that Lebanon and Jordan might also come under Nasser's domination. The pro-Western government of Lebanon requested aid against rebels, and the United States rushed in troops. At the same time Great Britain sent forces into Jordan. In the fall of 1958, when conditions became stabilized in Lebanon, the United States withdrew its troops. Iraq, however, continued to be a serious problem. Secretary Dulles, in order to balance its loss from the Baghdad Pact mutual defense organization, announced that the United States would assume full partnership in the alliance. But the withdrawal of Iraq from the alliance did not lead that country into Nasser's United Arab Republic as expected. The elements favoring this course soon fell from power in Iraq, and the danger in 1959 and after seemed to be that the country would swing into the Communist bloc. Reacting against the Communist trend in Iraq, Nasser veered back toward the West, and the United States again began plying him with favors. Conditions were thus unstable and uncertain in much of the Middle East.

The Communists Gain

The Eisenhower administration was hard pressed to contain the expansion of Communist power in the world, even without attempting the "roll-back" of which Dulles once had spoken. Indeed, before the end of the administration, the Communists appeared to be making further gains.

THE ROCKET RACE

The onslaught of Communist ideology and power was especially frightening because of the apparent failure of the United States to keep pace with the Soviet Union in the development of intercontinental ballistic missiles, a failure that the Russians tried to exploit throughout the world. In early 1957 the United States had appeared to be abreast or ahead of Russia in the development of guided missiles with nuclear warheads. Because of the potential horror of these weapons, both nations seemed ready to reach disarmament agreements during seven months of discussions in 1957 at a meeting of the United Nations subcommittee in London. The United States insisted upon schemes of strict inspection, including proposals for aerial photography over strips of each other's territory. To this the Soviet Union would not agree.

Then, in August, Russia announced that she had successfully tested an intercontinental ballistic missile. In contrast, the United States had successfully tested only intermediate-range missiles that traveled from 1,500 to 3,000 miles. The Russian claims received sobering confirmation in October when Soviet scientists, using a rocket booster engine more powerful than any yet developed in the United States, launched the first successful satellite, the "sputnik."

Khrushchev, who in a series of bold moves had just consolidated his power in the Kremlin, now issued a series of strong statements. The intent of his "sputnik diplomacy" was clearly to shake the Western alliance and impress neutral nations. The reaction within the United States, especially when the first American attempt to launch a much smaller satellite failed, was more one of angry fear than of congratulations to the Russian scientists. Three months later the United States began launching its own, smaller satellites.

As an indication of his concern, President Eisenhower, although recuperating from a mild stroke, flew to Paris (December 1957) to lend strong moral support at a NATO conference. In January 1958 he devoted almost his entire annual message to Congress to the armaments crisis and to the need to surpass Russia

Launching the First American Satellite

On January 31, 1958, four months after the Russians launched the first satellite —
three months after they sent up one so big that it contained a dog — the United
States, using a Jupiter-C launching vehicle, put into orbit the first American
satellite, called Explorer I. It was 80 inches long, 6 inches in diameter, and
weighed 30.8 pounds. In it were devices for measuring temperature, cosmic rays,
and the frequency of meteorite particles, and radios for transmitting the
measurements. (Official U.S. Army photo)

in providing aid for underdeveloped countries. He called upon an acquiescent Congress for heavy additional expenditures to rush development and construction of long-range missiles and of submarines and cruisers that could launch missiles. The first task confronting the nation was "to ensure our safety through strength," he pointed out. "But we could make no more tragic mistake than merely to concentrate on military strength. For if we did only this, the future would hold nothing for the world but an age of terror."

Meanwhile, extensive nuclear testing after 1954 by both the United States and Russia, climaxed by the Russian explosion of several "dirty" bombs, greatly increased the fallout of radioactive isotopes. Throughout the world there was a fear of possible harmful effects. "Any dose, however small, produces some biological effect and . . . this effect is harmful," the Joint Congressional Committee on Atomic Energy granted in a 1959 report. If testing were to continue at the same rate over the next two generations, the report warned, the average concentration of radioactive strontium in the bones would be close to what scientists had estimated would be the maximum permissible body burden. This threat, well before 1959, was bringing popular pressure for the curtailing of nuclear tests.

In the spring of 1958 Khrushchev announced a unilateral abstention from nuclear tests by Russia. This left Eisenhower with the choice of two courses. He could follow the reasoning of most officials in the Defense Department, who held that nuclear weapons were the only way in which the United States could counter the enormous land armies of Russia and China—and continue tests. Or he could promise to stop tests on the condition that Russia would agree to adequate inspection.

He decided upon the latter course and announced that the United States and its allies would suspend tests for one year beginning October 31, 1958. The suspension would continue on a year-to-year basis, provided a proper system of control could be developed and substantial progress could be made on disarmament negotiations. Russia, proclaiming that this was a Western trick, announced that it would resume testing. Nevertheless, President Eisenhower declared that for the time being the United States would continue its suspension of

tests as it sought some workable agreement with the Soviet Union. Representatives of the United States, Great Britain, and Russia met in Geneva and slowly, laboriously, tried to construct a regulatory treaty.

In 1959 Khrushchev made much propaganda use of the failure of the United States to catch up with Russia in astronautical feats. These feats obscured the fact that the "missile gap" between the two nations was not as great as had been feared two years earlier. The United States was successfully producing and testing its own missiles and developing plans for hiding and spreading the launching sites so that it would require ten times as many Russian missiles to destroy them. The success of the navy in constructing atomic-powered submarines that could launch missiles, and in bringing the submarines up through the ice at the North Pole, was a dramatic example of American achievement. The naval development of "Project Tepee," a radio-monitoring system that could detect any missile launchings anywhere in the world, was an indication of the technical advance of American defense.

If the Russians were to attack the United States, they could not expect their own cities to remain unscathed. The reverse held equally true—that American nuclear power would be incapable of destroying all the sites from which the Russians could launch missiles. The Congressional Joint Committee on Atomic Energy reported in August 1959 that an attack upon the United States, if it came, might kill 50 million people, seriously injure 20 million more, and destroy or render unusable for months half of the dwellings in the country. Crops would be contaminated and swept by fire. The only hopeful note was the assurance that bomb shelters for the entire population could reduce casualties by 25 or 30 percent.

FRIENDLY OVERTURES FAIL

Suddenly, in November 1958, Khrushchev precipitated a new crisis over Berlin, where the West's position was, as always, vulnerable. He asserted that conditions had changed so markedly in Berlin since the end of the war that the occupation agreements no longer applied. In six months he proposed to sign a separate peace treaty with the government of East

President Eisenhower on Berlin [1961]

Berlin is not so much a beleaguered city or threatened city as it is a symbol — for the West, of principle, of good faith, of determination; for the Soviets, a thorn in their flesh, a wound to their pride, an impediment to their designs.

The Soviets want to banish the Allies from West Berlin because, first, it is to them an unwelcome show place of Western freedom and prosperity in a region otherwise completely regimented and impoverished; and, second, because the opportunity it creates for the unhappy East Germans to escape to freedom emphasizes to the outside world the emptiness of the phrase "people's democracies." In the meantime, they use it as a pretext to create and intensify tensions and to try to divide the West. — Saturday Evening Post, *December 9, 1961.*

Germany, turning over to it all the Russian occupation functions in Berlin including control over the access routes that stretched 110 miles to West Germany.

The United States insisted that its treaty rights still held and undertook the twofold task of trying to maintain unity among its Western allies and of getting from the Soviet government concessions that would correspond to any that the United States might make. Neither task was easy. Russia made alternate proposals that were as unacceptable as the first demand had been, and Khrushchev manipulated the issue to try to force a summit meeting. The United States was not willing to go further than a foreign ministers' conference unless the Russians became more conciliatory. The Geneva sessions beginning in May 1959 were discouragingly unfruitful.

Meanwhile, the burden of conducting American foreign policy had shifted to a new Secretary of State, Christian Herter, when Dulles, dying of cancer, resigned in April 1959. Herter was a strong successor. He had capped his foreign service record as a young man with a successful career in politics. But he did not continue the one-man determination of foreign policy that had distinguished Dulles. President Eisenhower now assumed a larger measure of responsibility, and this pointed toward new interchanges at the top with the Russians.

Exchanges at lower levels had been going on at an increasing rate since the Geneva thaw of 1955. One of its few positive effects had been personal and cultural interchanges of musicians, dancers, students, and delegations of all kinds, climaxed in the summer of 1959 by a visit to the United States of Anastas Mikoyan, a So-

viet deputy premier, and to Russia of Vice President Nixon. The Russians demonstrated their wares at a fair in New York City, and the Americans at a corresponding fair in Moscow showed crowds of Russians the components of the high standard of living in the United States. While Nixon was at the fair, he engaged in informal debate with Khrushchev. The Russian press was for the most part hostile, but the crowds were friendly, and Khrushchev himself, while holding dogmatically to Soviet positions, seemed to demonstrate a keen interest in things American.

In August 1959 President Eisenhower announced that he would exchange visits with the Russian leader. The purpose in inviting Khrushchev, Eisenhower explained, was "to give him the opportunity to see what Americans are like" and "to give him, face to face, the basic convictions of our people on the major issues of the day." Khrushchev, during his travels in the United States, received on the whole a hearty welcome, despite the coldness of most American officials and the hostile demonstrations of certain groups, especially those sympathizing with the Hungarian rebels of 1956. He impressed Americans with his energy, toughness, and — except for a few petulant outbursts — good humor. Eisenhower, postponing his return visit, made tours of western Europe, southern Asia, and Latin America, to the cheers of enthusiastic crowds at almost every stop.

A second "summit" conference, to meet in Paris, was scheduled for May 1960. On May 1 an unarmed American U-2 plane was downed inside the Soviet Union. The American government at first denied, then acknowledged and attempted to justify the fact that the plane had been engaged in aerial reconnaissance of a kind the United States had been carrying on, systematically but secretly, for some time. At the Paris meeting, unsatisfied by Eisenhower's belated promise to discontinue flights over Russian territory, Khrushchev made the U-2 incident an occasion for denouncing Eisenhower and breaking up the conference.

Khrushchev also took back his invitation for Eisenhower to go to the Soviet Union. Eisenhower, having planned to stop in Japan on the way home from Russia, went ahead with arrangements for a Far Eastern trip in June. A new security pact, authorizing continued American bases in Japan, awaited ratification. Communist agitators now played upon the pacifisim of the Japanese people, a pacifism that American occupation policies earlier had stimulated. In Tokyo mobs began wild demonstrations against the pact, against Premier Nobusuke Kishi, who sponsored it, and against the Eisenhower visit. At the last minute, after the President had reached as far as Manila, his Japan appearance was called off. The Kishi government managed to put the unpopular treaty into effect; but throughout the world the Eisenhower administration could scarcely avoid a serious loss to American prestige, which already had been weakened by the administration's handling of the spy-plane affair.

DISGRUNTLED NEIGHBORS

The incessant threats against areas close to the Communist perimeter so occupied the American government and people that they paid scant attention to an area of vital worth to the United States and of growing vulnerability to Communist influence—the area to the south. One of the minor ironies of this hectic age was the erosion of the Good Neighbor feeling between Latin American nations and the United States during the very years when this country was extending much of the Good Neighbor policy to Europe and Asia.

On paper there was no deterioration. Quite the contrary; the Latin American nations signed new pacts and received additional forms of aid. They all became members of the United Nations. In 1947, at a conference at Rio de Janeiro, they drafted an Inter-American Treaty of Reciprocal Assistance, and the following year established an Organization of American States. The United States had abandoned the old unilateral Monroe Doctrine by entering into pacts and organizations providing for mutual action whether in defense, settlement of disputes, or economic cooperation.

Yet the overwhelming military and economic power of the "colossus of the North" remained. Latin Americans were not pleased when the United States brought its prestige to bear against the totalitarian dictator of Argentina, Juan D. Perón, in 1946–1947, even though the pressure failed. They were not much more pleased when the United States successfully brought pressure against a pro-Communist regime in Guatemala in 1954. But in the late fifties, when many of the nations overthrew dictators, the more common complaint was that the United States had been too friendly toward despots, as in Venezuela, and not enthusiastic enough about rebels like Fidel Castro, who came into power in Cuba in 1959, and who thereafter devoted himself to denunciations of "Yankee imperialism."

Above all, the problems from which Latin American peoples were suffering were economic. After the close of World War II, they could no longer sell raw materials from their farms and mines to the United States in such large quantities or at such favorable prices as before. The soaring costs of the American manufactured goods they imported further hurt them. At home they were undergoing a rapid industrial revolution, an accompanying social evolution, and an explosive population increase at the highest rate in the world, as much as 2.5 percent per year. Already their combined population had passed that of the United States. All these factors helped create acute internal problems.

Inevitably the United States would have to be involved in the solution of economic questions because the hostility of neighbors to the south would be potentially ruinous, and because the two areas had become increasingly interdependent economically. Trade with Latin America exceeded $8 billion a year by the end of the fifties, and accounted for a third of the imports and a quarter of the exports of the United States. In Latin America 80 percent of the foreign capital was American; it had a book value of about $9.5 billion. (This figure was sec-

Peruvians Threaten Nixon

On his goodwill tour of South America in 1958, Vice President Nixon was the target of violent anti-American demonstrations. When, on May 8, he appeared at San Marcos University in Lima, Peru, local police had difficulty in restraining the mob. The demonstrators threw stones, one of which grazed the Vice President's neck. (UPI)

ond only to the $13 billion invested in Canada, which was also unhappy about its economic relations with the United States.)

It seemed to Latin Americans that, despite these close economic ties, the United States was doing little specifically to help them solve their problems—to provide adequate capital for large-scale development, to stabilize raw materials at a profitable level, and to conquer inflation. They felt neglected as the American government poured billions into Europe and Asia while giving Latin America only a comparative pittance. Secretary Dulles was occupied elsewhere, and the Eisenhower administration,

under the influence of two successive conservative secretaries of the Treasury, was cold to requests for government loans for development. The festering economic ills and other grievances that could easily be focused against the United States were ready-made for the Communists. Exercising an influence out of proportion to their small numbers, they were active from Cuba to Guatemala and Argentina.

Despite riots and disorders, the Latin American discontent received little notice in the United States until May 1958, when Vice President Nixon was mobbed in Lima and Caracas. In the aftermath of the national shock, the State Department speeded changes in policy which were already slowly under way. This country helped Latin American nations negotiate export quota pacts among themselves to raise the price of coffee and some metals, and it expedited negotiations toward the establishment of a regional common market among the republics. When, in June 1958, the President of Brazil called for an Operation Pan-America to speed economic development, the American government agreed to furnish nearly half the capital for a new billion-dollar Inter-American Bank to make development loans. It also tried to improve public relations in a way Nixon had suggested by giving no more than a correct handshake to dictators but offering a warm embrace to democratic leaders.

The administration was increasing its attention to Latin America none too soon, since it was obvious that the well-disciplined, widely pervasive Communist activities throughout the area were receiving direction from Russia. Early in 1959 Latin American Communist leaders returned from attending the twenty-first party congress in Moscow and began the systematic denunciation of every point of the new United States program.

The full import of the Communist challenge to the south became clear in 1960. Fidel Castro, whose revolutionary accession to power had been cheered by Americans at the beginning of 1959, turned his administration increasingly to the left and indulged in shrill tirades against the United States. The Eisenhower administration, acting with restraint, was slow to retaliate economically until, in the summer of 1960, Castro systematically confiscated a billion dollars' worth of American property. At this point the United States stopped importing Cuban sugar at a subsidized price. Castro complained to the United Nations Security Council that the United States was engaging in economic aggression.

The Soviet leader Nikita S. Khrushchev proclaimed that the Monroe Doctrine was dead and that, if the United States were to intervene militarily, Soviet artillerymen could "support Cuba with rocket fire." In the fall of 1960 tension heightened as Castro tried to spread his revolution to neighboring republics. President Eisenhower established a naval patrol to prevent an invasion of Guatemala or Nicaragua. At the same time, secretly, Americans were training an anti-Castro Cuban force at a camp in Guatemala. In January 1961 Castro ordered the staff of the United States embassy in Havana cut from eighty-seven to eleven. The United States then severed diplomatic relations with Cuba. Soviet influence clearly extended to within ninety miles of the United States.

Selected Readings

The Truman Administration
R. F. Haynes, *The Awesome Power: Harry S. Truman as Commander in Chief* (1973); R. M. Freeland, *The Truman Doctrine and the Origins of McCarthyism* (1972); W. C. Berman, *The Politics of Civil Rights in the Truman Administration* (1971).

The Eisenhower Administration
D. D. Eisenhower, *The White House Years** (2 vols., 1963–1965); E. J. Hughes, *The Ordeal of Power* (1963); Richard Nixon, *Six Crises** (1962); J. T. Patterson, *Mr. Republican: A Biography of Robert A. Taft* (1972); J. R. Beals, *John Foster Dulles* (1959); Richard Goold-Adams, *J. F. Dulles: A Reappraisal* (1962); Louis Gerson, *American Secretaries of State: John Foster Dulles* (1967); T. Hoopes, *The Devil and John Foster Dulles* (1973).

The Cold War
G. F. Kennan, *American Diplomacy, 1900–1950** (1951); J. W. Spanier, *American Foreign Policy Since World War II** (1962); W. G. Carleton, *The Revolution in American Foreign Policy: Its Global Range** (1963); Norman Graebner, *Cold War Diplomacy: American Foreign Policy, 1945–1960** (1962); M. F. Herz, *Beginnings of the Cold War* (1960); D. F. Fleming, *The Cold War and Its Origins, 1917–1960* (2 vols., 1961), critical of the U.S.; J. and G. Kolko, *The Limits of Power: The World and United States Foreign Policy, 1945–1954** (1972); J. L. Gaddis, *The United States and the Origins of the Cold War, 1941–1947* (1973); T. G. Paterson, *Soviet-American Confrontation: Postwar Reconstruction and the Origins of the Cold War* (1973); L. S. Wittner, *Rebels Against War: The American Peace Movement, 1941–1960* (1969); David Wise and Thomas Ross, *The U-2 Affair* (1962).

Nuclear Power and Military Policy
H. A. Kissinger, *Nuclear Weapons and Foreign Policy* (1957); L. L. Strauss, *Men and Decisions* (1962); R. G. Hewlett and O. E. Anderson, Jr., *The New World* (1962); Herman Kahn, *On Thermonuclear War* (1960); M. D. Taylor, *The Uncertain Trumpet* (1960); H. L. Nieburg, *Nuclear Secrecy and Foreign Policy* (1964).

Communism and Anti-Communism
E. L. Shils, *The Torment of Secrecy* (1956); J. A.
Wechsler, *The Age of Suspicion* (1953); Whittaker
Chambers, *Witness* (1952); Alger Hiss, *In the Court of
Public Opinion* (1957); R. H. Rovere, *Senator Joe
McCarthy** (1959); C. P. Curtis, *The Oppenheimer
Case* (1955).

Germany
L. D. Clay, *Decision in Germany* (1950); Drew
Middleton, *The Struggle for Germany* (1949); R. H.
Jackson, *The Nürnberg Case* (1947); Eugene David-
son, *The Death and Life of Germany: An Account of
the American Occupation* (1959); J. E. Smith, *The
Defense of Berlin* (1963).

The Far East
E. O. Reischauer, *The United States and Japan**
(1957); R. A. Fearey, *Occupation of Japan* (1950);
F. S. Dunn, *Peace-Making and the Settlement with
Japan* (1963); Herbert Feis, *The China Tangle** (1953);
Tang Tsou, *America's Failure in China, 1941–1950*
(1963); David Rees, *Korea: The Limited War* (1964);
Carl Berger, *The Korea Knot: A Military-Political
History* (1957); G. D. Paige, *The Korea Decision, June
24–30, 1950** (1968); J. W. Spanier, *The Truman-
MacArthur Controversy and the Korean War** (1959);
A. D. Biderman, *March to Calumny* (1962), on "brain-
washed" American prisoners; Melvin Gurtov, *The
First Vietnam Crisis: Chinese Communist Strategy
and United States Involvement, 1953–1954* (1967).

The Near East
Nadav Safran, *The United States and Israel* (1963);
Hugh Thomas, *The Suez Affair* (1967); Herman Finer,
Dulles over Suez (1964).

Latin America
M. S. Eisenhower, *The Wine Is Bitter: The United
States and Latin America* (1963); B. F. Smith, *The
United States and Cuba: Business and Diplomacy,
1917–1960* (1960).

*Titles available in paperback.

The Politics of Plenty

Twenty-eight

Though the peril of nuclear annihilation hung over them, the majority of the American people, in the phrase of the time, "never had it so good." They were riding a wave of prosperity much higher and longer-lasting than any previous one in the history of the country. The boom, beginning in the 1940s, continued through the 1950s and the 1960s, with an occasional recession or minor slump but with no real depression. A generation grew up that had never experienced such a calamity and could not believe it possible.

Yet there was much to be apprehensive about, at home as well as abroad. The prosperity was largely due to the foreign dangers, for it was stimulated by government spending for defense, and there was reason to wonder how long the good times would last if by some chance there should be a sudden "outbreak of peace." And even while the prosperity lasted, a large minority of the people, perhaps as many as 30 million of them, had little or no share in it.

A Swedish sociologist, Gunnar Myrdal, well acquainted with life in the United States, was moved to write: "I draw the conclusion that the common idea that America is an immensely rich and affluent country is very much an exaggeration. American affluence is heavily mortgaged. America carries a tremendous burden of debt to its poor people. That this debt must be paid is not only a wish of the do-gooders. Not paying it implies a risk for the social order and for democracy as we have known it."

Especially disadvantaged were the Americans of African descent. In a country that professed devotion to the creed of liberty and equality, they suffered from limitations on both. This contradiction between profession and practice was the theme of an elaborate study, *An American Dilemma* (2 vols., 1944), which Myrdal and a team of American scholars had made of the Negro's place in the United States. Myrdal had

---

Poverty in Appalachia
More white than black Americans of the 1960s and 1970s lived in poverty, though proportionately the number of black poor was greater. Many of the poorest whites were to be found in Appalachia, the Appalachian Mountain area of the Southeast. Here poor white children are playing near the entrance to a Kentucky coal mine. (Magnum)

warned that, after the war, Negro Americans could be expected to demand the rights that so long had been systematically denied them.

In the war black troops fought along with white for the declared object of creating an international order in which the "four freedoms" would be secure. Then, in the cold war, the United States sought the support of dark-skinned peoples throughout the world. These peoples, emerging from colonialism in their own lands of Asia and Africa, provided inspiration for blacks in America who began to insist upon the freedom they had not yet fully won a century after their emancipation had been officially proclaimed.

With his "Fair Deal," President Truman had made an abortive effort to solve some of the most pressing of the domestic problems. President Eisenhower announced no comparable program, but his successors John F. Kennedy and Lyndon B. Johnson proposed reforms going beyond Truman's.

The "Middle of the Road"

In the 1950s the majority of the voters seemed more interested in preserving their own economic gains than in remaking society. Viewing themselves as moderates, they gave whole-hearted support to the moderate President, Dwight D. Eisenhower. As early as 1949 Eisenhower had indicated his own approach when, as president of Columbia University, he addressed the American Bar Association. "The path to America's future," he then said, "lies down the middle of the road between the unfettered power of concentrated wealth . . . and the unbridled power of statism or partisan interests."

BUSINESSMEN IN GOVERNMENT

Once in office, President Eisenhower set up a businessmen's administration. To his cabinet he appointed one of the highest-paid corporation lawyers in the country (Secretary of State John Foster Dulles), the president of General Motors (Secretary of Defense Charles E. Wilson), the president of Mark Hanna's former firm M. A. Hanna and Company (Secretary of the Treasury George Humphrey), a New England manufacturer, two automobile distributors, a conservative specialist in farm marketing, and the wife of a wealthy Texas publisher (Mrs. Oveta Culp Hobby, who had been wartime commander of the WACs and who was named to head the Department of Health, Education, and Welfare when it came into existence in 1953). Something of an exception was the Secretary of Labor, Martin P. Durkin, the president of the plumbers' union, who had backed Adlai Stevenson in the 1952 campaign. "Eight millionaires and a plumber," the *New Republic* disrespectfully remarked. At the hearing on his appointment, Wilson played into the hands of Democratic critics by testifying that he had long assumed that "what was good for our country was good for General Motors, and vice versa." A few days later, Stevenson declared: "While the New Dealers have all left Washington to make way for the car dealers, I hasten to say that I, for one, do not believe the story that the general welfare has become a subsidiary of General Motors."

President Eisenhower's system of administering the government gave special importance to this cabinet made up preponderantly of businessmen. Borrowing from earlier army experience, he established his assistant, Sherman Adams, former governor of New Hampshire, as a sort of chief of staff, and from Adams down through the cabinet he extended a chain of command. Through the cabinet, and through numerous new committees, administrators arrived at important policy decisions that they referred to the President, who relied heavily upon these recommendations.

"EISENHOWER PROSPERITY"

At the beginning of the new administration, Secretary of the Treasury George Humphrey undertook to restrict bank credit and thus prevent inflation. By the fall of 1953 the threat was one of deflation instead. When the economy slackened, Secretary Humphrey and the Federal Reserve Board reversed the scarce-money policies and eased credit. The Republican administration's first venture with the expedients of Keynesian economics (manipulating money and credit to control the business cycle) was a success. By the summer of 1955 the American economy was again booming.

In order to avoid strikes that might unsettle economic conditions, several large industries, led by the automobile manufacturers, made new concessions to organized labor. As early as 1948 Walter Reuther, the president of the United Automobile Workers, had obtained from General Motors, and later from other manufacturers, an "escalator clause" in contracts, providing for automatic increases or decreases in wages every three months as the consumers' price index rose or fell. In 1955 he demanded from the Ford Motor Company a guaranteed annual wage. Ford compromised by agreeing that workers should receive 65 percent of their net weekly wages for the first four weeks they were unemployed, and 60 percent for the next twenty-two weeks. General Motors followed. A few months later, steelworkers received from the American Can Company and the Continental Can Company the first guarantee of an annual wage.

The round of wage raises continued through 1956. After a five-week strike, steelworkers won a substantial gain, and the United Mine Workers without a strike obtained a 30-cents-an-hour increase. Factory workers' wages went up to approximately $80 per week. These wage increases, together with other factors, led to widespread wholesale price rises and a renewed threat of inflation.

In December 1955 the American Federation of Labor and the Congress of Industrial Organizations merged at the top into a new giant federation, the AFL-CIO. The powerful Teamsters' Brotherhood in 1957 became the focal point of a congressional investigation into labor racketeering. A Senate committee charged the president of the Teamsters, David Beck, with the misappropriation of over $320,000 in union funds. When Beck appeared before the committee, he refused to answer questions, invoking the constitutional protection of the Fifth Amendment against self-incrimination. Ultimately the committee brought forth so much evidence against Beck that he declined to run for reelection as president of the Teamsters. But at their convention the Teamsters defiantly elected, as their new president, James Hoffa, also under attack by the committee. His election resulted in the eviction of the Teamsters, the largest union in the United States, from the AFL-CIO. The congressional investigation led to the Labor Reform Act of 1959, which was intended to promote honest elections of union officials, safeguard union funds, ban Communist leaders, and restrict boycotting and picketing.

The great staples piled up in surplus, and from 1948 to 1956, farm prices dropped a third while the national income went up by half. In 1948 farmers received 8.9 percent of the national income; in 1956, only 4.1 percent. Farm population declined steadily, to 22,300,000 in 1956 — only a ninth of the nation. In that single year, one out of every eleven of the farm population either moved to a city or was absorbed in an expanding city. While farm produce prices fell, consumer food prices continued to rise. Mainly this was because distribution costs were steadily going up. The farmer was caught in a squeeze, as prices for his produce slipped while prices of what he bought gradually increased.

As surpluses of such agricultural staples as wheat and cotton piled up, the government sought to bolster the prices through $8 billion worth of purchases. In 1954 President Eisenhower and Secretary of Agriculture Benson proposed a shift away from rigid price supports to a flexible sliding-scale program. The purpose was to cut government losses and end artificiality in production and distribution. The 1955 harvest was the first to be grown under the new flexible system, but already Democratic politicians were denouncing flexible supports as ones that could only "flex" downward. Seeking to win the farm vote, in 1956 they wrote a bill providing for high price supports and a subsidy for farmers who let land lie fallow. They thought they had put President Eisenhower in an impossible position, and as they expected, he vetoed the bill. But in May 1956 he pulled out of the vetoed bill the provision for a "soil bank" of fallow land and threw it back at the congressional Democrats. In this form, Congress passed the bill and it became law. Under the 1956 program, farmers took 12.3 million acres out of production in return for payments of over $250 million.

In the realm of public power development, the administration demonstrated its friendliness toward private enterprise. The President in 1953 referred to expansion of the Tennessee Valley Authority as "creeping socialism." The administration sought to circumvent the TVA by contracting with the Dixon-Yates syndicate in 1954 to build a huge steam power plant on the banks of the Mississippi. The administration declared that the contract would save taxpayers an immediate $100 million in construction costs, but opponents pointed to the large profits that the syndicate would collect over many years. The power would cost the government $3.5 million per year more than TVA power. Ultimately in 1955, when the city of Memphis, Tennessee, offered to build the plant, the President retreated to the principle of decentralization and canceled the Dixon-Yates contract.

The Eisenhower administration proposed federal "partnership" with local public or private enterprise in power construction. Secretary of the Interior McKay thus permitted a private power company to plan three small power dams in Hell's Canyon on the Snake River, rather than obtain appropriations for one large federal multipurpose dam. In keeping with his feeling that development of resources should be decentralized, President Eisenhower signed a bill turning over to states offshore oil lands along the Gulf of Mexico and the Pacific coast.

While the Eisenhower administration moved toward the right, conciliating the Taft wing of the Republican party in Congress, the President retained the basic general welfare programs that had been enacted during the previous twenty years. He took a firm stand against so-called socialized medicine but proposed a public health-insurance program that would involve little more than limited underwriting of private insurance companies issuing health policies. Congress passed no health-insurance legislation, but in 1954 extended social security to 10 million more people, and unemployment compensation to an additional 4 million. In 1956 Congress authorized a ten-year highway building program for which it would allocate almost $25 billion.

This concept of the limited role of the federal government in providing for the general welfare was what Eisenhower referred to as "dynamic conservatism." It appealed to many members of Congress. During his first two years in office, when Congress was narrowly

Republican, the President was supported more often than not by a coalition of liberal Republicans and Democrats. Of eighty-three key issues brought to a vote in the 1953 session of Congress, the administration won seventy-four, but succeeded in fifty-eight of these only through Democratic support. After the elections of 1954 the Democrats controlled both the House and the Senate.

DECLINE OF McCARTHYISM

Among the politicians who, after the Communist victory in China, had encouraged and capitalized upon the American people's fear of Communism, none rose more sensationally than Senator Joseph R. McCarthy of Wisconsin. A Republican, McCarthy began in 1950 to charge that Communists and "fellow travelers" (sympathizers) dominated the State Department and shaped American foreign policy under the Truman administration. The Senate Foreign Relations Committee investigated and found not a single Communist or fellow traveler in the State Department. Nevertheless, millions were eager to believe McCarthy as he went on to make new and startling accusations more rapidly than they could be either substantiated or refuted. His followers applauded when he denounced as Communists or pro-Communists the "whole group of twisted-thinking New Dealers" who had "led America near to ruin at home and abroad." He got so much attention that "McCarthyism" became a synonym for hysterical anti-Communism. Only gradually after the Korean armistice was the nation relieved from the worst excesses of McCarthyism.

The hunt for subversives in the government, begun during the Truman years, was intensified early in the Eisenhower administration. Large numbers of employees resigned or were dismissed — a total of 2,200 according to an official report. But most of the serious security risks had already been removed in the Truman purge. A study of some 400 of the Eisenhower administration cases by the Fund for the Republic of the Ford Foundation indicated that in a majority of them the charges had been insupportable, and often reinstatement ultimately followed. In July 1955 the Congress established a bipartisan Commission on Government Security to reevaluate the security program.

The Army-McCarthy Hearings

During the 1954 televised hearings on alleged Communist influence in the Army, Senator Joseph McCarthy of Wisconsin uses a map to show the supposed distribution of Communists throughout the country, while the chief counsel for the Army, Joseph Welch, and (at the extreme left) the assistant counsel, James St. Clair, listen. Twenty years later St. Clair was to defend President Richard M. Nixon against an impeachment move arising from the Watergate affair. (UPI)

Senator McCarthy himself plummeted from the national limelight to relative obscurity. His downfall followed his serious blunder in obliquely attacking President Eisenhower and directly assailing Secretary of the Army Robert Stevens, in January 1954. The attacks led to congressional hearings, which turned into a great national spectacle viewed by millions over television. Many people for the first time saw McCarthy in action, as for thirteen days he bullied and harried Secretary Stevens, evading issues through irrelevant countercharges and insinuations, and interrupting to object at every point. As the public watched, McCarthy seemed to change from a national hero into something of a villain, then into a low buffoon. In December 1954 the Senate voted 67 to 22 to condemn him for conduct unbecoming a senator. He no longer had much of a following when he died in May 1957.

Remnants of the attitudes that had made possible the rise of McCarthy remained. There was, for example, the case of a consultant to the Atomic Energy Commission, J. Robert Oppenheimer, who had directed the wartime laboratory at Los Alamos that made the first atomic bomb. In 1950 he had opposed the development of a hydrogen bomb. The FBI in 1953 distributed to the White House and several government departments a report on Oppenheimer detailing his prewar associations with Communists. On order from President Eisenhower, a "blank wall" was placed between Oppenheimer and government secrets, pending hearings. A three-man board voted 2 to 1 against granting him security clearance; the AEC ratified the decision 4 to 1. Scientists were bitterly split over the wisdom of the decision.

The Supreme Court, as a result of the appointments of the Republican President, seemed to be moving toward a more liberal rather than conservative policy. In one case in 1957 it ruled that the government could not use secret FBI evidence against a defendant unless it was made available to his lawyers. Congress quickly passed legislation safeguarding FBI files. In four other cases the Court protected individuals who were suspected of being subversive against undue encroachment by federal or state power. In 1958 the Court ruled 5 to 4 that the State Department, in the absence of an act of Congress, was exceeding its authority in refusing passports to persons who failed to file affidavits "with respect to present or past membership in the Communist party." These decisions attracted relatively little attention compared with the Supreme Court rulings on desegregation.

DESEGREGATION BEGINS

A series of cases before the Supreme Court breaking down bit by bit racial segregation in public schools had been pressed by the National Association for the Advancement of Colored People since the late 1930s. Their target was a Supreme Court decision of 1896, *Plessy* v. *Ferguson*, which had interpreted the Fourteenth Amendment clause requiring that states give "equal protection of the laws" to mean that separate but equal facilities could be furnished to Negroes. Finally, the Supreme Court reversed this doctrine in the case of *Brown* v. *Board of Education of Topeka* in May 1954. Chief Justice Earl Warren (who had been appointed by President Eisenhower in 1953, after the death of Chief Justice Vinson) delivered the unanimous opinion of the Court: "We conclude that in the field of public education the doctrine of 'separate but equal' has no place. Separate educational facilities are inherently unequal." The Court called for the desegregation of schools "with all deliberate speed."

Some Southern and border states resorted to every possible legal device to avoid mixed schools. Each September mob action against integration in a few communities within the South attracted widespread attention throughout the world. By the fall of 1957, of some 3,000 biracial school districts in the South, a total of 684 had begun desegregation. Schools within these districts in large cities in the upper South

---

Brown et al. v. Board of Education of Topeka et al. [1954]

In approaching this problem, we cannot turn the clock back to 1868 when the [Fourteenth] Amendment was adopted, or even to 1896 when Plessy v. Ferguson was written. We must consider public education in the light of its full development and its present place in American life throughout the Nation. Only in this way can it be determined if segregation in public schools deprives these plaintiffs of the equal protection of the laws.

Today, education is perhaps the most important function of state and local governments. Compulsory school attendance laws and the great expenditures for education both demonstrate our recognition of the importance of education to our democratic society. It is required in the performance of our most basic public responsibilities, even service in the armed forces. It is the very foundation of good citizenship. Today it is a principal instrument in awakening the child to cultural values, in preparing him for later professional training, and in helping him to adjust normally to his environment. In these days it is doubtful that any child may reasonably be expected to succeed in life if he is denied the opportunity of an education. Such an opportunity where the state has undertaken to provide it, is a right which must be made available to all on equal terms.

We come then to the question presented: Does segregation of children in public schools solely on the basis of race, even though the physical facilities and other 'tangible' factors may be equal, deprive the children of the minority group of equal educational opportunities? We believe that it does. — Excerpt of opinion of the Supreme Court delivered by Chief Justice Earl Warren.

State of South Carolina, Resolution on Desegregation [1956]

For almost sixty years, beginning in 1896, an unbroken line of decisions of the [Supreme] Court interpreted the Fourteenth Amendment as recognizing the right of the States to maintain racially separate public facilities for their people. If the Court in the interpretation of the Constitution is to depart from the sanctity of past decisions and to rely on the current political and social philosophy of its members to unsettle the great constitutional principles so clearly established, the rights of individuals are not secure and government under a written Constitution has no stability. . . .

The educational opportunities of white and colored children in the public schools of South Carolina have been substantially improved during recent years and highly satisfactory results are being obtained in our segregated schools. If enforced, the decision of the Court will seriously impair and retard the education of the children of both races, will nullify these recent advances and will cause untold friction between the races. — Excerpt from Joint Resolution, February 14, 1956.

---

or the border area, like Washington, Baltimore, Louisville, and St. Louis, opened quietly on an integrated basis. But 2,300 districts, including all those in the deep South and in Virginia, remained racially separate. Some districts at-tempted desegregation on a very slow, "token" basis. One of these was Little Rock, Arkansas, where intervention by the governor and threats by a mob led President Eisenhower to send federal troops to maintain order.

Desegregation in Washington, D.C.
In the fall of 1954, following the Supreme Court decision against school segregation, McKinley Technical High School quietly opened on a basis of equality for all students regardless of color. Before this date, public schools in the nation's capital were segregated. (Wide World)

Pressure from growing blocs of Negro voters in the North, and from Negroes rising in economic status in the South, helped bring other changes. President Eisenhower completed the desegregation of the armed forces and tried to bring about greater integration in the government and the District of Columbia. "There must be no second-class citizens in this country," he wrote the Negro Representative Adam Clayton Powell. Representative Powell, ironically, was instrumental in killing President Eisenhower's school-aid program of 1956, which provided for grants of $250 million a year for five years to match state funds. Powell succeeded in amending the bill to ban racial segregation; Southern segregationists aligned themselves with Northern conservatives to defeat the bill.

Congress in August 1957, after debating sixty-three days, passed a new civil rights law—the first since Reconstruction—to give federal protection to Negroes wanting to vote. In eight Southern states with an adult Negro population of over 3,750,000, only 850,000 or 25 percent were registered and still fewer went to the polls. In a 1955 election in Mississippi, only about 1 percent of the adult Negroes had voted. The Civil Rights Act empowered the federal government to remove some of the obstacles that state and local officials were placing in the way of Negro registration and voting. Federal judges were authorized to enjoin state officials from refusing to register qualified persons. The judges could fine recalcitrant officials up to $300 and could sentence them to forty-five days in jail, without a jury trial.

With the Supreme Court ruling out school segregation and the Congress legislating for civil rights, it seemed that a "second Reconstruction" was beginning, one that would complete the task of emancipation left unfinished in 1877.

A SECOND TERM FOR IKE

In 1955 President Eisenhower was at the height of his popularity. Only the anti-third-term Twenty-second Amendment, ratified in 1951 as a belated slap at Roosevelt, seemed to bar him from staying in the White House as long as he chose. Apparently his health was excellent, but while vacationing in Colorado, on the morning of September 24, he suffered a heart attack.

The President began to make a promising recovery, but no one expected him to run for another term. In June, stricken a second time, he was operated upon for ileitis. Although the operation was serious, Eisenhower's advisers never let the question arise whether or not he would continue as a candidate—and except among some Democrats it seemed a matter above debate. At the Republican convention in San Francisco at the end of August, he and Vice President Nixon were renominated by acclamation. The proceedings seemed to some observers to reflect more the atmosphere of a coronation than a party convention. Regardless of Eisenhower's overwhelming popularity, Adlai Stevenson and Estes Kefauver fought vigorously for the Democratic nomination in state primary after primary. In the end, Stevenson triumphed at the Democratic convention and Kefauver became the vice-presidential nominee.

It was a rather dull campaign. Stevenson sought an issue by proposing that the United States agree to end hydrogen bomb tests. The average voter, relieved because the stalemate in nuclear weapons seemed to rule out a third world war, refused to worry about international affairs until actual shooting in the Suez area just before Election Day sent him to seek refuge with Eisenhower as commander in chief. Altogether, about 58 percent of the voters marked their ballots for Eisenhower, although he was sixty-six, the oldest man ever to be re-elected to the presidency, and had suffered two serious illnesses in little more than a year past. He received more than 35 million votes to only 26 million for Stevenson and carried forty-one states. It was not much of a triumph for the Republican party. The prestige of the President pulled some Republican congressmen to narrow victories, but the Democrats continued to control both houses of Congress.

During President Eisenhower's second administration, domestic policies were little changed. In 1957 Congress occupied itself largely with trying to slash the President's $71.8 billion budget, the largest in peacetime history. Even Secretary of the Treasury Humphrey (who resigned a few months later) joined in the onslaught against the "terrific" expenditures.

At the close of 1957 the nation skidded into the most serious recession since the war. By late spring of 1958 industrial production had dropped 14 percent below the level of a year earlier, and approximately 5 million workers were unemployed. Again the so-called built-in stabilizers of the economy, such as unemployment insurance payments to those out of work, somewhat softened the blow of the recession.

As Republicans prepared for the congressional campaign of 1958, they were handicapped by the persistence of economic trouble. Some of the more conservative Republican candidates, most notably Senate Minority Leader William Knowland, running for governor of California, centered their campaigns around attacks on organized labor. In some states they sought "right-to-work" laws to outlaw union shops (plants in which every employee hired must join the union). This onslaught, in most states, succeeded only in ensuring a large labor vote for Democratic candidates. The Republican party was also weakened by the revelation in the spring of 1958 that Sherman Adams, in effect the President's chief of staff, had received gifts from a New England textile manufacturer. Adams resigned in September, too late to benefit the party.

The result on November 4, 1958, was a Democratic landslide of impressive proportions. The Democrats won 13 additional seats in the Senate, giving them a 62 to 34 majority. They gained an added 47 seats in the House of Representatives, providing a majority of 282 to 153 — the largest margin since Roosevelt's 1936 victory.

The voter reaction in 1958 had slight effect upon the national administration in the two years that followed. President Eisenhower presented Congress in January 1959 with a $77 billion budget, which he promised would be in balance — a budget that northern Democrats decried as not sufficiently large in an expanding economy and not providing the services the nation needed. At first the Democrats in Congress gave promise of pushing far beyond the President's limited requests. As prosperity returned in the spring of 1959, however, public opinion began to react to the incessant warnings of the President and of conservative publicists that budget balancing was the only way to avoid another ruinous round of inflation. Eisenhower, acting more vigorously than in previous years, was able to marshal much public support and congressional voting strength for his conservative course, and Speaker Sam Rayburn and Senate Majority Leader Lyndon B. Johnson were more disposed to compromise than to throw their large Democratic majorities against him. As a result, Eisenhower succeeded in keeping down expenditures for inexpensive public housing for families displaced from slums and for other social services. He also succeeded in ending the 1960 fiscal year with a billion-dollar surplus. In the following year, he repeated the battle over the 1961 budget, which proposed expenditures of $70.8 billion and a surplus of $4.2 billion. But by the fall of 1960 the economy had again stalled into a recession; tax revenue declined, and the fiscal year ended with a serious deficit.

In his final State of the Union message, in January 1961, President Eisenhower granted that problems of recession and unemployment left little room for complacency. But he pointed out that during his eight years in office the inflationary spiral had all but ceased and that the nation's output of goods and services had increased 25 percent; the income of the average American family, 15 percent; and the real wages of workers, 20 percent. "In a united determination to keep this nation strong and free and to utilize our vast resources for the advancement of all mankind," he asserted, "we have carried America to unprecedented heights."

The "New Frontier"

KENNEDY OVER NIXON

The presidential election of 1960 was notable both for its remarkable closeness and for the relative sobriety with which the two major candidates addressed themselves to the issues.

Kennedy won the Democratic nomination only after a vigorous struggle in the primaries. A forty-three-year-old senator from Massachusetts and a Roman Catholic, he was thought to

"The world is very different now," said President John F. Kennedy in his inaugural address, January 20, 1961, "for man holds in his mortal hands the power to abolish all forms of human poverty and all forms of human life." To achieve the promise and avoid the peril was the twofold challenge of the time. This was what Kennedy called the "New Frontier" — a new challenge to the old pioneering instincts of Americans.

Two Presidential Candidates Debate on Television
*Before an estimated audience of 70 million viewers, the 1960 Republican nominee,
Vice President Richard M. Nixon, and the Democratic nominee, Senator John F.
Kennedy, participated in an unprecedented series of televised debates. Until then,
the lesser-known Kennedy had seemed the underdog. "It was the sight of the two
men side by side that carried the punch," Theodore H. White has written. "There
was, first and above all, the crude, overwhelming impression that side by side the
two seemed evenly matched—and this even matching in the popular imagination
was for Kennedy a major victory. Until the cameras opened on the Senator and the
Vice President, Kennedy had been the boy under assault and attack by the Vice
President as immature, young, inexperienced. Now, obviously, in flesh and
behavior he was the Vice President's equal."*—The Making of the President 1960
(New York: Atheneum, 1961), p. 288. (NBC)

be handicapped by his youth and his religion.
In the primaries he had to dispose of a fellow
senator, Hubert Humphrey of Minnesota, who
was considered more liberal than he. Then, at
the convention in Los Angeles, he had to overcome the powerful opposition of Lyndon B.
Johnson of Texas, the Senate majority leader.
In the 1930s, Johnson had been one of the cote-
rie of ardent New Dealers. By 1960, without
entirely abandoning his earlier allegiances, he
had become the most respected spokesman of
the industrialized and conservative South.
When Kennedy won the presidential nomination, he offered the vice-presidential nomina-

tion to Johnson, who accepted and campaigned
energetically.

The Republican nomination went almost
by default to Vice President Richard M. Nixon,
whom President Eisenhower favored. Nixon's
only rival, Governor Nelson Rockefeller of
New York, dropped out of the contest months
before the primaries. Henry Cabot Lodge,
ambassador to the United Nations, was nominated for Vice President.

Kennedy and Nixon represented the
broad moderate position within their respective parties, though Kennedy was slightly to the
left of center and Nixon slightly to the right. As

Vice President, Nixon had enjoyed eight years on the front pages and had even argued with Khrushchev in Moscow. Thus he was able to offer a continuation of President Eisenhower's "peace and prosperity," and—though he was only four years older than Kennedy—mature leadership.

When Kennedy challenged Nixon to a series of television debates, Nixon's advisers thought Kennedy would be no match for their man, and they agreed to four joint appearances. In the first debate, however, everything went wrong for Nixon. Not yet recovered from an illness, he appeared tired, haggard, and heavy-jowled, in contrast to Kennedy, who seemed relaxed, self-confident, and well informed—before an estimated 70 million television viewers. From then on, Kennedy seemed to take the lead from Nixon.

The business recession also hurt the Republicans. Nevertheless, in the closing days of the campaign, a vigorous Republican campaign drive, with the aid of President Eisenhower, brought a hairline decision at the polls. Out of 68,836,000 votes cast, Kennedy received 34,227,000 or 49.7 percent, and Nixon, 34,109,000 or 49.5 percent. (The remaining 502,000 votes were divided among thirteen minor candidates.)

Before the election, Kennedy had hoped that on taking office he could push through Congress a legislative program as sweeping as that of Franklin D. Roosevelt during the first hundred days of the New Deal. Kennedy did not abandon his reform plans, but the closeness of the decision led him to move with caution. Unlike the Eisenhower cabinet, which had predominantly represented business, the Kennedy cabinet balanced the economic and political as well as the regional interests in the nation. The most controversial of the appointments was that of Kennedy's thirty-five-year-old brother and campaign manager, Robert F. Kennedy, as attorney general.

Election of 1960

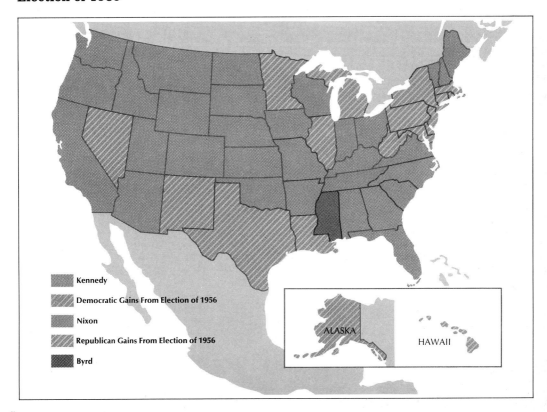

Kennedy

Democratic Gains From Election of 1956

Nixon

Republican Gains From Election of 1956

Byrd

ALASKA

HAWAII

THE KENNEDY PROGRAM

President Kennedy—the youngest man, except for Theodore Roosevelt, ever to occupy the White House—sent a record number of messages, twenty-five, to the first session of the Eighty-seventh Congress. Some called for long-range national undertakings: economic recovery and growth, health care for the aged, federal aid for schools, conservation and use of natural resources, highway construction, housing and community development.

The existence of a Democratic majority in each house did not mean that Kennedy could count upon an easy enactment of his program, since many Democrats were conservative and frequently voted with the Republicans.

By dint of persuasion and compromise he managed to obtain considerable legislation. An improvement in the minimum-wage law provided considerably less coverage than the President had wished, but it did bring an additional 3,624,000 workers under the law. It raised the minimum hourly pay rate, effective in several steps over two to four years, from $1.00 to $1.25. Another measure increased social security benefits substantially along the lines of the President's recommendations. The Housing Act of 1961 fully embodied his proposals, authorizing $4.9 billion in federal grants or loans over a four-year period for the preservation of open spaces in cities, the development of local mass transit systems, and the construction of middle-income housing. Congressional conservatives dealt the President two sharp setbacks when they defeated his bills to provide medical care for the aged and federal aid for school construction and teachers' salaries.

Kennedy obtained from Congress additional expenditures for unemployment compensation and aid to depressed areas—appropriations totaling $900 million. The only other large additions to the federal budget were $4 billion in defense spending to meet new challenges from Russia and large amounts of farm crop subsidies that had to be paid by virtue of earlier legislation. These expenditures were sufficient to bring about, well before the end of 1961, a substantial economic recovery.

But employment improved only slightly; in a time of record prosperity over 5 percent of the working force had no job. Out of a total of approximately 4.4 million unemployed (as of March 1962) between 1 and 2 million were for-

merly connected with eight industries in which the total number of jobs had declined from 7.5 million to 5 million in the years since World War II. Among these industries were textiles, coal, automobiles, and aircraft. The Kennedy administration tried to eliminate such unemployment through the retraining of dismissed workmen under the Manpower Training Bill and through the establishment of new industries in chronically depressed areas under the Area Redevelopment Act.

During his first two years in office, Kennedy emphasized that, because of the inflationary danger, the budget must be kept balanced. He also used his presidential power vigorously to try to prevent inflationary moves on the part of labor and industry. In the spring of 1962 he persuaded the United Steel Workers to accept a contract granting only small wage increases. When, almost immediately, United States Steel and most other companies unexpectedly announced 3.5-percent price increases, the President exploded with anger. During the three days that followed, he brought every variety of pressure he could muster, until the steel companies returned to their old prices. The cost to Kennedy was the hostility of the business community, which vented its anger upon him and blamed him for a stock-market drop a few weeks later. A year afterward, in the spring of 1963, when steel companies announced limited increases in prices, the President commented only that the companies had shown some restraint; he hoped the steel union and steel users would do likewise.

By January 1963 Kennedy had become convinced that the only way to stimulate economic growth and to reduce unemployment was a bold tax cut. He proposed to Congress a reduction of $13.5 billion in income taxes over a period of three years.

Kennedy was also becoming convinced that the government must do more than it had done for the Negroes—to whose votes he owed his narrow victory in the 1960 election. Nearly a decade after the Supreme Court's historic decision against segregation, the equal-rights movement was making little or no progress.

The National Association for the Advancement of Colored People (NAACP), which had led the cause, was still pressing lawsuits and seeking court orders, but more and more Negroes were growing impatient with its methods and were embittered by white obstruction of

**Martin Luther King Holding a Press Conference
at Birmingham, Alabama 1963**

*Throughout his years as head of the Southern Christian Leadership Conference,
King insisted that the civil rights movement must be nonviolent. He stated his
vision most vividly for America in August 1963 when during the "March on
Washington" he asserted from the steps of the Lincoln Memorial: "I have a dream
that one day this nation will rise up and live out the true meaning of its creed:
'We hold these truths to be self-evident, that all men are created equal.'. . . I have
a dream that my four little children will one day live in a nation where they will
not be judged by the color of their skin, but by the content of their character. This
is our hope. This is the faith that I go back to the South with—with this faith we
will be able to hew out of the mountain of despair a stone of hope." (Magnum)*

the cause. Blacks began to form more militant organizations. A desperate minority of perhaps 200,000 joined the Black Muslims and, in a spirit reminiscent of the Garvey black nationalism of the 1920s, proclaimed black supremacy and demanded a complete separation of the races. Others continued to struggle for integration but turned to direct action through new organizations such as the Congress of Racial Equality (CORE) and the Southern Christian Leadership Conference. The SCLC was led by an eloquent young Baptist minister, Dr. Martin Luther King, Jr., who had gained national and international fame as an advocate of passive resistance and, for his work, was to win the Nobel Peace Prize in 1964.

In the South, beginning in 1960, youthful blacks with some white sympathizers engaged in "sit-ins" to demand the right to eat in restaurants or at lunch counters or the right to use books in the main public libraries rather than in segregated branches. Negroes and whites went on "freedom rides" to desegregate inter-state buses and terminals. Thousands engaging in mass demonstrations accepted arrest; on several occasions the jails of Southern cities were filled to overflowing. Demonstrations spread to the North in mass attacks against de facto segregation in schools and housing and against the exclusion of all but a handful of Negroes from various kinds of employment. By the summer of 1963 the movement had reached such a peak that it was being proclaimed by news magazines as the "Negro revolution." More than 200,000 demonstrators (10 to 15 per-cent of them white) participated in a "March on Washington," converging on the Lincoln Me-morial.

In areas where federal power could be invoked, those protesting against segregation received the support of the Kennedy adminis-tration. Attorney General Robert F. Kennedy mustered federal force behind the integration of interstate transportation, and the President sent troops to the University of Mississippi to protect a Negro, James Meredith, who had been enrolled by order of a federal court. Throughout the South campaigns were under way to enroll Negro voters under the protec-tion of the civil rights legislation of 1957. As pressure intensified in 1963, President Kenne-dy threw the prestige of his administration be-hind the most comprehensive civil rights bill ever presented to Congress.

"LET US CONTINUE"

In the fall of 1963, though congressional con-servatives were blocking enactment of the two major bills in the New Frontier program, the civil rights and tax-cut measures, President Kennedy felt optimistic. He was looking ahead to the election of 1964, which most observers thought would result in his own reelection by a comfortable margin. He hoped that the election would bring to Washington a more liberal Con-gress.

To court Southern support, Kennedy visit-ed Florida and then Texas in November 1963. The Texas trip began well. On Friday, Novem-ber 22, as he drove through the streets of Dal-las, to the cheers of an enthusiastic crowd, the wife of Governor John Connally of Texas re-marked to him: "You can't say that Dallas isn't

friendly to you today." As Kennedy started to reply, he was hit in the neck by a bullet; anoth-er bullet struck the back of his head. His bleed-ing head cradled in the lap of his wife Jacque-line, he was rushed to a hospital.

An assassin, shooting three times in quick succession from a sixth-floor window, had killed President Kennedy and seriously wounded Governor Connally. Police arrested Lee Harvey Oswald, a self-styled Marxist who had once tried to expatriate himself in Russia, and charged him with the murder both of the President and a policeman. Piece after piece of circumstantial evidence seemed to tie Oswald to the murders, but through hours of question-ing he continued to protest his innocence. Two days after the shooting, while he was in the Dallas city jail, on his way to be transferred to the county jail, he was himself murdered by a Dallas night-club operator, before an incredu-lous national television audience. Inevitably rumors spread concerning the possibility that a ramifying plot lay behind President Kennedy's assassination. In an effort to eliminate uncer-tainties, a presidential commission headed-by Chief Justice Warren sifted through the evidence and several months later reported to the American people that Oswald had been a lone assassin.

About two hours after the assassination, Vice President Lyndon B. Johnson was sworn in as the thirty-sixth President of the United States. When he addressed a joint session of Congress on November 27, President Johnson expressed his main theme in the words "let us continue." The most fitting memorial to Kenne-dy, he reminded Congress, would be the enact-ment of the civil rights and tax bills and, in-deed, the whole agenda of the New Frontier.

The Eighty-eighth Congress responded and, in its 1964 session, enacted not only sever-al vital measures of the New Frontier program but also one of President Johnson's own rec-ommendations, an antipoverty bill. In getting the program adopted, the new President uti-lized to the utmost the formidable political skills he had perfected earlier as Senate majority leader. Not only did he conciliate and persuade congressional majorities; he also built a great national following.

From the outset, Johnson assiduously courted businessmen. Most of them were Re-publicans, and the proposal of a tax cut deliber-

President Johnson Takes the Oath of Office

With Mrs. Johnson (left) and Mrs. Kennedy at his side, Lyndon Baines Johnson took his oath of office as President on the afternoon of November 22, 1963, before Judge Sarah T. Hughes aboard the presidential airplane at Dallas, Texas. Johnson, born on a cattle ranch near Stonewall, Texas, on August 27, 1908, was of Confederate forebears, but considered himself more a Westerner than a Southerner. He had to bear the handicap of being regarded as a Southerner in national politics, even though he pointed with pride to his grandfather, who had been a Populist member of the Texas legislature, and his father, who had also served in the legislature and had been a firm opponent of the Ku Klux Klan. Johnson taught elementary school for a year after graduating from Southwest Texas State Teachers College, then became secretary to a Texas congressman. An ardent New Dealer, he was Texas director of the National Youth Administration and, after his election to the House of Representatives in 1937, a protégé of President Roosevelt. When Roosevelt died, Johnson said: "He was just like a daddy to me always." After an initial defeat, Johnson won election to the United States Senate in 1948 by a primary margin of eighty-seven votes. As senator from a state in which new business and industrial interests were increasingly powerful, Johnson came to be known less for his liberalism (which he continued to avow) than for his moderation. He liked to quote, as had his father, the words of the prophet Isaiah: "Come, let us reason together." An unparalleled master of the arts of political persuasion, Johnson rose to the position of Senate majority leader. Again and again he managed to bring together and to compromise the differences among Democratic senators from South and North. As Vice President, Johnson lacked the opportunity to practice these arts: he spent much of his time on missions outside the United States. When he was suddenly elevated to the Presidency, he pointed out to the Congress that he had taken the leadership in obtaining the civil rights acts of 1957 and 1960. Once again he undertook to bridge divisions of opinion in order to obtain constructive legislation. (Wide World)

ately creating a deficit in the budget at a time of prosperity went diametrically against their economic thinking. Nevertheless, after Congress passed the legislation early in 1964, the reduction of taxes seemed to stimulate an unprecedented continuation of prosperity and economic growth. By the beginning of 1965, the United States had experienced four years of boom without recession, a peacetime record since 1945. The rate of unemployment had dropped to about 5 percent for the first time in years.

To the delight of many businessmen, Johnson accompanied the lowering of taxes with the presentation of a federal budget smaller than they had anticipated for the 1965 fiscal year. Despite the overall cutback, he was able to increase expenditures on health, education, and welfare, through sharp limitation of the defense budget. While courting business, the administration remained on cordial terms with labor leaders. Workingmen shared in the boom as take-home pay rose 4 percent in 1964.

To aid those who were not sharing in the national prosperity, the President in January 1964 called upon Congress to enact a thirteen-point program that would declare "unconditional war on poverty." In August 1964 the anti-poverty bill was passed. It called for the establishment of VISTA, a volunteer corps of social workers, and for remedial education, vocational training, part-time employment for teen-agers and students, and federal grants to states or communities for local attacks on poverty. The initial budget was almost a billion dollars.

COMMITMENT TO EQUAL RIGHTS

Throughout the nation the problem of civil rights was closely related to that of poverty. A large proportion of the very poor were Negroes, unable either South or North to obtain adequately paid, secure employment. In cities like New York, Negroes (together with Puerto Ricans) filled a large number of badly paid service positions and jobs not requiring skill. The average Harlem family received $2,000 a year less in income than its white neighbors. Of the Negroes (largely youths) 13 percent were unemployed, since the poorer jobs were the sort being most rapidly eliminated by automation. Either through discrimination or through lack of training, young people were barred from more highly skilled work. Many Northern Negroes were crowded into substandard housing, and their children were enrolled in poor schools integrated only in name.

A number of young Northerners went to Mississippi in the summer of 1964 to enroll several thousand young Negroes in "Freedom Schools" and to conduct drives registering Negroes to vote. Three of the first civil rights workers to arrive disappeared; after some weeks the FBI found their bodies buried deep beneath an earthen dam.

As the struggle intensified, President Johnson threw his weight behind the comprehensive civil rights bill that Kennedy had presented to Congress. Bipartisan leadership in the Senate finally overcame Southern opposition. In June 1964, for the first time in history, the Senate voted to end a filibuster, so that the bill could be passed. The Civil Rights Act of 1964 strengthened earlier legislation to protect the voting rights of Negroes and to expedite the desegregation of schools. It also prohibited discrimination in public accommodations and facilities and in private employment.

After the act went into effect, Negroes ate with whites for the first time in some restaurants in the deep South, stayed in some hotels and motels, sat in "white only" sections of motion-picture theaters, and swam in previously segregated swimming pools. Compliance was not universal, and several test cases challenging the constitutionality of the law were brought before federal courts.

In 1965 violence again erupted in the South, especially in Selma, Alabama, where masses of Negroes and a few white sympathizers demonstrated in protest against registration procedures which kept Negroes off the voting rolls. The state police brutally broke up a parade, and assassins (said to be Klansmen) murdered two white civil rights workers from the North. To protect the demonstrators, President Johnson called up the Alabama National Guard. He also persuaded Congress to pass a bill guaranteeing the right to vote in presidential, senatorial, and congressional elections. This law provided for federal registration of voters in those states where there were literacy or other special tests for registering and where fewer than half of the people of voting age actually went to the polls.

ONE MAN, ONE VOTE

Meanwhile, constitutional amendments and court decisions were affecting, actually or potentially, the political rights of many Americans, both Negro and white.

The Twenty-third Amendment (1961) gave the franchise in presidential elections to residents of the District of Columbia. Home rule for Washington, which had the highest percentage of Negroes of any city in the country, continued to be withheld by Congress.

The Twenty-fourth Amendment (1964) gave symbolic, if not much practical, aid to Negro voters by providing that the right to vote in any primary or other federal election should not be abridged for failing to pay a poll tax. Most states in the deep South were using methods other than the poll tax to try to disfranchise Negroes.

An issue involving the rights of representation of a large part of the American electorate came before the Supreme Court in 1962, in a case involving the apportionment of legislative districts in Tennessee. Although the state constitution called for reapportionment every ten years, none had taken place since 1901, with the result that rural dominance in the legislature was out of all proportion to population. Moore County, with a population of 3,454, sent one legislator; Shelby County (Memphis), with 627,019 residents, sent only three. A vote in Moore County was worth more than sixty times as much as one in Shelby County. By a 6-to-2 decision, the Supreme Court gave the federal district court a mandate to order reapportionment if it found a violation of the Constitution. Similar inequities existed in a surprising number of other states; in all but six states, fewer than 40 percent of the population could elect a majority of the legislature. As a result of the Tennessee decision, many states quickly made some reapportionment of their legislative districts, either as a result of court action or as a means of forestalling it.

An even more important Supreme Court decision (in *Reynold* v. *Sims*, 1964) held that congressional districts within a state also must be substantially equal in population. The case before the court involved the congressional district containing the city of Atlanta, Georgia, a district that had a population of 820,000 as compared with the population of 270,000 in another Georgia district. Several state legislatures quietly initiated a counteraction by endorsing a constitutional amendment (proposed by the National Legislative Conference) which would negate federally enforced reapportionment. Within a few years, thirty-three legislatures had approved it. If one more should act, Congress would be required, according to the Constitution, to call a national convention to consider submitting the proposal to the states for their ratification. The movement lost its chief congressional sponsor, however, when Senator Everett Dirksen of Illinois died in 1969.

The "Great Society"

As he took up and expanded the Kennedy program, President Johnson restated the objective as the creation of the "Great Society." "For half a century we called upon unbounded invention and untiring industry to create an order of plenty for all our people," he declared in May 1964. "The challenge of the next half century is whether we have the wisdom to use that wealth to enrich and elevate our national life — and to advance the quality of American civilization."

But President Johnson himself was to jeopardize the "Great Society" program when, in 1965, he committed the country to large-scale war in faraway Vietnam.

JOHNSON THRASHES GOLDWATER

In the presidential campaign of 1964 the moderate liberalism for which Johnson had spoken confronted extreme conservatism.

In the years following the collapse of McCarthyism, militant conservatives in the United States had organized a number of action groups. The best known was the John Birch Society, whose founder, Robert Welch, called for the impeachment of Chief Justice Earl Warren and seemed to suspect the loyalty of even President Eisenhower. Senator Barry Goldwater of Arizona, though not himself a member of the so-called radical right organiza-

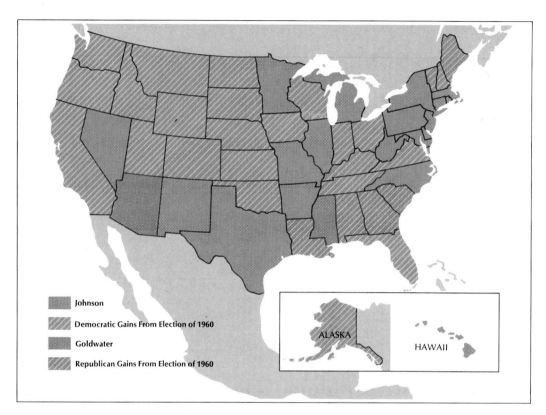

Johnson

Democratic Gains From Election of 1960

Goldwater

Republican Gains From Election of 1960

ALASKA

HAWAII

Election of 1964

tions, became the hero of most of these groups. In the Senate he had voted against tax reduction and against the antipoverty and civil rights bills.

At the Republican convention in San Francisco, the Goldwater forces were in complete command from the outset. They produced a platform conforming to their conservative philosophy and making no concessions to the moderate and liberal wings of the party. When Governor Nelson A. Rockefeller of New York tried to obtain a stronger civil rights plank, they hooted him down. Nor did Goldwater try to "balance the ticket" in his vice-presidential choice — Representative William E. Miller of New York stood staunchly to the right. Goldwater received tumultuous applause when, in his acceptance address, he declared: "I would remind you that extremism in the defense of liberty is no vice! And let me remind you also that moderation in the pursuit of justice is no virtue!"

As Senator Goldwater carried the Republican party far to the right, President Johnson tried to preempt not only the center of the road but also a wide strip to both the right and the left of it. Although he had been President for only nine months when the Democratic convention met at Atlantic City late in August 1964, he was firmly in control of his party. His main concern seemed to be to achieve as broad a consensus as possible in the platform. His supporters worked to minimize differences between the North and the South, especially over the seating of delegates. Delegates from Mississippi and Alabama were denied votes unless they pledged themselves to support the party's candidates in the November election, and most of them departed. Two votes were given to a Negro delegation representing the new Freedom Democratic party of Mississippi. In addition, the convention voted that in 1968 it would seat only those delegations that were chosen in a nondiscriminatory way.

The only drama in the convention concerned the question of whom President Johnson would ask the delegates to nominate for Vice President. Earlier he had eliminated one of the party's favorites, Attorney General Robert Kennedy, brother of the assassinated President. When Johnson, in person, revealed his choice to the convention, it was Senator Hubert Humphrey of Minnesota, identified with the liberal wing of the Democratic party.

Paradoxically, the campaign was one of the most hectic and yet one of the dullest ever to weary the electorate. In contrast to the comparatively precise debates of four years earlier, neither candidate ever went much beyond his acceptance speech. Yet each campaigned incessantly, often spanning the continent by jet in a day's appearances. Much of the Goldwater campaign centered upon charges of corruption and moral malaise in Washington. In mid-October, Johnson's chief White House aide was forced to resign because of personal scandal, but that same week the American people were even more startled by news of the precipitate removal of Nikita Khrushchev from the leadership of the U.S.S.R. New uncertainties abroad seemed to help drive the voters toward the President. Throughout the campaign President Johnson was as wary of making specific, detailed promises as Eisenhower had been in 1956 and Roosevelt in 1936; his best strategy seemed to be merely to gather the votes against Goldwater.

And gather them he did. He received more votes, over 42 million, and a larger plurality than any other candidate in history. On election night he told the American people that he regarded the overwhelming victory as a "mandate for unity." It gave him and the Democratic majority in Congress an opportunity to move on toward what he had been describing as the "Great Society," a society as free as it could be from poverty, prejudice, ignorance, and ugliness.

THE JOHNSON PROGRAM

When the Eighty-ninth Congress convened, President Johnson presented to it comprehensive proposals to make a beginning toward his long-range goals. With unprecedented speed, almost all of this far-ranging program became law. The overwhelmingly Democratic majorities in Congress, which had accompanied the landslide victory over Goldwater, were Johnson's to command.

A new immigration law, in response to the demands of urban and minority groups in America, abolished the inequities of the quota system established in the 1920s. The quota for England and Ireland of 83,000 persons per year had been seldom filled; that for Greece was only 308 persons. Gradually the government eliminated these quotas and began to allot visas not on a basis of national origins but giving preference on a basis of education and skills. Soon there were complaints that only an elite of professionals could enter the United States and that other nations, especially underdeveloped ones, were suffering a "brain drain" of their doctors, engineers, and highly educated specialists. In 1966 relatives of United States citizens began to receive preference, and a quota of 17,000 was set for professionals. Immigration from northwestern Europe declined and that from southern Europe and Asia increased.

Massive sustained federal aid to education at last began. President Johnson succeeded in circumventing the impasse in Congress over the question of whether parochial schools should receive a share of federal funds. He called for grants for text and library books for students in both public and parochial schools — and significantly the grants were to be made on the basis of the needs of individual students, not schools, a formula that the Supreme Court had approved when it applied to federal funds that were to provide milk or transportation to students. The Elementary and Secondary Education Act of 1965 and subsequent legislation gave aid to schools in both urban and rural areas in proportion to the number of poverty-stricken students in them. Federal funds purchased textbooks and library materials, financed special programs for adults and for the handicapped, and strengthened state educational agencies. Total federal expenditures in education and technical training rose from less than $5 billion in 1964 to more than $12 billion in 1967.

The establishment of Medicare for the 19 million Americans over sixty-five through the Medicare-Social Security Act of 1965 altered the lives of old people and had great impact upon American medicine. The debate over Medicare, which had been so bitter for twenty years, ended as the program went into effect. Expected resistance did not materialize. In the South, where hospitals had to accept desegregation in order to obtain funds, nearly nine-tenths of the hospitals complied. But numerous practical problems arose that made future adjustments likely. It was particularly difficult to institute the program in an era of rapidly rising costs. Objections to complicated paper work led more than half the nation's doctors to force patients to pay directly; patients were required to submit receipted bills for government reimbursement. The irritations were serious, but less important than the fact that large numbers of older people were receiving care that they could not previously have obtained or that would have exhausted their savings.

Rising costs also created problems for the Medicaid program, which was launched in 1968 to provide financial assistance to persons who were not old enough to qualify for Medicare but were too poor to pay their own medical bills. Under the Medicaid law each state was to set up its own plan, determining payments and standards of eligibility for them, and the federal government was to contribute from 50 to 80 percent of the expense. During the first year, however, the program cost the federal government more than ten times as much as had been expected. Congress and the state legislatures therefore changed their definition of the needy so as to make the benefits available to fewer people than had originally been covered.

Medicare and Medicaid were parts of the effort to eradicate the "pockets of poverty" within the prosperous nation. More than 9 mil-

By the 1960s, when President Johnson began his "war on poverty," the total family income of Americans had more than doubled since the depression decade of the 1930s. But shares of this income going to lower-income groups had increased only slightly. A great gap between the rich and the poor remained. In this chart the first "pie" shows the percentages of the total income for 1936 received by the poorest fifth of the people, the richest fifth, and the three fifths in between. The second pie reflects the same data for 1962. (Courtesy of W. E. Brownlee)

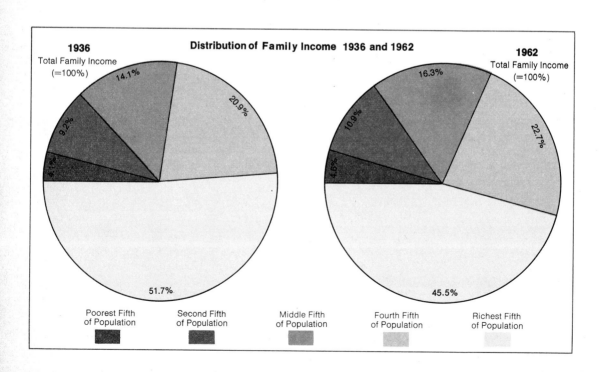

Distribution of Family Income 1936 and 1962

1936
Total Family Income (=100%)

14.1%
20.9%
9.2%
4.0%
51.7%

1962
Total Family Income (=100%)

16.3%
22.7%
10.9%
4.6%
45.5%

| Poorest Fifth of Population | Second Fifth of Population | Middle Fifth of Population | Fourth Fifth of Population | Richest Fifth of Population |

lion people classified as poor were receiving no aid from federal food programs, a Senate subcommittee learned. There was hunger in great cities, in Appalachia, the deep South, the Southwest, and on Indian reservations. Yet over 5 million people were receiving aid through federal food programs; either they were given food or could purchase it with reduced-cost stamps. Many millions were receiving other types of relief.

The poverty program of President Johnson, continuing and expanding that of Kennedy, approached the problem in numerous ways. By 1966 the Office of Economic Opportunity, established in 1964, had put about two-fifths of its budget into a variety of Community Action Programs. Another two-fifths went into youth programs—the Job Corps, Neighborhood Youth Corps, and College Work Study. Most of the remaining funds went into the Work Experience Program. VISTA (Volunteers in Service to America) served as a kind of Peace Corps at home.

While social security aided the considerable proportion of the poor who were aged, the Office of Economic Opportunity placed its emphasis upon helping the great numbers of poor among the young. The 1,000 core Community Action Programs were locally proposed and operated, in part by poor people themselves. Some of these programs not only gave poor people an opportunity to help themselves but gave them some feeling of political power. The job-training efforts, however, proved more expensive and less effective than had been predicted.

Especially among the urban Negro unemployed, the job-training programs were a disappointment. Although Negroes began to penetrate the ranks of the white-collar workers, the total numbers were small. Nominally, union restrictions against them no longer existed, yet few could gain employment as skilled, highly paid construction workers. Industries that might have hired Negroes were moving out of the cities, away from where they lived. The training programs could not easily provide the overall education and motivation that most of these unemployed Negroes lacked. A New York Negro woman declared in despair, "We are being trained for the unemployed."

While starting his "war on poverty," Johnson was escalating his war in Vietnam. The enormous costs of the latter made it more and more difficult to pay for the former.

BLACK POWER

The Negro population had been increasing more rapidly than the white population and had been shifting from the rural South to the cities throughout the nation, especially in the North. In 1910 only about a quarter of the Negroes lived in cities, and only a tenth outside the South; by 1966 69 percent were living in metropolitan areas; 45 percent were living outside the South. In several of the largest cities, the proportion of Negroes at least doubled between 1950 and 1968. Negroes constituted at least 30 percent of the population of seven of these cities and 66.6 percent of the population of Washington, D.C. A corresponding exodus of whites from the cities to the suburbs dramatically increased the areas of residential and school segregation in the "black ghettos."

While urban Negroes were sharing in the national prosperity, their proportional gains were decidedly less than those of the whites. Indeed, the gap between their incomes and those of whites was growing wider. Impatient urban Negroes, disappointed at the meager return that cooperation seemed to have brought them, began increasingly to turn toward other possible solutions: black power, separatism, or even violence.

With increasing rapidity after 1964, the United States moved into a double crisis, compounded of rioting in the poverty-stricken Negro areas in Northern cities and escalation of the intervention in Vietnam into a major—but stalemated—military confrontation. Each crisis interacted with the other. White college and university students and Northern liberals shifted their efforts from the civil rights drive in the South to concentrate on protest against the Vietnam War. Negroes in the rural South, and even more in the urban North, increasingly sought to take their destiny into their own hands through their own organizations, independent of aid or funds from whites.

The gradual shift from white participation and leadership to Negro domination of civil rights organizations was one indication of the new mood. The Congress of Racial Equality (CORE), founded in 1941–1942, had long been

Black Power: SNCC Paper

If we are to proceed toward true liberation, we must cut ourselves off from white people. We must form our own institutions, credit unions, co-ops, political parties, write our own histories, . . .

. . . on whatever level of contact . . . blacks and whites come together, that meeting or confrontation is not on the level of the blacks but always on the level of the whites. This only means that our everyday contact with whites is a reinforcement of the myth of white supremacy. Whites are the ones who must try to raise themselves to our humanistic level. We are not, after all, the ones who are responsible for a genocidal war in Vietnam; we are not the ones who are responsible for neocolonialism in Africa and Latin America; we are not the ones who held a people in animalistic bondage over 400 years. We reject the American dream as defined by white people and must work to construct an American reality defined by Afro-Americans. — Position paper by members of the Student Nonviolent Coordinating Committee, 1966.

---

the most interracial of the organizations, but by 1962 was predominantly Negro; after 1965 CORE allowed only Negro leadership in its chapters. At their height these organizations through direct action did succeed in obtaining some votes for Negroes and political participation, even in Alabama and Mississippi. In the North they helped force open new, desirable employment opportunities for adequately educated Negroes. But they could not change the inferior conditions under which most Negroes suffered. Their failure helped stimulate feelings of separateness and militancy among Negro youth in the large cities.

Out of James Meredith's march southward from Memphis, Tennessee, to Jackson, Mississippi, in June 1966 there grew the concept of black power. Politically it meant separate action through which blocs of Negro voters would win control in Northern ghettos or the Southern black belt. Economically it meant creating Negro business to serve Negroes. CORE and SNCC (the Student Nonviolent Coordinating Committee) became associated with the concept of black power — of Negro separateness. In some respects black power seemed to critics to be retrogressive, a harking back to the proposals of Booker T. Washington; it seemed to propose a withdrawal comparable to that which white racists had been demanding. Black militants replied that Negroes by themselves must attain economic and political parity with the white population before effective integration could take place.

On August 11, 1965, a Negro crowd had gathered in Watts, a Los Angeles suburb, to protest a traffic arrest; a policeman hit a bystander with his club, and several days of violence were touched off. Before the rioting was over, thirty-four people had been killed, hundreds wounded, and some $35 million in property destroyed. White Americans, hopeful that the civil rights movement was solving Negro problems, were shocked out of their optimism.

In the summer of 1966 there were forty-three outbreaks, with especially serious trouble in Chicago and Cleveland. In the summer of 1967 there were eight major riots. In the worst of these, at Detroit, forty-three persons (thirty-three Negroes, and ten whites) were killed. On their television screens, the people of the nation saw alarming scenes of arson, plunder, and military action. President Johnson, calling for law and order, warned also that the only genuine long-range solution must be an attack upon the conditions that were causing despair and violence. He appointed a group of distinguished citizens to a commission to investigate the disorders and recommend preventive measures for the future.

The report of the Commission on Civil Disorders, which appeared in the spring of 1968, deflated numerous wild stories: there had been few black snipers, and no organized conspiracy instigating and directing the riots. The report pointed to the complexities of the problems facing the occupants of the Negro ghettos, and it

Black Power: Commission's Report

What is new about "Black Power" is phraseology rather than substance. . . . The decade after World War I— which saw the militant, race-proud "new negro," the relatively widespread theory of retaliatory violence, and the high tide of the Negro-support-of-Negro-business ideology— exhibits striking parallels with the 1960's. . . .

Black Power rhetoric and ideology actually express a lack of power. The slogan emerged when the Negro protest movement was slowing down, when it was finding increasing resistance to its changing goals, when it discovered that nonviolent direct action was no more a panacea than legal action. . . . This combination of circumstances provoked anger deepened by impotence. Powerless to make any fundamental changes in the life of the masses—powerless, that is, to compel white America to make those changes—many advocates of Black Power have retreated into an unreal world, where they see an outnumbered and poverty-stricken minority organizing itself independently of whites and creating sufficient power to force white America to grant its demands. . . .

The Black Power advocates of today consciously feel that they are the most militant group in the Negro protest movement. Yet they have retreated from a direct confrontation with American society on the issue of integration and, by preaching separatism, unconsciously function as an accommodation to white racism. — Report of the National Advisory Commission on Civil Disorders, 1968.

recommended massive spending to erase these ghettos and the inequities their occupants suffered. "Only a commitment to national action on an unprecedented scale can shape a future compatible with the historic ideals of American society," the commission concluded. But Congress proceeded to cut rather than to increase spending for the alleviation of urban poverty.

In April 1968 the assassination of Dr. Martin Luther King, Jr., shocked the nation but did not alter the economizing mood of Congress. King, whose insistence upon Gandhi-like nonviolent techniques seemed old-fashioned to black militants, was preparing to lead a protest march on behalf of striking garbage workers in Memphis, Tennessee. While standing on a motel balcony, he was struck by a sniper's bullet and died within a few minutes. King's death touched off the most widespread rioting the nation had yet undergone in the Negro areas of cities from coast to coast. Looting and arson were endemic; forty persons were killed. Washington was the worst hit, as fires gutted buildings within sight of the Capitol and the White House. Yet within the Negro districts, innumerable residents worked doggedly to end the disorders. Simultaneously the nation mourned the assassinated leader, as King was given a funeral bringing together an assem-

blage of notables and receiving television coverage exceeded only by that of President Kennedy.

Within a week Congress responded by enacting the Civil Rights Act of 1968, which had been pending for two years. It outlawed racial discrimination in the sale and rental of four-fifths of all homes and apartments. But as poor people assembled in Washington a few weeks later in the campaign that King had been planning at the time of his death, Congress was still preoccupied with economy and little disposed to provide financial aid for them.

THE PAN-INDIAN MOVEMENT

The Indian population, growing much faster than the population as a whole, nearly doubled during the twenty years after 1950. By 1970 the total had reached about 800,000, of whom more than half lived on or near reservations and most of the rest in cities. The population increase had come in spite of a lower-than-average life expectancy. Indeed, the descendants of the aborigines were, as a group, much worse off than other Americans, even those of African descent. Annual family income for Indians was $1,000 less than for blacks, and the unemploy-

The Plight of the Indian

	American Indian	U.S.
Suicides (1970)	32.0 per 100,000	16.0 per 100,000
Life expectancy (1970)	47 years	70.8 years
Unemployment rate (1972)	45% estimated	5.8%
Median family income (1971)	$4,000	$9,867
Infant mortality (1970)	30.9 per 1,000 live births	21.8 per 1,000 live births
Percent entering college (1971)	18%	50%

ment rate for Indians was ten times the national rate. Suicides among Indian youth were one hundred times as frequent as among white youth.

Despite the 1924 grant of citizenship to all Indians, those on the reservations continued to be treated as "wards of the nation," with little or no control over their own affairs. They had been promised a New Deal in the Indian Reorganization Act of 1934, which had been ex-

pected to reverse the policy laid down in the Dawes Severalty Act of 1887. Presumably the Bureau of Indian Affairs would no longer try to make white farmers out of Indians but, under the 1934 law, would encourage the revitalization of aboriginal culture and tribal government. Congress failed to provide sufficient funds, however, to help the Indians advance very far in the new direction. Then, in 1953, Congress reverted to the old policy of forcing

Indians at Alcatraz
Indians occupying Alcatraz Island, the site of an abandoned federal prison in San Francisco Bay, to demonstrate for Indian rights, raise clenched fists as they vote down a proposal that they allow the island to be converted into a national park. Photograph taken April 8, 1970. (Wide World)

V. AFTER WORLD WAR II:
A Period of Experimentation

Plate 1: Willem de Kooning, UNTITLED
(Gift of Messrs. Julian J. & Joachim Jean Aberbach, New York; Brandeis University Art Collection)

Since World War II, the American artist has no longer needed to look to European sources for his training and standards. For the last thirty years, not Paris but New York City has been the center of artistic innovation.

The first movement to focus attention on the United States as the artistic center was Abstract Expressionism, a uniquely American invention, based on abstraction and reflecting the emotional intensity of the times. The movement can be traced to the early 1940s, and first appeared in the work of Jackson Pollock in the years immediately after the war. Pollock, whose earlier style had been influenced by the Regionalist Thomas Hart Benton, came in contact during this period with a group of European painters who had fled Nazi Germany and emigrated to New

Plate 2: George Tooker, THE SUBWAY
(Collection of the Whitney Museum of American Art, Juliana Force Purchase)

York. Many of these artists belonged to the school of Surrealism, which advocated the virtues of "automatic painting" – a technique in which the artist allows his subconscious mind to dictate the spontaneous execution of his painting. Utilizing this approach, Pollock and other members of the Abstract Expressionist group developed an explosively energetic style in which the act of painting, with its acceptance of the accidental and its fundamental expression of freedom, became the artist's primary objective.

Another leader of these "Action Painters," as they were called, was Willem de Kooning. De Kooning, like Pollock, emphasized the gestural approach in his large-scale compositions, but unlike Pollock, whose technique included the dripping and splashing of paint, de Kooning applied paint directly onto the canvas. In his painting "Untitled," 1962 *(Plate 1)*, the violent brush strokes seem in active conflict with each other. Although de Kooning gives no clue to a subject in this painting by way of a title, one senses the contours of a landscape in rhythms and movements of the painted surface.

The impact of Abstract Expressionism had international ramifications, and many European artists were deeply affected by the American experiment. But figurative art continued as a viable style for American painters in the postwar period, and although they remained in the shadow of the more robust abstractionists, these painters maintained an active realist tradition. The subject matter of the realists varied greatly, from representational scenes to symbolic images. A major contributor to the realist school in the early 1950s was George Tooker. In a number of his paintings Tooker created enigmatic compositions of people trapped by the complications of modern society. In his meticulously painted work of 1950 entitled "Subway" *(Plate 2)*, Tooker depicts a dreamlike world of multiple-perspective and repetitive elements focusing on the monotonous and often frightening experience of the urban environment.

In architecture, as in painting, the dislocation of the onset of World War II brought to America a number of Europe's outstanding designers. Among these was the former director of the German Bauhaus school of design and a leading figure in the International Style of architecture, Ludwig Mies van der Rohe. Mies settled in the United States in 1937 and his influence was felt almost immediately. The International Style featured large geometric forms, large areas of untextured surfaces, and the use of glass, steel, and reinforced concrete. The Miesan aesthetic of structural clarity, which emphasized the form as a reflection of its function and downplayed the use of purely

Plate 3: Philip Johnson, GLASS HOUSE, NEW CANAAN, CONNECTICUT *(Courtesy of Philip Johnson; Photo by Sandak)*

Plate 4: Eero Saarinen, ARMCHAIR
(Collection, The Museum of Modern Art, New York. Gift of the manufacturer, Knoll Associates, Inc. U.S.A.)

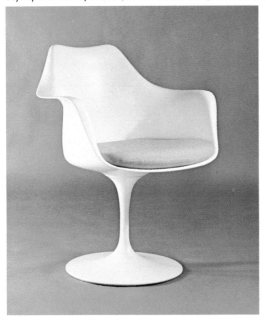

decorative detail, was adopted by a whole generation of American architects. One of Mies's earliest disciples was Philip Johnson, who, for his own home in New Canaan, Connecticut, designed his famous "Glass House" in 1949 *(Plate 3)*. Although the industrial-like steel frame and large glass panes would appear not to be a proper solution for a country house, the transparent walls help to integrate the park-like setting with the unobstructed space within. Only the brick service core and fireplace create a vertical interruption in an otherwise crystalline flow of space. The furniture for Johnson's Glass House was designed by his mentor Mies.

Another American architect whose early work was influenced by the International Style was Eero Saarinen. Saarinen won a number of important commissions in the early 1950s, and like many other modern architects, he also experimented in furniture design. In 1958 he developed the innovative concept of his single-pedestal chair *(Plate 4)*. By using the technique developed for processing lightweight plastics, Saarinen conceived of a shell-like form poised on a single shaft flowing out of a pedestal base. The elegant lines of this free-form object were made possible by the use of contemporary materials and technology.

Throughout the 1940s and 1950s Abstract Expressionism dominated the American art scene, but in the early sixties a number of reactions to the extremely personal styles of the action-oriented painters took place. One of the most significant was that of the Pop Art movement, which sought to reintroduce everyday reality into art. Led by Andy Warhol, these artists based their style on popular images from the mass media, often finding their subject matter in the advertisements, comic books, and billboards of the affluent American society.

A sculptor whose work has been associated with the Pop Art movement is George Segal. In such works as "The Diner," 1964–1966 (Plate 5), Segal has narrowed the division between art and life. The white plaster figures of his composition are cast from live

Plate 5: George Segal, THE DINER
(Collection, Walker Art Center, Minneapolis, Photographer: Eric Sutherland)

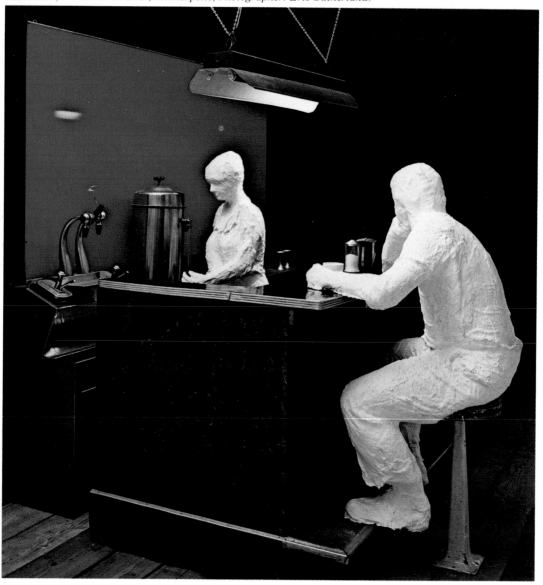

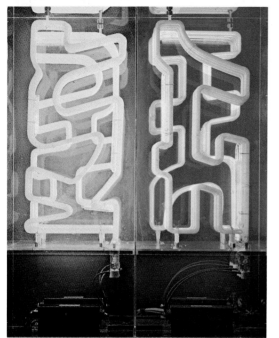

Plate 6: Chryssa, FRAGMENT FOR THE GATES TO TIMES SQUARE *(Collection of the Whitney Museum of American Art. Gift of Howard and Jean Lipman)*

models and placed in an everyday setting. By showing his figures in their natural environment, Segal continues in the long tradition of American genre art.

In recent years contemporary sculptors have freed themselves from traditional sculptural materials in their search for new means of expression. The Greek-born American sculptor Chryssa was inspired by the technology of modern advertising in her use of plastics and electronic circuits. Her large piece "Fragment for the Gates to Times Square," 1966 *(Plate 6)*, is composed of plexiglass cubes into which are placed a series of curved neon tubes, and the result is a rhythmic multicolored effect. The variety of new materials used to create these light-boxes reflects the expanded visual vocabulary of modern sculpture.

The 1960s witnessed a number of important architectural innovations. Many of the former disciples of Mies van der Rohe, including Johnson and Saarinen, rejected the severity of the International Style in favor of more

Plate 7: Paul Rudolph, ART AND ARCHITECTURE BUILDING, NEW HAVEN, CONNECTICUT *(Courtesy of Yale University)*

Plate 8: Kevin Roche, FORD FOUNDATION BUILDING, NEW YORK CITY *(ESTO for the Ford Foundation)*

sculptural and expressionistic designs. Although function continued to play a major role, new problems of mass and scale were explored in contemporary terms. The expressive power of architecture became a compelling concern of Paul Rudolph, who in his Art and Architecture Building at Yale University, 1962–1963 *(Plate 7)*, created an extremely dramatic structure. The vertical concrete piers of the exterior rise the full height of the building, contrasting in their massive form with the openness of the large plate glass windows. Rudolph's most imaginative innovation was his ability to create thirty-nine different levels in what appears from the exterior to be the space of seven stories. Although Rudolph's design has been severely criticized for its overly complicated maze-like interior plan, it has also received high praise for its relationship to its urban site and its concern for human scale.

Another architect of the sixties who attempted to redefine the traditional appearance of the multistoried building was Kevin Roche. In his Ford Foundation Building of 1967 in New York City *(Plate 8)*, Roche recognized the need to alleviate the density of the city block. His solution was to create a structure whose street façades are glass, allowing sunlight to illuminate the interior offices. The offices surround an inner garden court on two sides. This unique design provides a buffer from the bustle of the city street, while at the same time creating an oasis of green in the midst of the urban environment.

Although, as has been noted, many artists of the last decade have reacted strongly to the lack of recognizable objects in Abstract Expressionist painting, the nonrepresentational style has continued as one of the most important idioms in contemporary painting. A direction pursued by one group known as "Chromatic Abstractionists" was the exploration of the subtle, emotive power of large areas of pure color. Strongly influenced by Mark Rothko's richly atmospheric paintings of floating rectangles, the painter Morris Louis developed a style which relied entirely on the sensation of color. In his work entitled "Blue Veil," 1958–1959 *(Plate 9)*, Louis allowed the acrylic pigment to saturate the fabric of his unsealed canvas. The diaphanous veils of color, flowing together, evoke a mood of mystery and quiet contemplation.

In the last few years American painting has shown a renewed interest in photographic-like

Plate 9: Morris Louis, BLUE VEIL *(Courtesy of the Fogg Art Museum, Harvard University, Gift of Mrs. Culver Orswell and Gifts for Special Uses Fund)*

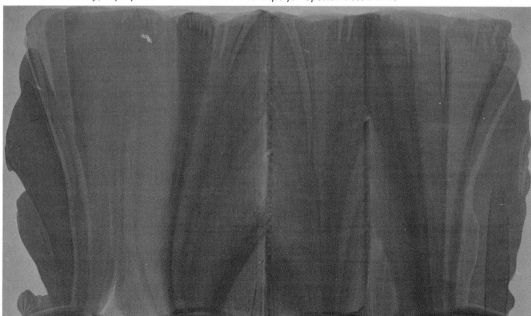

Plate 10: Jack Beal, STILL LIFE WITH PLANT AND MIRRORS
(Collection of the Whitney Museum of American Art. Neysa McMein Purchase Award)

realism. This trend has produced a variety of styles under such names as "Ultra-realism" or "Photo-realism," but the common denominator has been an intense fidelity to either photographic or real-life models. Many artists of this movement have utilized the commercial techniques of airbrush and enlargement grids as they translate to their canvas a sharply focused subject with every detail meticulously depicted.

Jack Beal's painting "Still Life with Plant and Mirrors," 1965 *(Plate 10)*, exemplifies the extreme complexity of these compositions. The subject is viewed from a slightly elevated position with the brightly colored pot and plant reflected in multiple mirrors at varying angles. The resulting effect is a dazzling pattern of shapes and forms.

American art in the last thirty years has been a succession of movements which has bordered on the chaotic. Experimentation in all the arts has presented the contemporary viewer with the persistent question of which of the various artistic movements has true historical significance and which will have enduring value. Only time and the opportunity for historical perspective will furnish the answers.

the Indians to adopt the white man's ways. A congressional resolution of that year declared the intention of terminating federal relations with the tribes and leaving them on their own. Thereafter relations with some tribes were terminated, among these the Menominee of Wisconsin, who saw their reservation converted into Menominee County. "Termination" led to further Indian impoverishment, both material and spiritual.

During the 1960s more Indians than ever before joined in a movement to bring all the tribes together and redress their common wrongs. In 1961 more than 400 members of 67 different tribes gathered in Chicago and drew up a Declaration of Indian Purpose, which stressed the "right to choose our own way of life" and the "responsibility of preserving our precious heritage." In 1964, while Congress was considering the Economic Opportunity Bill, hundreds of Indians and white sympathizers assembled in Washington to urge Congress to include Indians in the antipoverty program. After black militants had proclaimed black power as their aim, a number of young, college-educated Indians adapted the slogan to their own use and began to speak of red power. Some repudiated the name "Indian" — which, as they pointed out, whites had mistakenly given them — and insisted on being called "Native Americans" (a term that anti-immigrant whites had applied to themselves more than a century earlier).

Congress included Indians in the coverage of the Economic Opportunity Act, and for a time many of the reservation dwellers were allowed to plan and carry out their own antipoverty programs. Except for this, neither the Kennedy nor the Johnson administration did much more than the Eisenhower administration had done to meet the Indians' needs and demands. Johnson failed to give effect to his words of 1968: "I propose a new goal for our Indian programs: a goal that ends the old debate about 'termination' of Indian programs and stresses self-determination; a goal that erases old attitudes of paternalism and promotes partnership self-help."

Frustrated Indians turned more and more to direct action, to confrontations with whites, to defiance of state and federal authority. In 1968, Indian fishermen, seeking to exercise old treaty rights of fishing on the Columbia River and in Puget Sound, clashed with officials of the state of Washington. In 1969 a group of Indians of various tribes, to dramatize the plight of their people, landed on Alcatraz Island, the site of an abandoned federal prison in San Francisco Bay, and claimed the place "by right of discovery." The frustrations of many Indians found witty as well as angry expression in the writings of Vine Deloria, Jr., a Sioux, who titled one of his books *Custer Died for Your Sins* (1969).

THE SPANISH-SPEAKING MINORITY

Much more numerous than the descendants of North American tribes were the people of Latin American origin, most of whom also had Indian ancestors, and some of whom were at least partly of African descent. Numbering more than 9 million in 1970, the Spanish-speaking minority was, next to the American Negro minority, the largest in the country. The people of Puerto Rican background were concentrated mainly in New York, those of Cuban background mainly in Florida, and those of Mexican background mainly in California, Texas, and other states of the Southwest. The Mexican-Americans, totaling almost 7 million, included legal immigrants from Mexico, illegal immigrants ("mojados" or "wetbacks"), and temporary workers ("braceros") brought in under labor contracts, as well as descendants of families who had been living in Mexican territory at the time it was incorporated into the United States.

The Spanish-speaking peoples had suffered from various forms of discrimination, though they had not been consigned to separate schools. To advance their interests, many of them had joined organizations of one kind or another, but these were specialized or localized. During the 1960s, for the first time, large numbers of Mexican-Americans were brought together in a broad, inclusive "Chicano" (from "Mexicano") movement.

Its outstanding hero was César Chávez, an Arizona-born California farm worker. Its main focus, for the time being, was a farm workers' strike that Chávez called in 1965 and soon converted into a nonviolent crusade for social justice. He enlisted the cooperation of college students, churchmen and churchwomen, and civil rights groups, including CORE and SNCC. To bring pressure on employers, who brought in

Chicano Leader
*Evident in this picture is the magnetism of César Chávez, the labor organizer
who rose to be an outstanding hero of Mexican-Americans in the 1960s. He is
shown talking with grape workers at a California vineyard. (Paul Fusco from
Magnum)*

strikebreakers, he appealed for a nationwide
boycott of California table grapes. The boycott
gained the support of millions of sympathizers
throughout the country, but got no assistance
from the federal government, which increased
its purchases of grapes to be sent to American
troops in Vietnam. Chávez won a victory in
1970, when the growers of half of California's
table grapes signed contracts with his union.

WOMEN'S RIGHTS

American women in general could hardly be
called a minority, since 51 percent of the population was female; yet they suffered inequities
comparable to those imposed upon minority
groups, and women of these groups bore a
double burden of discrimination.

True, more and more job opportunities
were opening up for women, and an increasing
proportion of them, including wives and mothers, were working outside the home (fewer
than 25 percent of women over sixteen had
been counted as part of the labor force in 1940;
more than 43 percent were so counted in 1970).
But women were paid much less than men,
even for comparable work (in 1971, for men
employed full time, the median yearly pay was
$9,630; for women it was $5,700). Women had
fewer chances than men to make a professional
or managerial career. In the mid-1960s women
constituted only 7 percent of the nation's physicians and less than 4 percent of its lawyers, and
the proportion of women managers or owners
of businesses, already small, was actually declining. Women were being replaced by men in
top positions in schools, libraries, and social
work — which once had been considered wom-
en's fields.

In comparison with men, women were
receiving too little education, but in comparison
with their own career opportunities they were

receiving too much. They composed a smaller percentage of the college population in the 1950s than in the 1920s and were granted a smaller percentage of college degrees in 1960 than in 1930. During the 1960s they were earning only one in three of all B.A.s and M.A.s and only one in ten of the Ph.D.s. Yet the college graduates—like other, less well-educated women—often were handicapped in getting and holding outside employment because they had to carry the extra burden of bearing and rearing children and keeping house. Women with higher education seemed especially to resent the "double standard" that all women confronted in practically every aspect of life.

Educated women of the middle class took the lead (as they had done in earlier feminist crusades) in the dozens of "women's libera-

tion" movements that sprang forth in the 1960s. One of the most influential of the leaders was Betty Friedan, who in *The Feminine Mystique* (1963) denounced the American home as a "comfortable concentration camp" and called upon its inmates to free themselves. Friedan helped to found, in 1966, the most inclusive and effective of the new women's rights organizations, the National Organization for Women, or NOW. "There is no civil rights movement to speak for women, as there has been for Negroes and other victims of discrimination," the organizers of NOW declared, thus revealing that they, too, had been inspired, at least in part, by the example of the blacks. The organization's 1967 "bill of rights" demanded an Equal Rights Amendment to the Constitution— "Equality of Rights under the law shall not be

Abortion March
In the early 1900s, women's rights advocates demonstrated for the right to share in their own government by means of the vote. In the early 1970s some of them demanded the right to control their own bodies—through abortion. New York and a few other states responded with liberalized abortion laws. (Charles Gatewood)

denied or abridged by the United States on account of sex"—and Congress in 1970 approved the amendment and sent it to the states for ratification. NOW also called for enforcement of the 1964 Civil Rights Act, which prohibited discrimination in employment on account of sex as well as race, and "men wanted" and "women wanted" began to disappear from classified ads. Other NOW demands included the following: maternity leave for working women; public child-care centers, to enable mothers to compete more freely for jobs; absolute equality of educational opportunities at all levels; and the "right of women to control their own reproductive lives" through contraception and abortion.

NOW disclaimed any "enmity toward men" and advocated a "self-respecting partnership" with them, but some of the other liberation groups practically declared a war of the sexes. Some, resisting "male chauvinism," refused to let men open doors or light cigarettes for them. A few, protesting their treatment as mere "sex objects," publicly burned their brassieres or stripped off their clothes. Others forsook men and proclaimed themselves lesbians. The majority of American women, however, saw little need to support the feminist cause in any of its forms. A poll in 1970 put the question: "In your opinion, do women in the United States get as good a break as men?" Of the women replying, 65 percent said "Yes."

Selected Readings

Eisenhower
F. M. Shattuck, *The 1956 Presidential Campaign* (1960); Samuel Lubell, *The Revolt of the Moderates* (1956); R. H. Rovere, *Affairs of State: The Eisenhower Years* (1956); M. J. Pusey, *Eisenhower the President* (1956), very favorable; M. W. Childs, *Eisenhower, Captive Hero* (1956), rather critical; E. T. Benson, *Crossfire: The Eight Years with Eisenhower* (1962).

J. F. K. and L. B. J.
J. M. Burns, *John Kennedy: A Political Profile** (1959); T. H. White, *The Making of the President, 1960** (1961); A. M. Schlesinger, *A Thousand Days: John F. Kennedy in the White House** (1965); T. C. Sorensen, *Kennedy** (1965); William Manchester, *Death of a President** (1967); Tom Wicker, *JFK and LBJ: The Influence of Personality upon Politics* (1968); T. H. White, *The Making of the President, 1964** (1965); Rowland Evans and Robert Novak, *Lyndon B. Johnson: The Exercise of Power** (1966), critical; Robert Sherrill, *The Accidental President* (1967), critical.

Prosperity and Poverty
H. G. Vatter, *The U. S. Economy in the 1950's** (1963); Walter Heller, *New Dimensions of Political Economy* (1966); Gabriel Kolko, *Wealth and Power in America* (1962); Michael Harrington, *The Other America: Poverty in the United States* (1962); H. P. Miller, *Rich Man, Poor Man** (1964); Oscar Lewis, *La Vida: A Puerto Rican Family in the Culture of Poverty—San Juan and New York** (1966); H. M. Caudill, *Night Comes to the Cumberlands* (1963), on poverty in the Appalachians; J. D. Donovan, *The Politics of Poverty* (1967); Sar Levitan, *The Great Society's Poor Law: A New Approach to Poverty* (1969).

The Supreme Court
A. T. Mason, *The Supreme Court from Taft to Warren* (1958); J. D. Weaver, *Warren: The Man, the Court, the Era* (1967); W. F. Murphy, *Congress and the Court** (1962); R. G. Dixon, Jr., *Democratic Representation: Reapportionment in Law and Politics* (1968); R. B. McKay, *Reapportionment: The Law and Politics of Equal Representation* (1965); Loren Miller, *The Petitioners: The Story of the Supreme Court of the United States and the Negro* (1964); I. A. Newby, *Challenge to the Court: Social Scientists and the Defense of Segregation, 1954–1966* (1968).

Black Voices
M. L. King, Jr., *Stride Toward Freedom** (1958) and *Why We Can't Wait** (1964); James Baldwin, *The Fire Next Time* (1963); L. E. Lomax, *The Negro Revolt** (1963) and *When the Word Is Given: A Report on Elijah Muhammad, Malcolm X, and the Black Muslim World* (1963); *The Autobiography of Malcolm X** (1966); James Farmer, *Freedom—When?* (1966); Stokely Carmichael and C. V. Hamilton, *Black Power: The Politics of Liberation in America** (1967).

Civil Rights and Civil Disorders
Anthony Lewis, *Portrait of a Decade: The Second American Revolution* (1964); Louis Harlan, *Separate and Unequal** (1961), on segregated schools; A. P. Blaustein and C. C. Ferguson, *Desegregation and the Law** (1962); J. W. Silver, *Mississippi: The Closed Society** (1964); J. W. Anderson, *Eisenhower, Brownell, and the Congress: The Tangled Origins of the Civil Rights Bill of 1956–1957* (1964); D. M. Berman, *A Bill Becomes Law: The Civil Rights Act of 1960* (1962); A. I. Waskow, *From Race Riot to Sit-In: 1919 and the 1960's* (1966); James Peck, *Freedom Ride*

(1962); D. R. Matthews and J. W. Prothro, *Negroes and the New Southern Politics** (1966); N. V. Bartley, *The Rise of Massive Resistance: Race and Politics in the South During the 1950's* (1969); M. A. Schwartz, *Trends in White Attitudes Toward Negroes* (1967); Lee Rainwater and W. L. Yancey, *The Moynihan Report and the Politics of Controversy** (1967); *Report of the National Advisory Committee on Civil Disorders** (1968); A. Meier and E. Rudwick, *CORE: A Study in the Civil Rights Movement, 1942–1968* (1973); Richard Bardolph, *The Civil Rights Record* (1971).

Indians and Chicanos
Stan Steiner, *The New Indians** (1968); Vine Deloria, Jr., *Custer Died for Your Sins* (1969); H. W. Hertzberg, *The Search for an American Indian Identity: Modern Pan-Indian Movements* (1971); W. E. Washburn, *Red Man's Land / White Man's Law: A Study of the Past and Present Status of the American Indian* (1971); A. M. Josephy, ed., *Red Power** (1971); S. A. Levitan and B. Hetrick, *Big Brother's Indian Programs* (1972); Wayne Moquin, ed., *A Documentary History of the Mexican-Americans* (1971); Stan Steiner, *La Raza** (1970); M. S. Meier and F. Rivera, *The Chicanos: A History of Mexican Americans* (1972).

Woman's Place
W. H. Chafe, *The American Woman: Her Changing Social, Economic, and Political Roles, 1920–1970* (1972); Judith Hole and Ellen Levine, eds., *Rebirth of Feminism* (1972); Elizabeth Janeway, *Man's World, Woman's Place: A Study in Social Mythology* (1971); Juliet Mitchell, *Women's Estate* (1972).

*Titles available in paperback.

From Defiance to Détente?

Twenty-nine

"We face a hostile ideology—global in scope, atheistic in character, ruthless in purpose, and insidious in method. Unhappily the danger it poses promises to be of indefinite duration." So said President Eisenhower in the farewell address he directed to the American people shortly before leaving office in 1961. "A vital element in keeping the peace is our military establishment. Our arms must be mighty, ready for instant action, so that no potential aggressor may be tempted to risk his own destruction."

While warning of dangers from outside, President Eisenhower also drew attention to a possible threat arising within the nation. This was the threat of undue power accruing to the "military-industrial complex" that had developed to provide for the national defense. For the first time in their history, the American people had in their midst, on a permanent basis, the "conjunction of an immense military establishment and a large arms industry." Eisenhower did not fully describe the complex, but the military establishment consisted of the Armed Services, the Central Intelligence Agency, and other bodies provided for in the National Security Act of 1947. The arms industry included not only manufacturers of traditional armaments but also producers of a bewildering variety of new aviational, aerospace, electronic, chemical, and biological supplies. Supporting the industry and supported by it were certain labor unions and numerous scientific groups, many of these in universities that had government research contracts.

Under President Eisenhower's successors—Kennedy, Johnson, and Nixon—the United States continued to face a "hostile ideology" abroad. And the military-industrial complex continued to grow. It seemed to gain a greater and greater role in the determination of policy. Certainly it took a larger and larger share of the federal budget, leaving less and less for domestic needs, though these became increasingly serious. How

Peace March 1968
This peace march held in San Francisco in October 1968 was typical of the nationwide demonstrations against the Vietnam War. Students conducted frequent all-night teach-ins at their universities protesting the war; others went so far as to burn their draft cards. The varied backgrounds of the demonstrators were illustrated by the trial of several representative marchers ranging from a graduate student to one of the most prestigious physicians in the country, Dr. Benjamin Spock. (Photoreporters)

to provide for the national security while preserving and promoting individual freedom and opportunity — how to defend democracy without destroying it in the process — this was America's basic dilemma.

There was a ray of hope. Russia and China were ancient enemies, with differences of interest too profound to be patched over indefinitely by the shared ideology of Communism. By 1961, signs of serious conflict between the Soviet Union and the People's Republic had already begun to appear. If the conflict should worsen, one or both of the two Communist powers might be willing to seek or to accept improved relations with the United States. This prospect caused some Americans to look toward an eventual "détente," a relaxation of tensions in world politics. Actually, the most dangerous crisis between the United States and the Soviet Union was yet to come. By 1973, however, the achievement of some kind of détente seemed at last a real possibility.

Kennedy and Confrontation

In his inaugural address, President Kennedy had advised: "Let us never negotiate out of fear. But let us never fear to negotiate." During the next few years, as Russia and the United States faced one another over the issues of Berlin, Cuba, and nuclear testing, the spirit of negotiation was put to severe trials.

DIVERSIFIED DEFENSE

At the time Kennedy took office, the military establishment of the United States was spending half of the federal budget and nearly a tenth of the gross national product; it was directly employing 3.5 million people. The incoming President and his new Secretary of Defense, Robert McNamara, were as determined as President Eisenhower had been in his farewell address that this vast establishment should protect but not dominate the American nation. From the outset, McNamara established firm control over the enormous and complex Department of Defense. To the distress of some high-ranking officers and many congressmen, he brought in brilliant young civilians who, employing computers and cost-analysis techniques, plotted policy changes. He was accused of relying more upon civilian skills and problem-solving machines than upon military experience.

President Kennedy and Secretary McNamara built their plans upon the theory that the strength of thermonuclear weapons on the part of both the United States and Russia was sufficiently great to constitute a "mutual deterrent" against war. During the campaign of 1960 Kennedy had warned that the United States lagged behind Russia; soon after he took office his secretary of defense reported that the missile gap, if there was one, favored the United States. This nation, possessing sufficient striking power to destroy the Soviet Union several times over, was committed to staying ahead of Russia in missile and nuclear development. The new administration speeded the placing of nuclear-armed missiles in underground sites and the building of nuclear-armed Polaris submarines to rove the seas. These retaliatory weapons would guarantee that, if the United States suffered destruction, so would the attacking nation.

There was the assumption, however, that under the umbrella of the mutual deterrence of countering nuclear forces, the Communists would seek to gain new territories by subversion or by conventional warfare. Experts pointed to areas like South Vietnam to illustrate what they meant; nuclear deterrents were of no value there. So the President wished to develop forces expert in guerrilla and jungle warfare and equipped with special arms. A million American men were thus trained in "counterinsurgency." In addition, United States military missions aided other countries in establishing their own programs. During its first two years the administration also committed more of its defense expenditures to increasing its conventional forces. It raised the number of army combat divisions from eleven to sixteen and air force tactical wings from sixteen to twenty-one.

Since the inception of the Truman Doctrine (1947) and the Marshall Plan (1948), the United States had depended on economic aid as well as military power to defend many areas of the world against Communism. For both strategic and humanitarian reasons, President Eisenhower year after year requested and received huge appropriations for the mutual security program.

Most of the new, emergent nations in Asia and Africa were suffering from poverty and ignorance and from a growth in population so explosive that it canceled out gains in living standards. Many of these nations were ready to accept aid from the United States at the same time that they were also receptive to both aid and propaganda from Communist Russia and Communist China. Even before the end of the Eisenhower administration, the United States no longer insisted that the countries receiving economic assistance align themselves on the Western side. Their right to be neutral in the cold war was conceded.

President Kennedy continued and in some ways elaborated upon the policy of financial assistance abroad. He established the Agency for International Development (AID) to coordinate various projects and to explore means of making them more effective. He sponsored the so-called Alliance for Progress, which was not really an alliance but a set of agreements between the United States and Latin American governments for cooperative undertakings in Latin America. He also brought about the establishment of the Peace Corps, which trained and sent abroad thousands of specialists, mostly young people, to work for two years in underdeveloped areas.

The returns from foreign aid were debatable. The most successful of the programs — and the least expensive — was probably the Peace Corps. The Alliance for Progress was criticized by businessmen in the United States on the grounds that the administration's demands for tax and land reforms, as prerequisites to aid, were frightening investors away from Latin America. The Alliance was opposed by businessmen and landowners in Latin America on the grounds that, by demanding reforms, the United States was encouraging Communism. Foreign aid appeared to help in counteracting Russian influence in the emerging nations of Africa.

HEIGHTENING TENSION

The Cuban dictator Fidel Castro was drawing closer to Russia, heaping invective upon the United States, and exporting "Fidelismo" throughout Latin America. President Kennedy had declared: "Communist domination in this hemisphere can never be negotiated."

Once in office, Kennedy and his advisers faced the question of whether to go ahead with a project that the Eisenhower administration had begun. Under the direction of the Central Intelligence Agency, anti-Castro Cubans were secretly being trained and equipped in Central America for a landing in Cuba. They were intended to overthrow the Castro regime with the aid of discontented groups still on the island. Kennedy decided to authorize the invasion but refused to provide United States air support. On the morning of April 17, 1961, a force of about 2,000 rebels landed at the Bay of Pigs. No accompanying revolt, such as had been expected, took place in Cuba, and the invading rebels were left to the mercy of the Cuban army and air force. Within two days the beachhead was wiped out.

Throughout Latin America, and in many allied and neutral nations as well as Communist countries, the United States was the object of condemnation. This country reaped all the disadvantages and none of the potential advantages of the invasion attempt. President Kennedy retorted on April 20: "We do not intend to abandon [Cuba] to the Communists." But Castro moved rapidly toward aligning Cuba fully with the Soviet Union, proclaiming that it was a "socialist" state.

In the somber aftermath of the Bay of Pigs fiasco, President Kennedy in June 1961 met Premier Khrushchev in Vienna for a frank interchange of views. It was not encouraging. According to reports, Kennedy told Khrushchev that Russia wanted to trade an apple for an orchard, but the United States did not do business that way.

An ominous sequel to the conference was renewed Russian pressure upon Berlin, bringing with it the serious threat of nuclear war. On June 15, 1961, Khrushchev, who was then back in Russia, set a deadline for the settlement of the Berlin issue. "The conclusion of a peace treaty with Germany cannot be postponed any longer," he declared. "A peaceful settlement in

Europe must be attained this year." With or without the Western powers, he proposed to conclude a peace treaty with the East German government (the "German Democratic Republic"), which would then control access routes to West Berlin. As he well knew, the NATO powers did not possess conventional forces of sufficient strength to defend West Berlin and its access routes with any certainty of success. The defense of Berlin must rest upon the use of nuclear power, and Khrushchev acted as if he thought the United States would not risk the danger of world holocaust to defend Berlin.

What was pushing the Soviet Union toward this dangerous confrontation was the spectacular success of West Berlin as a "showcase of democracy" behind the Iron Curtain. East Germans could easily slip into West Berlin, though barbed wire and minefields prevented fugitives from crossing the rest of the border between Communist countries and western Europe. West Germany with its higher living standards and its demands for skilled workers and professional men was an irresistible lure to the poor, regimented East Germans.

Suddenly, before dawn on August 13, 1961, the East German government closed the border between East and West Berlin and in the next few days began erecting elaborate concrete block and barbed-wire barriers. East Germany was transformed into a vast concentration camp and West Berlin into a beleaguered island. Khrushchev had thus gained by a single act of force much that he had been seeking unsuccessfully at the conference table. The United States protested but was not ready to use armed force to destroy the new wall.

Fears of thermonuclear war ran so high throughout the United States that the nation faced seriously for the first time the problem of trying to construct fallout shelters sufficient to protect the entire population. There followed much controversy and some hysteria about shelters but little actual construction, despite the encouragement of the federal and state governments. Fears were intensified when the Soviet Union announced an extensive series of nuclear tests. During the autumn Russia exploded approximately fifty nuclear devices, one with an estimated force of sixty-five megatons—3,000 times more powerful than the Hiroshima bomb. The series as a whole produced double the amount of fallout of all previous atomic tests. The United States, fearing it would fall behind in the nuclear competition, announced it would resume tests underground and in outer space.

CUBA: THE MISSILE CRISIS

The Berlin crisis slowly subsided during the autumn of 1961, to be succeeded a year later by a new, more frightening encounter, this time in regard to Cuba. In mid-July 1962, shiploads of Russian technicians and equipment began arriving on the island, and in August more than 30 Soviet ships unloaded 2,000 technicians and instructors, together with fighter planes, surface-to-air missiles, and patrol boats with missiles. Photographic reconnaissance, which the United States was carrying out secretly around the periphery of Cuba, indicated, as Kennedy announced on September 4, that the armaments were solely defensive. "Were it otherwise," he declared, "the gravest issues would arise."

Refugees from Cuba brought reports, however, that Russia was also introducing offensive missiles into the island. Kennedy authorized photographic reconnaissance of all Cuba to ascertain if this was true. On October 14, a U-2 plane brought back incontrovertible evidence—photographs of new missile sites being rushed to completion. Why were the Russians engaged in this dangerous and expensive gamble? This was the first question that President Kennedy's advisers pondered as they began deliberations on October 16. The Russian move would more than redress the missile balance that had favored the United States. According to the London *Observer* (October 28, 1962): "Seen from the Pentagon, the two most alarming features of the missile build-up [in Cuba] were proximity and speed. Radar would give 15 minutes' warning of a missile attack from Russia, but only two–three minutes from Cuba. Medium-range missile bases can be constructed in hours or days. Within a month, if the U.S. sat tight, Russia could get 200–300 missiles in position—enough, at least in theory, to knock out a large part of the U.S. retaliatory forces in a surprise 'preemptive' attack."

How could the United States counter the Russian move? One of the two main alterna-

The Range of Cuban-Based Soviet Missiles

tives was to strike the bases from the air; the other was to blockade Cuba. The President and his advisers decided upon a "quarantine"—a blockade. Meanwhile, on October 18, Soviet Foreign Minister Gromyko called upon the President to assure him that Soviet assistance to Cuba was solely defensive.

On October 22, President Kennedy was ready to act. Appearing on television, he presented the photographic evidence of the missile sites and announced that the United States would establish a quarantine on all offensive weapons bound for Cuba. "This secret, swift and extraordinary build-up of Communist missiles—in an area well known to have a special and historical relationship to the United States and the nations of the Western hemisphere—is a deliberately provocative and unjustified change in the status quo which cannot be accepted by this country, if our courage and our commitments are ever again to be trusted by either friend or foe."

Several days of acute tension followed as the United States instituted its naval and air

A Cuban Medium-Range Ballistic Missile Launch Site
*This photograph shows the site at San Cristobal, Cuba, on October 25, 1962, at the
height of the crisis. Allen Dulles, former head of the Central Intelligence Agency,
has hinted that the requisite skill in identifying Soviet missile sites from
photographs had been acquired through data gathered by U-2 flights over Russia.
(U.S. Department of Defense)*

blockade, uncertain what would happen if a
Soviet vessel among the twenty-five bound for
Cuba should refuse to stop and should be sunk.
Some of the Soviet ships changed course or
stopped. But low-flying Navy P-8U planes
brought back evidence that work on the Soviet
bases continued at top speed.

'This evidence made especially unacceptable to the United States a proposal issued by U
Thant, acting secretary general of the United
Nations, after strong urging by unaligned nations. U Thant requested Russia to suspend
arms shipments, and he requested that the
United States suspend the blockade for two or
three weeks while negotiations took place.
Khrushchev accepted U Thant's suggestion,
but Kennedy declined.

All week long the United States negotiated
with Russia, and behind the stand of each side
was the threat of nuclear force. The United
States left no doubt that it was in earnest. The
navy established a 2,100-mile ring about Cuba,

employing 180 ships, including 8 aircraft carriers. The Strategic Air Command began "massive airborne" alerts on October 22, keeping
quantities of its heavy nuclear-armed B-52
bombers in the air at all times. Behind these
were 156 intercontinental ballistic missiles in
combat readiness and a fleet of Polaris submarines. Soviet miscalculation could bring a holocaust.

Late on the evening of October 26, President Kennedy received a long, rambling letter
from Khrushchev in which he compared the
United States and the Soviet Union to two men
tugging on a rope, pulling a knot tighter and
tighter until it could be cut only by a sword. In
effect, the letter said that if Kennedy would
cease tugging on his end, Khrushchev would
do likewise. The letter seemed to imply that
Russia would remove the missile bases provided the United States would promise not to invade Cuba. The next morning Moscow radio
broadcast quite a different proposal from

Khrushchev—that Russia would dismantle the bases in Cuba if the United States would withdraw its missile bases from Turkey.

Time was running out for the United States, and meanwhile in Cuba antiaircraft fire had downed one American plane and menaced others. Under these tense conditions, the President decided to accept Khrushchev's first offer and to ignore the second: if Khrushchev would remove the missiles, Kennedy proposed, the United States would end the blockade and not invade Cuba. The next day, October 27, Khrushchev accepted.

Though an armed clash had been avoided, trouble over Cuba by no means had been brought to an end. The Soviet Union did indeed remove the missiles and dismantle the bases, but Castro refused to allow on-the-spot inspection. Thousands of Soviet technicians remained, and although President Kennedy pressured Khrushchev to remove them, their return to Russia was slow. Cuban refugee groups, bewildered and angered by the no-invasion pledge, engaged in plots of their own against Castro and were resentful when the United States restrained them. In the immediate aftermath of the crisis, the national sentiment was one of profound relief, and President Kennedy's popularity rose.

LOOSENING OF ALLIANCES

While confronting one another over Cuba, the United States and the Soviet Union found themselves on the same side in a less serious and more remote crisis over India. The Chinese had launched surprise offensives along the Indian frontier. Already the Soviet Union was providing India with economic aid, and the United States now gave further assistance, ferrying weapons and other supplies in "flying boxcars" to the Himalayan front. Soon the Chinese agreed to negotiate their boundary dispute with India. The brief war had shown that, for the time being, Indo-American relations were close and cordial. It had also indicated that Russia and China were drawing further apart.

As relations between the Communist powers were being strained, so were those between the United States and one of its NATO allies—France. In western Europe the Marshall Plan had helped stimulate a recovery so

remarkable that by the 1960s some nations not only were more prosperous than ever before in their history but in percentage of annual growth were outstripping the United States. Their new economic power meant that, if they chose, they could either insist upon a more equal partnership or break loose to form a "third force" between the United States and Russia, such as some French leaders had long envisaged.

To strengthen western Europe against a possible Russian threat, the United States had encouraged the formation of the European Economic Community (or "Common Market"), in 1958. To give further encouragement, Kennedy in 1962 obtained from Congress authority to lower tariffs on trade with the Common Market countries. But President Charles de Gaulle of France jolted Kennedy's hopes for closer economic and political cooperation with Europe. In 1963, de Gaulle vetoed the British application to join the Common Market and did so because of the close British ties with the United States. He also proclaimed his opposition to American plans for creating a multination nuclear force within the North Atlantic Treaty Organization. He insisted upon creating a separate small nuclear force for France, in order to gain an independent voice in European policy. Later he recognized Red China, thus asserting an independent position in Asian affairs as well.

In the summer of 1963, perhaps in part because of growing trouble with China, the Soviet Union, after years of negotiation, agreed to a treaty banning atmospheric (but not underground) tests of nuclear weapons. The treaty, the first definite step in the direction of international arms reduction since the onset of the cold war, was ratified by almost every important country except Red China (who was preparing to test her own nuclear bomb), France, and Cuba. A notable thaw in the cold war followed. President Kennedy announced that the United States would be willing to sell large quantities of surplus wheat to the Russians, who were suffering from a shortage.

By 1964 many Americans were thinking hopefully of the prospect of a "détente" with the Soviet Union. But these prospects soon dimmed as the United States became more and more deeply involved in an anti-Communist crusade far from home in Southeast Asia.

Johnson's Dilemmas

During the presidential campaign of 1964 the Republican candidate, Senator Goldwater, urged that the United States take a much more active part in the war then going on between Communist North Vietnam and non-Communist South Vietnam. But President Johnson specifically repudiated the Goldwater policy. "There are those that say you ought to go north and drop bombs, and try to wipe out the supply lines, and they think that would escalate the war," Johnson declaimed in a campaign speech. "We don't want our American boys to do the fighting for Asian boys. We don't want to get involved in a nation [China] with 700 million people and get tied down in a land war in Asia."

In fact, Johnson himself was already preparing to enlarge the American role in Vietnam, and soon he was ordering bombs dropped on the north and was sending American boys by the hundreds of thousands to fight in that faraway land. As a consequence he lost all possibility of maintaining the "consensus" he had desired and of achieving the "Great Society" he had proclaimed. Never before had a President been elected by such a large popular majority, and never before had a President seen his popularity dwindle away so fast and so completely.

DOMINICAN INTERVENTION

While undertaking to prevent the spread of Communism in distant Asia, President Johnson faced what seemed like a new Communist threat much closer to home, in the Caribbean. There appeared to be a danger that a Castro-type government might be imposed upon the Dominican Republic, thus making that country a second Cuba. Johnson acted quickly to forestall the supposed Communist coup. In doing so, he laid himself open to charges of fostering imperialism and right-wing dictatorship.

After the assassination of the dictator General Rafael Trujillo in 1961, the Dominican Republic was slowly and painfully emerging from three decades of economic exploitation and political repression. The government of the democratically elected President, Juan Bosch, who was leftist though not Communist, floun-

dered. In 1963 a conservative military junta overthrew Bosch and, faring little better, became itself the target of unrest. There were rumors of Communist infiltration into the island. In the spring of 1965 when young military men sympathetic to Bosch rebelled against the junta, there was rioting, shooting, and looting in the streets of the capital, Santo Domingo.

Within the next few days, United States forces numbering 30,000 ashore and afloat helped restore order. In reply to criticisms that the United States had acted unilaterally, the President and Secretary of State Dean Rusk insisted that they had held preliminary consultations with other American states and that the need for sudden intervention to prevent loss of life arose too quickly for further reliance upon the Organization of American States.

The OAS did authorize the establishment of an Inter-American Peace Force. American troops, together with token forces from several other republics, donned blue and yellow OAS armbands, and served under the command of a Brazilian general. Bloody fighting continued for some days before order could be restored. More than a year later, on June 1, 1966, in a new presidential election, Bosch was defeated by a moderate candidate. The Peace Force was withdrawn in September 1966.

The United States achieved stabilization of the Dominican Republic only at the cost of much Latin American good will. In June 1965 a professor at the National University of Mexico wrote: "The way Juan Bosch has been treated and the clumsy invasion of the Dominican Republic have created more hatred toward the United States in Latin America than the combined anti-colonial propaganda of China and Russia."

INVOLVEMENT IN VIETNAM

The involvement of the United States in Vietnam had developed so slowly that when it began spectacularly to grow, in 1964 and 1965, few Americans could remember how it had originated.

After the close of World War II, Vietnamese nationalists, seeking independence from France, rallied around Ho Chi Minh, a Com-

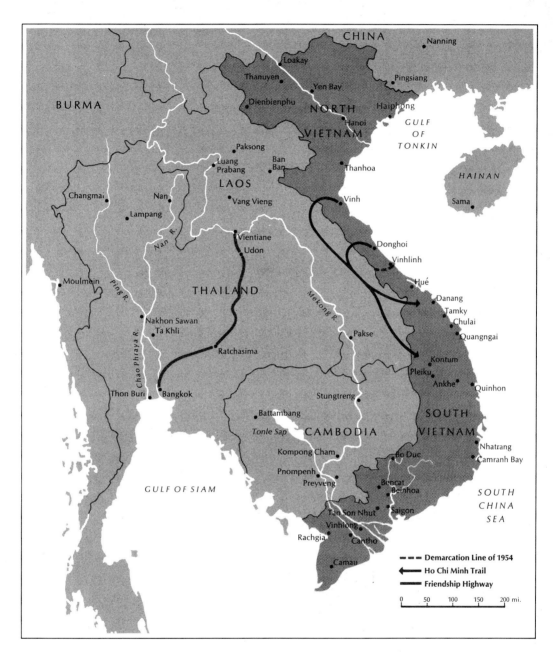

Vietnam

munist who during the war had led the anti-Japanese resistance and had cooperated with the Americans. Ho issued a declaration of independence echoing the American Declaration of 1776 and began negotiations with France. When negotiations broke down, Ho and his followers resorted to arms. The American government was little concerned until the fall of

Nationalist China and the outbreak of the Korean War. Then the Truman administration looked upon the French as manning a bastion to check the spread of Communism in Southeast Asia and began to send substantial aid. The Eisenhower administration increased the economic assistance and, when the French forces faced disaster in 1954, considered sending large-scale military aid as well. Eisenhower held back, however, because of the opposition of Congress and because of the refusal of Great Britain to cooperate.

There followed the 1954 settlements at Geneva, establishing Laos and Cambodia, and temporarily splitting Vietnam into a Communist north and non-Communist south until free elections could be held to unify the new nation. The United States did not participate in the negotiations or sign the agreements. It promised not to use force to upset them, but warned that "it would view any renewal of the aggression in violation of the . . . agreements with grave concern and as seriously threatening international peace and security." Subsequently, the State Department threw its influence against free elections, and they were never held.

The Eisenhower administration sought new arrangements to contain the Communists in Southeast Asia. Within two months of the Geneva agreements, Secretary Dulles succeeded in establishing the Southeast Asia Treaty Organization (SEATO), whose members agreed to consult one another regarding not only their own security but also the security of Laos, Cambodia, and South Vietnam. On October 23, 1954, President Eisenhower wrote the premier of South Vietnam, promising aid in return for certain reforms and offering to "assist the Government of Viet-Nam in developing and maintaining a strong, viable state, capable of resisting attempted subversion or aggression through military means." The SEATO treaty and President Eisenhower's letter were subsequently cited as the American commitments to assist South Vietnam — even though Dulles

Training Vietnamese Troops to Combat Communist Guerrillas
One of the most vital of the programs to counter Communist nibbling tactics was established in South Vietnam where a joint military assistance advisory group of the United States armed forces intensively trained Vietnamese armed forces in the use of American weapons and of limited warfare tactics against the Vietcong troops. Army Chief Warrant Officer Richard Parsons (standing right) instructs Vietnamese infantrymen on how to board an H-21C helicopter. (Official U.S. Army photo)

The Tonkin Gulf Resolution [August 1964]

. . . The Congress approves and supports the determination of the President, as Commander in Chief, to take all necessary measures to repel any armed attack against the forces of the United States and to prevent further aggression.

The United States regards as vital to its national interest and to world peace the maintenance of international peace and security in Southeast Asia. Consonant with the Constitution and the Charter of the United Nations and in accordance with its obligations under the Southeast Asia Collective Defense Treaty, the United States is, therefore, prepared, as the President determines, to take all necessary steps, including the use of armed force, to assist any member or protocol state of the Southeast Asia Collective Defense Treaty requesting assistance in defense of its freedom. . . .

---

himself had told the Senate Foreign Relations Committee, when seeking its approval of SEATO, that if there should be a "revolutionary movement" in Vietnam, the SEATO members "would consult together as to what to do about it . . . but we have no undertaking to put it down; all we have is an undertaking to consult."

While the United States sought stabilization, it claimed that North Vietnam continued to seek through guerrilla activity the conquest of Laos and South Vietnam. Political turbulence and the economic dissatisfaction of many South Vietnamese made possible the successful growth of bands of Vietcong (short for Viet Communists), which by 1959 were receiving training and supplies from North Vietnam. At the end of 1960 the Vietcong established the "National Front for the Liberation of South Vietnam." Making its forays at night, murdering headmen and terrorizing villages, the Vietcong succeeded in controlling large parts of the countryside. The government of South Vietnam was confined to the cities and main lines of communication.

Gradually the United States sent increasing aid to South Vietnam. Between 1954 and 1959, of $2.3 billion in aid, only two-fifths was military. American military advisers helped train the South Vietnam army. President Kennedy, inheriting the problem, tried to build more effective resistance in Vietnam, not only through military counterinsurgency, but also through gaining the support of the peasants. Vice President Johnson, visiting Saigon in May 1961, recommended aid but warned against direct military involvement: "American combat troop involvement is not only not required, it is not desirable. . . . Possibly Americans fail to

appreciate fully the subtlety that recently colonial peoples would not look with favor upon governments which invited or accept the return this soon of Western troops."

As political and military conditions in Vietnam continued to deteriorate, President Kennedy, despite his misgivings, added to the number of military advisers. By the time of his assassination in November 1963, the American personnel in that country had reached a total of 15,500. Reports from American officials in Vietnam were optimistic, though internal troubles there caused newspapermen to cable home dark predictions. A new era of even greater instability began in the fall of 1963 when the South Vietnamese army seized control of the government from the aristocratic nationalist Ngo Dinh Diem.

ESCALATING THE WAR

Despite growing difficulties in Vietnam, in the summer of 1964 they were overshadowed by the political campaign in the United States. The number of military advisers was up to 20,000, and on its way to 25,000. Then, in August, there occurred an episode that was to give legal grounds for the reshaping of the war: American destroyers on patrol in international waters in the Gulf of Tonkin reported that they had been attacked by North Vietnamese torpedo boats. (In 1968 Senator Fulbright, chairman of the Foreign Relations Committee, held hearings and sharply inquired about what had happened in the Tonkin Gulf. He raised the question of whether there actually had been an attack.) In 1964 President Johnson and Congress were in a mood to take stern measures.

Congress at the request of the President passed by a vote of 88 to 2 in the Senate and 416 to 0 in the House, a joint resolution "To promote the maintenance of international peace and security in Southeast Asia." The resolution authorized the President to "take all necessary measures" to protect American forces and "prevent further aggression" in Southeast Asia. Senators Wayne Morse and Ernest Gruening, the only two men in Congress to vote against the resolution, opposed it as being a "predated declaration of war power." Subsequently it did serve as legal authorization for the escalation of the conflict.

By the beginning of 1965 the Vietcong, aided not only by supplies but also by military units coming from North Vietnam along the jungle "Ho Chi Minh trail" through Laos, were in the ascendancy. The American "advisers" had gradually become combatants and were already suffering serious casualties. At this point the United States began a rapid build-up of troops in South Vietnam and the launching of regular bombing attacks upon supply depots, army camps, and transportation lines in North Vietnam. In 1965 United States armed forces in Vietnam grew from 23,000 to over 180,000; in 1966, the number was doubled; by the end of 1967, it was approaching an authorized half-million. Air sorties were intensified until the tonnage of bombs being dropped exceeded that in Europe during World War II. Casualties mounted. By every statistic, the Vietnam War was becoming one of the most serious in United States history.

According to Johnson, the purpose of this enormous effort was to stop aggression and preserve the freedom of the South Vietnamese people. "We want nothing for ourselves," he declared in 1965, "—only that the people of South Vietnam be allowed to guide their own country in their own way." Yet the Johnson administration supported the military dictatorship of General Nguyen Van Thieu, who in 1965 seized control of the South Vietnamese government.

The Debate on Vietnam [1965]

A great debate on the Vietnamese conflict is now raging all over the United States. It goes from the White House, Congress and the Pentagon to every home, office, factory, and farm. It is unresolved because the Government has not yet decided on its policy or, if it has, President Johnson is not telling the American people. The debate's subject, in its simplest form, is whether to fight a big war in Vietnam or to seek a way out through a combination of continuing defense and diplomatic negotiation.

The case for a vastly stepped-up American military commitment—as set forth . . . by military analyst Hanson W. Baldwin—is that the "Communist strategy of creeping aggression" must be stopped in Vietnam before it swallows all of Asia and the world. Under this theory, the United States should undertake saturation bombing of North Vietnam and send as many as a million American soldiers, sailors and fliers into a "war to win."

Such an approach discards any pretense that our objective in Vietnam is to protect the Vietnamese people; it turns the conflict into a naked ideological struggle that ignores all the deep cleavages recent years have brought in both the Communist and free worlds. Not one of our major allies in the West could be expected to endorse, much less actively assist, an American involvement so massive it would amount to a military occupation of leaderless South Vietnam. America's efforts to demonstrate the superiority of its social system by abolishing poverty and building a Great Society would vanish under the necessity for pouring our youth and treasure into a limitless solo adventure.—The New York Times, February 21, 1965.

While the United States increased its economic and military aid to the Thieu regime, the Soviet Union and the People's Republic of China provided larger and larger shipments of arms and other supplies to the Ho Chi Minh government of North Vietnam, and the North Vietnamese stepped up their military action and their assistance to the Vietcong. The American intervention seemed to be bringing together the rival Communist superpowers, who had a mutual interest in preventing a Communist defeat in Vietnam. There appeared to be a danger that, if the United States should press its intervention to the point of victory for Thieu, the Chinese might intervene with their own troops in Vietnam as they had done earlier in Korea.

On occasions, the United States limited or halted its bombings and other offensive actions in efforts to persuade the North Vietnamese to begin negotiations. Each time North Vietnam refused, for the most part adhering to the position that the United States must unconditionally and permanently end all bombing. At times a further stipulation was attached to this condition: all American forces were to leave Vietnam.

President Johnson and his advisers refused to end the bombing unconditionally and permanently. They pointed out that during each bombing halt at the time of a holiday truce the North Vietnamese rushed men and supplies southward or prepared for new attacks. American military leaders, following a policy of seeking out and destroying enemy forces, were confident at the beginning of 1968 that given sufficient men and matériel they could eventually triumph.

DEESCALATION BEGINS

In the United States, where television brought pictures of the cruelty and destruction of the war into every living room, the war became more and more unpopular. Liberals and university students participated vigorously in demonstrations, "teach-ins," and "sit-ins." Some young men burned their draft cards. Senator Fulbright and a group of his colleagues became bitter critics of President Johnson and Secretary of State Rusk. Public opinion polls indicated that a majority of Americans still endorsed the war, but it had become the transcendent issue in the nation.

The drain of enthusiasm accelerated rapidly in the early months of 1968. During a truce in the fighting to observe Tet—the Chinese New Year—the Vietcong suddenly struck in

---

Why We Were in Vietnam [1965]

Speaking at the Johns Hopkins University on April 7, 1965, shortly after deciding to send combat troops to South Vietnam, President Johnson said that the "deepening shadow of Communist China" was falling over Asia and that the trouble in Vietnam was "part of a wider pattern of aggressive purpose." He continued:

Why are we in South Vietnam?

We are there because we have a promise to keep. Since 1954 every American President has offered to support the people of South Vietnam. We have helped to build and we have helped to defend. Thus, over many years, we have made a national pledge to help South Vietnam defend its independence.

I intend to keep our promise.

To dishonor that pledge, to abandon this small and brave nation to its enemy—and to the terror that must follow—would be an unforgivable wrong.

We are there to strengthen world order. Around the globe—from Berlin to Thailand—are people whose well-being rests, in part, on the belief they can count on us if they are attacked. To leave Vietnam to its fate would shake the confidence of all these people in the value of American commitment. The result would be increased unrest and instability, or even war.

almost every city of South Vietnam. They were dislodged only after days of bitter fighting, great devastation, and heavy casualties. The single blow destroyed the homes of a half-million South Vietnamese. The Tet offensive intensified the opposition to the war on the part of a growing segment of the American voters.

In the fall of 1967 Senator Eugene Mc-Carthy of Minnesota had begun what seemed to be a futile protest campaign for the presidency. He had behind him only a handful of liberals and a growing group of enthusiastic students. In the first of the primary campaigns in New Hampshire, some of the young men cut their long hair and shaved their beards before ringing doorbells for McCarthy. In the voting, McCarthy was startlingly strong against Johnson, winning almost all of the delegates to the convention. The next day, Senator Robert Kennedy of New York, also a critic of the Vietnam War, announced his candidacy. There were indications that the challenge to President Johnson would be so strong that he might not be able to win renomination.

For months President Johnson had been considering a change in his course of action. On the evening of March 31, 1968, in a telecast to the nation, he suddenly announced that he was ordering a halt in the air attacks upon the populous areas of North Vietnam and was inviting the North Vietnamese to join him in a "series of mutual moves toward peace": "Tonight in the hope that this action will lead to early talks, I am taking the first step to de-escalate the conflict. We are reducing—substantially reducing—the present level of hostilities. And we are doing so unilaterally, and at once." At the close of his talk he made an announcement that removed any possibility that the deescalation could be looked upon as a political gesture: "I shall not seek and I will not accept the nomination of my party for another term."

The North Vietnamese government accepted President Johnson's invitation, and in May 1968 lengthy, fruitless negotiations began in Paris.

ELECTION OF 1968

During 1967 and 1968, the issues of the Vietnam War and urban violence became the focus of the preconvention presidential campaigns.

Significantly, the successful Republican contender, Richard Nixon, took no clear-cut stand on Vietnam. According to public opinion polls, he was running so far ahead in the first of the primary campaigns in New Hampshire that his principal opponent, Governor George Romney of Michigan, withdrew before the balloting. Nixon easily fended off last-minute threats from Governor Ronald Reagan of California on the right, and Governor Nelson Rockefeller of New York on the left, to win nomination on the first ballot. He chose Spiro Agnew, governor of Maryland, as his running mate.

The Vietnam debate, by contrast, wracked the Democratic party. After Johnson made his announcement not to run for another term, only Eugene McCarthy and Robert Kennedy (holding much the same views on Vietnam and domestic problems) were left to battle each other in the Democratic primaries. In late April, too late to become embroiled in the primaries, Vice President Humphrey entered the campaign. So many Democratic leaders in states without primaries backed Humphrey that he became an immediate favorite to win the nomination. Public attention focused on the primary contests. Kennedy won Indiana, lost Oregon to McCarthy, and then in the last primary in California, won again. At a Los Angeles hotel, on June 5, just after he had exhorted his cheering followers to seek victory with him at the Democratic convention, he was shot and killed by an assassin. National mourning for Kennedy brought a temporary cessation in the campaigning.

At the Democratic convention in Chicago, McCarthy (and some Kennedy followers backing Senator George McGovern of South Dakota) were unable to prevent the nomination of Humphrey on the first ballot. The critics of Humphrey, heir to administration policies, were bitter. Adding to their bitterness were the rough tactics of the Chicago police who shoved and harassed delegates and spectators to the convention, and before television cameras, clubbed and manhandled demonstrators in the streets of Chicago. An investigating committee subsequently referred to the violent police reactions to the taunts and attacks by the demonstrators as a "police riot." Through the campaign, Humphrey (although he had been distinguished for his liberalism throughout his political career) received little support from those who had followed McCarthy and Kennedy.

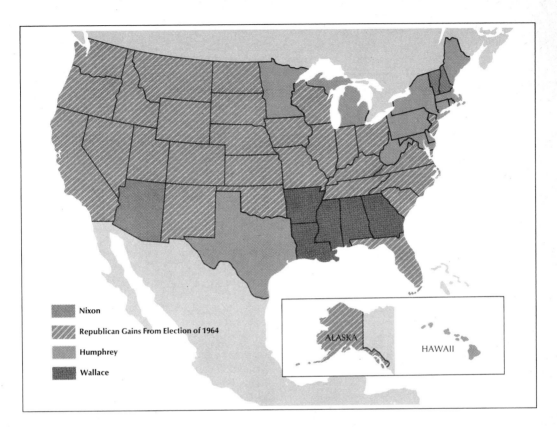

Nixon

Republican Gains From Election of 1964

Humphrey

Wallace

ALASKA

HAWAII

Election of 1968

The candidate who evoked the most enthusiastic responses and violent heckling wherever he spoke throughout the country was former Governor George Wallace of Alabama, running with General Curtis LeMay on the American Independent party ticket. "We are not talking about race," Wallace declared again and again, as he whipped up enthusiasm among audiences largely made up of white workers. General LeMay, who had been Chief of Staff of the Air Force, favored a hard line toward Vietnam. Public opinion polls showed Wallace at one point to be the favorite of a fifth of the voters; he hoped to throw the election into the House of Representatives. By Election Day his support had dropped substantially.

Neither of the major candidates evoked much enthusiasm. Nixon, campaigning methodically in almost computerized fashion, seemed far ahead from the outset. On the two main issues—law and order at home, and the Vietnam War—Nixon favored conciliation from

a position of strength. He declared in his acceptance address that he would heed "the voice of the great majority of Americans, the forgotten Americans, the non-shouters, the non-demonstrators, that are not racists or sick, that are not guilty of the crime that plagues the land." Regarding the Vietnam War, he pointed out that at every point he had been a critic of the administration, and Humphrey its defender; beyond that comment he made little commitment.

In contrast to Nixon's campaign, Humphrey's seemed lacking in both planning and finance. On Vietnam, he and his opponent differed little, but on the problem of poverty he pledged federal aid for a massive "Marshall Plan for the cities" in contrast to Nixon's insistence that private capital must help the poor to help themselves. During the last weeks of the campaign, Humphrey's standing in the public opinion polls increased markedly, and the statements of both candidates became sharper.

Yet, as the front runner, Nixon refused to debate on television. Both candidates were occupying middle positions, with Nixon to the right and Humphrey to the left of center.

By a fairly narrow margin of some 500,000 votes, out of more than 73 million cast, Nixon defeated Humphrey. The electoral vote was far more decisive, 302 for Nixon to 191 for Humphrey and 45 for Wallace. In his victory statement, Nixon returned to a theme he had frequently touched upon during the campaign and asserted that "the great objective of this Administration at the outset" would be "to bring the American people together."

Nixon and a New Balance

Even more than Presidents Kennedy and Johnson, President Nixon preoccupied himself with foreign affairs. In doing so he failed to "bring the American people together" and, instead, aroused increasing bitterness and division among them when he frustrated the hope for an early withdrawal from Vietnam. Nevertheless, he won widespread approval by finally withdrawing and by redirecting basic policy in such a way as to improve the prospects for moderating the cold war and for realizing what he hailed as a "generation of peace."

THE NIXON-KISSINGER APPROACH

On the basis of his earlier experience as Vice President, Nixon considered himself something of an expert in diplomacy. During his first term as President, he depended on Secretary of State William P. Rogers, a New York corporation lawyer, to administer the State Department and to carry out certain diplomatic missions. He also turned frequently to Secretary of Defense Melvin R. Laird, a former Wisconsin congressman, for advice. But he relied mainly on his special assistant for national security affairs, Henry A. Kissinger, a Harvard professor of international politics, for aid in both the making and the execution of policy. For four years, Kissinger's White House office overshadowed the Department of State. Then, after the inauguration of Nixon for a second term, the President put Kissinger at the head of the department. A refugee from Nazi Germany, Kissinger was the first German-born and the first Jewish Secretary of State (though a foreign-born Jew, Judah P. Benjamin, had been Secretary of State in the Confederacy during the Civil War).

Before his appointment as Nixon's security adviser, Kissinger in books and articles had criticized the assumptions on which American policy was based. To him, as well as to some other observers, it seemed that the developments of the 1960s had made obsolete the containment policy of the 1950s. The signs of growing antagonism between Communist China and Communist Russia belied the concept of a single, combined program of Communist aggression. No longer were there only two power centers, the United States and the Soviet Union; there were now at least three, with China, and potentially more than that, if western Europe and Japan were to be included. For this new "multipolar" world, Kissinger proposed a flexible, many-sided balance-of-power system to take the place of the rigid, two-sided system that had prevailed since the start of the cold war. In the new arrangement the United States would deal with Russia and China on the basis of practical interests rather than anti-Communist feelings.

Early in his first administration Nixon implied a change in policy when he put forth what he termed the Nixon Doctrine. The United States, he declared, would "participate in the defense and development of allies and friends" but would leave the "basic responsibility" to those friends themselves, especially when it came to actual fighting. In 1971 he clearly announced the new aim of a complex equilibrium: "It will be a safer world and a better world if we have a strong healthy United States, Europe, Soviet Union, China, Japan—each balancing the other, not playing one against the other, an even balance."

When Nixon decided to open relations with the Chinese People's Republic and to improve relations with the Soviet Union, his decision was in keeping with the new diplomacy that he and Kissinger had proposed. Meanwhile Nixon continued the war in Vietnam, though Kissinger believed that American involvement had been based on "an outmoded foreign policy concept." Nixon undertook to "Vietnamize" the war — that is, to shift the burden of actual combat from Americans to the South Vietnamese, in accordance with the Nixon Doctrine — but the process was painfully slow.

VIETNAMIZATION   1969–1972

Regarding Vietnam, Nixon said in May 1969 that he hoped to achieve "a peace we can live with and a peace to be proud of." He did not specify the kind of peace he had in mind, but presumably it would be one that kept in power the Thieu regime in Saigon. Whatever the details, his kind of peace, like Lyndon B. Johnson's, remained unacceptable to the Ho Chi Minh government of Hanoi. In Paris the talks

Vietnamese Children Flee Napalm
Terrified children with napalm burns run from the village of Trang Ban, southwest of Saigon in South Vietnam, when South Vietnamese government planes mistakenly drop fire bombs on the village, June 8, 1972. (UPI)

went on—among the representatives of the United States, South Vietnam, North Vietnam, and the National Liberation Front—but rumors of progress toward a settlement proved disappointing again and again. The demise of Ho Chi Minh, late in the summer, had no visible effect on either the Paris negotiations or the Vietnam bloodshed.

As the months passed and no end to the fighting appeared in sight, "Johnson's war" began to be looked upon as "Nixon's war," and its critics in Congress and throughout the country grew in numbers and determination. By the summer's end an opinion poll showed a clear majority of the American people believed the involvement in Vietnam was a mistake. Youthful peace advocates were planning a series of nationwide demonstrations to occupy one day in October, two days in November, three in December, and so on, until the United States was out of the war. Nixon turned opinion in favor of his Vietnam policy, however, by a televised speech on November 3, 1969. He said the "silent majority" agreed with him that a "precipitate withdrawal" would be "disastrous for the future of peace" in the world. Vice President Agnew afterward denounced the peace demonstrators as an "effete corps of impudent snobs" and reprimanded newspaper and television commentators for daring to question the Nixon policy.

Making a concession to the war's critics, Nixon had announced earlier the beginning of partial troop withdrawals, the first of which would reduce by 60,000 the United States force of about 540,000 men in Vietnam. These withdrawals, he explained, were steps toward the "Vietnamization" of the war. That is, the South Vietnamese themselves would be trained and equipped to take over the defense of their country as the American fighting men were gradually pulled out.

Nixon also sought to lessen opposition by reforming the draft, which because of its uncertainties and inequities added to the difficulty of justifying the sacrifice of American lives in a small and distant country. To its critics, the draft seemed all the worse because of the highhanded way in which it was administered. Its director persisted in advising local draft boards to punish antiwar demonstrators by conscripting them, even after a federal court had held this to be illegal. Nixon recommended that the conscription law be changed so as to provide

for a "draft lottery" that would take only nineteen-year-olds and would take them at random. Such a lottery went into effect in 1970. Going still further, Nixon urged the formation of an all-volunteer army, with improved pay and other incentives for enlistment. By 1973, Americans were no longer being drafted.

The Vietnamization plan was going so well, Nixon announced in April 1970, that he would bring home 150,000 additional men within a year or so. Suddenly, before the end of April, he broke the startling news that he had ordered American troops to cross into neutral Cambodia and, with their South Vietnamese allies, to seize military bases that the enemy had been using for operations in South Vietnam. He explained that "increased military aggression" by the Communists in Cambodia had begun to jeopardize the continuing success of the Vietnamization program.

Up to this point, Nixon said, it had been American policy "to scrupulously respect the neutrality" of Cambodia. What he did not tell the people was that the United States was already deliberately and systematically violating Cambodian neutrality. For more than a year he had personally authorized the secret bombing of suspected North Vietnamese bases on the Cambodian side of the border. For several years American ground forces had been carrying on clandestine operations in Cambodia and in Laos as well. If these facts had been made public at the time, the popular protest in the United States might have gone to even greater extremes than it actually went.

At the news of the Cambodian incursion, the languishing peace movement came to life with a more determined spirit than ever. On campuses all over this country, during May, youthful protesters demanded that the universities close down in a "strike" against the government's war policy. A radical minority resorted to violence, smashing windows and fire-bombing buildings. Policemen and national guardsmen arrived to face rock-throwing mobs, which they tried to disperse with tear gas and, in a few instances, with gunfire. Four students (all white) were shot and killed at Kent State University in Ohio, and two (both black) at Jackson State University in Mississippi. A few months later a physicist died when antiwar protesters set off an explosion that wrecked several buildings at the University of Wisconsin in Madison.

Kent State Killings
*Students at Kent State University, Kent, Ohio, come to the aid of
a fellow student who was wounded when, on May 4, 1970, national
guardsmen fired tear gas and then bullets, killing four students
and injuring several others. The guardsmen were on the campus to
put down antiwar demonstrations, which had culminated in the burning
of a university building. (UPI)*

After ending the invasion of Cambodia, in June 1970, Nixon launched an invasion of Laos, in February 1971. This time he sent no American ground troops (Congress in the Defense Appropriations Act of 1970 had prohibited their use in Laos) but gave American air support to the invading South Vietnamese army. "The South Vietnamese by themselves can hack it," he declared. This was a test of his Vietnamization program, and it proved a failure. Within a few weeks the badly mauled army scrambled back to the relative safety of South Vietnam.

American critics of "Nixon's war," like those of "Johnson's war," were appalled by the horrible sufferings it brought upon civilians, both South Vietnamese and North Vietnamese. Millions of them were deprived of life, health, shelter, or livelihood as a result of American action—napalm bombing, population transfer, village destruction, crop burning, and forest defoliation. Hundreds were shot or bayoneted by American soldiers, as in the "My Lai massacre" (March 16, 1968), for which Lieutenant William L. Calley, Jr., was convicted of premeditated murder in 1971.

Nixon had said the Calley case should be vigorously prosecuted, so that the incident would not "smear the decent men" who had gone to war in Vietnam. Continuing his troop withdrawals, he announced in January 1972 that the total of American troops in Vietnam would shortly be reduced to 69,000, the lowest figure in nearly seven years. As troops were withdrawn, American casualties in the war decreased, and so did the outcry at home. Yet, while taking out ground forces, Nixon was sending in more and more air and naval forces. Eventually he authorized the dropping of a greater tonnage of bombs than Johnson had, and these bombs killed far more civilians than the 102 that Calley was charged with murdering at My Lai. Nixon ordered his greatest escalation of the war against the Vietnamese Communists after he had dramatically displayed his friendship with the Chinese and Russian Communists.

RAPPROCHEMENT WITH CHINA

Until 1949 the United States had sought to maintain the Open Door policy in China. Then, after the Communists under Mao Tse-tung and Chou En-lai got control of the Chinese mainland, the doors were closed on both sides. The Peking government taught hatred of Americans and excluded them from the country. The Washington government prohibited trade between the United States and the Chinese mainland, refused to recognize the Mao regime, and opposed its being represented in the United Nations. Washington continued to treat Chiang Kai-shek, after his flight to the island of Taiwan, as an ally and as the rightful head of all China.

From 1949 to 1971, no American in national politics had opposed the recognition of the Peking government more resolutely than had Richard M. Nixon. Eventually, making a complete turnabout, he reopened relations in a spectacular display of presidential diplomacy.

Recognition was long past due. China was the largest nation in the world, with about a quarter of all the world's people. It was one of the nuclear powers, having set off its first atomic bomb in 1964 and its first hydrogen bomb in 1967. By making friends with the Peking leaders, Nixon could hope to get their cooperation in ending the Vietnam War. He could also hope to use China as a counterbalance to the Soviet Union and thus as a means of inducing in the Russians a conciliatory mood and hastening a détente. The Chinese leaders, for their part, were eager to have the United States as a potentiality in their own balance-of-power arrangement against the Soviet Union. They feared that the Russians might attack China in an attempt to destroy the Chinese nuclear installations.

Early in 1971 Nixon hinted at a change in American policy when, in a public statement, he used the legitimate name "People's Republic of China" for what he and other American officials always had called simply "Red China" or "Communist China." That spring the Peking government invited a team of American table-tennis players to visit China, and the Nixon administration gave them permission to go. Such "Ping-Pong diplomacy" led to speculation about higher-level contacts between the two countries but hardly prepared the American people for the startling announcement Nixon made in July. He said he himself had received an invitation to visit the People's Republic (an invitation that Kissinger had arranged on a secret trip to Peking) and would make the visit within the next several months.

To succeed in his new China policy, Nixon would have to approve the admission of the People's Republic to the United Nations. In the past the American delegates to the U.N. had repeatedly managed to prevent the seating of a Peking delegate, but the majorities on the American side had been growing smaller and smaller. Now the United States representative proposed giving a seat on the Security Council to the People's Republic while keeping a place for Nationalist China, that is, Taiwan. The Chinese Communists insisted, however, that the Chinese Nationalists must go. In October 1971 the United Nations admitted the People's Republic and expelled Nationalist China.

Nixon's China visit, when it finally came in February 1972, proved to be a theatrical success. For a whole week American television with Chinese cooperation followed the President and his entourage and explored various aspects of life in what had been to Americans a relatively unknown, mysterious land. Nixon was shown visiting the Great Wall and other tourist attractions, wining and dining with Communist dignitaries, exchanging pleasantries with party leader Mao Tse-tung and Premier Chou En-lai. Never before had a summit meeting been so elaborately staged or so extensively viewed. One effect was to reduce, if not to reverse, the anti-Chinese feelings that had been instilled in the American people for a generation.

The summit meeting was also something of a diplomatic success. In Peking the leaders of the two countries agreed to scientific, cultural, journalistic, and other exchanges and to the development of trade. They did not agree to the immediate establishment of formal rela-

Nixon in China
The first American President to visit China while in office, Nixon received a carefully staged welcome from the Chinese Communist leaders. On the day of his arrival, February 21, 1972, he was invited to review an honor guard of the Chinese army in company with Premier Chou En-lai. (UPI)

tions, with an exchange of ambassadors. The Communists, looking on Taiwan as part of their country, refused to accept an embassy from the United States so long as Taiwan had one. The United States must first break off diplomatic relations with Nationalist China. If the summit conferees arrived at any understanding in regard to the Vietnam War, they made no public announcement of the fact.

On subsequent journeys to Peking, Kissinger worked out details of trade arrangements and other matters and managed, as he put it, to "accelerate the normalization of relations." A year after the Nixon visit, the two countries agreed to set up "liaison offices" in each other's

capitals. Except in name, these offices practically amounted to embassies. The United States was expected soon to remove some of the 9,000 American troops on Taiwan. By 1973, it appeared that relations with China were getting back to normal, after nearly a quarter century of nonrecognition and estrangement.

DÉTENTE WITH RUSSIA

Nixon had been the first American President to make a trip, while in office, to China; he was the second to travel to Russia. His Russian visit, in May 1972, provided less drama, for there was less mystery about the Soviet Union, less to be revealed to the American public. Yet the summit conference in Moscow was even more important than the one in Peking, since the Soviet Union, like the United States, was a true superpower, and China, as yet, was not.

From both the Russian and the American points of view, the time was ripe for a move toward a new understanding. The Soviet government, under the leadership of Communist party chief Leonid Brezhnev, looked to the United States for possible future support against China, for aid in overcoming Russia's technological lag, and for wheat and other foodstuffs to make up for her serious crop shortages. Having achieved something like nuclear parity with the United States, the Russians also were interested in the economies of slowing down the arms race. Nixon and his advisers shared the desire for a limitation of nuclear armaments, wished to promote American trade, and hoped for Soviet cooperation in ending the war in Vietnam and preventing war in other parts of the world, especially in the Middle East.

By 1972 the United States still led the Soviet Union in the number of long-range planes kept in readiness for delivering nuclear bombs. Moreover, this country had almost twice as many submarines equipped with nuclear mis-

An English View of Détente
With President Nixon visiting the Russian Communist leader Brezhnev in 1972, and Brezhnev returning the visit in 1973, America's NATO allies became distrustful of the summit diplomacy between the two. Fears grew that Nixon was sacrificing the interests of the United States as well as those of NATO. These feelings are reflected in this cartoon, which appeared in the Daily Express *of London on June 25, 1973. (Cummings/London* Daily Express*)*

"Which rumour is true, Mr. Agnew? Is Russia about to become the 52nd State of America, or Mr. Nixon to become Vice-President of Russia after he's fired from the White House?"

siles. But the Soviet Union had moved ahead in regard to land-based intercontinental ballistic missiles, or ICBMs, which could carry nuclear explosives all the way from the one country to the other.

The two superpowers were engaged in a "doomsday game" of competition in the development of more and more deadly weapons and delivery systems—a game that could conceivably lead to mutual annihilation. Each of the two was testing a multiple independently targeted reentry vehicle, or MIRV, a device that could be sent into orbit and then directed back into the earth's atmosphere above the enemy's territory, where it would drop separate nuclear warheads on widely scattered targets. Each nation was also planning an antiballistic-missile system, or ABM, which was intended to protect population centers or ICBM emplacements against missile attack. In the ABM system, nuclear "antimissile missiles" would be launched to intercept and explode approaching enemy missiles before these could reach their targets. The Nixon administration's ABM project aroused considerable opposition in the United States. Critics said the ABM would have little effect on ICBMs and still less on MIRVs but would endanger civilians in its vicinity and would intensify the arms race.

Already the United States and the Soviet Union had taken a small step toward the control of nuclear weapons, a step beyond the 1963 treaty banning atmospheric tests. In the "nonproliferation" treaty of 1968 the two powers agreed to discourage the spread of nuclear weapon technology to nations not yet possessing it. Great Britain was the only other nuclear power to sign the treaty, but France and China were producing their own hydrogen bombs, and Israel and India (among other countries) appeared to be capable of doing so. The treaty, then, did not prevent a widening of the arms race, nor did it lessen the competition between the two front runners.

The two took a step toward lessening this competition when, in 1969, American and Russian diplomats met in Helsinki to begin discussion of a strategic arms limitation treaty, or SALT. After continuing their talks, in Vienna, for two years and a half, the negotiators arrived at a temporary agreement. This first-phase treaty, or SALT I, would limit each country to only two ABMs and the existing number of

ICBMs. The compromise would leave the United States superior in numbers of warheads and the Soviet Union, with its warheads of greater size, superior in total megatonnage. The limitations were to last for five years. Applying only to quantity and not to quality, they would do nothing to prevent a continuing and even heightening contest for arms improvements in the meantime.

At their Moscow meeting in 1972, Nixon and Brezhnev signed SALT I and several other agreements. One of these promised a vast expansion of trade through American tariff reductions and credit extensions. A gigantic "wheat deal" led immediately to the sale of about a fourth of the total American wheat supply at a bargain price, one well below the market price, and the American government was to make up the difference by means of subsidies to the American wheat sellers. The prospect of a reduction in arms spending, however, did not last long. After Nixon's return from Moscow, the administration asked Congress to approve the largest military budget ever except during a declared war.

In June 1973 Nixon welcomed Brezhnev to Washington for a round of partying and further negotiating. A series of new agreements confirmed and extended those of the previous year. The two countries pledged to abstain from nuclear war, to speed up the conclusion of SALT II for a permanent "freeze" on offensive nuclear arms, and to cooperate in various economic, scientific, and cultural fields. Toasting his Russian guest at a dinner, Nixon said: "The question is: Shall the world's two strongest nations constantly confront one another in areas which might lead to war, or shall we work together for peace?" The question remained to be answered, despite all the talk of détente.

EXIT FROM INDOCHINA

Nixon's China and Russia diplomacy gave him added strength in his conduct of the Vietnam War. Neither China nor Russia stopped sending military supplies to North Vietnam, but both powers indicated that there were limits to their aid. Apparently each was somewhat reluctant to risk damaging its new relationship with the United States.

Vietnam Cease-Fire Agreement [1973]

Following are some of the key provisions of the "agreement on ending the war and restoring peace in Vietnam" that American and Vietnamese representatives signed on January 27, 1973:

Article 1. "The United States and all other countries respect the independence, sovereignty, unity, and territorial integrity of Vietnam as recognized by the 1954 Geneva Agreements on Vietnam."

Article 5. "Within 60 days of the signing of this agreement, there will be a total withdrawal from South Vietnam of troops, military advisers, and military personnel . . . of the United States. . . ."

Article 8. "The return of captured military personnel and foreign civilians of the parties shall be carried out simultaneously with and completed not later than the same day as the troop withdrawal. . . ."

Article 9. "The South Vietnamese people shall decide themselves the political future of South Vietnam through genuinely free and democratic general elections under international supervision."

Article 15. "The reunification of Vietnam shall be carried out step by step through peaceful means on the basis of discussion and agreements between North and South Vietnam, without coercion or annexation by either party, and without foreign interference. . . . Pending the reunification . . . The military demarcation line between the two zones at the 17th parallel is only provisional and not a political or territorial boundary, as provided for in paragraph 6 of the Final Declaration of the 1954 Geneva Conference."

Between Nixon's China visit and his Russia visit, the fighting in Vietnam actually intensified, going in some respects to greater lengths than ever before. In March 1972 the North Vietnamese launched their heaviest attack since the Tet offensive of 1968. Well equipped with tanks and artillery, they crossed into South Vietnam and proceeded to overrun much of its territory. In April Nixon responded by sending B-52 bombers to strike near Hanoi and Haiphong, thus reversing Johnson's 1968 decision to deescalate the air war in the north. On May 8 – just before his scheduled trip to Peking – Nixon ordered the mining of Haiphong harbor and six other North Vietnamese ports, so as to prevent the delivery of war supplies by ship from China or the Soviet Union. Johnson had refrained from this extreme measure for fear it would provoke retaliation from one or both of those two countries. Now they confined themselves to comparatively mild protests.

In July 1972 the Paris peace negotiators (representing the two Vietnams, the Vietcong, and the United States) met for their 150th session, with no indication that, after four years, they were making any progress toward a settlement. It had recently come to light, however,

that Kissinger and North Vietnamese Foreign Secretary Le Duc Tho were meeting separately and secretly, and it was rumored that they were nearing a cease-fire agreement. "Peace is at hand," Kissinger finally announced on October 26, just before the American presidential election. The North Vietnamese government was ready and eager to accept the terms that Kissinger and Tho had arrived at, but President Thieu of South Vietnam raised objections, and Nixon refused to give his approval. On December 16, after Kissinger and Tho had broken off negotiations, Kissinger declared that the agreement was 99 percent complete, but he did not explain what the missing 1 percent consisted of.

The next day, December 17, without any announcement from the White House, American planes began to bomb North Vietnamese cities in the heaviest and most destructive raids of the entire war. The targets were docks, airfields, railyards, power plants, antiaircraft defenses, and the like, but these were located in or near residential areas, and homes, shops, schools, and even hospitals were hit. The destruction was achieved at considerable cost to the Americans. In the previous seven years of the Vietnam War, only one B-52 bomber had been lost in combat. Now, in two weeks of round-the-clock raiding, fifteen of the high-flying giant planes fell when struck by Russian-made surface-to-air missiles. On December 30 Nixon called off the bombing and announced that the North Vietnamese had consented to resuming the secret peace talks.

On January 27, 1973, representatives of the four parties (the United States and South Vietnam, North Vietnam and the "Provisional Revolutionary Government" of South Vietnam, that is, the Vietcong) signed an "agreement on ending the war and restoring peace in Vietnam." The main provisions of this agreement were the same as those of the October 1972 agreement, which Nixon had refused to approve. There was to be an immediate cease-fire, and within sixty days prisoners of war were to be returned and foreign military forces in South Vietnam were to be withdrawn. Contradictorily, both the South Vietnamese right of self-determination and the unity of all Vietnam, North and South, were recognized. Laos and Cambodia were to be evacuated, and their independence and neutrality were to be respected. An international commission was to supervise the cease-fire.

Nixon proclaimed that at last he had won a "peace with honor." In fact, he had gained two things in the peace arrangement. One was the return of several hundred American prisoners of war (whose numbers, incidentally, he had recently increased through the Christmas-season bombing and the exposure of downed B-52 crews to capture). The other gain for Nixon was to keep Thieu in power in South Vietnam for the time being. But Nixon had also yielded a lot in the truce terms. These included several references to the 1954 Geneva settlement, which the United States had never signed. They reconfirmed the Geneva principle of the ultimate reunification of Vietnam. That was what the North Vietnamese and the Vietcong had been fighting for, and at the time of the cease-fire they were in a strong position for achieving it, since they now occupied a large part of South Vietnam's territory.

Such were the inconclusive results of more than a decade of direct American military involvement in Vietnam, and they had been accomplished at a staggering cost. In money, this exceeded $100 billion for the United States

alone. In lives, it was approximately 1 million Vietnamese Communists, 200,000 South Vietnamese, and 55,000 Americans. Some 300,000 Americans were wounded, half of them seriously, and many of these permanently maimed. A total of about 3 million Americans served in the war, most of them unwillingly. Perhaps as many as 70,000 evaded service by dodging the draft or deserting after enlistment. Thousands of deserters and draft dodgers remained in hiding at home or in refuge abroad, particularly in Canada and Sweden, as Nixon with the backing of a public majority vowed to grant no amnesty. The psychological cost to Americans, both veterans and nonveterans, was incalculable. Never since the Civil War had the people been so badly divided. Understandably, the announcement of peace, after the longest war in American history, provoked no such demonstrations of popular rejoicing as had followed World War I and World War II.

There was no peace in Vietnam. The international commission, set up to supervise the cease-fire, was powerless to keep the Communists and the non-Communists apart. During the first year after the cease-fire the Vietnamese (both sides together) suffered more battle deaths than the Americans had suffered during the ten years before it. In Laos the fighting ended about a month after the cease-fire, when the Communists were left in control of more than half the country. In Cambodia the war continued, and American planes kept up and intensified their bombing in an effort to save the Lon Nol regime from its Communist enemies. Nixon refused to stop the bombing of Cambodia until Congress compelled him to do so.

Congress had been growing more and more critical of the President's assertion of warmaking powers without any congressional declaration of war, and both the Senate and the House had begun to consider proposals, mild at first, for holding him to constitutional limits. In 1969 the Senate advised the President that, in the future, he should get the approval of Congress before committing the United States to the use of armed forces abroad. In 1971 Congress repealed the 1964 Gulf of Tonkin resolution, which Johnson and Nixon had treated as the equivalent of a war declaration. Congress could have stopped the war by cutting off appropriations for it, but this would have been unpopular, since it would have looked like

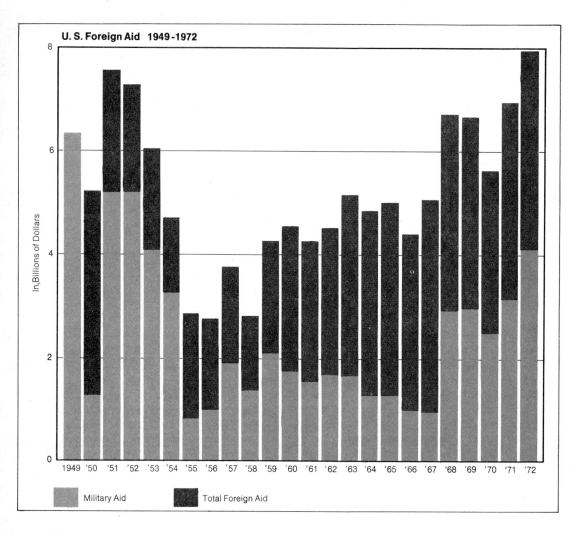

U. S. Foreign Aid 1949-1972

In Billions of Dollars

Military Aid   Total Foreign Aid

Since 1949 both the total amount expended to aid foreign countries and the proportion of this amount expended for military purposes have fluctuated from year to year. The nonmilitary expenditures have been intended chiefly to provide technical assistance, machinery, food, and capital loans. The growth in military aid after 1967 mainly reflects the increase in support for the government of South Vietnam.

abandoning American soldiers in the field. Nixon maintained that, as commander in chief, he had the power to use the armed forces as he saw fit in order to protect the troops while he was withdrawing them under his Vietnamization plan.

After the signing of the cease-fire and the withdrawal of the troops, Nixon no longer had that justification for waging war as he and his advisers saw fit. When he persisted in bombing Cambodia, despite congressional protests,

Congress set August 15, 1973, as a deadline for the cessation of all American military activity in Indochina, including the air warfare in Cambodia. Nixon discontinued the bombing only at the last minute.

Several months later Congress passed, over Nixon's veto, a measure intended to prevent a President from involving the country in future wars without congressional approval. Under this war-powers resolution of 1973, the President could order no troops into action without reporting to Congress, and he would have to halt the action immediately if Congress objected, or in ninety days if Congress failed to give its positive permission. The new law was a response to a growth in presidential power that Congresses as well as Presidents had been fostering for many years. Whether the measure was wise for the nuclear age, and whether it would work in any case, only time could tell.

OLD FRIENDSHIPS UNDER STRAIN

While relations with China and Russia were improving, relations with Japan, Western Germany, Great Britain, and other allies were getting worse.

The American conduct of the Vietnam War antagonized many Europeans. Some felt the United States was neglecting western Europe while preoccupying itself with Southeast Asia. Some were outraged by the warfare upon Vietnamese civilians, especially by the 1972 Christmas-season bombing of North Vietnamese cities.

The switch in American policy toward China and Russia disturbed the leaders of Japan and the western European countries. Japan, which had looked to the United States for security against China, now worried about the prospect of being abandoned. West Germany, under Chancellor Willy Brandt, approved of détente and was furthering it by making treaties with the Soviet Union and its Polish and East German satellites. To offset the risks of his new diplomacy, however, Brandt counted upon all-out American assistance in case of a Russian threat, and he wondered if he could be sure of such support after Nixon's negotiations with Brezhnev. British officials suspected that, in the negotiations, Nixon had gained less than he had given up. In general, the allies were uneasy at the thought of the United States going over their heads and dealing directly with the Communist powers.

Both American and European spokesmen pledged their respective governments' continued devotion to the North Atlantic Alliance as the alliance approached the twenty-fifth year of its existence. After the Vietnam cease-fire an American official said, "we have not been neglecting Europe. It is just a matter of Vietnam moving off the stage, and we now see that Europe is the center of the stage, as it normally is.". Kissinger declared 1973 to be "the year of Europe" and proposed a "new Atlantic Charter" that would include Japan. Nixon was expected to offset his summit diplomacy with China and Russia by going to Japan and Europe to conclude new understandings with them. But his trips were repeatedly postponed.

The constant repetition of mutual reassurances, on the part of American and European leaders, was itself a sign that NATO was in serious trouble. American leaders had to pay some attention to the voice of the people, and more and more the American people were questioning the necessity of keeping United States troops in Europe (most of them, about 215,000, in West Germany). In response to popular demand, some of the Democrats in Congress were proposing to compel a reduction in the number of American troops abroad.

Nixon, along with Brandt and other western European leaders, opposed the withdrawal of American forces from western Europe unless there should be a corresponding withdrawal of Russian forces from Eastern Europe. Nixon and Brezhnev, at their 1972 Moscow meeting, had agreed to the calling of a European security conference for the discussion of "mutual balanced force reductions" on both sides, and MBFR talks were getting under way in Vienna. Meanwhile the American government disagreed with its European allies about the sharing of NATO costs. The Nixon administration insisted that the allies, now that they were financially strong, ought to make larger contributions than they had been making to the common defense.

Toward the European Economic Community (the Common Market), the American government's attitude had become ambivalent by 1973. On the one hand, the United States still officially favored the strengthening of the EEC and approved its enlargement when Great Britain was finally admitted, along with Ireland and Denmark. On the other hand, the United States seemed to fear the economic competition of the EEC and complained that it was discriminating against American exports.

Already there was a crisis in trade and monetary relations between the United States and both Japan and Europe. For years, the American government and American citizens had been spending larger and larger quantities of dollars abroad, for tourist travel, foreign goods, capital investments, and economic and military aid. The expenditures on the Vietnam War, after its escalation in 1964, added greatly to the dollar outflow. All together, Americans spent far more in foreign countries than foreigners spent in the United States. Hence the balance of payments was upset, and the dollar tended to lose value in relation to foreign currencies.

To keep the various currencies in a stable relationship with one another, the gold standard had been reestablished and the International Monetary Fund had been set up at the end of World War II. The price of gold was then fixed (as it had been since 1934) at $35 an ounce – which meant that the dollar was worth 1/35 of an ounce of gold. The International Monetary Fund was to buy currencies when necessary to stop their decline in value, but the surplus of dollars proved too much for the Fund's resources. Foreign holders of excess dollars began to exchange them for gold, and by 1968 the United States was suffering a serious depletion of its gold supply. At that time, President de Gaulle of France was glad to see the United States financially weakened, but six other European governments joined with the American government in agreeing not to sell their gold to private buyers but to use it only for transactions among themselves. For these transactions, the price was kept at $35 an ounce. On the regular gold market it was allowed to rise and fall in accordance with supply and demand.

This two-price arrangement seemed to work for a time, as the exchange rate remained constant between the dollar and the yen, mark, pound, franc, and lira. But the balance-of-payments gap persisted and, to make up for it, the American government had to transfer gold to other governments. By 1971 the Nixon administration felt compelled to take drastic steps. It put a temporary 10 percent surcharge on imports. Then it stopped giving up gold in return for the dollars that foreign governments held. This meant that the exchange rates were no longer controlled, and the dollar price of other currencies, especially the mark and the yen, began to rise. Finally Nixon did what no President since Franklin D. Roosevelt had done – he officially devalued the dollar. He raised the official price of gold from $35 to $38 an ounce and thus reduced the gold content of the dollar from 1/35 to 1/38 of an ounce. In 1973

he further devalued the dollar, raising the gold price to $42.

Devaluation was intended to overcome the balance-of-payments deficit by causing Americans to buy less of foreign goods and services, and foreigners to buy more of American goods and services. But the deficit kept growing, and the dollar kept falling. By the summer of 1973 it was worth only a little more than half as many German marks as it formerly had been. To cut down imports, the Nixon administration threatened to raise tariffs and to impose other trade controls, while the Japanese and the Europeans protested. By this time, exports had begun to increase, with large shipments abroad of American wheat and other crops. Now, to cut down on exports and prevent shortages at home, the administration put limits on the foreign sale of farm commodities and steel scrap, thus provoking new protests, especially on the part of Japan.

The international trade and monetary system of the preceding quarter century appeared to have broken down, and economic conflicts between the United States and its allies were putting a serious strain on the alliances.

TROUBLE IN NONPOWER REGIONS

The Nixon-Kissinger theory of five power centers left a subordinate place for the nonpower regions of the world, the distinctly weaker countries of Latin America, Asia, and Africa. Yet clashes arising in these areas could jeopardize relations among the powerful, as the Vietnam War at times had seemed likely to do.

During Nixon's presidency, the relations of the United States with many of the Latin American countries deteriorated. At the outset his personal representative, Governor Nelson Rockefeller of New York, on a fact-finding tour, ran into popular hostility like that which Nixon himself had experienced when, as Vice President, he made a similar trip in 1958. Capitalizing upon the popular sentiment, new military governments in Peru and Bolivia seized the property of American corporations. The constitutionally elected government of the radical Salvador Allende did the same in Chile. In retaliation, Nixon undertook to block financial aid, from either American or international sources, to Chile and other countries that failed to compensate American property owners satisfactorily. It was revealed that officials of the International Telephone and Telegraph Company, an American-based multinational corporation having extensive holdings in Chile, had consulted with officials of the Central Intelligence Agency about possible methods of preventing Allende's election to the Chilean presidency. This revelation lent some credence to the charge, in 1973, after Allende's overthrow and death in a military coup, that the American government had connived with his opponents.

In Asia the Nixon administration reversed American policy toward India while reversing it toward China. Previous administrations had tried to encourage the development of India, the largest democracy in the world, as an offset to China, the largest Communist nation. They had also given arms aid to Pakistan, a military dictatorship, for defense against the Chinese. Pakistan had used its American equipment in clashes with India, however, and had become more and more friendly with China.

In 1971 the Pakistani ruler, Yahya Khan, ordered his armed forces to put down discontent in East Pakistan, and they attempted to do so by killing hundreds of thousands of civilians. Millions of East Pakistanis took refuge in India, where they constituted a grave burden for India's economy. India's Prime Minister, Indira Gandhi, turned to the Soviet Union for support, signed a friendship treaty with Brezhnev, and launched a war to detach East Pakistan from the rule of Yahya Khan. During this Indo-Pakistani war, Nixon wanted the United States to "tilt in favor of Pakistan," and he ordered an American fleet to the Bay of Bengal, thus giving Indians the impression that he was trying to intimidate them. India quickly won the war and proclaimed the independence of East Pakistan under the name of Bangladesh. The Nixon policy accomplished nothing except to reinforce the India-Russia alignment and lessen American influence on the Indian subcontinent.

The Middle East, the scene of continual fighting between Arabs and Israelis, presented a dilemma for the Nixon administration, as it had done for previous administrations. Israel (whose prime minister, Golda Meir, was a former Milwaukee schoolteacher) had many sympathizers, both Jewish and non-Jewish, within the United States. They could exert considerable pressure in American politics. The Arab countries could count upon no such American constituency, but they possessed two-thirds of the world's known oil reserves, and they occupied areas that were of strategic importance to the United States in its global conflict with the Soviet Union. So long as the United States backed the Israelis, it antagonized the Arabs and tended to throw them into the Russian embrace. If, however, the United States should discontinue its support, Israel might face destruction as an independent country.

Violence in the Middle East had been renewed in 1967, after a United Nations peacekeeping force had been withdrawn at the demand of Egypt. Expecting an attack from Egypt, which was well equipped with Russian arms, Israel struck and in the Six-Day War defeated Egypt, Jordan, and Syria and occupied parts of their territory. A 1967 U.N. resolution called upon Israel to withdraw her armed forces from the occupied territories, but recognized the right of every nation in the area to "live in peace within secure and recognized boundaries." Israel refused to budge without guarantees of her security. After the 1967 war Israel rearmed with American aid, and Egypt and Syria with Russian aid. Intermittent shelling and raiding went on across the borders between Israel and her neighbors.

The Nixon administration, at first, attempted an "even-handed" policy in the Middle East. Nixon hoped for a compromise that would satisfy both sides and make it unnecessary for Egypt or Syria to depend on the Soviet Union. The Russians cooperated to the extent of agreeing to U.N. mediation, which resulted only in a brief truce, in 1970. Then Palestinian Arabs, living as refugees in Jordan, revolted against Jordan's King Hussein, who was trying to stay on good terms with Israel and the United States. While Hussein was putting down the rebellion, Nixon made a display of naval strength in the Mediterranean Sea, presumably as a warning to Russia against allowing Egypt to intervene in Jordan. Thereafter the Soviet Union rapidly increased its naval force in the Mediterranean, and Russian ships soon outnumbered American vessels there.

After 1972 the détente between the United States and the Soviet Union could have been expected to defuse the explosive Middle Eastern situation. In October 1973, however, war again erupted, when on the Jewish holy day of

Peacemaking in the Middle East

In the spring of 1974, after repeated visits to Egypt, Israel, and Syria, Secretary of State Kissinger succeeded in working out a cease-fire between Egypt and Israel and then between Syria and Israel. After accepting his plan for troop disengagements along the Syrian border, Israeli leaders gave him their thanks at a farewell party in Jerusalem on May 29. He was photographed at the party with Israeli Premier Golda Meir and Religious Affairs Minister Yitzhak Rafael. (Wide World Photos)

Yom Kippur the Egyptians and the Syrians suddenly attacked. Both they and the Israelis quickly lost huge quantities of tanks, aircraft, and other equipment, and both the Russians and the Americans resorted to airlifts to make up for the losses. Only after the Israelis had got the upper hand did the Russians show any interest in ending the war. Then Kissinger and Brezhnev worked out and the U.N. Security Council adopted resolutions calling for an immediate cease-fire and for the beginning of peace negotiations on the basis of the 1967 resolution—which would presumably require Israel to give up most if not all of her 1967 conquests in return for some guarantee of her continued existence.

As the shooting died down, the American-Russian détente seemed belatedly to be having an effect in the Middle East. All at once Nixon made the startling announcement that he was putting American forces throughout the world on a stand-by alert. He was doing so, administration spokesmen said, because the Russians were increasing their already large naval force in the Mediterranean and were preparing to fly troops to the Middle East to enforce the cease-fire. The Russians sent no troops, and a new U.N. peacekeeping force began to arrive. Relaxing the alert, Nixon declared that the United States had just passed through its most dangerous war crisis since the Cuban missile crisis of 1962. "Without détente," he said, "we might have had a major confrontation in the Mideast."

While Egypt and Israel disputed over the details of the cease-fire and threatened to resume hostilities, the Arab countries announced plans to reduce oil production and to cut off petroleum sales to the United States. The Arabs intended, by withholding oil from Israel's friends, to pressure them into supporting a Middle Eastern settlement that would force Israel to leave the Arab territories she had conquered in 1967. Japan and western Europe, which had been getting respectively 82 percent and 72 percent of their petroleum from Arab sources, were much more vulnerable than was the United States, which had depended on those sources for only 11 percent of its supply. Understandably, Japan and the leading powers of western Europe were careful not to offend the Arabs. The United States seemed likely to become careful, too, as the American people increasingly felt the pinch of the oil embargo during the winter of 1973–1974.

Meanwhile the "Yom Kippur war" intensified the strains within the North Atlantic Alliance. None of the principal NATO allies had backed the United States in its support of Israel. During the airlift several of them had forbidden American transport planes to refuel in their territories or even to fly over them. After the war the Nixon administration made its anger known to the allies. They, in turn, complained that the American government had disregarded their desperate need for Arab oil and had failed to consult them about its intentions, particularly about its intention to order a world-wide military alert. The alliance now appeared to be more badly shaken than at any time since 1956, when France and Great Britain had joined Israel in invading Egypt, and the United States had sided with the Soviet Union in bringing about U.N. action against the invaders.

Selected Readings

Diplomacy in General
Seyom Brown, *The Faces of Power: Constancy and Change in United States Foreign Policy from Truman to Johnson* (1968); Gabriel Kolko, *The Roots of American Foreign Policy: An Analysis of Power and Purpose* (1969), a radical view; Crane Brinton, *The Americans and the French* (1968); R. J. Walton, *Cold War and Counter-Revolution: The Foreign Policy of John F. Kennedy** (1972); Henry A. Kissinger, *American Foreign Policy* (1969); Henry Brandon, *Retreat of American Power* (1973); Adam Yarmolinsky, *The Military Establishment: Its Impact on American Society* (1971); C. W. Pursell, Jr., *The Military Industrial Complex** (1973).

Foreign Aid
E. S. Mason, *Foreign Aid and Foreign Policy* (1964); D. A. Baldwin, *Economic Development and American Foreign Policy, 1943–1962* (1966); M. K. O'Leary, *The Politics of American Foreign Aid* (1967); W. D. Rogers, *The Twilight Struggle: The Alliance for Progress and the Politics of Development in Latin America* (1967).

Cuba and Santo Domingo
H. B. Johnson, *The Bay of Pigs* (1964); Elie Abel, *The Missile Crisis* (1966); Henry Pachter, *Collision Course* (1963), on the missile crisis; J. B. Martin, *Overtaken by Events* (1966); on the Dominican intervention; Dan Kurzman, *Santo Domingo: Revolt of the Damned* (1966).

Vietnam
David Halberstam, *The Making of a Quagmire* (1956); M. G. Raskin and B. B. Fall, eds., *The Vietnam Reader** (1965); J. W. Fulbright, ed., *The Vietnam Hearings** (1966); R. N. Goodwin, *Triumph or Tragedy: Reflections on Vietnam* (1966); G. M. Kahin and J. W. Lewis, *The United States in Vietnam* (1967); A. M. Schlesinger, Jr., *The Bitter Heritage: Vietnam and American Democracy, 1941–1966* (1967); Robert Shaplen, *Time Out of Hand: Revolution and Reaction in Southeast Asia* (1969); Seymour Hersh, *My Lai Four* (1970) and *Cover Up* (1972); Townsend Hoopes, *The Limits of Intervention* (1970); Telford Taylor, *Nuremberg and Vietnam: An American Tragedy** (1971); Neil Sheehan and others, *The Pentagon Papers** (1971); David Halberstam, *The Best and the Brightest* (1972).

Election of 1968
Stewart Alsop, *The Center: People and Power in Political Washington* (1968); T. H. White, *The Making of a President, 1968* (1969); J. McGinniss, *The Selling of the President, 1968* (1970); E. Mazo and S. Hess, *Nixon: A Political Portrait* (1968), a campaign biography; Jules Witcover, *The Resurrection of Richard Nixon* (1970) and *White Knight: The Rise of Spiro Agnew* (1972).

*Titles available in paperback.

Toward the Twenty-first Century

Thirty

On Sunday, July 20, 1969, slowly, cautiously, a white-clad figure climbed down from his spacecraft and extended a heavy, well-insulated boot toward the surface of the moon, while hundreds of millions of people throughout the world followed his movements on television or radio. As the astronaut, Neil Armstrong, placed both feet on the strange, finely powdered lunar soil, he said: "That's one small step for a man, one giant leap for mankind." A human being was standing where none had ever stood before—on land beyond the earth. A new age of interplanetary exploration had begun.

Most Americans rejoiced in the event as a triumph for humanity in general and for the United States in particular. But there were voices of dissent. Some Americans, especially among those of African ancestry, argued that the billions of dollars spent on traveling to the moon might better have been used for eliminating poverty from the earth. A Black Panther leader, Eldridge Cleaver, from his exile in Algeria, dismissed the lunar voyage as "a circus to distract people's minds from the real problems, which are here on the ground."

Certainly the moon landing, the result of cooperative efforts by thousands of scientists and technicians, provided a spectacular illustration of what sociologists call "cultural lag," that is, the failure of social and political development to keep up with technological advances. Man was acquiring the ability to visit other worlds before he had the capacity to put his own in order, with peace and plenty for its inhabitants. Another example of cultural lag was the exploitation of nuclear energy with no adequate arrangement of human power to control it. Still other examples were to be found in new production techniques that brought the promise of greater abundance and leisure without assuring that these benefits would be well distributed

Cars and the City
From one end of the country to the other, cities were ripped up and paved over to provide freeways and parking lots, but traffic congestion and air pollution remained. During the early 1970s, some 350,000 motor vehicles a day were passing over this Los Angeles freeway with its spectacular four-level interchange. (UPI)

and without making sufficient provision for the protection of the natural environment. Improvements in communication—the spread of the "mass media," especially television—only made the masses of the people even more aware of the stark contrast between affluence and poverty. Humanity needed inventions and achievements in society and government that would match those in science and technology.

Technology itself seemed to be approaching a crisis. The technological achievements of the past, bringing such a marvelous increase in the production of material things, had depended on an abundance of natural resources for raw material and for fuel. As the twentieth century reached its final quarter, signs of the near exhaustion of many resources began to appear. Unless new resources or new ways to utilize existing ones were found, the rising generation would face a period of scarcity instead of plenty, even in such a relatively rich country as the United States.

Meanwhile, as the country neared the 200th anniversary of its independence, the American people were confronted with a constitutional crisis. The Constitution had provided for a balanced government, with three equal and coordinate branches, but in recent years the executive branch had greatly overbalanced the legislative. Both national security and domestic welfare demanded a strong presidency. Constitutional and democratic government, however, required a controlled and responsible one.

The "New Federalism"

President Nixon, though full of ideas about foreign affairs, took office in 1969 without having given much thought to a domestic program. He favored what he called "reform," which seemed to mean a reversal of the policies his immediate predecessors had sponsored under the slogans of "the New Frontier" and "the Great Society." He looked for a slogan of his own and came up with "the New Federalism." This implied that he would, in his words, "reverse the flow of power and resources from the states and communities to Washington and start power and resources flowing back . . . to the people all over America."

THE IMPERIAL PRESIDENCY

In fact, while reversing certain policies, Nixon did not stop the trend toward the centralization of power. Rather, he encouraged a development that had been accelerating since the presidency of Franklin D. Roosevelt. With respect to domestic as well as foreign affairs, Nixon undertook to concentrate more and more authority in the White House.

"I've always thought this country could run itself domestically without a President," Nixon had said in 1967. "All you need is a competent Cabinet to run the country at home."

Actually, the cabinet had been losing influence on policy making ever since World War II, and it continued to do so under Nixon. His own cabinet was distinguished by little competence and still less continuity. He appointed few outstanding public figures to it, and during his first five years he made more changes in its membership than any other President had made during any length of time. For the most part, the members merely administered their own departments, seldom if ever consulting with one another as a group or even individually with the President. An exception was John Mitchell, Nixon's former law partner, his 1968 campaign manager, and from 1969 to 1972 his attorney general and chief adviser on politics. Mitchell had direct access to the White House.

Few other department heads, government officials of lesser rank, or congressmen or senators could approach the President directly. Almost all of them had to deal with him through his top White House aide, the "keeper of the gates," H. R. Haldeman, or through the chief of his domestic policy staff, John Ehrlichman. These two, old friends and veteran Nixon campaigners, now subject only to the President himself, ran the executive office with respect to domestic affairs from 1969 to 1973. The executive office was a large and rapidly swelling bureaucracy, whose numbers during that four-year period grew from 2,000 to more than 4,200.

By 1969 the domestic programs of the federal government and the agencies to administer them had become so numerous that they were difficult if not impossible for the President to control. As far back as the Truman and Eisenhower administrations a commission under former President Herbert Hoover had made proposals for reorganizing and streamlining the executive branch, but few of the proposals had been carried out. Now, on the advice of Roy Ash, a prominent businessman, Nixon proposed a new plan for bringing together the widely scattered threads of administration. The plan was to reorganize and enlarge the powers of the Bureau of the Budget, which had been set up during Harding's presidency to coordinate the requests of the various bureaus for appropriations from Congress. A new Office of Management and Budget, responsible to the President, was to oversee the financing and directing of all administrative agencies, including the formerly quasi-independent regulatory ones such as the Federal Power Commission. Congress approved the plan even though it meant that Congress would no longer be able to supervise the departments and commissions by negotiating directly with them in regard to their budget requests. These requests had to go through the Office of Management and Budget after it went into operation, in 1970.

Again acting on the advice of businessman Ash, Nixon proposed to reorganize and reduce the number of executive departments. When Congress failed to approve, the President in 1973 went ahead on his own, with a revised plan. By executive order he raised three of the department heads to the level of "presidential councillors" and directed that the others report to one of the three, who in turn would report to a presidential aide (Erhlichman). With the three councillors constituting a "super cabinet," the authority and prestige of the traditional cabinet would be still further reduced.

Nixon presented his reorganization measures as long overdue reforms that would bring businesslike efficiency to the government. They would, of course, enable the White House to manage more effectively the executive branch as a whole. But Nixon also claimed unprecedented authority for the presidential office in relation to the legislative branch, especially after his reelection in 1972. Asserting "executive privilege" seemingly without limit, he took the position that congressional committees could not question administrative officials without the President's consent. Implying that the President, not Congress, should have the power of the purse, he ordered administrative agencies not to spend appropriated money after Congress had overridden his vetoes of appropriation bills.

By the beginning of his second term, Nixon faced a congressional revolt. His critics in Congress — including some members of the Republican minority as well as the Democratic majority — talked of a constitutional crisis. For many years Congress had been allowing Presidents more and more discretion, particularly in foreign affairs (as seemed unavoidable in a nuclear age). Now Nixon, while stretching to the utmost his powers as commander in chief in Southeast Asia, was thought to be doing the same with his powers as chief executive at home. Unless Congress acted soon to regain its lost authority, some of the critics believed, the checks and balances of the Constitution would become meaningless in actual practice.

LAW AND ORDER

From the beginning of his first term, President Nixon hoped to alter the direction of the Supreme Court, which under Chief Justice Earl Warren had been actively enlarging the sphere of both personal liberty and civil rights. The Warren Court's decisions on civil rights had antagonized conservatives, particularly in the South, and the decisions on personal liberty had aroused advocates of "law and order" (one of Nixon's themes in the 1968 campaign) all over the country. Especially resented were the *Escobedo* and *Miranda* cases (1964, 1966), in which the judges had limited the power of local police to extract confessions from persons accused of crimes.

As Chief Justice Warren approached retirement, President Johnson had tried to replace him with Abe Fortas, whom Johnson earlier had appointed as an associate justice. Fortas, a liberal, could have been expected to keep the Court on essentially the same track it had been following under Warren. The Republicans in the Senate blocked the Fortas appointment and thus gave Nixon an opportunity to choose his own chief justice. Nixon — who insisted that it was "the job of the courts to interpret the law, not make the law" — chose a conservative strict constructionist who agreed with him. This was Warren Burger, who had served for thirteen years on the United States Court of Appeals for the District of Columbia and who had spoken out against what he considered the Supreme Court's protection of the rights of criminals. Burger's appointment received the prompt approval of the Senate.

Nixon soon had a chance to put another man of his choice on the Supreme Court, but this time he ran into difficulty and embarrassment. The opening occurred when Justice Fortas resigned after the revelation that he had received a salary payment from a foundation whose donor was under indictment for fraud. To take Fortas' place, Nixon named a federal circuit court judge from South Carolina, C. F. Haynsworth, who had the endorsement of the American Bar Association, but whose past decisions showed that he lagged considerably behind the Warren Court in his devotion to civil rights. Spokesmen for black organizations and for labor unions vociferously opposed the confirmation of Haynsworth. They were joined by others, including prominent members of Nixon's own party, when it was revealed that Haynsworth had sat on cases involving corporations in which he himself had a financial interest. His critics now said he was even more insensitive to possible conflicts of interest than Fortas had been. Eventually the Senate rejected the Haynsworth nomination, and Nixon then named G. Harrold Carswell, a judge of the Florida federal appeals court, who lacked Haynsworth's legal eminence and who was shown to have made racist statements in the past. When the Senate turned down Carswell also, Nixon angrily charged the Senate majority with bias against the South. The Senate finally accepted the appointment of Harry A. Blackmun, who, like Chief Justice Burger, came from Minnesota and had a reputation as a conservative jurist.

Before Nixon had been in office three years, two more Supreme Court vacancies arose, and again he ran into trouble in trying to fill them. The American Bar Association refused to endorse his first two choices, one of whom was a woman. Nixon then nominated, and the Senate approved, Lewis F. Powell, Jr., a Virginian and a former head of the American Bar Association, and William H. Rehnquist, assistant attorney general in the Nixon administration and a Goldwater Republican from

Arizona. "I shall continue to appoint judges," Nixon later said, "who share my philosophy that we must strengthen the peace forces against the criminal forces in America."

Through his four appointments to the Supreme Court, Nixon succeeded in changing its interpretations to some extent, at least in regard to criminal procedure. Usually his appointees voted together, and often Justice Byron White joined them to make a majority. With the cooperation of these five, the Court put new restrictions on the legal rights of defendants in criminal cases, even holding that a jury need no longer reach a unanimous verdict in order to convict. With White parting from the Nixon appointees, however, the Court in a five-to-four decision (*Furman* v. *Georgia,* 1972) banned capital punishment in states where juries could decide whether or not to impose it. With one or more of the new members concurring, the Court also diverged from Nixon's aims by giving some important decisions in favor of civil liberties and civil rights.

By 1969, a decade and a half after the Court's historic decision outlawing segregation, only about 20 percent of the black children in the South were attending mixed schools. Robert A. Finch—a civil-rights advocate whom Nixon had put in charge of the Department of Health, Education, and Welfare (HEW)—expressed determination to make the most of the government's power to withhold federal aid from schools whose authorities permitted no more than token integration. Finch indicated that he would not be satisfied with "freedom of choice" plans, which required the black child or his parents to take the initiative in seeking entrance to a school attended by whites. Then, in September 1969, the Nixon administration suddenly pulled back, ceased to insist on immediate steps toward integration, and granted Mississippi an additional delay in eliminating its dual school system. Several weeks later the Court overruled the administration and demanded that Mississippi integrate its schools "at once." But Nixon prevented the HEW Department from cutting off funds from noncomplying districts and continued to delay the carrying out of its desegregation plans. Finch and a number of other HEW officials soon left the department.

In many areas the achievement of racial balance in schools (so as to eliminate all racially identifiable ones) would require the transporting of children from one neighborhood to another. Busing to segregated schools was a common practice, but busing to integrated schools was quite another matter in the opinion of most whites (and some blacks). When federal courts began to order such busing, Nixon spoke out with the many who denounced it as unthinkable if not unconstitutional. Nevertheless, the Supreme Court unanimously upheld it in a 1971 case involving Charlotte, North Carolina. The next year Nixon tried, unsuccessfully, to induce Congress to pass an antibusing law. Meanwhile, opponents of busing in northern cities violently resisted court-ordered busing, those in Denver, Colorado, and Pontiac, Michigan, resorting to the fire-bombing of school buses. There was also resistance in the South,

but on the whole desegregation proceeded faster there than in the North. Before the end of Nixon's first term—thanks to the federal courts rather than the President—the proportion of Southern blacks in all-black schools had declined from about 80 to less than 20 percent.

Comparatively few blacks, North or South, approved of Nixon's policies in regard to schools or other matters. "For the first time since Woodrow Wilson," said an official of the National Association for the Advancement of Colored People, "we have a national administration that can be rightly characterized as anti-Negro." Nevertheless, during the first five years of Nixon's presidency, the country was spared the kind of racial violence that had been breaking out every summer for several years

Occupation of Wounded Knee

To draw attention to their demands for reform, members of the militant American Indian Movement (AIM) took over the tiny settlement of Wounded Knee on the Pine Ridge Reservation of the Sioux, in South Dakota. The AIM forces forbade federal agents to enter the place. In this picture, taken on March 11, 1973, an armed AIM guard holds four government officials and two farmers. The six were released after about an hour (UPI)

before 1969. The urban black communities had apparently come to the conclusion that rioting did them more harm than good.

The antiwar groups also calmed down after their campus eruptions at the time of the Cambodian invasion in 1970. Even the Christmas-season bombing of North Vietnam in 1972 provoked no riots. It was as if events had numbed the erstwhile protesters for peace.

But Indians resumed their demonstrations, sometimes with violence. At first, in 1969, the hopes of Indians had been raised when Nixon appointed a Mohawk-Sioux as Commissioner of Indian Affairs, and again in 1970 when Nixon promised Indians "self-determination without termination," that is, an increase in control over their own affairs and at the same time an increase in federal aid. The promises were not fulfilled, however, and among Indians anger and frustration took the place of hope. In November 1972 nearly a thousand protesters forcibly took over the Bureau of Indian Affairs building in Washington and, after six days, left it with damage to files and furniture that government officials estimated at $500,000 to $2 million. Later that winter members of the militant American Indian Movement occupied the hamlet of Wounded Knee on the Pine Ridge reservation in South Dakota, fortified the place (the site of a one-sided, bloody engagement between the United States cavalry and a group of Sioux in 1890), and held it for more than two months.

To deal with rioting and to put down "crime in the streets" — which were primarily state and local responsibilities — the Nixon administration gave millions of dollars to state and local law-enforcement agencies. Yet the number of crimes continued to go up, though at a decelerating rate. According to Federal Bureau of Investigation statistics, there were more than 6 million serious crimes committed in 1972, as compared with 4.5 million in 1968. That meant an increase of fully one-third in three years under Nixon. Though under the supervision of the federal government, the city of Washington itself remained unsafe, its downtown streets almost deserted at night.

THE GENERAL WELFARE

In dealing with the problem of poverty, Nixon appeared to follow a zigzag course. At first he saw himself as a conservative reformer who, like Queen Victoria's great prime minister Benjamin Disraeli, would outdo his political opponents in his concern for the poor and thus would win broad popular support. Eventually he went to the opposite extreme. At the beginning of his second term he announced his determination to put an end to what he called "condescending policies of paternalism."

By 1969 the existing welfare system, which had remained essentially unchanged since the time of the New Deal, was in serious need of reform. During the 1960s the number of persons receiving aid had doubled, from 1 to 2 million, and federal expenditures had increased from about $2 billion to nearly $18 billion. The welfare rolls had lengthened to the point where they included 6 percent of the population as a whole and a much higher proportion of the urban population, as high as 25 percent of the people of Newark, New Jersey. Approximately half of the recipients were black. Very few were employable men. Almost all were women or children or old, blind, or otherwise disabled persons. Among the worst faults of the existing program were the following: it denied benefits to families with able-bodied men, and so it induced husbands and fathers to desert; it denied benefits to the poor who were employed, and so it discouraged welfare recipients from accepting jobs.

In 1969 Nixon proposed a new Family Assistance Plan, which his special adviser on urban and poverty problems, Daniel P. Moynihan, had devised. Under the Moynihan plan, every unemployed family of four would receive at least $1,600 a year. The working poor would get this minimum and would be allowed to keep part of their pay until their earned income reached $4,000, when the benefits would be discontinued. To be eligible for relief, the able-bodied (women as well as men) would be required to work. The plan would add about 6 million people to the welfare rolls, and it would increase federal spending by about $4 billion annually. In keeping with Nixon's principle of the New Federalism, the states would take over an increased share of the responsibility for administering the program.

The Moynihan plan had much to recommend it, but it provoked a bitter controversy, both in and out of Congress. Black militants, welfare recipients, and social workers opposed it as inadequate. Congress neither adopted it nor agreed on a substitute, and Nixon himself soon lost interest in the plan. He turned to recommending, instead, that welfare expenditures be cut and that payments to "ineligibles" be stopped.

Already Nixon had begun to undo the Johnson poverty program by closing more than half of the Job Corps training centers. He also reduced spending on other social-welfare agencies, including the National Institute of Health. In his budget for 1973–1974 he proposed to abolish more than a hundred federal grant programs that were giving aid to the unemployed, the mentally ill, veterans, college students, small businessmen, and other groups. He also proposed to discontinue spending for urban renewal, to end assistance for hospital construction, and to reduce expenditures on lunches for schoolchildren. In 1973 he proceeded, without congressional approval, to break up the Office of Economic Opportunity, which had been the main agency of Johnson's "war on poverty."

To replace many of the federal grants for specific purposes, Nixon had been urging that the federal government transfer funds to the states and cities, which would then be responsible for their own social programs. Such "revenue sharing" he viewed as the finest example of the New Federalism in practice. Congress approved, and revenue sharing began in 1973, when the federal government turned about $5 billion over to state and local governments. Big-city mayors soon lost their enthusiasm for revenue sharing, since it promised them less money for dealing with urban problems than the specific grants, now being reduced or eliminated, had provided.

Nixon favored individual as well as local responsibility in overcoming poverty. To help Negroes help themselves, he advocated the encouragement of "black capitalism" through both public and private assistance to Negro-owned business enterprises. Some progress was made along this line.

While economizing on aid to the poor, Nixon was generous to large corporations, especially those in the aircraft industry. He endorsed federal spending to subsidize an airplane manufacturer in the development of a supersonic transport (SST), a large plane that would carry passengers faster than the speed of sound and would compete with craft under construction by the Soviet Union and, cooperatively, by Great Britain and France. President

Kennedy had put the government into the SST project, and by 1969 some $300 million of federal funds had already been contributed to it. President Nixon persuaded Congress to appropriate another $96 million for 1969–1970. Objections arose, however, on the grounds that the transport would never pay for itself and would damage the environment. Nixon suffered a personal defeat in 1971 when Congress killed the project by refusing to appropriate more money for it.

Many Americans had hoped that, once the United States was finally out of the Vietnam War, the government could cut its military spending and could afford to increase its domestic expenditures. Yet in his first postwar budget, the one for 1973–1974, Nixon not only demanded a reduction in domestic expenditures but also asked for an increase in military spending, from $74.8 billion to $79 billion. The extra money was to go largely for the development of new weapons and for pay raises to attract recruits to the all-volunteer armed forces.

THE NIXON ECONOMY

When Nixon talked of reducing expenditures on social programs, he justified it as a necessary means of controlling inflation and keeping prices within reason. He had inherited the inflation problem from his predecessor, Johnson, who had built up a tremendous inflationary pressure by increasing expenditures for both the Great Society and the Vietnam War. Nixon faced a dilemma, since rising prices could mean booming business, while deflationary policies might bring on widespread unemployment. In handling the problem he proved to be neither consistent nor successful.

At the outset, in 1969, Nixon announced a deflationary "game plan." He was going to maintain a balanced budget by spending less and taxing more, yet he signed a tax bill that enlarged exemptions and thus reduced revenue. He was also going to tighten bank credit and raise interest rates through the operations of the Federal Reserve System, and he succeeded in doing so. Nevertheless, prices continued to rise. At the same time unemployment also rose. The country began to suffer from "stagflation," stagnation and inflation together.

The Economic Stabilization Act of 1970 authorized the President to impose direct controls on prices and also wages if and when he saw fit to do so. Nixon said: "I will not take this nation down the road of wage and price controls, however politically expedient that may seem." One year later he put into effect a two-phase control system. In Phase I, to last for ninety days, nearly all wages and prices were frozen at their existing levels. In Phase II, to last indefinitely, most wage and price increases were kept within strict limits. Inflation now slowed down temporarily, but the business recession continued, and the unemployment rate rose to more than 6 percent of the labor force for 1971, as compared with less than 4 percent for 1969.

If these economic conditions had persisted, they might have threatened the reelection of Nixon in 1972. So, in 1971, he suddenly reversed his original game plan of tight credit and a balanced budget. He got from Congress a bill further reducing taxes. The Federal Reserve Board lowered interest rates and encouraged borrowing from banks. Government agencies began to spend at a rate of $1 billion a month more than had previously been planned. The Department of Agriculture increased its crop subsidies to farmers (for taking land out of production) from $3.1 billion to $4.1 billion a year. Altogether, the government paid out so much more than it took in that the deficit for 1972 was by far the largest for any year since World War II. By Election Day, incomes were up and unemployment was down. Politically, the combination of easy credit and deficit spending proved a great success.

The consequences, however, were disastrous for consumers. Foods and other raw materials were already becoming scarce throughout the world. Nixon's wheat deal with the Soviet Union made the food shortage worse than it would otherwise have been in the United States. The Russians took a fourth of the entire American crop (at a price well below the market price, the difference being paid by American taxpayers through export subsidies to American grain dealers). Meanwhile, food production in the United States was declining as a result of Nixon's election-year farm policy. By pushing exports and restricting output, the administration was decreasing the available supply of foodstuffs within the country. By loosening credit and pouring out money, it was increasing the effective demand. Thus it was creating an explosive inflationary force. At this critical moment, early in 1973, Nixon chose to discontinue the strict wage-price controls of Phase II, which he replaced with the flexible, largely voluntary guidelines of what came to be called Phase III.

There followed the most rapid and extreme rise in the cost of living since the end of World War II. Prices of meat and grain products soared the highest. Housewives tried, with only partial and temporary success, to bring down prices by boycotting meat. Responding to consumer protests, the administration finally put a ceiling on the retail prices of meat and other foods but not on the prices of livestock or grain. This haphazard attempt at price fixing only worsened the food shortage. Squeezed

---

The End of American Independence [1973]

Throughout its two centuries of existence, the United States has enjoyed an uncommon degree of national independence, in part because two vast oceans have isolated it from political conflicts in Europe and elsewhere and in part because it has been an essentially self-sufficient continental storehouse of energy fuels and raw materials.

Suddenly, this is beginning to change, and very rapidly. As recently as 1970 we were importing only a small fraction of our petroleum and only a few of the important minerals. By 1985 we will be importing well over half of our petroleum and will be primarily dependent on imports for nine of the thirteen basic minerals required by a modern industrial economy. The import bill for energy fuels and minerals, which totaled $8 billion in 1970, is projected to multiply severalfold by 1985. Within a fifteen-year span, scarcely half a generation, we will make the transition from being an essentially self-sufficient country to — at least in terms of raw materials — a have-not country. We do not yet appreciate the economic, social, and political consequences of this historically abrupt transition. — Lester R. Brown in Saturday Review/World, December 18, 1973.

between rising costs and fixed prices, some poultrymen killed baby chicks, and some packers and bakers went out of business.

Belatedly the government took measures for stimulating instead of retarding farm output. The administration advised farmers to plant grain and soybeans on millions of acres they had left idle the previous year in order to qualify for subsidies, and it began to sell its own stocks of grain. It planned to abandon gradually the crop controls and price supports for wheat, feed grains, and cotton, and to discontinue the purchase and storage of "surplus" crops. Thus it intended to change the basic agricultural policy that had prevailed ever since the New Deal. Presumably the nation's farmers were to be left, for the most part, to make their own decisions about what and how much to produce, as they had done before the 1930s.

After his reelection in 1972, Nixon ended the government's spending spree and renewed his demands for economizing on social programs. He opposed a tax increase and argued that, if an increase should become necessary, Congress would be to blame because of its extravagance. In order to forestall a recession, he now wanted to moderate the business boom that had been under way in 1972 and that was to last through most of 1973.

The prospects for continued prosperity received a jolt in the fall of 1973, when the Arab nations cut back their oil production and put an embargo on petroleum shipments to the United States. There had already been, in this country, scattered shortages of fuel oil during the winter of 1972–1973 and gasoline during the summer of 1973. For the winter of 1973–1974, a much greater and more general shortage was anticipated, but experts differed as to how great it would actually prove to be. Natural gas and electric power (produced largely with petroleum) were also in short supply. To meet the "energy crisis," the federal and state governments took a variety of steps. These included an appeal to homeowners to lower their thermostats, allotments of fuel to airlines and a consequent elimination of many flights, allocation of fuel oil and gasoline to dealers, a reduction of highway speed limits to fifty-five miles an hour, a ban on Sunday sales of gasoline, and a contingency plan for gasoline rationing. Prices of gasoline and fuel oil started to take a steep rise. The shortage threatened to curtail production

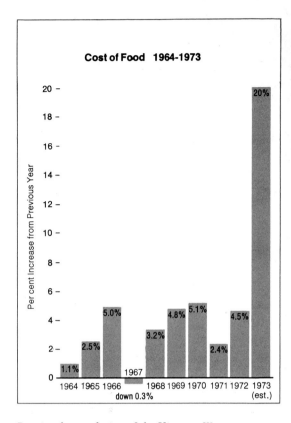

Cost of Food 1964-1973

Despite the escalation of the Vietnam War, food prices for American consumers rose only rather moderately until 1973. In that year, prices began to go up faster than at any time since immediately after the end of World War II. From a chart by J. Donovan. Time, August 27, 1973. (Reprinted by permission from TIME, The Weekly Newsmagazine; Copyright Time Inc.)

as well as transportation, since many industries depended directly or indirectly on petroleum for power, and others (such as those making or using plastics or synthetic fibers) depended on it also for raw material. By March 1974, the outlook was dim, with long lines of cars waiting for gas at filling stations in many parts of the country. The next month the prospect brightened, at least temporarily, when the Arab oil ban was lifted.

A TRIUMPHANT REELECTION

According to a 1970 book, the "real majority" in the United States was "unyoung, unblack, and unpoor." The mature, white, well-off citizens were most concerned about such things as

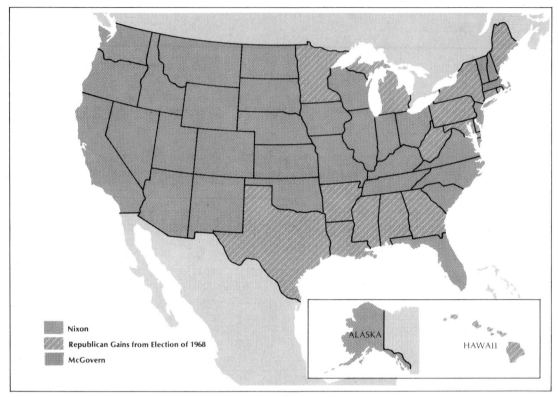

Election of 1972

Nixon

Republican Gains from Election of 1968

McGovern

ALASKA

HAWAII

campus protests, school integration, street crimes, and welfare costs. If these worried people could be induced to vote for Nixon, his reelection would be assured. This prospect formed the basis for the campaign strategy that Nixon's attorney general and political adviser, John Mitchell, adopted for 1972. In particular, Mitchell planned to attract to Nixon the voters who in 1968 had favored the American party candidate, George Wallace of Alabama. In addition to these Southern whites, the Republicans hoped to win over many Northern workers, especially the Catholics of immigrant background. Thus the Nixon forces might break up the already shaky Democratic coalition — which Franklin D. Roosevelt had put together in the 1930s — and replace it with a permanent Republican majority.

To Republican strategists it was hardly encouraging when, in 1970, Congress passed a bill to lower the voting age to eighteen. Nixon signed the bill, despite the widespread assumption that most of the young would vote Democratic. The Supreme Court ruled the new law

constitutional for federal but not for state or local elections. The Twenty-sixth Amendment, ratified in time for the elections of 1972, made eighteen the minimum age for voters in state and local as well as federal contests.

For the Republicans, the congressional elections of 1970 were also somewhat discouraging. Nixon put his own prestige at stake when he campaigned on behalf of Republican candidates, to denounce criminals and antiwar protesters, the "violent few." In San Jose, California, he taunted youthful demonstrators, who then threw stones and eggs at the presidential limousine. In Phoenix, Arizona, wildly gesticulating, he denounced the San Jose "terrorists." This performance was recorded and was nationally televised on election eve. It apparently did the Republicans little good. The next day they gained two seats in the Senate but lost nine in the House and also lost eleven state governorships.

Nixon's chances for reelection improved when, in May 1972, in a Maryland shopping center, a would-be assassin shot George Wallace, leaving him partially paralyzed and incapable of continuing his presidential campaign. Nixon's chances improved still further when, in July, the Democratic nominating convention met in Miami.

On the first ballot the convention chose George M. McGovern, an opponent of the Vietnam War and an advocate of a $1,000 yearly grant from the government to every citizen. While still a relatively unknown senator from South Dakota, McGovern had begun openly to seek the presidency far in advance, in January 1971. In the primaries he outdid the early favorite, Senator Edmund Muskie of Maine, and the previous candidate, Senator Hubert Humphrey of Minnesota. At the convention, McGovern benefited from reforms he himself had helped to bring about. The "McGovern rules"

were intended to make the convention broadly representative of the party by requiring certain proportions of women, blacks, and youths among the delegates. But the rules antagonized old-line politicians and had a very divisive effect on the party, especially when the convention unseated a powerful boss, Mayor Richard J. Daley of Chicago.

The very qualities that had brought McGovern the nomination—the qualities that appealed to liberals within the Democratic party—made him a weak candidate in the election. From the make-up of the convention, many voters got the impression that he was the candidate of hippies, aggressive women, and militant blacks. He offended many even among his adherents when—after the revelation that his vice-presidential choice, Senator Thomas Eag-

The Democratic Candidates   1972
In a jubilant mood, Senator George McGovern of South Dakota poses with his hand-picked running-mate, Senator Thomas Eagleton of Missouri, after their nomination in Miami. Their joy was not to last, as Eagleton soon withdrew from the ticket after the revelation that he had been treated for a nervous disorder, and McGovern went on, with Sargent Shriver as the vice-presidential candidate, to one of the most crushing defeats in American political history. (Wide World Photos)

leton of Missouri, had undergone treatments for an emotional disturbance—he at first said he stood "1,000 percent" behind Eagleton and then suddenly removed him from the ticket. During the campaign McGovern found it hard to maintain his credibility when he compared Nixon to Hitler and charged that the administration was the most corrupt in history. George Meany, head of the AFL-CIO, the nation's largest labor union, opposed McGovern, and so did all but a very few of the newspapers throughout the country.

While McGovern campaigned strenuously with limited financial resources, which came mainly from small contributors, Nixon (after a renomination, also in Miami, that was more a coronation than a contest) had an easy "noncampaign." He had the advantage of more money, most of it from large corporations, than any other presidential candidate had ever had at his disposal. Seldom appearing, Nixon was an "invisible candidate." His choice for a second time as Vice President, Spiro Agnew, together with other government officials, carried the campaign burden for Nixon, never mentioning him by name but always referring to him as "the President." The President now had only to reap the benefits of his recent policies. By virtue of his China and Russia visits and the Vietnam negotiations he appeared to be a bringer of peace. Since business was finally booming, he could be credited with prosperity. As a foe of busing for racial balance in schools, he had the gratitude of race-conscious whites. Through his "law and order" statements and his court appointments, he had made himself the apparent champion of peace at home as well as abroad.

Nixon won by one of the most decisive margins in history. He received the largest share of the popular vote (60.8 percent) of any candidate except Johnson (61.1 percent) in 1964. He received the largest proportion of the electoral vote (521 of 538) since Roosevelt (523 of 531) in 1936. McGovern carried only Massachusetts and the District of Columbia. He got little of the expected help from the newly enfranchised eighteen- to twenty-year-olds, as fewer than half of them bothered to go to the polls, and those who did divided their ballots almost evenly. He received a fairly solid black support, but scarcely more than half of the eligible blacks voted. He lost heavily among eth-

nic groups in the North and among whites generally in the South.

To judge by the presidential returns alone, it appeared that the Republicans had succeeded in their aim to replace the old Democratic coalition with a new one of their own. In the congressional elections, however, the Republicans had been deprived of two places in the Senate while gaining thirteen in the House, thus leaving the Democrats in control of the next Congress by margins of 57 to 43 and 243 to 192. So the returns as a whole hardly amounted to unqualified approval of the Republican party. Even the presidential victory, overwhelming though it was, probably meant less an endorsement of Nixon than a rejection of his opponent.

WATERGATE

As he began his second term, in January 1973, President Nixon stood at the height of his power and popularity. Soon his popularity, as measured by opinion polls, began to drop. It fell faster than that of any other President since such polls were first taken, in Franklin D. Roosevelt's time. Within a year, public confidence in Nixon was so low that serious doubts arose as to whether he should, or could, continue to lead the people. The reason for the sudden collapse of his prestige could be summed up in a word that became familiar to all newspaper readers and television viewers—"Watergate." That word designated a bewildering assortment of political scandals, the worst in American history.

The Watergate was a deluxe hotel-apartment-office complex in Washington. In it were located the headquarters of the Democratic National Committee. There, at about two o'clock in the morning of June 17, 1972, police arrested five men who had broken into the headquarters to "bug" them and to copy documents. Later two others were arrested, one of them the general counsel for Nixon's personal campaign organization, the Committee for the Re-election of the President (CREEP). Two months after the burglary, however, Nixon stated that "no one in the White House staff, no one in this Administration presently employed, was involved in this very bizarre incident." He added: "This kind of activity, as I have often

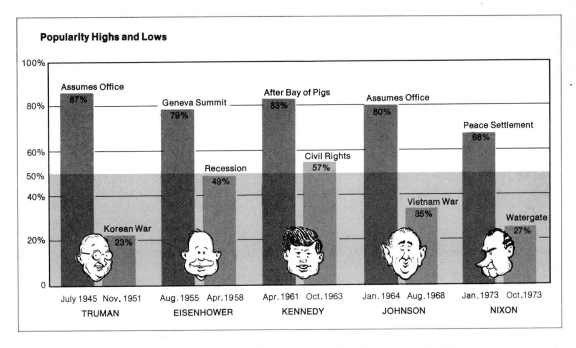

Popularity Highs and Lows

The bars indicate the percentage of people, as shown by Gallup opinion polls, who approved of the way the President was handling his job. Adapted from a chart prepared by J. Donovan and M. Witte and published in Time, July 30, 1973. (Reprinted by permission from TIME, The Weekly Newsmagazine; Copyright Time Inc.)

indicated, has no place whatsoever in our political process." His opponent, McGovern, tried in vain to make a campaign issue out of the crime.

When, after the election, the captured burglars went on trial, all but one of them pleaded guilty, and that one refused to talk. The Justice Department prosecutors failed to implicate anyone higher up than those arrested, but Federal District Judge John J. Sirica suspected that the whole truth had not been told. While sentencing the defendants to long terms in prison, Sirica intimated that if they would cooperate in getting at the truth, he would reduce the sentences. One of the defendants, James W. McCord, Jr., a former CIA agent and a "security coordinator" for CREEP, now agreed to testify before a federal grand jury and a Senate investigating committee, which was headed by Senator Sam J. Ervin of North Carolina. McCord led a long parade of witnesses who appeared, voluntarily or under subpoena, before the grand jury and the Ervin committee. The committee hearings, televised,

gave the public an opportunity to draw its own conclusions about the character and conduct of the men around the President. The testimony was so conflicting and confusing, however, that only with difficulty could the threads of the developing story be untangled.

Certain undisputed facts stood out. Nixon had been much concerned about the leaking of government secrets, especially the leaking of a Defense Department study of the Vietnam War, which The New York Times and other journals published as "The Pentagon Papers" in 1971. So, to plug the leaks, he set up and put Ehrlichman in charge of a special group of White House employees, who called themselves "the plumbers," and who tapped the telephones of newsmen and members of Kissinger's staff. Nixon ordered the plumbers to investigate the background of Daniel Ellsberg, the man responsible for leaking the Pentagon Papers. Using White House funds, two of the plumbers led a team of burglars who broke into the Los Angeles office of Ellsberg's psychiatrist

Watergate Hearings
Of the many witnesses who appeared before the Senate committee on the Watergate affair, as it held its televised hearings, John W. Dean III gave the fullest account of the White House involvements. Dean, a former attorney on Nixon's staff, charged that Nixon himself had taken part in the cover-up of the scandal. Here Dean begins his testimony with a lengthy prepared statement, on June 26, 1973. Second from the left at the table, his face partially hidden by a microphone, is Senator Sam J. Ervin of North Carolina, chairman of the committee. (UPI)

to search for Ellsberg's psychiatric files. Nixon was eager to prosecute and convict Ellsberg. While Ellsberg was on trial before a federal court, Nixon told Ehrlichman to approach the trial judge and find out if he would be interested in a promotion to the post of FBI director. The judge dismissed the case.

Four of the psychiatrist's office burglars, including the two leaders, took part, with CREEP financing, in the Watergate break-in. After the arrests, CREEP members and other government officials hastily destroyed a tremendous quantity of their records. Nixon told Haldeman and Ehrlichman to meet with top CIA officials, and the CIA director concluded that the White House was trying to "use" the agency as a means of slowing down an FBI probe and covering up CREEP activities. A

White House attorney suggested to one of the Watergate defendants that he, the defendant, would get a presidential pardon after a short time in prison if he would keep silent about his superiors' involvement in the affair. Nixon's personal attorney and other White House staffers covertly passed more than $400,000, mostly from Nixon campaign contributions, to the defendants, their families, and their lawyers.

Besides the Watergate burglary, CREEP agents had perpetrated a variety of "dirty tricks" before and during the campaign, the worst of them having been intended to destroy the reputation of Nixon's strongest potential rival, Senator Muskie, and thereby prevent his getting the Democratic nomination. "I have often thought we had too much money," one of Nixon's campaign workers said afterward.

Part of the money came from corporations that were making unlawful contributions, part of it from persons or groups who were receiving specific government favors. The Justice Department compromised an antitrust suit against the International Telephone and Telegraph Company after the ITT had agreed to contribute. The President raised price supports for milk after dairymen's organizations promised large payments. Attorney General Mitchell and Secretary of Commerce Maurice Stans interceded with the Securities and Exchange Commission on behalf of a disreputable financier who made a contribution. Mitchell and Stans were indicted, but were eventually acquitted.

A PRESIDENT RESIGNS

Still others among Nixon's friends, advisers, and aides were indicted on, and some of them were convicted of, charges growing out of illegal campaign activities. The question became more and more insistent: Was Nixon himself guilty? Did he authorize any of the illegal activities or any of the attempts to cover them up? Did he have any knowledge of the misdeeds or the cover-up and fail to act on his knowledge, fail to stop what was going on and see that those responsible were punished? (Misprision of felony is itself a crime.) In a succession of statements Nixon altered and added to his original story, but he continued to maintain that he was innocent of any wrongdoing. "I am not a crook," he declared at one news conference. There was a possible way of testing, at certain points, his veracity as against that of his accusers. At his direction—as one of the very few who knew about it revealed in the midst of the Senate hearings—hidden tape recorders had been recording White House conversations. But Nixon refused to give up the relevant tapes until after Judge Sirica had ruled that he must, and then Nixon's spokesmen let it be known that two of the most important tapes were nonexistent and a third had a peculiar gap in it. A team of experts concluded that part of this tape had been deliberately erased.

To a growing number of Americans it seemed that, at the very least, Nixon had shown remarkably poor judgment in choosing some of his subordinates. It turned out that he had certainly been no judge of character when

he twice endorsed Spiro Agnew for the vice presidency. Late in 1973 Agnew, the stern advocate of law and order, resigned as Vice President and pleaded nolo contendere (no contest) to a charge of income-tax evasion, the federal prosecutors agreeing in return to refrain from pressing charges of soliciting and accepting bribes. To replace Agnew, Nixon named the House Republican leader, Gerald Ford of Michigan. After a thorough investigation, Congress gave Ford its approval. He appeared to be, if not an imaginative or inspiring statesman, at least an honest politician.

With Ford as the prospective successor, old demands for the resignation or impeachment of Nixon were renewed. As 1974 began, Nixon still refused to resign. The Judiciary Committee of the House was busily gathering evidence for the decision whether or not to impeach. After requesting a number of the presidential tapes, the committee served the President with a subpoena when he refused to give them up. Finally, at the end of April, he responded, not by delivering the tapes, but by sending in and at the same time publishing 1200 pages of selected and edited transcripts. He and other Republican spokesmen claimed that these told the whole story of his relation to the Watergate scandal and completely exonerated him. Others, especially Democrats, drew a quite different conclusion. By a partisan vote, the committee ruled that Nixon had not made an adequate response to the subpoena.

By the summer of 1974, nine men—in addition to the "Watergate seven," the burglars and their accomplices—had confessed to or been convicted of Watergate-related offenses. These nine were former members of CREEP or of the White House staff, the highest ranking of them being Erlichman. Several others, including Haldeman and Mitchell, had been indicted and were awaiting trial. Nixon himself had been named as an "unindicted co-conspirator" by a federal grand jury.

For use as evidence in these cases the special prosecutor for the Justice Department, Leon Jaworski, asked for tape recordings of sixty-four White House conversations. Nixon refused to give them up, claiming that "executive privilege" justified him in thus protecting the confidentiality of his office. In the case of *United States* v. *Richard M. Nixon* the Supreme Court decided unanimously against the President in July 1974.

A few days later, after several months of thorough inquiry, the House Judiciary Committee voted to recommend three articles of impeachment. These charged that Nixon had (1) obstructed justice by helping to cover up the Watergate crimes, (2) misused federal agencies so as to violate the rights of citizens, and (3) interfered with congressional powers by refusing to turn over tapes and other materials that the committee had subpoenaed.

Though Nixon continued to assert his innocence, more and more signs of his complicity were coming to light. Newly released tapes proved what he had always denied—that he had been aware of and indeed had directed the Watergate cover-up from the beginning. With impeachment and conviction finally looming as unavoidable, he did what no President had ever done before. He resigned. Immediately, on August 9, 1974, Gerald Ford was sworn in as Nixon's successor. For the first time, there was a President who had not reached the office by going through a national election.

President Ford Addressing Congress
Gerald Rudolph Ford was sixty-one years old when he took office as President. Born in Omaha, Nebraska, he grew up in Grand Rapids, Michigan. After graduating from the University of Michigan, where he was a star football player, he earned a law degree at Yale. During World War II he served in the navy, rising to the rank of lieutenant commander. He was elected to the House of Representatives in 1948 and was reelected a dozen times after that. For nearly ten years, until he became Vice President, he was House minority leader. One of his first official acts after succeeding to the presidency was to name Nelson Rockefeller, a multimillionaire and former governor of New York, as Vice President. (Wide World Photos)

Articles of Impeachment [1974]

Article I. In his conduct of the office of President of the United States, Richard M. Nixon, in violation of his constitutional oath faithfully to execute the office of President of the United States and, to the best of his ability, preserve, protect, and defend the Constitution of the United States, and in violation of his constitutional duty to take care that the laws be faithfully executed, has prevented, obstructed, and impeded the administration of justice. . . .

Article II. . . . has repeatedly engaged in conduct violating the constitutional rights of citizens, impairing the due and proper administration of justice and the conduct of lawful inquiries, or contravening the laws governing agencies of the executive branch and the purposes of these agencies. . . .

Article III. . . . has failed without lawful cause or excuse to produce papers and things as directed by duly authorized subpoenas issued by the Committee on the Judiciary of the House of Representatives. . . .

In all of this, Richard M. Nixon has acted in a manner contrary to his trust as President and subversive of constitutional government, to the great prejudice of the cause of law and justice, and to the manifest injury of the people of the United States.

Wherefore, Richard M. Nixon, by such conduct, warrants impeachment and trial, and removal from office.

The Promise of Technology

Generation after generation, Americans had been preoccupied with material progress. Those of the late twentieth century saw technological achievements even more startling than those of earlier times. But people found it harder and harder to maintain the faith of their forefathers who had assumed that new inventions would almost automatically lead to a better life for everyone.

INNOVATIONS AND RESOURCES

A future of increasing abundance for the American people seemed to be promised by the continuing development of technical innovations summed up in the term "automation." Yet automation, like earlier phases of technical change dating back to the eighteenth century, threatened to create unemployment and social upheaval. Continuous automatic production was older than the term "automation," which a Ford Motor Company executive coined in 1946 to describe a system Ford was installing for the automatic handling of parts.

Essential to automation as it developed after World War II were electronic controls and the development of computer systems. The first electronic computer went into operation in 1946. Its name was descriptive: ENIAC, which stood for Electronic Numerical Integrator and Calculator. At first computers were large, cumbersome, and expensive, but the discovery that complicated electronic circuits, which had been assembled by hand, could be printed on cardboard or plastic and that compact durable transistors (invented in 1948) could replace fragile vacuum tubes made possible the rapid and spectacular advance in computer technology. By the end of the sixties, computers were a hundred times faster, ten times smaller in their electronic components, and provided information in a thousandth the time of earlier ones.

Computers, capable of answering in a few minutes problems that would require a thousand man-hours of calculation, were bringing a revolution in information processing. Jerome B. Wiesner, who had been President Kennedy's science adviser, described the change this way: "The computer, with its promise of a mil-lionfold increase in man's capacity to handle information, will undoubtedly have the most far-reaching consequences of any contemporary technical development. The potential for good in the computer, and the danger inherent in its misuse, exceed our ability to imagine."

Computers could give answers to innumerable informational problems previously so complex as to be unmanageable. They were helping industry control inventories to eliminate the periodic scarcity or glut that had contributed to irregularities in the business cycle. They could fly jet planes, guide rockets to the moon, or control almost any sort of machinery. They could, critics feared, through data storage on every individual, destroy privacy; through the tasks they could guide, they might create serious unemployment.

The bituminous coal industry was a spectacular example of what automation could mean. By the end of the 1940s, coal, being mined with some machinery, was being priced out of the market by cheaper petroleum and natural gas. In 1948 the United Mine Workers gave the operators freedom to automate in exchange for a royalty of 40 cents per ton to be paid into UMW welfare funds. The companies, investing $500 million in new machinery, automated the mines and laid off far more than half the workers. A quarter-million miners had lost their jobs; only 150,000 were kept at work. Yet the alternative, the president of the Princess Coal Company, pointed out, would have been bankruptcy for the bituminous coal industry. "We've lost major markets and must compete with other fuels that have tax advantages," he declared. "The fact that the price of coal at the mine has not gone up in the past ten years — during a period of inflation — is a major accomplishment."

Whether in the long run automation would mean chronic unemployment was not entirely clear. In agriculture and industry as well as mining, automatic machinery was displacing labor rather than creating jobs. Its effects upon other groups of workers — those employed as clerks, for example — remained to be seen. Yet overall, the first seven decades of the twentieth century had brought an enormous increase in output per man-hour without any corresponding rise in unemployment.

As production grew, the United States began to change from a "have" to a "have-not" nation in natural resources, but innovations postponed the danger of disastrous shortages. Between 1900 and 1950, the production of bituminous coal rose two and a half times, of copper three times, of iron ore three and a half times, and of crude oil thirty times. Although Gifford Pinchot, writing in the Progressive era, had feared that bituminous coal would soon be exhausted, exhaustion was still far off. In fact, the Department of the Interior was still researching new uses — such as liquefication and gasification — for bituminous coal. In 1877 Secretary of the Interior Carl Schurz warned of a "timber famine" only twenty years away, but according to a 1962 estimate forests at that time were growing at a rate that exceeded by 60 percent the amount of timber cut. Synthetic substances, plastics, and metals had cut the demand for forest products. As the rich iron deposits began to dwindle, steel companies developed processes to make use of lower-grade ore. Once the huge investment had been made in plants that produced high-grade pellets from taconite ores, the steel companies reaped the advantage of higher productivity from furnaces into which they fed the pellets. New ore deposits were opened in Labrador. The United States became the largest importer of copper, lead, and zinc, leading to a flow of dollars overseas.

Already the United States was beginning to develop electric power from atomic energy. Two small power plants were completed in 1957. In the future nuclear reactors were likely to produce electric power at competitive rates. Already steam plants fueled by oil, gas, or coal could produce electric power more cheaply than could be expected at the few major hydroelectric sites remaining in the United States.

SCIENTIFIC RESEARCH

Applications of scientific knowledge, both civilian and military, were being developed at such a rapid pace that they created a sharp pressure for additional basic research. In 1957 a Department of Defense research officer declared: "We have been chewing up the findings of basic research since World War II at a speed faster than they are being produced in the laboratories and ivory towers."

The chief agency for promotion of basic scientific research was the National Science Foundation. In 1945 Dr. Vannevar Bush, who had been wartime director of the Office of Scientific Research and Development, proposed the establishment of a peacetime government agency to promote basic research. The United States could no longer depend upon Europe, Bush warned. In 1950 Congress established the National Science Foundation, but limited its annual appropriations to $15 million per year and appropriated less than that until the 1956 fiscal year. In the 1959 budget, after the sputnik crisis, President Eisenhower asked for $140 million for the National Science Foundation. Thereafter its budget, and its impact upon scientific research, increased significantly.

Overall federal expenditures on research and development — no more than a tenth of it for basic research — rose so spectacularly that by the end of the sixties they totaled more than the entire federal budget before Pearl Harbor. These sums were so large that many universities were dependent upon them for a considerable portion of their budgets. Concentration of expenditures in a few universities (68 percent of federal research funds were going to twenty-five institutions) had important side effects.

Scientific and engineering work at Harvard and the Massachusetts Institute of Technology had helped attract science-based industry, especially in electronics, to Highway 128 ringing Boston; the University of California and Stanford had brought similar industry to the San Francisco Bay region. Understandably, there developed considerable pressure to allocate more scientific grants to the Middle West and other areas in the United States. The House Appropriations Committee forbade the granting of more than 10 percent of the National Science Foundation fellowships to the residents of any one state.

The most comprehensive and spectacular of basic research enterprises, in which the United States cooperated with sixty-two other countries including Russia, was the International Geophysical Year, from July 1, 1957, to the end of 1958. It involved exploring the globe from pole to pole and from ionosphere to core, and included the launching of satellites and the establishment of an American base at the

South Pole. The research in Antarctica developed into a long-range scientific program, centering in a permanent base at McMurdo Sound, which supplied a number of outlying stations. By international treaty, national territorial holdings and armaments were barred from the continent; the United States, the Soviet Union, and a number of other nations carried on scientific work and shared information without friction.

In medical research, the most important advance was the development of an effective polio vaccine by Dr. Jonas Salk of the University of Pittsburgh. The vaccine was first used on a large scale in 1955, and within two years the polio rate in the United States dropped 80 percent. Many of the most spectacular innovations were made possible by electronic or atomic advances. The transplant of kidneys and even of a human heart were aided by chemical treatment and radiation to prevent rejection of the new organ. A number of mechanical and electronic inventions—among them artificial kidneys and miniature electronic generators to keep a heart beating at the right pace—helped to save lives. The laser beam, a ray of concentrated light, became a tool of eye surgery to repair damage to the retina.

Advances in medical research contributed to a lengthening life span. In 1900 life expectancy at birth had been forty-nine years; by 1955 it was seventy years. Most of the gain was in reducing the death rate among infants and children. Older people did not live much longer than before. In 1900 a sixty-four-year-old person had a remaining life span ahead of him that averaged about twelve years; in the 1960s it averaged fourteen years. Even if the two prime killers of the aged, heart disease and cancer, were to be eliminated, life expectancy would not be greatly increased.

THE SPACE RACE BEGINS

The American government had shown little interest in space exploration until October 1957, when the Soviet Union put its first satellite, Sputnik I, into orbit. Already the United States was carrying on a program of rocket research under the direction of Wernher von Braun, a German-born expert whose team had designed and built for the Hitler regime the V-2 rockets

that devastated London during the final stages of World War II. As the Russians advanced into Germany in 1945, they captured a few of the top men and hundreds of the technicians engaged in the V-2 project. Braun and others turned themselves over to the United States Army. In the early postwar years, however, the Americans were slower than the Russians in using German expertise to produce ballistic missiles, and still slower in using it to develop space rockets.

"Our satellite program has never been conducted as a race with other nations," President Eisenhower declared as he congratulated the Soviet Union on the launching of Sputnik I. But most Americans, including prominent public figures, assumed that a race was indeed on, and the United States appeared to be lagging far behind. Sputnik II carried a dog into space in November 1957 while Braun and his co-workers were still trying to launch a tiny, three-pound sphere, which they did not succeed in orbiting until January 1958. In October of that year, twelve months after the appearance of Sputnik I, the American government set up the National Aeronautics and Space Administration (NASA) to coordinate the nation's space efforts, but gave it only a small budget.

By 1961, when Kennedy took over the presidency from Eisenhower, the United States appeared to be making some gains. This country was ahead of the Soviet Union in the number of satellites put into orbit—thirty-three to nine. The total weight of the nine Soviet satellites, however, was more than twice as great as that of all thirty-three American ones, and the Russians were rumored to be testing a five-ton spaceship that could take a man into orbit. To the Russians, Kennedy said in his inaugural: "Let us explore the stars together." But the Russians showed little interest in that. In April 1961 they sent the world's first cosmonaut, Yuri Gagarin, once around the earth. After reentering the atmosphere and parachuting to safety, Gagarin issued the boastful challenge: "Now let the other countries try to catch us."

Eight days after Garagin's flight (and just one day after the Bay of Pigs fiasco in Cuba) President Kennedy directed a memorandum to Vice President Johnson, whom he had named as chairman of an advisory Space Council. "Do we have a chance of beating the Soviets," Kennedy asked, "by putting a laboratory in space, or by a trip around the moon, or by a rocket to land on the moon, or by a rocket to go to the moon and back with a man?'' The best the United States could do for the time being was to propel Alan Shepard into a suborbital flight that went some 100 miles up to the edge of space and some 300 miles out into the Atlantic Ocean. Three weeks later, May 25, 1961, Kennedy appealed to Congress: "I believe this nation should commit itself to achieving the goal, before the decade is out, of landing a man on the moon and returning him safely to earth." Congress soon responded by making the first of the necessary appropriations.

The moon program, Project Apollo, was expected to cost $20 billion, ten times as much as the development of the atom bomb (but less than the Vietnam War was to cost for a single year). Advocates of the program maintained that it would be well worth the price on account of its scientific and economic benefits as well as its enhancement of national prestige. One space official declared: "Each improvement in our ability to fly unmanned and manned spacecraft results in a corresponding improvement in our ability to solve nature's mysteries."

TO THE MOON AND BEYOND

Until 1965 the United States continued to trail the Soviet Union in the launching of manned spacecraft, though not in the firing of unmanned satellites. A Russian cosmonaut circled the globe seventeen times (August 1961) before the first American, John Glenn, was put into space (February 1962), to return to earth after making only three orbits. Another and yet another American went around in one-man Mercury capsules similar to Glenn's, but the Russians kept the lead in flight endurance and took the lead in orbiting two vehicles close together, in launching two-man and then three-man craft, and in releasing a man from one of the ships to float in nothingness. But the United States was putting up, all together, more than twice as many satellites as was the Soviet Union. Some of these were intended for scientific purposes—to study solar radiation, the earth's magnetic field, and weather phenomena. Others, such as Telstar, facilitated around-the-world communication by telephone and television. Still others, such as the "eye in the sky" satellites Samos and Midas, gave the mili-

tary new means of observation or espionage. Meanwhile, from 1963 to 1965, the Americans discontinued manned flights and concentrated on the design and construction of improved space vehicles.

By 1965 the Americans were ready to achieve some firsts of their own with men in space. The new two-man Gemini, unlike the latest Soviet spaceships, was maneuverable; it was equipped with small rockets that could change its course in mid-orbit, as its pilots demonstrated on their first flight. On a second flight an astronaut stepped into space and, with a small oxygen-spitting gun, pulled the vehicle about on a tether. The third of the Geminis, orbiting for nearly 191 hours, broke the endurance record that the Russians had set. On a later launching, in 1966, a Gemini succeeded in overtaking an orbiting craft and joining up or "docking" with it—a maneuver essential for a moon trip. The United States now appeared to hold the lead in manned as well as unmanned flights.

The next stage involved the Apollo, a three-man spacecraft which, with over 2 million parts, was far more complicated than the Gemini or the Mercury. The project was set back and the nation was stunned when, early in 1967, a fire killed the three astronauts while they were rehearsing for the first Apollo take-off. While the craft was being redesigned and retested, a succession of Surveyors, unmanned, were being rocketed to the moon and were sending back tens of thousands of pictures of the lunar surface. One of the Surveyors landed on the moon and then took off from it, as a manned vehicle was scheduled to do eventually. In late 1968, after Apollo 7 had carried three men around the earth, Apollo 8 carried three others around the moon, the first men to leave the earth's gravitational field. During the next few months, Apollo 9 tested a lunar module (the landing craft that was to leave and rejoin the mother ship) in an earth orbit, and Apollo 10 tested one in a moon orbit.

". . . One Giant Leap for Mankind"
Astronaut Edwin "Buzz" Aldrin poses for a historic portrait photographed by the Apollo 11 Commander, Neil Armstrong. The surrealism of the fiction-like spacesuit and the starkness of the moon's landscape are brought to life by the astronauts' footprints and the reflection of the photographer and the lunar module as seen in Aldrin's visor. (NASA)

At last, in July 1969, Apollo 11 was blasted off on its epochal flight to land men on the moon. Ahead of them streaked a Russian spacecraft, Luna 15, heading for lunar orbit, but Luna carried no crew. Its launching seemed to show dramatically that, in space enterprises, the Soviet Union was still competing rather than cooperating—and now competing at a decided disadvantage. Not that sovereignty over the moon was at stake: by a treaty signed in 1966 the two superpowers had agreed that the moon should be a no man's land open to exploration and use by all nations. At issue were national prestige and (to the extent that the space programs yielded new techniques of warfare) military advantage.

The flight of Apollo 11 was a beginning, not an ending. During the next three years the United States launched a series of six additional Apollos, five of which succeeded in putting men on the moon, and all of which returned safely to the earth. Meanwhile both the United States and the Soviet Union sent space probes to Mars and Venus, and in 1973 the United States sent others to Jupiter and Mercury. Discontinuing lunar explorations for the time being, the Americans now concentrated their man-in-space efforts on experimental earth orbits. In 1973 they launched a two-story laboratory, Skylab, and three three-man crews in succession visited it to survey the earth's resources, test man's ability to live in space for long periods, and carry on other observations and experiments. At last, by an agreement of 1972, the Americans and the Russians were beginning to cooperate. They planned a joint earth-orbiting mission for 1975.

"There is no question but that we will go to Mars and colonize the moon, probably sooner than we now think," a NASA official said in 1972. "I think it will also become a reality that we'll pick up communications from other intelligence in the universe."

The Environment in Danger

"We have always assumed that progress and 'the good life' are connected with population growth," the President's Commission on Population Growth and the American Future reported in 1972. "If that were ever the case, it is not now. There is hardly any social problem confronting this nation whose solution would be easier if our population were larger."

THE CROWDING COUNTRY

In 1967 the demographic clock of the Census Bureau indicated that the population of the United States had passed the 200-million mark. In 1970 the census takers counted a total of 203,184,772. That was almost twice as large as it had been in 1920 and about 24 million larger than in 1960.

The rapid population growth after World War II belied the predictions of demographic experts who, on the basis of falling birth rates during the depression of the 1930s, had expected an early leveling-off. The baby boom of the 1950s caused pessimists to go to the opposite extreme. At the postwar rate of growth, some predicted, the population within 800 years would be so large that each American would have only one square foot of land to stand on. During the 1960s, however, the birth rate dropped even lower than it had been during the depression. By 1972 it was down to 2.11 per woman. This was a "zero population growth" rate, one that could mean eventually (after two more generations of childbearing women) just enough births to offset the number of deaths. Meanwhile the birth rate might rise again, and so population predicting remained as uncertain as ever.

Immigration accounted for less than a half million, or about 20 percent, of the population increase during the decade 1960–1970. The immigration act of 1965 eliminated the national-origins quota system, which had allowed only a certain percentage of each nationality to enter the country. The new law provided that, from 1969 on, there would be a ceiling of 120,000 on immigration from the Western Hemisphere and 170,000 from the rest of the world. The law allowed parents, spouses, and children of United States citizens to enter the country without regard to the overall limitations. There-

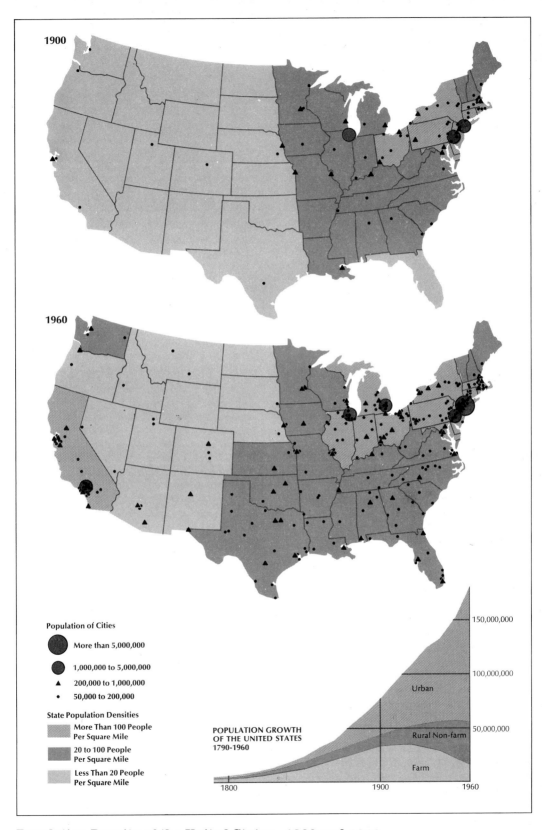

Population Density of the United States   1900 and 1960

after the largest numbers of immigrants no longer came from Canada and the United Kingdom but from Italy and the Philippines.

Mobility continued to characterize Americans, as it had always done. In 1970 more than one-fourth of the natives of the United States were living in a state other than the one they were born in (in 1850 the proportion had been about the same). During the 1960s, as during previous decades, the greatest interstate movement was to the Far West, especially to California, already the most populous state by 1960 and the home of nearly 20 million people in 1970. A reversal seemed under way in 1970 when, for the first time in a hundred years, as many people moved out of California as moved into it. From 1920 to 1960 so many blacks had left the South that the region lost more than it gained by migration, but during the 1960s it gained 1.8 million whites from the North while losing 1.4 million blacks to the North. As a whole, the black population grew 33 percent faster than the white during the decade and constituted about 11 percent of the nation's total population in 1970.

The flight from the farm continued, at an accelerating speed. In 1920 the people had been distributed about evenly between city and country. By 1970 the rural population had increased slightly, but the urban population had nearly tripled. The number of farms (and farmers) actually declined after 1935, from a peak of 6.8 million in that year to less than 3 million in 1970, and the figure was expected to be below 2 million by 1980. In 1970, some 63 million people were classified as rural (much the most of them nonfarm), about 62 million as strictly urban (living in cities proper), and 75 million as suburban.

RISE OF THE MEGALOPOLIS

During the decades after World War II, metropolitan areas expanded until they met and merged with one another. From north of Boston to south of Washington a single urban region—a megalopolis—was coming into being. From Raleigh to Greensboro and Charlotte, in a similar development on a smaller scale within North Carolina, an "urban crescent" or continuous series of thick settlements was developing. Elsewhere supercities of one kind or another were also taking form.

The proper governing of these areas was a problem. It was complicated by the escape of affluent whites from city jurisdictions and tax collectors to the suburbs, and by the concentration of poor blacks in the inner cities. While the city governments needed more and more financial resources, the tax basis was growing very slowly or actually shrinking.

Because individual metropolitan problems transcended city and sometimes state lines, special governmental authorities to deal with matters like harbor development or transit had come into existence. Together with traditional governments they led to a multiplicity of governmental agencies. Within the 212 standard metropolitan areas in the 1960s there were some 18,000 units of government, ranging from counties to school boards. There was little cooperation among them: most of these governments were ready to give little or no aid to the ailing cities. Many state, county, and suburban officials resisted the establishment of the federal Department of Housing and Urban Development, in 1965.

The problems with which metropolis and the merging megalopolis had to grapple were those long faced by city dwellers: improvement of housing, transportation, living conditions, educational and cultural opportunities, and above all the economic base for both the family and community; conversely, the elimination of pollution, blight, crime, and violence. The size of the new metropolitan areas made these problems far larger and sometimes more complex than in earlier generations.

Federally sponsored housing, which had originated three decades earlier in the New Deal era, together with the urban renewal programs developed after World War II, were good examples. Proponents of housing hoped through combining public and private funds to wipe out the blighted core of the metropolis; erect beautiful, modern structures; and in addition provide comfortable housing that families of varying incomes could afford. Much was achieved, but reality sometimes ran counter to the dream.

Federal aid in one form or another had helped make possible the vast growth of suburbia since 1945—and then the white exodus from cities into suburbs. By 1963, 5 million families owned houses built with FHA aid; millions more lived in houses financed through the GI Bill of Rights. Federal guarantees had helped

Some Favorable Aspects of Metropolitan Development [1966]

The American urban pattern, in which cities merge in great metropolitan belts, developed as a consequence of the efforts of economically free agents to maximize profits and amenities. In North America, therefore, the city is especially an economic entity. The American city is free, in an economic if not a political sense, to push its boundaries outward. It can preserve a kind of density balance in which individuals' preferences for space are accommodated and technology is used both to concentrate a high intensity of activities and to disperse places of residence. Given the extraordinary heterogeneity of the American population, it is possible that the sprawling development of American cities has actually relieved tension and reduced intergroup conflict by substituting a stratified spatial order for a genuine social accommodation. — John W. Dyckman, "Some Conditions of Civic Order in an Urbanized World," *Daedalus,* Summer 1966, p. 800.

---

27 million home owners to borrow money for repairs. The government encouraged the deposit of money in savings and loan associations which issued millions of mortgages, by insuring the deposits.

Simultaneously with the growth of suburbs, attempts were made to rejuvenate decaying central cities through federal aid. Urban renewal projects were to transform slums into business and cultural areas and above all into attractive apartment complexes. The new buildings were expected to bring a fivefold increase in taxes, thus helping to solve urban financial problems.

A small beginning during the New Deal had involved federal clearing of slums and construction of public housing. From 1937 on, the federal government helped cities in the undertaking. The 1949 legislation provided for a bold departure. The federal government would help cities finance the purchase of slum land, which would then be sold to private entrepreneurs at reduced costs. Federal loans or mortgage insurance gave these builders a further profit incentive. Thus private enterprise would be persuaded to rebuild the cities.

For five years the program made little progress and thereafter seemed most effective in producing profits for the entrepreneurs. There were numerous complaints that it was the land where the poorest people (often Negroes) lived that was being taken over, and that these people seldom received adequate housing elsewhere at rents they could afford. Sometimes land was cleared and left idle for years while builders were sought. Sometimes the new construction was a complex of luxury apartments, as in the West End of Boston.

Beautification, cleanliness, and safety were also problems requiring community and even national action. Cities in an affluent society produced ever-increasing quantities of waste. Keeping streets and vacant lots clean was relatively simple compared with disposing of the innumerable tons of sewage, garbage, and trash. In 1920 the average person threw away less than 3 pounds of refuse per day; by the mid-sixties he was discarding 4.5 pounds. Household and industrial waste had turned many of the nation's rivers into huge sewers. Smoke and fumes from industries, automobiles, incinerators, and burning dumps created acute smog hazards in widespread areas.

Maintenance of safety was an old problem that each generation faced anew. In 1967 the President's Commission on Crime declared that there was far more crime than ever reported to the police — three times as many burglaries, half again as many robberies, double the number of assaults. The commission observed: "The existence of crime, the talk about crime, the reports of crime, and the fear of crime have eroded the basic quality of life of many Americans." Nevertheless, some specialists doubted whether per capita crime rates had really risen in the 1960s.

THE TRANSPORTATION HEADACHE

Increasingly, after World War II, older modes of conveyance deteriorated. Streetcars, which had taken over America in the early years of the twentieth century, almost completely disappeared, to be supplanted by buses or additional subways. Transit lines, unable to meet rising

Troubles of Rapid Transit

To serve San Francisco and neighboring cities on both sides of San Francisco Bay, the Bay Area Rapid Transit (BART) District was formed to build and operate an ultra-modern, computer-controlled system, with automated high-speed trains. After long delays and unanticipated costs, the partially completed system was opened on September 11, 1972. Less than two weeks later, it had its first wreck, when the automatic controls failed and a train smashed through a sand embankment at the end of the line. (UPI)

costs with revenues that failed to keep pace, faced bankruptcy. Municipally owned systems ran heavier and heavier deficits. Between 1955 and 1965 the number of riders on public transit lines declined 25 percent. Railroads, to cut losses, tried to drop commuter services. The number of passengers commuting by train declined 45 percent between 1929 and 1963 and continued to decline thereafter. City dwellers and suburbanites depended more and more upon automobiles, which were quicker and more convenient. But automobiles required six to forty-five times more space on highways per passenger than did buses, and multiple-unit rail cars were even more efficient.

While public transportation languished, the federal government helped subsidize the building of 6,000 miles of expressways. This forced the leveling of countless blocks of urban buildings (including a disproportionate amount of poor peoples' housing), and other buildings were leveled to provide parking lots. As a consequence, still more automobiles poured into the cities, compounding traffic problems and, during public transportation strikes, creating chaos. An opposite approach at both the local and federal level was to try to improve public transit or even to develop new systems as, most spectacularly, in the San Francisco Bay region. In 1966 Congress created a new Department of Transportation.

National transportation problems were interrelated, as railroad passenger service rapidly declined, and trucks became an increasingly important factor in carrying freight. The large-scale program of turnpike building that

**Urban
Transportation
[1907–1966]**

In 1907 it was found that the average speed of horse-drawn vehicles through the city's streets was 11.5 miles per hour. In 1966 the average speed of motor vehicles through the central business district was 8.5 miles per hour — and during the mid-day crushes slower still. — A. E. Palmer, Jr., New York City Transportation Administrator, before a Senate subcommittee, November 16, 1967.

---

marked the first decade after World War II came to an end as thousands of miles of toll-free superhighways were built, beginning with the Interstate Highway Act of 1956, which set standards for the roads (no grade crossings, for example) and provided federal funds for 90 percent of the cost. For public transportation, Americans had to depend either upon buses or airlines.

By the mid-fifties, airlines, which had been luxury transportation before World War II, were carrying over 30 million passengers per year. By the mid-sixties, the figure had nearly quadrupled and was expected to double again within a decade. Especially along the northeast coast, the air lanes were so crowded that at the height of the evening rush, about 100 planes would be landing or about to land at the three major New York area airports, while another 250 private planes were also taking off or landing at these and smaller fields. Despite an occasional collision, and numerous near collisions, the airlines were able to boast a remarkable safety record. But the congestion of people at the major airports worsened with the appearance, in 1970, of the "jumbo jet" carrying more than twice as many passengers as any previous airliner.

For the future, when airlines might not be able to meet the passenger demands along the northeast corridor between Washington and Boston, the federal government was fostering high-speed train service which it hoped ultimately would carry passengers at 160 miles an hour. The Metroliner, with a speed of 120 miles an hour, was operating between New York and Washington by 1969. There might be a future along a few congested routes for rail passenger service of this sort. In the early 1970s a government-owned corporation, Amtrak, was running passenger trains on a number of railroad lines and was attracting more and more riders, despite the handicap of poor roadbeds

and rolling stock. The principal railroad companies of the Northeast were bankrupt or facing bankruptcy, however, and only massive federal aid could keep them in business.

THE COSTS OF ABUNDANCE

For the American people as a whole, the quarter century following World War II was a time of unprecedented enjoyment of material things. But abundance had its costs in the pollution of the environment and the depletion of natural resources. By the 1970s it had begun to appear that the age of plenty was about over and a new age of scarcity was at hand.

In the 1960s most Americans were still enjoying a living standard far higher than any they had previously known. Though the population had been growing, the output of goods and services had been growing much faster. Even allowing for the rise in prices and in taxes, the average person was better off than ever before. True, income continued to be very unevenly distributed, the top 5 percent of the people receiving 20 percent of the income. Some 40 percent of the people lived in what was considered "either poverty or deprivation" (which meant, as of 1960, having a family income of less than $6,000 a year). Yet workers were getting more pay for less work than in the past. With a forty-hour instead of a forty-four-hour week, and with paid vacations, the average industrial employee enjoyed much more free time than his father or grandfather had in 1900. Workers could afford to spend a smaller proportion of their wages for food, clothing, and shelter and a larger proportion for automobiles, appliances, medical care, recreation, and other luxuries. Even among families classified as living in "poverty" (having an income of less than $4,000 a year), 60 percent owned automobiles in 1960. In 1964, 93 percent of the homes, including those of the poor as well as the rich, contained television sets.

The goods that came forth in such abundance were produced by industries the ownership and control of which were more and more highly concentrated. In 1960 the eighty-seven largest corporations held 26 percent of the total of corporate assets, and in 1970 they held 46 percent. During the 1960s companies merged at a faster rate than ever, usually to form conglomerates. Many of these became "multinational" firms by acquiring subsidiaries in foreign countries. Corporations, "agrobusinesses," took over a larger and larger share of agriculture in the United States, and the average size of farms increased as the number of farms declined.

While consumers enjoyed the bounty that industry provided, a growing number of them complained that too many of the products were useless, dangerous, falsely advertised, overpriced, defective, or lacking in durability. The complaints resulted in an accelerating movement for consumer protection. As early as the 1920s the Consumers Union had begun to test products and issue reports on them. In 1966 Ralph Nader emerged as a leading advocate of the new consumerism when he published a book, *Unsafe at Any Speed,* exposing the built-in hazards of many American cars. Nader started a number of consumer organizations to bring public pressure on both business and government. One of these organizations reported in *The Monopoly Makers* (1973) that federal regulatory agencies often conspired with the industries they were supposed to regulate.

Public services were less plentiful than commercial services and commodities. As population grew, the construction and maintenance of schools, hospitals, streets, sewers, public housing, and other community facilities fell behind the mounting needs. The times were characterized by private wealth and public poverty. That was the theme of John K. Galbraith's widely quoted book *The Affluent Society* (1958). "The line which divides our area of wealth from our area of poverty," Galbraith wrote, "is roughly that which divides privately produced and marketed goods and services from publicly rendered services." The contrast was symbolized by the picture he described of a prosperous middle-class family driving in an air-conditioned car, over poorly paved and trash-littered streets and billboard-cluttered highways, to lunch on "exquisitely packaged food from a portable ice box" at a picnic spot beside a polluted stream.

There seemed to be, in some material respects, a lowering of the quality of American life, and for much of this the population growth itself was responsible. The results of growth, as the sociologist Dennis H. Wrong pointed out, included "traffic jams, spreading urban and suburban blight, the overcrowding and destruction of beaches, parks, and other outdoor recreational facilities, water shortages, air pollution," and "deterioration in professional and social services resulting from shortages of trained personnel."

The worsening pollution of the environment resulted not only from population growth but, much more, from the great increase in factory output and from the development of new industrial processes and products. The production of synthetic fibers, for example, used more energy and hence directly or indirectly yielded more pollutants than the production of cotton or wool. Synthetic detergents, plastic materials, and aluminum cans were not biodegradable as were the objects for which they were substituted.

One of the worst offenders, with regard to air pollution, was the automobile. Motor vehicle registrations, which had amounted to only 8,000 in 1900, rose from 31 million in 1945 to 109 million in 1970. Thus the number of vehicles grew by more than 300 percent while the number of people was growing by about 50 percent. Many of the newer cars and trucks had more powerful, higher-compression engines than earlier models and gave poorer mileage while using high-test gasoline that contained a lead compound, an additional pollutant.

The befouling of air and water posed an immediate threat to human well-being and an ultimate threat to human existence. Environmentalists raised a demand for government action, and Congress responded with the Clean Air Acts of 1963, 1965, and 1970. These encouraged states and municipalities to set up their own programs for controlling pollution from stationary sources and required car manufacturers to see that vehicle emissions were drastically cut by 1975. Pittsburgh had long since set an example for other municipalities by starting,

Air Pollution in New York

In any major American city the camera could underscore what gauges recorded: the serious pollution of the air, especially troublesome on windless days when an atmospheric inversion (a blanket of warmer air several hundred feet up) kept the pollutants from being dispersed. (New York Daily News)

in 1941, a smoke-abatement program which, by the 1950s, had changed the city from one of the smoggiest and grimiest to one of the cleanest. Most communities, however, were slow to act, though some of them experimented with methods of transforming waste into salable products—converting fly ash from incinerators into an ingredient for concrete, manufacturing fertilizer from garbage and sewage, and retrieving metal from dumps. Industrialists generally resisted the application of antipollution measures to their own industries, since such measures tended to raise production costs and lower profits.

The war effort of 1941–1945 had used up tremendous quantities of raw materials, and the ensuing production boom used up still larger quantities of resources, especially fossil fuel. After the war, Americans turned more and more away from coal to oil and natural gas for generating electrical energy as well as for heating houses and other buildings. Manufacturers of plastics, synthetic fibers, and petrochemicals demanded increasing quantities of petroleum as a raw material. Drivers of cars, trucks, and buses added greatly to the demand, and the air force added further with its fueling of bombers in Vietnam.

Signs of an approaching "energy crisis" appeared in the United States as early as the mid-1960s, with the sudden failures of the electrical supply and the temporary blackouts of New York City and other areas in the Northeast. The events of 1973–1974—the restrictions on oil exports by the Arabs and the fantastic price increases by the Arabs and other foreign producers—only made acute a condition that was already on the way to becoming chronic. For the indefinite future, Americans faced a recurring energy shortage. They could take little comfort in the probability that they would not be quite so bad off as the Europeans or the Japanese.

The United States still possessed considerable oil resources, already discovered or yet to be discovered, in addition to vast shale deposits

Strip Mining

Coal, lying just underground, remained abundant in various parts of the United States, but modern methods of removing the coal, though efficient, devastated the land. Here a mammoth strip shovel, as tall as a twenty-story building, is being operated in southeastern Ohio by the Hanna Coal Company. After viewing the scene from a plane—from which this photograph was taken, early in 1972—Governor John J. Gilligan said strip mines were making "Gobi Deserts" of Ohio. (Wide World Photos)

that eventually could be made to yield petroleum. The country had enough coal in the ground to last for centuries. It also had the capacity to build additional atomic-power plants. But the exploitation of petroleum, coal, or atomic fission endangered the environment in one way or another—through possible spills from drilling, damage to surroundings from oil transportation (as in the case of the Alaska pipeline to bring oil south from new Alaskan fields), destruction of mountains to get at shale, scarring of land by strip mining, pollution of air by the burning of low-grade coal, leakage of

radioactive wastes from an atomic reactor, or some even more deadly accident with an atomic-power plant.

In time the harnessing of the sun's rays might provide clean energy, but other resources would remain scarce in comparison with the abundant supplies of the past. Seemingly, as they advanced toward the twenty-first century, Americans would have to face the necessity of stabilizing their population, limiting their industrial growth, and changing their way of life so as to consume less of material goods.

Culture and Counterculture

After World War II the social and cultural life of Americans underwent noticeable changes. These, especially during the 1960s, seemed in some minds to portend the loss of moral values, the collapse of institutional authority, and the disintegration of society itself. Critics complained of a materialistic "consumer culture," a hedonistic "permissive society," and the "alienation" of children from parents and of individuals from the group. The changes, however, tended less in new and strange directions than in directions that already had long been set. Even the jeremiads were familiar. Complaints of the same tenor had been heard from time to time throughout the history of the American people and, indeed, the history of humankind.

THE "PERMISSIVE" SOCIETY

World War I had been followed, during the "roaring twenties," by deviations from traditional manners and morals, especially on the part of "flaming youth." World War II did not have so pronounced an immediate aftermath, but during the sixties, with the escalation of the Vietnam War, the deviations were even more spectacular. By the 1970s there were signs of a reaction away from some of the excesses.

"Togetherness" was a watchword of the 1950s, yet the family continued to lose its cohesion. By 1960, there was one annulment or divorce for every four marriages; by 1970, one for every three. Some attributed the rising divorce rate to the growing financial independence of women, more and more of whom were working outside the home. Yet the divorce rate, in 1970, was higher among the poor and the ill educated than among the better off and the better educated. It was higher for city dwellers than for rural folk, and much higher for nonwhites than for whites.

There was talk of a "sexual revolution" in the 1960s as sex relations outside of marriage appeared to become much more widespread than ever before. Presumably the oral contraceptive—"the pill"—encouraged extramarital intercourse by practically eliminating the risk of pregnancy. But studies by Dr. Alfred C. Kinsey and his Institute for Sex Research, at Indi-

Memorandum on Youth

I would assume that adolescents today and tomorrow are struggling to define new modes of conduct which are relevant to their lives. . . . Yet, this is within the context of two culture factors which seem to be extraordinary in the history of moral temper. One is the scepticism of all authority, the refusal to define natural authority (perhaps even that of paternal authority) and a cast of mind which is essentially anti-institutional and even antinomian. . . . The second factor is an extraordinary hedonism—using the word in the broadest sense—in that there is a desacralization of life and an attitude that all experience is permissible and even desirable. . . . At the same time society imposes new forms of specialization, of extending training, of new hierarchies and organizations. Thus, one finds an unprecedented divorce between culture and the society. And, from all indications, such a separation will increase. . . . In this respect, assuming this hypothesis is true, the greatest strains will be on the youth. This particular generation, like its predecessors, may come back to some form of accommodation with the society as it grows older and accepts positions within the society. But the experiences also leave a "cultural deposit" which is cumulative consciousness and—to this extent I am a Hegelian—is irreversible, and the next generation therefore starts from a more advanced position of alienation and detachment.—Erik H. Erikson, *Daedalus,* Summer 1967, pp. 860–863.

ana University, cast doubt on the idea of a re-volution. Kinsey's *Sexual Behavior in the Human Male* (1948) showed that, among the preceding generation of Americans, sex activity had been much more varied than laws or morals would have led anyone to believe. "People talk more freely about sex nowadays, and young people are far more tolerant and permissive regarding sex," Kinsey's successor observed in the 1960s. Yet, though premarital intercourse had increased, it had not risen suddenly or dramatically; "it has been on the rise ever since the turn of the century."

For some women, sexual freedom meant freedom from unwanted children, not only through contraception but, when necessary, through abortion. Advocates of abortion-on-demand asserted the right of a woman to control her own body. Opponents insisted on the right of the unborn to the enjoyment of life. A few states liberalized their laws so as to permit abortion under a wide range of conditions, but most of the states retained laws that made it difficult if not impossible — except for illegal and often dangerous practitioners. In 1973 the Supreme Court struck down those state laws that prohibited abortion during the first three months of pregnancy.

Freedom of sexual expression in words and pictures raised another constitutional issue, that of freedom of speech and the press. In 1957 the Supreme Court narrowed the legal definition of obscenity to include only those works that were morally offensive by prevailing national standards and were "utterly without redeeming social value." This decision put the burden of proof on local authorities in obscenity cases. It opened the way for an unprecedented flood of pornography. Vivid representations of sexual activity in all imaginable forms appeared in movies, plays, and books and magazines which mushrooming "adult" bookstores purveyed along with a variety of sexual devices. President Johnson appointed a Commission on Obscenity and Pornography to study the effects. The commission finally reported, in 1970, that "exposure to explicit sexual materials" apparently had little or nothing to do with causing emotional disorders, delinquency, or crime. The commission recommended the repeal of all laws forbidding the dissemination of such materials to consenting adults. Instead of acting on that recommendation, President Nixon denounced the report as

"morally bankrupt," and the Senate condemned it by a vote of 60 to 5. The Supreme Court, instead of further relaxing its stand, soon practically reversed itself. In 1973 it held that works were obscene if they lacked "serious literary, artistic, political, or scientific value" and if they were offensive by the standards of the local community. The burden of proof was now on the defendant, and local authorities here and there began successfully to prosecute.

Clothes may not make the man or woman, but changing styles of clothing seemed to reflect a changing relationship between women and men. In 1947 fashion designers decreed the "new look" of ankle-length skirts, and women meekly obeyed. Thereafter hemlines gradually rose until, in the late 1960s, they were much higher than they had been even during the 1920s. In 1971 the couturiers called for an end to "miniskirts" and to the even more abbreviated "hot pants" and for a return to long dresses, to mid-calf "midiskirts" or to full-length "maxiskirts." This time the women refused to heed. Instead, they turned to trousers and pant suits, or to blue jeans, which were already the uniform of the young, male and female alike. With young men and women wearing their hair to their shoulders, it was often hard to tell boy and girl apart — until, perhaps, one of them turned around and revealed a beard. The day of "unisex" seemed at hand, as distinctions of appearance if not also of role, became increasingly blurred. In the spirit of the time, homosexuals and lesbians came forth as never before to avow themselves openly and even proudly.

A great many middle-class young people, though by no means all of them, rejected the values as well as the clothes of adults. People spoke of the "generation gap" as if it were something entirely new. It did take new forms. Fringe groups, the "beatniks" of the 1950s and the "hippies" of the 1960s, went to extremes of unconventional dress and behavior. Drug use spread as growing numbers of youth retreated from a world they disliked. They were "turning on" (or, more accurately, turning off) by smoking marijuana, taking "mind-expanding" chemicals such as LSD, or injecting themselves with narcotics such as heroin. Blaring rock-and-roll music was a favorite with the young, along with ballads that, to a guitar accompaniment, protested against war, poverty, injustice, and the older generation, including everyone older than thirty. The youth movement reached a crescendo when, in August 1969, more than 300,000 gathered for a "rock festival" near Woodstock, New York, where most shed their inhibitions and many their clothing. The movement found a philosopher in Charles Reich, whose book *The Greening of America* (1970) praised "Consciousness III" as a new awareness, on the part of youth, of self as the only reality.

In the 1970s it appeared that young people were drawing away from their preoccupations of the previous decade. Some turned to religion of a traditional kind, the "Jesus freaks" singing, shouting, and clapping in the spirit of old-time revivalism. Others looked to even more unconventional cults. A sign of the changing times was the conversion of Rennie C. Davis. As a young radical, one of the "Chicago Seven," Davis had been charged (he was eventually acquitted) with inciting to riot at the Democratic national convention of 1968. Later he took up the mystical teachings of Maharaj Ji, a fifteen-year-old guru from India. In 1973 he proclaimed his love for the guru: "I would cross the planet on my hands and knees to touch his toe."

Leaders of the youth movement in the 1960s had rejected the past as "irrelevant." Now, in the 1970s, young people along with their elders acquired an enthusiasm for bygone decades, for the 1950s, the 1920s, or earlier periods. There developed a craze for reminders of what had come to seem like the good old days. This was reflected in art, dress, and the theater. It received a huge stimulus in 1974 from the promotion of a movie, *The Great Gatsby* (the third cinematic version of F. Scott Fitzgerald's 1925 novel), which drew large crowds eager to wallow in the sights and sounds of the 1920s. One might have concluded that, for many Americans of the 1970s, the past was more attractive than the present. Actually, such waves of nostalgia were not entirely new in American life. Previous generations, too, had looked back with longing beyond the immediate past to remoter and, in the haze of time, more glamorous eras.

The youth culture of the 1960s, in its various manifestations, had made so great an impression partly because young people were proportionally so numerous. With the aging of the population—with the disappearance of the youthful "bulge" in it—the influence of the young could be expected to decline.

EDUCATION AND RELIGION

After World War II, critics of public education charged that the schools were neglecting things of the mind in favor of athletics, band contests, vocational training, and "life adjustment." When the Soviet Union launched the first artificial satellite, sputnik, in 1957, many Americans assumed that the Russians had proved the superiority of their education in science and technology. A demand arose for fewer "frills" and more intellectual rigor, and school officials, teachers, and pupils responded. So did Congress. In 1958 it passed the National Defense Education Act, which provided for the spending of nearly a billion dollars over a four-year period to encourage the study of science, mathematics, and foreign languages.

Nevertheless, the schools continued to be criticized for their performance. At the end of the 1960s it appeared that 10 to 15 of every 100 pupils entering the fourth grade could not read (in ghetto schools, 35 to 50 of every 100). About 25 million adults in the nation as a whole were functionally illiterate, unable to comprehend a newspaper or magazine article or to fill out an application form. Most of these people were school dropouts.

With the gaining momentum of the civil rights movement, the emphasis of school reformers had shifted from academic excellence to equality of educational opportunity. This presumably would help the poor to rise out of poverty. But Christopher Jencks and seven associates at Harvard University's Center for Educational Policy Research questioned the assumption in a 1972 report. "If we want economic equality in our society," Jencks wrote, "we will have to get it by changing our economic institutions, not by changing the schools."

In fact, educational equality was yet to be tried. Annual expenditures per pupil ranged from a few hundred dollars in some schools to several thousand in others, even within the same state. Schools depended mainly on local property taxes, and resources therefore varied tremendously as between the poorest and the wealthiest districts. In the early 1970s, after the supreme court of California had declared the reliance on local school taxes unconstitutional in that state, suits were brought against similar financing arrangements in more than thirty other states.

The swelling enrollments of the 1950s and 1960s necessitated costly programs of school construction. At first the voters responded willingly by approving the issue of construction bonds, but eventually they grew more and more reluctant. In 1960 they approved nearly 90 percent of the bond issues put to referendums; in 1970, less than 47 percent. Undoubtedly the people were reacting against rising taxes, but they also seemed to be expressing a decline of confidence in the public schools.

During World War II, colleges and universities suffered from a loss of male students to the draft. The federal government helped many institutions by contracting with them to educate and train various kinds of specialists for the armed forces. After the war the government contributed to a sudden bulge in enrollments by paying the college expenses of veterans under the "GI Bill of Rights." During the 1950s and 1960s, attendance continued to swell, and at a faster rate than the college-age population, for a larger and larger proportion of young people were going on to secondary and higher education. Graduate and professional schools were especially thriving, as the demand for university teachers and other professional workers grew. The federal government heavily subsidized many programs that were directly or indirectly related to the national defense. State universities multiplied as teachers' colleges were converted into general colleges and these were raised, at least in name, to university status. Large campuses grew larger still— there were thirty-nine with more than 20,000 students in 1969 as compared with only two in 1941.

By the early 1970s the quarter-century-long academic boom appeared to be at an end. Federal support had been curtailed. Enrollments were leveling off and, in many institutions, even falling, while unemployment rose among holders of the Ph.D. and other advanced degrees. Private institutions, having had to raise tuition charges repeatedly in order to meet rising costs, had lagged far behind in the recruitment of students. Now many of the smaller and financially weaker private colleges faced the threat of extinction.

The first postwar generation of college students—especially the veterans, or GIs—seemed to be mainly interested in getting a degree in order to get ahead. A survey of members of the class of '49 concluded that they were "curiously old before their time" and were concentrating on the pursuit of economic security. Students of the 1950s also appeared to be looking ahead to jobs, especially corporation jobs. The prevailing campus spirit was quiet and conformist.

Then, in 1964, the campus of the University of California at Berkeley erupted, and during the next several years other large universities from coast to coast experienced a succession of student riots, with the rioters taking over and sometimes fire-bombing university buildings and "trashing" (vandalizing) business properties in the neighborhood. The rioters were giving expression to a variety of complaints—the impersonality of the gigantic and complex "multiversity," the irrelevance of its curriculum to their personal needs, its complicity in the Vietnam War (through war-related research and through the training of military officers in the ROTC), and its role as a bulwark of the socially unjust Establishment. Some of the rebels came from affluent families and were less preoccupied with upward striving than their successful fathers had been as college youths of the early postwar years. Other rebels, the blacks, were demanding the kind of college education that would enable them to rise in economic and social status and in self-esteem.

Colleges and universities responded to demands for "relevance" and personal involvement by relaxing requirements, adding courses in "black studies" and other contemporary concerns, and giving students some voice in administration. Some institutions, such as the City University of New York, adopted a policy of "open admissions," eliminating most entrance requirements.

During the postwar decade, church membership grew at about twice the rate of the population as a whole. This did not necessarily mean that Americans were becoming increasingly devout. When questioned, people generally identified themselves as Protestants, Catholics, or Jews, but relatively few expressed strong convictions. Many apparently referred to one faith or another as a means of indicating social background or of gaining, in an impersonal society, some sense of "belonging." Church attendance declined between 1958, when (according to a poll) 49 percent of the people were churchgoers, and 1972, when only 40 percent were. This, in turn, did not necessarily indicate a decline in religiosity. There were, indeed, signs of growing fervor on the part of groups who did not attend the traditional churches but who devoted themselves to Zen Buddhism, Hinduism, and other exotic faiths.

Churchmen, both Protestant and Catholic, were divided among themselves in regard to the mission of the church. Among Protestants, the most famous preacher, Norman Vincent Peale, wrote of religion as a force for success in the world (much as Bruce Barton formerly had done). The most popular revivalist, Billy Graham, offered a conventional message of individual salvation and, as a personal friend of Presidents Eisenhower and Nixon, associated with the politically powerful. But a spokesman for the World Council of Churches declared: "The Church must identify itself much more radically with the interests of the poor, the 'losers,' the outcasts and the alienated." While some Catholic priests revived the medieval practice of exorcising devils—and cooperated in the production of a 1973 movie on the theme, *The Exorcist,* a box-office hit—other priests, such as the brothers Philip and Daniel Berrigan, involved themselves in the antiwar movement and other social causes.

REFLECTIONS IN LITERATURE

The most prestigious figures in American writing, during the quarter century after World War II, were those who had made their reputations in earlier decades. Through the fifties, Ernest Hemingway and William Faulkner were two of the patriarchs of literature for the Western world as well as for the United States. Faulkner retained his master's touch in portraying the deep South he knew so well and through it viewing the world. Hemingway at times seemed to be parodying his earlier, virile, trenchant style, but produced one work in these years, *The Old Man and the Sea* (1952), that seemed destined to endure. It was the brief tale of an aged Cuban striving heroically, and unsuccessfully, to protect from the forays

of the sharks a huge fish he had caught. The poet Robert Frost seemed already a legendary figure before his death in 1963. After Eugene O'Neill's death in 1953, several of his previously unproduced plays ran for months on Broadway and on national tours.

By the sixties all these men of great reputation were gone. A large new generation of vigorous writers was attracting attention, but it was too soon to be sure which if any of them would win enduring top reputations. Among the novelists, their work ranged from the realism of John O'Hara and James Gould Cozzens, portrayers of the upper middle class, whose work seemed old-fashioned to younger critics, through a variety of newer styles and themes. The work of Robert Penn Warren, who won the Pulitzer Prize in both poetry and fiction, transcended Southern regionalism, but his most widely read novel, *All the King's Men* (1946), was a study of a political leader resembling Huey Long of Louisiana. In 1948 Norman Mailer produced the most acclaimed of the novels that came out of World War II, *The Naked and the Dead,* but in his subsequent work was more successful as a writer of nonfiction. J. D. Salinger through his account of the inward torture of an adolescent boy, *Catcher in the Rye* (1951), and subsequent stories about the precocious members of the Glass family (*Franny and Zooey,* 1962) became the spokesman for the generation of the 1950s.

Through the writings of several of the novelists ran a theme of alienation from, or at least serious questioning of, their culture. Saul Bellow began his work in this vein with *Dangling Man* (1944) and continued it in a number of successful novels, including *The Adventures of Augie March* (1953) and *Herzog* (1964). Nelson Algren, no admirer of middle-class values, wrote with blunt clarity about the flotsam of society, the men and women who had never had a chance, in his stories and novels, most notably, *The Man with the Golden Arm* (1949). Several Negro writers fell within this pattern. The most famous was James Baldwin, perhaps at his best in works of nonfiction like *The Fire Next Time* (1963); the most bitter, the poet and playwright, LeRoi Jones, especially effective in his one-act plays; and the most distinguished, Ralph Ellison, for a single novel, *Invisible Man* (1952). When the New York *Herald Tribune Book Week* in 1965 queried some 200 critics, authors, and editors, their consensus was that the work of fiction of the previous two decades most memorable and most likely to endure was *Invisible Man*. It is the sweeping, at times fantastic, drama of a young Negro's quest for identity. The novel that the critics listed second as most memorable was the polished social satire *Lolita* (1955) written by a Russian émigré, Vladimir Nabokov.

Among the novelists who emerged in the 1960s, perhaps the most notable were John Barth, Joseph Heller, Kurt Vonnegut, Jr., and Thomas Pynchon. Each dealt in his own way with what seemed to all of them like the cosmic absurdity of contemporary life. They were less interested in developing character or plot than in creating effects of intellectual ambiguity and emotional contradiction. In his mock-picaresque novel *The Sot-Weed Factor* (1961) Barth gave the impression that people could find no meaning in life except for the realization that they were merely acting their parts in a farce that had been written for them. In *Catch-22* (1964) Heller ridiculed the insanity and regimentation of war and, by implication, the insanity and regimentation of business society. In *Slaughterhouse-Five* (1969), his sixth novel, Vonnegut used his experience in World War II as a springboard for science fiction in which horror was mixed with humor. In his third novel, *Gravity's Rainbow* (1973), Pynchon made his central figure a German V-2 rocket of World War II. Baffling, jarring, full of complex symbolism, Pynchon's book gave an apocalyptic and paranoid vision of man's place in the universe. Some reviewers hailed it as the greatest American novel since *Moby Dick*.

Poetry, like painting, broke sharply with traditions after 1945. While poets like Frost and Carl Sandburg enjoyed fame in their old age, the liberal activism that moved poets like Archibald MacLeish during the depression and war years subsided after 1945. The newer poets moved away from public causes, toward the psychological and mythological, as did Randall Jarrell, or toward the autobiographical or confessional, as did Robert Lowell. Through much of this poetry ran a distaste for the established order. One critic, M. L. Rosenthal, suggests: "Behind it is the feeling, perhaps, that the humanistic way, which traditionally educated and romantic modern men still propose to protect, and indeed to project into a Utopian future, has already been defeated and is now no more than a ghost. It is that feeling which Robert Lowell in one of his poems calls, self-ironically, 'our universal *Angst*' — a heart-heavy realization that remorseless brutality is a condition not only of the physical universe but also of man himself."

CONSUMERS OF THE ARTS

Never had so many Americans shown so much interest in literature, art, and music as they did during the age of affluence that followed World War II. To some extent the federal and state governments encouraged cultural activity, the federal government establishing (1966) the Federal Arts and Humanities Endowments and a Federal Council on the Arts, and each of the states setting up its own arts council or commission. Some of the councils made financial grants, and private foundations provided more substantial sums. Most of the activity, however, was financed by individual spending.

The catering to cultural interests became a big business in itself, as statistics indicate. Between 1953 and 1960, expenditures on such interests rose by 130 percent, reaching an annual total of $3 billion. That was a larger sum than advertisers were spending on television commercials. In 1964, Americans paid the following amounts for certain cultural items: $1 billion for books, $600 million on musical instruments, $200 million on paintings or reproductions and art supplies, nearly $400 million to attend dramatic and musical performances, and $300 million to maintain art museums. By the end of the 1960s, total expenditures were approaching $7 billion a year. People were spending twice as much on the arts as on recreation in general and six times as much as on sports.

Nevertheless, the times were difficult for the performing arts, which suffered from rising costs, lagging attendance, and repeated deficits. A 1966 study showed that the nation was supporting only five full-time symphony orchestras, and the increase in attendance at concerts was somewhat slower than the increase in population. New York City accounted for nearly 40 percent of the receipts at musical performances and more than 50 percent of those at dramatic performances. The audiences represented only a very small and select portion of the people, consisting almost entirely of those with high incomes.

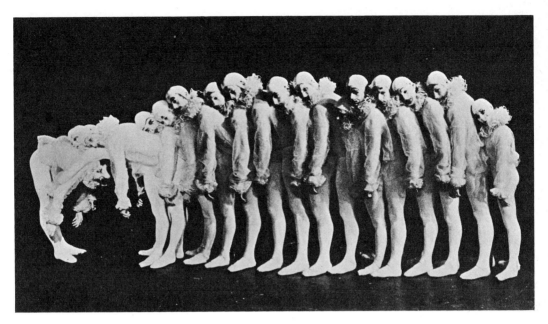

The Robert Joffrey Ballet
By the end of the 1960s a number of brilliant young companies were bringing both technical perfection and innovation to American ballets. (Herbert Migdoll)

Of all stage performances, musical comedies generally had the widest appeal. They constituted the American equivalent of a popular opera. Every few years an extremely successful one made its appearance: *Oklahoma!* in 1943, *My Fair Lady* in 1956, *West Side Story* in 1957, *Camelot* in 1960, *Hello Dolly* in 1963, and *Fiddler on the Roof* in 1964. *My Fair Lady* set a record for the longest Broadway run of a musical comedy. *Hello Dolly* broke that record and then was surpassed by *Fiddler on the Roof*, which in 1973 was still going strong.

Classical and popular music was available on improved, inexpensive phonograph records, the sales of which rose astronomically. In the 1940s, long-playing records of durable vinyl, turning at a speed of 45 or 33-1/3 revolutions per minute, began to replace the former short-playing, easily breakable 78 rpm disks. The quality of the reproduction was vastly improved, meanwhile, by the development of high-fidelity electronic recording and, during the 1950s, by the introduction of stereophonic sound. Together with television and both AM and FM radio, the improved phonographs provided good music to an audience vastly larger than that attending opera houses or concert halls.

THE ROLE OF TELEVISION

Television changed the leisure habits of the American people, made them better informed on the news and issues of the day, and even modified the patterns of American politics. In 1947 fewer than 10,000 people owned television sets with which they could view programs a few hours a day from a handful of stations. A decade later over 40 million sets in homes, hotels, and bars were tuned in to 467 stations. Motion-picture attendance dropped from a wartime high of 90 million a week to about 40 million. Not until the sixties did Hollywood begin to recuperate, by producing pictures that were better than before, or at least bolder. Professional sports, especially football and basketball, flourished as television brought them to millions of spectators at a time.

Television even more than radio meant mass communication to a nationwide audience. One musical show, telecast on 245 stations one night in March 1957 reached an estimated audience of 100 million—enough people to fill a Broadway theater every night for 165 years. Beginning with the 1952 campaign, television remade presidential elections as candidates began to make extensive and expensive use of the new medium. Radio was far from superseded, especially in the transistorized portable form that took over not only the United States but the entire world during these years.

Advertisers paid for the vast outpouring from commercial television and radio stations. They spent enormous sums to compete for the attention of the average television viewer who, surveys indicated, sat in front of his set as much as six hours a day. The manufacturers of one headache remedy, for example, spent nearly $750,000 in one month in 1958; their two nearest competitors spent a combined total of nearly $1 million that same month. In consequence, programs were patterned to draw the largest number of viewers, and when surveys indicated that the sets were tuned in elsewhere, the programs were ruthlessly pruned. Television lost one of its biggest sources of income when the federal government banned cigarette commercials after January 1, 1971.

One critic, Richard Schickel, commented that, to literate people, television was "an unparalleled purveyor of trash." Nevertheless, "we sit there, eyes glued to the set, watching this explication of the obvious in hateful fascination." A Canadian scholar, Marshall McLuhan, won a large following by extolling in confusing but thought-provoking prose the new era of mass media. He wrote, in *The Medium Is the Message* (1967): "The contained, the distinct, the separate—our western legacy—are being replaced by the flowing, the unified, the fused." The electronic medium of communication made its impressions all at once, he said, in contrast to the print medium, which made its impressions one after another. One reason for the generation gap and the youth revolt, he suggested, was the influence of the new medium on the young, who for the first time had been exposed to it in their formative years.

Foundations and the federal government tried to further the positive role of television. The Carnegie and Ford foundations proposed that educational stations be encouraged to take advantage of television's educational and cultural potentialities. The Public Broadcasting Act of 1967 authorized, though it provided no financing for, a noncommercial television network. Soon university-affiliated and other stations from coast to coast were providing high-quality theater, musical performances, and lecture courses with the cooperation of the Public Broadcasting System.

Commercial stations received and transmitted a large share of their programs from one or another of three great networks, the American Broadcasting Company, the National Broadcasting Company, and the Columbia Broadcasting System. These sources provided not only entertainment but also news and opinion for their affiliated stations. Bringing world events, or chosen segments of them, visibly into the home, the network programs had a much greater emotional impact (as in reporting the Vietnam War) than did newspaper accounts. A comparatively small number of prestigious commentators, outstanding among them Walter Cronkite of CBS, dominated the presentation of TV news. Hence questions arose regarding the breadth and balance of the coverage.

Vice President Agnew and other spokesmen for the Nixon administration, as well as Nixon himself, objected strongly to what they considered hostile treatment by the news media, especially television. Agnew demanded that commentators be "made more responsible to the views of the nation." The director of the White House Office of Telecommunications Policy attacked TV newsmen as "so-called professionals who confuse sensation with sense and who dispense elitist gossip in the guise of news analysis." He proposed a law that would put the responsibility on local stations for assuring "fairness," and the administration threatened to revoke the licenses of stations that failed to meet its standards.

An independent study (1973) by the Twentieth Century Fund concluded, however, that "presidential television" gave the President a great advantage over his critics. "Presidential television means the ability to appear simultaneously on all national radio and television networks at prime, large-audience evening hours, virtually whenever and however he wishes." Nixon exploited this advantage even more than his predecessors, taking as much TV time during his first eighteen months in office as Eisenhower, Kennedy, and Johnson together had taken during theirs. Congress, the courts, the opposition party could not keep up with the President in his ability to command free time on the air. Television appeared to be one of the factors that had increased the power of the executive as against that of the other branches of government.

Selected Readings

Nixon and Politics

Garry Wills, *Nixon Agonistes* (1970); Rowland Evans, Jr., and R. D. Novak, *Nixon in the White House: The Frustration of Power* (1971); R. J. Whalen, *Catch the Falling Flag* (1972); R. M. Scammon and B. J. Wattenberg, *The Real Majority* (1970); Samuel Lubell, *The Hidden Crisis in American Politics** (1970); L. K. Howe, ed., *The White Majority* (1970); Walter De-Vries and V. L. Tarrance, *The Ticket-Splitters* (1972); T. H. White, *The Making of the President, 1972* (1973); R. S. Anson, *McGovern* (1972), a campaign biography; H. E. Alexander, *Money in Politics* (1972); L. Baritz, ed., *The American Left: Radical Political Thought in the Twentieth Century* (1972); J. P. Diggins, *The American Left in the Twentieth Century** (1973).

Economic Policies

R. L. Miller, *The New Economics of Richard Nixon* (1972); Leonard Silk, *Nixonomics* (1972); F. F. Piven and R. A. Cloward, *Regulating the Poor: The Functions of Public Welfare* (1971); D. P. Moynihan, *The Politics of a Guaranteed Income: The Nixon Administration and the Family Assistance Plan* (1973); Walter Hickel, *Who Owns America?* (1971); J. K. Galbraith, *The New Industrial State** (1971); R. F. Buckthorn, *Nader, The People's Lawyer* (1972).

Population

B. J. Wattenberg and R. M. Scammon, *The U.S.A. An Unexpected Family Portrait . . . Drawn from the Census* (1965); L. H. and A. T. Day, *Too Many Americans* (1965); Conrad and I. B. Taeuber, *The Changing Population of the United States* (1958).

Interpretations of Society

David Riesman, *The Lonely Crowd** (1950); D. M. Potter, *People of Plenty: Economic Abundance and the American Character** (1954); J. K. Galbraith, *The Affluent Society** (1958); C. W. Mills, *The Power Elite** (1956); D. T. Bazelon, *Power in America* (1967); W. H. Whyte, *Organization Man** (1956); Vance Packard, *The Hidden Persuaders** (1957); Marshall McLuhan, *Understanding Media: The Extension of Man** (1964) and *The Medium Is the Message* (1967); Alvin Toffler, *Future Shock** (1970); W. L. O'Neill, *Coming Apart: An Informal History of America in the 1960's* (1971).

The City

Jean Gottman, *Megalopolis: The Urbanized Northeastern Seaboard of the United States* (1961); Martin Anderson, *The Federal Bulldozer: A Critical Analysis of Urban Renewal, 1949–1962** (1965); Charles Abrams, *The City Is the Frontier** (1965); R. C. Wood, *Suburbia: Its People and Their Politics* (1959); Wilfred Owen, *The Metropolitan Transportation Problem** (1966); Claiborne Pell, *Megalopolis Unbound: The Supercity and the Transportation of Tomorrow* (1966); Frank Graham, *Disaster by Default: Politics and Water Pollution* (1966); J. R. Lowe, *Cities in a Race with Time: Progress and Poverty in America's Renewing Cities* (1967); F. R. Harris and J. V. Lindsay, *The State of the Cities* (1972).

Culture

Ronald Berman, *America in the Sixties: An Intellectual History* (1968); Bernard Rosenberg and D. M. White, eds., *Mass Culture* (1957); K. S. Lynn, ed., *The Professions in America** (1965); John Burchard and Albert Bush-Brown, *The Architecture of America** (1961); W. J. Baumol and W. G. Bowen, *Performing Arts: The Economic Dilemma* (1966); Richard Kostelanetz, ed., *The New American Arts** (1965) and *On Contemporary American Literature** (1964); Stephen Stepanchev, *American Poetry Since 1945** (1965); Charles Rembar, *The End of Obscenity** (1968).

Youth and Education

E. H. Erikson, *Identity: Youth and Crisis* (1968); Kenneth Keniston, *The Uncommitted: Alienated Youth in American Society* (1965); Christopher Jencks and David Riesman, *The Academic Revolution* (1968); S. M. Lipset and S. S. Wolin, eds., *The Berkeley Student Revolt: Facts and Interpretations** (1965); J. B. Conant, *The American High School Today** (1959) and *Slums and Suburbs* (1964).

Science and Technology

D. K. Price, *The Scientific Estate* (1965); Gerald Holton, ed., *Science and Culture** (1965); Herbert Simon, *The Shape of Automation* (1966); William Francois, *Automation: Industrialization Comes of Age** (1964); H. H. Goldstine, *The Computer from Pascal to von Neumann* (1972).

To the Moon

Walter Sullivan, ed., *America's Race for the Moon** (1962); Jay Holmes, *America on the Moon* (1962); Hugh Odishaw, ed., *The Challenges of Space* (1962); L. S. Swenson and others, *This New Ocean: A History of Project Mercury* (1966); R. L. Rosholt, *An Administrative History of NASA, 1958–1963* (1966).

*Titles available in paperback.

Appendices

The Declaration of Independence

In Congress, July 4, 1776,

THE UNANIMOUS DECLARATION OF THE
THIRTEEN UNITED STATES OF AMERICA

When, in the course of human events, it becomes necessary for one people to dissolve the political bands which have connected them with another, and to assume, among the powers of the earth, the separate and equal station to which the laws of nature and of nature's God entitle them, a decent respect to the opinions of mankind requires that they should declare the causes which impel them to the separation.

We hold these truths to be self-evident, that all men are created equal; that they are endowed by their Creator with certain unalienable rights; that among these, are life, liberty, and the pursuit of happiness. That, to secure these rights, governments are instituted among men, deriving their just powers from the consent of the governed; that, whenever any form of government becomes destructive of these ends, it is the right of the people to alter or to abolish it, and to institute a new government, laying its foundation on such principles, and organizing its powers in such form, as to them shall seem most likely to effect their safety and happiness. Prudence, indeed, will dictate that governments long established, should not be changed for light and transient causes; and, accordingly, all experience hath shown, that mankind are more disposed to suffer, while evils are sufferable, than to right themselves by abolishing the forms to which they are accustomed. But, when a long train of abuses and usurpations, pursuing invariably the same object, evinces a design to reduce them under absolute despotism, it is their right, it is their duty, to throw off such government and to provide new guards for their future security. Such has been the patient sufferance of these colonies, and such is now the necessity which constrains them to alter their former systems of government. The history of the present King of Great Britain is a history of repeated injuries and usurpations, all having, in direct object, the establishment of an absolute tyranny over these States. To prove this, let facts be submitted to a candid world: —

He has refused his assent to laws the most wholesome and necessary for the public good.

He has forbidden his governors to pass laws of immediate and pressing importance, unless suspended in their operation till his assent should be obtained; and, when so suspended, he has utterly neglected to attend to them.

He has refused to pass other laws for the accommodation of large districts of people, unless those people would relinquish the right of representation in the legislature; a right inestimable to them, and formidable to tyrants only.

He has called together legislative bodies at places unusual, uncomfortable, and distant from the depository of their public records, for the sole purpose of fatiguing them into compliance with his measures.

He has dissolved representative houses repeatedly for opposing, with manly firmness, his invasions on the rights of the people.

He has refused, for a long time after such dissolutions, to cause others to be elected; whereby the legislative powers, incapable of annihilation, have returned to the people at large for their exercise; the state remaining, in the meantime, exposed to all the danger of invasion from without, and convulsions within.

He has endeavored to prevent the population of these States; for that purpose, obstructing the laws for naturalization of foreigners, refusing to pass others to encourage their migration hither, and raising the conditions of new appropriations of lands.

He has obstructed the administration of justice, by refusing his assent to laws for establishing judiciary powers.

He has made judges dependent on his will alone, for the tenure of their offices, and the amount and payment of their salaries.

He has erected a multitude of new offices, and sent hither swarms of officers to harass our people, and eat out their substance.

He has kept among us, in time of peace, standing armies, without the consent of our legislatures.

He has affected to render the military independent of, and superior to, the civil power.

He has combined, with others, to subject us to a jurisdiction foreign to our Constitution, and unacknowledged by our laws; giving his assent to their acts of pretended legislation:

For quartering large bodies of armed troops among us:

For protecting them by a mock trial, from punishment, for any murders which they should commit on the inhabitants of these States:

For cutting off our trade with all parts of the world:

For imposing taxes on us without our consent:

For depriving us, in many cases, of the benefit of trial by jury:

For transporting us beyond seas to be tried for pretended offences:

For abolishing the free system of English laws in a neighboring province, establishing therein an arbitrary government, and enlarging its boundaries, so as to render it at once an example and fit instrument for introducing the same absolute rule into these colonies:

For taking away our charters, abolishing our most valuable laws, and altering, fundamentally, the powers of our governments:

For suspending our own legislatures, and declaring themselves invested with power to legislate for us in all cases whatsoever.

He has abdicated government here, by declaring us out of his protection, and waging war against us.

He has plundered our seas, ravaged our coasts, burnt our towns, and destroyed the lives of our people.

He is, at this time, transporting large armies of foreign mercenaries to complete the works of death, desolation, and tyranny, already begun, with circumstances of cruelty and perfidy scarcely paralleled in the most barbarous ages, and totally unworthy the head of a civilized nation.

He has constrained our fellow citizens, taken captive on the high seas, to bear arms against their country, to become the executioners of their friends, and brethren, or to fall themselves by their hands.

He has excited domestic insurrections amongst us, and has endeavored to bring on the inhabitants of our frontiers, the merciless Indian savages, whose known rule of warfare is an undistinguished destruction of all ages, sexes, and conditions.

In every stage of these oppressions, we have petitioned for redress, in the most humble terms; our repeated petitions have been answered only by repeated injury. A prince, whose character is thus marked by every act which may define a tyrant, is unfit to be the ruler of a free people.

Nor have we been wanting in attention to our British brethren. We have warned them, from time to time, of attempts made by their legislature to extend an unwarrantable jurisdiction over us. We have reminded them of the circumstances of our emigration and settlement here. We have appealed to their native justice and magnanimity, and we have conjured them, by the ties of our common kindred, to disavow these usurpations, which would inevitably interrupt our connections and correspondence. They, too, have been deaf to the voice of justice and consanguinity. We must, therefore, acquiesce in the necessity which denounces our separation, and hold them as we hold the rest of mankind, enemies in war, in peace, friends.

We, therefore, the representatives of the United States of America, in general Congress assembled, appealing to the Supreme Judge of the world for the rectitude of our intentions, do, in the name, and by the authority of the good people of these colonies, solemnly publish and declare, that these united colonies are, and of right ought to be, free and independent states: that they are absolved from all allegiance to the British Crown, and that all political connection between them and the state of Great Britain is, and ought to be, totally dissolved; and that, as free and independent states, they have full power to levy war, conclude peace, contract alliances, establish commerce, and to do all other acts and things which independent states may of right do. And, for the support of this declaration, with a firm reliance on the protection of Divine Providence, we mutually pledge to each other our lives, our fortunes, and our sacred honor.

The foregoing Declaration was, by order of Congress, engrossed, and signed by the following members:

JOHN HANCOCK

New Hampshire

Josiah Bartlett
William Whipple
Matthew Thornton

Massachusetts Bay

Samuel Adams
John Adams
Robert Treat Paine
Elbridge Gerry

Rhode Island

Stephen Hopkins
William Ellery

Connecticut

Roger Sherman
Samuel Huntington
William Williams
Oliver Wolcott

New York

William Floyd
Philip Livingston
Francis Lewis
Lewis Morris

New Jersey

Richard Stockton
John Witherspoon
Francis Hopkinson
John Hart
Abraham Clark

Pennsylvania

Robert Morris
Benjamin Rush
Benjamin Franklin
John Morton
George Clymer
James Smith
George Taylor
James Wilson
George Ross

Delaware

Caesar Rodney
George Read
Thomas M'Kean

Maryland

Samuel Chase
William Paca
Thomas Stone
Charles Carroll,
    of Carrollton

Virginia

George Wythe
Richard Henry Lee
Thomas Jefferson
Benjamin Harrison
Thomas Nelson, Jr.
Francis Lightfoot Lee
Carter Braxton

North Carolina

William Hooper
Joseph Hewes
John Penn

South Carolina

Edward Rutledge
Thomas Heyward, Jr.
Thomas Lynch, Jr.
Arthur Middleton

Georgia

Button Gwinnett
Lyman Hall
George Walton

Resolved, That copies of the Declaration be sent to the several assemblies, conventions, and committees, or councils of safety, and to the several commanding officers of the continental troops; that it be proclaimed in each of the United States, at the head of the army.

The Constitution of the United States of America[1]

WE the People of the United States, in Order to form a more perfect Union, establish Justice, insure domestic Tranquility, provide for the common defence, promote the general Welfare, and secure the Blessings of Liberty to ourselves and our Posterity, do ordain and establish this CONSTITUTION for the United States of America.

Article I

SECTION 1.

All legislative Powers herein granted shall be vested in a Congress of the United States, which shall consist of a Senate and House of Representatives.

SECTION 2.

The House of Representatives shall be composed of Members chosen every second Year by the People of the several States, and the Electors in each State shall have the Qualifications requisite for Electors of the most numerous Branch of the State Legislature.

No Person shall be a Representative who shall not have attained to the Age of twenty-five Years, and been seven Years a Citizen of the United States, and who shall not, when elected, be an Inhabitant of that State in which he shall be chosen.

[Representatives and direct Taxes[2] shall be apportioned among the several States which may be included within this Union, according to their respective Numbers, which shall be determined by adding to the whole Number of free Persons, including those bound to Service for a Term of Years, and excluding Indians not taxed, three fifths of all other Persons.][3] The actual Enumeration shall be made within three Years after the first Meeting of the Congress of the United States, and within every subsequent Term of ten Years, in such Manner as they shall by Law direct. The Number of Representatives shall not exceed one for every thirty Thousand, but each State shall have at Least one Representative; and until such enumeration shall be made, the State of New Hampshire shall be entitled to chuse three, Massachusetts eight, Rhode-Island and Providence Plantations one, Connecticut five, New York six, New Jersey four, Pennsylvania eight, Delaware one, Maryland six, Virginia ten, North Carolina five, South Carolina five, and Georgia three.

When vacancies happen in the Representation from any State, the Executive Authority thereof shall issue Writs of Election to fill such Vacancies.

The House of Representatives shall chuse their Speaker and other Officers; and shall have the sole Power of Impeachment.

SECTION 3.

The Senate of the United States shall be composed of two Senators from each State, chosen by the Legislature thereof, for six Years; and each Senator shall have one Vote.

Immediately after they shall be assembled in Consequence of the first Election, they shall be divided as equally as may be into three Classes. The Seats of the Senators of the first Class shall be vacated at the Expiration of the second Year, of the second Class at the Expiration of the fourth Year, and of the third Class at the Expiration of the sixth Year, so that one-third may be chosen every second Year; and if Vacancies happen by Resignation, or otherwise, during the Recess of the Legislature of any State, the Executive thereof may make temporary Appointments until the next Meeting of the Legislature, which shall then fill such Vacancies.

No Person shall be a Senator who shall not have attained to the Age of thirty Years, and been nine Years a Citizen of the United States, and who shall not, when elected, be an Inhabitant of that State for which he shall be chosen.

---

[1]This version, which follows the original Constitution in capitalization and spelling, was published by the United States Department of the Interior, Office of Education, in 1935.
[2]Altered by the Sixteenth Amendment.
[3]Negated by the Fourteenth Amendment.

The Vice President of the United States shall be President of the Senate, but shall have no vote, unless they be equally divided.

The Senate shall chuse their other Officers, and also a President pro tempore, in the absence of the Vice President, or when he shall exercise the Office of President of the United States.

The Senate shall have the sole Power to try all Impeachments. When sitting for that purpose, they shall be on Oath or Affirmation. When the President of the United States is tried, the Chief Justice shall preside: And no person shall be convicted without the Concurrence of two thirds of the Members present.

Judgment in Cases of Impeachment shall not extend further than to removal from Office, and disqualification to hold and enjoy any Office of honor, Trust, or Profit under the United States: but the Party convicted shall nevertheless be liable and subject to Indictment, Trial, Judgment, and Punishment, according to Law.

SECTION 4.

The Times, Places and Manner of holding Elections for Senators and Representatives, shall be prescribed in each State by the Legislature thereof; but the Congress may at any time by Law make or alter such Regulations, except as to the Places of Chusing Senators.

The Congress shall assemble at least once in every Year, and such Meeting shall be on the first Monday in December, unless they shall by Law appoint a different Day.

SECTION 5.

Each House shall be the Judge of the Elections, Returns and Qualifications of its own Members, and a Majority of each shall constitute a Quorum to do Business; but a smaller number may adjourn from day to day, and may be authorized to compel the Attendance of absent Members, in such Manner, and under such Penalties, as each House may provide.

Each House may determine the Rules of its Proceedings, punish its Members for disorderly Behaviour, and, with the Concurrence of two thirds, expel a Member.

Each House shall keep a Journal of its Proceedings, and from time to time publish the same, excepting such Parts as may in their Judgment require Secrecy; and the Yeas and Nays of the Members of either House on any question shall, at the Desire of one fifth of those Present, be entered on the Journal.

Neither House, during the Session of Congress, shall, without the Consent of the other, adjourn for more than three days, nor to any other Place than that in which the two Houses shall be sitting.

SECTION 6.

The Senators and Representatives shall receive a Compensation for their Services, to be ascertained by Law, and paid out of the Treasury of the United States. They shall in all Cases, except Treason, Felony, and Breach of the Peace, be privileged from Arrest during their Attendance at the Session of their respective Houses, and in going to and returning from the same; and for any Speech or Debate in either House, they shall not be questioned in any other Place.

No Senator or Representative shall, during the Time for which he was elected, be appointed to any civil Office under the Authority of the United States, which shall have been created, or the Emoluments whereof shall have been increased, during such time; and no Person holding any Office under the United States shall be a Member of either House during his continuance in Office.

SECTION 7.

All Bills for raising Revenue shall originate in the House of Representatives; but the Senate may propose or concur with Amendments as on other bills.

Every Bill which shall have passed the House of Representatives and the Senate, shall, before it become a Law, be presented to the President of the United States; If he approve he shall sign it, but if not he shall return it, with his Objections, to that House in which it shall have originated, who shall enter the Objections at large on their Journal, and proceed to reconsider it. If after such Reconsideration two thirds of that House shall agree to pass the bill, it shall be sent, together with the objections, to the other House, by which it shall likewise be reconsidered, and if approved by two thirds of that House, it shall become a Law. But in all such Cases the Votes of both Houses shall be determined by Yeas and Nays, and the Names of the Persons voting for and against the Bill shall be entered on the Journal of each House respectively. If any Bill shall not be returned by the President within ten Days (Sundays excepted) after it shall have been presented to him, the Same shall be a Law, in like Manner as if he had signed it, unless the Congress by their Adjournment prevent its Return, in which Case it shall not be a Law.

Every Order, Resolution, or Vote to which the Concurrence of the Senate and House of Representatives may be necessary (except on a question of Adjournment) shall be presented to the President of the United States; and before the Same shall take Effect, shall be approved by him, or being disapproved by him, shall be repassed by two thirds of the Senate and House of Representatives, according to the Rules and Limitations prescribed in the Case of a Bill.

SECTION 8.

The Congress shall have Power To lay and collect Taxes, Duties, Imposts and Excises, to pay the Debts and provide for the common Defence and general Welfare of the United States; but all Duties, Imposts and Excises shall be uniform throughout the United States;

To borrow money on the credit of the United States;

To regulate Commerce with foreign Nations, and among the several States, and with the Indian Tribes;

To establish an uniform Rule of Naturalization, and uniform Laws on the subject of Bankruptcies throughout the United States;

To coin Money, regulate the Value thereof, and of foreign Coin, and fix the Standard of Weights and Measures;

To provide for the Punishment of counterfeiting the Securities and current Coin of the United States;

To establish Post Offices and post Roads;

To promote the Progress of Science and useful Arts, by securing for limited Times to Authors and Inventors the exclusive Right to their respective Writings and Discoveries;

To constitute Tribunals inferior to the Supreme Court;

To define and punish Piracies and Felonies committed on the high Seas, and Offenses against the Law of Nations;

To declare War, grant Letters of Marque and Reprisal, and make Rules concerning Captures on Land and Water;

To raise and support Armies, but no Appropriation of Money to that Use shall be for a longer Term than two Years;

To provide and maintain a Navy;

To make Rules for the Government and Regulation of the land and naval forces;

To provide for calling forth the Militia to execute the Laws of the Union, suppress Insurrections and repel Invasions;

To provide for organizing, arming, and disciplining the Militia, and for governing such Part of them as may be employed in the Service of the United States, reserving to the States respectively, the Appointment of the Officers, and the Authority of training the Militia according to the discipline prescribed by Congress;

To exercise exclusive Legislation in all Cases whatsoever, over such District (not exceeding ten Miles square) as may, by Cession of particular States, and the acceptance of Congress, become the Seat of the Government of the United States, and to exercise like Authority over all Places purchased by the Consent of the Legislature of the State in which the Same shall be, for the Erection of Forts, Magazines, Arsenals, Dock-yards, and other needful Buildings; — And

To make all Laws which shall be necessary and proper for carrying into Execution the foregoing Powers, and all other Powers vested by this Constitution in the Government of the United States, or in any Department or Officer thereof.

SECTION 9.

The Migration or Importation of such Persons as any of the States now existing shall think proper to admit, shall not be prohibited by the Congress prior to the Year one thousand eight hundred and eight, but a tax or duty may be imposed on such Importation, not exceeding ten dollars for each Person.

The privilege of the Writ of Habeas Corpus shall not be suspended, unless when in Cases of Rebellion or Invasion the public Safety may require it.

No bill of Attainder or ex post facto Law shall be passed.

No capitation, or other direct, Tax shall be laid unless in Proportion to the Census or Enumeration herein before directed to be taken.

No Tax or Duty shall be laid on Articles exported from any State.

No Preference shall be given by any Regulation of Commerce or Revenue to the Ports of one State over those of another: nor shall Vessels bound to, or from, one State, be obliged to enter, clear, or pay Duties in another.

No Money shall be drawn from the Treasury, but in Consequence of Appropriations made by Law; and a regular Statement and Account of the Receipts and Expenditures of all public Money shall be published from time to time.

No Title of Nobility shall be granted by the United States: And no Person holding any Office of Profit or Trust under them, shall, without the Consent of the Congress, accept of any present, Emolument, Office, or Title, of any kind whatever, from any King, Prince, or foreign State.

SECTION 10.

No State shall enter into any Treaty, Alliance, or Confederation; grant Letters of Marque and Reprisal; coin Money; emit Bills of Credit; make any Thing but gold and silver Coin a Tender in Payment of Debts; pass any Bill of Attainder, ex post facto Law, or Law impairing the Obligation of Contracts, or grant any Title of Nobility.

No State shall, without the Consent of the Congress, lay any Imposts or Duties on Imports or Exports, except what may be absolutely necessary for executing its inspection Laws: and the net Produce of all Duties and Imposts, laid by any State on Imports or Exports, shall be for the Use of the Treasury of the United States; and all such Laws shall be subject to the Revision and Control of the Congress.

No state shall, without the Consent of Congress, lay any duty of Tonnage, keep Troops, or Ships of War in time of Peace, enter into any Agreement or Compact with another State, or with a foreign Power, or engage in War, unless actually invaded, or in such imminent Danger as will not admit of delay.

Article II

SECTION 1.

The executive Power shall be vested in a President of the United States of America. He shall hold his Office during the Term of four years, and, together with the Vice President, chosen for the same Term, be elected, as follows:

Each State shall appoint, in such Manner as the Legislature thereof may direct, a Number of Electors, equal to the whole Number of Senators and Representatives to which the State may be entitled in the Congress: but no Senator or Representative, or Person holding an Office of Trust or Profit under the United States, shall be appointed an Elector.

[The Electors shall meet in their respective States, and vote by Ballot for two persons, of whom one at least shall not be an Inhabitant of the same State with themselves. And they shall make a List of all the Persons voted for, and of the Number of Votes for each; which List they shall sign and certify, and transmit sealed to the Seat of the Government of the United States, directed to the President of the Senate. The President of the Senate shall, in the Presence of the Senate and House of Representatives, open all the Certificates, and the Votes shall then be counted. The Person having the greatest Number of Votes shall be the President, if such Number be a Majority of the whole Number of Electors appointed; and if there be more than one who have such Majority, and have an equal Number of Votes, then the House of Representatives shall immediately chuse by Ballot one of them for President; and if no Person have a Majority, then from the five highest on the List the said House shall in the Manner chuse the President. But in chusing the President, the Votes shall be taken by States, the Representation from each State having one Vote; a quorum for this Purpose shall consist of a Member or Members from two-thirds of the States, and a Majority of all the States shall be necessary to a Choice. In every Case, after the Choice of the President, the Person having the greatest Number of Votes of the Electors shall be the Vice President. But if there should remain two or more who have equal votes, the Senate shall chuse from them by Ballot the Vice President.][4]

The Congress may determine the Time of chusing the Electors, and the Day on which they shall give their Votes; which Day shall be the same throughout the United States.

No person except a natural-born Citizen, or a Citizen of the United States, at the time of the Adoption of this Constitution, shall be eligible to the Office of President; neither shall any Person be eligible to that Office who shall not have attained to the Age of thirty-five years, and been fourteen Years a Resident within the United States.

[4]Revised by the Twelfth Amendment.

In Case of the Removal of the President from Office, or of his Death, Resignation, or Inability to discharge the Powers and Duties of the said Office, the same shall devolve on the Vice President, and the Congress may by Law provide for the Case of Removal, Death, Resignation, or Inability, both of the President and Vice President, declaring what Officer shall then act as President, and such Officer shall act accordingly, until the disability be removed, or a President shall be elected.

The President shall, at stated Times, receive for his Services a Compensation, which shall neither be increased nor diminished during the Period for which he shall have been elected, and he shall not receive within that Period any other Emolument from the United States, or any of them.

Before he enter on the execution of his Office, he shall take the following Oath or Affirmation: — "I do solemnly swear (or affirm) that I will faithfully execute the Office of President of the United States, and will, to the best of my Ability, preserve, protect, and defend the Constitution of the United States."

SECTION 2.

The President shall be Commander in Chief of the Army and Navy of the United States, and of the Militia of the several States, when called into the actual Service of the United States; he may require the Opinion, in writing, of the principal Officer in each of the executive Departments, upon any subject relating to the Duties of their respective Offices, and he shall have Power to Grant Reprieves and Pardons for Offenses against the United States, except in Cases of Impeachment.

He shall have Power, by and with the Advice and Consent of the Senate, to make Treaties, provided two-thirds of the Senators present concur; and he shall nominate, and by and with the Advice and Consent of the Senate, shall appoint Ambassadors, other public Ministers and Consuls, Judges of the supreme Court, and all other Officers of the United States, whose Appointments are not herein otherwise provided for, and which shall be established by Law: but the Congress may by Law vest the Appointment of such inferior Officers, as they think proper, in the President alone, in the Courts of Law, or in the Heads of Departments.

The President shall have Power to fill up all Vacancies that may happen during the Re-

cess of the Senate, by granting Commissions which shall expire at the End of their next Session.

SECTION 3.

He shall from time to time give to the Congress Information of the State of the Union, and recommend to their Consideration such Measures as he shall judge necessary and expedient; he may, on extraordinary occasions, convene both Houses, or either of them, and in Case of Disagreement between them, with respect to the Time of Adjournment, he may adjourn them to such Time as he shall think proper; he shall receive Ambassadors and other public Ministers; he shall take care that the Laws be faithfully executed, and shall Commission all the Officers of the United States.

SECTION 4.

The President, Vice President and all civil Officers of the United States, shall be removed from Office on Impeachment for, and Conviction of, Treason, Bribery, or other high Crimes and Misdemeanors.

Article III

SECTION 1.

The judicial Power of the United States, shall be vested in one supreme Court, and in such inferior Courts as the Congress may from time to time ordain and establish. The Judges, both of the supreme and inferior Courts, shall hold their Offices during good Behaviour, and shall, at stated Times, receive for their Services, a Compensation, which shall not be diminished during their Continuance in Office.

SECTION 2.

The judicial Power shall extend to all Cases, in Law and Equity, arising under this Constitution, the Laws of the United States, and Treaties made, or which shall be made, under their Authority; — to all Cases affecting ambassadors, other public ministers and consuls; — to all cases of admiralty and maritime Jurisdiction; — to Controversies to which the United States shall be a Party; — to Controversies between two or more States; — between a State and Citizens of another State;[5] — between Citizens of

---

[5]Qualified by the Eleventh Amendment.

different States, — between Citizens of the same State claiming Lands under Grants of different States, and between a State, or the Citizens thereof, and foreign States, Citizens or Subjects.

In all Cases affecting Ambassadors, other public Ministers and Consuls, and those in which a State shall be Party, the supreme Court shall have original Jurisdiction. In all the other Cases before mentioned, the supreme Court shall have appellate Jurisdiction, both as to Law and Fact, with such Exceptions, and under such Regulations as the Congress shall make.

The trial of all Crimes, except in Cases of Impeachment, shall be by Jury; and such Trial shall be held in the State where the said Crimes shall have been committed; but when not committed within any State, the Trial shall be at such Place or Places as the Congress may by Law have directed.

SECTION 3.

Treason against the United States, shall consist only in levying War against them, or in adhering to their Enemies, giving them Aid and Comfort. No Person shall be convicted of Treason unless on the Testimony of two Witnesses to the same overt Act, or on Confession in open Court.

The Congress shall have power to declare the Punishment of Treason, but no Attainder of Treason shall work Corruption of Blood, or Forfeiture except during the Life of the Person attainted.

Article IV

SECTION 1.

Full Faith and Credit shall be given in each State to the public Acts, Records, and judicial Proceedings of every other State. And the Congress may by general Laws prescribe the Manner in which such Acts, Records and Proceedings shall be proved, and the Effect thereof.

SECTION 2.

The Citizens of each State shall be entitled to all Privileges and Immunities of Citizens in the several States.

A Person charged in any State with Treason, Felony, or other Crime, who shall flee from Justice, and be found in another State, shall on demand of the executive Authority of the State from which he fled, be delivered up, to be removed to the State having Jurisdiction of the crime.

No Person held to Service or Labour in one State, under the Laws thereof, escaping into another, shall, in Consequence of any Law or Regulation therein, be discharged from such Service or Labour, but shall be delivered up on Claim of the Party to whom such Service or Labour may be due.

SECTION 3.

New States may be admitted by the Congress into this Union; but no new State shall be formed or erected within the Jurisdiction of any other State; nor any State be formed by the Junction of two or more States, or parts of States, without the Consent of the Legislatures of the States concerned as well as of the Congress.

The Congress shall have Power to dispose of and make all needful Rules and Regulations respecting the Territory or other Property belonging to the United States; and nothing in this Constitution shall be so construed as to Prejudice any Claims of the United States, or of any particular State.

SECTION 4.

The United States shall guarantee to every State in this Union a Republican Form of Government, and shall protect each of them against Invasion; and on Application of the Legislature, or of the Executive (when the Legislature cannot be convened) against domestic Violence.

Article V

The Congress, whenever two-thirds of both Houses shall deem it necessary, shall propose Amendments to this Constitution, or, on the Application of the Legislatures of two-thirds of the several States, shall call a Convention for proposing Amendments, which, in either Case, shall be valid to all Intents and Purposes, as part of this Constitution, when ratified by the Legislatures of three-fourths of the several States, or by Conventions in three-fourths thereof, as the one or the other Mode of Ratification may be proposed by the Congress; Provided that no Amendment which may be made prior to the Year One thousand eight hundred and eight shall in any Manner affect the first and fourth Clauses in the Ninth Section of the first Article; and that no State, without its Consent, shall be deprived of its equal Suffrage in the Senate.

Article VI

All Debts contracted and Engagements entered into, before the Adoption of this Constitution, shall be as valid against the United States under this Constitution, as under the Confederation.

This Constitution, and the Laws of the United States which shall be made in Pursuance thereof; and all Treaties made, or which shall be made, under the Authority of the United States, shall be the supreme Law of the Land; and the Judges in every State shall be bound thereby, any Thing in the Constitution or Laws of any State to the Contrary notwithstanding.

The Senators and Representatives before mentioned, and the Members of the several State Legislatures, and all executive and judicial Officers, both of the United States and of the several States, shall be bound by Oath or Affirmation to support this Constitution; but no religious Test shall ever be required as a qualification to any Office or public Trust under the United States.

Article VII

The Ratification of the Conventions of nine States shall be sufficient for the Establishment of this Constitution between the States so ratifying the same.

Done in Convention by the Unanimous Consent of the States present the Seventeenth Day of September in the Year of our Lord one thousand seven hundred and Eighty seven, and of the Independence of the United States of America the Twelfth. In Witness whereof We have hereunto subscribed our Names.[6]

George Washington
President and deputy from Virginia

New Hampshire

John Langdon
Nicholas Gilman

Massachusetts

Nathaniel Gorham
Rufus King

Connecticut

William Samuel Johnson
Roger Sherman

New York

Alexander Hamilton

New Jersey

William Livingston
David Brearley
William Paterson
Jonathan Dayton

Pennsylvania

Benjamin Franklin
Thomas Mifflin
Robert Morris
George Clymer
Thomas FitzSimons
Jared Ingersoll
James Wilson
Gouverneur Morris

Delaware

George Read
Gunning Bedford, Jr.
John Dickinson
Richard Bassett
Jacob Broom

Maryland

James McHenry
Daniel of
    St. Thomas Jenifer
Daniel Carroll

Virginia

John Blair
James Madison, Jr.

North Carolina

William Blount
Richard Dobbs Spaight
Hugh Williamson

South Carolina

John Rutledge
Charles Cotesworth Pinckney
Charles Pinckney
Pierce Butler

Georgia

William Few
Abraham Baldwin

[6]These are the full names of the signers, which in some cases are not the signatures on the document.

Articles in Addition to, and Amendment of, the Constitution of the United States of America, Proposed by Congress, and Ratified by the Legislatures of the Several States, Pursuant to the Fifth Article of the Original Constitution[7]

[Article I]

Congress shall make no law respecting an establishment of religion, or prohibiting the free exercise thereof; or abridging the freedom of speech, or of the press; or the right of the people peaceably to assemble, and to petition the Government for a redress of grievances.

[Article II]

A well regulated Militia, being necessary to the security of a free State, the right of the people to keep and bear Arms shall not be infringed.

[Article III]

No Soldier shall, in time of peace, be quartered in any house, without the consent of the Owner, nor in time of war, but in a manner to be prescribed by law.

[Article IV]

The right of the people to be secure in their persons, houses, papers, and effects, against unreasonable searches and seizures, shall not be violated, and no Warrants shall issue, but upon probable cause, supported by Oath or affirmation, and particularly describing the place to be searched, and the persons or things to be seized.

[Article V]

No person shall be held to answer for a capital or otherwise infamous crime, unless on a presentment or indictment of a Grand Jury, except in cases arising in the land or naval forces, or in

[7]This heading appears only in the joint resolution submitting the first ten amendments.

the Militia, when in actual service in time of War or public danger; nor shall any person be subject for the same offence to be twice put in jeopardy of life or limb; nor shall be compelled in any criminal case to be a witness against himself, nor be deprived of life, liberty, or property, without due process of law; nor shall private property be taken for public use, without just compensation.

[Article VI]

In all criminal prosecutions, the accused shall enjoy the right to a speedy and public trial, by an impartial jury of the State and district wherein the crime shall have been committed, which district shall have been previously ascertained by law, and to be informed of the nature and cause of the accusation; to be confronted with the witnesses against him; to have compulsory process for obtaining witnesses in his favour, and to have the Assistance of Counsel for his defence.

[Article VII]

In suits at common law, where the value in controversy shall exceed twenty dollars, the right of trial by jury shall be preserved, and no fact tried by a jury, shall be otherwise reexamined in any Court of the United States, than according to the rules of the common law.

[Article VIII]

Excessive bail shall not be required, nor excessive fines imposed, nor cruel and unusual punishments inflicted.

[Article IX]

The enumeration in the Constitution, of certain rights, shall not be construed to deny or disparage others retained by the people.

[Article X]

The powers not delegated to the United States by the Constitution, nor prohibited by it to the

States, are reserved to the States respectively, or to the people.

[Amendments I – X, in force 1791.]

[Article XI][8]

The Judicial power of the United States shall not be construed to extend to any suit in law or equity, commenced or prosecuted against one of the United States by Citizens of another State, or by Citizens or Subjects of any Foreign State.

[Article XII][9]

The Electors shall meet in their respective States and vote by ballot for President and Vice-President, one of whom, at least, shall not be an inhabitant of the same State with themselves; they shall name in their ballots the person voted for as President, and in distinct ballots the person voted for as Vice-President, and they shall make distinct lists of all persons voted for as President, and of all persons voted for as Vice-President, and of the number of votes for each, which lists they shall sign and certify, and transmit sealed to the seat of the government of the United States, directed to the President of the Senate; — The President of the Senate shall, in the presence of the Senate and House of Representatives, open all the certificates and the votes shall then be counted; — The person having the greatest number of votes for President, shall be the President, if such number be a majority of the whole number of Electors appointed; and if no person have such majority, then from the persons having the highest numbers not exceeding three on the list of those voted for as President, the House of Representatives shall choose immediately, by ballot, the President. But in choosing the President, the votes shall be taken by states, the representation from each state having one vote; a quorum for this purpose shall consist of a member or members from two-thirds of the states, and a majority of all the

states shall be necessary to a choice. And if the House of Representatives shall not choose a President whenever the right of choice shall devolve upon them, before the fourth day of March next following, then the Vice-President shall act as President, as in the case of the death or other constitutional disability of the President. — The person having the greatest number of votes as Vice-President, shall be the Vice-President, if such number be a majority of the whole number of Electors appointed, and if no person have a majority, then from the two highest numbers on the list, the Senate shall choose the Vice-President: a quorum for the purpose shall consist of two-thirds of the whole number of Senators, and a majority of the whole number shall be necessary to a choice. But no person constitutionally ineligible to the office of President shall be eligible to that of Vice-President of the United States.

[Article XIII][10]

SECTION 1.
Neither slavery nor involuntary servitude, except as a punishment for crime whereof the party shall have been duly convicted, shall exist within the United States, or any place subject to their jurisdiction.

SECTION 2.
Congress shall have power to enforce this article by appropriate legislation.

[Article XIV][11]

SECTION 1.
All persons born or naturalized in the United States, and subject to the jurisdiction thereof, are citizens of the United States and of the State wherein they reside. No State shall abridge the privileges or immunities of citizens of the United States; nor shall any State deprive any person of life, liberty, or property, without due process of law; nor deny to any person within its jurisdiction the equal protection of the laws.

[8]Adopted in 1798.
[9]Adopted in 1804.

[10]Adopted in 1865.
[11]Adopted in 1868.

SECTION 2.

Representatives shall be apportioned among the several States according to their respective numbers, counting the whole number of persons in each State, excluding Indians not taxed. But when the right to vote at any election for the choice of electors for President and Vice-President of the United States, Representatives in Congress, the Executive and Judicial officers of a State, or the members of the Legislature thereof, is denied to any of the male inhabitants of such State, being twenty-one years of age, and citizens of the United States, or in any way abridged, except for participation in rebellion, or other crime, the basis of representation therein shall be reduced in the proportion which the number of such male citizens shall bear to the whole number of male citizens twenty-one years of age in such State.

SECTION 3.

No person shall be a Senator or Representative in Congress, or elector of President and Vice-President, or hold any office, civil or military, under the United States, or under any State, who, having previously taken an oath, as a member of Congress, or as an officer of the United States, or as a member of any State legislature, or as an executive or judicial officer of any State, to support the Constitution of the United States, shall have engaged in insurrection or rebellion against the same, or given aid or comfort to the enemies thereof. But Congress may by a vote of two-thirds of each House, remove such disability.

SECTION 4.

The validity of the public debt of the United States, authorized by law, including debts incurred for payment of pensions and bounties for services in suppressing insurrection or rebellion, shall not be questioned. But neither the United States nor any State shall assume or pay any debts or obligation incurred in aid of insurrection or rebellion against the United States, or any claim for the loss or emancipation of any slave; but all such debts, obligations, and claims shall be held illegal and void.

SECTION 5.

The Congress shall have the power to enforce, by appropriate legislation, the provisions of this article.

[Article XV][12]

SECTION 1.

The right of citizens of the United States to vote shall not be denied or abridged by the United States or by any State on account of race, color, or previous condition of servitude—

SECTION 2.

The Congress shall have power to enforce this article by appropriate legislation.

[Article XVI][13]

The Congress shall have power to lay and collect taxes on incomes, from whatever source derived, without apportionment among the several States, and without regard to any census or enumeration.

[Article XVII][14]

The Senate of the United States shall be composed of two Senators from each State, elected by the people thereof, for six years; and each Senator shall have one vote. The electors in each State shall have the qualifications requisite for electors of the most numerous branch of the State legislatures.

When vacancies happen in the representation of any State in the Senate, the executive authority of such State shall issue writs of election to fill such vacancies: *Provided*, That the legislature of any State may empower the executive thereof to make temporary appointments until the people fill the vacancies by election as the legislature may direct.

This amendment shall not be so construed as to affect the election or term of any Senator chosen before it becomes valid as part of the Constitution.

[Article XVIII][15]

SECTION 1.

After one year from the ratification of this article the manufacture, sale, or transportation of

[12]Adopted in 1870.
[13]Adopted in 1913.
[14]Adopted in 1913.
[15]Adopted in 1918.

intoxicating liquors within, the importation thereof into, or the exportation thereof from the United States and all territory subject to the jurisdiction thereof for beverage purposes is hereby prohibited.

SECTION 2.

The Congress and the several States shall have concurrent power to enforce this article by appropriate legislation.

SECTION 3.

This article shall be inoperative unless it shall have been ratified as an amendment to the Constitution by the legislatures of the several States, as provided in the Constitution, within seven years from the date of the submission hereof to the States by the Congress.

[Article XIX][16]

The right of citizens of the United States to vote shall not be denied or abridged by the United States or by any State on account of sex.

Congress shall have power to enforce this article by appropriate legislation.

[Article XX][17]

SECTION 1.

The terms of the President and Vice-President shall end at noon on the 20th day of January, and the terms of Senators and Representatives at noon on the 3d day of January, of the years in which such terms would have ended if this article had not been ratified; and the terms of their successors shall then begin.

SECTION 2.

The Congress shall assemble at least once in every year, and such meeting shall begin at noon on the 3d day of January, unless they shall by law appoint a different day.

SECTION 3.

If, at the time fixed for the beginning of the term of the President, the President elect shall have died, the Vice-President elect shall become President. If a President shall not have been chosen before the time fixed for the be-

ginning of his term, or if the President elect shall have failed to qualify, then the Vice-President elect shall act as President until a President shall have qualified; and the Congress may by law provide for the case wherein neither a President elect nor a Vice-President elect shall have qualified, declaring who shall then act as President, or the manner in which one who is to act shall be selected, and such person shall act accordingly until a President or Vice-President shall have qualified.

SECTION 4.

The Congress may by law provide for the case of the death of any of the persons from whom the House of Representatives may choose a President whenever the right of choice shall have devolved upon them, and for the case of the death of any of the persons from whom the Senate may choose a Vice-President whenever the right of choice shall have devolved upon them.

SECTION 5.

Sections 1 and 2 shall take effect on the 15th day of October following the ratification of this article.

SECTION 6.

This article shall be inoperative unless it shall have been ratified as an amendment to the Constitution by the legislatures of three-fourths of the several States within seven years from the date of its submission.

[Article XXI][18]

SECTION 1.

The eighteenth article of amendment to the Constitution of the United States is hereby repealed.

SECTION 2.

The transportation or importation into any State, Territory, or possession of the United States for delivery or use therein of intoxicating liquors, in violation of the laws thereof, is hereby prohibited.

SECTION 3.

This article shall be inoperative unless it shall have been ratified as an amendment to the

[16]Adopted in 1920.
[17]Adopted in 1933.

[18]Adopted in 1933.

Constitution by conventions in the several States, as provided in the Constitution, within seven years from the date of the submission hereof to the States by the Congress.

[Article XXII][19]

No person shall be elected to the office of the President more than twice, and no person who has held the office of President, or acted as President, for more than two years of a term to which some other person was elected President shall be elected to the office of the President more than once.

But this Article shall not apply to any person holding the office of President when this Article was proposed by the Congress, and shall not prevent any person who may be holding the office of President, or acting as President, during the term within which this Article becomes operative from holding the office of President or acting as President during the remainder of such term.

This article shall be inoperative unless it shall have been ratified as an amendment to the Constitution by the legislatures of three-fourths of the several states within seven years from the date of its submission to the states by the Congress.

[Article XXIII][20]

SECTION 1.
The District constituting the seat of Government of the United States shall appoint in such manner as the Congress may direct:

A number of electors of President and Vice-President equal to the whole number of Senators and Representatives in Congress to which the District would be entitled if it were a State, but in no event more than the least populous State; they shall be in addition to those appointed by the States, but they shall be considered, for the purposes of the election of President and Vice-President, to be electors appointed by a State; and they shall meet in the District and perform such duties as provided by the twelfth article of amendment.

SECTION 2.
The Congress shall have power to enforce this article by appropriate legislation.

[Article XXIV][21]

SECTION 1.
The right of citizens of the United States to vote in any primary or other election for President or Vice President, for electors for President or Vice President, or for Senator or Representative in Congress, shall not be denied or abridged by the United States or any state by reason of failure to pay any poll tax or other tax.

SECTION 2.
The Congress shall have the power to enforce this article by appropriate legislation.

[Article XXV][22]

SECTION 1.
In case of the removal of the President from office or of his death or resignation, the Vice President shall become President.

SECTION 2.
Whenever there is a vacancy in the office of the Vice President, the President shall nominate a Vice President who shall take office upon confirmation by a majority vote of both Houses of Congress.

SECTION 3.
Whenever the President transmits to the President Pro Tempore of the Senate and the Speaker of the House of Representatives his written declaration that he is unable to discharge the powers and duties of his office, and until he transmits to them a written declaration to the contrary, such powers and duties shall be discharged by the Vice President as Acting President.

SECTION 4.
Whenever the Vice President and a majority of either the principal officers of the executive departments or of such other body as Congress may by law provide, transmit to the President Pro Tempore of the Senate and the Speaker of

[19]Adopted in 1951.
[20]Adopted in 1961.

[21]Adopted in 1964.
[22]Adopted in 1967.

the House of Representatives their written declaration that the President is unable to discharge the powers and duties of his office, the
Vice President shall immediately assume the
powers and duties of the office as Acting President.

Thereafter, when the President transmits
to the President Pro Tempore of the Senate
and the Speaker of the House of Representatives his written declaration that no inability
exists, he shall resume the powers and duties of
his office unless the Vice President and a
majority of either the principal officers of the
executive departments or of such other body
as Congress may by law provide, transmit
within four days to the President Pro Tempore of the Senate and the Speaker of the
House of Representatives their written declaration that the President is unable to discharge the powers and duties of his office.
Thereupon Congress shall decide the issue,
assembling within forty-eight hours for that
purpose if not in session. If the Congress, within twenty-one days after receipt of the latter
written declaration, or, if Congress is not in session, within twenty-one days after Congress is
required to assemble, determines by two-thirds
vote of both Houses that the President is unable to discharge the powers and duties of his
office, the Vice President shall continue to discharge the same as Acting President; otherwise, the President shall resume the powers
and duties of his office.

[Article XXVI][23]

SECTION 1.
The right of citizens of the United States, who
are eighteen years of age or older, to vote shall
not be denied or abridged by the United States
or by any State on account of age.

SECTION 2.
The Congress shall have power to enforce this
article by appropriate legislation.

[23]Adopted in 1971.

Sovereigns of England and Great Britain, 1485–1820

The ruler was King (or Queen) of England until 1707, except for the interegnum of 1649–1660, during which Oliver Cromwell made himself Lord Protector. The ruler was King (or Queen) of Great Britain after the union of England and Scotland in 1707, and King (or Queen) of Great Britain and Ireland after 1800.

Henry VII   *1485–1509*

Henry VIII   *1509–1547*

Edward VI   *1547–1553*

Mary I   *1553–1558*

Elizabeth I   *1558–1603*

James I (VI of Scotland)   *1603–1625*

Charles I   *1625–1649*

  Oliver Cromwell   *1650–1658*

  Richard Cromwell   *1658–1659*

Charles II   *1660–1685*

James II   *1685–1688*

William III and Mary II   *1689–1694*

William III   *1694–1702*

Anne   *1702–1714*

George I   *1714–1727*

George II   *1727–1760*

George III   *1760–1820*

Admission of States
to the Union*

1	Delaware	Dec. 7, 1787	26	Michigan	Jan. 26, 1837
2	Pennsylvania	Dec. 12, 1787	27	Florida	Mar. 3, 1845
3	New Jersey	Dec. 18, 1787	28	Texas	Dec. 29, 1845
4	Georgia	Jan. 2, 1788	29	Iowa	Dec. 28, 1846
5	Connecticut	Jan. 9, 1788	30	Wisconsin	May 29, 1848
6	Massachusetts	Feb. 6, 1788	31	California	Sept. 9, 1850
7	Maryland	Apr. 28, 1788	32	Minnesota	May 11, 1858
8	South Carolina	May 23, 1788	33	Oregon	Feb. 14, 1859
9	New Hampshire	June 21, 1788	34	Kansas	Jan. 29, 1861
10	Virginia	June 25, 1788	35	West Virginia	June 19, 1863
11	New York	July 26, 1788	36	Nevada	Oct. 31, 1864
12	North Carolina	Nov. 21, 1789	37	Nebraska	Mar. 1, 1867
13	Rhode Island	May 29, 1790	38	Colorado	Aug. 1, 1876
14	Vermont	Mar. 4, 1791	39	North Dakota	Nov. 2, 1889
15	Kentucky	June 1, 1792	40	South Dakota	Nov. 2, 1889
16	Tennessee	June 1, 1796	41	Montana	Nov. 8, 1889
17	Ohio	Mar. 1, 1803	42	Washington	Nov. 11, 1889
18	Louisiana	Apr. 30, 1812	43	Idaho	July 3, 1890
19	Indiana	Dec. 11, 1816	44	Wyoming	July 10, 1890
20	Mississippi	Dec. 10, 1817	45	Utah	Jan. 4, 1896
21	Illinois	Dec. 3, 1818	46	Oklahoma	Nov. 16, 1907
22	Alabama	Dec. 14, 1819	47	New Mexico	Jan. 6, 1912
23	Maine	Mar. 15, 1820	48	Arizona	Feb. 14, 1912
24	Missouri	Aug. 10, 1821	49	Alaska	Jan. 3, 1959
25	Arkansas	June 15, 1836	50	Hawaii	Aug. 21, 1959

*In the case of the first thirteen states, the date given is that of ratification of the Constitution.

Presidential Elections

Year	Candidates	Parties	Popular Vote	Electoral Vote
1789	**GEORGE WASHINGTON (Va.)***			69
	John Adams			34
	Others			35
1792	**GEORGE WASHINGTON (Va.)**			132
	John Adams			77
	George Clinton			50
	Others			5
1796	**JOHN ADAMS (Mass.)**	Federalist		71
	Thomas Jefferson	Democratic-Republican		68
	Thomas Pinckney	Federalist		59
	Aaron Burr	Dem.-Rep.		30
	Others			48
1800	**THOMAS JEFFERSON (Va.)**	Dem.-Rep.		73
	Aaron Burr	Dem.-Rep.		73
	John Adams	Federalist		65
	C. C. Pinckney	Federalist		64
	John Jay	Federalist		1
1804	**THOMAS JEFFERSON (Va.)**	Dem.-Rep.		162
	C. C. Pinckney	Federalist		14
1808	**JAMES MADISON (Va.)**	Dem.-Rep.		122
	C. C. Pinckney	Federalist		47
	George Clinton	Dem.-Rep.		6
1812	**JAMES MADISON (Va.)**	Dem.-Rep.		128
	De Witt Clinton	Federalist		89
1816	**JAMES MONROE (Va.)**	Dem.-Rep.		183
	Rufus King	Federalist		34
1820	**JAMES MONROE (Va.)**	Dem.-Rep.		231
	John Quincy Adams	Dem.-Rep.		1
1824	**JOHN Q. ADAMS (Mass.)**	Dem.-Rep.	108,740	84
	Andrew Jackson	Dem.-Rep.	153,544	99
	William H. Crawford	Dem.-Rep.	46,618	41
	Henry Clay	Dem.-Rep.	47,136	37
1828	**ANDREW JACKSON (Tenn.)**	Democrat	647,286	178
	John Quincy Adams	National Republican	508,064	83

*State of residence at time of election.

Year	Candidates	Parties	Popular Vote	Electoral Vote
1832	**ANDREW JACKSON** (Tenn.)	Democrat	687,502	219
	Henry Clay	National Republican	530,189	49
	John Floyd	Independent		11
	William Wirt	Anti-Mason	33,108	7
1836	**MARTIN VAN BUREN** (N.Y.)	Democrat	765,483	170
	W. H. Harrison	Whig		73
	Hugh L. White	Whig	739,795	26
	Daniel Webster	Whig		14
	W. P. Mangum	Independent		11
1840	**WILLIAM H. HARRISON** (Ohio)	Whig	1,274,624	234
	Martin Van Buren	Democrat	1,127,781	60
	J. G. Birney	Liberty	7,069	—
1844	**JAMES K. POLK** (Tenn.)	Democrat	1,338,464	170
	Henry Clay	Whig	1,300,097	105
	J. G. Birney	Liberty	62,300	—
1848	**ZACHARY TAYLOR** (La.)	Whig	1,360,967	163
	Lewis Cass	Democrat	1,222,342	127
	Martin Van Buren	Free-Soil	291,263	—
1852	**FRANKLIN PIERCE** (N.H.)	Democrat	1,601,117	254
	Winfield Scott	Whig	1,385,453	42
	John P. Hale	Free-Soil	155,825	—
1856	**JAMES BUCHANAN** (Pa.)	Democrat	1,832,955	174
	John C. Frémont	Republican	1,339,932	114
	Millard Fillmore	American	871,731	8
1860	**ABRAHAM LINCOLN** (Ill.)	Republican	1,865,593	180
	Stephen A. Douglas	Democrat	1,382,713	12
	John C. Breckinridge	Democrat	848,356	72
	John Bell	Union	592,906	39
1864	**ABRAHAM LINCOLN** (Ill.)*	Republican	2,213,655	212
	George B. McClellan	Democrat	1,805,237	21
1868	**ULYSSES S. GRANT** (Ill.)	Republican	3,012,833	214
	Horatio Seymour	Democrat	2,703,249	80
1872	**ULYSSES S. GRANT** (Ill.)	Republican	3,597,132	286
	Horace Greeley	Democrat; Liberal Republican	2,834,125	66
1876	**RUTHERFORD B. HAYES** (Ohio)	Republican	4,036,298	185
	Samuel J. Tilden	Democrat	4,300,590	184
1880	**JAMES A. GARFIELD** (Ohio)	Republican	4,454,416	214
	Winfield S. Hancock	Democrat	4,444,952	155

*State of residence at time of election.

Year	Candidates	Parties	Popular Vote	Electoral Vote
1884	**GROVER CLEVELAND (N.Y.)**	Democrat	4,874,986	219
	James G. Blaine	Republican	4,851,981	182
1888	**BENJAMIN HARRISON (Ind.)**	Republican	5,439,853	233
	Grover Cleveland	Democrat	5,540,309	168
1892	**GROVER CLEVELAND (N.Y.)**	Democrat	5,556,918	277
	Benjamin Harrison	Republican	5,176,108	145
	James B. Weaver	People's	1,041,028	22
1896	**WILLIAM McKINLEY (Ohio)**	Republican	7,104,779	271
	William J. Bryan	Democrat-People's	6,502,925	176
1900	**WILLIAM McKINLEY (Ohio)**	Republican	7,207,923	292
	William J. Bryan	Dem.-Populist	6,358,133	155
1904	**THEODORE ROOSEVELT (N.Y.)**	Republican	7,623,486	336
	Alton B. Parker	Democrat	5,077,911	140
	Eugene V. Debs	Socialist	402,283	—
1908	**WILLIAM H. TAFT (Ohio)**	Republican	7,678,908	321
	William J. Bryan	Democrat	6,409,104	162
	Eugene V. Debs	Socialist	420,793	—
1912	**WOODROW WILSON (N.J.)**	Democrat	6,293,454	435
	Theodore Roosevelt	Progressive	4,119,538	88
	William H. Taft	Republican	3,484,980	8
	Eugene V. Debs	Socialist	900,672	—
1916	**WOODROW WILSON (N.J.)**	Democrat	9,129,606	277
	Charles E. Hughes	Republican	8,538,221	254
	A. L. Benson	Socialist	585,113	—
1920	**WARREN G. HARDING (Ohio)**	Republican	16,152,200	404
	James M. Cox	Democrat	9,147,353	127
	Eugene V. Debs	Socialist	919,799	—
1924	**CALVIN COOLIDGE (Mass.)**	Republican	15,725,016	382
	John W. Davis	Democrat	8,386,503	136
	Robert M. LaFollette	Progressive	4,822,856	13
1928	**HERBERT HOOVER (Calif.)**	Republican	21,391,381	444
	Alfred E. Smith	Democrat	15,016,443	87
	Norman Thomas	Socialist	267,835	—
1932	**FRANKLIN D. ROOSEVELT (N.Y.)**	Democrat	22,821,857	472
	Herbert Hoover	Republican	15,761,841	59
	Norman Thomas	Socialist	881,951	—
1936	**FRANKLIN D. ROOSEVELT (N.Y.)**	Democrat	27,751,597	523
	Alfred M. Landon	Republican	16,679,583	8
	William Lemke	Union and others	882,479	—
1940	**FRANKLIN D. ROOSEVELT (N.Y.)**	Democrat	27,244,160	449
	Wendell L. Willkie	Republican	22,305,198	82

Year	Candidates	Parties	Popular Vote	Electoral Vote
1944	**FRANKLIN D. ROOSEVELT** (N.Y.)	Democrat	25,602,504	432
	Thomas E. Dewey	Republican	22,006,285	99
1948	**HARRY S TRUMAN (Mo.)**	Democrat	24,105,695	304
	Thomas E. Dewey	Republican	21,969,170	189
	J. Strom Thurmond	State-Rights Democrat	1,169,021	38
	Henry A. Wallace	Progressive	1,156,103	—
1952	**DWIGHT D. EISENHOWER** (N.Y.)	Republican	33,936,252	442
	Adlai E. Stevenson	Democrat	27,314,992	89
1956	**DWIGHT D. EISENHOWER** (N.Y.)	Republican	35,575,420	457
	Adlai E. Stevenson	Democrat	26,033,066	73
	Other	—	—	1
1960	**JOHN F. KENNEDY** (Mass.)	Democrat	34,227,096	303
	Richard M. Nixon	Republican	34,108,546	219
	Other	—	—	15
1964	**LYNDON B. JOHNSON** (Tex.)	Democrat	43,126,506	486
	Barry M. Goldwater	Republican	27,176,799	52
1968	**RICHARD M. NIXON** (N.Y.)	Republican	31,770,237	301
	Hubert H. Humphrey	Democrat	31,270,533	191
	George Wallace	American Indep.	9,906,141	46
1972	**RICHARD M. NIXON** (N.Y.)	Republican	47,169,911	520
	George S. McGovern	Democrat	29,170,383	17
	Other	—	—	1

Chief Justices of the United States

John Jay, *N.Y.* 1789–1795
John Rutledge, *S.C.* 1795
Oliver Ellsworth, *Conn.* 1795–1799
John Marshall, *Va.* 1801–1835
Roger B. Taney, *Md.* 1836–1864
Salmon P. Chase, *Ohio* 1864–1873
Morrison R. Waite, *Ohio* 1874–1888
Melville W. Fuller, *Ill.* 1888–1910

Edward D. White, *La.* 1910–1921
William H. Taft, *Ohio* 1921–1930
Charles E. Hughes, *N.Y.* 1930–1941
Harlan F. Stone, *N.Y.* 1941–1946
Fred M. Vinson, *Ky.* 1946–1953
Earl Warren, *Calif.* 1953–1969
Warren E. Burger, *Minn.* 1969–

Speakers of the House of Representatives

F. A. C. Muhlenberg, *Pennsylvania* 1789–1791
Jonathan Trumbull, *Connecticut* 1791–1793
F. A. C. Muhlenberg, *Pennsylvania* 1793–1795
Jonathan Dayton, *New Jersey* 1795–1799
Theodore Sedgwick, *Massachusetts* 1799–1801
Nathaniel Macon, *North Carolina* 1801–1807
Joseph B. Varnum, *Massachusetts* 1807–1811
Henry Clay, *Kentucky* 1811–1814
Langdon Cheves, *South Carolina* 1814–1815
Henry Clay, *Kentucky* 1815–1820
John W. Taylor, *New York* 1820–1821
Philip P. Barbour, *Virginia* 1821–1823
Henry Clay, *Kentucky* 1823–1825
John W. Taylor, *New York* 1825–1827
Andrew Stevenson, *Virginia* 1827–1834
John Bell, *Tennessee* 1834–1835
James K. Polk, *Tennessee* 1835–1839
R. M. T. Hunter, *Virginia* 1839–1841
John White, *Kentucky* 1841–1843
John W. Jones, *Virginia* 1843–1845
John W. Davis, *Indiana* 1845–1847
R. C. Winthrop, *Massachusetts* 1847–1849
Howell Cobb, *Georgia* 1849–1851
Linn Boyd, *Kentucky* 1851–1855
N. P. Banks, *Massachusetts* 1856–1857
James L. Orr, *South Carolina* 1857–1859
William Pennington, *New Jersey* 1860–1861

Galusha A. Grow, *Pennsylvania* 1861–1863
Schuyler Colfax, *Indiana* 1863–1869
James G. Blaine, *Maine* 1869–1875
Michael C. Kerr, *Indiana* 1875–1876
Samuel J. Randall, *Pennsylvania* 1876–1881
Joseph W. Keifer, *Ohio* 1881–1883
John G. Carlisle, *Kentucky* 1883–1889
Thomas B. Reed, *Maine* 1889–1891
Charles F. Crisp, *Georgia* 1891–1895
Thomas B. Reed, *Maine* 1895–1899
David B. Henderson, *Iowa* 1899–1903
Joseph G. Cannon, *Illinois* 1903–1910
Champ Clark, *Missouri* 1911–1919
Frederick H. Gillett, *Massachusetts* 1919–1925
Nicholas Longworth, *Ohio* 1925–1931
John Nance Garner, *Texas* 1931–1933
Henry T. Rainey, *Illinois* 1933–1934
Joseph W. Byrns, *Tennessee* 1935–1936
William B. Bankhead, *Alabama* 1936–1940
Sam Rayburn, *Texas* 1940–1947
Joseph W. Martin, Jr., *Massachusetts* 1947–1949
Sam Rayburn, *Texas* 1949–1953
Joseph W. Martin, Jr., *Massachusetts* 1953–1955
Sam Rayburn, *Texas* 1955–1961
John W. McCormack, *Massachusetts* 1961–1970
Carl Albert, *Oklahoma* 1970–

Presidents, Vice Presidents, and Cabinet Members

President	Vice President	Secretary of State	Secretary of Treasury	Secretary of War
1. George Washington, Federalist 1789	John Adams, Federalist 1789	T. Jefferson 1789 E. Randolph 1794 T. Pickering 1795	Alex. Hamilton 1789 Oliver Wolcott 1795	Henry Knox 1789 T. Pickering 1795 Jas. McHenry 1796
2. John Adams, Federalist 1797	Thomas Jefferson, Dem.-Rep. 1797	T. Pickering 1797 John Marshall 1800	Oliver Wolcott 1797 Samuel Dexter 1801	Jas. McHenry 1797 John Marshall 1800 Samuel Dexter 1800 R. Griswold 1801
3. Thomas Jefferson, Dem.-Rep. 1801	Aaron Burr, Dem.-Rep. 1801 George Clinton, Dem.-Rep. 1805	James Madison 1801	Samuel Dexter 1801 Albert Gallatin 1801	H. Dearborn 1801
4. James Madison, Dem.-Rep. 1809	George Clinton, Dem.-Rep. 1809 Elbridge Gerry, Dem.-Rep. 1813	Robert Smith 1809 James Monroe 1811	Albert Gallatin 1809 G. W. Campbell 1814 A. J. Dallas 1814 W. H. Crawford 1816	Wm. Eustis 1809 J. Armstrong 1813 James Monroe 1814 W. H. Crawford 1815
5. James Monroe, Dem.-Rep. 1817	D. D. Tompkins, Dem.-Rep. 1817	J. Q. Adams 1817	W. H. Crawford 1817	Isaac Shelby 1817 George Graham 1817 J. C. Calhoun 1817
6. John Quincy Adams, Dem.-Rep. 1825	John C. Calhoun, Dem.-Rep. 1825	Henry Clay 1825	Richard Rush 1825	Jas. Barbour 1825 Peter B. Porter 1828
7. Andrew Jackson, Democratic 1829	John C. Calhoun, Democratic 1829 Martin Van Buren, Democratic 1833	M. Van Buren 1829 E. Livingston 1831 Louis McLane 1833 John Forsyth 1834	Sam. D. Ingham 1829 Louis McLane 1831 W. J. Duane 1833 Roger B. Taney 1833 Levi Woodbury 1834	John H. Eaton 1829 Lewis Cass 1831 B. F. Butler 1837
8. Martin Van Buren, Democratic 1837	Richard M. Johnson, Democratic 1837	John Forsyth 1837	Levi Woodbury 1837	Joel R. Poinsett 1837
9. William H. Harrison, Whig 1841	John Tyler, Whig 1841	Daniel Webster 1841	Thomas Ewing 1841	John Bell 1841
10. John Tyler, Whig and Democratic 1841		Daniel Webster 1841 Hugh S. Legare 1843 Abel P. Upshur 1843 John C. Calhoun 1844	Thomas Ewing 1841 Walter Forward 1841 John C. Spencer 1843 Geo. M. Bibb 1844	John Bell 1841 John McLean 1841 J. C. Spencer 1841 Jas. M. Porter 1843 Wm. Wilkins 1844

President	Vice President	Secretary of State	Secretary of Treasury	Secretary of War
11. James K. Polk, Democratic 1845	George M. Dallas, Democratic 1845	James Buchanan 1845	Robert J. Walker 1845	William L. Marcy 1845
12. Zachary Taylor, Whig 1849	Millard Fillmore, Whig 1849	John M. Clayton 1849	Wm. M. Meredith 1849	G. W. Crawford 1849
13. Millard Fillmore, Whig 1850		Daniel Webster 1850 Edward Everett 1852	Thomas Corwin 1850	C. M. Conrad 1850
14. Franklin Pierce, Democratic 1853	William R. D. King, Democratic 1853	W. L. Marcy 1853	James Guthrie 1853	Jefferson Davis 1853
15. James Buchanan, Democratic 1857	John C. Breckinridge, Democratic 1857	Lewis Cass 1857 J. S. Black 1860	Howell Cobb 1857 Philip F. Thomas 1860 John A. Dix 1861	John B. Floyd 1857 Joseph Holt 1861
16. Abraham Lincoln, Republican 1861	Hannibal Hamlin, Republican 1861 Andrew Johnson, Unionist 1865	W. H. Seward 1861	Salmon P. Chase 1861 W. P. Fessenden 1864 Hugh McCulloch 1865	S. Cameron 1861 E. M. Stanton 1862
17. Andrew Johnson, Unionist 1865		W. H. Seward 1865	H. McCulloch 1865	E. M. Stanton 1865 U. S. Grant 1867 L. Thomas 1868 J. M. Schofield 1868
18. Ulysses S. Grant, Republican 1869	Schuyler Colfax, Republican 1869 Henry Wilson, Republican 1873	E. B. Washburne 1869 H. Fish 1869	G. S. Boutwell 1869 W. A. Richardson 1873 B. H. Bristow 1874 L. M. Morrill 1876	J. A. Rawlins 1869 W. T. Sherman 1869 W. W. Belknap 1869 A. Taft 1876 J. D. Cameron 1876
19. Rutherford B. Hayes, Republican 1877	William A. Wheeler, Republican 1877	W. M. Evarts 1877	J. Sherman 1877	G. W. McCrary 1877 A. Ramsey 1879
20. James A. Garfield, Republican 1881	Chester A. Arthur, Republican 1881	J. G. Blaine 1881	W. Windom 1881	R. T. Lincoln 1881
21. Chester A. Arthur, Republican 1881		F. T. Frelinghuysen 1881	C. J. Folger 1881 W. Q. Gresham 1884 H. McCulloch 1884	R. T. Lincoln 1881
22. Grover Cleveland, Democratic 1885	T. A. Hendricks, Democratic 1885	T. F. Bayard 1885	D. Manning 1885 C. S. Fairchild 1887	W. C. Endicott 1885
23. Benjamin Harrison, Republican 1889	Levi P. Morton, Republican 1889	J. G. Blaine 1889 J. W. Foster 1892	W. Windom 1889 C. Foster 1891	R. Proctor 1889 S. B. Elkins 1891
24. Grover Cleveland, Democratic 1893	Adlai E. Stevenson, Democratic 1893	W. Q. Gresham 1893 R. Olney 1895	J. G. Carlisle 1893	D. S. Lamont 1893
25. William McKinley, Republican 1897	Garret A. Hobart, Republican 1897 Theodore Roosevelt, Republican 1901	J. Sherman 1897 W. R. Day 1897 J. Hay 1898	L. J. Gage 1897	R. A. Alger 1897 E. Root 1899

President	Vice President	Secretary of State	Secretary of Treasury	Secretary of War
26. Theodore Roosevelt, Republican 1901	Chas. W. Fairbanks, Republican 1905	J. Hay 1901 E. Root 1905 R. Bacon 1909	L. J. Gage 1901 L. M. Shaw 1902 G. B. Cortelyou 1907	E. Root 1901 W. H. Taft 1904 L. E. Wright 1908
27. William H. Taft, Republican 1909	James S. Sherman, Republican 1909	P. C. Knox 1909	F. MacVeagh 1909	J. M. Dickinson 1909 H. L. Stimson 1911
28. Woodrow Wilson, Democratic 1913	Thomas R. Marshall, Democratic 1913	W. J. Bryan 1913 R. Lansing 1915 B. Colby 1920	W. G. McAdoo 1913 C. Glass 1918 D. F. Houston 1920	L. M. Garrison 1913 N. D. Baker 1916
29. Warren G. Harding, Republican 1921	Calvin Coolidge, Republican 1921	C. E. Hughes 1921	A. W. Mellon 1921	J. W. Weeks 1921
30. Calvin Coolidge, Republican 1923	Charles G. Dawes, Republican 1925	C. E. Hughes 1923 F. B. Kellogg 1925	A. W. Mellon 1923	J. W. Weeks 1923 D. F. Davis 1925
31. Herbert Hoover, Republican 1929	Charles Curtis, Republican 1929	H. L. Stimson 1929	A. W. Mellon 1929 O. L. Mills 1932	J. W. Good 1929 P. J. Hurley 1929
32. Franklin D. Roosevelt, Democratic 1933	John Nance Garner, Democratic 1933 Henry A. Wallace, Democratic 1941 Harry S Truman, Democratic 1945	C. Hull 1933 E. R. Stettinius, Jr. 1944	W. H. Woodin 1933 H. Morgenthau, Jr. 1934	G. H. Dern 1933 H. A. Woodring 1936 H. L. Stimson 1940
33. Harry S Truman, Democratic 1945	Alben W. Barkley, Democratic 1949	J. F. Byrnes 1945 G. C. Marshall 1947 D. G. Acheson 1949	F. M. Vinson 1945 J. W. Snyder 1946	R. H. Patterson 1945 K. C. Royall 1947 **
34. Dwight D. Eisenhower, Republican 1953	Richard M. Nixon, Republican 1953	J. F. Dulles 1953 C. A. Herter 1959	G. C. Humphrey 1953 R. B. Anderson 1957	
35. John F. Kennedy, Democratic 1961	Lyndon B. Johnson, Democratic 1961	D. Rusk 1961	C. D. Dillon 1961	
36. Lyndon B. Johnson, Democratic 1963	Hubert H. Humphrey, Democratic 1965	D. Rusk 1961	C. D. Dillon 1961 H. H. Fowler 1965	
37. Richard M. Nixon, Republican 1969	Spiro T. Agnew, Republican 1969 Gerald R. Ford, Republican 1973	W. P. Rogers 1969 H. M. Kissinger 1973	D. M. Kennedy 1969 J. B. Connally 1970 G. P. Shultz 1972	
38. Gerald R. Ford, Republican 1974				

**Lost cabinet status in 1947.

Attorney General	Postmaster General	Secretary of Navy	Secretary of Interior	Secretary of Agriculture	Other Members
(1.)* E. Randolph 1789 Wm. Bradford 1794 Charles Lee 1795	Samuel Osgood 1789 Tim. Pickering 1791 Jos. Habersham 1795	Established April 30, 1798	Established March 3, 1849		
(2.) Charles Lee 1797 Theo. Parsons 1801	Jos. Habersham 1797	Benj. Stoddert 1798			
(3.) Levi Lincoln 1801 Robert Smith 1805 J. Breckenridge 1805 C. A. Rodney 1807	Jos. Habersham 1801 Gideon Granger 1801	Benj. Stoddert 1801 Robert Smith 1801 J. Crowninshield 1805			
(4.) C. A. Rodney 1809 Wm. Pinkney 1811 Richard Rush 1814	Gideon Granger 1809 R. J. Meigs, Jr. 1814	Paul Hamilton 1809 William Jones 1813 B. W. Crowninshield 1814			
(5.) Richard Rush 1817 William Wirt 1817	R. J. Meigs, Jr. 1817 John McLean 1823	B. W. Crowninshield 1817 Smith Thompson 1818 S. L. Southard 1823			
(6.) William Wirt 1825	John McLean 1825	S. L. Southard 1825			
(7.) John M. Berrien 1829 Roger B. Taney 1831 B. F. Butler 1833	Wm. T. Barry 1829** Amos Kendall 1835	John Branch 1829 Levi Woodbury 1831 Mahlon Dickerson 1834			
(8.) B. F. Butler 1837 Felix Grundy 1838 H. D. Gilpin 1840	Amos Kendall 1837 John M. Niles 1840	Mahlon Dickerson 1837 Jas. K. Paulding 1838			
(9.) J. J. Crittenden 1841	Francis Granger 1841	George E. Badger 1841			
(10.) J. J. Crittenden 1841 Hugh S. Legare 1841 John Nelson 1843	Francis Granger 1841 C. A. Wickliffe 1841	George E. Badger 1841 Abel P. Upshur 1841 David Henshaw 1843 Thomas W. Gilmer 1844 John Y. Mason 1844			
(11.) John Y. Mason 1845 Nathan Clifford 1846 Isaac Toucey 1848	Cave Johnson 1845	George Bancroft 1845 John Y. Mason 1846			
(12.) Reverdy Johnson 1849	Jacob Collamer 1849	Wm. B. Preston 1849	Thomas Ewing 1849		*Secretary of Commerce and Labor* Established Feb. 14, 1903. G. B. Cortelyou 1903 V. H. Metcalf 1904 O. S. Straus 1907 C. Nagel 1909 (Department divided, 1913)
(13.) J. J. Crittenden 1850	Nathan K. Hall 1850 Sam D. Hubbard 1852	Wm. A. Graham 1850 John P. Kennedy 1852	A. H. Stuart 1850		
(14.) Caleb Cushing 1853	James Campbell 1853	James C. Dobbin 1853	Robert McClelland 1853		
(15.) J. S. Black 1857 Edw. M. Stanton 1860	Aaron V. Brown 1857 Joseph Holt 1859	Isaac Toucey 1857	Jacob Thompson 1857		

	Attorney General	Postmaster General	Secretary of Navy	Secretary of Interior	Secretary of Agriculture	Other Members
(16.)	Edward Bates 1861 Titian J. Coffey 1863 James Speed 1864	Horatio King 1861 Montgomery Blair 1861 William Dennison 1864	Gideon Welles 1861	Caleb B. Smith 1861 John P. Usher 1863		*Secretary of Commerce*
(17.)	J. Speed 1865 H. Stanbery 1866 W. M. Evarts 1868	W. Dennison 1865 A. W. Randall 1866	G. Welles 1865	J. P. Usher 1865 J. Harlan 1865 O. H. Browning 1866	Cabinet status since 1889	W. C. Redfield 1913 J. W. Alexander 1919 H. C. Hoover 1921 H. C. Hoover 1925 W. F. Whiting 1928 R. P. Lamont 1929 R. D. Chapin 1932 D. C. Roper 1933 H. L. Hopkins 1939 J. Jones 1940
(18.)	E. R. Hoar 1869 A. T. Ackerman 1870 G. H. Williams 1871 E. Pierrepont 1875 A. Taft 1876	J. A. J. Creswell 1869 J. W. Marshall 1874 M. Jewell 1874 J. N. Tyner 1876	A. E. Borie 1869 G. M. Robeson 1869	J. D. Cox 1869 C. Delano 1870 Z. Chandler 1875		H. A. Wallace 1945 W. A. Harriman 1946 C. W. Sawyer 1948 S. Weeks 1953 L. L. Strauss 1958 F. H. Mueller 1959 L. H. Hodges 1961 J. T. Connor 1965 A. B. Trowbridge 1967 M. H. Stans 1969 P. G. Peterson 1972 F. B. Dent 1973
(19.)	C. Devens 1877	D. M. Key 1877 H. Maynard 1880	R. W. Thompson 1877 N. Goff, Jr. 1881	C. Schurz 1877		
(20.)	W. MacVeagh 1881	T. L. James 1881	W. H. Hunt 1881	S. J. Kirkwood 1881		
(21.)	B. H. Brewster 1881	T. O. Howe 1881 W. Q. Gresham 1883 F. Hatton 1884	W. E. Chandler 1881	H. M. Teller 1881		
(22.)	A. H. Garland 1885	W. F. Vilas 1885 D. M. Dickinson 1888	W. C. Whitney 1885	L. Q. C. Lamar 1885 W. F. Vilas 1888	N. J. Colman 1889	
(23.)	W. H. H. Miller 1889	J. Wanamaker 1889	B. F. Tracy 1889	J. W. Noble 1889	J. M. Rusk 1889	
(24.)	R. Olney 1893 J. Harmon 1895	W. S. Bissell 1893 W. L. Wilson 1895	H. A. Herbert 1893	H. Smith 1893 D. R. Francis 1896	J. S. Morton 1893	*Secretary of Labor* Established March 4, 1913.
(25.)	J. McKenna 1897 J. W. Griggs 1897 P. C. Knox 1901	J. A. Gary 1897 C. E. Smith 1898	J. D. Long 1897	C. N. Bliss 1897 E. A. Hitchcock 1899	J. Wilson 1897	W. B. Wilson 1913 J. J. Davis 1921 W. N. Doak 1930 F. Perkins 1933
(26.)	P. C. Knox 1901 W. H. Moody 1904 C. J. Bonaparte 1907	C. E. Smith 1901 H. C. Payne 1902 R. J. Wynne 1904 G. B. Cortelyou 1905 G. von L. Meyer 1907	J. D. Long 1901 W. H. Moody 1902 P. Morton 1904 C. J. Bonaparte 1905 V. H. Metcalf 1907 T. H. Newberry 1908	E. A. Hitchcock 1901 J. R. Garfield 1907	J. Wilson 1901	L. B. Schwellenbach 1945 M. J. Tobin 1948 M. P. Durkin 1953 J. P. Mitchell 1953 A. J. Goldberg 1961
(27.)	G. W. Wickersham 1909	F. H. Hitchcock 1909	G. von L. Meyer 1909	R. A. Ballinger 1909 W. L. Fisher 1911	J. Wilson 1909	W. W. Wirtz 1962 G. P. Shultz 1969 J. D. Hodgson 1970 P. J. Brennan 1973
(28.)	J. C. McReynolds 1913 T. W. Gregory 1914 A. M. Palmer 1919	A. S. Burleson 1913	J. Daniels 1913	F. K. Lane 1913 J. B. Payne 1920	D. F. Houston 1913 E. T. Meredith 1920	*Secretary of Defense* Established July 26, 1947.
(29.)	H. M. Daugherty 1921	W. H. Hays 1921 H. Work 1922 H. S. New 1923	E. Denby 1921	A. B. Fall 1921 H. Work 1923	H. C. Wallace 1921	J. V. Forrestal 1947 L. A. Johnson 1949 G. C. Marshall 1950

	Attorney General	Postmaster General	Secretary of Navy	Secretary of Interior	Secretary of Agriculture	
(30.)	H. M. Daugherty 1923 H. F. Stone 1924 J. G. Sargent 1925	H. S. New 1923	E. Denby 1923 Curtis D. Wilbur 1924	H. Work 1923 R. O. West 1928	H. C. Wallace 1923 H. M. Gore 1924 W. M. Jardine 1925	R. A. Lovett 1951 C. E. Wilson 1953 N. McElroy 1957 T. S. Gates, Jr. 1959 R. S. McNamara 1961 C. Clifford 1968 M. R. Laird 1969 E. L. Richardson 1973 J. R. Schlesinger 1973
(31.)	W. D. Mitchell 1929	W. F. Brown 1929	C. F. Adams 1929	R. L. Wilbur 1929	A. M. Hyde 1929	
(32.)	H. S. Cummings 1933 F. Murphy 1939 R. H. Jackson 1940 F. Biddle 1941	J. A. Farley 1933 F. C. Walker 1940	C. A. Swanson 1933 C. Edison 1940 F. Knox 1940 J. V. Forrestal 1944	H. L. Ickes 1933	H. A. Wallace 1933 C. R. Wickard 1940	
(33.)	T. C. Clark 1945 J. H. McGrath 1949 J. P. McGranery 1952	R. E. Hannegan 1945 J. L. Donaldson 1947	J. V. Forrestal 1945 ††	H. L. Ickes 1945 J. A. Krug 1946 O. L. Chapman 1951	C. P. Anderson 1945 C. F. Brannan 1948	
(34.)	H. Brownell, Jr. 1953 W. P. Rogers 1957	A. E. Summerfield 1953		D. McKay 1953 F. Seaton 1956	E. T. Benson 1953	
(35.)	R. F. Kennedy 1961	J. E. Day 1961 J. Gronovski 1963		S. L. Udall 1961	O. L. Freeman 1961	
(36.)	N. de Katzenbach 1965 W. R. Clark 1967	L. F. O'Brien 1965 W. M. Watson 1968				
(37.)	J. N. Mitchell 1969 R. G. Kleindienst 1972 E. L. Richardson 1973 W. B. Saxbe 1973	W. Blount 1969 †††		W. J. Hickel 1969 R. C. B. Morton 1971	C. M. Hardin 1969 E. L. Butz 1971	

Secretary of Health, Education, and Welfare
Established April 1, 1953.
O. C. Hobby 1953
M. B. Folsom 1955
A. S. Flemming 1958
A. A. Ribicoff 1961
A. J. Celebrezze 1962
J. W. Gardner 1965
W. J. Cohen 1968
R. H. Finch 1969
E. L. Richardson 1970
C. W. Weinberger 1973

Secretary of Housing and Urban Development
Established September 9, 1965.
R. C. Weaver 1966
G. Romney 1969
J. T. Lynn 1973

Secretary of Transportation
Established October 15, 1966.
A. S. Boyd 1966
J. A. Volpe 1969
C. S. Brinegar 1973

*Numbers in parentheses indicate presidential administration.
**The postmaster general did not become a cabinet member until 1829.
††Lost cabinet status in 1947.
†††Discontinued in 1971.

Population of the United States

Division and State	1790	1800	1810	1820	1830	1840	1850	1860	1870
United States	3,929,214	5,308,483	7,239,881	9,638,453	12,866,020	17,069,453	23,191,876	31,443,321	39,818,449
GEOGRAPHIC DIVISIONS									
New England	1,009,408	1,233,011	1,471,973	1,660,071	1,954,717	2,234,822	2,728,116	3,135,283	3,487,924
Middle Atlantic	952,632	1,402,565	2,014,702	2,699,845	3,587,664	4,526,260	5,898,735	7,458,985	8,810,806
South Atlantic	1,851,806	2,286,494	2,674,891	3,061,063	3,645,752	3,925,299	4,679,090	5,364,703	5,853,610
East South Central	109,368	335,407	708,590	1,190,489	1,815,969	2,575,445	3,363,271	4,020,991	4,404,445
West South Central			77,618	167,680	246,127	449,985	940,251	1,747,667	2,029,965
East North Central		51,006	272,324	792,719	1,470,018	2,924,728	4,523,260	6,926,884	9,124,517
West North Central			19,783	66,586	140,455	426,814	880,335	2,169,832	3,856,594
Mountain							72,927	174,923	315,385
Pacific							105,871	444,053	675,125
NEW ENGLAND									
Maine	96,540	151,719	228,705	298,335	399,455	501,793	583,169	628,279	626,915
New Hampshire	141,885	183,858	214,460	244,161	269,328	284,574	317,976	326,073	318,300
Vermont	85,425	154,465	217,895	235,981	280,652	291,948	314,120	315,098	330,551
Massachusetts	378,787	422,845	472,040	523,287	610,408	737,699	994,514	1,231,066	1,457,351
Rhode Island	68,825	69,122	76,931	83,059	97,199	108,830	147,545	174,620	217,353
Connecticut	237,946	251,002	261,942	275,248	297,675	309,978	370,792	460,147	537,454
MIDDLE ATLANTIC									
New York	340,120	589,051	959,049	1,372,812	1,918,608	2,428,921	3,097,394	3,880,735	4,382,759
New Jersey	184,139	211,149	245,562	277,575	320,823	373,306	489,555	672,035	906,096
Pennsylvania	434,373	602,365	810,091	1,049,458	1,348,233	1,724,033	2,311,786	2,906,215	3,521,951
SOUTH ATLANTIC									
Delaware	59,096	64,273	72,674	72,749	76,748	78,085	91,532	112,216	125,015
Maryland	319,728	341,548	380,546	407,350	447,040	470,019	583,034	687,049	780,894
Dist. of Columbia		14,093	24,023	33,039	39,834	43,712	51,687	75,080	131,700
Virginia	747,610	880,200	974,600	1,065,366	1,211,405	1,239,797	1,421,661	1,596,318	1,225,163
West Virginia									442,014
North Carolina	393,751	478,103	555,500	638,829	737,987	753,419	869,039	992,622	1,071,361
South Carolina	249,073	345,591	415,115	502,741	581,185	594,398	668,507	703,708	705,606
Georgia	82,548	162,686	252,433	340,989	516,823	691,392	906,185	1,057,286	1,184,109
Florida					34,730	54,477	87,445	140,424	187,748
EAST SOUTH CENTRAL									
Kentucky	73,677	220,955	406,511	564,317	687,917	779,828	982,405	1,155,684	1,321,011
Tennessee	35,691	105,602	261,727	422,823	681,904	829,210	1,002,717	1,109,801	1,258,520
Alabama				127,901	309,527	590,756	771,623	964,201	996,992
Mississippi		8,850	40,352	75,448	136,621	375,651	606,526	791,305	827,922
WEST SOUTH CENTRAL									
Arkansas			1,062	14,273	30,388	97,574	209,897	435,450	484,471
Louisiana			76,556	153,407	215,739	352,411	517,762	708,002	726,915
Texas							212,592	604,215	818,579

EAST NORTH CENTRAL							
Ohio	45,365	230,760	581,434	937,903	1,519,467	1,980,329	2,339,511	2,665,260
Indiana	5,641	24,520	147,178	343,031	685,866	988,416	1,350,428	1,680,637
Illinois		12,282	55,211	157,445	476,183	851,470	1,711,951	2,539,981
Michigan		4,762	8,896	31,639	212,267	397,654	749,113	1,184,059
Wisconsin					30,945	305,391	775,881	1,054,670
WEST NORTH CENTRAL							
Minnesota						6,077	172,023	439,706
Iowa					43,112	192,214	674,913	1,194,020
Missouri		19,783	66,586	140,455	383,702	682,044	1,182,012	1,721,295
North Dakota								2,405
South Dakota								11,776
Nebraska							28,841	122,993
Kansas							107,206	364,399
MOUNTAIN							
Montana								20,595
Idaho								14,999
Wyoming								9,118
Colorado							34,277	39,864
New Mexico						61,547	93,516	91,874
Arizona								9,658
Utah						11,380	40,273	86,786
Nevada							6,857	42,491
PACIFIC							
Washington							11,594	23,955
Oregon						13,294	52,465	90,923
California						92,597	379,994	560,247

Division and State	1880	1890	1900	1910	1920	1930	1940	1950	1960	1970
UNITED STATES	50,155,783	62,947,714	75,994,575	91,972,266	105,710,620	122,775,046	131,669,275	150,697,361	179,323,175	203,211,926
GEOGRAPHIC DIVISIONS										
New England	4,010,529	4,700,749	5,592,017	6,552,681	7,400,909	8,166,341	8,437,290	9,314,453	10,509,367	11,841,663
Middle Atlantic	10,496,878	12,706,220	15,454,678	19,315,892	22,261,144	26,260,750	27,539,487	30,163,533	34,168,452	37,199,040
South Atlantic	7,597,197	8,857,922	10,443,480	12,194,895	13,990,272	15,793,589	17,823,151	21,182,335	25,971,732	30,671,337
East South Central	5,585,151	6,429,154	7,547,757	8,409,901	8,893,307	9,887,214	10,778,225	11,477,181	12,050,126	12,803,470
West South Central	3,334,220	4,740,983	6,532,290	8,784,534	10,242,224	12,176,830	13,064,525	14,537,572	16,951,255	19,320,560
East North Central	11,206,668	13,478,305	15,985,581	18,250,621	21,475,543	25,297,185	26,626,342	30,399,368	36,225,024	40,252,476
West North Central	6,157,443	8,932,112	10,347,423	11,637,921	12,544,249	13,296,915	13,516,990	14,061,394	15,394,115	16,319,187
Mountain	653,119	1,213,935	1,674,657	2,633,517	3,336,101	3,701,789	4,150,003	5,074,998	6,855,060	8,281,562
Pacific	1,114,578	1,888,334	2,416,692	4,192,304	5,566,871	8,194,433	9,733,262	14,486,527	20,339,105	25,453,688
Noncontiguous									858,939	1,068,943
NEW ENGLAND										
Maine	648,936	661,086	694,466	742,371	768,014	797,423	847,226	913,774	969,265	992,048
New Hampshire	346,991	376,530	411,588	430,572	443,083	465,293	491,524	533,242	606,921	731,681
Vermont	332,286	332,422	343,641	355,956	352,428	359,611	359,231	377,747	389,881	444,330
Massachusetts	1,783,085	2,238,947	2,805,346	3,366,416	3,852,356	4,249,614	4,316,721	4,690,514	5,148,578	5,689,110
Rhode Island	276,531	345,506	428,556	542,610	604,397	687,497	713,346	791,896	859,488	946,725
Connecticut	622,700	746,258	908,420	1,114,756	1,380,631	1,606,903	1,709,242	2,007,280	2,535,234	3,031,709
MIDDLE ATLANTIC										
New York	5,082,871	6,003,174	7,268,894	9,113,614	10,385,227	12,588,066	13,479,142	14,830,192	16,782,304	18,236,967
New Jersey	1,131,116	1,444,933	1,883,669	2,537,167	3,155,900	4,041,334	4,160,165	4,835,329	6,066,782	7,168,164
Pennsylvania	4,282,891	5,258,113	6,302,115	7,665,111	8,720,017	9,631,350	9,900,180	10,498,012	11,319,366	11,793,909
SOUTH ATLANTIC										
Delaware	146,608	168,493	184,735	202,322	223,003	238,380	266,505	318,085	446,292	548,104
Maryland	934,943	1,042,390	1,188,044	1,295,346	1,449,661	1,631,526	1,821,244	2,343,001	3,100,689	3,922,399
Dist. of Columbia	177,624	230,392	278,718	331,069	437,571	486,869	663,091	802,178	763,956	756,510
Virginia	1,512,565	1,655,980	1,854,184	2,061,612	2,309,187	2,421,851	2,677,773	3,318,680	3,966,949	4,648,494
West Virginia	618,457	762,794	958,800	1,221,119	1,463,701	1,729,205	1,901,974	2,005,552	1,860,421	1,744,237
North Carolina	1,399,750	1,617,949	1,893,810	2,206,287	2,559,123	3,170,276	3,571,623	4,061,929	4,556,155	5,082,059
South Carolina	995,577	1,151,149	1,340,316	1,515,400	1,683,724	1,738,765	1,899,804	2,117,027	2,382,594	2,590,516
Georgia	1,542,180	1,837,353	2,216,331	2,609,121	2,895,832	2,908,506	3,123,723	3,444,578	3,943,116	4,589,575
Florida	269,493	391,422	528,542	752,619	968,470	1,468,211	1,897,414	2,771,305	4,951,560	6,789,443
EAST SOUTH CENTRAL										
Kentucky	1,648,690	1,858,635	2,147,174	2,289,905	2,416,630	2,614,589	2,845,627	2,944,806	3,038,156	3,218,706
Tennessee	1,542,359	1,767,518	2,020,616	2,184,789	2,337,885	2,616,556	2,915,841	3,291,718	3,567,089	3,923,687
Alabama	1,262,505	1,513,401	1,828,697	2,138,093	2,348,174	2,646,248	2,832,961	3,061,743	3,266,740	3,444,165
Mississippi	1,131,597	1,289,600	1,551,270	1,797,114	1,790,618	2,009,821	2,183,796	2,178,914	2,178,141	2,216,912
WEST SOUTH CENTRAL										
Arkansas	802,525	1,128,211	1,311,564	1,574,449	1,752,204	1,854,482	1,949,387	1,909,511	1,786,272	1,923,285
Louisiana	939,946	1,118,588	1,381,625	1,656,388	1,798,509	2,101,593	2,363,880	2,683,516	3,257,022	3,641,306
Oklahoma		258,657	790,391	1,657,155	2,028,283	2,396,040	2,336,434	2,233,351	2,328,284	2,559,229
Texas	1,591,749	2,235,527	3,048,710	3,896,542	4,663,228	5,824,715	6,414,824	7,711,194	9,579,677	11,196,730
EAST NORTH CENTRAL										
Ohio	3,198,062	3,672,329	4,157,545	4,767,121	5,759,394	6,646,697	6,907,612	7,946,627	9,706,397	10,652,017
Indiana	1,978,301	2,192,404	2,516,462	2,700,876	2,930,390	3,238,503	3,427,796	3,934,224	4,662,498	5,193,669
Illinois	3,077,871	3,826,352	4,821,550	5,638,591	6,485,280	7,630,654	7,897,241	8,712,176	10,081,158	11,113,976
Michigan	1,636,937	2,093,890	2,420,982	2,810,173	3,668,412	4,842,325	5,256,106	6,371,766	7,823,194	8,875,083
Wisconsin	1,315,497	1,693,330	2,069,042	2,333,860	2,632,067	2,939,006	3,137,587	3,434,576	3,951,777	4,417,731

WEST NORTH CENTRAL										
Minnesota	780,773	1,310,283	1,751,394	2,075,708	2,387,125	2,563,953	2,792,300	2,982,483	3,413,864	3,804,971
Iowa	1,624,615	1,912,297	2,231,853	2,224,771	2,404,021	2,470,939	2,538,268	2,621,073	2,757,537	2,824,376
Missouri	2,168,380	2,679,185	3,106,665	3,293,335	3,404,055	3,629,367	3,784,664	3,954,653	4,319,813	4,676,501
North Dakota	36,909	190,983	319,146	577,056	646,872	680,845	641,935	619,636	632,446	617,761
South Dakota	98,268	348,600	401,570	583,888	636,547	692,849	642,961	652,740	680,514	665,507
Nebraska	452,402	1,062,656	1,066,300	1,192,214	1,296,372	1,377,963	1,315,834	1,325,510	1,411,330	1,483,493
Kansas	996,096	1,428,108	1,470,495	1,690,949	1,769,257	1,880,999	1,801,028	1,905,299	2,178,611	2,246,578
MOUNTAIN										
Montana	39,159	142,924	243,329	376,053	548,889	537,606	559,456	591,024	674,767	694,409
Idaho	32,610	88,548	161,772	325,594	431,866	445,032	524,873	588,637	667,191	712,567
Wyoming	20,789	62,555	92,531	145,965	194,402	225,565	250,742	290,529	330,066	332,416
Colorado	194,327	413,249	539,700	799,024	939,629	1,035,791	1,123,296	1,325,089	1,753,947	2,207,259
New Mexico	119,565	160,282	195,310	327,301	360,350	423,317	531,818	681,187	951,023	1,016,000
Arizona	40,440	88,243	122,931	204,354	334,162	435,573	499,261	749,587	1,302,161	1,770,900
Utah	143,963	210,779	276,749	373,351	449,396	507,847	550,310	688,862	890,627	1,059,273
Nevada	62,266	47,355	42,335	81,875	77,407	91,058	110,247	160,083	285,278	488,738
PACIFIC										
Washington	75,116	357,232	518,103	1,141,990	1,356,621	1,563,396	1,736,191	2,378,963	2,853,214	3,409,169
Oregon	174,768	317,704	413,536	672,765	783,389	953,786	1,089,684	1,521,341	1,768,687	2,091,385
California	864,694	1,213,398	1,485,053	2,377,549	3,426,861	5,677,251	6,907,387	10,586,223	15,717,204	19,953,134
NONCONTIGUOUS										
Alaska									226,167	300,382
Hawaii									632,772	786,561

Index

About the Authors

RICHARD N. CURRENT is University Distinguished Professor of History at the University of North Carolina at Greensboro. He is co-author of the Bancroft Prize-winning *Lincoln the President*. His books include: *Three Carpetbag Governors; The Lincoln Nobody Knows; Daniel Webster and the Rise of National Conservatism;* and *Secretary Stimson*. Professor Current has lectured on U.S. history in Europe, Asia, South America, Australia, and Antarctica. He has been a Fulbright Lecturer at the University of Munich and the University of Chile at Santiago, and has served as Harmsworth Professor of American History at Oxford. He is President of the Southern Historical Association.

T. HARRY WILLIAMS is Boyd Professor of History at Louisiana State University. He was awarded both the 1969 Pulitzer Prize and National Book Award for his biography of *Huey Long*. His books include: *Lincoln and His Generals; Lincoln and the Radicals; P.G.T. Beauregard; Americans at War; Romance and Realism in Southern Politics; Hayes of the Twenty-Third; McClellan, Sherman, and Grant; The Union Sundered;* and *The Union Restored*. Professor Williams has been a Harmsworth Professor of American History at Oxford and President of both the Southern Historical Association and the Organization of American Historians.

FRANK FREIDEL is Charles Warren Professor of History at Harvard University. He is writing a six-volume biography of Franklin D. Roosevelt, four volumes of which have been published. Among his other books are: *Our Country's Presidents; F.D.R. and the South;* and *America in the Twentieth Century*. He is co-editor of the 1974 edition of the *Harvard Guide to American History*, and Vice President of the Organization of American Historians. He is also a former president of the New England Historical Society.

This book was set on the Linofilm in Textype, a typeface designed primarily for printing textbooks and related works requiring intensive study and prolonged reading. Its letter shapes and word patterns have been authenticated by modern scientific research in readability. Its features of design give it optimum characteristics of visibility and speed of reading with a minimum of fatigue. Originally designed and cut for Mergenthaler Linotype in 1929.

Composed by American Can Co., Printing Division, Clarinda, Iowa; printed and bound by the Kingsport Press, Kingsport, Tenn.

Color essays printed by New York City Press, New York, N.Y.

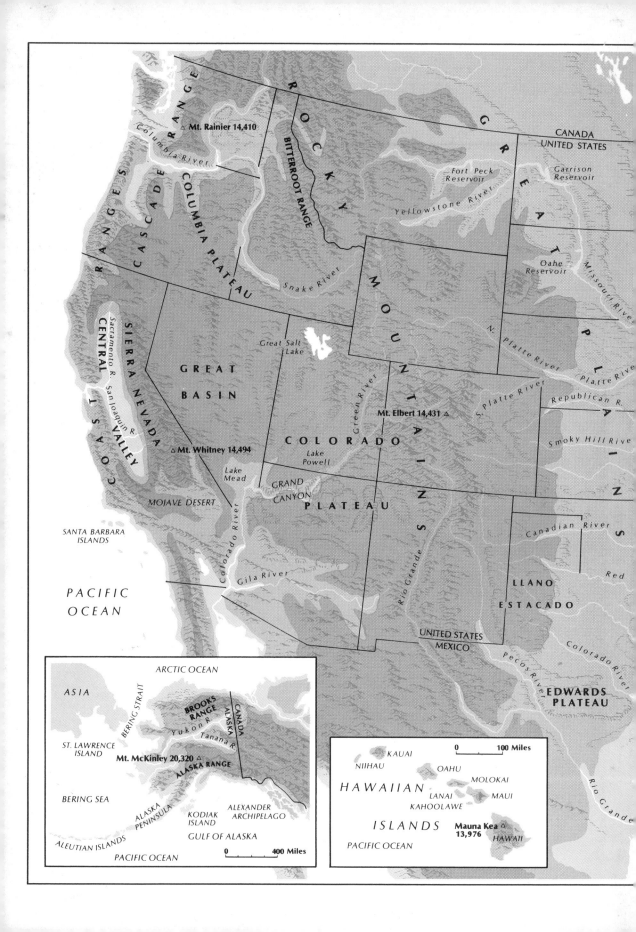

△ Mt. Rainier 14,410

CANADA
UNITED STATES

R O C K Y

Columbia River

BITTERROOT RANGE

Fort Peck
Reservoir

Garrison
Reservoir

Yellowstone River

Oahe
Reservoir

Missouri River

COLUMBIA PLATEAU

CASCADE RANGE

RANGES

Snake River

M O U N T A I N S

G R E A T

Sacramento R.
San Joaquin R.

CENTRAL

SIERRA NEVADA

VALLEY

GREAT

BASIN

Great Salt
Lake

Green River

Mt. Elbert 14,431 △

N. Platte River

Platte River

Republican R.

P L A I N S

C O A S T   R A N G E S

△ Mt. Whitney 14,494

C O L O R A D O

Lake
Powell

S. Platte River

Smoky Hill River

Lake
Mead

GRAND
CANYON

P L A T E A U

MOJAVE DESERT

SANTA BARBARA
ISLANDS

Colorado River

Gila River

Canadian River

Red

LLANO

ESTACADO

PACIFIC
OCEAN

Rio Grande

UNITED STATES
MEXICO

Pecos River

Colorado River

EDWARDS
PLATEAU

Rio Grande

ARCTIC OCEAN

ASIA

BERING STRAIT

BROOKS
RANGE

ALASKA
CANADA

Yukon R.

Tanana R.

ST. LAWRENCE
ISLAND

Mt. McKinley 20,320 △

ALASKA RANGE

BERING SEA

ALASKA
PENINSULA

KODIAK
ISLAND

ALEXANDER
ARCHIPELAGO

ALEUTIAN ISLANDS

GULF OF ALASKA

PACIFIC OCEAN

0   400 Miles

0   100 Miles

KAUAI

NIIHAU

OAHU

MOLOKAI

H A W A I I A N

LANAI

MAUI

KAHOOLAWE

I S L A N D S

Mauna Kea △
13,976

HAWAII

PACIFIC OCEAN